The choice is clear

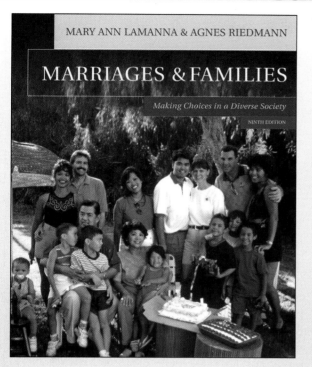

A changing society requires a marriage and family text that keeps pace with the rapidly evolving social world of the family. The best-selling *Marriages & Families: Making Choices in a Diverse Society* is that text. Mary Ann Lamanna and Agnes Riedmann's respected book has evolved over its nine editions to keep in step with the contemporary American family and scholarly interpretation of it.

The book's subtitle, *Making Choices in a Diverse Society,* illustrates the vast changes that have taken and continue to take place in marriages and families. With its inclusion of the latest research, and its emphasis on students being able to make choices in a diverse society, this is *the* leading text for gaining insights into today's marriages and families.

Explore this PREVIEW of the Ninth Edition of *Marriages & Families: Making Choices in a Diverse Society* and discover a text that is:

- **Current** The Ninth Edition is entirely up-to-date with the latest research and findings, all of which shed light on concepts and help students question assumptions and reconcile conflicting ideas and values as they make choices throughout their lives. *(See page 2)*
- **Balanced** The book's unparalleled blend of theory and application incorporates coverage of the broad spectrum of today's families: working parents, poor and minority families, single-parent families, remarried families, gay and lesbian couples, and other nontraditional families, as well as the classic nuclear family. *(See page 3)*
- **Accessible** Lamanna and Riedmann's narrative is as engaging as it is scholarly. With every chapter, students come to a better understanding that creating and maintaining marriages and families requires many personal choices made throughout the life span. And *Marriages & Families* is the perfect text whether you teach the course in a sociology or family studies program. *(See page 4)*
- **Enriched** Every new copy of the text is available packaged with free access to **Marriage&FamilyNow**™, an online tool that provides students with a *Personalized Study Plan* and the resources they need to master course concepts and material. Plus, you'll also have access to a comprehensive offering of ancillary materials that will enhance your teaching and your students' learning. *(See pages 5–7)*

Marriage & Family ⊛ Now™

THOMSON

★

WADSWORTH

With this Ninth Edition, Lamanna and Riedmann have thoroughly updated the text's research base and statistics, emphasizing cutting-edge research that addresses the diversity of marriages and families as well as many other topics. The authors' timely coverage offers insightful perspectives on diversity, including different ethnic traditions and marriage and family alternatives.

▶ **New!**

With the Ninth Edition, Lamanna and Riedmann add a new boxed feature that presents important demographic information about American families. Each *Facts About Families* section emphasizes the importance demography plays in the study of the family. These colorful, often multipage features include thought-provoking critical thinking questions that will spur students on to further exploration of such topics as:

- "American Families Today"
- "The Geography of Families"
- "Race/Ethnicity and Differential Fertility Rates"
- "Who Has HIV/AIDS?"
- "The Large and Increasing Number of Unmarrieds"
- "Fathers as Primary Parents"
- "Where Does the Time Go?"

Facts About Families — Who Has HIV/AIDS?[a]

Around 400,000 people are living with AIDS[b]: 42 percent black, 37 percent white, 20 percent Hispanic, and 1 percent each Asian/Pacific Islander and Native American/Alaska Native. The cumulative total of AIDS cases reported through 2003 is over 900,000, with more than 40,000 new cases diagnosed each year (U.S. Centers for Disease Control and Prevention 2004g, "Commentary" and Table 3).

Currently, around 800,000 people are infected with HIV, the largest number since the 1980s. On the positive side, infections are being caught in the early stages. On the other hand, the increase in infections suggests a growing sense of complacency among groups at risk of contracting the disease. "Because more effective treatments are available, there seems to be a perception, particularly in the gay community, that HIV is a manageable disease . . . I think the disease just doesn't have the fear that it once carried" (Dr.

a. The term "HIV/AIDS" is used in general references to this sexually transmitted disease. When speaking about numbers of cases, "HIV" (the virus which causes AIDS) and "AIDS" (the active disease) are often distinguished. Most of those who become infected with the HIV virus will progress to full-blown AIDS.

The incidence (number of new cases) and prevalence (current cases) of HIV-infection are only estimates, as there is no population-wide screening program. Many people who may be HIV-positive are not tested, and test results are not always reported consistently. Consequently, most of the data in these sections on the social distribution of HIV/AIDS are based on AIDS cases, as those are more definite in diagnosis and reported more accurately.

Robert Johnson, Director of the CDC's HIV and AIDS Prevention Division in O'Connor 2004, p. 28). Also, information efforts do not seem to be reaching minorities.

Primary risk groups Primary risk groups in the United States are men who have sex with men (MSM) (about 47 percent of cumulative AIDS cases through 2003). Intravenous drug users account for 27 percent of cases, and 7 percent are identified as men who have combined risks. Heterosexual transmission is the origin of 16 percent of AIDS cases.[b]

b. Woman-to-woman sex may carry some risk of HIV infection, although it is a rare occurrence (U.S. Centers for Disease Control and Prevention 2001a).

Heterosexual transmission is rising and is now the source of 34 percent of new HIV infections and of 90 percent of new HIV infections among teens (U.S. Centers for Disease Control and Prevention 2004g).

Age and HIV/AIDS HIV/AIDS has affected young and middle-aged adults the most. Almost three-fourths of AIDS cases to date were diagnosed in people in the twenty-five through forty-four age range. The proportion of HIV/AIDS cases among teenagers is small, around 1 percent (U.S. Centers for Disease Control and Prevention 2004g), but keep in mind that individuals who are older at diagnosis may have been infected as adolescents.

More AIDS infections are caught in the early stages now, thanks to the wide distribution of information about AIDS prevention and testing.

Table 9.1

The Desire to Stay Single Among Never-Married, Noncohabiting Individuals, by Age, Race/Ethnicity, and Sex

	WHITE MALES	BLACK MALES	HISPANIC MALES	WHITE FEMALES	BLACK FEMALES	HISPANIC FEMALES	TOTAL
Ages 19 to 35							
Percentage not desiring marriage	15.40	23.50	8.70	17.10	21.80	25.30	17.20
Number of all respondents	566	190	79	721	389	128	2,073
Ages 19 to 25							
Percentage not desiring marriage	12.60	22.80	6.80	11.20	12.70	13.10	12.60
Number of all respondents	291	97	50	288	149	51	926

Source: From "Racial and Ethnic Differences in the Desire to Marry," by Scott J. South, 1993, *Journal of Marriage and the Family,* 55 (2), 357–370. Copyright © 1993 by the National Council on Family Relations, 3989 Central Ave. NE, Suite 550, Minneapolis, MN 55421. Reprinted by permission.

Of course, the sex ratio for society *as a whole* does not tell the entire story. To get a better picture of how the sex ratio affects one's odds of marrying, we need to examine sex ratios within certain age groups—and, more specifically, sex ratios for *single* people within certain age groups. In the 1980s, the popular press made much of the idea that there weren't enough single, eligible men to go around. There still are far more women than men in older age groups. By the 1990s, however, there were more single men than single women in their twenties and early thirties (Weeks 2002). Whether due to a shortage of men or of women, in many social categories there just aren't enough eligible (heterosexual) mates, so in the musical chairs of marital pairings, some are left out.[4]

An additional reason for the growing proportion of singles in the United States involves changing atti-

Changing Attitudes Toward Marriage and Singlehood

Sociologist Scott South (1993) analyzed data from 2,073 never-married men and women aged nineteen to thirty-five who were not cohabiting. As part of the National Survey of Families and Households (NSFH), these singles were asked to respond to the statement "I would like to get married someday." They could answer with any one of the following: "strongly agree," "agree," "neither agree nor disagree," "disagree," or "strongly disagree." Notice that this question does not measure whether a person *expects* to marry, only whether she or he *would like* to marry.

Table 9.1 gives the percentages of respondents who did not agree with the statement. They either disagreed or answered that they could neither agree nor disagree. South cautions that this sample probably *overestimates* people's negative attitudes about marriage because only never-marrieds are included. Pr...

◀ **New!**

Chapter 9, "Alternatives to Marriage: Being Single, Cohabitation, and Domestic Partnerships" (formerly Chapter 7) extends the leadership role of Lamanna and Riedmann in their coverage of diversity, and includes the latest research on singles along with new studies on cohabitation. This important chapter examines what social scientists know about the large and growing number of singles and explores changing cultural attitudes about marriage and alternatives to marriage. A wealth of new data and research is incorporated into this chapter on topics such as:

- The popular press's reporting of single life
- Women's earning potential as it relates to their attitudes toward marriage
- Adoption among gay and lesbian couples
- Cohabitation among retirees
- Children in cohabitating families
- Domestic partner registration

Lamanna and Riedmann combine a scholarly and applied approach with a unique theme of making choices in today's diverse society. Their mainstream text achieves an excellent balance between the sociological and ecological theoretical perspectives, while including coverage of family dynamics and interpersonal relationships. A series of boxed features enhances this balanced approach and allows students to explore some of the most vital issues affecting today's marriages and families.

New!
Timely topics are found throughout the text in the boxed features, helping to draw students into the material while presenting the latest scholarship. These areas include "Safety and Risk in the Family Environment," covering the anxieties of today's parents, as well as specific concerns about crime and terrorism; "Challenges to Gender Boundaries"; "Pets as Family"; and "Test Tube Babies Grow Up."

Engaging boxed features are found throughout the text and include:

- **A Closer Look at Family Diversity**: These boxes draw on topics across a wide range of familial situations, demonstrating the true diversity of the modern family. Several of these boxes report on families in varied cultural settings and provide a valuable comparative.
- **As We Make Choices**: Highlighting the theme of the text, this feature emphasizes the hundreds of choices we make in our family lives and points out that each of these decisions is influenced by societal conditions and our own set of values.
- **Case Study**: With thought-provoking coverage of many issues facing American families today, the *Case Study* boxes reflect the range of experiences of individuals of all ages and backgrounds. These intriguing, first-person accounts balance and expand on topics presented in the chapters.
- **Issues for Thought**: These boxes highlight interesting factual information on public policy, social conditions, and individual decision making in areas such as partner choice, working out marital issues, having and raising children, and combining work with family. In many of these boxes, critical thinking questions are added to help students reflect upon the material, enhancing their ability to make informed choices throughout their own lives.
- **Focus on Children**: Highlighted by an icon, these sections focus on important material directly relating to children in families.

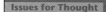

> *"[This text offers] superb integration of individual choice/experience with sociological research and theory."*
> **—Suzan Waller, Rose State College**

Issues for Thought

Safety and Risk in the Family Environment

Family ecology theory tells us to look at the environment surrounding the family. And what is that environment like in terms of risk and the perception of risk? The 9/11 terrorist attacks, Columbine school killings, and high-profile kidnappings lead us to consider our time and its dangers. Websites offer advice to parents on how to explain terrorism to children (useful websites, by the way, as terrorism remains a danger whose future scope is unknown).

At the same time, some social scientists speculate that fear may have outstripped the reality of risk. Historian Peter Stearns argues that Americans have become "anxious parents." Smaller families, which enhance the preciousness and per-

In his book *The Culture of Fear* sociologist Barry Glassner demythologizes some common fears about dangers to children, beginning with the urban myth of sabotaged Halloween candy. According to Glassner and others, kidnapping by a stranger, teen suicide, day-care abuse of children, teen births, adolescent drug use, in-school violence, and other juvenile violent crime are all threats that have either declined or been overstated as to frequency and upward trend (Glassner 1999; Leinwand 2002; Snyder and Sickmund 1999; "Teen Drug Use" 2003; Toppo 2003; U.S. National Center for Education Statistics 2004). We now have safety protections for children, such as car seats and bicycle helmets, that did not have

How much is a sense of environmental danger to children a question of perception rather than reality? Ironically, it appears that parents in low-crime areas are as likely to be fearful about dangers of the street as those whose children are in fact more exposed to dangerous surroundings. Michael Moore's *Bowling for Columbine* film crew, taken on a tour of South Central Los Angeles, observed that more children play in the street in this urban neighborhood than are allowed to in "wealthier white neighborhoods, where parents were more afraid to let their kids go out and play" (Barry Glassner in Ebner 2003).

In high-crime areas, parents often do keep their children inside, away from danger. Children and parents are essentially kept pris-

---

As We Make Choices

Learning to Love Yourself More

We all feel inadequate at times. What can you do with feelings of inadequacy besides worry about them? As one psychologist put it, "You can't just sit and psych yourself into high self-esteem" (Krueger 2003). However, people can work in many ways to improve their sense of self worth. For example, you may choose to do the following:

- Identify your best personality traits, such as curiosity, humor, or courage. Remember these when you face challenging situations, and try to find ways to manifest them.
- Pursue satisfying and useful occupations that realistically reflect your strengths and interests ("Young children make me nervous, but I'd like to teach, so I'll consider secondary or higher education").
- Use empathy, respect, courtesy, and kindness when interacting with others. In doing so, you affirm not only others but yourself.
- Try being more honest about yourself and open with people.
- Make efforts to appreciate the good things you have rather than focus on the more negative things in your life. Write a "gratitude list" of things that you can be grateful for.
- Avoid excessive daydreaming and fantasy living ("Boy, things would be different if only I were a little taller" or "If only I had not gotten married so young, things would be better").
- Volunteer. Studies show that volunteers tend to live longer and feel better about themselves.
- Expand your world of interest. Take a nonrequired course outside your major just for the fun of it, or develop a new hobby.
- "Keep on keeping on"—even when you are discouraged, realizing that one little step in the right direction is often good enough.
- Be satisfied about being smart *enough*, slender *enough*, or successful *enough* rather than imposing unrealistic standards on yourself. ("Easy does it.")
- Relax ("If I feel this way, it means this is a human way to feel, and everybody else has probably felt this way too at one time or another").
- Forgive somebody: "If physical exercise had a mental equivalent, it would probably be the process of forgiveness. Researchers continue to tally the benefits of burying the hatchet—lower blood pressure and heart rate, less depression, a better immune system and a longer life, among others" (Goodman 2004).
- Decide to be your own good friend, complimenting yourself when you do things well enough and not criticizing yourself too harshly.

Critical Thinking
You may recall from Chapter 3 that the interactionist theoretical perspective assumes that individuals develop identities and self-concepts through social interaction. How do the above suggestions illustrate this point?

Lamanna and Riedmann combine a scholarly and applied approach with a unique theme of making choices in today's diverse society. While built from a solid and visible research base, this mainstream text is written in a conversational style that makes the study of the family accessible *and* enjoyable.

THE UNMARRIED: REASONS FOR THEIR INCREASING NUMBERS **237**

Sex ratio

106
104
102
100
98
96
94

1800   1850   1900   1950 1997 2025
                                      2002
Year

FIGURE 9.3

Sex ratios in the United States from 1790 to 2002 and projections for 2025. Because 100 represents a balanced sex ratio—an e...
the curve a...
than wome...
more wome...

Sources: Calcu...
Bureau 2003a...

nineteenth...
States had...
more men...
to a lesser...
young wor...
is reversed...
greater im...
health. Sin...
have been...

The increase in the number and proportion of singles in our society is a result of many factors, including economic constrictions, improved contraception, an unequal sex ratio, and changing attitudes toward marriage and singlehood.

◄ Clarifying tables and figures and colorful photos are found throughout the book. Many of this edition's photo captions have been revised to include greater detail and to enhance critical thinking. And from the photos to the text narrative, the authors weave the text's theme of diversity throughout every chapter, helping students better appreciate the variety and diversity among families today.

Lesbian couples may take advantage of AID (artificial insemination by donor) technology so that one partner gives birth to a baby they both want. Research from more than 100 studies concludes that children of lesbian or gay male parents are generally well-adjusted and have no noticeable differences from children of heterosexual parents.

A dilemma faced by all parents of racial/ethnic identity—whether African American, Native American, Hispanic, Asian American, or multiracial—is to address the balance between loyalty to one's ethnic culture and individual advancement in the dominant society. Native Americans must choose between the reservation and its high poverty level and an urban life that is perhaps alienating but presents some economic opportunity.

"The text covers the full range of life experiences using theory and research to show how people's lives develop and evolve from childhood to the later adult years. The feedback from students is that they learn a lot, even though they thought they were pretty well educated in this subject matter."
—Frances Marx Stehle, Portland State University

"Hey, look -- Mom left us an internal memo."

Some children are in "self-care" after school, increasingly true in middle-class families.

"So what's your custody deal?"

◄ The authors are noted for their use of gentle humor and cartoons, many of them from *The New Yorker* magazine, to capture the variety and unexpected truths about families and our closest relationships.

One-of-a-kind teaching and learning resources help to optimize your time—and your students' learning opportunities.

Assign . . . Assess . . . Track Progress . . . Success!

Marriage & Family ● Now™

Marriage&FamilyNow™
http://sociology.wadsworth.com/lamanna_
riedmann9e/marriage_familynow
Packaged FREE with the text: **0-495-05388-0**

What do your students need to learn NOW?

Help your students take charge of their learning with **Marriage& FamilyNow™**—the first assessment-centered student learning tool for the marriage and family course! This powerful online tool provides students with a personalized, custom study plan based on a comprehensive set of assessments—and gives you the ability to track their progress.

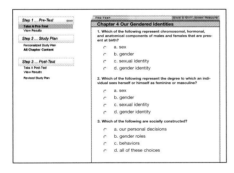

After taking a diagnostic *Pre-Test*, **Marriage& FamilyNow** generates a *Personalized Study Plan* for each student, providing interactive exercises, videos, and other resources to help them master course material— including an eBook linking students to the material they need to review. After reviewing the study plan, students can then take a *Post-Test* to monitor their progress in mastering the chapter concepts.

Online Study Tool

Marriage & Family ● Now™ Go to http://sociology.wadsworth.com to reach the companion website for your text and use the Marriage&FamilyNow access code that came with your book to access this study tool. Take a practice "pretest" after you have read each chapter, and then use the study plan provided to master that chapter. Afterward, take a "posttest" to monitor your progress.

References in the text to **Marriage &FamilyNow** direct students to the variety of resources they have access to with this powerful online learning companion.

Marriage&FamilyNow allows you to assign the *Pre-Test* and *Post-Test*—you can then keep track of student progress as assignment results flow automatically into the *Gradebook*. With this assistance in understanding of students' progress, you can easily identify concepts where your guidance will make a difference to students' success. The *Gradebook* can be exported into either WebCT® or Blackboard® applications. Your students can also use the program with no setup required from you. We encourage you to package **Marriage&FamilyNow** with each new copy of the text, at no additional cost to the student; use package **ISBN 0-495-05388-0**.

Book Companion Website
http://sociology.wadsworth.com/
lamanna_riedmann9e/

When you adopt *Marriages & Families: Making Choices in a Diverse Society,* you and your students will have access to a rich array of teaching and learning resources. This outstanding site features unique resources for students, including

- Chapter-by-chapter online tutorial quizzes
- A final exam
- Web links
- Flash cards
- Self-assessments

And for instructors, password-protected resources are available such as the **Instructor's Manual,** Microsoft® PowerPoint® lecture slides, chapter outlines, and more.

Also available . . .

InfoTrac® College Edition

The Wadsworth Marriage & Family Resource Center

See page 7 of this PREVIEW for details!

CLASS PREPARATION AND ASSESSMENT

Instructor's Manual/Test Bank
0-495-00109-0
by Kenrick Thompson, Arkansas State University Mountain Home. The **Instructor's Manual** contains resources designed to streamline and maximize the effectiveness of your course preparation, including *Lecture Outlines, Chapter Reviews, Student Activities,* and *Class Exercises/Discussion Questions.* The **Test Bank** offers approximately 100 test questions per chapter, in multiple-choice, true/false, completion, short-answer, and essay formats. The **Instructor's Manual** also includes a full answer key, and references to main text page numbers for answers to **Test Bank** questions.

ExamView

ExamView® Computerized Testing
0-495-00298-4
Create, deliver, and customize tests and study guides (both print and online) in minutes with this easy-to-use assessment and tutorial system. **ExamView®** offers both a *Quick Test Wizard* and an *Online Test Wizard* that guide you step-by-step through the process of creating tests, while its "what-you-see-is-what-you-get" interface allows you to see the test you are creating on the screen exactly as it will look when printed or displayed online. You can build tests of up to 250 questions using up to 12 question types. Using the complete word processing capabilities of **ExamView,** you can enter an unlimited number of new questions or edit existing questions.

COURSE MANAGEMENT

WebTUTOR™ ToolBox

WebTutor™ ToolBox on WebCT® and Blackboard®
Packaged with the text: WebCT: **0-495-05394-5**
Blackboard: **0-495-05393-7**
Preloaded with content and available via a free access code when packaged with this text, **WebTutor™ ToolBox** pairs all the content of the text's rich **Book Companion Website** with sophisticated course management functionality. You can assign materials (including online quizzes) and have the results flow automatically to your grade book. **WebTutor ToolBox** is ready to use as soon as you log on—or you can customize its preloaded content by uploading images and other resources, adding web links, or creating your own practice materials.

LECTURE TOOLS

JoinIn™ on TurningPoint®
0-495-12059-6
Thomson Wadsworth is now pleased to offer you book-specific **JoinIn™** content for Audience Response Systems tailored to *Marriages & Families: Making Choices in a Diverse Society,* **Ninth Edition.** This allows you to transform your classroom and assess your students' progress with instant in-class quizzes and polls. Our exclusive agreement to offer **TurningPoint®** software lets you pose book-specific questions and display students' answers seamlessly within the Microsoft® PowerPoint® slides of your own lecture, in conjunction with the "clicker" hardware of your choice. Enhance how your students interact with you, your lecture, and each other. *For college and university adopters only; contact your local Thomson representative to learn more.*

Multimedia Manager:
A Microsoft® PowerPoint® Tool
0-495-00297-6
This instructor resource includes book-specific Microsoft® PowerPoint® lecture slides, graphics from the book itself, the **Instructor's Manual** Microsoft® Word® documents, the book's **Test Bank,** dozens of video clips, and links to many of Wadsworth's important sociology resources. All of your media teaching resources in one place—culminating in a powerful, personalized, media-enhanced presentation.

CNN® Today Videos:
Marriage and Family
Volume V: **0-534-55271-4**
Volume VI: **0-534-61897-9**
Volume VII: **0-534-61900-2**
Each video in the series consists of approximately 45 minutes of footage originally broadcast on CNN within in the last several years and selected specifically to illustrate important sociological concepts in marriage and family. The videos are broken into short, two- to seven-minute segments that are ideal for classroom use as lecture launchers, or to illustrate key concepts. The high-interest clips are followed by questions designed to spark class discussion.

Transparency Masters
0-495-00449-9
This set of black-and-white masters consists of tables and figures from Wadsworth's marriage and family texts. Free to qualified adopters; contact your Thomson Wadsworth representative for details.

POWERFUL LEARNING RESOURCES ON THE WEB

InfoTrac® College Edition . . . *now with* InfoMarks™
Four months of free access with every new copy of
Lamanna and Riedmann's text! The **InfoTrac® College
Edition** online database is filled with more than 18
million reliable, full-length articles from 5,000
publications, **including tens of thousands of articles
from *The New York Times.*** Also included is access to
InfoMarks™, stable URLs that can be linked to articles,
journals, and searches. **InfoMarks** allows you to use a
simple "copy and paste" technique to create instant and
continually updated online readers, content services,
bibliographies, electronic "reserve" readings, and current topic sites. To help students use the research they
gather, their free four-month subscription to **InfoTrac
College Edition** includes access to **InfoWrite™**, a
complete set of online critical thinking and paper-writing
tools. (Certain restrictions may apply. For additional
information, please consult your local Thomson representative or visit **http://www.infotrac-college.com**.)
Not sold separately.

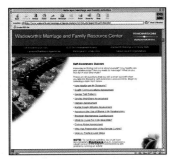

Wadsworth's Marriage and Family Resource Center
http://sociology.wadsworth.com
Combine Lamanna and Riedmann's text with the
Marriage and Family Resource Center's exciting range
of web resources, and you have greatly expanded your
students' learning opportunities. Accessible FREE via
Wadsworth's **Virtual Society** resource center and
requiring no password, this website includes self-
awareness quizzes, a GSS self-assessment activity,
marriage and family web links, and more. See the inside
back cover of this book for more information.

INVESTIGATION AND APPLICATION

Study Guide
0-495-03036-8 o Packaged with
the text, **0-495-05391-0**
*by Kenrick Thompson, Arkansas
State University Mountain Home.*
The **Study Guide** includes
learning objectives, chapter
summaries, key terms, and
extensive self-tests, including
multiple-choice, true/false,
completion, short-answer, and essay questions with a full
answer key and page references.

Telecourse Guide
0-495-03037-6
This **Telecourse Guide** is an essential resource that will
help students synthesize and evaluate information and
gauge their progress through the **Portrait of a Family**
telecourse. The **Telecourse Guide** includes an overview
of the telecourse material, key terms, reading assignments
and learning activities, self-tests, "viewing" questions that
focus student attention on key concepts addressed in the
video, and "decision" questions that ask students to
consider and apply concepts and ideas.

**Marriage and Family:
Using Microcase® ExplorIt®,
Third Edition**
0-534-60039-5 • Packaged with
the text, **0-495-05668-5**
*by Kevin Demmitt, Clayton
College & State University.*
With this workbook and
accompanying **ExplorIt®** software
and data sets, your students will
use national and cross-national survey to examine and
actively learn marriage and family topics. Included in
each workbook are a Windows® 95 and a DOS version of
the student **ExplorIt** software, an award-winning
program with a point-and-click interface that makes it
easy for students to analyze real data. Demmitt includes
16 active-learning exercises. Using aggregate data for the
United States and the world, students will explore
regional differences in teenage pregnancy, abortion,
working mothers, and divorce rates.

**Extension: Wadsworth's
Sociology Reader Database**
0-495-03089-9
The **Database** consists of approximately 100 articles—
both classic as well as contemporary—covering a broad
range of topics familiar to introductory sociology courses.

Student Resources

7

Lamanna and Riedmann's *Marriages & Families: Making Choices in a Diverse Society*, **Ninth Edition,** is available with a wide range of well-developed instructor and student resources including dynamic technology tools. All of these resources have been described in detail in the preceding pages. The purpose of this guide is to show how the rich ancillary materials can be used in conjunction with each chapter.

Chapter 1: Family Commitments: Making Choices in a Changing Society

Class Preparation / Lecture Tools	Testing Tools / Course Management	Student Mastery / Homework and Tutorials / Beyond the Book

Instructor's Manual with Test Bank
Contains lecture outlines, suggestions for class discussions, films and videos, chapter worksheets, and more for Chapter 1

Multimedia Manager Instructor's Resource CD-ROM
Allows you to create a media lecture for Chapter 1 using this Microsoft® PowerPoint® tool

Wadsworth's Sociology Video Library
Select a full-length video from the collection of Films for the Humanities.

Marriage & Family Transparency Masters 2006
A selection of quality transparencies from Wadsworth's texts

CNN® Today Videos
Marriage and Family Vols. V–VII

ExamView®
Computerized version of the Test Bank items for Chapter 1

WebTutor™ ToolBox
WebTutor™ Toolbox
Online course management tool for WebCT® or Blackboard® preloaded with text-specific content and media resources for Chapter 1

Marriage & Family Now™
An online diagnostic study tool for students to use without your help. Assign a *Pre-Test* and/or *Post-Test* and students' scores flow into the grade book. The program can be integrated with both WebCT® and Blackboard® course management platforms.

WebTutor™ Toolbox
Online course management tool for WebCT® or Blackboard® preloaded with text-specific content and media resources for Chapter 1

Study Guide
Chapter 1 includes a chapter summary, learning objectives, key terms, Internet and **InfoTrac® College Edition** exercises, and practice tests with multiple choice, true/false, short answer, and essay questions.

Book Companion Website
http://sociology.wadsworth.com/lamanna_riedmann9e/
Online quizzes, web links, and more for Chapter 1

Marriage & Family Now™
An online diagnostic study tool. Students take a *Pre-Test* and receive a *Personalized Study Plan.* Using their *Study Plan,* students can link to lecture outlines, study videos, and the textbook itself. An e-book is included!

InfoTrac® College Edition
Keywords: young adult, cohabitation

Chapter 2: American Families in Social Context

Class Preparation / Lecture Tools	Testing Tools / Course Management	Student Mastery / Homework and Tutorials / Beyond the Book

Instructor's Manual with Test Bank
Contains lecture outlines, suggestions for class discussions, films and videos, chapter worksheets, and more for Chapter 2

Multimedia Manager Instructor's Resource CD-ROM
Allows you to create a media lecture for Chapter 2 using this Microsoft® PowerPoint® tool

Wadsworth's Sociology Video Library
Select a full-length video from the collection of Films for the Humanities:
"The Changing Family and Its Implications"

Marriage & Family Transparency Masters 2006
A selection of quality transparencies from Wadsworth's texts

CNN® Today Videos
Marriage and Family Vol. V:
"Marriage & Family Demographics" (1:55);
"Household Incomes in the US" (2:14)

ExamView®
Computerized version of the Test Bank items for Chapter 2

WebTutor™ ToolBox
WebTutor™ Toolbox
Online course management tool for WebCT® or Blackboard® preloaded with text-specific content and media resources for Chapter 2

Marriage & Family Now™
This program is ready for your students to use without your help. Or, you can choose to incorporate the course management features of the platform to better administer your class and save yourself and your students valuable time. Assign a *Pre-Test* and/or *Post-Test* and students' scores flow into the grade book. The program can be integrated with both WebCT® and Blackboard® course management platforms.

WebTutor™ Toolbox
Online course management tool for WebCT® or Blackboard® preloaded with text-specific content and media resources for Chapter 2

Study Guide
Chapter 2 includes a chapter summary, learning objectives, key terms, Internet and **InfoTrac® College Edition** exercises, and practice tests with multiple choice, true/false, short answer, and essay questions.

Book Companion Website
http://sociology.wadsworth.com/lamanna_riedmann9e/
Online quizzes, web links, and more for Chapter 2

Marriage & Family Now™
An online diagnostic study tool. Students take a *Pre-Test* and receive a *Personalized Study Plan.* Using their *Study Plan,* students can link to helpful resources (lecture outlines, study videos, and the textbook itself) for material they need to review further. Students assess exactly what they need to know to succeed. An e-book is included!

InfoTrac® College Edition
Keywords: family + religion, multicultural + family

Chapter 3: Exploring the Family

Class Preparation / Lecture Tools

Instructor's Manual with Test Bank
Contains lecture outlines, suggestions for class discussions, films and videos, chapter worksheets, and more for Chapter 3

Multimedia Manager Instructor's Resource CD-ROM
Allows you to create a media lecture for Chapter 3 using this Microsoft® PowerPoint® tool

Wadsworth's Sociology Video Library
Select a full-length video from the collection of *Films for the Humanities:* "The Changing Family and Its Implications."

Marriage & Family Transparency Masters 2006
A selection of quality transparencies from Wadsworth's texts

CNN® Today Videos
Marriage and Family Vol. VI: "Polygamy in Utah" (3:48); "Operation Parenthood" (1:38)

Testing Tools / Course Management

ExamView

ExamView®
Computerized version of the Test Bank items for Chapter 3

WebTUTOR ToolBox

WebTutor™ Toolbox
Online course management tool for WebCT® or Blackboard® preloaded with text-specific content and media resources for Chapter 3

Marriage & Family Now™

This program is ready for your students to use without your help. Or, you can choose to incorporate the course management features of the platform to better administer your class and save yourself and your students valuable time. Assign a *Pre-Test* and/or *Post-Test* and students' scores flow into the grade book. The program can be integrated with both WebCT® and Blackboard® course management platforms.

Student Mastery / Homework and Tutorials / Beyond the Book

WebTutor™ Toolbox WebTUTOR ToolBox
Online course management tool for WebCT® or Blackboard® preloaded with text-specific content and media resources for Chapter 3

Study Guide
Chapter 3 includes a chapter summary, learning objectives, key terms, Internet and **InfoTrac® College Edition** exercises, and practice tests with multiple choice, true/false, short answer, and essay questions.

Book Companion Website
http://sociology.wadsworth.com/lamanna_riedmann9e/
Online quizzes, web links, and more for Chapter 3

Marriage & Family Now™

An online diagnostic study tool. Students take a *Pre-Test* and receive a *Personalized Study Plan.* Using their *Study Plan,* students can link to helpful resources (lecture outlines, study videos, and the textbook itself) for material they need to review further. Students assess exactly what they need to know to succeed. An e-book is included!

InfoTrac® College Edition
Keywords: biosocial + family, family + Russia

Chapter 4: Our Gendered Identities

Class Preparation / Lecture Tools

Instructor's Manual with Test Bank
Contains lecture outlines, suggestions for class discussions, films and videos, chapter worksheets, and more for Chapter 4

Multimedia Manager Instructor's Resource CD-ROM
Allows you to create a media lecture for Chapter 4 using this Microsoft® PowerPoint® tool

Wadsworth's Sociology Video Library
Select a full-length video from the collection of *Films for the Humanities:* "The Changing Role of Women"

Marriage & Family Transparency Masters 2006
A selection of quality transparencies from Wadsworth's texts

CNN® Today Videos
Marriage and Family Vol. V: "Becoming a House Husband" (3:37)

Testing Tools / Course Management

ExamView

ExamView®
Computerized version of the Test Bank items for Chapter 4

WebTUTOR ToolBox

WebTutor™ Toolbox
Online course management tool for WebCT® or Blackboard® preloaded with text-specific content and media resources for Chapter 4

Marriage & Family Now™

This program is ready for your students to use without your help. Or, you can choose to incorporate the course management features of the platform to better administer your class and save yourself and your students valuable time. Assign a *Pre-Test* and/or *Post-Test* and students' scores flow into the grade book. The program can be integrated with both WebCT® and Blackboard® course management platforms.

Student Mastery / Homework and Tutorials / Beyond the Book

WebTutor™ Toolbox WebTUTOR ToolBox
Online course management tool for WebCT® or Blackboard® preloaded with text-specific content and media resources for Chapter 4

Study Guide
Chapter 4 includes a chapter summary, learning objectives, key terms, Internet and **InfoTrac® College Edition** exercises, and practice tests with multiple choice, true/false, short answer, and essay questions.

Book Companion Website
http://sociology.wadsworth.com/lamanna_riedmann9e/
Online quizzes, web links, and more for Chapter 4

Marriage & Family Now™

An online diagnostic study tool. Students take a *Pre-Test* and receive a *Personalized Study Plan.* Using their *Study Plan,* students can link to helpful resources (lecture outlines, study videos, and the textbook itself) for material they need to review further. Students assess exactly what they need to know to succeed. An e-book is included!

InfoTrac® College Edition
Keywords: masculinity, feminism

Resource Integration Guide

9

Chapter 5: Loving Ourselves and Others

Class Preparation / Lecture Tools

Instructor's Manual with Test Bank
Contains lecture outlines, suggestions for class discussions, films and videos, chapter worksheets, and more for Chapter 5

Multimedia Manager Instructor's Resource CD-ROM
Allows you to create a media lecture for Chapter 5 using this Microsoft® PowerPoint® tool

Wadsworth's Sociology Video Library
Select a full-length video from the collection of *Films for the Humanities*

Marriage & Family Transparency Masters 2006
A selection of quality transparencies from Wadsworth's texts

CNN® Today Videos
Marriage and Family Vols. V–VII

Testing Tools / Course Management

ExamView

ExamView®
Computerized version of the Test Bank items for Chapter 5

WebTUTOR ToolBox

WebTutor™ Toolbox
Online course management tool for WebCT® or Blackboard® preloaded with text-specific content and media resources for Chapter 5

Marriage & Family ⊛ Now™
This program is ready for your students to use without your help. Or, you can choose to incorporate the course management features of the platform to better administer your class and save yourself and your students valuable time. Assign a *Pre-Test* and/or *Post-Test* and students' scores flow into the grade book. The program can be integrated with both WebCT® and Blackboard® course management platforms.

Student Mastery / Homework and Tutorials / Beyond the Book

WebTutor™ Toolbox
Online course management tool for WebCT® or Blackboard® preloaded with text-specific content and media resources for Chapter 5

Study Guide
Chapter 5 includes a chapter summary, learning objectives, key terms, Internet and **InfoTrac® College Edition** exercises, and practice tests with multiple choice, true/false, short answer, and essay questions.

Book Companion Website
http://sociology.wadsworth.com/lamanna_riedmann9e/
Online quizzes, web links, and more for Chapter 5

Marriage & Family ⊛ Now™
An online diagnostic study tool. Students take a *Pre-Test* and receive a *Personalized Study Plan.* Using their *Study Plan,* students can link to helpful resources (lecture outlines, study videos, and the textbook itself) for material they need to review further. Students assess exactly what they need to know to succeed. An e-book is included!

InfoTrac® College Edition
Keywords: intimacy, self-esteem, love

Chapter 6: Our Sexual Selves

Class Preparation / Lecture Tools

Instructor's Manual with Test Bank
Contains lecture outlines, suggestions for class discussions, films and videos, chapter worksheets, and more for Chapter 6

Multimedia Manager Instructor's Resource CD-ROM
Allows you to create a media lecture for Chapter 6 using this Microsoft® PowerPoint® tool

Wadsworth's Sociology Video Library
Select a full-length video from the collection of *Films for the Humanities:*
"Unsafe Sex and Its Consequences"

Marriage & Family Transparency Masters 2006
A selection of quality transparencies from Wadsworth's texts

CNN® Today Videos
Marriage and Family Vol. VI:
"Sex Talk with Teens" (1:29);
"Sexual Privacy and the State" (2:35);
"Changing Sexual Attitudes" (3:02)

Testing Tools / Course Management

ExamView

ExamView®
Computerized version of the Test Bank items for Chapter 6

WebTUTOR ToolBox

WebTutor™ Toolbox
Online course management tool for WebCT® or Blackboard® preloaded with text-specific content and media resources for Chapter 6

Marriage & Family ⊛ Now™
This program is ready for your students to use without your help. Or, you can choose to incorporate the course management features of the platform to better administer your class and save yourself and your students valuable time. Assign a *Pre-Test* and/or *Post-Test* and students' scores flow into the grade book. The program can be integrated with both WebCT® and Blackboard® course management platforms.

Student Mastery / Homework and Tutorials / Beyond the Book

WebTutor™ Toolbox
Online course management tool for WebCT® or Blackboard® preloaded with text-specific content and media resources for Chapter 6

Study Guide
Chapter 6 includes a chapter summary, learning objectives, key terms, Internet and **InfoTrac® College Edition** exercises, and practice tests with multiple choice, true/false, short answer, and essay questions.

Book Companion Website
http://sociology.wadsworth.com/lamanna_riedmann9e/
Online quizzes, web links, and more for Chapter 6

Marriage & Family ⊛ Now™
An online diagnostic study tool. Students take a *Pre-Test* and receive a *Personalized Study Plan.* Using their *Study Plan,* students can link to helpful resources (lecture outlines, study videos, and the textbook itself) for material they need to review further. Students assess exactly what they need to know to succeed. An e-book is included!

InfoTrac® College Edition
Keywords: college + sexual, sexual orientation

Chapter 7: Choosing a Marriage Partner

Class Preparation / Lecture Tools

Instructor's Manual with Test Bank
Contains lecture outlines, suggestions for class discussions, films and videos, chapter worksheets, and more for Chapter 7

Multimedia Manager Instructor's Resource CD-ROM
Allows you to create a media lecture for Chapter 7 using this Microsoft® PowerPoint® tool

Wadsworth's Sociology Video Library
Select a full-length video from the collection of *Films for the Humanities*

Marriage & Family Transparency Masters 2006
A selection of quality transparencies from Wadsworth's texts

CNN® Today Videos
Marriage and Family Vol. V:
"The Dating Class" (2:20);
"Internet Dating" (2:13)

Testing Tools / Course Management

ExamView

ExamView®
Computerized version of the Test Bank items for Chapter 7

WebTutor™ ToolBox

WebTutor™ Toolbox
Online course management tool for WebCT® or Blackboard® preloaded with text-specific content and media resources for Chapter 7

Marriage & Family Now™

This program is ready for your students to use without your help. Or, you can choose to incorporate the course management features of the platform to better administer your class and save yourself and your students valuable time. Assign a *Pre-Test* and/or *Post-Test* and students' scores flow into the grade book. The program can be integrated with both WebCT® and Blackboard® course management platforms.

Student Mastery / Homework and Tutorials / Beyond the Book

WebTutor™ Toolbox
Online course management tool for WebCT® or Blackboard® preloaded with text-specific content and media resources for Chapter 7

Study Guide
Chapter 7 includes a chapter summary, learning objectives, key terms, Internet and **InfoTrac® College Edition** exercises, and practice tests with multiple choice, true/false, short answer, and essay questions.

Book Companion Website
http://sociology.wadsworth.com/
lamanna_riedmann9e/
Online quizzes, web links, and more for Chapter 7

Marriage & Family Now™

An online diagnostic study tool. Students take a *Pre-Test* and receive a *Personalized Study Plan*. Using their *Study Plan*, students can link to helpful resources (lecture outlines, study videos, and the textbook itself) for material they need to review further. Students assess exactly what they need to know to succeed. An e-book is included!

InfoTrac® College Edition
Keywords: mate selection, interracial marriage

Chapter 8: Marriage, a Private and Public Relationship

Class Preparation / Lecture Tools

Instructor's Manual with Test Bank
Contains lecture outlines, suggestions for class discussions, films and videos, chapter worksheets, and more for Chapter 8

Multimedia Manager Instructor's Resource CD-ROM
Allows you to create a media lecture for Chapter 8 using this Microsoft® PowerPoint® tool

Wadsworth's Sociology Video Library
Select a full-length video from the collection of *Films for the Humanities:*
"Abortion and Divorce in Western Law"

Marriage & Family Transparency Masters 2006
A selection of quality transparencies from Wadsworth's texts

CNN® Today Videos
Marriage and Family Vol. V:
"Should the Government Encourage Marriage?" (3:15)

Testing Tools / Course Management

ExamView

ExamView®
Computerized version of the Test Bank items for Chapter 8

WebTutor™ ToolBox

WebTutor™ Toolbox
Online course management tool for WebCT® or Blackboard® preloaded with text-specific content and media resources for Chapter 8

Marriage & Family Now™

This program is ready for your students to use without your help. Or, you can choose to incorporate the course management features of the platform to better administer your class and save yourself and your students valuable time. Assign a *Pre-Test* and/or *Post-Test* and students' scores flow into the grade book. The program can be integrated with both WebCT® and Blackboard® course management platforms.

Student Mastery / Homework and Tutorials / Beyond the Book

WebTutor™ Toolbox
Online course management tool for WebCT® or Blackboard® preloaded with text-specific content and media resources for Chapter 8

Study Guide
Chapter 8 includes a chapter summary, learning objectives, key terms, Internet and **InfoTrac® College Edition** exercises, and practice tests with multiple choice, true/false, short answer, and essay questions.

Book Companion Website
http://sociology.wadsworth.com/
lamanna_riedmann9e/
Online quizzes, web links, and more for Chapter 8

Marriage & Family Now™

An online diagnostic study tool. Students take a *Pre-Test* and receive a *Personalized Study Plan*. Using their *Study Plan*, students can link to helpful resources (lecture outlines, study videos, and the textbook itself) for material they need to review further. Students assess exactly what they need to know to succeed. An e-book is included!

InfoTrac® College Edition
Keywords: sexual infidelity, gay marriage, martial satisfaction

Resource Integration Guide

11

Chapter 9: Alternatives to Marriage: Living Alone, Cohabitation, Domestic Partnerships, and Other Options

Class Preparation / Lecture Tools

Instructor's Manual with Test Bank
Contains lecture outlines, suggestions for class discussions, films and videos, chapter worksheets, and more for Chapter 9

Multimedia Manager Instructor's Resource CD-ROM
Allows you to create a media lecture for Chapter 9 using this Microsoft® PowerPoint® tool

Wadsworth's Sociology Video Library
Select a full-length video from the collection of *Films for the Humanities*

Marriage & Family Transparency Masters 2006
A selection of quality transparencies from Wadsworth's texts

CNN® Today Videos
Marriage and Family Vol. VI: "Same-Sex Marriage in Canada" (2:26)

Testing Tools / Course Management

ExamView

ExamView®
Computerized version of the Test Bank items for Chapter 9

WebTUTOR ToolBox

WebTutor™ Toolbox
Online course management tool for WebCT® or Blackboard® preloaded with text-specific content and media resources for Chapter 9

Marriage & Family Now™
This program is ready for your students to use without your help. Or, you can choose to incorporate the course management features of the platform to better administer your class and save yourself and your students valuable time. Assign a *Pre-Test* and/or *Post-Test* and students' scores flow into the grade book. The program can be integrated with both WebCT® and Blackboard® course management platforms.

Student Mastery / Homework and Tutorials / Beyond the Book

WebTutor™ Toolbox — WebTUTOR ToolBox
Online course management tool for WebCT® or Blackboard® preloaded with text-specific content and media resources for Chapter 9

Study Guide
Chapter 9 includes a chapter summary, learning objectives, key terms, Internet and **InfoTrac® College Edition** exercises, and practice tests with multiple choice, true/false, short answer, and essay questions.

Book Companion Website
http://sociology.wadsworth.com/lamanna_riedmann9e/
Online quizzes, web links, and more for Chapter 9

Marriage & Family Now™
An online diagnostic study tool. Students take a *Pre-Test* and receive a *Personalized Study Plan.* Using their *Study Plan,* students can link to helpful resources (lecture outlines, study videos, and the textbook itself) for material they need to review further. Students assess exactly what they need to know to succeed. An e-book is included!

InfoTrac® College Edition
Keywords: cohabitation, domestic partner

Chapter 10: To Parent or Not to Parent

Class Preparation / Lecture Tools

Instructor's Manual with Test Bank
Contains lecture outlines, suggestions for class discussions, films and videos, chapter worksheets, and more for Chapter 10

Multimedia Manager Instructor's Resource CD-ROM
Allows you to create a media lecture for Chapter 10 using this Microsoft® PowerPoint® tool

Wadsworth's Sociology Video Library
Select a full-length video from the collection of *Films for the Humanities*

Marriage & Family Transparency Masters 2006
A selection of quality transparencies from Wadsworth's texts

CNN® Today Videos
Marriage and Family Vol. V: "Adopting a Foster Child" (2:32); "Gay Parenting and In Vitro Fertilization" (2:44)

Testing Tools / Course Management

ExamView

ExamView®
Computerized version of the Test Bank items for Chapter 10

WebTUTOR ToolBox

WebTutor™ Toolbox
Online course management tool for WebCT® or Blackboard® preloaded with text-specific content and media resources for Chapter 10

Marriage & Family Now™
This program is ready for your students to use without your help. Or, you can choose to incorporate the course management features of the platform to better administer your class and save yourself and your students valuable time. Assign a *Pre-Test* and/or *Post-Test* and students' scores flow into the grade book. The program can be integrated with both WebCT® and Blackboard® course management platforms.

Student Mastery / Homework and Tutorials / Beyond the Book

WebTutor™ Toolbox — WebTUTOR ToolBox
Online course management tool for WebCT® or Blackboard® preloaded with text-specific content and media resources for Chapter 10

Study Guide
Chapter 10 includes a chapter summary, learning objectives, key terms, Internet and **InfoTrac® College Edition** exercises, and practice tests with multiple choice, true/false, short answer, and essay questions.

Book Companion Website
http://sociology.wadsworth.com/lamanna_riedmann9e/
Online quizzes, web links, and more for Chapter 10

Marriage & Family Now™
An online diagnostic study tool. Students take a *Pre-Test* and receive a *Personalized Study Plan.* Using their *Study Plan,* students can link to helpful resources (lecture outlines, study videos, and the textbook itself) for material they need to review further. Students assess exactly what they need to know to succeed. An e-book is included!

InfoTrac® College Edition
Keywords: multiple births, international adoption

Chapter 11: Raising Children in a Diverse and Multicultural Society

Class Preparation / Lecture Tools

Instructor's Manual with Test Bank
Contains lecture outlines, suggestions for class discussions, films and videos, chapter worksheets, and more for Chapter 11

Multimedia Manager Instructor's Resource CD-ROM
Allows you to create a media lecture for Chapter 11 using this Microsoft® PowerPoint® tool

Wadsworth's Sociology Video Library
Select a full-length video from the collection of *Films for the Humanities*.

Marriage & Family Transparency Masters 2006
A selection of quality transparencies from Wadsworth's texts

CNN® Today Videos
Marriage and Family Vol. V:
"Gay and Lesbian Adoption" (2:32)

Testing Tools / Course Management

ExamView®
Computerized version of the Test Bank items for Chapter 11

WebTutor™ Toolbox
Online course management tool for WebCT® or Blackboard® preloaded with text-specific content and media resources for Chapter 11

Marriage & Family Now™
This program is ready for your students to use without your help. Or, you can choose to incorporate the course management features of the platform to better administer your class and save yourself and your students valuable time. Assign a *Pre-Test* and/or *Post-Test* and students' scores flow into the grade book. The program can be integrated with both WebCT® and Blackboard® course management platforms.

Student Mastery / Homework and Tutorials / Beyond the Book

WebTutor™ Toolbox
Online course management tool for WebCT® or Blackboard® preloaded with text-specific content and media resources for Chapter 11

Study Guide
Chapter 11 includes a chapter summary, learning objectives, key terms, Internet and **InfoTrac® College Edition** exercises, and practice tests with multiple choice, true/false, short answer, and essay questions.

Book Companion Website
http://sociology.wadsworth.com/
lamanna_riedmann9e/
Online quizzes, web links, and more for Chapter 11

Marriage & Family Now™
An online diagnostic study tool. Students take a *Pre-Test* and receive a *Personalized Study Plan*. Using their *Study Plan*, students can link to helpful resources (lecture outlines, study videos, and the textbook itself) for material they need to review further. Students assess exactly what they need to know to succeed. An e-book is included!

InfoTrac® College Edition
Keywords: authoritative parenting, foster parents, child development

---

Chapter 12: Work and Family

Class Preparation / Lecture Tools

Instructor's Manual with Test Bank
Contains lecture outlines, suggestions for class discussions, films and videos, chapter worksheets, and more for Chapter 12

Multimedia Manager Instructor's Resource CD-ROM
Allows you to create a media lecture for Chapter 12 using this Microsoft® PowerPoint® tool

Wadsworth's Sociology Video Library
Select a full-length video from the collection of *Films for the Humanities:*
"Problems of Working Women"

Marriage & Family Transparency Masters 2006
A selection of quality transparencies from Wadsworth's texts

CNN® Today Videos
Marriage and Family Vol. VI:
"Stay-at-Home Dads" (3:48);
"Family-Friendly Employment" (1:37)

Testing Tools / Course Management

ExamView®
Computerized version of the Test Bank items for Chapter 12

WebTutor™ Toolbox
Online course management tool for WebCT® or Blackboard® preloaded with text-specific content and media resources for Chapter 12

Marriage & Family Now™
This program is ready for your students to use without your help. Or, you can choose to incorporate the course management features of the platform to better administer your class and save yourself and your students valuable time. Assign a *Pre-Test* and/or *Post-Test* and students' scores flow into the grade book. The program can be integrated with both WebCT® and Blackboard® course management platforms.

Student Mastery / Homework and Tutorials / Beyond the Book

WebTutor™ Toolbox
Online course management tool for WebCT® or Blackboard® preloaded with text-specific content and media resources for Chapter 12

Study Guide
Chapter 12 includes a chapter summary, learning objectives, key terms, Internet and **InfoTrac® College Edition** exercises, and practice tests with multiple choice, true/false, short answer, and essay questions.

Book Companion Website
http://sociology.wadsworth.com/
lamanna_riedmann9e/
Online quizzes, web links, and more for Chapter 12

Marriage & Family Now™
An online diagnostic study tool. Students take a *Pre-Test* and receive a *Personalized Study Plan*. Using their *Study Plan*, students can link to helpful resources (lecture outlines, study videos, and the textbook itself) for material they need to review further. Students assess exactly what they need to know to succeed. An e-book is included!

InfoTrac® College Edition
Keywords: family + time, children's household work

Resource Integration Guide

Chapter 13: Communication and Managing Conflict in Marriages and Families

Class Preparation / Lecture Tools	Testing Tools / Course Management	Student Mastery / Homework and Tutorials / Beyond the Book

Instructor's Manual with Test Bank
Contains lecture outlines, suggestions for class discussions, films and videos, chapter worksheets, and more for Chapter 13

Multimedia Manager Instructor's Resource CD-ROM
Allows you to create a media lecture for Chapter 13 using this Microsoft® PowerPoint® tool

Wadsworth's Sociology Video Library
Select a full-length video from the collection of *Films for the Humanities*

Marriage & Family Transparency Masters 2006
A selection of quality transparencies from Wadsworth's texts

CNN® Today Videos
Marriage and Family Vols. V–VII

ExamView

ExamView®
Computerized version of the Test Bank items for Chapter 13

WebTUTOR ToolBox

WebTutor™ Toolbox
Online course management tool for WebCT® or Blackboard® preloaded with text-specific content and media resources for Chapter 13

Marriage & Family ® Now™
This program is ready for your students to use without your help. Or, you can choose to incorporate the course management features of the platform to better administer your class and save yourself and your students valuable time. Assign a *Pre-Test* and/or *Post-Test* and students' scores flow into the grade book. The program can be integrated with both WebCT® and Blackboard® course management platforms.

WebTutor™ Toolbox WebTUTOR ToolBox
Online course management tool for WebCT® or Blackboard® preloaded with text-specific content and media resources for Chapter 13

Study Guide
Chapter 13 includes a chapter summary, learning objectives, key terms, Internet and **InfoTrac® College Edition** exercises, and practice tests with multiple choice, true/false, short answer, and essay questions.

Book Companion Website
http://sociology.wadsworth.com/
lamanna_riedmann9e/
Online quizzes, web links, and more for Chapter 13

Marriage & Family ® Now™
An online diagnostic study tool. Students take a *Pre-Test* and receive a *Personalized Study Plan.* Using their *Study Plan,* students can link to helpful resources (lecture outlines, study videos, and the textbook itself) for material they need to review further. Students assess exactly what they need to know to succeed. An e-book is included!

InfoTrac® College Edition
Keywords: marital satisfaction, couple communication

Chapter 14: Power and Violence in Marriages and Families

Class Preparation / Lecture Tools	Testing Tools / Course Management	Student Mastery / Homework and Tutorials / Beyond the Book

Instructor's Manual with Test Bank
Contains lecture outlines, suggestions for class discussions, films and videos, chapter worksheets, and more for Chapter 14

Multimedia Manager Instructor's Resource CD-ROM
Allows you to create a media lecture for Chapter 14 using this Microsoft® PowerPoint® tool

Wadsworth's Sociology Video Library
Select a full-length video from the collection of *Films for the Humanities*

Marriage & Family Transparency Masters 2006
A selection of quality transparencies from Wadsworth's texts

CNN® Today Videos
Marriage and Family Vol. V:
"Same-Sex Spousal Abuse" (2:13)

ExamView

ExamView®
Computerized version of the Test Bank items for Chapter 14

WebTUTOR ToolBox

WebTutor™ Toolbox
Online course management tool for WebCT® or Blackboard® preloaded with text-specific content and media resources for Chapter 14

Marriage & Family ® Now™
This program is ready for your students to use without your help. Or, you can choose to incorporate the course management features of the platform to better administer your class and save yourself and your students valuable time. Assign a *Pre-Test* and/or *Post-Test* and students' scores flow into the grade book. The program can be integrated with both WebCT® and Blackboard® course management platforms.

WebTutor™ Toolbox WebTUTOR ToolBox
Online course management tool for WebCT® or Blackboard® preloaded with text-specific content and media resources for Chapter 14

Study Guide
Chapter 14 includes a chapter summary, learning objectives, key terms, Internet and **InfoTrac® College Edition** exercises, and practice tests with multiple choice, true/false, short answer, and essay questions.

Book Companion Website
http://sociology.wadsworth.com/
lamanna_riedmann9e/
Online quizzes, web links, and more for Chapter 14

Marriage & Family ® Now™
An online diagnostic study tool. Students take a *Pre-Test* and receive a *Personalized Study Plan.* Using their *Study Plan,* students can link to helpful resources (lecture outlines, study videos, and the textbook itself) for material they need to review further. Students assess exactly what they need to know to succeed. An e-book is included!

InfoTrac® College Edition
Keywords: dating violence, sibling violence

Chapter 15: Family Stress, Crises, and Resilience

Class Preparation / Lecture Tools	Testing Tools / Course Management	Student Mastery / Homework and Tutorials / Beyond the Book

Class Preparation / Lecture Tools

Instructor's Manual with Test Bank
Contains lecture outlines, suggestions for class discussions, films and videos, chapter worksheets, and more for Chapter 15

Multimedia Manager Instructor's Resource CD-ROM
Allows you to create a media lecture for Chapter 15 using this Microsoft® PowerPoint® tool

Wadsworth's Sociology Video Library
Select a full-length video from the collection of *Films for the Humanities:* "Addiction: The Family in Crisis"

Marriage & Family Transparency Masters 2006
A selection of quality transparencies from Wadsworth's texts

CNN® Today Videos
Marriage and Family Vols. V–VII

Testing Tools / Course Management

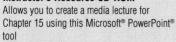
ExamView®
Computerized version of the Test Bank items for Chapter 15

WebTUTOR™ ToolBox
WebTutor™ Toolbox
Online course management tool for WebCT® or Blackboard® preloaded with text-specific content and media resources for Chapter 115

Marriage & Family ® Now™

This program is ready for your students to use without your help. Or, you can choose to incorporate the course management features of the platform to better administer your class and save yourself and your students valuable time. Assign a *Pre-Test* and/or *Post-Test* and students' scores flow into the grade book. The program can be integrated with both WebCT® and Blackboard® course management platforms.

Student Mastery / Homework and Tutorials / Beyond the Book

WebTutor™ Toolbox WebTUTOR™ ToolBox
Online course management tool for WebCT® or Blackboard® preloaded with text-specific content and media resources for Chapter 15

Study Guide
Chapter 15 includes a chapter summary, learning objectives, key terms, Internet and **InfoTrac® College Edition** exercises, and practice tests with multiple choice, true/false, short answer, and essay questions.

Book Companion Website
http://sociology.wadsworth.com/ lamanna_riedmann9e/
Online quizzes, web links, and more for Chapter 15

Marriage & Family ® Now™

An online diagnostic study tool. Students take a *Pre-Test* and receive a *Personalized Study Plan.* Using their *Study Plan,* students can link to helpful resources (lecture outlines, study videos, and the textbook itself) for material they need to review further. Students assess exactly what they need to know to succeed. An e-book is included!

InfoTrac® College Edition
Keywords: family stress, resilient family, vulnerable family

Chapter 16: Divorce: Before and After

Class Preparation / Lecture Tools	Testing Tools / Course Management	Student Mastery / Homework and Tutorials / Beyond the Book

Class Preparation / Lecture Tools

Instructor's Manual with Test Bank
Contains lecture outlines, suggestions for class discussions, films and videos, chapter worksheets, and more for Chapter 16

Multimedia Manager Instructor's Resource CD-ROM
Allows you to create a media lecture for Chapter 16 using this Microsoft® PowerPoint® tool

Wadsworth's Sociology Video Library
Select a full-length video from the collection of *Films for the Humanities:* "Children of Divorce"

Marriage & Family Transparency Masters 2006
A selection of quality transparencies from Wadsworth's texts

CNN® Today Videos
Marriage and Family Vol. V: "Divorce in the US" (2:20); "Renegotiating Your Divorce" (2:03)

Testing Tools / Course Management

ExamView®
Computerized version of the Test Bank items for Chapter 16

WebTUTOR™ ToolBox
WebTutor™ Toolbox
Online course management tool for WebCT® or Blackboard® preloaded with text-specific content and media resources for Chapter 16

Marriage & Family ® Now™

This program is ready for your students to use without your help. Or, you can choose to incorporate the course management features of the platform to better administer your class and save yourself and your students valuable time. Assign a *Pre-Test* and/or *Post-Test* and students' scores flow into the grade book. The program can be integrated with both WebCT® and Blackboard® course management platforms.

Student Mastery / Homework and Tutorials / Beyond the Book

WebTutor™ Toolbox WebTUTOR™ ToolBox
Online course management tool for WebCT® or Blackboard® preloaded with text-specific content and media resources for Chapter 16

Study Guide
Chapter 16 includes a chapter summary, learning objectives, key terms, Internet and **InfoTrac® College Edition** exercises, and practice tests with multiple choice, true/false, short answer, and essay questions.

Book Companion Website
http://sociology.wadsworth.com/ lamanna_riedmann9e/
Online quizzes, web links, and more for Chapter 16

Marriage & Family ® Now™

An online diagnostic study tool. Students take a *Pre-Test* and receive a *Personalized Study Plan.* Using their *Study Plan,* students can link to helpful resources (lecture outlines, study videos, and the textbook itself) for material they need to review further. Students assess exactly what they need to know to succeed. An e-book is included!

InfoTrac® College Edition
Keywords: joint custody, same-sex partners, separation, divorce, custody or visitation

Resource Integration Guide

Chapter 17: Remarriages and Stepfamilies

Class Preparation / Lecture Tools

Instructor's Manual with Test Bank
Contains lecture outlines, suggestions for class discussions, films and videos, chapter worksheets, and more for Chapter 17

Multimedia Manager Instructor's Resource CD-ROM
Allows you to create a media lecture for Chapter 17 using this Microsoft® PowerPoint® tool

Wadsworth's Sociology Video Library
Select a full-length video from the collection of *Films for the Humanities*

Marriage & Family Transparency Masters 2006
A selection of quality transparencies from Wadsworth's texts

CNN® Today Videos
Marriage and Family Vols. V–VII

Testing Tools / Course Management

ExamView

ExamView®
Computerized version of the Test Bank items for Chapter 17

WebTUTOR ToolBox

WebTutor™ Toolbox
Online course management tool for WebCT® or Blackboard® preloaded with text-specific content and media resources for Chapter 17

Marriage & Family ⊛ Now™
This program is ready for your students to use without your help. Or, you can choose to incorporate the course management features of the platform to better administer your class and save yourself and your students valuable time. Assign a *Pre-Test* and/or *Post-Test* and students' scores flow into the grade book. The program can be integrated with both WebCT® and Blackboard® course management platforms.

Student Mastery / Homework and Tutorials / Beyond the Book

WebTutor™ Toolbox WebTUTOR ToolBox
Online course management tool for WebCT® or Blackboard® preloaded with text-specific content and media resources for Chapter 17

Study Guide
Chapter 17 includes a chapter summary, learning objectives, key terms, Internet and **InfoTrac® College Edition** exercises, and practice tests with multiple choice, true/false, short answer, and essay questions.

Book Companion Website
http://sociology.wadsworth.com/
lamanna_riedmann9e/
Online quizzes, web links, and more for Chapter 17

Marriage & Family ⊛ Now™
An online diagnostic study tool. Students take a *Pre-Test* and receive a *Personalized Study Plan.* Using their *Study Plan,* students can link to helpful resources (lecture outlines, study videos, and the textbook itself) for material they need to review further. Students assess exactly what they need to know to succeed. An e-book is included!

InfoTrac® College Edition
Keywords: remarriage, stepfamily

Chapter 18: Aging Families

Class Preparation / Lecture Tools

Instructor's Manual with Test Bank
Contains lecture outlines, suggestions for class discussions, films and videos, chapter worksheets, and more for Chapter 18

Multimedia Manager Instructor's Resource CD-ROM
Allows you to create a media lecture for Chapter 18 using this Microsoft® PowerPoint® tool

Wadsworth's Sociology Video Library
Select a full-length video from the collection of *Films for the Humanities:*
"The Sandwich Generation: Caring for Both Children and Parents"

Marriage & Family Transparency Masters 2006
A selection of quality transparencies from Wadsworth's texts

CNN® Today Videos
Marriage and Family Vol. V:
"Sex Over 45" (2:02); Vol. VII:
"Dad's Biological Clock" (1:29)

Testing Tools / Course Management

ExamView

ExamView®
Computerized version of the Test Bank items for Chapter 18

WebTUTOR ToolBox

WebTutor™ Toolbox
Online course management tool for WebCT® or Blackboard® preloaded with text-specific content and media resources for Chapter 18

Marriage & Family ⊛ Now™
This program is ready for your students to use without your help. Or, you can choose to incorporate the course management features of the platform to better administer your class and save yourself and your students valuable time. Assign a *Pre-Test* and/or *Post-Test* and students' scores flow into the grade book. The program can be integrated with both WebCT® and Blackboard® course management platforms.

Student Mastery / Homework and Tutorials / Beyond the Book

WebTutor™ Toolbox WebTUTOR ToolBox
Online course management tool for WebCT® or Blackboard® preloaded with text-specific content and media resources for Chapter 18

Study Guide
Chapter 18 includes a chapter summary, learning objectives, key terms, Internet and **InfoTrac® College Edition** exercises, and practice tests with multiple choice, true/false, short answer, and essay questions.

Book Companion Website
http://sociology.wadsworth.com/
lamanna_riedmann9e/
Online quizzes, web links, and more for Chapter 18

Marriage & Family ⊛ Now™
An online diagnostic study tool. Students take a *Pre-Test* and receive a *Personalized Study Plan.* Using their *Study Plan,* students can link to helpful resources (lecture outlines, study videos, and the textbook itself) for material they need to review further. Students assess exactly what they need to know to succeed. An e-book is included!

InfoTrac® College Edition
Keywords: aging family, elderly caregiving

www.wadsworth.com

www.wadsworth.com is the World Wide Web site for Thomson Wadsworth and is your direct source to dozens of online resources.

At *www.wadsworth.com* you can find out about supplements, demonstration software, and student resources. You can also send e-mail to many of our authors and preview new publications and exciting new technologies.

www.wadsworth.com
Changing the way the world learns®

Marriages
& Families

MAKING CHOICES IN A DIVERSE SOCIETY

Ninth Edition

Mary Ann Lamanna
Emerita, University of Nebraska, Omaha

Agnes Riedmann
California State University, Stanislaus

THOMSON
WADSWORTH

Australia • Brazil • Canada • Mexico • Singapore • Spain
United Kingdom • United States

THOMSON

WADSWORTH

Marriages & Families: Making Choices in a Diverse Society, Ninth Edition

Mary Ann Lamanna and Agnes Riedmann

Sociology Editor: Robert Jucha
Development Editor: Sherry Symington
Assistant Editor: Elise Smith
Editorial Assistant: Christina Cha
Technology Project Manager: Dee Dee Zobian
Marketing Manager: Wendy Gordon
Marketing Assistant: Gregory Hughes
Marketing Communications Manager: Linda Yip
Project Manager, Editorial Production: Cheri Palmer
Creative Director: Rob Hugel
Print Buyer: Rebecca Cross

Permissions Editor: Joohee Lee
Production Service: Kathy Glidden, Stratford Publishing Services
Text Designer: Lisa Buckley
Photo Researcher: Terri Wright
Copy Editor: Karen Hansen
Illustrator: Judy Wingerter
Cover Designer: Yvo Riezebos
Cover Image: Myrleen Ferguson Cate / PhotoEdit
Cover Printer: Phoenix Color Corp
Compositor: Stratford Publishing Services
Printer: R.R. Donnelley/Willard

Printed in the United States of America
1 2 3 4 5 6 7 09 08 07 06 05

Thomson Higher Education
10 Davis Drive
Belmont, CA 94002-3098
USA

Library of Congress Control Number: 2005922106

Student Edition: ISBN 0-534-61859-6

DEDICATION

To our families, especially
Bill, Beth, Angel, Chris, Natalie, Alex, and Livia
Larry, Valerie, Sam, Janice, Simon, and Christie

About *the* Authors

Mary Ann Lamanna is Professor Emerita of Sociology at the University of Nebraska at Omaha. She received her bachelor's degree Phi Beta Kappa from Washington University (St. Louis) in political science, her master's degree in sociology (minor in psychology) from the University of North Carolina, Chapel Hill, and her doctorate in sociology from the University of Notre Dame.

Her teaching areas are family and gender, especially law and policy in those areas, and also population and social psychology. Research interests include family, reproduction, and gender and the law. In addition to this textbook, she has written *Emile Durkheim on the Family* (Sage 2002) and has articles in law, sociology, and medical humanities journals. Current research concerns the sociology of literature, specifically "novels of terrorism" and a sociological analysis of Marcel Proust's great novel *In Search of Lost Time*.

Professor Lamanna has two adult children, Larry and Valerie.

Agnes Riedmann is Professor of Sociology at California State University, Stanislaus. She attended Clarke College, Dubuque. She received her bachelor's degree from Creighton University and her doctorate from the University of Nebraska. Her professional areas of interest are theory and family. She is author of *Science that Colonizes: A Critique of Fertility Studies in Africa* (Temple University Press, 1993). Current research projects concern the sociology of demography and comparative family sociology. Dr. Riedmann has two children, Beth and Bill; two granddaughters, Natalie and Livia; and a grandson, Alex.

Brief Contents

Detailed Contents

How to Find the Appendices

The following appendices are available in full color on the Ninth Edition's book companion site at **http://sociology.wadsworth.com/lamanna_riedmann9e/**. To access the appendices, click on "Appendices" from the left navigation bar.

Appendix A	Human Sexual Anatomy
Appendix B	Human Sexual Response
Appendix C	Sexually Transmitted Diseases
Appendix D	Sexual Dysfunctions and Therapy
Appendix E	Conception, Pregnancy, and Childbirth
Appendix F	Contraceptive Techniques
Appendix G	High-Tech Fertility
Appendix H	Marriage and Close Relationship Counseling
Appendix I	Managing a Family Budget

Preface

As we complete our work on the ninth edition of *Marriages and Families*, we look back over eight earlier editions. Together, these represent over twenty-five years spent observing the contemporary American family. Not only has the family changed during this time, but so has social science's interpretation of it. It is gratifying to be a part of the enterprise of learning about the family and to share that knowledge with students.

Our own perspective on the family has developed and changed during this period. We have studied demography and history, and we have come to pay more attention to social structure in our analysis. In recent editions and in response to our reviewers, we have given more attention to the contributions of psychology, to the understanding of family interaction and its consequences, and to the analysis of gender. We have recognized the growing interest in biosocial perspectives. We have highlighted the family ecology perspective in keeping with the importance of social context and public policy. And we cannot help but be aware of the cultural and political tensions surrounding the family today.

We continue to affirm the power of families to direct the courses of their lives. But the American social milieu seems less unqualifiedly optimistic today than it did when we began this book. Consequently, we now give more attention to policies needed to provide support for today's families: working parents, families in poverty, single-parent families, families of varied racial/ethnic backgrounds, remarried families, same-sex couples, and other nontraditional families—as well as the classic nuclear family with one employed parent (not an easy choice today). Virtually all families need social policy support.

At the same time, a degree of stability has settled on the family. Divorce rates have stabilized and teen birth rates have declined dramatically. Couples seem to have adjusted to changing gender roles and have made individual accomodations to work-family strains despite weak institutional support.

Marriage and family values continue to be important in contemporary American life. Our students come to a marriage and family course because family life is important to them. Our aim now, as it was in the first edition, is to help students question assumptions and to reconcile conflicting ideas and values as they make choices throughout their lives. We enjoy and benefit from the contact we've had with faculty and students who have used this book. Their enthusiasm and criticism have stimulated many changes in the book's content. To know that a supportive audience is interested in our approach to the study of the family has enabled us to continue our work over a long period of time.

▪ The Book's Themes ▪

Several themes are interwoven throughout this text: people are influenced by the society around them as they make choices, social conditions change in ways that may impede or support family life, there is an interplay between individual families and the larger society, and individuals make family-related choices throughout adulthood.

Making Choices Throughout Life

The process of creating and maintaining marriages and families requires many personal choices, and people continue to make decisions, even "big" ones, throughout their lives.

Personal Choice and Social Life

Tension frequently exists between the individual and the social environment. Many personal troubles result from societal influences, values, or assumptions: inadequate societal support for family goals, and conflict between family values and individual values. By understanding some of these possible sources of tension and conflict, individuals can perceive their personal troubles more clearly and work constructively toward solutions. They may choose to form or join groups to achieve family goals. They may become involved in the political process to develop state or federal social policy supportive of the family. The accumulated decisions of individuals and families may also shape the social environment.

A Changing Society

In the past, people tended to emphasize the dutiful performance of social roles in marriage and in the family structure. Today, people are more apt to view marriages as committed relationships in which they expect to find companionship, intimacy, and support and often to become parents and share the responsibilities of rearing children. This book examines the implications of this shift in perspective. Individualism, economic pressure, time pressures, social diversity, and and an awareness of the risk of marital impermanence are features of the social context in which personal decision making takes place today. As fewer social guidelines seem fixed, personal decision making becomes even more challenging.

The Themes Throughout the Life Course

The book's themes are introduced in Chapter 1, and they reappear throughout the text. We developed these themes by looking at the interplay between findings in the social sciences and the experiences of the people around us. Ideas for topics arose from the needs and concerns we perceived. We observed many changes in the roles people play and in the ways they relate to one another. Neither the "old" nor the "new" roles and relationships seemed to us as stereotyped or as free of ambivalence and conflict as is often indicated in books and articles. The attitudes, behavior, and relationships of real people have a complexity that we have tried to portray in this book. Interwoven with these themes is the concept of the life course—the idea that adults may change through reevaluation and restructuring throughout their lives. This emphasis on the life course creates a comprehensive picture of marriages and families and enables us to cover topics that are new to marriage and family texts. This book makes these points:

- People's personal problems and their interaction with the social environment change as they and their marriages and families grow older.
- People reexamine their relationships and their expectations for relationships as they and their marriages and families mature.
- Because marriage and family forms are more flexible today, people may change the style of their marriages and families throughout their lives.

Marriages and Families Making Choices

Making decisions about one's marriage and family, either knowledgeably or by default, begins in early adulthood and lasts into old age. People choose whether they will adhere to traditional beliefs, values, and attitudes about gender roles or will adopt more flexible roles and relationships. They may rethink their values about sex and become more knowledgeable and comfortable with their sexual choices.

Women and men may choose to remain single or to marry, and they have the option today of staying single longer before marrying. Single people make choices about their lives ranging from decisions to engage in sex only in marriage or committed relationships, to engage in sex for recreation, or to abstain from sex altogether. In the courtship process, people choose between the more formal customs of dating and the less formal "getting together."

Once individuals choose their partners, they have to decide how they are going to structure their marriages and families. Will the partners be legally married? Will theirs be a dual-career marriage? Will they plan periods in which just the husband or just the wife works interspersed with times in which both work? Will they have children? Will they use the new reproductive technology to become parents? Will other family members live with them—parents, for example?

They will make these decisions not once, but over and over during their lifetimes. Within a marital or other couple relationship, partners choose how they will deal with conflict. Will they try to ignore conflicts and risk the prospect of devitalized relationships? Will they vent their anger in hostile, alienating, or physically violent ways? Or will they practice bonding ways of communicating and fighting—ways that emphasize sharing and can deepen intimacy?

How will the partners distribute power in the marriage? Will they work toward a no-power relationship, in which the individual is more concerned with helping and supporting the other than with gaining a power advantage? How will the partners allocate work responsibilities in the home? What value will they place on their sexual lives together? Throughout their experience, family members continually face decisions about how to balance each one's need for individuality with the need for togetherness.

Parents also have choices. In raising their children, they can choose the authoritative parenting style, for example, in which parents define themselves as having more experience than their youngsters and take an active role in responsibly guiding and monitoring their children, while simultaneouly striving to develop supportive, mutually cooperative family relationships.

Many spouses face decisions about whether to divorce. They weigh the pros and cons, asking themselves which is the better alternative: living together as they are or separating? Even when a couple decides to divorce, there are choices to make, whether consciously or not: Will they try to cooperate as much as possible or insist on blame and revenge? What living and economic support arrangements will work best for themselves and their children? How will they handle the legal process? The majority of divorced individuals eventually face decisions about remarriage. In the absence of cultural models, they choose how they will define step-relationships.

Then, too, as more and more Americans live longer, families will "age." As a result, more and more Americans face issues concerning giving—and receiving—family eldercare. When families encounter crises—and every family will face *some* crises—members must make additional decisions. Will they view each crisis as a challenge to be met, or will they blame one another? What resources can they use to handle the crisis?

An emphasis on knowledgeable decision making does not mean that individuals can completely control their lives. People can influence but never directly determine how those around them behave or feel about them. Partners cannot control one another's changes over time, and they cannot avoid all accidents, illnesses, unemployment, deaths, or even divorce. Society-wide conditions may create unavoidable crises for individual families. However, families *can* control how they respond to such crises. Their responses will meet their own needs better when they refuse to react automatically and choose instead to act as a consequence of knowledgeable decision making.

◾ Key Features ◾

As marriages and families have evolved over the last twenty-five years, so has this text. Its subtitle, *Making Choices in a Diverse Society*, illustrates the vast changes that have taken place over the last decade. With its thorough updating and inclusion of current research, plus its emphasis on students' being able to make choices in an exceedingly diverse society, this book has become an unparalleled resource for gaining insights into today's marriages and families.

Over the past eight editions, we have had three goals in mind for student readers: first, to help them better understand themselves and their family situations; second, to make students more conscious of the personal decisions that they will make throughout their lives and of the societal influences that affect those decisions; third, to help students better appreciate the variety and diversity among families today. To these ends, this text has become recognized for its accessible writing style, up-to-date research, well-written boxed features, and useful chapter learning aids.

Up-to-Date Research and Statistics

As users have come to expect, we have thoroughly updated the text's research base and statistics, emphasizing cutting-edge research that addresses the diversity of marriages and families, as well as all other topics. In accordance with this approach, users will notice many entirely new tables and figures. Revised tables and figures have been updated with the latest available statistics, including data from the U.S. Census Bureau or other governmental agencies, as well as survey and research data.

Boxed Features

The several themes described earlier are reflected in the boxed features.

AS WE MAKE CHOICES. We highlight the theme of making choices with a group of boxes throughout the text, for example, "Ten Rules for a Successful Relationship, "Selecting A Child Care Facility," and "Community Resources for Eldercare." These boxes emphasize human agency and are designed to help students through crucial decisions.

A CLOSER LOOK AT FAMILY DIVERSITY. In order to accomplish our third goal, we have presented the latest research and statistical information on diverse family forms, lesbian and gay male families, and families of diverse race and ethnicity. We have consciously integrated these materials throughout the textbook, always with an eye toward avoiding stereotypical, simplistic generalizations and, instead, explaining data in sociological and sociohistorical context. Besides integrating information on ethnic diversity throughout the text proper, we have a series of boxes titled "A Closer Look at Family Diversity," for example, "Diversity and Child Care" or "Strategies for Dealing with Others' Disapproval When You're in an Interracial Relationship."

CASE STUDIES. Agnes Riedmann talked with individuals of all ages about their experiences in marriages and families. These interviews appear as boxed-feature excerpts, balancing and expanding topics presented in the chapters. Some student essays also appear as case study boxes. We hope that the presentation of these individuals' stories will help students to see their own lives more clearly and will encourage them to discuss and reevaluate their own attitudes and values. An example is one student's essay, titled "My (Step)Family."

ISSUES FOR THOUGHT. These boxes feature research designed to spark students' critical thinking and/or discussion. One box explores "Subcultures with Norms Contrary to Sexual Exclusivity." Additionally, a box on "Meddling with Nature" discusses ethical issues involved in the use of reproductive technology.

FACTS ABOUT FAMILIES. These boxes present demographic and other factual information on focused topics such as family members' time use: "Where Does The Time Go?" Two other examples discuss "Fathers As Primary Parents" and "Remarriage and Race/Ethnic Diversity."

FOCUS ON CHILDREN. A sixth important feature, which is not specifically a box, is called Focus on Children. When you see this icon, you are being alerted to important material related to children. We added this focus for several reasons. First, the amount of news on children's issues, including such things as their abuse and neglect, their living in poverty, and their growing up in neighborhoods plagued by crime, gave rise to concern about the extent to which America's children today are

well nurtured. We wanted to encourage students to examine the condition of children today from a sociological perspective. We continue to hope that, as a consequence, students will be able to make informed decisions now and in the future.

In addition, the sociology of the child has become increasingly important as an area of scholarly interest: hence, we wanted to include additional coverage on children in order to help professors bring more of this material into their courses.

▪ Chapter Learning Aids ▪

We have devised a series of chapter learning aids to help students comprehend and retain the material they read.

- **Chapter opening quotations** set the stage for the material in the chapter. While understandable at first glance, the quotations are designed to gain meaning as students absorb the material presented in the chapter.

- **Footnotes**, although not overused, are presented when we feel that a point needs to be made but might disrupt the flow of the text itself.

- **Chapter Summaries**, called In Sum, have been reformatted into bulleted, point-by-point summaries of the key material in the chapter.

- **Key Terms** alert students to the key concepts presented in the chapter. A full glossary is provided at the end of the text.

- **Questions for Review and Reflection** have been created by the authors to assist students in reviewing the material. Thought questions encourage students to think critically and to integrate material from other chapters with that presented in the current chapter.

- **Suggested Readings** give students ideas for further reading on topics and issues presented in the chapter.

▪ Key Changes in This Edition ▪

This edition includes many key changes, some of which are outlined below.

In the eighth edition, we added two new chapters: Chapter 2, "American Families in Social Context" and a second new chapter, "Aging Families." In the ninth edition we have reconceptualized the chapter on singles. This chapter—Chapter 9 in this edition—is now titled "Alternatives to Marriage: Being Single, Cohabitation, and Domestic Partnerships." We have made this change in response to the transformation of these family forms and alternatives from interesting but infrequent choices to virtually mainstream options.

Meanwhile, we have substantially revised each and every chapter. Every chapter is updated with the latest research throughout. In addition, we mention some (but not all!) specific changes here:

Chapter 1, "Family Commitments: Making Choices in a Changing Society," has a new box discussing "Pets as Family"—*are* they family, or not? The "Facts About Families" box has been updated, with new information on cohabiting families and same-sex partner families. The chapter's discussion of the "politics" of the family—that is conflicting views on structural and cultural changes in the family—is brought up to date. Chapter 1 continues to present the choices and life course themes of the book, as well as pointing to the significance of larger social forces for the family.

Chapter 2, "American Families in Social Context," has a new box on regional differences in family indicators, "The Geography of Families." The chapter includes more on families in diverse racial/ethnic settings, including multicultural families.

Chapter 3, "Exploring the Family," now includes more material on the transition to adulthood and the addition to the family life cycle of an "emerging adulthood" stage. An "Issues for Thought" box addresses "Safety and Risk in the Family Environment," including such topics as the anxiety of today's parents generally, as well as specific concerns about crime and terrorism. Theoretical perspectives are now summarized in a chart of key concepts and research applications.

In Chapter 4, "Our Gendered Identities," the "intersex" movement is discussed in a box on "gender boundaries." Some individuals are born with characteristics of both sexes, while others consciously choose to change their sexual and gender identity. Chapter 4 includes an updated discussion of the women's and men's movements, which have undergone considerable change and development since their inception.

Chapter 5, "Loving Ourselves and Others," is updated throughout with increased sensitivity to our discussion of the concept, *self-esteem*. In light of the controversy surrounding that concept, we have chosen instead to speak of "self worth."

Chapter 6, "Our Sexual Selves," presents new developments in research and policy on adolescent sexuality and sex education. The section on AIDS has been shortened, with the demographics of AIDS placed into a "Facts about Families: Who Has HIV/AIDS" box, improving the flow of the chapter and its focus on family relations.

Chapter 7, "Choosing a Marriage Partner," features a shortened discussion of the traditional exchange and more material on bargaining in a changing society. This chapter has new sections on the intergenerational transmission of divorce risk and on minimizing the potentially negative impact that mate selection can have on marital happiness and longevity.

Chapter 8, "Marriage, A Private and Public Relationship," has an up-to-date discussion of the legalization of marriage for same-sex couples.

Chapter 9, "Alternatives to Marriage: Living Alone, Cohabition, Domestic Partnerships, and Other Options," has been reframed from a discussion of being single to highlight the concept of *continuum of attachment*. Now, coupled alternatives to marriage are consciously discussed as such.

Chapter 10, "To Parent or Not To Parent," (formerly Chapter 12) has been much revised to incorporate new developments and trends. Two theoretical perspectives on motivation for parenthood are introduced; the *value of children perspective* and the *social capital perspective*. Some sections have been reorganized: "Remaining Childfree" is moved to the major section on "The Decision to Parent or Not to Parent." A new 'Options and Circumstances' section looks at one-child families, postponement of parenthood, nonmarital births, and stepparents' decisions about having children. The nonmarital birth section includes cohabiting parents, teen parents, older mothers, and single-mothers-by-choice.

There is a new box on parents and children in reproductive technology families. And for the first time, census data on adoption is available, so that is included.

Chapter 11, "Raising Children in a Diverse and Multicultural Society" (formerly Chapter 13), has been somewhat reconceptualized. After describing the authoritative parenting style, we note its acceptance by mainstream experts in the parenting field. We then present a critique, that questions whether this parenting style is universally appropriate or whether it is simply a white, middle-class pattern that may not be so suitable to other social contexts.

Chapter 12, "Work and Family" (formerly Chapter 14), includes a new box and a new table on time spent with children and on household chores, and other matters. There is more on "househusbands" and on "sequencing moms," who drop out of the labor force but plan to return when children are older. There is also more on working at home.

The chapter continues to examine the persistence of gender differences in the "second shift" of housework and child care and the wage gap between men and women. We continue to follow the National Institute of Child Health and Human Development study of child care, and consider children's outcomes in an "As We Make Choices" box.

Chapter 13, "Communication and Managing Conflict in Marriages and Families," (formerly Chapter 10) has been somewhat reorganized in order to place greater emphasis on family cohesion as a function of positive couple communication and to offer more on supportive couple communication in general, rather than simply with regard to disagreements or conflict.

Chapter 14, "Power and Violence in Marriages and Families" (formerly Chapter 11), sees a consolidation of the classic research on family power, with a more explicit connection to current research. The future of marital power is considered. The effect of immigration status on family power and violence has received more attention in this edition.

In the section on family violence, the controversial question of gender symmetry in intimate partner violence is considered. There is more material on same-sex partner violence and sibling violence as well.

Chapter 15, "Family Stress, Crises, and Resilience," incorporates the concept of *family resilience* during times of family stress and crisis. Here you will find a new box, "Issues for Thought: Sudden Health: the Experience of Families with a Member Who Has Surgery to Correct Epilepsy."

Chapter 16, "Divorce: Before and After" (formerly Chapter 15), sharpens the contrast in assessments of divorce outcomes made by notable researchers Judith Wallerstein and E. Mavis Hetherington. Marital separation is introduced as a new topic. The issue of parental relocation after divorce has an expanded discussion, with new information on legal

developments and research. There is more on joint custody, noncustodial parents, no-fault divorce, and grandparent visitation rights, and new research on adult children of divorce. The case study, "The Family as a Child-Raising Institution" is moved from Chapter 3 to Chapter 16.

Chapter 17, "Remarriages and Stepfamilies," (formerly Chapter 16) is on remarriages, emphasizing the plural to demonstrate that remarriages are not all alike. We also give greater attention in this edition to the "nuclear-family model monopoly," whereby the cultural assumption is that the first-marriage family is the "real" model for family living, with all other family forms viewed as deficient. As well as being completely updated, this chapter contains a new table (Table 16.2) with data from the National Longitudinal Survey of Youth (NLSY) on children's economic well-being before and after a custodial parent's remarriage.

Chapter 18, "Aging Families," has been updated throughout with the latest research.

All the appendices have been updated. For example, material on sexually transmitted diseases other than AIDS has been expanded in response to reviewers' comments. An updated discussion of birthing looks at the relative merits of the medical and natural childbirth models and the preferences of today's mothers.

▪ Supplements ▪

This new edition is accompanied by a wide array of supplements prepared to create the best learning environment inside as well as outside the classroom for both the instructor and the student. All the continuing supplements for *Marriages and Families: Making Choices in a Diverse Society*, Ninth Edition, have been thoroughly revised and updated, and several are new to this edition.

Supplements for the Instructor

Instructor's Manual with Test Bank. Written by Kenrick S. Thompson, Arkansas State University Mountain Home, this Instructor's Manual with Test Bank offers a wide range of resources to help you teach your course including lecture outlines, classroom discussion and lecture suggestions, student activities, classroom discussion questions, a list of film and video resources, chapter review worksheets, and Internet and InfoTrac® College Edition exercises. The Instructor's Manual also includes 50 to 60 multiple-choice and 15 to 20 true-false questions for each chapter, all with answers and page references. It also includes 10 to 15 completion questions, 3 to 5 short-answer questions, and 3 to 4 essay questions for each chapter.

ExamView Computerized Testing for Macintosh and Windows. Create, deliver, and customize printed and online tests and study guides in minutes with this easy-to-use assessment and tutorial system. ExamView includes a Quick Test Wizard and an Online Test Wizard to guide instructors step by step through the process of creating tests. The test appears onscreen exactly as it will print or display online. Using ExamView's complete word processing capabilities, instructors can enter an unlimited number of new questions or edit questions included with ExamView.

JoinIn™ on TurningPoint®. Transform your lecture into an interactive student experience with *JoinIn*. Combined with your choice of keypad systems, JoinIn turns your Microsoft® PowerPoint® application into audience response software. With a click on a handheld device, students can respond to multiple choice questions, short polls, interactive exercises, and peer review questions. You can also take attendance, check student comprehension of concepts, collect student demographics to better assess student needs, and even administer quizzes. In addition, there are interactive text-specific slide sets that you can modify and merge with any your own PowerPoint lecture slides. This tool is available to qualified adopters at **http://turning-point.thomsonlearningconnections.com**.

Multimedia Manager Instructor Resource CD: A 2005 Microsoft® PowerPoint® Link Tool. With this one-stop digital library and presentation tool, instructors can assemble, edit, and present custom lectures with ease. The MultiMedia Manager contains figures, tables, graphs, and maps from this text, pre-assembled Microsoft PowerPoint lecture slides, video clips from DALLAS TeleLearning, ShowCase presentational software, tips for teaching, the instructor's manual, and more.

Transparency Masters for Marriage and Family 2006, consisting of black-and-white tables and figures from Wadsworth's 2006 Marriage and Family texts is also available to help you prepare your lecture presentations.

CNN Today® Video Series: Marriage and Family, Volumes V-VII. Illustrate the relevance of marriage and family to everyday life with this exclusive series of videos for the Marriage and Family course. Jointly created by Wadsworth and CNN, each video consists of approximately 45 minutes of footage originally broadcast on CNN and specifically selected to illustrate important sociological concepts.

Supplements for the Student

Access to **Marriage & FamilyNow** is web-based and FREE with every new copy of this text—all you need to do is order the access code, and your students are in! This powerful and interactive resource allows students to gauge their own unique study needs by taking a diagnostic text. It then presents a personalized Study Plan that helps them focus their study time on the concepts they most need to master. With the program's unique diagnostic quizzes and study plan, your students will quickly begin to maximize study time and get one step closer to success! Included in the Study Plan is an eBook that links students directly to the material in the chapter where they need further review. Other resources include illustrating videos, lecture slides, web links, and interactive exercises. Instructors can use Marriage&FamilyNow for course management, or they can send students to the program on their own, with no set-up required. Visit **http://sociology.wadsworth.com** to view a brief demonstration.

Study Guide. Written by Kenrick S. Thompson of Arkansas State University Mountian Home, this Study Guide includes a Chapter Summary, Learning Objectives, Key Terms, Key Term completion exercises, Internet and InfoTrac College Edition activities, and Key Theoretical Perspectives for each chapter. The guide also contains practice tests consisting of 10 to 15 true-false questions and 20 to 25 multiple-choice questions, with answers and page references, as well as 3 to 5 short-answer and 3 to 5 essay questions.

Portrait of a Family: Telecourse Guide. Written especially for students who use Lamanna and Riedmann in conjunction with the "Portrait of a Family" telecourse, this study guide is designed to connect the readings and viewing componenets of the course. For each lesson, the guide includes chapter overviews, chapter objectives, key terms, reading assignments, video viewing questions, decision questions, practice tests, and additional learning activities.

Marriage and Family: Using Microcase® ExplorIt®, Third Edition, written by Kevin Demmitt of Clayton College, is a software-based workbook that provides and exciting way to get students to view marriage and family from the sociological perspective. With this workbook and the accompanying ExplorIt software and data sets, your students will use national and cross-national surveys to examine and actively learn marriage and family topics. This inexpensive workbook will add an exciting dimension to your marriage and family course.

Internet-Based Supplements

InfoTrac College Edition. Available as a free option with newly purchased texts, InfoTrac College Edition gives instructors and students four months of free access to an extensive online database of reliable, full-length articles (not just abstracts) from thousands of scholarly and popular publications going back as many as 22 years. Among the journals available 24/7 are *American Journal of Sociology, Social Forces, Social Research,* and *Sociology.* InfoTrac College Edition now also comes with InfoMark™, a tool that allows you to save your search parameters, as well as save links to specific articles. (Available to North American college and university students only; journals are subject to change.)

WebTutor™ Toolbox on Blackboard and WebCT offers web-based software for students and instructors that takes a course beyond the classroom to an anywhere, anytime environment. Students gain access to to the rich content from our book companion websites. Available for WebCT and Blackboard only.

Companion Website for *Marriages and Families: Making Choices in a Diverse Society,* Ninth Edition (http://sociology.wadsworth.com/lamanna _riedmann9e/. The book's companion site includes chapter-specific resources for instructors and students. For instructors, the site offers a password-protected instructor's manual, PowerPoint presentation slides, and more. For students, there is a multitude of text-specific study aids, including the following:

- Tutorial practice quizzes that can be scored and emailed to the instructor
- Web links
- InfoTrac College Edition exercises
- Flash cards

- MicroCase Online data exercises
- Crossword puzzles
- Virtual Explorations
- A GSS Self-Assessment activity
- Self-awareness quizzes

▪ Acknowledgments ▪

This book is a result of a joint effort on our part; neither of us could have conceptualized or written it alone. We want to thank some of the many people who helped us. Looking back on the long life of this book, we acknowledge Steve Rutter for his original vision of the project and his faith in us. We also want to thank Sheryl Fullerton, Serina Beauparlant, and Eve Howard, who saw us through earlier editions as editors and friends.

As has been true of our past editions, the people at Wadsworth Publishing Company have been professionally competent and a pleasure to work with. We are especially grateful to Bob Jucha, Sociology Editor, who has guided our recent revisions; Sherry Symington, Development Editor, who worked with us "hands-on" throughout this edition; and Christina Cha, Sociology Editorial Assistant, who managed the mansucript as a practical matter.

Cheri Palmer, Senior Production Project Manager, oversaw the process of moving the book from manuscript to print and was ready to ensure communication among the many people who worked on the book. Elise Smith, Assistant Editor, had responsibility for the fine array of print supplements that are available with this ninth edition of *Marriages and Families,* and Dee Dee Zobian, Technology Project Manager, developed the Web-based materials. Joohee Lee, Permissions Editor, made sure we were accountable to other authors and publishers when we used their work.

Kathy Glidden of Stratford Publishing Services led a production team whose specialized competence and coordinated efforts have made the book a reality. Kathy was excellent to work with; always available and responsive to our questions, supportive when we felt overwhelmed by time pressures, and helpful when we needed to make last-minute changes. She managed a complex production process smoothly and effectively to ensure a timely completion of the project and a book whose look and presentation of content are very pleasing to us—and, we hope, to the reader.

The production effort also included Karen Hansen, copyeditor, who did a fine job of improving our draft manuscript. Terri Wright and Austin McCrae of Terri Wright Design, worked with us to find photos that captured the ideas we presented in words; and Judy Wingerter designed the figures, converting numbers into pictures. Ellen Keelan proofread the book pages, and Lee Sender composed the index. Lisa Buckley developed the overall design of the book.

Once it is completed, our textbook needs to find the faculty and students who will use it. Wendy Gordon, Marketing Manager at Wadsworth, and Christine Davis of Two Chicks Marketing captured the essence of our book in the various marketing materials that present our book to its prospective audience. Linda Yip, Marketing Communication Manager, oversaw this process, aided by Annabelle Yang, Marketing Assistant.

Closer to home, Agnes Riedmann wishes to acknowledge her late mother, Ann Langley Czerwinski, Ph.D., who helped her significantly with past editions. Sam Walker has contributed to each edition of this book through his enthusiasm and encouragement for Mary Ann Lamanna's work on the project. Larry and Valerie Lamanna and other family members have enlarged their mother's perspective on the family by bringing her into personal contact with other family worlds—those beyond the everyday experience of family life among the social scientists!

Reviewers gave us many helpful suggestions for revising the book. Peter Stein's work as a thorough, informed, and supportive reviewer throughout previous editions has been an especially important contribution. Although we have not incorporated all suggestions from reviewers, we have considered them all carefully and used many. The review process makes a substantial, and indeed essential, contribution to each revision of the book.

Ninth Edition Reviewers

Sylvia M. Asay, University of Nebraska-Kearney
Nicole Banton, Seminole Community College
Theodore N. Greenstein, North Carolina State University
Marsha McGee, University of Louisiana-Monroe
Junelyn Peeples, Chaffey Community College
Frances Marx Stehle, Portland State University
Suzan Waller, Rose State College
Toni Zimmerman, Colorado State University

Eighth Edition Reviewers

Scot Allgood, Utah State University; Sampson Lee Blair, Arizona State University; Elisabeth O. Burgess, Georgia State University; Carole M. Carroll, Middle Tennessee State University; Genie H. Dyer, Baylor University; Mark G. Eckel, McHenry County College; Ron J. Hammond, Utah Valley State College; Peter Stein, William Paterson University; Wen-hui Tsai, Indiana University—Purdue University Fort Wayne.

Seventh Edition Reviewers

Elisabeth O. Burgess, Georgia State University; Carol S. Campbell, McNeese State University Janet Cosbey, Eastern Illinois University; Gary Cutchin, Virginia Commonwealth University; Frances Dumas-Hines, Bowling Green State University; John Holian, Cuyahoga Community College; Larry Horn, Pierce College; Bernita Quoss, University of Wyoming; Rhonda A. Richardson, Kent State University; Carl A. Ridley, University of Arizona; and Sheila Walker, Scripps College.

Students and faculty members who tell us of their interest in the book are a special inspiration. To all of the people who gave their time and gave of themselves—interviewees, students, our families and friends—many thanks.

Chapter 1

Family Commitments:
Making Choices in a Changing Society

Today's Americans are cautious and apprehensive—and at the same time creative and hopeful—about marriages and families. On the one hand, most of us still hope to experience ongoing happiness in committed unions and families. And there *are* long-term, happy marriages (Wallerstein and Blakeslee 1995).

Yet we have reason to wonder about the chances of finding such happiness. Some who would like to marry or form a committed relationship have not yet found partners. Moreover, the high divorce rate has called into question the stability of marriage. New books that talk about "conjugal succession," a series of marriages for each person (Paul 2002, p. 251), echo concerns expressed as early as the 1970s.

We remain hopeful about family commitment; families are central to society as an institution and to our everyday lives. Families are commissioned with the pivotal tasks of raising children and providing continuing intimacy, affection, and companionship to members. But hoping alone won't make enduring or emotionally satisfying families. Maintaining a family requires both commitment and knowledge of what you're doing. This theme is a good part of what this book is about. We will return to it later in this chapter and throughout the text. Right now, though, we need to discuss what a family is.

▪ Defining Family ▪

What is a **family**? In everyday conversation we make assumptions about what families are or should be. Traditionally, both law and social science have specified that the family consists of people related by blood, marriage,

An indirect indicator of the centrality of the family to American life is the degree to which family themes are used as advertising motifs. The grandparent-grandchild relationship is evoked in the first photo, while the text of the second describes the family life of the father and the child pictured in the photo.

A Closer Look at Family Diversity

Which of These Is a Family?

A husband and wife and their offspring.

A single woman and her three young children.

A 52-year-old woman and her adoptive mother.

A man, his daughter, and the daughter's son.

An 84-year-old widow and her dog, Fido.

A man and all of his ancestors back to Adam and Eve.

The 1979 World Champion Pittsburgh Pirates (theme song: "We Are Family").

Three adult sisters living together.

Two lesbians in an intimate relationship and their children from a previous marriage of one woman and a

previous relationship of the other woman with a male friend.

Two children, their divorced parents, the current spouses of their divorced parents, and the children from previous marriages of their stepparents.

A child, his stepfather, and the stepfather's wife subsequent to his divorce from the child's mother.

Two adult male cousins living together.

A 77-year-old man and his lifelong best friend.

A childless husband and wife who live 1,000 miles apart.

A widow and her former husband's grandfather's sister's granddaughter.

A divorced man, his girlfriend, and her child.

Both sets of parents of a deceased married couple.

A married couple, one son and his wife, and the latter couple's children, all living together.

Six adults and their 12 young children, all living together in a communal fashion.

Critical Thinking

Identify which groups you consider to be a family. What is it that makes them "family" or "not family"?

Source: From *Family Theories: An Introduction,* by James K. White and David M. Klein, p. 22. Copyright © 2002 by Sage Publications, Inc. Reprinted by Permission.

---

or adoption. Some definitions of the family have specified a common household, economic interdependency, and sexual and reproductive relations (Murdoch 1949). The U.S. Census Bureau defines a family as two or more people who share a **household**, that is, reside together, and who are related by blood, marriage, or adoption (McFalls 2003). (To think more about this question, you might want to examine "A Closer Look at Family Diversity: Which of These Is a Family?")

In their classic work *The Family: From Institution to Companionship* (1945), Burgess and Locke think of the family as a **primary group**—a term coined by early sociologist Charles Cooley (1909) to describe any group in which there is a close, face-to-face relationship.[1] In a primary group, people communicate with one another as whole human beings. They laugh and cry to-

gether, they share experiences, and they quarrel, too, because that's part of being close. Primary groups can give each of us the feeling of being accepted and liked for who we are.

Burgess and Locke gave us a definition of the family that described some family relationships. But their view of family interaction was more limited than current views. It assumed that family interaction occurred primarily in the context of traditional (heterosexual, married-couple, gender-differentiated) social roles, rather than in emphasizing spontaneity, individuality, and intimacy. Today's social scientists continue to recognize the family's important responsibility in performing necessary social roles, such as child rearing, economic support, and domestic maintenance. But many social scientists (including us) place more emphasis on companionship and emotional support. Moreover, today family members are not necessarily bound to each other by legal marriage, by blood, or by adoption but may experience family relationships and commitment in other forms (Struening 2002, p. 15).

---

1. Another example of a primary group relationship is a close friendship. In contrast, a **secondary group** is characterized by more distant, practical, and unemotional relationships as, for example, in a professional organization or business association.

A primary group is a small group marked by close face-to-face relationships. Group members share experiences, express emotions, and, in the ideal case, know they are accepted and valued. In many ways, families, friends, and teams are similar primary groups: Joys are celebrated spontaneously, tempers can flare quickly, and expression is often physical.

© Jeff Greenburg/PhotoEdit

Burgess and Locke specified that family members "constitute a household." We would expand their definition to include, for example, commuter couples, noncustodial parents, parents with adult children living elsewhere, extended kin such as aunts and uncles, and adult siblings and stepsiblings. In other words, the term "family" can identify relationships beyond partners, parents, and children living in one household.

There Is No Typical Family

Until recently, Judeo-Christian tradition, the law, and societal attitudes converged into a fairly common expectation about what form the American family should take. This **nuclear family** model—husband, wife, and children in an independent household—is often called "traditional," but it is also termed "modern" because it emerged with modern industrial society.

Figure 1.1 and "Facts About Families: American Families Today" show us that families today are very different from their mid-twentieth-century counterparts. Today, only 7 percent of families fit the 1950s ideal of intact marriage, children, and husband-breadwinner and homemaker-wife (AmeriStat Staff 2003f). Instead, there is a proliferation of different family forms: two-earner, single parent, stepfamilies, cohabiting couples, gay, and lesbian families, for example. A family need not include all the roles we might think of—husband, wife, children. Single-parent households and childless unions are families. And roles may be nontraditional. Put another way, social scientists no longer assume that a family has a male breadwinner and a female homemaker; dual-career and reversed-role (working wife, househusband) combinations are also families.

As Figure 1.1 shows, the most common household type today is that of married couples without children because the children have grown up and left or because the couple has not yet had children or doesn't plan to. Only a third of all households include children under eighteen. Just under a quarter of households are nuclear families of husband, wife, and children; this compares to 44 percent in 1960 (Casper and Bianchi 2002, p. 8).

The increasing family diversity that we see now has led some scholars to refer to today's family as the *postmodern family*. Indeed, some theorists argue that the concept of "family" no longer has any objective meaning and that "the new family diversity [is] 'an intrinsic feature . . . rather than a temporary aberration of contemporary family life'" (Stacey 1996, p. 37, quoting Castro Martin and Bumpass 1989, p. 49).

New Definitions of the Family

Not only social scientists are rethinking the family. As families have become less traditional, the legal definition of a family has become more flexible. Law, government agencies, and to some extent private bureaucracies such as insurance companies, must make decisions about what a family is. If zoning laws, rental practices, employee privileges, and insurance policies

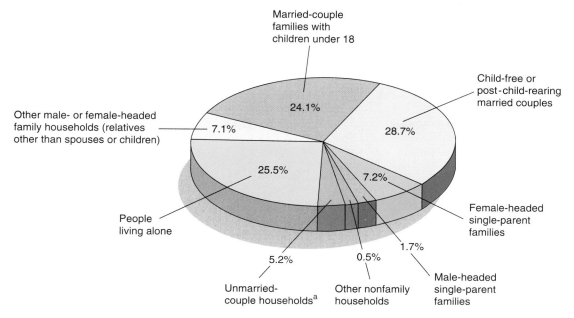

Married-couple families with children under 18

Child-free or post-child-rearing married couples

Other male- or female-headed family households (relatives other than spouses or children)

24.1%

28.7%

7.1%

25.5%

7.2%

People living alone

Female-headed single-parent families

5.2%

0.5%

1.7%

Unmarried-couple households[a]

Other nonfamily households

Male-headed single-parent families

FIGURE 1.1

The many kinds of American households, 2000. A *household* is a person or a group of people who occupy a dwelling unit.

(Source: Simmons and O'Connell 2003; U.S. Census Bureau 2002, Tables 50, 51)

a. Unmarried-couple households may be composed of two male partners (5.5 percent); two female partners (5.4 percent); or a heterosexual couple (89.1 percent). The Census Bureau classifies unmarried-couple households as "nonfamily households."

cover families, decisions must be made about which groups of people can be considered a family.

Some employers have sought to redefine *family* in applying their benefits policies. More than 7,000 employers now offer domestic partner health benefits, including more than 200 Fortune 500 companies, 10 state governments, and 130 city and county governments (Human Rights Campaign 2004). Federal practices permit low-income unmarried couples to qualify as families and live in public housing. A number of cities and states have expanded their definitions of the family, either voluntarily or because courts have ordered them to (e.g., *Braschi 1989*). In 2003, the state of California passed a law granting domestic partners who register with the state many of the same rights and responsibilities as married couples (Lucas 2004).

Some courts have determined that unmarried heterosexual, gay, or lesbian couples; elderly people and their caregivers; handicapped people who live together; and even co-resident groups of students constitute families (e.g., *Glassboro v. Vallorosi 1990; V.C. v. M.J.B. 2000*). According to one state supreme court, "the val-

ues attached to family life, although properly attributed to the nuclear family model, can exist in other settings, including families created by unmarried persons regardless of their sexual orientation" (New Jersey Supreme Court Justice Virginia Long in *V.C. v. M.J.B. 1990*). In defining family, judges who depart from a traditional definition have used the criteria of common residence and economic interdependency along with the more intangible qualities of stability and commitment (*Dunphy v. Gregor 1994*). From this point of view, the definition of family "should not rest on fictitious legal distinctions or genetic history, but instead should find its foundation in the reality of family life. . . . [It] is the totality of the relationship as evidenced by the dedication, caring and self-sacrifice of the parties which should, in the final analysis, control" (Judge Vito Titone in *Braschi v. Stahl Associates Company 1989*).[2]

_____

2. Further issues arise in court cases involving adoption, child custody, or reproductive technology. Courts must decide if the family is biologically or socially based (Burbach and Lamanna 2000; Dolgin 1997). This issue will be discussed further in Chapter 10.

Facts About Families

American Families Today[a,b]

What do U.S. marriages and families look like today? The demographic data presented in this box are generalizations that do not take into account differences among sectors of American society. In Chapter 2 we will explore that social diversity in detail. But for now, let's look at these overall statistics. Although statistics can't tell the whole story of the family, they are an important beginning.

Critical Thinking

After you read these facts about families, what did you think about today's American family? What do you see as the strengths and weaknesses of the contemporary American family?

1. *Fewer people are currently married.* Only 52 percent of American households[c] contained a married couple in 2002, compared to 71 percent in 1970 (U.S. Census Bureau 1998, Table 69; 2003a, Table 66). Among adults in 2002, 59 percent are currently married, while 24 percent have never married; 10 percent are divorced, and 7 percent widowed. By comparison, in 1970, 69 percent of women and 75 percent of men were married; fewer than 5 percent were divorced or separated (U.S. Census Bureau 1989a, Table 50; 2003a, Table 61).

2. *People have been postponing marriage in recent years.* In 2000, the median age at first marriage was 25.1 for women, 26.8 for men, compared to 20.8 for women and 23.5 for men in 1970 (and slightly lower than that in the 1950s). Still, around 90 percent of Americans will marry (Fields 2003; Fields and Casper 2001; Goldstein and Kenney 2001; Kreider and Fields 2002, p. 17; U.S. Census Bureau 1998, Table 159).

3. *Cohabitation has emerged as a lifestyle intermediate between marriage and singlehood.* From 1990 to 2000 there was a 72-percent increase in the number of unmarried-couple households (Simmons and O'Connell 2003). "Increasing rates of cohabitation have largely offset decreasing rates of marriage" (Bramlett and Mosher 2001, p. 2). Unmarried-couple families are only 5 percent of households at any one time, but more than 50 percent of first marriages were preceded by cohabitation.

    More than 40 percent of heterosexual cohabiting couples lived with children under eighteen in 2000. These might be children of the couple or children from a previous marriage or relationship of one or both of the partners (Simmons and O'Connell 2003; Smock and Gupta 2002).

4. *Some cohabitants maintain gay and lesbian domestic partnerships.* Not all cohabiting couples are heterosexual. Almost 600,000 same-sex couple households were reported to the 2000 census (United States Census Bureau 2003a, Table 69).[d] Twenty-two percent of male same-sex partner households and 34 percent of female same-sex households include children (Simmons and O'Connell 2003).

5. *The number of people living alone is substantial.* Single-person households now represent a quarter of American households (U.S. Census Bureau 2003a, Table 66). Delayed marriage is a contributing factor, as is the comparatively good health and economic situation of older people, which enables unmarried

seniors to choose to live independently.

    Because of the increased number of people living alone and the smaller number of children per family, the average size of a U.S. household dropped from 3.14 people in 1970 to 2.58 in 2002 (U.S. Census Bureau 1998, Table 69; U.S. Census Bureau 2003a, Table 66).

6. *Many adult children live with their parents.* Of young adults aged 18–24, 56 percent of men and 43 percent of women lived with parents in 2000. Other young adults are more apt to cohabit or to live with roommates or others than to live alone (or with spouses) (Casper and Fields 2001).

7. *There are other multigenerational households.* Some 3.7 percent of all households are multigenerational. They are more likely to be found in areas of new immigration; areas where there are housing shortages or high costs; and areas where there are high proportions of unwed mothers who live with their families.

    The most common form of multi-generational household (65 percent) is that of a grandparent providing a home for an adult child and grandchildren. Some 2 percent of multi-generational households contain four generations (Simmons and O'Neill 2001).

8. *A much higher proportion of older men than older women are married* (80 percent of men aged 65–74 compared to 55 percent of women in that age group). Women in that age group are more likely to be widowed (31

percent) than men (9 percent) (U.S. Census Bureau 2003a, Table 63). Older Americans are most likely of all age groups to be living alone. Only 20 percent of seniors lived with relatives (AmeriStat Staff 2003e; Bianchi and Casper 2000; U.S. Census Bureau 2003a, Table 67).

9. *Parenthood is increasingly postponed and fertility has declined.* From a high point of 3.6 children per woman in 1957, the *total fertility rate* dropped to 1.7 in 1976 (Weeks 2002, p. 238). It then rose and has been around two children per woman for a decade and a half (Hamilton, Martin, and Sutton 2003).[e]

Childlessness has increased in recent decades. Of women aged 40–44 in 1998, 19 percent had not borne children. This contrasts with 10 percent in 1976 and is similar to the rate of childlessness among Depression-era women. Rates of childlessness seem to be leveling off now, though, rather than increasing (Bachu and O'Connell 2000).

A more common pattern is delayed childbearing. The twenties are still the most fertile ages for women, but a striking shift toward births in older age groups has occurred. Along with this we see more frequent multiple births, more common among older mothers and those who have employed fertility drugs (Martin, Hamilton, Ventura, Menacker, Park, and Sutton 2002; Ventura, Hamilton, and Sutton 2003).

10. *More births are to unmarried mothers than in the past.* Presently about one-third of births are to unmarried mothers. That compares to 18 percent in 1980 and 4 percent in 1950.

But *the nonmarital birth rate has remained stable for the last decade.* And keep in mind that many unwed births occur to co-

habiting couples (Martin et al. 2002; Hamilton, Martin, and Sutton 2003; Ventura and Bachrach 2000). Births to teens are at "historic low levels" (Ventura et al. 2003).

11. *There are now fewer children and more elderly.* Children under 18 composed 26 percent of the U.S. population in 2002, a substantial drop from 1960, when 36 percent of the population were children. Fewer than half (46 percent) of all married-couple households contain children (Conlin 2003b; Fields 2003; Simmons and O'Connell 2003).

12. *Divorce rates have stabilized, although they remain at high levels.* The divorce rate, which had risen slowly from the nineteenth century onward, doubled from 1965 to the end of the 1970s. Then it began to drop, falling almost 25 percent between 1980 and 2001 (Bianchi and Casper 2000, Fig. 2; U.S. Census Bureau 1998, Table 163; 2003a, Table 126).

The majority of married adults, however, have married only once, and most of those who divorced are currently remarried. Still, nearly half of recent first marriages are likely to end in divorce (Kreider and Fields 2002).[f]

13. *Remarriage rates have declined, but remain high.* Three-quarters of divorced women remarry within ten years—81 percent of younger women and 68 percent of those who are over 25 when they divorce. Remarriage rates of men are even higher (Bramlett and Mosher 2001).

 FOCUS ON CHILDREN Perhaps the greatest concern Americans have about contemporary family change is its impact on children. Let us take a look at these family data from the child's

perspective, that is, the living arrangements of children.

14. *A majority of children live in two-parent households.* Despite the visibility of divorce, nonmarital births, and single-parent households, "two married parents are the norm" (Bernstein 2003). In 2002, 69 percent of children under 18 lived with two parents (3 percent were unmarried). Twenty-eight percent lived in single-parent households (23 percent with mother; 5 percent with father), and the other 4 percent did not live with a parent. Of those not living with any parent, the largest group of children (44 percent) was cared for by relatives, while others were in foster care or other nonfamily arrangements (Fields 2003).

15. *Over the last five years the proportion of children living in single-parent families has stabilized.* Single-parent households grew rapidly in the first half of the 1990s. Since then the percentage of children in single-parent households has declined slightly, although it is still about 10 percent higher than in 1990. Twenty-eight percent of America's children live in single-parent households. There are four times as many single-mother households as single-father households (Fields 2003; O'Hare 2001b).

The census category "single-parent family household" obscures the fact that there may be other adults present in that household—grandparents or other relatives, for example. It is also the case that some households defined by the Census Bureau as single-parent households are actually two-parent households. In 33 percent of "single-father" households and 11 percent of "single-mother" *continued* households there is a cohabiting partner. The Census Bureau assumes that such a partner functions as a second parent (Fields 2003, pp. 4–5).

16. *There is considerable variation in children's living arrangements.* First of all, living in a two-parent household does not necessarily mean the child is living with two biological parents in an intact first marriage. A 1996 study (the latest detailed data available) reporting the living arrangements of children in two-parent households found 88 percent of children living with their biological parents (some unmarried), 7 percent with biological mother and stepfather, 2 percent with biological father and stepmother, 1 percent with adoptive mother and father, 1 percent with adoptive father and biological mother, and smaller numbers with an adoptive mother and biological father or an adoptive parent and a stepparent.

   Moreover, a snapshot taken at one time understates family instability (Raley and Wildsmith 2004). A child may live in an intact two-parent family, a single-parent household, with a cohabiting parent, and in a remarried family in sequence. An earlier study estimated that half of children would live in a single-parent household at some point in their lives. On average, a child can expect to spend 3 years in a single-parent household, 1.5 years with a cohabiting parent, and 11.5 years with married parents (perhaps including a stepparent) (Bumpass and Lu 2000).

17. *Children are more likely to live with a grandparent today than in the recent past.* In 1970, 3 percent of children lived in a household containing a grandparent, but by 2002 that rate had more

than doubled, to 8 percent. In about a quarter of the cases, grandparents had sole responsibility for raising the child; neither parent was in the household. Many households containing grandparents are **extended family households** that include other relatives (Bryson and Casper 1999; Fields 2003).

18. *Most parents are working parents.* In 2002, only 7 percent of households were married-couple households with children *in which only the father was employed* (AmeriStat Staff 2003f). Two-thirds of children in two-parent households have two working parents. Children in single-parent households are even more likely to be living with employed parents: 89 percent of those in father-only households; 77 percent in mother-only households (Fields 2003).

19. *Children are more likely than the general population or the elderly to be living in poverty.* In 2002, the poverty rate of children stood at 16.7 percent, whereas that of the general adult population was 10.6 percent and that of the elderly 10.4 percent. Although the current child poverty rate represents a considerable decline from the 1983 peak of 22.3 percent, it is higher than it was in 1970 (Proctor and Dalaker 2003). We will discuss the economic circumstances of families in Chapters 2 and 12.

a. Percentages may not total exactly 100 percent due to rounding error.

b. The data we present are drawn from U.S. government reports and from surveys. The release of data typically lags its collection by a year or more. Thus data that may appear less timely to the reader may actually be the very latest data available. This is especially true regarding data on marriage and divorce because the Census Bureau ceased publishing such reports in the early nineties. The best available

data on marriage and divorce comes from a 1996 survey of individuals about their marital history (Bramlett and Mosher 2001; Kreider and Fields 2002).

c. The Census Bureau uses the term **household** for any group of people residing together. Not all households are families by the Census Bureau definition—that is, persons related by blood, marriage, or adoption (McFalls 2003).

   Talking about *households* presents a picture of how all people in the United States live. Data on *families,* by definition, do not include those not living in family settings. Figures will be different depending on whether *household* or *family* is the unit of analysis. For example, single-parent family households were 9 percent of all *households* in 2002, but 13 percent of all *families* (U.S. Census Bureau 2003a, Table 66).

d. This represents a substantial increase over 1990. The increase may be due to a major change in the census procedure for tallying same-sex households. Or it may represent a real increase in gay and lesbian households or a greater willingness of gay/lesbian partners to report their relationship to the Census Bureau.

   In the 1990 census, most of those respondents who checked "spouse" as the category of person with whom they shared a household, but were of the same sex as that person, were counted as married. The sex of one or the other was arbitrarily changed to make the couple heterosexual. In the 2000 census, the format was clearer so that gay and lesbian partners were more likely to select the *unmarried partner* category to identify their relationship. If they were of the same sex, but selected the spouse category, they were classified as unmarried partners (U.S. Census Bureau 2001).

e. The *total fertility rate* for a year is a calculation that represents the number of births that women would have over their reproductive lifetimes if all women at each age had babies at the rate current for each age group. *Replacement level* is the average number of births per woman needed to replace the population.

f. It is difficult to be precise about the likelihood of divorce for those currently married or about to marry because of differences among generations, the absence of detailed statistics, differences in risk between first and later marriages, and the uncertainty of future developments. Divorce rates are discussed in more detail in Chapter 16.

Family change has become the stuff of talk radio, academic analysis, and political debate. Critics have described it as "family breakdown." Others argue that today's "postmodern family condition" is simply the newest development in the historical evolution of family life (Stacey 1996).

We, the authors, have worked to balance in this text an appreciation for flexibility and diversity in family structure and relations—and for freedom of choice—with the increased concern of many social scientists about what they see as diminished marital and child-rearing commitment. We have adopted a definition of the family that combines elements of some of the definitions discussed here. A family is any sexually expressive or parent–child or other kin relationship in which people—usually related by ancestry, marriage, or adoption—(1) form an economic unit and care for any young, (2) consider their identity to be significantly attached to the group, and (3) commit to maintaining that group over time. This definition combines some practical and objective criteria with a more social–psychological sense of family identity.

We hope our definition and the others presented here will stimulate your thoughts and discussion about what a family is. Ultimately, there is no one correct answer to the question "What is a family?" In fact, when asked to list their family members, some of our students include their dogs, cats, or other pets. Are pets family members? The box "Issues for Thought: Pets as Family?" poses this question.

To a significant extent, the diversity that we see in families today is a result, over time, of people making personal choices about marital or other intimate commitments, raising children, and providing material and emotional support to each other in relationships that they identify as "family." We turn now to a discussion of such choices.

© Michael Heron/CORBIS

In a world of demographic, cultural, and political changes, our views of family structure and life cycle have begun to broaden. For example, today there are more single-parent families, gay partners and parents, remarried families, and families in which adult children care for their aging parents. Whatever their form, families can remain a center of love and support.

The Freedom and Pressures of Choosing

This text is different from others you may have read. It is not intended specifically to prepare you for a particular occupation. Instead, it has three other goals: (1) to help you understand yourself and your family situations; (2) to help you appreciate the variety and diversity among families today; and (3) to make you more conscious of the personal decisions you must make throughout your life and of the societal influences that affect those decisions. As families have become less rigidly structured, people have made fewer choices "once and for all." Of course, previous decisions do have consequences that may limit later choices. Nevertheless, many people re-examine their decisions about family—and face new choices—throughout the course of their lives. Thus, choice is an important emphasis of this book.

One advertisement portrays a happy gay family, making the statement that this is a home like any other. Advertisers have departed from the safe image of the nuclear family to portray nontraditional family forms, as well as family crises such as divorce, as we see in the other photo (Lauro 2000a).

The best way to make decisions about our personal lives is to make them knowledgeably. It helps to know something about all the alternatives; it also helps to know what kinds of social pressures affect our decisions. As we'll see, people are influenced by the beliefs and values of their society. In a very real way, we and our personal decisions and attitudes are products of our environment.

But in just as real a way, people can influence society. Individuals create social change by continually offering new insights to their groups. Sometimes social change occurs because of conversation with others.

Sometimes it requires forming social organizations and becoming politically involved. Sometimes it involves many people living their lives according to their values even when these differ from more generally accepted group or cultural norms.

We can apply this view to the phenomenon of living together, or cohabitation. Forty years ago, it was widely accepted that unmarried couples who lived together were immoral. But in the seventies, some college students challenged university restrictions on cohabitation, and subsequently many more people than before—students and nonstudents, young and

Families are commissioned with the pivotal tasks of raising children and providing members with ongoing intimacy, affection, and companionship. Family members consider their identity to be significantly attached to the group.

old—chose to live together. As cohabitation rates increased, societal attitudes became more favorable. Over time, cohabitation has become "mainstream" (Smock and Gupta 2002). Many religions and some individuals do continue to object to cohabitation outside marriage. Still, it is now easier for people to choose this option. We are influenced by the society around us, but we are also free to influence it. And we do that every time we make a choice.

Personal Troubles and Societal Influences

People's private lives are affected by what is happening in the society around them. Many of their personal troubles are shared by others, and these troubles often reflect societal influences.[3] When a family breadwinner cannot find work, for example, the cause may not lie in his or her lack of ambition but rather in the economy's inability to provide a job. The difficulty of jug-

gling work and family is not usually just a personal question of individual time management skills but of society-wide influences—the totality of time required for employment, commuting, and family care in a society that provides limited support for working families (Hochschild 1997).

This text assumes that people need to understand themselves (and their problems) in the context of the larger society. Individuals' choices depend largely on the alternatives that exist in their social environment and on cultural values and attitudes toward those alternatives. Moreover, if people are to shape the kinds of family living they want, they must not limit their attention to their own marriages and families. Making knowledgeable family decisions increasingly means getting involved in national and local political campaigns, finding out what candidates have in mind for families, and writing and phoning government representatives once they are in office. One's role as a family member, as much as one's role as a citizen, has come to require participation in public-policy decisions so as to create a desirable context for family life and family choices. Although no social policy can guarantee "ideal" families, such policies may contribute to a good foundation for family life.

---

3. This theme is drawn from C. Wright Mills, *The Sociological Imagination.* In Mills's words, people must begin to grasp the "problems of biography, of history, and of their interactions within a society" (1973 [1959], p. 6).

Pets as Family?

There are no statistics on pets in the "Facts About Families" box. Should there be? Dogs and cats are called "companion pets." Are they also "real" family members?

Pets are present in 62 percent of American households; more than one-third of U.S. households have a dog, and around one-third have at least one cat. Larger households, presumably those with children, are the most likely to have pets. More than 90 percent of people who own pets think of them as part of the family (Gardyn 2002; "Pet Lovers" 2002; U.S. Census Bureau 2003a, Table 1242).

People talk to their pets and believe that they understand. Stores carry greeting cards for pets to "send" to their humans on important family occasions ("Pet Lovers" 2002). A large majority of dog and cat owners refer to themselves as "mommy" or "daddy" with reference to their pets (Block 2002; Gardyn 2002). Couple break-ups have resulted in pet-custody disputes, sometimes decided on a "best interest of the pet" standard ("Pet Custody" 2000).

Although the very wealthy are not as likely as the upper-middle class to own pets, for the most part, the more a family earns, the more likely it is to have a pet (U.S. Census Bureau 2003a, Table 1242). Some pet owners take their animals to day care, vacation spas, psychotherapy, acupuncture, massage, swimming lessons, and photo shoots (Alexander 2003; Gardyn 2002). Health care for a pet can involve a $1,200 MRI or kidney transplant (Brody 2001; "DC Suburb" 2002). So it may not be too surprising that some owners buy pet health insurance—or set up trust funds to care for a pet after their death (Brody 2001; Willing 2002).

One reason pet owners are willing to spend money on pet health care is because losing a pet can be very painful (Doka 1989). Recognizing this, greeting card companies now market sympathy cards for grieving pet owners, who sometimes attend professional therapy or support groups. As one owner explained, "A lot of people don't get it, when you try to relate how you bonded with an animal" ("Pet Lovers" 2002). In some states, a bereaved owner may sue for emotional suffering or loss of companionship if a pet is accidentally or intentionally killed by a third party (Williams 2003).

Thus it does appear that for some, pets are "family." A study of children and pets finds that pets perform certain support functions for children, particularly as providers of comfort and esteem and as an audience for secrets (McNicholas and Collis 2004). Pets seem to increase family adaptability and reduce stress. Studies suggest that the presence of pets can help when owners are lonely or depressed, or during a family crisis (Allen 2002). Administrators of homes for the elderly have noted that a pet brightens the setting and improves residents' emotional well-being. In the words of one veterinary researcher, "Clearly, dogs are assuming more importance in people's lives, in many cases taking the place of family" (Gail Golab in Egan 2001, p. 24).

However, as the emergence of pets-as-family continues and especially as spending on pets grows, some are uneasy about giving so much attention to animals when the needs of society's children are so great. Another, more philosophical, concern involves pet owners' anthropomorphism—acting as if their animals were truly human. As one veterinarian has noted, it used to be that "'a pet was a pet' and 'there was a very clear boundary as to what you would do' [when a pet got sick]" (Veterinarian Robert Gilbert in Brody 2001, p. 4). Now people are less inclined to think of the family dog or cat as "just an animal." (There is also some concern for the pets' well-being. Katz [2003] worries about the pressures placed on pets and the potential for mistreatment that could occur when owners become disappointed that their needs are not met.)

With increasing examples of pets filling empty spots in today's families, some observers have begun to look at what thinking of one's pet as "family" says about the family itself. Caroline Knapp's *Pack of Two* (1999) points to changes in the family—more people living alone, delayed marriage, cohabitation, and the deferral of parenthood—that have opened a void that pets may fill. "The fragmentation of the traditional family and the swelling ranks of singles, and empty nesters . . . has created a deep longing for child substitutes and the unquestioning devotion offered by pack animals" (Iovine 2002, p.6; also Albert and Bulcroft 1988). In *The New Work of Dogs* (2003) journalist Jon Katz argues that dogs used to have work responsibilities, tending sheep and the like. Now companion animals have an important new role—that of sustaining the mental health and emotional equilibrium of their owners in an era of work pressures and insecure family lives.

Critical Thinking

Do you think of pets as family members? Dogs, cats, or any and all pets? Is it appropriate to broaden the definition of *family* to include other than humans? What changes in the family may have encouraged changes in our attitudes about pets?

Social Influences and Personal Choices

Social factors influence people's personal choices in three ways. First, it is always easier to make the common choice. In the 1950s and early 1960s, when people tended to marry earlier than they do now, it was more difficult for women to remain single after graduation and for men to remain unmarried past their mid-twenties. Now, staying single longer is a more comfortable choice.

A second way that social factors can influence personal choices is by expanding people's options. For example, the availability of effective contraceptives makes limiting one's family size, if desired, easier than in the past. New forms of reproductive technology provide new options for parenthood. We are presently watching to see how state and federal courts and legislatures will affect individuals' options concerning same-sex marriage or domestic partnerships.

Third, social factors can also limit people's options. As one example, American society has never offered polygamy (more than one spouse) as a legal option. Those who would like to form plural marriages risk prosecution (Janofsky 2001). More broadly, economic changes of the last thirty years, which make well-paid employment more problematic and higher education more essential, have influenced individual choices to delay marriage (Sassler and Goldscheider 2004).

Extended education, delayed marriage, and high housing costs, among other financial pressures, have made it more common for young adults to continue to live with their parents or to move back home. There is less of a "generation gap" between parents and children today—they seem to enjoy each other's company.

▪ Making Choices ▪

All people make choices, even when they are not aware of it. Let's look more closely at two forms of decision making—choosing by default and choosing knowledgeably—along with the consequences of each. One effect of taking a course in marriage and the family may be to make you more aware of when choices are available and how a decision may be related to subsequent options and choices.

Choosing by Default

Unconscious decisions are called **choosing by default**. Choices made by default are ones that people make when they are not aware of all the alternatives or when they pursue the proverbial path of least resistance. If you're taking this class, for example, but you're unaware that a class in modern dance (which

you would have preferred) is meeting at the same time, you have chosen not to take the class in modern dance. But you have done so by default because you didn't find out about all the alternatives before you registered.

Another kind of decision by default occurs when people pursue a course of action primarily because it seems the easiest thing to do. Sometimes, college students choose their courses or even their majors by default. They try to register only to find that the classes they had planned to take are closed. So they register for something they hadn't planned on, do well enough, and continue in that program of study.

Many decisions concerning marriages and families are also made by default. For example, spouses may focus on career success to the neglect of their relationship simply because this is what society expects of them. Strong day-to-day pressures on the job may erode family time. The goal of spending more time with the family is on the horizon but is never reached because it is not consciously planned for.

Although most of us have made at least some decisions by default, almost everyone can recall having the opposite experience: choosing knowledgeably. Figure 1.2, "The Cycle of Knowledgeable Decision Making," maps this process.

FIGURE 1.2

The cycle of knowledge-able decision making.

(Source: Adapted from *Shifting Gears,* by Nena O'Neill and George O'Neill, p. 167, 1974. Copyright © 1974 by Nena O'Neill and George O'Neill. Reprinted by permission of the publisher, M. Evans and Company, New York, NY.)

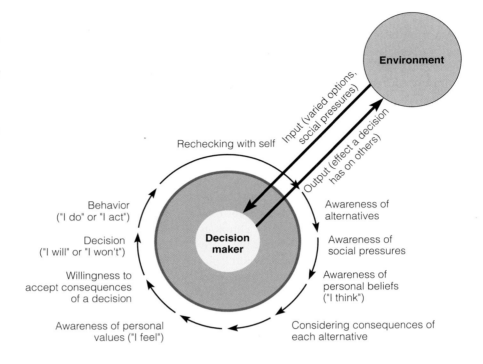

Choosing Knowledgeably

Today, society offers many options. People can stay single, cohabit, or marry. They can form communal living groups or family-like ties with others. They can decide to divorce or to stay married. Couples or individuals can have children biologically, with the aid of reproductive technology, or through adoption. They can parent stepchildren or foster children. One important component of **choosing knowledgeably** is recognizing as many options or alternatives as possible. This text is designed in part to help you do that.

A second component in making knowledgeable choices is recognizing the social pressures that may influence personal choices. Some of these pressures are economic, whereas others relate to cultural norms that are often taken for granted. Sometimes people decide that they agree with socially accepted or prescribed behavior. They concur in the teachings of their religion, for example. Other times people decide that they strongly disagree with socially prescribed beliefs, values, and standards. Whether they agree with such standards or not, once people recognize the force of social pressures, they are free to choose whether or not to act in accordance with them.

An important aspect of making knowledgeable choices is considering the consequences of each alter-

native rather than just gravitating toward the one that initially seemed most attractive. For example, a couple deciding whether to move so that one partner can be promoted or take a new job may want to list the consequences. In the positive column, one partner may have a higher position and earn more money, and the region to which the couple would move may have a nicer climate. In the negative column, the other partner may have to disrupt his or her career, and both may have to leave relatives. Listing positive and negative consequences of alternatives—either mentally or on paper—helps one see the larger picture and thus make a more knowledgeable decision.

Part of this process requires becoming aware of your values and choosing to act consistently with them. Contradictory sets of values exist in American society. For example, standards of nonmarital sex range from abstinence to sex in committed relationships to sex for recreation only. Contradictory values can cause people to feel ambivalent about what they want for themselves.

Clarifying one's values involves cutting through this ambivalence in order to decide which of several standards, for example, are more strongly valued. It is important to respect the so-called gut factor—the emotional dimension of decision making. Besides rationally considering alternatives, people have subjec-

Midlife changes can be both exhilarating and intimidating, as these college students have probably found. Certainly the decision of a middle-aged adult to earn a college degree involves many emotional and practical changes. But by making knowledgeable choices—by weighing alternatives, considering consequences, clarifying values and goals, and continually rechecking—personal decisions and changes can be both positive and dynamic.

© Curtis Willocks/Brooklyn Image Group

tive (often almost visceral) feelings about what feels right or wrong, good or bad. Respecting one's feelings is an important part of making the right decision. Following one's feelings can mean grounding one's decisions in a religious or spiritual tradition or in one's cultural heritage, for these have a great deal of emotional power and often represent deep commitments.

Another important component of decision making is rechecking. Once a choice is made and a person acts on it, the process is not necessarily complete. As Figure 1.2 suggests, people constantly recheck their decisions throughout the entire decision-making cycle, testing these decisions against their experiences and against any changes in the social environment.

Underlying this discussion is the assumption that individuals cannot have everything. Every time people make an important decision or commitment, they rule out alternatives—for the time being, and perhaps permanently. People cannot simultaneously have the relative freedom of a child-free union and the gratification that often accompanies parenthood.

In some respects, though, people can focus on some goals and values during one part of their lives, then turn their attention to different ones at other times. Four decades ago, we used to think of adults as people who entered adulthood in their early twenties, found work, married, had children, and continued on the same track until the end of the life course. That view has changed. Today we view adulthood as a time

with potential for continued personal development, growth, and change.

In a family setting, development and change involve more than one individual. Multiple life courses must be coordinated, and if one member changes, that affects the values and choices of other members of the family. Moreover, life in American families reflects a tension in American culture between family solidarity and individual freedom.

▪ A Family of Individuals ▪

Americans place a high value on the family. Ninety-one percent of Americans report that family relations are extremely important to them (Bogenschneider 2000, p. 1138). **Family values** such as family togetherness, stability, and loyalty focus on the family as a whole. Many of us have an image of the ideal family in which members spend considerable time together, enjoying one another's company. For many of us, the family is a major source of stability. We tend to believe that the family is the group most deserving our loyalty. Those of us who married vowed publicly to stay with our partners as long as we live. We expect our partners, parents, children, and even our more distant relatives to remain loyal to the family unit. Placing family well-being over individual interests and preferences is termed **familism**.

Families as a Place to Belong

Whether families are traditional nuclear families or newer in form, they create a place to belong in at least two ways. They create boundaries, and they serve as a repository or archive of family memories and traditions.

BOUNDARIES Families create **boundaries**, both physical and psychological, between themselves and the rest of the world. Whether in multiple- or single-family dwellings, families mark off some physical space that is private and theirs alone. Family members determine "what kinds of things are allowed to enter the family space and under what conditions and what kinds of items are simply not permitted admission" (Kantor and Lehr 1975, p. 68).

With an idea of how the external world resembles and differs from the family interior, family members screen off certain aspects of the larger, outside culture. For example, they put up fences so that they can barbeque or sunbathe in privacy, and they prevent certain people, books, pictures, words, and topics of conversation from entering the family interior. Some families decide to home-school children rather than send them to public or private schools. Families living in dangerous neighborhoods may routinely accompany children or other family members as they move about the neighborhood or city (Burton and Jarrett 2000, p. 1123).

At the same time, family boundaries create a space in which members can relax and be themselves. They are **backstage**, so to speak, and can let go of the polite and restrained dress and demeanor called for in public places, workplaces, and schools. In his classic *The Presentation of Self in Everyday Life* (1959), sociologist Erving Goffman used the terminology of the theater to convey concepts of social interaction. *Frontstage* is what we show the public. *Backstage* is the private sphere, where we can be informal, relaxed, and authentic. Families may have their own code words based on some shared experience. They may eat peanut-butter-and-pickle sandwiches or pigs' feet, favorite foods that would draw comment outside the family. They may make up "house rules" for games and sports. They may quarrel but quickly cover up their anger if an outsider arrives.

ARCHIVAL FAMILY FUNCTION A second way that families create a place to belong is by performing an **archival family function**. That is, families create, store, preserve, and pass on particular objects, events, or rituals that members consider relevant to their personal identities and to maintaining the family as a unique experiential reality or group. The archives contain a variety of symbols:

> There are snapshots of happy times, posed and unposed (apparently never snapshots of sad times); family movies of celebrations or rites of passage or vacations; . . . artifacts from infancy or childhood transmuted into relics of lost and sweet identities; symbols of recognition and achievement such as diplomas; . . . pointed anecdotes about infancy or youth which reinforce a particular identity as the reckless one, the always helpful one, or the unlucky one ("Remember the time you accidentally broke two of Mr. Jones's porch windows!"); and various . . . symbols which function almost like debts binding one to past relationships with the implication of potential future obligations ("Here is part of the plaster cast from your left leg which you broke in sixth grade, when I had to care for you at home for six weeks—remember that when I am unable to walk around by myself anymore"). (Weigert and Hastings 1977, p. 1174)

But just as family values permeate American society, so also do **individualistic (self-fulfillment) values**. These American values encourage people to develop an *individualistic orientation;* that is, people think in terms of primarily personal—as opposed to communal or group—happiness and goals. An individualistic orientation gives more weight to the expression of individual preferences and the maximization of individual talents and options. However, an individualistic orientation can also put great stress on family relationships when there is little emphasis on contributing to other family members' happiness or postponing personal satisfactions in order to attain family goals.

Expressing our individuality within the context of a family requires us to negotiate innumerable day-to-day issues. How much privacy can each person have at home? What things and places in the family dwelling belong just to one particular individual? What family activities should be scheduled, how often, and when? What outside friendships and activities can a family member sustain?

Families are composed of individuals, each seeking self-fulfillment and a unique identity, but they also offer a place to learn and express togetherness, stability, and loyalty. Families also perform a special archival function: Events, rituals, and histories are created and preserved, and, in turn, become intrinsic parts of each individual. These sisters are sharing memories recorded in family photos.

© Mark Romaine/Stock Connection

Family Rhythms of Separateness and Togetherness

In every family, members regulate personal privacy (Kantor and Lehr 1975). Members come together for family activities, such as eating dinner and playing games or watching television, but they also need and want to spend time alone. Being shortchanged on privacy or living in a crowded household is associated with irritability, weariness, family violence, poor family relationships, and emotional distance from one's spouse (Gove and Hughes 1983; Maxwell 1996).

Time represents another important dimension of family life. Each family member has personal feelings about time. Staying at a party until the wee hours might feel good to one spouse, but the other might prefer to call it quits earlier. Working out a common rhythm for dialogue, sexual expression, and joint activities can be difficult for spouses—for example, when a "night person" marries a "morning person."

In all intimate relationships, partners alternately move toward each other, then back away to reestablish a sense of individuality or separateness. The needs of individuals vary, of course, and so do the temporary or permanent balances that couples and families strike

between togetherness and individuality: "Family life in any form has both costs and benefits. . . . Belonging to any group involves loss of personal freedom" (Chilman 1978). The juxtaposition of opposing values—familism and individualism—creates in society and in ourselves a tension that we must resolve. Where are our solutions leading us?

"Family Decline" or "Family Change"?

As students interested in the family, you are no doubt aware of the current debate over the family. "Many argue that family life has been seriously degraded by the movement away from marriage and traditional gender roles. Others view family life as amazingly diverse, resilient, and adaptive to new circumstances" (Bianchi and Casper 2000, p. 3).

According to demographer Tom Smith, "Marriage has declined as a central institution under which households are organized and children are raised" (quoted in "Marriage Wanes" 1999). Some scholars worry about "the growing disconnect between children and marriage, with fewer adults holding the view that the main purpose of marriage is to rear children. Instead, marriage is prized for meeting the emotional and sexual needs of the couple" (Adams 2003). Sociologist Norval Glenn states his view:

> I believe that marriage should be satisfying to the spouses. . . . [However,] I do not give the spouses' needs and desires priority over the needs of their children or over the social need for the proper socialization of children. Second, I do not believe that each spouse's giving priority to his or her own needs, deemphasizing duty and obligation in marriage, and giving up the ideal of marital permanence will maximize the happiness and satisfaction of American adults. (1987, pp. 350–51)

Scholars and advocates with a "**family decline**" perspective point to what they see as a cultural change accentuated by the self-indulgence of the baby boom generation. Family scholar Barbara Dafoe Whitehead writes: "Beginning in the late 1950's, Americans began to change their ideas about the individual's obligations to family and society. . . . [T]his change was away from an ethic of obligation to others and toward an obligation to self" (1996, p. 4). There is concern that the pursuit of self-realization underlies the increase in divorce and unmarried parenthood and has undermined responsible parenting (Yorburg 2002, p. 33).

Not every family expert concurs that the family is in decline: "**family change**," yes, but not necessarily "family decline." These family scholars would argue that, in many ways, families are better off than in the past. In the nineteenth or early twentieth centuries, families were more apt to live in extreme poverty. Families were often broken up by illness and death, and children sent to orphanages, foster homes, or already burdened relatives. Single mothers, as well as wives in lower-class, working-class, and immigrant families, were not home with children, but went out to labor in factories, workshops, or domestic service. Nonmarital pregnancy rates were higher in the 1950s than they are today (Coontz 1992; Yorburg 2002).[4]

Scholars and policymakers with a "family change" perspective do not ignore the difficulties which divorce and nonmarital parenthood present to families and children. But they argue that it makes more sense to provide support to families as they exist today rather than to attempt to turn back the clock to an idealized past.

Many scholars and policymakers argue further that family values of commitment and responsibility have not changed much. Data from a longitudinal study suggests that an earlier upward trend in individualism has reversed since the early seventies; the "historical trend is toward greater collectivism" (Bengtson, Biblarz, and Roberts 2002, p. 119). But families are struggling with new economic and time pressures which affect their ability to realize their values. These scholars "believe that at least part of the increase in divorce, living together, and single parenting has less to do with changing values than with inadequate support for families in the U.S., especially compared to other advanced industrial countries" (Yorburg 2002, p. 33). Many European countries, for example, have family leave policies that enable parents to take time off from work to be with young children and that provide more generous economic support for families in crisis.

Sociologists Paul Amato and Alan Booth present a mixed picture (1997). They do see America's children as "at risk"—a generation "growing up in an era of family upheaval"—but refuse to place blame on individuals' supposedly self-centered choices. And they find some changes to be good ones—for example, the increased levels of education in our society. Parents' education is positively associated with better outcomes for children. Amato and Booth's research also indicates that the nontraditional gender roles increasingly adopted by American families have had no negative effect on child outcomes. Responsible social science research requires careful analysis, not only of individualism but also of social and economic forces affecting the family.

For those concerned about family change over the past several decades, there may be some encouraging signs. The divorce rate has declined somewhat over the last twenty-five years. The rate of nonmarital childbearing has leveled off and there has been a dramatic decline in teen birth rates (See "Facts About Families"). As demographers Suzanne Bianchi and Lynne Casper observe: "Our rhetoric about the dra-

---

4. A relative (Raymond) of one of the authors, born in 1904, lost his mother at age seven. Relatives urged that Raymond and his siblings be placed in an orphanage, but his father kept them at home and eventually remarried. The father died when Raymond was 15. Raymond continued to live with his stepmother, who was a most caring and supportive figure, but she soon died as well. He then lived with a series of older siblings, who pressured him to drop out of high school. Raymond persisted in working to support his continued education and eventually became a physician (Ritter 1990).

George and Gaynel Couran were married in 1916. "That was the girl for me. I got the woman I wanted," said George at the couple's eightieth wedding anniversary. Judging by her expression, Gaynel undoubtedly got the man she wanted. The Courans learned to balance individualism and familism over the course of their marriage.

© AP Wide World Photos

matically changing family may be a step behind reality. Recent trends suggest a quieting of changes in the family, or at least of the pace of change" (2000, p. 3).

Individualism, Familism, and Partners

Still, shifts in the balance of individuality and familism have meant that family lives have become less predictable than at mid-twentieth century. The course of family living results in large part from the decisions and choices that two adults make, moving in their own ways and at their own paces through their own lives. Assuming that partners' respective beliefs, values, and behaviors mesh fairly well at the point of marriage, any change in either spouse is likely to adversely affect the fit. One consequence of ongoing developmental change in two individuals is that a marriage is no longer as likely to be permanent, as we'll see in Chapter 16. If one or both change considerably over time, they may grow apart instead of together. A challenge for contemporary relationships is to integrate divergent personal change into the relationship while nurturing any children involved.

How can partners make it through such changes and still stay together? Two guidelines may be helpful. The first is for people to take responsibility for their own past choices and decisions rather than blaming previous "mistakes" on their mates. The second is for individuals to be aware that married life is far more complex than the traditional image commonly por-

trayed. It helps to recognize that a changing spouse may be difficult to live with for a while. A relationship needs to be flexible enough to allow for each partner's individual changes—to allow family members some degree of freedom.

At the same time, we must remind ourselves of the benefits of family living and the commitment necessary to sustain it. Individual happiness and family commitment are not inevitably in conflict; research shows that a supportive marriage has a significant positive impact on individual well-being (Waite and Gallagher 2000). Nevertheless, we will continue to explore the tension between individualism and familism in American values throughout this text.

Marriages and Families: Four Themes

In this chapter we have defined the term family and discussed decision making and diversity in the context of family living. We can now state explicitly the four themes of this text.

1. Personal decisions must be made throughout the life course. Decision making is a trade-off; once we choose an option, we discard alternatives. No one can have everything. Thus, the best way to make choices is knowledgeably.

2. People are influenced by the society around them. Cultural beliefs and values influence our attitudes and decisions. Societal or structural conditions can limit or expand our options.

3. We live in a changing society, characterized by increased ethnic, economic, and family diversity; by increased tension between familistic and individualistic values; by decreased marital and family permanence; and by increased political and policy attention to the needs of children. This dynamic situation can make personal decision making more difficult than in the past and more important.

4. Personal decision making feeds into society and changes it. We affect our social environment every time we make a choice. Making family decisions can also mean choosing to become politically involved in order to effect family-related social change. Making family choices consciously, according to our values, gives our family lives greater integrity.

In Sum

- This chapter introduced the subject matter for this course and presented the four themes that this text develops. The chapter began by addressing the challenge of defining the term *family*.

- In "Facts About Families: American Families Today," we pointed to statistical evidence that we live in a changing society. Family diversity has progressed to the point that there is no typical family form today.

- Our culture values both familism and individualism. Whether individualism has gone too far and led to "family decline" is a matter of debate. Even though families fill the important function of providing members a place to belong, finding personal freedom within families is an ongoing, negotiated process.

- Marriages and families are composed of separate, unique individuals. Human beings have creativity and free will: nothing they think or do is totally programmed.

- At the same time, all the individuals in a particular society share some things. They speak the same language and have some common attitudes about work, education, and marriages and families. Moreover, within a socially diverse society such as ours, many individuals are part of a racial, ethnic, or religious community or social class that has a distinct family heritage.

- It is now widely recognized that change and development continue throughout adult life. People make choices, either actively and knowledgeably or by default, that determine the courses of their lives. People must make choices and decisions throughout their life course. Those choices and decisions are limited by social structure and at the same time are causes for change in that structure.

- Because adults change, marriages and families are not static: Every time one individual in a relationship changes, the relationship changes, however subtly. Throughout this text we will discuss some creative ways in which partners can alter their relationship in order to meet their changing needs.

- We continue our examination of the family in Chapter 2 by looking at the social context in which families make choices.

Key Terms

archival family function	family decline
backstage	family values
boundaries	household
choosing by default	individualistic (self-
choosing knowledgeably	fulfillment) values
extended family households	nuclear family
familism	primary group
family	secondary group
family change	

Questions for Review and Reflection

1. Without looking to find ours, write your definition of family. Now compare yours to ours. How are the two similar? How are they different? Does your definition have some advantages over ours?

2. What important changes in family patterns do you see today? Do you see positive changes, negative changes, or both? What do they mean for families, in your opinion?

3. What are some examples of a personal or family problem that is at least partly a result of problems in the society?

4. Do you want your family life to be similar to or different from that of your parents? In what ways?

5. **Policy Question.** Are there changes in law and social policy that you would like to see put in place to enhance family life?

Suggested Readings

Amato, Paul R., and Alan Booth. 1997. *A Generation at Risk: Growing Up in an Era of Family Upheaval.* Cambridge, MA: Harvard. This research-based book examines the impact on children of twentieth-century family change. Some assumptions are challenged; some fears are confirmed.

Coontz, Stephanie. 1992. *The Way We Never Were: American Families and The Nostalgia Trip.* New York: Basic. Social historian Coontz presents the argument that our image of past family stability and satisfaction is not accurate. The realistic historical detail of this book is excellent as background for the family issues of today.

Pleck, Elizabeth H. 2000. *Celebrating the Family: Ethnicity, Consumer Culture, and Family Rituals.* Cambridge, MA: Harvard. A fascinating historical account of family rituals. As families have changed from colonial times onward, so have their celebrations.

Struening, Karen. 2002. *New Family Values: Liberty, Equality, and Diversity.* Lanham, MD: Rowman and Littlefield. Makes the case that a changed family in a changed world is consistent with American values. Proposes directions for public policy in support of families.

U.S. Census Bureau. 2003a. *The Statistical Abstract of the United States.* Washington, DC: **www.census.gov/ stat_abstract**. A compendium of government statistics on the family and many other topics. Useful reference tool.

Waite, Linda J., and Maggie Gallagher. 2000. *The Case for Marriage: Why Married People Are Happier, Healthier, and Better Off Financially.* New York: Doubleday. This book presents a strong defense of the traditional family from a "family decline" perspective. Covers a variety of family issues, not only marriage.

Yorburg, Betty. 2002. *Family Realities: A Global View.* Upper Saddle River, NJ: Prentice Hall. Goes beyond the American family to look at the global context of family change and diversity.

Virtual Society: The Wadsworth Sociology Resource Center

 Go to the Sociology Resource Center at **http:// sociology.wadsworth.com** for a wealth of online resources, including a companion website for your text that provides study aids such as self-quizzes for each chapter and a practice final exam, as well as links to sociology websites and information on the latest theories and discoveries in the field. In addition, you will find further suggested readings, flash cards, MicroCase online exercises, and appendices on a range of subjects.

Online Study Tool

Marriage&Family®Now™ Go to **http://sociology .wadsworth.com** to reach the companion website for your text and use the Marriage&FamilyNow access code that came with your book to access this study tool. Take a practice pretest after you have read each chapter, and then use the study plan provided to master that chapter. Afterward, take a posttest to monitor your progress.

Search Online with InfoTrac College Edition

For additional information, exercises, and key words to aid your research, explore InfoTrac College Edition, your online library that offers full-length articles from thousands of scholarly and popular publications. Click on *InfoTrac College Edition* under *Chapter Resources* at the companion website and use the access code that came with your book.

- Search keywords: *young adult; transitional adulthood;* and *twenties.* Look at a few of these articles. Limit your search to the years 2000 and after. Do you find a discussion of how the lives of twenty-somethings have changed in the last few decades?

- Search keyword: *cohabitation.* Next, do a limit search and enter the dates 1980 and 2002 to look at articles on cohabitation written more than twenty years apart. Do the numbers of articles differ for 1980 and 2002? Does the tone of the articles change over time?

American Families *in* Social Context

FAMILIES ARE FAMILIES, RIGHT? WELL, yes and no. All families do some important things for their members. Family members make commitments to one another and share an identity. Yet Chapter 1 showed us that families are not all alike in form. We also saw in Chapter 1 that social factors influence our personal options and choices. Put another way, individuals and families vary as a result of the social settings in which they exist. Sociologist C. Wright Mills (1959) argued in *The Sociological Imagination*, now considered a classic, that the society in which we live (what Mills referred to as "history") so thoroughly influences our individual lives (our "biographies") that we really can't understand our personal lives or family lives without paying attention to our social environment.

In this chapter, we will explore in greater detail the social context in which today's family members live out their opportunities and choices. Here we'll examine the variations in family life that are associated with race/ethnicity, immigration, religion, geographical region, and the events of our nation's recent history. We'll also look at how the economy affects families and at the impact of new technologies.

This chapter focuses on U.S. society, but we need to point out that social–historical circumstances and technological change affect families in other societies and cultures. Many European nations, as well as Japan, Canada, and Australia, to name only a few, face challenges caused by society-wide and global developments.

We begin with a look at how historical events in the United States have affected family life.

▪ Historical Events ▪

Specific historical events and conditions—war and economic depression, for example—affect options, choices, and the everyday lives of families. In the twen-tieth century, American family life has been a different experience in the Great Depression, during World War II, the optimistic fifties, the tumultuous sixties, the economically constricted seventies and eighties, the time-crunched nineties, and the current era of a globalized economy.

In the Depression years, couples delayed marriage and parenthood and had fewer children than they wanted (Elder 1974). During World War II, married couples were separated for long periods. Married women were encouraged to get defense jobs and to place their children in day-care centers. Some husbands and fathers were casualties of war. Families in certain nationality groups—all Japanese and some Italians—were sent to internment camps and had their property seized even though many were U.S. citizens or long-term residents (Taylor 2002c; Tonelli 2004).

The end of the war was followed by a spurt in the divorce rate, when hastily contracted wartime marriages proved to be mistakes or extended separation led couples to grow apart. World War II was also followed by an uptick in marriages and childbearing. In the 1950s, family life was not overshadowed by national crisis. In those prosperous times, people could afford to get married young and have larger families. The GI Bill enabled returning soldiers to get a college education, and the less well-educated could get good jobs in automobile and other factories as the economy boomed. Men earned a "family wage" (enough money to support a family) and children were cared for by stay-at-home mothers. Divorce rates slowed their long-term increase. The expanding economy and government subsidies for housing and education provided a sound basis for family life (Coontz 1992).

Today, a man is far less likely to earn a family wage. Partly for that reason, more wives seek employment, including mothers of infants and preschool children. Moreover, the feminist movement opened opportunities for women and changed ideas about women's and men's roles in the family and workplace. (Gender will be discussed in more detail in Chapter 4, work and family in Chapter 12.) Educational careers were extended and marriage delayed for both sexes, as young people prepared for a competitive economic environment.

In the 1960s and 1970s, marriage rates declined and divorce rates increased dramatically—perhaps in response to a declining job market for working-class men, the increased economic independence of women,

During World War II, married couples were separated and children did not see their fathers for long periods.

and the cultural revolution of the sixties, which encouraged more individualistic perspectives. These trends, as well as the sexual revolution, contributed to a dramatic rise in nonmarital births.

The present historical moment is one of adaptation to these rather profound cultural changes and to economic ups and downs much affected by **globalization** of the economy, as jobs may migrate from the U.S. to other countries, while skilled and unskilled workers migrate to the U.S. (Baca Zinn and Pok 2002). Immigration to the United States, a strong force for change, has been shaped by historical events in other countries, as well as economic pressures. Also of powerful significance today is the "war on terror." The September 11, 2001, attacks on the United States created a pervasive sense of insecurity, triggered new overseas wars, and led to a debate about what changes in our way of life might be necessary.

Of course, the family has faced the necessity of adapting to demographic, social, economic, and political change throughout its history. Families have also

coped with externally induced crises, as those who remember World War II can tell us (Witchel 2001).

▪ Age Structure ▪

Historical change involves not only specific events but also the basic facts of human life. One of the most dramatic developments of the twentieth century was the increased longevity of our population. Life expectancy in 1900 was forty-seven years, but an American child born in 2001 is expected to live to seventy-seven (Arias 2004, Table 12).

Aging itself has changed. Disability rates of the elderly have been steadily declining; the years that have been added to our lives have been healthy and active ones (Cahan 2001; Himes 2001a, p. 21). Survival to older ages has meant that men and women over sixty-five are now more likely to be living with spouses than in the past. For those without spouses, maintaining an independent residence has become more feasible economically and in terms of health. (Chapter 17 discusses aging families.)

Family life will be profoundly affected by this changing demography. Among the positive consequences of increased longevity are more years invested in education, longer marriages (for those who do not divorce), a longer period during which parents and children interact as adults, and a long retirement during which family activities and other interests may be pursued or second careers launched. More of us will have longer relationships with grandparents (Bianchi and Casper 2000, p. 6).

At the same time, the increasing numbers of elderly people must be cared for by a smaller group of middle-aged and young adults. The smaller family sizes of today will result in fewer adults who can share caregiving responsibilities in the future. Moreover, divorce and remarriage may change family relationships in ways that affect the ability and willingness of adult children to care for their parents (Ganong, Coleman, McDaniel, and Killian 1998; Himes 2001a, p. 37). The impact of a growing proportion of elderly will also be felt economically. As the ratio of retired elderly to working-age people grows, so will the problem of funding Social Security and Medicare.

At the other end of the age structure, the declining proportion of children is likely to affect public policy support for families raising children. As the large baby boom cohort ages, the ratio of children to elderly will continue to drop. Fewer children may mean less attention and fewer resources devoted to their needs in a society under pressure to provide care for the elderly. As the proportion of children declines, "adults are less likely to be living with children, . . . neighborhoods are less likely to contain children, and . . . children are less likely to be a consideration in daily life. . . . [T]he need and concerns of children . . . gradually may be receding from our consciousness" (Whitehead and Popenoe 2001, p. 15). Only 20 percent of those eligible to vote have children (Conlin 2003b).

The historical moment and a society's age structure affect family life, but so does the family's place within our culturally diverse society. Racial/ethnic heritage affects preferences, options, and decisions. The growth of immigration in recent decades should increase the impact of ethnicity on family life because new immigrants retain more of their ethnic culture than do those who have been in the United States longer. Religion and regional location may also be associated with differences in family life.

■ Race and Ethnicity ■

To begin, we need to consider what is meant by **race** and **ethnicity**. The term *race* implies a biologically distinct group, but scientific thinking rejects the idea that there are separate races distinguished by biological markers. Features, such as skin color, that Americans use to place someone in a racial group are superficial, genetically speaking. Instead, race is a social construction reflecting how Americans think about race ("Genetically, Race Doesn't Exist" 2003).

In this text, we use the racial/ethnic categories formally adopted by the U.S. government because we draw on statistics collected by the Census Bureau and other government agencies. The 2000 census employed five major racial categories: (1) white, (2) black or African American, (3) Asian, (4) American Indian or Alaska Native, and (5) Hawaiian or other Pacific Islander (U.S. Office of Management and Budget 1999).[1] In the census, racial identity is based on self-

report. In 2000, individuals were permitted to indicate more than one race, but only 2.4 percent did so (Jones and Smith 2001).

You'll notice that Latinos are not listed as a racial category. That's because Hispanic or Latino is considered an *ethnic* identity, not a *race*. Ethnicity has no biological connotations, but refers to culture. For census purposes, there are two ethnic categories: Hispanic and non-Hispanic. Hispanics may be of any race (U.S. Census Bureau 2003b).[2]

The Census Bureau does *not* include Islamic, Muslim, or Arab as a separate major racial/ethnic category. More than one million Americans identified themselves as of Arab ancestry in the last census (de la Cruz and Brittingham 2003).

In a final distinction, African Americans, Hispanics, American Indians, Asians, and Hawaiians and other Pacific Islanders are often grouped into a category termed **minority group** or **minority**. This conveys the idea that persons in those groups experience some disadvantage, exclusion, or discrimination in American society as compared to the dominant group: non-Hispanic white Americans.[3] One may argue that no category system can truly capture cultural identity—or argue, on the other hand, that we are all "Americans." Nevertheless, we need to make use of data collected in this format by the government and other researchers in order to inform ourselves about family patterns. At the same time, keep in mind that

---

1. Prior to 2000, Hawaiian and Pacific Islanders were included in an "Asian and Pacific Islander" category. Racial categorization has varied throughout American history. See Pollard and O'Hare 1999, pp. 8–9.

2. The racial composition of the Latino population is not knowable with certainty. Latino countries of origin typically have more nuanced racial vocabularies than does the United States. Moreover, some Latinos view their ethnic identity as a racial one (AmeriStat Staff 2001; Fears 2003). The racial self-identification of those who indicate an Hispanic ethnic identity is: just under 50 percent white, 2.7 percent black, and 47 percent "some other race." Demographers infer from these responses that 90 percent of Hispanics would be classified as "white" (Kent et al. 2001).

   In many statistical analyses, Hispanics are separated out from other whites so that *non-Hispanic white* and *Hispanic* become separate categories.

3. "*Minority*" in this context does not have its everyday meaning of fewer than 50 percent. Regardless of size, if a group is distinguishable and in some way disadvantaged within a society, it is considered by sociologists to be a *minority group* (Ferrante 2000). Examples of groups that are considered minority groups despite being a numerical majority are South African blacks, who compose about four-fifths of the population of that country, and women, who are more than 50 percent of the U.S. population, yet less advantaged than males in terms of occupational status and income.

   The term *minority* has become a contested one, viewed by some as demeaning, as ignoring differences among groups, and as ignoring variation in the self-identities of individuals (Wilkinson 2000).

The child population of the United States is more racially and ethnically diverse than the adult population and will become even more diverse in the future.

© Charles Thatcher/Getty Images

categories of race and ethnicity are social constructions, concepts that do not by any means capture the reality of identity and cultural experience.

Now it's time to use these racial/ethnic categories to explore distinctive features of family life in various social settings.[4] In doing so, we turn to research rather than rely on stereotypes or assumptions about differences—which may be mistaken.

The United States is an increasingly diverse nation. By 2050, non-Hispanic whites are expected to be only half the population. Presently, racial/ethnic minorities compose almost one-third of the population. In 2002, the nation was 68 percent non-Hispanic white; 12.7 percent black; 4 percent Asian; 1 percent American Indian/Alaska Native; and less than 1 percent Native Hawaiian and other Pacific Islander. The Hispanic population has increased dramatically, and Hispanics are now 13.4 percent of the population, surpassing blacks as the largest racial/ethnic group after whites. Hispanics' increasing numbers derive from immigration and from fertility rates that are higher than those of blacks or whites (Bergman 2004; U.S. Census Bureau 2003a, Table 13).

Black, Asian, and Hispanic populations are further diversified by ethnicity and nationality; for example, there are Caribbean and African blacks as well as those descended from slave populations. *Within* each major racial/ethnic category, there are often significant differences in family patterns, as Figure 2.1 illustrates.

The child population is even more diverse at 61 percent non-Hispanic white; 17 percent Hispanic; 15 percent black; 3 percent Asian and Pacific Islander; 1 percent American Indian and Alaska Native; and 0.1 percent Native Hawaiian and other Pacific Islander (Lugaila and Overturf 2004, Table 3). Much of the growth of the child population between 1990 and 2000 occurred among groups other than non-Hispanic whites (O'Hare 2001a).

African American Families

African Americans are increasingly split into a middle class that has benefitted from the opportunities opened by the civil rights movement and a substantial sector that remains disadvantaged. More than one-half of all black married couples had incomes of $50,000 or more in 2001, and one-quarter had incomes of $75,000 or more (McKinnon 2003). Yet a higher proportion of black children (32 percent) than those of other racial/ethnic groups lives in poverty (Proctor and Dalaker 2003, Table A-2). This includes 47 per-

---

4. Totals for racial/ethnic groups may not always add up to 100 percent due not only to rounding errors, but also to the difficulty of classifying individuals into the current complex multicategory system used for race and ethnicity.

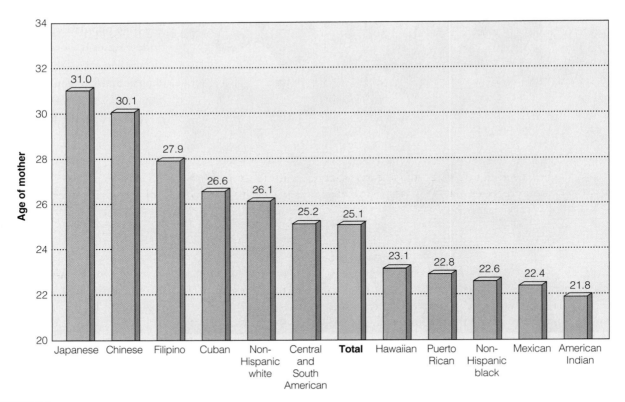

FIGURE 2.1

Mean age of mother at first birth by race and Hispanic origin: United States, 2002. This graph indicates the average age of mothers at the birth of their first child for a variety of racial/ethnic groups. It illustrates the point that differences in family patterns exist *within* major racial/ethnic groups. For example, Japanese-American women are, on average, thirty-one when they have their first child, while Hawaiian women are twenty-three.

Source: Martin et al. 2003, Figure 5.

cent of children in female-headed families. Only 11 percent of black children in married-couple families are poor (Lugaila and Overturf 2004, Figure 5). The impact of racial discrimination and economic disadvantage on African American families is further indicated by the fact that blacks are more than twice as likely as whites to suffer the death of an infant (Kochanek and Smith 2004).

Childbearing and child rearing are increasingly divorced from marriage. True of all racial/ethnic groups, this trend is pronounced among blacks, with 68.4 percent of births to unmarried mothers in 2002 (Martin et al. 2003). Black divorce rates are higher (Nock 2003a), although the more substantial differ-

ence between blacks and whites is that blacks are far more likely to have never married (McKinnon 2002). As a consequence, only 35 percent of African American children are living with married parents, compared to 76 percent of white (non-Hispanic) and 65 percent of Hispanic children. Eighty-three percent of Asian children, 62 percent of Hawaiian/Pacific Islander children, and 52 percent of American Indian children reside in married-couple homes, (Lugaila and Overturf 2004, Table 2; PHC-T-30 Census 2000).

Differences between African Americans and whites in the proportion of two-parent families are not new, but as recently as the 1960s, more than 70 percent of black families were headed by married couples. In

2002, only 48 percent were. Between 1975 and 2002, the proportion of never-married blacks increased and the proportion currently married decreased. Most of the change occurred before the late nineties (Ameri-Stat Staff 2003a, 2003f; Clayton and Moore 2003; Franklin 1997; "Married Households" 2003; McKinnon 2003; Taylor 2002a).

Experts do not agree on the cause of the decline in marriage and two-parent families among African Americans. The argument that African Americans value marriage less has been contradicted by research that shows either no difference or that blacks ascribe greater importance to marriage (Oropesa and Gorman 2000; Taylor 2002a; Tucker 2000).

Given similar values regarding marriage, some suggest that the source of differences in marital patterns is economic. Our economy's shift away from manufacturing has meant the elimination of the relatively well-paying entry-level positions that once sustained black working-class families. Low levels of black male employment and income may preclude marriage or doom it from the start (Wilson 1987; Taylor 2003).

African American women have traditionally been employed, and they may be less dependent on the earnings of a spouse for economic survival. But the *economic independence* explanation of low marriage rates is not supported by research; it appears that the better their earnings, the more likely black women are to marry (Tucker 2000). Research also indicates that the availability of welfare is not a significant factor in a black woman's decision to marry (Teachman 2000).

Another possible explanation for the lower marriage rates of African Americans is the **sex ratio**, the number of eligible men available for women seeking marital partners. High rates of incarceration, what some black scholars call "the prisonization of black America" (Clayton and Moore 2003, p. 85),[5] as well as poorer health and higher mortality have taken many African American men out of circulation.

More generally, poverty and racism continue to create stress on many African American families (Staples 1999c). Segregation persists in much of everyday life even in the suburban middle-class settings to which many African Americans have moved (el Nasser 2001; Scott 2001b). "The upward strides of many African Americans into the middle class have given the illusion that race cannot be the barrier that some make it out to be. The reality, however, is that even the black and white *middle classes* remain separate and unequal" (Pattillo-McCoy 1999, p. 2). Middle-class blacks have comparatively lower-status jobs and incomes and must cope with housing segregation and neighborhoods that often have higher crime rates, poorer schools, and fewer services.

Parents, however, utilize socialization strategies that do not vary by race so much as by class. Annette Lareau's research on black and white children found that "the role of race in children's daily lives was less powerful than I expected" (2002, p. 773). White and black middle-class parents exhibited similar strategies in parenting so as to provide their children with educational, social, and developmental advantages intended to facilitate their educational and career success.

The emphasis in many scholarly and policy analyses of the African American family is on the "crisis" of marriage among blacks (Clayton and Moore 2003, p. 85), and we have reported that here. At the same time, African American scholars rightly complain of "sweeping generalizations" and "pejorative characterizations" (Taylor 2002a, p. 19) that often reflect a research focus on lower-income blacks in the inner city. (In Chapter 3 we discuss the methodology of research on racial/ethnic families.) Recent research gives more attention to middle-class blacks (e.g., Pattillo-McCoy 1999) and also gives us more nuanced portraits of those families not organized around a married couple.

Sociologist Jennifer Hamer (2001) undertook a qualitative study of eighty-eight lower-income black fathers living away from their children. These fathers view spending time with children, providing emotional support and discipline, and serving as role models and guides as among their most important parental functions, although they also tried to do what they could by way of economic support. Speaking more generally, Crosbie-Burnett and Lewis (1999) argue that the experience of African American families raising children in non-nuclear family settings may serve

5. "Racial profiling, mandatory minimum sentences, and especially the disparities in drug laws [which penalize crimes involving drugs typically used by blacks more harshly than those used by whites] have had a dramatic effect on the incarceration rates of young males, especially in urban inner-city neighborhoods" (Clayton and Moore 2003, p. 86). African Americans are 13 percent of drug users, but represent 35 percent of drug arrests and 53 percent of drug convictions ("Incarceration and Fewer Jobs" 2003). Sentences are longer for possession or distribution of crack cocaine (a "black" drug) than for powder cocaine (a "white" drug). See Clayton and Moore for an extensive discussion and critique of explanations of African American incarceration rates and their impact on the family.

as a model for Euro-American families, which are themselves becoming increasingly nontraditional.

As a family system, African American families are child-focused. Blacks are disposed to accept children regardless of circumstances: "Children are prized" (Crosbie-Burnett and Lewis 1999, p. 457). In a child-focused family system, the extended family and community are involved in caring for children; their survival and well-being do not depend on the parents alone. Middle-class as well as lower-socioeconomic-status blacks are more embedded in kin networks. They have a "sense of responsibility that extends beyond the boundaries of the nuclear family unit" (Uttal 1999, p. 855).

With regard to couple dynamics, we find that married blacks have more egalitarian gender roles than do whites, characterized by role flexibility and power sharing. Other research finds that African American men do more housework and are more supportive of working wives than other men, but are traditional in other respects. Child socialization is less gender differentiated in African American families (McLoyd et al. 2000, Taylor 2002).

As we write, the direction of change in the circumstances of African American families is uncertain. There has been a small but steady rise in the percentage of black families headed by married couples since 1996. "'It is reflecting the consolidation of a stable kind of middle class, which has grown because of the economy of the 1990s'" (Demographer Roderick Harrison in "Married Households" 2003). At the same time, the median income of African Americans declined from 2000 to 2002 (DeNavas-Walt et al. 2003, Table 1).

Latino (Hispanic) Families[6]

Latinos are now the largest racial/ethnic group in the United States after non-Hispanic whites. Although the first Spanish settlements in what is now the United States date back to the sixteenth century, many Latinos are recent immigrants from Mexico, Central America, the Caribbean, or South America. About two-thirds of the current Latino population are immigrants or children of immigrants, while one-third were born in the United States to U.S.-born parents (del Pinal and

Singer 1997, p. 2). More than half (53 percent) of the recent growth of the Hispanic population is due to international migration, while births to those already here make up 47 percent of the increase (Bernstein and Bergman 2003). Latino families may be binational. **Binational families** are those in which some family members are American citizens or legal residents, while others are undocumented, i.e., not legally in the United States and subject to sudden deportation (Baca Zinn and Pok 2002, p. 90, citing Chavez 1992). Families of immigrants are discussed in the box: "A Closer Look at Family Diversity: Family Ties and Immigration."

Some 29 percent of Latino children are poor compared to 18 percent of all children (Bernstein and Bergman 2003; Proctor and Dalaker 2003). Even in married-couple families, almost 20 percent of children are poor, due to the relatively low earnings of employed Hispanic parents. Educational levels are low; only 57 percent of Latinos have graduated from high school. This may be due not only to language barriers for more recent immigrants, but also to an "Hispanic culture of hard work" that draws Latinos into the labor force early to contribute to family welfare ("Hispanic Nation" 2004; Lugaila and Overturf 2004; Proctor and Dalaker 2003; Ramirez and de la Cruz 2003; U.S. Census Bureau 2003a, Table 227).

Latinos are about as likely as the U.S. average to be married and significantly less likely to be divorced. Latinos are also less likely to have cohabited than non-Hispanic whites or blacks (U.S. Census Bureau 2003a, Tables 53, 58). The Hispanic population is young—34 percent are under eighteen and only 5 percent are over sixty-five (Ramirez and de la Cruz 2004). Sixty-three percent of Hispanic children are living with married-couple parents; 25 percent with single mothers (some of whom are cohabiting); and 5 percent with single fathers (of whom almost half are cohabiting) (Fields 2003, Figure 1).

We tend to think about Latino families in terms of familistic values, which place extended family commitment above individual preference. A Catholic religious heritage offers a ready explanation for high Hispanic fertility rates. Cultural traditions of gender roles, in which patriarchal men make all the family decisions while women are self-sacrificing, have been assumed. But Latino scholars and other researchers have begun to move away from those images, asking whether these stereotypes represent present-day reality (McLoyd

---

6. Latino has become the preferred term to indicate Spanish heritage. The U.S. government still uses Hispanic in data presentation, although both terms were offered as choices in the 2000 census.

Family Ties and Immigration

Today there is more racial and ethnic diversity among American families than ever before, and much of this diversity results from immigration. The United States admits approximately one million legal immigrants each year. Since 1965, Asia and Latin America and the Caribbean—not Europe—have been the major sending regions. In addition to legal immigration, estimates are that there are seven to nine million **undocumented immigrants** residing in the United States. The vast majority of these are from Mexico, Central America, and the Caribbean, but there are also substantial numbers from such countries as Canada, Poland, and Ireland ("Illegal Immigrant Population 2001"; Martin and Midgely 2003). **Immigrant stock**—that is, immigrants and children of immigrants—now constitutes about one-fifth of the U.S. population (Martin and Midgely 2003; Rumbaut 1999b).

Why do immigrants choose to come here? For the most part, immigrants leave a poorer country for a richer one. The household economics of migration may encourage a rural Mexican family, for instance, to send a daughter to Mexico City to be a secretary and a son to Los Angeles to be a day laborer. Typically, the children send money home so that the family may plant a new kind of crop, for example, or buy farm equipment or a television set, build a house, pay for the education of younger children, or bring other family members to the U.S.

Another type of immigrant is the highly educated professional, a doctor or computer specialist, let's

say, who cannot find suitable employment in his or her home country. Finally, many refugees have arrived here and spread out across the United States to areas which previously had little immigration. Nebraska, for example, is home to clusters of Afghani, Cuban, Hmong, Serbian, Somali, Sudanese, Soviet Jewish, and Vietnamese refugees and to Mexicans and Central Americans who have come to work in the meatpacking plants.

Immigrants may be single individuals or they may be young or middle-aged married adults who migrate with spouses or children or who plan to bring them here. As immigrants establish themselves, they begin to send for their relatives, and ethnic kin or community networks develop. Every major U.S. city today is truly multicultural, characterized by disparate ethnic neighborhoods.

One feature of recent immigration is that immigrants may have transnational identities and families. With modern communication and transportation, and because much immigration is from geographically "convenient" countries, such as Mexico, migrants often maintain close ties with relatives in the home country. A **transnational family** is one that maintains significant contact with two countries: the country of origin and the United States. Such contact may involve back-and-forth changes of residence; visits, especially to celebrate holidays or to attend family events; business dealings; money transfers to family members and to assist the community of origin; placement of children with relatives in the other country;

and seeking marital partners in the home country.

The foreign-born population is a diverse group, but on average poorer, more likely to be in the work force, and younger than the general population. Many are in the childbearing years, and one-fifth of current births are to foreign-born women. Immigrant children and U.S.-born children of immigrants are the fastest-growing segment of the U.S. child population (Rumbaut 1999b). Children of immigrants are most likely (81 percent) to be living in two-parent families. Education varies, but two-thirds of immigrants have graduated from high school, and they are as likely to be college graduates as native-born Americans. One-third of foreign-born Americans have become naturalized citizens (Bernstein 2002; Martin and Midgely 2003; Schmidley 2003; U.S. Federal Interagency Forum 2003).

The increase in immigrant families has led policy makers and others to consider many issues. Five percent of American children speak a language other than English at home and do not speak English well (U.S. Federal Interagency Forum on Child and Family Statistics 2003). Some school districts have bilingual education programs, others teach English as a second language, and still others offer no special help at all. How best to educate immigrant children—many of them already U.S. citizens and many more on the path toward naturalization—is a matter of public debate (Navarro 2001). Some research indicates that the children themselves have a preference for English (Rumbaut 1999a).

continued

Another issue is whether, on balance, immigrant families are an asset or a liability to the nation's economy. The latest research suggests that there is a small net uptick to the Gross Domestic Product and a moderation of prices due to corporate savings from lower wages paid to immigrant workers. This leads to a concern about whether wages would be generally higher for all workers without the availability of cheaper immigrant labor. At least one study provides some evidence to the contrary, however ("NE-UNL Study" 2003).

Immigrant families pay payroll, property, and sales taxes while having very limited access to government benefits.[a] But these costs and benefits are not evenly distributed. Most immigrant family tax dollars go the federal government, whereas the costs of immigrants' schooling or emergency health care are largely paid by local governments. Whether immigration is a net gain or loss regarding taxes and benefits depends on the age

a. Illegal immigrants pay taxes but are not entitled to most government services; emergency health care and children's elementary and secondary education are the exceptions. There are also some limitations on benefits for legal residents who are not citizens.

and occupational level of the immigrant. Probably more is spent to aid elderly and less-educated immigrants, while younger, more-educated immigrants will pay more in taxes than they gain in benefits (Martin and Midgely 2003). Whatever our views on immigration policy, immigrants are generally responsible family members doing what they can to improve their family lives.

The degree to which immigrant families should adapt to American culture is one that different people, in and outside of immigrant communities, have different views on. Cultural differences may enrich the American experience, as has always been the case: foods, festivals, music, art, and dance. Some cultural differences in family patterns are more controversial and, in fact, may be contrary to American law. Immigrants are more apt to use corporal punishment than are native-born American parents, perhaps in ways that violate American child-abuse laws. Sophisticated children may themselves report parental punishment as child abuse (Waters 1997). Parents from societies in which a village collectively supervises children may give young children freedom to wander, a practice that is a safety risk in an American city and may also lead to a citation for child neg-

lect (Aksamit 2001). The arranged marriages of underage girls is another practice taken for granted in some cultures, where fourteen to seventeen is a normal age for marriage for women. In the United States, this custom is a violation of American law (Buttry 2001a, 2001b; Detzner and Xiong 1999).

The freedom of American children and youth may be very disturbing to parents who come from more conservative cultures. One of the adjustment problems of immigrant families is the **role reversal** that may occur when children learn the English language and American ways faster than their parents and, thus, become the family leaders. These youths become **cultural brokers**, managing interaction with bureaucracies and the larger society (Baca Zinn and Pok 2002; Hedges 2000). Parents may resent their dependency and step up their assertion of authority, while children believe they are receiving mixed messages.

Marriages of recent immigrants seem less egalitarian than those of couples of similar ethnic background whose families have been in the United States longer (Pozzetta 1991). The concept of family choice on which this book is framed may be alien to cultures in which family

et al. 2000). Are family patterns and relationships determined by an inherited Latino culture? Or are they more affected by economy and social structure in the United States?

Latino and other social scientists now tend to argue that many Latino family patterns—as well as those of whites and other racial/ethnic groups—are shaped by "structural forces that place families in different social environments." These scholars emphasize adaptive strategies: How people with severely constrained options nevertheless forge family lives that are suited to their needs and social settings (Baca Zinn and Pok 2002, p. 97; Baca Zinn and Wells 2000, p. 268; McLoyd et al. 2000).

Vega (1995) refers to the "plasticity of Latino family forms" (p. 14), which include fostering of children and female-headed families as well as classic two-parent nuclear and complex extended families incorporating godparents. Hispanic households are larger in size than those of any other racial/ethnic group (Fields 2003, Table AVG1). But the extended households of immigrants tend to dissolve into nuclear family units with time. Relatives tend to continue to live near one another and engage in mutual aid.

There is enormous diversity within the Latino population because Mexican Americans, Puerto Ricans, Cubans, and Central Americans have different histories and different resources—and often different

life is experienced as carrying on tradition and accepting the decisions of family heads.

Yet migration is likely to change husband-wife roles. Male heads of household may lose status when male privilege and authority here is not what it was in the home country. Moreover, many formerly middle- and upper-class males must take jobs at a much lower level, compounding their status loss (Liu, Lamanna, and Murata 1979; Buriel and DeMent 1997; García Coll and Magnuson 1997). "Men try to continue in that traditional role once they move to a western culture," states the husband of a female Nigerian doctor who is now the family breadwinner. "But the wife is pushing for more independence, more of a partnership" (Prue 2003). Women, who usually enter the labor force after coming to the U.S., begin to experience an independence and autonomy that carries over into the negotiation of new roles and patterns of family life (Hondagneu-Sotelo and Messner 1994).

Meanwhile, things may also be changing in the home country. Younger couples in Mexico are likely to have a "companionate marriage" ideal, in which reproduction is subordinated to marital intimacy. Men and women in Mexican trans-national families, while not necessarily having equal and similar roles, have moved far from the more traditional roles of their parents (Hirsch 2003).

It may be difficult to supervise children in the new setting. The hard work and long hours that immigrant parents typically put in may give them little time to watch over children. Post-traumatic stress for families that have experienced war and violence creates additional difficulties. Some families have been separated, as parents come to the United States, leaving children behind in the care of relatives for long periods, engaging in "transnational motherhood" (Hondagneu-Sotelo and Avila 1997). Children may be resentful and less inclined to obey when they finally join their parents in the United States. Children of immigrants may make unfavorable comparisons of their stoic and practical parents to the more openly emotional and expressive American families they see (perhaps only on TV). Parents, in turn, fear their children's loss of traditional culture (Pyke 2003). Perhaps the family members who have most difficulty with immigration are the elderly from traditional cultures where children provide a home for aging parents. These elderly will not nec-essarily receive what they provided for their own parents from their now-American adult children, who wish homes of their own (Mui 1996). Still, the foreign-born are far more likely (43 percent) to care for older relatives than are people born in the United States (20 percent) (Lewin 2001c). Sometimes this means caregiving from a distance or through visits to the home country (Baldock 2000).

Immigrants bring many strengths to this country: the "immigrant ethos" of strong family ties and high aspirations, hard work, and achievement (Waters 1997, p. 79). Children in immigrant families put more time in on homework and have higher GPAs than the U.S. average. Immigrants exhibit a strong devotion to family and community, respect for work and education, good health, spirituality, and low crime rates (Waters 1997; Detzner and Xiong 1999).

Critical Thinking

What are some strengths exhibited by immigrant families? What are some challenges they face?

At the societal level, what benefits does recent increased immigration offer the U.S.? What challenges does it bring?

family patterns. Mexican Americans are more "married" than other disadvantaged groups in the U.S.; Cuban and Mexican marriage and marital dissolution rates are similar to those of whites. Puerto Ricans share a Caribbean tradition of informal marriage (i.e., cohabitation that resembles marriage). Mexican American birth rates are among the highest in the U.S., while those of Cubans are among the lowest. More than 40 percent of births to Latina women are to unmarried women. Mexican American women typically have their first child in marriage, while Puerto Rican women are especially likely (59 percent) to be unmarried at a child's birth, perhaps a consequence of the Caribbean pattern of acceptance of informal marital ties. At the same time, the assumption that Latinos are conservative on sexual and reproductive issues is supported by survey results indicating high rates of disapproval of abortion and of opposition to the legalization of homosexual relations and same-sex marriage (Baca Zinn and Pok 2002, Baca Zinn and Wells 2000, "Hispanics Back Big Government" 2003; Martin et al. 2003, McLoyd et al. 2000, Perez 2002, Rodman 1971, Taylor 2002b, Vega 1995). Interestingly, Central American, Cuban, and Mexican immigrants all have lower **infant mortality rates** than non-Hispanic whites despite higher levels of poverty and lower levels of education and income (Matthews, Menacker, and MacDorman 2003, Table D). One possible explanation,

© Royalty Free/Getty

Latina women do not necessarily limit their lives to traditional roles. They enter the labor force and undertake important activities in the community.

besides extended family support, is that Latinas are more likely to refrain from smoking, drinking, and drug use.

Gender roles are an area of family change that has been shaped by immigration. In the United States, regardless of cultural ideals about the importance of women's maternal and domestic roles, Latina wives must typically enter the labor force to contribute to the family economy. That leads to increased autonomy and independence, and a stronger voice in family decisions. On average, Mexican immigrant women in this country have less power than men in terms of decision making and the division of household labor, but more power than in Mexico. There is great variation in the relationships of Latino married couples, ranging from patriarchy to egalitarianism (Baca Zinn and Pok 2002;

Baca Zinn and Wells 2000, Hirsch 2003, Hondagneu-Sotelo and Messner 1994, McLoyd et al. 2000, Vega 1995).

Studies comparing African Americans, Mexican Americans, and whites found that Mexican American men, like black men, place a high value on marriage (Tucker 2000). Latinos have nevertheless been affected by the trends toward lower rates of marriage or later marriage that are seen among other racial/ethnic groups including whites (del Pinal and Singer 1997). One researcher detects a "growing ambivalence among some Latinas about marriage in the face of the conflicts generated through increased women's economic power and traditional gender role beliefs" (Tucker 2000, p. 180).

Asian and Pacific Islander Families[7]

Asian/Pacific Islanders are the fastest growing of all racial/ethnic groups, although their numbers are relatively small (Bernstein and Bergman 2003). Asian Americans are often termed a "model minority" because of their strong educational attainment, high representation in managerial and professional occupations, and family incomes which are the highest of all racial/ethnic groups (DeNavas-Walt et al. 2003, Table 1).

Asians indeed have some favorable family indicators. Their divorce rate is lower than that of other groups (Reeves and Bennett 2003). Asian American children are very likely (83 percent) to be living in married-couple families (Lugaila and Overturf 2003, Table PHC-T-30). Infant mortality rates are low (lower than those of whites) and teen birth rates and nonmarital births are also very low (Kochanek and Smith 2004; Martin et al. 2003; Matthews et al. 2003, Table D). Asian Americans are most likely of all groups to be caring for older family members (AARP 2004). Asian American women have a total fertility rate (1.82) that is lower than that of the United States as a whole (Martin et al. 2003, Table 4).

As with all racial/ethnic groups, there is considerable within-category diversity. Overall statistics mask the disadvantage of several subgroups, notably Pacific Islanders and Southeast Asians. Hawaiians, for example, have an infant mortality rate (7.8) that is well

---

7. The previous "Asian/Pacific Islander" census category was divided in the 2000 census into "Asian" and "Hawaiian Native and other Pacific Islander." We will present a few statistics separately for the two groups, but for the most part, data analyses combine the two.

above that of the overall rate of Asian/Pacific Islanders (Matthews et al. 2003). And while Asians are most likely of all racial/ethnic groups to have incomes of $75,000 or more, to have high levels of education, and to be concentrated in managerial and professional occupations, Asian/Pacific Islanders are also more likely than whites to be poor (Reeves and Bennett 2003).

Discrimination and hostility toward Asians still exist, but at the same time, Asian Americans have high rates of intermarriage and are less residentially segregated than most other racial/ethnic groups (Ishii-Kuntz 2000; Lee 1998). In the more successful sectors of the Asian American population, individuals and families may suffer from comparisons to the "model minority" image. Some children and young people are poor, not academically successful, in conflict with parents, and/or from divorced families. Thirteen percent of Asian American children live in single-mother households (Fields 2003; Ishii-Kuntz 2000; Lee 1998). Even advantaged youth may feel marginalized at school and among peers (Purkayastha 2002).

Still, Asian American families are more cohesive and less individualistic than are white families. Average family size (those living together) is 3.4, compared to 3.0 for non-Hispanic white families (Fields 2003, Table AVG2). Scholars explain the survival of extended family commitment among Asian Americans in the U.S. less by cultural heritage than by the need for family cohesion in the face of economic pressures and discrimination against Asian immigrants (Taylor 2002b). Indo-American families are strongly transnational, maintaining cohesive relations with the home country through visits, business linkages, remittances, and marriage arrangements (Purkayastha 2002).

Ironically, some scholars credit the increased independence of Asian women in the United States to discrimination. To begin with, the image of Asian women as subordinated to men in patriarchal households was not always the reality. In the United States, Asian women entered the labor force because of the low wages of men. As well, the internment of Japanese-American citizens and legal residents during World War II undercut men's patriarchal authority over both women and children. Contemporary Japanese married couples evidence greater equality than in the past, although there is still a gendered division of labor (Takagi 2002). Male dominance may continue to be characteristic of more recent immigrants and some

subgroups, but not of Chinese, Japanese, and Koreans (Ishii-Kuntz 2000).

American Indian (Native American) Families[8]

A unique feature of Native American families is the relationship of tribal societies to the U.S. government. In the latter half of the nineteenth century, Indians were forcibly removed to reservations. Assimilation policies led to the creation of boarding schools, where young Indian children were placed for years with little contact with family or tribe. American Indians were encouraged to seek better conditions for their infants by placing them for adoption with white families; many of those adoptions appear in retrospect to have been forced or fraudulent (Fanshel 1972). Given the history of Native American oppression "it is not surprising . . . that American Indians suffer the highest rates of most social problems in the U.S." (Willeto and Goodluck 2004).

In the 1960s, American Indians successfully advocated for their rights, and a degree of tribal sovereignty was formalized in federal law. The Indian Child Welfare Act of 1978 gave tribes communal responsibility for tribal children. For example, a biological mother who wishes to relinquish a child for adoption cannot make those arrangements on her own; the tribe must agree and may, in fact, wish to place the child on the reservation rather than in a white adoptive home ("Navajo Tribal Court" 1988; Egan 1993).

American Indian households have incomes that are significantly lower than those of whites or Asians, though slightly higher than those of Latinos and African Americans. One-quarter of Native Americans had incomes of more than $50,000 (in 1999), but poverty rates of children are also high, even in married-couple families. The child poverty rate reaches 50 percent in female-headed families (Lugaila and Overturf 2004, Figure 5; U.S. Census Bureau 2003a, Table 680). The Indian infant mortality rate is high (9.7) compared to the overall U.S. rate of 7.0 (Matthews et al. 2003).

American Indians tend to marry at younger ages than do blacks or whites, and they have a higher rate of

---

8. Alaska Native tribes are included in a census category termed "American Indian and Alaska Native." For convenience and because little research has been done on Alaska Natives, we will refer to "Native Americans" or "American Indians."

Many social factors condition people's options and choices. One such factor is an individual's place within our culturally diverse society. These rural Navajo reservation children are learning to weave baskets to sell to tourists. Even within a racial/ethnic group, however, families and individuals may differ in the degrees to which they retain their original culture. Many Navajo live in urban settings off the reservation or go back and forth between the reservation and towns or cities.

© Phil Schermeister/CORBIS

cohabitation than other racial/ethnic groups. More than half of married American Indians have spouses who are not Native Americans. A higher proportion of Indians than blacks or whites are divorced (Kreider and Simmons 2003, Table 1; Pollard and O'Hare 1999; Yellowbird and Snipp 2002).

In 2000, 29 percent of American Indian and Alaska Native children lived with mother only and 10 percent with father only, while 52 percent lived with two parents. Another 10 percent did not live with either parent (Lugaila and Overturf 2004, Table 2-PHC-T-30). Children and youth often move between households of extended family members, and, given the high rates of alcoholism on the reservation, children may be placed with foster families, Indian or non-Indian (Lobo 2001). In common with other economically disadvantaged groups, American Indians have high rates of adolescent births, but overall birth rates are less than the U.S. average (Fields and Casper 2001; Martin et al. 2003, Table 4; Yellowbird and Snipp 2002).

Native American culture gives great respect to elders as leaders and mentors. Older women may also be relied upon for care of grandchildren. Conversely,

Native American families take care of the elderly, although they are finding that more difficult to do when so many adults live off the reservation. Acculturation seems to have lessened the dominant position of men in the family. The increase in female-headed families has been "the most significant role change in recent times," and one that has enhanced female authority and status in the family and the tribe (Yellowbird and Snipp 2002, p. 243).

How Indian families live depends on the tribe and on whether they live on or off the reservation. Surprisingly, given the historic and symbolic importance of the reservation, 60 percent of American Indians live in urban areas (Willeto and Goodluck 2004). They may often return to the reservation on ceremonial occasions; to visit friends and family; as a refuge in times of hardship; and to expose their children to tribal traditions. Because of their high rates of intermarriage and because of mobility of residence between the reservation and the city, American Indians have complex racial/cultural identities. Self-identity does not always match tribal registration (Snipp 2002).

Dorothy Miller developed a typology to explore the relative influence of Indian and mainstream American culture on urban Indian families. **Miller's typology of urban Native American families** posits a continuum from traditional to transitional to bicultural to marginal families. **Traditional families** retain Indian ways, with minimal influence from the urban settings they live in. **Bicultural families** develop a successful blend of native beliefs and the adaptations necessary to live in urban settings. **Transitional families** have lost Indian culture and are becoming assimilated to the white working class. **Marginal families** have become alienated from both Indian and mainstream cultures. In her empirical research, Miller found bicultural and marginal families to be most common, as transitional and traditional families move toward the bicultural model (Miller 1979, cited in Yellowbird and Snipp 2002, pp. 239–243).

White Families

Non-Hispanic whites continue to be the numerical majority in the United States, 68 percent of the population (U.S. Census Bureau 2003a, Table 13). Because whites are the taken-for-granted category, we tend not to see anything distinctive about white families or to consider them part of a spectrum of diversity. Whites are "the ground from which everyone else differs" (Levine 1994, p. 22).

White families are largely of European descent and so are sometimes termed *Euro-American* families. Studies of working-class families and rural families are usually based on whites. There have been other studies of family life in specific European-American ethnic groups. Much that is written about "the family" or "the American family" is grounded in patterns common among middle-class whites. But the concept of "white families" has not really been considered except for the presentation of government statistical data.

In those terms, the non-Hispanic white family, compared to most other racial/ethnic groups, appears more likely to be a married couple and less likely to have family members beyond the nuclear family residing with it. Whites are older than other groups, on average, and have lower fertility rates, so white families are less likely than Hispanic or black families to have children under eighteen living at home. White families have higher incomes than all groups but Asians, and lower poverty rates than all other racial/ethnic groups. White women are less likely than black and Hispanic women to bear children as teenagers or to have nonmarital births. In 2002, 76 percent of white children

lived with two parents, compared to 63 percent of Hispanic children and 35 percent of black children.

In terms of family structure and economic resources, then, white children and families are more advantaged. Yet the ties that provide mutual support and care of younger and older members are not as strong. White respondents reported less caregiving to aging family members; they are also less likely to rely on family members as child-care providers (AARP 2004; DeNavas-Walt et al. 2002; Dalaker and Proctor 2003; Lugnaila and Overturf 2004, Table 2-PHC-T-ep; Martin et al. 2003; U.S. Census Bureau 2003a, Tables 13, 71; Uttal 1999). Residential separation of whites from other racial/ethnic groups continues even in suburban settings (Frey 2002).

As "white studies" programs emerged in universities in the last few decades, scholars and students began to consider whether there is anything distinctive about being white. One theme that appears in the literature is "privilege," the idea that non-Hispanic whites have advantages in our society that go unnoticed by them (McIntosh 2004). Another theme that emerged from interviews is the identification of white families with some of the cultural patterns brought about by modernity and capitalism. A hallmark of the white family is the "private" family life that is affordable for middle-class families (Frankenberg 1993, pp. 192, 197, 200), who are not so often dependent on extended kin or as deeply involved in an ethnic community.

In the future, more white Americans may begin to think about identity in racial/ethnic terms, as high levels of immigration and the increasing visibility of "people of color" challenge an unconscious assumption that "American" equals "white" (Rubin 2004). At the same time, there is as much diversity among white families as there is within other broad racial/ethnic groups.

Multicultural Families[9]

Golfer Tiger Woods's emergence as a celebrity made interracial and interethnic families visible. Multiracial and multiethnic families are created by marriage, by

9. Measuring multiracial identity is difficult. Sample surveys taken before the 2000 census to try out various ways of asking about multiracial identity indicated that a straightforward question would not work. A decision was made to allow respondents to check more than one race in the 2000 census. However, only around 2.5 percent of the population did so (Grieco and Cassidy 2001; Jones and Smith 2001). Keep in mind that "Hispanic" is an ethnic, not racial, category, so is not included in the calculation of respondents who identify with two or more races.

establishment of an unmarried-couple household, and by adoption of children who are of a different race than their new parents. Since colonial times there has been racial mixing in the U.S. in marriage and other sexual and reproductive relationships (Davis 1991). Recent high levels of immigration, as well as political and cultural change, have created a situation in which the former dichotomy of black and white has expanded into a multiplicity of racial/ethnic identities and combinations.

About 7 percent of married-couple households include spouses whose racial/ethnic identities (regarding racial self-identification and Hispanic heritage) differ as reported to the 2000 census. This pattern was even more common in households of unmarried couples. Fifteen percent of opposite-sex partners and male same-sex partners and 13 percent of female partners reported different racial/ethnic identities (Simmons and O'Connell 2003).

However, only a small percentage of *individuals* claim a multiracial identity. Only 2.4 percent of the population checked more than one race in the 2000 census. Four percent of children were reported to be of two or more races (Jones and Smith 2001; Lugaila and Overturf 2004, Table 3). The proportion of multiracial children in the population is likely to increase; between 1977 and 1997 the percentage of babies born to people of different races more than doubled (Pollard and O'Hare 1999, Box 2).

As yet, we have had few studies focused on multiracial/multiethnic families in all their complexity. Interracial marriage has been the subject of some research (discussed in detail in Chapter 8). A *Washington Post* national survey of 540 interracial married or cohabiting couples tells us that families have been accepting, on the whole. African American/white couples have encountered more difficulty in marriage or with parents than have Asian/white or Latino/non-Hispanic white couples (Fears and Dean 2001; "Race and Ethnicity in 2001" 2001).

Tensions may arise out of cultural differences within families, and issues may need to be worked out before a couple and their children can reap the benefit of their rich cultural mix. Yet by and large, the *Washington Post* survey indicates that interracial couples are positive about the benefits of diversity. They believe that their children are more advantaged than disadvantaged by their multicultural heritage.

Recent research addresses the question of the racial identity of those who have parents of two races.

Surveys (177 respondents) and interviews (25 participants) of biracial students at a community college and an urban university found four ways of dealing with racial identity among students with one black and one white parent. The most common identity was a *border identity*. Fifty-eight percent of those surveyed believed that their biracial background placed them between social categories. They drew from both heritages. A difficulty in maintaining a border identity is that it was sometimes difficult to get this identity validated by others.

Seventeen percent of respondents had a *singular identity*, that is, they identified as *either* black (13 percent) *or* white (4 percent), but did not also ground their identity in the other race. Thirteen percent claimed a *protean identity;* that is, their sense of identity varied with the context—whichever social group they were interacting with at the time. They operated as insiders in both racial groups. Finally, 4 percent could be described as having a *transcendent identity*. They argued that they (and others) had no race; rather, all people should be seen as unique individuals (Rocquemore and Brunsma 2001).

We might wonder whether singular racial/ethnic identities will eventually become obsolete if interracial/interethnic marriages increase and children of those marriages adopt a multicultural identity.

■ Other Social Characteristics ■

Religion

Religious heritage is a significant influence on family life, ranging from what holidays are celebrated to the placement of family relations into a moral framework. Looking at religion over the life course, family scientist Elizabeth Miller finds that religion offers rituals to mark such important family milestones as birth, coming of age, marriage, and death. Religious affiliation provides families with a sense of community, support in times of crisis, and a set of values that give meaning to life (Miller 2000). Membership in religious congregations is associated with age and life cycle; young people who have not been actively religious tend to become so as they marry and have children (Stolzenberg, Blair-Loy, and Waite 1995).

The U.S. is among the most religious of modern industrial nations. Eighty percent of American adults surveyed in 2001 indicated a religious identification

At Arlington National Cemetery, Buddhist monks escort the coffin of an American soldier killed in Iraq. Immigration has contributed to increasing religious diversity in the U.S. There has been a Buddhist presence in the United States since at least the nineteenth century, and Buddhist practices have been followed by many Americans of non-Asian backgrounds. But the number of Buddhists more than doubled from 1990 to 2001 as the Asian American population increased through immigration.

© AP/Wide World Photos

(U.S. Census Bureau 2003a, Table 79). The historically dominant religion in the United States has been Protestantism, especially "mainstream" denominations such as Presbyterianism, Methodism, and Episcopalianism. In examining the impact of religion on family life, however, researchers tend to find other religious groups more interesting.

Earlier work focused on how Catholics and Jews differed from Protestants in their family patterns. The formalities of doctrine have not always had the effect we might assume on family-related behavior. Catholics, for example, appear to have shifted from traditional church teachings to modern conceptualizations of family and sexuality (Goldman 1992; D'Antonio et al. 1996; Davidson et al. 1997). High fertility used to be a hallmark of Catholic families, but no longer; Catholic fertility now parallels that of the general population. But studies still find contemporary Catholics to be different from Protestants in their more communal, rather than individualistic, world view (Greeley 1989).

Encouragement of large families by the Church of Jesus Christ of Latter-day Saints (LDS, formerly termed "Mormon") is reflected in the distinctly high fertility of the state of Utah (Martin et al., Table 10). Conservative Christian (including LDS) religions reject homosexuality perhaps more strongly than some others, although younger people are more liberal ("Born Again Adults Remain" 2001). Adherents of these religions favor more traditional gender roles. The Southern Baptist convention, for example, issued a declaration that wives should "submit" to their husbands (Niebuhr 1998). Conservative Protestant Christians and Latter-day Saints, as well as Catholics, are strongly opposed to abortion. Members are not always in conformity with their church's teachings. But religious influences tend to be powerful enough to produce differences in responses to surveys about attitudes and values in many family-related areas. Religious values and teaching may, in turn, influence views on public policy, as "growing levels of concern with

© Sergio Dorantes/CORBIS

In this photo of a Saudi Muslim family, the young woman's Western dress and uncovered hair suggest that cultural beliefs and norms concerning women's dress and behavior have been negotiated in a nontraditional direction within this family—a conclusion that reflects the interactional perspective (discussed in Chapter 3). Some modern young Muslim women, however, have recently adopted the head scarf to express an intensified identification with Islam in the context of experiences of discrimination or challenge to their religious community.

family decline [in the 1980s and 1990s] . . . were disproportionately concentrated among evangelical Protestants" (Brooks 2002, p. 207).

Religion affects family life in complex and perhaps unexpected ways. Conservative Christians accept a symbolic traditionalism of "headship," the man as head of the family. At the same time, in day-to-day family life, decision making seems egalitarian. Women believe they benefit from the headship concept because they perceive it as providing them with love, respect, and security. They also point to the doctrine of "mutual submission," which fosters negotiation between husband and wife. Moreover, there is a diversity of viewpoints on gender roles *within* the evangelical community (Gallagher and Smith 1999; Bartkowski 2001; Dollahite 2002). Researchers find a similar diversity among Latter-day Saints women (Beaman 2001).

With regard to marital stability, "born-again" Christians are far less likely than other Americans to enter cohabiting relationships, but their divorce rates do not differ ("Born Again Adults Less" 2001). Religion may be associated with child-rearing practices. Conservative Protestants appear more likely than the general population to emphasize obedience and to use physical punishment. At the same time, they seem more emotionally expressive in their child rearing, and more likely to praise and hug their children. It also appears that conservative Protestant fathers are more likely than mainstream Protestant or unaffiliated fathers to engage in one-on-one interaction with children in leisure activities, projects, homework help, and just talking. They are more likely than religiously unaffiliated fathers to have dinner with children and to participate in youth activities as coaches or leaders. Catholic fathers follow the same pattern of involvement (Wilcox 1998, 2002).

Those religions such as Islam that depart from a Christian tradition have the added burden of raising

Geographic location can affect chances to marry. When many young singles leave farms and small towns to live and work in the city, it becomes difficult for those who remain on the farm to find a mate. The man pictured here likes his farming life but wishes he could share it.

© Ed Lallo/Index Stock Imagery/PictureQuest

children in a society that does not support their faith; this could be said of conservative Protestant groups as well. Interfaith marriages provide a similar challenge. More than half of Jews do not have Jewish spouses, and in those mixed marriages, more than two-thirds of children are not being raised as Jews (Stern 2003). Holidays may be difficult because outsiders may expect Muslim or Jewish children to join in Christian celebrations. Some religious groups consider Halloween to be satanic and do not permit their children to celebrate it. Religiously mixed couples may experience tension over how to celebrate the holidays as a family (Haddad and Smith 1996; Horowitz 1999).

Issues other than holiday celebrations may be involved. Conservative Christians may not permit their children to date (Goodstein 2001). Islamic families provide an example of the difficulty of maintaining a religiously appropriate family life in the context of a culture that does not share their beliefs. For Muslims, dating, marital choice, child rearing, employment of women, dress, and marital decision making are all religious issues. As one Muslim mother stated to a researcher:

> I think that integration into the non-Muslim environment has to be done with the sense that we

have to preserve our Islamic identity. As long as the activity or whatever the children are doing is not in conflict with Islamic values or ways, it is permissible. But when we see it is going to be something against Islamic values, we try to teach our children that this is not correct to our beliefs and practices. They understand it and they are trying to cope with that. (Haddad and Smith 1996, p. 19)

For other religions, as well, finding a balance between participation in the larger society and preserving unique values and behaviors and a sense of community is a challenge in a society characterized by religious freedom rather than a religious establishment. Yet that freedom seems to be cherished by virtually all religious groups in the United States.

Region

In national elections, commentators point to regional differences in party affiliation and voting patterns. When we consider *family* diversity, we usually don't think of regional variation. Yet certain family patterns do seem to vary around the country, as the box "Facts About Families: The Geography of Families" indicates.

The Geography of Families

Let's take a look at regional differences in family patterns. The Census Bureau identifies four regions: Northeast, Midwest, South, and West, and also reports some county-by-county data. Academic researchers also undertake studies that make regional comparisons.

Traditional Families. The first map shows state variation in the proportion of traditional families (a married couple and their own children). Parts of the West seem to have the strongest concentration of such families. Overall we find that 8.23 percent of households in the West are traditional family households, compared with 6.48 percent in the Northeast and 6.15 percent in the South, with the Midwest having the least representation of traditional families. (Does this last number surprise you? What might explain it?)

Unwed Partners. Cohabitation has become relatively common even in conservative regions. In fact, the increase in the 1990s was most dramatic in the Bible Belt and Great Plains.

Same-Sex Partner Households. The second map in Figure 2.2 indicates the prevalence of gay/lesbian couple households. These seem most concentrated in the Northeast, Georgia and Florida in the South, and in a large part of the West, though not the same part of the West that has a strong presence of traditional households.

Divorce. Divorce rates are highest in the West and South, lowest in the Northeast and Midwest. Only one Northeastern state and one Midwestern state have divorce rates above the U.S. average, while 70 percent of Southern states and 80 percent of Western states have rates higher than average.

Children's Living Arrangements. More children in the West are living in unmarried partner households: 6.2 percent, compared to 5.8 percent in the Northeast, 5.7 percent in the Midwest, and 5.3 percent in the South.

While the South has the fewest children in unmarried partner households, it also has the highest percentage of children not living in a married-couple family. The South has by far the highest proportion of female single-parent households.

Poverty and Labor Force Participation. The South also has the highest proportion of children living in poverty: 19.5 percent, compared to 18.5 percent for the West, 16.1 percent in the Northeast, and a substantially lower 14.3 percent in the Midwest. And a child in the South is almost half again as likely to have parents *not* in the labor force (18.1 percent) as a child in the Midwest (12.6).

Corporal Punishment. A parent in the South is more apt to favor corporal punishment than those in other regions. Some 80 percent of Southern parents agree that it is "sometimes necessary to discipline with a good hard spanking," while only about 60 percent of New England parents agree. In actual practice the two regions are not far apart, as only 40 percent of Southerners and 36 percent of New England parents "ever spanks." New England parents tend to be yellers (56 percent) compared to Southern parents (48 percent).

Sexuality. The South tends to be most conservative in agreeing that sex should be limited to marriage (40 percent) and in opposing the legalization of "homosexual relations" (32 percent) or same-sex mar-

riage (29 percent). The Northeast and the West are least disapproving of nonmarital sex (26 percent and 29 percent). The West is most likely to favor the legality of gay/lesbian relationships (59 percent) and same-sex marriage (40 percent), with the Northeast not far behind.

Nevertheless, Southerners are almost as likely as those in other regions to agree (90 percent) that contraception is an appropriate topic for sex education in the eleventh and twelfth grades. While that is lower than the 93 percent in the Northeast and West who favor contraceptive education, perhaps what is most striking is the high level of support for contraceptive education in all regions.

Teen Pregnancies and Births. However, the South and the West had higher pregnancies and birth rates for women fifteen through seventeen than did the Northeast and Midwest.

Gender Roles. Gender roles are hard to characterize, although there are regional differences. The South continues to be the most conservative region, but has become much less so since the seventies; differences between Southerners and non-Southerners in gender role attitudes are now small. A high proportion of women in the South, as elsewhere, work outside the home, and Southerners do not differ much from respondents in other regions as to whether an employed woman can be a good mother. Still, Southerners are more apt to agree with the general statement that women should refrain from working outside the home and much more likely to see the realm of politics as a man's world (Rice and Coats 1995; Twenge 1997a). Differences between the South and other regions are attributed to the more conservative political climate of the

South; the association of conservative attitudes toward women with fundamentalist Protestantism, which is a strong presence in the region; and a "Southern Belle mentality" (Rice and Coates 1995, p. 754).

Other Family Indicators. Regions are rather similar in terms of the number of children in a family; the percentage of adults who are married; and the proportion of children living with at least one of their parents, which clusters around 90 percent.

We have not attempted to systematically explain *why* these differences between regions exist, as that is too complex a task for a brief summary. They are likely due to differences in the historical experience of regions and cultural differences resulting from those histories. Differences may reflect the population composition of a region in terms of age, race/ethnicity, and religion, as well as the nature of the economy.

Critical Thinking

Have you lived in more than one region of the country? If so, did it seem to you that there were differences in family patterns and "family values" in these different locations?

Pick one of the family patterns discussed in the box and think about how you might explain regional variation. Or think about a region and speculate about reasons for the cluster of family patterns associated with that region.

(Sources: AmeriStat Staff 2003f; Fields 2001; Harden 2001; Landry, Darroch, Singh, and Higgins 2004; Lugaila and Overturf 2004; Rice and Coates 1995; Roseamilia and Van Willigen 2002; Smith and Gates 2001; U.S. Census Bureau 2003a, Tables 68, 126; "Views on Homosexuality" 2003.)

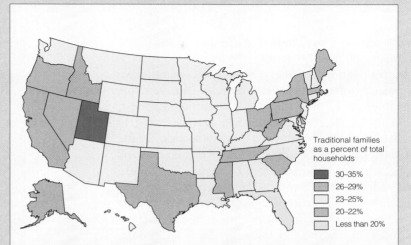

Regional variation in the traditional American household: 2000. A "traditional household" is defined as a married couple with children under 18. The map shows the variation among states in the percentage of all households that are traditional households. There is also a great deal of variation within each state.

Source: U.S. Census Bureau 2003a, Table 68.

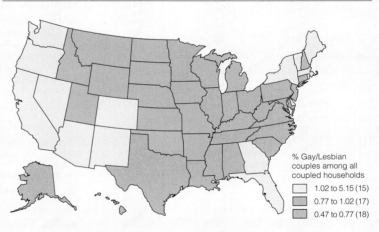

Percentage of gay/lesbian couples among all coupled households: 2000. Fifty States and the District of Columbia.

Source: David M. Smith and Gary J. Gates. Gay and Lesbian Families in the United States: Same-Sex Unmarried Partner Households, Washington, D.C. Human Rights Campaign, 2001. Figure 1, p. 11.

FIGURE 2.2

The Geography of Families—These maps illustrate regional variation in such indicators of family life as the percentage of traditional households and the percentage of gay/lesbian couples.

The Economy and Social Class

In this section we will look at the economic well-being of American families as we examine the social-class context of family life. **Social class**, one's overall status in a society (often measured in terms of education, occupation, and income), may be as important as race or ethnicity in affecting people's choices. We tend to think of the United States as a classless society. Yet **life chances**—the opportunities one has for education and work, whether one can afford to marry, the schools that children attend, and the family's health care—all depend on family economic resources. Lifestyles vary by social class, and so may family patterns. For instance, attitudes, behaviors, and the experiences of middle-class blacks differ from those of poor African Americans (Billingsley 1992). A study of parental socialization of children found class to be more important than race in terms of parental values and interactions with their children (Laureau 2003).

Class differences in economic resources affect the timing of leaving home, marriage, and caretaking responsibilities:

> An elderly widow with a paid-off house and investments can afford home health care; her children and grandchildren need not organize themselves around her care. In contrast, a family sharing a grandmother's subsidized housing becomes homeless on her death, and the mother, who has already lost many work days because of the grandmother's illness, may be fired while apartment hunting. (Kliman and Madsen 1999, p. 93)

Economic Change and Inequality

Economists are divided as to whether the increasing globalization of the economy—with more "outsourcing" of U.S. jobs overseas and the replacement of manufacturing by service jobs—is rendering the economic foundation of the family more precarious or is opening new opportunities. While the U.S. economy was good for many Americans during the 1990s, others are experiencing increased job insecurity, loss of benefits, longer workdays, and more part-time and temporary work (Teachman, Tedrow, and Crowder 2000).

The overall trend in household income has been upward, though falling back during periods of reces-

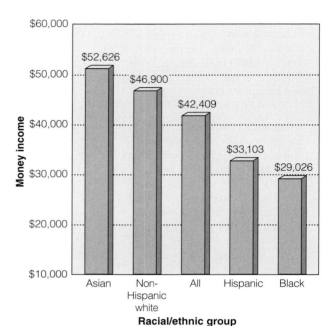

FIGURE 2.3

Median household money income by race and Hispanic origin of householder: 2002.

Source: Adapted from DeNavas-Walt, Cleveland, and Webster, Figure 1. Comparable data are not available for American Indian/Alaska Natives or for Native Hawaiians and Other Pacific Islanders. In 1999, American Indians had median incomes slightly greater than those of blacks, while Native Hawaiian and Other Pacific Islander incomes were slightly higher than the figure for all households, but significantly below Asian median income (U.S. Census Bureau 2003a, Table 680).

sion. But clearly, the distribution of income in the United States is highly unequal. In 2002, the top 20 percent of U.S. families received almost half (49.7 percent) of the nation's total income, while the poorest 20 percent of Americans received just 3.5 percent. Over the past thirty years, the inequality gap has grown; the rich have gotten richer, and the poor have gotten poorer. Income varies by race and ethnicity (see Figures 2.3 and 2.4), but all middle to lower groups show moderate gains at best over the long term. Most of the gain has accrued to those with a college education (Day and Cheeseman 2002; DeNavas-Walt et al. 2003, Table A-3; Scott 2001a).

Women gained more during this period, while men's wages were largely stagnant (Kilborn 2002). Still, access to a male wage remains an advantage. Experts debate the extent to which changes in the distribution of family structures—i.e., more female-headed single-parent households—have contributed to poverty

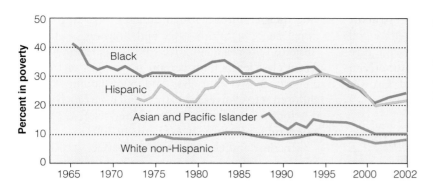

FIGURE 2.4

Poverty rates by race and Hispanic origin: 1965–2002.

Sources: Lichter and Crowley 2002, Figure 3, with additional data from Procotor and Dalaker 2003, Table 1.

levels (Lichter and Crowley 2002; Lichter, Graefe, and Brown 2003). Incomes do vary by family type. Married-couple families with wives in the labor force have the highest family incomes ($70,834 in 2001), compared to married-couple families in which the wife is not in the labor force ($40,782) or male-headed ($36,590) or female-headed families ($25,745) (U.S. Census Bureau 2003a, p. 472, Table 690).

Poverty rates fell dramatically in the 1960s and have risen and fallen again since then. Only in 2000 did the overall poverty rate descend below its previous low point of 8.7 in 1974, though it has risen again, to 9.6 percent in 2002 (Proctor and Dalaker 2003, Table A-3).

In many respects, the second half of the 1990s brought an increase in living standards in terms of income, housing, education, and automobile ownership. The 2000 median household income matches the highest ever recorded, though it declined in 2001 and 2002. Americans overall are better off economically than they were in the 1970s. But incomes have grown little for the middle class and the working poor; programs of assistance for the poor have been cut, and there is increased economic risk and volatility and uncertainty about the future of such benefits as pensions and health insurance (Hacker 2004; Kilborn and Clemetson 2002). Some 12 percent of families were classified as "working poor" (at least one wage earner), and these low-wage earners find it difficult to afford even a one- or two-bedroom apartment (Clemetson 2003; U.S. Bureau of Labor Statistics 2003b).

While child poverty is down, it is above the levels of the 1960s and 1970s and higher than poverty rates in other wealthy industrialized nations ("Living in Poverty" 2002; Madrick 2002). One in six children is in poverty. Black children have a poverty rate of 31.5 percent (in 2002), Hispanic children are at 28.6 percent, non-Hispanic white children at 9.4 percent, while Asian children have a poverty rate of 11.7 percent (Proctor and Dalaker 2003). The income of a number of black families has risen, but conditions at the lowest economic levels have not shown improvement, nor have blacks at higher income levels acquired assets that compare with those of non-Hispanic whites. Black gains have seemed fragile, as median household income dropped back during the recent recession (Crockett 2003).

Furthermore, a new book argues that the middle-class two-income household is not so secure as one would think. It takes two incomes to provide what one did thirty years ago. Housing costs in safe neighborhoods have risen dramatically, as has the cost of college education. Even seemingly affluent two-income families are at risk of financial failure in the event of unexpected misfortune. Married couples with children are twice as likely to file for bankruptcy as childless couples (Warren and Warren 2003). "They're middle-class couples who are in deep financial trouble in large part because they have kids" (Surowiecki 2003).

Money may not buy happiness, but it does afford a myriad of options: sufficient and nutritious food, comfortable residences, better health care, keeping in touch with family and friends through the Internet, education at prestigious universities, vacations, household help, and family counseling. Researchers dispute the degree to which money alone accounts for child outcomes in poor families or whether there are other differences in parenting or other conditions of socialization that are more significant once the basic necessities of food and housing are provided (Duncan and Brooks-Gunn 2002; Mayer 1997).

We do need to think about public resources, which some observers see as on the decline—support for education, for example. While the 1996 restructuring of "welfare" has led to a decline in welfare rolls without, overall, the disastrous results predicted, it remains to be seen what will happen in the future (Duncan and Brooks-Gunn 2002; Lichter and Crowley 2002).

Blue-Collar and White-Collar Families

In examining social class, social scientists have often compared blue-collar and white-collar workers in terms of values and lifestyles. Working-class people, or blue-collar workers, are employed as mechanics, truckers, machine operators, and factory workers—jobs typically requiring uniforms or durable work clothes. Some jobs, such as police officer, occupy a sort of intermediate position. White-collar workers include professionals, managers, clerical workers, salespeople, and so forth, who have traditionally worn white shirts to work.

Social scientists do not agree on whether blue- and white-collar workers have become increasingly alike in their values and attitudes in recent decades. To complicate matters, the nature of some blue-collar jobs has changed dramatically with the advent of computerized manufacturing, while some professions—medicine, for example—have lost ground in terms of income and autonomy. White-collar job security has been eroded by changes in the economy, and middle-class families are "increasingly vulnerable" to financial misfortune, particularly when overloaded with consumer debt (Sullivan, Walker, and Westbrook 2000, p. 22).

But blue- and white-collar employees may continue to look at life differently even at similar income levels. Regarding marriage, for example, working-class couples tend to emphasize values associated with parenthood and job stability and may be more traditional in gender-role ideology. White-collar couples are more inclined to value companionship, self-expression, and communication. Middle-class parents value self-direction and initiative in children, whereas parents in working-class families stress obedience and conformity (Hochschild 1989; Laureau 2003b; Luster, Rhoades, and Haas 1989; Smith 1999, pp. 12–19). Middle-class parenting strategies also include involving children in a myriad of stimulating activities and lessons to enhance their development. While there is no doubt that middle-class parents pro- vide their children with advantages regarding educational success, health care, and housing, sociologist Annette Lareau's qualitative study of parenting at different class levels finds certain advantages accruing to children in working-class and poor families. These children see relatives frequently and have much deeper relationships with cousins and older relatives, as well as less time-pressured lives (Laureau 2003a).

Income and class position may affect access to an important feature of contemporary society: technology. Computers and the Internet, other technology, and related developments in medicine are not evenly distributed across our society. Nine in ten family households with incomes of more than $75,000 have a computer, and eight in ten have Internet access. Comparable figures for family households with incomes of less than $25,000 are three in ten and two in ten (Newburger 2001).

■ Technology and the Family ■

Technology has always affected family life, from prehistoric discoveries of fire and stone tools to the present. The invention of the automobile changed courtship from a process closely supervised by family and community to one conducted by young people on their own.

Recently, links between family and technology have taken the form of electronic devices and biomedical breakthroughs, which offer hope and expanded options while creating new arenas of decision making. Technology has influenced how family members communicate with one another, as well as matters of life and death (e.g., reproductive technology and organ transplants).

Communication Technology

Computer-based technology and hand-held devices enable family members to remain in touch when, for example, they are traveling, serving in the military, or as noncustodial parents living in another city. Parents can go over homework or discuss a child's concerns. Locally, they can keep pace with children's movements around town by means of cell phone check-ins. Parents at work can monitor or communicate with their children through cell phones, pagers, and the Internet. With communication technology, parents can feel

These days, family members who are apart stay in touch through e-mail and other electronic means. Many in this generation of college students maintain daily contact with parents.

"Don't forget to click Reply."

more secure about their child's safety and well-being, while children can contact parents when they need help, advice, or permission to proceed. Young adults in college or otherwise away from their parents can keep in touch by e-mail or cell phone (Alvord 2003b; Jackson 2002).

Some concern has been expressed that parents may rely too much on these forms of contact; children may lose by not having time where they just talk with their parents (Schneider, Waite, and Dempsey 2000). Some psychologists and educators have seen constant parental availability to children as a developmental disadvantage: "It prevents our kids from learning life skills they need to succeed in the real world. There are times they need to ad lib. There are times they need to wait. There are even times they need to turn to someone else—another family member, a teacher, a neighbor—and ask for help" (Wise 2000, p. 15).

Going away to college is fast becoming a different experience, as parents and children now seem to communicate daily by phone or e-mail. Some college counselors (and social scientists) see this as a developmentally inappropriate dependency, and one which might limit a full immersion into college life. Others see simply another step in the evolution of intergenerational relations. Children of baby boomers seem to be

closer to parents and to have more in common with them than was true of the baby boomers and their parents (Lewin 2003a; Schouten 2003; Vanderkam 2003).

E-mail supports communication within the extended family. Family photos may be sent instantly, and families may develop their own websites. Almost 60 percent of respondents to one survey reported that with e-mail and the Internet, they communicate more with significant family members (Harmon 1998; Raney 2000).

Of course, modern forms of communication may compete with the family. They keep family members at work even while in family settings. It has also been alleged that computers, the Internet, and e-mail may be so absorbing that attention is drained from normal family interchange. Some research suggests that "computer addiction" is not that common. A majority of survey respondents reported increased sociability, not less (Raney 2000; Guernsey 2001). But a recent survey (Nie, Hillygus, and Erbring 2002) found the reverse, and no definitive conclusion seems possible at the moment.

The Internet may help form families. Prospective parents now search for adoptable children on the Internet (Sink 2000). Internet contacts have also become a way of forming romantic relationships that sometimes ripen into marriage. Self-disclosure seems to occur earlier in online relationships (Hughes and Hans 2001; Morris 1999b). Needless to say, however, the person who seems so attractive in e-mail may not be so in person. Conversely, expectations may be so high that a person met through an e-mail is rejected when this person might be pursued if met in person (Cohen 2001b). Dating partners may find it easier to break up in e-mail (Boland 2000).

For those looking for marital matches with people of their own racial/ethnic background, specialized websites may help. South Asians, who have high rates of Internet connectivity as well as a tradition of formal matchmaking, find that websites provide a network of American- and Asian-based potential partners and a control over the situation that they seek in preference to casual dating (Jana 2000). Silicon Valley—the world of computer and Internet workers—is another locus of busy professionals and computer ease that fosters matchmaking websites (Stone 1999). Religious niche matchmaking sites give singles the option of looking for a partner from their faith community (Parnes 2001).

As noted in Chapter 8, concern has been expressed about Internet "affairs" that may threaten a marriage even if not consummated sexually or advanced by an in-person meeting (Hughes and Hans 2001). At the same time, technology may keep family bonds intact when disruption occurs. Courts sometimes order videoconferencing and more routinely require that e-mail, instant messaging, and private phone lines be provided to keep children of divorce in touch with noncustodial parents (Flaherty 2001).

Electronic Surveillance

Thanks to modern technology, parents may check on children, partners check on their spouses or lovers, and families check on hired caregivers. The ubiquitous teen cell phone may serve as monitoring device and safety precaution. With a cell phone, the youth may call for a ride or help in a risky situation. Yet parents may call or page often to check on an adolescent, and teens may resent this: "Now it's like I have kind of a dog chain on. If she pages me, I have to call her back. She always has some kind of access to me . . . like my personal space is being invaded" (quoted in Hafner 2000, p. D–1).

For smaller children there is the baby monitor, bringing an infant's cries to parents' attention. Parents

may also monitor children's safety and the quality of hired caregivers through video monitoring. Although they may make parents feel more in control, such surveillance systems create ethical issues if unknown to the target. Many child-care centers now provide Internet transmission of video scanning of the children's activities (Morris 1999a). Those services are typically very visible; their public relations value is the point.

Homing devices or special cell phones enable parents to check a youth's whereabouts directly (Harmon 2003; Talbot 2002a; Armstrong 2003). Chips planted on the cars of teenage drivers permit a parent to monitor a child's location (or at least the car's location) for safety reasons, or because the parent believes the youth to be so troubled that drastic action is called for. Home drug testing may be used by a concerned or suspicious parent ("Who Needs Doctors?" 1998).

Adults may be electronically tracked as well, or their phone calls tapped or e-mail or Internet traffic monitored by computer software. One woman bought a program to check on her adolescent daughter's e-mail only to discover that her husband was having affairs; the marriage broke up (Anderson 2000).

How do people feel about being watched? Often resentful. More generally, the implied need for electronic security may create an atmosphere of apprehension or of unknown danger. Paradoxically, surveillance may be liberating for a special category of people: the vulnerable elderly. Seniors may be able to live on their own longer with the aid of surveillance technology and other technological support (Long 2002; Raymond 2002).

Biomedical Technology

Transplantation of organs and bone marrow to save lives has become almost routine. But transplantation requires a donor. Because a match is needed for best results, those who are genetically close to the patient (family members) are the best donors. Willingness to donate kidneys or bone marrow and positive feelings in the aftermath are the most common responses among potential donors (Simmons 1991). But not all family members or their spouses are willing. A family member's refusal to be tested may create tension in family relations. Whether a parent should give consent for a child to donate a kidney is another sticky ethical issue, as is the conception of a child for the sole purpose of providing tissue or an organ for a sick older sibling (Belkin 2001).

In situations where family donor matches prove impossible, families have gone online to seek bone marrow donors. The Internet has expanded the network through which donors may be recruited (Pollak 2000).

Biomedical developments seem to leap out of the headlines with great frequency. We may expect new arenas of biomedical technology to create new issues for family decision making. (Reproductive technology and genetic testing are discussed in Chapter 10).

Technology: Pros, Cons, and Change

A particular technology usually has both benefits and costs. The videoconferencing that keeps parents in touch with children after divorce, a positive development, may seem intrusive to the noncustodial parent as the camera sweeps around his or her space. Technology may disrupt the family when the unforeseen consequences of using it are negative. Discovery that a couple's child of the marriage is not the biological child of the husband is one striking example.

Technology confronts families with new decisions: about medical treatment and the use of reproductive technology; about investigating suspicions of other family members; about risking a meeting with an In-

ternet contact; about what to do with knowledge of teen children's movements or knowledge of family genetic risks; about paying attention (or not) to work-related communication while at home; about how much time parents should invest in monitoring children.

Technology may transform family relationships. E-mail is predicted to enhance the father's communicative role with children and others. Separate e-mail accounts for parents may make father–child contacts more distinct than when Mom spoke for the parent couple in letters or phone calls (Bold 2001). Moreover, people who tend to communicate in a less open, elaborative style (typically males) expand their expressive communication in e-mail (Cohen 2001a).

Technology may subvert other roles and stereotypes. An older person who masters the Internet may feel empowered compared to age-mates. On the other hand, an older parent may find his or her central role in the family eroded now that adult children can easily communicate directly with one another, bypassing the parent (English-Lueck 2001).

Looking back, we can see that while new technologies may affect the family, the process of adapting to technology is not a new experience for families. What needs to happen, though, is that families need to be aware of the role that technology plays in the social environment of the family.

In Sum

- Families exist in a social context that affects many aspects of family life.
- Historical events and trends have affected family life over the last century. These include economic and cultural trends, as well as wars and other national crises.
- The age structure affects family patterns and social policy needs regarding families. The proportion of older Americans in the population is increasing, so we may anticipate growing responsibilities for the older generation. The proportion of children in the population is decreasing, leading to questions about the future of society's commitment to children.
- Race and ethnicity shape family life because African American, Latino, Asian, American Indian/Alaska Native, Native Hawaiian and other Pacific Islander, and

white families have some differences in structure, resources, and culture. The increasing rate of racial/ethnic intermarriage suggests that more families in the future will be multicultural.

- Immigration has risen to a level that contributes visibly to the diversity of family life.
- Religious traditions and prescriptions shape family life. In studying the family, we are apt to take more notice of religions that maintain distinctive family norms.
- The economy has a strong impact on family life. Americans do not like to acknowledge class differences, but the possession or lack of economic resources affects family options. So do differences in values and preferences that characterize blue-collar and white-collar sectors of society.
- Technological developments have made significant changes in family life, with new options and new

responsibilities. Electronic communication, surveillance technology, and biomedical developments mean that families have new decisions to make.

- Exploring the social context highlights some constraints on American families. Even though individuals may be limited in their choices by social conditions, becoming conscious of social influences permits a more knowledgeable choice. It also minimizes self-blame for what may be a socially structured lack of options and may inspire collective effort to alter social conditions.

- The first two chapters of this book have examined specific forms and patterns of American family life. In the next chapter we take a more abstract look at families through the lens of family theory. We also explore the ways in which social scientists study the family using various methodologies.

Key Terms

binational family	traditional
cultural broker	transitional
ethnicity	minority
globalization	minority group
immigrant stock	race
infant mortality rate	role reversal
life chances	sex ratio
Miller's typology of urban	social class
Native American families:	transnational family
bicultural	undocumented immigrant
marginal	

Questions for Review and Reflection

1. Describe one specific social context of family life presented in the text. Does what you read match what you see in everyday life?

2. What are some significant aspects of the family lives of immigrant families? Do you think immigrant families will change over time? How?

3. In the everyday lives of families (yours or those you observe), what economic pressures, opportunities, and choices do you see?

4. Would you be willing to donate a kidney to a sibling? Why or why not? Do you think it would be okay to conceive a child to become a bone marrow donor for another child of the family?

5. **Policy Question.** Which age group is increasing as a proportion of the U.S. population, children or the elderly? What social changes might occur as a result? What social policies do we need to maintain or develop to care for children and the elderly?

Suggested Readings

Hirsch, Jennifer S. 2003. *A Courtship after Marriage: Sexuality and Love in Mexican Transnational Families.* Berkeley, CA: University of California Press. Exemplifying the theme "We are not like our parents," this study of a Mexican migrant community examines changes in marriage, sexual relations, reproduction, and gender roles.

Mintz, Steven, and Susan Kellogg. 1988. *Domestic Revolutions: A Social History of American Family Life.* New York: Free Press. Comprehensive history of the American family from colonial times onward. Treats regional and racial/ethnic differences in historical context.

Newman, Katherine. 1993. *Declining Fortunes: The Withering of the American Dream.* New York: Basic. The economy has been up and down since Newman published her study of families affected by economic decline. The book is still relevant in showing the impact of unemployment, rising housing costs, and other economic pressures on families.

Pattillo-McCoy, Mary. 1999. *Black Picket Fences: Privilege and Peril among the Black Middle Class.* Chicago: University of Chicago Press. An in-depth ethnographic study of black middle-class families in Chicago, whose theme is the "privilege and peril" of black middle-class youth.

Taylor, Ronald L. 2002c. *Minority Families in the United States: A Multicultural Perspective*, 3rd ed. New York: Prentice Hall. Includes good discussions of minority families in general, as well as essays on black, Hispanic, Asian, and Native American families and ethnic divisions within the major categories.

Turow, Joseph, and Andrea L. Kavanaugh, eds. 2003. *The Wired Homestead: An MIT Press Sourcebook on the Internet and the Family.* Cambridge, MA: MIT Press. Readings on the impact of the Internet on family life.

Annie E. Casey Foundation **http://www.aecf.org** The Annie E. Casey Foundation website features its "Kids Count" data project. Kids Count compiles data on children: the social conditions in which they live and indicators of their well-being. Includes state-by-state data that enable exploration of this level of social diversity.

Virtual Society: The Wadsworth Sociology Resource Center

 Go to the Sociology Resource Center at **http:// sociology.wadsworth.com** for a wealth of online resources, including a companion website for your text that provides study aids such as self-quizzes for each chapter and a practice final exam, as well as links to sociology websites and information on the latest theories and discoveries in the field. In addition, you will find further suggested readings, flash cards, MicroCase online exercises, and appendices on a range of subjects.

Online Study Tool

Marriage & Family ⊛ Now™ Go to **http://sociology .wadsworth.com** to reach the companion website for your text and use the Marriage&FamilyNow access code that came with your book to access this study tool. Take a practice pretest after you have read each chapter, and then use the study plan provided to master that chapter. Afterward, take a posttest to monitor your progress.

Search Online with InfoTrac College Edition

For additional information, exercises, and key words to aid your research, explore InfoTrac College Edition, your online library that offers full-length articles from thousands of scholarly and popular publications. Click on *InfoTrac College Edition* under *Chapter Resources* at the companion website and use the access code that came with your book.

- Search keywords: *multiracial, multiethnic, or multicultural + family*. Look for articles on families that have a multicultural heritage. How are families affected by their linkages to multiple racial/ethnic groups?

- Search keywords: *religion + family*, or substitute the name of a particular religious group. Does the number of articles you find indicate that researchers are interested in this topic? What religious groups seem to get most attention in conjunction with their family life?

Chapter **3**

Exploring the Family

There is nothing so practical as a good theory.

KURT LEWIN

Wᴴᴇɴ ᴡᴇ ʙᴇɢɪɴ ᴀ ᴄᴏᴜʀsᴇ ᴏɴ ᴛʜᴇ family, we are eager to have our questions answered:

- "What's a good family?"
- "How do I make that happen?"
- "Whom should I choose?"
- "What do I need to know to be a good parent?"

And:

- "What's happening to the family today?"

In Chapter 1, we outlined some trends in family life, and some changes and developments you may have learned about from the media or deduced from observing life around you. In Chapter 2, we looked at social variation in family life and family change. But what these changes mean—how to interpret them—is not always so easy. There are many visions of the family, and what an observer reads into the data depends partly on his or her perspective.

For some, these trends mean that the family is "declining," whereas for others, the family is simply "changing." From politicians, we hear about family trends with words such as *conservative* or *liberal* attached. But in forming their interpretations, social scientists often use the more formal vocabulary of social theory and research methodology to characterize marriage and family patterns.

This chapter invites you to share this way of seeing families. First, we look at some theoretical perspectives that shape our thinking about families. Then we consider the knotty problem of studying a phenomenon as close to our hearts as family life.

Theoretical Perspectives on the Family

Theoretical perspectives are ways of viewing reality. They are lenses through which observers organize and interpret what they see. A theoretical perspective leads researchers to identify those aspects of families that are of interest to them and suggests explanations for why family patterns and practices are the way they are.

There are a number of different theoretical perspectives on the family. We shall see that what is significant about families varies from one perspective to the next. Sometimes, the perspectives complement one another and may appear together in a single piece of research. In other instances, the perspectives compete with one another, a situation that may lead analysts and policy makers to a heated debate. All this may frustrate students who grope for the one "correct" answer. Instead, it is useful to think of a theoretical perspective as a point of view. As we move around an object and see it from different angles, we have a better grasp of what it is than if we look at it from a single, fixed position.

In this chapter, we describe eight theoretical perspectives on the family: family ecology, family development, structure–functionalism, the interactionist perspective, exchange theory, family systems theory, feminist perspectives, and biosocial perspectives. Table 3.1, "Theoretical Perspectives on the Family," presents a summary of these theoretical perspectives. We will see that each perspective not only illuminates our understanding in its own way but has also emerged in its own social and historical context.

The Family Ecology Perspective

The **family ecology perspective** explores how a family influences and is influenced by the environments that surround it. We use the family ecology perspective throughout this book when we stress that society does not determine family members' behavior but does present limitations and constraints for families as well as possibilities and opportunities.

Every family is embedded in "a set of nested structures, each inside the next, like a set of Russian dolls" (Bronfenbrenner 1979, quoted in Bubolz and Sontag 1993, p. 423; see Figure 3.1). At the foundation is the *natural physical–biological environment*—climate, soil, plants, animals, etc. The *human-built environment* develops when nature is altered by human action. As modern human settlement occurs, for example, roads and houses are built, and utility lines are strung. Commerce and industry develop and may in turn affect the natural environment. The *social–cultural environment* is entirely a human creation and consists of cultural values, cultural products like language and

Table 3.1

Theoretical Perspectives on the Family			
Theoretical Perspective	**Theme**	**Key Concepts**	**Current Research**
Family Ecology	The ecological context of the family affects family life and children's outcomes.	Natural physical–biological environment; Human-built environment; Social–cultural environment	Family policy; Neighborhood effects
Family Development	Families experience predictable changes over time.	Family life cycle; Developmental tasks	Transition to adulthood
Structure–Functional	The family performs essential functions for society.	Social institution; Family structure; Family functions	Cross-cultural and historical comparisons
Interactionist	The internal dynamics of the family as a group of interacting individuals shape the family.	Interaction; Self-concept; Identity; Meaning	Family rituals; Meanings assigned to domestic work
Exchange Theory	The resources that individuals bring to a relationship or family affect formation, continuation, and nature of a relationship.	Resources; Costs and rewards; Exchange balance; Power and decision making	Family power; Entry and exit from marriage; Family violence
Systems Theory	The family as a whole is more than the sum of its parts.	System; Equilibrium; Boundaries; Family therapy	Family efficacy and crisis management; Family boundaries
Feminist Perspectives	Gender is central to the analysis of family; male dominance in family and society is oppressive of women.	Male dominance; Power and inequality; Sex/gender systems	Work and family; Domestic violence; Family power; Advocacy of women's issues
Biosocial Perspectives	Evolution of the human species has put in place certain biological endowments that shape and limit family choices.	Evolutionary heritage; Genes; Inclusive fitness	Correlations between biological markers and family behavior; Evolutionary explanations for gender differences and sexuality

law, and social and economic systems. All parts of the model are interrelated and influence one another (Bubolz and Sontag 1993).

The ecology of families may be analyzed at various levels, from the neighborhood (Burton and Jarrett 2000) to the global level (Goode 1993). The increasing *globalization* of the sociocultural environment of families, for example, means that job opportunities for American family members are affected by the decisions of multinational corporations about where to place their operations. And the 9/11 terrorist attacks on the United States, which have affected American family life in countless ways, are part of a global conflict.

The family ecology perspective emerged in the latter part of the nineteenth century, a period marked by social concern about the health and welfare of families. After losing ground to other theories, the family ecology model resurfaced in the 1960s with increased awareness of the interdependence of families and their political and economic environments (Bubolz and Sontag 1993). For instance, the Head Start program, part of President Lyndon Johnson's War on Poverty in the 1960s, was largely propelled by the perspective of family ecology.

The family ecology model is once again prominent in research and in political discussion and debate

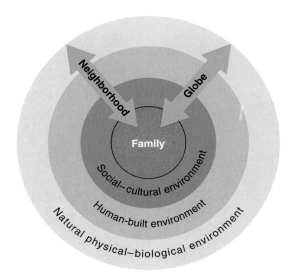

FIGURE 3.1

The family ecology perspective. The family is embedded in natural physical–biological, human-built, and social–cultural environments.

Source: Adapted with permission from "Human Ecology Theory," pp. 419–448 in *Sourcebook of Family Theories and Methods,* ed. by Pauline G. Boss et al. Copyright © 1993, Kluwer Academic/Plenum Publishers.

(Booth and Crouter 2001). An exploration of the ecological setting of the family may identify important factors in effective neighborhood and community support for families. The relationship of work and family life, discussed in Chapter 12, is another ecological focus. So is the recent interest in families with incarcerated members. (See "When A Parent Is in Prison" in Chapter 15.) And part of the ecology of the family today is the perception of risk in local or global settings. (See "Issues for Thought: Safety and Risk in the Family Environment.")

Furthermore, today's family ecologists, in an increasingly global society, stress the interdependence of all the world's families—not only with one another but also with our fragile physical–biological environment. In this vein, the Family Energy Project at Michigan State University has studied families' energy usage and conservation of energy (Bubolz and Sontag 1993). But while it is crucial, the interaction of families with the physical–biological environment is beyond the scope of this text. Here our interest centers on families enmeshed in their sociocultural environments.

FAMILY POLICY The ecology model's focus on how various sociocultural environments affect families leads to an interest in *family policy*. In a narrow sense, **family policy** is all the procedures, regulations, attitudes, and goals of government that affect families. More generally, family policy concerns itself with the circumstances in the broader society that affect the family. American families worry about making ends meet: how we will support ourselves, find comfortable housing, educate (or feed) our children, get affordable health care, finance our old age. Poverty is a real problem for many U.S. families, and research suggests that deep poverty in early childhood affects outcomes for children (Duncan and Brooks-Gunn 2002). Family ecologists might point out that the United States provides fewer services to families than does any other industrialized nation, while Western Europe offers many examples of a successful partnership between government and families in the interests of family support.

The ecology perspective encourages researchers and policy makers to investigate what might be done to create environments that improve families' quality of life. How can families become activists for the kinds of changes they want?

Given the social and political diversity in American society, all parents or political actors are unlikely to agree on the best course of action. For example, with five million children home alone after school each week ("Facts About Child Care" 1998), providing adequate child care is an important issue in the United States today. But how should it be done? The liberal national organization Children's Defense Fund has urged increases in day-care funding that would, among other things, expand the availability of after-school programs ("Child Care NOW" 1998). Meanwhile, the Family Research Council, a conservative national organization, proposes a "Family Time" child-care policy. Designed to "facilitate parental child rearing," this policy would double tax credits for families with children and legislate flextime in some workplaces ("'Family Time' Child Care Policy" 1998).

Americans are divided on what "family" means in a policy sense. Some argue that only heterosexual, nuclear families should be encouraged, whereas others believe in supporting a variety of families—single-parent or gay and lesbian families, for example (Bogenschneider 2000; Waite 2001). Indeed, the diversity of family lifestyles in the United States makes it ex-

People in this neighborhood join together in activities of benefit to all. This group is organizing a Neighborhood Watch program.

tremely difficult to develop a national family policy that would satisfy all, or even most, of us.

Then, too, more government help to families would be costly, hence sure to be opposed in this era of increased hostility to taxes. On the other hand, the estimated costs of not having family programs may be higher. Disadvantaged children may eventually cost society more in unemployment compensation and incarceration expenses than would preventive investments in support of these children and their families.

THE NEIGHBORHOOD Family policy is usually pursued at the national or state level, in terms of legislation and new programs. Social scientists have recently become interested in the local ecology of families (Scanzoni 2001a). Neighborhoods are especially important for the well-being and development of teenagers, who spend much time outside the house (Kurz 2002). It's been assumed that in the past there were neighborhoods

> where there were many children and parents considered the neighborhood safe enough so that children could be allowed simply to "go out

to play." Nowadays most neighborhoods, even in small towns, have many fewer children, also there are fewer neighbors home during the day to keep a watchful eye on children. . . . And parents are almost universally concerned about the safety of their children with strangers who come into the neighborhood. (Maccoby 1998)

Social scientists have examined both inner-city and suburban neighborhoods. Glen Elder and colleagues (Elder, Eccles, Ardett, and Lord 1995) studied low-income inner-city parents. They found less collective support available to African American parents and fewer programs available for their children, even compared to low-income white parents in inner-city settings. "Parents who live in neighborhoods where social cohesion is low and poverty is high must make sizeable investments of personal energy and ingenuity to ensure a protective community for their children" (Elder et al. p. 782, citing Walker and Furstenburg 1994). Elder et al. noted that those African American parents who successfully involved themselves in the community had a strong sense of efficacy. But the challenge was considerable, because poor mothers typically have more hours of work, less flexibility, more

Issues for Thought

Safety and Risk in the Family Environment

Family ecology theory tells us to look at the environment surrounding the family. And what is that environment like in terms of risk and the perception of risk? The 9/11 terrorist attacks, Columbine school killings, and high-profile kidnappings lead us to consider our time and its dangers. Websites offer advice to parents on how to explain terrorism to children (useful websites, by the way, as terrorism remains a danger whose future scope is unknown).

At the same time, some social scientists speculate that fear may have outstripped the reality of risk. Historian Peter Stearns argues that Americans have become "anxious parents." Smaller families, which enhance the preciousness and perceived vulnerability of each child; urbanization and its mythic dangers; and increased media portrayal of danger has led to a general "culture of fear" (Glassner 1999) that makes "anxiety about children . . . a central matter in twentieth-century American culture" (Fass 2003a; Stearns 2003).

In his book *The Culture of Fear* sociologist Barry Glassner demythologizes some common fears about dangers to children, beginning with the urban myth of sabotaged Halloween candy. According to Glassner and others, kidnapping by a stranger, teen suicide, day-care abuse of children, teen births, adolescent drug use, in-school violence, and other juvenile violent crime are all threats that have either declined or been overstated as to frequency and upward trend (Glassner 1999; Leinwand 2002; Synder and Sickmund 1999; "Teen Drug Use" 2003; Toppo 2003; U.S. National Center for Education Statistics 2004). We now have safety protections for children, such as car seats and bicycle helmets, that previous generations did not have (Moretti 2002). With regard to terrorism or war, a survey suggests that except for children in the New York City area (Kleinfield 2002), children's fears are more local than global, including concerns about school bullying (Edwards 2003).

How much is a sense of environmental danger to children a question of perception rather than reality? Ironically, it appears that parents in low-crime areas are as likely to be fearful about dangers of the street as those whose children are in fact more exposed to dangerous surroundings. Michael Moore's *Bowling for Columbine* film crew, taken on a tour of South Central Los Angeles, observed that more children play in the street in this urban neighborhood than are allowed to in "wealthier white neighborhoods, where parents were more afraid to let their kids go out and play" (Barry Glassner in Ebner 2003).

In high-crime areas, parents often do keep their children inside, away from danger. Children and parents are essentially kept prisoner in their own homes, likely a necessary strategy, but one that is problematic in terms of child development and community responsiveness to problems (Fox 2000; Marriott 1995). It is important to consider that extended deep poverty may pose as great a risk to

night jobs, and little money for household help compared to professional mothers, and so have less time available for proactive parenting and community involvement (Kurz 2002).

Surprisingly—given the reputation of suburbs as lacking the sense of community of traditional urban neighborhoods—researchers have found some close-knit neighborhoods in suburban areas that perform the thought-to-be-lost function of "bringing up kids together" (Bould 2003). Typically, these are racially homogeneous neighborhoods, with stay-at-home moms, who bonded when children were small and who continue to have a level of trust that permits families to

monitor and discipline each other's children. Bould ponders the trade-off this seems to require in terms of women's role choices and neighborhood diversity.

The family ecology perspective sensitizes us to significant politico-economic and sociocultural issues that may not be addressed in other theories. It turns our attention to what may be done about social problems that affect the family, whether through "civil society," neighbors and citizens coming together, or through strategies of formal policy development and lobbying for change.

A weakness of the family ecology perspective is that it is so broad and inclusive that virtually nothing is

children's well-being (Elder, Eccles, Ardett, and Lord 1995). In fact, poverty and violence go together, and "children living in poor neighborhoods are disproportionately exposed to high levels of community violence . . . as a routine feature of the child's social ecology" (Fox 2000, p. 166).

An increasing number of children are living in "severely distressed neighborhoods" of high poverty, high proportions of female-headed households, high rates of high school dropouts, and low rates of male employment (O'Hare and Mather 2003). Parents generally employ "neighborhood survival tactics" of setting rules, evaluating their children's peers, checking in via cell phones and pagers, encouraging children to bring friends home, and involving children in activities to keep them off the street and away from questionable peers (Kurz 2002; Letiecq and Koblinsky 2001, 2004). But we must look to public policy to do more to make areas safer.

In ecological settings with fewer obvious dangers, one must consider what an overly strong parental response to risk communicates to children. If they are given to believe that people in general mean them harm; if parental surveillance is constant; if children are unreasonably

limited in the environments they are permitted to explore, how can they not develop a high anxiety about living and acting in the everyday world?

Ironically, past risks are often ignored when present-day America is viewed as a dangerous place for children. Journalists have taken note of the low-key response of older Americans to terrorism, a "been there, done that" attitude (Gross 2001). Well, those who were children in the 1940s lived through World War II in homes whose windows were shielded in the evenings with blackout curtains in the expectation that the Nazis might bomb American cities. They were asked to sacrifice normal food and activities and to do real work on behalf of America's war project through Victory gardens, scrap collecting, and selling war bonds and stamps. Children of the 1950s had their "duck and cover" drills when nuclear war seemed a real possibility. "Those who have 'already had to manage dangers and disturbances . . . are more resilient,'" according to sociologist Todd Gitlin (in Gross 2001).

It appears we cannot ever completely shield children from global or local dangers. A *realistic* analysis of risk; collecting information on

strategies appropriate in dangerous neighborhoods—or safer ones (Brody 2003b); a plan for talking with children about protection from salient risks; and a "check it out" attitude toward scary media stories would seem to be a good parental approach.

To return to the terrorism theme, such danger as we face now is difficult to address with children because the drama and magnitude of the World Trade Center deaths must be put next to the vagueness of future threats. The Iraq war may have activated children's fears (Elias 2003a). The work of Judith Myers-Walls on "Talking to Children About Terrorism and Armed Conflict" (2002 and www.ces.purdue.edu/terrorism) offers a model that may well be applied to the risks discussed here as well as to others.[a]

a. Many of the other references cited in this box offer good suggestions for parents.

Critical Thinking

What risks to children do you see in family environments with which you are familiar?

How should parents communicate with children about risk in high-risk neighborhoods? In low-risk neighborhoods?

left out. More and more, however, social scientists are exploring family ecology in concrete settings. They are also going beyond the former focus of family ecological theory on poverty and disadvantage to look at the ecological settings of more privileged families. Examining the kinds of economic and social advantages enjoyed by the middle and upper levels of society may provide insight into the conditions that would enable *all* families to succeed. Moreover, there are sometimes elements in an upper-socioeconomic-level environment—excessive achievement pressure or the isolation of children from busy, achievement-oriented parents—that may be problematic (Luthar 2003). In any

case, pointing to the ecology of family life challenges the notion that satisfaction and success are due solely to individual effort (Marks 2001).

The Family Development Perspective

Whereas family ecology analyzes family and society (and even the physical–biological environment) as interdependent parts of a whole, the **family development perspective** emphasizes the family itself as its unit of analysis. The concept of the family life cycle is central here, based on the idea that the family changes in predictable ways over time.

THE FAMILY LIFE CYCLE Typical stages of family life are marked off by (1) the addition or subtraction of family members (through birth, death, and leaving home), (2) the various stages that the children go through, and (3) changes in the family's connections with other social institutions (retirement from work, for example, or a child's entry into school). These stages of family development are termed the **family life cycle**. Ideally they succeed one another in an orderly progression and have their requisite **developmental tasks**, challenges that must be mastered in one stage for a successful transition to the next.

Various versions of the stages of the family life cycle have been offered, but there is some convergence on a six- to eight-stage model (Aldous 1996; Duvall and Miller 1985; Rodgers and White 1993). The family begins with marriage and the establishment of an independent residence for the couple. The *newly established couple* stage comes to an end when the arrival of the first baby thrusts the couple into the *families of preschoolers* stage. Entry of the oldest child into school brings about further changes in family life, as *families of primary school children* need to coordinate schedules with another social institution and parents are faced with the task of helping their children meet the school's expectations. *Families with adolescents* may be dealing with more complex problems involving adolescent sexual activity or drug and alcohol abuse. Children become increasingly expensive during this stage, and anticipated college costs add to parents' financial pressures.

Families in the middle years help their offspring to enter the adult world of employment and begin their own family formation. Later, these parents return to a couple focus with (if they are fortunate!) the time and money to pursue leisure activities. Still later, *aging families* must adjust to retirement and perhaps health crises or debilitating chronic illness. The death of a spouse marks the end of the family life cycle (Aldous 1996).

The family development perspective emerged and prospered from the 1930s through the 1950s—an era in which the taken-for-granted family was nuclear: two monogamous heterosexual parents and their children. Accordingly, the model assumed that family life follows certain conventional patterns: Couples marry, and marriage precedes parenthood; families are nuclear and reside independently from other relatives; all families have children; fathers are employed and mothers are not; parents remain together for a lifetime. Of course today—and, in fact, in the past as well—many of us do not proceed so predictably along these well-marked paths.

Critics have noted the white, middle-class bias of the family life cycle perspective (Hogan and Astone 1986). Due to economic, ethnic, and cultural differences, two families in the same life cycle stage may actually be very different from each other in many respects. For these reasons, the family development perspective in its traditional form is less popular now than it once was.

Meanwhile, family development theorists continue to see the model as useful (Mattessich and Hill 1987, p. 445). Despite growing diversity and broader time frames, there is still a sense in our society of a right time to have a child or retire. And the family development perspective has been used effectively as a research framework. One interesting, though small, study (twenty families) examined family boundaries over the life cycle—ties to kin and friends—by looking at families' photo albums. Families were very closed during the preschool years, reaching out more to friends and kin when the children entered school. Kin ties became especially important later in the family life cycle (Gardner 1990).

TRANSITION TO ADULTHOOD A current area of research is the transition to adulthood. This is the period of transition between adolescence and adulthood that essentially precedes the family life cycle as defined above. It is a question of *individual* maturation rather than *family* development, yet, it is foundational to the family.

Scholars have become aware of the historical contingency of the family life cycle (Shanahan 2000). In different historical periods and for different generations, "normal" timing of the family life cycle has varied. In the post–World War II era, marriage and parenthood typically occurred at a much younger age than today. The transition to adulthood has become elongated and now is completed much later. "'There used to be a societal expectation that people in their early twenties would have finished their schooling, set up a household, gotten married, and started their careers. . . . But now that's the exception rather than the norm'" (sociologist Frank Furstenberg, Jr. in Lewin 2003a).

The extended family—grand-parents, aunts, and uncles—is often an important source of security. Extended families meet most needs in a tra-ditional society—economic and material needs and child care, for example—and they have strong bonds. In urban societies, specialized institutions such as factories, schools, and public agencies often meet practical needs. But extended families may also help one another materi-ally in urban society, especially during crises.

© Sybil Shackman

Today the late teens and twenties—perhaps even the early thirties—are typically "a period of frequent change and exploration." The concept of **emerging adulthood** conveys this sense of ongoing change and development, "a time of life when many different directions remain possible, when little about the future has been decided for certain, when the scope of independent exploration of life's possibilities is greater for most people than it will be at any other period of the life course" (Arnett 2000a).

Ironically, as the arrival at adulthood has been postponed for many and seems to provide a new freedom of choice, new pressures have arisen for the early birds. Having a baby in one's twenties, for example, may be seen as "out of step," a risky life course move (Jong-Fast 2003). This does suggest the utility of the life course perspective. The notion that doing something "on time"—or not—makes a difference suggests that, in fact, there *are* culturally defined family life cycle expectations.

THE UTILITY OF THE FAMILY LIFE CYCLE
The family development perspective has been made more useful by modifications that recognize racial/ethnic and other family variations such as child-free

unions, single parenthood, divorce, adoption, gay/lesbian families, and working couples (Rodgers and White 1993; Slater 1995; Aldous 1996; Brodzinsky, Smith, and Brodzinski 1998, Chapter 3; and Carter and McGoldrick 1999). Defining the family life cycle in terms of children and the child-rearing stage, and carefully distinguishing those areas of family life that are logically related to these stages, is one way in which family scientists tinker with the family development perspective to match it to the empirical reality of families today.

The Structure–Functional Perspective

The **structure–functional perspective** sees the family as a social institution that performs certain essential functions for society. Social **institutions** are patterned and predictable ways of thinking and behaving—beliefs, values, attitudes, and norms—that are organized around vital aspects of group life and serve essential social functions; that is, they meet the needs of members and enable the society to survive.

In the structure–functional perspective, the family is the institution commissioned to perform some basic social functions. **Family structure**, or the form of the

In today's impersonal world, the family has grown more important as a source of emotional support. Family members cannot fulfill all of one another's emotional needs, but committed family relationships can and do offer important emotional security.

© 2002 Elyse Lewin Studio Inc./Getty Images

family, varies according to the society in which it is embedded. In preindustrial or traditional societies, the family structure was extended to involve whole kinship groups and performed most societal functions. In industrial or modern societies, the typical family structure is more often nuclear (husband, wife, children) and has lost many functions (Goode 1963). Nevertheless, in contemporary society, the family remains principally accountable for at least three important **family functions**: to raise children responsibly, to provide economic support, and to give emotional security.

FAMILY FUNCTION 1: TO RAISE CHILDREN RESPONSIBLY If a society is to persist beyond one generation, it is necessary that adults not only bear children but also feed, clothe, and shelter them during their long years of dependency. Furthermore, a society needs new members who are properly trained in the ways of the culture and who will be dependable members of the group. All this requires that children be responsibly raised. Virtually every society places this essential task on the shoulders of families—either extended or nuclear.

Accordingly, a related family function has traditionally been to control its members' sexual activity. Although there are several reasons for the social control of sexual activity, the most important one is to ensure that reproduction takes place under circum-

stances that guarantee the responsible care and socialization of children. Even though one-third of U.S. births are to single women (see Chapter 1), the universally approved locus of reproduction remains the married-couple family. For this reason, there is renewed, concerted effort on the part of politicians and others to keep married couples together. Nevertheless, in the United States, the child-rearing function is often performed by divorced or never-married parents.

FAMILY FUNCTION 2: TO PROVIDE ECONOMIC SUPPORT A second family function involves providing economic support. For much of history, the family was primarily an economic unit rather than an emotional unit. The family was the unit of economic production in societies with agriculture, craft, and earlier industrial or commercial economies (Shorter 1975; Stone 1980). Although the modern family is no longer a self-sufficient economic unit, virtually every family engages in activities aimed at providing for such practical needs as food, clothing, and shelter.

Family economic functions now consist of earning a living outside the home, pooling resources, and making consumption decisions together. In assisting one another economically, family members create some sense of material security. For example, mates may offer each other a kind of unemployment insurance. And family members care for one another in additional practical

"This family is <u>way</u> too functional."

This cartoon pokes fun at the image of smoothly working families presented by structure–functional theory. Perhaps the comment will lead to family interaction that will produce some changes desired by the speaker. At the same time, the family may continue to perform essential family functions.

ways, such as nursing and transportation during illness. Chapter 12 explores how individuals integrate work and family, and Chapter 18 discusses family caregiving.

FAMILY FUNCTION 3: TO GIVE EMOTIONAL SECURITY While historically the family was a pragmatic institution involving its material maintenance, in today's world, the family has grown more important as a source of emotional security (Berger, Berger, and Kellner 1973; Giddens 2003). This is not to say that families can solve all our longings for affection, companionship, and intimacy. They cannot. (Sometimes, in fact, the family situation itself is a source of stress, as we'll discuss in Chapters 14 and 15.) Neither is it true that family members or intimate partners never experience loneliness—or that they can fulfill all of one another's emotional needs. But families and committed intimate relationships may offer important emotional support. The broader family network—grandparents, grown sisters and brothers, aunts and uncles—is often

an important source of emotional security. Family may mean having a place where you may be yourself, even sometimes your worst self, and still belong.

The structure–functional perspective calls attention to cross-cultural variations in family structure. As it dominated family sociology in the United States during the 1950s, however, the structure–functional perspective emphasized the heterosexual nuclear family as the "normal" or "functional" family structure. Furthermore, the structure–functional perspective argued the functionality of specialized gender roles: the *instrumental* husband-father, who supports the family economically and wields authority inside and outside the family, and the *expressive* wife-mother-homemaker, whose main function is to enhance emotional relations at home and socialize young children (Parsons and Bales 1955). These views fit nicely into a post-World War II society, characterized by an expanding economy in which a man's wage could support a family. Moreover, whereas many women had been gainfully employed during World War II as well as during the preceding Depression years, a return to "normal" after the war meant an emphasis on traditional husband–wife roles (Kingsbury and Scanzoni 1993). (Gender is discussed more fully in Chapter 4).

Much of the current debate over "family decline" may be better understood once one has a grasp of the structure–functional perspective. Those who argue that the family is in decline or "breaking down" see the nuclear family as an essential structure for performing necessary social functions, but one that is losing ground (Popenoe 1993, 1996). In contrast, a "family change" perspective emphasizes the historical and cross-cultural variation in family structures and the effective performance of family functions by a variety of family types (Coontz 1992; Scanzoni 2004; Stacey 1993). Both sides would agree that many families in our contemporary society do depart from the nuclear family structure.

The structure–functional perspective has been criticized for giving us an image of smoothly working families characterized by shared values, while overlooking gender inequality and power issues, spousal or parent–child conflict, and even family violence. The perspective has been further criticized because it generally fails to recognize that what is functional for one group or category of people may not be so for others. And structure–functionalism does not take into consideration racial/ethnic or class variation in family structures. Nonetheless, virtually all social scientists assume the one basic premise underlying structure–functionalism: that families are an important social institution performing essential social functions.

The Interactionist Perspective

Unlike the three theoretical orientations that we have already described, the **interactionist perspective** looks at internal family dynamics. This point of view explores the interaction of family members—that is, the back-and-forth talk, gestures, and actions that go on in families. Members respond to what other members say (verbally or nonverbally) and do. These interchanges take on a reality of their own; they construct or create a family. Put another way, something called "family" emerges from the relationships and interactions among family members. Unlike structure–functionalism, which posits a standard family form, the interactionist perspective refuses to identify a "natu-

ral" family structure. The family is not a stock social unit but the creation of its participants as they spontaneously relate to one another.

Based on the work of Charles Horton Cooley (1909) and George Herbert Mead (1934), the interactionist perspective was an important theoretical orientation in sociology during the 1920s and 1930s, when the family studies field was establishing itself as a legitimate social science. The orientation remains a popular and fruitful one.

Interactionists assume that an individual develops a **self-concept** (the basic feelings people have about themselves, their abilities, and their worth) and an **identity** (a sense of inner sameness developed by individuals throughout their lives) through social interaction. Families shape the identities and self-concepts of all their members, including adults. The self, in turn, is able to assess and assign meaning and value to ongoing family activities and relationships. Family identity and traditions emerge through interaction, with the growth of relationships and the creation of rituals (Bossard and Boll 1943; Fiese et al. 2002).

A related concept is that of **meaning**, or what a given activity or statement conveys symbolically. For example, a man's or woman's domestic work may symbolize love and family caring (Nippert-Eng 1996), or it may be seen as boring and unappreciated, and therefore demeaning. The difference in meaning has much to do with spouses' satisfaction with their division of labor.

Thinking about families in interactionist terms, researchers investigate questions such as the following: How do two separate individuals interact in a marriage or a committed partnership to fashion a couple identity (Berger and Kellner 1970)? Conversely, how is the couple identity dismantled through divorce (Vaughan 1986)? How do families define the appropriateness of feelings (Hochschild 1979)? How do family members communicate intimacy? What acts or objects symbolize a family's idea of itself? How are family roles constructed and learned (LaRossa and Reitzes 1993)? By what process do family members arrive at more or less shared goals, beliefs, values, and norms (LaRossa and Reitzes 1993)?

An often-voiced criticism of the interactionist perspective is that interactionism makes intuitive sense but is difficult to test empirically. A related criticism is that because it is qualitative and relatively subjective,

This extended African American family is celebrating Kwanzaa, created in the 1960s by black militant Ron Karenga based on African traditions. An estimated ten million black Americans now celebrate Kwanzaa as a ritual of family, roots, and community. The experience of adopting or creating family rituals fits the interactionist perspective on the family.

the research connected with the interactionist perspective lacks rigor. Perhaps a more serious criticism is that interactionism overestimates the power of individuals to create their own realities, ignoring the extent to which humans inhabit a world not of their own making. However, the intersection between family preferences and norms of the wider world may be a focus of interesting research. Sociologist Kristin Park studied the interaction strategies employed by those who have a stigmatized family identity, the voluntarily childless. Some couples employed defensive strategies, making a claim of biological inability to have children. Others aggressively asserted the merits of a child-free life style (Park 2002).

Interactionists have not always been sensitive to cultural variation, instead taking interaction to be the same in all settings. This theoretical perspective needs to be expanded to consider an important question: "How do geography, race/ethnicity, class, gender, age, and time relate to family interaction?" (LaRossa and Reitzes 1993, 136). How do families change—or avoid changing—in the wake of societal change or a personal crisis (LaRossa and Reitzes 1993)?

Exchange Theory

Exchange theory grew out of the application of an economic perspective to social relationships. Developing around 1960 and flourishing during the 1960s and 1970s, this orientation focuses on how individuals' personal resources, such as education, income, physical attractiveness, and personality, affect their formation of and continuation in relationships and their relative positions in families or other groups. The basic premise is that people use their resources to bargain and secure advantage in relationships. In a family, the exchange of rewards and costs among participants in a relationship or family unit may affect power and influence in the family, the household division of labor, and commitment to the relationship. Exchange transactions form and stabilize a relationship or group (Becker 1991; Sabatelli and Shehan 1993).

Relationships based on equal or equitable (fair, if not actually equal) exchanges thrive, whereas those in which the **exchange balance** feels consistently one-sided are more likely to dissolve or be unhappy. Whether an unhappy couple divorces or remains married can be analyzed in exchange terms (Brehm et al. 2002; Sprecher and Schwartz 1994; Van Yperen and Brunk 1990).

Exchange theory must fight the human tendency to see family relationships in far more romantic and emotional terms. Yet dating relationships, marriage and other committed partnerships, divorce, and even parent–child relationships show signs of being influenced by the relative assets of the parties. Money is power, and the children of wealthier parents are more likely to share their parents' values, for example (Luster, Rhoades, and Haas 1989). Marriages tend to take place between people of equal status (see Chapter 7). Decision making within a marriage, as well as decisions to divorce and responses to domestic violence, are affected by the relative resources of the spouses. People without resources or alternatives to a relationship defer to the preferences of others and are less likely to leave a relationship.

As applied to the family, exchange theory is subject to the criticism that it assumes a human nature that is unrealistically rational. In practice, researchers who explore rewards, costs, and interdependence do consider the emotional attachment and commitment that make couples concerned about their *partners'* rewards as well as their own. But they also note that inequality and/or an unfavorable balance of rewards and costs may erode positive feelings over the long term (Brehm et al. 2002).

Family Systems Theory

Family systems theory, like interactionism, is an umbrella term for a wide range of specific theories that look at the family as a whole. Originating in natural science, systems theory was applied to the family by psychotherapists and was then adopted by family scholars and practitioners in other disciplines.

Systems theory uses the model of—a system! Like an organic system (the body) or a mechanical or a cybernetic system (a computer), the parts of a family make a whole that is more than the sum of the parts. A family functions regularly in a certain way; emotional expression and behavior of family members tend to persist. Put another way, systems tend toward equilibrium. Like a computer program directing a space vehicle, information about behavior provides feedback to the system, which then adjusts itself. Change in the external environment or in one of the internal parts sets in motion a process to restore equilibrium (Whitchurch and Constantine 1993).

What this means in a family is that there is pressure on a changing family member to revert to his or her original behavior within the family system. For change to occur, the family system as a whole must change; indeed, that is the goal of family therapy based on systems theory. The family may see one member as the problem, but if the psychologist draws the whole family into therapy, the family system should begin to change as a result. Without therapeutic intervention, families may replicate problem behaviors over the generations. Similarly, it might be unrealistic for a spouse to attempt to resolve marital difficulties by leaving the family (by divorcing). An individual may recreate or enter a family system similar to the one that she or he left. Family systems can survive divorce.

Social scientists have moved systems theory away from its therapeutic origins to use it in a more general analysis of families. They have been especially interested in how family systems handle information, deal with problems, respond to crises, and regulate contact with the outside world. Family boundaries, as well as the closeness or distance of family members from one another, are important issues in systems theory (Kantor and Lehr 1975).

Criticism of the family systems perspective relates to its nonspecificity: So the family is a system—then what? In working concretely with families in therapy, however, this approach may be very useful to both therapists and clients. If family members come to understand how their family system operates, they may use this knowledge to achieve desired goals.

Systems theory does not take note of social structure (the class system or race/ethnicity) but presumes instead that families are families the world over. Transactions with a particular family's external world of work, school, religious affiliation, and **extended family** may be addressed, but the structure of economic opportunity and other features of the larger society are not analyzed. Systems theory tends to diffuse responsibility for conflict by attributing dysfunction to the system. This makes it difficult to extend social support to victimized family members while establishing legal accountability for others, as in incest or other domestic violence (Stewart 1984).

But systems theory often gives family members insight into the effects of their behavior and is a good analytic tool. It may make visible the hidden benefits or costs of certain family patterns. For example, doctors were puzzled by the fact that death rates were higher among kidney dialysis patients with supportive families. Family systems theorists attributed the higher rates to the unspoken desire of the patients to lift the burden of care from the close-knit family they loved (Reiss, Gonzalez, and Kramer 1986).

Feminist Perspectives

For decades, sociologists talked about how traditional family roles were functional for society, ignoring in the process the politics of gender. The central focus of **feminist perspectives** is on gender issues. Although there are many variations within the feminist perspective, a unifying theme is that male dominance in family and society is oppressive to women.

Moreover, the feminist perspective brings attention to women and their experiences (Osmond and Thorne 1993). Women's domestic work was largely invisible in social science until feminist theories began to treat household labor as work that has economic value. In the 1960s and subsequently, the application of feminist perspectives has permitted us to see some things about families that had been overlooked before. Social scientists became aware of wife abuse, marital rape, child abuse, and other forms of domestic vio-

lence. These family behaviors had been there all along, but not remarked upon or treated as social problems.

For the most part, feminist theories derive from the broader **conflict perspective**. One way of thinking about the conflict perspective is that its position is the opposite of functional theory: Not all of a family's practices are good; not all family behaviors contribute to family well-being; what is good for one family member is not necessarily good for another. Family interaction may include domestic violence as well as holiday rituals—sometimes both on the same day.

Unlike the perspectives already described, which were developed primarily by academic theorists and researchers, feminist theories emerged from political and social movements over the past forty years. As such, the mission of feminist theory is to use knowledge to actively confront and end the oppression of women and related patterns of subordination based on social class, race/ethnicity, age, or sexual orientation. Feminist theorizing has contributed to political action regarding gender and race discrimination in wages; divorce laws that disadvantage women; sexual and physical violence against women and children; and reproductive issues, such as abortion rights and the inclusion of contraception in health insurance. Feminist perspectives promote recognition and support for women's unpaid work; the greater involvement of men in housework and child care; efforts to fund quality day care and paid parental leaves; and transformations in family therapy so that counselors recognize the reality of gender inequality in family life and treat women's concerns with respect (Goldner 1993).

Feminist perspectives are frequently under fire from conservative media, politicians, religious leaders—and some academics. Family scholars Blankenhorn (1995) and Popenoe (1996) fear that feminism may have taken women's rights too far, resulting in harmful effects on children, who spend much time in child care when mothers are employed outside the home. Too high divorce rates, too many single-parent families—in short, "family breakdown" is sometimes attributed to women's economic and psychological independence.

Feminists maintain that these assertions of a negative impact of feminism on the family are biased and do not take into account other interpretations of family change (Fox and Murry 2000). That feminists value female caregiving in the family is not acknowledged. Moreover, from the feminist perspective, championing the traditional nuclear family at the cost of women's equality and well-being is unconscionable. Feminists argue that there is more than one effective way to structure family life.

Biosocial Perspectives

The **biosocial perspective** on the family, also termed *sociobiology* or *evolutionary psychology*, is characterized by "concepts linking psychosocial factors to physiology, genetics, and evolution" (Booth, Carver, and Granger 2000, p. 1018). This perspective argues that humans' evolutionary biology (that is, human anatomy/physiology, genetics, and hormones) affects much of human behavior and, more specifically, many family-related behaviors.

This perspective has its roots in Charles Darwin's *The Origin of Species* (1859). Darwin proposed that species evolve according to the principle of *survival of the fittest:* Only the stronger, more intelligent, and adaptable members of a species survive to reproduce, a process whereby the entire species is strengthened and prospers over time. Much of contemporary human behavior is explained as having evolved in ways that most effectively accomplish the task of transmitting successful behavior patterns encoded in the genes (Dawkins 1976). For instance,

> We are all descended from generations and generations of people who looked after their children. People who could think of better things to do than look after crying, demanding infants and who abandoned them, also tended to have few or no descendants, so their genes died out. It is therefore not surprising to sociobiologists that our societies are full of examples of people looking after, and looking out for, their children. (Wallace and Wolf 1999, pp. 385–386)

In the contemporary version of evolutionary theory, it is the survival of one's *genes*, termed **inclusive fitness** (Hamilton 1964), that is important. Behavior is thought to be oriented to the survival and reproduction of other close kin as well as direct descendants.

The biosocial perspective presumes that certain human behaviors, because they evolved for the purpose of human survival, are both "natural" and difficult to change. For example, in this perspective it is maintained that traditional gender roles evolved from patterns shared with our mammalian ancestors and useful in early hunter–gatherer societies. Gender differences—males allegedly more aggressive than females, and mothers more likely than fathers to be primarily responsible for child care—are seen as anchored in hereditary biology and as such, difficult to change (Rossi 1984; Udry 1994, 2000).

Sociobiological explanations are offered for other contemporary family patterns. For example, research suggests that children are more likely to be abused by nonbiologically related parents or caregivers than by biological parents. The biosocial perspective explains this situation by arguing that parents "naturally" protect the carriers of their genetic material (Gelles and Lancaster 1987).

Sociobiologists are careful to point out that biological predisposition does *not* mean that a person's behavior cannot be influenced or changed by social structure. Working together with biology, culture influences human behavior. "Nature" (genetics) and "nurture" (culture) are seen as interacting to produce human attitudes and behavior (Udry 1994; Wallace and Wolf 1999).

Over the past twenty-five years, the biosocial perspective has emerged as a significant theoretical perspective on the family. Researchers have employed a biosocial perspective to examine such family phenomena as sexual bonding, decisions about whether to have children, parenting behavior, parent–child attachment, gender differences in children and adults, sexual development and behavior, courtship and mate selection, and marital stability and quality (Booth, Carver, and Granger 2000).

Nevertheless, it is very important to realize that biological theories of human behavior have in the past been used to justify systems of inequality and oppression. As a result, many scholars are concerned about the possibility of deterministic interpretations of biological influence. For example, biosociologists have questioned the validity of nonreproductive partner relationships, as well as mothers being employed (Daly and Wilson 2000). As a second example, while he acknowledges that there are many successful stepfamilies and adoptions, Popenoe (1994) nevertheless finds these family forms to be unsupported by our evolutionary heritage and concludes that "we as a society should be doing more to halt the growth of stepfamilies" (p. 21). How strong the evidence is to support

These folks are waiting patiently for medical attention in a neighborhood clinic. How might scholars from different theoretical orientations see this photograph? *Family ecologists* might remark on the quality of the facilities—or speculate about the family's home and neighborhood—and how this affects family health and relations. Scholars from the *family development* perspective would likely note that this woman is in the child-rearing stage of the family life cycle. *Structure-functionalists* would be quick to note the child-raising (and, perhaps, expressive) function(s) that this woman is performing for society. *Interactionists* would be more inclined to explore the mother's body language: What is she saying nonverbally to the child on her lap? What is he saying to her? *Exchange theorists* might speculate about this woman's personal power and resources relative to others in her family. *Family system theorists* might point out that this mother and child are part of a family system: Should one person leave or become seriously and chronically ill, for example, the roles and relationships in the entire family would change and adapt as a result. *Feminist theorists* might point out that typically it is mothers, not fathers, who are primarily responsible for their children's health—and ask why. The answer from a *biosocial perspective* would be that women have evolved a stronger nurturing capacity that is hormonally based.

© Martin Rodgers/Stock Boston

such claims is questionable. Hence, it is not surprising that biosocial perspectives have been politically and academically controversial.

Still, social science researchers are doing some interesting work from a biosocial perspective, and an "explosion" of biosocial research on the family is anticipated in the next decade (Booth, Carver, and Granger 2000, p. 1018). Family scholars and those who use their research should be careful to avoid interpretations shaped by ideological bias—whether this is a presumption that biology is destiny or a contrary postulate, that biosocial perspectives are inherently invalid. In this text, we explore and appraise the biosocial perspective when discussing gender (Chapter 4), extramarital sex (Chapter 8), and children's well-being in stepfamilies (Chapter 17).

▪ Studying Families ▪

In exploring families, social scientists employ both theory and research. In fact, theory and research are, ideally at least, closely integrated, with theory directing us to the topics we should study and the concepts and methods we should use to do so.

The great variation in family forms and the variety of social settings for family life mean that few of us can rely on firsthand experience alone in studying the family. Although we "know" about the family because we have lived in one, our **experiential reality**—beliefs we have about the family—may not be accurate. We may also be misled by media images and common sense—what everybody "knows." Everybody knows, for example, that the American family is a nuclear one—or else that it is dying. This **agreement reality**—what members of a society agree is true—may misrepresent the actual experience of families (Babbie 1992, p. 17).

We turn now to consider the difficulties inherent in studying the family and then to a presentation of various methods used by social scientists. Although imperfect, the methods of scientific inquiry may bring us a clearer knowledge of the family than either personal experience or speculation based on media images. Scientific methods represent a form of agreement reality that sets special standards for the acceptance of statements about the family.

The Blinders of Personal Experience

Most people grow up in some form of family and know something about what marriages and families are. But while personal experience provides us with information, it may also act as blinders. We assume that our own family is normal or typical. If you grew up in a large family, for example, in which a grandparent or an aunt or uncle shared your home, you probably assumed (for a short time at least) that everyone had a big family. Perceptions like this are usually outgrown at an early age, but some family styles may be taken for granted or assumed to be universal, though they are not. Some families talk and argue loudly, for example, while in other families controversial topics are avoided. The members of your family may spend a lot of time alone, perhaps reading, whereas in other families it may be cause for alarm if a family member—adult or child—is not talking to others around the kitchen table.

Personal experience, then, may make us believe that most people's family lives are similar to our own when often this is not the case. We may be very committed to the view of family life shaped by our experiences and our own choices.

In looking at marriage and family customs around the world, we can easily perceive the error of assuming that all marriage and family practices are like our own. But not only do common American assumptions about family life not hold true in other places, they also frequently don't even describe our own society. Lesbian or gay male families; black, Latino, and Asian families; Jewish, Protestant, Catholic, Latter-day Saints (Mormon), Islamic, Buddhist, and nonreligious families; upper-class, middle-class, and lower-class families all represent some differences in family lifestyle. How-

ever, the tendency to use the most familiar yardstick for measuring things is a strong one; even social scientists fall victim to it. (See "A Closer Look at Family Diversity: Studying Ethnic Minority Families" for a look at how social scientists have begun to address the problems of cultural bias.)

Scientific Investigation: Removing Blinders

Seeing beyond our personal experience involves learning what kinds of families other people are experiencing, and with what consequences. To do this, we rely on data gathered systematically from many sources through techniques of **scientific investigation**, from which it is often possible to generalize. These techniques—surveys, laboratory observation and experiments, naturalistic observation, case studies, longitudinal studies, and historical and cross-cultural data—will be referred to throughout this text, so we will briefly describe them now.

SURVEYS **Surveys** are part of our everyday experience. When conducting scientific surveys, researchers either engage in face-to-face or telephone interviews or distribute questionnaires to be answered and returned. Questions are often structured so that after a statement (such as "I like to go places with my partner"), the respondent has answers from which to choose. Common survey responses are: "always," "usually," "sometimes," "not very often," and "never." Researchers spend much energy and time wording such *closed-ended* questions so that, as much as possible, all respondents will interpret questions in the same way.

Survey questions may also be *open-ended*. For example, the question might be "How do you feel about going places with your partner?" or "Tell me about going places with your partner." Many social scientists and respondents alike believe that open-ended questions give those answering more opportunity to express how they really feel or what they actually believe than do more structured questions, which require people to choose from a predetermined set of responses.

Once the returns are in, survey responses are tallied and statistically analyzed, usually with computer software programs. After the survey data have been analyzed, the scientists conducting the research begin to draw conclusions about respondents' atti-

A Closer Look at Family Diversity

Studying Ethnic Minority Families

Just a few decades ago, white, middle-class (often male) scholars conducted the preponderance of theorizing and research on families. But as men and women from diverse racial/ethnic backgrounds came into the field of family studies, they pointed out how limited, and hence biased, our theoretical and research perspectives have been. In this chapter, for example, we noted the white, middle-class bias in family development theory as it was originally formulated as well as the cultural assumptions of the structure–functional perspective.

To begin to understand the question of bias, we might think of theory and research on racial/ethnic minority families as falling into one of three frameworks: cultural equivalent, cultural deviant, and cultural variant (Allen 1978). The **cultural equivalent** approach emphasizes those features that racial/ethnic minority families have in common with mainstream white families. An example would be the finding that middle-class black parents treat their children much the same way as do middle-class white parents (Laureau 2002).

The **cultural deviant** approach views the qualities that distinguish minority families from mainstream families as negative or pathological. An example would be analysis that laments the high prevalence of female-headed families among blacks compared with non-Hispanic whites or Asians.

The **cultural variant** approach calls for making culturally and contextually relevant interpretations of minority family lives. For example, a substantial proportion of these single-mother households contain other adults who take part in rearing the children in many cases (Manning and Smock 1997). A classic example of research from a cultural variant perspective is Carol Stack's (1974) participant observation study of a black community; her book *All Our Kin* emphasizes previously ignored strengths in extended African American families.

In the first two approaches, white mainstream families are considered the standard against which "other" or "less valid" families are compared, either favorably or unfavorably—a situation conducive to bias. In the third and preferred approach, minority families are studied on their own terms. Comparisons may be made *within* those groups (for example, comparing urban Native American parenting styles with those of American Indians on reservations).

The cultural variant approaches may lead to "reverse theorizing." Ideas, insights, and concepts developed in the study of families that vary from the majority group are applied to enrich family studies more generally. For example, while we may take for granted the advantages of the middle-class household, Annette Laureau (2003a) points to the rich family life of working- and lower-class children, whose parents are less focused on educational and achievement goals and activities and who have more time to spend with relatives.

The *kin scripts* theoretical framework, which developed out of research on black extended families, may be applied to kin relations in other racial/ethnic settings (Dilworth-Anderson, Burton, and Johnson 1993). Such concepts as *kin-work*, the labor that extended family members engage in to help each other survive, and *kin-scription*, the recruitment of family members to do kin-work, enable us to see those activities in white families, Latino families, etc.

Critical Thinking

Does your family heritage or your observation of families make you aware of some family patterns that you would see as different from common American assumptions about families? How could these observations be applied to help researchers learn more about families in a variety of family settings?

---

tudes and behavior. Then the researchers must decide to whom their conclusions are applicable. Do they apply only to those who are in the sample studied, or more generally, to other people similar to the research participants?

In order to ensure that their conclusions may be *generalized* (applied to people other than those directly questioned), survey researchers do their best to ensure that their respondents constitute a *representative sample* of the people they intend to draw conclusions about. Popular magazine surveys, for example, are seldom representative of the total American public. A survey on attitudes about premarital sex in *Cosmopolitan* or *Playboy* will likely yield different findings than one in

Family Circle or *Reader's Digest*. In the same way, results from a survey in which all respondents are young, white, middle-class college students cannot be considered representative of Americans in general. So researchers and political pollsters may use *random samples*, in which households or individuals are randomly selected from a comprehensive list (see Babbie 2003 for a more detailed discussion). A random sample is considered to be representative of the population from which it is drawn. A national random sample of approximately 1,500 people may validly represent the U.S. population. Sets of data already collected and archived may also be used by those doing research on the family (Walker 2001).

Survey research has certain advantages over other inquiry techniques. The main advantage is uniformity. Also, surveys are a relatively efficient means of gathering large amounts of information. And, provided the sample is designed to be accurately representative, conclusions drawn from that information may be applied to a large number of people.

Surveys have disadvantages, too. Because they ask uniform or standardized questions, surveys may miss points that respondents consider important. Surveys neither tell us about the context in which a question is answered nor guarantee that in a real-life situation a person will act in a manner consistent with the answer given to the interviewer. Other disadvantages of surveys result from respondents' tendency to say what they think they *should* say, rather than what they in fact believe. If asked whether or how often physical abuse occurs in the home, for example, those who often engage in family violence might be reluctant to say so.

A further disadvantage of surveys is the tendency of respondents to forget or to reinterpret what happened in the past. (Because of this tendency, social scientists recognize the value of longitudinal studies—studies in which the same group of respondents is surveyed or interviewed intermittently over a period of years.) Another disadvantage of surveys is that depending on the sex, age, race, and style of the person questioning you, you might tend, even without knowing it, to give a certain response. Scientists call this tendency *interview effects of an interviewer*. A forty-five-year-old male, for example, asked about his experience with sexual impotence, may be expected to reply differently to a male interviewer of twenty than he would to one of sixty—or to a female of any age.

LABORATORY OBSERVATION AND EXPERIMENTS Because of the relative ease of conducting surveys, the flexibility of the format, and the availability of samples (even a classroom sample may provide some useful information), surveys have been the primary source of information about family living. Other techniques are also used, however. In laboratory observation or an experiment, behaviors are carefully monitored or measured under controlled conditions. These methods are particularly useful in measuring physiological changes associated with anger, fear, sexual response, or behavior that is difficult to report verbally. In family problem solving, for example, families may be asked to discuss a hypothetical case or to play a game while their behavior is observed and recorded.

In an **experiment**, subjects from a pool of similar participants will be randomly assigned to groups (*experimental* and *control groups*) that will be given different experiences (*treatments*). Families whose child is undergoing a bone-marrow transplant may be asked to participate in an experiment to determine how they may best be helped to cope with the situation. One group of families may be assigned to a support group in which the expression of feelings, even negative ones, is encouraged (Experimental Group 1). Another set of families may be assigned to a group in which the emphasis is on providing factual information about transplantation and maintaining a positive, cheerful outlook (Experimental Group 2). A third group of families may receive no special intervention (Control Group). If at the conclusion of the experiment the groups differ in attitudes and behavior according to some measures of coping behavior, mental health, and family functioning, then this outcome is presumed to be a result of the experimental treatment. Put another way, because no other differences are presumed to exist among the randomly assigned groups, the results of the experiment provide evidence of the effects of the therapeutic interventions.

A true experiment has these features of random assignment and experimental manipulation of the important variable. **Laboratory observation**, on the other hand, simply means that behavior is *observed* in a laboratory setting, but it does not involve random assignment or experimental manipulation of a variable.

The experiment described above takes place in a field (real-life) setting, but experiments are often conducted in a laboratory setting because researchers have more control over what will happen. They have more chance to plan the activities, measure the results, determine who is involved, and eliminate outside influences. In the previous example, families might have obtained additional personal counseling on their own, which would affect the results, or they may have attended the group only infrequently.

Experiments, like other methods, have both advantages and disadvantages. One advantage of experiments is that social scientists may observe human behavior directly, rather than depending, as they do in surveys, on what respondents *tell* them. The experimenter may control the experience of the subjects and may ensure, to some extent, the initial similarity of subjects in the two groups. A disadvantage of this research technique is that the behaviors being observed often take place in an artificial situation, and whether an artificial or simulated testing situation is analogous to real life is almost always debatable. A family asked to solve a hypothetical problem through group discussion may behave differently in a formal laboratory experiment than they would at home around the kitchen table discussing a real problem.

Another limitation in social research is that the subject pool is often drawn from college classrooms and is therefore not representative of the general population. Sometimes, "volunteer" participants must participate in an experiment for class credit or are subjects who have responded to financial incentives; in such cases, the authenticity of results is often in question. And volunteer subjects may be very different from their peers who decide not to participate.

NATURALISTIC OBSERVATION Many aspects of human behavior and interaction just don't lend themselves to study in laboratory settings, so social scientists use another technique in an attempt to overcome artificiality. In **naturalistic observation**, the researcher lives with a family or social group or spends extensive time with family or group members, carefully recording their activities, conversations, gestures, and other aspects of everyday life. The researcher attempts to discern family interrelationships and communication patterns and to draw implications and conclusions from them for understanding family behavior in general.

The principal advantage of naturalistic observation is that it allows us to view family behavior as it actually happens in its own natural—as opposed to artificial—setting. The most significant disadvantage of this tool is that findings and conclusions may be highly subjective. That is, what is recorded, analyzed, and assumed to be accurate depends on what one or very few observers think is significant. Another drawback to naturalistic observation is that it requires enormous amounts of time to observe only a few families. And these families may not be representative of family living in general. Perhaps because of these disadvantages, relatively few studies use this technique.

Still, Fred Davis's (1991) study of the families of polio victims, first published in 1963, remains an important piece of observational research that provides useful insights into family dynamics. It may become even more relevant because, as medical science has enabled more children to survive serious illness, they and their families will live with crisis and chronic disease for an extended period. This study is a good example of the *interactionist* theoretical perspective, which is often the framework for naturalistic observation.

An especially important use of naturalistic observation has been in research on racial/ethnic communities or in other settings not easily accessible by survey or experimental research. Studies such as anthropologist Carol Stack's (1974) participant observation of families in a lower-class black community and sociologist Arlie Hochschild's (1997) study of family members at work and home give us the context in which families live their lives. They often reveal that families play an active role in using the resources of their social environment to shape their destinies.

CLINICIANS' CASE STUDIES A fourth way that we get information about families is from **case studies** compiled by clinicians—psychologists, psychiatrists, marriage counselors, and social workers—who counsel people with marital and family problems. As they see individuals, couples, or whole families over a period of time, these counselors become acquainted with communication patterns and other interactions within families. Clinicians offer us knowledge about family behavior and attitudes by describing cases to us or by telling us about their conclusions based on a series of cases.

The advantages of case studies are the vivid detail and realistic flavor that enable us to experience vicariously the family life of others. The insights of clinicians may be helpful. But case studies also have important weaknesses. There is always a subjective or personal element in the way the clinician views the family. Inevitably, any one person has a limited viewpoint. Clinicians' professional training may also lead them to overemphasize or underemphasize certain aspects of family life or to mistake cultural patterns for psychological truths. Psychiatrists, for example, used to assume that the assertiveness or career interests of women caused the development of marital and sexual problems.

Another potential bias of case studies is that people who present themselves for counseling may differ in important ways from those who do not. Most obviously, they may have more problems. For example, throughout the 1950s psychiatrists reported that gays and lesbians in therapy had many emotional difficulties. Subsequent studies of gay males not in therapy concluded that gays were no more likely to have mental health problems than were heterosexuals (American Psychological Association 2001).

LONGITUDINAL STUDIES **Longitudinal studies** provide long-term information about individuals or groups, as a researcher or research group conducts follow-up investigations (by means of interviews or questionnaires) for several years after the initial study. Observational or experimental studies could be repeated, but this is rarely done.

Ongoing research by Booth, White, and colleagues, in which adults who were married at the time of the first survey in 1980 were reinterviewed three more times during the 1980s and 1990s, is a good example of longitudinal research. The researchers traced the demographic and relationship patterns affecting marital quality and stability, divorce, and remarriage. In 1992 and 1995, the now-grown children (over age eighteen) of these marriages were interviewed, and information about their educational and occupational attainment and family status was added to the study (Booth, Johnson, White, and Edwards 1985; White and Keith 1990; Amato and Booth 1997; and many other articles). Publication of studies based on statistical analysis of this data set continues.

A difficulty encountered in longitudinal studies, besides the almost prohibitive cost, is the frequent loss of subjects due to death, relocation, or loss of interest. Social change occurring over a long period of time may make it difficult to ascertain what, precisely, has influenced family change. Yet cross-sectional data (one-time comparison of different groups) cannot show change in the same individuals over time.

HISTORICAL AND CROSS-CULTURAL DATA Analyzing historical records is a research approach that came to attention beginning in the 1960s with some interesting work by social historians in France (Ariès 1962) and England (Laslett 1971). Whether done by historians or other social scientists, historical research continues to be an important method of family research.

Zelizer's (1985) study of insurance documents and other historical materials conveys the changing status of the child from economic asset to emotional asset. Linda Gordon's (1988) research using social agency files from the early twentieth century reveals how lower- and working-class women used social agencies to cope with domestic violence, child sexual abuse, and other family problems. Historical studies of marriage and divorce in the United States give us a picture of the past, which is not always as we thought it was in terms of stability and harmony (Cott 2000; Hartog 2000).

Drawbacks of historical research are the unevenness and unavailability of data. Scholars must rely on only those data to which they have access. Typically, the upper classes, who had both the leisure and resources to record their activities, are overrepresented. But historical scholars have been very creative. Hanawalt (1986) constructed a rich picture of the medieval family from an examination of death records. Demographic and economic data and legal records are especially useful for analyses of the family institution (see Glendon 1989). Scholars are on less solid footing in describing intimate family matters because they must rely on materials such as individuals' diaries, which may not be representative of the period. More recently, however, the use of these personal materials has been defended, and the results have challenged earlier historians' assumptions that premodern family life lacked emotional intimacy (Osment 2001). Sociologists, especially those who place more emphasis on cross-cultural comparison than we are able to do in this text, continue to look to anthropological fieldwork as well as survey data for information on family life and structure in societies in both developed and developing nations. Access can be a problem for those studying contemporary families, and is likely to be affected by the political relations among nations. It is only since the Soviet Union opened to the West, for example, that scholars have been able to analyze families in Russia and the other former Soviet republics (Maddock et al. 1993). Conversely, in recent years in the United States, funding has been restricted or access limited for certain populations, particularly minors, or when the topic of research is viewed as controversial (e.g., Herbert 2003; Navarro 2004).

The Application of Scientific Techniques

All research tools represent a compromise. Each has its special strengths and weaknesses. However, the strengths of one research tool may make up for the weaknesses of another. For example, findings that result from direct observations supplement survey reports in an important way. Whereas the former allow scientists to observe actual behavior among a limited number of people, surveys provide information about attitudes and reported behavior of a vast number of people. To get around the drawbacks of each technique, social scientists may combine two or more tools in their research. Ideally, a number of scientists examine one topic by several different methods. In general, the scientific conclusions in this text result from many studies and from various and complementary research tools. Despite the drawbacks and occasional blinders, the total body of information available from sociological, psychological, and counseling literature provides a reasonably accurate portrayal of marriage and family life today.

In Sum

- Different theoretical perspectives—family ecology, family development, structure–functional, interactionist, exchange, family systems, feminist, and biosocial—illuminate various features of families and provide a foundation for research.

- The structure–functional theoretical perspective draws attention to functions performed by the family. Cross-cultural comparisons show us that assumptions about family structure, family functions, and family ways of courtship, marriage, gender, parenting, and kinship based on our own culture are limited. Family life is quite diverse across cultures.

- How do we know what families are like? We can call upon personal experience for the beginning of an answer to this question. But everyone's personal experience is limited. Scientific investigation—with its various methodological techniques—is designed to provide a more effective and accurate way of gathering knowledge about the family.

- Methodologies and resources for studying the family include surveys, laboratory observation and experiments, naturalistic observation, clinicians' case studies, longitudinal studies, and historical and cross-cultural data.

Key Terms

agreement reality	experiment
biosocial perspective	extended family
case study	family development perspective
conflict perspective	
cultural deviant	family ecology perspective
cultural equivalent	family function
cultural variant	family life cycle
developmental task	family policy
emerging adulthood	family structure
exchange balance	family systems theory
exchange theory	feminist perspective
experiential reality	human-built environment

identity
inclusive fitness
institution
interactionist perspective
laboratory observation
longitudinal study
meaning
natural physical–biological
  environment

naturalistic observation
scientific investigation
self-concept
social-cultural environment
structure–functional
  perspective
survey
theoretical perspective

Questions for Review and Reflection

1. Choose one of the theoretical perspectives on the family, and discuss how you might use it to understand something about life in *your* family.

2. Choose a magazine photo, and analyze its content from a structure–functional perspective. (*Hint:* Together the people in the photo may constitute the group under analysis, with each person meeting certain of the group's needs, or functional requisites.) Then analyze the photo from another theoretical perspective. How do your insights differ depending on which theoretical perspective is used?

3. Why is the family a major social institution? Does your family fulfill each of the family functions identified in the text? How?

4. Review the techniques of scientific investigation, and discuss why science is often considered a better way to gain knowledge than is personal experience alone. When might this not be the case?

5. **Policy Question.** What aspect of family life would it be helpful for policy makers to know more about as they make law and design social programs? How might this topic be researched? Is it controversial? If yes, why?

Suggested Readings

Bogenschneider, Karen. 2002. *Family Policy Matters: How Policymaking Affects Families and What Professionals Can Do.* Mahwah, NJ: Lawrence Erlbaum. Good resource for those who would like to read more about family policy.

Booth, Alan, and Ann C. Crouter, eds. 2001. *Does It Take A Village? Community Effects On Children, Adolescents, and Families.* Mahwah, NJ: Lawrence Erlbaum. Readings which report and discuss research on the neighborhood

and community context and suggest ways of improving these family settings.

Greenstein, Theodore N. 2001. *Methods of Family Research.* Thousand Oaks, CA: Sage. Discusses the application of standard research methods to the study of the family.

Ingoldsby, Bron B., and Suzanne R. Smith, eds. 2005. *Families in Global and Multicultural Perspective,* 2nd ed. Thousand Oaks, CA: Sage. Cross-national comparisons organized topically, e.g., gender relations and family power; families in later life; etc. Good complement to the North American focus of our text.

Ingoldsby, Bron B., Suzanne R. Smith, and J. Elizabeth Miller. 2004. *Exploring Family Theories.* Los Angeles: Roxbury. Good summary of most of the theories discussed in this chapter and some others. Appropriate for undergraduate students.

Stack, Carol. 1974. *All Our Kin: Strategies for Survival.* New York: Harper & Row. An example of participant observation research that conveys what the experience is like. Exemplifies the *cultural variant* approach to research on ethnic minority families, and shows how new theoretical perspectives may emerge to better describe ethnic minority families.

Virtual Society: The Wadsworth Sociology Resource Center

 Go to the Sociology Resource Center at **http:// sociology.wadsworth.com** for a wealth of online resources, including a companion website for your text that provides study aids such as self-quizzes for each chapter and a practice final exam, as well as links to sociology websites and information on the latest theories and discoveries in the field. In addition, you will find further suggested readings, flash cards, MicroCase online exercises, and appendices on a range of subjects.

Online Study Tool

Marriage & Family ⊚ Now™ Go to **http://sociology .wadsworth.com** to reach the companion website for your text and use the Marriage&FamilyNow access code that came with your book to access this study tool. Take a practice pretest after you have read each chapter, and then use the study plan provided to master that chapter. Afterward, take a posttest to monitor your progress.

Search Online with InfoTrac College Edition

For additional information, exercises, and key words to aid your research, explore InfoTrac College Edition, your online library that offers full-length articles from thousands of scholarly and popular publications. Click on *InfoTrac College Edition* under *Chapter Resources* at the companion website and use the access code that came with your book.

- Search keywords: *biosocial + family*. See what new developments are taking place in research on the family from a biosocial perspective.

- Search keywords: *family* + the name or adjective for a country or geographic area (for example, *Russia* or *African*). Explore cross-cultural diversity in families.

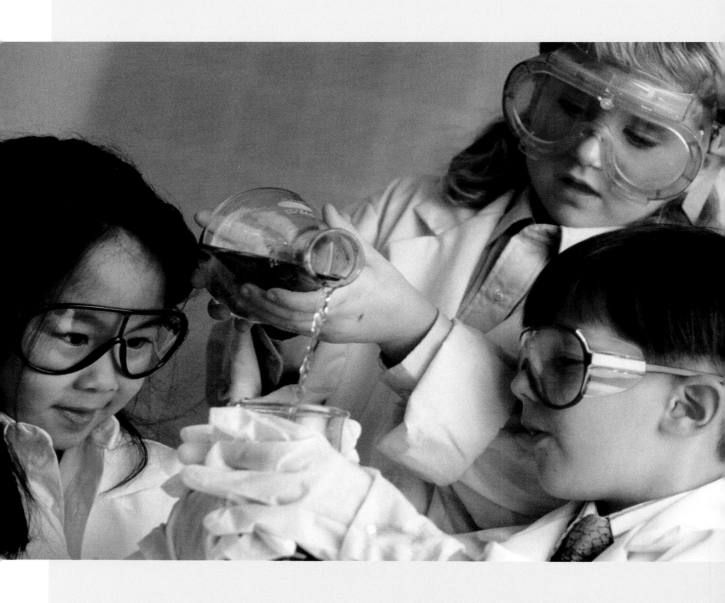

Our Gendered Identities

Women are creating a new world, restructuring and reinventing social institutions around the globe.

NANCY FELIPE RUSSO,
Psychology of Women Quarterly

Many of the changes happening to the family are problematic and difficult. But surveys . . . show that few want to go back to traditional male and female roles.

ANTHONY GIDDENS,
Runaway World

GENDER INFLUENCES VIRTUALLY every aspect of people's lives and relationships. Regarding gender attitudes and behaviors, this is an ambivalent time. On the one hand, it is now taken for granted that women have careers and that most will work after they become mothers. Examples of women in nontraditional roles abound: women as astronauts, CEOs, and officers and enlisted personnel in the military. On the other hand, the media and research explore the continuing disadvantage faced by women and the uncertainty that many women have about their choices and the ability to realize them.

Men have begun to consider where they stand as well—in relationships, in the family, and at work. Some men have begun to move into traditional female occupations, and married fathers are doing more at home than they used to (Armour 2003; Coltrane 1996).

Research shows that American attitudes have grown more liberal regarding men's and women's roles. Few agree, for example, that "sons in a family should be given more encouragement to go to college than daughters," an expression of **"traditional sexism"** (Sherman and Spence 1997). Traditional sexism is the belief that women's roles should be confined to the family and that women are not as fit as men for certain tasks or for leadership positions. Such beliefs have declined since the 1970s (Twenge 1997a, 1997b).

But now a more subtle **"modern sexism"** has replaced traditional sexism. It takes the form of agreement with statements like: "Discrimination in the labor force is no longer a problem" and "In order not to appear sexist, many men are inclined to overcompensate women" (Tongas et al. 1995; Campbell, Schellenberg, and Senn 1997). Modern sexism denies that gender discrimination persists and includes the belief that women are asking for too much—a situation that results in resistance to women's demands (Swim, Aikin, Hall, and Hunter 1995; Swim and Cohen 1997; Faludi 1991).

Although gender expectations have changed and continue to change, they have obviously not done so completely. Men face conflicting expectations in changing times. While 70 percent of people surveyed believe making money and cooking family meals should be equally shared by men and women, 25 percent to 30 percent think a gendered division of labor should continue (Felto 2002). It's still true that living in our society is a different experience for males and females. In this chapter, we will examine various aspects of gender, especially those that more directly affect committed relationships and families. In doing so, we'll consider personality traits and cultural scripts typically associated with masculinity and femininity. We'll describe male dominance, discuss the possible influence of biology, and examine the socialization process as we explore whether people learn to behave as either females or males, or whether they are born that way. We'll consider the ambiguity of the boundary between male and female, masculine and feminine. We'll discuss the lives of adults as they select from options available to them. And we'll examine the social movements that have arisen around gender issues. We'll speculate about what the future may hold.

▪ Gendered Identities ▪

We are using the term *gender* rather than *sex* for an important reason. The word **sex** refers only to male or female anatomy and physiology. Sex includes the different chromosomal, hormonal, and anatomical components of males and females that are present at birth. We use the term **gender** (or **gender role**) far more broadly—to describe societal attitudes and behaviors expected of and associated with the two sexes. Gender,

More and more women are entering nontraditional occupations such as the military.

as distinguished from sex, involves socially constructed roles regarding what it means to be masculine or feminine.[1] Another concept, **gender identity**, refers to the degree to which an individual sees herself or himself as feminine or masculine based on society's definitions of appropriate gender roles (Burke and Cast 1997).

A further complication of the analysis of sex and gender occurs because a small number of people are born with ambiguous sexual characteristics or are uncomfortable with their gender of birth, as discussed in "Issues for Thought: Challenges to Gender Boundaries."

Gender Expectations

Earlier chapters pointed out that our personal decisions, attitudes, and behaviors are influenced by our social environment, which we in turn influence and shape. The interactionist perspective (see Chapter 3) encourages us to recognize that our culture and the social arrangements surrounding us are not "natural," but rather are socially constructed. Gender roles, attitudes, and behaviors are socially constructed as well. People **internalize** others' expectations regarding gender. By acting accordingly, they reinforce those expectations for themselves, for others around them, and for all who will follow them in subsequent generations. On the contrary, people who refuse to act in accord with gender expectations precipitate change. Let's examine the predominant gender expectations in our culture.

You can probably think of some characteristics typically associated with being feminine or masculine. Stereotypically masculine people are often thought to have **agentic** (from the root word *agent*) or **instrumental character traits**: confidence, assertiveness, and ambition that enable them to accomplish difficult tasks or goals. A relative absence of agency characterizes our expectations of women, who are thought to embody **communal** or **expressive character traits**: warmth, sensitivity, the ability to express tender feelings, and placing concern about others' welfare above self-interest.[2]

Cultural Messages

The ways in which men are expected to show agency and women expressiveness are embedded in the culture around us. Let's examine some of our cultural messages about masculinity and femininity.

MASCULINITIES In writing about men and gender, we need to state the obvious: Men are not all alike. Recognizing this, scholars have begun to analyze **masculinities** in the plural, rather than the singular—a recent and subtle change meant to promote our appreciation for the differences among men. Anthropologist David Gilmore (1990), having examined expectations

---

1. The distinction between *sex* and *gender,* first made by sociologist Ann Oakley (1972), is a dominant perspective in social science (Laner 2003). But not all social theorists agree with this conceptualization. Judith Butler (1990) argues that the two are essentially one—gender—and others agree that the biological as well as behavioral aspects of sex are socially constructed (Creswell 2003).

2. Talcott Parsons, a prominent structure-functionalist in the 1950s (see Chapter 3 of this text), helped to establish these gender expectations (Parsons and Bales 1955, pp. 22–23, 101).

Issues for Thought

Challenges to Gender Boundaries

We take for granted that sex is a dichotomy: You are either male or female. Yet somewhere between 1 percent and 4 percent of live births are **intersexual**—that is, the children have some anatomical, chromosomal, or hormonal variation from the male or female biology that is considered "normal" (Fausto-Sterling 2000; Laner 2003; Preves 2003; Sax 2002): "Chromosomes, hormones, the internal sex structures, the gonads and the external genitalia all vary more than most people realize" (Fausto-Sterling 2000, p. 20).

In the 1950s, psychologist John Money and his colleagues at Johns Hopkins University began the study of intersex babies (then termed *hermaphrodites*). In this clinical program, hermaphrodites were assigned a gender identity, and parents were advised to treat them accordingly. They typically underwent surgery to give their genitals a closer approximation to the assigned gender.

Recently, intersexuality has emerged as an area of political activism through the formation of the Intersex Society of North America in 1993. Members have demonstrated against arbitrary gender assignment and the surgical "correction" of intersexed infants, arguing instead for the acceptance of gender ambiguity (Preves 2002). Some medical ethicists now take the position that "the various forms of intersexuality should be defined as normal" (Lawrence McCullough, quoted in Fausto-Sterling 2000, p. 21).

Similarly, although some **transsexuals** (who have been raised as one sex, while emotionally identifying with the other) still wish surgery to conform their bodies to their gender identity, others "are content to inhabit a more ambiguous zone" (p. 22). They may adopt the dress and demeanor of the sex with which they identify, vary their appearance and self-presentation, or adopt a style that is not gender-identified. The term **transgendered** describes an identity adopted by those who are uncomfortable in the gender of their birth. They may be in transition to a new gender or simply wish to continue to occupy a middle ground. "Some people think it's important to be seen as a specific gender; that's not me," says a Wesleyan college student (in Bernstein 2004, p. ST-1).

Some universities have established nongendered housing at the request of transgendered students. Some bureaucratic forms now include a "transgender" box as well as those for "male" and "female," suggesting the beginning of societal accommodation to a more complex sex/gender system. The biological, psychological, and social realities presented by intersexed or transgendered individuals are political challenges to the notion that there are clearly demarcated masculine and feminine genders and gender roles.

Critical Thinking

Have transgendered individuals been politically visible in your campus or community? What are your own thoughts as to whether gender is a dichotomy or can be a continuum along which individuals may vary?

for men cross-culturally, argues that what is common among the world's concepts of masculinity—and what separates these from cultural messages regarding women—is that a man must somehow prove that he is a "real man" whereas a women is allowed to take gender for granted.

How do men go about demonstrating their manhood? Early in the study of gender, sociologists Deborah David and Robert Brannon (1976) pointed to four masculine "scripts" that our culture provides as guidelines. The first was *no sissy-stuff*, according to which men are expected to distance themselves from anything considered feminine. In a second cultural message, a man should be occupationally or financially successful, a *big wheel*. Third, a man is expected to be confident and self-reliant, even tough—a *sturdy oak*.

A fourth cultural message emphasizes adventure, sometimes coupled with violence and/or the need to outwit, humiliate, and defeat. Adult men *give 'em hell* in barroom brawls, contact sports, and war. If a male finds that legitimate avenues to occupational success are blocked to him because of, for example, social class or racial/ethnic status, he might "make it" through an alternative route, through physical aggression, rapping, or striking a "cool pose." The latter involves dress and postures manifesting fearlessness and detachment, adapted by some racial/ethnic minority males for emotional survival in a discriminatory and hostile society (Majors and Billson 1992). A corresponding stereotypical white working-class male response to economic disadvantage and social change involves a denigrating and hostile critique of blacks, other minorities, and women or the "hypermasculinity [of] shop floors, motorcycle clubs, and urban gangs" (Pyke 1996, p. 53; Fine et al. 1997).

During the 1980s, another cultural message emerged and was lauded by many (including us) as the preferred option for men. According to this message, the "liberated" male is emotionally sensitive and expressive, valuing tenderness and equal relationships with women (Messner 1997, pp. 36–38, 41).

Yet another transformation of the ideal male image has occurred according to some commentators. In response to the terrorist attacks of 9/11 we see "the return of manly men":

> They are the knights in shining fire helmets. They are the welders, policemen, and businessmen with can-do attitudes who are unafraid to tackle armed hijackers . . . The operative word is men. Brawny, heroic, manly men. . . . stoic, muscle-bound and exuding competence from every pore. (Brown 2001, p. WK-5)

Perhaps "'the idea that, due to technological advances, men no longer needed physical strength. . . . look[s] different now,'" says David Blankenhorn of the Institute of American Values (in Brown 2001, p. 5). Cultural messages are complex, for 9/11 also brought us some examples of American men shedding tears in public. Men not known for their warm emotionality—New York Mayor Rudolph Giuliani, for example—did not hide their mourning of the loss of friends, colleagues, and family members (Wax 2001).

Indeed, divergent cultural messages—coupled with the male's need to prove his manhood—contribute to men's sometime ambivalence and confusion in today's changing society (Gilmore 1990; Gerson 1993), a point explored later in this chapter.

FEMININITIES There are a variety of ways of being a woman, according to cultural messages. The pivotal expectation in **femininities** for a woman requires her to offer emotional support. Traditionally, the ideal woman was physically attractive, not too competitive, a good listener, and adaptable. Considered fortunate if she had a man in her life, she acted as his helpmate, aiding and cheering his accomplishments. In addition to caring for a man, a woman was expected to be a good mother and put her family's and children's needs before her own. The "strong black woman" cultural message combined assertiveness, independence, employment, and child care (Basow 1992, p. 132).

A feminine expectation that has emerged as women entered the workforce and the feminist movement developed is that of the "professional woman": independent, ambitious, self-confident. This cultural model may combine with the traditional one to form the "superwoman" message, according to which a good wife and/or mother also efficiently attains career success or supports her children by herself. An emerging female expectation is the "satisfied single": a woman (either heterosexual or lesbian, usually employed, and perhaps a parent) who is quite happy not to be in a serious relationship with a male.

A theme that has wound through cultural images of femininity is the good girl/bad girl or virgin/whore theme. Women have traditionally been stereotyped as either sexually conservative or sluts.

GENDER EXPECTATIONS AND DIVERSITY This view of men as instrumental and women as expressive was based primarily on people's images of white, middle-class heterosexuals. But there are racial/ethnic variations in gender expectations. For example, African American males and females are thought to be more similar to one another in terms of expressiveness and instrumental competence than are non-Hispanic whites (Canary and Emmers-Sommer 1997). Compared to white men, black men are viewed as more emotionally expressive. Compared to white women, black women are viewed as less passive and less dependent. Latinas and Asian women are stereotyped as being more submissive than non-Hispanic white women. Latino men are stereotyped as extremely patriarchal, following a **machismo** cultural ideal of extreme masculinity and male dominance (Hondagneu-Sotelo 1996; McLoyd et al. 2000). In addition to racial/ethnic components, there are age, class, and sexual orientation differences in gender expectations.

Research indicates that racial/ethnic differences in role expectations and behaviors, particularly for males, are actually not as strong as either stereotypes or sociohistorical perspectives have suggested. The preeminence of the male provider role is a powerful theme in *all* racial/ethnic groups (e.g., Taylor, Tucker, and Mitchell-Kernan 1999). African American families have "flexible family roles," but the male's involvement in child care and other expressive roles does not have the same priority as the provider role, despite the difficulty encountered by African American males in fulfilling this role.

Black men and women express preferences for egalitarian relationships (Kane 2000). African American men are more supportive of employed wives than white men are. Yet, gender ideology among African Americans does differentiate the sexes by the importance of the male provider role, with corresponding emotional effects on the marriage when he is not so successful. Women are likely to perform more of the household labor than men (though African American men do more than white men) (Blee and Tickameyer 1995; Orbuch and Eyster 1997; Haynes 2000). African American men show up as more conservative than white men in other ways—for example, in a stronger conviction that men and women are essentially different: Men are "manly," and women are "womanly," or soft and feminine (Haynes 2000, p. 834).

Similarly complex gender patterns are observed in Latino families. For example, Mexican American women carry the primary responsibility for housework and child care (Coltrane 1996). But roles have been modified in the migration process and with women's entry into the labor force. Mexican American women do more housework and child care than men, but less than their counterparts in Mexico. And they have more influence over household decisions (Hondagneu-Sotelo and Messner 1999; Hondagneu-Sotelo 1996).

These are but a few examples of the complexity of role expectations and behavior in real-life families.

To What Extent Do Women and Men Follow Cultural Expectations?

Thus, it is one thing to recognize cultural images but another to follow them. Consequently, we may ask this question: To what extent do individual men and women exhibit gender-expected behaviors?

In adult life, women seem to have greater connectedness in interpersonal relations and to enter the caregiving professions in greater numbers than men, while men are more socially dominant, physically aggressive, and interested in competitive, achievement-oriented occupations (Beutel and Marini 1995). But there is great individual variation, and the situational context accounts for much of the apparent difference between men and women (Myers 2002, Chapter 5). Although some research finds women more concerned about others' well-being than men and men more competitive than women (Beutel and Marini 1995), generally the **gendered** expectations we've discussed fit an overlapping pattern (Basow 1992).

We can visualize the extent to which females and males actually differ on a trait as two overlapping normal distribution curves (see Figure 4.1). For example, although the majority of men are taller than the majority of women, the area of overlap in men's and women's heights is considerable. Furthermore, the shaded area in Figure 4.1 indicates that some men are shorter than some women. It is also true that differences among women or among men (*within-group variation*) are usually greater than the differences between men and women (*between-group variation*).

We also need to recognize that gender traits are sometimes thought to be opposite and mutually exclusive—that is, we may think that a person cannot be both masculine and feminine. But this is not the case.

FIGURE 4.1

How females and males differ on one trait, height, conceptualized as overlapping normal distribution curves. Means (averages) may differ by sex, but trait distributions of men and women occupy much common ground.

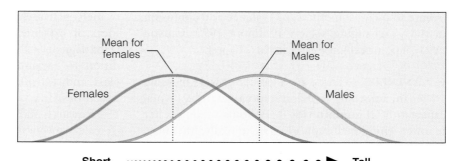

"It's her first bench-clearing brawl."

Traditional stereotypes of children define males as aggressive and competitive and girls as sensitive and concerned for others. Real behavior is far more varied than these stereotypes, however, and depends very much on the situation.

Indeed, fairly recent descriptions by college students of "typical" men and women overlap considerably (De Lisi and Soundranayagam 1990).

Moreover, acting according to cultural expectations may be situational (Wagner and Berger 1997). The same woman may speak forcefully when in a job interview and demurely when on a date, for example. A man who suffers pain without wincing on a football field may cry in response to a family death or other tragedy. Then too, beginning in the 1970s, researchers (Bem 1975, 1981; Swim 1994) have found that about half of American individuals actually see themselves as having both agentic/instrumental and communal/expressive traits.

Finally, as we discuss later in the chapter, the opportunities available in the social structure affect the options of men and women, and ultimately their behaviors as they adapt to those options. Virtually all societies, including our own, are structured around some degree of male dominance.

Male Dominance

On an interpersonal level, **male dominance** describes a situation in which the male(s) in a dyad or group assume authority over the female(s). On the societal level, male dominance is the assignment to men of greater control and influence over society's institutions.

Research shows that on an interpersonal level, males in groups tend to dominate verbally. Men talk louder and longer, interrupt other speakers, and control conversational topics more than women do. Also, females restrict themselves more in claiming personal space, smile more when smiling is not related to happiness, and touch others less in groups, but are touched more. Although these findings may reflect personality differences, they also indicate male–female status differences (Henley and Freeman 1995). On an institutional level, male dominance is evident in politics, religion, and the economy. In fact, "in no known

© Carol Halebian

Nydia Velázquez is the first Puerto Rican-born woman to be elected to Congress. Although the number of female senators and members of the House of Representatives has increased in recent years, women remain a minority in positions of political power.

societies do women dominate men" (Myers 2002, p. 182).

MALE DOMINANCE IN POLITICS Before 1992, there had never been more than two women among our 100 U.S. senators. As of 2001, there were 13 women in the Senate and 62 in the House of Representatives; women compose 14 percent of Congress (U.S. Census Bureau 2003a, Table 408). Democratic congresswoman Nancy Pelosi is minority whip, the highest minority party position in the House of Representatives. Yet women "on the Hill" are still an obvious minority and generally have more difficulty than men gaining access to power positions.

Beginning with the Clinton administration and continuing under President Bush, women have been more visible in the executive branch of government. Condoleeza Rice, an African American woman, has served as national security adviser. The Supreme Court now has two women justices (of nine). One can see considerable progress, though not parity. Still, surveys

report that 92 percent of the public say they would be willing to vote for a woman for president, compared to 53 percent thirty years earlier (Newport, Moore, and Saad 1999).

MALE DOMINANCE IN RELIGION Religion displays male dominance as well. Although most U.S. congregations have more female than male participants, men more often hold positions of authority, while women perform secretarial, housekeeping, and low-level administrative chores. Women have entered the pastorate in Protestant Christian churches and have become rabbis in Reform Jewish congregations, but in both cases remain a minority. Women are prohibited from holding Catholic clerical or lay deacon positions. A majority of U.S. Catholic laypeople (Davidson et al. 1997, p. 45) and U.S. Catholic theologians (Woodward 1997) believe the Catholic church should ordain women priests, but the Vatican disagrees.

The effects of personal religious involvement on women's daily lives are complex. On the one hand, the growth of evangelical Protestantism, Islamic funda-mentalism, and the Latter-day Saints (Mormon) church, along with the charismatic renewal in the Catholic church, has fostered a traditional family ideal of male headship and a corresponding rejection of feminist-inspired redefinitions of family roles. On the other hand, actual practice seems more egalitarian than formal doctrine. Some feminist evangelicals mingle the two movements. Other evangelical and charismatic women redefine male authority to foster greater male involvement in the household, more open communication, and shared decision making (Stacey 1990; Gallagher and Smith 1999). There is a feminist movement among Arab Muslim women who seek to combine their religio-cultural heritage with equal rights for females (Tucker 1993).

MALE DOMINANCE IN THE ECONOMY Al-though the situation is changing, men as a category have been and continue to be dominant economically. For example, in 2002, women who were employed full time earned 77 percent of what men employed full time did. When differences in years of experience, hours per year, time out of the labor force, industry, occupation, race, marital status, and job tenure are all taken into account, women's earnings were 80 percent of men's in 2000 (Weinberg 2004). The remaining 20-percent difference in earnings is unexplained and may be due, at least partially, to discrimination.

Younger women earn a larger proportion (82 per-cent) of what men do. Black (91 percent) and Hispanic (88 percent) female/male comparisons are more favor-able than those of non-Hispanic whites (78 percent), But this is primarily because black and Hispanic men have much lower earnings than do white men (Di Na-tale and Boraas 2002; U.S. Census Bureau 2003a, Table 641).

Even in the same occupational categories, women earn less than men. For instance, in 2000, in the high-est paying occupation, that of physician, women made $80,000 while men earned $140,000 on average. The difference is thought to be related to choice of occupa-tional specialty and practice setting (for example, pedi-atrics, which pays less, is a popular choice of female physicians). Female professionals generally made 67 percent of what their male counterparts did in their longest-held job. Similarly, women's earnings in mana-gerial occupations were 65 percent of men's (U.S. Census Bureau 2003a, Table 642; Weinberg 2004). To some extent, these differences reflect the type of pro-fessional and management jobs that women hold. Men's and women's employment remains segmented into dual labor markets, with women in a narrower range of jobs offering fewer benefits and advancement opportunities.

The earnings gap between men and women has narrowed some in recent decades. Unfortunately, this narrowing is due as much to falling wages for men as it is to rising wages for women (DiNatale and Boraas 2002). Since the 1970s, highly paid industrial produc-tion has declined, white-collar corporate structures have grown leaner, and the labor force has become in-creasingly characterized by lower-paying, less-secure jobs. Except for the college-educated, male workers across the wage hierarchy have suffered declining or stagnant earnings (White and Rogers 2000).

Men continue to dominate corporate America. In 2000, only 5.2 percent of the highest-earning executives in Fortune 500 companies were women ("Women Still Lag" 2004). Although racism blocks the path to management for nonwhite or Hispanic men, both racism and sexism block the path for non-white and Hispanic women, who hold only 1.3 percent of executive positions (Solis and Oldham 2001). Asian American women are most likely of all women to be in management and professional roles ("Women Still Lag" 2004). (Chapter 12 explores men's and women's work in more detail.)

We have been discussing male dominance in the United States today, which of course is more moderate than in our past or compared to some other contem-porary societies. Still, cross-culturally and historically, it appears that virtually all societies have been charac-terized by some degree of male dominance. This leads us to ask whether male dominance might be anchored in biology. Put another way, is what Sigmund Freud once proposed true—that "anatomy is destiny"?

■ Is Anatomy Destiny? ■

We need to ask which aspects of gender-associated be-havior depend on physiology and which are socially shaped. For example, about 80 percent of adult Ameri-can females shave their body hair (Basow 1991). Is this behavior genetic in females, or learned? More seri-ously, are males biologically destined to be more agen-tic, instrumental, and dominant than females? Or are their different behaviors and statuses the products of social organization, power, and social learning?

Biologically Based Arguments

Advocates of a biological basis for gender-related differences invoke various arguments to support their contentions. Some social scientists, as well as biologists, have adopted biological theories of gender.

BIOLOGICALLY BASED THEORIES Biological theories of gender difference were initially offered by primatologists (termed "ethologists") who study human beings as an evolved animal species (e.g., Tiger 1969). Tiger, who primarily studied baboons, found males to be dominant and argued that Homo sapiens inherited this condition through evolutionary selection. Newer data on nonhuman primates have challenged these conclusions as socially constructed myths—"politics by other means" (Haraway 1989)—or as biased science at best. Primate species vary in their behavior, and within species there is some environmentally shaped variation (Wood and Eagly 2002, p. 721). These facts suggest that male and female behavior is not differentiated in a consistent way in the animal species most closely related to humans.

A subsequent biological theory of gendered behavior focused on genes. In this view, in order to continue their genes, individuals act to maximize their reproduction or that of close kin. Different strategies characterize males (who seek to impregnate many females) and females (who seek the best conditions in which to nurture their small number of children) (Dawkins 1976).

Other evolutionary perspectives focus on the hunting–gathering era of early human evolution. Men, because of their greater physical strength and their freedom from reproductive responsibility, were able to hunt. But women, who might be pregnant or breast-feeding, gathered food that was naturally available close to home while they also cared for children. These circumstances elicited different adaptive strategies and skills from men and women that then became encoded in the genes—greater aggression and spatial skills for men, nurturance and domesticity for women. According to this perspective, these traits remain part of our genetic heritage and are today the foundation of gender differences in personality traits, abilities, and behavior (Maccoby 1998, Chapter 5).

The genetic heritage is expressed through **hormonal processes**.[3]

Another area of biological research and theorizing on gender differences has to do with brain organization and functioning. *Brain lateralization* refers to the relative dominance and the synchronization of the two hemispheres of the brain. Some scientists have argued that male and female brains differ due to greater amounts of testosterone secreted by a male fetus. Male fetuses are exposed to relatively large amounts of testosterone at mid-pregnancy, resulting not only in the masculinization of their genitals, but also, according to this theory, an organization of brain structure that gives rise to "masculine" behavior and abilities. As a result, different sides of the brain may be dominant in males and females, or males and females may differ in the degree to which the two brain halves work together. These differences are thought to account for differences in verbal and mathematical ability and visual/spatial skills (Blum 1997; Springer and Deutsch 1994).

Overall, brain lateralization studies have produced conflicting—and unconvincing—evidence concerning sex differences in brain organization or a connection to verbal, spatial, or mathematical abilities (Kimmel 2000a, pp. 30–33; Rogers 2001; Wood and Eagly 2002, p. 720). Furthermore, gender differences in measured math ability and achievement have declined dramatically, arguing against a biological explanation (Hyde, Fennema, and Lamon, 1990; Marecek 1995; Rogers 2001, p. 33).

Many contemporary biologists have relinquished biologically deterministic models in their thinking about gender and family. They present an evolutionary theory of gender and family that acknowledges strong environmental effects on all animal behavior. These more sophisticated theories point to some features

---

3. **Hormones** are chemical substances secreted into the bloodstream by the endocrine glands; they influence the activities of cells, tissues, and body organs. Sex hormones are secreted by male or female gonads, or sex glands. The primary male sex hormones are androgens. Testosterone, produced in the male testes, is an androgen. Testosterone levels in males peak in adolescence and early adulthood, then slowly decline throughout the rest of a man's life. Females secrete testosterone and other androgens also, but in smaller amounts. The primary female hormones are estrogen and progesterone, secreted by the female ovaries.

Sex hormones influence *sexual dimorphism,* differences between the sexes in body structure and size, muscle development, fat distribution, hair growth, voice quality, etc. The degree to which hormones produce gender-differentiated behavior is disputed.

that characterize humans uniquely: extensive paternal investment in children, ongoing (rather than seasonal) sexual relations, and the importance of kin-based social networks, which support the long developmental period needed for human progeny to "acquire sociocompetitive competencies" (Geary and Flinn 2001, p. 7). Biologists also note the reduction of sex differences in physical size in the course of hominid evolution. (*Hominid* refers to the primate species that were the immediate predecessors of humans.) Although molecular geneticist Dean Hamer (Hamer and Copeland 1998) continues to assert a very strong role for genes in shaping gender patterns, neither he nor most other biologists see genes as sole determinants of human behavior. Much current biological theorizing leaves plenty of room for culture (e.g., Geary and Flinn 2001; Emlen 1995). It is safe to say that there is convergence on the opinion that in gender, as well as other behavior, biology interacts with culture in complex and constantly changing ways that cannot be reduced to biological determinism.

THEORIZING BY SOCIAL SCIENTISTS Meanwhile, in sociology, biosocial theorists point to evolution, to behavioral endocrinology (hormones), and to behavioral genetics as influences on family-related behavior (Booth, Carver, and Granger 2000; see also Chapter 3 of this text). They point to studies, such as that of Booth and Dabbs (1993), which suggest that those men with higher testosterone levels may be less likely to marry. If they marry, they may experience a lower quality of spousal interaction, be more likely to report hitting or throwing things at their wives, be more likely to have extramarital sex, and be more likely to divorce.

Biosocial theories of gender are supported by research, such as a study of preschoolers, which found that girls' tendency to engage in gender-related activities (or not) seemed more related to mothers' testosterone levels during pregnancy than to the sex composition of the family, the traditionality of parents' roles, or presence of a male partner in the home. Interestingly, boys' behavior did *not* seem to be related to prenatal levels of mothers' testosterone levels. Researchers attributed this to the strong peer and parental pressure on boys to display traditional masculine behavior; these social pressures overshadowed any effect of prenatally produced biological differences among boys (Hines et al. 2002).

Psychologist Eleanor Maccoby, earlier associated with a review of research on sex differences that found them few and mostly unimportant (Maccoby and Jacklin 1974), has now come to see biology as grounding some childhood differences between the sexes, as well as children's tendency to prefer sex-segregated play. She sees certain sex-differentiated patterns—boys' rough play, earlier separation from adults, poor impulse control, and competition-seeking behavior, and girls' interest in young infants, earlier verbal fluency, and earlier self-regulation—as biologically based. She attributes these differences to *prenatal* hormonal priming, noting that hormonal levels *during childhood* do not match these observed patterns, nor do hormonal levels vary much by sex until adolescence. It is worth noting that she sees the biological influence as very specific: *not* marking the existence of generalized sex differences.

The most developed biosocial gender theory is that of demographer J. Richard Udry. His theory relies on differences in male and female levels of testosterone and other hormones and posits a "primate model" for some sex differences in behavior. Udry conducted studies of women whose mothers' levels of prenatal androgens (testosterone) had been recorded. These women were surveyed about their lives at around ages 27–30. Udry concluded that differences in prenatal hormone exposure predicted differences in indicators of "behaviors on which men and women typically differ" (Udry 2000, p. 445).

Udry labels his theory an interactive one that recognizes the interaction of biology and sociology. But, in fact, his theory seems rather biologically deterministic. "Humans form their social structures around gender because males and females have different and biologically influenced behavioral predispositions. Gendered social structure is a universal accommodation to this biological fact" (p. 454).

Udry's paradigm has been severely criticized by feminists on methodological and theoretical grounds, as well as for its social implications (Kennelly, Merz, and Lorber 2001; Miller and Costello 2001; Risman 2001; and see his response, Udry 2001). According to Miller and Costello, "Small variations in brain morphology cannot explain phenomena such as wage level, who drives on a date, or division of labor in the home" (2001, p. 594). Udry's theory ignores areas of social life, abilities, and personality where the sexes are similar. His work does not address cross-cultural variation,

Native Americans, members of what were once hunting and gathering and hoe cultures, have a complex heritage that varies by tribe but may include a matrilineal tradition in which women owned, and may still own, houses, tools, and land. Native American women's political power declined with the spread of Europeans into their territories and the subsequent reorganization of Indian life by federal legislation in the 1920s. Recently, Native American women have begun to regain their power: A woman, Wilma Mankiller, has served as principal chief of the Cherokee Nation. (Her surname derives from warrior ancestors.)

nor does it acknowledge that the life choices of women have been limited by gender stratification in society.

Society-Based Arguments

In arguing against a biological determinism of whatever sort, sociologists point to instances in which gender-expected behaviors have "clearly followed no logical pattern based on biological differences" (Huber 1989, p. 111). Most modern jobs, for example, do not require the greater upper-body strength of men or their greater physical aggressiveness. Much research on this question does *not* find the differences expected from hypotheses about the behavioral impact of testosterone (Hines et al. 2002). Even the notion that

prehistoric societies were characterized by male hunters and female gatherers has been challenged. In surviving preliterate societies, women do much of the heavy labor and carrying of heavy burdens, and in some societies women hunt small game. In their review of studies of nonliterate societies, Wood and Eagly found that most societies do have a gendered division of labor, but one that varies considerably in the tasks assigned to women and men (Blum 1997, pp. 270–276; Maccoby 1998, p. 2; Wood and Eagly 2002).

It is very difficult to explain short-term change—such as we have seen since the 1970s—by stable biological differences. According to a society-based perspective, it is **structural constraints**—"the established and customary rules, policies, and day-to-day practices that affect a person's life chances" (Ferrante 2000, p. 348)—that produce the gendered behavior that we see. From this perspective, biological theories of gender are essentially ideological (Lewontin 1992), having the effect of obscuring the social construction of gender and thus presenting gender differences as inevitable, not amenable to political challenge and social change (Kennelly, Merz, and Lorber 2001).

There are a variety of social structural perspectives on gender, and we are going to explore one in detail. **Huber's theory of gender stratification** gives great weight to the economic basis of a society, examining three stages—*foraging and hoe societies, agricultural societies*, and *industrial societies*—that vary considerably in the roles and status assigned to men and women.

FORAGING AND HOE SOCIETIES In both foraging (hunting and gathering) and hoe societies (where digging sticks were used to break ground for minimal levels of cultivation), food production was relatively compatible with pregnancy, childbirth, and breast-feeding; thus, women played an important part in the economy. Among foragers, 60 percent to 80 percent of the food comes from gathering activities performed predominantly by women, and both sexes may hunt small game (Linton 1971). With women fully participating economically, males are less dominant than in agricultural or industrial societies (Chafetz 1988).

AGRICULTURAL SOCIETIES Agricultural societies, based on plow cultivation, the domestication of animals, and land ownership (hoe cultivators were nomadic), developed about 5,000 years ago. Plow agriculture requires greater physical strength, full-time labor, and work located farther from the family dwelling, conditions less compatible with pregnancy and nursing (Basow 1992, p. 108). Although women continued to contribute significantly to the family economic enterprise (Huber 1986), men did the plowing and other heavy work, thereby making women's productive labor less visible. About this time, *patriarchy*—a form of social organization based on the supremacy of fathers and inheritance through the male line—became firmly established. As it became possible to accumulate wealth through large landholdings, concern with property inheritance—and hence with the legitimacy of offspring—increased the social control exerted over women, particularly in non-European areas.

INDUSTRIAL SOCIETIES With industrialization, beginning about 200 years ago in Europe, economic production gradually shifted from agriculture to mechanized production of manufactured goods. The status of women declined further as industrialization separated work from home and family life, transferring work traditionally done by women (such as clothing production) from homes to factories. Since factory-based industrial work could not easily be combined with domestic tasks and the supervision of children, women at home no longer contributed directly to economic production; their indirect contribution to the economy through domestic support and reproduction of the labor force became virtually invisible.

In the middle and upper classes, an ideology of **separate spheres** arose to support this separation of men's and women's roles. Men came to be seen as possessing the instrumental traits referred to earlier, as being more comfortable than women with the competition and harshness of the world outside the home. Middle- and upper-class (white) women were "angels of the house," whose delicacy and passivity were appropriate to their more sheltered lives.[4] Women's submissiveness and emotional sensitivity, the expressive qualities described earlier, supposedly enabled them both to provide a haven for their wage-earner husbands and to bring up innocent children (Cancian 1987). These breadwinner and housewife roles applied mainly to middle- and upper-class white men's and women's work—and for only a brief period, from the late nineteenth century to the mid-twentieth century. Most immigrant, black, and working- and lower-class women did not have the housewife option, but instead needed employment in domestic service, factories, or in home-based activities such as piecework performed for money. Nevertheless, although the traditionally idealized portrait of men, women, work, and personality is changing, we have retained remnants of it to the present.

POSTINDUSTRIAL SOCIETIES In the present day, we go beyond Huber's three-fold typology into an economy and society termed **postindustrial** because it is dominated by information-based and service work,

---

4. We should note that some women were able to use the moral authority given to them by a separate-spheres ideology to lead antislavery campaigns, temperance crusades, and suffrage movements. Also during this era, some women advocated radical changes in society and the family (Rossi 1973).

not the manufacture of things. *Processing ideas and information* in complex areas (e.g., media, law, financial services, computer technology) and *providing services* that range from medical care to telemarketing dominate the economy now. Huber's thesis that economic arrangements underlie gender ones still holds, however. As a postindustrial labor force is more inclusive of women, so also does it minimize gender differentiation and spur changes in gender roles. Ironically, biosocial theories of gender have recently become more prominent in the social sciences.

The Interaction of Culture and Biology

Very probably, biology and society interact to create **gender-linked characteristics and roles**. For example, men's greater average physical strength, a result of higher testosterone levels, may have resulted in force and/or threats of force to effect some degree of male dominance in past and some present societies. But, as we have seen, the various forms of economic organization either mitigated or exaggerated male dominance.

Most biologists of human behavior today concede the interaction of biology and environment, although they tend to give greater emphasis to biology (Eagly 1995). Many sociologists, on the other hand, take a strongly social constructionist view of gender (Risman 1998) even while recognizing some biological foundation for human behavior. Support exists for the proposition that gender-linked characteristics result from the interaction of cultural pressures and biological processes, which has reciprocal effects.

The relationship between hormones and behavior goes in both directions: what's happening in one's environment may influence hormone secretion levels. Several small studies have found that the hormonal levels of new fathers undergo changes parallel to those associated with maternal behavior (lower testosterone and cortisol and detectable levels of estradiol) (Berg and Wynne-Edwards 2001). Testosterone rises in men in response to an athletic or other competition or in response to insults (Woods and Eagly 2002, pp. 701–02).

> Biological development never unfolds within a vacuum: it is always subject to social and environmental inputs. If . . . we treat infant boys and infant girls differently from birth, for example, by holding girls more than we do boys, the differential treatment they receive may alter their neurological development. (Brody 1999, p. 103)

It's important to recognize that cultural learning may either exaggerate or minimize whatever genetic tendencies exist.

▪ Gender and Socialization ▪

Social structure and societal values influence how we behave. As people in a given society learn to talk, think, and feel, they *internalize* (make their own) cultural expectations about how to behave. The process by which society influences members to internalize attitudes and expectations is called **socialization**.

The socialization process is an important concept in the interactional theoretical perspective (see Chapter 3). Interactionists point out that individuals do not automatically absorb, but rather negotiate, cultural attitudes and roles. Therefore, gendered behavior varies from individual to individual. Nevertheless, in various ways society encourages people to adhere, often unconsciously, to culturally acceptable gender roles. We'll examine in detail how language, family, and school function in gender socialization.

The Power of Cultural Images

Our cultural images in language and in the media convey the gendered expectations described earlier in this chapter. You are no doubt aware of the many—and sometimes controversial—efforts to make our language less gender-oriented over the past three decades by substituting, for example, "mail carrier" for "mail man." But our language also continues to accentuate male–female differences rather than similarities (Adams and Ware 1995). Soon after birth, most infants receive either a masculine or a feminine name.

Besides first names, titles, adjectives, nouns, and verbs remind people that males and females differ—and in stereotypic ways. A new mother may be told that she has either a "*lovely* girl" or a "*strong* boy." In her book about the differences in masculine and feminine communication styles, linguist Deborah Tannen writes the following:

> If I wrote, "After delivering the acceptance speech, the candidate fainted," you would know I was talking about a woman. Men do not faint; they pass out. (Tannen 1990, pp. 241–242)

The media promote gender stereotypes as well. Children's programming more often depicts boys than

Children learn much about gender roles from their parents, whether they are taught consciously or unconsciously. Parents may model roles and reinforce expectations of appropriate behavior. Children also internalize messages from available cultural influences and materials surrounding them.

© David Young-Wolff/PhotoEdit

girls in dominant, agentic roles (Carter 1991). On music videos, females are likely to be shown trying to get a man's attention. Some videos broadcast shockingly violent misogynous (hatred of women) messages. In TV commercials, men predominate by about nine to one as the authoritative narrators or voiceovers, even when the products are aimed at women (Craig 1992; Kilbourne 1994).

Cultural images in the media and language help to socialize individuals to expected gender attitudes and roles. They do so by portraying what is "normal" and by influencing socializing agents, such as our parents, peers, and teachers. We turn now to a brief examination of socialization theories.

Theories of Socialization

How do cultural ideas about gender get incorporated into personality and behavior? We don't have a definitive answer to that question because there are a number of competing theories of gender socialization, each with some supporting evidence (Hines et al. 2002).

SOCIAL LEARNING THEORY Much of what we have just described fits a **social learning theory** in which children learn gender roles as they are taught by

parents, schools, and the media. Children imitate models for behavior and are rewarded by parents and others for whatever is perceived as sex-appropriate behavior.

As children grow older, toys, talk of future careers or marriages, and admonitions about "sissies" and "ladies" communicate parents' ideas about appropriate behavior for boys and girls. The *rewards and punishments,* however subtle, that parents assign to gender roles are sometimes seen to be the key to behavior patterns. Other theorists emphasize the significance of parents as *models* of masculine and feminine behavior, although researchers have found little association between children's personalities and parents' characteristics. Fathers seem to have stronger expectations for gender-appropriate behavior than do mothers (Losh-Hesselbart 1987; Andersen 1988).

SELF-IDENTIFICATION THEORY Some psychologists think that what comes first is not rules about what boys and girls should do but rather the child's awareness of being a boy or a girl. In this **self-identification theory**, children categorize themselves as male or female, typically by age three. They then identify behaviors in their families, in the media, or elsewhere that are appropriate to their sex and adopt those behaviors.

In effect, children socialize themselves from available cultural materials. This perspective, developed by psychologist Lawrence Kohlberg (1966), may account for the fact that boys without a father in the home may be just as masculine as boys in intact families (Andersen 1988).

GENDER SCHEMA THEORY Somewhat similar to self-identification theory, gender schema theory posits that children develop a framework of knowledge (a **gender schema**) about what girls and boys typically do (Bem 1981). Children then use this framework to organize how they interpret new information and think about gender. Once a child has developed a gender schema, the schema influences how she or he processes new information, with gender-consistent information remembered better than gender-inconsistent information. For example, a child with a traditional gender schema might generalize that physicians are men even though the child has sometimes had appointments with female physicians. Overall, gender schema theorists see gender schema as maintaining traditional stereotypes.

CHODOROW'S THEORY OF GENDER Sociologist Nancy Chodorow (1978) has constructed a theory of gender that combines psychoanalytic ideas about identification of children with parents with an awareness of what those parents' social roles are in our society. According to Chodorow, infants develop a "primary identification" with the person primarily responsible for their early care. Later, children must learn to differentiate psychologically and emotionally between themselves and their primary caregiver.

Cross-culturally and historically, children's primary caregivers are virtually always female. Both daughters and sons make their primary identification with a female; as a result, the task of separation is more difficult for a boy. Because a daughter is developing a gender identity similar to her principal caregiver's (her mother), she can readily model her mother's behavior. But a boy cannot model his mother's behavior and also develop a culturally consistent gender identity. He learns instead that he is "not female." He must suppress "feelings of overwhelming love, attachment, and dependence on his mother" (Thurman 1982, p. 35). The stress of separation from mother is heightened for boys in cultures such as ours, where open expression of loss is discouraged as inappropriate for males (Kantrowitz and Kalb 1998; Pollack 1998).

Chodorow attributes differences between adult men and women to this divergence in the early socialization experiences of boys and girls. Boys are disappointed and angry at the necessary—but abrupt and emotionally charged—detachment from their mother. Gradually, however, they come to value their relatively absent fathers as models of agency, independence, and "the superiority of masculine . . . prerogatives" (Thurman 1982, p. 35). Conversely, "relatedness," or expressiveness, is allowed and fostered among girls.

Research does not strongly support Chodorow's theory, and in an era of numerous single-parent families and changing parental roles, it seems less applicable. Nevertheless, Chodorow has been very influential in academic thinking and policy perspectives on gender.

In fact, all of the gender socialization theories presented seem plausible, but none has overwhelming research support. We'll turn now to some empirical findings regarding gender socialization.

Girls and Boys in the Family

FOCUS ON CHILDREN Until recently, most studies on gender socialization were conducted on non-Hispanic white families. This research practice has begun to change, and the results are interesting. One study of black families, for example, indicated that both sons and daughters are socialized toward independence, employment, and child care (Hale-Benson 1986). Because most of the classic research presented in this section has focused on middle-class whites, findings may or may not apply to other racial/ethnic or class categories. (Racial/ethnic and class variation in child rearing will be discussed in Chapter 11.)

From the 1970s on, parents have reported treating their sons and daughters similarly (Maccoby and Jacklin 1974; Antill 1987). "[T]he specialization of men for dominance and women for subordination that emerged [as a socialization pattern] in patriarchal societies has eroded with the weakening of gender hierarchies in postindustrial societies" (Wood and Eagly 2002, p. 717).

Differential socialization still exists, but is typically subtle and less deliberate. Encouragement of gender-typed interests and activities continues. A study of 120 babies' and toddlers' rooms found that girls had more dolls, fictional characters, children's furniture, and the color pink; boys had more sports equipment, tools, toy vehicles, and the colors blue,

titudes and skills of tenderness or nurturance (Kindlon and Thompson 1998; Pollack 1998).

Beginning when children are about five and increasing through adolescence, parents allocate household chores—both the number and kinds—to their children differentially, according to the child's sex. With African American children often an exception, Patricia will more likely be assigned cooking and laundry tasks; Patrick will find himself painting and mowing (Burns and Homel 1989; McHale et al. 1990). Because girls' chores are typically daily and boys' sporadic, girls spend more time doing them—a fact that "may convey a message about male privilege" (Basow 1992, p. 131). Interestingly, the number of girls and boys in a family apparently influences how chores are distributed. For example, families with all girls more readily assign traditional male-child tasks to girls than do families with at least one boy. And the age and gender of siblings are important. Research has found that when an older sibling is of the same sex, play activities tend to be gender-stereotyped; if the other sibling is of the other sex, cross-sex play is common (Brody and Steelman 1985).

Although relations in the family provide early feedback and help shape a child's developing identity, play and peer groups become important as children try out identities and adult behaviors.

Play and Games[5]

Boys and girls tend to play separately and differently (Maccoby 1998). Girls play in one-to-one relationships or in small groups of twosomes and threesomes; their play is relatively cooperative, emphasizes turn taking, requires little competition, and has relatively few rules. In "feminine" games like jump rope or hopscotch, the goal is skill rather than winning (Basow 1992). Boys more often play in fairly large groups, characterized by more

Toys send messages about gender roles. What does this toy say?

Courtesy Deb Glover and Celeste Wheeler

red, and white. And most parents, especially fathers, discourage their children, especially sons, from playing with opposite-gender toys (Bussey and Bandura 1999; Feldman 2003, p. 207; Lytton and Romney 1991; Pomerleau et al. 1990).

Exploratory behavior is more encouraged in boys than girls (Feldman 2003, p. 207). Toys considered appropriate for boys encourage physical activity and independent play, whereas "girls' toys" elicit closer physical proximity and more talk between child and caregiver (Caldera, Huston, and O'Brien 1989). Even parents who support nonsexist child rearing for their daughters are often concerned if their sons are not aggressive or competitive "enough"—or are "too" sensitive (Pleck 1992). Girls are increasingly allowed or encouraged to develop instrumental attitudes and skills. Meanwhile, boys are still discouraged from, or encounter parental ambivalence about, developing at-

5. The role of play is an important concept in the interactionist perspective, particularly in symbolic interaction theory, developed by philosopher George Herbert Mead (see Chapter 3 of this text). **Play**, in Mead's theory, is not idle time, but rather a significant vehicle through which children develop appropriate conceptions of adult roles, as well as images of themselves. In interaction theory, one's self-concept, including one's sense of masculinity and femininity, depends on the responses of significant others: emotionally important people such as parents. Playmates are an important influence as well. A boy or girl begins to see himself or herself as competent or as delicate and nurturing, depending on the comments of parents and playmates.

fighting and attempts to effect a hierarchical pecking order. Boys also seem to exhibit high spirits and having fun (Maccoby 1998). From preschool through adolescence, children who play according to traditional gender roles are more popular with their peers; this is more true for boys (Martin 1989).

Sex segregation at play and leisure begins in preschool and intensifies in elementary school. In identifying "two cultures of childhood" (Maccoby 1998, p. 32), psychologist Eleanor Maccoby argues that these different styles of play may be anchored in biology and that contrasting play styles lead to the separation of boys and girls, who find their same-sex peers more attractive playmates. (She also notes that context is everything: Boys' and girls' behavior varies greatly with social context.)

Differences in childhood play and games work to teach boys and girls divergent attitudes, skills, and gendered identities. The process is reinforced in schools.

Socialization in Schools

FOCUS ON CHILDREN

School organization, classroom teachers, and textbooks all convey the message that boys are more important than girls. Indeed, there is considerable evidence that the way girls and boys are treated differently in school is detrimental to both genders (AAUW 1992; Sadker and Sadker 1994; Pollack 1998; Kindlon and Thompson 1998). Let's consider each element of the educational system in turn.

SCHOOL ORGANIZATION In 1999, 73 percent of all public school employees were women, but only about half of the principals and assistant principals were women, and fewer than half of officials and administrators (46 percent). Eighty-seven percent of elementary teachers were women, compared to 58 percent of secondary teachers. And almost 90 percent of teacher aides and 96 percent of clerical and secretarial staff were female. These 1999 numbers represent a change toward greater balance since 1982, when only 21 percent of principals and 49 percent of secondary teachers were women (U.S. Census Bureau 2003a, Table 252). Still, with men in positions of authority (principals, superintendents), women in positions of service (teacher's aides, secretaries), and men more visible in the upper grade levels, school organization models male dominance.

TEACHERS' PRACTICES Research shows that teachers pay more attention to males than to females, and males tend to dominate learning environments from nursery school through college (Lips 1995). Researchers who observed more than 100 fourth-, sixth-, and eighth-grade classes over a three-year period found that boys consistently and clearly dominated classrooms. Teachers called on and encouraged boys more often than girls. If a girl gave an incorrect answer, the teacher was likely to call on another student, but if a boy was incorrect, the teacher was more likely to encourage him to learn by helping him discover his error and correct it (Sadker and Sadker 1994). Compared to girls, boys are more likely to receive a teacher's attention, to call out in class, to demand help or attention from the teacher, to be seen as model students, or to be praised by teachers. Boys are also more likely to be disciplined harshly by teachers (Pollack 1998; Gurian 1996; Kindlon and Thompson 1998).

In subtle ways, teachers may reinforce the idea that males and females are more different than similar. There are times when boys and girls interact together relatively comfortably—in the school band, for example. But especially in elementary schools, many cross-sexual interaction rituals such as playground games are based on and reaffirm boundaries and differences between girls and boys. Sociologist Barrie Thorne (1992) calls these rituals **borderwork**. Between 1976 and 1981, Thorne spent eleven months doing naturalistic or participant observation (see Chapter 3) in two elementary schools, one in California and one in Michigan. In classrooms, teachers often pitted girls and boys against each other in spelling bees or math contests.

AFRICAN AMERICAN GIRLS, LATINAS, AND ASIAN AMERICAN GIRLS IN MIDDLE AND HIGH SCHOOL Journalist Peggy Orenstein (1994) spent one year observing in two California middle schools, one mostly white and middle class and the other predominantly African American and Hispanic and of lower socioeconomic status. Orenstein found that in both schools, girls were subtly encouraged to be quiet and nonassertive whereas boys were rewarded for boisterous and even aggressive behaviors.

However, African American girls were louder and less unassuming than non-Hispanic white girls when they began school—and some continued along this path. In fact, they called out in the classroom as often

Are boys behaving differently than girls in this photo? How does this fit with the discussion of gender and socialization in school?

as boys did. But Orenstein noted that teachers' reactions differed. The participation, and even antics, of white boys in the classroom were considered inevitable and rewarded with extra attention and instruction, whereas the assertiveness of African American girls was defined as "menacing, something that, for the sake of order in the classroom, must be squelched" (p. 181). Orenstein further found that Latinas, along with Asian American girls, had special difficulty being heard or even noticed. Probably socialized into quiet demeanor at home and often having language difficulties, these girls' scholastic or leadership abilities largely went unseen. In some cases, their classroom teachers did not even know who the girls were when Orenstein mentioned their names.

In high school, Latina girls experience cross-pressures when the desire to succeed in school and move on to a career is in tension with the traditional assumption of wife and mother roles at a young age. Twenty-six percent do not finish high school, compared to 13 percent of black and 7 percent of white girls. Factors such as poverty and language barriers, as well as the pressure to contribute to the family, affect the educational attainment of both boys and girls. But young Latinas, especially recent immigrants, seem torn between newer models for women as mothers *and* career women and the traditional model of marriage and homemaking (Canedy 2001). Nevertheless, the majority of Latinas and Latinos finish high school.

PROGRAMS AND OUTCOMES One concern related to schooling has been whether girls are channeled into or themselves avoid the traditionally masculine areas in high school study. A recent review of 1,000 research studies (AAUW Education Foundation 1999) reports that high school boys and girls now take similar numbers of science courses, but boys are more likely to take all three core courses: biology, chemistry, and physics. Girls enroll in Advanced Placement (AP) courses in greater numbers than boys, including AP biology. But fewer girls than boys get high enough scores on AP tests to get college credit. Girls take fewer computer courses, and they cluster in traditional female occupations in career-oriented programs.

WOMEN AND MEN IN COLLEGE Many women, especially those returning to college and/or working in less gender-friendly corporate environments, find the college environment liberating. Women have been the majority of college students since 1979, and among young adults 25–29, women are slightly more likely to have a college degree. This is a relatively recent development, so that when older adults are included (*all* men and women over 25), men still hold slightly more bachelor's degrees (29 percent compared to 25 percent for women) ("People: Gender" 2003; Spraggins 2003).

Greater numbers in college do not mean that women have attained complete equality on campus, however. In 2001, men received a slight majority of first professional and doctoral degrees, while women received 59 percent of M.A. degrees (U.S. Census Bureau 2003a, Table 298). A minority of college teachers are women; women compose 41 percent of all college faculty and 37 percent of those with full-time positions (U.S. Census Bureau 2003a, Table 295).

Women comprise the majority of college students in all racial/ethnic groups (and racial/ethnic minorities are presently 28 percent of students at degree-granting institutions) (U.S. Census Bureau 2003a, Table 280; U.S. National Center for Educational Statistics 2002, Table 206). Still, racial/ethnic minority students have fewer role models and suffer from the racism sometimes directed at them at predominantly white colleges (Waters 2004, pp. 423–424). Of full-time faculty in 1999, 34 percent were white non-Hispanic women; 3 percent black women; 1 percent Hispanic women; 2 percent Asian/Pacific Islander women; and American Indian women were less than 1 percent of the faculty (U.S. National Center for Education Statistics 2001, Table 224).

Moreover, men's harassment of campus women continues (Dziech 2003). In the media, high-profile examples of sexual exploitation and rape by male students or campus guests (Bloomberg News 2004; Schemo 2003) appear side by side with stories of universities' efforts to strictly limit relationships of students and faculty (Rimer 2003) as a means of controlling sexual harassment of students by faculty.

What About Boys?

Girls have long been the primary focus of attention in examining the possible bias of educational institutions. The previous sections

make a good case for such concern, and the 1994 Gender Equity Act declares girls an "under-served population." But despite the litany of difficulties girls and women may face in educational settings, all this is by way of identifying problems that need attention. In fact, girls and women are doing well, on the whole. Women and girls "are on a tear through the educational system. . . . In the past 30 years, nearly every inch of progress . . . has gone to them" (Thor Mortenson of the Dell Institute for the Study of Opportunity in Higher Education, in Conlin 2003a, p. 76).

In recent years, attention has turned to boys. Some writers attack the "myth of girls in crisis" (Sommers 2000a, p. 61). Sommers's critique goes beyond a concern for balance to argue that there is a "war on boys" (2000b). In Sommers's view, boys are actively discriminated against by the educational establishment: "[B]oys are resented, both as the unfairly privileged sex and as obstacles on the path to gender justice" (2000b, p. 60; 2000a, p. 23).

Sommers and others have some valid points. They point to the declining male share of college enrollments and note that on a number of indicators, girls do better in school: better grades, higher educational aspirations, greater enrollment in AP and other demanding academic programs. Currently, girls are even more likely to outnumber boys in higher-level math and science courses, student government, honor society, and student newspaper staffs. More boys fall behind grade level and more are suspended, and they are far more likely to be shunted into special education classes or to have their inattentive and restless behavior defined as deviant and be medicated. Indicators of deviant behavior—crime, alcohol, and drugs—show more involvement by boys. To the argument that boys do better on SAT and other standardized tests, Sommers responds that the pool of girls taking the test is more apt to include disadvantaged and/or marginal students, whereas their male counterparts do not take these exams. Boys have a greater incidence of diagnosis of emotional disorders, learning disorders, attention-deficit disorders, and teen deaths (Conlin 2003a; Goldberg 1998; Sommers 2000a, 2000b). The "gender gap" in current bachelor's degrees is noted. In every racial/ethnic group, women receive more degrees ("A Widening Gulf" 2003).

Other analysts do not necessarily share Sommers's allegations of active discrimination against boys. But they argue that attention to girls' educational needs

"We don't believe in pressuring the children. When the time is right, they'll choose the appropriate gender."

and the success of men in the work world tended to obscure boys' problems in school. They see a mismatch between typical boy behavior—high levels of physical activity and more challenges to teachers and school rules—and school expectations about sitting still, following rules, and concentration (Poe 2004). Moreover, a survey by the Public Education Network (Metropolitan Life Insurance Company 1997) found that 31 percent of boys in grades 7–12 felt that teachers do not listen to them, compared to 19 percent of girls.

What to do? Sommers can be described as an antifeminist, and she believes that a deteriorating situation among boys is an outcome of feminist efforts not only to advance girls but also to encourage nonsexist child rearing and to denigrate "male culture" by treating "normal" male exuberant play as deviant behavior. Sommers proposes single-sex schools; restoration of a competitive, structured, and achievement-oriented environment; and elimination of attempts to get boys to express their emotions (Sommers 2000a, 2000b).

Other approaches to concerns about boys are exactly opposite to the approach of Sommers. A group at the Harvard School of Education led by educational

psychologist Carol Gilligan proposes a reform based on the notion that boys are at risk because they are separated from mothers earlier than girls and because a hypermasculine culture of emotional repression, competition, and glorification of war compromises their humanity. She would encourage boys to develop their sensitive side (cited in Goldberg 1998). Psychiatrist William Pollack's perspective is that "what we call . . . normal boy development . . . not only isn't normal, but it's traumatic and that trauma has major consequences" (quoted in Goldberg 1998, p. A–12; see also Kimmel 2001).

But to express vulnerability runs the risk of victimization. Boys, particularly racial/ethnic minority youth, face a dilemma in that acting tough to protect themselves is threatening to adults (psychologist Dan Kindlon, cited in Goldberg 1998). One effort suggested by this line of thought is to decrease tolerance for bullying (Kimmel 2001). Other proposals include (1) accepting a certain level of boys' rowdy play as not deviant, (2) more active learning-by-doing to permit physical movement in classroom settings, and (3) activities shared by boys and girls and boy–girl dialogues about gender (Thompson and Kindlon 1999). The bottom line may be the observation by Marie C. Wilson, president of the Ms. Foundation for women: "We'd be so naive to think we could change the lives of girls without boys' lives changing" (quoted in Goldberg 1998, p. A–12). It may be that "girls and boys are on the same side in this issue."

In this section on socialization, we have examined how socialization shapes gender identities and gendered behavior. Socialization throughout infancy, childhood, and adolescence is an obvious influence on the development of gender roles in the adult women and men we see around us. Socialization continues throughout adulthood as we negotiate and learn new roles—or as those already learned are renegotiated or reinforced.

But socialization is not the final answer to the role that gender plays in our lives. The varied opportunities we encounter as adults influence the adult roles we choose and play out and the qualities and skills we develop. And that, in turn, comes from the gender structure of society: "The complex political, economic, psychological, and social relations of men and women in society" (Andersen 1988, p. 76, in Hall 2000, p. 102).

▪ Gender in Adult Lives ▪

In this section, we examine various aspects of gender in adults' lives today. One of the most dramatic changes of the last decades has been the rapid shift in what the culture expects of men and women. This includes changes in work and family roles, and, more generally, changes in cultural definitions of "femininities" and "masculinities." Old patterns may be difficult to alter. This is true for both women and men, who may be torn between newer ideas and what they have learned to value from the past. But new roles promise some rewards.

Gender and Stress

Traditional gender roles result in some characteristic stresses. Oriented to others at the expense of self, many women have felt depressed, bored, empty, dissatisfied with life, inadequate, and excessively guilty. Suicide attempts are more common among women than men (although men are more likely to succeed and therefore have a higher suicide rate). Women also experience higher rates of mental illness and eating disorders, and are particularly prone to depression (Basow 1992; Bower 1995). Traditional sex roles are hazardous to women's health.

Traditional gender expectations are hazardous to men as well. Overemphasis on productivity, competition, and achievement creates anxiety or emotional stress, which may contribute to men's shorter life expectancy through higher rates of heart disease. Physically dangerous behaviors, notably smoking, unsafe driving, drug use, and violence, shorten men's lives, and there may be biological differences that affect survival. For much of this century, the gap in longevity between men and women grew, increasing from two years in 1900 to more than seven in 1970. (See Figure 4.2.) The gap has been declining since then; nevertheless, women presently outlive men by 5.2 years ("Gender Differences" 2001; Kochanek and Smith 2004).

The masculine role not only requires that men undergo pressure to "prove it"—but also encourages them to discount or ignore their anxiety and physical symptoms of stress, illness, or pain. Men are encouraged to hide emotions of vulnerability, tenderness, and warmth when they are in public. When hiding tender feelings, men may not share their inner selves, a situation that may lead to hidden depression, which, in turn, may be acted out with violence (Real 1997). Following traditional gender role expectations, men may block avenues to intimacy, isolating themselves. Meanwhile, psychological and other research tells us that both agency (instrumental roles) and communal (expressive roles) are required for optimum well-being (Helgeson 1994).

Gender and Personal Change

Sometimes in response to these stresses—and also in response to available options—adults reconsider earlier choices regarding gender roles. For example, a small proportion of men choose to be full-time fathers and/or househusbands. Others may effect more subtle changes, such as breaking through previously learned isolating habits to form more intimate friendships and deeper family relationships.

That choices in adult development and social roles are contingent on opportunity and, to some degree, chance is illustrated by Kathleen Gerson's research on women's and men's role choices. Gerson (1985) studied sixty-three women who were between ages twenty-seven and thirty-seven when interviewed in

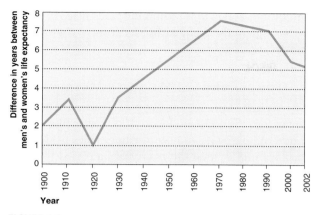

FIGURE 4.2

Gender differences in life expectancy at birth, United States, 1900–2002. This graph shows the number of years by which women's life expectancy exceeds that of men. A female born in 2002, for example, can expect to live 5.2 years longer on average than a male born in the same year.

In earlier centuries, women had high death rates because they often died in childbirth. After maternal mortality declined due to changes in medical practice, women's life expectancy began to exceed men's, and it increased more rapidly than men's throughout most of the twentieth century. (The high rate of deaths for both men and women during the flu epidemic of the early twentieth century was an exceptional break in this pattern.) Men's higher rates of smoking, drug use, violence, and other risk-taking behavior affected their mortality negatively, while women's healthier life styles (less smoking and risk-taking) and more frequent visits to health care providers, as well as a biological advantage in hormonal protection against chronic diseases, were to their advantage as chronic disease became the major causes of death. Recently, men have adopted healthier lifestyles, especially reduced rates of smoking, which has lowered their mortality. That, and women's increased smoking and perhaps stresses related to labor force participation have brought the sexes closer together in terms of life expectancy.

Source: Adapted from *Population Today* (Aug/Sept. 2001), p. 11, with additional data from Minino and Smith 2001, p. 2; Kochanek and Smith 2004, Table 6. Courtesy of the Population Reference Bureau.

1978–1979. Extensive and repeated interviews enabled Gerson to construct life histories and to trace gender-related decisions made in adulthood, particularly decisions about work and motherhood.

The women fell into four groups: Two groups of women made role choices early in life and held to them. The other two groups are more interesting for our purposes. These women had entered young adulthood with clear expectations for their lives. One set planned a rather conventional marriage and family; work would be an interim activity. The other group gave high priority to careers, regardless of any hopes for marriage and children.

But their lives turned out to be quite different from their expectations. Sometimes women who had planned careers met obstacles, often overt or covert discrimination. They became pessimistic about their chances of realizing their original goals. Or they fell into very satisfying relationships and may also have found domesticity and children to be more enjoyable than they had expected. These circumstances combined to channel their movement into more traditional family lifestyles. Here is one example:

> Vicki was never especially oriented toward motherhood. Instead, since she was old enough to know who the police were, she wanted to be a policewoman. . . . Forced to take the best job she could find after high school, Vicki became a secretary-clerk. She also took the qualifying exam for police work and passed with high marks. No jobs were available [at that time], however. . . . In the meantime, she met and married Joe. . . . She ultimately grew to hate working, for it usually involved taking orders from bosses she did not respect. . . . After the birth of her first child, Vicki discovered that staying at home to rear a child was more important than her succession of boring, deadend jobs. By her mid-thirties, she was a full-time mother of two. Today she has given up hope of becoming a policewoman, but in return for this sacrifice she feels she has gained the secure home life she never knew as a child. (Gerson 1985, pp. 18–19)

Vicki's story illustrates a point we made earlier: Individuals may choose only options that are available in their society. At the time Vicki sought a job as a policewoman, probably few women were being hired. Now women are routinely hired as police officers, partly as a consequence of the courts' support for affirmative action hiring practices. This change indicates that it is possible to create options through changes in public policy. Making choices about family life may include political activity directed toward creating those choices.

Several years after her study of women, Gerson (1993) turned her attention to men's changing lives. She interviewed 138 men, mostly in their thirties, and found that, like women, they were reexamining choices made when they were younger. Subsequent changes often involved family roles, a point we will return to throughout this text. But some of these men had also changed their attitudes toward masculinity in general. In one example, Carlos, a Mexican American social worker, recalled his earlier days:

> When I was in high school, I was more of a traditional Hispanic male—sort of macho. At least, I was playing with that idea. A relationship started that was more of a traditional relationship. I expected that person to give to me more than I gave [her]. It was almost like a fetch-me type of relationship. I think if we had lived together, she would have cooked, cleaned the house, raised the kids.

A growing sense of discomfort led Carlos to later reject this cultural message:

> I felt that I wouldn't want to be treated that way, and I shouldn't treat someone else that way. I saw there could be an abuse of the traditional male role, and also I saw limitations in that type of relationship. The woman is limited within the family, and the man gets locked into an image I didn't enjoy. At that point, I pretty much decided that the type of person I wanted to be did not match with the traditional Hispanic role model. (quoted in Gerson 1993, p. 159)

The import of Gerson's two studies for our understanding of change over the course of life is that childhood socialization and early goals do not necessarily predict adult lifestyles. The adult life course is determined by the interaction of the individual's goals, values, abilities, and motivation with the opportunities that present themselves. Throughout adulthood, individuals make a series of choices about their lives. Different individuals respond differently to those options that are the product of a particular time. The development of adult life is a process of ongoing decision and choice, early choices shaping later ones, within the possibilities of a society at a particular historical time. Both men and women may rethink gender roles in adulthood. Today that rethinking takes place in a society considerably changed by the women's movement and responses to it.

Options and the Women's Movement

The separate-spheres ideology of gender retained its power into the 1950s and early 1960s, as media glorification of housewife and breadwinner roles made them seem natural despite the reality of increased women's employment. But contradictions between what women were actually doing and the roles prescribed for them became increasingly apparent. Higher levels of education for women left college-educated women with a significant gap between their abilities and the housewife role assigned to them (Friedan 1963). Employed women chafed at the unequal pay and working conditions in which they labored and began to think that their interest lay in increasing equal opportunity.

Further, the civil rights movement of the 1960s provided a model of activism. In a climate in which social change seemed possible, changes in the economic situation of women precipitated a social movement—the *second wave* of the women's movement.[6] This movement challenged the heretofore accepted traditional roles and strove to increase gender equality.

Women vary in their attitudes toward the women's movement. Some women of color and white working-class women may find the movement irrelevant to the extent that it focuses on psychological oppression or on professional women's opportunities rather than on "the daily struggle to make ends meet that is faced by working class women" (Aronson 2003, p. 907). Black women have always labored in the productive economy under duress or out of financial necessity and did not experience the enforced delicacy of women in the Victorian period. Nor were they ever housewives in large numbers, so the feminist critique of that role may seem irrelevant (Hunter and Sellers 1998).

Chicano/Chicana (Mexican American) activism gave *la familia* a central place as a distinctive cultural value. Latinos of both sexes placed a high value on family solidarity, with individual family members' needs and desires subsumed to the collective good so that Chicana feminists' critiques of unequal gender re-

---

6. The *first wave* of the women's movement in the United States occurred from about the latter half of the nineteenth century until about 1920, when women obtained the right to vote.

lations in *la familia* often met with hostility (Segura and Pesquera 1995).

African American and Latino women consider racial/ethnic as well as gender discrimination in setting their priorities (Amott and Matthaei 2004). In some ways, such as their experience with racial/ethnic discrimination and their relatively low wages, Chicanas are more like Mexican American men, who are also subordinated, than they are like non-Hispanic white women. Nevertheless, a Chicana feminism emerged during the 1960s and 1970s. Generally, Chicanas support women's economic issues, such as equal employment and day care, while showing less support for abortion rights than do Anglo women. Latinas formed some grassroots community organizations of their own to offer social services such as job training, community-based alternatives to juvenile incarceration, and bilingual child development centers. The Mexican American Women's National Association was established in 1974 (Segura and Pesquera 1995).

African American women are more critical of gender inequality than are white women (Kane 2000). A National Urban League report states that "a feminist perspective has much to offer Black America" (West 2003). African American women and men are more likely (more than 80 percent) than whites to endorse political organizing for women's issues (Hunter and Sellers 1998). Sixty-eight percent of Latina women (n = 354) and 63 percent of African American women (n = 352) surveyed in 2001 by Princeton Survey Research Associates as part of a national sample of 2,329 "strongly agree" that there is a need for a women's movement today (Center for the Advancement of Women 2003).

There are other variations in attitudes toward the women's movement. Some women deplore the rise of feminism and encourage traditional marriage and motherhood as the best path to women's self-fulfillment (Marshall 1995; Enda 1998; Passno 2000). Many feminists, however, would define the movement as one that advances the interests and status of women as mothers and caregivers, as well as workers (Coburn 1999). Surveys in the 1980s indicate that large majorities reject the notion that the women's movement is anti-family (Hall and Rodriguez 2003).

The media often assert that a younger "post-feminist" generation does not support a women's movement. The assumption is that they may have a negative image of feminism as driven by hostility toward men, and a perception that feminist activists have been too drawn away from their personal lives. Younger women may, on the contrary, be latently feminist, but believe that goals have been achieved. Or they may simply be too busy with work and family to have the time to be active. Differences of opinion among women on issues related to sexuality and reproduction are undoubtedly divisive.

Research suggests that "post-feminism" is a myth. Hall and Rodriguez, who did an extensive review of survey data, found an increase in support for the women's movement from the 1970s and 1980s to the middle or late 1990s. Young adults 18–29 reported more favorable attitudes than older cohorts. Some approval is backward looking, recognizing that feminism has been "very important in helping women achieve equality with men in the last century" (Hall and Rodriguez 2003, p. 895; Aronson 2003). Some surveys indicate that women find the movement more relevant for others than for themselves (Hall and Rodriguez 2003). Most recent research finds a complex array of definitions of feminism and positions with regard to feminism, one article constructing a four-fold typology (Aronson 2003), another a six-fold typology (Center for the Advancement of Women 2003).

In noting the "increased heterogeneity in . . . conceptions of feminism," Schneider, Freese, and Powell comment: "One might note that many of the ideologies associated with feminism have become relatively common place and speak to the success of feminism in attaining much broader acceptance of gender equality" (2003, pp. 619–20). Although not all supporters of the women's movement self-identify as feminists, a majority (54 percent) "say that being a feminist is an important part of who they are" (Center for the Advancement of Women 2003). Overall, "80 percent say the women's movement has improved status for women."

Despite considerable progress, both men and women who choose nontraditional roles may still experience discrimination and negative sanctioning. The stresses that women (and men) face in combining work and family have not been adequately dealt with. Some 60 percent of women surveyed in 2001–2003 agree that "there is a need for a revitalized women's movement to push for changes that benefit women" (Center for the Advancement of Women 2003).

And what issues might today's women be especially interested in? Figure 4.3 presents the results of

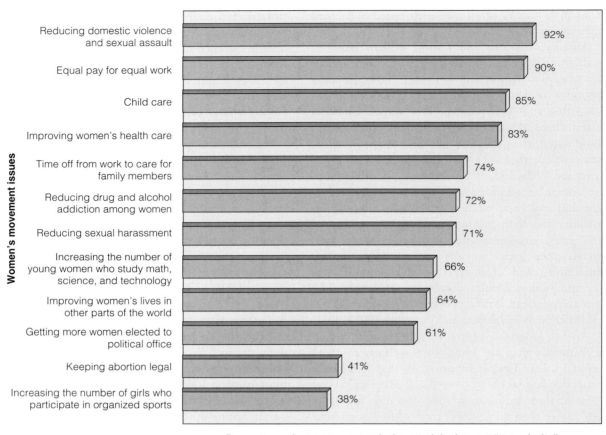

Percentage of women surveyed who rated the issue a "top priority"

FIGURE 4.3

"Top Priority" issues that the women's movement should focus on according to survey respondents in 2003. The survey of more than 3,300 women was conducted for the Center for the Advancement of Women by Princeton Survey Research Associates.

Source: Center for the Advancement of Women 2003, p. 11. www.advancewomen.org.

the CAW 2003 survey, indicating those issues which are reported as top priorities.

The Men's Movement

As the women's movement encouraged changes in gendered cultural expectations and social organization, some men responded by initiating a men's movement. The first National Conference on Men and Masculinity was held in 1975 and has been held almost annually ever since. The focus of the men's movement is on changes that men want in their lives and how best to get them. One goal has been to give men a forum—in consciousness-raising groups, in men's studies college

courses, and, increasingly, on the Internet—in which to air their feelings about gender and think about their life goals and their relationships with others.

Kimmel (1995) divides today's men's movement into three fairly distinct camps: antifeminists, profeminists, and masculinists. *Antifeminists* believe that the women's movement has caused the collapse of the natural order, one that guaranteed male dominance, and they work to reverse this trend. The National Organization for Men (NOM) opposes feminism, which it claims is "designed to denigrate men, exempt women from the draft and to encourage the disintegration of the family" (Siller 1984, quoted in Kimmel 1995, p. 564). Some antifeminists' responses emphasize "men's rights," especially fathers' rights, and not feeling guilty in relationships with women.

According to Mark Kann, men's self-interest may lead to an antifeminist response even among men who wish women well in an abstract sense:

> I would suggest . . . that men's immediate self-interest rarely coincides with feminist opposition to patriarchy. Consider that men need money and leisure to carry out their experiments in self-fulfillment. Is it not their immediate interest to monopolize the few jobs that promise affluence and autonomy by continuing to deny women equal access to them? Further, men need social space or freedom from constraints for their experiments. Why should they commit themselves to those aspects of feminism that reduce men's social space? It is one thing to try out the joys of parenting, for example, but quite another to assume sacrificial responsibility for the pains of parenting. Is it not men's immediate self-interest to strengthen the cultural presumption that women are the prime parents and thus the ones who must diaper, chauffeur, tend middle-of-the-night illnesses, launder, and so forth? (Kann 1986, p. 32)

Profeminists support feminists in their opposition to patriarchy. They analyze men's problems as stemming from a patriarchal system that privileges white heterosexual men while forcing all males into restrictive gender roles. In 1983, profeminist men formed the National Organization for Changing Men (changed in 1990 to the National Organization for Men Against Sexism, or NOMAS), whose purposes are to transcend gender stereotypes while supporting women's and gays' struggles for respect and equality (Doyle 1989).

The newer *masculinists*, who emerged in the early 1990s, tend not to focus on patriarchy as problematic (although they might agree that it is). Instead, masculinists work to develop a positive image of masculinity, one combining strength with tenderness. Their path to this is through therapy, consciousness-raising groups, and rituals. The latter encourage men to release the "wild man" from within the socialized or "civilized" man. Through rituals, men get in touch with their feelings and heal the buried rage and grief caused by the oppressive nature of corporate culture, the psychological and/or physical absence of their fa-

thers, and men's general isolation due to a learned reluctance to share their feelings. Robert Bly's *Iron John* (1990) is a prominent example of the ideas of this camp. Retreats ("wildman gatherings") encourage men to overcome the barriers to intimate friendships with one another (Kimmel 1995).

In examining men's movements and their goals, it is important to appreciate that men's social situations vis-à-vis traditional roles are as diverse as women's. The idea of a universal patriarchy and male dominance is challenged by the obvious point that all men are not privileged in the larger society (Connell 1995), whether or not they are so in gender relations. "When race, social class, sexual orientation, physical abilities, and immigrant or national status are taken into account, we can see that in some circumstances 'male privilege' is partly—sometimes substantially—muted" (Baca Zinn, Hondagneu-Sotelo, and Messner 2004, p. 170, citing Kimmel and Messner 1998).

Ambivalence, Confusion—and Hope

In the 1970s, profeminist social scientists typically proposed androgyny as an answer to the stresses and inequalities that result from traditional masculine and feminine expectations and conditions. **Androgyny** (formed from the Greek words *andro* for man and *gune* for woman) is the social and psychological condition by which individuals think, feel, and behave both instrumentally and expressively (Bem 1975). In other words, androgynous people evidence the positive qualities associated with both masculine and feminine roles. An androgynous man or woman could be both achievement-oriented and emotionally nurturing.

More recently, feminists have disagreed about androgyny as a model for women. *Equal rights feminists* continue to emphasize equal treatment of men and women and to encourage nonsexist child rearing that would produce similarity in personality between men and women. *Cultural feminists* celebrate a "women's culture" (whether its origin is biology or socialization or both) that downplays individual ambition and instead emphasizes communitarian values and women's nurturing capacity (Fox-Genovese 1991; Fineman 1991; Weisberg 1993). Men's movement activists continue to explore what masculinity means. But the fact remains that in a modern, complex society such as ours, people need to be assertive and self-reliant and also to depend on one another for intimacy and

Cartoon by Anne Gibbons, from Roz Warren [Ed.], *Men From Detroit, Women From Paris*, p. 100. Crossing Press. Reprinted by permission of Anne Gibbons.

emotional support (Helgeson 1994). Allowing people both to develop their talents fully and to be emotionally expressive can greatly expand the range of behaviors and possibilities open to everyone.

Ironically, however, that very expansion in the range of people's opportunities may lead to mixed feelings and conflicts, both within ourselves and between men and women as we confront the "lived messiness" of gender in contemporary life (Heywood and Drake 1997, p. 8). Stay-at-home moms may worry about the family budget and about their options if their marriages fail or if they desire to work when children are older. They may feel others consider them to be uninteresting or incompetent. Women who are employed may wish they could stay home full time with their families or at least have less-hectic days and more family time. Moreover, a wife's career success and work demands may lead her into renegotiating gender boundaries at home, and that may produce domestic tension.

Modern men may be torn between egalitarian principles and the advantages of male privilege. For one thing, husbands are still expected to succeed as principal family breadwinners—even in an economy that makes this increasingly difficult. The "new" man is expected to succeed economically *and* to value relationships and emotional openness. Although women want men to be sensitive and emotionally expressive, they also want them to be self-assured and confident. Men often face prejudice when they take jobs traditionally considered women's, such as day-care workers (Campbell 1991). They may encounter more resistance than women when they try to exercise "family-friendly" options in the workplace (Hochschild 1997).

These conflicts are more than psychological. They are in part a consequence of our society's failure to provide support for employed parents in the form of adequate maternity and paternity leave or day care, for example. American families continue to deal individually with problems of pregnancy, recovery from childbirth, and early child care as best they can. Adequate job performance, let alone career achievement, is difficult for women under such conditions regardless of ability. Declining economic opportunities, coupled with criticisms of patriarchy sparked by the women's movement, lead some men to feel unfairly picked on (Scott 1992). Perhaps more common is the ambivalence of a man who wants his wife and daughters to have the same opportunities he does and who is willing to pitch in at home—but who envies the freedom from domestic cares and ability to concentrate on work of a man in a more traditional household.

Today's men, like today's women, find it difficult to have it all. If women find it difficult to combine a sustained work career with motherhood, men face a conflict between maintaining their privileges and enjoying supportive relationships. But many "will find that equality and sharing offer compensations to offset their attendant loss of power and privilege" (Gerson 1993, p. 274).

In Sum

- Roles of men and women have changed over time, but living in our society remains a different experience for women and for men. Gendered cultural messages and social structure influence people's behavior, attitudes, and options. Women tend to be seen as more expressive, relationship-oriented, and "communal"; men are considered more instrumental or agentic.

- Generally, traditional masculine expectations require that men be confident, self-reliant, and occupationally successful—and engage in "no sissy stuff." During the 1980s, the "liberated male" cultural message emerged, according to which men are expected to value tenderness and equal relationships with women.

- Traditional feminine expectations involve a woman's being a man's helpmate and a "good mother." An emergent feminine role is the successful "professional woman"; when coupled with the more traditional ones, this results in the "superwoman."

- Individuals vary in the degree to which they follow cultural models for gendered behavior. The extent to which men and women differ from each other and follow these cultural messages can be visualized as two overlapping normal distribution curves.

- Although there are significant changes, male dominance remains evident in politics, in religion, and in the economy.

- There are racial/ethnic and class differences in stereotypes, as well as some differences in actual gender and family patterns. This and other diversity has come to be expressed in reactions to and participation in the women's and men's movements.

- Biology interacts with culture to produce human behavior, and the two influences are not really separable. Sociologists give considerable attention to the socialization process, for which there are several theoretical explanations. Underlying both socialization and adult behavior are the social structural pressures and societal constraints that shape men's and women's choices and behaviors. These have changed under different economic systems.

- Turning our attention to the actual lives of adults in contemporary society, we find women and men negotiating gendered expectations and making choices in a context of change at work and in the family. New cultural ideals are far from realization, and efforts to create lives balancing love and work involve conflict and struggle, but promise fulfillment as well.

Key Terms

agentic (instrumental) character traits

androgyny

borderwork

Chodorow's theory of gender

communal (expressive) character traits

femininities

gender

gendered

gender identity

gender-linked characteristics and roles

gender role

gender schema

hormonal processes

hormones

Huber's theory of gender stratification

  foraging and hoe societies

  industrial societies

internalize

intersexual

machismo

male dominance

masculinities

modern sexism

play

postindustrial

self-identification theory

separate spheres

sex

socialization

social learning theory

structural constraints

traditional sexism

transgender

transsexual

Questions for Review and Reflection

1. What are some characteristics generally associated with males in our society? What traits are associated with females? How do these affect our expectations about the ways that men and women should behave?

2. Which theory of gender socialization presented in this chapter seems most applicable to what you see in the real world? Can you give some examples from your own experience of gender socialization?

3. How have traditional gender roles been stressful for men and women? How have changing roles altered the stresses on men and women?

4. Women and men may renegotiate and change their gendered attitudes and behaviors as they progress through life. What evidence do you see of this in your own or others' lives?

5. Policy Question. Describe the women's movement and the men's movement. What family law and policy changes that have occurred in recent years do you think are related to these movements?

Suggested Readings

Andersen, Margaret L., and Patricia Hill Collins, eds. 2004. *Race, Class, and Gender: An Anthology*, 5th ed. Belmont, CA: Wadsworth. A compendium of articles on gender in diverse settings.

Bartkowski, John P. 2001. *Remaking the Godly Family: Gender Negotiation in Evangelical Families*. Piscataway, NJ: Rutgers. Interesting study of the variation in gender identities and roles within a religious group presumed to be monolithically traditional.

Coltrane, Scott. 1996. *Family Man: Fatherhood, Housework, and Gender Equity*. New York: Oxford. Takes a broad perspective about men's involvement in families, connecting men in families to economy and culture, historically and in the present. Written in a very readable style.

Hurtado, Aída. 2003. *Voicing Chicano Feminisms: Young Women Speak Out on Sexuality and Identity*. New York: New York University Press. Reports on a qualitative study of 101 Chicanas between the ages of 20 and 30, who speak about family, work, self, sex, and politics.

Kimmel, Michael. 2000. *The Gendered Society*. New York: Oxford. Comprehensive exploration of gender in society, including the topics of education, work and family, and intimate relations. Kimmel finds men and women "more alike . . . than different" and considers the prospects of a "degendered society."

Messner, Michael A. 1997. *The Politics of Masculinity: Men in Movements*. Thousand Oaks, CA: Sage. Written by a profeminist male, this book describes a broad spectrum of men's movements and organizations.

Preves, Sharon E. 2003. *Intersex and Identity: The Contested Self*. Piscataway, NJ: Rutgers. A study of intersexed individuals, along with background information on physiology, conceptualization, clinical response, and political advocacy regarding intersexuality.

Virtual Society: The Wadsworth Sociology Resource Center

Go to the Sociology Resource Center at **http://sociology.wadsworth.com** for a wealth of online resources, including a companion website for your text that provides study aids such as self-quizzes for each chapter and a practice final exam, as well as links to sociology websites and information on the latest theories and discoveries in the field. In addition, you will find further suggested readings, flash cards, MicroCase online exercises, and appendices on a range of subjects.

Online Study Tool

Marriage & Family ⊛ Now™   Go to **http://sociology.wadsworth.com** to reach the companion website for your text and use the Marriage&FamilyNow access code that came with your book to access this study tool. Take a practice pretest after you have read each chapter, and then use the study plan provided to master that chapter. Afterward, take a posttest to monitor your progress.

Search Online with InfoTrac College Edition

 For additional information, exercises, and key words to aid your research, explore InfoTrac College

Edition, your online library that offers full-length articles from thousands of scholarly and popular publications. Click on *InfoTrac College Edition* under *Chapter Resources* at the companion website and use the access code that came with your book.

- Search keywords: *masculinity, men's roles.*
- Search keywords: *feminism, feminist.*
- Search current or recent years to see what developments may have occurred since this *Marriages and Families* textbook went to press.

Loving Ourselves *and* Others

> *To love fully and deeply puts us at risk. When we love we are changed utterly.*
>
> BELL HOOKS
>
> *The science of today puts kindness ahead of romance.*
>
> DEBORAH BLUM,
> *cited in Neimark (2003)*

I N A 2001 GALLUP POLL, more than half of American adults said they believed in "love at first sight," and almost three-quarters said they believed in "one true love" (Carlson 2001). We all want to be loved. But when asked what love is, most of us have trouble answering. Love *is* difficult to define; in attempting to do so, we "toy with mystery" (Peck 1978).

In this chapter, we'll discuss the need for loving in today's society and describe one writer's view of some forms that love takes. We'll examine what love is (and isn't). We'll explore the idea that, because love involves the will, "love implies choice. We do not have to love. We choose to love." We *practice*, or *do* love (Carter 2001). And we can learn to love (Jaksch 2002). We begin by looking at what love means in an impersonal, modern society.

Personal Ties in an Impersonal Society

We say that modern society is impersonal because so much of the time we are encouraged to think and behave in ways that deny our emotional need to be cared for and to care for others (Bellah et al. 1985; Real 2002). An impersonal society exaggerates the rational and economic aspects of human beings but tends to ignore people's feelings and their need for affection and human contact.[1] For example, we expect people

to leave their friends and relatives to move to job-determined new locations because job mobility is an economically efficient way of organizing production and management. Our society places greater value on achievement and consumerism than on the attitudes and behaviors necessary to maintain a long-term loving relationship (Lewis, Amini, and Lannon 2000; Love 2001).

Furthermore, some observers argue that many Americans—especially young people—have grown increasingly cynical, calculating, and distrustful of others over the past two decades (Bulcroft 2000; Dowd and Pallotta 2000). This situation sets up a paradox: Our need for love is heightened while loving becomes more difficult (Alper 2003). Yet most people continue to search for at least one caring person with whom to share their private time. Some find love and nourish it; some don't discover love at all. But we all need love—not only to receive it but also to give it (Gold and Rogers 1995). Physicians and psychologists point out that loving acts, both given and received, enhance physical health and are essential for emotional survival (Ciaramigoli and Ketcham 2000; Fletcher 2002; Lewis, Amini, and Lannon 2000; Stratton 2003).

What Is Love?

Love exists between parents and children, and between people of the same and opposite sexes. Love may or may not involve sexuality. When it does involve sexuality, "romantic" love can be heterosexual or homosexual. Psychoanalyst Rollo May defines love as "a delight in the presence of the other person and an affirming of his [or her] value and development as much as one's own" (1975, p. 116). Feminist theorist bell hooks defines love as "the will to nurture one's own or another's spiritual growth, revealed through acts of care, respect, knowing, and assuming responsibility" (2000, p. 136). We include these definitions here because we like them and think they complement ours. We define **love** as a deep and vital emotion that satisfies certain needs, combined with a caring for and acceptance of the beloved and resulting in an intimate relationship. We'll discuss each part of this definition.

Love Is a Deep and Vital Emotion

An **emotion** is a strong feeling, arising without conscious mental or rational effort, which motivates an

---

1. This impersonality of modern society has been a principal concern of sociologists (see Durkheim 1893; Berger, Berger, and Kellner 1973; Hochschild 2003; Simmel 1950; Weber 1948) since sociology first appeared as a distinct discipline in the Western world, roughly at the time of the Industrial Revolution.

Love is a deep and vital emotion, combined with a caring for and acceptance of the beloved, and resulting in an intimate relationship. Defined this way, love is increasingly important in an impersonal society such as ours.

individual to behave in certain ways. Anger, reverence, and fear are emotions that evoke certain behaviors. When people feel joy, for instance, they may beam, even "jump for joy." Love is also an emotion that evokes behavior. Loving parents are motivated to see what is wrong if their child begins to cry.

Historically, in many cultures, love has been seen as a dangerous threat to the legal and moral order. This is because love, being a strong emotion, can lead individuals to challenge the norms of their society or kinship group (Goode 1968). For instance, a parent who loves a son deeply may discourage him from going to war for his country. Romantic lovers, such as Romeo and Juliet, may form unions that are not sanctioned by their kinship group (Goode 1968). Chapter 7 explores the issue of arranged versus "love" marriages.

Love Satisfies Legitimate Personal Needs

Human beings need recognition and affection, and a second element of love is that it fills this basic need.

Giving and receiving love enables people to fulfill their needs for nurturance, creativity, and self-revelation (Lewis, Amini, and Lannon 2000).

It's all very well to state that a person's emotional needs can be fulfilled by love, but what kind of—and how many—needs can we expect to be satisfied? Psychologists stress that being loved cannot fulfill all needs, and they distinguish between legitimate and illegitimate needs.

LEGITIMATE NEEDS Sometimes called "being needs," **legitimate needs** arise in the present rather than out of deficits accumulated in the past (Crosby 1991, pp. 50–51). Ongoing social and emotional support is certainly a legitimate human need (Strobe and Strobe 1996). People can legitimately expect emotional support and understanding, companionship, and often sexual sharing from their partners. But they should not expect their partners to make them feel lovable or worthwhile. Indeed, achieving a sense of individuality and personal identity is a step that best precedes relationship formation (Vannoy 1991; Cramer 2003). People's legitimate need in loving becomes the desire to share themselves with loved ones to enrich their—and their loved ones'—lives (Maslow 1943).

ILLEGITIMATE NEEDS Sometimes called "deficiency needs," **illegitimate needs** arise from feelings of self-doubt, unworthiness, and inadequacy (Crosby 1991). Often, people who feel deficient count on others to convince them that they are worthwhile (Cramer 2003; "Low Self-esteem" 2003). "If you are not eternally showing me that you live for me," they seem to say, "then I feel like nothing" (Satir 1972, p. 136). They strive to borrow security from others.

To expect others to fill such needs is asking the impossible: No amount of loving will convince a person that he or she is worthwhile or lovable if that person doesn't already believe it. Hence, illegitimate needs for affection are insatiable. However, love does satisfy legitimate needs.

Love Involves Caring and Acceptance

A third element of love is the acceptance of partners for themselves and "not for their ability to change themselves or to meet another's requirements to play a role" (Dahms 1976, p. 100). People are free to be themselves in a loving relationship, to expose their feelings, frailties, and strengths (Armstrong 2003). Related to this acceptance is caring, or empathy—the concern a person has for the partner's growth and the willingness to "affirm [the partner's] potentialities" (May 1975, p. 116; Jaksch 2002). Psychologist Erich Fromm (1956) chastises Americans for their emphasis on wanting to *be loved* rather than on learning to *love*. Many of our ways to be loved or make ourselves lovable, Fromm writes, "are the same as those used to make oneself successful, 'to win friends and influence people.' As a matter of fact, what most people in our culture mean by being lovable is essentially a mixture between being popular and having sex appeal" (p. 2). Showing empathy, of course, is something very different (Ciaramigoli and Ketcham 2000).

Rollo May defines empathy, or caring, as a state "composed of the recognition of another; a fellow human being like one's self; of identification of one's self with the pain or joy of the other" (1969, p. 289). Each partner tries to understand and accept how the

This chapter focuses on romantic love, or love with a sexual component. However, love also exists, of course, between individuals who are not romantically involved, such as between siblings.

© Ghislain & Marie David de Lossy/Getty Images

other perceives situations and people. As an example, if your loved one tells you that he or she dislikes a friend of yours, the accepting response is not "That's impossible!" but "Tell me why." This doesn't mean that you, too, have to decide to dislike your friend. But even when loved ones do not share or condone specific attitudes and behavior, they accept each other as people (Dahms 1976, pp. 100–101).

Furthermore, caring and acceptance involve *honoring*, or "conferring distinction" upon one's beloved:

Honor is not judgmental. Honor does not involve the belief that your opinions, concerns, and desires are somehow superior to your partner's. Honor does not involve getting your mate to see things your way. . . . Honor is a "lifting up," a holding up of your mate with reverence. (Smalley 2000, p. 10)

Do Men and Women Care Differently?

Research shows that both women and men value psychic as well as sexual intimacy ("Emotional Intimacy" 2003; Hook et al. 2003; Sprecher and Toro-Morn 2002). Note, however, that desiring or experiencing feelings of intimacy and expressing those desires or feelings are not the same thing. Sociologists have observed that in our society, women verbally express feelings of love more than men do. Research indicates that women today do not believe that they should be more self-sacrificing in relationships (Heiss 1991). However, their socialization has been directed more strongly to attachment than to autonomy. Women have been raised to be more aware of their feelings and how to communicate them. Men may more often be baffled by questions about inner feelings (Real 2002).

Seeking emotional satisfaction in marriage and other romantic relationships has been part of a general contemporary trend toward self-development and the cultivation of emotional intimacy for both sexes. But men were not as well prepared as women for these new expectations. Earlier, before the nineteenth century, men's and women's domestic activities involved economic production, not personal intimacy. With the development of separate gender spheres in industrializing societies during the nineteenth century, *love* and *feeling* became the domain of women, whereas *work* was seen to be the appropriate masculine mode. As a result of this historical legacy, we have come to see men as less well equipped for the emotional relatedness considered essential to the companionate model of marriage that emerged in the twentieth century (Real 2002).

Sociologist Francesca Cancian (1987) maintains that men are equally loving but that in our society, women, not men, are made to feel primarily responsible for love's endurance or success. Furthermore, love is expressed mostly verbally in our society—i.e., on feminine terms—and women are the more verbal sex. Nonverbal expressions of love that men may make, such as doing favors or reducing their partners' burdens, are not credited as love. This situation results in *both* partners feeling manipulated and powerless. "The consequences of love would be more positive if love were the responsibility of men as well as women and if love were defined more broadly to include instrumental help as well as emotional expression" (Cancian 1985, p. 262).

Cancian also argues that a more balanced view of how love is to be expressed—one that includes masculine as well as feminine elements—would find men equally loving and emotionally profound. Less abstractly, a lover could consider the possibility that the partner expresses love differently and accept such differences, or else negotiate change openly. It is possible that as gender roles continue to change, men and women will develop more balanced capacities for autonomy and intimacy, "the very capacities necessary for sustaining the loving relationships on which marriages now depend" (Vannoy 1991, p. 262).

Love and Intimacy: Commitment to Sharing

Love involves **intimacy**—"an interpersonal process that involves the expression and sharing of emotions, communication of personal feelings and information, development of shared affection, support, and feeling closely connected with another person" (Wagner-Raphael, Seal, and Ehrhardt 2001, p. 243), together with the willingness to commit oneself to that person despite the need for some personal sacrifices. We'll look more closely at two elements of this definition: first, the experience of sharing intimacy, and second, the **commitment** involved in intimacy. Then we'll look at the triangular theory of love, which puts it all together.

PSYCHIC AND SEXUAL INTIMACY Intimacy involves sharing. This sharing may take place on two often overlapping planes. At one level is **sexual intimacy**. In popular terminology, people who have a sexual relationship are "intimate" with each other. At another level is **psychic intimacy**: people engaging in self-disclosure. That is, they share their thoughts, feelings, goals, and needs (Smalley 2000). This is the sense in which we use the term here. Although sexual intimacy may either result from or lead to psychic intimacy, the two concepts are not synonymous. Strangers and people who like each other may enjoy

Love involves intimacy, the capacity to share one's inner self with someone else and to commit oneself to that person despite the need for some personal sacrifices. But love—and commitment—aren't meant to be all work. Love needs to feel supportive, at least most of the time, and fun, at least sometimes.

sexual intimacy. Those who share with and accept each other experience psychic intimacy. They engage in the "work of attention": making the effort to set aside existing preoccupations in order to listen to each other (Peck 1978, p. 120; Armstrong 2003). Research on married couples indicates that partners who are self-disclosing and openly express feelings of love to each other perceive their marriages to be more intimate and score high on measures of marital adjustment (Love 2001; Smalley 2000; Waring, Schaefer, and Fry 1994). Psychic and/or sexual intimacy enhances feelings of attachment, which in turn strengthens the will to commit (Hein 2000).

COMMITMENT In love, committing oneself to another person requires the determination to develop a relationship "where experiences cover many areas of personality; where problems are worked through; where conflict is expected and seen as a normal part of the growth process; and where there is an expectation that the relationship is basically viable and worthwhile" (Altman and Taylor 1973, pp. 184–187; Armstrong 2003). The case study "Sharon and Gary: Discovering Love after Twenty-Five Years" illustrates commitment.

Committed lovers have fun together; they also share more tedious times. They express themselves freely and authentically (Smalley 2000). Committed partners do not see problems or disagreements as indications that their relationship is over. They view their relationship as worth keeping, and they work to maintain it in spite of difficulties (Love 2001). Commitment is characterized by this willingness to work through problems and conflicts as opposed to calling it quits when problems arise. In this view, commitment involves consciously investing in the relationship. Committed partners "regularly, routinely, and predictably attend to each other and their relationship no matter how they feel" (Peck 1978, p. 118).

THE TRIANGULAR THEORY OF LOVE Psychological research expands upon these notions. Psychologist Robert Sternberg believes that the qualities most important to a lasting relationship are not so visible in the early stages. In his research on relationships varying in length from one month to thirty-six years, he found three components of love: intimacy, passion, and commitment.

According to **Sternberg's triangular theory of love, intimacy** "refers to close, connected, and bonded feelings in a loving relationship. It includes feelings that create the experience of warmth in a loving relationship . . . [such as] experiencing happiness with the loved one; . . . sharing one's self and one's possessions with the loved one; receiving . . . and giving emotional support to the loved one; [and] having intimate communication with the loved one." **Passion** "refers to the drives that lead to romance, physical attraction, sexual consummation, and the like in a loving relationship." **Commitment**—actually, the "decision/commitment component of love"—consists of "two aspects, one short-term and one long-term. The short-term one is the decision that one loves someone. The long-term aspect is the commitment to maintain that love"

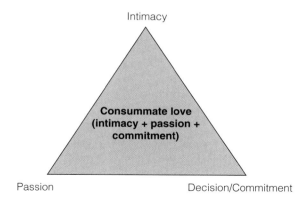

Intimacy

Consummate love
(intimacy + passion +
commitment)

Passion   Decision/Commitment

FIGURE 5.1

The three components of love: triangular theory.

Source: Adapted from "Triangular Love," by Robert J. Sternberg, 1988a
fig. 6.1, p. 121. In Robert J. Sternberg and Michael L. Barnes (Eds.) *The
Psychology of Love.* Copyright © 1988 Yale University Press. Adapted by
permission.

(Sternberg 1988a, pp. 120–121). **Consummate love**
(see Figure 5.1), composed of all three components,
is "complete love, . . . a kind of love toward which
many of us strive, especially in romantic relationships"
(p. 129).

The three components of consummate love develop at different times, as love grows and changes:
"Passion is the quickest to develop, and the quickest to
fade. . . . Intimacy develops more slowly, and commitment more gradually still" (Sternberg, quoted in Goleman 1985). Passion, or "chemistry," peaks early in the
relationship but generally continues at a stable, although fluctuating, level and remains important both
to our good health (Kluger 2004) and to the long-term
maintenance of the relationship (Love 2001, Montgomery and Sorell 1997, Smalley 2000). Intimacy,
which includes conveying and understanding each
other's needs, listening to and supporting each other,
and sharing common values, becomes increasingly important as time goes on. In fact, psychologist and marriage counselor Gary Smalley (2000) argues that a
couple is typically together for about six years before
they feel safe enough to share their deepest relational
needs with one another. Commitment is essential;
however, commitment without intimacy and some
level of passion is hollow. In other words, all these elements of love are important. And because these com-

ponents not only develop at different rates but also
exist in various combinations of intensity, a relationship is always changing, if only subtly (Sternberg
1988b).

Social scientists find Sternberg's theory conceptu-
ally appealing, and reviews of a number of theories of
love and their measures identify similar elements
(Armstrong 2003, Hein 2000, Jaksch 2002). Generally, commitment has been found to be the factor that
is most predictive of happiness in relationships. Of
course, the triangular theory of love is not the only
way of looking at love. One interesting typology, developed by social scientist John Alan Lee, looks at the
wide variation in love styles.

Six Love Styles

Loving relationships may take many forms or personalities, just as the individuals in a relationship may.
John Alan Lee (1973) classified six love styles, initially
based on interviews with 120 respondents, half of
them male and half female. All were heterosexual,
white, and of Canadian or English descent. Lee subsequently applied his typology to an analysis of gay relationships (Lee 1981). Researchers have developed a
Love Attitudes Scale (LAS): eighteen to twenty-four
specific questions to measure Lee's typology (Hendrick, Hendrick, and Dicke 1998). Although not all
subsequent research has found all six dimensions, this
typology of love styles has withstood the test of time
and has proven to be more than hypothetical (Borello
and Thompson 1990, Frey and Hojjat 1998).

Love styles are distinctive characteristics or personalities that loving or lovelike relationships may
take. The word *lovelike* is included in this definition
because not all love styles amount to genuine loving as
we have defined it. Moreover, people do not necessarily confine themselves to one style or another; they
may incorporate different aspects of several styles into
their relationships. In any case, these love styles tell us
that people may love passionately, quietly, pragmati-
cally, playfully, and self-sacrificingly.

EROS **Eros** (AIR-ohs) is a Greek word meaning
"love"; it forms the root of our word *erotic.* This love
style is characterized by intense emotional attachment
and powerful sexual feelings or desires. When erotic
couples establish sustained relationships, these are

Case Study

Sharon and Gary:
Discovering Love After Twenty-Five Years

Married at ages sixteen and eighteen, respectively, Sharon and Gary were together nearly twenty-five years and had four children before separating for ten months. After the separation they got back together, publicly restating their wedding vows in a religious ceremony. Here they talk about what commitment to loving means to them.

Interviewer: How did you two get back together?

Sharon: Connection. For me, it was that I had to be connected. I just need someone regular to check in with, to have dinner with, to care where you are and what you are doing.

Gary: For me, it was just love. For a long time I didn't love Sharon after we got married, and then I grew to love her very much. Then when we separated—it was both of our idea to separate—I think once she moved out it was an empty place. I knew

that I just needed her back. I needed to have her there to share my love with her. It kinda took her moving out to really find that, to determine that was what I wanted.

Sharon: I think our troubles started when we got married. I was pregnant, our parents didn't approve, and we both thought we were doing the right thing. We tried for years to do the right things, and it wasn't quite right. A lot of things we never talked about and buried, they got deep . . . he told me he didn't love me when we first got married. . . . I got married because I loved him like crazy and I knew I could make it work. I tried really hard. I did all the right things. I thought if we had a child it would tie us together.

Gary: I got married because it was the honorable thing to do. I don't regret being married. I don't regret being married as young as I was. . . . It took a few years, and I ended up loving her.

Interviewer: You got to know Sharon?

Gary: I don't know if I've ever got to know Sharon. Probably the last year I have got to know Sharon more than I had up until then.

Interviewer: Why's that?

Gary: That's because we didn't say nothing. We could argue, and neither one of us would tell why we were mad or what the problem was.

Sharon: We didn't argue that much either.

Gary: No.

Sharon: Just glaring, that kind of stuff. . . . We were young, and I used to cry for his attention. And when I cried, he left. A few of those and you think, "What good is this doing me?" So I quit crying.

Gary: Well, if I had known what else to do, I probably would have done that. Today I give her a hug and try

characterized by continued active interest in sexual and emotional fulfillment, plus the development of emotional rapport. Romeo and Juliet, who fell in love on first meeting, were erotic lovers, as are an older couple you may know who seem endlessly fascinated by each other. A sample question on the Love Attitudes Scale designed to measure eros asks the respondent to agree or disagree with this statement: "My partner and I have the right chemistry between us." Agreement would indicate erotic love (Hendrick, Hendrick, and Dicke 1998).

STORGE Storge (STOR-gay) is an affectionate, companionate style of loving. This love style focuses on deepening mutual commitment, respect, friendship over time, and common goals. Sexual intimacy comes about as partners develop increasing understanding of each other. The storgic lover's basic attitude to his or her partner is one of familiarity: "I've known you a long time, seen you in many moods" (Lee 1973, p. 87). In other words, my partner is my friend. Storgic lovers are likely to agree that "Genuine loving involves caring for awhile" and that "I always expect to be friends

to hold her. Back then, you know, laughter was easier.

Sharon: I don't remember if I ever told him what I needed then or not. I don't think so. I just wanted comfort and understanding, I guess. I think I usually cried over something—lack of money or fears.

Gary: We had plenty of all that.

Sharon: I found out with the separation, though; finally, I realized that Gary loved me. The turning point was when Gary made a commitment to help me get into the apartment. It made me look at him differently. It was the commitment; it was obvious that he cared—and not for his own personal thing. He wasn't just saying to get out. He was saying, "I want you to be well." He came to help me do that.

Interviewer: What did he do?

Sharon: Painted, laid carpet and ripped wallpaper, those things.

Gary: I was doing that because I cared about her. It surprised me that it was the turning point because I was helping her get out. We had set this date that she had to be moved, but where she was moving to—it was next to impossible to move in there at that date. So we set another

week, and we cleaned and got the place ready for her. That was the time that she decided that I cared for her.

Sharon: I remember it was a Sunday that I first got into the apartment where I was going to move to. It was pretty awful. I called Gary and said could I have another week, and he came over and brought breakfast. . . .

Interviewer: Why did you guys have a public ceremony when you got back together?

Gary: I think one of the reasons that I wanted it was because there were a lot of our friends who knew what had gone on between us. I just wanted them to be part of our getting back together. . . . It was very touching to me, very emotional. We never had anything like this. We got married by the justice of the peace—very cold, very. I don't know who was the witness now, just some person in the courthouse at the time. . . . That wasn't emotional; it was cold. It was just: "Let's get this over with so people can start counting the months." And hoping that the baby would come up a month late or something.

Sharon: This time we invited our whole church and our whole square-

dance club and our whole group of people that we both work with. . . . We called our parents and asked for their blessing.

Gary: What they wanted to do was to make believe that we had already done this twenty-five years ago.

Sharon: But it was important that they came this time.

Gary: [At this ceremony,] I felt a lot of love. We had it taped. I've watched the tape lots of times already. In the tape I see it. Sharon's trying to hold this thing together. She doesn't want to cry. She is just trying to hold a stiff lip, you know, and keep this thing going. You can see every once in a while, when I would break down and cry, she would try to stiffen up for the whole bunch.

Sharon: Sometimes I do that too well.

Critical Thinking

How does Gary and Sharon's story illustrate the idea of commitment in loving? How does it illustrate Francesca Cancian's (1985) view that men love differently than women do and that a more balanced view of what loving is would find men equally loving?

with the one I love" (Hendrick, Hendrick, and Dicke 1998).

PRAGMA **Pragma** (PRAG-mah) is the root word for *pragmatic*. Pragmatic love emphasizes the practical element in human relationships, particularly in marriages. Pragmatic love involves rational assessment of a potential partner's assets and liabilities. Here, a relationship provides a practical base for both economic and emotional security. Arranged marriages are often examples of pragma. But so is the person who decides very rationally to get married to a suitable partner. LAS questions that measure pragma are "A main consideration in choosing a partner is/was how he/she would reflect on my family" and "I tried to plan my life carefully before choosing a partner" (Hendrick, Hendrick, and Dicke 1998).

AGAPE **Agape** (ah-GAH-pay) is a Greek word meaning "love feast." Agape emphasizes unselfish concern for the beloved's needs even when that requires some personal sacrifice. Often called *altruistic love*,

© Arthur Tilley/Getty Images

Agape is a love style that emphasizes unselfish concern for another's needs. Often called altruistic love, agape emphasizes nurturing. This love style exists between partners and also between and among other family members and friends.

agape emphasizes nurturing others with little conscious desire for return other than the intrinsic satisfaction of having loved and cared for someone else. The sexual component of love seems less important in agape. Agapic lovers would likely agree that they "would rather suffer myself than let my partner suffer" and that "I try to always help my partner through difficult times" (Hendrick, Hendrick, and Dicke 1998).

LUDUS **Ludus** (LEWD-us) focuses on love as play or fun. Ludus emphasizes the recreational aspects of sexuality and enjoying many sexual partners rather than searching for one serious relationship. Of course, ludic flirtation and playful sexuality may be part of a more committed relationship based on one of the other love styles. LAS questions designed to measure ludus include the following: "I enjoy playing the game of love with a number of different partners"; "I try to keep my partner a little uncertain about my commitment to him/her" (Hendrick, Hendrick, and Dicke 1998).

MANIA **Mania**, a Greek word, designates a wild or violent mental disorder, an obsession or craze. Mania rests on strong sexual attraction and emotional intensity, as does eros. However, it differs from eros in that manic partners are extremely jealous and moody, and their need for attention and affection is insatiable. Manic lovers alternate between euphoria and depression. The slightest lack of response from the love partner causes anxiety and resentment. Manic lovers would be likely to say that "When my partner doesn't pay attention to me, I feel sick all over" or "I cannot relax if I feel my partner is with someone else" (Hendrick, Hendrick, and Dicke 1998). We may learn of manic love in the news when a relationship ends violently.

These six love styles represent different ways that people may feel about and behave toward each other in lovelike relationships. In real life, a relationship is never entirely one style, and the same relationship may be characterized, at different times, by features of several styles. Lovers may be erotic or pragmatic. Loving may assume qualities of quiet understanding and respect, along with playfulness. How do these love styles relate to relationship satisfaction and to the continuity of marriage and other intimate relationships?

Psychologists Marilyn Montgomery and Gwendolyn Sorell (1997) administered the LAS to 250 single college students and married adults of all ages. Among other things, they found that erotic love attitudes existed throughout marriage and were related to high marital satisfaction. Agapic attitudes were also positively associated with relationship satisfaction (Neimark 2003). Interestingly, Montgomery and Sorell found storge to be important only in marriages with children. Ludus did not affect satisfaction with a relationship among singles. However, at least as measured by the LAS (which emphasizes ludic lovers' lack of commitment), ludic attitudes are associated with diminished marital satisfaction. We turn now to an examination of two things love isn't.

"Damn it, Ethel, all I'm asking you for is one lousy kidney!"

■ Two Things Love Isn't ■

Love is not inordinate self-sacrifice. And loving is not the continual attempt to get others to feel or do what we want them to—although each of these ideas is frequently mistaken for love. We'll examine these misconceptions in detail

Martyring

Love isn't martyring. **Martyring** involves maintaining relationships by consistently ignoring one's own legitimate needs while trying to satisfy virtually all of a partner's needs, even illegitimate ones. Martyring differs from agapic love, described above. Agapic love involves giving much attention to the needs of a beloved with joy—and *not* ignoring one's own legitimate needs at the same time. Periods of self-sacrifice are necessary through difficult times, but as a premise of the relationship, excessive self-sacrifice or martyring is unworkable. Martyrs may have good intentions, believing that love involves doing unselfishly for others without voicing their own needs in return. Consequently, however, martyrs seldom feel that they receive genuine affection. Martyrs may

- Be reluctant to suggest what they would like (concerning recreation or entertainment, for example) and leave decisions to others.

- Allow others to be constantly late for engagements and never protest directly.

- Work on helping loved ones develop talents and interests while ignoring or neglecting their own.

- Be sensitive to others' feelings and problems while hiding their own disappointments and hurts.

Although it may sound noble, there's a catch to martyring. Believing that they're not receiving much emotional support, martyrs grow angry, although they seldom express their anger directly. (In Chapter 13, we will discuss how unexpressed anger can damage a loving relationship.) Martyrs may think "it is better to be wanted as a victim than to not be wanted at all" (Szasz 1976, p. 62). The reluctance of martyrs to express legitimate needs is damaging to a relationship, for it prevents openness and intimacy.

Martyring has other negative consequences. Social psychologists have been researching the concept of equity, the balance of rewards and costs to the partners in a relationship. In love relationships and marriage, as well as in other relationships, people seem most comfortable when things feel generally fair or equitable—when, over time, partners are reasonably well balanced in terms of what they are giving to and getting from the relationship (Risman and Johnson-Sumerford 1998).

Manipulating

Manipulators follow this maxim: If I can get him/her to do what I want done, then I'll be sure he/she loves me. **Manipulating** means seeking to control the feelings, attitudes, and behavior of your partner or partners in underhanded ways rather than by assertively stating your case. Manipulating is not the same thing as love. Manipulators may

■ Ask others to do things for them that they could do for themselves, and generally expect to be waited on.

■ Assume that others will (if they "really" love them) be happy to do whatever the manipulators choose, not only regarding recreation, for example, but also in more important matters.

■ Be consistently late for engagements ("if he [or she] will wait patiently for me, he [or she] loves me").

■ Want others to help them develop their interests and talents but seldom think of reciprocating.

Manipulators, like martyrs, may not believe that they are lovable or that others can really love them, and this may be why they feel a continual need to test their partner. Aware that they are exploiting others, habitual manipulators may experience guilt and try to relieve this guilt by minimizing or finding fault with their loved one's complaints. "You don't really love me," they may accuse. Manipulating, like martyring, can destroy a relationship.

You may have already noticed that martyring and manipulating complement each other. Martyrs and manipulators are often attracted to each other, forming what family counselor John Crosby (1991) calls **symbiotic relationships**, in which each partner expects the other to provide a sense of meaning or purpose. Often, such symbiotic relationships are quite stable, although at the same time they can be unhappy—maybe even dangerously violent. Should one symbiotic partner learn to stand on his or her own feet, the relationship is less likely to last. Manipulating and martyring are both sometimes mistaken for love.[2] But

they are not love, for one simple reason: Both relationships share a refusal to accept oneself or one's partner realistically. The next section examines a personal characteristic that many psychologists (although not all) believe to be a prerequisite for loving: self-esteem.

■ Self Worth as a Prerequisite ■ to Loving

"I'm more interested," writes Leo Buscaglia, "in who is a loving person. . . . I believe that probably the most important thing is that this loving person is a person who loves him [or her] self" (1982, p. 9). **Self worth**, or self-esteem,[3] is part of a person's self-concept; it involves feelings that people have about their own value. Psychologist Nathaniel Branden has described self worth as "the disposition to experience oneself as competent to cope with the basic challenges of life and as worthy of happiness" (1994, p. 21). And what is happiness? Psychologist Martin Seligman argues that authentic happiness does not result simply from having a

---

2. Students reading this section sometimes ask whether martyring is the same as being co-dependent. The answer is *yes, pretty much.* **Co-dependents** have been defined as "persons who gravitate toward relationships with exploitative or abusive partners around whom they organize their lives and to whom they remain strongly committed despite the absence of any identifiable rewards or personal fulfillment for themselves" (Wright and Wright 1999,

p. 528). We, the authors, have not until now used the term *co-dependency* in any edition of this textbook because the concept is controversial among professional social scientists. A grassroots concept that originally emerged in self-help groups to describe spouses and children of alcoholics/addicts, co-dependency has typically been dismissed as unscientific by professionals. Critics argue that the concept is too general either to be empirically tested or to permit useful treatment planning for therapists. However, the concept of co-dependency has begun to find its way into respected family therapy journals, and research has begun to investigate it (Wells, Glickauf-Hughes, and Jones 1999; Wright and Wright 1999; Dear and Roberts, 2002).

3. The concept of *self-esteem* is controversial among psychologists and others today (Owens 2001). Some "postmodern" philosophers and psychologists argue that there is no such thing as a constant self; hence, there can be no such thing as global self-esteem (Cravens 1997). Other critics see the self-esteem movement, which began in the United States after World War II, as too individualistic and leading to self-absorption, which in turn discourages people from taking any real interest in social or political issues (Bellah et al. 1985). Furthermore, psychologists who study violence have argued that parents' and teachers' efforts to promote self-esteem in children can actually foster its opposite, narcissism, and that narcissism can lead to violent outbursts (Bushman and Baumeister 1998; Fink 2003; Goode 2002). Nevertheless, much research has been done on self-esteem, and the majority of psychologists, especially counseling psychologists, continue to research and find use in the concept (Durm, Giddens, and Blakenship 1997; Jacobvitz and Bush 1996; Jezl, Molidor, and Wright 1996; Longmore and Demaris 1997; Page, Stevens, and Galvin 1996; Rugel and Martinovich 1997). Having considered the arguments, we continue to explore the concept of self-esteem in this edition.

"pleasant life," characterized by self-centered pleasures or acquiring things like a new car stereo. Instead, we attain authentic happiness by developing our strengths and devoting ourselves to meaningful work or other activities and to family life or some other cause greater than ourselves, such as improving the environment (Lawson 2004b).

Accordingly, Branden (1994) argues that beliefs and feelings about one's self worth are a *consequence*, not simply an uncontrollable condition or a narcissistic focus on self. A sense of self worth results from actual, real accomplishments, not simply from hearing or telling oneself that one is, for example, "special" (K. Johnson 1998). Because self worth is a consequence of all the things we do, we can enhance it by working to develop our talents, by affirming or supporting others, and by doing things that contribute to our communities (Katz 1998; Neimark 2003). Accordingly, Branden (1994) has identified the following six "pillars" or practices that enhance our feelings of self worth:

1. Being aware of what's going on around us, or living consciously (p. 67)
2. Being a friend to myself, or self-acceptance (p. 94)
3. Being willing to take responsibility for my actions and for attaining my goals, or self-responsibility (p. 185)
4. "Honoring" our wants, needs, and values, and seeking "appropriate forms of their expression in reality," or self-assertiveness (p. 118)
5. Setting realistic goals and working toward their achievement, or living purposefully (p. 130)
6. Practicing behavior that is congruent with my values, or personal integrity (p. 143)

"As We Make Choices: Learning to Love Yourself More" gives suggestions for enhancing self-esteem.

Self-Love Versus Narcissism

In discussing feelings of self worth, or self-esteem, we need to distinguish between well-grounded *self-love* and its opposite, *narcissism* (Slater 2002). Self-love enhances a person's capacity to love others. People commonly confuse self-love with conceit—a self-centered, selfish outlook (Katz 1998; Fink 2003). But psychologists point out that self-love and narcissism are opposites. **Narcissism** is characterized by an exaggerated

concern with one's own self-image and how one *appears* to others, not with one's own or others' true feelings. That is, narcissism is concerned chiefly with oneself, without regard for the well-being of others. Narcissists are often smug, acting as if they are superior. Many psychologists believe that such attitudes and behaviors actually result from *low* self-esteem (Begley 1998; Slater 2002). Whether people genuinely love themselves—as opposed to being narcissistic—affects their personal relationships.

Self-Esteem and Personal Relationships

Research indicates that self-esteem does a lot to influence the way people respond to others (Jezl, Molidor, and Wright 1996; Longmore and Demaris 1997; Rugel and Martinovich 1997). For instance, psychologist Brad Bushman, who has conducted a recent study of what he calls "unjustified and unstable self-esteem" (i.e., narcissism), argues that "narcissists are supersensitive to criticisms or slights because deep down they suspect that their feeling of superiority is built on quicksand" (quoted in Begley 1998; Bushman and Baumeister 1998, p. 227).

People with sufficient self-esteem are likely to be more responsive to praise, whereas men and women without much self-esteem "are forever on the alert for criticism . . . and remember it long afterward." People sufficient in self-esteem are better at picking up signs of interest from other people and responding to them genuinely, whereas people low in self-esteem often miss such cues and, in general, are "set for rejection" (Walster and Walster 1978, pp. 54–55; Cramer 2003; Duck 1998, 1999; Murray, Holmes, and Griffin 2000). Then too,

> When we develop a good sense of ourselves—intimacy with what is within—we are able to express ourselves creatively, bond with others, and risk being genuinely vulnerable. We can have our needs met if only for the simple reason that we know what they are. (Hein 2000, p. 2)

And finally, the more that people can accept themselves, the more that they can accept others.

Emotional Interdependence

Besides self-esteem, or self-love, a quality necessary for loving is the ability to be emotionally interde-

As We Make Choices

Learning to Love Yourself More

We all feel inadequate at times. What can you do with feelings of inadequacy besides worry about them? As one psychologist put it, "You can't just sit and psych yourself into high self-esteem" (Krueger 2003). However, people can work in many ways to improve their sense of self worth. For example, you may choose to do the following:

- Identify your best personality traits, such as curiosity, humor, or courage. Remember these when you face challenging situations, and try to find ways to manifest them.

- Pursue satisfying and useful occupations that realistically reflect your strengths and interests ("Young children make me nervous, but I'd like to teach, so I'll consider secondary or higher education").

- Use empathy, respect, courtesy, and kindness when interacting with others. In doing so, you affirm not only others but yourself.

- Work to develop the skills and interests you have rather than fret about those you don't.

- Try being more honest about yourself and open with people.

- Make efforts to appreciate the good things you have rather than focus on the more negative things in your life. Write a "gratitude list" of things that you can be grateful for.

- Avoid excessive daydreaming and fantasy living ("Boy, things would be different if only I were a little taller" or "If only I had not gotten married so young, things would be better").

- Volunteer. Studies show that volunteers tend to live longer and feel better about themselves.

- Expand your world of interest. Take a nonrequired course outside your major just for the fun of it, or develop a new hobby.

- "Keep on keeping on"—even when you are discouraged, realizing that one little step in the right direction is often good enough.

- Be satisfied about being smart *enough*, slender *enough*, or successful *enough* rather than imposing unrealistic standards on yourself. ("Easy does it.")

- Touch and be touched. Give someone a hug or pat on the back; get a massage or shampoo.

- Relax ("If I feel this way, it means this is a human way to feel, and everybody else has probably felt this way too at one time or another").

- Forgive somebody: "If physical exercise had a mental equivalent, it would probably be the process of forgiveness. Researchers continue to tally the benefits of burying the hatchet—lower blood pressure and heart rate, less depression, a better immune system and a longer life, among others" (Goodman 2004).

- Decide to be your own good friend, complimenting yourself when you do things well enough and not criticizing yourself too harshly.

Critical Thinking

You may recall from Chapter 3 that the interactionist theoretical perspective assumes that individuals develop identities and self-concepts through social interaction. How do the above suggestions illustrate this point?

Sources: Goodman 2004; Hamachek 1971, 1992; Lawson 2004b; Neimark 2003; Slater 2002.

pendent. Interdependence is different from both dependence and independence. **Dependence** involves reliance on another or others for continual support or assurance, coupled with subordination—being easily influenced or controlled by those who are also greatly needed. **Independence**, on the other hand, involves self-reliance and self-sufficiency and may imply that the individual functions in isolation from others. It emphasizes separation from others.

Loving is different from both dependence and independence as we have defined them. Loving is **interdependence**, a relationship in which individuals retain a degree of autonomy and sense of self, yet simultaneously make strong commitments to each other (Carter 2001). Regarding interdependence, therapist John Crosby has distinguished between A-frame (dependent), H-frame (independent), and M-frame (interdependent) relationships. **A-frame relationships**

Love is a process of discovery, which involves continual exploration, commitment, and sharing.

are symbolized by the capital letter *A:* Partners have a strong couple identity but little sense of themselves as individuals. Like the long lines in the letter *A*, they lean on each other. The relationship is structured so that "if one lets go, the other falls" (Crosby 1991, p. 55). And that is exactly what happens when only one partner outgrows his or her dependency in a martyr–manipulator relationship.

H-frame relationships are structured like a capital *H:* Partners stand virtually alone, each self-sufficient and neither influenced much by the other. There is little or no couple identity and little emotionality: "If one lets go, the other hardly feels a thing" (Crosby 1991, p. 55). **M-frame relationships** rest on interdependence: Each partner has an adequate sense of self (unlike in the A-frame relationship), and partners experience loving as a deep emotion (unlike in the H-frame relationship). The relationship involves mutual influence and emotional support. In a recent qualitative study of 108 heterosexual and same-gender couples of various race/ethnicity and religious backgrounds, researchers found that a moderate degree of personal autonomy actually facilitated couple intimacy:

> Maintaining interpersonal boundaries in these relationships apparently helped to sustain a sense of psychological intimacy; that is, individuals felt "safe" in revealing their inner thoughts and feelings because they could count on a partner to respect their separateness and to accept, if not understand, them. (Mackey, Diemer, and O'Brien 2000, p. 206)

EMOTIONAL INTERDEPENDENCE AND AT-TACHMENT Psychology and counseling psychologists often analyze an individual's relationship in terms of that person's attachment style. This perspective, known as **attachment theory**, holds that during infancy and childhood a young person develops a general style of attaching to others. Once a youngster's attachment style is established, she or he unconsciously applies that style to later, adult relationships.

An individual's primary caretakers (usually parents and most often mother) exhibit a "style" of attachment with the young child. (Chapter 11 explores the roles of fathers and mothers in our society.) The three basic styles of attachment are **secure**, **insecure/anxious**, and **avoidant**. Children who can trust that a caretaker will be there to attend to their practical and emotional needs develop a secure attachment style. Children who are, or feel, uncared for or abandoned develop either an insecure/anxious or an avoidant attachment style. In adulthood, a secure attachment style involves trust that the relationship will provide necessary and ongoing emotional and social support. An insecure/anxious attachment style entails concern that the beloved will disappear, a situation often characterized as "fear of abandonment." An adult with an avoidant attachment style dodges closeness and genuine intimacy either by evading relationships altogether or demonstrating ambivalence, seeming preoccupied or otherwise establishing distance in intimate situations (Benoit and Parker 1994; Fletcher 2002; Hazen and Shaver 1994). Individual or relationship therapy may help people change their attachment style (Fuller and Fincham 1997; Furman and Flanagan 1997).

Correlating attachment theory with Crosby's relationship typology, described above, a secure attachment style would characterize partners in an emotionally interdependent (Collins and Feeney 2000; LaGuardia, Ryan, Couchman, and Deci 2000), or M-frame, relationship. An insecure/anxious attachment style would likely be evidenced in partners engaged in an A-frame (dependent) relationship. An avoidant style would characterize partners in an independent (Murray, Holmes, and Griffin 2000), or H-frame, relationship. We will now discuss how love happens.

▪ Love as a Discovery ▪

Psychologists warn that romantically inclined individuals who insist on waiting for their ideal lover to come around the next corner may wait forever—and miss opportunities to love real people who may already be in their lives. However, even when it is easily found, love needs to be continuously discovered. The words *discover* and *find* have similar meanings. But to discover

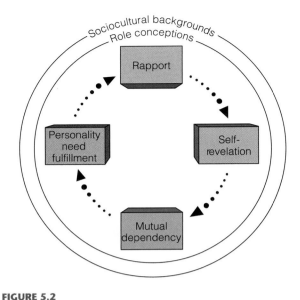

FIGURE 5.2

Reiss's wheel theory of the development of love.

Source: From *Family Systems in America, 3E,* by I. Reiss © 1980. Reprinted with permission of Wadsworth, an imprint of the Wadsworth Group, a division of Thomson Learning. Fax 800-730-2215.

involves a process, whereas to find refers to a singular act. Loving is a process of discovery. It is something people must do—and keep doing—rather than just a feeling they come upon (Love 2001; Smalley 2000). In Erich Fromm's words, love is "an activity, not a passive affect; it is a 'standing in,' not a 'falling for'" (1956, p. 22). It's fine to say that love is a process of discovery. But that doesn't answer the question of how love happens. To describe the process of love's development, social scientist Ira Reiss has proposed what he calls the "wheel theory of love."

The Wheel of Love

According to Reiss's theory, there are four stages in the development of love, which he sees as a circular process—a **wheel of love**—capable of continuing indefinitely. The four stages—rapport, self-revelation, mutual dependency, and personality need fulfillment—are shown in Figure 5.2, and they describe the span from attraction to love.

RAPPORT Feelings of rapport rest on mutual trust and respect. People vary in their ability to gain rapport with others. Some feel at ease with a variety of people;

others find it hard to relax with most people and have difficulty understanding others.

One factor that may make people more likely to establish rapport is similarity of background—social class, religion, and so forth, as Chapter 7 points out. The outside circle in Figure 5.2 is meant to convey this point. But rapport can also be established between people of different backgrounds, who may perceive one another as an interesting contrast to themselves or see qualities in one another that they admire (Reiss and Lee 1988).

Meanwhile, Robert Sternberg (1998), whose triangular theory of love is described earlier in this chapter, has a complementary view on developing rapport. According to Sternberg, people have ideas, or stories, about how a love relationship will be. For example, the travel love plot sees partners beginning an exciting journey together; the garden story views a relationship as needing to be nourished; and the business story always considers the financial implications of the relationship as well as other things. Individuals with the same love stories are likely to develop rapport.

SELF-REVELATION Self-revelation, or **self-disclosure**, involves gradually sharing intimate information about oneself. People have internalized different views about how much self-revelation is proper. The middle circle, "Role Conceptions," signifies that ideas about social class-, ethnic-, or gender-appropriate behaviors influence how partners self-disclose and respond to one another's self-revelations and other activities.

For most of us, falling in love produces anxiety. We fear that our love won't be returned. Maybe we worry about being exploited or are afraid of becoming too dependent. One way of dealing with these anxieties is, ironically, to let others see us as we really are and to share our motives, beliefs, and feelings. As reciprocal self-revelation continues, an intimate relationship may develop while a couple progresses to the third stage in the wheel of love: developing interdependence, or mutual dependency.

MUTUAL DEPENDENCY In this stage of a relationship, the two people desire to spend more time together and thereby develop the kind of interdependence or, in Reiss's terminology, mutual dependency, described in the discussion of M-frame relationships. Partners develop habits that require the presence of both partners. Consequently, they begin to depend on

or need each other. For example, watching videos or DVDs may begin to seem lonely without the other person because enjoyment now depends not only on the movie but on sharing it with the other. Interdependency leads to the fourth stage: a degree of mutual personality need fulfillment.

PERSONALITY NEED FULFILLMENT As their relationship develops, two people find that they satisfy a majority of each other's emotional needs. As personality needs are satisfied, greater rapport is developed, which leads to deeper self-revelation, more mutually dependent habits, and still greater need satisfaction. Reiss uses the term *personality need fulfillment* to describe the stage of a relationship in which a stable pattern of emotional exchange and mutual support has developed. The relationship meets both partners' basic human needs, both practical and emotional.

Returning to Reiss's image of this four-stage process as a wheel, then, the wheel turns indefinitely in a lasting, deep relationship. Or the wheel may turn only a few times in a passing romance. Finally, the wheel can reverse itself and turn in the other direction. As Reiss explains, "If one reduced the amount of self-revelation through an argument . . . that would affect the dependency and need-fulfillment processes, which would in turn weaken the rapport process, which would in turn lower the revelation level even further" (1988).

Keeping Love

The wheel theory suggests that once people fall in love, they may not necessarily stay in love. Relationships may "keep turning," or they may slow down or reverse themselves. Sometimes love's reversal, and eventual break-up, is a good thing: "Perhaps the hardest part of a relationship is knowing when to salvage things and when not to" (Sternberg 1988a, p. 242). Chapter 7 explores this issue more fully. But here we want to point out that being committed is not always noble, as in cases of relationships characterized by violence or consistent verbal abuse, for example (partner abuse is discussed in Chapter 14).

That said, keeping a supportive love relationship is not automatic; "you have to *make* it last" (Love 2001, p. viii). How? A good start is to recognize that we may not have an accurate idea of what real love is (Love 2001). We may have grown up with poor role

Finding love is a beginning. **Keeping** love involves recognizing the importance of the relationship, ongoing supportive communication, and a conscious decision to spend time together. These behaviors result in mutuality, or partners' meeting many of each other's legitimate needs.

modeling on the part of our parents (Zimmerman and Thayer 2004). But regardless of how our parents behaved, maintaining love involves being aware of the many erroneous cultural myths that delude us about love. Marriage and relationship therapist Patricia Love has identified the following misconceptions that limit our ability to maintain love:

- *Misconception 1.* Infatuation equals love; chemistry is all that matters.
- *Misconception 2.* If it isn't perfect, it wasn't meant to be.
- *Misconception 3.* You can't rekindle passion; once love dies, you can never get it back.
- *Misconception 4.* There is one true soul mate for everyone; if you meet the right person, you will live happily ever after.
- *Misconception 5.* Love conquers all; if a relationship is tough, it means you have the wrong partner.

- *Misconception 6.* Love is a static state; once you fall in love, you get on a high and stay there forever.
- *Misconception 7.* Love is a feeling, and you either have it or you don't. (Adapted from Love 2001, Chapter 1)

We will respond to these misconceptions now.

INFATUATION IS BUT A BEGINNING Many social scientists and others strongly criticize the way that American culture tends to equate love with infatuation, or chemistry. "Every pop-cultural medium portrays the heights of adult intimacy as the moment when two attractive people who don't know a thing about each other tumble into bed and have passionate sex" (Lewis, Amini, and Lannon 2000, p. 207). As one marriage counselor describes her experience,

A couple of years ago HBO was premiering *Bridges of Madison County* and touting it as "the love story of the century." The first time I heard that ad I thought to myself: "This is great job security. As long as our society believes that *Bridges of Madison County* is the love story of the century, I will have a job!" If a brief, clandestine encounter is equated with true love, no wonder marriage is in trouble. (Love 2001, p. iv)

Infatuation "merely brings the players together" (Lewis, Amini, and Lannon 2000, p. 206–207). We need to move from infatuation to "the deep connection that is the hallmark and destination of true love" (Love 2001, p. xi).

LOVE IS NOT PERFECT AND DOESN'T CONQUER ALL Nevertheless, "the fact is that love grows in response to getting your needs met" (Love 2001, p. xi). What's the difference? The disparity between these two thoughts lies in the dual ideas of (1) being realistic, and (2) mutuality. **Being realistic** means that you don't expect your partner to meet *all* of your needs *all of the time*. While it's important not to confuse love with martyring, as discussed earlier in this chapter, no one person can meet all of even our legitimate needs (Jaksch 2002). So one aspect of discovering love involves finding ways to get some of our needs met outside the relationship—by extended family, friends, work, or other activities. Another realistic requirement for getting your needs met, of course, is to know what they are and be able and willing to express them.

Mutuality refers to both partners meeting one another's needs. Psychologist Gary Smalley (2000) describes this situation as "constantly recharging your mate's 'needs battery'":

> Human beings have internal "needs batteries," and our actions produce either positive or negative "charges" to our mate's battery. Loving attention given to each other's needs undoubtedly has a positive effect, while selfish, draining charges have a negative effect. (p. 8)

When each partner attends to the other, "both thrive" (Lewis, Amini, and Lannon 2000, p. 208).

LOVE INVOLVES MUCH MORE THAN A FEELING YOU GET Lovers don't automatically live happily ever after. What can help to make it happen? First, partners need to recognize the importance of their relationship. Keeping love may demand seeing your relationship as priceless—worth whatever it takes to nurture or strengthen it (Smalley 2000). Discovering love also requires ongoing, supportive communication, discussed at length in Chapter 13. "Knowing ourselves is one task of adulthood, and communicating that knowledge is the task of forming a relationship"

(Hein 2000, p. 3). Third, keeping love entails being kind, not rude, as well as cultivating feelings of joy when connecting with one's mate (Neimark 2003). Of course, listening is important, a skill discussed further in Chapter 13. Fourth, counselors suggest scheduling play into your relationship and planning surprises (Lawson 2004b). Although they needn't cost money, occasionally shared new activities or experiences may be a good idea (Aron, Norman, Aron, McKenna, and Heyman 2000).

Then too, "Relationships live on time. . . . Some couples cannot love because the two simply don't spend enough time in each other's presence to allow it" (Lewis, Amini, and Lannon 2000, p. 205). Spending time together, committing to learn to know each other over time, and committing to self-disclosure involve risks—risks that some social scientists see men and women today as less willing to take (Bulcroft 2000). Recently, social scientists have argued that benevolent, loving relationships require some things that might sound old-fashioned—virtues such as prudence, humility, tolerance, gratitude, justice, charity, and forgiveness (Ciaramigoli and Ketcham 2000; Jeffries 2000; Slater 2002). In Chapter 6, we'll discuss sexual expressions of love.

In Sum

- Love is a deep and vital emotion resulting from significant need satisfaction, coupled with caring for and acceptance of the beloved, and resulting in an intimate relationship.

- Loving is a caring, responsible, and sharing relationship involving deep feelings, and it is a commitment to intimacy.

- Intimacy involves disclosing one's inner feelings, a process that is always emotionally risky.

- Loving also takes the ability to be emotionally interdependent, an acceptance of oneself as well as a sense of empathy, and a willingness to let down barriers set up for self-preservation.

- In an impersonal society, love provides an important source of fulfillment and intimacy.

- Genuine loving in our competitive society is rare and difficult to learn.

- Our culture's emphasis on self-reliance as a central virtue ignores the fact that all of us are interdependent. We rely on parents, spouses or partners, other relatives, and friends far more than our culture encourages us to recognize (Cancian 1985, pp. 261–262).

- Loving is one form of interdependence.

- Despite its importance, love is often misunderstood.

- Love should not be confused with martyring or manipulating.

- There are many contemporary love styles that indicate the range that lovelike relationships—not necessarily love—can take.

- John Lee lists six love types: eros, or passionate love; storge, or friendship love; pragma, or pragmatic love; agape, or altruistic love; ludus, or love play; and mania, or possessive love.

- A sense of self worth is important to loving.

- We *can* learn to love, even if it's difficult. A first step is knowing what love and loving are.
- People discover love; they don't simply find it. The term *discovering* implies a process, and to develop and maintain a loving relationship requires seeing the relationship as valuable, commitment to mutual needs satisfaction and self-disclosure, supportive communication, and time together.

Key Terms

A-frame relationships
agape
attachment theory
avoidant attachment style
being realistic
co-dependents
commitment
commitment (Sternberg's theory)
consummate love
dependence
emotion
eros
H-frame relationships
illegitimate needs
independence
insecure/anxious attachment style
interdependence
intimacy
intimacy (Sternberg's theory)

legitimate needs
love
love styles
ludus
mania
manipulating
martyring
M-frame relationships
mutuality
narcissism
passion (Sternberg's theory)
pragma
psychic intimacy
secure attachment style
self-disclosure
self worth
sexual intimacy
Sternberg's triangular theory of love
storge
symbiotic relationships
wheel of love

Questions for Review and Reflection

1. What kinds of needs can a love relationship satisfy? What needs can never be satisfied by a love relationship?
2. Sternberg offers the triangular theory of love. What are its components? Are they useful concepts in analyzing any love experience(s) you have had?
3. Describe Reiss's wheel theory of love. Compare it to your idea of how love develops.

4. What is the difference between self-love and narcissism? How is each related to a person's capacity to love others?
5. **Policy Question.** Discuss the social-cultural irony involved in the facts that (1) loving is increasingly important for emotional survival; and (2) our popular culture generates myths, or misconceptions, that make it difficult to love authentically.

Suggested Readings

Ciaramigoli, Arthur P., and Katherine Ketcham. 2000. *The Power of Empathy: A Practical Guide to Creating Intimacy, Self-Understanding, and Lasting Love in Your Life*. New York: Dutton. Written for the popular audience by a practicing psychologist, this book argues that developing empathy and its eight "expressions"—honesty, humility, acceptance, tolerance, gratitude, faith, hope, and forgiveness—is both self-healing and a prerequisite to discovering love.

Duck, Steve. 1999. *Relating to Others*, 2nd ed. Philadelphia: Open University Press. This well-known social psychologist explores many topics, such as self-esteem and attachment theory.

Fromm, Erich. 1956. *The Art of Loving*. New York: Harper & Row. A classic, this book talks about love as an active choice to care for another person.

hooks, bell. 2000. *All About Love*. New York: HarperCollins. The African American feminist theorist's treatise on the need for loving behavior in today's society and culture.

Peck, M. Scott, M.D. 1978. *The Road Less Traveled: A New Psychology of Love, Traditional Values and Spiritual Growth*. New York: Simon & Schuster. More contemporary than *The Art of Loving* (Fromm), this popular work speaks of love as active, willful, disciplined, committed, and attentive.

Powell, John. 1969. *Why Am I Afraid to Tell You Who I Am?* Niles, IL: Argus Communications. A book about self-understanding and the development of intimacy.

Smalley, Gary. 2000. *Secrets to Lasting Love: Uncovering the Keys to Life-Long Intimacy*. New York: Simon & Schuster. One of many recent books written for a mass audience by psychiatrists, psychologists, or practicing relationship counselors on how to keep a loving relationship alive and well.

Virtual Society: The Wadsworth Sociology Resource Center

Go to the Sociology Resource Center at **http://sociology.wadsworth.com** for a wealth of online resources, including a companion website for your text that provides study aids such as self-quizzes for each chapter and a practice final exam, as well as links to sociology websites and information on the latest theories and discoveries in the field. In addition, you will find further suggested readings, flash cards, MicroCase online exercises, and appendices on a range of subjects.

Online Study Tool

Marriage & Family ⊛ Now™   Go to **http://sociology.wadsworth.com** to reach the companion website for your text and use the Marriage&FamilyNow access code that came with your book to access this study tool. Take a practice pretest after you have read each chapter, and then use the study plan provided to master that chapter. Afterward, take a posttest to monitor your progress.

Search Online with InfoTrac College Edition

For additional information, exercises, and key words to aid your research, explore InfoTrac College Edition, your online library that offers full-length articles from thousands of scholarly and popular publications. Click on *InfoTrac College Edition* under *Chapter Resources* at the companion website and use the access code that came with your book.

- Search keywords: *intimacy, self-esteem, love.*

Our Sexual Selves

I have a fancy body.

FRED ROGERS,
Mr. Rogers' Neighborhood

The real issue isn't making love; it's feeling loved.

WILLIAM H. MASTERS AND
VIRGINIA E. JOHNSON,
The Pleasure Bond

FROM CHILDHOOD TO OLD AGE, PEOPLE are sexual beings. Sexuality has a lot to do with the way we think about ourselves and how we relate to others. It goes without saying that sex plays a vital role in marriages and other relationships. Despite the pleasure it may give, sexuality may be one of the most baffling aspects of ourselves. In our society, sex is both exaggerated and repressed; rarely is it treated naturally. For this reason, people's sexual selves may be sources of ambivalence, even discomfort. Finding mutually satisfying ways of expressing our sexuality may be a challenge.

In this chapter, we will define sexual orientation and examine various cultural messages regarding men's and women's sexuality. We will discuss sex as a pleasure bond that requires open, honest, and supportive communication, and then look at the role sex plays throughout marriage. We will look at the impact of the emergence of HIV/AIDS as a pandemic disease and consider its effects on relationships. Finally, we will examine ways that politics and religion have combined to influence sexual expression in our society today.

Before we discuss sexuality in detail, we want to point out our society's tendency to reinforce the differences between women and men and to ignore the common feelings, problems, and joys that make us all human. The truth is, men and women aren't really so different. As Appendix A[1] illustrates, many physiologi-

cal parts of the male and female genital systems are either alike or directly analogous. Furthermore, as Appendix B illustrates, the patterns of sexual response are similar in men and women. Space limits our ability to present much detail on the various possibilities of sexual expression (kissing, fondling, cuddling, even holding hands), but keep in mind that intercourse, or coitus, is not the only mode of sexual relating.

Sexual Development and Orientation

Knowledge about children's sexual development and the emergence of sexual orientation is sketchy to begin with and, furthermore, not agreed upon by pediatricians, child development experts, or other researchers.

Children's Sexual Development

FOCUS ON CHILDREN We may agree that "human beings are sexual beings throughout their entire lives" (DeLamater and Friedrich 2002, p. 10). As early as twenty-four hours after birth, male newborns get erections, and infants may touch their genitals. In a study of almost 1,000 children in Minneapolis and Los Angeles, pediatric researchers found that young children often exhibit overtly sexual behaviors. The researchers' concern was to establish a baseline of "normative" sexual behavior, that is, to indicate to parents, social workers, and others the normality of children's sexual interest.

Reports by "primary female caregivers" using the Child Behavior Checklist and Child Sexual Behavior Inventory indicate that between the ages of two and five, a substantial number of children engage in "rhythmic manipulation" of their genitals, which the researchers term "natural form of sexual expression" (DeLamater and Friedrich 2002, p. 10). They may also try to look at others who are nude or undressing or try to touch their mother's breasts or genitals. Forty-four percent of two-to-five-year-old girls and 42 percent of boys have touched their mother's breasts, for example, whereas 27 percent of both sexes tried to look at nude people. Sixty percent of boys and 44 percent of girls in this age group touched their own sex organs (Friedrich et al. 1998, Tables 3 and 4). There were few sex differences overall.

Children also "play doctor," examining each others' genitals. Researchers are interested in these

---

1. In addition to the contents of this chapter, seven online appendices give information on sexual and reproductive topics: **Appendix A:** Human Sexual Anatomy, **Appendix B:** Human Sexual Response, **Appendix C:** Sexually Transmitted Diseases, **Appendix D:** Sexual Dysfunctions and Therapy, **Appendix E:** Conception, Pregnancy, and Childbirth, **Appendix F:** Contraceptive Techniques, and **Appendix G:** High-Tech Fertility.

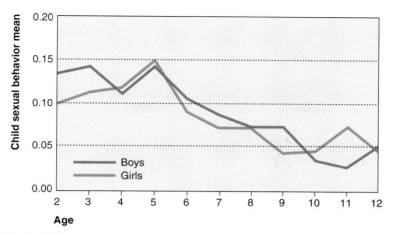

FIGURE 6.1

Mean *Child Sexual Behavior Index* scores for boys and girls aged two through twelve. The graph lines indicate the proportion of the children in the study who have engaged in such sexual behaviors as showing interest in their genitals, touching themselves, trying to look at others who are nude or undressing, or trying to touch their mother's breasts.

Source: Friedrich et al. 1998, Figure 1.

physical manifestations of childhood sexual development. But they place this in context, noting that overall sensual experiences from infancy onward shape later sexual expression, while attachment to parents in infancy and childhood provides the emotional security essential to later sexual relationships (DeLamater and Friedrich 2002; Friedrich et al. 1998; Marano 1997).

As Figure 6.1 shows, sexual behavior peaks at age five, declining thereafter until sexual attraction first manifests itself around age eleven or twelve. Children are maturing earlier than in the past. Earlier puberty may be due to improved nutrition, increased obesity in children, environmental exposure to estrogen-stimulating chemicals, or to family stress (Brody 1999; Belkin 2000a; "Study: Male Puberty" 2001). As the age of puberty has declined, the age at marriage has risen, leaving a more extended time period during which sexual activity may occur among adolescents, as well as unmarried young adults.

Sexual Orientation

As we develop into sexually expressive individuals, we manifest a sexual orientation. **Sexual orientation** refers to whether an individual is drawn to a partner of the same sex or the opposite sex. **Heterosexuals** are attracted to opposite-sex partners and **homosexuals** to same-sex partners.[2] **Bisexuals** are attracted to people of both sexes. A person's sexual orientation does not necessarily predict his or her sexual behavior; abstinence is a behavioral choice, as is sexual expression with partners of the nonpreferred sex. All these terms designate one's choice of sex partner only, not general masculinity or femininity or other aspects of personality.

We tend to think of sexual orientation as a dichotomy: One is either "gay" or "straight." Actually, sexual orientation may be a continuum. Freud and many present-day psychologists and biologists maintain that humans are inherently bisexual; that is, we all may have the latent physiological and emotional structures necessary for responding sexually to either sex. From the interactionist point of view (Chapter 3), the very concepts "bisexual," "heterosexual," and "homo-

2. Everyday terms are "straight" (heterosexual), "gay," and "lesbian." The term "gay" is synonymous with "homosexual" and refers to males or females. But often "gay" or "gay male" is used in reference to men, while "lesbian" is used to refer to gay women. The Committee on Lesbian and Gay Concerns of the American Psychological Association (1991) prefers the terms "gay male" or "gay man" and "lesbian" to "homosexual" because the commission thinks that the latter term may be associated with negative stereotypes.

sexual" are social inventions. They emerged in the late nineteenth century in scientific and medical literature (Seidman 2003, pp. 46–49, 56–58). While same-sex sexual relations existed all along, the conceptual categories and the notion of sexual orientation itself were cultural creations. Developing a sexual orientation today may be influenced by the resultant tendency to think in dichotomous terms: individuals may sort themselves into the available categories and behave accordingly. In time, social pressures to view oneself as either straight or gay may inhibit latent bisexuality (Gagnon and Simon 2005).

The question why some individuals develop a gay sexual orientation has not been definitively answered—nor do we yet understand the development of heterosexuality. Among gays, sexual identity, through a sense of being different, might have been felt in childhood, but a conscious self-identification as gay commonly occurs in late adolescence (at seventeen for males, on average, at eighteen for females). Same-sex sexual activity typically begins earlier than that for males, at age fifteen, while women's initial experiences tend to occur around age twenty. "Coming out"—identifying oneself as gay to others—occurs in adulthood on average (Greenberg, Bruess, and Haffner 2002, p. 411).

Deciding who is to be categorized as **gay** or **lesbian**—how much experience? how exclusively homosexual?—is difficult, and with possible concealment of sexual orientation by survey respondents, this precludes any certain calculation of how many gays and lesbians there are in our society. Until fairly recently, it was stated that about 10 percent of adult individuals are gay or lesbian. However, the National Health and Social Life Survey (Laumann et al. 1994) suggests that the proportion of homosexual individuals in the population is probably lower. An analysis of combined NHSLS data and University of Chicago National Opinion Research Center (NORC) survey data finds that 4.7 percent of men have had some same-sex experience since age 18, while 2.5 percent had exclusively same-sex experience over the last year. Three and a half percent of women report some adult same-sex experience, while for 1.4 percent, experience has been exclusively same sex over the last year. In terms of self identification, 1.8 percent of men and 0.6 percent of women describe themselves as gay or lesbian. Additionally, 0.7 percent of men with bisexual experience report themselves to be gay and 0.5 percent of bisexual women (Black et al. 2000). As a bottom-line figure,

Smith and Gates (2001), looking at these and other data, estimate that approximately 5 percent of the U.S. population over eighteen is gay or lesbian.

The existence of a fairly constant proportion of gays in virtually every society—in societies that treat homosexuality harshly as well as those that treat it permissively—suggests a biological imperative (Bell, Weinberg, and Hammersmith 1981). Some anatomical and genetic research claims a possible relationship between physiology and sexual orientation (LeVay and Hamer 1994; Hamer and Copeland 1998), although other researchers failed to find the same result (Goode 1999). No specific genetic differences between heterosexuals and gays have been conclusively established (Greenberg et al. 2002, p. 367).

Based on studies by themselves and colleagues, Bailey, Bobrow, Wolfe, and Mikach (1995) claim "empirical support for partial genetic transmission of both male and female sexual orientation," whereas "no existing theory of parent-to-child environmental transmission has received unambiguous support" (p. 125). Several sociologists agree that the Bailey and colleagues' study of gay men and their sons "provides evidence of a moderate degree of parent-to-child transmission of sexual orientation" (Stacey and Biblarz 2001, p. 171). Yet, a majority of children raised in lesbian families self-identified as heterosexual in adulthood (Golombok and Tasker 1996, p. 8) as did 90 percent of gay men's sons (Bailey et al. 1995). Virtually all the studies of child sexual development attempting to determine the origin of sexual orientation have methodological limitations (according to reviews by Rogers 2001 and Stacey and Biblarz 2001): "Research and theory on sexual development remain . . . rudimentary" (Stacey and Biblarz 2001, p. 178).

It may not be clear to what extent, if at all, sexual orientation is genetic in origin; nevertheless, we each make choices regarding many aspects of sexual expression. We negotiate decisions within the parameters established by society. The next section takes a look at how sexuality and society interface.

Theoretical Perspectives on Human Sexuality

We saw in Chapter 3 that there are various theoretical perspectives concerning marriage and families. The same is true for human sexuality. We can, for example, look at sexuality using a *structure–functional* perspective. In this case, we see sex as a focus of norms designed to regulate sexuality so that it serves the societal function of responsible reproduction. From a *biosocial perspective*, we consider that humans—like the species from which they evolved—are designed for the purpose of transmitting their genes to the next generation. They do this in the most efficient ways possible. A woman, regardless of how many sex partners she has, can generally have only one offspring a year, so she must be more discriminating when choosing a partner. For a man, each new mate offers a real chance for carrying on his genetic material into the future. According to the biosocial perspective, men are inclined toward casual sex with many partners, whereas women are inclined to be selective and monogamous (Dawkins 1976).

Yet, as social scientists, we see the remarkable cross-cultural and historical variation in the meaning and expression of sexuality, as well as the bargaining about sex that goes on between individuals. Two ways of looking at sexual relations are *exchange theory* and *interaction theory*.

The Exchange Perspective: Rewards, Costs, and Equality in Sexual Relationships

From one *exchange theory* perspective (exchange theory is discussed generally in Chapter 3), women's sexuality and associated fertility are resources that can be exchanged for economic support, protection, and status in society. But an exchange theory perspective that brings sex closer to our human experience is the **interpersonal exchange model of sexual satisfaction** (Lawrance and Byers 1995), anchored in Thibaut and Kelley's (1959) exchange theory.

In the interpersonal exchange model of sexual satisfaction, satisfaction is seen to depend on the *costs* and *rewards* of a sexual relationship, as well as the participant's *comparison level*—what the person expects out of the relationship. Also important is the *comparison level for alternatives*—what other options are available, and how good are they compared to the present relationship? Finally, in this day and age, expectations are likely to include some degree of *equality*.

Research to test this model found that these elements of the relationship did indeed predict sexual satisfaction in married and cohabiting couples and dating

partners, as did the quality of the intimate relationship generally (Lawrance and Byers 1995; Byers, Demmons, and Lawrance 1998).

The Interactionist Perspective: Negotiating Cultural Messages

The interaction perspective (see Chapter 3) emphasizes the interpersonal negotiation of relationships in the context of sexual scripts: "*That* we are sexual is determined by a biological imperative toward reproduction, but *how* we are sexual—where, when, how often, with whom, and why—has to do with cultural learning, with meaning transmitted in a cultural setting" (Fracher and Kimmel 1992).

As with gender roles, the way that people think and feel about sex has a lot to do with the messages society gives them (Longmore 1998). Cultural messages give us legitimate reasons for having sex, as well as who should take the sexual initiative, how long a sexual encounter should last, how important it is to experience orgasm, what positions are acceptable, and whether it is appropriate to masturbate, among other things.

An **interactionist perspective on human sexuality** holds that women and men are influenced by the **sexual scripts** (Gagnon and Simon 2005) that they learn from their culture. They then negotiate the particulars of their sexual encounter and developing relationship (Stein 1989, p. 7).[3]

Sex partners assign meaning to their sexual activity—that is, sex is symbolic of something, which might be affection, communication, recreation, or play, for example (Lally and Maddock 1994). Whether or not they each give their sexual relationship the same meaning has a lot to do with satisfaction and outcomes. For example, if one is only playing while the other is expressing deep affection, trouble is likely. A relationship goal for couples becoming committed is to establish a joint meaning for their sexual relationship.

---

3. In her thoughtful article, sociologist Arlene Stein (1989) notes some limitations of an interaction theory of sexuality. She takes the position that on the one hand, the notion that sexuality is "socially constructed and has no existence apart from its cultural content" (p. 1) probably understates biology and certainly differs from "the fact that most people experience their sexuality as a powerful, natural, and unchanging force" (p. 2). Moreover, an interactionist theory fails to explain what accounts for particular cultural scripts and resistance to them: "a conception of power and the element of resistance to power . . . the open or covert social struggles . . . attending definitions of sexuality" (p. 11).

Morning on the Cape by Leon Kroll.

Sex has different cultural meanings and plays a different role in different social settings. In the United States (and elsewhere), messages about sex have changed over time.

Changing Cultural Scripts

From colonial times until the nineteenth century, the purpose of sex in America was defined as reproduction. A new definition of sexuality emerged in the nineteenth century and flourished in the twentieth. Sex became significant for many people as a means of communication and intimacy (D'Emilio and Freedman 1988). We will explore the cultural messages of several historical periods in the United States in more detail.

EARLY AMERICA: PATRIARCHAL SEX In a patriarchal society, descent, succession, and inheritance are traced through the male genetic line, and the socioeconomic system is male dominated. Sex is defined as a physiological activity, valued for its procreative potential. **Patriarchal sexuality** is characterized by many beliefs, values, attitudes, and behaviors developed to protect the male line of descent. Men are to control women's sexuality. Exclusive sexual possession by a man of a woman in monogamous marriage ensures that her children will be legitimately his. Men are thought to be born with an urgent sex drive, whereas women are seen as naturally sexually passive; orgasm is expected for men but not for women. Unmarried men and husbands whose wives do not meet their sexual needs may gratify those needs outside marriage. Sex outside marriage is wrong for women, however.

Although it has been significantly challenged, the patriarchal sexual script persists to some extent and corresponds to traditional gender expectations (see Chapter 4). If masculinity is a quality that must be achieved or proven, one arena for doing so is sexual accomplishment or conquest. A 1992 national survey by the National Opinion Research Center (NORC) at the University of Chicago, based on a representative sample of 3,432 Americans aged 18–59, found that men were considerably more likely than women to perform, or "do," sex. For example, more than three times as many men as women report masturbating at least once a week. Three-quarters of the men reported always reaching orgasm in intercourse, while the fraction for women was nearer to one-quarter. Men are also much more likely to think about sex (54 percent of men and 19 percent of women said they think about it at least once a day) and to have multiple partners. Men are also more excited by the prospect of group sex (Laumann et al. 1994). One might return to a biosocial perspective to explain these differences except that they are less pronounced among the youngest cohort.

THE TWENTIETH CENTURY: THE EMERGENCE OF EXPRESSIVE SEXUALITY A different sexual message has emerged as the result of several societal changes, including the decreasing economic dependence of women and the availability of new methods of birth control. Because of the emphasis on couple intimacy in recent decades, women's sexual expression has been more encouraged than it had been earlier (D'Emilio and Freedman 1988). **Expressive sexuality** sees sexuality as basic to the humanness of both women and men; there is no one-sided sense of ownership. Orgasm is important for women as well as for men. Sex is not only, or even primarily, for reproduction, but is an important means of enhancing human intimacy. Hence, all forms of sexual activity between consenting adults are acceptable.

THE 1960S SEXUAL REVOLUTION: SEX FOR PLEASURE Although the view of sex as intimacy continues to predominate, in the 1920s an alternative message began to emerge wherein sex was seen as a legitimate means to individual pleasure, whether or not it was embedded in a serious couple relationship. Probably as a result, the generation of women born in the first decade of the twentieth century showed twice the incidence of nonmarital intercourse[4] as those born earlier (D'Emilio and Freedman 1988). Further liberalization of attitudes and behaviors characterized the sexual revolution of the 1960s.

What was so revolutionary about the sixties? For one thing, the birth control pill became widely available; as a result, people were freer to have intercourse with more certainty of avoiding pregnancy. At least for heterosexuals, laws regarding sexuality became more liberal. When the 1960s began, for instance, the sale or provision of contraception was illegal in some

---

4. "Nonmarital" sex refers to sexual activity by people who are not married to each other, whether they have never married or are divorced, widowed, or even currently married (although we usually use the term "extramarital sex" for this last situation). "Nonmarital sex" replaces the previously common term "premarital sex." "Premarital" connotes the anticipation of marriage, reflecting the fact that before the sexual revolution a substantial portion of nonmarital sexual activity took place between people who were formally engaged, informally pledged to marry, or who would subsequently marry.

Table 6.1

Sexual Experience of High School Students, 2003, by Race/Ethnicity and Gender

| | PERCENTAGE WHO . . . | | | |
| | "EVER HAD SEXUAL INTERCOURSE" | | "ARE CURRENTLY SEXUALLY ACTIVE" | |
Ethnicity	Males	Females	Males	Females
White	41%	43%	29%	33%
Black	74%	61%	54%	44%
Hispanic	57%	46%	39%	36%

Source: U.S. Centers for Disease Control and Prevention 2004n, "Youth Risk Behavior Survey, 2003" Tables 42, 44.

states. But the U.S. Supreme Court decision in *Griswold v. Connecticut* (1965) stated a right of "marital privacy," the idea that sexual and reproductive decision making belonged to the couple, not to the state. This concept of "privacy" was extended to single individuals and minors by subsequent decisions (*Eisenstadt v. Baird* 1972; *Carey v. Population Services* 1977).

Americans' attitudes and behavior regarding sex changed during this period. For instance, in 1959 about four-fifths of Americans surveyed said they disapproved of sex outside marriage. By 1972, only 36 percent said it was "always wrong" (Smith 1999, p. 8). Not only did attitudes become more liberal and information more solidly grounded, but behaviors (particularly women's behaviors) changed as well. The rate of nonmarital sex and the number of partners rose, while age at first intercourse dropped. The trend toward higher rates of nonmarital sex has continued, with 81 percent of unmarried women aged 20–29 no longer virgins (Tanfer and Cubbins 1992, from the National Survey of Unwed Women), while 88 percent of unmarried men 20–39 were sexually experienced (Billy, Tanfer, Grady, and Keplinger 1993, from the National Survey of Men).

Today, sexual activity often begins in the teen years. In 2003, almost half (46.7 percent) of high school students had had sexual experience (U.S. Centers for Disease Control and Prevention 2004n). For the vast majority (85 percent) of teens, the first sexual experience was with a romantic partner. Some 9 percent of students were forced to have sex (Ryan, Manlove, and Franzella 2003). Table 6.1 shows the percentages of sexually experienced teens in each of the

Self-disclosure and physical pleasure are key qualities in building sexually intimate relationships. Tenderness is a form of sexual expression valued not just as a prelude to sex but as an end in itself.

© Paul Fusco/Magnum Photos

major racial/ethnic groups. Black male and female students are the most likely to be sexually experienced and currently sexually active according to the Youth Risk Behavior Surveillance Survey, a national high-school-based survey conducted by the U.S. Centers for Disease Control and Prevention (CDC). Not surprisingly, sexual experience increases with age (Terry and Manlove 2004).

In recent years, sexual activity has declined among youth, and that is especially true for black youth. A number of possible reasons for the decline have been suggested: fear of sexually transmitted diseases; a cultural backlash against the sexual revolution; a general conservatism; the success of sex education and teen outreach programs. Studies suggest males have changed more than females (Risman and Schwartz 2002, p. 18). In 2003, more than half of high school males reported themselves to be virgins (U.S. Centers for Disease Control and Prevention 2004b, Table 42). The decline in sexual activity, which predates the creation of "abstinence only" sex education programs, is one of the reasons for the decrease in teen pregnancy and births (Dailard 2003). (The topic of teen pregnancy is discussed in Chapter 10.) At the same time that they avoid genital intercourse, an unknown number of teens seem to be engaging in oral sex. Teens seem con-

fused about what sexual "abstinence" is. Some equate sex to genital intercourse while not considering oral and anal contacts to be "sex" (Schemo 2000b). Some 55 percent of those who described themselves as virgins had engaged in oral sex (Dailard 2003; Denizet-Lewis 2004; Prinstein, Meade, and Cohen 2003).

Perhaps the most significant change ushered in by the sexual revolution, among heterosexuals at least, has been in marital sex. "Today's married couples have sexual intercourse more often, experience more sexual pleasure, and engage in a greater variety of sexual activities and techniques than people surveyed in the 1950s" (Greenberg et al. 2002, p. 437). In the NORC study, 88 percent of married partners said they enjoy great sexual pleasure (Laumann et al. 1994).

THE 1980S AND 1990S: CHALLENGES TO HET-EROSEXISM If the sexual revolution of the 1960s focused on freer attitudes and behaviors among heterosexuals, more-recent decades have expanded that liberalism to encompass lesbian and gay male sexuality. Until several decades ago, most people thought about sexuality almost exclusively as between men and women. In other words, our thinking was characterized by **heterosexism**—the taken-for-granted system of beliefs, values, and customs that places superior value on heterosexual (as opposed to homosexual) behavior and that denies or stigmatizes nonheterosexual relations. However, since "Stonewall" (a 1969 police raid on a U.S. gay bar) galvanized the gay community into advocacy, gay males and lesbians have not only become increasingly visible but have also challenged the notion that heterosexuality is the one proper form of sexual expression.

Although the percentage of gay men and lesbians in our society is relatively small, political activism has resulted in gays' greater visibility. Gay men and lesbians have won legal victories, new tolerance by some religious denominations, greater understanding on the part of some heterosexuals, and sometimes positive action by government. Some states and communities have passed sexual orientation anti-discrimination laws. Corporations also are increasingly likely to enact anti-discrimination policies (Human Rights Campaign 2003).

The public's attitudes toward homosexuality, while never as favorable as toward nonmarital sex generally, became generally more favorable in the 1990s after earlier high rates of disapproval. In the early 1970s, about 70 percent thought homosexual relations were "always wrong," rising to 76–77 percent in the mid-eighties. In 1986 the Supreme Court decision in *Bowers v. Hardwick* declined to extend privacy protection to gay male or lesbian relationships, and homosexual conduct remained criminalized in some states.

Disapproval rates began to fall in 1992 so that by 1998, 56 percent of a national sample of Americans (still a majority of the population) found homosexuality "always wrong" (Loftus 2001). Then in a 2003 case, the Supreme Court reversed its earlier decision, striking down a Texas law criminalizing homosexual acts, thus legalizing same-sex sexual relations: "The petitioners are entitled to respect for their private lives. The state cannot demean their existence or control their destiny by making their private sexual conduct a crime" (*Lawrence v. Texas* 2003).

But right after the *Lawrence* decision, attitudes toward homosexuality became more unfavorable. In May 2003, 60 percent of Americans thought "homosexual relations between consenting adults" should be legal. By July this figure had dropped to 48 percent, suggesting a backlash to the decision. A slight rebound to 52 percent favoring decriminalization of homosexual relations had occurred by May 2004 (Moore 2004; Newport 2003a, 2003b).

Lesbian and gay male unions and families have become increasingly visible over the past decade. Meanwhile, discrimination and controversy persist.

Americans are more likely to approve of civil rights protections for gays and lesbians than of a gay or lesbian lifestyle, and that approval has continued to strengthen since the 1970s. In 2004, 89 percent of Americans surveyed by the Gallup Poll agreed that "homosexuals . . . should have equal rights in terms of job opportunities" (Moore 2004).

Americans are divided over whether gay men and lesbians choose their sexual orientation, a split that shapes attitudes. People who see being gay as a choice are less sympathetic to lesbians or gay men regarding jobs and other rights (Loftus 2001). The American Psychological Association, as well as the U.S. Surgeon General, take the position that sexual orientation is not a choice and cannot be changed at will (APA 2001; U.S. Surgeon General 2001, p. 4).

We are currently experiencing a challenge to heterosexism, but the goals of this challenge—equal treatment and acceptance for lesbians and gay males—have hardly been accomplished. A recent survey reported that almost two-thirds of gays and lesbians who had "come out" found acceptance by their families, and 76 percent of gays, lesbians, and bisexuals say there is more acceptance today (Kaiser Family Foundation 2001). Nevertheless, **homophobia**—viewing homosexuals with fear, dread, aversion, or hatred—is still present in American society. A survey conducted in 2000 found that 74 percent of gays and lesbians re-

Table 6.2

How the Public Views Gay Issues

	PERCENT WHO AGREE	
	GP[1]	LGB[1]
How much discrimination, if any, do you think there is against gay men and lesbians?—"Some" or "A lot"	78%	97%
Compared to a few years ago, do you think there is more acceptance . . . less acceptance of gays and lesbians . . . or the same amount?—"More acceptance today"	64%	76%
Do you think the government is doing too much, too little, or about the right amount to protect gay men and lesbians from prejudice and discrimination?—"Too little"	40%	90%
Do you think that in general gays and lesbians are born with their sexual orientation or that it develops as a result of some other factors such as upbringing or environment?—"Born"[2]	21%	43%
Would you favor or oppose a . . . federal law that would mandate increased penalties for people who commit *hate crimes* out of prejudice towards gays and lesbians?—"Favor"	73%	95%

[1] GP = general public; LGB = lesbians, gay males, and bisexuals
[2] Response categories were: "Born," "Develops," or a "Combination." Forty-nine percent of the general public and 51 percent of LGB respondents responded "Combination."

Note: Based on two 2000 surveys: (1) general public (national sample survey; n = 2,283 adults) and (2) a random sample of gays, lesbians, and bisexuals in fifteen metropolitan areas thought to contain concentrations of gays (n = 405).

Source: Kaiser Family Foundation 2001.

ported experiencing prejudice, 32 percent in the form of physical violence (Kaiser Family Foundation 2001).

As Table 6.2 shows, the views of the general population are different from those of gay men and lesbians on many issues. Ninety percent of lesbians, gays, and bisexuals think that the government is doing "too little" to protect gay men and lesbians, while only 40 percent of the general public agrees. Other comparisons of the views of lesbians, gays, and bisexuals with those of the general public are presented in Table 6.2. (Figures 8.2 and 8.3 in Chapter 8 also present information on attitudes toward lesbians and gays.)

Constructing Gay Male and Lesbian Identities Amid Homophobia One result of homophobia is that gay males and lesbians may have to negotiate, or construct, their sexual identities amid hostility and maintain them within the context of a "deviant" subculture. According to one model (Troiden 1988, pp. 41–58), this process occurs in four stages: sensitization, identity confusion, identity assumption (acceptance and "coming out"), and commitment to homosexuality as a way of life.

Sensitization occurs before puberty. At this time, most children assume they are heterosexual (if they think about their sexuality at all). But future homosexuals, feeling sexually marginal, have experiences that sensitize them to subsequent definitions of themselves as lesbian or gay: "I wasn't interested in boys (girls)"; "I didn't express myself the way other girls (boys) would."

Identity confusion occurs in adolescence as lesbians and gays begin to see that their feelings, fantasies, or behaviors might be considered homosexual. Because the idea that they might be homosexual goes against previously held self-images, identity confusion (inner turmoil and uncertainty) results. Some assume anti-homosexual postures or establish heterosexual involvements to eliminate their "inappropriate" sexual interests: "I thought my homosexual feelings would go away if I dated a lot and had sex with as many women as possible" or "I thought my attraction to women was a passing phase and would go away once I started having intercourse with my boyfriend" (Troiden 1988, p. 48). In fact, three-quarters of lesbians responding to a magazine survey by *The Advocate*, a gay publication, reported having had sex with men (Remez 2000).

Identity assumption, which occurs during or after late adolescence, involves developing both a self identity and a presented identity—presented among other homosexuals at least—as homosexual. In one writer's description of this stage,

> you are quite sure you are a homosexual and you accept this fairly happily. You are prepared to tell a few people about being a homosexual but you carefully select whom you will tell. You adopt an attitude of fitting in where you live and work. You can't see any point in confronting people with your homosexuality if it's going to embarrass all concerned. (Cass 1984, p. 156, quoted in Troiden 1988, p. 53)

The final stage, *commitment*, involves the decision to accept homosexuality as a way of life. At this point, the costs are lower and the rewards greater for remaining a homosexual than for trying to function as a heterosexual. Having "come out," even to nonhomosexuals, "you are happy about the way you are but feel that being a homosexual is not the most important part of you. You mix socially with homosexuals and heterosexuals [with whom] you are open about your homosexuality" (Cass 1984, p. 156, quoted in Troiden 1988, p. 57).

The above analysis treats the development of gay male and lesbian sexual identities as similar processes. Nevertheless, lesbian and gay male behaviors are different in some respects.

Comparing Gay Male and Lesbian Sexual Behaviors

In a large national sample of 12,000 volunteers from the Seattle, San Francisco, and Washington, DC, areas, sociologists Philip Blumstein and Pepper Schwartz (1983)[5] compared four types of couples: heterosexual marrieds, cohabiting heterosexuals, gay male, and lesbian. They found that gay male and lesbian relationships differ; that lesbian couples consist of two women and gay couples of two men is significant. Gay men are more accepting of nonmonogamous relationships than are lesbians—or heterosexuals (Christopher and Sprecher 2000). They have more transitory sex than lesbians; casual sex among lesbians is relatively rare. Gay male sexuality is more often "body-centered"

(Ruefli, Yu, and Barton 1992), and lesbian sexuality is more person-centered. In fact, Blumstein and Schwartz (1983) described lesbian relationships as the "least sexualized" of the four kinds of couples in terms of frequency (although it may be difficult to compare these different forms of sexual expression; Frye 1992). Nevertheless, lesbians report greater sexual satisfaction than do heterosexual women: "Their greater tenderness, patience, and knowledge of the female body are said to be the reasons" (Konner 1990, p. 26).

We have discussed differences, but patterns of sexual frequency and satisfaction in gay and lesbian relationships resemble those of heterosexual marriage in some ways. In all couple types studied by Kurdek (1991)—gay, lesbian, heterosexual cohabitants, and married couples—within each group, sexual satisfaction was associated with general relationship satisfaction and with sexual frequency.

THE TWENTY-FIRST CENTURY: RISK, CAUTION—AND INTIMACY While pleasure seeking was the icon of sixties' sexuality, caution in the face of risk characterizes contemporary times. The risk of disappointment and heartbreak in sexual relations invested with romantic feelings is nothing new. But in an age of HIV/AIDS, sex now carries the risk of death. The proportion of teen boys and girls who are sexually active has shown a downward trend in the last few years (Santelli, Lindberg, Abma, McNeely, and Resnick 2000). Caution flags are also up in a generation of young adults that grew up with parental divorce and is now pressed for time, whether in building a professional career or working two jobs to make ends meet.

Yet most unmarried young adults engage in sexual relations—and there are more of them than in the past due to delayed marriage. According to one study, motivations include: "feeling nurturing toward one's partner," "emotionally valuing one's partner" (especially true of women), and "experiencing pleasure" (Christopher and Sprecher 2000, p. 1010, citing Hill and Preston 1996).

Although "most never married young adults accepted premarital coitus and were sexually active, [research findings] . . . concurrently demonstrate that some young adults remain virgins" (Christopher and Sprecher 2000, p. 1009). A study of college students suggests that women tend to refrain from sexual activity because of an absence of love, a fear of pregnancy or **sexually**

---

5. Although the Blumstein and Schwartz study was published in 1983 and researched before that, a recent review article concluded that it "continues to be the most extensive study on the sexuality of gay and lesbian couples to date" (Christopher and Sprecher 2000, p. 1007).

"How about a kiss?"

transmitted diseases (STDs), or a belief system that endorses nonmarital virginity. Men's hesitancy to pursue sexual involvement comes more often from feeling "inadequate or insecure" (Christopher and Sprecher, p. 1009, citing Sprecher and Reagan 1996).

Noncohabiting but sexually active singles have lower rates of activity than do either married or cohabiting singles (Christopher and Sprecher 2000). A number of singles have multiple partners over time; perhaps a third of young adult women had more than one partner during the year prior to one survey, while 45 percent of men did (Laumann et al. 1994).

Today, there is risk in a sexual encounter, and critiques of sexual liberation point to the disadvantage for women (Shalit 1999). At the same time, a more liberal sexual environment offers some potential for expressive sexuality and true sexual intimacy. A fiercely repressive sexual socialization seems a thing of the past. People now have more knowledge of the principles of building good relationships (whether or not they always succeed in putting them into practice). Now that the possibility of satisfying sexual relationships seems more attainable, how do men and women negotiate those sexual relationships?

Negotiating (Hetero)sexual Expression[6]

Despite the fact that relationships between the sexes are generally more equal today than in the past, many—though assuredly not all—women and men today may have internalized divergent sexual scripts, or messages. Today's heterosexuals negotiate sexual relationships in a context in which new expectations of equality and similarity coexist within a heritage of gender-related difference. Men are more accepting of recreational sex; about one-third "strongly favor recreational sex" whereas less than a quarter of women do (Schwartz and Rutter 1998, Figure 2.5, p. 46). Studies continue to show that women are more interested than men in romantic preliminaries (Purnine and Carey 1998). Women may feel lonely and psychologically separated from task-oriented, emotionally reserved male partners, whereas men feel that their female partners ask too much emotionally (Tannen 1990; Gray 1995).

---

6. The idea that sexual expression is negotiated was developed in regard to heterosexual relationships; this principle may be applied to gay and lesbian relationships.

A research project designed to test the persistence of male dominance in dating assigned men and women to play nontraditional roles in conversations about having sex (women were to initiate a request for sex while men were to respond). The research participants found, for the most part, that they simply couldn't do it! (Gilbert, Walker, McKinney, and Snell 1999). "Some [heterosexual] men were concerned that refusing . . . sexual intimacy [when a woman asked] would mean they were gay or would be perceived as gay (p. 770). It was difficult to get women—but not men—role players to talk about wanting sex.

Still, "the pressure on men to be more sensitive, less predatory, and less macho has been mounting for several decades" (Schwartz and Rutter 1998, p. 48). For both sexes, "'relational sex'—sex in the context of a relationship—is the preferred model of sex for both men and women" (p. 45, citing Laumann et al. 1994). After the sexual revolution of the 1960s, men did become more interested in communicating intimately through sex, whereas women showed more interest than before in physical pleasure (Pietropinto and Simenauer 1977).

Masters and Johnson argue that more-equal gender expectations lead to better sex: "The most effective sex is not something a man does to or for a woman but something a man and a woman do together as equals" (1976, p. 88). From this point of view, the female not only is free to initiate sex but also is equally responsible for her own arousal and orgasm. The male is not required to "deliver pleasure on demand" but can openly express his spontaneous feelings.

This discussion points again to the fact that cultural messages vary and that sexual relationships are negotiated in this social context. Sociologist Ira Reiss developed a fourfold classification of societal standards for nonmarital sex that illustrates these varied messages.

Four Standards of Nonmarital Sex

Reiss's (1976) four standards—abstinence, permissiveness with affection, permissiveness without affection, and the double standard—were originally developed to apply to premarital sex among heterosexual couples. However, they have since been applied to nonmarital sexual activities generally.

ABSTINENCE The standard of **abstinence** maintains that regardless of the circumstances, nonmarital

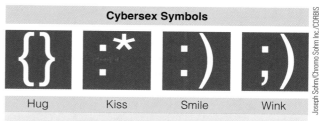

Cybersex Symbols

| Hug | Kiss | Smile | Wink |

Joseph Sohm/Chromo Sohm Inc./CORBIS

Cybersex. Is it sex—cyberstyle—or is it abstinence? From an interactionist perspective, we might say that society is still constructing the answer. But we've already constructed the beginnings of a cyber-sex language.

intercourse is wrong for both women and men. Many contemporary religious groups, especially the more-conservative Christian and Islamic communities, encourage abstinence as a moral imperative. However, a Gallup Poll taken in 2000 found that 60 percent of Americans do *not* agree that it is wrong to have sexual relations before marriage (38 percent agree) (Saad 2001a).

There are other reasons for adopting an abstinence standard. Some women have withdrawn from nonmarital sexual relationships entirely, because of or in order to avoid bad experiences. Celibacy can be conceptualized as "the right to say no" (Johnson 1990; Stark 1997)—to withdraw from sexual risk, at least for a time, rather than feeling vulnerable in the open sexual climate of the sexual revolution (Shalit 1999). Abstinence for teens and unmarried young adults receives support from counselors and feminists as a positive choice (Whitman 1997). These experts are concerned about pressures on young people to establish sexual activity before they're ready, or about pressures for men and women to engage in sexual relationships when they don't want to. In fact, there has been a recent increase in virginity among teenagers (Christopher and Sprecher 2000). Generally, teens who do not engage in sexual activity give conservative values or fear of pregnancy, disease, or parents as their reasons (Blinn-Pike 1999).

PERMISSIVENESS WITH AFFECTION The standard of **permissiveness with affection** permits nonmarital intercourse for both men and women equally, provided they have a fairly stable, affectionate relationship. This standard may be the most widespread sexual norm among unmarrieds. In a 1997 national poll by *U.S. News & World Report* magazine, a majority of respondents under the age of forty-five said that adult, nonmarital sex "generally benefits people" in addition to offering sexual pleasure. A majority also felt that having had a few sexual partners makes it easier for a person to choose a sexually compatible spouse (Whitman 1997). The previously mentioned NORC survey concluded that we have sex mainly with people we know and care about. Seventy-one percent of Americans have only one sexual partner in the course of a year (Laumann et al. 1994).

PERMISSIVENESS WITHOUT AFFECTION Sometimes called recreational sex, **permissiveness without affection** allows intercourse for women and men regardless of how much stability or affection is in their relationship. Casual sex—intercourse between partners only briefly acquainted—is permitted. This standard reminds us of the argument by historians D'Emilio and Freedman (1988) that, from about the 1920s, American sex began increasingly to be seen as an avenue for individual pleasure. A small study (forty-one women and sixty-four men) of mostly white college students who engage in casual sex suggests a variety of motives. Some motives are indeed individualistic—feelings of sexual desire; a search for physical pleasure—and some involve situational factors, notably alcohol use or a partner's perceived attractiveness. Men also spoke of status enhancement and peer group pressures, while women sometimes engaged in casual sex hoping that it would lead to a longer-term relationship (Regan and Dreyer 1999).

The increased placement of sex into a relational context may have led to some rejection of this standard. Sex education, family life education, media coverage of the psychology of relationships, religious efforts, and fear of HIV/AIDS and other sexually transmitted diseases may have had an effect. In any case, surveys show that in 1975, half of U.S. college freshmen approved of casual sex; today the figure is 41 percent (Sengupta 1997).

At the same time, a recent *New York Times* article describes a pattern among adolescents termed "friends with benefits" (Denizet-Lewis 2004). Teens may "hook up" casually for sexual encounters with friends and acquaintances, completely outside of a romantic

relationship context. In fact, that seems partly the point. Teens who feel themselves to be unready for romance and commitment explore their sexuality in what is intended to be an emotionally neutral context; of course, it doesn't always work out that way. Sexual activity does not necessarily move to genital intercourse; oral sex is quite common. The article received a great deal of attention, but, as a set of journalistic interviews rather than a social science study, it cannot tell us whether "friends with benefits" is a common practice.

THE DOUBLE STANDARD According to the **double standard**, women's sexual behavior must be more conservative than men's. In its original form, the double standard meant that women should not have sex before or outside of marriage, whereas men could. More recently, the double standard has required that women be in love to have sex, or at least have fewer partners than men have.

Throughout the 1980s, researchers found the double standard to be declining and reported expectations to be similar for men and women (Sprecher, McKinney, and Orbuch 1987; Sprecher 1989). Nevertheless, there is also evidence that, at least among some young people, the double standard remains alive and well. In her naturalistic observation of mostly white, middle-class students in a California middle school, Peggy Orenstein (1994) describes an episode in an eighth-grade sex education class on sexually transmitted diseases. "What a slut," cries out one boy about a woman described as having had sex with three men. Responses to a similar hypothetical case of a man with five sexual encounters? Some boys strike "macho poses" and point at themselves, while others take bows. The girls remain silent (p. 61).

Men and women may have different expectations, with men exposed to cultural conditioning that encourages them to separate sex from intimacy, while among women, sexual expression more often symbolizes connection with a partner and communicates intimacy. The more-restrained sexual standards of women are attributed to a legacy of differential socialization and perhaps to greater religiosity as well (Tanfer and Cubbins 1992). One observer also argues that women are less likely to have control over a sexual encounter. Gender differences in permissiveness may reflect differences in social power and vulnerability, prompting a woman's strategy of self-protection through adherence to conventional moral expectations (Howard 1988).

Race/Ethnicity and Sexual Expression

We've been comparing men and women, heterosexuals and gays. Are there any differences among racial/ethnic groups in sexual expression?

Much research has been done on youth of varying racial/ethnic background. Table 6.1 reports differences in the sexual experience of high school students. Among adults, most work has been done on African American sexuality. Studies comparing African Americans to whites find that African Americans have sex earlier, more often, with more sexual partners, and with a greater prominence of the double standard. *However,* these conclusions are based on research on lower-class men (and adolescents) and are, to say the least, insufficient to support valid conclusions about African American sexual expression more generally (Bowser 1999, pp. 130–131). At least one sex researcher (Belcastro 1985) has argued that African Americans and non-Hispanic whites are more similar than dissimilar in their sexual behavior. Recent research on married couples finds that frequency of sex does not vary significantly with race, social class, or religion (Christopher and Sprecher 2000).

Being "respectable" is important to both adult and teen African American women (Weinberg and Williams 1988). But factors other than sexual attitudes may shape relationships. One group of researchers (Fullilove et al. 1990) thinks black women are currently vulnerable to sexual exploitation. Economic needs—but even more than that, the valuing of "interconnectedness" with others that is so culturally important—may lead women to establish sexual relationships even when there is limited availability of marriageable males (Wyatt, Myers, Ashing-Giwa, and Durvasula 1999). Those black men who are relatively unable to secure employment and to make sufficient income to support families are less likely to form a permanent romantic or marital attachment and more likely to press women for casual sex (Staples 1994).

Gay/lesbian sexuality, like heterosexual behavior, has been explored among African Americans mostly in the context of problems (e.g., AIDS) and at the lower end of the social scale. (See "Studying Racial/Ethnic Minority Families" in Chapter 3). Social scientists writing about gay black male sexuality believe it is not as visible as among whites because blacks may find white gay subcultures alien, and they may tend to be integrated into heterosexual communities and extended families that strongly disapprove of homosexuality. As part of that social integration, black gay men may be more likely to be bisexual than exclusively homosexual and less likely to assert a gay identity even when engaged primarily in same-sex relations (Cochran and Mays 1999). This pattern of engaging in sex with other men while maintaining a straight masculine identity has been labeled "the down low." It has become a privately expressed identity and noted as a cultural pattern by the media (Denizet-Lewis 2004).

Black lesbians are relatively invisible due to their smaller numbers, their identification in the black community, and their integration into family relationships. The black lesbians in a descriptive qualitative study of 530 lesbians and 66 bisexual women were well-educated, middle-class women in their thirties, who first became conscious of their attraction to women at around age fourteen, with first same-sex sexual experience at age nineteen. Their adult relationships have been generally satisfying and close (Mays and Cochran 1999).

The problem in discussing racial/ethnic variation in sexual expression is that it is difficult to find a research base for drawing conclusions about African American sexual expression that is not heavily influenced by myths, stereotypes, unrepresentative samples, and a focus on youth and social problems, or is simply insufficient (Bowser 1999; Staples 1999a, pp. 40–41). Even less information exists about sexual expression among other racial/ethnic groups other than whites. Research is still needed on "sexual development and behavior patterns across the life cycle, for diversified cultural groups in diversified geographic regions" (Belcastro 1985, p. 56).

We turn now from group comparisons concerning sex to present an overview of sexual relations during the course of a marriage.

Sexuality Throughout Marriage

It might surprise you that various aspects of nonmarital sex are more likely to be studied than are those within marriage (Greenberg et al. 2002, p. 437). One aspect of marital sex that has consistently been researched is sexual frequency: How often do married couples have sex, and what factors affect this frequency? Before we get to the answers, we need to say something about how the information is gathered.

How Do We Know What We Do? A Look at Sex Surveys

Chapter 3 points out that a *Playboy* magazine survey about sex would yield different results from one in *Family Circle* magazine. Neither survey could be taken as representative of the American population. In serious social science, researchers strive for *representative samples*—survey samples that reflect, or represent, all the people about whom they want to know something.

The pioneer research surveys on sex in the United States were the Kinsey reports on male and female sexuality (Kinsey, Pomeroy, and Martin 1948, 1953) of the 1940s and 1950s. Kinsey believed that a statistically representative survey of sexual behavior was impossible because many of the randomly selected respondents would refuse to answer or would lie, so he used volunteers.

More recent scientific studies on sexual behavior have used random samples. In 1992, the National Opinion Research Center (NORC) at the University of Chicago conducted interviews with a random (and thus representative) sample of 3,432 Americans, aged eighteen to fifty-nine—the National Health and Social Life Survey (Laumann et al. 1994). Respondents were questioned in ninety-minute face-to-face interviews, enabling the interviewer to better judge the honesty of the respondents' answers, always a concern for social scientists. Furthermore, 80 percent of the randomly selected people agreed to be interviewed—an impressively high response rate. NORC's findings may be generalized to the U.S. population under age sixty with a high degree of confidence. Indeed, the results have been welcomed as the first-ever truly scientific nationwide survey of sex in the United States. Because the NORC sample included only people under sixty, it cannot tell us anything about the sexual activities of older Americans.

Another study of sex among marrieds (Call, Sprecher, and Schwartz 1995) sought to compensate for the NORC study's deficiencies by using another national data set, the National Survey of Families and Households (NSFH). In 1987–88 the NSFH staff,

affiliated with the University of Wisconsin, did in-person interviews with a representative national sample of 13,000 respondents aged eighteen and over (Sweet, Bumpass, and Call 1988), and the survey was repeated in 1992–94. Considered very reliable, the NSFH data are used as a basis for analysis regarding many topics discussed in this text.

Conclusions based on survey research on sensitive matters such as sexuality must always be qualified by an awareness of their limitations—the possibility that respondents have minimized or exaggerated their sexual activity or that people willing to answer a survey on sex are not representative of the public. Nevertheless, with data from national samples such as the NSFH and the NORC study, we have far more reliable information than ever before. Appreciating both the strengths and weaknesses of the data, let us examine what we know about sexuality in American marriages.

How Often?

Social scientists are interested in sexual frequency because they like to examine trends over time and to relate these to other aspects of intimate relationships. For the rest of us, "How often?" is typically a question motivated by curiosity about our own sexual behavior compared to others. Either way, what do we know?

In the NORC survey, the average frequency of sex for sexually active, married respondents under age sixty was seven times a month. About 40 percent of marrieds said they had intercourse at least twice a week (Laumann et al. 1994). Of course, these figures are averages: "People don't have sex every week; they have good weeks and bad weeks" (Pepper Schwartz, quoted in Adler 1993).

So does the ratio of good to bad weeks change over the course of a marriage? Yes: You have fewer good weeks (sorry).

FEWER GOOD WEEKS To examine sexual frequency throughout marriage, Call, Sprecher, and Schwartz (1995) looked at the responses of 6,785 marrieds with a spouse in the household (and 678 respondents who were cohabiting) in the NSFH data set described above. Like researchers before them, they found that sexual activity is highest among young marrieds. About 96 percent of spouses under age twenty-five reported having had sex at least once during the previous month. The proportion of sexually active spouses

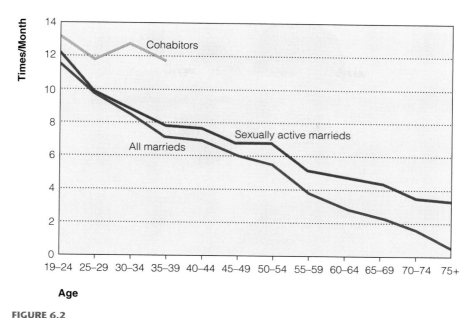

FIGURE 6.2

Frequency of sex last month by age and marital status.

Source: From "The Incidence and Frequency of Marital Sex in a National Sample," by Vaughn Call, Susan Sprecher, and Pepper Schwartz, 1995, p. 646. *Journal of Marriage and the Family,* 57 (3) (August), 639–652. Copyright © 1995 by the National Council on Family Relations, 3989 Central Ave. NE, Suite 550, Minneapolis, MN 55421. Reprinted by permission.

gradually diminished until about age fifty, when sharp declines were evident. Among those fifty to fifty-four years old, 83 percent said they had sex within the previous month; for those between sixty-five and sixty-nine, the figure was 57 percent; 27 percent of respondents over age seventy-four reported having had sex within the previous month.

Figure 6.2 shows the mean (average) frequency of sexual intercourse during the month prior to the interview by age (and marital status). When examining Figure 6.2, note that the researchers report separate means for all the marrieds in the sample and then for the sexually active spouses only. (The figure also shows frequency rates for cohabitors.) The average number of times that married people under age twenty-five had sex is about twelve times a month. That number drops to about eight times a month at ages thirty through thirty-four, then to about six times monthly at about age fifty. After that, frequency of intercourse drops more sharply; spouses over age seventy-four average having sex less than once each month.

It used to be that describing sexuality over the course of a marriage would be nearly the same as discussing sex as people grow older. Today this is not the case. Many couples are remarried, so that at age forty-five, or even seventy, a person may be newly married. Nonetheless, we may logically assume that young spouses are in the early years of marriage.

Young Spouses

Young spouses have sexual intercourse more frequently than do older mates. Young married partners, as a rule, have fewer distractions and worries. The high frequency of intercourse in this age group may also reflect a self-fulfilling prophecy: These couples may have sex more often partly because society expects them to.

On average, as people get older they have sex less often (Call, Sprecher, and Schwartz 1995). But physical aging is not the only possible explanation for the decline of sexual activity over time, particularly with regard to couples who are still young. After the first few years, couples can expect sexual frequency to decline (Smith

Intimacy and sexuality require communication—physical as well as verbal—from both partners. Sexuality has become more expressive and less patriarchal in the United States, and each generation finds itself reevaluating sexual assumptions, behaviors, and standards.

© Jeff Greenberg/PhotoEdit

2003a). Why so? It seems that a frequency pattern is set the first year. And "from then on almost everything—children, jobs, commuting, housework, financial worries—that happens to a couple conspires to reduce the degree of sexual interaction while almost nothing leads to increasing it" (Greenblatt 1983, p. 294).

Researchers have begun to wonder how sexual relations in early marriage might differ between couples who have established a sexual relationship before marriage and those who did not (Sprecher 2002), but there has been little examination of the transition from premarital to marital sex.

Spouses in Middle Age

Despite declining coital frequency, respondents in one small study emphasized the continuing importance of sexuality. Participants pointed to the total marital relationship rather than just to intercourse—to such aspects as "closeness, tenderness, love, companionship and affection" (Greenblatt 1983, p. 298)—as well as other forms of physical closeness such as cuddling or lying in bed together. In other words, with time, sex may become more broadly based in the couple's relationship. During this period, sexual relating may also become more sophisticated, as the partners become more experienced and secure.

Greenblatt's was a small sample (thirty men and fifty women), though a random sample. But similar to Greenblatt's findings, the NSFH study (whose results are illustrated in Figure 6.2) found that marital satisfaction was the second largest predictor of sexual frequency (after age). Unhappy marriages were associated with a lower sexual frequency (Call, Sprecher, and Schwartz 1995). We should be clear that it is impossible to determine which factor is cause and which is effect here: Does a lower level of marital satisfaction cause a couple to have sex less often, or is it the other way around? Another point: Middle-aged couples are apt to be more sexually active now than in the past. Over the past several decades, each age cohort has been somewhat more active than its predecessor. What appears to be declining frequency of sex with age is in part a generation-by-generation change toward heightened sexual activity (Carpenter, Nathanson, and Kim 2002).

"Looks like the Wilsons are putting a little excitement back in their marriage."

© 1993 Artemus Cole. Reprinted with permission.

Older Partners

In our society, images of sex tend to be associated with youth, beauty, and romance; to many young people, sex seems out of place in the lives of older adults. Not too many years ago, public opinion was virtually uniform in seeing sex as unlikely—even inappropriate—for older people. With Masters and Johnson's work in the 1970s indicating that many older people are sexually active, public opinion began to swing the other way. Then, in the 1980s, researchers began to caution against the romanticized notion that biological aging could be abolished (Cole 1983, pp. 35, 39). Of course, physical changes associated with aging do affect sexuality (Christopher and Sprecher 2000, p. 1002). Health concerns that may particularly affect sexual activity include diabetes and vascular illnesses, prostate problems, the need to take pain-killing drugs, and perhaps—contrary to the reassuring statements that we sometimes read—hysterectomies. Sexual functioning may also be impaired by the body's withdrawal of energy from the sexual system in order to address any other serious illness.

Some older partners shift from intercourse to petting as a preferred sexual activity. On the other hand, sexual intercourse does not necessarily cease with age. Half of married people sixty or older have had sex in the last month and one quarter of those seventy-six and older (Treas 2004). Among the sexually active, 90 percent said they found their mates "very attractive physically" (Greeley 1991). You can see in Figure 6.2 that, for older respondents, among whom the proportion of sexually inactive couples is large, the mean average frequency seriously understates what is happening in sexually active marriages; sexually active spouses over age seventy-four have sex about four times a month. Indeed, retirement "creates the possibility for more erotic spontaneity, because leisure time increases" (Allgeier 1983, p. 146).

When health problems do not interfere, both women's and men's emotional and psychological outlooks are as important as age in determining sexual functioning. Factors such as monotony, lack of an understanding partner, mental or physical fatigue, and overindulgence in food or alcohol may all have a profound negative effect on a person's capacity for sexual expression. Another important factor is regular sexual activity (Masters and Johnson 1966)—as in "use it or lose it."

What About Boredom?

Jokes about sex in marriage are often about boredom. And among social scientists, an explanation for the decline in marital sexual frequency (apart from the recognized factors associated with the aging process) is **habituation**—the decreased interest in sex that results from the increased accessibility of a sexual partner and the predictability in sexual behavior with that partner over time. Decreases due to habituation seem to occur early in the marriage; sexual frequency declines sharply after about the first year of marriage no matter how old (or young) the partners are. The reason for "this rather quick loss of intensity of interest and performance" appears to have two components: "a reduction in the novelty of the physical pleasure provided by sex with a particular partner and a reduction in the perceived need to maintain high levels of sexual behavior" (Call, Sprecher, and Schwartz 1995, p. 649).

FIRST-MARRIEDS COMPARED WITH REMARRIEDS AND COHABITORS To study the habituation theory, researchers examined the effects on coital frequency of remarriage and of cohabiting. Remarried respondents reported somewhat higher rates of sex frequency compared with people in first marriages who were the same age, and this was particularly true for those under age forty. Because people who remarry do renew the novelty of marital sex with a new partner, this finding is evidence for the habituation hypothesis, although it could also be true for other reasons (Call, Sprecher, and Schwartz 1995).

Unfortunately, the NSFH sample did not have enough cohabiting respondents over age thirty-five to allow for statistical analysis of older partners. Among those aged thirty-five and younger, Figure 6.2 indicates that cohabiting respondents had considerably higher intercourse rates than did legal spouses of the same age. This finding supports the idea that legal marriage lessens a person's interest in sex by legitimating it, making it seem expected rather than spontaneous. However, this difference could also be at least partly explained by cohabitors' generally more permissive sexual attitudes and values (Call, Sprecher, and Schwartz 1995).

Sexual Satisfaction in Marriage and Other Partnerships

All this discussion of coital frequency may tempt us to forget that committed partners' sexuality is essentially about intimacy and self-disclosure. In other words, sex between partners—heterosexual partners and gay and lesbian partners as well—both gives pleasure and reinforces their relationship. A recent study found that those who "reported both the greatest emotional satisfaction and the greatest physical pleasure in their intimate relationships were those who were partnered in a monogamous relationship" (Hendrick 2000, p. 4). Another study comparing cohabiting, married, and single individuals found that cohabiting and married individuals had the highest—and equal—levels of physical pleasure, with emotional satisfaction with sex greatest among married people (Waite and Joyner 2001).

Despite declining sexual frequency, sexual satisfaction remains high in marriages over the life course (of course, the less satisfied may have opted for divorce); 88 percent report that they are "extremely" or "very physically pleased" (Laumann et al. 1994; also Christopher and Sprecher 2000, p. 1003). General satisfaction with sexual relationships was also characteristic of gay and lesbian couples.

▪ Sex as a Pleasure Bond ▪

The convergence of sexual satisfaction with general satisfaction serves to support Masters, Johnson, and Kolodny's (1994) view that sex is a **pleasure bond** by which partners commit themselves to expressing their sexual feelings with each other.

In sharing sexual pleasure, partners realize that sex is something partners do with each other, not to or for each other. Each partner participates actively, as an equal in the sexual union. Further, each partner assumes **sexual responsibility**—that is, responsibility for his or her own sexual response. When this happens, the stage is set for conscious, mutual cooperation. Partners feel freer to express themselves sexually. Such expression may not be as easy as it seems, for it requires a high degree of self-esteem, the willingness to transcend gendered expectations, and the ability to create and maintain an atmosphere of mutual cooperation. We'll look at each of these elements in turn.

Sexual Pleasure and Self-Esteem

Research shows a correlation between sexual satisfaction and self-esteem (Wiederman and Hurst 1998; Larson et al. 1998). High self-esteem is important to pleasurable sex in several ways. First, self-esteem allows a person the freedom to receive pleasure. People who become uncomfortable when offered a favor, a present, or praise typically have low self-esteem and have trouble believing that others think well of them. This problem is heightened when the gift is sexual pleasure. People with low self-esteem may turn off their erotic feelings because unconsciously they feel they don't deserve them.

Self-esteem also allows individuals to acknowledge and accept their own tastes and preferences. This is vital in sexual relationships because there is a great deal of individuality in sexual expression. An important part of sexual pleasure lies in doing what one wants to—not necessarily doing things the ways others do them.

Third, self-esteem provides us the freedom to search for new pleasures. As we've seen, some individuals let their sexual relationship grow stale because they do not accept or appreciate their own sexuality and their need to experiment and explore with their partner.

Fourth, high self-esteem lets each of us ask our partner to help satisfy our preferences. In contrast, low self-esteem may lead a person to be defensive about her or his sexuality and reluctant to express valid human needs. In fact, people with low self-esteem may actively discourage their partners from stimulating them effectively (Burchell 1975).

Finally, high self-esteem allows us to engage in **pleasuring**: spontaneously doing what feels good at the moment and letting orgasm happen (or not), rather than working to produce it. Masters and Johnson (1976), who initiated contemporary sex therapy, point out that trying too hard may cause sexual problems. They use the term **spectatoring** to describe the practice of emotionally removing oneself from a sexual encounter in order to watch and judge one's productivity, and they state that this practice can be self-inhibiting.

Sexual Pleasure and Gender

Another important element in making sex a pleasure bond is the ability to transcend gender stereotypes. For instance, a man may reject tender sexual advances and activities because he believes he has to be emotionally unfeeling or be the initiator of sexual activity.

© The Newark Museum/Art Resource, NY

Likewise, women may have trouble in receiving or asking for pleasure because they feel uncomfortable or guilty about being assertive. Many women have been culturally conditioned to put their partner's needs first, so heterosexual women may proceed to intercourse before they are sufficiently aroused to reach climax. Then they are less likely to enjoy sex, which can detract from the experience for both partners.

Sex can be more effective as a pleasure bond when the partners appreciate any real gender differences that may exist and also transcend restrictive gender stereotypes (Money 1995). To do this, partners must be equal and must communicate in bonding rather than alienating ways.

Communication and Cooperation

A third element in sharing sex as a pleasure bond is communication and cooperation. Partners may use conjugal sex as an arena for power struggles, or they may cooperate to enrich their sexual relationship and to nurture each other's sexual self-concept. To create a cooperative sexual atmosphere, partners must be willing to clearly communicate their own sexual needs and to hear and respond to their partner's needs and preferences as well.

When conflicts arise—and they do in any honest sexual relationship—they need to be constructively negotiated. For example, one partner may desire to have sex more frequently than the other does, which could cause the other to feel pressured. The couple might agree that the partner who wants sex more often should stop pressing, and the other partner promises to consider what external pressures such as workload might be lessening his or her sexual feelings.

Other couples might have conflicts over whether to engage in oral–genital sex. It is important to communicate about such strong differences. Sometimes, a couple can work out a compromise; in other cases, compromise may be difficult or impossible. Therapists generally agree that no one should be urged to do something that he or she finds abhorrent. (And labeling partners "perverted" or "prudish" obviously does not contribute to a cooperative atmosphere.)

Open communication is important not only in resolving conflicts but also in sharing anxieties or doubts. Sex is a topic that is especially difficult for many people to talk about, yet misunderstanding about sex may cause stress in a relationship. Good sex is not something that just happens when two people are in love. Forming a good sexual relationship is a process that necessarily involves partners in open verbal and nonverbal communication. To have satisfying sex, both partners need to tell each other what pleases them.

Some Principles for Sexual Sharing

Some important principles may be distilled from the previous discussion to serve as guidelines for establishing and maintaining a nurturing, cooperative atmosphere even when a couple can't find a compromise that suits them both.

Partners should avoid passing judgment on each other's sexual fantasies, needs, desires, or requests. Labeling a partner or communicating nonverbally that something is disgusting or wrong may lower a person's sexual self-esteem and destroy the trust in a relationship. Nor should partners presume to know what the other is thinking or feeling, or what would be good for the other sexually. In a cooperative relationship, each

"Hey look, before this goes any further, I should probably tell you we're married."

partner accepts the other as the final authority on his or her own feelings, tastes, and preferences.

Another principle is what Masters and Johnson (1976) call the "principle of mutuality." Mutuality implies that "all sexual messages between two people, whether conveyed by words or actions, by tone of voice or touch of fingertips, be exchanged in the spirit of having a common cause." Mutuality means "two people united in an effort to discover what is best for both" (p. 53).

An attitude of mutuality is important because it fills each partner's need to feel secure, to know that any sexual difficulties, failures, or misgivings will not be used against him or her: "Together they succeed or together they fail in the sexual encounter, sharing the responsibility for failure, whether it is reflected in his performance or hers" (pp. 57, 89).

A final principle of sexual sharing is to maintain a **holistic view of sex**—that is, to see sex as an extension of the whole relationship rather than as a purely physical exchange, a single aspect of marriage. One woman described it this way:

I don't quite understand these references to the sex side of life. It is life. My husband and I are first of all a man and a woman—sexual creatures all through. That's where we get our real and central life satisfactions. If that's not right, nothing is. (quoted in Cuber and Harroff 1965, p. 136)

Recognizing its holistic emotional value is one way to keep marital sex pleasurable. Another is a commitment to discovering a partner's continually changing fantasies and needs. For, as one writer put it, besides a partner's fairly predictable habits and character, "there is also a core of surprises hidden in us all that can become an inexhaustible source of freshness in life and love" (Gottlieb 1979, p. 196).

Deepening the commitment to sharing and cooperation may make sex a growing and continuing pleasure bond. This does not mean that a couple will regularly have great sex by some external standard. It means that each partner chooses to try—and keep on trying—to say more and to hear more.

Making the Time for Intimacy

Just as it is important for families to arrange their schedules so that they may spend time together, it's also important for couples to plan time to be alone and intimate (Masters, Johnson, and Kolodny 1994). Planning time for intimacy involves making conscious choices. For example, partners may choose to set aside at least one night a week for themselves alone, without work, movies, television, the DVD player, the computer, another couple's company, or the children. They do not have to have intercourse during these times: They should do only what they feel like doing. But scheduling time alone together does mean mutually agreeing to exclude other preoccupations and devote full attention to each other.

Two sex therapists advise couples to reserve at least twenty-five minutes each night for a quiet talk, "with clothes off and defenses down" (Koch and Koch 1976, p. 35). This last suggestion may be easier for parents with young children who are put to bed fairly early. A common complaint from parents of older children is that the children stay up later; by the time the children have become teenagers, the parents no longer have any private evening time together even with their clothes on. One woman, after attending an education course for parents, found a solution:

Our house shuts down at 9:30 now. That doesn't mean we say "It's your bedtime, kids. You're tired

and you need your sleep." It means we say, "Your dad (or your mom) and I need some time alone." The children go to their rooms at 9:30. Help with homework, lunch money, decisions about what they'll wear tomorrow—all those things get taken care of by 9:30 or they don't get taken care of.

Boredom with sex after many years in a marriage may be at least partly the consequence of a decision by default. Therapists suggest that couples may avoid this situation perhaps by creating romantic settings—a candlelit dinner or a night away from the family at a motel—or by opening themselves to new experiences, such as describing their sexual fantasies to each other, reading sex manuals together, or renting an erotic movie. (The important thing, these therapists stress, is that partners don't lose touch with either their sexuality or their ability to share it with each other.) Therapists also point out that just because spouses find they don't desire sex together much anymore does not mean they no longer love each other.

We have been talking about human sexual expression as a pleasure bond. It is terribly unfortunate that sexuality can also be associated with disease and death. Indeed, the fact that it is so difficult to make this transition points to the multifaceted, sometimes even contradictory, nature of contemporary human sexual expression.

Sexual Expression, Family Relations, and HIV/AIDS and Other Sexually Transmitted Diseases

HIV/AIDS has now been known for almost twenty-five years. The HIV, or "human immunodeficiency virus," which produces AIDS, has existed longer than that, but it was only in 1981 that AIDS suddenly emerged as the cause of a rapidly increasing number of deaths. AIDS is a viral disease that destroys the immune system—AIDS stands for "acquired immune deficiency syndrome."

The HIV virus is transmitted through the exchange of infected body fluids—hence the need for protection during sex with HIV-positive partners.

HIV may also be transmitted from mothers to infants during pregnancy and through sharing needles with infected drug users. ("Facts About Families: Who Has HIV/AIDS?" presents some detail on the demographics of HIV/AIDS.) With a lowered resistance to disease, a person with AIDS becomes vulnerable to infections and diseases that other people easily fight off; the immediate cause of death from AIDS is often a rare form of pneumonia or cancer.

Because of its lethal character—a total of 524,000 deaths in the United States through 2003 (U.S. Centers for Disease Control and Prevention 2001g)—we give most attention in this chapter to HIV/AIDS. But other sexually transmitted diseases have the power to significantly affect lives and relationships. Not including AIDS, more than sixty-five million Americans currently live with **sexually transmitted diseases (STDs)**[7] while nineteen million new cases arise each year, about half of which will become chronic. The number of syphilis and gonorrhea cases has declined, but genital herpes, chlamydia, and human papilloma virus, among others, are widespread (U.S. Centers for Disease Control and Prevention 2004b, 2004c, 2004d, 2004e) and can have powerful effects on health and reproduction. Needless to say, they have an impact on sexual relationships. Appendix C describes various STDs and presents information on transmission, prevention, and treatment.

A theme of this text is that sociocultural conditions affect people's choices. We can examine how HIV/AIDS, as a societal phenomenon, has changed the consequences of decisions about sexual activity. The essay in Appendix C, "As We Make Choices: HIV/AIDS—Some Precautions," discusses some guidelines for sexual and family relationships in the age of AIDS.

HIV/AIDS and Heterosexuals

Although men may contract HIV/AIDS from sexual intercourse with infected women, transmission from men to women is higher because of anatomical differences.

Heterosexual adults may be responding to the threat of AIDS with changed behavior (Mosher and Pratt 1993; Ku, Sonenstein, and Pleck 1995). Sexually active singles may now want to have a longer period of acquaintance before initiating sexual contact, hoping to experience greater attraction, security, or commitment before deciding that sex is worth it. Some opt for periods of celibacy. At the same time, women, teens, and older Americans, especially, may not perceive their risk. Given the increasing heterosexual transmission of HIV/AIDS, "women should embrace a philosophy of always protecting themselves from HIV" ("A Third 2004"). Perhaps 20 percent of gay men marry at least once (Buxton 1991). Consequently, some heterosexual women may be regularly exposed to the virus if their husbands are sexually active with men.

HIV/AIDS and Gay Men

Many gay men modified their sexual behavior in the 1980s. Multiple, frequent, and anonymous sexual contacts had been common elements of lifestyle and sexual ideology for many gays (Blumstein and Schwartz 1983). But attitudes and behavior changed enough, at least among men in their thirties and over, to have dramatically reduced the incidence of new cases among gay males for a time.

The decline of deaths, due to new medications, has meant that for many, AIDS has become a chronic disease rather than a death sentence. As the mood in the gay community has lightened, some gay men have returned to unprotected sex with many and anonymous partners. These practices may include men who know that they are HIV-positive (Sanchez 2002). Moreover, "a lot of younger men have grown up from the time they were eight years old hearing on television about gay men and HIV. They have seamlessly integrated being gay with having HIV" (Walt Odets, quoted in Hagar 1995, p. 10). One gay activist has expressed concern that drug ads with pictures of relatively hearty gay men conveys a misleading message about the difficulties of living with AIDS, a message that may reduce caution and prevention (Fierstein 2003).

HIV/AIDS Means New Family Crises

Some families will face crises and loss because of AIDS. Telling one's family members that one has HIV/AIDS is a crisis in itself. Due to shame about the disease, some relatives grieve amid a shroud of secrecy, thereby isolating themselves.

---

7. The term *sexually transmitted infections (STIs)* is also used and is equivalent to *sexually transmitted diseases (STDs)*.

In addition, HIV/AIDS victims and their families and friends are living with the burden of personal care for friends, lovers, or family members with AIDS. Unattached AIDS victims may return home to live with parents or siblings. Especially in geographically distinct gay/lesbian communities, responsibility accrues to lesbians as well as to gay men. Lesbians in the San Francisco area, for example, often have close ties with gay men and may consider them members of their families.

Some married heterosexuals have lost partners to the disease or are helping infected partners fight health battles. AIDS contracted from a blood transfusion means a prolonged medical battle for the partner, and perhaps children who may be infected; this is less likely now.[8] But it is a tragedy that may be shared. AIDS resulting from drug use frequently occurs in transient relationships, but in marital settings it often indicates a family that has many problems. In cases in which a partner (more often the husband) develops AIDS from sex outside the relationship, the marriage may end. As more senior citizens develop AIDS, grandparents may fear that they will be stigmatized by their grown children and isolated from their grandchildren (Stock 1997).

The burdens of AIDS are not all emotional, nor do they involve only physical care of victims; some are financial. New drug therapies may cost thousands of dollars a year. AIDS patients may be unable to work and lose health insurance as well as income. (Some government programs now exist to assist with costs.) Being HIV-positive or having AIDS has led to being fired, although favorable decisions have now been rendered in discrimination cases brought under the Americans with Disabilities Act (ACLU 2001).

HIV/AIDS and Children

Most children with AIDS contracted it from their mothers during pregnancy, at birth, or through breast milk. This form of AIDS transmission has declined dramatically due to pregnant women's (voluntary) pre-natal HIV testing and the subsequent administration of prenatal drug therapies when necessary. African American and Hispanic women, who have the highest rates of AIDS, are less likely to receive the early and adequate prenatal care which is increasingly effective in treating perinatal HIV/AIDS.

Women who have tested positive for HIV/AIDS are not always willing to give up the prospect of motherhood; some are deciding to have children after diagnosis now that the risk of transmission may be drastically reduced by medication (Villarosa 2001). Approximately 6,000 HIV-infected women give birth each year.

Men with HIV are beginning to hope for parenthood also, with procedures designed to minimize transmission to a female partner.[9] This is still controversial, but the American Society for Reproductive Medicine has declared that providing these services is acceptable practice (Kolata 2002a).

Children with AIDS have a unique array of treatment requirements and are often in the hospital (Klass 1989). Some were abandoned by their parents to hospital care. Others are raised by grandparents or foster parents (Lee 1994). A new set of problems has arisen as AIDS babies enter their teens. Clinical professionals report serious behavior, emotional, and cognitive problems among some of the AIDS babies who have survived to adolescence. Public health workers are starting to take note of the teens' needs for services (Villarosa 2002c).

HIV/AIDS and other sexually transmitted diseases are more than a medical or a family problem—they are conditions imbued with social meanings and consequences. As we will see in the next section, politics enters into decisions about policy related to HIV/AIDS as well as other STDs—and about sexuality in general.

▪ Platform and Pulpit ▪

Political and religious conflict over sexuality characterized the 1980s and 1990s and continues to do so.

---

8. Initially, many cases of AIDS arose through infection from blood transfusions, but this mode of transmission declined after 1985, when donated blood began to be rigorously screened for HIV. Blood transfusion accounted for only 1 percent of cumulative cases as of 2000 (U.S. Centers for Disease Control and Prevention 2001b, Table 5).

9. A technique called "sperm washing" separates the sperm from the seminal fluid containing the virus. Another approach is to test men who are on HIV-suppressing drugs and to use their semen if there is no detectable virus. Fertility clinicians vary in their assessment of the risks involved and in their willingness to offer their services (Kolata 2002a).

Facts About Families | Who Has HIV/AIDS?[a]

Around 400,000 people are living with AIDS[8]: 42 percent black, 37 percent white, 20 percent Hispanic, and 1 percent each Asian/Pacific Islander and Native American/Alaska Native. The cumulative total of AIDS cases reported through 2003 is over 900,000, with more than 40,000 new cases diagnosed each year (U.S. Centers for Disease Control and Prevention 2004g, "Commentary" and Table 3).

Currently, around 800,000 people are infected with HIV, the largest number since the 1980s. On the positive side, infections are being caught in the early stages. On the other hand, the increase in infections suggests a growing sense of complacency among groups at risk of contracting the disease. "Because more effective treatments are available, there seems to be a perception, particularly in the gay community, that HIV is a manageable disease . . . I think the disease just doesn't have the fear that it once carried" (Dr.

More AIDS infections are caught in the early stages now, thanks to the wide distribution of information about AIDS prevention and testing.

a. The term "HIV/AIDS" is used in general references to this sexually transmitted disease. When speaking about numbers of cases, "HIV" (the virus which causes AIDS) and "AIDS" (the active disease) are often distinguished. Most of those who become infected with the HIV virus will progress to full-blown AIDS.

The incidence (number of new cases) and prevalence (current cases) of HIV-infection are only estimates, as there is no population-wide screening program. Many people who may be HIV-positive are not tested, and test results are not always reported consistently. Consequently, most of the data in these sections on the social distribution of HIV/AIDS are based on AIDS cases, as those are more definite in diagnosis and reported more accurately.

Robert Johnson, Director of the CDC's HIV and AIDS Prevention Division in O'Connor 2003, p. 28). Also, information efforts do not seem to be reaching minorities.

Primary risk groups Primary risk groups in the United States are men who have sex with men (MSM) (about 47 percent of cumulative AIDS cases through 2003). Intravenous drug users account for 27 percent of cases, and 7 percent are identified as men who have combined risks. Heterosexual transmission is the origin of 16 percent of AIDS cases.[b]

b. Woman-to-woman sex may carry some risk of HIV infection, although it is a rare occurrence (U.S. Centers for Disease Control and Prevention 2001a).

Heterosexual transmission is rising and is now the source of 34 percent of new HIV infections and of 90 percent of new HIV infections among teens (U.S. Centers for Disease Control and Prevention 2004g).

Age and HIV/AIDS HIV/AIDS has affected young and middle-aged adults the most. Almost three-fourths of AIDS cases to date were diagnosed in people in the twenty-five through forty-four age range. The proportion of HIV/AIDS cases among teenagers is small, around 1 percent (U.S. Centers for Disease Control and Prevention 2004g), but keep in mind that individuals who are older at diagnosis may have been infected as adolescents.

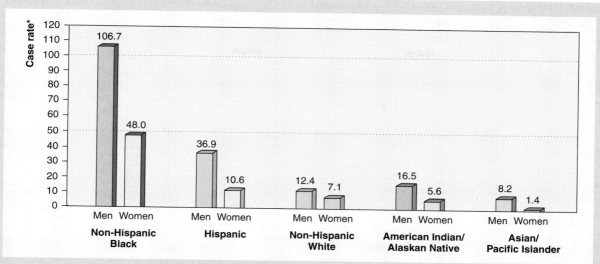

FIGURE 6.3

Rate of AIDS cases reported among adults and adolescents by race/ethnicity and gender, 2002.

* Number of cases per 100,000 in respective racial/ethnic and gender group.

Source: U.S. Centers for Disease Control and Prevention 2004a, Table 4.

There is concern that HIV/AIDS is spreading among adolescents and young adults (Lerner 2003).

Expanded testing and treatment of HIV-infected pregnant women have lowered the rate of new cases of prenatal transmission to fewer than 1 percent of births to infected women (Villarosa 2001). There were only 59 new cases of AIDS in children in 2002 (U.S. Centers for Disease Control and Prevention 2004g, Table 3).

We seldom think of AIDS as affecting older individuals, but around 5 percent of cases are found among those aged fifty-five through sixty-four. Only 1 percent of AIDS cases are reported for individuals aged sixty-five and older, but that is almost 13,000 cases among senior citizens (U.S. Centers for Disease Control and Prevention 2004g, Table 3). Currently, there are efforts to create programs to educate older Americans about risks and precautions concerning HIV/AIDS (Villarosa 2003).

Gender and HIV/AIDS Women constitute 18 percent of AIDS cases cumulatively, although they are an estimated one-third of new HIV infections. Cumulatively, 53 percent of AIDS cases among women arose from heterosexual contact and 43 percent from intravenous drug use. The dominant source of AIDS among males is having sex with other men (59 percent), with intravenous drug use and heterosexual contacts also significant causes of infection (U.S. Centers for Disease Control and Prevention 2004g, Table 3).

Race/Ethnicity and HIV/AIDS Racial and ethnic minorities have been disproportionately affected by HIV/AIDS. Rates of AIDS cases diagnosed in 2002 were highest among non-Hispanic blacks, with the rate for Hispanics also high. American Indians have a slightly higher rate than non-Hispanic whites, while Asians and Pacific Islanders have the lowest rate of AIDS cases (U.S. Centers for Disease Control and Prevention 2004g, Table 5). When we examine those rates by gender within race/ethnic categories, we see that within every category, men have much higher rates of AIDS than women. (See Figure 6.3.)

Critical Thinking

Pick one of the above demographic categories—for example, teen women. What ideas can you think of for an HIV/AIDS prevention program for this group? You may want to consult the essay "HIV/AIDS—Some Precautions" in Appendix C on the website.

That has changed the context in which individuals make decisions about sexual expression, as well as public policy regarding sexuality and reproduction.

One of the most striking changes over the past several decades has been the emergence of sexual and reproductive issues as political controversies. On the one hand, a loose coalition of religious fundamentalists and political conservatives believes that the U.S. government and American social institutions should operate according to traditional principles of sexual morality. On the other side are liberal religious and secular individuals and organizations with a different set of values—more open to nonmarital sexuality, for example. Public health professionals approach policy from a research-based and pragmatic perspective as to effective means to achieve sexual and reproductive health goals.

Controversies over AIDS—and especially over how to educate youth about AIDS, and sex education in general—illustrate the conflict between a morally neutral and pragmatic public health policy and a religious fundamentalist moral approach. Conservative religious leaders, who for religious reasons oppose nonmarital sexual relationships or homosexuality, may rule out certain AIDS preventive measures such as condoms, as well as explicit sex education. Other issues engendering political conflict include abortion and the recognition of same-sex relationships through domestic partnerships or marriage. (Same-sex marriage and domestic partnerships are discussed in Chapters 8 and 9).

Conservatives use political processes to try to shape public policy on sex matters in a conservative direction, while those with more liberal views and/or public health perspectives resist these initiatives. Political controversy has influenced both research and education about sexuality in the United States over the last few decades.

Politics and Research

The need for more comprehensive and current data on sexual behavior twice led to unsuccessful efforts to mount federally funded national sample surveys to be conducted by teams of well-respected social scientists. Congress canceled a pilot study on the grounds that a sex survey would be too controversial. (NORC conducted the much smaller survey without federal funds.) A planned survey of 24,000 teens in grades 7 to 11 was also cancelled ("U.S. Scraps" 1991). Ironically, comparisons with other countries suggest that our society's tendency to deny sexuality at the same time we encourage it sends mixed messages that, among other negative consequences, probably help account for the unusually high rates of teen pregnancy and abortion in the United States (Risman and Schwartz 2002).

Recently, the politicization of research has taken another form. Some reports of research that does not support the government position on an issue have been removed from government websites or changed after their initial posting. For example, a review of many studies which concluded that abortion does *not* cause breast cancer (contradicting the position of the right to life movement) was removed from the National Cancer Institute website. Research on sex education which found that providing information about contraception to teens does *not* increase their sexual activity was removed from the U.S. Centers for Disease Control and Prevention website. The CDC fact sheet on condoms was changed to de-emphasize the protective value of condoms vis-a-vis HIV infection. Also, government research funding for "controversial" topics has been denied despite favorable review by granting agency experts in the field (Clymer 2002; Herbert 2003; Navarro 2004).

Politics and Sex Education

In the 1980s, then-Surgeon General C. Everett Koop, himself a fundamentalist Christian and political conservative, was moved by public health concerns to propose explicit education about AIDS to children as young as nine, including the topics of homosexuality, genital intercourse, and condoms (Koop n.d.). A later Surgeon General encountered a hostile reception ("White House Distances" 2001) when he released a report calling for a more comprehensive program of sex education than federal policy supported (U.S. Surgeon General 2001).

Current controversy centers on whether sex education should be "abstinence only" or "abstinence plus" (also termed "comprehensive"). Since 1996, the federal government has taken the official position that abstention from sexual relations unless in a monogamous marriage is the only protection against sexually transmitted disease and pregnancy—and that absti-

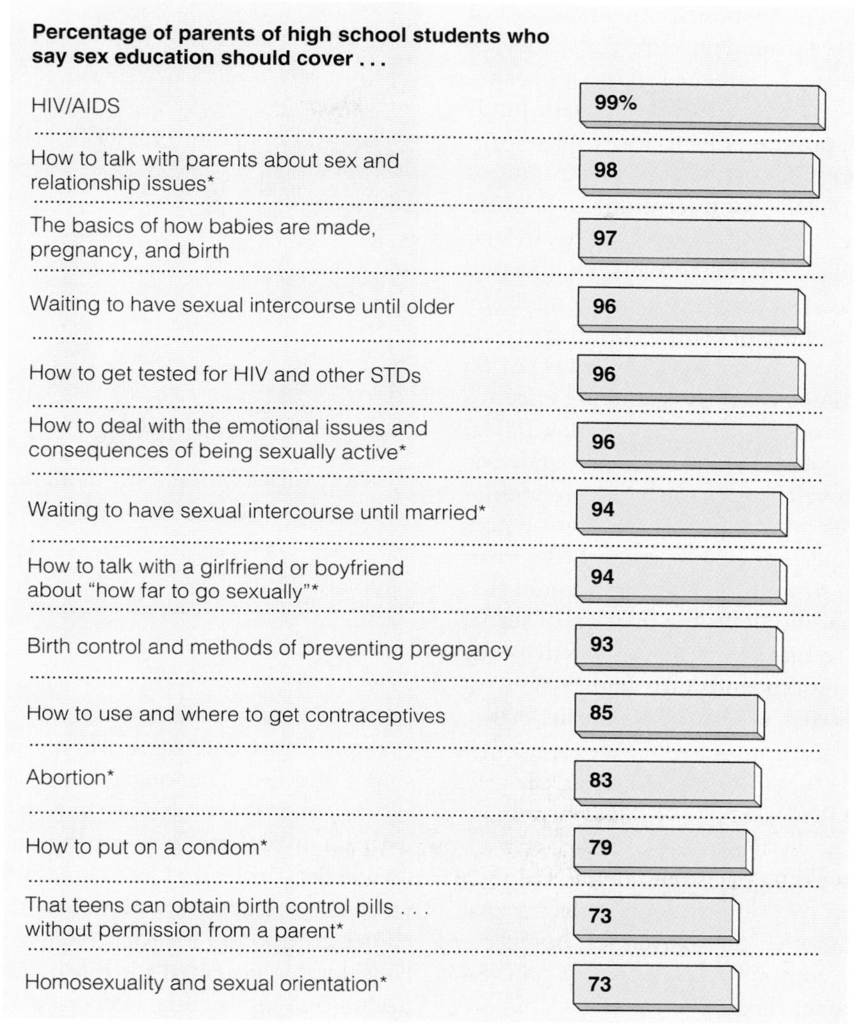

Percentage of parents of high school students who say sex education should cover . . .

HIV/AIDS	99%
How to talk with parents about sex and relationship issues*	98
The basics of how babies are made, pregnancy, and birth	97
Waiting to have sexual intercourse until older	96
How to get tested for HIV and other STDs	96
How to deal with the emotional issues and consequences of being sexually active*	96
Waiting to have sexual intercourse until married*	94
How to talk with a girlfriend or boyfriend about "how far to go sexually"*	94
Birth control and methods of preventing pregnancy	93
How to use and where to get contraceptives	85
Abortion*	83
How to put on a condom*	79
That teens can obtain birth control pills . . . without permission from a parent*	73
Homosexuality and sexual orientation*	73

FIGURE 6.4

What parents want sex education to teach their children.

* Questions marked with an asterisk were asked of only half the sample.

Source: Survey of 1,001 parents of children in 7th to 12th grade sponsored by NPR/Kaiser Family Foundation/ Kennedy School of Government (NPR et al. 2004). The survey was conducted Sept./Oct. 2003. The high school parent sub-sample = 450.

nence is the only morally appropriate principle of sexual conduct. "Abstinence-only" programs may mention contraception, if at all, only to cite allegedly high failure rates. Programs are urged to convey to students that nonmarital sex for people *of any age* is likely to have harmful physical and psychological effects (Brody 2004a; Dailard 2002).

Surveys of parents indicate that they prefer that an "abstinence-plus" sex education be presented in the schools, one that would include contraception and AIDS prevention as well as promotion of abstinence. As Figure 6.4 indicates, more than 80 percent of parents support teaching about birth control, and 73 percent want sex education to cover sexual orientation

(NPR/Kaiser Family Foundation/Kennedy School of Government 2004). Yet around one-third of school sex education programs are "abstinence only," a proportion that seems to be increasing as government funding is limited to such programs.

Research indicates that comprehensive sex education programs (that include contraception) do not lead to any earlier commencement of sexual activity; in fact, research indicates that comprehensive sex education delays the start of sexual activity. "Encouraging abstinence and urging better use of contraception are compatible goals" (Kirby 2001, p. 18). There is as yet no evidence that "abstinence-only" programs are effective in delaying sex or preventing pregnancy (Brody 2004a; Dailard 2002; Kirby 2002). While abstinence-only education has yet to prove effective, early research found that virginity pledges taken in certain circumstances seemed to delay adolescent sexual activity (Bearman and Brückner 2001). More recent research found that while virginity pledges do delay the iniation of sexual activity, once these teens become sexually active they do so without precautions and have higher rates of pregnancy and STDs than other teens (Altman 2004b).

Today's society offers individuals divergent sexual standards, from casual sex to abstinence. So making knowledgeable choices—and assuming responsibility—are a must.

▪ Sexual Responsibility ▪

People today are making decisions about sex in a climate characterized by political conflict over sexual issues. Premarital and other nonmarital sex, homosexuality, abortion, and contraception represent political issues as well as personal choices.

Both public and private communication must rise to new levels, as potential sexual partners talk about sex and disease, precautions and risk, and sexual history and sexual practices. The AIDS epidemic has brought the importance of sexual responsibility to our attention in a dramatic way.

In such a climate, making knowledgeable choices is a must. Because there are various standards today concerning sex, each individual must determine what sexual standard he or she values, which is not always easy. Today's adults may be exposed to several different standards throughout the course of their lives because different groups and individuals adhere to various standards. Even when people feel they know which standard they value, applications to particular situations may be difficult. People who believe in the standard of sexual permissiveness with affection, for

example, must determine when a particular relationship is affectionate enough.

Making these choices and feeling comfortable with them requires recognizing and respecting your own values, instead of just being influenced by others when in a sexual situation. Anxiety may accompany the choice to develop a sexual relationship, and there is considerable potential for misunderstanding between partners. This section addresses some principles of sexual responsibility that may serve as guidelines for sexual decision making.

One obvious responsibility concerns the possibility of pregnancy. Partners should plan responsibly whether, when, and how they will conceive children and then use effective birth control methods accordingly. (Chapter 10 and Appendices E, F, and G provide information on the reproductive process, birth control, and reproductive technology.)

A second responsibility concerns the possibility of contracting sexually transmitted diseases (STDs) or transmitting them to someone else. Individuals should be aware of the facts concerning HIV/AIDS and other STDs. They need to assume responsibility for protecting themselves and their partners. They need to know how to recognize the symptoms of an STD and what to do if they get one. (See Appendix C)

A third responsibility concerns communicating with partners or potential sexual partners. In one study, 35 percent of men reported lying to a partner in order to have sex with her, and 60 percent of women thought they had been lied to. Such lies involved overstating love and caring, denying other simultaneous relationships, and reporting fewer sex partners than was true (Goleman 1988b). Emotional harm from misrepresentation may be more serious than rejection due to a genuine change of heart.

People should be honest with partners about their motives for wanting to have sexual relations with them. As we've seen in this chapter, sex may mean many different things to different people. A sexual encounter may mean love and intimacy to one partner and be a source of achievement or relaxation to the other. Honesty lessens the potential for misunderstanding and hurt between partners. People should treat each other as people rather than things—as people with needs and feelings.

A fourth responsibility is to oneself. In expressing sexuality today, each of us must make decisions according to our own values. A person may choose to follow values held on the basis of religious commitment or put forth by ethicists or by psychologists or counselors. People's values change over the course of their lives, and what's right at one time may not be satisfying later. Despite the confusion caused both by internal changes as our personalities develop and by the social changes going on around us, it is important for individuals to make thoughtful decisions about sexual relationships.

Sex has an enormous potential for good in bringing pleasure and intensifying couple intimacy. Having cautioned about risk and responsibility, let's close with the voice of one of sociology's founders, writing in the late nineteenth century as a modern sensibility developed: "[T]he sex act . . . produces . . . the most intimate communion that can exist between two conscious beings" (Emile Durkheim in "L'education Sexuelle" 1911).

In Sum

- Social attitudes and values play an important role in the forms of sexual expression that people find comfortable and enjoyable.

- Despite decades of conjecture and research, it is still unclear just how sexual orientation develops and whether it is genetic or socially conditioned. Recent decades have witnessed political and other challenges by gay activists (and some others) to heterosexism and to one of its consequences, homophobia.

- Whatever one's sexual orientation, sexual expression is negotiated amid cultural messages about what is sexually permissible or desirable. In the United States, these cultural messages have moved from patriarchal sex, based on male dominance and reproduction as its principal purpose, to a message that encourages sexual expressiveness in myriad ways for both genders equally.

- Four standards of nonmarital sex are abstinence, permissiveness with affection, permissiveness without affection, and the double standard—the latter diminished since the 1960s, but still alive.

- Marital sex changes throughout the life course. Young spouses have sex more often than do older mates. Although the frequency of sexual intercourse declines over time and the length of a marriage, some 27 percent of married people over age seventy-four are sexually active.

- Making sex a pleasure bond, whether a couple is married or not, involves cooperation in a nurturing, caring relationship. To fully cooperate sexually, partners need to develop high self-esteem, to break free from restrictive gendered stereotypes, and to communicate openly.

- HIV/AIDS has had an impact on relationships, marriages, and families.

- Sexuality and sexual expression are public issues at present. The social institutions of religion, law, and politics are arenas of dispute over values and policies regarding sex.

- Whatever the philosophical or religious grounding of one's perspective on sexuality, there are certain guidelines for personal sexual responsibility that we should all heed.

Key Terms

abstinence

bisexual

double standard

expressive sexuality

gay

habituation

heterosexism

heterosexual

HIV/AIDS

holistic view of sex

homophobia

homosexual

interactionist perspective on human sexuality

interpersonal exchange model of sexual satisfaction

lesbian

patriarchal sexuality

permissiveness with affection

permissiveness without affection

pleasure bond

pleasuring

sexual orientation

sexual responsibility

sexual scripts

sexually transmitted disease (STD)

spectatoring

Questions for Review and Reflection

1. Give some examples to illustrate changes in sexual behavior and social attitudes about sex. What might change in the future?

2. Do you think that sex is changing from "his and hers" to "theirs"? What do you see as some difficulties in making this transition?

3. Discuss the principles for sexual sharing suggested in this chapter. Are there any you would add or subtract? What about the premises of sexual responsibility? Do you agree with the list?

4. How do you think HIV/AIDS affects sex and sex relationships—or does it?

5. Policy Question. What role, if any, should government play regarding sex education, research and information on sex, and sexual regulation?

Suggested Readings

Boston Women's Health Book Collective. 1998. *Our Bodies, Our Selves for the New Century.* New York: Simon and Schuster. Manual of women's health and sexuality that has gained enormous respect from the user public. Similar books have appeared for parents, gays, heterosexual men, teens, and children.

Colombo, Luann. 1999. *How to Have Sex in the Woods.* New York: Random House. This book is but one example of the many "how-to" books on sex to be found in bookstores. They are too numerous and diverse for us to pick one or a few to recommend—usefulness and appeal depend on your sexuality, relationship status, and personal taste.

Francoeur, Robert T., and William J. Taverner. 2000. *Taking Sides: Clashing Views on Controversial Issues in Human Sexuality*, 7th ed. New York: McGraw-Hill. Presents both sides of controversies in various areas of human sexuality.

Greenberg, Jerrold S., Clint E. Breuss, and Debra W. Haffner. 2002. *Exploring the Dimensions of Human Sexuality.* Sudbury, MA: Jones and Bartlett. Thorough, comprehensive, yet user-friendly textbook on human sexuality and reproduction. Use as a reference or read it from cover to cover.

Michael, Robert T., John H. Gagnon, Edward O. Laumann, and Gina Kolata. 1994. *Sex in America: A Definitive Survey.* A concise version of the NORC study of sexual practices in the United States (Laumann et al. 1994). Written for a popular audience with lots of good examples.

Go Ask Alice!

http://www.goaskalice.columbia.edu

This is a health question-and-answer Internet service produced by Columbia University's Health Education Program. Answers questions from college and high school students, parents, teachers, professionals, older adults, and others on every conceivable health topic, including relationships, sexuality, sexual health, and emotional health.

Alan Guttmacher Institute

http://www.guttmacher.org or www.agi-usa.org

Alan Guttmacher Institute is the research arm of the Planned Parenthood Federation. The site includes fact sheets on various sexual and reproductive topics, as well as *Perspectives on Sexual and Reproductive Health*, a bimonthly periodical that summarizes relevant current research, policy, and law.

Virtual Society: The Wadsworth Sociology Resource Center

Go to the Sociology Resource Center at **http://sociology.wadsworth.com** for a wealth of online resources, including a companion web site for your text that provides study aids such as self-quizzes for each chapter and a practice final exam, as well as links to sociology websites and information on the latest theories and discoveries in the field. In addition, you will find further suggested readings, flash cards, MicroCase online exercises, and appendices on a range of subjects, including Appendix A, "Human Sexual Anatomy"; Appendix B, "Human Sexual Response"; Appendix C, "Sexually Transmitted Diseases"; and Appendix D, "Sexual Dysfunction and Therapy."

Online Study Tool

Marriage & Family ⊛ Now™   Go to **http://sociology .wadsworth.com** to reach the companion website for your text and use the Marriage&FamilyNow access code that came with your book to access this study tool. Take a practice pretest after you have read each chapter, and then use the study plan provided to master that chapter. Afterward, take a posttest to monitor your progress.

Search Online with InfoTrac College Edition

For additional information, exercises, and key words to aid your research, explore InfoTrac College Edition, your online library that offers full-length articles from thousands of scholarly and popular publications. Click on *InfoTrac College Edition* under *Chapter Resources* at the companion web site and use the access code that came with your book.

- Search keywords: *college + sexual.* Seek articles on sexual activity and sexual relationships of college students.

- Search keywords: *sexual orientation.* Look for articles that address this topic. Do a "limit search" for articles published in 2004 or 2005.

Choosing *a* Marriage Partner

"The Pasture"
I'm going out to clean the pasture spring;
I'll only stop to rake the leaves away
(And wait to watch the water clear, I may):
I sha'n't be gone long—You come too.

I'm going out to fetch the little calf
That's standing by the mother. It's so young.
It totters when she licks it with her tongue.
I sha'n't be gone long—You come too.

ROBERT FROST
From The Poetry of Robert Frost

ABOUT 90 PERCENT OF AMERICANS marry (see "Facts about Families: American Families Today" in Chapter 1). The vast majority of us value having one special relationship with a person we love best. This often means selecting someone, usually of the opposite sex, with whom to become both emotionally and sexually intimate. In American or Western culture this relationship is supposed to have a romantic quality. It may lead to marriage.

However, many people in the world expect love to develop after marriage. Today this is true for some immigrant groups in the United States. As we'll see, only recently in history have people even begun to equate the two concepts of love and marriage. Although love is usually an important ingredient, successful marriages are also based on such qualities as the partners' common goals and needs, their maturity, and the soundness of their reasons for marrying.

You'll recall that Chapter 5 examines developing a loving relationship with an intimate partner. In the following pages we'll examine patterns by which the majority of individuals in our society choose marriage partners. We'll look at some social variables that may influence choice of a spouse and marital stability. We'll also examine the role of cohabitation in selecting a spouse. First, we'll explore the idea that love and marriage go together and look at different ways that spouses may be selected for marriage.

■ Love—and Marriage? ■

That marriages should involve romance and lead to personal satisfaction is a uniquely modern—and Western—idea. (By *Western* we mean the culture that developed in Western Europe and now characterizes that region and Canada, the United States, Australia, New Zealand, and other societies shaped by Western European culture.) According to an American song made popular by Frank Sinatra, "love and marriage go together like a horse and carriage." The obvious meaning in this phrase is that love is a necessary factor in marriage. You may also notice a second assumption: Love, the horse, goes *before* marriage, the carriage. Not all cultures adhere to these assumptions about "love marriages," however.

Arranged Marriages

In much of the world, particularly in parts of Europe, Asia, and Africa that are less Westernized, parents arrange their children's marriages.[1] In **arranged marriage**, there are various ways that future spouses can be brought together. Traditionally, the parents of both prospective partners (often with other relatives' or a paid matchmaker's help) work out the details and then announce the upcoming marriage to their children. The children may have little or no say in the matter, and they may not meet their future spouse until the wedding (Tepperman and Wilson 1993; Ingoldsby

---

1. In some arranged marriages a traditional pattern for mate selection developed, such as marriage between cousins. Some cultures practice *sororate* and/or *levirate* arrangements. These terms refer to remarriage practices after a first spouse's death. In sororate cultures, a sister replaces a deceased wife. More widely practiced has been the levirate. Under this system, a woman's brother-in-law replaces her deceased husband.

There are various reasons for the sororate and the levirate. For one thing, these practices assured that any property agreements made by the two families in the first marriage would continue. In the case of the levirate, a wife was typically the property of her husband; therefore, she would be inherited, along with other possessions, by her brother-in-law. Also, it was understood that women needed to be taken care of and that a brother-in-law should assume that responsibility. It has been reported that the levirate has been practiced by Afghans, Abyssinians, Hebrews, Hindus, and some Native American and African groups, among others (Ingoldsby 1995a).

The man on the decorated horse is an investment banker from New York who has traveled to Jaipur, India, to marry a native Asian Indian woman. The marriage had been arranged in India by the groom's mother. The couple will return to New York to live. "I always knew I'd probably end up getting married to someone who wasn't very American, because I'm not myself in some ways," he said.

© Edward Keating/NYT Pictures

1995a). However, today it is more common for the children to marry only when they themselves accept the parents' choice. Marriages like these are sometimes called "assisted marriages" (Alvarez 2003).

The fact that marriages are arranged doesn't mean that love is completely ignored by parents. Indeed, marital love may be highly valued. However, couples in arranged marriages are expected to develop a loving relationship after the marriage, not before (Tepperman and Wilson 1993). In some societies, such as India, parents typically check prospective partners' astrological charts to assure future compatibility (Ingoldsby 1995a, p. 149).

Arranged marriage developed in collectivist societies based on strong extended family ties.[2] In these societies, marriage unites not just two people but two kinship groups as well (Sherif-Trask 2003). Because a marriage joins two families, selecting a suitable mate is a "huge responsibility" not to be left to the young people themselves (Tepperman and Wilson 1993, pp. 73–74). Analyzing arranged marriage in Bangladesh, sociologist Ashraf Uddin Ahmed (1993) notes that "Love marriage is thought to be disruptive to family ties, and is viewed as a children's transference of the loyalty from a family orientation to a single person, ignoring obligations to the family and kin group for personal goals" (p. 76). Moreover, it is often assumed that an infatuated young person may choose a partner who will make a poor spouse. ("Smoke Gets in Your Eyes," warns an old American song.)

Taking a functional perspective (see Chapter 3), Ahmed concludes that arranged marriage performs the following functions, among others:

1. affirms and strengthens parents' power over their children
2. helps keep the family traditions and value systems intact
3. helps consolidate and extend family property
4. enhances the value of the kinship group
5. helps young people avoid the uncertainty of searching for a mate (1993, p. 74)

2. You may recall that Chapter 3's "A Closer Look at Family Diversity" contrasts individualistic societies and collectivist societies. In individualistic societies, the main concern is with one's own self-actualization and interests. In collectivist societies, people identify with and conform to the expectations of their extended kin. Western societies are characterized as individualistic (Hofstede 1980), and individualism is positively associated with valuing romantic love (Dion and Dion 1991).

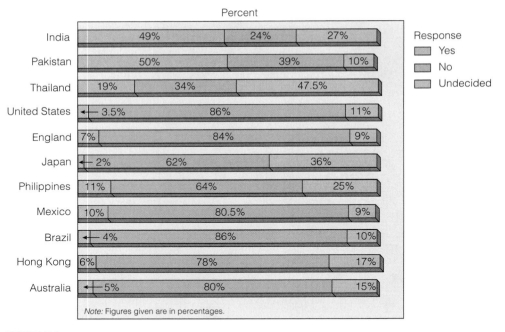

FIGURE 7.1

Responses to question: "If a man (woman) had all the other qualities you desired, would you marry this person if you were not in love with him (her)?"

Source: Adapted from "Love and Marriage in Eleven Cultures," by R. Levine, S. Sato, T. Hasimoto, & J. Verma, 1995, *Journal of Cross-Cultural Psychology,* 26 (5), pp. 554–571. Copyright © 1996 by Sage Publications, Inc. Reprinted by permission.

Despite its functions, arranged marriage is changing as the world's cultures become increasingly Westernized—that is, adopt Western or American beliefs, values, and norms. For example, in Thailand most young people choose their own spouse, but at the same time they need their parents' approval in order to have the traditional wedding ceremony. If their parents are not supportive, the couple may elope, and there is an institutionalized method for elopement:

> This elopement pattern often follows its own elaborate ritual, in which the couple runs away to a nearby village only to return after a short stay of a few days or weeks. Then the young man begs forgiveness from the young woman's parents. The parents nearly always agree to forgive, and typically an abbreviated ceremony is held. (Cherlin and Chamratrithirong 1993, p. 86)

With global Westernization, "love marriages" are replacing arranged marriage as the preferred way to select mates throughout the world (Sherif-Trask 2003). For instance, in the 1980s in Sri Lanka, researchers asked respondents whether they were in arranged marriages. Among those who were wed before 1940, 80 percent of the marriages had been arranged. Of those married in the early 1980s, only about one-quarter were arranged (Caldwell et al. 1993).

In another study (Levine et al. 1995), researchers asked 497 male and 673 female urban university undergraduates in ten countries and in Hong Kong the following question: If a man (woman) had all the qualities you desired, would you marry this person if you were not in love with him (her)? The results are presented in Figure 7.1. As you can see from that figure, of the eleven societies sampled, students in Pakistan were most likely to answer *yes;* 50.4 percent of them did so. Japanese students were least likely to say *yes,* but more than one-third (35.7 percent) said they were undecided. In the United States, often considered the most individualistic society in the world, only 3.5 percent of the students said they would marry someone with whom they were not in love, and the highest proportion (85.9 percent) said that no, they would not.

Although the arranged marriage of this Syrian couple may be a world apart from the freely chosen marriage of this couple in the United States, bargaining has occurred in both of these unions. In arranged marriages, families and community do the bargaining, based on assets such as status, possessions, and dowry. In freely chosen marriages, the individuals perform a more subtle form of bargaining, weighing the costs and benefits of personal characteristics, economic status, and education.

The United States is an example of what cross-cultural researchers call a **free-choice culture**: People freely choose their own mates. Immigrants who come to the United States from more collectivist cultures, in which arranged marriages have been the tradition, face the situation of living with a divergent set of expectations for selecting a mate. Some immigrant parents arrange for spouses from their home country to marry their offspring. This is one type of **cross-national marriage**. Either the future spouse comes to the United States to marry the young person, or the young person travels to the home country for the wedding ceremony, after which the newlyweds usually live in the United

States (Dugger 1998). In this case, the marriage is typically characterized by the greater Westernization of one partner (the young person who has lived in the United States) and the spouse's simultaneous need to adjust to an entirely new culture and to marriage (Cottrell 1993).

Some children of immigrant parents will follow their parents' expectations and participate in arranged unions. Others will not. The case study "An East Indian–American Student's Essay on Arranged Marriages" illustrates this point. Arranged marriage was practiced throughout most of the world into the twentieth century—and in Western Europe well into the eighteenth century. The following section explores

Case Study

An East Indian–American Student's Essay on Arranged Marriages

The college student who wrote the following essay (in 1997) is the daughter of East Indian immigrants to California. Her essay points out that arranged marriages are experienced by some people in the United States today and also that arranged marriage is changing.

Normally [in the United States] when two people decide whether to get married they think about how much they love each other. This, however, is not the case in arranged marriages. . . . I interviewed a classmate, my parents, and my friend who have had marriages arranged for them. After interviewing these people I realized that not all arranged marriages work the same way. I will first discuss what I learned from my classmate.

My heart goes out to her. From what she told me, she has had to live a hard and lonely life because her parents wanted her to marry someone whom she did not love. Her mother is Portuguese and her father is Italian. When she was 14 years old, her father arranged for her to marry a 32-year-old man.

Actually, this man was first supposed to marry her older sister. Unfortunately, her sister died before the marriage went through. Since their father had already paid a dowry of money and land to the [prospective] groom, he decided to marry his younger daughter to this man.

My classmate never got a chance to meet her soon-to-be-husband. She had a picture of him and was told she could meet him on their wedding day. She was shocked and angry. . . . In an attempt to be in control of her own life, she refused to marry this man. For this reason she was beaten and whipped by her father. To this day she has scars on her back from her father's whip.

She left her parents to live with her godparents until she was able to support herself. She has been disowned by her own family. She has been taken out of her family's will; she has been told that she is a disgrace to the family. . . . Although she feels sorry for hurting her parents and going against their wishes, she does not regret what she did. She feels that people should have a

choice of whom they marry. She said, "You should always be true to your heart, don't ever cheat yourself." . . . She had a bad experience with arranged marriages and therefore wouldn't recommend them to anyone.

My parents, on the other hand, had an arranged marriage 23 years ago and are still married to this day. Their wedding day was the first time they saw each other, and even then it was just a quick glance. A mutual friend of both families mentioned to both [sets of] parents that their kids would be a good match. So my mom's parents went and interviewed my dad, without my mom being there. My grandparents took into consideration various things like my dad's height, weight, education, family background, age, income, house, and health. . . .

My dad's parents did the same thing to my mom. They went to see her without my dad to see whether they liked her. One of their main concerns was what their grandchildren would look like. So they wanted a tall, pretty, healthy wife for their son. Both sets of parents

how the idea of love before marriage developed in Western Europe.

"Love" Marriages

How did our notion of romantic love come about, and why is it assumed to be the basis for weddings in our society?

Courtly love (or romantic love) flourished during the Middle Ages. Most marriages in the upper levels of society during this period were based on pragmatic considerations involving property and family alliances (Stone 1980). Tender emotions were expressed in nonmarital relationships in which a knight worshipped his lady, and ladies had their favorites. These relationships involved a great deal of idealization, were not necessarily sexually consummated, and certainly did not require the parties to live together. In time, the ideology of romantic love was adapted to a situation for which it was probably much less suitable—marriage.

As urban economies developed and young people increasingly worked away from home, arranged mar-

agreed to the other's child, and the deal was made.

Both sets of my grandparents went home to tell their son and daughter that they were getting married. There were no questions asked by my parents. Out of respect for their parents, they agreed to be married. Actually, this is incorrect, because they didn't really agree; they couldn't have agreed [because] they were never asked. Basically they weren't given an option. However, neither of my parents argued; they just went along with their parents' wishes.

When I asked my parents if they were disappointed when they first saw each other on their wedding day, they said no. They did not fall in love at first sight either, but they thought their parents did a good job in finding them a spouse. . . .

I do believe that my parents love each other, not the way I love my husband, but they have more of a Pragma style of love [see Chapter 5] that emphasizes the practical, or pragmatic, element in human relationships and involves the rational assessment of a potential partner's assets and liabilities. Neither of my parents regret marrying each other even though they really didn't have much of a choice. They are happy with their lives, their children, and each other. . . .

As I mentioned earlier, my parents got married 23 years ago.

Arranged marriages in the East-Indian culture are a lot different today than they were back then. I have friends my own age who have had arranged marriages. Now they get the opportunity to actually meet the person whom their parents have in mind for them. Better yet, they get to decide whether or not they want to marry that person.

A friend of mine just went to India with her parents to get married. Once she got there she discovered that her family members had already picked out about fifteen different men from whom she could choose. She interviewed all of them with her parents. She crossed off the names of the ones she wasn't interested in and had a second interview with the remaining men on her list. With three men left on her list after the second interview, her parents decided that she could meet these men alone without any parent chaperons. . . .

She ended up liking one of them. She said she was very attracted to him. He was a dentist, tall, had a nice body, very polite, and treated her like a princess. She married this guy and brought him over to California. She couldn't be happier. She told me that she doesn't think that she would have ever been able to find such a wonderful husband without the help of her family. She is very grateful to them.

As for my two brothers and me, my parents have not necessarily expected us to have an arranged marriage. But before we do get married they want us to possess the best qualities, mainly a high education, good manners, respect for others, and high self-esteem which will enable us to choose a partner of equal qualities. . . . I did not have an arranged marriage. I married my husband because I truly loved him. However, before I made the decision to get married, I did try to make sure that we would be compatible and have similar goals.

I sometimes wonder what it would be like to have an arranged marriage. What would the wedding night be like? How could two people who don't really know each other or love each other make love? I did not feel comfortable enough to ask my parents or my friend about this. But it is something that I wonder about.

Critical Thinking

How do the arranged marriages that this student describes illustrate a collectivist society? How does each arranged marriage differ from the others described? Would you characterize the writer's friend's marriage as arranged, free-choice, or somewhere in between? Why? What are some advantages of arranged marriage? Some disadvantages? How do you think arranged marriage is changing, as a result of Westernization?

riages gave way to marriages in which individuals selected their own mates. Sentiment rather than property became the basis for unions (Shorter 1975). The strong emotional and personal qualities of romantic love were in keeping with the individualism and introspection characteristic of the evolving Protestant capitalistic society of Western Europe (Stone 1980).

In the absence of arranged marriages, love provided motivation for choosing mates and forming families, and thereby served important social functions. This continues to be true. The connection between love and marriage serves to harness unpredictable feelings for the service of society (Goode 1959; Greenfield 1969).

Intense romantic feelings may serve to get a married couple through bad times and are associated with greater marital happiness (Udry 1974; Wallerstein and Blakeslee 1995). However, the idealization and unrealistic expectations implicit in the ideology of romantic love may also cause problems. Many Americans expect romance to continue not only through courtship but in marriage, too. Combining the practical and economic elements of marriage with developing intimacy and love is, historically speaking, a new goal. Whether marriages are arranged or are "love" unions, we can think of choosing a marital partner as taking place in a "marriage market."

▪ The Marriage Market ▪

Imagine a large marketplace in which people come with goods to exchange for other items. In nonindustrialized societies, a person may go to market with a few chickens to trade for some vegetables. In modern societies, people attend hockey-equipment swaps, for example, trading outgrown skates for larger ones. People choose marriage partners in much the same way: They enter the **marriage market** armed with resources—their (or their children's, in the case of arranged marriages) personal and social characteristics—and then bargain for the best buy they can get.

We have seen that in many other cultures, parents arrange their children's marriages. Parents go through a bargaining process not unlike what takes place at a traditional village market. They make rationally calculated choices after determining the social status or position, health, temperament, and, sometimes, physical attractiveness of their prospective son- or daughter-in-law. In such societies the bargaining is obvious. Professional matchmakers often serve as investigators and go-betweens, just as we might engage an attorney or a stockbroker in an important business deal.

Sometimes, as in the Hmong culture, the exchange involves a **bride price**, money or property that the future groom pays the future bride's family so that he can marry her. More often the exchange is accompanied by a **dowry**, a sum of money or property brought to the marriage by the female. As one example, Asian Indians have traditionally practiced the dowry system. A woman with a large dowry can expect to marry into a higher-ranking family than can a woman with a small dowry, and dowries are often increased to make up for qualities considered undesirable (Kaplan 1985, pp. 1–13). For instance, parents in eighteenth-century England increased the dowries of daughters who were pockmarked.

The difference between arranged marriages and marriages in free-choice cultures seems so great that we are inclined to overlook an important similarity: Both involve bargaining. What has changed in free-choice societies is that individuals, not the family, do the bargaining.

Exchange Theory

The ideas of bargaining, market, and resources used to describe relationships such as marriage come to us from **exchange theory**, discussed in Chapter 3. Recall that the basic idea of exchange theory is that whether or not relationships form or continue depends on the rewards and costs they provide to the partners. Individuals, it is presumed, want to maximize their rewards and avoid costs, so when there are choices, they will pick the relationship that is most rewarding or least costly. The analogy is to economics, but in romantic and marital relationships individuals are thought to have other sorts of resources to bargain besides money: physical attractiveness, personality, family status, skills, emotional supportiveness, cooperativeness, intellect, originality, and so on. Individuals also have costly attributes: being irritable or demanding, ineptitude, low social status, geographic inaccessibility (a major consideration in modern society), and so on. If each individual adopts a strategy of maximizing outcomes, then stable relationships will tend to exist between people who have like amounts of resources because they will strike a fair balance or bargain.

One weakness of exchange theory is its assumption of rationality. Are people actually so calculating about rewards and costs, even at an unconscious level? Further, in an exchange analysis, what is rewarding and what is costly? It varies with the individual.

Descriptions of exchange behavior are reminiscent of traditional arranged marriages. Nevertheless, even for the majority of Americans who choose their own partners, we present an exchange perspective as a useful tool. In fact, the basic structures of American life channel men and women into roles that have certain consequences for marital partnerships. We need to be aware of an underlying exchange structure of intimate relationships and marital ties. We'll look now at an exchange version of marital choice.

The Traditional Exchange

Individuals may bargain such characteristics as social class, age, physical attractiveness, and education, but the basic marital exchange traditionally has been related to gender. Historically, women have traded their ability to bear and rear children and perform domestic duties, along with sexual accessibility and physical attractiveness, for a man's protection, status, and economic support. Even though more and more women are gaining status by means of their own careers or professions, many women continue to expect greater financial success from their future husbands than vice versa and perhaps to attain a higher status by marrying than they would have as single individuals supporting themselves (Buss, Shackelford, Kirkpatrick, and Larsen 2001; Twenge 1997b). For example, for some women, being a school principal's wife may offer higher status than being a teacher or secretary.

Evidence from classified personal ads shows that the traditional exchange still influences heterosexual relationships. Men are more likely to advertise for a physically attractive woman and women for an economically stable man (Buss et al. 2001, p. 496). Moreover, the traditional exchange characterizes marriages in many immigrant groups that have recently arrived in the United States (Hill, Ramirez, and Dumka 2003).

Both women and men can experience gender-related disadvantages in the traditional exchange. For one thing, men can exchange their occupational *potential* for marital security, taking their time to shop for a partner. Women, on the other hand, lose an important advantage with time, because a female's traditional bargaining assets of physical attractiveness and childbearing capacity are given less value as she ages. Nevertheless, in a poor economy, men have disadvantages as well. National data that looked at black, Hispanic, and white males found that the probability of a man's getting married largely depends on his earning power (Manning and Smock 2002). Hence, in tough economic times the traditional exchange may work against males who would like to marry but cannot find good jobs.

THE MARRIAGE GRADIENT Closely related to the traditional exchange is a phenomenon called the **marriage gradient**—the tendency for women to marry "up" with regard to age, education, occupation, and earning potential. The marriage gradient has traditionally helped to shape marital choice.[3] For example, in about 57 percent of U.S. married couples, the husband is two or more years older than his wife; however,

the wife is older in only 11 percent of today's unions (U.S. Census Bureau 2000, Table 56). And it's curious that the marriage gradient is at work with such an apparently inconsequential factor as height; in a heterosexual relationship, a male is expected to be taller than a female.

More consequential for marriage and family dynamics is that in more than two-thirds of dual-earner marriages today, the husband earns more than his wife (AmeriStat 2003d). Much of this difference is due to societal and family dynamics *after* marriage, as discussed in Chapter 12. However, we can also assume that the marriage gradient is at work, encouraging at least some women to prefer men who make more than they do. Where the marriage gradient persists with regard to education and earning potential, the practice sets the stage for greater marital power for husbands than for wives, because educational attainment and earnings are related to power in marriages. Marital power is fully explored in Chapter 14.

Bargaining in a Changing Society

"As gender differences in work and family roles blur, individuals' criteria for an acceptable mate are likely to change" (Raley and Bratter 2004, p. 179). For instance, research that looked at mate preferences in the United States over the past sixty years shows that men and women—but especially men—have increased the importance they put on potential financial success in a mate, while domestic skills in a future wife have declined in importance (Buss et al. 2001; Siegel 2004).

This trend is apparent with regard to education. Rather than marrying "down" in education, as might be expected in the traditional exchange, college-educated men are now more likely to marry college-educated women. Researchers suggest that this situation is due to "increasing competition in the marriage market for wives with good prospects in the labor market" (Mare 1991, p. 15; Raley and Bratter 2004). When social scientists examine exchange in light of today's job market and changing gender roles, some see continuing disadvantages for women, others speculate that new limitations for both men and women are emerging, and still others point to positive outcomes.

CONTINUING DISADVANTAGES FOR WOMEN This view pays attention to the substantial inequalities that remain, particularly women's marginal position in

---

3. Note that the marriage-gradient process takes place within culturally accepted limits. Regarding age, for example, most marriages are characterized by an age difference of no more than three or four years (U.S. Census Bureau 2000, Table 56).

"We'll always have the food court."

the economic system (Wax 1998). Although women have entered the labor market in large numbers, their jobs and incomes are inferior, on average, to those of men. Although social expectations are generally moving toward androgyny, men continue to hold the advantage regarding access to financial security and status. Meanwhile, many of the bargaining chips that women have traditionally brought to the marriage market—children, domestic services, sexual accessibility—have been devalued because they are now available to unmarried men as well as to husbands (Sassler and Goldscheider 2004, p. 140).

EMERGING NEW LIMITATIONS FOR BOTH MEN AND WOMEN Meanwhile, if not only women, but also men, express a desire to marry "up," the pool of eligibles in the marriage market becomes seriously unbalanced. "If both men and women hope to improve their financial status by marrying a higher-earning spouse, it will take longer for both to find a suitable mate and more people will never marry" (Raley and Bratter 2004, p. 175). Analyzing National Survey of Family and Households (NSFH) data (see Chapter 2), sociologists R. Kelly Raley and Jenifer Bratter found that both men and women "are most willing to marry someone with more education or who earns more money" (2004, p. 175). Meanwhile, since the 1980s, even for some college graduates, many available jobs neither pay well nor offer benefits, such as health insurance. Therefore, "having a job might no longer be enough" to be a good prospective mate (Sassler and Goldscheider 2004, p. 143). In the estimation of Raley and Bratter, "[T]he mate selection process might have changed in ways that make it difficult for young adults to find a good match, especially during their early 20s. . . . If both sexes are looking to marry hypergamously, there is a mismatch between the preferences of men and women" (2004, p. 168).

POSITIVE OUTCOMES Nevertheless, some social scientists have pointed out that as gender roles become more alike, exchange between partners may increasingly include "expressive, affective, sexual, and companionship resources" for both partners. In fact, a high-earning woman might bargain for a nurturing, although lower-wage-earning, husband (Sprecher and Toro-Morn 2002). More often, as women approach occupational and economic equality with men, the exchange can become more symmetrical, with women and men increasingly looking for similar characteristics—emotional sensitivity and earning potential—in each other (Buss et al. 2001). Marriages based on both partners' contributing roughly equal economic and status resources are more egalitarian. Changes in men's roles toward greater emotional expressiveness may improve marital communication and satisfaction.

The fact that college-educated women and men tend to marry each other, as discussed above, raises another factor shaping marital choice—the tendency of people to marry others with whom they share certain social characteristics. Social scientists term this phenomenon *homogamy*.

Homogamy: Narrowing the Pool of Eligibles

Not everyone who enters the marriage market is equally available to everyone else. Americans, like many other people, tend to make marital choices in socially patterned ways, viewing only certain others as potentially suitable mates. The market analogy would be to choose only certain stores at which to shop. For each shopper there is a socially defined **pool of eligibles**: a group of individuals who, by virtue of background or birth, are considered most likely to make compatible marriage partners.

Americans tend to choose partners who are like themselves in many ways. This situation is called **homogamy**: People tend to marry people of similar race, age, education, religious background, and social class. For instance, not only do college graduates more often marry each other; so do people without college educations (Albrecht et al. 1997; Qian 1998). Analysis of census data has found evidence of increased educational homogamy since the 1930s (Qian 1998). As another example, traditionally, the Protestant, Catholic, and Jewish religions, as well as the Muslim and Hindu religions, have all encouraged **endogamy**: marrying within one's own social group. (The opposite of endogamy is **exogamy**, marrying outside one's group, or **heterogamy**, marrying someone dissimilar in race, age, education, religion, or social class.) Age and educational heterogamy have been more pronounced among blacks than among whites, partly because an "undersupply" of marriageable black men prompts black women to marry down educationally and to marry considerably older or younger men (Surra 1990, p. 848).

In spite of the trend toward less religious homogamy and a lessened tendency of European Americans—such as Irish, Italians, or Poles—to marry within their own ethnic group, homogamy is still a strong force (Kalmijn 1998). In 2002, only about 6 percent of U.S. marriages involved spouses of different races or a Hispanic married to a non-Hispanic (U.S. Census Bureau 2003a, Table 62). With regard to racial/ethnic intermarriage, 98 percent of non-Hispanic whites marry other non-Hispanic whites, and 94 percent of African American couples are racially homogeneous (Qian 1997). About 60 percent of Asian Americans and 75 percent of Hispanics marry within their group (del Pinal and Singer 1997, p. 29). However, nearly 54 percent of Native Americans marry outside their race, and more than 80 percent of Arab Americans marry outside their ethnicity, mostly to whites (Pollard and O'Hare 1999; Kulczycki and Lobo 2002).

Social scientists point out that although people today are marrying across small class distinctions, they still are not doing so across large ones. For instance, individuals of established wealth seldom marry the poor. All in all, an individual is most likely to marry someone who is similar in basic social characteristics. Let's look at a hypothetical case to see why this may be so.

Reasons for Homogamy

Rose is attracted to Alexander (and vice versa), who is a college student (like herself), two years older, and single. Rose's parents are upper-middle class. They live in the expensive section of her hometown, have a housekeeper, drink wine with their meals, and frequently have parties by their pool. Catholic, they go to Mass every Sunday. Alexander's parents are upper-lower class. They are separated. His mother lives in an apartment and works as a checker in a supermarket. The family drinks soft drinks at mealtime, then watches TV. They believe in "being good people," but do not belong to any organized religion.

How likely is it that Rose and Alexander will marry? If they do marry, what sources of conflict might occur? We can help to answer these questions by exploring four related elements that influence both initial attraction and long-term happiness. These elements—geographic availability, social pressure, feeling at home, and a fair exchange—are important reasons that many people are homogamous.

These Hmong immigrants in St. Paul, Minnesota, are celebrating the Hmong New Year, which also serves as a courting ritual. As in Laos, teenagers line up— boys on one side, girls on the other—and play catch with desirable potential mates. Catching the ball begins conversation. Tossing the ball gives girls a chance to meet boys under conditions approved by their parents. In Minnesota, however, the traditional Laotian black cloth ball is often replaced with a fluorescent tennis ball (Hopfensperger 1990, p. 1B). Because virtually all participants are Hmong, the ritual helps to ensure racial/ethnic homogamy.

GEOGRAPHIC AVAILABILITY **Geographic availability** (traditionally known as **propinquity** in the marriage and family literature) has typically been a reason that people tend to meet others who are a lot like themselves. Geographic segregation, which can result from discrimination or from strong community ties, contributes to homogamous marriages. Intermarriage patterns within the American Jewish community are an example. Until the 1880s, the small size of this group and its geographic dispersal limited the availability of Jewish marriage partners and led to frequent marriages with non-Jews. The large Jewish migration from eastern Europe that began in the late nineteenth century changed this pattern. Immigrants tended to settle together in Jewish neighborhoods; for this reason, among others, intermarriage rates dropped (William Petschek National Jewish Family Center 1986). Only about 6 percent of Jews married non-Jews in the late 1950s. Now that the barriers that used to exclude Jews from certain residential areas and colleges are gone, about half marry Gentiles (Stern 2003).

Geographic availability also helps to account for educational (Stevens 1991) and social-class homogamy. Middle-class people live in neighborhoods with other middle-class people. They socialize together and send their children to the same schools; upper- and lower-class people do the same. Unless they had met in a large, public university or online, it is unlikely that Alexander and Rose would have become acquainted at all.

Racial/ethnic and educational homogamy are strong forces in marriages, partly because people who share these social characteristics tend to "feel at home" together. Social pressure also plays a part and, despite some changes, may remain a significant factor.

© Lonnie Duka/Index Stock Imagery

Today, first encounters may occur in cyberspace, and people meet others as far away as other countries.[4] Curiously, however, the Internet may actually encourage homogamy among some ethnic groups, such as Jews, who can advertise online for dating partners of the same ethnicity (e.g., www.jewishconnect.com). Moreover, online daters' mutual ability to access the Internet and then to travel, if necessary, to meet each other face-to-face assures some degree of educational and/or financial homogamy.

SOCIAL PRESSURE A second reason for homogamy is social pressure. Our cultural values encourage people to marry others socially similar to themselves and discourage marrying anyone too different: Rose's parents, friends, and siblings are not likely to approve of Alexander because he doesn't exhibit the social skills and behavior of their social class (Blackwell 1998). Meanwhile, Alexander's mother and friends may say to him, "Rose thinks she is too good for us. Find a girl more like our own kind."

Sometimes, social pressure results from a group's concern for preserving its ethnic or cultural identity.

When young Jews, particularly college students, began to intermarry more often in the 1960s, Jewish leaders became concerned (Stern 2003; "Tracing" 2003). Recent immigrants, such as various Arab, Asian, or Hispanic groups, may pressure their children to marry within their own ethnic group in order to preserve their unique culture (Kitano and Daniels 1995; Lee 1998; "One Hundred Questions" n.d.). Whether blatant or subtle, social pressure toward homogamy can be forceful. As discussed in Chapter 1, making knowledgeable choices involves recognizing the strength of social pressures and deciding whether to act in accordance with them.

FEELING AT HOME People often feel more at home with others from similar education and class or ethnic backgrounds; couples from different social groups may struggle to communicate and may feel uncomfortable (Blackwell 1998). With regard to social-class differences, Alexander is likely to have different attitudes, mannerisms, and vocabulary from Rose. Rose won't know how to dress or behave in Alexander's hangouts and among his friends. Each may feel uncomfortable and out of place in the surroundings the other considers natural.

Members of the same ethnic group may also share common memories or experiences such that being

---

4. We know of no research on the effect of the Internet on homogamous relationships or marriages, and we'd like to suggest that this question would be a good one for future research—perhaps yours.

together provides them a sense of mutual understanding and comfort. For instance, in an assigned essay, Hmong student True See Chang described his family's 1975 exodus from Laos, his southeast Asian homeland, as the United States withdrew from the war in Vietnam:

> It was dreadful now that everyone was trying to find their loved one or observing the war zones left behind by the American soldiers to the Vietnamese and the Communist Lao government. My father came back from the war headquarters to find his home torn apart and in ruins. My mother desperately searched for him in the crowd. . . . Within the next hour, the soldiers from the government will [sic] come and execute everyone who did not leave. In desperation, everyone packed up what they could carry and headed toward the Mekong River to cross over into Thailand. Those who refused to leave were never heard from again. (Chang 1999)

Chang may feel more at home with a partner who shares his cultural background and understands these historical events because of similar personal experiences. Researchers have come to similar conclusions regarding Holocaust survivors (Lev-Wiesel and Amir 2003).

STRIKING A FAIR EXCHANGE As previously noted, exchange theory suggests that people tend to marry others whose social currency—social class, education, physical attractiveness—is similar to their own.

The questions that people ask on first meeting point up their concern with each other's exchange value. They want to know whether their prospective dates are married or single, where they are employed, whether they attend college and where, what they plan to do upon graduation, where they live, and perhaps what kind of vehicle they drive. If prospective partners are single, they will be asked whether they are divorced or still single and, especially in the case of women, whether they have children and, if so, how many.

If meeting in the marriage market can sound like a job interview, maybe that's because in at least one important way it is: The goal is to strike a fair exchange. And even without the benefit of interviews, people learn to discern the social class of others through mannerisms, language, dress, and a score of other cues.

We've discussed some reasons for homogamy, but, as we pointed out earlier in this chapter, not all marriages are homogamous. *Heterogamy* refers to marriage between those who are different in race, age, education, religious background, or social class.

Examples of Heterogamy

How does marrying someone from a different religion, social class, or race/ethnicity affect a person's chances for a happy union? In answer to this, we first examine interfaith marriages, then look at interclass partnerships, and finally at interracial and interethnic unions.

INTERFAITH MARRIAGES It is estimated that about 30 percent of Jewish, 20 percent of Catholic, 30 percent of Mormon, 40 percent of Muslim, up to 40 percent of Catholic, and a higher percentage of Protestant adults and children in the United States live in interfaith or interdenominational households (Adler 1997a; D'Antonio, Hoge, Meyer, and Davidson 1999). Being highly educated seems to lessen individuals' commitment to religious homogamy (Petersen 1994).

Marriages are less homogamous if we consider couples' religion before the wedding. Many partners who originally differed in religion switch to make their religion the same as their future spouse's (Shatzmiller 1996). Religions that see themselves as the one true faith and people who adhere to a religion as an integral component of their ethnic/cultural identity (for example, some Catholics, Jews, and Muslims) are more likely to press a prospective spouse to convert (Smits, Ultee, and Lammers 1998). Often, religious bodies are concerned that children born into the marriage will not be raised in their religion (Adler 1997a).

Some switching, no doubt, also takes place because partners agree with the widely held belief that interreligious marriages tend not to be as successful as homogamous ones—a belief supported by research (Heaton and Pratt 1990; Maneker and Rankin 1993). One probable reason that religious homogeneity improves chances for marital success involves value consensus. Religion-based values and attitudes may come into play when negotiating leisure activities, child-raising methods, investing and spending money, housework, and appropriate roles for wives and husbands (Curtis and Elison 2002; Heaton and Pratt 1990). Meanwhile, analysis of data from a national random telephone survey of U.S. Christian households concluded that while marital satisfaction was less for interdenominational couples, the difference dis-

As this Jewish and Christian couple illustrates, when elements of propinquity and cultural pressure are overcome, heterogamous marriages do take place. Although some research shows that homogamous unions tend to be more stable than interreligious or interracial ones, a heterogamous couple may hold common values that will transcend differences in background, religion, or race.

© Ellen Denuto/Index Stock Imagery

appeared when the interdenominational couple had good communication skills and similar beliefs about child raising (Williams and Lawler 2003). One research team has attributed differences in marital happiness associated with religious homogeneity almost entirely to the positive effect of church attendance: Homogamously married partners go to church more often and at similar rates and, as a result, show higher marital satisfaction and stability (Heaton and Pratt 1990). Another study (Sheehan, Bock, and Lee 1990) used General Social Survey data from the National Opinion Research Center to compare Catholics in heterogeneous marriages with those in homogamous ones. Heterogamously married Catholics went to Mass less frequently, but this did *not* reduce marital satisfaction. These researchers concluded that

> the effect of church attendance on marital satisfaction in the general population may be due more to the integrative properties of couple-centered organizational participation than to the religious nature of the activity. Heterogamous couples in which one spouse is Catholic are unlikely to attend church together, and may compensate for this by engaging in other couple-centered activities that are equally effective in promoting marital solidarity. (p. 78)

In general, however, religious homogamy may "create a more integrated social network of relatives, friends,

and religious advisors" (Heaton and Pratt 1990, p. 192). This is also true, as is pointed out later in this section, for interracial marriages.

INTERCLASS MARRIAGES What about the marital satisfaction of partners in interclass unions? Researchers have tended to ignore this question in recent decades, focusing instead on interracial and interethnic unions (Kalmijn 1998). However, they have defined the concept of **hypergamy**—improving one's social and/or economic status by marrying up. The opposite, **hypogamy**, involves marrying down.

One study of marriage in urban Chicago (Pearlin 1975) found that partners experienced more stress in class-heterogamous unions. Maybe not surprisingly, the spouse who had married down was more stressed than the one who had married up. However, it is important to note that the relationship between stress and marrying down existed only when status striving was important to the individual. Those people for whom status was important and who had married down perceived their marriages more negatively—as less reciprocal, less affectionate, less emotionally supportive, and with less value consensus—than did those who had married up. In an exchange framework, the partner who had married down had not struck a good bargain in an important matter. For people for whom status was *not* important, neither marrying up nor down produced any difference in their evaluation of their marriages.

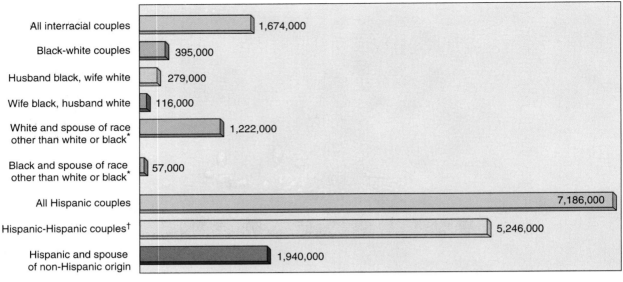

*Neither white nor black, but Asian, Native American, Aleut, Pacific Islander.

†Persons of Hispanic origin may be of any race.

FIGURE 7.2

Number of interracial and Hispanic–non-Hispanic married couples, 2002.

Source: U.S. Census Bureau 2003a, Table 62.

INTERRACIAL/INTERETHNIC MARRIAGES **In-terracial marriages** include unions between partners of the white, African American, Asian, or Native American races with a spouse outside their own race. Hispanics are not a separate race, but rather an ethnic group (see footnote 2, Chapter 2). Unions between Hispanics and others, as well as between different Asian/Pacific Islander or Hispanic ethnic groups (such as Thai–Chinese or Puerto Rican–Cuban), are considered **interethnic marriages**.

In June 1967 *(Loving v. Virginia)*, the U.S. Supreme Court declared that interracial marriages must be considered legally valid in all states. At about the same time, it became impossible to gather accurate statistics on interracial marriages. Many states no longer require race information on marriage registration forms, so these data are incomplete at best.

Available statistics show that the proportion of interracial and interethnic marriages is small (about 6 percent) but has steadily increased since 1970 (U.S. Census Bureau 1994a, Table 62; 2003, Table 62). If we count cohabiting couples, the proportion would be slightly higher because cohabiting couples are less homogamous than married couples (Heaton and Albrecht 1996).

Of all interracial (this does not count Hispanic–non-Hispanic) marriages in 2002, about 24 percent (395,000 couples) were black–white. The remainder, for the most part, were various combinations of whites or blacks with Asians, Native Americans, and others (see Figure 7.2). Seventy-one percent of black–white marriages involve black men married to white women (U.S. Census Bureau 2003a, Table 62).

Table 7.1 gives 1990 percentages of racially homogeneous marriages by education levels in the United States for couples in their twenties. As you can see from Table 7.1, whites and blacks are more inclined than are Hispanics or Asian Americans to marry within their racial/ethnic group. Education makes little difference in whether whites marry within their race. Among African American women who marry, education makes little difference in whether they do so within their race. However, college-educated black men are more likely than black men with less education to marry outside their race (Crowder and Tolnay 2000); the respective proportions of homogamous marriages are 90 percent compared with 94 percent.

Higher education decreases the likelihood that Hispanic men and women will marry homogamously. For example, 76 percent of Hispanic men with no high

Table 7.1

Percentage of Racially Homogamous Marriages, by Educational Attainment, for Married Individuals Aged 20–29 in 1990					
	EDUCATIONAL ATTAINMENT				
1990	No High School Diploma	High School Diploma	Some College	College Degree and More	Total
Whites					
Men (%)	98	98	98	98	98
Women (%)	97.5	98	98	98	98
African Americans					
Men (%)	94	93	91	90	92
Women (%)	97	97	97	96	97
Hispanics					
Men (%)	76	67	55	41	64
Women (%)	78	66	55	34	62.5
Asian Americans					
Men (%)	0	21	31	52	39
Women (%)	14	11	32	42	33.5

Source: Adapted from "Breaking the Racial Barriers: Variations in Interracial Marriage between 1980 and 1990" by Z. Qian, 1997, *Demography* 34 (2), 263–276. Copyright © 1997 by Population Association of America.

school diploma marry Hispanic women, while just 41 percent of Hispanic men with a college degree do so. However, Asian Americans show a different pattern: The highly educated are more likely to marry within their race (Qian 1997). Furthermore, Hispanics who marry outside their particular ethnic group (such as Mexican, Puerto Rican, Cuban, or Central–South American) are more likely to marry non-Hispanics than to marry other Hispanics of a different ethnicity (del Pinal and Singer 1997, pp. 28–29). This pattern is also true for Asian Americans (Fong and Yung 1995). For example, the majority of Koreans marry within their own ethnic group. When they do not, however, they are far more likely to marry non-Hispanic whites than to marry Chinese, Japanese, or Vietnamese partners (Hwang and Aguirre 1997). Many interethnic unions such as those between different Hispanic groups (for example, Colombian- and Mexican-American) or between Asian groups (for example, Chinese- and Japanese-American) go mostly unnoticed in the general society. Nevertheless, marriages like these do indeed cause partners to address cultural differences (Clemetson 2000).

Much attention has been devoted to why people marry interracially. One apparent reason among racial/ethnic groups that are relatively small in number is simply that they are more likely than larger racial/ethnic groups to interact with others of different races. This situation explains much of the reason why Asian Americans, for example, have lower homogamy rates than do whites, blacks, or Hispanics (Hwang and Aguirre 1997). Similarly, black–white marriages may be more numerous today simply because the races are interacting more ("Why Interracial" 1996; Yancey and Yancey 1998; Staples 1999c).

Another explanation is the **status exchange hypothesis**: the argument that an individual might trade his or her socially defined superior racial/ethnic status for the economically or educationally superior status of a partner in a less-privileged racial/ethnic group (Kalmijn 1998). Applying the status exchange hypothesis to black–white intermarriage would suggest marrying up socioeconomically on the part of a white person who, in effect, trades socially defined superior racial status for the economically superior status of a middle- or upper-middle-class black partner. Little research has been done to test this hypothesis, but a recent study of intermarriage among native Hawaiians, Japanese, Filipinos, and Caucasians in Hawaii supports the hypothesis (Fu and Heaton 2000). As a result of

© Frank Siteman/Index Stock Imagery

Not wanting to limit their social contacts—including potential marriage partners—to socially similar people, many Americans enter into ethnically heterogamous unions. Although many people may retain a warm attachment to their racial or ethnic community, and some ethnic groups strongly value homogamy, social and political change has been in the direction of breaking down those barriers. People committed to an open society find intermarriage to be an important symbol, whether or not it is a personal choice, and do not wish to discourage this option.

nese, native Hawaiians and Filipinos had to have higher economic or educational status than those who married within their own ethnic group. At the same time, Japanese and Caucasians who married native Hawaiians or Filipinos were "of lower status in their own group" (p. 53).

Some people believe that those with privileged racial/ethnic status marry interracially because of rebellion and hostility, guilt, or low self-esteem. Such explanations smack of racism and are not supported by research (Davidson 1992). Meanwhile, some African American sociologists have expressed concern about black men—especially educated black men—choosing spouses from other races (Crowder and Tolnay 2000; Staples 1994, 1999a). For example, Robert Davis, a past president of the Association of Black Sociologists, believes that black men are inclined to see white women as "the prize." In fact, he told a reporter for *Jet* magazine, "Some Black men will jump over three successful Black women just to be with a White woman" (Davis, quoted in "Why Interracial" 1996). Meanwhile, some African American women view black males' interracial relationships as "selling out"—sacrificing allegiance to one's racial heritage in order to date someone of higher racial status (Paset and Taylor 1991). In a paper on this topic, a female Mexican American student wrote the following:

> It is not just in the African-American community that this is happening. . . . I have noticed when a Mexican-American man gets educated, he usually ends up dating and marrying an Anglo female. Being with an Anglo female is more of a trophy to the Mexican man. . . . I would like to meet an educated Mexican male and date him but there are not that many around. I am not totally set on just dating a Mexican male, but you hardly see white males dating other races. Sometimes it seems there is little hope for Hispanic and African-American females to ever find a good partner. (Torres 1997)

Having said this, we note that at least one study of forty black–white interracially married couples found, simply, that "with few exceptions, this group's motives for marriage do not appear to be any different from those of individuals marrying . . . within their own race." The most common motives by far were love and compatibility (Porterfield 1982, p. 23).

historical events and cultural definitions, native Hawaiians and Filipinos have lower ethnic status in Hawaii than do Japanese or Caucasians. Examining marriage certificates in Hawaii from 1983 to 1994, the researchers found that to marry a Caucasian or a Japa-

Heterogamy and Marital Stability

Marital success can be measured in terms of stability—whether or how long the union lasts—and the happiness of the partners. Marital stability is not synonymous with marital happiness because, in some instances, unhappy spouses remain married, whereas less unhappy partners may choose to separate. In general, social scientists find that marriages that are homogamous in age, education, religion, and race are the most stable (Kalmijn 1998).

Meanwhile, just as information on interracial/interethnic marriages is incomplete, so is information on their divorces. Only about half the states and the District of Columbia report race/ethnicity on divorce records. What evidence we have is conflicting on whether interracial/interethnic marriages are more or less stable than intraracial/intraethnic unions. And although we have some census data on Hispanics who marry outside their ethnic group (Figure 7.1), we do not know the divorce rates for these interethnic couples.

We can offer at least three explanations for any differences in marital stability that may exist. First, significant differences in values and interests between partners can create a lack of mutual understanding, resulting in emotional gaps. One in-depth study of seventeen married interracial couples concluded that from the view of outsiders, the union is interracial. From the inside, however, the spouses themselves may see their union as "cross-cultural" (Johnson and Warren 1994).

Second, such marriages may create conflict between the partners and other groups, such as parents, relatives, and friends. Continual discriminatory pressure from the broader society may create undue marital stress. As one interracially married husband put it, "People's heads almost whiplashed off their necks when we walked down the street together" (quoted in Romano and Trescott 1992, p. 91). If they lack a supporting social network, partners may find it more difficult to maintain their union in times of crisis. "A Closer Look at Family Diversity: Strategies for Dealing with Others' Disapproval When You're in an Interracial Relationship" describes ways that interracial couples respond to other people's objections.

Finally, a higher divorce rate among heterogamous marriages may reflect the fact that these partners are likely to be less conventional in their values and behavior. Such unconventional people may divorce more readily than others.

Heterogamy and Human Values

It is important to note the difference between scientific information and values. Social science can tell us that the stability of heterogamous marriages may be lower than that of homogamous marriages, but many people do not want to limit their social contacts—including potential marriage partners—to socially similar people. Although many people may retain a warm attachment to their racial or ethnic community, and some ethnic groups strongly value homogamy, social and political change has been in the direction of breaking down those barriers. People committed to an open society find intermarriage to be an important symbol, whether or not it is a personal choice, and do not wish to discourage this option (Moran 2001).

From this perspective, we can think of the negative data on heterogamy and marital stability not as discouragements to marriage, but in terms of their utility in helping couples be aware of possible problems. Intermarrying couples such as Alexander and Rose may anticipate and talk through the differences in their lifestyles.

The data on heterogamy may also be interpreted to mean that common values and lifestyles contribute to stability. A heterogamous pair may have common values that transcend their differences in background. Furthermore, some problems of interracial (or other heterogamous) marriages have to do with social disapproval and lack of social support from either race. But individuals can choose to work to change the society into one in which heterogamous marriage will be more accepted and hence will pose fewer problems.

Moreover, to the degree that racially, religiously, or economically heterogamous marriages increase in number, they are less likely to be troubled by the reactions of society. Again, we see that private troubles—or choices—are intertwined with public issues; social changes are needed to make heterogamous marriages work. Some ethnic groups strongly value homogamy. Meanwhile, it is also true that if people are able to cross racial, class, or religious boundaries and at the same time share important values, they may open doors to a varied and exciting relationship.

Falling in love in a society such as ours, which emphasizes individualism and free choice of marriage partners, whether homogamous or heterogamous, usually involves developing an intimate relationship and establishing mutual commitment. The next section examines these ideas.

A Closer Look at Family Diversity

Strategies for Dealing with Others' Disapproval When You're in an Interracial Relationship

How do people in interracial dating relationships or marriages deal with the negative reactions they encounter from others? In a small, qualitative study, two researchers (Hill and Thomas 2000) asked four white and three black women in black–white heterosexual relationships to answer this question. The study used the interactionist perspective, described in Chapter 3. Six of the seven women in the study were married, and all of them had relationships lasting from three to twenty-six years.

After interviewing the seven women, the researchers categorized their responses as follows: (1) blocking strategies, (2) transforming strategies, and (3) generating strategies.

BLOCKING STRATEGIES
Blocking strategies are used to deflect negative responses from others either by *screening, discrediting,* or *directly confronting* the offending person or persons. A black woman described her screening activities this way:

> The friends I have now . . . are all [supportive]. If they're not, then I don't . . . hang out with them anymore. . . . And if they're talking about, "I hate this person 'cause this person is White" or "How can you trust White people?" . . . then that's just the end. (p. 196)

Discrediting includes thinking or saying things like "It's probably their own insecurities" or "I feel sorry for

people who have attitudes like that—they don't know any better" (p. 196). A woman who had been married more than twenty years described how, early in her relationship, she and her husband directly confronted offending others:

> People would look at us. And it would be obvious that they would be staring. . . . So [he] wouldn't hesitate . . . to just look straight at them and say, "Take a picture—it'll last longer." . . . He wanted me to do that. (p. 196)

This respondent explained that her husband wanted her to confront others because it "was a way of my saying that I was not ashamed of being with him."

Courtship in a Free-Choice Society

As romantic love has come to be associated with marriage, the responsibility for finding marital partners has increasingly fallen to individuals themselves. Typically in free-choice cultures, a wedding takes place only after a relationship has developed.

Developing the Relationship

In the United States, sociologists and social psychologists have been interested in how relationships develop during courtship. What first brings people together? What keeps them together?

AT FIRST MEETING: PHYSICAL ATTRACTIVE-NESS AND RAPPORT The majority of couples meet

for the first time in face-to-face encounters, such as when participating in a favorite activity or as students. But today, many people meet through newspaper singles ads, videodating services, or online (Cullen 2004). However individuals meet, what is it that draws one to another? When the first meeting is face-to-face, very often the answer is physical attractiveness (Buss 1994; Cowley 1996). Both women and men tend to see more socially desirable personality traits in people who are physically attractive, and an examination of research studies on mate preferences since 1939 shows that physical attractiveness has increased as a value over the past sixty years (Buss et al. 2001). In a 1999 Gallup poll of American adults, seven out of ten said that physical attractiveness is important today in terms of "happiness, social life, and the ability to get ahead." Nineteen percent of those polled said they would consider plastic surgery to improve their appearance

TRANSFORMING STRATEGIES

Blocking strategies simply defend individuals against other people's disapproving reactions, but **transforming strategies** reinterpret negative responses to define them differently. One transforming strategy that the researchers found was to redefine the situation from enduring others' hostility to being a role model. As one woman explained, "We do everything we can to project a positive image and try to be friendly to people." Another woman said, "We've always tried to be very visible . . . 'cause we wanted to show that we're okay, we don't fight, we're not high. Our kids are very respectful" (p. 197).

Furthermore, partners in interracial relationships, when out in public but not together, are often **masked**: Others don't know they are interracially involved. Being masked can expose a partner to stinging comments from the unwitting. The women redefined these masked situations from being misunderstood and vulnerable to being in disguise and detecting

racism. One respondent explained her strategy this way:

> I always think it's fun, when I first meet somebody, for them not to know I'm in an interracial relationship. . . . I always play that little game and listen for things they'll say before they find out and then listen after they find out and see how their reaction differs. (p. 197)

Another who used this strategy said, "It's funny to me 'cause I don't tell people until they see him. And they're like, 'You didn't tell us your husband was White.' [I respond,] 'I didn't ask you what color yours is'" (p. 197).

GENERATING STRATEGIES

Generating strategies are not direct reactions to any specific encounter but develop to generate partners' empowered feelings about their relationship. Cultivating close friend-and-family ties with those who are accepting of the relationship is a generating strategy. The study's couples also actively developed connections with other interracial families. As one woman said, "You feel comfortable being

around other mixed families because it makes you see that you're not alone . . ." (p. 197).

In discussing their findings, Hill and Thomas point out that each of their respondents had experienced some disapproval but actively worked to empower herself in her relationship. Findings from this study "indicate both a common theme of contending with racism and a diversity of successful outcomes" (p. 199).

Critical Thinking

This research focused on black–white interracial couples. To what extent do you think the concepts that Hill and Thomas developed might also apply to other interracial or to interethnic couples? Hill and Thomas discuss people's disapproval of interracial relationships as racism. Are there situations in which disapproving of an interracial or interethnic relationship would not stem from racism, in your opinion? Why or why not? When would you define disapproval as racist?

(Newport 1999).[5] Physical attractiveness is especially important in the early stages of a relationship (Buss et al. 2001).

Physical appeal and other readily apparent characteristics serve to attract people to each other and to spark an interest in getting acquainted, which leads to an initial contact (Buss 1994). But whether this initial interest develops into a prolonged attachment depends on whether the two people can develop rapport: Do

they feel at ease with each other? Are they free to talk spontaneously? Do they feel they can understand each other? When two people experience rapport, they may be ready to develop a loving relationship. Common values appear to play an important role, though whether in early stages only or throughout courtship is not clear. Couples also seem to be matched on sex drive and interest in sex (Murstein 1980), as well as on what sex means to them (Lally and Maddock 1994), suggesting that this is an important sorting factor.

Development of a face-to-face romantic relationship moves from initial encounter, often based on physical attractiveness, to discovery of similarities and self-disclosure, but meeting for the first time online is a bit different (Mulrine 2003). Internet relationships progress through "an inverted developmental sequence." That is, without first seeing one another, two people who find each other intriguing or interesting

---

5. A side effect of the media's and our general culture's increased emphasis on physical attractiveness—for women and, more recently, for men—is that men are increasingly dissatisfied with their appearance. In a 1999 Gallup poll that asked, "All in all, are you satisfied with how attractive you are, or do you often wish you could be more attractive?" 17 percent of men said they wished they were more attractive—up from 12 percent in 1990 (Newport 1999). In light of this, it is hardly surprising that the cosmetic and plastic surgery industries are growing for men as well as for women (Condor 2000; Davis and Vernon 2002; Haiken 2000).

Physical attraction may draw people together initially. After rapport develops, individuals who are considering marriage gradually filter out those who they believe would not make the best spouse.

gradually get to know one another through keyboard discussions. Over time, e-mails become more intimate, and a powerful rapport may be established:

> Intriguingly, unlike face-to-face relating, the importance of physical attractiveness as a relationship determinant, is minimized by the ability to know someone through intense mutual self-disclosure and intimate sharing of private world-views. In the end, with the presence of such heightened self-disclosure, these individuals may arrange to meet one another, occasionally with highly sexualized outcomes. (Merkle and Richardson 2000, p. 189)

Sociologist Andrea Baker sees the Internet "as a haven for the shy." In the words of a twenty-nine-year-old New Yorker interviewed for an article in *Time* magazine, "All of a sudden, there's a forum for meeting people that doesn't involve alcohol or staying out till 4 in the morning" (Kirn 2000, p. 73). (However, it's important to note here that meeting on the Net can be risky; e-mail dates can lie about themselves. Furthermore, counselors and others warn that the first several physical meetings should be arranged in the daytime and in public places, such as coffee shops, in order to protect oneself against possible physical danger.)

AS THE RELATIONSHIP PROGRESSES The wheel theory of love (Reiss and Lee 1988), described in Chapter 5, explains the role of rapport in the development of a relationship. It suggests that mutual disclosure, along with feelings of trust and understanding, are necessary early steps. As you may recall, this theory also posits that an important phase in developing love is "mutual need satisfaction." Along this line, social scientist Robert Winch (1958) once proposed the **theory of complementary needs**, whereby we are attracted to partners whose needs complement our own. Sometimes this is taken to mean that, psychologically, opposites attract. This idea makes intuitive sense to many of us, but social science researchers have found very little evidence to support complementary needs theory (Klohnen and Mendelsohn 1998). Some "needs theorists" argue that we are attracted to others whose strengths are *harmonious* with our own so that we are more effective as a couple than either of us would be alone (Epstein, Evans, and Evans 1994).

ASSORTIVE MATING—A FILTERING PROCESS Whatever the case regarding complementary or harmonious needs, individuals gradually filter out those in their pool of eligibles who, they think, would not make the best spouse. Research has consistently shown that people are willing to date a wider range of individuals than they would become engaged to or live with, and they are willing to live with a wider range of persons than they would marry (Jepsen and Jepsen 2002; Schoen and Weinick 1993). For instance, one study has found that women are less likely to consider the economic prospects of their male partners when deciding whether to cohabit than when deciding about marriage (Manning and Smock 2002). Social psychologists call this process **assortive mating**. As an

© Bob Winsett/Index Stock Imagery

example of assortive mating, we saw earlier in this chapter that men today are more likely than in the past to sift, or sort out, women with poor financial prospects and less likely to sort out messy housekeepers. Some social scientists have proposed that people go through a three-stage filtering sequence, called **SVR**—for **stimulus–values–roles** (Murstein 1986).

In the *stimulus stage*, interaction depends upon physical attraction. In the *values stage*, partners compare their individual values and determine whether these are appropriately matched. For instance, they might explore their views on marital fidelity, abortion, racism, the value of a college education, the environment, personal ambition, and work. Today it's not uncommon for a couple to explore whether both partners value getting married at all (to anyone) or would prefer an ongoing, unmarried relationship (Marech 2004a). If both partners find a satisfactory degree of values consensus, they proceed to the final stage, that of exploring *role compatibility*. Here the prospective spouses test and negotiate how they will play their respective marital and leisure roles (Houts, Robins, and Huston 1996). It is possible, of course, that the courtship process will break down at either the values or the role compatibility stage; if it does not, however, the assumption is that the filtering process ends with one chosen partner.

Relationships leading to marriage do not always show these rational characteristics, however. In lengthy interviews with 116 individuals in "premarital relationships," two social scientists examined the process by which these partners gradually committed to marriage (Surra and Hughes 1997). From the interviews, the researchers classified the respondents' relationships in two categories: *relationship-driven* and *event-driven*.

Relationship-driven couples followed the rationally evolving pattern described above. But in event-driven relationships, partners vacillated between commitment and ambivalence. Often they disagreed on how committed they were as well as why they had become committed in the first place. The researchers called this relationship type event-driven because events—fighting, discussing the relationship with one's own friends, and making up—punctuated each partner's account.

It's probably no surprise that event-driven couples' satisfaction with the relationship fluctuated over time. Often recognizing their relationships as rocky, they do not necessarily break up, because positive events (for example, a discussion about getting married or an ex-

pression of approval of the relationship from others) typically follow negative ones.

Attachment Theory

Attachment theory (also discussed in Chapter 5) posits that during infancy and childhood, individuals develop a general style of attaching to others (Bowlby 1969, 1982; Fletcher 2002). Responding to and modeling their primary caretakers, children learn and gradually take for granted one of three attachment styles: secure, insecure/anxious, or avoidant. Children who trust that their needs will be met form a secure attachment style; children who feel abandoned are likely to acquire an insecure/anxious or an avoidant attachment style. By adulthood, these attachment styles—partly conscious and partly unconscious—have generated broad expectations about oneself and one's partner in close relationships. Adults with a secure attachment style are inclined to trust that their relationships will provide ongoing emotional support. Adults with an insecure/anxious attachment style worry that their beloved will leave or betray them, a situation often described as "fear of abandonment." Adults with an avoidant attachment style duck, or evade, emotional closeness (Fletcher 2002; Main 1996; Simpson and Rholes 1998).

Applying attachment theory to our current discussion about getting to know a partner and gaining commitment, we might presume that persons with secure attachment styles would have little ambivalence about commitment. Those with insecure or distant attachment styles would be more likely to have dating relationships beset by conflicts about emotional closeness and commitment. The vast majority of psychological research on relationships is done on college students, and we can't be sure whether the findings also apply to older persons. But in one study, research on eighteen- and nineteen-year-olds in their first years of college found that those with less-secure attachment styles had more trouble managing conflict in their romantic relationships (Creasey, Kershaw, and Boston 1999). Similar to partners in the event-driven relationships described in the section above, less-secure individuals would be expected to waver between commitment and ambivalence, a conflict-causing situation.

Psychologists using attachment theory would explain event-driven (as well as relationship-driven) relationships as influenced by early childhood experiences. Meanwhile, sociologists have wondered to what extent society's courtship process encourages conflict and ambivalence about making commitments. In the next section, we discuss American **courtship**, the process through which the couple develops a mutual commitment. We contrast getting together and cohabitation.

Getting to Know Someone and Gaining Commitment

Traditionally courtship has had two purposes: (1) for romantic partners to try to get to know each other better, and (2) to gain each other's progressive commitment to marriage.

These two purposes can be at odds. On the one hand, courtship is supposed to lead to self-disclosure and intimacy (Campbell 2004). On the other hand, gaining a partner's commitment to marriage often involves marketing oneself in the best possible package. In the next sections, we will contrast three styles of courtship that are familiar to Americans today: the traditional ritual of dating, getting together, and cohabitation. We will see that each of these courtship styles emphasizes one over the other of these two purposes: self-disclosure and marketing oneself.

DATING AND "GETTING TOGETHER" The dating system emerged in our society at the beginning of the twentieth century, prevailed through the 1950s and early 1960s, became less popular in the late 1960s and early 1970s, and appears to have become somewhat popular again since the 1980s. Dating consists of an exclusive relationship developed between two people through a series of appointed meetings. Of course, dating can be just for fun! However, when they lead to marriage, dating relationships develop through evolving, progressive commitment, along with increasing emphasis on sexual exclusivity.

By the 1970s, an alternative to dating had emerged—"getting together" (Libby 1976). **Getting together** is a courtship process in which, unlike dating, groups of women and men congregate at a party or share an activity. Getting together de-emphasizes relating solely to one member of the opposite sex. In getting together, females may play a similar role to males, initiating relationships and suggesting activities. Meetings are often less formal than in the traditional date.

These changes in how women and men relate to one another are associated with changing attitudes toward marriage itself. Remaining single, at least for a

© Peter Langone/Index Stock Imagery

The dating tradition that began in the early twentieth century continues to exist, although there's no doubt that it has changed some. Meanwhile, relationships that are based on more casual forms of getting together have emerged. As a courtship process, "getting together" may allow for greater spontaneity and openness. If intimacy does develop, then individuals may already have a strong sense of each other's personality, moods, and values.

good part of one's twenties, is an attractive alternative for many today. As a result, people who are freed somewhat from the pressure to date and to marry can be more casual and spontaneous with each other. They are less likely to focus so intensely on being liked or accepted by the other person and more likely to see each other in a variety of settings and moods (Murstein 1986, p. 67).

As a courtship process, getting together places less emphasis on the end result, marriage, than dating does. Ironically, this de-emphasis may be effective, as it allows people to choose partners whom they really know and could be happily married to.

MARGARET MEAD'S CRITICISMS OF DATING AS COURTSHIP In 1949, anthropologist Margaret Mead severely criticized the dating pattern that had emerged in the United States. She perceived the process not as one in which two people genuinely try to get to know each other, but rather as a competitive game in which Americans, preoccupied with success, try to be the most popular and have the most dates. Sociologist Willard Waller (1937) had earlier termed this "rating and dating."

Mead saw at least two major problems in dating. First, it encourages men and women to define heterosexual relationships as situational, rather than ongoing: "You 'have a date,' you 'go out with a date,' you groan because 'there isn't a decent date in town'" (Mead 1949, p. 276). Because dating is formalized, women and men—even as they approach marriage—see each other only at appointed times and places. Partners look and behave their best during a date; they seldom share their "backstage behavior."[6]

Second, sex becomes depersonalized and genitally oriented, rather than oriented to the whole person; that is, the salient question becomes whether a couple "went all the way"—or whether the male is "getting any"—rather than how much emotional and sensual rapport the partners share. In a similar spirit, though not connected to Mead's writings that we know of, some fundamentalist Christian writers propose a different courtship pattern. Here, "If a young man is interested in a young woman, he starts by praying about the relationship. With a go-ahead from the Lord and his parents, he then approaches the girl's parents." Before the couple begins spending time together, the young woman's father and the interested young man spend time getting to know each other. Parents of both parties would focus on their child's prospective partner's "spiritual depth, strong biblical character, financial responsibility, sexual and emotional purity, and the ability to lead a simple practical life." Courtship activities would often involve family activities, not just couple activities (Ryan and Ryan 1995, p. 12).

Mead's criticisms of dating led her to propose instead what she called the **two-stage marriage**. As the name suggests, two-stage marriage consists of two sequential types of marriage, each with a different license, different ceremony, and different responsibilities. The first stage, called *individual marriage*, involves "serious commitment . . . in which each partner would have a deep and continuing concern for the happiness of the other" (Mead 1966, p. 50). It limits responsibilities, however, because the couple agrees not to have children during this time. The second stage, *parental marriage*, would follow only if the partners decided they wanted to continue their relationship and share the responsibility of children. Mead's proposal is much like the choice that some couples make today to live together to assess their compatibility before marrying. We now turn to what has in many cases become another form of courtship—cohabitation (Teachman 2003).

Cohabitation and Marriage

Since the 1970s, the proportion of marriages preceded by cohabitation has grown steadily so that by 1995, this was true of a majority of marriages (Bumpass and Sweet 1989; Bumpass and Lu 2000). However, cohabitation serves different purposes for different couples: Living together "may be a precursor to marriage, a trial marriage, a substitute for marriage, or simply a serious boyfriend–girlfriend relationship" (Bianchi and Casper 2000, p. 17). Cohabitation as an alternative to marriage is explored in Chapter 9. This section addresses cohabitation as courtship. We will explore answers to two questions: (1) What are the odds of a cohabiting relationship ending with marriage? and (2) How does cohabiting affect marital quality later?

COHABITATION AND THE LIKELIHOOD OF MARRIAGE During the 1990s, the proportion of cohabitors who eventually married their partners declined (Seltzer 2000, p. 1252). As discussed in Chapter 9, this is probably because cohabiting has become more socially acceptable, a cultural change that "contributes to a decline in cohabiting partners' expectations about whether marriage is the 'next step' in their

---

6. Using the interactionist theoretical perspective (Chapter 3), sociologist Erving Goffman (1959), in *The Presentation of Self in Everyday Life,* differentiated between people's frontstage and backstage behavior. Frontstage behavior is what we show the public; backstage behavior is more private. We can think of individuals' grooming rituals—shaving, doing their hair, applying makeup—as taking place backstage. They are preparations for meeting one's audience. Developing intimacy involves gradually allowing another person to see more of one's backstage behavior.

Table 7.2

Cohabiting Couples: The Varied Paths They Take				
		OUTCOME OF RELATIONSHIP AFTER 5 TO 7 YEARS		
Type of Relationship in 1987–1988	All Couples Percent	Still Live Together[1]	Married[2]	Separated[3]
All unmarried couples	100	21	40	39
Substitute for marriage	10	39	25	35
Precursor to marriage	46	17	52	31
Trial marriage	15	21	28	51
Co-residential dating	29	21	33	46

Note: Couples were interviewed between 1987 and 1988, and again from 1992 to 1994.

[1] Couple was still cohabiting at the time of the second survey.
[2] Got married some time between the two surveys (may or may not be currently married).
[3] No longer cohabiting.

Source: L. M. Casper and L. C. Sayer, "Cohabitation Transitions: Different Attitudes and Purposes, Different Paths." (Paper presented at the annual meeting of the Population Association of America, Los Angeles. March 2000.) Reprinted with permission from the Population Reference Bureau.

own relationship" (p. 1249). What are the odds these days of a cohabiting relationship ending with marriage?

Demographers surveyed cohabiting couples in 1987–1988 and then again between 1992 and 1994. Some of the results are summarized in Table 7.2. When first surveyed, 46 percent of the respondents defined their cohabiting relationship as a "precursor to marriage," and another 15 percent said they were in a "trial marriage." (Very probably, those who saw their relationship as a "precursor to marriage" had already decided that their partner would be their future spouse, whereas those who said that they were in a "trial marriage" were less sure.) When surveyed again five to seven years later, a little more than half (52 percent) of the couples who had seen cohabiting as a precursor to marrying had done so; however, almost one-third of them (31 percent) had separated. Another 17 percent were still cohabiting. Of those who had said they were in a trial marriage, 28 percent were married five to seven years later, while slightly more than half (51 percent) had separated. The researchers concluded that "Those with the strongest commitment to one another and to marriage were most likely to get married" (Bianchi and Casper 2000, p. 17).

We might further conclude from these findings that there is a slightly higher than even chance that people who live together with the belief that their arrangement is a "precursor to marriage" will indeed marry. The odds are considerably lower for those who

cohabit as a "trial marriage." Interestingly, more survey respondents who characterized their relationship as a trial marriage were separated five to seven years later (51 percent) than were those who said they were simply in a co-residential dating relationship (46 percent). Why might this be? One hypothesis is that couples who said they were in a trial marriage responded that way because they were indeed wary about their compatibility, a wariness that proved to be warranted. Then too, we cannot tell from the data presented here to what extent coupled partners agreed with each other on their reasons for cohabiting. Hence, a second hypothesis would be that couples who said they were in trial marriages experienced conflicts over commitment to marriage—and more so than those who saw their relationship simply as co-residential dating. For those who do marry, how does cohabiting affect marital quality?

COHABITATION AND MARITAL QUALITY In line with Margaret Mead's assumption, many people today follow the intuitive belief that "cohabitation is a worthwhile experiment for evaluating the compatibility of a potential spouse, [and therefore] one would expect those who cohabit first to have even more stable marriages than those who marry without cohabiting . . ." (Seltzer 2000, p. 1252). Perhaps surprisingly, however, there has been little research on whether cohabitation that is limited only to one's future spouse increases the odds of marital success. At this time, we can report that analysis of a nationally representative sample of 6,577 women who married for the first time between 1970 and 1995 has found that premarital cohabitation that was limited to the woman's future husband did not increase the couple's likelihood of divorce (Teachman 2003).

Meanwhile, research over the past twenty years consistently shows that marriages preceded by more than one instance of cohabitation are more likely to end in separation or divorce than marriages in which the spouses had not previously cohabited at all (DeMaris and MacDonald 1993; Dush, Cohan, and Amato 2003; Seltzer 2000; Teachman 2003). Why might serial cohabitation before marriage be related to lower marital stability? Hypotheses to answer this question can be divided into two categories, both of which are supported to some degree by recent research studies.

First, the **selection hypothesis** assumes that individuals who choose serial cohabitation (or who "select" themselves into cohabiting situations) are different from those who do not; these differences translate into higher divorce rates. For instance, one study has found that men and women who choose to cohabit have less effective problem-solving and communication skills (Cohan and Kleinbaum 2002). Why this is so is unclear. Furthermore, those who choose serial cohabitation before they marry may have more negative attitudes about marriage in general and more accepting attitudes toward divorce.

Second, the **experience hypothesis** posits that cohabiting experiences themselves affect individuals so that, once married, they are more likely to divorce (Seltzer 2000, p. 1253). For example, serial cohabitation may adversely affect subsequent marital quality and stability inasmuch as the experiences actually weaken commitment because "'successful' cohabitation demonstrates that reasonable alternatives to marriage exist" (Thomson and Colella 1992, p. 266). More generally, there is evidence that "young adults become more tolerant of divorce as a result of cohabiting, whatever their initial views were," possibly because "cohabiting exposes people to a wider range of attitudes about family arrangements than those who marry without first living together" (Seltzer 2000, p. 1253). One recent, important study found little support for the *selection hypothesis* but significant evidence to support the *experience hypothesis* (Dush, Cohan, and Amato 2003).

We will end this section by pointing out that researchers have only begun to investigate how and why cohabiting couples decide whether to marry; whether cohabiting with only one's future spouse serves as an effective courtship practice; or how marriage changes, if it does, a formerly cohabiting couple's behavior and feelings about the relationship. A student reading this text might one day design research to answer one or more of these questions.

We have looked at dating, getting together, and cohabiting as courtship processes. Next we turn to a brief discussion of intimate violence during courtship.

Courtship Violence

Research suggests that physical violence occurs in about one-fifth of cohabiting and in 20 to 40 percent of dating relationships (DeMaris 2001; Simons, Lin, and Gordon 1998)—a high, "most surprising incidence" to sociologists when they first uncovered dating violence in the 1980s (Johnson and Ferraro 2000, p. 951). Courtship violence can also occur after breaking up (Langhinrichsen-Rohling, Palarea, Cohen, and Rohling 2000). Most of this aggression consists of pushing, grabbing, or slapping. Nevertheless, between 1 and 3 percent of college students have reported experiencing severe violence, such as beatings or assault with an object. Both genders engage in physical aggression. However, women are apt to report pushing or slapping a man, whereas men are more likely to report beating up a date or threatening her with a weapon (Makepeace 1981; Riggs 1993). "With regard to injury, the more serious physical consequences of male-to-female violence are well-established" (Johnson and Ferraro 2000, p. 952). Due to stereotypes, research on courtship violence has been neglected for some ethnic groups, such as Asian Americans, although it does exist (Yoshihama, Parekh, and Boyington 1991).

Dating violence is typically accompanied by verbal or psychological abuse (Hogben and Waterman 2000) and tends to occur over jealousy, with a refusal of sex, after excessive drinking of alcohol, or upon disagreement about drinking behavior (Makepeace 1981, 1986). One study that examined a sample of 411 heterosexual cohabiting couples, who were part of the National Survey of Families and Households (NSFH), found that severe violence on the part of the male did tend to dissuade the couple from marrying and also tended to encourage the couple's breaking up. However, less-severe violence, as well as violence by the female, was not associated with breaking up (DeMaris 2001).

Researchers have found it discouraging that about half of dating relationships continue after the violence rather than being broken off (Levy 1991). Indeed, this finding that violent dating relationships continue was part of the surprise mentioned above. Given that the economic and social constraints of marriage are not usually applicable to dating, researchers have wondered why these relationships persist. Some evidence suggests that having been physically abused by one's father is highly related to men's—but not women's—verbal and physical abuse of one's dating partner (Alexander, Moore, and Alexander 1991; Dutton 2003). In a longitudinal study of 116 teenage boys, social scientists found that boys who experienced little involvement or support from their parents were more likely to begin abusing illegal drugs. The drug abuse then led to violence on dates. Also, boys who had often received physical or corporal punishment from their fathers were more likely to be violent on dates (Simons, Lin, and Gordon 1998). According to one study (Ronfeldt, Kimerling, and Arias 1998), men who were dissatisfied with the power they felt in their dating relationships were more likely to be verbally or physically violent toward their dates.

What are some early indicators that a dating partner is likely to become violent eventually? Social scientists David Island and Patrick Letellier (1991) have addressed this question. They intended their counsel for gay male readers, but what they say can apply more broadly. A date who is likely to someday become physically violent often, though not necessarily, exhibits one or more of the following characteristics:

1. handles ordinary disagreements or disappointments with inappropriate anger or rage
2. has to struggle to retain self-control when some little thing triggers anger
3. goes into tirades
4. is quick to criticize or to be verbally mean
5. appears unduly jealous, restricting, and controlling
6. has been violent in previous relationships (Island and Letellier 1991, pp. 158–166)

We have been discussing violence in courtship. We turn now to a related topic, date rape, which often occurs in less involved relationships.

DATE RAPE Most rape victims know their rapists (Cowan 2000). **Date rape** or **acquaintance rape**—being involved in a coercive sexual encounter with a date or other acquaintance—emerged as an issue on college campuses over the past two decades, but date rape no doubt plagued the dating scene for a long time before that (Friedman, Boumil, and Taylor 1992). Often, excessive use of alcohol is involved (Cue, George, and Norris 1996). Findings from various research studies over the past decade show that sexually coercive men tend to dismiss women's rejection messages regarding unwanted sex and differ from noncoercive men in their approach to relationships and sexuality: They date more frequently; have higher numbers of sexual partners, especially uncommitted dating relationships; prefer casual encounters; and may "take a predatory approach to their sexual interactions with women."

Closely related to the concept of date rape is sexual coercion. Very recently some researchers have begun to look at female-initiated sexual coercion, and they've found that it does indeed exist—although significantly fewer women than men are sexually coercive, and when they are coercive, they use less-forceful techniques. Moreover, when men are victims of non-violent sexually coercive pressure, they experience less shorter-term emotional upset as a consequence of their experience than do women. Men's experiences with being coerced most often do not advance beyond kissing or fondling, whereas women's most often result in intercourse (Christopher and Sprecher 2000, p. 1012).

The feminist movement and other social changes have transformed dating into a somewhat more egalitarian experience with some features of the pattern we call *getting together*. But research indicates considerable confusion, mistrust, and uncertainty about what rules and preferences are operating in a given situation. Such misunderstanding may contribute to date rape (Gibbs 1991)—although we do not want to understate the force and coercion very often characterizing date rape. In one study, half of the freshman and sophomore college women interviewed reported unwanted attempts at intercourse by males of their acquaintance.

© Phi Kappa Phi Fraternity

At its 1985 national convention, members of the national Pi Kappa Phi Fraternity unanimously adopted a resolution not to tolerate any form of sexually abusive behavior on the part of their members. The fraternity also produced this poster and distributed it to all its chapters. The illustration is a detail from the painting *The Rape of the Sabine Women*. Beneath the large message a smaller one reads, "Just a reminder from Pi Kappa Phi. Against her will is against the law."

sponses, which were largely passive and accepting; 37 percent did nothing. Only a minority gave a strong verbal (26 percent) or physical response (14 percent). Half of the attacks succeeded; the stronger the victim's response, the less likely it was that the attempted rape was completed. None of the women reported the attack to the authorities, and half talked to no one about it; the remainder told friends. Only 11 percent ended the relationship, whereas almost three-quarters either accepted or ignored the attack. Fifty percent continued to be friends (25 percent) or dating or sex partners (25 percent). Most blamed themselves at least partially (Murnen, Perot, and Byrne 1989).

One reason that date- or acquaintance-rape victims may be tempted to blame themselves has to do with **rape myths**: beliefs about rape that function to blame the victim and exonerate the rapist (Cowan 2000). Rape myths include the ideas that (1) the rape was somehow provoked by the victim (for example, she "led him on" or wore provocative clothes); (2) men cannot control their sexual urges, a belief that consequently holds women responsible for preventing rape; and (3) rapists are mentally ill, a belief that encourages potential victims to feel safe with someone they know, no matter what (Cowan 2000). In at least two fairly recent studies, males attributed more responsibility to the victim—and less to the perpetrator—than women did (Hinck and Thomas 1999; Workman and Freeburg 1999). However, neither male nor female college students are as likely to believe rape myths as they were in the past. Increasingly, college men report that they recognize the male's responsibility for rape; this finding may be evidence that campus rape-prevention information and workshops make a difference (Domitrz 2003; Hinck and Thomas 1999).

This discussion of intimate violence during courtship raises the question of deciding to break up—whether the relationship is abusive or not. Indeed, making a conscious decision about marrying a dating or cohabiting partner raises the possibility of *not* marrying. Letting go of a relationship can be painful. Next, we'll look at the experience of breaking up.

Breaking Up

Psychologist Lawrence Kurdek (1995a) has applied exchange theory to determine whether couple relationships continue. (Exchange theory is described in

These were usually (83 percent) men they knew at least moderately well. One-third of these attempts were accompanied by "strong" physical force, and another third by "mild" physical force. The women seemed constrained by traditional roles in their re-

"Put me on your do-not-call list."

Chapter 3.) According to the exchange perspective, couples choose either to stay committed or to break up by weighing the rewards of their relationship against its costs. As partners go through this process, they also consider how well their relationship matches an imagined, ideal one. Partners also contemplate alternatives to the relationship, the investments they've made in it, and barriers to breaking up. (We will see in Chapter 16 that this perspective is also used when examining people's decisions about divorce.) Using this scheme, Kurdek developed a questionnaire to measure a couple's relationship commitment. The following are some questions from Kurdek's measure (respondents could strongly agree, agree, remain neutral, disagree, or strongly disagree):

Rewards:
One advantage to my relationship is having someone to count on.

Costs:
It takes a lot for me to be in my relationship.

Match to Ideal Comparison Level:
My current relationship comes close to matching what I would consider to be my ideal relationship.

Alternatives:
As an alternative to my current relationship, I would like the freedom to do what I want to do whenever I want to do it.

As an alternative to my relationship, I would like to date someone else.

Investments:
I've put a lot of energy and effort into my relationship.

A part of me is tied up in my relationship.

Barriers to Breaking Up:
It would be difficult to leave my partner because of the emotional pain involved.

I would find it difficult to leave my partner because I would feel obligated to keep the relationship together. (p. 263)

When a partner's rewards are higher than the costs, when there are few desirable alternatives to the relationship, when the relationship comes close to one's ideal, when one has invested a great deal in the relationship, and, when the barriers to breaking up are perceived as high, an individual is likely to remain committed. However, when costs outweigh rewards, when there are desirable alternatives to the relationship, when one's relationship does not match one's ideal, when little has been invested in the relationship in comparison to rewards, and when there are fewer barriers to breaking up, couples are more likely to do so.

Although breaking up is hard to do at any time, break-ups before marriage are generally less stressful than divorce. Nevertheless, the act of breaking up can be an ordeal (Amatenstein 2002). Sometimes a break-up is followed by unwanted phone calls, unwanted in-person encounters, or stalking. As you might guess, those who initiate the break-up are less likely to engage in these unwanted pursuits than are those who have been left behind (Langhinrichsen-Rohling et al. 2000). Sociologist David Knox (1975), in a classic statement mirrored by contemporary counselors, offers the following guidelines for ending a relationship:

1. Decide that terminating the relationship is what you really want to do.

2. Assuming you have definitely determined to break up, prepare yourself for wavering—but don't change your mind.

3. Plan the break-up discussion with your partner in person, but at a location from which you can readily withdraw.

4. Explain your reasons for breaking up in terms of your own values, rather than pointing out what you think is wrong with the other person.

5. Seek out new relationships.

Item 5 is also good advice for those who have recently been broken up with. A few recent studies have found that some ex-partners forge supportive post-dating relationships that satisfy legitimate needs, such as friendship and shared history (Foley and Fraser 1998; Langhinrichsen-Rohling et al. 2000).

Until now we have been discussing why and how relationships proceed to marriage. We assume that people in the marriage market hope to choose a partner with whom they can develop a harmonious, stable spousal relationship. The final section of this chapter looks at how selecting a spouse is related to marital quality and stability.

Mate Selection and Marital Stability

Sociologist Norval Glenn recently made "a plea for greater concern about the quality of marital matching" (2002). Psychologists and counselors advise choosing a mate who is integrated into society by means of school, employment, a network of friends, and/or family ties, and who demonstrates a sense of self-worth (not narcissism, as discussed in Chapter 5) (Cotton, Burton, and Rushing 2003). Sociological research shows that marriages are more likely to be stable when partners are in their mid-twenties or older and when the spouses' parents have not been divorced. We'll explore these points here.

Age at Marriage and Marital Stability

Marriages that occur when individuals are over twenty-five may be slightly more stable than those that take place in their early twenties, but the most significant distinction is between teenage and all other marriages (Heaton 2002). Ten years after their weddings, 48 percent of unions of women who were under age eighteen at marriage have divorced, compared with 40 percent of marriages among women who were eighteen or nineteen years old on their wedding day. Twenty-nine percent of marriages among women who were twenty to twenty-four on their wedding day have dissolved after ten years; the figure is 24 percent for women at least twenty-five years old at marriage (Bramlett and Mosher 2001, p. 5).

Low socioeconomic origins, coupled with school failure or lack of interest in school, are associated with early marriages. Higher fertility and economic deprivation are also associated with early marriages (Hayes 1987; Teti and Lamb 1989). (However, a study of Hmong Americans [Hutchinson and McNall 1994] suggested that this overall conclusion may not apply to all ethnic groups; ethnic groups that encourage early marriage and are psychologically supportive and economically helpful to newlyweds may not experience such negative consequences of young marriages.)

Age itself is probably not the key variable in determining the likelihood of a marriage's succeeding. Rather, it seems likely that one's age at marriage is associated with other elements contributing to marital instability, such as parental dissatisfactions accompanying early marriage; social and economic handicaps;

lowered educational achievement (South 1995); premarital pregnancy or the female's attitude toward the pregnancy condition; courtship histories, including length of acquaintance and engagement; personality characteristics; and the rapid onset of parental responsibilities. Social scientists generally maintain that people who marry young are less apt to be educationally, financially, or psychologically prepared to select a mate or to perform marital roles. What if a prospective spouse is from a divorced family?

The Intergenerational Transmission of Divorce Risk

"Studies based on large national samples consistently show that parental divorce increases the risk of marital instability in offspring" (Hetherington 2003, p. 325; Teachman 2004). When both spouses come from a divorced family, the probability of their own divorce is still higher (Amato 1996; Amato and DeBoer 2001; Diekmann and Engelhardt 1999; Hetherington 2003; Wolfinger 1999, 2000).[7] Family scholars refer to this phenomenon as the **intergenerational transmission of divorce risk**: A divorced parental family transmits to its children a heightened risk of getting divorced. Noting that "apparently, there is something in the divorce experience beyond that of parental conflict that exacerbates problems in stability in intimate relations in offspring" (Hetherington 2003, p. 326), researchers have identified various explanations for the intergenerational transmission of divorce risk. For one thing, children of divorce are more likely to evidence other factors associated with getting divorced. For instance, they are more likely to leave home early, become teenage parents, and exhibit "higher levels of antisocial behavior" (Hetherington 2003, p. 326).

In addition, the following four hypotheses have been suggested to explain the intergenerational transmission of divorce risk. Children of divorce are more likely to get divorced themselves because they have

1. more—and more serious—personality problems
2. neither been exposed to nor learned supportive communication or problem-solving skills
3. less commitment to the relationship itself
4. more accepting attitudes toward divorce (Dunne, Hudgins, and Babcock 2000; Hetherington 2003; Hetherington and Kelly 2002)

After what we've said here, it's important to emphasize that it is not true that children of divorce will themselves *necessarily* divorce (Zimmerman and Thayer 2004). Research shows that a supportive, well-adjusted partner "can play a protective role" to minimize the intergenerational transmission of divorce risk. Prominent researcher on children of divorce E. Mavis Hetherington (2003) has described her findings on this point:

> Under conditions of low stress with a supportive partner, there was no difference in couple instability between the offspring of divorced and nondivorced parents. For these well-married youths in a benign environment, no intergenerational transmission of marital instability was found. Under conditions of high stress, there was a marginally significant trend for the offspring of divorced parents, even with a supportive partner, to show somewhat more marital instability than those from nondivorced families. (p. 328)

MATE SELECTION RISK Mate selection plays a part in the intergenerational transmission of divorce risk because individuals from divorced families are themselves more inclined to have the characteristics described above and also to choose partners who have them. Hetherington (2003) reports her findings concerning "**mate selection risk**" as follows:

> Youths from divorced families were more likely to select high-risk partners who were also from divorced families and who were impulsive, socially irresponsible, and had a history of antisocial behaviors such as alcohol and drug abuse, minor misdemeanors, troubles with the law, problems in school and at work, fighting, and an unstable job history. (p. 328)

Other research has found that *mate selection risk* may apply to adult children of alcoholics as well as to those of divorce (Olmsted, Crowell, and Waters 2003; Watt 2002). What can one do to minimize the mate selection risk?

7. We have seen that serial cohabitation prior to marriage is statistically associated with the union's ending in divorce. One recent analysis of 1995 nationally representative data from the National Survey of Family Growth has found that "With the exception of parental death, . . . any time spent in an alternative family [such as cohabitation] increases the likelihood that a woman forms a union with characteristics that decrease the likelihood of a successful union" (Teachman 2004, p. 86). Why this is the case is not clear. We expect that research on this topic will grow as more children raised in cohabiting households reach adulthood and enter the marriage market.

Minimizing Mate Selection Risk

A first step in minimizing mate selection risk is to let go of misconceptions we might have both about love itself and choosing a partner. Chapter 5 explores various misconceptions about discovering love. It's also true that in the absence of adequate role models for maintaining a supportive marriage, many of us may embrace misconceptions about finding a partner. For instance, we might believe one or more of the following:

1. Until I find the perfect person to marry I should not get married . . .

2. Until I feel completely confident as a future spouse, I should not get married . . .

3. I can be happy with anyone I choose to marry, if I work hard enough . . .

4. Falling in love with someone is sufficient reason for me to marry that person. (Cobb, Larson, and Watson 2003, p. 223)

However, no one—neither oneself nor a prospective spouse—is "perfect in every way" (Cobb, Larson, and Watson 2003, p. 223). At the same time, working things out requires both partners' willingness and ability to do so; just one's own willingness to work hard at a marriage is not enough. Selecting a partner wisely involves balancing the insistence on perfection against the need to be thoughtful. Finally, if having fallen in love is assumed to be enough to make a marriage last, then other important partner qualities may not be taken into account (Cobb, Larson, and Watson 2003).

"Generally, marriages that have built up positive emotional bank accounts through respect, mutual support and affirmation of each other's worth are more likely to survive" (Hetherington 2003, p. 322). Research suggests that the best way to counteract the intergenerational transmission of divorce risk is to look for a socially responsible, respectful, and supportive mate who demonstrates good listening and problem-solving skills (Hetherington 2003).

Equally important, research findings also point to looking for a mate with values and attitudes similar to one's own because like values and attitudes are strong predictors of marital happiness and stability (Larson and Holman 1994; Cobb, Larson, and Watson 2003). For example, do the prospective spouses agree on whether they want children and/or whether they would be willing to adopt a child?

The section "Some Questions to Ask" in Chapter 8 gives other ideas on assessing your own and a prospective spouse's values and attitudes. Of course, it's important to be truthful when relating with a potential spouse, as well as ascertaining how truthful one's partner is being (Campbell 2004). Some couples in the marriage market today go to counselors, not after they have decided definitely to marry, but to assess their commitment to marriage and future compatibility (Marech 2004a).

In Chapter 8, we turn to an examination of marriage as both a public and a private relationship.

In Sum

- The association of love and marriage is characteristic of modern culture. As they modernize, increasingly more cultures accept the idea of love and marriage.

- Historically, in Western cultures, marriages were often arranged in the marriage market, as business deals. In some of the world that is less Westernized, some marriages are still arranged. Some immigrant groups in the United States (and other Westernized societies) today practice arranged or "assisted" marriage.

- Social scientists typically view people as choosing marriage partners in a marriage market; armed with resources (personal and social characteristics), they bargain for the best deal they can get.

- Although things are certainly changing with the trend toward androgyny, some aspects of the traditional marriage exchange (a man's providing financial support in exchange for the woman's childbearing and child-rearing capabilities, domestic services, and sexual availability) remain.

- The marriage gradient—the traditional tendency for women to marry up with regard to age, education, and occupation—also shapes marital options, albeit to a weakening extent today, compared to the past.

- An additional factor shaping marital choice is homogamy, the tendency of people to marry others with whom they share certain social characteristics. Despite the trend toward declining homogamy, it is still a strong force, encouraged by geographical availability, social pressure, and feeling at home with people like ourselves.

- Physical attractiveness, coupled with attitudes either supporting or not supporting homogamy, helps explain our attraction to others.

- Three patterns of courtship familiar in our society are dating, getting together, and cohabitation.

- About half of cohabiting couples who see their relationship as a precursor to marriage eventually do marry.

- Serial cohabiting (although not necessarily cohabiting before marriage only with one's future spouse) has been shown to increase the likelihood of divorce. The suggested reasons for this involve the *selection hypothesis* and the *experience hypothesis*.

- Two important factors related to marital stability are mate selection risk and a couple's age at marriage. People who marry too young are less likely to stay married, perhaps partly because they are less likely to choose a socially responsible and emotionally supportive partner.

- Some courting relationships will end in break-ups.

Key Terms

arranged marriage	free-choice culture
assortive mating	generating strategies
blocking strategies	geographic availability
bride price	getting together
courtly love	heterogamy
courtship	homogamy
cross-national marriage	hypergamy
date rape (acquaintance rape)	hypogamy
dowry	interethnic marriage
emotional maturity	intergenerational transmission of divorce risk
endogamy	interracial marriage
exchange theory	marriage gradient
exogamy	marriage market
experience hypothesis	masked

mate selection risk	stimulus–values–roles (SVR) theory of courtship
pool of eligibles	theory of complementary needs
propinquity	transforming strategies
rape myth	two-stage marriage
selection hypothesis	
status exchange hypothesis	

Questions for Review and Reflection

1. How are marriages in a free-choice culture or society similar to arranged marriages? How are they different? What role does the marriage market play in both types of partner selection?

2. Explain reasons why marriages are likely to be homogamous. What difficulties are people in heterogamous relationships likely to face? Why do you think homogamous marriages are more stable than heterogamous marriages? Does this necessarily mean that homogamous marriages are more successful? Why or why not?

3. Why did Margaret Mead criticize the dating pattern that had emerged in the United States? What problems did she think were caused by dating? Do we still face these problems today?

4. If possible, talk to a few married couples you know who lived together before marrying, and ask them how their cohabiting experience influenced their transition to marriage. How do their answers compare with the survey findings presented in this chapter?

5. **Policy Question.** What does the idea that "normal" men are capable of date rape or acquaintance rape say about gender scripts today and whether, how, and how much they are changing? What social policies presently exist to discourage date rape? What new policies might be enacted to further discourage date rape?

Suggested Readings

Colorful Couples

http://www.kudoku.com/colorful/

The website of an organization of interracial couples for heterogamous couples of all backgrounds.

Crohn, John. 1995. *Mixed Matches: How to Create Successful Interracial, Interethnic, and Interfaith Relationships.* New York: Fawcett Columbine. Crohn is a psychologist and therapist who gives good advice based on his clinical experience.

Kalmijn, Matthijs. 1998. "Intermarriage and Homogamy: Causes, Patterns, Trends." Pp. 395–422 in *Annual Review of Sociology*, vol. 24. Thorough and clearly written essay and literature review on homogamy, both historically and cross-culturally.

Moran, Rachel F. 2001. *Interracial Intimacy: The Regulation of Race & Romance*. Chicago: University of Chicago Press. Historical overview of miscegenation laws and their aftermath, as well as positive analysis and discussion of the potential emotional advantages of racial heterogamy.

Regan, Pamela C. 2003. *The Mating Game: A Primer on Love, Sex, and Marriage*. Newbury Park, CA: Sage. Comprehensive review of the social science literature on love, sexuality, and mate selection.

Rothman, Ellen K. 1984. *Hands and Hearts: A History of Courtship in America*. New York: Basic. A historical account of American courtship.

Simpson, J., and R. Rholes. 1998. *Attachment Theory and Close Relationships*. New York: Guilford. Good summary and explication of attachment theory and research, focusing on how attachment styles affect adult intimacy and relationships.

Zimmerman, Jeffrey, and Elizabeth Thayer. 2004. *Adult Children of Divorce: How to Overcome the Legacy of Your Parents' Breakup and Enjoy Love, Trust, and Intimacy*. Oakland, CA: New Harbinger Press. A self-help book written by two psychologists, this work examines the impact of having divorced parents on adult children and then explores ways to heal and build positive, supportive relationships and relationship skills.

Virtual Society: The Wadsworth Sociology Resource Center

Go to the Sociology Resource Center at **http://sociology.wadsworth.com** for a wealth of online resources, including a companion website for your text that provides study aids such as self-quizzes for each chapter and a practice final exam, as well links to sociology websites and information on the latest theories and discoveries in the field. In addition, you will find further suggested readings, flashcards, and MicroCase online exercises, and appendices on a range of subjects.

Online Study Tool

Marriage & Family ⊛ Now™ Go to **http://sociology .wadsworth.com** to reach the companion website for your text and use the Marriage&FamilyNow passcode that came with your book to access this study tool. Take a practice pretest after you have read each chapter, and then use the study plan provided to master that chapter. Afterward, take a posttest to monitor your progress.

Search Online with InfoTrac College Edition

For additional information, exercises, and key words to aid your research, explore InfoTrac College Edition, your online library that offers full-length articles from thousands of scholarly and popular publications. Click on *InfoTrac College Edition* under *Chapter Resources* at the companion website and use the passcode that came with your book.

- Search keywords: *mate selection, interracial dating, interracial marriage, homogamy.*

Marriage, *a* Private *and* Public Relationship

Because the family is so central to human life, no one can be neutral about its future prospects.

WILLIAM J. DOHERTY

Marriage is not an answer, but a search, a process, a search for life, just as dialogue is a search for truth.

SIDNEY JOURARD

Y OU'LL RECALL THAT IN CHAPTER 1, we defined *families* as kin relationships in which people form an economic unit and care for their young, consider their identity to be significantly attached to the group, and are committed to maintaining that group over time. Although the situation is less clear-cut than two decades ago, marriage remains the most socially acceptable—and stable—gateway to family life.

Despite wide variations, all marriages have one very important element in common: the commitment that partners make—and make *publicly*—to each other and to the institution of marriage itself. Indeed, "Marriage is not just about love and intimacy between two adults. It is an institution" (Seidman 2003, p. 123). This is why we say that getting married—as opposed to "just" living together, for example—is both a private and a public relationship.

In the discussions that follow, we'll look at how getting married announces a personal life-course decision to one's relatives, to the community, and, yes, to the state. We'll ask which couples should be allowed to legally proclaim their commitment as we examine the public debate over whether the right to marry legally should extend to lesbian and gay couples.

Then we'll turn to a discussion of marriage as a more private relationship between partners. How does that private relationship reflect spouses' personal choices, made either actively or by default? The kind of relationship a couple shares is largely a product of the values, expectations, and efforts partners invest in it. One way to design and retain the kind of relation-

ship that spouses want, as we shall see, is to be adaptable. Marrying is a trade-off. Brides and grooms discard prior alternatives and publicly proclaim that they are no longer available in the marriage market. This is one expectation inherent in the traditional *marriage premise* that permanence and sexual exclusivity are fundamental to marriage.

We begin by discussing marriage as a social institution that involves a publicly proclaimed *marriage premise*. After that, we explore the relationship between marriage and kinship.

The Marriage Premise: ▪ Permanence and ▪ Sexual Exclusivity

Why does a marriage require a wedding? Why does a wedding require witnesses and a license from the state? The government, representing the community, is legally involved in all weddings because a marriage is necessarily a community, or public, concern. Put another way, the state, or community, has a stake in who gets married (as well as in whether spouses are allowed to divorce).

Over the past several hundred years, the state has become involved in marriages largely because the community has a stake in an essential social function: children being responsibly cared for. Historically marriage has performed a second social function of providing economically for family members (see Chapter 3). As a result, virtually all social scientists agree that families are an important **social institution**—a system of patterned and predictable ways of thinking and behaving concerning important aspects of people's lives.[1]

For many (although not all, as we shall see) social scientists and policy makers, the family as a social institution rests on the **marriage premise** of permanence and sexual exclusivity. By getting married, the majority of American partners vow to work hard to ensure that their relationship continues. Furthermore, virtually all married individuals have promised sexual exclusivity. We can look more closely at the two important elements of this definition: permanence and primariness.

---

1. Social scientists typically point to five major social institutions: family, religion, government or politics, the economy, and education.

Marking a couple's commitment, weddings are public events because the community has a stake in marriage as a social institution.

© Royalty-Free Image Source, London

Expectations of Permanence

As a community event, a wedding traditionally marks a bride and groom's passage into adult family roles. And with few exceptions, marriages were always thought of as permanent, lifelong commitments. Although it is statistically less permanent now than it has ever been in our society, marriage, more than any other relationship, holds the hope for permanence. The marriage contract remains a legal contract between two people that cannot be broken without permission of society or the state. Most religions urge permanence in marriage.

In our society, couples usually vow publicly to stay together "until death do us part" or "so long as we both shall live." People enter marriage expecting—hoping—that mutual affection and commitment will be lasting. But as far back as 1949, Margaret Mead pointed to the "great contradictoriness" in American culture. People "are still encouraged to marry as if they could count on marriage's being for life, and at the same time they are absorbing a knowledge of the great frequency of divorce." Today "marriage *may* be

for life, *can* be for life, but also may not be" (Mead 1949, pp. 335, 338). The recognition of this cultural contradiction is a step toward self-understanding and helps in making personal choices about permanence in marriage.

Expectations for permanence derive from the fact that, historically, marriage has been a practical social institution. Economic security and responsible child rearing required marriages to be permanent, and even at the turn of the twentieth century, parents only occasionally outlived the departure of their last child from home to become a couple household again. Today, as we've seen in earlier chapters, marriage is somewhat less important for economic security, but remains significant for responsible child raising (Furstenberg 2003; Rector and Pardue 2004). Meanwhile, another function of marriage—providing ongoing emotional support and love—has become key for most people.

Marital relationships can more often be permanently satisfying, counselors advise, when spouses learn to care for the "unvarnished" other, not a "splen-

"That's for staying married for thirty-five years to a difficult woman."

did image" (Van den Haag 1974, p. 142). In this regard, sociologist Judith Wallerstein, reflecting on her own marriage of fifty years, writes:

> I certainly have not been happy all through each year of my marriage. There have been good times and bad, angry and joyful moments, times of ecstasy and times of quiet contentment. But I would never trade my husband, Robert, for another man. I would not swap my marriage for any other. This does not mean that I find other men unattractive, but there is all the difference in the world between a passing fancy and a life plan. For me, there has always been only one life plan, the one I have lived with my husband. (Wallerstein and Blakesley 1995, p. 8)

Getting married can encourage partners to commit themselves to building an ongoing love relationship and history together. Some social scientists and policy makers, concerned that so many marriages end in divorce or separation despite vows of permanence, have proposed ways to encourage marital permanence.

SOCIAL POLICIES DESIGNED TO ENCOURAGE MARITAL PERMANENCE A central theme of this text is that society influences individuals' options and thereby impacts people's decisions. Recognizing this, some policymakers have proposed ways to promote marital permanence. For instance, many religions insist on premarital counseling, discussed in more detail later in this chapter, and offer voluntary marriage enrichment programs (see, for example, "Case Study: Making A Marriage Encounter Weekend" in Chapter 13). Moreover, some legislators and conservative Christian organizations advocate *covenant marriage* ("Covenant Marriages Ministry" 1998; Sanchez, Nock, Wright, and Gager 2002).

Covenant Marriage **Covenant marriage** is a fairly new type of legal marriage in which the bride and groom agree to be bound by a marriage "covenant" (stronger than an ordinary contract) that will not let them get divorced as easily as is presently allowed. Three states have enacted a covenant marriage law—Louisiana in 1997, Arizona in 1998, and Arkansas in

2001. At least twenty-five other states have considered, but failed to pass, covenant marriage laws (Gardiner, Fishman, Nokolov, Glosser, and Laud 2002). Relatively few couples in the states where it is available have opted for covenant marriage (Sanchez et al. 2002).

How does covenant marriage work? Before their wedding, couples in states with the covenant marriage option are required to choose between two marital contracts, conventional or covenant. Under today's no-fault divorce laws (discussed at length in Chapter 16), which apply to conventional marriages in all fifty states, either spouse can divorce the other at relatively short notice, without showing that anyone was "at fault" for causing the marriage relationship to deteriorate. Under Louisiana's covenant marriage contract, couples are required to get premarital counseling and may divorce only after being separated for at least two years or if imprisonment, desertion for one year, adultery, or domestic abuse is proved in court. In addition, a covenant couple must submit to counseling before a divorce (Olson 1998).

Typically, fundamentalist religionists are enthusiastic about covenant marriage, and feminists are not (Hawkins, Nock, Wilson, Sanchez, and Wright 2002; Sanchez et al. 2002). Critics warn that covenant marriage could result in emotional blackmail: A partner might be pressured into the contract and later regret it (Olson 1998). Critics also point out that proving adultery or domestic abuse in court may be difficult and expensive—and that living in a violent household can be deadly (Gelles 1996). Moreover, some religious authorities have expressed concern that covenant marriage laws, in effect, set up a two-tiered marriage structure that makes a noncovenant marriage second class, however valid and sacramental it may be.[2] The Catholic church has declined to endorse covenant marriage for this reason. Meanwhile, various other state and federal initiatives have been enacted to encourage spouses to stay together.

State and Federal Marriage Initiatives States have long been invested in marriage. For example, all states have requirements regarding the issuance of marriage licenses. Ten states require blood tests for various communicable diseases, while most states require waiting periods—ranging from seventy-two hours to

six days—between the license application date and its receipt or between receipt of the license and the wedding (Gardiner et al. 2002).

More recently, states have promoted marriage education, some offering incentives for couples to participate. At least two states (Indiana and Mississippi) require premarital counseling, and several others have proposed similar legislation (Hawkins et al. 2002). Michigan has introduced a bill to offer a tax credit to couples who take part in marriage education or enrichment programs. Other state initiatives include home visitation programs for families that might be targeted for a variety of reasons, such as a birth to a teenager or an unstable marriage; mentoring, marriage counseling, communications skills, and anger management workshops; state-funded resource centers that provide information on marriage; and state websites that include marriage enrichment information and links to service-related sites (Gardiner et al. 2002).

These more recent state marriage initiatives largely began after 1996, when Congress passed the Personal Responsibility and Work Opportunity Reconciliation Act. That federal law authorized the Temporary Assistance for Needy Families (TANF), or "welfare reform," program and stated the goal, among others, of encouraging the formation and maintenance of two-parent families. As a consequence, states were allotted federal monies to enact programs that would bolster marital permanence. (TANF is also addressed in Chapter 11.)

In 2004, as part of TANF's required reauthorization, George W. Bush introduced the President's Healthy Marriage Initiative. Designed "to promote healthy marriage as a part of welfare reauthorization," proponents argue that "accurate information on the value of marriage in the lives of men, women, and children," along with marriage-skills education

> will enable couples to reduce conflict and increase the happiness and longevity of their relationship. . . . The marriage program will encourage couples to reexamine and improve their relationships and plan wisely for the future. . . . The program will also provide marriage-skills education to married couples to improve their relationships and to reduce the probability of divorce. (Rector and Pardue 2004)

Because state and federal marriage initiatives proceed from "welfare reform" legislation, their focus has been primarily on low-income Americans. Meanwhile,

2. Sociologist Amitai Etzioni sarcastically referred to the choice between conventional and covenant marriage as one between "marriage lite" or "marriage plus" (Etzioni 1997).

critics suggest that—especially among this group—efforts to strengthen marriage must recognize and address the significant economic barriers to happy, permanent unions. As we pointed out in Chapter 1, many policymakers maintain that family formation and maintenance is not simply a question of values or motivation. Instead, families are struggling with economic and time pressures that get in the way of their ability to realize family values (Yorburg 2002). In the words of demographer Frank Furstenberg,

> Restoring marriage to an institution of enduring, compassionate relationships will require more than sanctimonious calls for traditional, communitarian, and family values. We should back up our words with resources. This includes moving toward a society that offers secure, remunerative jobs, as well as better child-care options and more flexible schedules so people can accept those jobs. Otherwise, the institution of marriage as we knew it in [the twentieth] century will in the 21st century become a practice of the privileged. (Furstenberg 2003, p. 197)

Expectations of Sexual Exclusivity

Marriage typically involves **expectations of sexual exclusivity**, in which spouses promise to have sexual relations only with each other: "Many people still feel that the self-disclosure involved in sexuality symbolizes the love relationship and therefore sexuality should not be shared with extramarital partners" (Reiss 1986, pp. 56–57). Sexual exclusivity emerged as a cultural value in traditional society to maintain the patriarchal line of descent; the wedding ring placed on the bride's finger by the groom symbolized this expectation of sexual exclusivity on her part. Although historically polygamy was common (remember the Old Testament patriarchs), the Judeo-Christian tradition extended expectations of sexual exclusivity to include both husbands and wives. For example, the Book of Common Prayer asks both partners to "forsake all others."

Taboos against extramarital sex are widespread among the world's cultures, although the proscription against extramarital sex is stronger in the United States than in many other parts of the world. About 70 percent to 80 percent of Americans believe that extramarital sex is "always harmful to a marriage" or "always wrong" (Adler 1996a; Christopher and Sprecher 2000). However, there are exceptions to our cultural

expectation in the United States for sexual exclusivity, and some of these exceptions are touched on in "Issues for Thought: Subcultures with Norms Contrary to Sexual Exclusivity."

COHABITATION AND SEXUAL EXCLUSIVITY
It is important to note that cohabiting couples generally expect each other to be sexually faithful (Treas and Giesen 2000). Like marrieds, cohabitors may be much distressed by a partner's affair. However, there is empirical evidence that the rate of sexual infidelity is higher among cohabitors than among marrieds (Christopher and Sprecher 2000, p. 1006). These points highlight two important facts. First, marriage continues to be qualitatively different from other sexual relationships, even cohabiting. Second, marriage—because it is a public institution, embedded in the broader community—involves more responsibilities than do other sexual relationships.

The topic of extramarital sex is explored more fully later in this chapter. Here we note that maintaining the marriage premise involves not only the personal or private decisions of married partners but also the more public pressures that exercise social control. In many traditional societies, social control over a married couple has been exercised by the spouses' kin (Adams 1971).

▪ Marriage and Kinship ▪

Who are your kin? Anthropologists have defined *kinship* as the social organization of the entire family, including blood (**consanguineous**) relatives and **conjugal** relationships acquired through marriage.[3] Parents and grandparents are consanguineous relations; spouses and in-laws are conjugal relatives; aunts and uncles may be either. Certain rights and obligations accompany one's kinship status. For example, you may expect your grown sister or brother to attend your wedding or graduation.

As you may have already noticed, the concept of kinship is closely related to that of *extended family*. An extended family includes parents and children, along with other relatives, such as in-laws, grandparents, aunts

---

3. The word *consanguineous* comes from the Latin prefix *com,* which means "joint," and the Latin word *sanguineus,* which means "of blood." The word *conjugal* comes from the Latin word *conjugere,* which means "to join together."

The Dinner Quilt, *Faith Ringgold, 1986.*

and uncles, and cousins. Some groups, such as African Americans, Hispanics, and gay male and lesbian families, also have "fictive" or "virtual" kin—friends who are so close that they are hardly distinguished from actual relatives.

Meanwhile, it may be the case that every society has a **dominant dyad**—a centrally important dyad, or twosome, that symbolizes the culture's basic values and kinship obligations (Hsu 1971). At least among white, middle-class Americans, the husband–wife dyad is expected to take precedence over any others. According to sociologist Talcott Parsons (1943), the American kinship system is generally not based on vital extended family ties. Parsons writes that kinship in the United States is instead comprised of "interlocking conjugal families" in which married people are common members of their **family of orientation** (the family they grew up in) and of their **family of procreation** (the one formed by marrying and having children). Parsons views the husband–wife bond and the resulting family of procreation as the most meaningful "inner circle" of Americans' kin relations, surrounded by decreasingly important outer circles. However, Parsons points out that his model characterizes mainly the American middle class. Recent immigrants and lower socioeconomic classes, as well as upper-class families, still rely on meaningful ties to their extended kin.

Although the situation is changing, the extended family (as opposed to the married couple or nuclear family) has been the basic family unit in the majority of non-European countries (Ingoldsby and Smith 1995). Extended families have declined greatly in significance for white middle-class Americans, but they continue to be comparatively important for various European ethnic families, such as Italians, and for African American, Hispanic, Asian American, and Native American families as well. This situation follows from the fact that family norms result both from cultural influences and from economic or other concrete options and demands (McLoyd et al. 2000).

For instance, Hispanics today do not necessarily subscribe to the middle-class norm of the primary conjugal bond; *la familia* ("the family") means the extended as well as the nuclear family. Like the Italians that Gans (1982 [1962]) studied in the 1960s, many Mexican Americans and other Hispanics live in comparatively large, reciprocally supportive kinship networks. For example, most Puerto Rican families live in "ethnically specific enclaves" (largely in New York City) and rely more on extended, consanguineous kin than on conjugal ties (Wilkinson 1993). Puerto Ricans are similar to working-class African Americans in this way.

Recent Asian immigrants are also likely to emphasize extended kin ties over the marriage relationship

Issues for Thought

Subcultures with Norms Contrary to Sexual Exclusivity

Despite the fact that a very substantial majority of Americans value monogamy as a cultural standard, there are subcultural exceptions. This box examines three of these subcultural exceptions—swinging, polyamory, and polygamy.

Swinging

Swinging is a marriage arrangement in which couples exchange partners in order to engage in purely recreational sex. Swinging gained media and research attention as one of several "alternative lifestyles" in the late 1960s and early 1970s (Rubin 2001). At that time it was estimated that about 2 percent of adults in the United States had participated in swinging at least once (Gilmartin 1977).

Although little research has been done on swinging in the past few decades, "lifestyle practitioners," as some swingers now prefer to be called, still exist as a minority subculture. It has been estimated that there are about three million married swingers in the United States, an increase of about one million since 1990. Some of this growth is probably due to the Internet, which "may have replaced magazines in linking potential participants to one another" (Rubin 2001, p. 722).

Interestingly, as a category, swingers tend to be middle-aged, middle-class, and more otherwise socially and politically conservative than one might expect (Jenks 1998; Rubin 2001). Swingers emphasize the lifestyle's positive effects—variety, for example. Former swingers who have given up the lifestyle point to problems with jealousy, guilt, competing emotional attachments, and fear of being discovered by other family members, friends, or neighbors (Macklin 1987).

Polyamory

Polyamory refers to marriages in which one or both spouses retain the option to sexually love others in addition to their spouse. According to Rubin, "Polyamorists are more committed to emotional fulfillment and family building than recreational swingers" (2001, p. 721). Evolving from the sexually open marriage movement, which received considerable publicity in the late 1960s and 1970s, polyamorous spouses agree that each may have openly acknowledged sexual relationships with others while keeping the marriage relationship primary. Unlike in swinging, outside relationships can be emotional as well as sexual. Couples usually establish limits on the degree of sexual and/or emotional involve-

ment of the outside relationship, along with ground rules concerning honesty and what details to tell each other (Macklin 1987, p. 335; Rubin 2001).

Spouses in polyamorous unions often say that the arrangement has many personal and relationship benefits. They also report complications: jealousy, guilt, difficulty in apportioning time and attention, pressure from the extramarital partner, need for continuous negotiation and accommodation, and loneliness when the spouse is not home. This is a tall order and may be why many sexually open marriages have difficulties (Masters, Johnson, and Kolodny 1994) or apparently become monogamous after a period of time.

Advocacy of polyamory and swinging is largely a product of the pre-AIDS era. Today, a couple considering a sexually nonexclusive marriage must take into account not only personal values and relationship management challenges, but also the increased risk of being infected with HIV/AIDS: "However, the fear of disease has apparently not inhibited the recent growth of swinging" (Rubin 2001, p. 723). Condoms are available at swing clubs, and it has been reported that some polyamorists practice "safe sex

(Glick, Bean, and Van Hook 1997). Among Chinese and Japanese Americans, *hsiao* defines the dominant dyad—that of adult child (especially son) and aging parent (especially father). *Hsiao* requires that an adult child provide aid and affection to parents even when this might conflict with marital obligations (Lin and Liu 1993).

In the following, a Vietnamese refugee describes his reaction to U.S. housing patterns, which reflect nuclear family norms and husband–wife as the dominant dyad:

Before I left Vietnam, three generations lived together in the same group. My mom, my family

circles" in which only those who have tested negatively for sexually transmitted diseases may participate (Rubin 2001).

Polygamy

The term **polygamy** means more than one spouse at a time for a partner of either sex. **Polygyny** refers to multiple wives for a man, and **polyandry** refers to multiple husbands for one wife. Polygyny has been very common throughout history as a permissible pattern in many cultures. Where permitted, though, it is not always that frequent, for many men cannot afford multiple wives. Polyandry is rare and tends to exist in very poor societies in which female infanticide is practiced to reduce the number of mouths to feed, with the result that there are not enough women to go around for marriage in adulthood. It is also practiced when brothers share a wife—again, often because of economic constraints (Stephens 1963).

Polygamy has been illegal in the United States since 1878, when the U.S. Supreme Court ruled that freedom to practice the Mormon religion did not extend to having multiple wives (*Reynolds v. United States* 1878). Although the Church of the Latter-day Saints (LDS) no longer permits polygamy, there are dissident Mormons (not recognized as LDS by the mainstream church) who follow the traditional teachings and take multiple wives (Woodward 2001, p. 50). They tend to live in remote areas for fear of prosecution, but occasionally members of these families have talked to the media to explain and advocate their lifestyle.

Some multiple wives have argued that polygyny is a feminist arrangement because the sharing of domestic responsibilities benefits working women (Johnson 1991; Joseph 1991).

Polygamy has not received the public acceptance that heterosexual and even homosexual cohabitation have. Bigamy is vigorously prosecuted. Yet civil libertarians argue that the Supreme Court should rescind its *Reynolds* decision on the grounds that the right to privacy permits this choice of domestic lifestyle as much as any other.

Meanwhile, African American sociologist Joseph Scott (1980, 1999) has studied what he terms "polygamy" among American blacks. In the African American polygamous family, two (or more) women maintain separate households and are independently "pair-bonded to a man whom they share and who moves between . . . households as a husband to both women" (Scott 1980, p. 43). In view of the particularly unbalanced sex ratio among blacks, Scott suggests that "the only way many black women may have men permanently in their lives would be to share them with women who already have them as husbands or friends" (1980, p. 48).

Scott interviewed twenty-two African American women who either were or had been in a polygamous relationship. Half the women were single (consensual wives), and half were married (legal wives). Their relationships varied in length from two to twelve years. These women tended to be young, to be of low socioeconomic status, and to have experienced premarital pregnancies

for which they were ill prepared. Consensual wives saw the single black men available to them as unreliable compared to those already married (Scott 1980, 1999). Most of the legal wives became involved in polygamy because their husbands had other close female companions before marriage and kept them. Generally, they accepted their situations as inevitable, "given the scarcity of what they call 'good men.' . . . They all shared the view that if their husbands maintained their economic priorities to their legal families, this was evidence of their giving priority to the legal marriages themselves" (Scott 1980, p. 60; 1999).

Critics question whether polygamy among African Americans is freely chosen or imposed on the women by circumstance and men's behavior (Staples 1985). Scott replies to the critics that, in fact, the polygamy is consensual (that is, agreed to by the women) and that these unions are socially recognized as legitimate family constellations in the black community. Even though polygamy may be a logical solution to the lack of adult black males in urban settings, "many are concerned about the vulnerability of the mother/child units in 'man sharing' and see the pattern as one more instance of the exploitation of poor women" (Peters and McAdoo 1983, pp. 302–303).

Critical Thinking

What do you think about these exceptions to monogamy? Are there some that seem reasonable to you while others do not? Why?

including wife and seven children, my elder brother, his wife and three children, my little brother and two sisters—we live in a big house. So when we came here we are thinking of being united in one place. But there is no way. However, we try to live as close as possible. (quoted in Gold 1993, p. 303)

American housing architecture is similarly discouraging to many Muslim families—from India, Pakistan, or Bangladesh, for example—who would prefer to live in extended households (Nanji 1993).

All of this is not to say that extended family members are irrelevant to non-Hispanic white families in the United States. For instance, a study of 451 rural

Midwestern white families found that, in general, disagreements with in-laws negatively influenced the spouses' marital satisfaction and commitment to the union, as well as the marriage's stability (Bryant, Conger, and Meehan 2001). Nuclear families maintain significant emotional and practical ties with extended kin, such as parents-in-law (Lee, Spitze, and Logan 2003). However, as families become more urban, the power of kin to exercise social control over family members generally declines. The following section explores the social change from traditional expectations concerning marriage and families to those of contemporary industrialized societies.

Social Change: From ▪ Marriage As Institution ▪ to Pluralistic Families

Social scientist William Doherty (1992), among others (e.g., Farrell 1999), has documented an historical change from marriage as a *social institution* to marriage as *"psychological."* Doherty proceeds to characterize families in today's highly industrialized societies as *pluralistic*, a term that he uses to describe a situation similar to the "postmodern family," described in Chapter 1. This section examines Doherty's argument.

Marriage As a Social Institution

According to Doherty,

> the institutional family represented the age-old tradition of a family organized around economic production, kinship network, community connections, the father's authority, and marriage as a functional partnership rather than a romantic relationship. . . . Family tradition, loyalty, and solidarity were more important than individual goals and romantic interest. (1992, p. 33)

Institutional families can be characterized by *responsibility*, their principal value.

However, as urbanization and individualism (see Chapter 1) emerged gradually over the past several centuries, kinship ties weakened while values of self-actualization and individual achievement emerged (Smolka 2001). "In the culture of individualism, . . . relationships are based on 'contracts'—what people can do for each other, rather than on traditional

'covenants'—virtually unbreakable commitments based on loyalty and responsibility " (Doherty 1992, p. 34).

The Psychological Marriage

By the 1920s in the United States, family sociologists had begun to note a shift away from "institutional marriage," and in 1945, the first sociology textbook on the American family (by Ernest Burgess and Harvey Locke) was titled *The Family: From Institution to Companionship.*

The emergent "companionate," or *psychological marriage*

> was a more private affair than its predecessor—more nuclear, more mobile, less tied to extended-kin networks and the broader community. It aspired to something unprecedented in human history: a family based on the personal satisfaction and fulfillment of its individual members in a nuclear, two-parent arrangement. (Doherty 1992, p. 34)

As described in Chapter 7, marriage in an individualized society came to be based on love and attraction, not necessarily on child raising or economic responsibilities. Meanwhile, psychological marriage was built upon distinct, so-called "complementary," gender roles. The chief value of the psychological marriage was satisfaction.

Meanwhile, Doherty argues, a fundamental society-wide contradiction between the ideal of "a mutually satisfying, intact, nuclear family" and actual gender inequality sowed the seeds for family change:

> When the social changes of the 1960s challenged the Psychological Family under the banners of gender equality and personal freedom, the Psychological Family began to give way as a normative ideal in American society. . . . By the late 1980s, the Psychological Family, itself a radical shift from the Institutional Family, had given way to its successor, the Pluralistic Family. (1992, p. 35)

An illustration of the tension between mutual satisfaction within psychological marriage and issues of gender equality is explored in "As We Make Choices: Getting Married—and Changing Your Name?"

We will consider the pluralistic family shortly. But first we'll look at some ways that social scientists have examined relationships within the psychological marriage.

To varying degrees, Americans think of marriage as primarily based on psychological factors, such as emotional satisfaction. However, virtually all marriages combine elements of pragmatism and emotional sharing. This Russian-immigrant couple, who owns and operates a small grocery store in Los Angeles, is an example.

© Michael Newman/PhotoEdit

MARRIAGE RELATIONSHIPS WITHIN THE PSYCHOLOGICAL FAMILY Forty years ago, family sociologist Jesse Bernard noted what she called a **parallel relationship pattern** among spouses in the working class; she distinguished this pattern from the **interactional relationship pattern** of middle-class marriages. In the interactional pattern, which dominates Americans' goals for marriage today, partners expect companionship and intimacy as well as more practical benefits. In a parallel relationship, the husband was expected mainly to be a hardworking provider and the wife was expected to be a good housekeeper and cook: "Companionship in the sense of exchange of ideas or opinions or the enhancement of personality by verbal play or conversation is not considered a basic component in this pattern" (Bernard 1964, p. 687). Today these social-class distinctions are less apparent as more and more working-class couples count on the interactional pattern. Meanwhile, we should not forget that marriage often offers practical advantages as well.

The Pluralistic Family

As is explored in Chapter 1, the *pluralistic* family has no one structure or form. After all,

> Family forms do not arrive and evaporate overnight; they just become more or less norma-

tive over time. In the late 20th century, the Psychological Family hasn't died; it has just become one family among others. The chief value—[emotional] satisfaction—continues to be prominent in the Pluralistic Family, but it is now supplemented by a new family value for the postmodern age—flexibility. (Doherty 1992, p. 36)

In other words, families may now take many forms, as we saw in Chapter 1. Doherty adds that flexibility "does not mean, however, that anything goes; all family forms should be judged by how well they provide commitment, care, and community for their members" (p. 9). While they may be changing, the values associated with family-as-institution have not disappeared. Nevertheless, Doherty writes that "tolerance and diversity, rather than a single family ideal, characterize the Pluralistic Family" (1992, p. 35).

As an example, "Gay marriage might not have gained political traction in the United States were it not for broader changes in the American family"—that is, from family as institution to the pluralistic family (Seidman 2003, p. 125). Today it would be difficult to escape the public debate over whether, on the one hand, family as institution is inappropriately threatened or, on the other hand, tolerance for diversity is fitting when the issue is legal marriage for same-sex couples.

As We Make Choices

Getting Married— and Changing Your Name?

If you're married, did you change your last name on your wedding day? If you're not married but plan to marry someday, do you think you'll change your name? If you have answered "yes" to either of these questions, there's a good chance you're female. Custom and law have traditionally required wives to take their husbands' names at marriage. It is now legal in every state for a wife to keep her given name. However, as recently as the 1970s, several states refused to let married women keep their names (Scheuble and Johnson 1993). The norms in our society continue to encourage brides to change their names, despite changing gender roles (Scheuble and Johnson 1993; Twenge 1997b). Even stronger norms discourage grooms from changing (or "giving up") their surnames.

Meanwhile, it is not only custom and gender roles that affect individuals' choices about married names. Changing—or not changing—one's name is also symbolic of what marriage means to people. In a study at the University of Michigan (Twenge

1997b), 153 young women enrolled in an introductory psychology course were questioned about their preferences for married last names. The sample was 19 percent African American, 6 percent Hispanic, 15 percent Asian, and 60 percent non-Hispanic white. Virtually all were middle- or upper-middle class. Ninety-eight percent identified themselves as heterosexual, and 98 percent were unmarried. The women were asked to choose one of seven options for their own name after marriage and one of six options for their future children's names. Table 8.1 shows the results.

Nearly 60 percent said that they would take their husband's name, compared to about 10 percent who said they planned to keep their own name for all purposes. Another 4 percent thought that both spouses should hyphenate their names. More than twice as many young women (8.2 percent) planned to hyphenate their name but did not expect their husband to hyphenate his. With regard to future children's names, nearly 80 percent of the

coeds expected their children to have their husband's name, while 12 percent said their children would have a hyphenated name.

The researcher asked the students to explain in their own words the reason for their choices. Those who said they would take their husband's name often gave tradition as a reason—for example, "Traditionally, that's the way it is supposed to be." These women also indicated that taking their husband's name symbolized romantic conjugal bonding: "The same last name would symbolize this 'two becoming one' idea"; "I think that we will be together as one now and I can share his last name" (p. 424).

The women who said they would do something other than take their husband's last name often explained their need to retain a sense of personal identity. Typical responses included "My last name is important to me, because that represents *me* and everything I worked for and accomplished in my life, and I will *not* entirely give up my identity for a man" and "It makes no sense to give up my identity just because I marry.

Same-Sex Couples and Legal Marriage

"Despite unfriendly social conditions," many gay male and lesbian couples live together in long-term, committed relationships (Patterson 2000; Seidman 2003, p. 123).[4] Partners may exchange vows or rings or both (Marech 2004b). Couples may publicly declare their

commitment in ceremonies among friends or in some congregations and churches, such as the Unitarian Universalist Association or the Metropolitan Community Church, the latter expressly dedicated to serving the gay community (Demian 2003c, 2004a). Catholics

---

4. Same-sex couples living together in long-term, committed relationships is not a recent development. According to social historian Samuel Kader (1999), same-sex committed couples date back to the Old Testament, and commitment ceremonies between same-

sex partners were not unknown in early Christianity. More recently, scholars "have uncovered a long and complicated history of gay relationships in nineteenth-century America. Sometimes women passed as men to form straight-seeming relationships; sometimes men or women lived together as housemates but were really lovers; sometimes individuals would marry but still carry on romantic, sometimes life-long same-sex intimate relationships" (Seidman 2003, p. 124).

Table 8.1

Young Women's Preferred Name Choice at Marriage (Sample *n* = 153)

CHOICES FOR OWN LAST NAME	PERCENTAGE CHOOSING OPTION
Take husband's name	59.5
Keep my own name for all purposes	9.8
Use my name for professional purposes, husband's for social	13.7
Hyphenate my name, but not expect him to hyphenate his	9.2
Hyphenate my name, and he will hyphenate his	3.9
Husband and I will choose new name and both use	0.7
Other	3.3
CHOICES FOR CHILDREN'S LAST NAME	
Husband's name	79.6
My name	0.7
Hyphenated name	12.1
Daughters will have my name, sons my husband's	0.7
New name	0.7
Other	3.9

Source: Jean M. Twenge, 1997, "Mrs. His Name: Women's Preferences for Married Names," *Psychology of Women Quarterly* 21, Table 1, p. 422. Reprinted with permission from Blackwell Publishing.

It is sexist, archaic, and illogical." Some women who preferred to keep their names explained that the decision was related to their ethnicity and culture. As one Latina wrote, "I want to keep my last name because it reflects my culture, which is part of who I am" (p. 424).

As Table 8.1 shows, the students were more likely to choose their husband's last name for their children than for themselves. Those who said that their children should have their husband's last name explained that this was traditional and would generally be easier and avoid confusion. A woman who hoped to give her children hyphenated names explained that "Their names should be a combination of our last names, since that is what they are, a combination of the two of us" (p. 425).

An earlier study surveyed both female and male students in a small Midwestern college in 1990. In that study, the women students thought of more good reasons for the bride to keep her name than the men did. Probably not surprisingly, women who planned to marry later and/or to have a professional career were more likely not to want to change their names. Women who planned to marry earlier and have larger families were more likely to plan to change their name (Scheuble and Johnson 1993).

Critical Thinking

If you are single and plan to marry, what do you want to do about your last name at the wedding? If you are presently married, did you keep or change your surname? What does doing so symbolize, do you think? How does the question whether a bride should change her name reflect the tension within *psychological marriage* between gender equality and expectations for a love-based relationship?

have access to a union ceremony designed by Dignity, a Catholic support association, although these unions are not recognized by the Catholic church ("What Is Dignity?" 2004). Secular commitment ceremonies for gay and lesbians have become common enough to have sparked a number of "wedding"-planning businesses for same-sex couples in the United States and abroad (Pink Weddings 2004; Two Brides 2004).

In addition, gay and lesbian couples may establish families with children by becoming parents through adoption, foster care, planned sexual intercourse, or artificial insemination (Bell 2003; Gomes 2003; John-son and O'Connor 2002). Courts vary in their receptiveness to such families. For example, the state of Florida prohibits gay or lesbian couples from adopting children (De Valle 2004; Rostow 2004), while other courts increasingly permit a lesbian to adopt her partner's children (e.g., *In re-Petition of L. S. and V. L. for the Adoption of T. and of M.* 1991) or grant joint adoption to gay male couples ("Lesbian and Gay Rights" 2001). As a further example, the New Jersey Supreme Court ruled in 2000 that a co-parenting lesbian is entitled to visitation rights after the relationship ends even though she is not a biological parent of the child

(Levinson 2001). However, many other jurisdictions refuse custody or visiting rights to a gay/lesbian co-parent when the couple breaks up ("Lesbian and Gay Rights" 2001). That courts become involved in parenting issues involving same-sex couples supports the point that the government has a stake in children's being raised responsibly. A related question is whether the government should allow legal marriage for gay male and lesbian couples.

A Legal Maze

In 2000, the Netherlands became the first country to allow same-sex partners to marry under the same legal code as any couple (Deutsch 2000). Three years later, Belgium became the second (Demian 2004b). Several other countries, most of them northern and western European, now legally recognize lesbian/gay unions by granting same-sex couples a new marital status variously called "life partnerships," "registered partnerships," or "civil solidarity pacts" (Demian 2002, 2004b; "Marriage Law Status" 1999).[5] During 2003 and 2004, several Canadian provinces ruled to permit legal same-sex marriage (Demian 2004b).[6] Meanwhile, the United Nations Commission on Human Rights has not been able to pass a resolution to add sexual preference as a reason that people's human rights must not be violated. The motion was dropped "in the midst of intense pressure" from the Vatican and the Conference of Islamic States ("United Nations Drops" 2004). We can conclude that the **culture war**—intense conflict over matters concerning human sexuality and gender—is global.

What about the United States? The 1974 U.S. Supreme Court decision in *Singer v. Hara* defined marriage as a union between one man and one woman.

Nevertheless, the federal government has traditionally recognized the right of individual states to create, interpret, and enforce laws regarding marriage and families. Consequently, the battle over legal marriage for same-sex couples has largely been fought within individual states. *U.S. News & World Report* writer Angie Cannon has described the question of same-sex, legal marriage in the United States as "a legal maze—and more to come" (Cannon 2004). In this section, we do our best to wind through the maze. As we do, we'll need to keep in mind some points about how our government works. These can be found in the accompanying footnote.[7]

MASSACHUSETTS Since May 2004, gay and lesbian couples have been allowed to marry legally in one state, Massachusetts (Abraham and Klein 2004). However, whether they will be allowed to marry there legally after 2006 remains to be seen. How can this be?

In 2003, the Massachusetts Supreme Judicial Court ruled that barring lesbians and gays from legal marriage was unconstitutional because it discriminates against same-sex couples. The court then ordered the Massachusetts state legislature to find a way to remedy this situation. When the Massachusetts Senate asked the Court for an advisory opinion on the constitutionality of a proposed law that would continue to bar same-sex couples from legal marriage but would also create "civil unions" with all the same benefits, the Court answered that

> segregating same-sex unions from opposite-sex unions cannot possibly be held rationally to advance or preserve [the public goal of promoting]

---

5. For a detailed account of developments regarding same-sex legal marriage around the world, see Demian 2004b. "Legal Marriage Report: Global Status of Legal Marriage." Partners Task Force for Gay & Lesbian Couples. <http://www.buddybuddy.com/mar-repo.html>

6. U.S. citizens are allowed to marry in the Canadian provinces of British Columbia, Ontario, and Quebec. However, upon their return to the United States, their unions are unlikely to be recognized by either the federal government or the vast majority of state governments ("What Do" 2004). "Another complication arises if a couple wishes to divorce. They would not be able to do so in their resident state if their state did not recognize the marriage in the first place. To get a divorce, one of the partners would need to reside in Canada for a year" (Demian 2004d). For these reasons, gay rights activists have published Internet advisories for U.S. citizens deciding about going to Canada to wed (Demian 2004d).

7. A civics lesson in a family sociology textbook? In this case, it seems necessary. Keeping the following points in mind will help as we wind our way through the "legal maze" that characterizes the issue of legal marriage for gay and lesbian couples:

- Individual state legislatures have the right and duty to pass laws regarding marriage for citizens of their state.
- In addition to the U.S. Constitution, each state has a state constitution (although the U.S. Constitution has power over states and state constitutions).
- State Judicial Courts determine whether laws passed by the state's legislature are constitutional under their current state constitutions.
- State constitutions, as well as the U.S. Constitution, may be amended, or changed, to reflect the will of the majority of people under their jurisdiction.
- A constitutional amendment overrides a court's ruling that upheld the previous (non-amended) constitution.

With these facts in mind, we can better navigate the legal maze that currently characterizes same-sex marriage in the United States.

During February and March 2004, 4,161 lesbian and gay couples were married in San Francisco's city hall. Pundits called these weddings acts of "civil marriage disobedience." (See "A Closer Look at Family Diversity: Civil Marriage Disobedience.") The state of California did not recognize these marriages and stopped the weddings after about six weeks.

© AP/Wide World Photos

stable adult relationships for the good of the individual and of the community, especially its children. ("Same-Sex Marriage" 2004)

Given this response, Massachusetts apparently had no option but to issue marriage licenses to same-sex couples.

However, in March 2004, the state's legislators voted to begin the process of enacting a state constitutional amendment banning legal marriage for same-sex couples.[8] In the same bill, the legislators voted to establish "civil unions" for gay and lesbian couples (Klein 2004). If the amendment passes, the Massachusetts Supreme Judicial Court will be obligated to uphold the amended constitution, thereby *denying* (rather than demanding, as in its 2003 decision) legal marriages for gay and lesbian couples. Because a state constitutional amendment must be approved by Massachusetts voters, who will not vote on the issue until November 2006, same-sex marriages may be legal in Massachusetts for only two and one-half years—but indefinitely if the constitutional amendment fails to pass (Bayles 2004).

---

8. As of March 1, 2004, four states—Alaska, Hawaii, Nebraska, and Nevada—had expressly defined marriage as between a man and a woman in their state constitutions. Eighteen more states had proposed similar state constitutional amendments (National Conference of State Legislatures 2004).

EARLIER LEGAL STRUGGLES—HAWAII, VERMONT, AND ALASKA The Massachusetts situation is the latest legal struggle in a debate that began in the early 1990s when same-sex couples in Hawaii, Vermont, and Alaska sued for access to legal marriage. Generally, these lawsuits, like the one in Massachusetts, argued that marriage laws that require spouses to be heterosexual are unconstitutional because they discriminate against same-sex couples. Hawaii's final court ruling in 1999 denied legal marriage to gays or lesbians but offered them instead the option to become "reciprocal beneficiaries," explained below. That same year, Vermont's State Supreme Court ruled that same-sex couples must be afforded the same rights and benefits as opposite-sex couples, but allowed the Vermont legislature to provide a "civil union" law, rather than issue legal marriage licenses for same-sex couples (Demian 2001). In Alaska, the couple who filed the lawsuit decided not to pursue it after a 1998 state ballot measure prohibited any legal recognition of same-sex marriage.

RECIPROCAL BENEFICIARIES AND CIVIL UNIONS Hawaii's Reciprocal Beneficiaries Law and Vermont's Civil Union Act allow any two single adults—including same-sex partners or blood relatives, such as siblings or a parent and adult child—to have access to virtually all marriage rights and benefits on the state level, but none on the federal level (Partners Task Force for Gay & Lesbian Couples 2000a). For instance, reciprocal beneficiaries in Hawaii and "next of kin" under Vermont's civil union legislation have rights to joint property and tenancy, inheritance without a will, and hospital visitation and health care decisions for their partners. However, these couples cannot collect federal Social Security benefits upon a partner's death, nor can a non-U.S. partner become a U.S. citizen upon becoming a "reciprocal beneficiary" or joining a "civil union."

DOMESTIC PARTNERS Meanwhile, many cities, states, and the U.S. House of Representatives, as well as many businesses, have passed *domestic partner* laws (discussed in detail in Chapter 9 "As We Make Choices: Some Advice on the Legal Side of Living Together"). According to this concept, unmarried couples may register their partnership and then receive many (although not all) of the legal benefits of marriage. Besides practical benefits such as joint health or auto insurance or bereavement leave, registering as domestic partners can have emotional significance for some same-sex couples, who do so as a way of publicly expressing their commitment (Ames 1992). But registering as domestic partners lacks the deep symbolism of marriage. Meanwhile, as local governments enact more domestic partner laws, the federal government passed the Defense of Marriage Act in 1996.

THE FEDERAL DEFENSE OF MARRIAGE ACT (DOMA) States usually recognize one another's legal decisions; this principle of reciprocity would require a state to recognize a legal marriage performed in another state. However, in order to allow states *not* to follow the principle of reciprocity regarding same-sex marriages, the United States passed the 1996 Defense of Marriage Act (DOMA). At the time, many legislators and others were afraid that same-sex marriage might be legalized in Hawaii (it has not been, as we saw above) and that other states would be required to recognize same-sex marriages performed there.

The **Defense of Marriage Act** is a federal statute declaring marriage to be a "legal union of one man and one woman," and relieving states of the obligation to grant reciprocity, or "full faith and credit," to marriages performed in another state (Hatfield 1996; Purdum 1996). Largely as a result of the Defense of Marriage Act, by February 2004, thirty-nine states

had passed laws refusing to recognize a marriage obtained by gay or lesbian couples in another state (National Conference of State Legislatures 2004b) (see Figure 8.1).

A PROPOSED AMENDMENT TO THE UNITED STATES CONSTITUTION In response to the highly publicized same-sex weddings in San Francisco during February and March 2004, (see "A Closer Look at Family Diversity: Civil Marriage Disobedience") and to the developments in Massachusetts, described above, President George W. Bush announced his support for an amendment to the United States Constitution that would define marriage as between one man and one woman (Page and Benedetto 2004). The proposed amendment would ban same-sex marriage in the United States while allowing states to create "civil unions" or domestic partnerships (Allen and Cooperman 2004).

From legal marriage for same-sex couples in Massachusetts to a possible constitutional amendment that would ban same-sex marriages across the country, the details of this "legal maze" point up the serious public divide regarding marriage for lesbians and gays. We turn now to this public debate.

The Debate over Legal Marriage for Same-Sex Couples

"Take a Stand for Marriage!" urges the conservative Family Research Council website (**http://www.frc.org**), one of several that gives directions on ways to speak out against same-sex marriage. Other websites, such as Gay & Lesbian Advocates & Defenders (GLAD) or the Partners Task Force for Gay and Lesbian Couples, advocate for the other side (**http://www.glad.org/; www.buddybuddy.com**). Having first emerged as a remote possibility in the 1970s, legal marriage for gay and lesbian couples "became a front-line issue" after 1991 when gay activists formed the Equal Rights Marriage Fund (Seidman 2003).

ARGUMENTS FOR LEGAL MARRIAGE AS HETEROSEXUAL ONLY Not all religions or religious leaders oppose legal same-sex marriage ("Religious Leaders Descend" 2004). However, for religious fundamentalists and other conservative groups, the move to legalize marriage is an "attempt to deconstruct traditional morality" (Smolowe 1996a; Wilson 2001).

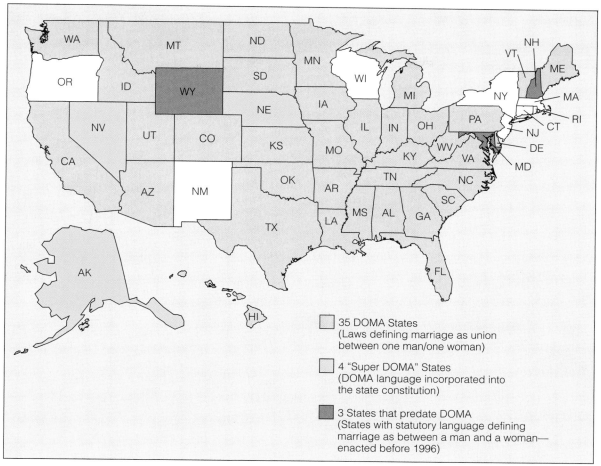

FIGURE 8.1

State Defense of Marriage Acts (DOMAs) as of February 2004.

Source: National Conference of State Legislatures. http://www.ncsl.org.

Those who favor defining legal marriage as only heterosexual argue that only heterosexual marriage has deep roots in history, as well as in the Judeo-Christian and other religious traditions (Dalley 2004).

They further claim that only heterosexual married parents can provide the optimum family environment for raising children and that legalizing same-sex marriage would weaken an institution already threatened by single-parent families, cohabitation, and divorce (McClusky 2004; Seidman 2003). Some contend that, "Even more ominously, permitting gays to marry would open the door for all sorts of people to demand the right to marry—polygamists, children, friends, kin—even more than two partners" (Seidman 2003,

p. 128).[9] Finally, they argue that legal marriage for same-sex couples is unnecessary, given "compromise" legislation, like that in Vermont and Hawaii, which gives virtually all the rights of marriage to same-sex couples without the title "married" or "spouse" (Seidman 2003).

---

9. This fear is not entirely unfounded. In 2004, attorneys filed suit in Utah, arguing that the state's ban on polygamy violated Mormons' First Amendment right to practice their religion. Six months before, the U.S. Supreme Court had struck down laws criminalizing sodomy. At that time, the Supreme Court said that gays are "entitled to respect for their private lives." The Utah suit requests the same considerations for proponents of bigamy (Sage 2004).

A Closer Look at Family Diversity

Civil Marriage Disobedience

On February 12, 2004, San Francisco's newly elected Mayor Gavin Newsom surprisingly ordered the San Francisco County clerk to issue civil marriage licenses to same-sex couples. Explaining the move, Newsom said, "I took the oath of office . . . and swore to uphold California's Constitution, which clearly outlaws all forms of discrimination. Denying basic rights to members of our community will not be tolerated" (quoted in Romney 2004).

The first pair to marry were lesbian activists Del Martin, 83, and Phyllis Lyon, 79. The two had been in a committed relationship for 51 years. Over the following two days, in what San Francisco newspapers called a "mad dash to get hitched," a "gay-marriage tsunami," and a "watershed moment," 940 same-sex couples got married in San Francisco's city hall (Chiang and Rubenstein 2004; Herel 2004). At times the waiting line curled around the block outside. Inside, the building smelled of wedding cakes and fresh flowers, sent from anonymous well-wishers around the world to "any couple who is getting married at San Francisco's City Hall."

But according to California state law, same-sex couples do not have the right to marry. In fact, it seemed probable that all of these marriage licenses would one day be revoked. As one California resident put it, "I call [the weddings] 'Newsom unions' because it's something between marriage and civil unions, but it's not the law" (quoted in Konrad 2004). In 2000, California voters had approved a state initiative declaring that marriage be only between a man and a woman. But throughout February and into March of 2004, the civil marriage movement—which came to be called "civil marriage disobedience"—spread from the "liberal bubble" of San Francisco to other parts of the country (Demian 2004c; Romney 2004). For instance,

- The city of Portland, Oregon, began to issue marriage licenses to lesbian and gay couples. By the end of the first day, 422 same-sex licenses had been issued in the Portland area's Multnomah County ("Multnomah County" 2004; "Seattle Same-Sex Couples" 2004).

- The county clerk of Sandoval County, New Mexico, pronouncing that she saw nothing in New Mexico law to prevent it, issued marriage licenses to sixty-seven same-sex couples (Marech 2004c).

- The mayor of New Paltz, New York, officiated at the marriages of twenty-five same-sex couples ("N.Y. Gay-Marriage Mayor Charged" 2004).

- The mayor of Ithaca, New York, announced that the town clerk

ARGUMENTS FOR LEGAL SAME-SEX MARRIAGE Virginia resident Peggy Hein was the lesbian partner for eighteen years of Sheila Neff, who was killed in the 9/11 attack on the Pentagon in Washington, DC. But Peggy Hein will not receive any survivor benefits. Under Virginia law, only a surviving spouse, close relative, or legal dependent of a deceased victim can receive survivor benefits. Furthermore, Sheila Neff had life insurance but had never specified a beneficiary. Because she was not legally married, the life insurance money did not go to Peggy Hein ("Lesbian Survivor" 2002). Lesbians and gay men who favor legalized same-sex marriage argue that denying them the right to marry legally violates the United States Constitution because it discriminates against a category of citizens. Legal marriage yields economic and other practical advantages. For instance, marrieds can sometimes lower their taxes by filing a joint return; if one spouse dies or is disabled, the other is entitled to Social Security benefits; legal partners can inherit from each other without a will; spouses are immune from subpoenas requiring testimony against each other; the immigrant spouse of a U.S. citizen can, more readily than otherwise, become a citizen him/herself. In areas without domestic partner laws, some employers offer health insurance to an employee's legal spouse and dependents.

When one or both partners suffer from serious illness, the protections of marriage could prove highly beneficial. For instance, a hospital may allow visiting rights only to next of kin. Indeed, the U.S. General Accounting Office has identified more than 1,000 federal laws in which marital status is a factor. These include veterans' benefits; Social Security and related

would accept marriage license applications from same-sex couples (Demian 2004c).

- The mayor of Nyack, New York, announced that his village would respect the legal marriages of same-sex couples performed in other states or countries because he believed that gay couples should be treated equally (Demian 2004c).
- The City Council of San Jose passed a motion to recognize the marriages of city workers who had married in San Francisco (Konrad 2004).
- The mayor of Seattle signed an order granting city benefits to same-sex couples with marriage licenses from other states (Demian 2004c).
- Nine city mayors, including those of Chicago, Minneapolis, and Salt Lake City, announced their support for granting same-sex marriage licenses.
- In New York City, demonstrators stood on the steps of City hall, demanding that Mayor Michael Bloomberg follow San Francisco's lead and order the city clerk to issue same-sex marriage licenses (Roskoff 2004).

Meanwhile, California governor Arnold Schwarzenegger, appearing on NBC's *Meet the Press,* "warned of anarchy and deadly consequences if the San Francisco marriages were not stopped" (Roskoff 2004). And various regional authorities squelched the "anarchy" (Faust 2004). The California Supreme Court ordered a halt to San Francisco's same-sex marriages. In New Mexico, the same day that licenses began to be issued, the state's Attorney General stated that the marriages were invalid because his legal staff understood marriage in New Mexico to be "between a man and a woman." (Demian 2004c). In New Platz, New York, the twenty-five couples who had been "married" had not secured licenses. Because marrying someone who does not have a license is a misdemeanor, the local district attorney charged the mayor who had officiated at the marriages with criminal misconduct ("N.Y. Gay-Marriage Mayor Charged" 2004). In April 2004, Oregon stopped issuing same-sex marriage licenses (Hunter 2004).

Before the San Francisco weddings were stopped, 4,161 couples from the city and around the world had obtained marriage licenses. Many others were left waiting in line (Demian 2004c). The same day that the marriages were halted, six same-sex couples filed suit in the San Francisco County Superior Court asking the state to require that marriage licenses use gender-neutral language and be made available to gay and lesbian couples (Demian 2004c). The California courts agreed to hear the case.

Critical Thinking

Do you approve or disapprove of legal marriage for same-sex couples? Do you believe that it is discriminatory to deny civil marriage licenses to gays or lesbians? Explain why you believe as you do. Is civil disobedience warranted in this case? Why or why not?

---

programs, such as housing and food stamps; employment benefits; immigration and naturalization laws; financial disclosure and conflict of interest legislation; and crimes and family violence legislation, among others (Butz 2004; U.S. General Accounting Office 1997).

Furthermore, proponents of gay and lesbian rights argue that creating domestic partnerships or civil unions, while not allowing marriage for same-sex partners, creates a "separate but equal" situation that has already been declared unconstitutional by the U.S. Supreme Court regarding racially segregated schools (Williams 2004). Also, denying lesbians and gay men the right to marry implies that they are "second-class citizens," not as valuable as heterosexuals (Belluck 2004; Seidman 2003). "Gays and lesbians were raised in the same culture [as] everyone else," notes gay historian Eric Marcus. "When they settle down they want gold bands [and] legal documents" (quoted in Salholz 1993). This is one opinion. Actually, gays and lesbians themselves have been divided somewhat on the desirability of legalized same-sex marriage ("Gays Want the Right" 2004).

DISSENTING ARGUMENTS AMONG LESBIANS AND GAY MEN Although this is not so true today as it was ten years ago, some gays and lesbians have themselves opposed legal same-sex marriage. Generally, they have objected to mimicking a traditionally patriarchal institution based on property rights and institutionalized husband–wife roles. Opponents have also objected to giving the state power to regulate primary adult relationships. Furthermore, they have stressed that legalizing same-sex unions would further

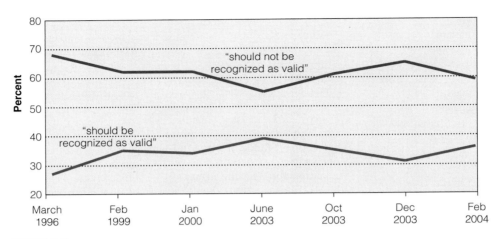

FIGURE 8.2

Responses to the question "Do you think marriages between homosexuals should or should not be recognized by the law as valid, with the same rights as traditional marriages?" March 1996 to February 2004.

Source: Newport 2004a. Data from "Constitutional Amendment Defining Marriage Lacks 'Supermajority' Support." The Gallup Organization, Gallup News Service. February 25. http://www.gallup.com.

stigmatize any sex outside marriage, with unmarried lesbians and gay men facing heightened discrimination ("Monogamy: Is It?" 1998; Seidman 2003). Then too, some same-sex partners question the advantage of joining an institution that seems to have many problems. As one lesbian explained, "One of the reasons I don't like to associate with marriage is because heterosexual marriage seems to be in trouble. It's like booking passage on the *Titanic* (quoted in Sherman 1992, pp. 189–190). Having gotten a sense of the debate over same-sex marriage within the gay/lesbian community, we turn to an examination of U.S. public opinion more generally.

Public Opinion on Same-Sex Marriage

Attitudes toward gay rights generally became more liberal during the 1990s. Gallup polls showed a gradual increase—from 38 percent in 1992 to 52 percent in 2001—in agreement with the idea that being gay or lesbian is an "acceptable alternative lifestyle" (Newport 2001). However, beginning about July 2003, when gay rights issues became more prominent in the news media, support for gay and lesbian rights and lifestyles dropped somewhat ("Opposition" 2003). As Figure 8.2 shows, the percentage of Americans who said that same-sex marriages should be legally valid

generally rose to a high of 39 percent in June 2003, but subsequently fell to 31 percent in December 2003. After that, the figure rose again to 36 percent in February 2003 (Newport 2004a). Attitudes toward gay and lesbian civil rights and lifestyles seem to decline as media attention to gay rights issues increases. Gary Bauer, president of the conservative activist organization American Values argues that "The more that the movement demands the endorsement of the law and the culture, the more resistance there will be" (Page 2003). Whether in the future Bauer will prove to be right remains to be seen.

In the most recent Gallup polls available at this writing, about one-third of Americans said that they favor legal marriage for same-sex couples, while 63 percent said that same-sex marriage should not be legal (see Figure 8.3). Asked whether they would favor or oppose a law that would allow same-sex couples to legally form civil unions, giving them some of the legal rights of married couples, but without the label "marriage," 34 percent favored and 41 percent opposed civil unions. Given the opportunity to express "no opinion," about one-quarter said that they had "no opinion either way" ("American Public Opinion" 2004).

Meanwhile, about half of Americans favor a United States Constitutional amendment that would define marriage as necessarily heterosexual (Newport 2004b). When President George W. Bush called upon Congress to pass such an amendment, "defining and protecting marriage as a union of a man and woman as husband and wife," he further noted that "An amendment to the Constitution is never to be undertaken lightly" (quoted in Newport 2004a).[10] Indeed, as you can see in Figure 8.3, Americans are less likely to support a U.S. Constitutional amendment defining marriage as heterosexual than they are to oppose legal marriage for same-sex couples.

A poll by CBS News that asked Americans whether they think of marriage as mostly a legal matter or as mostly a religious matter found that one-third saw marriage as mostly a legal matter while more than half (53 percent) saw it as mostly a religious matter ("Opposition" 2003). Perhaps not surprisingly, those who view marriage as primarily religious are less likely to favor same-sex, legal marriage. About one-quarter of those who see marriage as primarily religious favor legal marriage for same-sex couples, compared with about half of those who see marriage as mainly a legal matter ("Opposition" 2003). Males, older Americans, those living in the Midwest and in the South, those who define themselves as conservative or Republican, who have a high school education or less, and who attend church weekly are most likely to support a United States Constitutional amendment that would define marriage as between one man and one woman (Newport 2004a).

Whether one's commitment is same-sex or heterosexual, caring about marriage involves making choices. Sometimes these choices involve public activism toward one's goals—working for passage of the Defense of Marriage Act or, alternatively, pushing for the legal right to full-fledged marriage for same-sex couples. At other times, choices about marriage and family involve more personal ones, concerning, among other things, how we treat others in our own relationships. The following section examines the impact of some of these more personal choices on marital happiness and satisfaction.

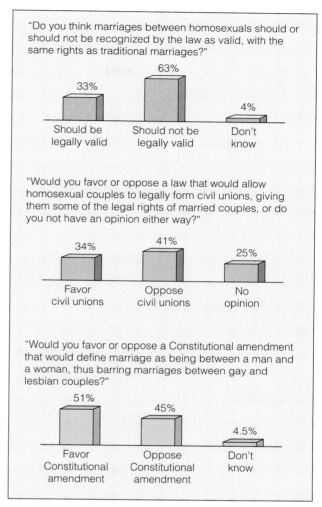

FIGURE 8.3

American public opinion regarding legal marriage and civil unions for same-sex couples, and regarding a United States Constitutional Amendment that would define marriage as necessarily heterosexual—i.e., between a man and a woman.

Sources: "American Public Opinion, Gallup poll conducted in January–February 2004"; 2003; Newport 2004a, 2004b.

---

10. Because the originators of the U.S. Constitution intended for amendments not to be undertaken lightly, they made it very difficult to pass a U.S. Constitutional amendment. Passing a U.S. Constitutional amendment requires a two-thirds majority in both the United States House of Representatives and Senate. Then the amendment must be approved by three-fourths of the states.

Marital Satisfaction and Choices Throughout Life

Our theme of making choices throughout life surely applies both to couples preparing for marriage and the early years of marriage. We'll look at these two topics here, and then discuss some ongoing decisions that couples make throughout the course of their marriage.

Preparation for Marriage

Given today's high divorce rate, clergy, teachers, parents, policy makers, and others have grown increasingly concerned that individuals be better prepared for a marital relationship. Family life education courses, which take place in high school and college classrooms, are designed to prepare individuals for marriage. Increasingly, such programs are designed to be meaningful to a variety of racial/ethnic groups (Duncan, Box, and Silliman 1996). Premarital counseling, which often takes place at churches or with private counselors, is specifically oriented to couples who plan to marry. For example, many Catholic dioceses require premarital counseling before a couple may be married by a priest. Catholic dioceses have also organized weekend engagement encounters during which couples who plan to marry learn about and discuss various aspects of married life. Such programs are designed and generally conducted by professionally trained people. Other churches have adopted these programs, and some couples may seek premarital counseling on their own initiative. Illustrating the connection between private lives and public interest, a few states now legally require premarital counseling, as we saw earlier in this chapter.

Premarital counseling has two goals: first, to evaluate the relationship with the possibility of deciding against marriage, and, second, to sensitize partners to potential problems and to teach positive ways of communicating about and resolving conflicts. Even though common sense suggests that these kinds of programs help, they have seldom been scientifically evaluated in terms of their impact on subsequent marriages. Nevertheless, family experts see these programs as important, especially for adult children of troubled, dysfunctional, or divorced families (Markman, Stanley, and Blumberg 1994; Russo 1997). Psychologist Scott Stanley identifies four benefits of premarital education:

(a) it can slow couples down to foster deliberation, (b) it sends a message that marriage matters, (c) it can help couples learn of options if they need help later, and (d) there is evidence that providing some couples with some types of

premarital training . . . can lower their risks for subsequent marital distress or termination. (2001, p. 272)

Premarital education or counseling may help make the first years of marriage go more smoothly.

The First Years of Marriage

In the 1950s, marriage and family texts characteristically referred to the first months and years of marriage as a period of adjustment, after which, presumably, spouses had learned to play traditional marital roles. Today we view early marriage more as a time of role *making* than of role *taking*.

Role making refers to modifying or adjusting the expectations and obligations traditionally associated with a role. Role making involves issues explored more fully in other chapters of this text. Newlyweds negotiate expectations for sex and intimacy (Chapter 6), establish communication (Chapter 13) and decision-making patterns (Chapter 14), balance expectations about marital and job responsibilities (Chapter 12), and come to some agreement about childbearing (Chapter 10) and how they will handle and budget their money (Knudson-Martin and Mahoney 1998; Burke and Cast 1997). When children are present, role making involves negotiation about parenting roles (Chapter 11). Role-making issues peculiar to remarriages are addressed in Chapter 17. Generally, role making in new marriages involves creating, by means of communication and negotiation, identities as married persons (Rotenburg, Schaut, and O'Connor 1993). One aspect of this process involves decisions about keeping or changing one's last name. This issue is explored in "As We Make Choices: Getting Married—and Changing Your Name?" The time of role making is not a clearly demarcated period but rather continues throughout marriage.

Although the early stages of marriage are not a distinct period, social scientists and others continue to talk and write about them as such (Bulcroft, Smeins, and Bulcroft 1999). One thing we know is that this period tends to be the happiest, with gradual declines in marital satisfaction afterward (Glenn 1998). (Perhaps this is where we get the popular expression "The honeymoon's over.") Why this is true is not clear. One explanation points to life-cycle stresses as children arrive and economic pressures intensify; others simply assume that courtship and new marriage are periods of

The early stages of marriage tend to be the happiest, as couples have time to enjoy each other and to pursue common interests. During this time, couples also need to establish a sense of solidarity and to modify competing interpersonal ties.

emotional intensity from which there is an inevitable decline (Whyte 1990, pp. 190–195; Glenn 1998).

We do know something about the structural advantages of early marriage, and it is likely that these contribute to high levels of satisfaction. For one thing, partners' roles are relatively similar or unsegregated in early marriage. Spouses tend to share household tasks and, because of similar experiences, are better able to empathize with each other. But early marriage is not characterized only by happiness. Couples must also accomplish certain tasks during this period. In general, "the solidarity of the new couple relation must be established and competing interpersonal ties modified" (Aldous 1978, p. 141; Rotenberg, Schaut, and O'Connor 1993). Getting through this stage requires making requests for change and negotiating resolutions, along with renewed acceptance of each other. Indeed, recent research by psychoanalyst John Gottman shows that communication as newlyweds tends to influence the later happiness—and even the permanence—of the

marriage (Gottman et al. 1998). The couple constructs relationships and interprets events in a way that reinforces their sense of themselves as a couple (Wallerstein and Blakeslee 1995).

Creating Couple Connection

In Chapter 5 we saw that sociologist Francesca Cancian (1985) views love as combining both instrumental and affectionate qualities. Similarly, a marriage relationship fulfills both practical and intimacy needs. Meanwhile, partners who desire enduring emotional relationships must keep their relationship as a high priority. Research shows that spouses who together pursue leisure activities that they both enjoy are not only more compatible but also more satisfied with their marriage (Crawford, Houts, Huston, and George 2002). Assuredly for wives, time spent together is important to marital happiness (Gager and Sanchez 2001). An important psychologist and expert on marital communication, John Gottman, offers this advice:

> Happy, solid couples nourish their marriages with plenty of positive moments together. . . . Too often, families lead complex—even grueling—lives in which they sacrifice the happy times for more materialistic, fleeting goals. . . . Sundays at the office take the place of Sundays at the park. But if you want to keep your marriage alive, it's essential to rediscover—or perhaps simply make time for—those experiences that make you feel good about your spouse and your marriage. (1995, p. 223)

Comparative analysis of data collected from national samples in 1980 and 2000 revealed that spouses spend less time interacting with each other now than they did twenty-five years ago. (However, their reported marital satisfaction had not declined significantly, partly because they were more satisfied with the decision-making equality in their marriage [Amato, Johnson, Booth, and Rogers 2003].) Nevertheless, increased emphasis on other matters, such as job pressures and long work hours or children's needs, can result in exhaustion and slow emotional erosion (Roberts and Levenson 2001; Sternberg 1988b).

Keeping one's marriage vital requires that partners consciously and continuously strive to maintain intimacy, which can entail "an enormous investment: in time, effort, and priorities. In other words, an emo-

© Henley & Savage/CORBIS

tionally meaningful relationship does not often develop 'by drift or default'" (Cuber and Harroff 1965, pp. 142–145). Clearly, the nature and quality of a marital relationship has a great deal to do with the choices that partners make. One important set of decisions concerns sexual exclusivity.

Making Choices about Sexual Exclusivity

Although a large majority of Americans publicly disapprove of extramarital sex, in practice the picture is somewhat different. Statistics are probably less than totally accurate because they are based on what people report: Some spouses hesitate to admit an affair; others boast about affairs that didn't really happen. Nevertheless, in an important U.S. national survey on sexuality undertaken in the 1990s (see Chapter 6), one-quarter of all husbands and 15 percent of wives ages eighteen through fifty-nine reported having had at least one affair. Among men in their fifties, the figure was 37 percent (Laumann et al. 1994). Social scientists F. Scott Christopher and Susan Sprecher (2000), reviewing 1990s research on extramarital sex, concluded that studies in the 1990s found lower extramarital sex rates than in earlier studies. "Nonetheless, these percentages translate into a significant number of Americans who have experienced sex with someone other than their spouse at least once" (Christopher and Sprecher 2000, p. 1006).

Moreover, the 1990s saw the emergence of a new brand of marital infidelity—adultery on the Net, or **cyberadultery**. It may be that, for some people, two potentially addictive attractions—the Internet and sex—interact to make "cyber-sexual compulsivity" difficult to just say no to (Glass 1998; Maheu and Subotnik 2001). In a typical cyberadulterous scenario, a married person wanders into a computer chat room, becomes enamored with a cyberpartner, and may—or may not—eventually meet the cyberpartner in person. Meanwhile, experts and aggrieved spouses have found themselves trying to define just what *is* sexual infidelity in the computer age. Is virtual sex real? Does infidelity have to be physical? Whatever the ultimate answers, there is evidence that cyberinfidelity has resulted in the breakup of at least some marriages ("The Dark Side" 1997).

Then too, gender differences are evident in any discussion of extramarital sex (Harris 2003a). More

husbands (about 23 percent according to one national survey) than wives (about 12 percent) have had an affair sometime during their marriage (Wiederman 1997). If a wife has an affair, she is more likely to do so because she feels emotionally distanced by her husband. Men who have affairs are far more likely to do so for the sexual excitement and variety they hope to find (Masters, Johnson, and Kolodny 1994, pp. 494, 499). Then too, "Men feel more betrayed by their wives having sex with someone else; women feel more betrayed by their husbands being emotionally involved with someone else" (Glass 1998, p. 35).

REASONS FOR EXTRAMARITAL AFFAIRS—TWO THEORETICAL PERSPECTIVES Interestingly, research suggests that although dissatisfaction with one's marriage plays a part in a spouse's decision to have extramarital sex, other factors are also important; marital dissatisfaction may play only a small role (Christopher and Sprecher 2000, p. 1006; Treas and Giesen 2000). We can look briefly at two theoretical perspectives used to shed light on why a spouse might choose to have an affair.

Evolutionary Psychology: a Biosocial Perspective You may recall that Chapter 6 discussed evolutionary psychology's argument that human sexual behavior may be partly genetically influenced. From this point of view, men are genetically more likely to be unfaithful because of an evolutionary predisposition to fertilize as many female eggs as possible. Women, on the other hand, because pregnancy and delivery are far more time- and energy-consuming than the act of conception, are genetically more reluctant to engage in casual sex (Buss 1994; Wright 1994b). This biosocial perspective on affairs is highly controversial (see also the discussion of the biosocial perspective in Chapter 3). Exchange theory is another somewhat controversial perspective used to explain sexual infidelity.

Exchange Theory You may recall from Chapter 3 that a basic idea in exchange theory (also called rational choice theory) is that people use their resources rationally to bargain and secure advantage in relationships. Also, as individuals, people are inherently interested in maximizing their rewards or pleasures and minimizing their costs or pain. A related idea is that the more often or easily a person experiences some pleasure, the less valuable it becomes. For example, a hot fudge sundae is really great if you haven't had one for a while, but if you indulge in one daily, it becomes less enjoyable—or valuable—to you. A second related idea is that the more a person invests in something, the more valuable it will be to her or him. So if you have to walk ten miles through thunder and lightning for the hot fudge sundae, it will seem more valuable to you than if your local ice cream parlor is just beneath your second-floor apartment.

Sociologist Chien Liu (2000) applied these principles to extramarital sex. Liu noted that husbands engage in extramarital affairs more often than do wives (see below) and that a vast amount of research consistently finds that wives invest more than husbands do in the expressive, or relationship, dimension of marriage. Next, Liu argued as follows:

> [M]arital sexual actions between a husband and a wife initially bring about a relatively high level of satisfaction. . . . [But as] marital sex increases, the level of satisfaction lowers. . . . [O]ther things being equal, over the course of a marriage a rational actor would become more likely to engage in extramarital sex [because the pleasure] . . . of a sexual action with an old partner is lower than that of a sexual action with a new partner. (pp. 365–366)

Liu argued that the above analysis more often applies to husbands, because a wife's relatively high investment in the marital sex relationship counterbalances the fact that her husband is a familiar partner.

We have examined two theoretical perspectives on causes for infidelity; the remainder of our focus will be on empirical findings regarding causes for affairs. We will note that many of the points below can be explained by exchange theory.

CAUSES FOR AFFAIRS—EMPIRICAL FINDINGS

Some extramarital affairs are brief; others are more enduring (Glass 1998, 2003). Many *short-term affairs* are "situation specific": a fling while attending an out-of-town meeting, or a surprise telephone call from a former boyfriend or girlfriend that leads to sex but ends as abruptly as it began (Masters, Johnson, and Kolodny 1994, pp. 483–486). Other short-term affairs are motivated by the need for conquest (a new "notch on his or her gun barrel") or to get revenge for a spouse's real or imagined injustices. Husbands are more likely to engage in conquest affairs while wives

are more likely to have anger/revenge affairs. Another type of short-term affair precedes a possible divorce; predivorce affairs are "like test flights—transient forays into the world of sex outside marriage as a prelude to making the final decision to terminate a relationship that is already on a shaky foundation" (Masters, Johnson, and Kolodny 1994, p. 489).

A final type of short-term affair is the male bisexual affair. While a wife's bisexual affair is more likely to be long term, a husband's bisexual affair(s) are much more likely to be quick and anonymous. Male bisexual affairs may occur among husbands who are predominantly heterosexual but are occasionally drawn to the danger, variety, or intrigue of same-sex relations as a means of experiencing a different form of sexual excitement. On the other hand, there are married men who might appear to be heterosexual but who are really closeted gay men using marriage to hide their sexual orientation (Masters, Johnson, and Kolodny 1994, p. 489).

Long-term affairs tend to be more complex than short-term liaisons (Glass 1998, 2003). Masters, Johnson, and Kolodny include the following types, depending on their purpose: hedonistic, marriage maintenance, intimacy reduction, and reactive affairs.

Hedonistic affairs rarely lead to emotional entanglements:

> The affair is an indulgence, a creative act of playfulness, an oasis of sensual energy in a world fogged over by trivial details of everyday life. . . . The participants often have happy and sexually fulfilling marriages of their own. (Masters, Johnson, and Kolodny 1994, p. 492)

Marriage maintenance affairs are convenient arrangements that provide something that is missing from the marriage, such as kinky sexual experimentation. By supplying this element, the affair actually stabilizes the marriage and makes it less likely that a marital breakup will occur: "Although common wisdom has it that affairs often lead to marital dissolution, we have encountered hundreds of marriages that were held together and solidified by affairs" (Masters, Johnson, and Kolodny 1994, p. 491).

Intimacy reduction affairs are undertaken by spouses who are ambivalent about the intimacy demanded by their husband or wife. Creating a safety zone of emotional distance within the marriage, the affair serves as a buffer against too much closeness:

When tension and anxiety over too much intimacy mount, it can be defused by more involvement with the affair. In contrast, when enough emotional space has developed in the marriage for it to feel comfortable, rather than smothering, the affair may be ignored for awhile, since there is at least temporarily safe harbor at home. (Masters, Johnson, and Kolodny 1994, p. 492)

Reactive affairs are motivated by a spouse's desire to be reassured amid changing life circumstances. For instance, a middle-aged husband who is feeling over the hill may seek to prove his youthfulness by having an affair with a younger woman. Or a wife may rediscover her sexuality once her children have left home and opt for the excitement of extramarital sex. A wife's bisexual affair often fits this category (Masters, Johnson, and Kolodny 1994, p. 493).

Finally, the book *Not Just Friends* (2003), by the late psychotherapist and researcher Shirley Glass, a recognized expert on marital affairs, contends that there is a "new infidelity." In this situation, a well-meaning partner, absorbed at work and harried at home, never intended to be unfaithful but unwittingly slips into a passionate extramarital connection before realizing it.

EFFECTS OF EXTRAMARITAL AFFAIRS Extramarital sex *can* have positive effects (Cano and O'Leary 1997; Hein 2000). As we have seen, for example, an affair can sometimes help keep a marriage together by filling a need or reducing intimacy anxiety. But recognizing that affairs can have a positive side is hardly the whole story: "We are firmly convinced that the downside of extramarital sex usually looms larger than any potential benefits" (Masters, Johnson, and Kolodny 1994, p. 502).

First, an affair that is nonconsensual involves deceit and can be considered a form of theft: "What is stolen is the bond of trust and its attendant consent to mutual vulnerability between spouses" (Masters, Johnson, and Kolodny 1994, p. 503; Glass 2003). The discovery of a spouse's affair often results in jealousy, shock, and outrage, setting off a series of negative consequences that reverberate over time through the course of the marriage (Aune and Comstock 2002; Harris 2002, 2003b).

Moreover, affairs victimize the uninvolved partner without giving her or him prior warning or any way to avoid being injured (Cano and O'Leary 1997). Not only have trust been eroded and feelings been hurt, but the uninvolved spouse may also have been exposed to various sexually transmitted diseases—not a rare occurrence. For many spouses, concern about AIDS heightens anger and turmoil over affairs (Adler 1996a). The uninvolved spouse may feel exploited financially as well, because what were thought to be joint funds have been unilaterally spent on dinners, gifts, hotel rooms, or weekends away.

JEALOUSY **Jealousy** is strong emotional pain, anger, fear, and uncertainty arising when a valued relationship is threatened or perceived to be threatened. Sociologist Ira Reiss sees a spouse's jealousy as "a boundary-setting mechanism." When boundaries are violated (in this case, those circumscribing the married couple as primary), "jealousy occurs and indexes the anger and hurt that are expected to be activated by a violation of an important norm" (1986a, p. 47).

Research has found differences in how men and women experience and react to jealousy (Harris 2003a; Nannini and Meyers 2000). Men are more reactive to the sexual threat, whereas women are more anxious about losing a primary relationship. Women, being more likely to monitor relationships, are more apt to try to change to please their partner so as to avoid the threat of another relationship. However, men are more likely to seek solace or retribution in alternative relationships (Cano and O'Leary 1997). Several research projects suggest that those who already feel insecure or have poor self-images are more inclined toward jealousy (Macklin 1987; Buunk 1991; Cano and O'Leary 1997).

Although marital jealousy can probably never be completely eliminated, mutually supportive encouragement may lessen feelings of insecurity and jealousy. Also, nurturing one's self-esteem may allay unwarranted jealousy (Cano and O'Leary 1997). In sum, jealousy, like pain, needs to be viewed as a warning signal. Jealousy may mean that one or both partners' interests in outside activities need to be counterbalanced with activities within the relationship.

RECOVERING FROM AN EXTRAMARITAL AFFAIR Given that affairs do occur, many people will have to think about this issue when they discover that their spouse has had (or is having) one. The unin-

There are many types of extramarital affairs, just as there are different reasons for having an affair. Although an affair may have positive consequences for the individuals involved, and even for the marriage, the negative effects are likely to outweigh any positive ones. This couple is in marriage counseling to deal with the aftermath of an extramarital affair.

volved mate will need to consider how important the affair is relative to the marital relationship as a whole. Can she or he regain trust? In some cases, the answer is "no"; trust never gets reestablished, and the heightened suspicion gets incorporated into other problems the couple might have (Levine 1998).

Whether trust can be reestablished depends on several factors. One is how much trust there is in the first place. One researcher (Hansen 1985) has suggested that for this reason, new relationships may be especially vulnerable to breaking up after an affair. But many couples do recover from an affair, although "it's hard to do without a therapist" (Glass 1998, p. 44). Therapists suggest that doing so requires that the offending spouse

- apologize sincerely and without defending her or his behavior
- allow and hear the verbally vented anger and rage of the offended partner (but not permit physical abuse)

- allow for trust to rebuild gradually and to realize that this may take a long time—up to two years or more
- do things to help the offended partner to regain trust—keep agreements, for example, and call if he or she is running late

Meanwhile, the offended spouse needs to decide whether she or he is committed to the marriage and, if so, needs to be willing to let go of resentments as this becomes possible. Finally, the couple should consider marriage counseling (described in Appendix H). According to Shirley Glass, "The affair creates a loss of innocence and some scar tissue. I tell couples things will never be the same. But the relationship may be stronger" (1998, p. 44).

On the one hand, data on extramarital affairs suggest that, although lifelong fidelity is not always practiced, specific acts of infidelity may not be routine or continual. The data on extramarital sex suggest that today, as in the past, many spouses are torn between

"We are gathered here to join together this man and this woman in matrimony—a very serious step, with far-reaching and unpredictable consequences."

lifelong commitment to a sexually exclusive marriage and desire for outside sexual relationships (Levine 1998). For the majority of mates, however, the decision to marry involves the promise to forego other sexual partners. If we interpret fidelity to mean a primary commitment to one's partner and the relationship, then maintaining *emotional* intimacy becomes essential to being "faithful." Without continued intimacy and self-disclosure, partners may not remain in love or keep a central place in each other's lives (Hein 2000).

This section has addressed extramarital sex from the married couple's point of view. There is some research, though, on the "other woman" (not to imply that there is never the "other man"—just that we know of no research on him). Sociologist Laurel Richardson (1985) interviewed fifty-five women from varied social backgrounds—high school graduates and women with postgraduate degrees, skilled workers and professional and managerial women, traditional women and feminists—who were having affairs with married men. For the most part, the woman did not intend to have the affair; it developed inadvertently out of sustained work or social contact. Once begun, it seemed a rational solution to the woman's dilemma: how to meet her emotional, sexual, and companionship needs in the absence of marriage.

To sum up, marriage entails making ongoing choices about permanence and sexual exclusivity. Getting married is a public statement that a couple intends to do so. Nevertheless, we saw in Chapter 1 that as people change throughout life, the kind of relationship they need also changes. Thus, marriages need to be adaptable if they are to continue to be satisfying to changing partners.

Creating Adaptable Marriage Relationships

For years, writes psychoanalyst Sidney Jourard,

> spouses go to sleep night after night, with their relationship patterned one way, a way that perhaps satisfies neither—too close, too distant, boring or suffocating—and on awakening the next morning, they reinvent their relationship *in the same way.* (1976, p. 231)

People change, however, and—if the marriage is to be permanent—spouses need to envision marriage as able to allow for such change.

An option is to actively pursue an **adaptable marriage relationship**, one that allows and encourages partners to grow and change. In an adaptable marriage, spouses' roles may be renegotiated as the needs of each change (Scarf 1995). Some people may have an intuitive knack for achieving this kind of marriage. But again, we want to stress the way in which decisions, in the absence of conscious reflection, are often made by default. Hence, we would encourage spouses to talk to each other about the following questions at various times throughout their marriage.

Talking about the marriage that you and your partner want and expect may point up differences, many of which can be worked out. Then too, if dating or engaged couples uncover basic value differences and cannot work them out—for example, about whether or not to have children—it would probably be better to end their relationship before marriage than to commit themselves to a union that cannot satisfy either of them. Openly and honestly discussing matters like the ones that follow is important in maintaining a mutually supportive relationship.

Some Things to Talk About

1. When should a marriage be dissolved and under what conditions? How long and in what ways would you work on an unsatisfactory relationship before dissolving it? If you live in a state where it is available, might the two of you consider a covenant marriage—or not? Why?

2. What are your expectations, attitudes, and preferences regarding sex? Are there sexual activities that you consider distasteful and would prefer not to engage in? How would you expect to deal with either your own or your partner's sexual dysfunction if that occurred?

3. Do you want children? If so, how many, and how would you like to space them? Whose responsibility is birth control, and what kind of contraception will you use? What is your attitude toward unwanted pregnancy? Abortion? Adoption? Having a child who might result from an unwanted pregnancy?

4. If you have children, how will you allocate child-rearing responsibilities and tasks? Will either spouse be primarily responsible for discipline? What are some of your values about child raising?

5. Will decisions be made equally? Will there be a principal breadwinner, or will partners equally share responsibility for earning money? How will funds be allocated? Will there be his, her, and our money? Or will all money be pooled? Who is the owner of family property, such as family business(es), farms, or other partnerships?

6. Will there be a principal homemaker, or will domestic chores be shared?

7. What about religious values? Do you expect your partner to share them? Will you attend religious services together? How often? If you are of a different religion from your mate, where will you worship on special religious holidays? What about the children's religion?

8. What are your educational goals? What educational goals do you expect your partner to have? Under what circumstances could you or your partner put aside wage-earning or housekeeping responsibilities to pursue advanced education?

9. How will you relate to your own and to your spouse's relatives? How do you expect your partner to relate to them? Will you expect to share many or most activities with relatives? Or do you prefer more couple togetherness, discouraging activities with relatives?

10. How much time and how much intimate information will you share with friends other than your partner? What is your attitude toward friendships with people of the opposite sex? How about Internet (cyberspace) friends? Would you ever consider having sex with someone other than your mate? If so, under what circumstances? How would you react if your partner were to have sex with another person?

11. How much time alone do you need? How much are you willing to allow your partner? Will you buy a larger house or rent a bigger apartment so that each partner may have private space?

12. Will you purposely set aside time to talk to each other? What topics do you like to talk about? What topics do you dislike? Are you willing to try to become more comfortable about discussing these? If communication becomes difficult, will you go to a marriage counselor? If so, what percentage of your income would you be willing to pay for marriage counseling?

13. What kinds of vacations will you take? Will you take couple-only vacations? Will you take separate vacations? If so, how often and what kind?

14. What are your own and your partner's personal definitions of *intimacy*, *commitment*, and *responsibility*?

In talking with each other, partners need to try to keep an open mind and use their creativity. Maintaining a happy marriage is challenging, if only because two people, two imaginations, and two sets of needs are involved. Differences *will* arise because no two individuals have exactly the same points of view. (Some methods for reconciling these differences and other conflicts—as well as for communicating in positive ways generally—are discussed in Chapter 13.)

In Sum

- Marriage has changed—and continues to change—from marriage-as-institution to psychological marriage to pluralistic, or postmodern families.

- Although marriage is less permanent and more adaptable than it has ever been, it is still both a private relationship and a public proclamation of a couple's intention to adhere to the marriage premise that traditionally involves expectations for permanence and sexual exclusivity.

- As both of these expectations come to depend less on legal definitions and social conventions, partners need to invest more effort in sustaining a marriage.

- Congruent with the emergence of the pluralistic (or postmodern) family, we are witnessing a national and global debate over whether legal marriage should be extended to include lesbians and gay men.

- Although the state of Massachusetts presently allows legal marriage for same-sex couples, this situation could change due either to revised Massachusetts state legislation or a federal Constitutional amendment.

- Extramarital affairs break the norm of sexual exclusivity, inherent in the marriage premise.

- Two theoretical perspectives used to explain extramarital affairs are evolutionary psychology (a biosocial perspective) and exchange theory.

- There is society-wide concern about preparation for marriage. Premarital counseling and family life education are two approaches that have been developed, but we need more research data on their effectiveness.

- Partners change over the course of a marriage, so a relationship needs to be adaptable if it is to continue to be emotionally satisfying.

Key Terms

adaptable marriage relationship
conjugal relatives
consanguineous relatives
covenant marriage
culture war
cyberadultery
Defense of Marriage Act
dominant dyad
expectations of sexual exclusivity
la familia
family of orientation
family of procreation
interactional relationship pattern
jealousy
marriage premise
parallel relationship pattern
polyamory
polyandry
polygamy
polygyny
role making
social institution
swinging

Questions for Review and Reflection

1. Discuss the marriage premise, with its expectations of permanence and sexual exclusivity. How does the marriage premise affect one's personal marital relationship?

2. Describe adaptable marriages and discuss ways to create one.

3. This chapter lists topics that are important to discuss before and throughout one's marriage. Which do you think are the most important? Which do you think are the least important? Why?

4. Describe the arguments in favor of and against covenant marriage. With which side of the controversy do you agree?

5. **Policy Question.** Do you think that legalizing same-sex marriage is a good idea? Give arguments based on facts to support your opinion.

Suggested Readings

Association for Couples in Marriage Enrichment

http://www.marriageenrichment.com/

Website of and for couples in the national/international Marriage Enrichment Association, which encourages ongoing marital commitment.

Bulcroft, Kris, Linda Smeins, and Richard Bulcroft. 1999. *Romancing the Honeymoon: Consummating Marriage in Modern Society.* Thousand Oaks, CA: Sage. Contemporary review of the literature and theoretical discussion on early marriage, particularly the honeymoon as important to marriage and family development.

Farrell, Betty G. 1999. *Family: The Making of an Idea, an Institution, and a Controversy in American Culture.* Boulder, CO: Westview Press. A family scholar at Pitzer College, Farrell presents accessible, but scholarly and balanced (neither obviously conservative nor liberal), "essays" on family-as-institution and implications of family change for childhood, adolescence, adult married life, and old age.

Mackey, Richard A. 1997. *Gay and Lesbian Couples: Voices from Lasting Relationships.* Westport, CT: Praeger. Even when they cannot marry legally, many gay and lesbian couples forge lasting relationships, and the couples in this book describe their relationships.

Partners Task Force for Gay & Lesbian Couples

http://www.buddybuddy.com/

Current information on issues of legal marriage for same-sex couples.

Rutgers National Marriage Project

http://marriage.rutgers.edu

Conservative/centrist research and family policy site of "The National Marriage Project," headquartered at Rutgers University and co-directed by David Popenoe (see Chapter 1).

Wallerstein, Judith S., and Sandra Blakeslee. 1995. *The Good Marriage: How and Why Love Lasts.* New York: Houghton Mifflin. These two marriage counselors and researchers offer their own typology of marriage relationships and list tasks that every couple needs to accomplish in a long-term, successful union.

Virtual Society: The Wadsworth Sociology Resource Center

 Go to the Sociology Resource Center at **http://sociology.wadsworth.com** for a wealth of online resources, including a companion website for your text that provides study aids such as self-quizzes for each chapter and a practice final exam, as well as links to sociology websites and information on the latest theories and discoveries in the field. In addition, you will find further suggested readings, flash cards, MicroCase online exercises, and appendices on a range of subjects.

Online Study Tool

Marriage & Family ⊛ Now™ Go to **http://sociology.wadsworth.com** to reach the companion website for your text and use the Marriage&FamilyNow access code that came with your book to access this study tool. Take a practice pretest after you have read each chapter, and then use the study plan provided to master that chapter. Afterward, take a posttest to monitor your progress.

Search Online with InfoTrac College Edition

For additional information, exercises, and key words to aid your research, explore InfoTrac College Edition, your online library that offers full-length articles from thousands of scholarly and popular publications. Click on *InfoTrac College Edition* under *Chapter Resources* at the companion website and use the access code that came with your book.

■ Search keywords: *sexual infidelity, marital satisfaction, gay marriage.*

Alternatives
to Marriage:
Living Alone, Cohabitation, Domestic Partnerships, and Other Options

Marital status may reflect an outdated set of categories. When asked whether they are married, divorced, separated, never married, or widowed, more and more people find that none of these categories accurately describe their situation. . . . Some people have a partner they are living with, but not in a traditional heterosexual marriage. Others have a partner outside the household. Some live in a household with other adults but without significant social attachments to them.

CATHERINE ROSS,
Journal of Marriage and Family, 1995

FIFTY YEARS AGO the majority of Americans thought of themselves as either married or single. But the distinction between marriage and singlehood has become blurred over the past several decades. As a result, sociologist Catherine Ross (1995) has suggested that we need to reconceptualize marital status as a **continuum of social attachment**. You can think of a continuum as a line between two opposites; the points on a continuum are not simply black or white but are shades of gray.

Factors such as age, sex, residence, religion, and economic status contribute to the diversity and complexity of single life. An elderly man or woman existing on Social Security payments and meager savings has a vastly different lifestyle from two single professionals living together in an urban area. Single life in small towns differs from that in large cities. Then too, the experience of singlehood, or being unmarried, differs according to whether one is single by choice, or voluntarily single, or whether one is involuntarily single— unmarried but would like to be otherwise (Stein 1981).

In this chapter we will examine what social scientists know about the large and growing number of singles: the never-married, the divorced, and the widowed. We'll look at changing cultural attitudes about marriage and discuss reasons that more people today are choosing alternatives to marriage, such as cohabitation or domestic partnerships. We will also look at gay male or lesbian singles and at the lifestyles of singles who live alone or with their parents. Many college students today think of "being single" as not being in a romantic relationship. By this way of thinking, a person in a serious dating relationship or individuals "living together" would not be single. To social scientists, however, *single* still means *unmarried*, and we, the authors, use these two terms interchangeably. Sometimes when we discuss reasons for singlehood and how the unmarried live, we will consider only those who have never married; other times we will consider factors applying to all singles, whether divorced, widowed, or never-married. To begin, we examine some reasons for the increasing number of unmarrieds today.

The Unmarried: Reasons for Their Increasing Numbers

The number of singles, or unmarrieds, in the United States has risen strikingly over the past fifty years (see "Facts About Families: The Large and Increasing Numbers of Unmarrieds").

Throughout the first half of the twentieth century, the trend was for more and more people to marry and at increasingly younger ages.[1] In the 1960s that trend reversed, and since that time the trend has been for more and more American adults to be categorized by the U.S. Census Bureau as single. Before about 1960, family sociologists described a standard pattern of marriage at about age twenty for women and twenty-two for men (Aldous 1978). About 80 percent of these unions lasted until the children left home (Scanzoni 1972).

Today, in contrast, we see an increasing number of never-married young adults and of formerly married singles, as Figure 9.1 illustrates. The increase in young singles over the past four decades reverses a downward trend lasting from 1900 to 1960. At least four social factors may encourage young people today to postpone marriage or not to marry at all. First, changes in the economy may make early marriage less attractive, a point that is explored in Chapter 8 as well as later in this chapter. Second, improved contraception may contribute to the decision to delay getting married.

---

1. For men, median age at first marriage in 1890—the year when the government first began to calculate and report this statistic—was 26.1. For both women and men, median ages at first marriage fell from 1890 until 1960, when they began to rise again.

The increase in the number and proportion of singles in our society is a result of many factors, including economic constrictions, improved contraception, an unequal sex ratio, and changing attitudes toward marriage and singlehood.

With effective contraception, sex without great risk of unwanted pregnancy is possible outside marriage, and at least one researcher has found evidence that women "substitute premarital liaisons for marriage early in the adult life course" (Gaughan 2002, p. 407).

The Sex Ratio

A third reason for the growing proportion of singles is demographic—that is, related to population numbers. The **sex ratio** is the ratio of men to women in a given society or subgroup of a society.[2] Throughout the

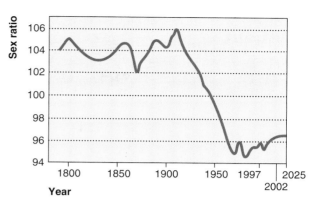

FIGURE 9.3

Sex ratios in the United States from 1790 to 2002 and projections for 2025. Because 100 represents a balanced sex ratio—an equal number of men and women—the parts of the curve above the 100 line mean there are more men than women; portions below that line mean that there are more women than men.

Sources: Calculated from U.S. Census Bureau 2000, Table 14; U.S. Census Bureau 2003a, Table 11.

nineteenth and early twentieth centuries, the United States had more men than women, mainly because more men than women migrated to this country and, to a lesser extent, because a considerable number of young women died in childbirth. Today this situation is reversed due to changes in immigration patterns and greater improvement in women's health than in men's health. Since World War II, which ended in 1945, there have been more women than men (see Figure 9.3). In the year 2000, for example, there were about 95 men for every 100 women, whereas in 1910 there were nearly 106. The sex ratio was 100, or "even," in about 1948.

Sex ratios can affect the odds of finding a spouse (Albrecht and Albrecht 2001).[3] Sex ratios differ somewhat for various racial/ethnic categories. For instance, at younger ages the sex ratio is lower for blacks and Native Americans than for Hispanics or non-Hispanic whites. Beginning with middle age, however, there are increasingly fewer men than women in every racial/ethnic category. If each of these people wished to marry, many women would be left out, increasingly so in the older age groups.

---

2. The sex ratio is expressed in one number: the number of males for every 100 females. Thus, a sex ratio of 105 means there are 105 men for every 100 women in a given population. More-specialized sex ratios may be calculated: for example, the sex ratio for specific racial/ethnic categories at various ages or the sex ratio for unmarried people only.

---

3. Moreover, as is discussed in Chapter 7, not only the relative number of eligible men is salient; their employment prospects also affect women's chances for marrying (South and Lloyd 1992b).

Facts About Families

The Large and Increasing Numbers of Unmarrieds

The number of unmarrieds over age seventeen has jumped from about twenty-five million at the turn of the twentieth century to nearly eighty-six million at present. Singles have increased in absolute numbers partly because the population as a whole has grown. But singles have also increased as a relative proportion of the population—from 28 percent of the total population in 1970 to 39.5 percent in 2002 (U.S. Census Bureau 2003, Table 61). (See Figure 9.1.)

Figure 9.2 compares marital status proportions for non-Hispanic white, Hispanic, and African American women and men. As you can see in Figure 9.2, African Americans are more likely to be never-married and less likely to be married than whites. The percentage for Hispanics falls somewhere in between. African Americans are slightly more likely than non-Hispanic whites to be divorced; the proportion divorced is lowest among Hispanics, an indication of their strong cultural commitment to lifelong marriage, among other possible reasons (Oropesa, Lichter, and Anderson 1994). The fact that Hispanics are less likely to be widowed reflects the fact that, as a category, they are younger, on average, than either non-Hispanic whites or African Americans.

The Never-Married

There is a growing tendency for young adults to postpone marriage until they are older. By 2000, the median age at first marriage for both men and women had risen, to 25.1 for women and 26.8 for men (Fields and Casper 2001, Figure 3). For women, this figure is as high as

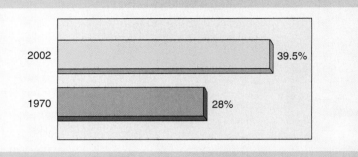

FIGURE 9.1

Unmarried adults as a percentage of all adults: 1970 and 2002.

Sources: Saluter and Lugaila 1998, Figure 1; U.S. Census Bureau 2003a, Table 61.

any figure ever recorded. The highest median age at first marriage ever recorded for men was 27.1, in 1996 ("Estimated Median Age" 1999).

As a consequence of postponing marriage, the number of singles in their twenties has risen dramatically. In 1970, 36 percent of women aged twenty through twenty-four were single; by 2002, that figure had risen to 74 percent. Even though larger numbers of men than women have traditionally remained single in their twenties, the ranks of single men aged twenty through twenty-four have nevertheless increased from 55 percent in 1970 to 85 percent in 2002 (Saluter and Lugaila 1998, Table B; U.S. Census Bureau 2003, Table 63).

This rate of singlehood is striking when compared with the 1950s, but not so unusual in a broader time frame. That is, the percentage of never-married men and women aged twenty through twenty-four today is comparable to the proportion of young adults never married at the turn of the twentieth century (Haines 1996).

The Divorced

The growing divorce rate has contributed to the increased number of singles. In 2002, 8.6 percent of men and 11.3 percent of women aged eighteen and over were divorced. These proportions show a sharp increase from 1980, when 3.9 percent of adult men and 6 percent of adult women were divorced (U.S. Census Bureau 2000, Table 53; U.S. Census Bureau 2003, Table 61). Although the divorce rate is no longer rising, it is stable at a high level, and the divorced will continue to be a substantial component of the singles population.

The Widowed

Unlike the other singles categories, the proportion of widowed women and men has remained about the same since 1980—between 2 percent and 2.7 percent for men and about 10.5 percent for women (U.S. Census Bureau 2003, Table 61). Death rates declined throughout the twentieth century, reducing the chances of widowhood for the young and middle-aged. However,

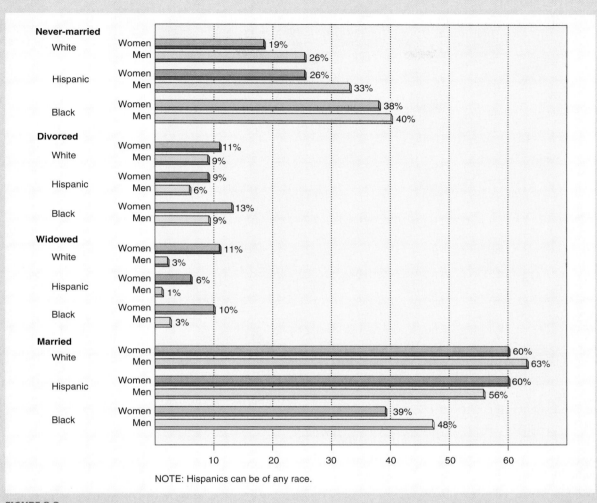

FIGURE 9.2

Marital status of U.S. population, age 18 and over, 2002, by race/ethnicity.

Source: U.S. Census Bureau 2003a, Table 61.

the proportion of older people in the population has increased, and an older person has a greater risk of losing a spouse.

Women are much more likely to be widowed than men. As shown in Figure 9.2, this is true across racial/ethnic categories. This difference is due to women's greater longevity and their lower likelihood of remarrying after the death of a spouse. Thirty-one percent of women sixty-five through seventy-four are widowed, compared to 9 percent of men. Of women seventy-five years old and over, 61 percent are widowed (U.S. Census Bureau 2003, Table 63). Widowhood is not a status of choice, although those who are widowed may experience some positive aspects of independent living. (Chapter 18 discusses the experience of widowhood.)

Critical Thinking

How has the growing number of unmarrieds affected American society, do you think? On the one hand, what changes in *cultural attitudes* have helped to cause the high proportion of unmarrieds today? On the other hand, what *structural factors* have helped to cause the high proportion of unmarrieds today? Besides the fact that they are not married, what (if anything) might the divorced or the widowed have in common with the never-married?

Table 9.1

The Desire to Stay Single Among Never-Married, Noncohabiting Individuals, by Age, Race/Ethnicity, and Sex

	WHITE MALES	BLACK MALES	HISPANIC MALES	WHITE FEMALES	BLACK FEMALES	HISPANIC FEMALES	TOTAL
Ages 19 to 35							
Percentage not desiring marriage	15.40	23.50	8.70	17.10	21.80	25.30	17.20
Number of all respondents	566	190	79	721	389	128	2,073
Ages 19 to 25							
Percentage not desiring marriage	12.60	22.80	6.80	11.20	12.70	13.10	12.60
Number of all respondents	291	97	50	288	149	51	926

Source: From "Racial and Ethnic Differences in the Desire to Marry," by Scott J. South, 1993, *Journal of Marriage and the Family,* 55 (2), 357–370. Copyright © 1993 by the National Council on Family Relations, 3989 Central Ave. NE, Suite 550, Minneapolis, MN 55421. Reprinted by permission.

Of course, the sex ratio for society *as a whole* does not tell the entire story. To get a better picture of how the sex ratio affects one's odds of marrying, we need to examine sex ratios within certain age groups—and, more specifically, sex ratios for *single* people within certain age groups. In the 1980s, the popular press made much of the idea that there weren't enough single, eligible men to go around. There still are far more women than men in older age groups. By the 1990s, however, there were more single men than single women in their twenties and early thirties (Weeks 2002). Whether due to a shortage of men or of women, in many social categories there just aren't enough eligible (heterosexual) mates, so in the musical chairs of marital pairings, some are left out.[4]

An additional reason for the growing proportion of singles in the United States involves changing attitudes toward marriage and singlehood, discussed in the following section. As American culture gives greater weight to personal autonomy (Thornton and Young-DeMarco 2001), many find singlehood more desirable than marriage.

Changing Attitudes Toward Marriage and Singlehood

Sociologist Scott South (1993) analyzed data from 2,073 never-married men and women aged nineteen to thirty-five who were not cohabiting. As part of the National Survey of Families and Households (NSFH), these singles were asked to respond to the statement "I would like to get married someday." They could answer with any one of the following: "strongly agree," "agree," "neither agree nor disagree," "disagree," or "strongly disagree." Notice that this question does not measure whether a person *expects* to marry, only whether she or he *would like* to marry.

Table 9.1 gives the percentages of respondents who did not agree with the statement. They either disagreed or answered that they could neither agree nor disagree. South cautions that this sample probably *overestimates* people's negative attitudes about marriage, because only never-marrieds are included. Presumably, the marrieds have generally positive feelings about marriage. (This overestimation is especially apparent for Hispanic females, a large majority of whom are married.)

Although most people *do* want to marry, 17 percent of these respondents do not. Why not? First, compared with married people, singles hold more individualistic than familistic values. For example, we saw in Chapter 5 that young, never-married singles are more likely to have ludic, or playful, love styles and less likely to have agapic, or unselfish, love styles than are marrieds (Montgomery and Sorell 1997). As Table

---

4. Then too, calculation of the availability of mates is complicated by the tendency of men to be two to three years older than the women they marry and by the fact that individuals seek mates within *local* markets; thus, the latest available nationally aggregated figures presented here may not apply to certain specific regions (Lichter, LeClere, and McLaughlin 1991).

"This next one goes out to all those who have ever been in love, then become engaged, gotten married, participated in the tragic deterioration of a relationship, suffered the pains and agonies of a bitter divorce, subjected themselves to the fruitless search for a new partner, and ultimately resigned themselves to remaining single in a world full of irresponsible jerks, noncommittal weirdoes, and neurotic misfits."

9.1 shows, singles may intensify their individualistic attitudes the longer they remain unmarried. Of those under age twenty-six, 12.6 percent did not want to marry, but when singles up to age thirty-five are included, the proportion rises to 17.2 percent (South 1993). Furthermore, the high divorce rates have left many gun-shy.

Sociologists have applied the exchange theoretical perspective (see Chapter 3) to this question of less-favorable attitudes about marriage. They argue that singles weigh the costs against the benefits of marrying (McGinnis 2003). Then too, because society has grown more and more accepting of cohabitation while marriage has become less strongly defined as permanent, "marriage offers fewer benefits relative to cohabitation now than in the past" (Seltzer 2000, p. 1249).

One reason for the declining perceived advantages of marriage is that society today views being single as an optional rather than a deviant lifestyle. During the 1950s, social scientists and people in general tended to characterize singles as neurotic or unattractive (Kuhn 1955, cited in Stein 1976, p. 521). That view has changed so much that today the popular press enthusiastically runs stories about those who are "embracing the solo life" (Sanders 2004) and happily examines the lifestyles of the "Quirkyalones: They're hip, they're single, and they don't need you" (Hurwitt 2004; Sanders 2004). Socially accepted alternatives to permanent marriage—being divorced, cohabiting, and permanent singlehood—have indeed emerged.

Furthermore, getting married is no longer the principal way to gain adult status. Data from the National Survey of Families and Households show that, increasingly, "twentysomethings" leave their parental home for reasons other than marriage. Before 1936, 40 percent of men and about two-thirds of women who left their parental home did so in order to marry. By the 1980s, only 10 percent of men and one-third of women left home for marriage. Today, 45 percent of young men and 39 percent of young women say they first left home for other reasons, often "to gain independence." As more and more young people choose to claim independence simply by moving out of their parental homes, marriage loses its monopoly as the way to claim adulthood (Booth, Crouter, and Shanahan 1999; Furstenberg, Jr., et al. 2004; Teachman, Tedrow, and Crowder 2000).

Another national survey, the General Social Survey (GSS), conducted by the National Opinion Research Center (NORC), found that people now see becoming self-supporting as the first transition to adulthood, followed by no longer living with one's parents, having a full-time job, completing school, being able to support a family financially, and—sixth in the list—getting married (Smith 2003b). Then too, many young adults experience less parental pressure to marry than young people did in the past (Bumpass, Sweet, and Cherlin 1991).

Feminist social scientist Barbara Ehrenreich (1983) traced the historical development of what she called the "breadwinner revolt" among men from the 1950s through the 1980s. She argued that through the 1940s, men demonstrated their masculinity through family breadwinning—that is, by establishing and providing for a family. Beginning in the 1950s, divergent cultural factors, from the *Playboy* magazine mystique to the counterculture, have legitimated singlehood for men. Sociologist Kathleen Gerson (1993) has argued that changes in our economy have made family breadwinning more difficult, hence less attractive, to a growing number of men. Also, the fact that many men's earning potential has declined, relative to women's, may make marriage less attractive to women (Manning and Smock 2002; Raley and Bratter 2004; Sassler and Goldscheider 2004). Moreover, women have increasingly challenged men's privileges in marriage. Men differ in their responses to these changes. Many will marry, but others will eschew commitment, either permanently or at least "for now" (Dowd and Pallotta 2000).

Simultaneously, expanded educational and career options for women and, consequently, their growing commitment to paid work have given women increased economic independence. One result is that more *women* are voluntarily choosing singlehood—and like it (Swartz 2004). Sociologist Frances Goldscheider has called women's growing lack of interest in marriage a revolution. In particular, middle-aged, divorced women with careers tend to look on marriage skeptically, viewing it as a bad bargain once they have gained financial and sexual independence. For example,

a forty-nine-year-old divorced female executive says she loves eating popcorn for dinner rather than cooking as she used to when she was married. Once divorced, she said, "I could do anything I wanted for the first time in my life" (in Gross 1992b).

In sum, it appears that much of the increase in singlehood (1) represents a return to long-term patterns of late marriage at the turn of the century; (2) results from economic disadvantage and/or a low sex ratio, which prevent a portion of the population from marrying; and (3) results from changing attitudes toward marriage and singlehood. Other reasons for the increase in the number and proportion of unmarrieds in our society include the high likelihood and acceptance of heterosexual cohabitation, discussed later in this chapter, as well as a high divorce rate (see Chapter 16) and the possibilities for parenting—by means of artificial insemination, for example—available to single women (see Chapter 10).

African American Singles

Sociologist Robert Staples, who has specialized in research on African American families, addresses singlehood among blacks. Staples (1999a) notes the high value placed on marriage in the black community, despite popular perceptions to the contrary. When measured by surveyed attitudes, "the degree of attachment to marriage among black Americans is similar to that of white Americans" (Bramlett and Mosher 2001, p. 2).

At the same time, African Americans have shared in the recent trend toward greater singlehood. In fact, the proportion of married African Americans has declined sharply, from 64 percent in 1970 to 42 percent in 2002. This figure compares with 58 percent for Hispanics and 61 percent for whites (U.S. Census Bureau 1998, Table 61; 2003, Table 61). (See also Figure 9.2.)

Scholars have been puzzled by the fact that black marriage rates are substantially lower than those of other groups. Staples (1999a) explored demographic reasons for African American singlehood. For one thing, there are more black women than men available because young black men have relatively high mortality rates and are more likely to be imprisoned or to join the military.[5] In addition, the rate of homosexuality of

---

5. Much could be said about the reasons for this, but it ultimately points to the impact of discrimination. See Staples (1999a) for a more-detailed discussion.

African Americans are considerably more likely to be single than are people in other racial/ethnic groups. Among other reasons, differences in family patterns between blacks and others reflect structural factors, such as an unequal sex ratio and low employment for African American men.

black men exceeds that of black women, and more African American men than women have married partners of other races (Crowder and Tolnay 2000). When we recognize that many lower-class, never-married black males are poorly educated and unemployed, and therefore unable to support a family,[6] it becomes apparent that choices are limited for black women wanting black men as marriage partners.

College-educated black women have difficulty finding black mates of similar educational background (Chambers 2003; Raley 1996; South and Lloyd 1992a). Black men, especially the highly educated and professionally successful, have significantly higher rates of intermarriage than black women; this situation is another factor that limits African American women's marriage opportunities (Crowder and Tolnay 2000). Furthermore, according to Staples, the sex ratio imbalance (see Table 9.1) means that "middle-class black men are able to screen out certain types of women"— perhaps those who are poorer (McLaughlin and Lichter

1997) or more assertive. Some other scholars of black families concur that, overall, "the lower the sex ratio (the scarcer men are), the more favorable the relationship outcomes men can negotiate." Consequently, African American men "are more reluctant to enter long-term relationships," whereas black women "are predicted to receive fewer rewards for conforming to traditional family roles, and will be forced to consider nontraditional paths of marriage and family formation" (Kiecolt and Fossett 1995, pp. 123–124). Indeed, there is evidence that if "desirable" men are available (Staples 1994, p. 15), black single women may be more desirous of marriage than are black single men (South 1993).

As Table 9.1 shows, among never-married African Americans between ages nineteen and twenty-five, black *men* are far less desirous of marriage than are black women. While not as dramatic, this difference is true for the entire sample of respondents ages nineteen through thirty-five. Moreover, single black males are considerably less likely than their non-Hispanic white counterparts to desire marriage: 15.4 percent of single non-Hispanic white men do not want to marry, compared to 23.5 percent of single African American men.

When considering responses to additional survey questions (besides the one about desiring to marry), the researcher who analyzed these data found that black men were more worried than non-Hispanic whites that they would not be able to hang out with their friends after marriage. Furthermore, African American men did not expect to improve their sex life with marriage, whereas other men did. Using an exchange perspective, South assumed that single people weigh the costs against the benefits of potential marriage and argued that men who think their living standards will improve with marriage are more likely to want to marry. In large part, black men have less desire to marry than do other men (or black women) because they expect marriage to have a less positive—or a more negative—impact on their personal friendships and sex life (South 1993).

The unequal sex ratio among African Americans, as well as black men's high rates of unemployment, underemployment, military service, imprisonment, and other structural factors, works against black people's marrying and contributes to their higher rates of singlehood (Furstenberg 2001). However, socioeconomic factors alone do not explain this situation. For instance, it is important to note that the marriage rate

6. The male provider role is part of many African Americans' expectations of marriage in its ideal form. But often this ideal is not realizable for lower-class men. Anthropologist Elliot Liebow's classic study of "corner men" in Washington, DC, depicts the frequently unsuccessful struggle of these men to find jobs and maintain marriages (Liebow 1967).

for Mexican Americans more closely resembles that for non-Hispanic whites "despite economic conditions that closely approximate those of African Americans" (Oropesa, Lichter, and Anderson 1994). Demonstrating that, along with other structural factors, the uneven sex ratio does make a difference in blacks' likelihood for remaining single, demographer R. Kelly Raley (1996) also shows that when black *couples* are compared with non-Hispanic white *couples*, blacks are more likely to cohabit rather than to marry. Furthermore, cohabiting unions more quickly lead to marriage for whites than for blacks (Manning and Smock 1996; Rendall 1999).

Besides structural reasons for high rates of African American singlehood, it may also be true that culture plays a part (Ruggles 1994; Manning and Landale 1996; Stokes and Chevan 1996). As we noted in Chapter 1, the pattern of high singlehood among black Americans may indicate divergent social norms between blacks and whites. The pattern among black families of combining parenthood with singlehood has been traced as far back as 1850 among free blacks (Ruggles 1994). Then too, any stigma related to non-marital childbearing may be smaller among blacks than among other racial/ethnic groups (Brien, Lillard, and Waite 1999). Staples argues that among African Americans, "The role of mother is regarded as more important than any other role, including that of wife" (1994, p. 12).

Furthermore, African Americans are more likely than whites to highly value and gain social and emotional support from extended family relationships (Raley 1995). "Among Blacks, households centered around consanguineal relatives have as much legitimacy (and for most people, as much respectability) as family units as do households centered around conjugal unions" (Sudarkasa 1981, p. 55; 1993). Sociologist Steven Ruggles (1994) concludes the following:

> All things considered, the cultural explanations appear just as persuasive as the economic ones. It is likely that there have been persistent differences between blacks and whites in norms about residence with spouses and children. Given the radical differences in their backgrounds and experiences, it would be remarkable if African-Americans and white Americans in 1880 had an identical set of family values. European norms transmitted by American masters under slavery

doubtless influenced the black family, but the experience of slavery and African traditions were probably just as important. (p. 148)

We should note that the analysis in this section proceeds from the *cultural variant* approach to research on ethnic minority families, not from the *cultural deviant* approach (Dilworth-Anderson, Burton, and Johnson 1993; see also Chapter 3's "A Closer Look at Family Diversity: Studying Ethnic Minority Families"). We need to consider how the singlehood patterns of diverse racial/ethnic groups vary from one another (the cultural variant approach) without falling into the temptation of seeing one pattern as necessarily deviant, negative, or pathological. ("A Closer Look at Family Diversity: The Meaning of Cohabitation Among Diverse Racial/Ethnic Groups" further explores racial/ethnic differences in singlehood.)

This analysis reminds us that singlehood may be freely chosen, imposed by a structural lack of options, self-imposed, or a result of some combination of these. Again we see the theme that whereas the social structure influences people's decisions, people do have choices to make. An African American woman who faces the fact that there are fewer black men of marriageable age may choose to create a satisfying single life, to marry an African American man who is not as liberated or successful as she would like, to marry a man of another race, or to establish a lesbian relationship. Of course, women of all racial/ethnic groups may have parallel choices to make. We turn now to an examination of singles' income, followed by a look at the various living arrangements of singles in the United States today.

▪ Income and Singlehood ▪

There is evidence that occupation and income are related to marital status. As you can see in Table 9.2, married couples earn considerably more than singles, and this is true even if both spouses are not in the paid labor force. Singles who are not living with any other relatives earn significantly less, with single women earning the least. Married people are more likely to have white-collar jobs and higher incomes than are singles, regardless of age and education.

Moreover, sociologist Peter Stein (2001), among others, sees singles as being discriminated against in

The Meaning of Cohabitation Among Diverse Racial/Ethnic Groups

You probably have an idea what cohabitation means or symbolizes to you. Without thinking about it, you may assume that living together signifies the same thing to virtually all Americans. But researchers who have studied cohabitation among various racial/ethnic groups have uncovered interesting differences (Martin 2002). One study analyzed data from two large, national surveys to examine how living together influences the likelihood that the couple will marry if the woman becomes pregnant. These researchers compared this situation among mainland Puerto Ricans, non-Hispanic whites, and African Americans. They found that pregnant non-Hispanic white cohabitors were more likely to get married than premaritally pregnant white women who were not cohabiting. But pregnant black cohabitors were no more likely to marry than if they had not been living together. And Puerto Rican pregnant women were *less* likely to marry if they were cohabiting when they became pregnant than if they had not been cohabiting at the time of conception (Manning and Landale 1996).

The researchers concluded that these differences must be explained at least partly by cultural differences. For non-Hispanic whites, cohabitation signifies mainly a transitional stage before marriage. But living together does not necessarily mean the same thing for African Americans or Puerto Ricans. The researchers pointed out that black women are less likely than either of the two other groups to be in any union (cohabitation or marriage) when they become mothers.

Meanwhile, Puerto Rican women have a long history of **consensual marriages** (heterosexual, conjugal unions that have not gone through a legal marriage ceremony). The tradition of consensual marriages probably began among Puerto Ricans due to lack of economic resources necessary for marriage licenses and weddings: "Although nonmarital unions were never considered the cultural ideal, they were recognized as a form of marriage and they typically produced children" (Manning and Landale 1996, p. 65). Therefore, cohabitation symbolizes a committed union much like marriage for Puerto Ricans; hence, they don't feel the need to marry legally should the woman become pregnant because they have already defined themselves as (consensually) married.

The researchers point out that "the rise of cohabitation has taken place in very different family contexts for various racial and ethnic groups . . . [and] plays a very different role in the family patterns of these two disadvantaged groups, illustrating clearly the importance of the cultural context to contemporary union and childbearing behavior" (Manning and Landale 1996, p. 75).

Another researcher used the National Survey of Families and Households (NSFH) data to examine normative or cultural beliefs about cohabitation among mainland Puerto Ricans, Mexican Americans, and non-Hispanic whites (Oropesa 1996). Of the three groups, Mexican Americans were most likely to agree that "It is better to get married than go through life being single." Puerto Ricans followed, with non-Hispanic whites least likely to agree. In response to the statement "It's all right for an unmarried couple to live together if they have no plans to marry," Puerto Ricans were most likely to agree, followed by non-Hispanic whites, and, last, by Mexican Americans.

From this and other evidence, Oropesa deduced that Mexican Americans weigh marriage very positively compared to being single— and marriage plans significantly increase Mexican Americans' approval of living together. These findings are especially strong for foreign-born Mexican Americans. Oropesa concluded that her results pointed to cultural norms as reasons for these differences.

As we saw above, mainland Puerto Ricans often define living together as a form of committed marriage (consensual marriage). Hence, they would not be expected to object to cohabitation, even without formal marriage plans. Meanwhile, "in keeping with their cultural heritage, marriage is often portrayed as an affirmation of womanhood for Mexican American girls. [Especially foreign-born] girls were traditionally socialized to believe that marriage 'is part of God's plan' and should be their 'major life objective'" (Oropesa 1996, pp. 59–60).

In conclusion, cultural factors play a part in how people define situations and events such as cohabitation. Our diverse American society encompasses many ethnic groups with family and cultural norms that sometimes differ from one another: "Clearly, attention to traditional family practices is necessary to understand racial and ethnic differences in family formation patterns" (Manning and Landale 1996, p. 75).

Critical Thinking

How do the facts presented here illustrate the interactionist perspective, explained in Chapter 3?

Table 9.2

Median Annual Household Income of Singles Compared with Marrieds, 2002	
Married-couple families	$61,254
Male householder, wife absent	41,711
Female householder, husband absent	29,001
Unmarried households	25,402
Male householder	31,404
Female householder	20,913

Source: U.S. Census Bureau 2003c, "Income in the United States: 2002." Current Population Reports # P60-221, Table 3.

subtle ways in the workplace. For one thing, "The assumption in many corporations and companies is that all employees will sooner or later pair off." Then too,

> We have found that managers tend to view singles as having more free time and prime candidates for weekend work in labs, computer centers, etc. The needs of single employees tend not to be seen as genuine as those of marrieds. It is also assumed, of course, that singles can travel more easily than marrieds.
>
> And what about gay or lesbian singles in the workplace? Do they present themselves as being straight, making up stories about heterosexual partners, or do they come out in the workplace? And if they do, at what costs? (Stein 2001)

Then too,

> In the workplace, unmarried people wind up making an average 25 percent less than married colleagues for the same work because of the marriage-centric structure of health care, retirement, and other benefits, calculates Thomas F. Coleman, a lawyer who heads the Los Angeles-based American Association for Single People. (Conlin 2003b, p. 107)

Satisfaction with single living depends to some extent on income, for financial hardships can impose heavy restrictions. Many single women, especially those with children, just do not make enough money (Mink 1998; Wallis 1999). These women head single-parent families rather than engaging in the stereotypical singles lifestyle characterized by personal freedom and consumerism. Many work two relatively low-paying jobs, one full-time and one part-time, then take care of their homes and children. For them, "career advancement" means hoping for a small annual raise or just hanging on to a job in the face of growing economic insecurity. Pursuing higher educational opportunities means rushing to class one evening a week after working all day and making dinner for the children. For reasons that we will examine in detail throughout this book, many women's experiences as heads of single-parent households can be aptly described, in economist and policy scholar Sylvia Hewlett's words, as "a lesser life" (1986).

The Various Living Arrangements of Nonmarrieds

As unmarrieds make choices about their living arrangements, we see the variety of singles' lives. Some live alone; some live with parents; some live in groups or communally; some cohabit with partners of the same or opposite sex. We look now at this variety of domestic arrangements. In the process we will find that the distinction between being single and being married is not that sharp, for people who are legally single tend to be embedded in families of one form or another.

Living Alone

The number of one-person households has increased dramatically over the past thirty years. Individuals living alone now make up one-quarter of U.S. households—up from just 8 percent in 1940 (U.S. Census Bureau 1989a, Table 61; 2003a, Table 65). The likelihood of living alone increases with age and is markedly higher for older woman than for older men. For instance, in 2002, the proportions of Americans living alone increased from 6 percent among those twenty through twenty-four years old, to 9 percent for those thirty-five through forty-four, to 24 percent for those sixty-five through seventy-four, to 40 percent of those seventy-five years old and over (U.S. Census Bureau 2003, Table 64). Between ages sixty-five and seventy-five, women are about twice as likely as men to live alone. After age seventy-five, women are about three times as likely as men to live alone (Saluter and Lugaila 1998, Table F).

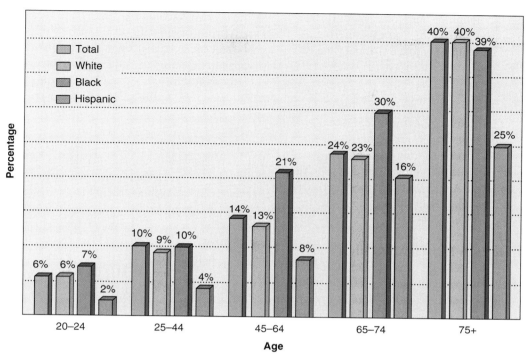

FIGURE 9.4

Percentage of people over 19 years old living alone, by race/ethnicity, 2002.

Source: Calculated from U.S. Census Bureau 2003a, Table 64.

Figure 9.4 gives the percentage of people over age nineteen living alone, by race/ethnicity. As you can see from Figure 9.4, Hispanics of all ages are less likely to live by themselves than are either blacks or non-Hispanic whites. We can hypothesize that Hispanic culture, which encourages more collectivist, family living (familism), influences Hispanics' and their relatives' living choices. It is also clear from Figure 9.4 that people are more likely to live by themselves as they get older. This is particularly true for women, who are more likely to become widowed. (Older families are the subject of Chapter 18.)

Although living alone can be lonesome, we need to remember that aloneness (being by oneself) and loneliness (a subjective sensation of distress) are different. One can feel lonely in the presence of others, even a spouse, and happy alone. Moreover, living alone does not necessarily imply a lack of social integration or meaningful connections with others (Ross 1995).

Nevertheless, singles have tended to report feeling lonely more often than have marrieds (Kim and McKenry 2002; Shostak 1987). Poor and older singles

are especially likely to be lonely, perhaps because the low incomes and ill health that tend to accompany old age make socializing very difficult. Besides age and income, being single as a result of divorce apparently affects loneliness (Menaghan and Lieberman 1986). Meanwhile, during the past several decades, young single adults have been more and more likely to live with their parents.

Living with Parents

A growing proportion of young adults are living with one or both parents. In 1940, the proportion of adults under age thirty living with their parents was quite high. Sociologists Paul Glick and Sung Ling Lin suggest why:

> The economic depression of the 1930s had made it difficult for young men and women to obtain employment on a regular basis, and this must have discouraged many of them from establishing new homes. Also, the birth rate had been low for several years; this means that fewer homes

were crowded with numerous young children, and that left more space for young adult sons and daughters to occupy. (Glick and Lin 1986a, p. 108)

Some of these same reasons apply to young people today (Booth, Crouter, and Shanahan 1999; Cohen and Casper 2002). Demographer Frank Furstenberg explains that young single adults are "accurately seeing that if they ever want to buy a house, if they're ever going to get married, if they even want a car, they're going to have to save. And, in effect, their families [with whom they reside] are subsidizing that saving" (quoted in De Vise 2004).

Table 9.3 lists the percentages of young adults living with their parents in 1960 and currently. In Table 9.3, we see that the percentage of young adults living at home has increased moderately since 1960. By 2000, more than half of young adults aged eighteen through twenty-four (57 percent of women and 47 percent of men) lived with their parents (Bianchi and Casper 2000, Figure 4).

Table 9.3

Young Adults Living with One or Both Parents, by Age, United States, 1960, 1995, and 2000		
	PERCENTAGE LIVING WITH THEIR PARENTS SEX AND YEAR	
	18–24	25–34
Total		
1960	43	9
1995	53	12
2000	52	*
Men		
1960	52	11
1995	58	15
2000	57	*
Women		
1960	35	7
1995	47	8
2000	47	*

*Data for 2000 unavailable for age category 25–34.

Sources: U.S. Census Bureau 1988, Table A–6; 1997a, Table 65; Bianchi and Casper 2000, Figure 4.

The postponement of marriage has meant a longer period of singlehood. Housing in urban areas may be so expensive that singles cannot maintain their own apartments. Some ethnic groups, such as Mexican Americans and Hmong, expect single women to reside with their parents until marriage. Unmarried women who have babies, especially those who became mothers in their teens, may be living with parents (London 1998). Others may return after divorce, as may divorced men as well. Interestingly, singles are less likely to return home when their parents have been divorced or remarried (Goldscheider and Goldscheider 1998).

Just as economic considerations, the need for emotional support, or the need for help with child rearing may lead young singles to choose living with parents, similar pressures may encourage singles to fashion group or communal living arrangements.

Group or Communal Living

Groups of single adults and perhaps children may live together. Most often, these situations may be defined as simple roommate arrangements. However, a minority of group houses purposefully share aspects of their lives in common. **Communes**—that is, situations or places characterized by group living—have existed in American society throughout its history. Like communes elsewhere, they have been enormously varied in their structure and family arrangements.[7] As part of "the sixties" countercultural movement, a number of communal families were established, and this mode of living became a highly visible family alternative to the conventional nuclear family.

Living communally has declined in the United States from its highly visible and idealized status in the 1960s, but many communes that were established in

---

7. In some communes, such as the Israeli kibbutzim (Spiro 1956) and nineteenth-century American groups such as the Shakers and the Oneida colony (Kephart 1971; Kern 1981), all economic resources are shared. Work is organized by the commune, and commune members are fed, housed, and clothed by the community. Other communes may have some private property; even some Israeli farming cooperatives that superficially resemble kibbutzim have private land plots, although members share a communal life (Schwartz 1954).

There is also variation in sexual arrangements among communes, ranging from celibacy to monogamous couples (the kibbutzim and some communes in this country) to the open sexual sharing found in both the Oneida colony and some modern American groups. Children may be under the control and supervision of a parent, or they may be more communally reared, with a deemphasis on biological relationships and responsibility for discipline and care vested in the entire community.

the 1960s still exist (Miller 1999). And new, small-scale and nonideological versions of communal living have surfaced as singlehood has increased and as our population ages. Communal living, either in single houses or in co-housing complexes that combine private areas with communal kitchens (Ravo 1993), may be one way to cope with some of the problems of aging, singlehood, or single parenthood. In a small but growing number of co-housing complexes, people of different sexes and diverse ages may choose to reside together as a solution to economic and other practical concerns, such as in-home child care ("Communal Living" 1998).

As with any living arrangement, communal living has positives and negatives. Single mothers may get help, but may also relinquish some parental control. And, as one might expect, agreeing on standards for privacy, housekeeping, and noise may be a source of conflict among members. Still, communal living represents an attempt to provide people with greater opportunities for social support, companionship, and personal growth.

Financial considerations and the need for social support may also encourage dating singles to share households. We explore cohabitation, or living together, later in this chapter. But here we turn our attention to another domestic arrangement of some people who are, for the most part, legally categorized as "single"—gay and lesbian partners.

Gay and Lesbian Partners

A Web search for gay and lesbian organizations yielded organizations for blacks, Latinos/as, Jews, and Muslims, among others. Lesbian and gay singles make up a diverse category of all ages (Price 2000) and racial/ethnic groups.

Until the 2000 census, the U.S. Census Bureau did not ask questions about co-residence in such a way that same-sex couples could be identified. For this reason, earlier census statistics do not tell us much about the domestic arrangements of gays and lesbians, and comparing estimates from before 2000 with census data from the year 2000 is inappropriate (U.S. Census Bureau 2001).[8]

Many gay and lesbian couples live together and share sexual and emotional commitment (Patterson 2000). From a variety of national surveys, demographers estimate that about 28 percent of gay men and 44 percent of lesbians are "currently partnered" (Black, Gates, Sanders, and Taylor 2000, p. 143). Some have married legally in the state of Massachusetts, although there are legal challenges to their marital status. (Legal same-sex marriage is explored in Chapter 8.) Others may consider themselves married as a result of personal ceremonies in which they exchange vows or rings or both, or they may form more public unions, religiously recognized by the Metropolitan Community Church or the Unitarian Universalist Church, for example.

Enough same-sex couples are establishing families with children—by becoming parents through adoption, foster care, planned sexual intercourse, or artificial insemination—that some observers now point to a "gay baby boom" (Bell 2003; Johnson and O'Connor 2002). According to the 2000 census (see Figure 9.5), more than one-third (34.3 percent) of female, and close to one-quarter (22.3 percent) of male, same-sex couple households now include children under age 18— some born to the union and many others from prior heterosexual relationships. Despite this situation, "little is known about the impact of child rearing on same-gender couples compared to the literature examining the impact of children on traditional married couples across the family life cycle" (Means-Christensen, Snyder, and Negy 2003).

Courts vary in their receptiveness to same-sex families with children. More and more permit a lesbian to adopt her partner's children (e.g., *In re-Petition of L. S. and V. L. for the Adoption of T. and of M.* 1991) or grant joint adoption to gay male couples ("Lesbian and Gay Rights" 2001). In the year 2000, the New Jersey Supreme Court ruled that a co-parenting lesbian is entitled to visitation rights after the relationship ends

---

8. Until the 2000 census, the census definition on which calculations of unmarried couples were based was as follows: An unmarried-couple household that contained two adults, not related and of opposite sex, but no additional adults; and any children present are under fifteen. In the 1980s, this measure became popularly known as POSSLQ (pronounced "PA-sul-cue"): Partners of the Op-

posite Sex Sharing Living Quarters. This concept and its acronym became culture fixtures of the time, as demonstrated by book titles in the 1980s such as *There's Nothing That I Wouldn't Do if You Would Be My POSSLQ* and *Will You Be My POSSLQ?* (Casper and Cohen 2000, p. 237).

Besides cohabiting couples, this census measure could include tenant and roomer, caregivers of the disabled or handicapped, and roommates of the opposite sex. But until the 2000 census, this figure excluded gay and lesbian couples and heterosexual cohabiting couples who had other adults living with them (Saluter 1994, p. 7). However, different statistical processing steps used in the 2000 census have made it more possible to identify gay/lesbian households (U.S. Census Bureau 2001).

even though she is not a biological parent of the child (Levinson 2001). However, many other jurisdictions refuse custody or visiting rights to a gay/lesbian co-parent when the couple breaks up ("Lesbian and Gay Rights" 2001).

Meanwhile, same-sex parents emphasize their similarity to heterosexual parents: "We're not dykes on bikes or men in drag. We go to story time at the library and worry about all the same food groups" (Bell 2003). Social science researchers generally conclude that children raised in same-sex families differ little from those raised in heterosexual homes (Stacey and Biblarz 2001), and the American Association of Pediatrics officially supports gay and lesbian couples' adopting and having children (Belge 2004).

With regard to the couple themselves, more and more businesses and government bodies have created domestic partner laws and policies, discussed in a later section of this chapter. Domestic partner arrangements extend some or many (but not all) of the legal benefits of marriage, such as health insurance and bereavement leave, to unmarried same- or opposite-sex partners (Demian 2004e).

In many (other than legal) respects, same-sex relationships are similar to heterosexual ones. For example, research indicates that the need to resolve such issues as sexual exclusivity, division of labor, and power and decision making is not much different in gay or lesbian pairings than in heterosexual pairings or marriage (Peplau 1981; Harry 1983). Psychologist Lawrence Kurdek has conducted considerable research on gay and lesbian couples. In one study comparing cohabiting gay male, lesbian, heterosexually married, and dating couples, Kurdek concluded that the gay and lesbian couples experienced relationship quality similar to that of the marrieds (Kurdek 1995a). An earlier study directed by Letitia Peplau (1981), based on questionnaires administered to 128 gay men, 127 lesbians, and 130 unmarried heterosexual women and men found that both heterosexuals and gay people struggle to balance "the value placed on having an emotionally close and secure relationship" with that of "having major interests of . . . [one's] own outside the relationship [and] a supportive group of friends as well as . . . [one's] romantic sexual partner" (p. 33). Regarding gay people's similarities with—or differences from—heterosexuals, Peplau concluded:

> We found little evidence for a distinctive homosexual "ethos" or orientation toward love rela-

"We're a traditional gay couple—we don't have kids."

> tionships. There are many commonalities in the values most people bring to intimate relationships. Individual differences in values are more closely linked to gender and to background characteristics than to sexual orientation. (Peplau 1981, p. 33)

Blumstein and Schwartz's study (1983) of married heterosexual couples, unmarried heterosexual cohabitants, and gay male and lesbian couples reached a similar conclusion: Gender is a more important determinant of the nature of couple relationships than is sexual orientation (see also Chapter 6).

Kurdek's (1989b) study of a nonrandom, convenience sample of seventy-four gay male and forty-five lesbian couples found lesbian couples to have "enhanced relationship quality" (p. 55). Like the other researchers, he attributes the lesbian couples'

> greater relationship satisfaction, stronger liking of their partners, greater trust, and more frequent shared decision making . . . to *both* partners having been socialized to define themselves in terms of relationships with others, to regulate interactions with others on the basis of care and nurturance, to be sensitive to the needs and feelings of others and to suppress aggressive and competitive urges which may result in social isolation. (Kurdek 1989b, p. 55)

More-recent research on gay male couples found that for older couples, relationship satisfaction was related to sexual satisfaction. However, for younger men, rela-

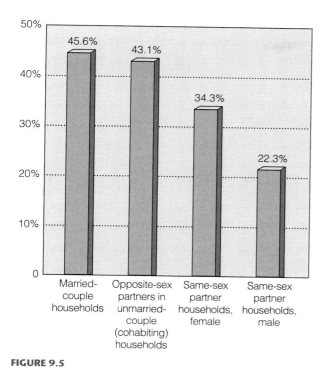

FIGURE 9.5

Percent of U.S. households with children under 18, 2000.

Note: Unmarried partners' children refers to sons/daughters of householder and to other children not related to the household.

Sources: Simmons and O'Connell 2003; "What Happened?" 2003.

tionship satisfaction was more often related to psychological intimacy (Deenen, Gijs, and van Naerssen 1994).

Although there may be no distinct homosexual "ethos," gay male and lesbian relationships do differ from others in two important ways. First, gay male and lesbian partners tend to be more autonomous than heterosexual spouses (Kurdek 1998). Second, gays and lesbians are less likely to adopt traditional masculine and feminine roles in their relationships (Reimann 1997). Instead, couples assume a pattern characterized by more equality and role sharing than in heterosexual marriages (Rosenbluth 1997). One reason many gay relationships are relatively egalitarian is that pairings of two men or two women generally provide members of the couple with similar incomes, whereas a heterosexual couple tends to be characterized by higher income, and therefore more power, for males (Harry 1983). (Chapter 14 addresses the association of income equality with egalitarian decision making.)

Same-sex partners, like unmarrieds in other situations, search for a community of friends and neighbors. Many find community in urban areas that have concentrations of other gays and lesbians, along with strong activist organizations. But lesbians and gays do live in smaller towns (Oswald and Culton 2003) and, like heterosexual singles, they have also been moving to the suburbs. As a former candidate for Congress in a San Francisco Bay Area suburb commented, "There are still people who clearly want to live in the gay ghettoes. . . . But a whole lot more . . . want to lead their lives like other people lead their lives" (Tom Nolan, quoted in Gross 1991b, p. E–16).

Cohabitation

Cohabitation, or singles' living together, gained widespread acceptance over the past forty years so that today heterosexual cohabitants express "little concern with cohabitation being a moral issue or with the disapproval of parents or friends" (Bumpass, Sweet, and Cherlin 1991, p. 921). Some cohabitants may consider their lifestyle a means of courtship, as discussed in Chapter 7. Other cohabitants view living together as a long-term alternative to legal wedlock (Booth and Crouter 2002; Seltzer 2000). As one cohabitant explained:

> We've been together 10 years. We met at college. . . . When we first met, we were talking about music and classes and where we were from, and it didn't really occur to us to talk about marriage. We graduated and started living together. What we realized after a while is that while marriage wasn't something that either of us was thinking about, it was something that was a big deal to other people. . . . We never say never, but we certainly don't have any plans to [marry]. We're very happy being unmarried to each other. (in Sachs, Solot, and Miller 2003)

The cohabitation trend spread widely in the 1960s, took off sharply in the 1970s, and has risen steadily ever since, as Figure 9.6 illustrates. Today approximately 5.5 million U.S. heterosexual couples cohabit (Schneider 2003). This figure represents a 72-percent increase in the number of unmarried-couple households between 1990 and 2000 (Simmons and O'Connell 2003). Although only about 7 percent of the population is currently cohabiting, just over 40 percent of women aged fifteen through forty-four

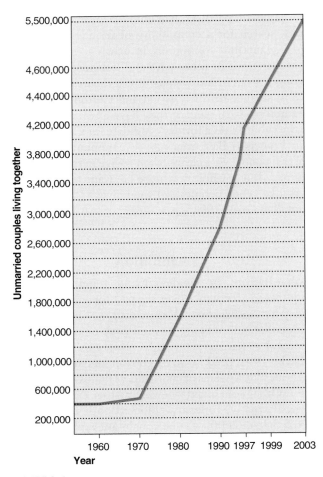

FIGURE 9.6

Unmarried couples living together in the United States, 1960–2003.

Sources: Glick and Norton 1979; U.S. Census Bureau 2000, Table 57; Schneider 2003; Simmons and O'Connell 2003.

Table 9.4

Selected Characteristics of Unmarried-Couple Households, 2002	
Cohabitants with one or more children under age 18	40%
Age of cohabitants*	
Under 25	18%
25–44	57%
45–64	20%
65+	5%

Sources: U.S. Census Bureau 2000, Table 57; Simmons and O'Connell 2003.

*Data for age of cohabitants are for 1999, the latest available at this printing.

have cohabited at some time in their lives. Many cohabitants have been previously married, then divorced, or (less often) widowed. Indeed, cohabitation is now more frequent among the divorced than the never-married (U.S. Census Bureau 2000, Table 58).

Although the prevalence of cohabiting declines with education (U.S. Census Bureau 2000, Table 58), people from all social, educational, and age groups have experimented with this family form (Smock 2000). While approximately 75 percent of cohabitants are under age forty-five (see Table 9.4), the proportion of middle-aged cohabitors has increased over the past

two decades. Also, older retired couples have found that living together without being legally married may be economically advantageous, as financial benefits contingent on not marrying are retained. Approximately 5 percent of cohabitants are age sixty-five and over—a 50-percent increase over the past fifteen years ("Numbers" 2004; U.S. Census Bureau 2000, Table 57).

Unmarried couples are generally less homogamous than marrieds (Jepsen and Jepsen 2002) and twice as likely as married couples to be interracial (Fields and Casper 2001, Table 8). Indeed, cohabitants are more likely than others to be nontraditional in many ways, including attitudes about gender roles, and to have parents with nontraditional attitudes (Axinn and Thornton 1993; Booth and Amato 1994a) and/or who have divorced (Teachman 2004).

People's reasons for living together outside of legal marriage include the wish not to make the strong commitment that marriage requires and the belief that legal marriage may signify loss of identity (Willetts 2003) and stifle communication and equality between partners (Steinhauer 1995; Moore, McCabe, and Brink 2001). Whether an early beginning to marriage or an alternative lifestyle, "cohabitation is very much a family status, but one in which the levels of certainty about commitment are less than in marriage" (Bumpass, Sweet, and Cherlin 1991, p. 913; Bianchi and Casper 2000). On average, cohabiting relationships are relatively short-term. Half last less than one year, because the couple either break up or marry (Bumpass and Lu 2000). On the other hand, in one

As We Make Choices

Some Advice on the Legal Side of Living Together

When unmarried partners decide to move in together, they may encounter regulations, customs, and laws that cause them problems, especially if they're not prepared (Demian 2003b; Lankford 2002). There are no absolutely firm legal guidelines to follow. State laws vary, and new court decisions may effect changes. But a look at some of the changes and potential trouble spots may help.

Residence

When renting an apartment or house, renters usually must sign a lease. This is a legal contract, and failure to abide by it may result in eviction. Many leases specify how many people will live in the rental unit. For a single person who later decides to take in a friend, an objecting landlord may prove troublesome.

When two or more unmarried people are looking for a place, landlords may ask each of them to sign the lease so that everyone involved is held individually responsible for its terms, including the total rent. This may also be true for utilities. Conversely, if an unmarried partner's name is not on the lease, she or he may not be entitled to continue living in the rental unit if something happens to the nominal renter.

People who are legally unrelated also need to check zoning laws before renting or buying a house. The zoning laws of many cities require occupants in single-family residence areas to be of a certain number and relationship. These laws are being challenged with increasing frequency, but it would be wise to check out your local situation.

Bank Accounts

There are no legal restrictions against an unmarried couple's opening a joint bank account. It's important to realize, though, that one of the couple may then withdraw some or all of the money without the other's approval.

Power of Attorney for Finances

"One simple thing that all same-sex [and heterosexual cohabiting] couples should do is prepare a durable power of attorney for finances," advises Pam Rhode, president of Myvesta, a nonprofit consumer education organization. "Otherwise, if you get sick it's up to a court to decide who is in control of your finances. And quite often it's not someone you would have picked" (quoted in "Financial Agreements" 2004).

A power of attorney for finances allows the authorized partner to:

- Make payments on credit card and other bills
- Run the partner's business
- File taxes
- Write checks on the partner's account
- Apply for insurance benefits
- Act on any other financial affairs that are specified in the document (Demian 2003b)

Credit Cards and Charge Accounts

Unmarried couples may find it difficult to open joint charge accounts. Creditors may not want to take a risk on the stability of the relationship, for fear that bills may not be paid if the relationship ends. If a store or a utility company does issue a two-name account, both partners are legally responsible for all charges made by either of them, even if the relationship has ended. And creditors generally will not remove one person's name from an account until it is paid in full.

Property

When unmarrieds purchase a house or other property such as home furnishings together, it is a good idea to have a written agreement about what happens to the purchase should one partner die or the couple break up. If the property is held in "joint tenancy with the right of survivorship" and one dies, the other would take ownership without probate. Hawaii's 1997 Reciprocal Beneficiaries law and Vermont's Civil Union legislation, passed in 2001, grant joint tenancy rights for eligible unmarried couples (Partners Task Force for Gay & Lesbian Couples 2000a, 2001).

If partners don't want one partner's share of the property to go to the other person, it can be held as "tenants in common," which means that it would go into the estate to be distributed according to a will. In either case, if a partner decides to sell, a buyer will want both names on the transfer of title or on the deed. Except in Hawaii and Vermont, which now allow for inheritance without a will (Partners Task Force for Gay & Lesbian Couples 2000a, 2001), surviving partners who do

continued

not have legal title to the couple's possessions or property must establish a legal right to ownership in order to keep the property. It is important to check with a lawyer to be sure that one will be entitled to assert ownership of joint property upon the death of other owners. Meanwhile, keep in mind that under joint title ownership, creditors could take one partner's property if the other partner gets into problems with debts.

Insurance

Anyone may buy life insurance and name anyone else as the beneficiary. However, insurance companies sometimes require an "insurable interest," generally interpreted to mean a conventional family tie. Moreover, the routine extension of auto and home insurance policies to "residents of the household" cannot be presumed to include nonrelatives; one should check with the company about terms of the policy. Domestic partner laws and company policies frequently extend health insurance coverage to an employee's partner.

Wills and Living Trusts

"If you have no will or living trust when you die, your property will pass to those people named by law as intestate heirs—usually legal spouses, children, parents, and other [blood] relatives. As a result, your surviving partner may end up with nothing, and even lose property he or she paid for by being unable to demonstrate ownership" (Demian 2003b). Therefore, it's

good planning for each partner to have a properly drawn-up will. Often, telling relatives or friends what to do in case of death doesn't work out. Because handwritten wills are not recognized in some states, it's good to obtain a lawyer's advice.

An alternative to a traditional will is a living trust. This is a legal document naming yourself as the trustee and sole controller of your own property but also providing for a cotrustee, who would only take over the property upon your death or disability.

> Living trusts offer a number of estate planning benefits unavailable with wills . . . [They can be] advantageous to same-sex couples because, in most states, a trust need not be publicly recorded as a will must be. Consequently, it can provide some protection against contests by hostile blood relatives. (Demian 2003b)

Health Care Decision Making

Any individual has the right to refuse treatment, but anyone too ill to be legally competent must have an agent to act for him or her in medical decision making. Most cohabitants want their partners to play this role. The catch is that to hospitals and doctors, "family" may mean spouses, parents, adult children, or siblings but not unmarried partners or close friends. In other cases, however, medical personnel are more than willing to accept the significant other preferred by the patient.

Laws in most states now offer a good solution to this uncertainty. A person may designate a decision

maker through use of a "durable power of attorney for health care." Among other rights and responsibilities, the person designated may authorize medical treatment if you are incapacitated and be given first priority in visitation if you become a patient (Demian 2003b). Check local laws for the specifics of appointing a person of your choice to make health care decisions on your behalf. The Hawaii Reciprocal Beneficiaries and the Vermont Civil Union laws entitle same-sex partners and cohabitors to be notified of a partner's condition, visit the hospital, and make medical decisions for the partner (Partners Task Force for Gay & Lesbian Couples 2000a, 2001).

Children

Children born to unmarried couples bring new legal issues of rights and responsibilities. Most states provide that children become legitimized if the natural parents marry or if the father accepts the child into his home or acknowledges the child as his, even though he doesn't marry the mother. Even though the question of legitimacy no longer has the significance it once did, cohabiting heterosexual parents would be wise to formally acknowledge paternity in conformity with the laws of their state. This step is crucial in obtaining child support from an unmarried father. In fact, more and more states require that paternity be established for all newborns for precisely this reason.

Recognition of an unmarried father's interest in custody or visitation

recent national survey, 39 percent of unmarried couples remained together after five to seven years (Bianchi and Casper 2000, p. 17). Nevertheless, "Compared with married couples, cohabitors are much more likely to break up" (Seltzer 2000, p. 1252).

Uncertainty about commitment may be one reason that, compared to marrieds, cohabitants pool their

finances to a lesser extent (Heimdal and Houseknecht 2003; Kenney 2004); say that they are less happy with their relationships and find them less fair (Skinner, Bahr, Crane, and Call 2002); report a higher incidence of depression than marrieds (Kim and McKenry 2002; Lamb, Lee, and DeMaris 2003); and have more sex outside the relationship than marrieds do (Treas and

of children was established in 1972 in the case of *Stanley v. Illinois* (405 U.S. 645), so the unwed mother is no longer entitled to sole disposition of the child in many states. Although the courts have placement discretion, couples should stipulate in writing that custody is to go to the father (if so desired) if the mother dies. In virtually all states, written agreements may not adversely affect a minor's right to child support (Greenstein 2001).

Increasingly, courts permit a lesbian partner to adopt the biological child of the other partner or will grant joint adoption to same-sex couples, ensuring legal parenthood to both members of the couple raising a child ("Lesbian and Gay Rights" 2001). Courts have also permitted lesbian co-parents to sue for visitation rights if a couple breaks up after parenting one partner's biological child. Although the legal situation for parenthood is likely to continue evolving in this direction, by and large, biology, legal adoption, and/or marriage have traditionally been—and in many cases continue to be—everything. The legal rights of "biological strangers" to continue associating with children whom they have socially parented are tenuous ("Lesbian and Gay Rights" 2001).

Unmarried parents to one partner's child should consider the following three documents:

- a Co-parenting Agreement that spells out the rights and responsibilities of each partner "and

requires enforcement through private mediation"
- a Nomination of Guardianship that adds language to a will or living trust and nominates the co-parent as the child's guardian in the event of the biological parent's death
- a Consent to Medical Treatment form that gives the co-parent the right to authorize medical procedures for a child (Demian 2003b)

Breaking Up

An advantage that people sometimes see in cohabiting is avoiding legal hassles in the event of a breakup. But if couples do not take care to stipulate in writing—and preferably with an attorney's assistance—paternity, property, and other agreements, legal hassles *may* result (Greenstein 2001). The parties may find that they have legal obligations typically associated with marriage (*Marvin v. Marvin* 1976).

The *Marvin* case established that nonmarital partners may claim property and support if their explicit or implicit contract (the verbal or written understanding underlying their union) established these obligations. It is important to note that child support can never be determined by contract; it is considered an unqualified entitlement of the child.

Another complication for couples intending to remain unmarried is **common law marriage**, a legal doctrine under which couples who live together for a certain period of time (which varies by state) and

"hold themselves out" to be husband and wife are legally married. The majority of states have abolished common law marriage; lawyers and courts tend to consider the concept obsolete. However, common law marriage could be invoked and become an important element in a dispute between parties (Willetts 2003). Again, check your state's laws, including states where you might spend extensive vacation or work time (Demian 2003a).

To summarize the legal side of living together, individuals must decide how they want to live, based on their needs, values, and goals. In so doing, they should be aware of the laws of their state. At the present time there are discrepancies between how people live (social reality) and the law. People may make choices that seem reasonable to them and that conform to their values—in insurance or property rights while cohabiting, for example—only to find they are not protected as they thought they were. The burden is on individuals to stay informed. At the same time, laws and policies seem to be in the process of changing to meet the needs of today's variety of families. (See also Demian 2003b, "Legal Precautions to Protect Your Relationship" at **http://buddybuddy.com/protect.html**, and/or attorney Frederick Hertz's *Living Together: A Legal Guide for Unmarried Couples*, Nolo Press, 2001, and/or **www.Myvesta.org** for online publications regarding the legal side of unmarried living together.)

Giesen 2000). There is also evidence of considerable domestic violence in cohabiting relationships (Brownridge and Halli 2002; DeMaris 2001)—more than among marrieds or dating partners. This situation may also be due to relatively low commitment (Johnson and Ferraro 2000) and to conflict over "rights, duties, and obligations" (Magdol et al. 1998, p. 52).[9]

9. A study of 411 heterosexual cohabiting couples who participated in the National Survey of Families and Households found that when a male's violence was more severe than his partner's, the couple was more likely to separate. However, when a female's violence was equal to or more severe than her partner's, the couple was more likely to delay marriage, although not necessarily to separate (DeMaris 2001).

Meanwhile, perhaps one in four American children "will live in a family headed by a cohabiting couple at some point during childhood" (Graefe and Lichter 1999, p. 215). As Figure 9.5 shows, more than 40 percent of cohabiting households contain children under age eighteen—a proportion that approaches the percentage of married-couple households with children (Simmons and O'Connell 2003; "What Happened?" 2003). Although the majority of children in cohabiting households were born in marriages that preceded the current cohabiting relationship (Wineberg and McCarthy 1998), about one-sixth of these children were born to the cohabiting couple.

By the mid-1990s, the proportion of nonmarital births to cohabiting heterosexual couples reached about 40 percent (Sigle-Rushton and McLanahan 2002; Raley 2001). As cohabitation becomes increasingly acceptable, "A nonmarital conception may precipitate a cohabitation, just as it may precipitate a marriage" (Brien, Lillard, and Waite 1999, p. 537; Musick 2002). Meanwhile, however, analysis from the National Survey of Family Growth shows that many— perhaps the majority—of births to cohabitors were planned by the already cohabiting couple (Manning 2001). Research from at least two national samples has found this situation to be more characteristic of black and of Hispanic cohabitors than of whites (Manning 2001; Musick 2002). One scholar has concluded that, at least for Hispanics, "Cohabitation seems well integrated into the family life . . . sharply increasing the chances of having a birth, especially a planned birth" (Musick 2002, p. 926).

Because cohabiting couples are significantly less likely to stay together than marrieds, it has been noted that children in cohabiting-couple families "will experience rapid subsequent changes in family status" (Graefe and Lichter 1999; see also Glenn 2001; Raley and Wildsmith 2004). Meanwhile, "Residential and other household changes associated with the formation of new partnerships may disrupt well-established patterns of [parental] supervision" (Thomson, Mosley, Hanson, and McLanahan 2001, p. 378). Accordingly, some family scholars have begun to publish findings that lead to concern regarding outcomes for adolescents and younger children living in cohabiting families (Booth and Crouter 2002; Brown 2004). For example, research that compared economically disadvantaged six- and seven-year-olds from families of various forms found more problem behaviors among

Cohabitation is increasingly becoming a legitimated alternative to marriage. Some evidence of this development is the fact that 43.1 percent of heterosexual cohabiting households include children under age eighteen, compared with 45.6 percent of married-couple households. According to Pamela J. Smock, associate director at the Institute for Research at the University of Michigan, Ann Arbor, cohabiting "has become the typical and, increasingly, the majority experience of persons before marriage and after marriage" (quoted in "What Happened?" 2003).

children in unmarried families, including cohabiting unions (Ackerman, D'Eramo, Umylny, Schultz, and Izard 2001).

Another study has found that adolescent and young adult children who had lived with a cohabiting parent were more likely to experience earlier premari-

City of Ashland, Oregon

CERTIFICATE OF DOMESTIC PARTNERSHIP

We, The Undersigned, Declare That:
❖ We are residing together and sharing the common necessities of life.
❖ We are not married.
❖ We are both at least 18 years of age.
❖ We are not related by blood kinship closer than would bar marriage in the State of Oregon and are mentally competent to consent to contract.
❖ We are each other's sole domestic partner and intend to remain so indefinitely and are responsible for each other's common welfare.
❖ We are ineligible under the laws of the State of Oregon to be married to each other.

As Domestic Partners formally recognized in this Domestic Partnership we:
1. Agree to file a Statement of Termination of Domestic Partnership, if the partnership is terminated or any of the facts set forth above change.
2. Understand that the registration of the Certificate of Domestic Partnership creates a domestic partnership of continuous duration until either of the partners files a Statement of Termination or upon the death of either partner. In the case of such death, no statement is required to be filed.
3. Affirm that neither of us has filed a Statement of Termination within the last six months.
4. Understand that any employer who suffers any loss because of false statements contained in the Certificate of Domestic Partnership may have cause to bring a civil action against the partners to recover losses.
5. Understand that we have a choice to formally file the registration or to retain the registration for our own records. We understand that formally filed registrations are public information and may be viewed by the public.

We do hereby swear or affirm that the information stated above is true and correct to the best of our knowledge.

_____   _____
Signature   Signature
_____   _____
Name (Print)   Name (Print)
Subscribed and sworn to (or affirmed) before me on _____ by _____ and
_____

                                                                      _____
Certificate No. _____   Notary Public for the state of Oregon
                                                                      My Commission Expires: _____
                                                                      City of Ashland Title: _____

© City of Ashland, Oregon

More and more city and state governments, as well as federal agencies and many major corporations, offer the option for heterosexual or same-sex couples to register as domestic partners. A domestic-partner certificate usually indicates joint residence and finances, as well as including a statement of loyalty and commitment, and grants unmarried partners some legal rights traditionally restricted to marrieds.

tal intercourse (Albrecht and Teachman 2003). Still another study (Manning and Lamb 2003), using national data from the National Longitudinal Study of Adolescent Health, found higher rates of delinquent behaviors and school suspension, coupled with lower academic achievement and expectations for college among adolescents from cohabiting households, when compared with those in married, two-biological-parent families. Interestingly, having a cohabiting male in the household who is not the biological father appears not to enhance adolescents' outcomes when compared with living in a single-mother household (Manning and Lamb 2003; see also Brown 2004).

When responding to surveys, people are articulate about their reasons for cohabitation, but accounts of how cohabitation begins suggest that cohabiting does not always result from a well-considered choice. Like some of the decisions previously discussed, it may also happen by default. As one college student explained, "It just got to be too much bother to go home every morning" (Macklin 1983).

Counselors stress the importance of being fairly independent before deciding to cohabit, understanding one's motives, having clear goals and expectations, and being sensitive to the needs of one's partner. This is especially necessary when children are involved. For individuals who are not prepared, living together may lead to "misunderstanding, frustration, and resentment" (Ridley, Peterman, and Avery 1978, p. 129).

Domestic Partners

Although some unmarried couples want to avoid the obligations of marriage, many would like to reap the practical benefits of marriage (Willetts 2003). Same-sex and heterosexual couples who reside together may not have access to joint health care, auto and home insurance, family or bereavement leave, or other benefits supportive of a commitment to a partner. However, over the past decade, more and more cities, states, federal agencies, and major corporations and businesses have established the concept of "domestic partner" and offer this status to their members/employees (Demian 2004e).

Unmarried couples may register their partnership and then enjoy some (although not necessarily all) rights, benefits, and entitlements that have traditionally been reserved for marrieds. The definition of **domestic partner** usually includes criteria of joint residence and finances, as well as a statement of loyalty and commitment. Using 1990 U.S. Census data, demographers have calculated that only 1.4 percent of the nation's work force would be eligible for and need domestic-partner benefits—so these benefits "won't break the bank" (Gates 2001). Domestic partner laws or policies are a particular boon to gay and lesbian couples, who may not be legally allowed to marry. However, they meet the needs of heterosexual unmarried couples as well. In fact, 70 percent to 90 percent of people registering domestic partnerships have been heterosexual couples.

Registering as domestic partners has an emotional significance for some (Willetts 2003). In cities and states that have established domestic-partner registration but have not accorded partners any privileges, couples come in to register anyway as a way of expressing their commitment to a nonmarital partner (Demian 2004e).

Looking at singles who live with domestic partners, in communal groups, or with their parents, we realize that the distinction between married and single is no longer very clear. Many singles are embedded in families. Then too, there are married couples who live apart in commuter marriages (see Chapter 12), postdivorce families in which no-longer-married individuals still function as a couple, and married couples who are emotionally or sexually estranged. In other words, being married does not *necessarily* embed one in a day-to-day, supportive relationship or family, while being single does not *necessarily* imply being physically or emotionally alone. Keeping these points in mind, we now examine what we know about the life satisfaction of the legally single.

Singlehood and Life Satisfaction

Looking at life satisfaction among American adults, surveys since the 1970s have consistently found that, in general, singles of both sexes have been less likely than marrieds to say that they were happy with their lives (Glenn and Weaver 1988; Lee, Seccombe, and Shehan 1991). Married living has some clear mental health benefits compared to singlehood (Kim and McKenry 2002; Waite 1995; Waite and Gallagher 2000). For example, married people are less likely to be depressed, abuse alcohol, or commit suicide (Kim and McKenry 2002; Stack and Wasserman 1993).[10] Evidence shows that marriage has physical health benefits as well (Waite and Gallagher 2000; Wickrama et al. 1997; Murphy, Glaser, and Grundy 1997). In the words of demographer Linda Waite, "There's something about being married that makes people work better. We're group-living animals, and we're hard-wired to bond" (in Angier 1998). Some research (Kurdek 1991) has found cohabitants to be midway between unattached singles and marrieds in mental and physical well-being (Kurdek 1991), while other studies have shown no difference between cohabitants and other singles, "suggesting that the protection effects of marriage are not as applicable to cohabitation" (Kim and McKenry 2002, p. 905).

However, marriage also involves a set of obligations and the responsibility of coping with both the burdens of other family members and the disappointments and tragedies that come with family life. Increasingly, individualistic Americans may find these obligations more emotionally stressful than in the familistic past (Gove, Style, and Hughes 1990). Hughes and Gove (1989) note that social scientists have tended to focus on the benefits of social integration and ignore its costs, and that there are some areas in which those living alone are consistently better off than the married. They point to less irritation; widowed people living alone have higher self-esteem than when living with others; and the never-married report a greater sense of control over their lives.

---

10. We need to caution here that association between two variables does not necessarily prove causality. Marriage may be associated with lower alcohol abuse, not because being married encourages moderation, but because alcoholics are more likely to be divorced and/or less likely to get married in the first place. Bottom line: Marrying a person who abuses alcohol or other drugs is very unlikely to sober her or him up.

While there is undeniable evidence for the physical and psychological benefits of marriage, unattached singles do point to benefits of their lifestyle. Among these are less irritation with co-resident family members and a greater sense of control over their lives. Moreover, when we think of singlehood as a continuum, we realize that not all singles—even those who live alone—are socially unattached, disconnected, or isolated. Maintaining close relationships with family and friends is associated with positive adjustment and satisfaction among singles.

Furthermore, when we think of singlehood as a continuum, as discussed at the beginning of this chapter, we realize that not all singles are socially unattached, disconnected, or isolated. In Ross's (1995) research with a nationally representative sample of 2,031 adults who were interviewed by telephone in 1990, people in close relationships—whether married or not and whether living alone or not—were significantly less depressed than those with no intimate partner at all. Moreover (and this is important!), the relationship between being involved and not being depressed held *only* for those in happy, or supportive, arrangements (see also Wickrama et al. 1997). Research biologist Ingrid Waldron found that marriage

was related to better overall health for women who were not employed outside their homes, though not for employed women. "We suspect that it's a matter of social support," Waldron explained. "You can get that support from your husband, or you can get it from being around other adults at work, but having it seems to be the key" (in Angier 1998).

Choice and Singlehood

Whether a person is single by choice affects satisfaction with singlehood. In 1983 and 1984, social scientist Barbara Levy Simon (1987) interviewed fifty never-married New York City women born between 1884 and 1918. She found thirty-six who had freely and deliberately chosen singlehood. All said they were happy and satisfied. Thirty-four expressed antimarriage sentiments. As one woman put it,

> Men? Men have been important to me all my life. I have had friendship and love and sex with men since I was a young thing in Detroit. . . . You see, dear, it's *marriage* I avoid, not men. Why would I ever want to be a wife? . . . A wife is someone's servant. A woman is someone's friend. (in Simon 1987, pp. 31–32)

Predictably, the twelve women who were single involuntarily gave a less rosy picture of never-married life. Of these, seven said conflicts between caring for elderly parents and the demands of finances ended their marriage plans. These women remained somewhat bitter, resenting siblings' failure to help out and/or the inflexibility of their suitors (Simon 1987, p. 51). As one self-reported unhappy thirty-nine-year-old woman (with a master's degree in music and self-employed as a freelance musician) put it, "I have always been brought up to believe that I would be taken care of by a husband. I just assumed that it would happen and it is not happening" (in Holmes 1983, p. 115).

Maintaining Supportive Social Networks

Although individuals may be single for many reasons, they cannot remain happy for long without support from people they are close to and who care about them (Kraus et al. 1993). "It's the 10 to 20 percent of people who say they have nobody with whom they can share their private feelings or who have close contact with others less than once a week who are at most risk"

(quoted in Goleman 1988a, p. 21). Such isolation increases feelings of unhappiness, depression, and anxiety (Umberson et al. 1996), whereas the social support that results from being socially connected "seems to keep stress responses . . . from running amok," according to UCLA psychologist Shelley Taylor (quoted in "Save the Date" 2004). Perhaps the greatest challenge to unmarried individuals of both genders is the development of strong social networks. Maintaining close relationships with parents, brothers and sisters (Weaver, Coleman, and Ganong 2003), and friends is associated with positive adjustment and satisfaction among singles.

A crucial part of one's support network is valued same-sex friendships. Research on a national sample of 3,617 individuals interviewed in 1986 concluded that, of various types of social support, friends may be the best: "Friends may provide a nonjudgmental source of support and provide support because they choose to, not because it is expected. Other types of support are not filling this same role" (Cotton 1999, p. 231).

Despite changing gender roles, unmarried men are, as a group, less likely to cultivate psychologically intimate relationships with their siblings (Weaver, Coleman, and Ganong 2003) or same-sex friends. They may believe that they shouldn't bother other men when they feel low, or they may fear that intimate sharing with another man might be interpreted as gay behavior (Monroe, Baker, and Roll 1997). Should he have one or more, a man may be more open and disclosing with a woman friend (Wagner-Raphael, Seal, and Ehrhardt 2001). In general, "The thinness of men's friendships with each other [compared to women's] and the ways that they seem to be constantly undermined through competition and jealousy are distinctive features of modern society" (Seidler 1992, p. 17).

For singles, it's important to develop and maintain supportive social networks of friends and family. Single people place high value on friendships, and they are also major contributors to community services and volunteer work.

Single men, more than single women, may feel—and be—socially isolated.

In addition to same-sex friendships, other sources of support for singles include opposite-sex friendships (either sexual or nonsexual), group-living situations, and volunteer work. Singles may also reach out to their families of origin. Barbara Simon studied fifty never-marrieds old enough to be retired and found that they received a great deal of support from their families, especially in middle and old age. Families helped in crises, whether of health, disability, or economic loss. Black women are especially likely to be embedded in extended families, regardless of class.

In later life, single women were likely to set up joint living arrangements with siblings, something they would have been reluctant to do earlier. Twenty-three of the fifty women whom Simon studied were living with a brother or sister in retirement. But ties outside the family remained important. Simon (1987,

pp. 53–54) found among the fifty elderly women she interviewed that "perhaps the most common thread of identity" these women shared was "their view of themselves as members of a group *larger than* their own families." Asked what had given their lives meaning, forty-five emphasized religious, political, or humanitarian volunteer work. One woman who had been a Big Sister to sixteen Puerto Rican children over the past twenty-three years explained proudly that "all Puerto Rican kids are *my* family. . . . Of those sixteen children I have been a buddy to over the years, not one of them has gotten into trouble" (quoted in Simon 1987, p. 54). Contributing an average of eighteen hours weekly, these women

think of themselves as members of an integrated moral world in which their commitments to their work, their family, their friends, their neighborhood, and their society flow from one passion—the desire to be a responsible and responsive actor in the world. (Simon 1987, p. 56)

Social support is necessary for feeling positive about and generally satisfied with being single, whether living alone or not ("Save the Date" 2004). In his review of the seventh edition of this textbook, Peter Stein (2001) noted that

Much has changed in [the singles] population since I first wrote about single women and men, but the major issues of acceptance, friendship, loneliness, and community are still there. Yet this continues to be an under-researched area of sociology!

However one chooses to live the single life, maintaining supportive social networks is important.

In Sum

- Since the 1960s, the number of unmarrieds has risen dramatically. Much of this increase is due to young adults' postponing marriage, coupled with the rise in the incidence of cohabitation.

- Although there is a growing tendency for young adults to postpone marriage, this is not a new trend but a return to a pattern that was typical early in the twentieth century.

- One reason people are postponing marriage today is that increased job and lifestyle opportunities may make marriage less attractive.

- The low sex ratio—fewer men for women of marriageable age—has also caused some women to postpone marriage or put it off entirely.

- Attitudes toward marriage and singlehood have changed, so that being unmarried is now viewed not so much as deviant but as a legitimate choice.

- The limits that marriage puts on individuality may also seem more constraining to today's Americans.

- More and more young unmarrieds are living in their parents' homes; this is usually at least partly a result of economic constraints.

- Some singles have chosen to live in communal or group homes.

- Some unmarrieds live together in gay male or lesbian unions; a little more than one-third of lesbian and nearly one-quarter of gay male households include children either from the same-sex union or from a previous (often heterosexual) relationship.

- A substantial number of heterosexual unmarrieds (about 7 percent) are cohabiting.

- As heterosexual cohabitation becomes more acceptable, more and more cohabiting households include children either born to the union or from a previous relationship.

- The relative instability of heterosexual cohabiting unions has led to some, apparently warranted, concern for the outcomes of children living in cohabiting families.

- Research has consistently found marrieds to be physically and psychologically healthier and happier than singles. However, marriage may not necessarily *cause* better health; this statistical relationship may reflect the fact that healthier people are more likely to get and stay married.

- However one chooses to live the single life, it is important to maintain supportive social networks.

Key Terms

cohabitation

common law marriage

commune

consensual marriage

continuum of social attachment

domestic partner

sex ratio

single

Questions for Review and Reflection

1. How do economics and income affect a single person's life?

2. Individual choices take place within a broader social spectrum—that is, within society. How do social factors influence an individual's decision about whether to marry or to remain single?

3. What are the particular circumstances constraining African American women who are single and would like to marry?

4. What do you see as the differences—advantages or disadvantages—of cohabitation compared to marriage?

5. **Policy Question.** Review the cultural divergent, cultural variant, and cultural deviant models of family research described in Chapter 3's "A Closer Look at Family Diversity: Studying Ethnic Minority Families." Apply these models to the singlehood topics discussed in this chapter.

Suggested Readings

Alternatives to Marriage Project

http://www.unmarried.org

A national, nonprofit organization for unmarried people, including cohabiting couples. Publishes a newsletter to which you can subscribe. "Hot topics" include cohabitation, living single, domestic-partner benefits, legal issues, and unmarried parenting, among others.

Booth, Alan, and Ann C. Crouter. 2002. *Just Living Together: Implications of Cohabitation for Children, Families, and Social Policy.* Mahwah, NJ: Lawrence Erlbaum Associates. Published as a result of the annual conference sponsored by the Population Research Institute at Pennsylvania State University, this book examines the historical and cross-cultural foundations of cohabitation with a focus on the long- and short-term impacts of cohabitation on children's well-being, and policy implications.

Goldscheider, Frances K., and Calvin Goldscheider. 1999. *The Changing Transition to Adulthood: Leaving and Returning Home.* Thousand Oaks, CA: Sage. The Goldscheiders are both professors at Brown University. They explore the many issues concerning young adults' leaving—and sometimes returning to—their parental homes and compare experiences across U.S. races/ethnicities and subcultures.

Miller, Timothy. 1999. *The 60s Communes: Hippies and Beyond.* New York: Syracuse University Press. A social historian and professor of religious studies, Miller "surveys the broad sweep of this great social yearning from the first portents of a new type of communitarianism in the early 1960s through the waning of the movement in the mid-1970s." Scholarly, serious, and interesting.

Singles Groups USA

http://www.singlesgroupsusa.com/

At this site, you can conduct a search for singles organizations and adventure groups by state, and find out about singles travel and cruises to tropical destinations, among other things.

Waite, Linda J., and Maggie Gallagher. 2000. *The Case for Marriage: Why Married People Are Happier, Healthier, and Better Off Financially.* New York: Doubleday. Sociologist Linda Waite, affiliated with the Institute of American Values, makes an empirically supported argument that the state of marriage benefits spouses. Written for the general public. Interesting and readable.

Virtual Society: The Wadsworth Sociology Resource Center

Go to the Sociology Resource Center at **http://sociology.wadsworth.com** for a wealth of online resources, including a companion website for your text that provides study aids such as self-quizzes for each chapter and a practice final exam, as well as links to sociology websites and information on the latest theories and discoveries in the field. In addition, you will find further suggested readings, flash cards, MicroCase online exercises, and appendices on a range of subjects.

Online Study Tool

Marriage & Family ⊛ Now™ Go to **http://sociology.wadsworth.com** to reach the companion website for your text and use the Marriage&FamilyNow access code that came with your book to access this study tool. Take a practice pretest after you have read each chapter, and then use the study plan provided to master that chapter. Afterward, take a posttest to monitor your progress.

Search Online with InfoTrac College Edition

For additional information, exercises, and key words to aid your research, explore InfoTrac College Edition, your online library that offers full-length articles from thousands of scholarly and popular publications. Click on *InfoTrac College Edition* under *Chapter Resources* at the companion website and use the access code that came with your book.

■ Search keywords: *cohabitation, domestic partner.*

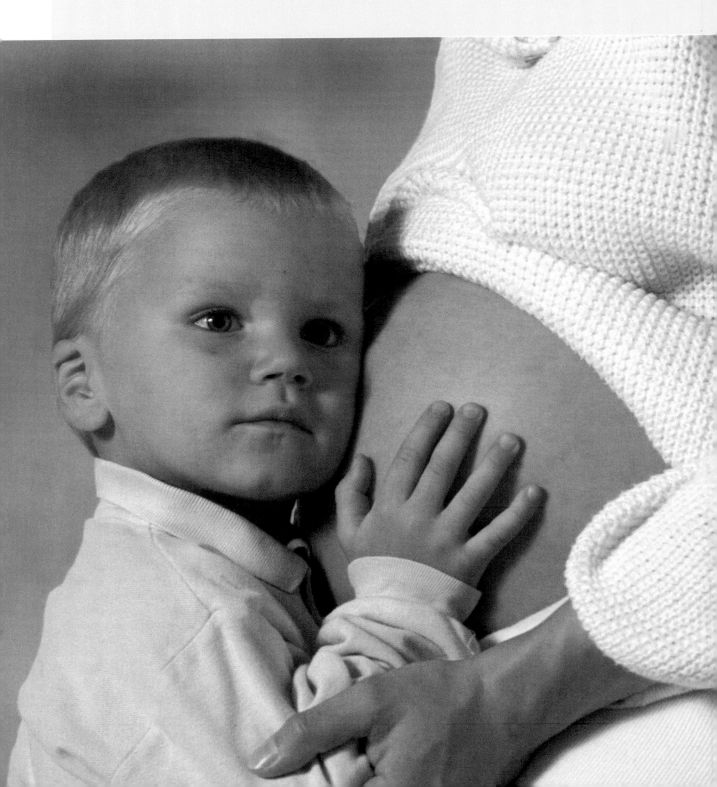

To Parent *or* Not *to* Parent

> *And now I want a child. And I want that*
> *child to carry me in his head forever, and to*
> *love me forever. . . . Is that a sentence of life*
> *imprisonment? A lifetime of love? The way*
> *the world is structured?*
>
> JOYCE CAROL OATES,
> *Do With Me What You Will*

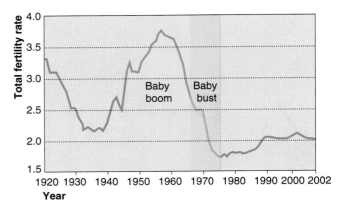

FIGURE 10.1

Total fertility rate, United States, 1920–2002.

Source: Courtesy of the Population Reference Bureau. "U.S. Fertility Trends: Boom and Bust and Leveling Off" 2001. www.prb.org/AmeristatTemplate; Martin, Hamilton, and Ventura 2001, p. 4; Martin et al. 2003, Table 9.

THERE MAY BE SOMEONE WHO'S BEEN adopted in your class, perhaps by parents of another race. There may be someone in your class who is thinking about infertility treatment. Or who is thinking about having an abortion. Or about having a first child. Or about whether to have children ever. Or about having and raising an only child, or a larger family. All these decisions focus on some aspect of whether (or how) to become a parent. They are very personal choices, but in this chapter we'll see that they are nevertheless influenced by the society around us.

Significant changes have taken place in American childbearing patterns over the past decades. For one thing, the average number of children an American woman bears over a lifetime has declined. For another, women are having children at later ages. And finally, childlessness—either by choice or by circumstance—is more common today.

The U.S. **total fertility rate (TFR)**—the number of births a typical woman will have over her lifetime[1]—dropped sharply from a high of more than 3.5 in 1957 to the lowest level ever recorded (1.738) in 1976. In recent years, the total fertility rate has fluctuated around 2.0; that is, on average, American women are now having around two children each (Martin et al. 2003; and

see Figure 10.1). At the same time, choosing not to be a parent is more acceptable today.

As overall fertility[2] levels have dropped, childbearing has increasingly shifted to later ages. Married women are waiting longer to have their first babies. Women in their thirties who had postponed parenthood are now having first, second, and, in some cases, third children, and some are becoming mothers for the first time in their forties (Martin et al. 2003). At the same time, childlessness seems higher now than in the recent past. In 2002, 18 percent of women aged forty through forty-four were childless, about twice the percentage of childless women in that age group in 1976 (Downs 2003).

These points describe the sum total of many couple and individual decisions. Throughout this chapter we'll be looking at the choices that individuals and couples

---

1. The total fertility rate (TFR) for a given year is an artificial figure arrived at through complex mathematical calculations. In common sense terms, the TFR indicates how many children an average woman would have if present trends continue. It is the figure most used in this textbook to grasp trends in fertility and family size. Another measure of fertility is the number of births per 1,000 population, the *crude birth rate*. Birth rates may be computed for various sectors of the population, for example, unmarried women, white women, etc.

---

2. The term *fertility* is used by demographers to refer to actual births. Even though everyday language uses the term *fertility* to mean ability to reproduce, the technical term used in social science for reproductive capacity is *fecundity*.

The terms *infecundity* and *sterility* describe the physical inability to have children. More commonly, the term infertility or *involuntary infertility* is used to describe the situation of a couple or individual who would like to have a baby but cannot. Physicians consider a woman infertile if she has tried for twelve months to become pregnant without success (Weeks 2002, p. 167). A woman or a couple may experience infertility as they try to have another child after having had one or more biological children. Physicians call this *subfecundity* or *secondary infertility*.

have about whether or not to have children and how many. Among other things, we'll see that modern scientific and technological advances have both increased people's options and added new wrinkles to their decision making. We'll see, too, that technological progress does not mean that people can exercise complete control over their fertility. To begin, we'll review fertility trends in the United States in more detail. Then we'll examine the decision whether or not to become a parent.

Fertility Trends in the United States

Lower U.S. fertility appears to be a major change when we compare current birth rates to those of the 1950s. But the decline in fertility is actually a continuation of a long-term pattern dating back to about 1800. Alternatives to the motherhood role began to open up with the Industrial Revolution and the resulting creation of a labor force that worked in production outside the home (see Chapter 12). Previously, in a preindustrial economy, women could combine productive work and motherhood. But when work moved from home to factory, the roles of worker and mother were not so compatible. Consequently, as women's employment increased, fertility declined.

Another change affecting fertility over time has been declining infant mortality, a result of improved health and living conditions. Gradually, it became unnecessary to bear so many children to ensure the survival of a few. Changes in values accompanying these transformations made large numbers of children more costly economically and less satisfying to parents.

In the face of the long-term decline over the past two centuries, it is the upswing in fertility in the late 1940s and 1950s that requires explanation. It appears that those who had grown up during the Great Depression, when family goals were limited by economic factors, found themselves as adults in an affluent economy. They were able to fulfill dreams of a happy and abundant family life to compensate for deprivations suffered as children (Easterlin 1987). Marriage and motherhood became dominant cultural goals for American women; men also concentrated their attention on family life. This generation produced what is now called the baby boom, having more than three children, on average, and sometimes more.

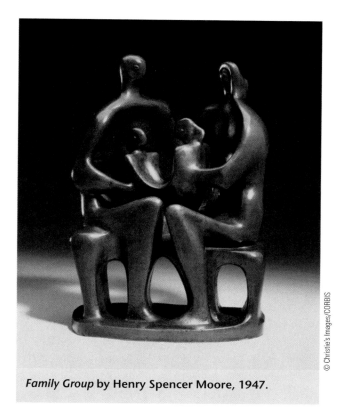

Family Group by Henry Spencer Moore, 1947.

© Christie's Images/CORBIS

Family Size

Women born during the Depression years of the 1930s favored larger families than had been the case in immediately preceding decades. Today a two-child preference dominates Americans' preferences (Stewart 2002). In 2000, only 11 percent of women who had completed their childbearing had four or more children, compared to more than three times that percentage in 1976 (Bernstein 2002). Improvements in contraception have enabled couples to attain the desired number of children with greater certainty (see Appendix F, "Contraceptive Techniques").

The total fertility rate in the United States has never dropped as low as those of some European and Asian countries,[3] so a current question regarding

---

3. The decline in the birth rate has been a worldwide trend. Many European industrialized nations now have total fertility rates that are far below the population replacement level of 2.1 and well below those of the United States. For example, the total fertility rate is 1.7 in the United Kingdom, 1.5 in Sweden, 1.3 in Italy, 1.2 in Spain, 1.3 in Japan, and even 1.8 in China (Population Reference Bureau 2001).

© Joel Gordon

Native American women who live on reservations have significantly higher fertility than those who do not. Differential birth rates reflect the fact that people in various cultures have different beliefs and values about having children.

American fertility is why the United States still has higher fertility than other countries with parallel levels of economic development (Riche 2000, p. 6). Historically, American fertility was higher than that of Europe (Weeks 2002, p. 236), so there may be cultural factors at work that social scientists have not yet identified. Moreover, our racial/ethnic minority population has relatively high fertility rates, as do immigrants. European nations and many others have family-support policies and programs that are far stronger than those in the United States. But Europe

has struggled with high unemployment rates for many years, Japan has been in economic recession, and housing is cramped and expensive in both areas (Riche 2000). The U.S. economy has been better on these factors, although it is characterized by substantial inequality.

Some wonder whether the situation will change in a way that will lead to lower fertility here, comparable to that of Western European countries. Indeed, fertility rates have continued to decline since 1990 for all U.S. racial/ethnic groups (Martin et al. 2003). Sociologists Lynn White and Stacy Rogers (2000), writing on the economic circumstances of the family, note that

> for the past 2 decades, American families in the middle of the income distribution masked men's stagnating wages by reducing the number of children and increasing wives' labor force participation. . . . With these strategies already implemented, economic inequality may seem more visible and problematic in the future. Will Americans, like the Japanese and many Europeans, cut fertility even further, to an average of little over one child? (p. 1048)

Differential Fertility Rates

Not surprisingly, fertility rates vary among segments of the U.S. population, as fertility rates have social, cultural, and economic origins. Usually, more highly educated and well-off families have fewer children. Although they have more money, their children are also more costly, for these parents expect to send their children to college and to provide them with expensive experiences and possessions. Moreover, people with high education or income have other options besides parenting. They may be involved in demanding careers or enjoy travel, activities that they weigh against the greater investment of time and money required in parenting more children. The tendency for the more highly educated and wealthier in any group to have fewer offspring is characteristic of all racial groups in the United States.

Differential birth rates also reflect the fact that beliefs and values about having children vary among cultures—see "Facts About Families: Race/Ethnicity and Differential Fertility Rates" for a discussion of fertility among the diverse racial/ethnic groups of the United States.

Multiple Births

Do you see parents pushing twin strollers in the mall? One of the striking developments in American women's fertility patterns in recent decades has been the dramatic increase in multiple births. Not only are there more twins, but more triplets and higher-order births as well. As the numbers of multiples have grown, so have organizations to bring them together to share common concerns and joys. Commercial products and websites market to parents of multiples.

Fewer than 20 percent of multiple births are the result of natural conception, while the rest are owing to later age at conception or the use of reproductive technology and other infertility treatments (Martin and Park 1999; Martin et al. 2003). Decision making about having children now takes place at a time of more reproductive options than ever before. This observation highlights the point that in the early twenty-first century, parenthood is a choice, made in a social context. We now focus on people as they make their decisions about becoming parents.

The Decision to Parent or Not to Parent

The variations in birth rates just described reflect decisions shaped by values and attitudes about having children. But in traditional society, couples didn't decide to have children. Children just came, and preferring not to have any was unthinkable.

Earlier in the twentieth century, family planning efforts focused on the timing of children and family size rather than on whether to have them. Now choices include "if" (that is, whether to have children) as well as "when," "how many," and "how."

Although social change and technology provide more choices, they also present dilemmas. It is not always easy to choose whether to have children, how many to have, when to have them, and what reproductive technology to use in the event of infertility. Not all choices can be realized, whether they reflect a desire to have children or to avoid having children.

The extent to which people today consciously choose (or reject) parenthood or experience it as something that simply happens to them is uncertain. Certainly, educated and affluent people have more control

over their lives generally, so they may be more apt to approach parenthood as a conscious choice. Among others—teenagers, for example—parenthood is usually less thought out. Some people may be philosophically disinclined to plan their lives (Luker 1984). For whatever reason, in a 1995 survey, women respondents reported that almost 50 percent of the pregnancies they had experienced in the previous year were unintended—71 percent of those mistimed, and 29 percent unwanted (Santelli et al. 2003).[4] Nevertheless, more so than in the past, our society presents the possibility of choice and decision making about parenthood. The decision to parent (and if so, when) or not to parent is one in which many couples and individuals invest a great deal of thought and emotion.

In the following pages, we'll look more closely at some of the factors involved in an individual's or couple's decision making about whether to become a parent: first, the social pressures, and then the personal pros and cons.

Social Pressures to Have Children

We see in Chapter 9 that single people in our society may feel strong pressures to conform by marrying. The same kinds of pressures may exist for married people who don't want to have children.

Our society still has a **pronatalist bias**: Having children is taken for granted, whereas not having children seems to need a justification (May 1997). Moreover, since everyone has been a child and most people were raised with siblings, families with children seem altogether normal. Eighty-three percent of American women say being or becoming a mother is important to their identity (Center for the Advancement of Women 2003, p. 8). Some scholars believe pronatal pressures are becoming stronger now that the countercultural trends of the 1960s and 1970s have been replaced by a cultural emphasis on "family values" (Bulcroft and Teachman 2004; Park 2002).

Some of the strongest pressures may come from a couple's parents. Hopeful prospective grandparents

---

4. See Santelli et al. 2003 for a discussion of how "unintended" has been defined, and the limitations of research on unintended pregnancy. Recent research (Hummer, Hack, and Raley 2004) suggests that pregnancies reported as unintended or unwanted are associated with poorer outcomes.

Facts
About
Families

Race/Ethnicity and Differential Fertility Rates

As Figure 10.2 shows, women in the various U.S. racial/ethnic groups vary quite a bit in the number of children they have and the age at which they bear children. Here we look at fertility patterns among the major American racial/ethnic groups.

Fertility Rates Among Non-Hispanic Whites. Fertility patterns of the non-Hispanic white population are very similar to those described for the total population, although slightly lower. The TFR for whites in 2002 was 1.83 compared to 2.01 for the total population (Martin et al. 2003). Because the white population was historically such a large part of the total population, the explanations offered for historical changes in fertility apply to changes in fertility among non-Hispanic whites.

Fertility Rates Among African Americans. Most racial/ethnic minority populations in the United States have fertility rates that are higher than those of non-Hispanic whites, and that is true of African American women at the present time. Earlier in our history, in the late eighteenth century, white and black women appear to have borne children at approximately the same rates. At about that time, the white

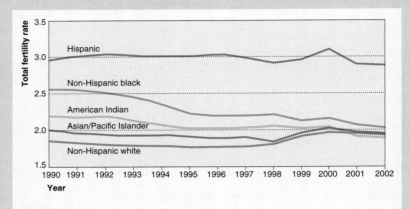

FIGURE 10.2

Total fertility rate by race/ethnicity, United States, 1990–2002.

Source: Courtesy of the Population Reference Bureau. "U.S. Fertility Rates Higher Among Minorities" 2001. www.prb.org/AmeristatTemplate; Martin, Hamilton, and Ventura 2001, p. 4; Martin et al. 2003, Tables 4 and 9.

population began to reduce its fertility, and by the end of the nineteenth century, childbearing among whites had declined significantly. The birth rate among blacks did not decline much until after 1880, when it began to drop rapidly. By the 1930s, it was close to that of whites.

Since then, trends in black fertility have generally paralleled those among whites, though at a higher level. Black fertility rates increased during the post-World War II baby boom and decreased after the late 1950s. The total fertility rate for non-Hispanic African Americans was 2.0 in 2002, as compared to a TFR of 1.83 for non-Hispanic whites (Martin et al. 2003, Table 9).

Earlier we suggested that since about 1800, expanding opportunities and changing values have made large numbers of children less economically rewarding and less

are not always subtle: One gave his wife a grandmother photo album for Christmas, even though his childless daughter and her husband were not aware of any grandchildren on the way!

Still, the expectation for married couples to have children is much less pronounced than in the past. For example, the term *child-free* is often used now in-

stead of the more negative-sounding term *childless.*[5] Some observers, in fact, argue that U.S. society has become antinatalist—that is, against having children or,

---

5. Each term conveys an inherent bias. For that reason and because there are no easy-to-use substitute terms, we use both *childless* and *child-free* in this text.

personally satisfying to individuals. Although economic and social pressures on families can impel them to limit fertility—as the sharp drop in fertility during the Depression indicates—long-term decline in birth rates is mostly a consequence of increased opportunity for economic advancement, more easily taken advantage of by small families (Weeks 2002). When individuals have satisfying options other than parenthood, they typically choose to limit their childbearing. The differences in fertility decline between white and black populations in this country suggests that although education and other opportunities opened up for whites with the Industrial Revolution earlier in the nineteenth century, they did not do so for blacks until well after the Civil War.

With regard to the current fertility rate among black Americans, the same differential opportunity explanation holds true (Moore, Simms, and Betsey 1986). Nevertheless, African American fertility rates declined by almost 25 percent in the 1990s and into the current century (Martin et al. 2003).

Fertility Rates Among Latinos. Latinos (termed Hispanics in government statistical documents) have the highest fertility rate of any U.S. racial/ethnic group. Their TFR of 2.72 in 2002 was almost 50 percent higher than that of non-Hispanic white women. Rates for Mexican American women are the highest among Hispanics, while women of

Puerto Rican and Cuban background have moderate total fertility rates of around 1.94. Women of other Central American and South American background have fertility rates just slightly lower than those of Mexican American women (Martin et al. 2003, Table 9).

Reasons for the high birth rates include the fact that Hispanics migrate from nations with high birth rates and still-powerful Catholic and rural traditions that value large families. Large families may serve important functions, especially in poorer families. A child might be an insurance policy against a parent's old age in a society without bureaucratized welfare systems such as Social Security—those norms may be carried over to the United States. Even while children are growing up, their earnings might be an important part of the family income (Collins 1999, p. 202).

Moreover, the lifetime fertility of Latinas varies strongly with their educational attainment, and Spanish-origin women are relatively more concentrated in the lower educational categories (Bean and Tienda, 1987, cited in Vega 1990, p. 1017). Similarly, on average (Cubans excepted), Latino families have lower incomes and higher rates of poverty than the non-Hispanic white population; these are also factors associated with higher fertility.

Finally, Latinos are younger, with more concentration in childbearing ages (McLoyd et al. 2000). Latina women, especially Mexican Americans, typically begin having children

at younger ages (Ventura, Martin, Curtin, Menacker, and Hamilton 2001, Table 9). Latinas in their early twenties have a much higher fertility rate than women this age in other racial/ethnic groups (Downs 2003).

Asian American/Pacific Islander Fertility. Asian American/Pacific Islander and Native American births are a relatively small proportion of U.S. births. Asian/Pacific Islander women have a comparatively low TFR (1.82) (Martin et al. 2003, Table 4). There is considerable variation by country of origin. Moreover, as immigrants assimilate, their birth rates converge with those of whites (Hwang and Saenz 1997).

Native American Fertility. Fertility rates of Native Americans/Alaska Natives declined by almost 25 percent since 1990, to a TFR of 1.74 in 2002 (Martin et al. 2003, Table 4). Native American women who live on reservations have significantly higher fertility than those who do not (Taffel 1987), probably for the reasons of limited educational and economic opportunity noted earlier.

Critical Thinking

The total fertility rate, which is an approximation of average family size, is lower in all racial/ethnic groups that it was during the baby boom era (1946–1964). Why do you think this is so? Does it have to do with economic pressures? Changing attitudes toward children? Or something else?

at least, not doing all it can to support parents and their children.

Is American Society Antinatalist?

Some family policy scholars view American society as characterized by **structural antinatalism** (Huber

1980), insufficiently supportive of parents and children. Sociologists Janet Hunt and Larry Hunt express concern about a future in which they anticipate:

a widening gap in the standard of living between parents and non-parents. . . . Those with children will tend to have lower incomes [as careers

The numbers of twins, triplets, and higher-order births have increased dramatically since 1980. Families raising two or more children who are the same age gain the attention of onlookers when they are out-and-about—and they face challenges at home. As their numbers have grown, so have organizations to bring them together to share common concerns and joys.

are impeded by family responsibilities], in addition to absorbing the expenses of children, and will fall further and further behind their child-free counterparts. (Hunt and Hunt 1986, p. 283; see also King 1999)

Critics point out that compared to other nations at our economic level, nutrition, social service, financial aid, and education programs directly affecting the welfare of children are not adequate (Children's Defense Fund 1998; Hewlett and West 1998). Nor do we provide paid parental leave or other support for parents of young children, as many other countries do. Children in the United States are more likely to be poor than in comparable countries (Population Reference Bureau 2002, 2003).

In sum, there are social pressures to have children, but other features of our society make parenthood less than automatic. Of course, the decisions that people

make should reflect not only external social pressures but also their own needs, values, and attitudes about becoming parents. In the next sections, we will look at some of the advantages and disadvantages associated with parenthood.

Motivation for Parenthood

FOCUS ON CHILDREN   Traditionally, children were viewed as economic assets; in a farm economy, more hands added to the work that could be produced in the fields and kitchens. Generally, however, the shift from an agricultural to an industrial society and the development of compulsory education have transformed children from economic assets to economic liabilities. But as their economic value declined, children's emotional significance to parents increased, partly because declining infant mortality rates made it safe to become attached to children, to invest in them

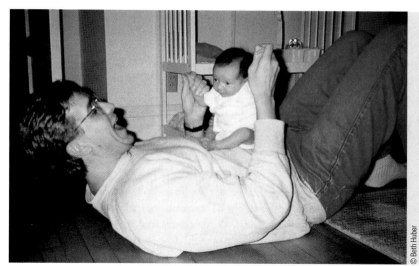

Children can bring vitality and a sense of purpose into a household. Having a child also broadens a parent's role in the world: Mothers and fathers become nurturers, advocates, authority figures, counselors, caregivers, and playmates.

emotionally. Parents' desire was for "a child to love" (Zelizer 1985, p. 190).

In a study of 100 white working-class and middle-class biological and adoptive parent couples in the Midwest, coauthor Mary Ann Lamanna (1977) found parents reporting a variety of emotional satisfactions from having children. Many stated that children gave their lives meaning and purpose, a sense of destiny. Children provided a sense of continuity of self—as one parent put it, "the advantage of seeing something of yourself passed on to your children."

Others reported that their satisfaction is in belonging to a close family unit, which they associate with having children, not just with being married. As one parent commented, "Since the daughter, we all do things together more than we used to—the zoo, picnics, and things like that." Many parents in the study enjoyed the satisfaction of nurturing the emotional and physical growth of their children. Others spoke of the joy of loving and being loved by their children. In her study of men's feelings about family and work, sociologist Kathleen Gerson (1993) found that some men value close relationships with their children because they missed having a close emotional bond with their own fathers. Others seemed to find that children offered them an emotional base that work or romantic relationships could not promise (p. 177).

In having children, parents can find a satisfaction that is lacking in their jobs. Family life also offers an opportunity to exercise a kind of authority and influence that one may not have at work (Hoffman and Manis 1979). Children add considerable liveliness to a household, and they have fresh and novel responses to the joys and vexations of life. In sum, children "are capable of bringing profound meaning and purpose into people's lives" (Groat et al. 1997, p. 571). This idea that children bring unique benefits to parents has been termed the **value of children perspective** on motivation for parenthood.

The *value of children perspective* represented by Lamanna's study (also Hoffman and Manis 1979) has more recently been supplemented by a **social capital perspective**[6] on the benefits of parenthood:

> Parenthood intensifies interaction with, and assistance from, other family members. It facilitates exchanges with neighbors and other community members. . . . [P]arenthood can bring parents into an extensive and supportive network. (Schoen and Tufis 2003, p. 1032)

Research suggests that the anticipated social capital benefits of parenthood may be one motivation for childbearing, not only for married but also for unmar-

---

6. We usually think of *capital* as money. But more generally, the term refers to a resource that can be used to one's benefit. Social capital, then, refers to social ties that are or can be helpful resources.

ried prospective parents. Analysis of responses from a subsample of 1,155 unmarried women in the National Survey of Families and Households (NSFH) found that nonmarital conceptions occurred more often to women who anticipated social capital benefits from children (Schoen and Tufis 2003).

Costs of Having Children

Although the benefits of having children can be immeasurable, the experience can also be costly. On a purely financial basis, children decrease a couple's level of living considerably. In husband–wife families with two children, an estimated 42 percent of household expenditures are attributable to children. The average cost of raising a child born in 2001 to age eighteen is estimated at $231,470 for middle-income families (Lino 2002, Tables 11 and 12).

Added to the direct costs of parenting are **opportunity costs**: the economic opportunities for wage earning and investments that parents forgo when rearing children. These costs are felt most by mothers. A woman's career advancement may suffer as a consequence of becoming a mother in a society that does not provide adequate day care or a flexible workplace. A couple in which one partner quits work to stay home with a child or children faces loss of up to half or more of its family income (Longman 1998). The spouse (more often the woman) who quits work also faces lost pension and Social Security benefits later. All in all, in our society there is "a heavy financial penalty on anyone who chooses to spend any serious amount of time with children" (Crittenden 2001 p. 6). Conversely, the loss of free time is one important cost of trying to lead two lives, as a family person and as a career person (Groat et al. 1997).

Parents in Lamanna's study identified some noneconomic costs of having children: Children add tension to the household and restrict parents' activities outside the home. They require a daily routine that can limit parents' spontaneity. Children also make for substantial additional work—not only physical care but also the work of parenting: guiding the child's social and emotional growth and dealing with anxiety about such pitfalls to healthy development as school difficulties and drug use. Added to these emotional costs is the parent's recognition that once assumed, the parent status is one that a person cannot easily escape.

All in all, "from the day children are born they become a source of joy and a source of burdens for their parents (Nomaguchi and Milkie 2003, p. 372).

How Children Affect Marital Happiness

Marital strain is considered to be a common cost of having children. Evidence shows that children—especially when they are young—stabilize marriage; that is, parents are less likely to divorce. But a stable marriage is not necessarily a happy one: "[C]hildren have the paradoxical effect of increasing the stability of the marriage while decreasing its quality" (Bradbury et al. 2000, p. 969). A major review of the research in this area finds that not only do parents report lower marital satisfaction than nonparents, but the more children there are, the lower marital satisfaction is (Twenge, Campbell, and Foster 2003).

Many, though certainly not all, couples report that the happiest time in marriage was before the arrival of the first child and after the departure of the last. Spouses' reported marital satisfaction tends to decline over time whether they have children or not. But serious conflicts over work, identity, and domestic responsibilities can erupt with the arrival of children. A study that followed Swedish couples through the parenting years found that while at any one time the majority of parents described their marriages favorably, the marital relationship became less harmonious over time, disharmony peaking at the child's ages of ten through twelve (Stattin and Klackenberg 1992). The couple's relationship is especially affected if one or both partners are not cooperative in their parenting (Belsky and Hsieh 1998).

When they have children, spouses may find that they begin responding to each other in terms of more traditional role obligations (Nock 1998c), and that in turn affects marital happiness negatively (Coltrane 1990). Spouses, who now are not only busier as parents but also more dissimilar in their dominant roles, begin to do fewer things together and to share decision making less (Bird 1997). While parenthood is viewed positively and increases life satisfaction, research indicates that positive feelings about children are not sufficient to offset the negative effects on marital happiness of changes in marital structure brought about by the arrival of children (Tsang, Harvey, Duncan, and Sommer 2003; White, Booth, and Edwards 1986). Dissatisfaction with one's marriage after the arrival of the first child seems more pronounced and longer lasting for wives than for husbands (Glenn 1990, p. 825).

A comprehensive review of the research (Twenge et al. 2003) noted that the negative effects of children on marital satisfaction seem to be stronger for younger cohorts. Perhaps couples today experience a greater "before-after" contrast when children arrive. They have often married and become parents later in their lives, and so experienced a great deal of personal freedom and a career focus for many years. Women's roles, especially, have changed, leaving a bigger gap between the child-free working-woman's lifestyle and that of a new mother. In general, the increased individualism of our culture may make day-to-day responsibility for the care of young children seem less natural than in the 1950s, when social obligations were culturally dominant (Turner 1976).

Even though the addition of a child necessarily influences a household, the arrival of a child is less disruptive when the parents get along well and have a strong commitment to parenting. One longitudinal study shows that the drop in marital satisfaction is less for couples who were happy before the birth and actively planned for the infant (Cowan and Cowan 1992). And new friendship networks, such as with other parents, may provide some of the social support previously given by one's spouse (Roxburgh 1997). (Chapter 11 looks more closely at the relationships between parents and their children.)

Remaining Child-Free

We have been discussing factors that influence the decision whether to have children (or not). At present, it looks like almost 20 percent of women born in the late 1950s will be childless. Although childlessness is higher than it was at mid-century, it seems to have stabilized and is not likely to rise further in the near future (Bachu 1999a; Downs 2003).

Childlessness can be the result of choice or circumstance, and there is often some ambiguity about the "decision" to remain child-free. For some, it represents an early commitment not to have children. For many, it is a gradual decision over time. For still others, it is a decision by default, as age or relationship status lead eventually to realization that one will not have children.

Involuntary childlessness, the result of infertility or other adverse circumstances, is discussed later in this chapter. Here we examine **voluntary childlessness**, the choice of 6.6 percent of American women in a 1995 survey (latest data available), an increase from 2.6 percent in 1978 (Bulcroft and Teachman 2004; Park 2002).

An increase in voluntary childlessness is ascribed to the social changes of recent decades. The rise of feminism challenged the inevitability of the mother role. More than 70 percent of women surveyed in 2001 said "no" to the question of whether "a woman need[s] the experience of motherhood to have a complete life," including 69 percent of mothers (Center for the Advancement of Women 2003, p. 8). Greater ability to control fertility; greater participation of women in paid employment; and—for some men and women—concern about overpopulation and the environment or an ideological rejection of the traditional family are all factors in some people's decisions (Gillespie 2003; Paul 2001).

The voluntarily childless have more education, and more are likely to have managerial or professional employment. They have higher incomes, are less religious, more likely to be firstborns, and less traditional in gender roles. When we move from demographics to examine the experience, we learn that individuals who choose to remain childless are usually neither frustrated nor unhappy (Veevers 1980). Voluntarily childless couples typically have vital relationships. Often they believe that adding a third member to their family would change the character of their intense personal relationship.

Child-free women tend to be attached to a satisfying career. Childless couples value their relative freedom to change jobs or careers, move around the country, and pursue any endeavor they might find interesting (Dalphonse 1997). A study comparing 74 voluntarily child-free women and men with 127 fathers and mothers found that the child-free couples felt negatively stereotyped by society (as did other interviewees some years later [Park 2002]). But they were more satisfied with their relationship as a couple than the parents were (Somers 1993). One study of childless, older women has found that they have developed a strong network of friends over the years and are not necessarily isolated or regretful (Rubinstein et al. 1991).

REMAINING CHILDLESS: THE "DECISION"
There have been very few recent studies on the child-

free choice, and older research is still being cited in research reviews (e.g., Bulcroft and Teachman 2004). Research as does exist shows that not all childless couples are equally committed to remaining child-free (Nason and Poloma 1976; Veevers 1980). A fairly recent study (Heaton, Jacobson, and Holland 1999) attempted to get at the degree to which intentions do change about having or not having children. This study used data from a two-stage survey of men and women who themselves or whose female partners were under forty. In the follow-up, the individuals were classified into five categories. Forty-five percent were postponers, who had not yet had children, but intended to. Twenty-five percent were intentional parents; they had had a child since the first round of data collection.

Of the remaining groups, 13 percent expressed an intention to have children when surveyed earlier, but now had decided against it or become undecided. Seven percent had initially expressed a commitment to being child-free, and they were consistent in adhering to that decision. Six percent had not intended to have children but did anyway or were now thinking about it. The more highly educated individuals were least likely to change their minds.

WOMEN'S AND MEN'S REASONS From the few studies of couples who decided not to have children, we can draw the following tentative conclusions:

1. It is often the woman who first takes the child-free position (Seccombe 1991). Typically, she is an achievement-oriented only child or a firstborn who had to help raise her younger brothers or sisters.

2. Men who want to remain childless tend to be more confident about their decision than women, who express more ambivalence. Men in egalitarian marriages may prefer having fewer or no children over sharing the work of raising them (Gerson 1993). One study, however, found egalitarian men *more* likely than traditional men to express a positive intention to become a parent, perhaps because they anticipated more involvement with their children and found that attractive (Kaufman 2000).

3. When a couple disagrees about having children, substantial conflict may occur before this issue is resolved. It is, of course, possible that it cannot be resolved. Partners sometimes use prolonged postponement to avoid confronting the issue of permanent childlessness, although they eventually realize that they will not have children.

Two conclusions here: The vast majority of adults of reproductive ages have or want to have children. The second point: "[F]ew early childbearing intentions appear to be hard and fast" (Heaton et al. 1999, p. 539).

Having Children: Options and Circumstances

Discussions about having children often evoke images of a young, newly married couple. More and more, however, as the discussion of the changing life course in Chapter 3 suggests, decisions about becoming parents are being made in a much wider variety of circumstances. In this section we address childbearing with reference to postponing parenthood; the one-child family; nonmarital childbearing; and decisions about having children in stepfamilies. Gay and lesbian parenthood is discussed in Chapter 11.

The Timing of Parenthood

Teen birth rates have declined, and births to women in their twenties, the primary ages for childbearing, now constitute just over half of all births in the United States. Meanwhile, birth rates for women in their thirties and forties have increased dramatically (Martin et al. 2003). Birth rates for men over forty-five—that is, the rate at which older men have fathered children—have increased by almost 20 percent since 1980 (Martin et al. 2003, Table 20). What are the factors producing this change, and how do early and late parenthood look as choices at the present time?

POSTPONING PARENTHOOD Later age at marriage and the desire of many women to complete their education and become established in a career appear to be important factors in the high levels of postponed childbearing.[7] Both sexes remain longer in the "emerg-

---

7. In addition to delayed first-time parenthood, some births to older women (and men) follow the breakup of marriages or other relationships (Brown 2000; Carnoy and Carnoy 1995).

ing adulthood" stage of the life course (see Chapter 3), enjoying a greater degree of personal freedom and ability to concentrate on career than is possible after family responsibilities are assumed. Then too, with the availability of reliable contraception and the promise of assisted reproduction technology, people can now plan their parenthood for earlier or later in their adult lives.

But fertility declines with age, for men as well as women, although less dramatically for men. Older mothers have higher rates of premature or low-weight babies and multiple births—all risks for learning disabilities and health problems. Older mothers also have higher rates of miscarriage, and both sexes run a greater risk of conceiving children with certain genetic defects (Brody 2002, 2004d; Tough et al. 2002; Henderson and Barkham; "Older Moms" 1999). Physicians advise that pregnancy risk factors should not deter women who want children from having them at older ages: "The take-home message is that while a lot of complications of labor and pregnancy are increased . . . the vast majority of [older mothers] do perfectly fine" (Dr. William Gilbert, quoted in "Older Moms" 1999).

Still, a more intense concern about the dangers for women of postponing parenthood emerged with the publication of economist Sylvia Ann Hewlett's book *Creating a Life* (2002) based on her survey of 1,168 older "high achieving career women" (women in the top 10 percent of earners). Hewlett found a high rate of childlessness among successful managerial and professional career women, most of whom had not intended to be childless.

Hewlett's interpretation of this undesired outcome is that the women were too focused on building their careers while ignoring their personal lives, with the assumption that it was easy enough to have children later in life. Hewlett notes the lack of policy support for working mothers as a factor in women's decisions to establish their careers before becoming parents. Nevertheless, she blames what she sees as contemporary feminism's lack of interest in motherhood, as well as women's too-individualistic attitudes, for their fate. To avoid childlessness, Hewlett suggests that women start their families earlier by planfully seeking a husband while in their twenties, a time when there are more prospective spouses available and when women, just beginning their careers, may be less threatening to men. Hewlett advises that "giving pri-

© Rob Lewine/CORBIS

Many couples today are postponing parenthood into their thirties, sometimes later.

ority to establishing a stable, loving relationship early on might be worth the effort even if this involves surrendering part of one's ego" (p. 199).

Hewlett's caution about fertility decline and the limits of reproductive technology are valid. Professional medical societies had initiated programs to publicize these facts (Kalb 2001; Brody 2002). But critics of Hewlett's book (Chira 2002; Flanagan 2002; Pollitt 2002) argue that the real problem is the failure of policy support for working families (see Chapter 12). Also, needless to say, it is uncertain as to whether a planful "let's get married" agenda would result in a good marriage. And the implication that women need to minimize their career interests is surprising in this era of generally advancing gender equality.

EARLY PARENTHOOD Now that postponing parenthood to the thirties is increasingly common, early parenthood tends to be seen as the more difficult path (Jong-Fast 2003). Choosing early parenthood means more certainty of having children, but young parents may have to forego some education and get a slower start up the career ladder. Early parenthood can create strains on a marriage if the breadwinner's need to support the family means little time to spend at home, or if the parents lack the maturity needed to cope with family responsibility (Poniewozik 2002). And of course, couples who start early on children usually start late on saving for college or retirement and work harder and longer to meet family needs (Strauss 2002; Tyre 2004).

EARLY AND LATE PARENTHOOD: A TWO-SIDED COIN What do early and late parenthood look like from the inside? Whereas early first-time parents in one study "couldn't remember a time when they weren't parents," postponers reported a sharp sense of before and after (Daniels and Weingarten 1980). Early mothers' identities seemed much more dominated by their maternal role, while later mothers' identities were more variegated (Walter 1986).

Women who postponed parenthood found that combining established careers with parenting created unforeseen problems. Career commitments may ripen just at the peak of parental responsibilities. Those who set their careers aside temporarily to be full-time mothers met with criticism from their work colleagues and peers. Those who continued to work, even though many reduced their hours, felt that they missed important time with their children or were generally overloaded (Daniels and Weingarten 1980).

On the other hand, late mothers had more confidence in their ability to manage their changed lives because of the organizational skills they had developed in their work. They also had more money with which to arrange support services. And they felt confident of their ability as parents (Walter 1986). Psychiatrists speak of the maturity, patience, and good parenting skills of later-life parents (Tyre 2004). A book based on interviews with a nonrandom set of older fathers, mostly white and middle class, found that men who had children in later life expressed a great deal of joy in parenthood, particularly if they had given priority to jobs with earlier-born children (Carnoy and Carnoy 1995).

Late parents reported their impatience for the empty-nest stage of life, when they could return to the personal privacy and freedom from responsibility they enjoyed before their children were born. Early first-time parents, on the other hand, felt that they reaped definite pluses both early and later (Daniels and Weingarten 1980). As one woman, who had been a first-time mother in her early twenties and was now older and a systems analyst, said:

> I like the fact that my children are as old as they are, and that I'm as young as I am and my career is so open ahead of me. I'd hate to be in my career position, wanting to have children and not knowing when to make the break. (Daniels and Weingarten 1980, p. 60)

Early mothers also felt that they had had more spontaneity as youthful parents (Walter 1986). "We wanted to be young parents [said one mother]. . . . We didn't want to be 60 when they got out of high school" (Poniewozik 2002, pp. 56–57). For older parents, there is a sense of limited time with children that both increases pleasure in parenting—"Everything is more precious"—and creates anxiety about the future—"How long am I going to be here?" (parents, quoted in Walter 1986, p. 83).

Being born to older parents affects children's lives as well. They usually benefit from the financial and emotional stability that older parents can provide and the attention given by parents who have waited a long time to have children: "Children of older parents are more likely to take center stage" (Yarrow 1987, p. 17, citing Iris Kern). But children of older parents can also experience anxiety about their parents' health and mortality. Parents may become frail while children are still young, before they have established themselves in their adult lives (Yarrow 1987).

If prospective parents seek to time their parenthood to be early or later in life, it's important to have an awareness of the trade-offs we've described—plus an understanding that having children is a challenge at any age!

The One-Child Family

Some prospective parents consider the challenges of parenthood daunting, but also reject the idea of child-

© Laura Dwight/CORBIS

Some families choose to have only one child, a decision that can ease time, energy, and economic concerns. There may be extra pressure on only children, and they do not experience sibling relationships. But only children tend to receive more personal attention from parents, and parents may enjoy their child more when they do not feel so overwhelmed as they might with more offspring to care for.

lessness. For them, the solution is the one-child family. In 2002, 17 percent of women aged forty through forty-four had just one child (Downs 2003).

The proportion of one-child families in America appears to be growing due to at least three factors: (1) the high cost of raising a child through college, (2) women's increasing career opportunities and aspirations, and (3) the choice to have just one child becomes easier to make as more couples do so. Divorced people may end up with a one-child family because the marriage ended before more children were born.

Negative stereotypes present only children as spoiled, lonely, dependent, and selfish. To find out whether there was any basis for this image, psychologists in the 1970s produced a staggering number of studies: "The overall conclusion: There are no major differences between only children and others; no negative effects of being an only child can be found" (Pines 1981, p. 15; also Falbo 1976 and Hawke and Knox 1978). Since the 1970s, research in this area has sharply diminished.

ADVANTAGES Parents with only one child report that they can enjoy parenthood without feeling overwhelmed and tied down. They have more free time and are better off financially than they would have been with more children (Downey 1995). Researchers have found that family members shared decisions more equally and could afford to do more things together (Hawke and Knox 1978).

Research shows that the child in a one-child family has some advantages over children with siblings. In a study using a national sample of more than 24,000 eighth-graders surveyed in 1988, sociologist Douglas Downey (1995) found that only children were significantly more likely to talk frequently with their parents; to have attended art, music, or dance classes outside of school; and to have visited art, science, or history museums. Furthermore, parents of only children had higher educational expectations for their child, were more likely to know their child's friends and the friends' parents, and had more money saved for their child's college education.

DISADVANTAGES There are disadvantages, too, in a one-child family. For the children, these include the obvious lack of opportunity to experience sibling relationships, not only in childhood but also as adults. They may face extra pressure from parents to succeed. Only children are sometimes under an uncomfortable amount of parental scrutiny. As adults they have no help in caring for their aging parents. Disadvantages for parents include the fear that the only child might be seriously hurt or might die and the feeling, in some cases, that they have only one chance to prove themselves good parents.

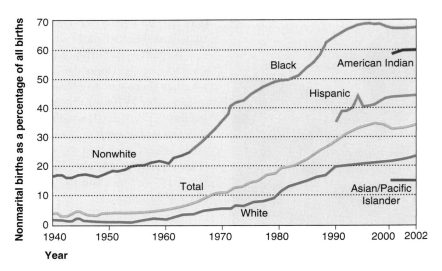

FIGURE 10.3

Births to unmarried women as a percentage of all births by race and ethnicity, 1940–2002. This figure illustrates the percentage of total births that are to unmarried women in each category, each year. Before 1964, data for blacks were combined with those of other nonwhites, but blacks were 90 percent of that category. Hispanic data are available only for 1990 onward. American Indian and Asian/Pacific Islander data are available only from 2000.

Source: Thornton and Freedman 1983, p. 22; U.S. Census Bureau 1995, Table 94; Ventura, Martin, Curtin, and Mathews 1998, Table C; Ventura and Bachrach 2000, Table 4; Ventura, Martin, Curtin, Menacker, and Hamilton 2001, p. 9; Martin, Hamilton, and Ventura 2001, Table 5; U.S. Census Bureau 2003a, Tables 84 and 91; Martin et al. 2003, Table 17.

Pregnancy Outside Marriage

As with births to married couples, births to unmarried individuals or couples may or may not have been intended. More and more, however, it seems that cohabiting couples and some unmarried individuals are intentional parents. In this section, we look at the demographics of nonmarital births and also at some of the settings in which nonmarital births take place.

In 2002, 34 percent of all births were to unmarried women. Although nonmarital birth rates have declined from their all-time high in 1994, childbearing in marriage declined even more, leaving births outside of marriage a larger proportion of total births (Martin et al. 2003). Figure 10.3 shows the percentage of children born to unmarried mothers since 1940. In 1940, fewer than 4 percent of all births were to unmarried women. The current figure represents a profound change in our society over the past fifty years or so.

Biologically, women mature earlier today,[8] but they marry later and are more likely to divorce than in the past, so they spend more years at risk of a nonmarital pregnancy if sexually active (as three-quarters of adult unmarried women are). They are much less likely now to marry upon the discovery of a nonmarital pregnancy (Ventura and Bachrach 2000).

Almost 40 percent of births to unmarried women in 2002 were to non-Hispanic white mothers (Martin et al. 2003, Table 17). But when we look at the *proportion* of nonmarital births in each racial/ethnic category, the picture looks somewhat different. As Figure 10.3 shows, in 2002, 68 percent of African Amer-

---

8. The average age of the onset of menstruation was almost seventeen in nineteenth-century Europe; in the United States today, the average age is about twelve (Alvardo 1992). Some recent research suggests that puberty now begins even earlier, but the research is disputed (Kolata 2001).

ican births, 60 percent of American Indian births, 44 percent of Hispanic births, 23 percent of non-Hispanic white births, and 15 percent of Asian/Pacific Islander births occurred outside marriage (Martin et al. 2003).

The nonmarital birth rate of African American women has actually declined substantially. After peaking in 1989, the nonmarital birth rate declined 27 percent between 1990 and 2002. This decline has reduced the difference between black and white rates considerably, although African American nonmarital birth rates remain well above those of white women.

Despite the decline in the nonmarital birth rate, the *proportion* of nonmarital births among African American women remains high for several reasons. First, the overall length of time that African American women spend in marriage has shortened dramatically; that is, fewer black women are married throughout their childbearing years. Second, fertility has declined more among married than among unmarried black women, which results in a shift in the proportion of total births that are to unmarried women. For many black women, marriage and parenthood have become separate experiences (Cherlin 1981; Martin et al. 2003; Ventura and Bachrach 2000).

Hispanic women have a high level of cohabitation, and children are often born in those unions (Ventura, Martin, Curtin, and Mathews 1998; Manning 2001). Nonmarital birth rates of Hispanic women are highest of any racial/ethnic group, but so are marital births, so that nonmarital births remain a smaller proportion of the total (Martin et al. 2003).

NONMARITAL BIRTHS TO COHABITANTS AND OTHER UNMARRIED COUPLES Childbearing in a cohabiting relationship is increasingly common.

> Fertility during cohabitation continues to account for almost all of the recent increases in nonmarital childbearing. . . . Cohabitation . . . has increasingly become a setting for family formation, . . . a two-parent family union in which to have and raise children outside of marriage. (Manning 2001, p. 217)

Indeed, the birth rate of cohabiting women is essentially the same as that of women living with a husband (Downs 2003). Some cohabiting families have been established by previously married women. Previously

married women have high rates of cohabitation and high fertility. Twenty percent of women give birth postmaritally and "a substantial proportion" of those births are to cohabiting couples (Brown 2000, p. 520). Also, childbearing among lesbians has increased, often in committed couple settings. Cohabiting families are discussed extensively in Chapter 9.

It is now realized that even less visibly attached unmarried parents may have a more regular relationship than previously thought. The Fragile Families study (McLanahan, Garfinkel, Reichman, and Teitler 2001) found in an analysis based on 1,764 new mothers in seven cities that the vast majority of new parents (82 percent) described themselves as "romantically involved on a steady basis." "The myth that unwed fathers are not around at the time of the birth could not be further from the truth" (McLanahan et al. 2001, p. 217). Nevertheless, involvement of the fathers is likely to decline over time, given their limited resources (Wu and Wolfe 2001). McLanahan and her research colleagues encourage policy support for "fragile families."

NONMARITAL BIRTHS TO OLDER SINGLE MOTHERS Although unwed birth rates are highest among young adult women (aged twenty through twenty-four), they have increased dramatically for older women in recent years. Rates for unmarried women aged thirty through thirty-four increased by 90 percent between 1980 and 1998. The increase in childbearing among older single women is largely a white phenomenon (Ventura and Bachrach 2000, Table 3).

As opportunities grow for women to support themselves and as the permanence of marriage becomes less certain, there is less motivation for a woman to avoid giving birth out of wedlock, because she cannot count on lifetime male support for the child even if she marries. Furthermore, stigma and discrimination against unwed mothers have lessened. Still, because the burden of responsibility for support and care of the child remains on the mother, overall, "the economic situation of older, single mothers is closer to that of teen mothers than that of married childbearers the same age" (Foster, Jones, and Hoffman 1998, p. 163).

There is a category of older single mothers who may be better off than that—**single mothers by choice**. The image is that of an older woman with an education, an established job, and economic resources,

Studies have shown that unmarried partners who have a higher level of commitment and a greater sense of self-esteem and acceptance of their sexuality are more likely to use contraceptives. Birth rates of teen women have declined, and effective use of contraception is a major factor in this decline.

who has made a choice to become a single mother. Not having found stable life partners, yet wanting to parent, women make this choice as they see time running out on their "biological clock."

Whether this is a significant development in terms of numbers is uncertain (Musick 2002). However, in two small studies of single mothers by choice (Bock 2000; Mannis 1999), researchers interviewed women who adopted children or who purposefully became pregnant. These mothers, usually over age thirty, saw themselves as responsible, emotionally mature, and financially capable of raising a child. Rather than viewing themselves as alternative lifestyle pioneers, they saw their choice as conforming to normal family goals. In fact, their decisions to become single mothers were well-accepted by family, friends, employers, clergy, and physicians.

These were white, middle-class, educated women who insisted on the great difference between themselves and "welfare" or teen mothers. What, in fact, are the realities of teen parenthood today?

NONMARITAL BIRTHS TO ADOLESCENTS Public concerns about outcomes for the children of unmarried parents intensify when the mother is a teenager. The words *teenage pregnancy* have been asso-

ciated with the word *problem* since most of us can remember.

Adolescent birth rates rose in the late 1960s as sexual behavior liberalized. However, by the time a "teen pregnancy epidemic" was identified in the mid-1970s, those birth rates had already begun to decline. The teen birth rate is now less than half what it was at its peak in 1957. The teen abortion rate dropped also. Adolescents, in other words, are having fewer pregnancies. They are using contraception more regularly, and teen sexual activity has leveled off. Declines in the adolescent birth rate in the 1990s and since have been especially large for young black women (Ventura, Mathews, and Hamilton 2001; Martin et al. 2003).

Nevertheless, the United States still has by far the highest teen pregnancy, abortion, and birth rates of any industrialized country (Ventura, Mathews, and Hamilton 2001), and teen pregnancy is still problematic. In the 1950s, when teen birth rates were actually higher, most teen mothers were either already married or they married before the child's birth. A strong economy provided young fathers with jobs that could support a family while teen wives remained at home caring for children. In other words, adolescent parents married and easily stepped into adult roles, forming two-parent families that were indistinguishable from those of older couples. Women were not expected to be employed or to get extensive education to prepare for a lifelong career, while young men held good jobs without higher education, even if they did not complete high school.

Today we live in a different world. As Figure 10.4 indicates, most teen women giving birth are not married, and so they lack the economic support of a spouse and the practical assistance and psychological support of a co-parent. Women as well as men need more education now, and women are expected to seek employment (Mauldon 2003). But that is difficult to manage for a young, usually poor, mother on her own. Teenage parents today, especially those with more than one child, face a bleak educational future, a stunted career, and a very good chance of living in poverty, compared with peers who do not become parents as teenagers (Nock 1998a; Zabin et al. 1992). Teen mothers are less likely than their counterparts to marry eventually, and teen marriages have higher divorce rates (Manning 1993). Prospects for the children of teen parents included lower academic achievement and a tendency to repeat the cycle of early unmarried pregnancy (Hayes 1987; Alexander and Guyer 1993).

There has been some revisionist thinking about the association between teen childbearing and these negative outcomes. First of all, some research suggests that a background of economic or racial/ethnic disadvantage may be playing a larger role than age-at-parenthood in shaping a teen mother's limited future (Geronimus 1991; Gueorguieva et al. 2001; Mauldon 2003; Turley 2003). Secondly, the research has illustrated that teen parents are quite varied in their experiences and educational and work aspirations (Camarena et al. 1998). Outcomes of teen parenthood vary, and are not by any means uniformly negative. One longitudinal study of black teen mothers from low-income families in Baltimore concluded that

> [W]hile early childbearing increases the risk of ill effects for mother and child, it is unclear that the risk is so high as to justify the popular image of the adolescent mother as an unemployed woman living on welfare with a number of poorly cared-for children. To be sure, teenage mothers do not manage as well as women who delay childbearing, but most studies have shown that there is great variation in the effects of

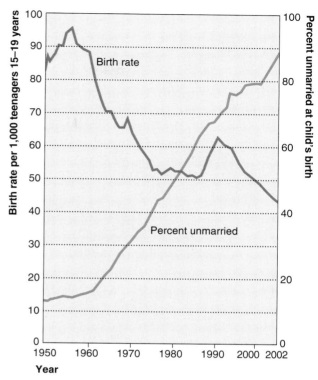

FIGURE 10.4

Birth rate for teen women fifteen through nineteen years and percentage of teen births that are to unmarried teenagers, 1950–2002.

Source: Ventura, Mathews, and Hamilton 2001, Figure 1; Downs 2003, Figure 1.

teenage childbearing. (Furstenberg, Brooks-Gunn, and Morgan 1987, p. 142)

Social scientists and others have pointed to the ongoing need for support programs to help young parents and to help their families help them (Leitch 1998; Mauldon 2003). Teen fathers need to be included in such programs and services. Support programs in the schools and other programs targeted to teen parents have, in fact, produced good outcomes.

Stepparents' Decisions About Having Children

When people remarry or form a new committed partnership, they have decisions to make about having children together. Does it make a difference whether one or both partners already have children? The answer to that question is: yes.

A study of more than 2,000 couples drawn from a national sample—National Survey of Family and Households data—found that individuals living with a second spouse or partner were most likely to want to have a child if there were no stepchildren of either partner (Stewart 2002). Desire for another child was lower for cohabiting couples than married ones. If *both* partners already had children, an intention to have another child was especially low, with one exception.

Because of the symbolic importance of joint parenthood, if the couple did not have a biological child, they were very likely to intend to have one. If they already had a shared child, couples were less likely to want to have additional children—*unless* they had only *one* shared child. In that case they were likely want to have another baby—the two-child norm at work.

▪ Preventing Pregnancy ▪

Falling birth rates from the nineteenth century onward indicate that people did not always want to have as many children as nature would make possible. As early as 1832 a book describing birth control techniques and devices was published in the United States. The diaphragm was invented in 1883 and was a common method of birth control for married couples (Weeks 2002, pp. 180–81; 530–31), as was the condom. But it was not until the contraceptive pill became available in the 1960s, that women could be more certain of controlling fertility, and they did not need male cooperation to do so.

Primacy of the pill as a means of birth control shifted the locus of responsibility for contraception to the woman. The long-awaited "male pill" is still on the drawing board ("The Quest Is On" 2004). (Appendix F, "Contraceptive Techniques," describes the various methods of birth control, their effectiveness, and any risks associated with them.)

Whatever methods are available, use of contraception takes place in a relationship context that affects not only choice of methods but also whether contraception is used at all. As one example, teenagers who had a long relationship before commencing a sexual relationship were more apt to use contraception at first sex. (Manlove, Ryan, and Franzetta 2003).

The physical and opportunity costs of children tend to be higher for women than for men, married or unmarried, and family planning services have always been oriented to women as a clientele. More recently, the reproductive health needs of men have received attention from family planning organizations, but they have not yet seen adequate development, and men are typically unaware of their availability where they do exist (Finer, Darroch, and Frost 2003). New research and services have targeted adolescent young men as an approach to adolescent pregnancy prevention (Marsiglio 2003; Marsiglio and Hutchinson 2002).

▪ Abortion ▪

Effective contraception prevents the potential problems associated with pregnancy outside of marriage. When contraception isn't used or fails, however, many women who don't want to remain pregnant decide to have an abortion. We will look next at this option, an extremely controversial social issue.

Abortion is the expulsion of the embryo or fetus from the uterus either naturally (spontaneous abortion or miscarriage) or medically (surgically or drug-induced abortion). This section addresses **induced abortion**.[9] Thirty percent of American women have had an induced abortion at some point in their lives (Henshaw 1998, p. 24).

Abortion decisions are primarily made within the context of unmarried, accidental pregnancy. However, some married couples may consider aborting an unwanted pregnancy if, for example, they feel that they have already completed their family or could not manage or afford to raise another child. The question of abortion can also arise for couples who, through prenatal diagnosis techniques, find out that a fetus has a serious defect.

Around a quarter of pregnancies ended in abortion in 2000. Some 1,315,000 legal abortions were performed in the United States in that year, down from a peak of about 1.6 million in 1990. The rate of abor-

---

9. For detailed descriptions of the various options in abortion procedures, see *Our Bodies, Ourselves for the New Century,* by the Boston Women's Health Book Collective (1998), Chapter 17 or Greenberg, Bruess, and Haffner 2002. Updated information may become available on medical websites.

In our society, sexuality and reproduction have become increasingly politicized. Nowhere is this more apparent than in the intensely heated pro-life/pro-choice debate over abortion, one of the most polarizing issues in America today.

tions per 1,000 women aged fifteen through forty-four (childbearing age) has been falling since 1980 (Jones, Darroch, and Henshaw 2002; U.S. Census Bureau 2003a, Table 102). "Although further decreases in unintended pregnancies can help the downward trend in U.S. abortion rates continue, some women will still turn to abortion, either to resolve an unintended pregnancy or to deal with a change in circumstances following an intended conception (Jones et al. 2002, p. 234).

In 2000, more than four-fifths of abortions were obtained by unmarried women. More than half (56 percent) were obtained by women in their twenties, almost 20 percent by teens. White women account for the greatest number of abortions (41 percent of total abortions, compared to 32 percent for blacks, 20 percent for Hispanics, 6 percent for Asian/Pacific Islanders, and 1 percent for Native Americans (Jones et al. 2002, Table 1). But the percentage of pregnancies that are terminated by abortion (the *abortion ratio*) is highest among black and Asian/Pacific Islander women. Researchers conclude that "women who have abortions are diverse, and unintended pregnancy leading to abortion is common in all population subgroups" (Jones et al. 2002, p. 232). Still, women in poverty account for a disproportionate share of abor-

tions. Just under half (48 percent) of women obtaining abortions have had a previous abortion (U.S. Census Bureau 2003a, Tables 102 and 103).

The Safety of Abortions

Abortion is now a safe medical procedure when it is performed in a hospital or a clinic in the first trimester, as almost 90 percent of abortions are. Abortions in the second trimester are about ten times more dangerous than those performed in the first trimester.

Research indicates that abortion has no impact on the ability to become pregnant—sterility following abortion is very uncommon—and there is virtually no risk to future pregnancies from a first-trimester abortion of a first pregnancy (Boston Women's Health Book Collective 1998, p. 407).[10]

---

10. The question of a link between abortion and breast cancer has been raised by the pro-life movement (Brind 2002; and see Malec 2003). A panel assembled by the National Cancer Institute to review the research concluded that there is no association between induced abortion and breast cancer (Altman 2003; Collaborative Group on Hormonal Factors in Breast Cancer 2004; U.S. National Cancer Institute 2003).

The Politics of Abortion

Throughout world history, abortion has been a way of preventing birth. The practice was not legally prohibited in the United States until the mid-nineteenth century. Laws prohibiting abortion stood relatively unchallenged until the 1960s, when an abortion reform movement succeeded in modifying some state laws to permit abortions approved by physicians on a case-by-case basis. The movement culminated in the 1973 U.S. Supreme Court decision *Roe v. Wade*, which legalized abortion throughout the United States.[11]

As virtually everyone is aware, pro-choice and pro-life activists—those who favor or oppose legal abortion—have made abortion a major political issue. Legislation and other public policy responses to abortion have been shaped by this struggle, as has been the availability of abortion services. Abortion was never widely available outside of urban areas. Now states have placed various restrictions on access to abortion. Moreover, the scaling back of training in abortion procedures in medical education as a consequence of political pressures means that as current providers age out or become discouraged by social pressures and threats to their lives, the practical effect is to reduce abortion options (Feldt 1998). Although clinic violence is down, women arriving for abortion appointments must usually pass a gauntlet of picketers (Zernike 2003b).

At the same time that the Supreme Court has upheld many state restrictions on abortion, it has not outlawed the procedure. Nor has a constitutional amendment to criminalize abortion made it through Congress.[12] The result is that abortion continues to be legally available, as pro-choice advocates wish, while the goals of pro-life advocates have been partially reached through legal and practical restrictions on abortion availability. This has some correspondence with the centrist position of the American public, which favors abortion under certain circumstances.

---

11. Contrary to what some people may think, *Roe v. Wade* did not legalize any and all abortions in any and all situations. *Roe v. Wade* allows abortion to be obtained without question in the first trimester of pregnancy, but abortion is subject to regulation of providers and procedure in the second trimester and may be outlawed by states after fetal viability (when the fetus is able to live outside the womb), which occurs in the third trimester.
12. The implications of the recently passed federal law banning "partial birth abortion" are not clear as we complete work on this edition of *Marriages and Families* because the law is being reviewed by higher courts.

Table 10.1

Percentage of U.S. Adults Approving of Abortion Under Certain Circumstances

ABORTION SHOULD BE LEGAL . . .	
When the woman's life is endangered	85%
When the woman's physical health is endangered	77
When the pregnancy was caused by rape or incest	76
When the woman's mental health is endangered	63
When there is evidence that the baby may be physically impaired	56
When there is evidence that the baby may be mentally impaired	55
When the woman or family cannot afford to raise the child	35

Source: Gallup poll, Jan. 10–12, 2003 (Saad 2003).

Social Attitudes About Abortion

According to a 2003 Gallup poll, the majority of Americans believe that *Roe v. Wade* should remain the law of the land. Support for abortion is heavily qualified, however, with only 24 percent believing that abortion should be legal in all circumstances, another 14 percent in most circumstances, 42 percent in only a few circumstances, and 18 percent believing abortion should be illegal in all circumstances. Table 10.1 shows the particular circumstances that influence people's attitudes about abortion.

Forty-six percent of respondents (in 2001) described themselves as pro-choice, while 46 percent chose the pro-life label (Saad 2002). Public opinion approval of abortion differs sharply by the trimester of pregnancy. First-trimester abortion was approved by two-thirds of poll respondents, while later-stage abortions were disapproved by more than two-thirds (Saad 2003). Few abortions (0.17 percent) take place in the third trimester of pregnancy (Jones, Darroch, and Henshaw 2002).

Approval of abortion seems to be decreasing among younger people. A 2003 national survey of college freshman conducted by UCLA found that 55 percent support legal abortion, compared to 64 percent ten years earlier: "We're the first generation to be more pro-life than our parents," said one freshman (Rosenberg 2004).

The Emotional and Psychological Impact of Abortion

What all this public discussion about abortion means for individuals is that women making decisions about abortion today do so in a far more political climate than in earlier decades. It's safe to say that for most women (and for many of their male partners), abortion is an emotionally charged, often upsetting, experience. Some women report feeling guilty or frightened, a situation that can be heightened by demonstrators outside abortion clinics. Emotional stress is more pronounced for second-trimester than earlier abortions and for women who are uncertain about their decision (Boston Women's Health Book Collective 1998, pp. 406–408). Women from religious denominations or ethnic cultures that strongly oppose abortion may have more negative and mixed feelings after an abortion, but outcomes are more complex than that, as they seem to depend also on the woman's emotional well-being prior to having the abortion (Russo and Dabul 1997).

Some women have reported that the decision to abort enhanced their sense of personal empowerment (Boston Women's Health Book Collective 1998, pp. 406–407). Research has found positive educational, economic, and social outcomes for teen women who resolve pregnancies by abortion rather than giving birth. In one study, "those who obtained abortions did better economically and educationally and had fewer subsequent pregnancies than those who chose to bear children" (Holmes 1990). For many women, having an abortion probably results in mixed feelings.

The decision to abort is often very difficult to make and act on. But according to a longitudinal study of almost 5,000 black and white women, the emotional distress involved in making the decision and having the abortion does not typically lead to severe or long-lasting psychological problems (Russo and Dabul 1997; see also Adler et al. 1992; Russo and Zierk 1992; O'Malley 2002). The American Psychiatric Association and the American Psychological Association have taken the position that the alleged psychiatric disorder of "abortion trauma" does not exist (O'Malley 2002). It is important to make a distinction between negative feelings and psychiatric problems. The consensus at present is that there is no clear relationship of abortion to mental health (Lee 2003).

Regardless of this background information, women (and men) making decisions about abortions are most likely to make them in accordance with their values. A detailed review of religiously or philosophically grounded moral and ethical perspectives on abortion is outside the scope of this text, but as we note in Chapter 1, values provide the context for such decisions.

Involuntary Infertility and Reproductive Technology

For some, concern about fertility means avoiding unwanted births. Other couples and individuals face a different problem. They want to have a child, but either they cannot conceive or they cannot sustain a full-term pregnancy. We turn now to the issue of involuntary infertility.

As medically defined, **involuntary infertility** is the condition of wanting to conceive and bear a child but being physically unable to do so. It is usually diagnosed in terms of unsuccessful efforts to conceive for at least twelve months or the inability to carry a pregnancy to full term. "For most women and their partners, infertility is a major life crisis" (Boston Women's Health Book Collective 1998, p. 532).

The Social and Biological Context of Infertility

Infertility problems are attributed to the male partner in 40 percent of the cases and to the female partner in 40 percent of the cases; the remaining 20 percent are attributed to both partners or considered to be of unknown origin (Becker 2000).[13] About half of couples defined as infertile will eventually conceive and deliver, with or without medical intervention (Boston Women's Health Book Collective 1998, p. 532).

Through advances in health and medicine, the incidence of involuntary infertility declined during most of the twentieth century (Mosher and Pratt 1990). In recent years, infertility has increased slightly—from 8 percent of women aged fifteen through forty-four in the 1980s to an estimated 10 percent in 1995 (latest

---

13. The physiology of conception, pregnancy, and childbirth is described in Appendix E and should be referred to in conjunction with this section. For a more detailed technical discussion of infertility, see Greenberg, Bruess, and Haffner 2002; Becker 2000; or current books on the subject addressed to a lay (nonmedical) audience.

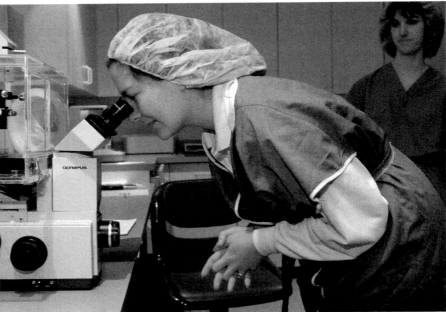

This physician, an infertility specialist, is looking through the microscope to examine donor eggs, which will be used in treating a couple's infertility. Infertility treatments are increasingly high-tech—and costly; nevertheless, they are more and more seen as a normal means of reproduction.

© Annie Griffiths Belt/CORBIS

data); that is more than six million women (Chandra and Stephen 1998).[14] Infertility has become more visible because the present tendency to postpone childbearing until one's thirties or even forties creates a class of infertile potential parents who are intensely hopeful and also financially able to seek treatment.

Anthropologist Gay Becker undertook an ethnographic study of infertility treatment, conducting 500 interviews and doing field observation over a four-year period. The study included 143 women and 134 men and is a good source of information about the experience of infertility and its treatment.

When faced with involuntary infertility, an individual or a couple experiences a loss of control over life plans and feels helpless, defective, angry, and often guilty. While men and women may differ in their spe-

cific responses to infertility, both are very affected emotionally by the challenge to taken-for-granted life plans and their sense of manhood or womanhood (Becker 2000). Research based on a random sample of 580 Midwestern women found motherhood to be a primary identity, such that women who had experienced infertility and had never become mothers showed higher levels of distress than comparison groups of women with no fertility problems or those who eventually became mothers despite such problems (McQuillan, Greil, White, and Jacob 2003). For men, issues of masculinity came to the fore in their preference for keeping the infertility problem secret or presenting it as the wife's. They were also more ambivalent than their partners about infertility treatment and more likely to end treatment sooner than their partners, even without success (Throsby and Gill 2004).

The psychological burden of infertility may fall especially hard on professional, goal-oriented individuals. These people "have learned to focus all their energies on a particular goal. When that goal becomes a pregnancy that they cannot achieve, they see themselves as failures in a global sense" (Berg 1984, p. 164). Besides having an effect on each partner's self-esteem, the situation can hurt their relationship (Becker 2000).

---

14. Neither modern contraceptives (other than possibly a no-longer-used version of the IUD) nor abortion impair fertility. New factors contributing to infertility include the rising incidence of STDs, which can damage the reproductive systems of women and sometimes men. Exposure to various drugs, chemicals, and radiation can also cause infertility, and smoking and excessive exercise (which inhibits ovulation) may contribute to it. There has been a concern that various environmental pollutants are lowering males' sperm counts, but newer research has found no change in sperm quality over almost sixty years ("American Sperm" 2000).

SEEKING INFERTILITY SERVICES Many couples only gradually become aware that unlike other couples they know who are publicly planning their pregnancies without apparent difficulty, they themselves remain without desired children. It is at this point that couples are likely to seek a medical solution to their problem (Matthews and Matthews 1986).

Almost half (44 percent) of fertility-impaired women sought medical help in 1995 (the latest year for which data are available). They were more often white (75 percent) and typically older (twenty-five through forty-four), married, better educated, and with higher family incomes than those not seeking treatment. But 20 percent of those using infertility services were not married, and 11 percent were poor (Chandra and Stephen 1998). With regard to race, few social science data exist, but individuals and physicians have pointed out the difficulty that blacks may have in obtaining certain infertility services, notably sperm or egg donations when a donor of their own race is sought—there are few donors ("Infertile Black Couples" 1999). Moreover, African Americans have tended to view high-tech infertility treatments as "a white thing." Even though blacks' infertility rate is higher than that of non-Hispanic whites, childless African Americans tend to perform parenting roles in extended families or through fostering friends' children rather than by pursuing infertility treatments (Sanders 1992).

After initial testing, the next step is to explore medical procedures involving drug therapies or donor insemination, in vitro fertilization, and related techniques (see Appendix G). Fertility treatment is stressful. The procedures can be uncomfortable, and scheduling sex for the main purpose of reproduction can feel depersonalizing and can also add conflict to a relationship (Becker 1990, 2000). As one wife explained:

> All the things you read about—that men feel like they are just a tool. You have to have an erection and ejaculate at a certain time whether you want to or not. He has said to me in times out of genuine anger, "I feel like all you want me for is to make a baby. You don't really want me, you just want me to do it." (Becker 1990, p. 94)

Going through infertility treatment is costly. A current controversy involves whether employee health

"I told my parents that if grades were so important they should have paid for a smarter egg donor."

insurance should cover it. As of 2001, only fourteen states required insurance companies to offer policies that cover infertility treatment (National Conference of State Legislatures 2004a). Would-be parents who cannot afford in vitro fertilization clash with corporations and health policy analysts concerned about health insurance costs. Some among the public view having children as a personal choice that calls for no societal support. Advocates of insurance coverage argue instead that infertility coverage is minimally costly and that "the right to have a family is no different than the right to chemotherapy so someone can live five more years to see a son or daughter graduate from high school" (Applebly 2001, p. 2-B)

Infertility treatment can be successful, but often it is not. When it is not, couples are faced with yet another decision—whether, or when, to quit trying. Said one husband, "The technology . . . has given us so many options that it is hard to say no" (quoted in Stolberg 1997a, p. A–1). Still, more and more, **assisted reproductive technology (ART)** has become a normal

Issues for Thought

Meddling with Nature

A set of issues concerning reproductive technology involves whether the unlimited technological alteration of nature in this way is prudent or ethically sound. Catholic theology, grounded in the natural law tradition, views reproductive technology as a violation of the natural order. One does not need a natural law philosophy to feel a bit uneasy about some of the implications of reproductive technology.

There are now some 400,000 frozen human embryos left over from couples' infertility treatment (Weiss 2003a). Several divorced couples' disagreements over whether their frozen embryos may be used by one of the parties to bear children have had to be resolved by the courts (Dolgin 1997, pp. 156–174; *J.B. v. M.B. and C.C.* 2001). Broader debates exist over whether the frozen embryos should be discarded, used in stem cell research, or transferred to other couples—and who should make those decisions

Even **embryo adoption**—one couple's unneeded frozen embryos are used to enable another couple to have a child—presents problems despite its benign intent. This form of reproduction has not been addressed legislatively by any state. In the absence of statutory regulation, biological parents may wonder if they might be sought out later by their "children," while the new parents may feel that their children are not wholly theirs. In fact, some parents who permitted their embryos to be "adopted" specifically mandate that the adopting couple maintain contact with them (Stolberg 2000). Embryo adoption has also become a political issue in that the Bush administration has funded a promotional campaign, while pro-choice activists and others are wary of an adoption analogy that treats frozen embryos as children ("Some Groups" 2002).

With reproductive technology we are faced with the question of how

old is too old to become a mother. By using a younger woman's eggs, some women past menopause—one as old as sixty-three (Budd 2002)— have carried and delivered infants. Older mothers who bear children this way are likely to be financially stable, but a mother giving birth in her fifties will be seventy when her child graduates from high school. This has always been true for fathers, of course, who can remain fertile to older ages. It is only a mother's aging that tends to be questioned, says older mom and therapist Micky Doxbury (in Rubin 2003).

Reproduction can and has extended beyond the grave, as some surviving spouses, partners, or parents have wished to use frozen sperm or embryos to produce the children or grandchildren they might have had if death had not intervened. The American Society of Reproductive Medicine now has a "Posthumous Reproduction" protocol providing guidelines for physicians receiving such requests

part of reproduction. In 2001, there were more than 100,000 ART procedures, which resulted in more than 40,000 infants (Wright et al. 2004).

Reproductive Technology: Social and Ethical Issues

Reproductive technologies enhance choices and can reward infertile couples with much-desired parenthood. They enable same-sex couples or uncoupled individuals to become biological parents. But reproductive technologies have tremendous social implications for the family as an institution and raise serious ethical questions as well. The box "Issues for Thought:

Meddling with Nature" discusses some of the implications of reproductive technology, as biological limits formerly taken for granted are transgressed. The following sections explore the commercialization of reproduction, inequality of access to reproductive technology, and the parent-child relationships created by reproductive technology.

COMMERCIALIZATION OF REPRODUCTION A general concern is that the new techniques, when performed for profit, commercialize reproduction. Prospective parents and their bodies are treated as products and thereby dehumanized (Rothman 1999).

(Andrews 1999). Some men in the military have had sperm frozen before deploying overseas as a precaution against exposure to biochemical hazards that might affect their fertility (Alvord 2003a), and men about to undergo cancer treatment have done the same. One man interviewed by Gay Becker in her study of those in infertility treatment suggested that "Twenty years from now people will automatically bank their sperm and their eggs in their early twenties, then go on with their lives until they are much older, when they are ready to have kids" (Charlie, in Becker 2000, p. 7).

One departure from nature is already quite common—large numbers of multiple births. At present, more than half of ART births are multiples (Wright et al. 2004). Concern about the possibility of adverse outcomes for multiples (higher risk of death or disability), as well as the strain on parents, has led the American Society of Reproductive Medicine to recommend implantation of fewer embryos at a time, specifically two to five. Though voluntary, these guidelines seem to have had some influence; in 2001, the average number of embryos implanted was three ("Study: Multiple" 2004). But prospective parents often do not agree to that, as they wish to maximize their chances of having a child by having more embryos implanted. Moreover, there is an economic incentive for clients of infertility services to pressure physicians to implant more embryos at a time since health insurance usually does not cover the cost (Olson 2002). Countries or American states that subsidize reproductive technology have a lower rate of multiples (Leigh 2004; Reynolds et al. 2003).

Ethicists are also addressing the possibility that in the future, prospective parents may be able to choose the traits they want in a biological child—customizing, as it were. Sex selection is one version of this—already possible through selective abortion, although that is thought to be infrequent in the United States. Now reproductive clinics claim the capability of sperm-sorting techniques or selection of embryos to produce girls with 91-percent reliability and boys with 76-percent reliability. Eventually, it might be possible to screen for other traits. In fact, some infertility clinics market sperm and eggs from donors who have "desirable" characteristics or experiment with mixing sperm and eggs to produce embryos with certain traits (Friend 2003; Kalb 2004; Kolata 1997). These possibilities are met with the argument from ethicists that "offspring [should be accepted] for themselves and not their non-essential characteristics" (Talbot 2002b, p. 25).

Critical Thinking

We "meddle with nature" all the time, as we use health care treatment to prevent disease, forestall death, and improve quality of life. Is reproductive technology any different?

Would you use reproductive technology to try to have children of a certain sex? With certain physical or mental qualities? What reproductive technologies, if any, do you think should *not* be made available to the public?

An example is the selling of eggs or sperm to for-profit fertility clinics and the marketing of sperm or eggs with certain donor characteristics such as IQ, intelligence, and physical attractiveness. Reports of fraud, overstatement of positive outcomes, failure to warn about the risk of multiple births, and other professional violations in fertility centers (Leigh 2004) make it important to understand that an individual seeking treatment is in fact a consumer and should interview the doctor and investigate the facility.

INEQUALITY ISSUES Reproductive technologies raise social class and other inequality issues. Assisted reproductive technology is usually not affordable by those with low incomes. By and large, after initial diagnosis, lower-income couples do not go on to more advanced (and expensive) treatment. Said one woman, "There need to be some options for people like us who don't have money sitting in the bank" (Becker 2000, p. 20).

WHO IS A PARENT? With donor insemination, courts have had to address the question "Who is the father?" Many states have laws by which sperm donors, with the exception of the husband, have no parental rights. But donors have occasionally attempted to assert parental rights in situations where they know the child's parents, and courts have sometimes recognized their rights (Peres 1997).

Furthermore, surrogacy, along with embryo transfer, creates the possibility that a child could have three mothers (the genetic mother, the gestational mother, and the social mother), as well as two fathers (genetic and social). In such a situation, how do courts define the "real" parents (Schwartz 2003)?[15]

Reproductive Technology: Making Personal Choices

We should note that the concerns about reproductive technology described in the previous section and in the box "Issues for Thought: Meddling with Nature" are articulated primarily by medical and public health professionals, academics, and policy analysts. For the most part, prospective parents themselves are more focused on their desire for a child and not so inclined to view ART with a critical eye—at least not initially.

Choosing to use reproductive technology depends on one's values and circumstances. Religious beliefs and cultural values influence decisions.[16] Fertility treatment can be financially, physically, and emotionally draining. The need for frequent physician's visits can interfere with job obligations, and infertility treatment can lead to tensions in a marriage.

---

15. Legislation in Sweden and court decisions in the United Kingdom have given children the right to obtain identifying information about a donor. Some American sperm clinics have responded to the *identity release movement* by developing *open sperm donor* programs, which agree to make information available to the child at eighteen; offer photos of the donor; or at a minimum, offer genetic/health information. Some previously anonymous donors and their biological offspring have met, arranging meetings through the clinic when there is mutual agreement to do so (Villarosa 2002b; Talbot 2001). The American Fertility Society recommends against secrecy: "It's no longer possible to think of sperm donation without thinking of what the child it produces may someday want" (Talbot 2001, p. 88). See Dolgin 1997, Chapters 6 and 7, for an extended discussion of the varied decisions courts have made regarding the rights of biological and social parents in these and other situations.

16. The Catholic church prohibits all forms of reproductive technology, including donor insemination (Congregation for the Doctrine of the Faith 1988; McCormick 1992). The Jewish tradition requires physical union for adultery and so does not define DI as adulterous. But Judaism does view masturbation as sinful. Hence, a man's obtaining sperm either to sell or to artificially inseminate his wife is morally problematic; this is true of Catholic teaching as well (Newman 1992). Some interpretations of Protestantism, on the other hand, note that the Bible sees infertility as cause for sorrow and exalts increasing human freedom beyond natural barriers (Meilander 1992).

Those who are successful are euphoric: "Our son is so gorgeous!" marveled one mother (McCarthy, quoted in Halpern 1989b, p. 151). Children born through the use of in vitro fertilization or donor sperm seem to be thoroughly normal, as the research reported in "Facts About Families: 'Test-Tube' Babies Grow Up" shows us.

For some who had hoped to become parents, infertility treatment eventually became the problem instead of the solution. Coming to terms with infertility has been likened to the grief process, in which initial denial is followed by anger, depression, and usually ultimate acceptance: "When I finally found out that I absolutely could not have children . . . it was a tremendous relief. I could get on with my life" (Bouton 1987, p. 92). Some people gradually choose to define themselves as permanently and comfortably child-free. A second way to get on with life yet retain the hope of parenthood is through adoption. Indeed, some couples explore adoption options even as they continue infertility treatments (Becker 2000).

▪ Adoption ▪

The U.S. Census looked at adoption for the first time in 2000. In that year, there were more than two million adopted children in U.S. households, about 2.5 percent of all children. In terms of *numbers* there are more adopted children in non-Hispanic white families (more than 70 percent of all adopted children). But Asian/Pacific Islander families have the highest *rate* of adoption relative to their population.

More girls than boys are adopted. Women, especially single women, prefer to adopt girls, and girls are more likely to be available for adoption. Ninety-five percent of Chinese babies available for adoption, for example, are girls (Fields 2001; Kreider 2003; U.S. Census Bureau 2004).

Census data do not distinguish adoptions by biological relatives or stepparents from non-relative adoptions. But earlier research found that a majority of adopted children were related to their adopted parents by blood or marriage. Most commonly, those who adopted unrelated children have no other children, have impaired fertility, and have used infertility services. They are more likely to be older, highly educated, and to have higher incomes (Chandra,

Facts About Families

"Test-Tube" Babies Grow Up

Louise Brown, the first baby conceived through the use of in vitro fertilization (IVF), turned twenty-five in 2003, and Elizabeth Carr, the first American IVF baby, is now twenty-two and a college graduate. In vitro fertilization and other assisted reproductive technologies are the "new normal." That is, there are now more than one million living IVF children, and almost 50,000 are born worldwide every year (Szabo 2004a; Weiss 2002). "New reproductive technologies . . . have come to be viewed as simply another means of conception" (Becker 2000, p. 19).

How normal are the children produced by the use of such assisted reproductive technology (ART) as in vitro fertilization (IVF), donor insemination (DI), egg donation, and embryo transfer? Medically, the use of ART involves a greater risk of low birth weight, birth defects, developmental delay, or a greater, though infrequent, incidence of some rare diseases ("Abnormalities Cause"

2003; Brown 2002; Kolata 2002b; Schieve et al. 2002; Stromberg et al. 2002; and Weiss 2002). Nevertheless, 94 percent of all full-term IVF singletons had normal birth weight and 91 percent, no major birth defects.

What one may especially want to know about assisted reproduction children is what they are like psychosocially? And are their parents able to relate to them in a "normal" way? Major longitudinal studies of in vitro fertilization and donor insemination children have been conducted in Britain and in some other European countries. The researchers followed the children to age twelve and compared IVF and DI children to adopted and naturally conceived children. On a variety of measures obtained from parents, teachers, and the children themselves, the researchers concluded that the reproductive technology children were functioning well and did not differ from naturally conceived or adopted children

in their psychosocial adjustment (Golombok, Brewaeys, Giavazzi, Guerra, MacCallum, and Rust 2002; Golombok, Cook, Bish, and Murray 1995; Golombok, MacCallum, and Goodman 2003; Golombok, MacCallum, Goodman, and Rutter 2002; McMahon et al. 2003; also Chan, Raboy, and Patterson 1998). All in all, careful, well-designed longitudinal studies of ART children and their families conducted by different sets of researchers are unanimous in finding ART children to be thoroughly normal. "Test-tube" babies are developing normally as they grow into adolescence.

Critical Thinking

Do you know anyone who is an ART child and has discussed it with you? Do you know any parents or would-be parents who have used reproductive technology? What were their experiences with ART?

Abma, Maza, and Bachrach 1999; Kreider 2003). To encourage more adoption, there is now a federal tax credit of $10,000 toward adoption expenses for low- and middle-income parents. Corporations sometimes subsidize adoptions by their employees (Block 2003).

Some children are adopted informally—that is, children are taken into a parent's home, but the adoption is not legally formalized. **Informal adoption** is most common among Alaska Natives, blacks, and Hispanics (Kreider 2003).

Adoptions increased through much of this century and reached a peak in 1970. But the number has declined since (Bachrach et al. 1990). Fewer infants are available due to more effective contraception and le-

galized abortion. And white unmarried mothers, those most likely to relinquish their infants in the past, are now likely to keep their babies.

Adoptions by lesbian co-parents have been attempted in many states. When one partner is the biological parent of a lesbian couple's child, the other would often like to establish a legal relationship to the child through adoption. Courts in various states have rendered diverse decisions in these cases, and the law remains unsettled ("Across the USA: Indiana" 2003; McKee and Booth 1999; Rodier 2000). Some states have prohibited adoption by gays (ACLU 2004a). Where the practice has not been made illegal, a majority of adoption agencies will place a child with gay or lesbian parents (Peterson 2003a).

Some couples pursue international adoption. A second option is to adopt difficult-to-place or "special needs" children—those who are older, are nonwhite, come with siblings, and/or are disabled.

The Adoption Process

The experience of legal adoption varies widely across the country, partly because it is subject to differing state laws. Adoptions may be public or private. *Public adoptions* take place through licensed agencies. *Private adoptions* (also called *independent adoptions*) are arranged between adoptive parent(s) and the biological (or birth) mother, usually through an attorney. Legal fees and the birth mother's medical costs are usually paid by the adopting couple.

Because there is no central registry of available babies, adopting couples must themselves search for a woman who is willing to relinquish her child, by contacting doctors, lawyers, or social workers or by placing newspaper ads or web listings. Would-be adoptive parents present themselves to best advantage, for they are "buyers" in a sellers' market (Mansnerus 1998, 2001).

Licensed agencies offer counseling and inform both relinquishing and adopting parents of their legal rights. However, agencies have been criticized for cumbersome bureaucratic procedures and unrealistic standards of income, housing, and lifestyle for prospective adoptive parents. Waiting periods may be long, and older prospective adoptive parents are likely to be screened out. (Williams 1992).

Private adoptions offer birth and adopting parents more personal control. But they can be expensive for an adopting couple. Moreover, private adoptions may render both the birth and adoptive parents more vulnerable to exploitation. The birth mother may feel manipulated into relinquishing her baby. Or, even after her medical and living expenses during pregnancy have been paid by prospective parents, the birth mother might capriciously choose a different adoptive couple or else decide to keep her baby (Crossen 1990).

More and more, adoptions are open; that is, the birth and adoptive parents meet or have some specific knowledge of each other's identities. Even when an adoption is closed, as adoptions were until recently, some states now have laws permitting the adoptee access to records at a certain age or under specified conditions. Advocacy groups of adoptees support granting access to records. Meanwhile, those who encourage adoption over abortion fear that pregnant women will choose the latter unless they are guaranteed confidentiality, and some adoptive parents and birth parents find open records threatening. In forty-four states, adoption records remain sealed (Dusky 2003; Robbins 2001). Nevertheless, in recent years, there have been more and more **adoption reunions** (the meeting of birth parents, most often the mother, with the biological child), as adopted children or birth mothers find ways to get information. Adoption reunions have various outcomes, some extremely positive and others disappointing (March 1997; Gladstone and Westhues 1998).

A concern that arose in recent decades because of some high-profile cases is whether birth parents can claim rights to a biological child after the child has been adopted. In those cases, a nonmarital biological father had not given consent or even been notified, and he was able to assert his parental rights (Burbach and Lamanna 2000). However, of all domestic adoptions, fewer than 1 percent are ever contested by biological parents (Ingrassia 1995a).

Another concern of prospective adoptive parents has to do with the adjustment of adopted children—are they likely to have more problems than other children? Research suggests that adopted children, especially males, are at higher risk of problems in school achievement and behavior, psychological well-being, and substance use. A recent careful study, based on a large, nationally representative sample, confirms earlier findings of small to moderate differences between adopted children and nonadopted children (those living with biological and/or stepparents). The authors recommend more long-term support for adoptive families (Miller, Fan, Christensen, Grotevant, and van Dulmen 2000).

Adoption of Racial/Ethnic Minority Children

Today, two in ten adopted children are of a different race than one or both of their parents (Kreider 2003). The family diversity created by transracial adoption seems in tune with the increasing diversity of American society (Pertman 2000). Yet it has been controversial.

In 1971, agencies placed more than one-third of their black infants with white parents (Nazario 1990b). At that time, the number of black adoptive homes was much smaller than the number of available children, while the reverse was true for whites. But interracial adoptions, having increased rapidly in the 1960s and early 1970s, were much curtailed after 1972, when the National Association of Black Social Workers strongly objected. Suggesting that transracial adoption amounted to cultural genocide, racial/ethnic minority advocates expressed concern about identity problems and the loss of children from the black community (Simon and Altstein 2002). Native American activists have successfully asserted tribal rights and collective interest in Indian children. In addition to identity concerns, they expressed the fear that coercive pressures might be put on parents to relinquish their children in order to provide adoptable children to white parents. Indeed, this practice had been pervasive through the 1960s (Fanshel 1972).[17]

As a result of this controversy, adoption agencies shied away from transracial adoption for many years. In the late 1980s only about 8 percent of adoptions were interracial, usually adoption by white parents of mixed-race, African American, Asian, or Native American children (Bachrach et al. 1990). Congress had the last word on this matter, however. The Multi-Ethnic Placement Act (1994) and the Adoption and Safe Families Act (1997) now prohibit delay or denial in the placement of children on the basis of race, color, or national origin of the parents.

Some important long-term studies suggest that transracial adoption has proven successful for most parents and children, including with regard to racial issues. Sociologist Rita Simon and social work professor Howard Altstein followed interracial adoptees from their infancy in 1972 to adulthood, with contacts in 1979 and 1984. They were able to locate eighty-eight of the ninety-six families from the 1984 phase of the study for their latest book (2002). They concluded that, as adolescents and later, transracially adopted children "clearly were aware of and comfortable with their racial identity" (p. 222).

Another longitudinal study of transracial (white parents and African American, Asian, and Latino children) and in-race adoptions (white parents, white children) followed the children from the mid-seventies to their early twenties in 1993. There were no differences in adjustment or problem behavior. Such adjustment difficulties as did exist among the transracially adopted children tended to be connected to racial issues—discrimination and "differentness" of appearance. Not surprisingly then, researchers found that neighborhood made a difference within the transracial adoptee group; those who were reared in mixed-race neighborhoods were more confident in their racial identity (Feigelman 2000).

Some researchers have suggested that rather than causing serious problems, transracial adoptions may produce individuals with heightened skills at bridging cultures. In the words of one researcher, "the message of our findings is that transracial adoption should not be excluded as a permanent placement when no appropriate permanent inracial placement is available" (Simon 1990).

Adoption of Older Children and Disabled Children

Together with certain racial/ethnic minorities, children who are no longer infants and disabled children make up the large majority of youngsters now handled by adoption agencies (Finley 2000). Special needs adoptions are pursued not only by couples who are infertile, but also for altruistic motives. Gay men have adopted infants with HIV/AIDS, for example (Morrow 1992). National adoption exchanges for children with Down's syndrome and spina bifida have waiting lists of would-be parents. In some cases, lesbian and gay male couples adopt such hard-to-place children because law or adoption agency policy denies them the ability to adopt other children.

The majority of adoptions of older and disabled children work out well. But disruption and dissolution rates rise with the child's age at adoption. Among adoptions generally, only about 2 percent of agency adoptions end up being *disrupted adoptions* (the child is

---

17. The Indian Child Welfare Act of 1978 requires that "adoptive placement be made with (1) members of the child's extended family, (2) other members of the same tribe, or (3) other Indian families" so as "to protect the rights of the Indian child as an Indian and the rights of the Indian community and tribe in retaining its children in its society." In practice, outcomes of contested adoption cases have depended on the parents' attachment to the reservation and other circumstances. Tribes have also agreed to placements with white guardians or adoptive parents when they have believed it to be in the child's best interest.

returned to the agency before the adoption is legally final) or *dissolved adoptions* (the child is returned after the adoption is final). But 4.7 percent of adoptions of children aged three to five at adoption, 10 percent of those aged six to eight years, and perhaps as high as 40 percent of children adopted between the ages of twelve and seventeen are disrupted or dissolved (Barth and Berry 1988; Sachs 1990; Seelye 1998).

What causes these disrupted and dissolved adoptions? For one thing, some children available for adoption may be emotionally disturbed or developmentally impaired due to drug- or alcohol-addicted biological parents or to physical abuse from biological or foster parents (Avery 1997). Furthermore, older children have often undergone more broken attachments previously, as they have been moved from one foster home to another or through disrupted adoption attempts. Some develop **attachment disorder**, defensively shutting off the willingness or ability to make future attachments to anyone (Barth and Berry 1988). Observers have seen attachment disorder among recent adoptees from Romania and other Eastern European orphanages (Mainemer, Gilman, and Ames 1998).

Moreover, some parents may be persuaded to accept an older or disabled child without being properly advised of potential problems. For example, prospective parents might be told that a child is mildly hyperactive when in truth the problems are much worse, ranging from the child's showing virtually no emotion to destructive rampages—behaviors with which parents are unprepared to cope (Fishman 1992). For adoptive parents of children with attachment disorder, their emotional and behavioral problems can be extremely difficult to deal with. An adopted child's health conditions and psychiatric problems can be extremely expensive for adoptive parents to treat.

Adoption professionals point out that parents are willing to adopt all kinds of children, as long as they know what they are getting into (Groze 1996). Prospective adoptive parents need to think carefully about what they can handle. Those who imagine themselves accepting the child as she or he is need to know, in as much detail as possible, what that really means in daily life. Agencies have increasingly tried to gain information about the circumstances of the pregnancy and the child's early life and to match children's backgrounds with couples who know how to help them (Ward 1997).

International Adoptions

International adoption has grown dramatically in recent years; about 18,000 adoptions in 2000 were of children from outside the country. Almost half of all children who have been adopted from overseas by American parents (48 percent) were from Asia, especially from Korea and China, 33 percent from Latin America, and 11 percent from Europe. (Kreider 2003).

International adoptions can pose some of the same problems as the adoption of older children, for conditions in homes and institutions overseas may not be ideal beginnings. Prenatal care might have been lacking, or the mother may have had drug or alcohol problems. The child might have passed through a series of temporary placements (Greene 2000) or been in an understaffed and negligent institution.

Parents who have adopted internationally have encountered all kinds of difficulties: the expense of travel to a foreign country—and getting time off from work to go to the child's country for an extended stay; difficulty with negotiations and paperwork in a foreign language, and the need to rely on translators and brokers; the uncertainty about being able to choose a child, as opposed to having one thrust upon the parent; the occasional unexpected expansion of adoption fees or expected charitable contributions; the ambivalence and reluctance of a nation to place its children abroad; and the complete failure to bring home a child. The biological mother's consent is an issue in overseas adoptions because it is more difficult to be sure that the mother has willingly placed her child for adoption. Romania recently placed a moratorium on adoptions, fearing corruption of their entire system (Bartholet 1993; Bogert 1994; Knox 2004). Some experts believe that international adoptions are more likely to be troubled ones, especially with children adopted from Eastern Europe. But the vast majority of international adoptions are successful (Seelye 1998).

Despite difficulties, those who adopt internationally say they made this choice for several reasons. They are more apt to be able to adopt a healthy infant, with a shorter wait and often fewer limits in terms of age or marital status. The adoption is perceived to be less risky in that there is little likelihood of a birth mother seeking to reclaim the child (Zuang 2004). To what degree racial preferences enter into the choice of international adoption is difficult to determine.

In this photo, taken in Plainview, Nebraska, four-year-old adopted daughter Natalie has just been sworn in as a new U.S. citizen. Since 2001, children adopted internationally by U.S. citizens receive their American citizenship automatically.

© Jeff Beiermann/Omaha World Herald

Today, there are not only more agencies for arranging international adoptions, but there are also more resources for coping with any post-adoption difficulties. There are now specialists in "adoption medicine," who can address medical and cognitive problems of children adopted overseas (Tuller 2001). There are "culture camps" (Chappell 1996), schools (Zhao 2002), and other resources for bridging the cultural gap for a child raised in America, but conscious of having started life in another country. Most parents try very hard to maintain a bicultural identity for the child (Brooke 2004), and some undertake travel to the child's country of origin. Sometimes, though, internationally adopted children just want to simply be the American child that they also are (Dewan 2000).

International adoption produces more and more multicultural families in an increasingly multicultural America. The many media photos of happy adoptive parents and children tell a story of hopes for parenthood that are realized.

In Sum

- Today, individuals have more choice than ever about whether, when, and how many children to have.
- Although parenthood has become a choice, the majority of Americans continue to value parenthood. Only a small percentage expect to be childless by choice.
- Nevertheless, it is likely that changing values concerning parenthood, the weakening of social norms prescribing marriage and parenthood, a wider range of alternatives for women, the desire to postpone marriage and childbearing, and the availability of modern contraceptives and legal abortion will result in a higher proportion of Americans remaining childless or having only one child.
- Some observers believe that societal support for children is so lacking in the United States that it amounts to structural antinatalism. They point to the absence of a society-wide program of health insurance and health care for children, to workplace inflexibility, to the lack of affordable quality day care, and to the absence of paid maternal or paternal leave, as is provided in Europe and elsewhere.

- Children can add a fulfilling and highly rewarding experience to people's lives, but they also impose complications and stresses, both financial and emotional.

- Birth rates have declined for married women, and many women are waiting longer to have their first child. Although nonmarital birth rates have risen in recent decades, teen birth rates have declined. Pregnancy outside of marriage has become increasingly acceptable, but some unmarried pregnant women choose abortion.

- Deciding about parenthood today can include consideration of postponing parenthood; a one-child family; nonmarital births; having new biological children in stepfamilies; adoption; and infertility treatment.

Key Terms

adoption
adoption reunions
assisted reproductive
 technology (ART)
attachment disorder
embryo adoption
fecundity
fertility
induced abortion
infecundity
informal adoption
involuntary infertility
opportunity costs (of
 children)
pronatalist bias
single mothers by choice
social capital perspective
 (on parenthood)
sterility
structural antinatalism
total fertility rate (TFR)
value of children perspective
 (on parenthood)
voluntary childlessness

Questions for Review and Reflection

1. What are some reasons that there aren't as many large families as there used to be?

2. Discuss the advantages and disadvantages of having children. Which do you think are the strongest reasons for having children? Which do you think are the strongest reasons for *not* having children?

3. How would you react to becoming the parent of twins? Triplets? More? If your choice is to take fertility treatments that pose a risk of multiple births or to not have children at all, what would you do—and why?

4. Which reproductive technology would you be willing to use? In what circumstances?

5. **Policy Question.** How is a pronatalist bias shown in our society? Are there antinatalist pressures? What policies might be developed to support parents? Are there any special policy needs of nonparents? Why might a society's social policies favor parents over nonparents?

Suggested Readings

Bartholet, Elizabeth. 1993. *Adoption and the Politics of Parenting*. Boston: Houghton Mifflin. Interesting combination of personal experience, social policy, and academic reflection on parenthood. Bartholet, a Harvard law professor, is both a biological parent and an adoptive parent.

Becker, Gay. 2000. *The Elusive Embryo: How Women and Men Approach Reproductive Technology*. Berkeley and Los Angeles: University of California Press. An anthropologist does ethnographic research on reproductive technology, exploring the experiences of men and women using infertility services.

Casey, Terri. 1998. *Pride and Joy: The Lives and Passions of Women Without Children*. Hillsboro, OR: Beyond Words. Collection of interviews with twenty-five purposefully child-free women who are happy with their decisions.

Nachman, Patricia Ann. 1997. *You and Your Only Child: The Joys, Myths, and Challenges of Raising an Only Child*. New York: HarperCollins. Readable discussion and some advice on parenting an only child.

Child Welfare League of America

http://www.cwla.org

"Oldest and largest national nonprofit organization developing and promoting policies and programs to protect America's children and strengthen America's families." A good source of information on adoption.

Human Rights Campaign

www.hrc.org/family

This gay/lesbian/bisexual advocacy organization has an extensive web section on "family," including detailed advice on reproduction and adoption.

Resolve: The National Infertility Association

http://www.resolve.org

A nonprofit organization dedicated to providing "timely, compassionate support and information to people who are experiencing infertility and to increase awareness of infertility issues through public education and advocacy."

Virtual Society: The Wadsworth Sociology Resource Center

 Go to the Sociology Resource Center at **http:// sociology.wadsworth.com** for a wealth of online resources, including a companion website for your text that provides study aids such as self-quizzes for each chapter and a practice final exam, as well as links to sociology websites and information on the latest theories and discoveries in the field. In addition, you will find further suggested readings, flash cards, MicroCase online exercises, and appendices on a range of subjects. Appendixes relevant to Chapter 10 include Appendix E, "Conception, Pregnancy, and Childbirth"; Appendix F, "Contraceptive Techniques"; and Appendix G, "High-Tech Fertility."

Online Study Tool

Marriage & Family⊛Now™ Go to **http://sociology .wadsworth.com** to reach the companion website for your text and use the Marriage&FamilyNow access code that came with your book to access this study tool. Take a practice pretest after you have read each chapter, and then use the study plan provided to master that chapter. Afterward, take a posttest to monitor your progress.

Search Online with InfoTrac College Edition

For additional information, exercises, and key words to aid your research, explore InfoTrac College Edition, your online library that offers full-length articles from thousands of scholarly and popular publications. Click on *InfoTrac College Edition* under *Chapter Resources* at the companion website and use the access code that came with your book.

- Search keywords: *multiples* or *multiple births*. See if research articles present the difficulties or the satisfactions of multiple births, or both.
- Search keywords: *international adoption*. International adoption is a rapidly emerging area of research interest—see what has been learned since this textbook was published.

Chapter 11

Raising Children *in a* Diverse *and* Multicultural Society

> *I see children as kites. You spend a lifetime trying to get them off the ground. . . . Finally they are airborne. . . .*
>
> ERMA BOMBECK

FOR MOST OF HUMAN HISTORY, ADULTS raised children simply by living with them and thereby providing examples and socialization to eventual adult roles. From an early age, children shared the everyday world of adults, working beside them, dressing like them, sleeping near them.

The concept of childhood as different from adulthood did not emerge until about the seventeenth century, according to historian Phillipe Ariès (1962). For religious reasons (to be able to read the Bible) and because of generally improving conditions in industrializing societies, education became increasingly available to all children, not just those of the wealthy. As children spent more of their time in school, they were gradually drawn away or segregated from the adult world. Although children may continue to do household chores, the move to school has been a move away from participation in the everyday lives of adults. One result is that today we regard children as people who need special training, guidance, and care.

But at the same time, our society does not offer parents, stepparents, or others acting as parents much psychological or social support. Indeed, American society is often indifferent to the needs of parents, including the economic support of families with children (Kost 2001). The rate of child poverty in the United States exceeds that of the nation as a whole and is considerably higher than in other wealthy industrialized nations ("Living in Poverty" 2002; Madrick 2002). Furthermore, except for some renewed interest in the nation's schools, the mood of the country and politicians seems not to favor social programs for children (Seccombe 2000).

In this chapter, we will discuss a limited range of parenting issues. We'll begin by looking at some difficulties of parenting. Next, we'll examine the roles of mothers and fathers, describe parenting styles, then examine parenting over the life course. We'll see that parenting takes place in social contexts that vary with regard to parents' marital status, social class, and racial/ethnic background. We'll describe three newly visible parenting environments: gay male/lesbian parents, grandparents as parents, and foster parents. (The special concerns of divorced single parents are discussed in Chapter 16; those of stepfamilies are considered in Chapter 17. Particular issues regarding children in cohabiting families are addressed in Chapter 9.) Here we discuss some common parenting issues and consider how parents can make relationships with their children more satisfying.

▪ Parents in Modern America ▪

Although raising children may be a joyful and fulfilling enterprise, parenting today takes place in a social context that can make child raising an enormously difficult task. Today's parents face a myriad of questions and dilemmas that parents just a few decades ago would not have imagined: Should I have my baby boy circumcised? Can I trust my child's babysitter? Should I let my child walk to school? How do I monitor my child's surfing the Net? Should I believe the teacher or doctor who says my child is hyperactive or bipolar and needs medication? Should I home-school my child? Should I allow guns in the house? What if I discover that my child is using illegal drugs? What should I tell my child about terrorism?

We would not want to point out the difficulties of today's parents without first noting some advantages. In many respects, technology has vastly improved health care over the past several decades, and parents now have higher levels of education and are likely to have had some exposure to formal knowledge about child development and child-raising techniques. Many fathers are more emotionally involved than they were several decades ago (Gerson 1997; Rane and McBride 2000). The Internet offers countless sources of information for parents dealing with a myriad of situations, including, for example,

- raising children with disabilities (Educational Resources Information Center, www.Ericec.org; *www.childrenwithdisabilities.ncjrs.org*)
- parenting biracial or multiracial children (Family Matters!, *www.parenting-child-development.com*)
- being a lesbian or gay parent (Family Pride Coalition, *www.familypride.org*)
- parenting a gay or lesbian child (Parents, Families and Friends of Lesbians and Gays, *www.pflag.org*)
- serving as a foster parent (Foster Parents Library, *www.fostercare.org*)

- maintaining a parent–child relationship while in prison (Child Welfare League of America, *www.cwla.org/programs/incarcerated*) (Chapter 15's "Issues for Thought: When a Parent Is in Prison" also addresses this issue.)

Then too, e-mail can make keeping in touch with children, parents, and extended family both easier and more likely, especially for fathers (Bold 2001) or parents of children away at college (Lewin 2003b).

Nevertheless, the family ecology theoretical perspective (see Chapter 3) leads us to point to ways that the larger environment makes parenting especially difficult today. Here we list eight features of the social context of child raising that can make modern parenting difficult:

1. In our society, the parenting or stepparenting role typically conflicts with the working role, and employers place work demands first (Ryan 1999). Also, the homework and extracurricular activities of school-age children demand a significant amount of support and time from parents who are already overloaded (Balli, Demo, and Wedman 1998; Kantrowitz and Wingert 2001). Two-thirds of a national representative sample of 1,607 American parents or guardians who had children between age five and seventeen living with them and were telephone-surveyed by the research organization Public Agenda said that they worry either "some" or "a lot" about juggling the demands of work and family (see Figure 11.1). (Chapter 12 presents work–family conflicts in more detail.)

2. Parenting today requires learning attitudes and techniques that are different from those of the past. There is greater emphasis on using positive communication techniques, for example, with corporal punishment criticized (Straus 1994). Moreover, today's parents are probably judged by higher standards than those of the past. For instance, raising children who can succeed in college is often an expectation rather than an option.

3. Today's parents raise their children in a pluralistic society, characterized by diverse and conflicting values. Parents are only one of several influences on children. Others are schools, peers, television, movies, music, rented videos, books, the Internet, travel, and, yes, drug dealers. As Figure 11.1

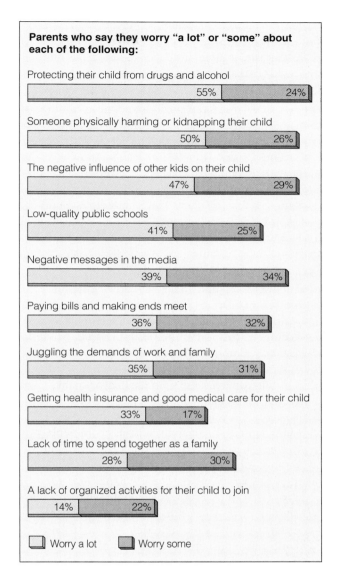

FIGURE 11.1

Parents who say they worry "a lot" or "some" about each of these potential hazards.

Source: Steve Farkas, Jean Johnson, and Ann Duffett, *A Lot Easier Said Than Done: Parents Talk about Raising Children in Today's America.* Public Agenda: A Report prepared for State Farm Insurance, 2002.

shows, 39 percent of American parents today say they worry "a lot" about negative messages in the media, while another 34 percent say that they worry "some." More than half (55 percent) worry a lot about protecting their children from drugs and alcohol. Nearly half (47 percent) worry "a lot"—and another 29 percent worry "some"—about the negative influence of other kids on their child (Farkas, Johnson, and Duffett 2002).

4. The emphasis on the malleability of children tends to make parents feel anxious and guilty about their performance. Even as biologists claim to have found genes that influence a child's aggressiveness, risk taking, or future addictions (Wright 1998), psychologists have publicized the fact that parents influence their children's math and language abilities, behaviors, and self-esteem (Nash 1997; Brazelton 1997). Parents may lose confidence, believing that they will make mistakes with dire consequences.

5. Child-raising experts sometimes disagree among themselves (Family Science Network 1998; Murkoff 2000). Over the years, they have shifted their emphasis from one recommended child-raising technique to another. For example, today there is debate among child psychologists concerning disciplinary techniques, such as timeouts, withholding privileges, slapping hands, or spanking (Larzelere et al. 1998). (But the issue of whether spanking is ever appropriate is addressed later in this chapter.) As one journalist has commented, "A new theory will change our attitudes about child raising—we don't know what it is yet, but there always is one" (Adler 1998, p. 57). And given that values shape ideas about what children should grow up to be like as adults—or what parents might do to get them there—parents and child-raising experts may have conflicting perspectives.

6. Today's parents are given full responsibility for raising successful or good children, but their authority is often put to question. The state may intervene in parental decisions about schooling, discipline and punishment, and medical care (LeMasters and DeFrain 1989; Jervey 2004).

    As an example, at least ten states and several cities have passed laws that require parents to "exercise reasonable control over their children," with sanctions for parents ranging from compulsory counseling to jail time (Smolowe 1996b).

7. That people live longer today than in the past means that many parents, especially mothers, are responsible not only for working outside the home

and child care but also for the needs of aging parents. Middle-aged parents in this **sandwich generation** may find themselves especially pressed as role conflicts arise between parenting and elder care. Caring for aging parents is further addressed in Chapters 15 and 18.

8. Divergent family forms may cause parents special difficulties just because these forms are different from the idealized norm of the intact, nuclear family. Divorced parents and stepfamilies must cope with different rules at home as children go back and forth between homes or are now living with stepsiblings raised with different rules. There is likely to be lingering emotional distress to cope with (Wallerstein and Blakeslee 1989), and perhaps continued legal struggles as well.

    Grandparent families (families in which a grandparent acts as the primary parent for grandchildren) face special challenges. Gay male and lesbian parents face the questions of schools, neighbors, and their children's playmates; perhaps legal challenges; and the need to work out their position as parents with respect to sexuality and gender-role issues (Stacey 1999). And despite growing equality and similarity of the sexes in daily life, our society combines an ambivalent commitment to equality with a continuing sense that the mother's role and the father's role are different (Kurz 1997).

As a result of all these factors, becoming a parent may be more difficult than anticipated (Nordin 2000).

Transition to Parenthood

Interviews in two hospitals' labor and delivery units with eighty-eight mothers and seventy-five fathers of firstborns found that "nearly all of the fathers" and two-thirds of the mothers expressed worry or concern about becoming parents: "[T]he concerns voiced by the greatest number of fathers related to his ability to 'take good enough care' of his child . . . and his ability to 'keep your kids safe.' . . . Among mothers, concerns about safety and finding childcare predominated" (Fox, Bruce, and Combs-Orme 2000, p. 126).

Once they get their babies home, new fathers and mothers report being bothered by the baby's interruption of such activities as sleeping, going places, and sexual expression. When a new mother's expectations about how much the father will be involved with the

The transition to parenthood can be difficult for a number of reasons, including upset schedules and lack of sleep. It can help to remember that babies have different temperaments: some are "easy," others "difficult." Many fathers today are more involved with day-to-day parenting activities than in the past— a situation that increases marital satisfaction and both parents' confidence.

© Chad Ehlers/Index Stock Imagery

baby are met, the transition to parenthood is easier (Fox et al. 2000).

Thirty years ago, in what has become a classic analysis that still applies, social scientist Alice Rossi (1968) analyzed the **transition to parenthood**, comparing the circumstances involved in assuming the parent role with those of other adult roles, such as worker or spouse. The transition to parenthood, Rossi asserts, is more difficult than the transition to either of these other roles for several reasons:

1. Cultural pressure encourages adults to become parents even though they may not really want to. But once a baby is born to married or, to a lesser degree, to cohabiting couples, there is little possibility of undoing the commitment to parenthood.

2. Most first parents approach parenting with little or no previous experience in child care.

3. Unlike other adult roles, the transition to parenting is abrupt. New parents suddenly are on twenty-four-hour duty, caring for a fragile and mysterious and utterly dependent infant.

4. Adjusting to parenthood necessitates changes in the couple's emotional and sexual relationship (Savage 2003). In general, husbands can expect to receive less attention from their wives. Employed wives who have established fairly egalitarian relationships with their husbands may find themselves in a different role, particularly if they

quit working to become full-time homemakers (see Chapter 10).

Research supports the continued general validity of Rossi's analysis (Wallace and Gotlib 1990).[1] Along with other factors, this situation can cause post-partum depression in about 10 percent of new mothers (Formichelli 2001). It helps to know that babies are different from one another even at birth; the fact that one baby cries a lot does not necessarily mean that he or she is receiving the wrong kind of care. From birth, infants have different "readabilities"—that is, varying clarity in the messages or cues they give to tell caregivers how they feel or what they want (Bell 1974).

Babies also have different temperaments at birth (Hayden 2000). Some are "easy," responding positively to new foods, people, and situations, and transmitting consistent cues (such as tired cry or hungry cry). Other infants are more "difficult." They have irregular habits of sleeping, eating, and elimination, which sometimes extend into childhood; they may adapt slowly to new situations and stimuli; and they

---

1. Meanwhile, a point not mentioned by Rossi (because it was not so true in the 1960s) is that more of today's parents will be caring for fragile infants. Smaller and smaller infants are surviving, thanks to modern technology. But they remain in the hospital in intensive care for some time after birth, may need special care, are likely to suffer some disability, and do not fit easily into a family routine (Rosenthal 1991).

may seem to cry endlessly, for no apparent reason. Still other babies, of course, are neither easy nor particularly difficult (Crouter and Booth 2003; Thomas, Chess, and Birch 1968). Meanwhile, it may help to keep in mind that, according to a review of research throughout the 1990s, "it appears that after an initial disruption, most couples . . . seem to be doing well" (Demo and Cox 2000, p. 878). Feeling support of family and friends helps (Bost, Cox, and Payne 2002).

Mothers and Fathers: Images and Reality

If we look at men and women as parents, we find a range of ideas and practices.

Old and New Images of Parents

Our cultural tradition stipulates that mothers assume primary responsibility for child raising (Cancian and Oliker 2000). In the United States, the mother is expected to be the child's primary *psychological parent*, assuming the major emotional responsibility for the safety and upbringing of her children (Tavris 1992). The "enduring image of motherhood" includes the idea that "A woman enjoys and intuitively knows what to do for her child; she cares for her child without ambivalence or awkwardness" (Thompson and Walker 1991, p. 91). This traditional image of motherhood persists, even when Mom is employed. And what about fathers?

GOOD DAD—BAD DAD Fathers were once thought to be mainly providers or breadwinners, not necessarily competent or desirous of nurturing children on a day-to-day basis (Gerson 1997). Succeeding the breadwinner-only father, we now have the opposite images of the "good dad" and the "bad dad" (Furstenberg 1991)—the "new father" and the "deadbeat dad," as they have been termed in the media.

On the one hand, "new" fathers not only take financial responsibility for their children but also are actively involved in child care (Thompson and Walker 1991). Meanwhile, "Another scenario focuses on . . . 'deadbeat dads.' From this vantage point, a growing group of men"—including some middle-class, divorced fathers who can well afford to support their children economically—"are eschewing even minimal

responsibility for their children" (Gerson 1997, p. 119; Blankenhorn 1995).

However, unwed, noncustodial, poverty-level fathers may not have the means to support their children financially. And

Child support policy does not allow fathers to substitute the provision of in-kind services when circumstances prevent their economic support. For example, absent, unemployed fathers are not permitted to provide child care that might allow the mother to continue working and reduce the cost of such care to her in place of their child support payment. . . . The potential use and effect of alternative forms of support by the absent father is unknown. . . . Thus, the role of breadwinner is the most visible socially prescribed duty of the paternal role in the American construction of fatherhood. While its successful performance is critical to the economic well-being of children, its primacy tends to relegate [poverty-level] fathers to a peripheral function in their child's development. (Kost 2001)

Furthermore, racial/ethnic stereotyping gives us an exaggerated, negative image of African Americans and Latinos as parents: black matriarchs; aloof or absent black fathers; macho, authoritarian Latino fathers (Gibbs 1993; Cose 1994b). But, because they are exaggerated, these

images are myths: black couples share child raising no less, and perhaps more, than white couples, and black husbands are as intimately involved with their children as white husbands, although it is more difficult for them to provide for and protect their children. (Thompson and Walker 1991, p. 91)

Recent research, especially on fathers, has "alerted us to the historical flexibility of fatherhood" (Marsiglio, Amato, Day, and Lamb 2000, p. 1175) and of motherhood as well (Arendell 2000). In other words, throughout history parents have never completely conformed with dominant cultural images. Contrary to stereotypes, there are women who do not want to care for children, "and many men do" (Cancian and Oliker 2000, p. 48). (See "Facts About Families: Fathers As Primary Parents.") With an idea of our varied cultural images of fathers and mothers, we'll look briefly at what mothers and fathers actually do.

Facts About Families

Fathers As Primary Parents

Some fathers who serve as primary, or principal, parents are single, usually divorced but also possibly never-married or widowed. A single custodial father may be cohabiting or not. Other men serving as primary parents are stay-at-home married fathers with wives in the labor force. Compared to mothers, the proportion of fathers who serve as the principal parent is small. However, there has been a significant increase in their numbers over the past twenty years. Take a look at the following facts:

1. About 5 percent of all U.S. children under age fifteen—or 3.3 million children—are living with single fathers (Fields 2003, p. 5).

2. About 1.1 million children under age fifteen live with a single father who is cohabiting (Fields 2003, p. 5).

3. About 5 percent of black and Hispanic children live with single fathers, compared with 4 percent of non-Hispanic white children and 2 percent of Asian and Pacific Islander children (Fields 2003, Figure 1).

4. Another 1.5 million children under age fifteen are living in two-parent families with a stay-at-home father (Fields 2003, p. 10).

5. Among these children, about 336,000 had fathers who told the U.S. Census Bureau that their primary reason for staying home was to "care for home and family" (Fields 2003, Table 5).

6. Some stay-at-home, married fathers have been laid off and decided to stay out of the workforce. Others have wives who had earned more than they were and began to question the logic of spending money on day care

and sending the children away to day care when one of them could stay at home. Others are "trailing husbands," who follow their wives to new career positions (Conlin 2001).

7. Whether married or single, fathers as primary parents report facing isolation and stereotypes (Allen 2001).

8. In response, primary-parent fathers have begun to organize support groups, often on the Internet (*http://www.dadstayshome. com; http://slowlane.com*).

Critical Thinking

How might the higher visibility of fathers as primary parents change neighborhoods? What might be some similarities between single-parent fathers and single-parent mothers? Some differences?

Mothers and Fathers: What Do They Do?

Mothers typically engage in more hands-on parenting and take primary responsibility for children, whereas fathers are often viewed as helping (Hochschild 1989; Arendell 2000; Cancian and Oliker 2000). As Figure 11.2 makes clear, "Despite much attention in recent years to the so-called 'new, nurturing father' and some change on men's part, women still do most child raising (and homemaking)" (Arendell 2000, p. 1198). (But see "Case Study: A Full-Time Father's Story" for an exception.) As one example, mothers in two-parent families are far more likely than fathers to attend school conferences and class events and to serve as school volunteers (U.S. Census Bureau 2000, Table 256). Then too, a mother may try to manage her child(ren)'s relationship with their father by encouraging father–child activities and constructing for them a positive image of him (Seery and Crowley 2000). The

intense daily contact with children is viewed ambivalently by mothers: as a source of great life satisfaction but also a source of a great deal of frustration and stress (Arendell 2000).

In the past, research on parent roles viewed fathers as financial providers, disciplinarians, and "playmates," while mothers were seen mainly as "caregivers and comfort givers" (Thompson and Walker 1991, pp. 91–92). But as women have entered the labor force in greater numbers, many men have been encouraged by their family's need and the redefinition of male roles (see Chapter 12) to want to play a larger part in the day-to-day care of the family (Bulanda 2004). Doing errands, planning, sharing activities, and teaching their children, married fathers—although, as a group, still less emotionally involved than mothers—are more and more invested in their children (Marsiglio et al. 2000; Strand 2004; Yeung, Sandberg, Davis-Kean, and

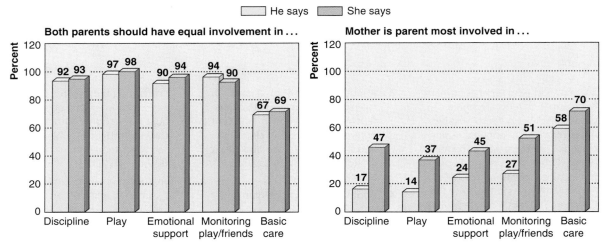

FIGURE 11.2

Who *should* do vs. who *does* the most parenting?

Source: M. Milke, S. M. Bianchi, M. Mattingly, and J. Robinson, "Fathers' Involvement in Childrearing: Ideals, Realities, and Their Relationship to Parental Well-Being." Revised version of a paper presented at the American Association for Public Opinion Research, Portland, Oregon, May 18–21, 2000.

Hofferth 2001). Today's fathers tend to compare themselves favorably to their own fathers, who were generally much less involved with their children (Adler 1996b). Less caught up with their daughters than with their sons, fathers become more involved in instruction and discipline of all their offspring as their children grow older (Updegraff, McHale, Crouter, and Kupanoff 2001).

At the same time—partly because of "daily hassles" such as health concerns, job dissatisfactions, hassles from the boss, transportation problems, use of drugs or alcohol, not enough money, problems with one's partner/wife, and not getting enough sleep (Fagan 2000)—more and more divorced or unwed fathers are distancing themselves from their children (Blankenhorn 1995), neither seeing them nor supporting them:

> There are two sides to male liberation. As men have escaped from the excessive burdens of the good provider role, they have been freed to participate more fully in the family. They have also been freed from family responsibilities altogether. (Furstenberg 1992, p. 347)

One result is the recent push by some interest groups, such as the National Fatherhood Initiative, to reemphasize "responsible fathering" (Doherty, Kouneski, and Erickson 1998) and the provider role of fathers as

valued and necessary (Marsiglio et al. 2000; Christiansen and Palkovitz 2001). Meanwhile, some couples are truly sharing parenthood.

Sharing Parenthood

Diane Ehrensaft (1990) searched for "new" parents to learn more about them. She interviewed and observed forty shared-parenting couples in the San Francisco Bay Area and some other large urban centers or academic communities. She defined **shared parenting** not in terms of time, but rather as an identity. Her central question was this: Were both father and mother **primary parents**—a couple "mothering together"—rather than one parent and one helper?

Three factors affected both parents' commitment to shared parenting. First, many couples were strongly influenced by the feminist movement. Second, many of the fathers were in occupations related to children, such as academic child psychology. Finally, both parents tended to have good job security, so they could risk the displeasure of their supervisors in giving time to parenthood.

Nevertheless, there was a tendency to backslide as the husband's income outpaced the wife's. Finally, mothers, more than fathers, engaged in "worrying" (anticipating and coping with problems) and gave

Case Study

A Full-Time Father's Story

Bob is thirty-one, comes from a working-class background, and has been married seven years. At the time of this interview, he had just gotten out of the Air Force and was collecting unemployment benefits. His wife is a clerical worker. His future goal, he said, is to be a child psychologist. He has two children—Tim, six, and a daughter, Nicole, eighteen months. His father deserted his family when Bob was a baby, and he feels he suffered greatly as a result. Here he describes what it's like for him to be a temporary househusband and full-time father.

Today I took a bunch of kids from my son's school to the zoo. Kindergartners. You know I like kids (*laughs*). . . . It was something hectic. The kids, they all want to run six different ways. They were climbing over the fences and through the fences to the elephants. . . .

I think fathers should be more involved with their kids when it is possible. In fact, a couple of mothers commented [at the zoo] that they were happy to see a father along for a change. I never had a father. . . . I'm determined that my son and I should have time together—which is tough when I'm working. . . . [But for a while now] I've got the two kids. I fix them lunch and all that. You fix a can of soup, you give her half, you give him half. Hers you don't have any soup in it—just noodles and stuff because she eats with

her fingers and you don't want any soup in there. And while they're eating I usually get dressed to take them out. And after they're done eating, I dress them.

I change her diaper and dress her and I dress my kid for school and take him to school. And while the kid's at school, we go somewhere like the park—me and my baby. . . . There aren't too many dads in the park, I'll tell you. Most of them are out working. I get some strange looks once in a while, but it doesn't bother me. It really doesn't. Besides, if some fox comes by, I'll just tell her my wife and I were divorced and I got the kids, right? (*laughs*). . . . Then about two thirty, quarter to three, I drive over to the school from the park, and it's time for him to get out. Not the stereotype, you'd think, huh?

Sometimes it's a pain, you know. I can't get anything done. And there's a lot of things I could do, but it's really a chore to keep track of the baby. She's at the age now where she wants outside all the time, and it's really a hassle. I mean I'll bring her in the back door, and while you're locking the back door, she goes out the front. She's one door to the other, and she's out again. Yesterday our son came in, yelling, "She's out walking down the sidewalk!" She was having herself a good old time. . . . I would do it [though] anytime I was off work because, well, I look at the economical

aspects. I can't afford to pay for child care when I'm at home. It's much, much cheaper for me to go ahead and do it myself, and it's not really that much of a hassle . . . unless you've gotta go to the library or something like that. You can't drag them with you because—I took them to the library to get some books and I about went nuts chasing the little one around the shelves. She's really too young to understand "Now you stay there!" And she smiles and she's gone by the time you can turn around. . . .

I'm going to keep doing this until my twenty-six weeks is up or I find a job. I'm not saying I'm not looking for a job now, but I am saying I'll probably keep doing this all the twenty-six weeks. . . . I love those kids to pieces. I can just sit there and just look at them, and just smile inwardly at what they do, you know. I don't know if it detracts from my image or anything. . . .

Critical Thinking

In what ways might Bob and his wife's arrangement be better than day care, do you think? Not as good as day care? As a parent, what would you do differently from Bob? What do you like about Bob's style of fathering? Do you think Bob is a househusband and full-time father now only because of economics? What else might motivate him?

more attention to the "psychological management" of children. They devoted more attention than their husbands did to the child's clothing or birthday parties, for example. There was a tendency for mothers to "take over" in these areas. Meanwhile, other research shows that when mothers see fathers as competent parents—

and when fathers believe that their wives have confidence in them—fathers are more likely to be highly involved (Fagan and Barnett 2003; Pasley, Futris, and Skiller 2002).

The couples in Ehrensaft's study felt that their relationship was strengthened by sharing such an im-

© Laura Dwight

Many relationship dynamics affect parenting. Fathers and mothers not only relate individually to their children and to each other but also relate as co-parents to their children, as do the parents of this joyful dancer.

portant family activity as parenting. Generally, research shows that shared parenting decreases children's behavior problems (Amato and Rivera 1999) and increases partners' feelings of competence as parents and spouses' marital satisfaction (Ehrenberg, Gearing-Small, Hunter, and Small 2001; Kluwer, Heesink, and Van de Vliert 2002). (However, Ehrensaft noted some potential strains of shared parenting. Couples had very little time alone. Ehrensaft speculated that this could represent avoidance of the marital relationship, leaving a vacuum that would be difficult to deal with at the empty-nest stage of family life.) Shared parenting is probably more satisfying for parents and effective for children when both parents use an authoritative parenting style (Lindsey and Mize 2001).

▪ Authoritative Parenting ▪

Children's needs differ according to their age. For instance, in order to establish the basic human trust that is a prelude to normal development, infants need to bond with a consistent and dependable caregiver (Karen 1994; Brazelton and Greenspan 2000). Like anyone else, they need positive, affectionate, intimate relationships as well as encouragement, conversation, and variety in their environment in order to develop emotionally and intellectually (Brazelton and Greenspan 2000; Khaleque and Rohner 2002). (Discipline is never appropriate for babies.) Preschool children need opportunities to practice motor development as well as wide exposure to language, especially when people talk directly to them (Cowley 2000). They also need consistent, clear definitions of what behavior is acceptable (Dinkmeyer, McKay, and Dinkmeyer 1997).[2]

School-age children need to practice accomplishing goals appropriate to their abilities (Hofferth and Sandberg 2001) and to learn how to get along with

---

2. Limits are best set as house rules and stated objectively in third-person terms. A parent may say, for example, "Chairs are for sitting in, not for jumping on." With preschoolers, limits need to be set and stated very clearly: A parent who says "Don't go too far from home" leaves "too far" to the child's interpretation. "Don't go out of the yard at all" is a wiser rule. As the child learns to distinguish what is "too much," limits may be more flexible.

others.[3] They also need to feel they are contributing family members by being assigned tasks and taught how to do them. (Those who are not given responsibility for their share of household chores may have trouble feeling that they belong, or they may become demanding because they have learned to belong as consumers rather than as productive family members [Dinkmeyer, McKay, and Dinkmeyer 1997].) Adolescents need firm guidance, coupled with emotional support, as they search for identity and begin to define who they are and will be as adults (Collins 1990; Steinberg 1990). They also need to learn effective methods for resolving conflict (Tucker, McHale, and Crouter 2003). While the majority of teenagers do not cause familial "storm and stress" (Larson and Ham 1993), the teen years do have the special potential of creating conflict between parent and child (Booth, Carver, and Granger 2000).[4] Despite these age-related differences, virtually all children benefit from authoritative parenting.

From one point of view, there are as many parenting styles as there are parents. Nevertheless, parents and stepparents will gradually establish a **parenting style**—a general manner of relating to and disciplining their children. We can distinguish among authoritarian, laissez-faire, and authoritative parenting styles (Baumrind 1978). The **authoritarian parenting style** is characterized as low on emotional nurturing and support but high on parental direction and control. The authoritarian parent's attitude is "I am in charge and set/enforce the rules, no matter what." Characterized as emotionally aloof or harsh, parents using this style often use physical or otherwise harsh punishment (Manisses Communications Group 2000).

In contrast, the **laissez-faire parenting style** is permissive, allowing children to set their own limits with little or no parental guidance. This parenting style, while low on parental direction or control, may be high on parental emotional nurturing—a situation that "leads to the classic 'spoiled child.'" This parenting style is characterized by the statement "I often give in to my child's arguing, whining, and other demands."

A variant of the laissez-faire parenting style is low on both parental direction and emotional support—a situation of emotional neglect. This style is characterized by the statement "I spend little time with my child" or "I feel overwhelmed and am almost ready to give up on my child" (Manisses Communications Group 2000, p. S1). Both authoritarian and laissez-faire parenting styles are associated with children's and adolescents' depression and otherwise poor mental health, low school performance, behavior problems, high rates of teen sexuality and pregnancy, and juvenile delinquency (Longmore, Manning, and Giordano 2001; Morris et al. 2002; Parcel and Dufur 2001).

Child psychologists prefer the **authoritative parenting style**. This style, described as "warm, firm, and fair" (Gray and Steinberg 1999), combines emotional nurturing and support with parental direction. Authoritative parenting involves encouraging the child's individuality and accepting the child's personality, talents, and emerging independence, while also consciously setting and enforcing rules and limits (Brooks and Goldstein 2001; Ginott, Ginott, and Goddard 2003). The authoritative parent monitors the child's activities and behavior, and gives appropriate consequences for misbehavior.

As the child grows older, the authoritative parent increasingly considers the child's point of view when setting rules. I-statements (see Chapter 13) from parent to child can help. For example, "I get angry when you leave the car without gas in it, and I go out to work and find the tank empty." Or "I was worried because I hadn't heard from you." ("As We Make Choices: Communicating with Children—How to Talk So Kids Will Listen and Listen So Kids Will Talk" offers some important advice on parenting.)

Authoritative parents would agree with the statements "I communicate rules clearly and directly," "I consider my child's wishes and opinions along with my own when making decisions," "I value my child's school achievement and support my child's efforts," and "I expect my child to act independently at an age-

---

3. One particular area of conflict is between siblings. Parents should recognize the inevitability of sibling rivalry and make an effort *not* to overrespond by punishing competitiveness. Children should be encouraged to work out disputes by themselves whenever possible (Felson and Russo 1988). Having said this, we need to emphasize that physical violence *should* be kept in check by parents. Research on family violence (Straus, Gelles, and Steinmetz 1980) indicates that violence between siblings, particularly boys, and some of it quite serious, is the most pervasive form of family violence. Parents should provide children with an environment in which nonviolent methods of solving conflicts are learned (Gelles and Straus 1988).

4. Nevertheless, in reviewing the research on adolescence during the 1990s, sociologist Frank Furstenberg (2000) noted that "the vast majority of articles and studies of youth are focused on the problematic features of adolescence and explicitly on problem behavior" (p. 900). Hence, "too little recognition has been accorded to the obvious fact that most adolescents make it to adulthood relatively unscathed and prepared to accept and assume adult roles" (p. 903).

As We Make Choices

Communicating with Children— How to Talk So Kids Will Listen and Listen So Kids Will Talk

Either knowledgeably or by default, we choose how we communicate with children. There are more and less effective ways to communicate, so a knowledgeable choice would probably involve choosing more, not less, effective ways. What are some of these methods?

Helping Children Deal with Their Feelings

Children—even adult children— need to have their feelings accepted and respected.

1. *You can listen quietly and attentively.*

2. *You can acknowledge their feelings with a word.* "Oh . . . mmm . . . I see. . . ."

3. *You can give the feeling a name.* "That sounds frustrating!"

4. *You can give the child his wishes in fantasy.* "I wish I could make the banana ripe for you right now!" Or "I wish I could make your boss give you the promotion you want."

5. *You can note that all feelings are accepted, but certain actions must be limited.* "I can see how angry you are at your brother. Tell him what you want with words, not fists."

Engaging a Child's Cooperation

1. *Describe what you see, or describe the problem.* "There's a wet towel on the bed."

2. *Give information.* "The towel is getting my blanket wet."

3. *Say it with a word.* "The towel!"

4. *Describe what you feel.* "I don't like sleeping in a wet bed!"

5. *Write a note* (above towel rack): Please put me back so I can dry. Thanks!
Your Towel

Instead of Punishment

1. *Express your feelings strongly— without attacking character.* "I'm furious that my saw was left outside to rust in the rain!"

2. *State your expectations.* "I expect my tools to be returned after they've been borrowed."

3. *Show the child how to make amends.* "What this saw needs now is a little steel wool and a lot of elbow grease."

4. *Give the child a choice.* "You can borrow my tools and return them, or you can give up the privilege of using them. You decide."

5. *Take action.* Child: "Why is the tool box locked?" Father: "You tell me why."

6. *Problem solve.* "What can we work out so that you can use my tools when you need them and

appropriate level" (Manisses Communications Group 2000, p. S1). Believing that the parent can be counted on for direction and assistance if needed, the child likely views the authoritative parent as loving, responsive, and involved (Gray and Steinberg 1999). Regardless of ethnicity, parental education, or family structure, authoritative parents tend to have children who do better in school and are socially competent, with relatively high self-esteem and cooperative, yet independent, personalities (Amato and Fowler 2002; Brooks and Goldstein 2001; Crosnoe 2004).

However, we need to note that more and more scholars of color view the authoritarian/laissez-faire/authoritative model as biased and ethnocentric or Eurocentric. These scholars argue that the model uses European, white, middle-class parenting beliefs, values, and behaviors as the standard to which all others are—usually unfavorably—compared (McLoyd et al. 2000; Greenfield and Suzuki 2001). This point is developed throughout the section "Racial/Ethnic Diversity and Parenting," later in this chapter. The next section focuses on the question of whether spanking is ever appropriate.

Is Spanking Ever Appropriate?

A cross-cultural study that compared aggressiveness among American, Swedish, German, and Indonesian

so that I'll be sure they're here when I need them?"

Encouraging Autonomy

1. *Let children make choices.* "Are you in the mood for your gray pants today or your red pants?"

2. *Show respect for a child's struggle.* "A jar can be hard to open. Sometimes it helps if you tap the side of the lid with a spoon." "A tax return can be hard to fill out. Sometimes it helps to tear it into a million pieces and drop them from an airplane."

3. *Don't ask too many questions.* "Glad to see you. Welcome home."

4. *Don't rush to answer questions.* "That's an interesting question. What do you think?"

5. *Encourage children to use sources outside the home.* "Maybe the pet shop owner would have a suggestion."

6. *Don't take away hope.* "So you're thinking of trying out for the play! That should be an experience."

Praise and Self-Esteem

Instead of evaluating, describe.

1. *Describe what you see.* "I see a clean floor, a smooth bed, and books neatly lined up on the shelf." Or "I see your car parked exactly where we agreed it would be."

2. *Describe what you feel.* "It's a pleasure to walk into this room!" Or "I've enjoyed learning a little about the music you like."

3. *Sum up the child's praiseworthy behavior with a word.* "You sorted out your pencils, crayons, and pens, and put them in separate boxes. That's what I call *organization*!"

Freeing Children from Playing Roles

1. *Look for opportunities to show the child a new picture of himself or herself.* "You've had that toy since you were three, and it looks almost like new!"

2. *Put children in situations in which they can see themselves differently.* "Sara, would you take the screwdriver and tighten the pulls on these drawers?"

3. *Let children overhear you say something positive about them.* "He held his arm steady even though the shot hurt." Or "She's back home for a while, and I do enjoy her company."

4. *Model the behavior you'd like to see.* "It's hard to lose, but I'll try to be a sport about it. Congratulations!"

5. *Be a storehouse for your child's special moments.* "I remember the time you. . . ."

6. *When the child acts according to the old label, state your feelings and/or your expectations.* "I don't like that. Despite your strong feelings, I expect sportsmanship from you."

Source: Excerpts from Rawson Associates/Scribner, an imprint of Simon & Schuster, from *How to Talk So Kids Will Listen and Listen So Kids Will Talk,* by Adele Faber and Elaine Mazlish. Copyright © 1980 by Adele Faber and Elaine Mazlish.

children (Farver et al. 1997) found that American children were the most aggressive. This situation is a product of our generally violent culture. But one specific cause, according to some social scientists, may be Americans' habit of spanking their children (Straus 1999a).

Spanking refers to hitting a child with an open hand without causing physical injury. It is estimated that more than 90 percent of U.S. parents spank their children, at least occasionally. Analysis of data from the 13,000 respondents in the National Survey of Families and Households (see Chapter 6) shows that about one-third of fathers and 44 percent of mothers had spanked their children during the week prior to being interviewed.

Boys, especially those under age two, are spanked the most often. Children over age six are spanked less often, but some parents spank their children during early adolescence. Mothers spank more often than fathers. African American mothers, but not fathers, spank more frequently than most other racial/ethnic groups. Younger, less-educated parents in larger households with more children and less social support, parents who argue a lot with their children, and those with a fundamentalist religious orientation are more likely to spank. "It is clear . . . that wide variations in the incidence of spanking and extensive differences in its intensity are certainly prevalent" (Day, Peterson, and McCracken 1998, p. 91).

Authoritative parents are emotionally involved with their children, setting limits while encouraging them to develop and practice their talents.

Pediatricians and social scientists have conflicting opinions about whether it is appropriate ever to spank a child. A leading domestic violence researcher, sociologist Murray Straus (1996, 1999a), advises parents never to hit children of any age under any circumstances. Research by Straus and his colleagues shows that children who have been spanked by their parents—even if infrequently and by parents who are otherwise loving—are more likely later to cheat or tell lies, bully or be cruel or mean to others, disobey in school, and misbehave in other ways (Straus and Mouradian 1998).

Furthermore, being spanked in childhood is linked to depression, suicide, alcohol or drug abuse, and physical aggression against one's parents in adolescence and to abusing one's own children and violence against an intimate partner in adulthood (Straus 1999; Swinford, DeMaris, Cernkovich, and Giordano 2000). Straus argues that spanking teaches children a "hidden agenda"—that it is all right to hit someone and that those who love you hit you. This confusion of love

with violence sets the stage for spouse abuse. Then too, "the more parents rely on corporal punishment to deal with misbehavior, the less opportunity the child has to observe, participate in, and learn nonviolent modes of influencing the behavior of another person" (Straus and Yodanis 1996, p. 828).

However, some researchers contend that Straus and others may be oversimplifying, hence overstating, the case. Psychologist Marjorie Gunnoe (cited in Gilbert 1997) theorizes that spanking is most likely to result in children's aggressive behavior only when they perceive being spanked as an aggressive act. She hypothesizes that children under age eight tend to think it is their parent's right to spank them; older children, who are less willing to accept parental authority, are more likely to see being spanked as aggressive. Gunnoe also hypothesizes that African American children are more inclined than others to see spanking as acceptable, because spanking is generally accepted in the black community.[5]

Nevertheless, child-raising experts find many reasons to discourage spanking. For one thing, physical punishment "may interfere with the development of a child's conscience. *Spanking relieves guilt too easily:* The child, having paid for the misbehavior, feels free to repeat it (Ginott, Ginott, and Goddard 2003, p. 133, italics in original). Many parents feel that when all else fails, spanking works (although spanking can also encourage a child to misbehave further, even immediately). But research shows that spanking is seldom more effective than timeouts. Straus has argued that spanking usually accompanies other, more effective discipline methods such as explaining or depriving privileges. These nonspanking discipline methods are effective by themselves, and parents should be encouraged to follow the principle of "just leave out the spanking part" (Straus 1999a, p. 8).

Consensus statements drafted at the 1996 Conference of the American Academy of Pediatrics advise that children under two years old and adolescents should *never* be spanked. Spanking can cause physical

---

5. Some members of other nonwhite racial/ethnic groups, particularly recent-immigrant parents, apparently agree. Harvard sociologist Mary C. Waters, who has interviewed West Indian immigrants in New York City, reports that corporal punishment was the central issue for them: "When I asked what's different about the United States, they said, 'The state comes between you and your children. Americans don't discipline their children well, and when you do it the right way [spank or beat them], there's the danger your kids can call social services on you'" (Waters, quoted in Dugger 1996).

Children have a certain degree of resilience, which is enhanced by strong familial bonds. Although these children experience economic hardship, the self-esteem they gain through their family and friends can help them in becoming self-confident adults.

injury in the former and is known to promote aggression in the latter (Gilbert 1997). Straus would go further, suggesting that "there should be a notice on all birth certificates such as: WARNING: SPANKING HAS BEEN DETERMINED TO BE DANGEROUS TO THE HEALTH AND WELL BEING OF YOUR CHILD—**DO NOT EVER, UNDER ANY CIRCUMSTANCES SPANK YOUR CHILD**" (1999, p. 7, capitalization and bold emphasis in the original).

The Resilient Child

This textbook is written for people interested enough in parenting and family life to take a course. But no one is perfect; most parents have failings of one sort or another. Parents may encounter serious problems in their lives, problems that affect their children: poverty, discrimination, divorce, unemployment, legal and financial conflicts, scandal, sudden change of residence, crime victimization, military service, war, death, mental illness, drug or alcohol abuse, or family violence.

The hope that research in child development offers to parents who make mistakes is that children can be surprisingly resilient (Furstenberg and Hughes 1995; Rubin 1997; Brooks and Goldstein 2001). As an example, a long-term study was conducted in Hawaii based on a sample of all the children (698) born on the island of Kauai in 1955—one-half of whom were in poverty, and one-sixth of whom were physically or intellectually handicapped. A smaller group of 225 children was identified as being at high risk of poor developmental outcomes. Researchers found that even one-third of this last group "grew into competent young adults who loved well, worked well, played well, and expected well" (Werner 1992, p. 263). The researchers spoke of a "self-righting tendency" whereby children lucky enough to have certain characteristics—a sociable personality, self-esteem derived from a particular talent, a support network, and, above all, a good relationship with at least one caring adult—emerged into adulthood in good shape (Werner 1992; Werner and Smith 2001).

Risk is risk, but hope is not unrealistic (Brooks and Goldstein 2001). Other research indicates that "[a]dults who acknowledge and seem to have worked through difficulties of their childhood are apparently protected against inflicting them on their children"

(Belsky 1991, p. 124). There is also evidence that a conscientious **para-parent**—an unrelated adult who informally plays a parentlike role for a child—can generate a resilient child (Johnson 2000; Soukhanov 1996).[6] We turn next to an examination of parenting differences related to social class.

▪ Social Class and Parenting ▪

As Chapter 2 points out, virtually all life experiences (and opportunities, or "life chances") are mediated or influenced by social class—one's overall status in a society, often measured by educational achievement, occupation, and/or income. Parenting is no exception (Bornstein and Bradley 2003). You'll recall a theme of this text: Decisions are influenced by social conditions that limit or expand a decision maker's options. This section examines some ways that the conditions of social class affect a parent's options and decisions.

The Family in an Unpredictable Economy

After World War II and until the mid-1970s, a majority of (Caucasian) Americans experienced job security and higher wages as they benefited from the postwar economic boom. However, since the mid-1970s—and dramatically, since the terrorist attacks of September 11, 2001—the U.S. economy has been much less predictable. This has meant declining economic security for many American families (Crouter and Booth 2004; Teachman, Tedrow, and Crowder 2000). The rise of a service (as opposed to an industrial) economy has spelled lower wages for many workers. Although some service jobs—those that involve technological expertise or a fairly high level of education—pay well, many new jobs in data entry and word processing that accompany the information age are low-paying, with few benefits and limited prospects for advancement (Seccombe 2000).

Analysis of income data over the past thirty-five years reveals another feature affecting families' sense of well-being—increased inequality (White and Rogers 2000). The wealthy have gained while the less well-off have become even more so (Teachman, Tedrow, and Crowder 2000). As discussed in Chapter 2, the unequal distribution of income—or "inequality gap"—in the United States[7] has grown.

As Chapter 2's Figure 2.3 shows, when family incomes are compared, Asian and non-Hispanic white families are economically better off than others. They are even more relatively well-off when assets (such as home and savings and investments) are considered (Crockett 2003). The relatively low wages associated with service jobs and periodic unemployment have hurt non-Hispanic white families to an even greater extent than they have the white majority.

Meanwhile, the recent years have been characterized by continued downsizing, which has severely affected both white-collar and blue-collar jobs. Many high- and mid-level managers in "dot coms" and other corporations (those employees with technical expertise and college educations) and factory workers alike have found it difficult to find and/or hold jobs (White and Rogers 2000, p. 1039).

Poverty-Level Parents

Four million U.S. children under age six live below poverty level. Of those between ages six and seventeen, another 7.6 million live in poverty (U.S. Census Bureau 2000, Table 697). Children living in poverty sometimes do not have enough to eat; have more physical health, socioemotional, and behavioral problems; and do less well in school than do other children (Seccombe 2000; White and Rogers 2000). Poor children may drop out of school to try to help their families; this is one explanation for the relatively high dropout rate of Latino youth (Huston, McLoyd, and Coll 1994).

The overall poverty rate was close to 25 percent in 1959, but beginning with President Lyndon Johnson's "War on Poverty" in the 1960s, the poverty rate dropped consistently during the 1970s to a low of 11 percent. It began to rise in the late 1970s, fell again

---

6. One form of *para-parent* can be the "social father." Notably, research that examined the role of "social father"—"a male relative or family associate who demonstrates parental behaviors and is like a father to the child"—and social fathers' influence on preschoolers' development found that "male relative social fathers are associated with higher levels of children's school readiness, whereas mothers' romantic partner social fathers are associated with lower levels of emotional maturity" (Jayakody and Kalil 2002, p. 504).

7. In 2002, the top 20 percent of U.S. families received almost half (49.7 percent) of the nation's total income, while the poorest 20 percent of Americans received just 3.5 percent.

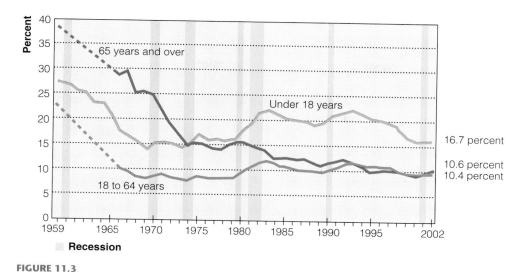

FIGURE 11.3

U.S. poverty rates by age, 1959 to 2002.

Note: Data for people eighteen to sixty-four and sixty-five and older are not available from 1960 to 1965.

Sources: Proctor, Bernadette D., and Joseph Dalaker. 2003. "Poverty in the United States: 2002." Current Population Reports P60–222. Washington, DC: United States Census Bureau.

in the 1990s, and was 12.1 percent in 2002—up from 11.7 percent in 2001 (Proctor and Dalaker 2003). If we include those "near poor" who are just above the official poverty line, the figure rises to approximately 16 percent (U.S. Census Bureau 2003, Table 700). Children make up 39 percent of the poor. In recent years, poverty rates have declined for African Americans and Hispanics. Nevertheless, in 2002, 31.5 percent (nearly one-third) of African American and 28.6 percent of Hispanic children lived in poverty (Proctor and Dalaker 2003). As Figure 11.3 shows, the child poverty rate (at 16.7 percent in 2002) is not only greater than that of the nation as a whole, but also well above that of adult Americans, including those aged 65 and older.

We may be inclined to think of family poverty in terms of black or Hispanic families, but even more poor children are white. Despite higher *rates* of non-Hispanic white poverty, white families predominate in sheer numbers. White people make up 69 percent of the poor (U.S. Census Bureau 2003, Table 700). (But a South Dakota county covering most of the Pine Ridge Indian reservation is typically one of the poorest coun-

ties in the United States [e.g., Kilborn 1992b], calling our attention to the high unemployment on the reservation and a poverty rate among Native Americans/ Alaska Natives (25.7 percent) that is the highest of all racial/ethnic groups [U.S. Census Bureau 2003, Table 697].) Moreover, the majority of poor families have at least one working parent (U.S. Census Bureau 2003, Tables 701 and 707).

"WELFARE REFORM" The 1996 Personal Responsibility and Work Opportunity Act, or "welfare reform bill," effectively ended the federal government's sixty-year guarantee of assisting low-income mothers and children. The federal Aid to Families with Dependent Children (AFDC) program ended in 1997, and a different federal program, **Temporary Assistance for Needy Families (TANF)**, ensued. Under the new legislation, assistance is limited to five years for most families, with most adult recipients required to find work within two years.

"Welfare reform" was partly motivated by the belief that cutting welfare aid to single mothers would result in fewer female-headed families. However, research suggests that this may not be the case (Meckler 1999). The majority of mothers on welfare may be committed to work, but many lack job skills, and many more face problems with job, day-care, or transportation availability (Monroe and Tiller 2001). The long-term consequences of TANF remain to be seen (Duncan and Brooks-Gunn 2002; Lichter and Crowley 2002), but organizations such as the National Coalition for the Homeless argue that welfare changes have increased poverty and family homelessness ("Homeless Families with Children" 2001).

THE WORKING POOR The majority of poor parents live in rented homes, apartments, or motel rooms and are employed (Ehrenreich 2001). These "working poor" have minimum- or less-than-minimum-wage jobs with irregular and unpredictable hours and no medical insurance or other benefits. Working full time at minimum wage does not earn a parent enough money to live above the poverty line (Clemetson 2003; Seccombe 2000).

Nearly 12 percent of all children (8 percent of white, 14 percent of black, and 23 percent of Hispanic children) have no health insurance, either public or private (Federal Interagency Forum 2004, Table ECON5.A). Meanwhile, children living in poverty—more often disabled or chronically ill than other children—have expensive health care needs that are not always or completely covered by welfare or other social services (Lukemeyer, Meyers, and Smeeding 2000). Many poor families move often from city to city to move in with relatives or to search for jobs. This makes it difficult for a parent to establish support systems and hinders children's chances for school continuity and success (Molyneux 1995).

Assuredly, raising children in poverty is qualitatively different from doing so otherwise. Poverty-level parents and their children have poorer nutrition; more illnesses such as asthma, which has been associated with household cockroaches (Cowley and Underwood 1997; Crouter and Booth 2004); schools that are less safe; and limited access to quality medical care (Barton 1999). A parent's not feeling well must make raising children in poverty conditions even more difficult than it would be otherwise (Klebanov, Brooks-Gunn, and Duncan 1994): "Economic insecurity, underemployment, and joblessness, on top of years of defeats and dashed hopes, have proven devastating to poor families" (Sugrue 1999, p. 245). Items that other Americans take for granted, such as relatively safe, gang-free

© Ewing Galloway / Index Stock Imagery

Raising children while in poverty is a very different experience from parenting in wealthier social classes. Besides concerns for basic necessities, such as food, clothing, shelter, and health care, poverty-level parents may live in depressingly blighted neighborhoods.

neighborhoods, are often unavailable (O'Hare and Mather 2003), and parental control is harder to achieve in neighborhoods characterized by antisocial behavior (Simons, Lin, Gordon, Brody, and Conger 2002).[8]

Nevertheless, poverty-level parents have actively worked to make many poor neighborhoods safer (Letiecq and Koblinsky 2001). And it is important to point out that some parents and children living in poverty do overcome severe hardships (Kozol 2000). One longitudinal, qualitative study of preschoolers born to low-income adolescent mothers found that

---

8. In the words of one college student, "When I was young, gunshots could be heard three to four times a week. It was no big deal unless there were repeated gunshots. Most often it was just a few shots. But there were times when gunfire could be heard throughout the night." This student's family moved from an impoverished, crime-ridden neighborhood to one a little bit safer. "Even though it felt safer," according to the student, "I remember seeing chalk outlines from the night before" ("Growing Up in the Inner City" 1998). Some parents respond to this environment by keeping their children inside the house as much as possible, a situation the children often call "lockdown," a term "snatched from the grim lexicon of prison life" (Marriott 1995, p. 56).

children of mothers whose parenting style was generally authoritative made a better adjustment to school (Luster, Bates, Fitzgerald, Vanderbelt, and Key 2000).

HOMELESS FAMILIES Over the past two decades a shortage of affordable housing has helped create a significant and visible number of homeless families—a phenomenon that twenty-five years ago would have been unthinkable.

Declining wages have put housing out of reach for many families: in every state, metropolitan area, county, and town, more than the minimum wage is required to afford a one- or two-bedroom apartment at Fair Market Rent. In fact, the median wage needed to afford a two-bedroom apartment is more than twice the minimum wage ("Homeless Families with Children" 2001).

Partly as a result of changes to the welfare laws (Seccombe 2000; Quindlen 2001), described above, approximately 40 percent of the homeless today are mothers and children, with children under age eighteen making up about one-quarter of the homeless. Families with children are among the fastest-growing segments of the homeless population ("Who Is Homeless?" 2004).

Homeless parents, especially those who have been without housing for a longer period of time, move often and have little in the way of a helpful social network ("Homeless Families with Children" 2001). "Length-of-stay restrictions in shelters, short stays with friends and relatives, and/or relocation to seek employment make it difficult for homeless children to attend school regularly" ("Education of Homeless Children and Youth" 2001). It is difficult to imagine raising children while living on the street. For example, carefully monitoring children's homework becomes an impossible expectation for a parent whose concern is finding the children's next meal or keeping them warm (Lindsey 1998). (For more examples, see Chapter 15's A Closer Look at Family Diversity: Stressor Pile-Up Among Single-Mother Families in Homeless Shelters.)

Blue-Collar, or Working-Class, Parents

Blue-collar, or working-class, families have traditionally taken their designation from the primary breadwinner (traditionally the husband-father or stepfather), who is employed in blue-collar work: factory produc-

tion, maintenance, construction, truck driving, or appliance repair, for example. Protected by powerful trade unions, blue-collar families once enjoyed fairly high wages, benefits such as seniority, pensions, paid vacations, and fully covered medical care. But blue-collar parents have declined both in number and in resources (Rubin 1999).

Blue-collar/working-class parents are more likely than middle- and upper-class parents to be strict disciplinarians, expecting conformity, obedience, neatness, and good manners from their children (Kohn 1977; Luster, Rhoades, and Haas 1989). More likely than wealthier parents to use physical (corporal) punishment (Straus and Stewart 1999), their parenting style may often best be described as authoritarian.[9]

Because finances are an issue, blue-collar/working-class parents have been more likely to push their offspring into independent adulthood earlier than have middle- or upper-middle-class parents. Meanwhile, being ambitious for their children, they may well encourage them to go to college even though they themselves are usually not college graduates. This means that their children might eventually adopt different values and behaviors—from how to spend leisure time to political or religious values—and this may create strain between a family's generations.

Another interesting observation is that the employed wives of blue-collar husbands often have white-collar office jobs and are hence exposed to middle-class values. This can make for a "value stretch" between blue-collar men and their mates: Husbands may value a more restrictive parenting style than do their wives (LeMasters and DeFrain 1989).

Middle- and Upper-Middle-Class Parents

Incomes have grown little for middle-class parents, who have experienced increased economic uncertainty: For example, can they pay off their credit card debt or count on continued health insurance or pension benefits (Hacker 2004; Kilborn and Clemetson 2002; Warren and Tyagi 2003)? Upper-middle-class

---

9. During the second half of the twentieth century, child development advice became widely dispersed through the popular media. Despite a convergence of available professional information about child raising across social classes, educational, neighborhood/community, and extended-family differences continue to result in different social classes' receiving different information regarding child rearing. Also, parents in different social classes may interpret the same professional advice in different ways (Walsh 2002).

"So many toys—so little unstructured time."

parents, on the other hand, may not have significant family wealth but do earn high salaries as corporate executives and professionals: physicians or attorneys, for example. Other professionals, such as college professors, accountants, engineers, architects, and psychotherapists, may not earn quite so much money but have a comfortable income that supports an upper-middle-class lifestyle.

Upper-middle-class parents have the money to fit the idealized cultural image of the self-sufficient nuclear family (Cancian and Oliker 2000, p. 44). For instance, one married parent in this social class is more likely than in lower social classes to embrace the option of not working outside the home (Wallis 2004). Indeed, upper-middle-class families have considerably more options than do those in lower social classes. They can better afford to choose the neighborhood in which they want to raise their children, for instance. They can send their offspring away to college and sometimes to private schools. On a different level (but one that points up the myriad of daily-life advantages), upper-middle-class parents can hire personal parenting coaches (Harvey 2002) or household help; or they can purchase an automobile for their adolescent so that sharing a parent's car is unnecessary.

Despite these differences—worries about financial security among middle-class parents versus enough money to support various options among upper-middle-class parents—these families' parenting styles tend to be more alike than different. While working-class parents tend to emphasize obedience and conformity, middle- and upper-middle-class parents foster language and critical thinking skills, self-direction, and initiative in their children (Laureau 2003b; Smith 1999). Tending to adopt a more authoritative parenting style, emphasizing a child's happiness, creativity, achievement, and independence, they are generally less restrictive and more "affectionate and responsive" (Belsky 1991, p. 122). As a group, they have the material and educational resources to better prepare their children for occupational success. (For one thing, better-educated parents are more likely to discourage their children from watching television while encouraging them to read or study [Hofferth and Sandberg 2001].)

THE "HURRIED CHILD" Upper-middle-class parents sometimes place too many demands on their children by engaging them in all sorts of private lessons, extracurricular activities associated with school or church, and organized recreational programs. According to one critic, such parents may be determined to raise "trophy kids" (Kirn and Cole 2001; Zimmerman 2004). But "scheduled hyperactivity" (Kantrowitz 2000b)—or "hyper-parenting" (Rosenfeld and Wise 2001)—can produce the "over-scheduled," or "hurried child," who is forced to assume too many challenges and responsibilities too soon (Elkind 1988; Rosenfeld and Wise 2001). Hurried children may achieve in adult ways at a young age, but they also acquire the stress induced by the pressure to achieve (Kantrowitz and Wingert 2001; Noonan 2001). Or they may "drop out" and abandon goal-directed academic and/or extracurricular activity.[10]

Despite their best efforts, upper-middle-class parents cannot ensure that each child will eventually enjoy a position in the upper-middle class. An executive's child will more than likely have to finish college and maybe even attain a higher degree in order to match the parent's occupational status. Related to this is the problem of how to teach a child raised in relative affluence to live in less luxurious conditions should she or he be unable to afford luxury in adulthood (LeMasters and DeFrain 1989).

This section has described various parenting issues associated with different social classes, regardless of ethnicity. The next section addresses racial/ethnic diversity with regard to raising children.

Racial/Ethnic Diversity and Parenting

Chapter 2 points out that social class may be more important than race in terms of parental values and interactions with their children (Laureau 2003b). At the same time, social scientists do look at how various U.S. ethnic groups evidence culturally specific parenting styles. Much of this research used the *cultural equivalent* approach (described in Chapter 3's "A Closer Look at Family Diversity: Studying Ethnic Non-Hispanic White Families"), which compares ethnic non-Hispanic white family practices with those of white mainstream families. For example, a study found that Vietnamese American high schoolers are more likely than most American teens to get homework help from their older siblings—a culturally expected practice that is important to Vietnamese students' school success (Bankston 1998). A few studies have used the *cultural variant* approach; comparisons are made within the ethnic group itself. For instance, a qualitative study of forty immigrant Asian Indian families found that more-acculturated, or Americanized, fathers were

more engaged in their young children's lives (Jain and Belsky 1997). We may expect more studies like these in the future (Demo and Cox 2000). The major focus of this section, however, is on the particular challenges faced by racial/ethnic minority parents in the United States today.

As a beginning, we need to note that there is considerable overlap among class and racial/ethnic categories. The upper class is almost entirely white. The upper-middle class, still overwhelmingly white, now includes substantial numbers of people of color, particularly Asians. Other Asians, especially Southeast Asians, remain in lower social classes. Many African American families are now solidly middle class (Dent 1992). African Americans, Native Americans, Latinos, and some Asians are heavily represented in the working class and overrepresented in the poverty ranks. Within the broad "poverty" category, blacks are much more likely to live in neighborhoods of "extreme poverty," those where two-fifths of the population is poor. It is important to remember, though, that a majority of African Americans are now members of the working or middle class (Staples 1999b).

African American Parents and Children

Evidence suggests that African American (as well as Hispanic and Asian American) parents' attitudes, behaviors, and hopes for their children are similar to those of other parents in their social class (Julian, McKenry, and McKelvey 1994). Middle-class parents of all racial/ethnic groups are more alike than different, and so are poverty-level parents. Upper-middle-class black parents perform their role differently from working-class black parents (Bluestone and Tamis-LeMonda 1999) or those living below poverty level.

Nevertheless, the impact of race remains important. For instance, even when social class is taken into account, it appears that more African American parents than parents in other ethnic groups spank their children: "There is debate over whether the approval and use of [corporal punishment] by African Americans is a legacy of their culture prior to enslavement or a legacy of the physical brutality to which African Americans were subjected during slavery . . ." (Straus and Stewart 1999, p. 67). But the cultural equivalent approach that compares African American parents to other ethnic groups can be seen as Eurocentric. Spanking may not have the same negative effects on African American children as it does on European

---

10. Parents can help not only by checking on whether they have realistic expectations for their children but also by moderating unreasonable outside demands. Some Minnesota parents have created an organization called "Family Life 1st!" that encourages and supports parents who want to do less car-pooling to children's organized activities and have more unscheduled family time (Kantrowitz 2000).

© Robert Llewelyn/Imagestate

Negative racial stereotypes give us images of aloof, or absent, African American fathers. But African American parents' attitudes, behaviors, and hopes for their children are similar to those of other parents in their social class. Many African American families are now solidly middle- or upper-middle class, but they and their children continue to be vulnerable to discrimination, a situation that virtually all parents in racial/ethnic non-Hispanic white groups face.

American children. Among African Americans, physical punishment is more acceptable and hence more likely to be viewed as an appropriate display of positive parenting both by the parent and by the child (McLoyd et al. 2000, p. 1082).

Besides putting up with research findings that are possibly biased against them (Pyke 2000a), parents of color face additional challenges. The African American middle class remains vulnerable to discrimination in employment and housing. The status of middle-class black parents does not suffice to protect them from demeaning or suspicious behavior on the part of whites (Staples 1999b, p. 284). Even so simple a matter

as buying toys becomes problematic. Black dolls only? Should the child choose? What if the choice is a white Barbie doll?

Native American Parents and Children

Native American parents have been described as exercising a laissez-faire parenting style, bordering on—if not actually—neglectful. However, describing Native American parenting in this way may smack of Eurocentrism. Traditionally, Native American culture has emphasized personal autonomy and individual choice, even for children. Before the arrival of Europeans and for some time thereafter, Native Americans successfully raised their children by using example and "light discipline" and by "persuasion, ridicule, or shaming in opposition to corporal punishment or coercion." Native Americans continue to "respect children enough to allow them to work things out in their own manner" (John 1998, p. 400).

Given the problems of substance abuse and high teenage suicide rates documented among Native American youth ("American Indians" 1992; John 1998), we might conclude that the traditional method of raising Native American children is no longer effective, due to changes in the broader society:

> Back when [today's] elders were growing up, the family was much closer, was more organized and protective, combined discipline with permissiveness better than today, and had the advantage of having parents (particularly the mother) around the home. (John 1998, p. 401)

However, valuing their cultural heritage, many Native Americans have been reluctant to assimilate into the broader society—and this reluctance may mean a rejection of the authoritative parenting style advised by European American psychologists. Meanwhile, suicide prevention has become a top priority in many tribes, with the use of tribal elders "to help mitigate the loss of parental involvement and early nurturant figures in the lives of Native American adolescents" (John 1998, p. 404).

Hispanic Parents and Children

In 1998, among eighteen- to twenty-four-year-olds, more than one-third (34.4 percent) of Hispanics had not completed high school and were not enrolled, compared with 17.1 percent of blacks and 13.7 percent of whites (U.S. Census Bureau 2000, Table 290). Dropping out of school is related to poverty. But, at 21.4 percent, the poverty rate for Hispanics is slightly below that of African Americans' 22.7 percent (U.S. Census Bureau 2003, Table 700), and African Americans have a significantly lower high school dropout rate. Some think the lower educational levels of Hispanics can partly be explained by the fact that many immigrants from Mexico arrive here looking for little more than jobs that require unskilled labor (Becerra 1998, p. 162). The phenomenon may also result from Mexican Americans' comparing their achievements and standard of living in the United States to past conditions in Mexico. Current well-being and even a partial high school education seem so superior that young Mexican Americans may not be inclined to persevere through high school and into college (Suro 1992).

Then too, Hispanics' relatively low educational attainment may be associated with difficulty in speaking English. Looking at school readiness skills among three- to five-year-olds, 25 percent of both blacks and whites can recognize all their letters, while just 14 percent of Hispanic children can. Sixty percent of black and white children between three and five years old can count to twenty, while just 40 percent of Hispanic children can. It appears that the difference is due to whether the child's mother's home language is English. Children whose mother does not speak English at home are, on average, about half as well prepared for school as other American children (U.S. Census Bureau 2000, Table 258; 2003, Table 238).

Mexican American parents teach their children the traditions and values of their cultures of origin (McLoyd et al. 2000) while often coping with a generational gap that may include differential fluency and different attitudes toward speaking Spanish (Anti-Defamation League of B'nai B'rith 1981; Becerra 1998). As in other bicultural families, conflicts may extend into many matters of everyday life: "My mother would give me these silly dresses to wear to school, not jeans," complains a fifteen-year-old Mexican American female (Suro 1992, p. A–11).

Hispanic parents have been described as more authoritarian than white parents. However, as with African Americans, it may be that this description is Eurocentric and therefore inaccurate. The concept of **hierarchical parenting**, which combines warm emotional support for children with a demand for significant respect for parents and other authority figures, including older extended family members, may more aptly apply to Hispanic parents. Hierarchical parenting is designed to instill in children a more collective value system (see Chapter 9) rather than the relatively high individualism favored by European Americans (McLoyd et al. 2000, p. 1082).

Asian American Parents and Children

Compared to the average of 25 percent for all Americans over twenty-five years old, 42 percent of Asians have completed four years of college or more (U.S. Census Bureau 2000, Table 249). Ironically, the Asian American parenting style, characterized by some researchers as authoritarian (Greenfield and Suzuki 2001) and even hostile (McBride-Chang and Chang 1998), has not generally been credited with children's educational success. So researchers have explained Asian American children's high school performance by arguing that peers in their ethnic group strongly support academic success (McBride-Chang and Chang 1998; McLoyd et al. 2000). Finding this explanation inadequate and ethnocentric, a few Asian American social scientists have offered alternative concepts that emphasize the indigenous **Confucian training doctrine**, named after the sixth-century Chinese social philosopher Confucius, who stressed (among other things) honesty, sacrifice, familial loyalty, and respect for parents and all elders. Like the *hierarchical parenting* concept suggested for Hispanic parents, the Confucian training doctrine blends parental love, concern, involvement, and physical closeness with strict and firm control (Chao 1994; McBride-Chang and Chang 1998).

Meanwhile, because Asian American children have achieved above-average education levels in the United States and have done relatively well in the professions, they are thought to have few problems. Nevertheless, like other ethnic minorities, they have suffered from discrimination (Fernandez 1998). Furthermore, Asian American youths must contend with high expectations created by the stereotyping of Asians as a "superminority" (Wong et al. 1998).

Parents and Multiracial Children

According to the 2000 census, which was the first to offer citizens the option of identifying themselves as more than one race, there are nearly seven million Americans of mixed race. Of those, more than 40 percent are children under age eighteen. Chapter 7 explores homogamy versus heterogamy in marriage; as racial heterogamy slowly loses its taboo, the number of multiracial births is expected to climb (Dunnewind 2003). The greatest number of multiracial births is to black–white couples, followed by Asian–white and then Native American–white couples. Other interracial births occur as well, of course, such as babies born to Native American–black or Native American–Asian couples (Kalish 1995).

Raising biracial or multiracial children has challenges peculiar to it, although not without rewards as well. For instance, "Some children of mixed parentage can experience racial abuse, both verbal and physical, within their family settings, most commonly by a white parent or relative, although occasionally the ethnic minority family members" (Barter 1999, p. 2). Another challenge may be tension between parents—and between parents and children—over cultural values and attitudes: "Black parents may teach their biracial children to grow up to be Black and proud, but society teaches that to be Black is to be an inferior person. . . . Yet a white parent may have trouble instilling 'white cultural pride' in the child." As one wife put it, "I have nothing against teaching him Black pride, but I am a white person. . . . In this racist society I'm not even permitted to feel good about being white and teach my child that it's okay that he has a part of whiteness in him as well" (Luke 1994, p. 58, citing Ladner 1984):

> Such contradictory identity positions that parents in fact embody, illustrate the conflicts and paradoxes many interracial parents face. Hence, the complexity of parenting in these contexts is a profoundly different emotional, cultural, and political experience for either parent, particularly when the family includes biracial and monoracial children. (Luke 1994, p. 58)

One psychologist surveyed multiracial adults and asked whether they thought that their parents had been prepared to raise children of mixed race. The majority did not believe so (Dunnewind 2003). Today, however, there are more resources for parents raising multiracial children. The following are four tips from one of these resources (Nakazawa 2003):

- "Encourage children to be proud of all their racial background. Encouraging them to identify with only one race 'is all but guaranteed to set them up for a state of inner turmoil and identity problems over the long haul'. . . .

- "Watch for two pivotal 'pressure points' children will face: grade school (usually third or fourth grade), when teasing starts and multiracial children realize that others see them as different; and the early teen years, as they struggle to fit in socially and find their identities. . . .

- "Understand that racial identity is fluid during adolescence, with a teen changing from one primary racial affiliation to another. [Among other reasons,] this is a way to fit into racial groupings at school. . . .

- "Stress the positives. Multiracial children often demonstrate greater creativity and flexibility because they use more than one culture's approach to life's challenges" (Dunnewind 2003, citing and quoting Nakazawa 2003).

For other intermarried parents, the challenge may be about what religion the children will be raised in or how to teach the children one's native tongue: "As the trend toward increased rates of racial and ethnic intermarriage continues, it will become increasingly important to understand what factors promote resilience among such families, given the unique challenges they confront" (McLoyd et al. 2000, p. 1074).

Religious Minority Parents and Children

Ethnicity is often associated with religious belief. Chinese Americans may be Buddhists, for example, and Asian Indian Americans may be Hindu or Sikh. In a dominant Christian culture, diverse ethno-religious affiliations affect parenting for many Americans. For instance, there is a strong tradition in Islam, known as *hadith*, that frowns on singing other than to recite the required Muslim daily prayers; at Christmastime, Muslim children may be invited—at school or in their neighborhoods—to join in Christmas (or winter) carols (Connell 1993).

Meanwhile, Muslims have their own holy days, such as Ramadan, which are little appreciated by the majority American culture. Then too, traditional Muslims, particularly women, dress differently than do the majority of Americans. Wearing flowing robes and, more often, headscarves or veils (called *hijab*), Muslims report that they fear ridicule and face discrimination from employers and others (Witt and Roberts 1997; Harden and Sengupta 2001).

Parents of minority religions in America hope that their children will remain true to their religious

In this Modesto, California, mosque—as in mosques across the United States—Muslims gather for daily prayers at morning, noon, and night. Muslim parents hope that their children will remain true to their religious tradition. Meanwhile, like parents of other minority religions in the United States, they must help their children face fear of ridicule and actual discrimination.

heritage, even amid a majority culture that seldom understands (Winston 1998) and, in fact, is sometimes threatening (Lee 2001).[11] One solution has been the emergence of religion-based summer camps for children of Jewish, Buddhist, Muslim, Hindu, Sikh, and Zoroastrian parents (Lieblich 1998).

Raising Children of Racial/ Ethnic Identity in a Racist and Discriminatory Society

Whatever its social class, the family of racial/ethnic identity—whether black, Native American, Hispanic, Asian American, or multiracial—must serve as an insulating and advocating environment, as much as possible shielding children from and/or confronting racial slurs and injustices. Raising children in a white-dominated society creates situations that white families never encounter, regardless of their social class

(McLoyd et al. 2000). For instance, various forms of racism persist in our nation's schools ("Black Parents Fight" 2004; Owo 2004). On a more personal level, a parent of a child of color must decide whether to warn the youngster who is going off to school for the first time about the possibility of classmates' racial slurs (Ambert 1994).

As a result, parents are acutely concerned about the need to develop adequate self-esteem in their children, along with pride in their cultural heritage. Some parents in families of racial/ethnic identity decide not to discuss racism or discrimination with their children; they do not want them to become unnecessarily bitter or resentful. Instead, these parents prepare to help their offspring cope with racism when it arises (Moore 1993; White 1993). Others believe it is important to teach their youngsters the history of discrimination against them.

Parents do not necessarily agree on the best approach to racial issues. About one-third of African American parents do not attempt any explicit racial socialization. Others differ as to whether they emphasize forewarning or take a more militant position toward the elimination of social inequality (Taylor et al. 1991;

11. This desire that their children maintain their ethno-religious heritage is a principal reason for some immigrant parents' preference that their children marry homogamously, sometimes in arranged marriages (see Chapter 7).

A dilemma faced by all parents of racial/ethnic identity—whether African American, Native American, Hispanic, Asian American, or multiracial—is to address the balance between loyalty to one's ethnic culture and individual advancement in the dominant society. Native Americans must choose between the reservation and its high poverty level and an urban life that is perhaps alienating but presents some economic opportunity.

© Branson Reynolds/Index Stock Imagery

A dilemma faced by all parents of racial/ethnic identity is to address the balance between loyalty to one's ethnic culture and individual advancement in the dominant society. For instance, in many ethnic families the dialect or language spoken at home is neither used nor respected in the larger society. Hence, in order to succeed educationally and occupationally, children must become bilingual or forsake the language of their ancestors.

Valuing one's cultural heritage, while simultaneously being required to deny or "rise above" it in order to advance, poses problems both for individuals and between parents and their children. Native Americans must choose between the reservation and its high poverty level (some have 90-percent unemployment [Bedard 1992, p. 99]) and an urban life that is perhaps alienating but presents some economic opportunity. Latinos may see a threat to deeply cherished values of family and community in the competitive individualism of the mainstream American achievement path (McLoyd et al. 2000). Asian Americans may live out the "model minority" route to success but experience emotional estrangement from still-traditional parents or identity problems as they feel pressured to cultivate their Asian ethnicity but also to downplay it (Kibria 2000). And Asian American parents may be dismayed by their children's lack of interest in the history of their homeland or failure to respect their elders (Gorman 1998).

Having explored the class and racial/ethnic diversity of U.S. parents, we turn now to a discussion of three newly visible parenting environments: gay male and lesbian parents, grandparent parents, and foster parents.

McLoyd et al. 2000, p. 1085–1086). We might conclude that

> In the socialization of children there is some tension between teaching an unclouded knowledge of racism's realities and communicating a sense of personal strength and capability. Black children should be taught that there are major barriers, but they also need to be taught that they can be overcome—a difficult balancing act for parents. (Feagin and Sikes 1994, p. 314)

Newly Visible Parenting Environments

The three parenting environments discussed in this section are newly visible in our society, although they certainly are not new in fact. One reason that these parenting environments—gay and lesbian parents, grandparent parents, and foster parents—are more visible today is that their numbers have increased over the past two decades. A second reason that they are more visible now is that they are less stigmatized than in the past, so people are talking publicly about being parents, being children, and having been children in these parenting environments.

Gay Male and Lesbian Parents

Gay and lesbian parents have not only become increasingly visible but have also increased significantly in number (Bell 2003). Gay men and lesbians become parents in various ways. A significant number have been married, and some have children from those marriages. Lesbian and gay parents of children from previous, heterosexual marriages often face custody issues, which have had various resolutions.

Gays and lesbians have also sought parenthood as adoptive parents and as birth parents, as one lesbian partner gives birth to a baby they both parent. Artificial insemination by donor (AID), discussed in Chapter 10 and Appendix G, "is largely accredited for the 'lesbian baby boom' on the West Coast" since the mid-1970s (R. L. Taylor 1997a, p. 85). This baby boom includes not only lesbian co-parents but an array of combinations of lesbian mothers and biological fathers, surrogate mothers, and gay biological fathers (less frequent) (Patterson 2000). A family studies professor describes the diversity apparent in her own lesbian family as follows:

> My partner and I live with our two sons. Our older son was conceived in my former heterosexual marriage. At first, our blended family consisted of a lesbian couple and a child from one partner's previous marriage. After several years, our circumstances changed. My brother's life partner became the donor and father to our second son, who is my partner's biological child. My partner and I draw a boundary around our lesbian-headed family in which we share a household consisting of two moms and two sons, but our extended family consists of additional kin groups. For example, my former husband and his wife have an infant son, who is my biological son's second brother. All four sets of grandparents and extended kin related to our sons' biological parents are involved in all our lives to varying degrees. These kin comprise a diversity of heterosexual and gay identities as well as long-term married, ever-single, and divorced individuals. (Allen 1997, p. 213)

Research from an accumulation of more than 100 studies finds children of gay male and lesbian parents to be well-adjusted, with no noticeable differences from children of heterosexual parents (Perrin 2002,

Lesbian couples may take advantage of AID (artificial insemination by donor) technology so that one partner gives birth to a baby they both want. Research from more than 100 studies concludes that children of lesbian or gay male parents are generally well-adjusted and have no noticeable differences from children of heterosexual parents.

Chapter 5).[12] Nor are they more likely to be gay as adults (Patterson 2000). They may, however, encounter challenges from friends, classmates, or teachers. Indeed, an ongoing challenge to same-sex parents involves determining whether and how to explain the child's family situation to others. Regarding relationships with schools, the Family Pride Coalition urges same-sex parents to

> Tell the teachers who is in your family and names your children use to identify them, and provide a

12. Although not necessarily refuting these findings, sociologists Judith Stacey and Timothy Biblarz (2001) question the research methodologies of many studies that show no differences between children raised by "lesbigay" parents and those raised by heterosexual parents and urge more rigorous research to assess possible differences and what might be their causes.

Issues for Thought

Growing Up in a Household Characterized by Conflict

Many social scientists have found that a home characterized by significant, ongoing conflict has a negative impact on the couple's children (Siegel 2000). Researchers divide children's behavior problems into two categories: externalizing (aggression, lying, cheating, running away from home, disobeying at school, delinquency) and internalizing (withdrawal, depression, and anxiety). At least since the 1980s, researchers have consistently found a link between marital conflict and both types of behavior problems in children (Dukes 2003; Erel and Burman 1995).

One study (Buehler et al. 1998) sampled 337 sixth- through eighth-grade girls and boys, aged ten through fifteen, in Utah and Tennessee. Three-quarters of the children were non-Hispanic white, 12 percent were Hispanic, and 13 percent represented other racial/ethnic groups. Most families were middle class; 85 percent of the children had their own bedroom, for example. The parents of 87 percent of the children in the sample were married. The parents' average education level was somewhere between high school graduate and some college.

The students were asked to fill out questionnaires that assessed their behavior and any conflict between their parents. Externalizing behavior problems were measured by students' agreeing or disagreeing with statements such as "I cheat a lot" or "I tease others a lot." Internalizing behavior problems were measured by students' agreeing or

disagreeing with statements such as "I am unhappy a lot" or "I worry a lot." The children were also asked how often their parents disagreed on certain topics. Then they were asked about the style of their parents' conflict. Overt parental conflict styles involved such things as the parents' calling each other names, telling each other to shut up, or threatening each other in front of the child. Covert parental conflict styles included such things as trying to get the child to side with one parent and asking the child to relay a message from one parent to the other because the parents didn't want to talk to each other.

The researchers found that conflict between parents was far from the only cause of children's behavior problems. Nevertheless, for both girls and boys, the researchers did find a strong correlation between interparental conflict and behavior problems. This relationship held true regardless of whether the parents were married or divorced. When parents displayed an overt conflict style, the youth were more likely to report externalizing behavior problems; this relationship was stronger for fifth graders than it was for eighth graders. When parents displayed a more covert conflict style, the youth were more likely to report internalizing behavior problems. In the researchers' words, "The results of our study confirm previous findings that hostile and sometimes violent ways of managing interparental disagreements place youth at risk for problem behaviors" (p. 130).

In another study of fifty-five Caucasian middle- and upper-middle-class five-year-olds (twenty-six girls and twenty-nine boys) and their married mothers, the mothers completed questionnaires on parent–child relations and interparental arguing that were mailed to them at home. Later, the mothers took their children to be observed in a university laboratory setting. The researchers found that marital discord was positively related both to children's externalizing and internalizing behavior problems. However, this research also showed that the interparental conflict influenced a child's behavior *indirectly:* Marital discord negatively affected parental discipline and the parent–child relationship more generally; this situation negatively affected the child's behavior. The researchers concluded that "if parents are able to maintain good relations with children in the face of marital conflict, the children may be buffered from the potential emotional fallout of the conflict" (Harrist and Ainslie 1998, p. 156; Buehler and Gerard 2002).

Generally, these two studies and others (Cummings, Goeke-Morey, Papp, and Dukewich 2002; Katz and Woodin 2002) show that choices about one's marital relations, conflicts, and conflict styles affect not only the spouses but their children as well. Whether children are better off in two-parent conflict-habituated households or in single-parent households is discussed in Chapter 16.

glossary of correct terms for lesbian and gay families. Give the library a list of books, videos and other resource materials. . . , and encourage school administrators and librarians to purchase these material for the school. (Brickley, Gelnaw, Marsh, and Ryan 1999)

In many cities there are workshops for lesbians wanting to get pregnant, for gays and lesbians who want to parent together, and for gay male parents. There are also discussion groups on raising children and choosing child care, along with play groups and organized events for children of gay parents. Then too, "Contrary to stereotypes of these families as isolated from families of origin, most reported that children had regular (i.e., at least monthly) contact with one or more grandparents, as well as with other adult friends and relatives of both genders" (Patterson 2000, p. 1062).

Grandparents as Parents

More than 3.6 million children under age eighteen are living in a grandparent's household. These grandchildren—and great-grandchildren—represent about 5 percent of all children under eighteen (Fields 2003, Table 3). Some experts predict that these figures will rise as changes in welfare laws, discussed earlier in this chapter, limit parents' welfare benefits. In accordance with "welfare reform," several states require single teen mothers to reside with their parents (the baby's grandparents) in order to receive government assistance (McDonald and Armstrong 2001):

> In the context of marital instability. . . , it is clear that grandparents and step-grandparents are becoming increasingly important family connections. . . . Two-fifths of divorced mothers move during the first year of the divorce. . . , and most of these move in with their parents while they make the transition to single parenting. (Bengston 2001, p. 7)

Individuals who have grandchildren living in their homes are not always primary parents; single mothers who also reside in the household usually assume the role of primary parent (Caputo 2001; and see Fields 2003, Table 3). Nevertheless, many grandparents do serve as the grandchild's principal parent. A grandparent's assuming the role of primary parent may often be

viewed as a family crisis; handling family crises creatively is addressed in Chapter 15. Abuse of alcohol and drugs, particularly crack, along with the rapid spread of AIDS—combined with teen pregnancy, abuse, neglect, abandonment, incarceration, and sometimes murder—account for more than 80 percent of grandparent families (Jendrick 1993; Holloway 1994; Toledo and Brown 1995, p. 13).

Using data from the 1998 National Longitudinal Survey of Youth, social scientist Richard Caputo concluded that, compared with other parents, grandparents who are raising their grandchildren tend to be "less educated, much younger at the time of the birth of their first child, and 2 to 4 times as likely to be female, single, black, poor and unemployed" (Caputo 2001, p. 541). About one-fifth of those who are raising grandchildren live below poverty level (Haskell 2003). However, contrary to stereotypes, a grandparent's (often a single grandmother's) assuming full-time responsibility for a grandchild's upbringing is limited neither to racial/ethnic minorities nor to inner-city settings (Toledo and Brown 1995; Rosenfeld 1997).

According to Sylvie de Toledo, a social worker whose nephew was raised by her mother after her sister's suicide and who founded a support group, Grandparents as Parents (GAP) as a result,

> Sometimes the call comes at night, sometimes on a bright morning. It may be your child, the police, or child protective services. "Mama, I've messed up . . ." "We're sorry. There has been an accident . . ." "Mrs. Smith, we have your grandchild. Can you take him?" Sometimes you make the call yourself—reporting your own child to the authorities in a desperate attempt to protect your grandchild from abuse or neglect. Often the change is gradual. At first your grandchild is with you for a day, then four days, a month, and then two months as the parents slowly lose control of their lives. You start out baby-sitting. You think the arrangement is temporary. You put off buying a crib or moving to a bigger apartment. Then you get a collect call from jail—or no call at all. (Toledo and Brown 1995, p. 9)

At other times the change is more sudden, as when a grandchild's parents are killed in an auto accident, for example.

Becoming a primary parent requires adjustment for grandparents. Their circle of friends may change or dwindle because no one else in the grandparent's peer group has children, and the grandparent is older than parents with children. And living with children in the house is an adjustment after years of not doing so. Moreover, a grandmother's work life may change. She may retire early, reduce her work hours, or try to negotiate more flexible ones. On the other hand, she may return to work to have money to raise the child. In either case, the grandparent's finances may suffer, although states offer some financial compensation to grandparents who are officially serving as foster parents. Realizing that "the social problems that led to the phenomenon of grandparents raising grandchildren are not likely to disappear in the near future," social service agencies across the country are initiating educational programs for grandparents acting as parents (Targ and Brintnall-Peterson 2001).

Foster Parents

Every state government has a department that monitors parents' treatment of their children. An example is California's Department of Child Protective Services. When state or county officials determine that a child is being abused or neglected, they can take temporary or permanent custody of the child and remove her or him from the parental home to be placed in **foster care**. Some foster care takes place in **group homes**, where several children are cared for around-the-clock by paid professionals who work in shifts and live elsewhere.

A significant portion of foster care is **family foster care**—foster care that takes place in a trained and licensed foster parent's home. The goal of family foster care is to provide "planned, time-limited, substitute family care for children who cannot be adequately cared for at home" (Baum, Crase, and Crase 2001, p. 202). Some specialized foster family homes are available for children with specific and complex emotional or medical needs (Ward 1998). Then too, a fairly new development in foster parenting, **formal kinship care**, is out-of-home placement with biological relatives of children who are in the custody of the state (Scannapieco, Hegar, and McAlpine 1997): "In California, almost half of the 100,000 foster placements are with relative caregivers, mostly grandparents" (Goodman and Silverstein 2001, p. 557).

It is estimated that between 500,000 and 700,000 U.S. children are in foster care (U.S. Department of Health and Human Services 1997). Largely due to the effects of parental drug abuse on the child before and/or after the child's birth, a disproportionately high percentage of children living below or near the poverty level are foster children (Barton 1999). Foster children have up to seven times more serious chronic health, emotional, developmental, and cognitive problems than poor children not in foster care (Baum, Crase, and Crase 2001). Foster parents may be married or single, are of all social classes, and may or may not be employed outside the home (Foster Care Project 1998). Among others, motivations for becoming a foster parent include religious reasons, wanting to help fill the community's need for foster homes, enjoying children and hoping to help them, providing a companion for one's only child or for oneself, and earning money. Some foster parents had childhood experiences with foster care: They were foster children themselves, or their own parents fostered children.

Some foster parents see fostering as a step toward adopting either the child they are fostering or a different child (Baum, Crase, and Crase 2001). While family reunification is the goal in foster parenting, many children—for the most part, the developmentally neediest—remain in foster care indefinitely, and some are available for adoption. (Adoption of children with special needs is addressed in Chapter 10.)

As wards of the court, foster children are financially supported by the state. Technically not salaried, foster parents are "reimbursed" in regular monthly stipends by the government. While there is a popular belief that foster families "do it just for the money," the reimbursement is not large and is even inadequate for many foster parents, who report spending significant amounts of their own money to get needed clothes, toys, and services for their foster children (Barton 1999). In the case of kinship foster care, relatives often need tangible items such as beds, food, and clothing as foster care begins. Ongoing needs include information regarding how the case is progressing through the child welfare agencies involved, day care, and counseling for the child (Davidson 1997).

There is a shortage of foster parents today (Baum, Crase, and Crase 2001). Furthermore, as many as 40 percent of foster parents stop fostering within their first year (Barbell 1996). There are several reasons for this. First, some foster parents report difficulties in dealing with the bureaucracy of the social services system. Second, even trained and licensed foster parents are not always equipped to handle the children's demanding needs, including health care (Barton 1999) and school-related problems (Noble 1997). Third, there is little distinction, or social respect, associated with being a foster parent (Rindfleisch 1999).

About 40 percent of foster children eventually go onto welfare rolls or into prison. (But more than half do not!) More than half (54 percent) finish high school, and about half (49 percent) are gainfully employed as adults (Toth 1997). We end this section with the words of Jo Ann Wentzel, senior editor of the magazine *Parenting Today's Teen* and foster mother to more than seventy-five children over the course of her career:

> I don't regret anything I've ever done for any of my [foster] kids. I do not for one minute believe I replaced their parents. When they left our house to return to their birth parents, they may have soon forgot me, but some of them never did. . . . Every once in a while, a kid will track me down and leave a cryptic message on my answering machine, which says, I know I was a pain-in-the-butt when I lived with you but I really learned a lot from you. . . . Or maybe they will tell me about their successes and claim it was because of something we did or said. They tell me they called because they wanted us to know they turned out good [sic] or because they respected our opinion on something. (Wentzel 2001, p. 2)

The next section explores relationships between parents and adult children.

■ Parents and Adult Children ■

Parents with Young Adult Children

Parenting does not end when a child reaches eighteen, twenty-one, or even twenty-five or older; children benefit from parents' emotional support and encouragement through their twenties and after (Ingersoll-Dayton, Neal, and Hammer 2001). One study that analyzed National Survey of Families and Households (NSFH) data (see Chapter 6) concluded that as adolescents make the transition to adult roles, parent–child relations grow closer, more supportive, and less conflicted (Aquilino 1997). Just listening and using other positive communication skills (described in Chapter 13) can help. (It also helps not to jump to conclusions.

A child who calls in desperation because his or her marriage is breaking up may *not* be asking to move home.) Parents can help to replenish self-confidence in frustrated children by reminding them of their past successes and commenting on the strength and skills they demonstrated (Haines and Neely 1987). A parent might say, for example, "I remember your persistence as you worked toward first chair in band." A grieving young adult will need to be informed that what she or he is feeling is normal.

At times, parents may choose to confront their adult children: "It sounds as if drinking is beginning to cause problems for you," or "It sounds as if you feel stuck in a job you don't like." Serious problems, such as dealing with an adult child's chronic depression or chemical addiction, require counseling and/or support groups designed for this purpose.

SHARING THE HOUSEHOLD More and more young adult children either do not leave the family home or return to it—after college, after divorce, or upon finding first jobs unsatisfactory. As noted in Chapter 1, 56 percent of men and 43 percent of women between ages eighteen and twenty-four live with their parents (Casper and Fields 2001). Unemployment and underemployment, along with a decline in affordable housing, make launching oneself into independent adulthood especially difficult today (Goldscheider 1997).

Parents who anticipated increased intimacy or personal freedom may be disappointed when the nest doesn't empty. When parents share their homes with adult children, the relationship is often characterized by ambivalence (Luscher 2002; Pillemer and Suitor 2002), but it will probably be enhanced if parents relinquish at least some parental authority and recognize that their children's attitudes and values may differ from their own (Miller and Glass 1989). However, relinquishing parental authority does *not* mean allowing absolutely any behavior to go on in the family home. For instance, parents who believe that premarital sex or alcohol or other drug usage is always unwarranted have the right to disallow it under their roof ("Not in Our House" 2001). The relationship will probably be more positive when the adult child is more responsible—older, in school, or employed (White and Rogers 1997). In general, parents should feel comfortable in setting reasonable household expectations. One way to do this is to negotiate a parent–adult child residence-sharing agreement.

PARENT–ADULT CHILD RESIDENCE-SHARING AGREEMENTS Some issues to address and negotiate are the following:

1. How much money will the adult child be expected to contribute to the household? When is it to be paid? Will there be penalties for late payment?

2. What benefits will the child receive? For example, will the family's laundry soap or anything in the refrigerator be at the child's disposal?

3. Who will have authority over utility usage? Who will decide, for instance, when the weather warrants turning on an air conditioner or where to set the thermostat?

4. What are the standards for cleanliness and orderliness? For instance, what precisely is the definition of "leaving the bathroom (or kitchen) in a mess"?

5. Who is responsible for cleaning what and when? What about yard work?

6. Who is responsible for cooking what and when? Will meals be at specified times? Will the adult child provide his or her own food?

7. How will laundry tasks be divided?

8. If the adult child owns a car, where will it be parked? Who will pay the property taxes and insurance?

9. What about noise levels? How loud may music be played and when? If the noise associated with an adult child's coming home late at night disturbs sleeping parents, how will this problem be solved?

10. What about guests? When are they welcome, with how much notice, and in what rooms of the house? Will the home be used for parties? (First, though, what *is* a party? Three guests? Six? Five hundred?)

11. What arrangement will be made for informing other household members if one will be unexpectedly late? (As an adult, the child should have a right to come and go as he or she pleases. But courtesy requires informing others in the household of the general time when one may be expected home. This avoids unnecessary phone calls to every hospital emergency room in the region.)

12. What about using the personal possessions of other members in the household? May a mother borrow her adult daughter's clothes without asking, for example?

13. If the adult child has returned home with children, who is responsible for their care? How often, when, and with how much notice will the grandparents babysit? Who in the household may discipline the children? How, when, and for what?

Although a residence-sharing agreement can help temporarily, the goal of the majority of parents is for their adult children to move on. Accomplishing this may be complicated by differing ideas on just what a parent owes an adult child. Our culture offers few guidelines about when parental responsibility ends or how to withdraw it.

Independent Adults and Their Parents

Relationships between parents and their children last a lifetime (Kaufman and Uhlenberg 1998). In discussing child raising throughout this chapter, we have taken the perspective of the older generation looking at the younger. But as parents, children, and their children grow older, things change.

Marriage, and then parenthood, redefine the relationship between parents and children. Typically, the parent–child tie moves from one of dependence to interdependence at this point (Cooney 1997, p. 458). For many mothers and daughters, motherhood for the daughter creates a closer bond than had existed in adolescence—perhaps ever—as these women, who may have very different views and styles, may now have something very important in common (Kutner 1990d).

Adults' relationships with their parents range from tight-knit, to intimate but distant, to nonintimate but sociable, to obligatory, to detached (Silverstein and Bengston 1997). In some families the reality of past abuse, a conflict-filled divorce, or simply fundamental differences in values or lifestyles make it seem unlikely that parents and children will spend time together (Kutner 1990a; Kaufman and Uhlenberg 1998). Money matters can also cause tension (Kutner 1990c). Meanwhile, an interesting qualitative study of adults who had moved at least 200 miles from their parents found that the majority were comfortable with the distance and/or with their relationships with their parents. Others yearned to be reunited. Most kept in touch by telephone (Climo 1992). And now, of course, e-mail is available.

Good parenting involves adequate economic resources, being involved with the child, using supportive communication, and having support from family and/or friends. There is evidence that using supportive parenting techniques is intergenerationally transmitted, or passed on from parent to adult child.

Toward Better Parent–Child Relationships

Studies generally show that good parenting involves at least four factors: (1) adequate economic resources; (2) being involved in a child's life and school; (3) using supportive, rather than negative, communication between partners (Jenkins 2000; Krishnakumar and Buehler 2000) and in the family more generally (Hofferth and Sandberg 2001); and (4) having support from family and/or friends (Scanzoni 2001). There is evidence that using supportive parenting techniques is intergenerationally transmitted, or passed on from parent to adult child (Zeng-Yin and Kaplan 2001).

Over the past thirty years, many, varied national organizations have emerged to help parents with the parent–child relationship (Matthews and Hudson 2001). One program is Thomas Gordon's Parent Effectiveness Training (PET), which applies the guidelines for no-win intimacy to the parent–child relationship (Gordon 2000). Another is Systematic Training for Effective Parenting (STEP). Both STEP and PET combine instruction on effective communication techniques with emotional support for parents. These programs are offered in many communities, and related books are also available. In addition to national organizations, countless local and community programs, as well as professional websites, have emerged that teach various facets of parent education, particularly to teen and low-income parents (Mertensmeyer and Fine 2000; Walker and Riley 2001) and also, most recently, for grandparents as parents (Landry-Meyer 1999). Some of these programs are especially designed by and intended for particular racial/ethnic groups (Kumpfer and Tait 2000).

Furthermore, parents need to be willing to seek professional help when their efforts seem to be unsuccessful. Problems are best addressed early in the child's life, when intervention or the changes parents make in response to advice will have the most effect (research evidence supports this truism [Brody 1991]). In addition to gaining self-acceptance and knowledge of good parenting techniques, parents can involve other members of their communities in child raising (Scanzoni 2001). "Pediatrics is politics," the late pediatrician Benjamin Spock once said (quoted in Maier 1998). He meant that good parenting makes for better communities—and more supportive communities make for better parents.

Then, too, parents can not only encourage more cooperation among friends and neighbors but also work together toward creating safer, more child-friendly neighborhoods (Furstenberg 2001a). For instance, parents might exchange homework help—"I'll help Johnny with math on Tuesday evenings if you'll help Mary with English"—and of course form car pools for children's lessons and activities. Such practical exchanges provide the occasion for children to form supportive relationships with other adults, who serve as para-parents or mentors (Bould 2003). Another source of support is the community itself: teachers, school counselors and principals, police officers, adolescents' employers, the library, the Internet, and the public in general (Warren and Cannan 1997; McCurdy and Daro 2001; Miller 2003).

In Sum

- The family ecology theoretical perspective reminds us that societywide conditions influence the relationship, and these factors can place extraordinary emotional and financial strains on parents.

- This chapter began by presenting some reasons why parenting and stepparenting can be difficult today. Some things noted are that work and parent roles often conflict.

- Although more fathers are involved in child care today, mothers are the primary parent in the vast majority of cases and continue to do the majority of day-to-day child care.

- Not only mothers' but fathers' roles can be difficult, especially in a society like ours, in which attitudes have changed so rapidly and in which there is no consensus about how to raise children and how mothers and fathers should parent.

- Middle-aged parents, especially mothers, may be sandwiched between dependent children on one hand and increasingly dependent, aging parents on the other.

- Child psychologists prefer the authoritative parenting style, although some scholars of color describe the authoritarian/laissez-faire/authoritative parenting style model as ethnocentric or Eurocentric.

- The need for supportive—and socially supported—parenting transcends social class and race or ethnicity. At the same time, we have seen that parenting differs in some important ways, according to economic resources, social class, and whether parent and child suffer discrimination due to religion, racial/ethnic status, or sexual orientation of the parents.

- Raising children while in poverty is a very different experience from parenting in wealthier social classes. Besides concerns for basic necessities, such as food, clothing, shelter, and health care, poverty-level parents may live in depressingly blighted neighborhoods.

- Three newly visible parenting environments involve gay/lesbian parents, grandparents as parents, and foster parents.

- To have better relationships with their children, parents need to recognize their own needs and to avoid feeling unnecessary guilt; to accept help from others (friends and the community at large as well as professional caregivers); and finally, to try to build and maintain flexible, intimate relationships using the techniques suggested in this chapter, along with those suggested in Chapter 13.

Key Terms

authoritarian parenting style	laissez-faire parenting style
authoritative parenting style	para-parent
Confucian training doctrine	parenting style
family foster care	primary parents
formal kinship care	sandwich generation
foster care	shared parenting
grandparent families	Temporary Assistance for Needy Families (TANF)
group home	transition to parenthood
hierarchical parenting	

Questions for Review and Reflection

1. Describe reasons why parenting can be difficult today. Can you think of others besides those presented in this chapter?

2. Compare these three parenting styles: authoritarian, authoritative, and laissez-faire. What are some empirical outcomes of each? Which one is recommended by most experts? Why?

3. How does parenting differ according to social class? Use the family ecology theoretical perspective to explain some of these differences.

4. What unique challenges do African American, Native American, Hispanic, and/or Asian American parents face today, regardless of their social class? How would *you* prepare an immigrant child or a child of color to face possible discrimination?

5. Policy Question. Choose one of the three newly visible parenting environments discussed in this chapter (i.e., lesbian/gay male families, grandparents as parents, or foster parents) and describe some social policies that could benefit the children in these families.

Suggested Readings

Brooks, Robert, and Sam Goldstein. 2001. *Raising Resilient Children: Fostering Strength, Hope, and Optimism in Your Child.* New York: Contemporary. Written for parents, this book is encouraging and informative, with topics such as how to change the negative ways you might speak to your child and loving and disciplining your children in ways that help them feel appreciated.

Ginott, Haim G., Alice Ginott, and H. Wallace Goddard. 2003. *Between Parent and Child: The Bestselling Classic that Revolutionized Parent-Child Communication.* New York: Three Rivers Press. Originally published in 1965, renowned psychologist Dr. Haim Ginott's true classic did indeed revolutionize parent-child communication. Now revised and updated, this book is worth reading, now more than ever.

Gordon, Thomas. 2000. *Parent Effectiveness Training: The Program for Raising Responsible Children.* New York: Three Rivers Press. Another highly praised and respected classic by a well-known and respected licensed psychologist. Introduces and explains, with concrete examples, the methods of PET (Parent Effectiveness Training).

Hewlett, Sylvia Ann, and Cornell West. 1998. *The War Against Parents: What We Can Do for America's Beleaguered Moms and Dads.* Boston: Houghton Mifflin. Overview of economic, cultural, and public policy issues related to parenting. Addresses and evaluates both liberal and conservative perspectives on the family.

Kozol, Jonathan. 2000. *Ordinary Resurrections: Children in the Years of Hope.* New York: Crown. Description of children's everyday lives in poverty; a call to social action that would address this situation, but with focus on individual parents and parent figures whose dedication lessens the negative effects of poverty on children.

Parenting Resources for the Twenty-first Century
http://www.parentingresources.ncjrs.org

Website maintained by the National Criminal Justice Reference Service (NCJRS) that links parents with information on a wide spectrum of parenting/child-care issues.

Statistics on Children
http//www.childstats.gov/

Federal government website with a wealth of statistics on U.S. children from various national surveys, such as the National Assessment of Educational Progress, and from federal agencies such as the U.S. Census Bureau.

Virtual Society: The Wadsworth Sociology Resource Center

 Go to the Sociology Resource Center at **http://sociology.wadsworth.com** for a wealth of online resources, including a companion website for your text that provides study aids such as self-quizzes for each chapter and a practice final exam, as well as links to sociology websites and information on the latest theories and discoveries in the field. In addition, you will find further suggested readings, flash cards, MicroCase online exercises, and appendices on a range of subjects.

Online Study Tool

Marriage & Family ⊛ Now™ Go to **http://sociology .wadsworth.com** to reach the companion website for your text and use the Marriage&FamilyNow access code that came with your book to access this study tool. Take a practice pretest after you have read each chapter, and then use the study plan provided to master that chapter. Afterward, take a posttest to monitor your progress.

Search Online with InfoTrac College Edition

For additional information, exercises, and key words to aid your research, explore InfoTrac College Edition, your online library that offers full-length articles from thousands of scholarly and popular publications. Click on *InfoTrac College Edition* under *Chapter Resources* at the companion website and use the access code that came with your book.

- Search keywords: *authoritative parenting, foster parents, child development.*

Work *and* Family

She picks a field to purchase; out of her earnings she plants a vineyard. . . . She fears not the snow for her household; all her charges are doubly clothed. . . . Her children rise up and praise her; her husband too, extols her.

Proverbs

PROVIDING AND CARING FOR ALL FAMILY household members, including dependents and the elderly, is integral to our definition of families (and to the functional theoretical perspective on families; see Chapter 3). Until recently, historically speaking, cooperative labor for survival was the dominant purpose of marriage. And it took place within the household. The woman described above is the "ideal wife" of preindustrial times, for women as well as men engaged in economically productive labor not limited to the personal care of family members.

"Where do you work?" is a new question in human history. Only since the Industrial Revolution has working been considered separate from family living, and only since then have the concepts "employed" and "unemployed" emerged. With the Industrial Revolution, economic production moved outside the household to factories, shops, and offices. For those who remained in the home (usually wives and mothers), working in the public sphere was beyond their experience and took on an aura of mystery. To those who labored outside the home and earned money (mainly husbands), partners who stayed at home seemed unproductive; they were not "employed." "His" work was in the public sphere, for money; "her" work was in the private sphere of the household, for free. Spouses' work roles were quite distinct.

Today, although occupational segregation and sex discrimination in employment persist, the trend is away from distinguishing work based on sex. A majority of married women work outside the home. Many chapters in this book discuss social change and how it affects people's attitudes and family life. This chapter looks at one aspect of modern living that is profoundly affecting marriages and families: the movement of women into the labor force. We'll explore traditional employment patterns that have characterized our soci-

ety until recently, then look at newer patterns and the interrelationship of work and family roles for both women and men. We'll see that the trend toward women's working outside the home offers new options for families. And with new options come new responsibilities for making knowledgeable decisions. To begin, we will examine the concept of "labor force" as a social invention.

The Labor Force— A Social Invention

Although human beings have always worked, it was not until the industrialization of the workplace in the nineteenth century that people characteristically became wage earners, hiring out their labor to someone else and joining a **labor force**. The labor force, then, is a social invention.

The Labor Force in Postindustrial Society

Gradually throughout the twentieth century, our society has moved from an industrial one that manufactured products to a postindustrial one that transmits information and offers other services. Eighty percent of America's jobs are now in the service sector (Leonhardt 2001). While some of these jobs are very good ones, many of the jobs created by the service economy pay less than did industrial work. Many are part time and offer no employee benefits such as contributions to retirement or health care (Taylor 1997b; Booth, Crouter, and Shanahan 1999). Although other factors are involved as well, American workers' earnings for all but the college-educated have declined or stagnated since 1973. One way that families have adapted to this decline is for both wives and husbands to be employed (White and Rogers 2000).

However, employees are increasingly aware that they are replaceable, if not dispensable. Partly in order to compete with foreign markets and partly to maintain corporate profits in an uncertain economy, employers have reduced costs by streamlining operations. One way they have done that has been to let some workers go. By the 1990s, job security had become an issue even for highly educated managerial employees. "Downsizing" (job cuts) continued even in the rebounding economy of the late 1990s (Uchitelle 1998b; Ryan 1999).

Many Americans find their positions or careers challenging and satisfying, not only in the professions or the corporate world but in manufacturing and related economic sectors as well. Some jobs that were formerly manual or craft jobs in manufacturing or construction design have been computerized in a way that makes them more mentally challenging and less physically demanding (Gans 1996). But a significant (and growing) proportion of workers have difficulty finding personal satisfaction or security in their jobs. This is not only true at lower occupational levels, but also in the professions such as medicine (because the opportunity for independent decision making is receding); nursing (where short staffing places pressure on floor nurses); and law and on Wall Street (where the "best" jobs require a sixty- to eighty-hour workweek and "part time" is a forty-hour workweek) (Abelson 1998; Ryan 1999).

Moreover, especially in single-parent families and for couples where both partners are employed and have dependents, the separation of work from family living creates role conflict and tension. Increasingly, stressed and overloaded workers juggle what have become conflicting obligations: *providing for* and *caring for* family members.

It is in this context that we explore the relationship between work and family. We will look first at what has been the traditional work model in industrialized society.

The Traditional Model: Provider Husbands and Homemaking Wives

Until fairly recently, a husband has been not only culturally, but legally, expected to be his family's principal breadwinner. Wives were culturally and legally bound to husband care, house care, and child care (Weitzman 1981; Coltrane 1996; Hays 1996).

Men and the Provider Role

What sociologist Jessie Bernard terms the **good provider role** for men emerged in this country during the 1830s. Before then, a man was expected to be "a good steady worker," but "the idea that he was the provider would hardly ring true" (Bernard 1986, p. 126). The good provider role lasted into the late 1970s. Its

end, again according to Bernard, was officially marked when, in the 1980 U.S. census, a male was no longer automatically assumed to be head of the household. Indeed, the proportion of married-couple families in which men are the sole breadwinner has declined from 42 percent in 1960 to 20 percent in 2000 (Wilkie 1991; U.S. Bureau of Labor Statistics 2004a).

Although the role of family wage earner is no longer reserved for husbands, many Americans still believe that the man should be the principal provider for his family (Crowley 1998). Sociologist Jane Hood (1986) identified three provider role systems in dual-worker marriages. They vary according to the couples' attitudes toward husbands' and wives' responsibilities. Some working couples see their roles in terms of a main provider/secondary provider division. For the **main/secondary provider couple**, providing is the man's responsibility; the home is the woman's. Whatever wages her employment brings in are nice, but extra. In the two other models, the wife's income is essential to the couple's finances. In a **co-provider couple**, both partners are seen as equally responsible for providing. In the **ambivalent provider couple**, the wife's providing responsibilities are not clearly acknowledged (Johnson et al. 1992). To these provider role systems we would add the **role-reversed provider couple**, in which the husband is mainly responsible for homemaking and child care while the wife is the principal breadwinner.

We have no national data on the relative numbers of each of these types, but a random sample study done in Maine found that about 15 percent of all two-earner unions are co-provider couples (Potuchek 1997). Government data indicate that 7 percent of married-couple families are role-reversed so far as *employment* is concerned, with the wife but not the husband employed (U.S. Bureau of Labor Statistics 2004a, Table 2). Looking at the relative earnings of employed couples, the BLS estimates that 20 percent to 25 percent of married couples are role-reversed, with the wife the primary earner and husband a secondary earner (Winkler 1998).

Overall, whether single or married, parent or not, men work more hours than women and are more likely (87 percent) to work full time than women (72 percent) (U.S. Bureau of Labor Statistics 2003c, Table 1; 2004b). Men continue to be primary breadwinners in the majority of couples, and most men identify with this role (Coltrane 2000).

© 1992. Carnegie Museum of Art, Pittsburgh

Robert Gwathmey, American, 1903–1988. *Hoeing,* **oil on canvas.**

[S]ocietal notions of the meaning of work for men and women are still quite distinctive. Both men and women may view working as a choice for women, even when the woman has no real alternative to being employed. In contrast, there is a strong societal imperative for men to be employed outside the home, and those who choose not to do so are viewed skeptically. (Taylor, Tucker, and Mitchell-Kernan 1999, p. 356)

Traditional attitudes toward the provider role are more characteristic of African Americans than whites, which may reflect the role's greater precariousness in a context of limited opportunities for many Hispanic and nonwhite men. Minority women (or others), who typically have greater labor force attachment, may define themselves as "helpers" in order to respect spouses' pride (Taylor et al. 1999, pp. 356–357). In terms of our typology, they are ambivalent providers.

REWARDS AND COSTS The good provider role entailed both rewards and costs for men. The husband exchanged breadwinning for the wife's homemaking skills and child rearing, and more general care and emotional support. Rewards of the provider role also included social status outside the family and greater authority in the family.

A serious cost was that the good provider role encouraged a man to put all of his "gender-identifying eggs into one psychic basket"; that is, "Men were judged as men by the level of living they provided" (Bernard 1986, p. 130). Failure, or even mediocre performance in the role, meant one had failed as a *man* (Bernard 1986; Crowley 1998). In fact, men's success—as measured in terms of employment and higher earnings—still seems to be important in "facilitating marriage and enhancing marital stability" (Bianchi and Casper 2000, p. 31).

It is difficult to live up to societal expectations that may not mesh with the reality of economic opportunities. This situation is especially applicable to blue-collar and racial/ethnic minority husbands in the late twentieth- and early twenty-first-century economy (Gerson 1993; Grimm-Thomas and Perry-Jenkins 1994).

Meanwhile, social scientist Joseph Pleck has argued that "the most obvious and direct effect" of the male's breadwinning role is "the restricting effect of the male occupational role on men's family role" (1977, p. 420; Coltrane 1996). Husbands who want to share household work and child care will not find it easy to do so while continuing as the primary breadwinner. "Society hasn't lowered its level of job performance, but it has raised its expectations of our roles in our children's lives," said a Los Angeles lawyer and father (Gregg 1986, p. 48; Berry and Rao 1997). For this reason, partners who want to create new options for themselves need to work for changes in the public and corporate spheres, an option explored later in this chapter.

MEN AND THE PROVIDER ROLE TODAY Some husbands today are rejecting the idea that dedication to one's job or occupational achievement is the ultimate indicator of success (Booth and Crouter 1998). Some are choosing less competitive careers and are spending more time with their families. Four-fifths of men aged twenty through thirty-nine who were interviewed in 2000 rated a work schedule that would give them more family time as a more desirable job quality than challenging work or high income. Seventy percent of these younger men said they would exchange money for time with their families—compared to 26 percent of men over sixty-five. This suggests an important generational change and one that may be owing to the fact that a substantial majority of the younger men (70 percent) had working mothers (Grimsley 2000).

Meanwhile, there is an effort on the part of some social scientists (e.g., Christiansen and Palkovitz 2001) to change the *meaning* of the standard male provider role so that it is seen to be as much a form of family work and fathering as "hands-on" parenting. They argue that providing should be conceptualized as a form of parental involvement, which not only brings resources to the family but also models a work ethic: "[v]aluing what fathers provide may give fathers an emotional base that will allow them to be involved in other ways with their families" (p. 102).

Men with children work increased hours compared to childless men, on average. Still, it appears that there are two distinct models for the father role as regards providing. Some fathers (*good providers*) work *more* hours than childless men, while others (*involved*

fathers) work *fewer* hours. A man's ideological commitment to one or the other role makes a difference. And "it seems clear that a shift away from the provider role and toward the involved father role [has occurred] in recent years" (Kaufman and Uhlenberg 2000, p. 934). Thus, some fathers try to decrease the demands of the workplace in order to participate more at home.

HOUSEHUSBANDS Although they are a small minority, some men have relinquished breadwinning to become **househusbands**: men who stay home to care for the house and family while their wives work. About 5 percent of fathers are stay-at-home dads (U.S. Bureau of Labor Statistics 2004a, Table 4). Although few men make this choice, some 24 percent of men polled in 2000 said they would prefer to stay home and take care of the house and family (Saad 2001b).

Men may relinquish employment as a positive choice: the desire to spend more time with their children. Or, they may not be employed because of poor health or disability, or their loss of a job may have developed into long-term unemployment. Men may be dissatisfied with the competitive grind or the nature of their work, and find themselves in a situation—a working wife who earns enough to support the family or an early retirement package—that permits them to seek new options (Hagenbaugh 2002; Shellenbarger 2002; Tyre and McGinn 2003). Some couples may size up the situation and recognize that the woman is more desirous of pursuing a career, or has a higher-earning career, and/or is more successful than the man, and they can decide as a couple to reverse roles. For a variety of reasons, including the demise of secure employment at all economic levels, labor force participation rates have fallen for men (Krueger 2004).

As it happens, gay male couples with children often (26 percent) include a stay-at-home parent: "To some gay men, the idea of entrusting the care of a hard-won child to someone else seems to defeat the purpose of parenthood" (Bellafante 2004). These couples will, of course, have a male earner, and that points to the fact that the options for men who would like to give more time to families are limited by the simple fact that in our society men typically earn more than women do. Consequently, whatever their preferences, many heterosexual couples find themselves needing to encourage the man's dedication to his job or career in the interests of the family's overall financial well-being (Casper and O'Connell 1998).

While fathers who are primary parents express more sense of isolation than stay-at-home mothers and may experience the loss of a career-based identity, being a househusband is not the lonely choice it once was. Local groups, national organizations, and Internet chat rooms bring househusbands together, and mothers at home are more welcoming of their male counterparts than they used to be. As with many aspects of family life, choice is the key to a man's satisfaction with the househusband role, as is mutual understanding by the couple about the specifics of their division of labor (Eveld 2003; Marin 2000; Shellenbarger 2002; Spragins 2002). Chapter 11 further explores stay-at-home fathers.

The next section examines wives' traditional work role.

Doris Lee, American, 1905–1983. *Thanksgiving,* **1935. Oil on canvas.**

© The Art Institute of Chicago

Women as Full-Time Homemakers

Historically, the homemaker, or housewife—the married woman who remains in the home to do housework and rear children—is a modern role. Before industrialization, women produced goods and income by working on the family farm and later by taking in boarders or providing baking or laundry services. As the Industrial Revolution removed even those economic activities from the household, women could less easily combine work in the economy with the care of children and home. At the same time, the increase in real income produced by the Industrial Revolution made it possible for many wives to devote their time solely to housekeeping and child care. The era of the housewife extended from the latter half of the nineteenth century until World War II. As late as 1940, only a small minority (14 percent) of married women were in the labor force (Thornton and Freedman 1983, p. 24).

Of course, not all married women were housewives. In the early twentieth century:

> observers noted that millions of immigrant and minority mothers, and mothers in the lower working class were employed. Their inability to adopt the middle class ideal of stay-at-home mothering and breadwinner fathering was understandable, particularly in light of the economic marginality of lower class husbands. . . . It was not until American middle-class, mostly White, mothers entered the work force en masse [after World War II] that many researchers

turned attention to the issue of working mothers, however. (Edwards 2001, p. 183)

In 2002, 60 percent of married women were in the labor force (U.S. Census Bureau 2003a, Table 589). Women who head single-parent households are even more likely to work outside the home; 72 percent were in the labor force in 2003 (U.S. Bureau of Labor Statistics 2004a). Figure 12.1 shows the overall participation of women in the labor force from 1900 through 2002. Although the trend has been for wives to join the labor force, nevertheless, about one-third of married women with children are full-time homemakers (U.S. Bureau of Labor Statistics 2004a).

THE ECONOMIC BENEFITS AND STATUS OF HOMEMAKING The economic benefits of a full-time homemaker to her family have been evaluated in many ways.[1] Considering motherhood and housewifery to be "a skilled mid-level management job," sociologist Ann Crittenden finds $60,000 to be a "sensible estimate" of a housewife's economic worth (Lobb 2002).

Even these calculations ignore important economic benefits to society provided by homemakers. For example, older wives often provide nursing services for their husbands or other relatives. But work

---

1. Economists have interested themselves in this issue, often as a service to insurance companies or personal-injury trial attorneys who want to establish the projected value of the loss of services of a disabled or deceased homemaker.

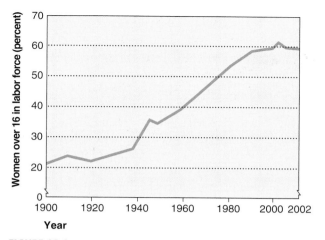

FIGURE 12.1

The participation of women over age sixteen in the labor force, 1900–2002.

Sources: Thornton and Freedman 1983; U.S. Census Bureau 1998, Table 645; 2000, Table 644; 2003a, Table 589; "Record Number of Women" 2001 (Population Reference Bureau/AmeriStat).

that is directly productive (and paid for) is more highly valued and rewarded in most industrialized societies. Therefore, it is not surprising to find that the job of homemaker has ambiguous status and low economic rewards.

Since homemaking is not formal employment, no financial compensation is associated with this position. A wife, even one who participates in her husband's career,[2] has an uncertain claim to the resulting economic rewards—during the marriage, after divorce, or after the husband's death. Her Social Security benefit based on her husband's earnings record will be half the amount that he receives. Even a wife currently working may not establish an adequate Social Security record due to years out of the labor force or in part-time work while engaged in childbearing and child rearing.

---

2. Among some business, professional, and political families, wives are expected to help their husbands professionally by cultivating appropriate acquaintances and by being charming hostesses and companions. Wives in two-person single careers typically do volunteer work in the arts and for charitable organizations; they may also provide their husbands with career support services such as word-processing, bookkeeping, researching, and writing. These wives are part of a **two-person single career**; their contributions advance their husbands' careers and benefit their spouses' employers. The wife of the eminent founder of sociology in France, Emile Durkheim, did editorial work on his journal *Année Sociologique,* as well as taking complete charge of household and children (Lamanna 2002).

Steps could be taken to address this inequity. Changes in the Social Security system favorable to homemakers have been proposed, but not enacted. Other changes regarding inheritance and property rights are gradually moving the law toward an economic partnership concept of matrimony (Weitzman 1985). Marital dissolution laws generally provide for "equity" in the distribution of marital property and now include pensions in that marital property (Buehler 1995, p. 106; see Chapter 16 for more detail on the economic outcomes of divorce).

HOMEMAKERS BY CHOICE An essential feature of the housewife role is constant availability to meet others' needs. Housewives report a lower sense of being in control of their lives than do employed women (Bird and Ross 1993). In fact, the more time that is spent in housework, the more depressive symptoms appear in both men and women (Glass and Fujimoto 1994). A survey of nearly 18,000 readers of *Parents* magazine found 62 percent of full-time mothers answering that their biggest stress was not having enough time with other adults or feeling that their role is not valued by society (Louv 1996).

But clearly, a significant proportion of homemakers enjoy their work (Glass 1992). And a number of employed women would rather be full-time homemakers but do not have this option because of financial constraints. In a Gallup poll of adult women in 2001, 53 percent said they preferred to work outside the home, while 45 percent said they would rather stay home and take care of house and family. Among women presently employed, only 59 percent said they would continue if they had a choice (Saad 2001b). The critical difference between full-time homemakers who enjoy their work and those who don't is choice (Klein et al. 1998). Satisfied homemakers are women who are exercising their preference to work in the home.

As full-time homemaking has become a minority pattern rather than the taken-for-granted role of adult women, reasons for this preference are more consciously thought through. One small study of housewives elicited two major themes. These mothers, college-educated women who had been employed prior to parenting, wished to stay deeply involved in their children's daily lives and did not anticipate that this would change as the children grew older. They had also assessed their situations and were pessimistic about the chances of getting their husbands to share

One key to finding satisfaction in a full-time homemaker role is choice. Women who choose to work as homemakers and who do not face economic constraints are often comfortable with and enjoy their role.

housework and child care if they went to work. Staying at home is one response to our society's pervasive lack of support for working mothers. And although these women exhibited considerable confidence about their ability to reenter the labor market successfully, they saw paid employment as unsatisfying, preferring to pursue other activities, such as arts and crafts, as a supplement to domesticity (Milner 1990).

Some contemporary housewives consider the housewife role a stage in the life course (Uchitelle 2002), and we'll say more about that later in this chapter. We turn now to an examination of women's place in the labor force.

▪ Women in the Labor Force ▪

As Figure 12.1 shows, women's participation in the labor force has increased greatly since the beginning of the nineteenth century. Industrialization gave rise to bureaucratic corporations, which depended heavily on paperwork. Clerical workers were needed, and not enough men were available. Some industries, such as textiles, sought workers with a dexterity thought to be possessed by women. The expanding economy needed more workers, and women were drawn into the labor force in significant numbers beginning around 1890.

This trend accelerated during World War I and the Great Depression, then slowed following World War II. As soldiers came home to jobs, the government encouraged women to return to their kitchens. Despite cultural pressures against employment of women, however, the number of wage-earning women rose again. Beginning in about 1960, the number of employed women began to increase rapidly. As the 1970s brought a decline or stagnation of men's earnings and economic uncertainty spread to sectors that had been doing relatively well, more families turned to a second earner. Material expectations for quality of life increased as well, with larger homes and more consumer goods becoming the norm, along with college education for the kids. Also, the growth in the divorce rate left women uncertain about the wisdom of remaining out of the labor force and hence dependent on a husband's earnings. By 1979, a majority of married women were employed outside the home (see Figure 12.2). Economic uncertainty and the economic squeeze on even middle-class families have continued to fuel the entry of women into the labor force (Edwards 2001).

Throughout most of this period, the largest group of wage-earning women was young (aged twenty through twenty-four), and relatively few women worked during child-rearing years. The picture has changed in the decades since 1950. While many mothers remained at home while children were small, Figure 12.2 shows that by 1970, half of wives with children between ages six and seventeen earned wages, and that figure increased to 77 percent in 2002.[3]

---

3. The fact that this figure surpasses the number of married working women with no children younger than eighteen reflects the older age of that group and a generational difference from younger women in both employability and attitudes about being employed.

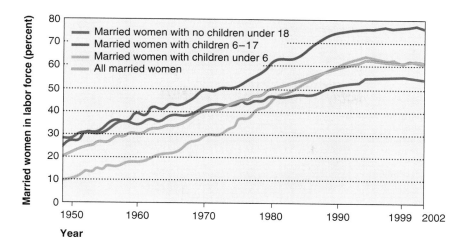

FIGURE 12.2

Participation in the labor force on the part of married women, 1948–2002.

Sources: Thornton and Freedman 1983; U.S. Census Bureau 1998, Table 655; 2000, Tables 653 and 654; 2003a, Tables 575, 595, and 597.

Mothers of young children were the last women to move into employment outside the home. They have been entering the labor force in increasing numbers; as Figure 12.2 illustrates, more than 60 percent of wives with children under age six in 2003 were paid employees. In fact, in 2002, 55 percent of married mothers of children under age one had joined the labor force; this compares to 31 percent of mothers of infants in the labor force in 1976, the year this statistic was first compiled (Downs 2003; O'Connell 2001).

As women moved into the labor force, they fueled a revival of a feminist movement that had been dormant for many years. Jobs and careers for women—at least as an option—came to be seen as desirable in themselves. While these labor force trends are generally true for all women, the *rate* of increase has been greater for white women than black women, who historically had been more likely to work for wages. Now, white women—with a labor force participation rate of 60 percent—are catching up to black women (at 62 percent). Because they are the largest population segment, it was "the growing employment of [white married] mothers of preschoolers [that] especially marked the demise of the male-breadwinner system, in which those previously most likely to depend on a husband's income, no longer did so" (Edwards 2001, p. 183). The labor force participation rate of Latinas has traditionally been lower than non-Hispanic white women's, but their labor force participation rate rose from 47 percent in 1980 to 58 percent in 2002 (U.S. Census Bureau 2003a, Table 588).

Women's Market Work

The pronounced tendency for men and women to be employed in different types of jobs is termed **occupational segregation**. Although more and more women are working, many of them earn low wages. Figure 12.3 depicts the major occupational categories of employed women for 2002. The situation has improved since 1980, when two-thirds of employed women were clerical workers, saleswomen, or service personnel, and only 7 percent were managers (Hacker 1983). But female workers remain concentrated in low-paying occupations. As you can see in Figure 12.3, 40 percent of all employed women are clerical or service workers. Only 15 percent of employed women are in executive, managerial, or administrative positions, and 19 percent are in professional work (U.S. Census Bureau 2003a, Table 615). Asian American (41 percent) and white women (39 percent) are most likely to hold managerial or professional jobs, while Native American and African American (30 percent) and Hispanic (23 percent) women are less likely to ("Women Still Lag" 2004).

Jobs typically held by men and women differ within major occupational categories, with men more

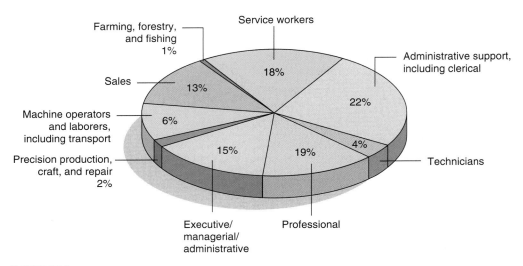

FIGURE 12.3

The jobs women hold, 2002. The percentages in each sector of the pie chart tell us the kinds of jobs that are held by women. For example, 19 percent of women have professional employment, while 18 percent are in service occupations.

Source: Based on data from the U.S. Census Bureau 2003a, Table 615.

likely to hold the upper-level jobs within each sector (Weinberg 2004). Even though women constituted 55 percent of all professionals in 2002, they occupied the lowest-paying ranks. For example, 75 percent of teachers were female, while 43 percent of college professors were women. More than 90 percent of RNs (nurses) are women; 52 percent of pharmacists; and 31 percent of physicians (U.S. Census Bureau 2003a, Tables 295, 615). As managers, women tend to be in staff rather than line positions—that is, in human resources or communications departments rather than in the operating divisions from which senior management is usually chosen ("Middle Ranks" 1999).

Women-dominated professions tend to be service or support professions, often related to women's traditional home or clerical work: health care, teaching, social work, library work, and recreation. In medicine, women tend to be in pediatrics, anesthesiology, and psychiatry. In academia, women are more apt to occupy the especially low-paid, part-time positions (Roos and Jones 1993).

The Wage Gap

Differences in earnings persist in comparisons of employed women and men. In virtually all occupations, women earn less than men ("hazardous material removal worker" is one of the exceptions [Weinberg 2004, Table 7]). Women who worked full time in 2003 earned seventy-seven cents for every dollar earned by men (DeNavas-Walt, Proctor, and Mills 2004). The **wage gap** (the difference in earnings between men and women) varies by race and ethnicity. In groups where men typically have lower wages, women's earnings compared to men's are relatively higher. Hispanic women's wages were 87 percent of Hispanic men's, while African American women earned 84 percent of what African American men did in 2002 (U.S. Bureau of Labor Statistics 2004c). As Figure 12.4 shows, the wage gap has closed over the years since 1960, but it remains substantial.

The wage gap varies considerably depending on occupation, and tends to be greater in the more elite, higher-paying occupations. For example, the median earnings of women physicians are $88,000, while male physicians' median earnings are $140,000 (Weinberg 2004).

Whether the wage gap is due to discrimination or represents "the personal choices of some men and many women who want or need a job that fits their family obligations" is disputed (Boraas and Rodgers 2003, p. 14). Do women's family responsibilities lower

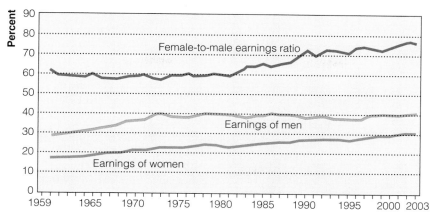

FIGURE 12.4

Female-to-male earnings ratio and median earnings of full-time, year-round workers fifteen years old and over by sex: 1960–2003. Women's earnings compared to men's have increased since 1980, but have not reached parity. Their relative earnings declined in 2003 for the first time in four years.

Source: DeNavas-Walt, Proctor, and Mills 2004, Figure 2.

their career achievement, and if so, is the pay gap a result of personal choice?

The concept of **motherhood penalty** describes the fact that motherhood has a tremendous negative lifetime impact on earnings. One study found that childless women earn 90 percent of what males with comparable education earn (Waldfogel 1997, 1998). Other research has found that the motherhood penalty increases with the number of children. Furthermore, the motherhood penalty has not declined over time despite women's increasing education, attachment to the labor force, and, presumably, less discrimination and more opportunities open to women to advance their careers (Budig and England 2001; Avellar and Smock 2003).

Another study, conducted by the U.S. General Accounting Office (a study conducted by the U.S. General Accounting Office (2003), based on data from the Panel Study of Income Dynamics for workers for the years 1983–2000) did find that work patterns accounted for much of the difference between the earnings of women and men. Women had fewer years of work experience, worked fewer hours per year, were less likely to work full time, and left the labor force for longer periods than men. Work productivity may be affected by a mother's sense of constant responsibility for children. One mother says that no matter what she is doing

at work, "I'm thinking, 'Is Colin going to eat lunch?' 'Is Kara going out on the playground and does she have the right coat?'" (interview in Orenstein 1998, p. 48). Mothers may be tired, worried, distracted, or saving up energy for the home front (Budig and England 2001).

But 20 percent of the difference between men's and women's earnings was left unexplained when these and other relevant variables (industry, specific occupation, race, marital status, and job tenure) were taken into account. Left open is whether the difference is due to discrimination or to unknown other factors. The researchers concluded that "It is difficult to evaluate this remaining portion. . . . [A]n earnings difference that results from individuals' decisions about how to manage work and family responsibilities may not necessarily indicate a problem unless these decisions are not freely made. On the other hand, an earnings difference may result from discrimination in the workplace or subtler discrimination about what types of career or job choices women can make" (U.S. General Accounting Office 2003, p. 3).

Many women do *perceive* themselves to be discriminated against in employment. Two-thirds surveyed by the Gallup poll do not think women have the same job opportunities as men (Saad 2001b).

The relative share of child care and domestic work carried by men and women (to be discussed later in

Women in blue-collar jobs are still a minority, although more women *are* entering these jobs— and they tend to pay better than traditional women's jobs in service or clerical work.

this chapter) plays a role as well. "Until men take on close to an equal role at home, the pattern will be difficult to break," comments economist Anne Preston, author of yet another study finding a motherhood penalty (in Kleiman 2003, p. D-1). She concludes from her study of men and women with science degrees that employers perceive women to be less committed to the job, anticipating that they will be spending more time than men on child-care responsibilities. Women are then given "low commitment, low salary jobs," while men get the better ones. Preston urges that the wage gap be addressed by encouraging men to take on a greater share of child care. "Once men start taking over these activities in large numbers, the workplace norms of commitment will change, or at least will be applied more equitably" (Preston 2003, p. 39).

Researchers Budig and England point out that society as a whole benefits from mothers' work:

> Good parenting . . . increases the likelihood that a child will grow up to be a caring, well-behaved, and productive adult. This lowers crime rates, increases the level of care for the next generation, and contributes to economic productivity. Most of those who benefit—the future employers, neighbors, spouses, friends, and children of

the person who has been well-reared—pay nothing to the parent. Thus, mothers pay a price in lowered wages for doing childrearing, while most of the rest of us are "free riders" on their labor. (2001, p. 205)

The future is difficult to predict. On the one hand, women's increased entry into professional and managerial tracks suggests a more substantial future presence in those jobs. Yet the difficulty of combining work and family responsibilities, a burden that most often falls unevenly on women, still seems to present a formidable barrier to equal occupational status and income.

Two-Earner Marriages— Work/Family Options

As recently as 1968, there were equal proportions of dual-earner and provider–housewife couples: 45 percent of each (Hayghe 1982). Today, **two-earner marriages**, in which both partners are in the labor force, are the statistical norm among married couples (U.S. Bureau of Labor Statistics 2003a). An employed wife contributes a significant amount to her family's income, and a growing number earn more than their husbands do (AmeriStat 2003d). Still, because of the differential between women's and men's jobs and pay, employed wives contribute on the average only about 35 percent of the family income (Table 750; Winkler 1998).

Even though we may tend to think of two-earner couples as ones in which both partners are employed nine to five, spouses display considerable flexibility in how they design their two-earner unions. (Single-parent-headed households, of course, have more constraints on their choices.) In this section we examine the various ways in which couples choose to structure their work commitments and family life: the two-career marriage, part-time employment, shift work, working at home, and temporarily leaving the labor force.

Two-Career Marriages

Careers differ from *jobs* in that they hold the promise of advancement, are considered important in themselves— not just a source of money—and demand a high degree of commitment. Career men and women work in occupations that usually require education beyond the bachelor's degree, such as medicine, law, academia, financial services, and corporation management.[4]

The vast majority of two-earner marriages would not be classified as *dual career* because the wife's or the husband's employment does not have the features of a *career*. Nevertheless, the dual-career couple is a powerful image. Most of today's college students view the **two-career marriage** as an available and workable option.

Increasingly, however, experts are pointing out, and couples are realizing, that expecting to "have it all" in a two-career marriage, particularly one with children, may be unrealistic. For two-career couples with children, family life can be hectic, as partners juggle schedules, chores, and child care. Career wives, in particular, often find themselves in a paradoxical situation. The career world tends to view the person who splits time between work and family as being less than professional, yet society encourages working women to do exactly that (Hochschild 1997).

Part-Time Employment

Of 18,000 mothers surveyed by *Parents* magazine, nearly two-thirds (61 percent) said that if they could do anything they wished, they would have a part-time job (Louv 1996). Although only 29 percent of employed married women with children and 18 percent of other mothers are working part time (under thirty-five hours a week), many mothers scale back their employment while children are preschoolers. Two-thirds of all mothers of preschool children did not work full time in 2003, almost evenly divided between those not employed at all and those working part time (U.S. Bureau of Labor Statistics 2004a, Table 5). "Most married mothers have not traded raising their own children for paid work" (Bianchi and Casper 2000, p. 33).

Research shows that mothers employed part time are more traditional and more similar to full-time homemakers than to full-time employed mothers in their attitudes about wife and mother roles (Glass 1992; Muller 1995), although some women are channeled into part-time work because they cannot find full-time jobs and/or adequate child care.

Greater family and personal time is a clear benefit of part-time employment, but there are costs. As it exists now, part-time work seldom offers job security or benefits such as health insurance. And part-time pay is rarely proportionate to that of full-time jobs. For example, a part-time teacher or secretary usually earns well below the wage paid to regular staff. In higher-level professional/managerial jobs, a different problem appears. To work "part time" as an attorney, accountant, or aspiring manager is to forgo the salary, status, and security of a full-time position and still to put in forty hours a week or more (Abelson 1998).

Shift Work

Sometimes one or both spouses engage in **shift work**, defined by the Bureau of Labor Statistics as any work schedule in which more than half an employee's hours are before 8 A.M. or after 4 P.M. It has been estimated that in one-quarter of all two-earner couples, at least one spouse does shift work, and one in three if they have children (Presser 2000). Some spouses use shift work for higher wages or to ease child-care arrangements (Hertz 1997).

But not only do they face physical stress with night work or frequently changing schedules; shift work also reduces the overlap of family members' leisure time, and that can affect the marriage: "To the extent that social interaction among family members provides the 'glue' that binds them together, we would expect that the more time spouses have with one another, the more likely they are to develop a strong commitment to their marriage and feel happy with it" (Presser 2000, p. 94). Analysis of responses of 1,668 individuals in a national survey found that—all things equal—a partner's doing shift work reduced satisfaction with the sexual relationship and increased the probability of divorce (White and Keith 1990). A later study also found shift work associated with a higher risk of divorce, though only for couples with children and only for work at late-night hours (Presser 2000).

Home-Based Work

Seven percent of the labor force was self-employed in 2002 (U.S. Census Bureau 2003a, Tables 587, 604). Many, though assuredly not all, of the self-employed today work from home (Shellenbarger 1998). Home-based work (working from home, either for oneself or for an employer) has increased over the past decades.

---

4. Higher-income men tend to be married to higher-income women, as the tendency to marry homogamously (see Chapter 7) would suggest. One of the effects of the trend toward dual-earner families is increasing inequality between families with two high-status, high-paying careers and those with two poorly paid jobs (Samuelson 1997; Winkler 1998). Families depending on one woman's income fare even worse.

Home-based work used to involve *piecework*, sewing or flower-making, for example. This mode of home production is declining due to competition from low-wage workers overseas. It still exists, particularly in the assembly of medical kits, circuit boards, jewelry, and some textile work. Nowadays, some states regulate home-based piecework, and require payment of workers' compensation and unemployment benefits ("At-Home Workers" 2003). Other home-based businesses include the direct selling of cosmetics, kitchenware, and other products.

Home-based work now includes working from home for an employer, perhaps through telecommuting—connecting to the office, customers, clients, or others by the Internet, telephone, videoconferencing, or other means. In 2001, some twenty million people did work at home as part of their primary job (30 percent of these were self-employed) (U.S. Bureau of Labor Statistics 2002a).

For some, it is a way to integrate work and family activities. Just under half of home-based, self-employed people are women (U.S. Census Bureau 2000, Table 661), and the reason women give most often for working at home is "competing domestic demands, such as taking care of children or household chores" ("Both Sexes" 1990). One study (Hill, Hawkins, and Miller 1996) compared 157 home-based teleworkers for a major corporation with 89 office workers from the same company. Almost three-quarters of the teleworkers reported benefiting from the arrangement. Remarking on the advantages of flexibility, mothers of young children were the most likely to be favorable: "I can take care of the sick child and get my work done. A win–win situation" (p. 297).

As the author of a study of women in a home-based direct-selling business noted, however, "many women soon discovered . . . that they had exchanged one set of challenges for another. Mothers employed at home report problems with interruptions. And like full-time homemakers, they are often asked to do chores for extended kin and others—for example, to run errands for relatives, to watch neighbors' children when bad weather closes the school, or to keep an eye out for the older kids" (Kutner 1988b).

A study comparing teleworkers to office-based employees found that both worker categories reported putting in about fifty-two hours a week, with those at home working slightly more than the office-based employees. Teleworkers were no more likely than the office workers to feel they had enough time for family life.

Some said that they tended to work more hours than they would otherwise, "instead of taking time to enjoy the family" (Hill, Hawkins, and Miller 1996, p. 297). Indeed, work–family flexibility may be a double-edged sword. The families of some teleworkers "struggled because workplace and schedule flexibility blurred the boundaries between work and family life" (p. 293). As one teleworker said, "I am always at work" (p. 298). Home-based workers faced the same tension between career-advancement—which required putting in long work hours—and family time as did employees working in a more conventional setting (Berke 2003).

Those who work at home can pursue either *integrative* or *compartmentalizing* strategies in terms of placing boundaries between domesticity and work (Berke 2003; Felstead and Jewson 2000; Nippert-Eng 1996). An integrative strategy is characterized by using domestic space as a worksite (rather than setting aside a room for an office), having children present, tolerating interruptions, working a shorter week, and doing more household chores. Those home workers who compartmentalize may set aside a separate space for work, have a separate work phone line, hire a sitter, and/or schedule specific work hours. Women are more likely than men to adopt an integrative strategy (Beach 1989). But the choice also varies by "occupation, work organization . . . gender, family structure, spouses' wage work, one's parenting role, and domestic labor role" (Nippert-Eng 1996, p. 14, quoted in Berke 2003). Given the recent increase in home-based work, we can anticipate that more research will be done in the future on this work choice.

Leaving the Labor Force and Reentry

A common pattern among marrieds after World War II was for the wife to be employed full time until shortly before the birth of her first child and then to permanently leave the full-time labor force. Later, women began returning to work when their children graduated from high school, and still later, after their children began elementary school. In 1988, for the first time, a majority of new mothers reentered the labor force in the year after their child's birth (Downs 2003, Figure 2). Despite motherhood, these women's employment was virtually continuous.

Now observers think they see a new pattern, which one journalist has called **sequencing moms**: mothers who choose to leave paid employment in order to spend some years at home raising children (Armour

2004). A *New York Times* article announced "The Opt-Out Revolution"—women graduates of elite universities who begin to successfully climb the career ladder, then quit to stay home when they have children. As one of them said, "I wish it had been possible to be the kind of parent I want to be and continue with my legal career. But I wore myself out trying to do both jobs well." Said another, "I like life's rhythms when I'm nurturing a child." Many of these women plan to reenter the labor force at some point. As one mother explained, "This is not permanent. . . . You're working. Then you're not working. Then maybe you're working part time or consulting. Then you go back. This is a chapter, not the whole book" (Belkin 2003, p. 46, 58).

Data indicate that women in the twenty-five through forty-five age bracket "are now more likely than they were in the past to describe staying at home as a phase in a life that gives equal importance to paid employment" (Uchitelle 2002, p. C1). This is especially true for college-educated women and for those whose husbands earn enough to support the family during the wife's at-home phase.

> Distrustful of dawn-to-dusk child care and unable to negotiate flexible work schedules, a growing number of women are conducting their lives in chapters, devoting their adulthood largely to careers but taking time off to be full-time mothers while their children are young. (Uchitelle 2002, p. C1)

Sequencing moms who've been interviewed report being pleased with their decision. As one explained, "[W]e had money, but someone else was raising our kids. . . . I just feel like a new person. After working so hard and being so stressed for years, I really appreciate the small things in life, like the first smile" (Armour 2002, p. B-2).

There may be additional reasons for a mother's putting her career on hold. Job dissatisfaction may be one. Economists who have studied women's employment find that barriers to career advancement remain. Lack of society-wide support for employed women—in terms of parental leave with pay, flexible time schedules, or reasonable work expectations—makes combining work and family difficult. This situation is aggravated by the lingering inequity between spouses regarding housework and child care (Pearson 2003; Rose and Hartmann 2004). Another reason for the emerging sequencing-mom pattern has to do with

"I'm off now to reproduce—but I'll be back!"

traditional gender roles. In our society, becoming a mother gives women an option that men are less likely to see as possible: "When a man gets dissatisfied with his job, he has to stick it out" (Belkin 2003, p. 8).

The down side to exercising the sequencing-mom alternative involves concerns about career reentry. At least one expert has warned that sequencing moms may be overly optimistic: "These women may think they can get back in. . . . but it's harder than they anticipate" (quoted in Belkin 2003, p. 58). A lot depends on the economy and the need for workers. It may very well be that with the education and skill levels that characterize women who choose this option, employers will cheerfully adapt to the sequencing-mom pattern. In fact, there are search firms that specialize in mothers who are reentering the labor force (Armour 2004). Needless to say, sequencing moms need to keep up their skills and maintain their networks, perhaps by consulting or working part time as they prepare to return to paid employment ("Playing Catch-up" 2004).

So far, it is journalists, not academic researchers, who are exploring the sequencing-mom phenomenon, and they have interviewed primarily educated, professional, or managerial women. Although not indicated by scientific research, it's possible that there has been a shift in values and goals over the past twenty years:

> A younger generation of workers watched their mothers strive to raise children while ascending the corporate ladder, but they've decided they don't want the same stress. Many still want a career *and* a family. But unlike the Baby Boom women before them, they don't want them at the same time." (Armour 2002, p. B-1)

Meanwhile, a majority of women still plan to return to work within the first year after their baby is born—and each cohort of American women has evidenced higher participation in the labor force than the previous one (Uchitelle 2002).

■ Unpaid Family Work ■

The discussion of the ways that two-earner couples organize their provider and family roles indicates that unpaid family work is indeed a factor to be considered. This section examines that unpaid family work.

Unpaid family work involves the necessary tasks of attending to both the emotional needs of all family members and the practical needs of dependent members (such as children or elderly parents), as well as maintaining the family domicile.

Caring for Dependent Family Members

As discussed in Chapter 11, our cultural tradition and social institutions give women principal responsibility for raising children. This situation has not changed even as more and more mothers have entered the labor force. Moreover, our culture designates women as "kinkeepers" (Hagestad 1986), whose job it is to keep in touch with—and, if necessary, care for—parents, adult siblings, and other relatives. The vast majority of informal elderly care is provided by female relatives, usually daughters and (albeit less often) daughters-in-law (Keith 1995; Globerman 1996). Women, more so than men, feel obliged to care for frail parents and experience guilt when they do not (McGrew 1998).

Family responsibilities and resources in meeting the needs of elderly, ill, or disabled family members are topics included in Chapters 15 and 18, while many of the chapters deal with the emotional aspects of family life. In this chapter we look more closely at housework and child care.

Housework

Utopians and engineers alike once shared a hope that advancing technology and changed social arrangements would make obsolete the need for families to cook, clean, or mind children (Hayden 1981). But collective arrangements proposed by utopians and early feminists never caught on. And servants, who had done much of the work for earlier middle-class housewives, entered factory work or took other, better jobs, and middle-class women were left to do their own house-

According to traditional roles, wives are the principal homemakers and husbands the primary economic providers. Even as the majority of wives are employed outside the home today, they continue to do more of the housework.

© Juan Silva/Getty Images

work (Cowan 1983). Technology seems merely to have raised the standards rather than making housework less time-consuming. For example, instead of changing clothes at infrequent intervals, we now do so daily (Cowan 1983).

Ever since immigration laws were changed in the 1960s, increased immigration has provided a class of women who will do child care and cleaning for affluent, dual-career families. But since it is primarily upper-middle-class women who rely on paid help, other contemporary women spend as much time on housework as did women in earlier times.

For women—but not men—marriage increases household labor hours. The number of children in the family is associated with both women's and men's household work. Although men with children spend more time on household labor than those without, children's impact on women's housework time is greater; the result is a larger gap between mothers and fathers than between child-free partners (Shelton 1992, pp. 67–68).

WHO DOES HOUSEWORK? Despite changing attitudes among couples and media portrayals of two-earner couples who share housework, women in fact continue to do more of it. While the gap has lessened (Artis and Pavalko 2003), data from about 8,500 participants in a University of Michigan study found that women, on average, spend twenty-seven hours a week on housework (compared to forty hours in 1965), while men increased their housework time from twelve hours in 1965 to sixteen hours in 1999 (Institute for Social Research 2002). There has been virtually no change in their hours of housework since 1990 (Peterson 2002).

A researcher commenting on the Michigan study said: "Women have shown a massive decline in the time spent in housework and a massive increase in paid work. Men have picked up a bit of the slack at home, but at some point have said, 'I've put the dishes in the dishwasher five nights this week. What else do you want from me?'" (Peterson 2002, p. D-06). Husbands are typically more willing to do child care—especially "fun" activities—than housework (Berk 1985; Hochschild 1989).

Still, the Michigan researchers believe that "the gap will continue to close as society moves closer to the notion that there is not men's work and women's work, but just different kinds of work that is shared by both sexes" (in Peterson 2002, p. D-06). (See Table 12.1 for a comparison of the time husbands and wives spend on specific household tasks.)

RACE/ETHNICITY AND OTHER FACTORS In some ethnic groups, such as Vietnamese and Laotian, housework is significantly shared, if not by husbands, by household members other than the wife/mother

Table 12.1

Average Hours Spent on Housework by Women and Men, Ages 25 to 64, 1965 and 1995						
	HOURS PER WEEK				**RATIO OF WOMEN'S HOURS TO MEN'S**	
	WOMEN		**MEN**			
Household task	**1965**	**1995**	**1965**	**1995**	**1965**	**1995**
Total housework	30.0	17.5	4.9	10.0	6.1	1.8
Core housework	26.9	13.9	2.3	3.8	11.9	3.7
Cooking meals	9.3	4.6	1.1	1.6	8.8	2.8
Meal clean-up	4.5	0.7	0.5	0.1	9.9	5.4
Housecleaning	7.2	6.7	0.5	1.7	15.5	3.8
Laundry, ironing	5.8	1.9	0.3	0.3	22.1	6.9
Other housework	3.1	3.6	2.6	6.2	1.2	0.6
Outdoor chores	0.3	0.8	0.4	1.9	0.7	0.4
Repairs, maintenance	0.4	0.7	1.0	1.9	0.4	0.4
Garden, animal care	0.6	0.8	0.2	1.0	2.4	0.8
Bills, other	1.8	1.3	0.9	1.5	2.0	0.9
Number of women/men	579	493	469	359		

These data (the latest detailed data available) show us the kinds of work men and women do at home. The *total housework* line tells us that women spent less time on housework in 1995 than they did in 1965, while men spent more time on housework in 1995 than they used to. The *ratio of women's hours to men's* column shows whether it is women or men who spend more time on a particular task, and how great the difference between the sexes is. (If the number is above 1, that indicates that *women* are spending more time; if it is below 1, that means *men* are.) Women spend much more time than men on "core housework," ranging from almost three to almost seven times as much. Men spend more time than women on "other housework."

Source: Adapted with permission from Bianchi & Casper, "American Families," *Population Bulletin* 55 (4), Table 7, © 2000 Population Reference Bureau.

(P. Johnson 1998). Among blacks, other family members are likely to share domestic work: adult children living at home, extended kin, and nonresident fathers (Coltrane 2000). The latter may provide child care or help with repairs.

Research on racial/ethnic differences finds that the pattern of men's spending less time than women in housework occurs in white, black, and Hispanic families. However, black men spend more time in unpaid family work than do white men (Shelton and John 1993; John, Shelton, and Luschen 1995; Orbuch and Eyster 1997). One explanation offered for black men's greater participation in housework is that they have more egalitarian attitudes, at least in this domain, and that African American wives are more likely to be employed and to have earnings that are closer to equality compared to their husbands than is true for other groups (Coltrane 2000). However, when factors other than race/ethnicity that affect men's household labor were taken into account—such as age, number of children, sex-role attitudes, and wives' sex-role attitudes—race/ethnicity was no longer so significantly associated with household labor time (Shelton and John 1993). In other words, the differences among white, black, and Hispanic men's household labor time may reflect other differences among them, as well. Further research will be needed to resolve the differences among these studies.

Research regarding Latino couples is mixed, with some studies showing no difference from the white division of household labor, while others show that Latino men do slightly more (Coltrane 2000). Blue-collar men do more housework than middle-class white-collar men despite being more likely to express a traditional gender ideology—the wife's earnings are more essential to the family (Hochschild 1989).

Participation in household labor is generally related to the degree of equality of earnings between the spouses and the proportionate share of those earnings produced by the wife. But when men are unemployed they may actually do less (Coltrane 2000). It may be that being a breadwinner is so symbolically important that unemployed family men are reluctant to do anything that might seem to undermine their manhood, such as labor traditionally considered women's work (Shelton and John 1993). This pattern of less housework time also characterizes those men whose wives earn more than they do, perhaps for the same reason (Brines 1994; Hochschild 1989; Tichenor 1999; see also Kroska 1997).

IS HOUSEWORK VANISHING? The University of Michigan researchers use the term "vanishing housework" in noting that as men and women are both putting in more hours of employment, the total amount of time a couple spends on housework has declined. One of the ways in which families have adjusted to women's entry into the labor force is to scale down what is thought necessary—assisted by microwaves, fast food, and so forth, and sometimes by using paid services.

> There's . . . reason to believe . . . low levels of family-performed housework will persist . . . since our research shows that most people rate routine housework as the least enjoyable use of their time. (Researcher Frank Stafford in Peterson 2002, p. D-06)

Another reason for the decline in housework may be a related change in culture. A study which looked at different cohorts of women finds that younger women do less housework, suggesting that "Socialization about family life, gender, and household labor may have been substantially different for newer cohorts" (Artis and Pavalko 2003, p. 758).

THE SECOND SHIFT Housework—even with the decline of recent decades—remains substantial. Including child care, many employed wives (and some husbands) put in what sociologist Arlie Hochschild calls a **second shift** of unpaid family work that amounts to an extra month of work each year (Hochschild 1989). The second shift for women means a "leisure gap" between husbands and wives, as the latter sacrifice avocational activities (Schnittger and Bird 1990), leisure—and sleep—to accomplish unpaid family work (Hochschild 1989; Shelton 1992). Women interviewed by sociologist Arlie Hochschild

> tended to talk more intently about being over-tired, sick, and "emotionally drained." . . . They talked about how much [sleep] they could "get by on.". . . These women talked about sleep the way a hungry person talks about food. (Hochschild 1989, p. 9)

Women's revolutionary entry into the labor force would seem to require a concurrent restructuring of household labor. Husbands *are* doing somewhat more around the house than twenty years ago. But "women continue to feel responsible for family members' well-being and are more likely than men to adjust their work and home schedules to accommodate others"

© The Modesto Bee

After a long day on the job, Cabral and Denys get some sleep on the seventeen-mile shuttle bus trip from the plant to Moline, Illinois, where they live. Longer hours of employment mean that time families spend on housework is "vanishing."

(Coltrane 2000, p. 1212). Hochschild (1989) calls this situation a **stalled revolution**.

Ways in which individual families manage during this stalled revolution vary. Some wives scale back their paid work, and others quit entirely. These may seem the best choices, given the options. But the reality is that "no-fault divorce laws combined with rising divorce rates have substantially increased the risks for women [who remain out of the labor force or reduce their employment options]" (Peterson 1989, p. 2). Another strategy is to lower housework standards and food preparation time after a wife becomes employed (Shelton 1990), as changes in housework time suggest has happened.

Some two-earner couples hire household help, especially in upper-income white families, and purchase the services of immigrant, racial/ethnic minority, and working-class people for housekeeping and child-care work or other chores (Coltrane 2000). Researchers note that women are more often the coordinators of paid services as well as doing more housework themselves (Thompson 1991).

Another housework option might appear to be help from children. Some studies find that children in single-parent families, especially, help significantly with housework, while others find that children in married-couple families do more work. In any case, "while many children do some household labor . . . their contribution is typically occasional and their time investment small" (Shelton and John 1996, p. 311; also Coltrane 2000, pp. 1225–1226).

Generally, husbands follow "the path of least resistance" (Peterson and Gerson 1992, p. 532). To secure her spouse's help with the second shift, a wife must take the initiative, in essence demanding his participation (Hochschild 1989; Guelzow, Bird, and Koball 1991). She must be willing to truly share decisions about children and housework. Some wives are reluctant to relinquish the centrality and decision-making role or to loosen their standards and preferences for how things should be done, and that may discourage husband participation (Allen and Hawkins 1999).

WHY WOMEN DO THE HOUSEWORK Household labor is of keen interest to social scientists because struggles over who does it are central to analyses of gender and class. We might apply the *conflict* and *feminist* theoretical perspectives discussed in Chapter 3 to this issue. Doing so would mean arguing that (1) women are more likely than men to do housework—and other unpaid family labor—because they have less power in their families (Shelton and John 1996, pp. 303–304; Coltrane 2000, p. 1215) and (2) that paid caregivers, who typically receive low wages, are likely to come from more-disadvantaged social sectors.

Other related perspectives on the division of household labor have emerged.[5] One view, the **time availability perspective**, holds simply that the partner with more time does the housework (England and Farkas 1986). Expanding on this idea, the **rational investment perspective** argues that couples attempt to maximize the family economy by trading off between

---

5. See Artis and Pavalco 2003, pp. 747–748, or Coltrane 2000, pp. 1212–1217, for a more comprehensive discussion than we can present here.

Children do some household labor, but it is more often a socialization device or family group activity than a substantial sharing of parents' household tasks.

time and energy investments in paid market work and unpaid household labor (Becker 1991). Spouses agree that each partner will spend more time and effort in the activities at which she or he is more efficient.

The **resource hypothesis** suggests that a partner's household labor is a consequence of her or his resources compared to those of the other. Thus, the partner with higher resources (such as greater income or long-term earning potential) will have more power and hence spend less time on housework. The earnings difference *is* associated with the housework split, but the resource hypothesis leaves a substantial amount

of the difference between men's and women's housework time unexplained (Shelton 2000, pp. 348–350).

In principle, both the rational investment perspective and the resource hypothesis are gender neutral: Either husband or wife might invest more time and energy in the labor force and less in housework. But as we have already seen, husbands are likely to be receiving higher salaries than are their wives even within an occupational grouping. Men invest relatively more time in the labor force. As a result, husbands are likely to have more status and power in marriages and can therefore resist housework demands (Coverman 1985).

The **ideological perspective** points to the effects of gendered cultural expectations on household labor (Shelton and John 1996, 2000). In the ideological perspective, who does the housework at least partly reflects stereotypes and norms about "who should do what" (Berk 1985). Women's and men's attitudes—especially men's—are associated with the division of household labor. Some research has found that more highly educated husbands are more willing to do housework, a finding in support of the ideological perspective inasmuch as more education results in less traditional gender attitudes (Ross 1987). On the other hand, even egalitarian men do not do an equal share of the housework (Shelton 2000, p. 348).

Findings from the National Survey of Families and Households and some other research support all of the perspectives to some degree: "This suggests that the division of household labor is the result of multiple causal forces. Who does what around the house is shaped by time availability, relative resources, and ideology" (Coltrane and Ishii-Kuntz 1992, p. 53; Kroska 2004; Orbuch and Eyster 1997; Shelton 2000; Shelton and John 1996).

A final perspective on the household division of labor is the **gender construction perspective**, sometimes termed *doing gender*. Drawn from symbolic interaction theory (see Chapter 3), it looks to the *meaning* of housework, rather than the practicalities of time and income, to explain a gendered division of labor. Performing certain household tasks considered traditionally masculine or feminine may reinforce a masculine or feminine gender identity (Coltrane 2000, p. 1213). "Housework is not just the performance of basic household tasks but it is also a symbolic expression of gender relations, particularly between wives and husbands" (Artis and Pavalco 2003, p. 748).

For some homemakers, the perception of 'home' is of "the world where we carry out the private search for intimacy" (Nippert-Eng 1996, p. 22). Their enjoyment of domestic work relates to their belief that "performing family work is a way of showing care for loved ones" (Grote, Naylor, and Clark 2002, p. 520). Gender ideology plays a role for more traditional women—for them, housework has a "moral quality" (Stevens, Kiger, and Riley 2001, p. 524).

A REINFORCING CYCLE Still, economics are important. When we consider men's and women's paid and unpaid work, it becomes apparent that a **reinforcing cycle** emerges: For a number of reasons, which we have already explored, men employed full time average higher earnings than women employed full time. Because most husbands actually or potentially earn more than their wives, couples allow her paid work role to be more vulnerable to family demands than his. This situation, in turn, has the effects of lowering the time and energy a wife spends in the labor force and of giving employers reason to pay women less than men. This lower pay, coupled with society's devaluation of family in favor of job demands, encourages husbands to see their wives' work (paid and unpaid) as less important than their own—and to conclude that they really shouldn't be asked to take responsibility for homemaking. Disproportionately burdened with household labor, wives find it difficult to invest themselves in the labor force to the same degree that husbands do (Zvonkovic et al. 1996). This situation remains true even for the majority of two-career couples, including physicians married to one another (Grant et al. 1990).

FAIRNESS AND MARITAL HAPPINESS A conclusion easily drawn from research is that employed women are carrying an unfair share of domestic tasks. But do couples themselves see it that way? That depends on the meaning of household work to the couple and what they consider "fair."

While, overall, unequal shares of household labor are associated with marital dissatisfaction, this relationship is altered by perceptions of fairness. Citing a number of studies, Frisco and Williams (2003) found perceived fairness to be more strongly associated with marital happiness (and, in their own study, with the likelihood of divorce) than differences in actual hours spent in domestic work. To a wife or woman partner, a man's taking up *some*, if not an equal share of, household tasks may signify caring.

Interesting is that men and women perceive "fair share" differently. Of those men in dual-earner families who perceived that they were doing *more than their fair share*, 43 percent were actually doing *less than half* of the housework. In other words, they did not think it would be fair for them to do as much as half the housework. Meanwhile, of women who perceived themselves to be doing a *fair* share, almost two-thirds are doing *all or more* of the housework. An uneven split seems fair to them (Frisco and Williams 2003). (The Frisco and Williams study uses the *Marital Stability over the Life Course* data set; White and Booth 1991.) Probably what is happening is that both men and women have in mind as a standard of comparison the breadwinner–housewife model. Men, then, are doing more, while women are unloading some of their former responsibility. That seems "fair."

Feeling competent and being considered competent by wives seems to make housework more enjoyable for men, hence fairer. And men may lump housework and employment together and add that up to feel the total burden of family responsibility is a fair one (Lavee and Katz 2002). Indeed, the University of Michigan time study found that women averaged fifty-one hours, while men averaged fifty-three in total hours spent on employment plus domestic work (Johnson 2002).

In the next section, we will examine how partners juggle household labor demands, along with employment.

Juggling Employment and Unpaid Family Work

The concept of juggling implies a hectic and stressful situation. Virtually all research and other writings on the subject suggest that today's typical American family is a hectic one (e.g., Hochschild 1989, 1997). This is particularly true when there are children in the home.

The Speed-Up of Family Life

For one thing, working people are spending significantly more hours at work (Schor 1991). American workers lead the industrial world in the number of hours worked ("Some Noses" 2004). About 30 percent

Family life has increasingly become characterized by not having enough time for everything that must get done.

© Steve Liss/Getty Images

We will look now at how children in two-earner marriages are doing.

How Are Children Faring?

FOCUS ON CHILDREN

Before women with children entered the work force in large numbers, working mothers were considered problematic by child development experts and the public. Now they are taken for granted. A 2001 survey of women (not all of them mothers) found more than 90 percent in agreement with the statement that a woman can be a good mother and have a successful career (Center for the Advancement of Women 2003). A recent study draws the conclusion that maternal employment does not cause behavior problems in children (Vander Ven, Cullen, Carrozza, and Wright 2001), and another study of more than 6,000 children studied at age twelve found no difference between the children whose mothers were employed or not employed during the child's first three years (Harvey 1999).

of all employees now work more than forty hours per week. Five percent of the labor force held two or more paid jobs in 2002 (U.S. Census Bureau 2003a, Table 602, 608).

While individuals interviewed by the Gallup poll are divided on whether or not they have enough time to do what they want (see Table 12.2), about 60 percent of those aged eighteen through forty-nine—the ages of employment and active parenting—say they do not have enough time (Saad 2004). Working parents report chronic fatigue and being at "the breaking point" (Hancock 1995; Gibbs and Duffy 1996; Morin and Rosenfeld 1998). For a majority of Americans, rest and relaxation time, time for friends, hobbies, and even time for sleep is not what they would like it to be (Saad 2004; and see Table 12.2). "Facts About Families: Where Does the Time Go?" describes how employed parents spend their time on an average day.

Sociologist Arlie Hochschild's (1989) qualitative study of fifty two-earner couples pointed to the frantic pace and sense of pressure for everyone involved, but especially for mothers and for children, whose harried mothers often rushed them: "Hurry up! It's time to go," "Finish your cereal now," "You can do that later," "Let's go!" . . . "Let's see who can take their bath the quickest!" (quoted in Hochschild 1989, pp. 9–10).

Table 12.2

Do Americans Feel That They Have Enough Time, or Not?			
GALLUP POLL RESPONSES TO THE FOLLOWING QUESTION: GENERALLY SPEAKING, DO YOU HAVE ENOUGH TIME TO DO WHAT YOU WANT TO THESE DAYS, OR NOT?			
December 2003	**Right Amount**	**Too Little**	**Too Much**
In general	52%	48%	—
Your family	66%	29%	4%
Friendships or other personal relationships	58%	37%	4%
Sleep	57%	39%	4%
Household chores	55%	27%	17%
Internet use (users only)	55%	26%	17%
Your job (employed only)	54%	4%	41%
Relaxing or doing nothing	45%	44%	11%
Hobbies	40%	51%	5%
Reading	38%	54%	7%
Personal exercise and recreation	37%	59%	3%
Watching television	50%	16%	32%

Data were collected by the Gallup poll from a national sample of 1,011 adults, Dec. 11–14, 2003.

Source: Adapted from Saad 2004.

Facts About Families — Where Does The Time Go?

We've talked about employment and household labor. What do people do with the rest of their time? And how does it all add up?

An American Time Use Survey was conducted in 2003 by the U.S. Bureau of Labor Statistics (2004a). Some 21,000 people were asked to keep time diaries, recording what activities they engaged in and for how much time. The reports of these many individuals were averaged to come up with typical days for different groups.

Let's look at employed parents of children under eighteen and see what happens in an average day. Well, there are the basics. Just over an hour (1.12 hours) was spent in *eating and drinking*. Around nine hours (8.97) were spent in such *personal care* activities as sleeping, bathing, dressing, and health care.

Work averaged six and a half hours (6.49) for men, and four and a half (4.64) for women (remember that some people work part time and also that all days are not work days). On average, employed women spent over two hours (2.05) on *household activities*—the domestic labor we have talked about—while these tasks occupied almost an hour and a quarter (1.22) of men's time.

These totals did not include child care, which fell into the category of

caring for and helping household members, a category which also included helping adult members of the household, perhaps with medical needs. Women spent an hour and a half (1.56) on caring for household members, while men spent less than an hour (.85).

Shopping—*purchasing goods and services,* as the survey termed it— took almost an hour of an employed mother's daily time (.91), while fathers devoted two-thirds of an hour to shopping (.65). Men were able to devote more of their time to *leisure and sports* (4.07 hours) than women (3.49 hours). The most common use of leisure time for all was watching television.

Men and women participated in *organizational, civic, and religious activities* at about the same rate, each spending about a third of an hour on an average day. Men and women alike spent an average of .18 hour in *caring for and helping nonhousehold members* and in *educational activities. Telephone calls, mail, and e-mail* communication rounded out the day (at .07 hour for men and .14 hour for women), while some time (.14 hour) was spent on unspecified *other activities.*

So what does it all mean? Despite amounts of time in some categories so small as to seem trivial, we can see

some interesting things in these figures. The American Time Use Survey shows that women spend 75 percent more time than men in the care of the household and its members, adding one more study to those which show a gender disparity. However, men spent 40 percent more time working than did women.

In other areas, there is little difference in time use between men and women. The time men and women devote to organizational, civic, religious, and educational activities and to helping nonhousehold members is similar. Still, men have more leisure time, while women do more shopping (more likely to be grocery shopping than "fun" shopping). Women spend twice as much time as men in communication activities and more time on personal care, a large portion of which is sleeping.

Critical Thinking

How do you spend *your* time? Has the time you spend in various activities changed throughout your life? These data are for employed people who have children at home. If your situation is different, is your time use different as well?

Source: *American Time Use Survey* 2003. U.S. Bureau of Labor Statistics 2004b, Tables 1 and 6.

Overall, this continues to be the prevailing view. Employed mothers foster independence in their children and are especially good role models for adolescent daughters (Wilkie 1988). Furthermore, the economic benefit to children of working mothers cannot be overlooked. Family income tends to be favorably associated with various child outcome measures. Important for parents, though, is keeping their child's needs in the forefront in the face of daily pressures. Recent studies have found that mothers who work part

time are better at this than those who work full time— and may indeed spend more time helping their children with homework than even full-time homemakers (Muller 1995).

A survey of children provides encouraging news. This 1997–1998 national survey found that of 1,023 seventh- to twelfth-grade children, 67 percent "graded" fathers A or B, and 76 percent graded mothers A or B on a question about working parents' attention to their children. Seventy-seven percent of fathers and 84 percent of mothers were graded A or B on "being able to attend important events in your life." Children of employed and stay-at-home mothers did not differ in their answers to questions about too little time with moms (Galinsky 1999).

"The puzzling thing about the reallocation of mothers' time to market work is that it appears to have been accomplished with little effect on children's well-being," noted sociologist Suzanne Bianchi in her presidential address to the Population Association of America (Bianchi 2000). Employed parents, especially those employed full time, do spend less time with children than parents who are not employed, according to a National Survey of Parents, a national sample survey conducted in 2000 (Milkie et al. 2004; see Table 12.3 for details about time spent with children). Nevertheless, a variety of studies indicate that parents today spend as much or more time with children as in the past (Milkie 2004). Before the era of working mothers, so-called full-time mothers did not spend all their time with children, but devoted more time than today's mothers to household work or volunteer work. And some of those mothers—of larger families, especially—made use of paid help in caring for children.

Employed mothers today consciously strive to make time for children by reducing housework, personal leisure, or volunteer work or by working part time or leaving the labor force when children are small. Also, the smaller size of today's families has enabled parents to give more attention to each child. Fathers are spending more time with children than in the past, adding to parental time with children (Bianchi 2000).

These results present an optimistic and reassuring view of how children of working parents are faring. But despite the favorable data on time spent with children, almost half the parents in national sample surveys (the National Survey of Parents and the General Social Survey conducted by the University of Chicago) felt they did not spend enough time with them.

A study by University of Michigan researchers suggests that "the time-squeeze felt by parents trying to juggle the demands of work and family is increasingly being transferred to their children's lives. . . . [A]s parents' lives have become more hectic, those of their children are becoming more tightly organized." Children are spending more time on school, organized sports, chores, and going with their parents on errands rather than engaging in unstructured play or organizing their own activities with other children (Holmes 1998).

Table 12.3

Amount of Time Parents Spend with Children: The National Survey of Parents

	HOURS PER WEEK
All Parents	42.7
Gender	
Mothers	50.2
Fathers	33.4
Age of Youngest Child	
Preschool (ages 0–5)	50.8
School age (ages 6–12)	38.2
Adolescent (ages 13–17)	30.3
Employment Status	
Not employed	63.8
Part time (1–34 hours)	49.3
Full time (over 34 hours)	36.5
Marital Status	
Married parent	43.5
Single parent	40.3
Spouse's Work Hours (for married parents)	
Spouse not employed	36.0
Spouse employed part time (1–34 hours)	37.9
Spouse employed full time (over 34 hours)	46.2

Based on a national sample survey of 1,200 parents in 2000. Mothers and fathers are from different households.

Source: From Melissa A. Milkie, et al., "The Time Squeeze: Parental Statuses and Feelings about Time With Children." Journal of Marriage and the Family 66: 739–761. Copyright © 2004 by the National Council on Family Relations, 3989 Central Ave., NE, Suite 550, Minneapolis, MN 55421. Reprinted by permission.

We turn now to the question of how parents are faring as they juggle paid and unpaid work.

How Are Parents Faring?

This chapter focuses on work and family in marriages (rather than other family forms) for two reasons. First, the vast majority of research on the interface between paid employment and family labor concerns marrieds (Crouter and Helms-Erikson 1997); second, single parenting is addressed in some detail in Chapter 16. But for a moment, we want to point to the situation of single parents.

WORK, FAMILY, AND THE SINGLE PARENT
The following experience captures the work–family conflict for single custodial parents:

I am stopped dead on the San Francisco Bay Bridge. . . . I have not moved for twenty minutes. . . . I was due to pick up my four-year-old son at five o'clock. The hands are crawling past six o'clock, seven o'clock, eight o'clock. Finally the cars break free and I race to the baby-sitter's house. She primly informs me that she had no idea where I was and she has called the police to take my son. . . . The police have determined that I am clearly not a fit mother and will no longer be allowed to take care of him.

This is my recurring nightmare. It is founded in a real incident which occurred ten years ago when I was living through a painful divorce and trying to learn the difficult role of single-parent working mother. The real-life incident did not end disastrously; the baby-sitter was merely annoyed. But clearly the sharp anxiety and profound feelings of inadequacy which were evoked by that very troubled period have not yet been put to rest. (Mason 1988, pp. 11–12)

The University of Michigan study found that single-parent mothers spend nine hours weekly in parent–child activities, while two-earner, two-parent families spend about nineteen hours in combined time, and two-parent, breadwinner–housewife families spend twenty-two hours (Holmes 1998). Trying to do everything involved in parenting in half the time takes its toll on employed single parents.

OTHER WORKING PARENTS Although the rough edges of the work–family conflict may be particularly sharp for single parents, two-earner marriages assuredly have them also. Whether one is single or married, "career and family involvement have never been combined easily in the same person" (Hunt and Hunt 1986). Higher education and family life may present the same conflict. A married student writes:

A student, like myself, has homework and projects that need many more hours to complete than time allotted. How can I save up energy at school to be ready for [coming home to my family]. . . . I feel guilty because I cannot give my children the attention they need. I try to lend half of myself to them and half to my school work. This does not include time for my husband. (Vance 1998)

The media have given us the new man, the baby boom era (or younger) husband who shares wage-

This father has chosen to make use of an opportunity to spend time with his family.

earning and family responsibilities on an egalitarian basis and relates warmly to his children. Indeed, more fathers are taking off work following the birth of a child, and they are more visible in parenting classes, in pediatricians' offices, and dropping off and picking up children in day-care centers (Levine, cited in Lawson 1990). But "the image of the new man is like the image of the supermom: it obscures the strain" (Hochschild 1989, p. 31).

The man who gives family priority may have to deal with challenges to his masculinity or resentment from co-workers, whether parents or not. In her most recent book on work–family tensions and corporate family policies, sociologist Arlie Hochschild gave her chapter on men who took paternity leave the sardonic title "Catching Up on the Soaps" (1997, p. 115) to capture the pressures these men felt from workmates and supervisors. Employers may not see unpaid family work as important and do not believe that employees,

What's missing from this picture? Two-career marriages often rely on household help, not pictured here.

© Ron Chapple/Getty Images

especially males, should allow family responsibilities to interfere with labor force involvement (Hochschild 1997). As a result, some husbands report having lied to bosses or taking other evasive steps at work to hide conflicts between job and family. One man told his boss that he has "another meeting" so that he can leave the office each day at 6 P.M.: "I never say it's a meeting with my family."

The previous discussion applies to working parents generally. In the next section, we will look at some stresses peculiar to two-career marriages—keeping in mind the distinction between *two-earner* couples and *two-career* couples made earlier in the chapter.

Two-Career Marriages— Juggling Even Faster

Twenty-eight years ago, Hunt and Hunt (1977) noted that dual-career families require a support system of child-care providers and household help that depends heavily on ability to pay, which is inherently limited to a small number of families. Today's two-career union is premised on the existence of a labor pool of low-paid, but highly dependable, household help. The vast majority of such help is provided by women, many of whom have their own families to worry about (Romero 1992). (See "A Closer Look at Family Diversity: Diversity and Child Care.") Even parents who can afford to pay for it find that locating such help may be difficult.

Two careers requiring travel may present added problems as parents "scramble to patch things together" for overnight child care (Shellenbarger 1991b). Two-career partners need the dexterity to balance not only career and family life, but also her and his careers so that both spouses prosper professionally in what they see as a fair way. The balance between partners may be upset by career fluctuations as well as family time allocations. The contrast between one career that is going well and one that is not may be hard on the partner on the down side. But the marriage may "operate as a buffer, cushioning the negative impacts of failures or reversals in one or the other career" (Hertz 1986, p. 59). When the marriage is rewarding, compromises, such as turning down opportunities that would require relocation, are acceptable because of the importance given to marriage as well as career.

Hertz (1986) found that the two-career couples she studied were realistic, though sometimes regretful, about some benefits of the traditional relationships they are giving up. Although men acknowledged that their wives provided less husband care and support, they appreciated the excitement, and also the status, associated with an achieving wife. Some of them had considered or made career changes that would not have been possible if wives had not been successful wage earners. Both partners claimed fulfillment from and assigned emotional meaning to an egalitarian dual-career marriage: "She has a sense of a full partnership and she should" (in Hertz 1986, p. 75).

Commitment was perceived as truer: "Working . . . has decreased my dependence. . . . That makes it into much more of a voluntary relationship than an involuntary one of my staying with him because I need to stay with him. He's not staying with me because he's obligated to somehow, and it just makes it into a much clearer situation" (in Hertz 1986, p. 75). Very visible to Hertz was the way in which communication was enhanced by similar lives, making possible a higher level of mutual support than in conventional couples: "These couples . . . [had] a different level of understanding about each other's lives, a level that is intimate and empathic" (p. 77).

The couples studied by Hertz did report conflict over balancing time, commitment, and career moves. Indeed, the geography of two careers presents a significant challenge to couples.

THE GEOGRAPHY OF TWO CAREERS Because career advancement often requires geographic mobility—and even international transfers—juggling two careers may prove difficult for marrieds or committed partners. A career move for one partner may make the other a **trailing spouse** who relocates to accommodate the other one's career. Increasingly, couples turn down transfers because of two-career issues. As a result, some large companies now offer career-opportunity assistance to a trailing spouse, such as hiring a job search firm, intercompany networking, attempts to locate a position for the spouse in the same institution, or career counseling (Lublin 1992).

Although wives still move for their husband's careers more often than the reverse (Shihadeh 1991), the number of trailing husbands has increased. Counselors who work with trailing husbands note that these men have few role models and must confront norms and social pressures that conflict with their decisions. Financial pressures when a trailing spouse cannot find a job may intensify the strain. But more two-career marriages today are based on a conscious mutuality to which partners have become accustomed by the time a career move presents itself. Such couples are less likely to have problems with a female-led relocation than are more traditional marrieds. For many spouses, trailing is preferable to commuting, another solution to the problem of career opportunities in two locations.

TO COMMUTE OR NOT TO COMMUTE? Social scientists have called marriages in which spouses live apart **commuter marriages**. The vast majority of

The second shift is probably more enjoyable when shared by both partners.

commuting couples would rather not do so, but endure the separation for the sake of career or other goals. Since research began on commuter marriages in the early 1970s, social scientists have drawn different conclusions. Some studies suggest that the benefits of such marriages—greater economic and emotional equality between spouses and the potential for better communication—counter their drawbacks. Other research suggests a different view, focusing on difficulties in managing the lifestyle. One conclusion to be drawn from the research is that commuters who are able to have frequent reunions are happier with the lifestyle than those who cannot.

One study (Bunker et al. 1992) compared life satisfaction for 90 commuting and 133 single-resident, two-career couples. Almost three-fourths of the commuters saw their partner weekly. The researchers were surprised to find that the commuters experienced less stress and overload than the single-residence couples: "Perhaps there is some restructuring in the commuting two-residence couple that simplifies life or perceptions of it. Perhaps short separations facilitate compartmentalization, allowing commuters to keep

A Closer Look at Family Diversity

Diversity and Child Care

FOCUS ON CHILDREN Every weekday evening in affluent homes across America, two groups of women trade places. Mothers who follow careers come home and the women who are paid to care for their children prepare to depart or step aside. . . .

For Ruth Sarfaty, 31 years old, a Manhattan public relations executive with a 2 1/2 year-old daughter, the other woman is Cheryl Ryan, 40, a mother of five from Trinidad. "I'm completely dependent on her," said Ms. Sarfaty, whose husband is a real estate broker. "She's in my home more than I am. We could not earn a living without her." Yet, fundamental as these arrangements may be, there are few working relationships that are more ambiguous, complex or ultimately fragile. . . . There are rarely credentials or contracts. Many caregivers are . . . [undocumented immigrants] who are grateful for work that is paid for off the books.

A Gamble, and for Low Pay

[In-home caregivers are poorly paid, on average]. . . . Sixty-two percent

leave their jobs each year. "It's a gamble," Professor [Edward] Zigler said, "If you get a wonderful one, it's like having a new, valued family member. If you get an awful one, you and your child are in trouble." But for women who pursue demanding careers that involve long workdays and irregular hours or travel, in-home care is more than a luxury. . . . [Thus, c]aregivers can wield tremendous power over these women: "You think, if the nanny is happy, the baby is happy. If the baby's happy, you're happy. If you're happy, your husband's happy."

When problems come up, they can throw a family into chaos. Stories of caregivers' abrupt departures abound. . . . Even if the arrangement is running smoothly, women who employ caregivers often wonder about their influence. . . . "You're always re-evaluating the choice," said Rhea Paul, a professor of speech and hearing science at Courtland State University, Oregon, who has hired a grandmother from the Netherlands to care for her three children. "Every day you come home and ask yourself: 'Am I doing the right thing?'" . . .

Special Fabrics of Living

Women who strive to be model mothers learn to make accommodations as their children and caregivers develop their own rituals. Amy Samuelson's 3-year-old son, Zachary, has looked forward to weekly outings to McDonald's with his caregiver. Ms. Samuelson, who is a nutritionist, said, "It's not my favorite place, but it's important to Zachary. . . ."

Such domestic arrangements, while unfamiliar to many professional women, have long been a part of the fabric of life for the wealthiest Americans and for white Southern families. . . . Today, while there are no reliable estimates of the number of in-home caregivers, it seems clear that not enough skilled ones are available. Caregivers often tell of being approached in playgrounds with their charges by other mothers seeking to lure them away from their employer.

Yet for all the demand, many caregivers complain bitterly about how they are treated. "In this country baby sitting is not seen as a job," said a Jamaican caregiver who keeps a photograph of her employ-

work life and family life in well-separated spheres, and to confront the demands of each role in alternation rather than simultaneously" (p. 405). Then, too, the commuter couples had significantly fewer babies and young children than did single-resident couples; commuter marriages probably work better in the absence of dependent children (Stern 1991).

Generally, the researchers concluded that commuting has both rewards and costs. Commuters reported more satisfaction with their work life than did single-residence, two-career respondents, but commuters were significantly less satisfied with their part-

ner relationships and family life (Bunker et al. 1992). Some commuters say they can put their respective careers first for only so long before their relationship frays: "Career-wise it was absolutely fantastic," said one spouse who had given it up. "Personally, it was absolutely horrible" (in Stern 1991, p. B3). Consider the following example:

Michael and Judy Casper intended to celebrate their 25th wedding anniversary last month with a three-week vacation in Alaska. But their conflicting careers scotched the trip. Michael couldn't get

er's child on her dresser at home along with a photograph of her own son. . . .

"It's long hours," said Marie Gaston, 50, who works as a live-in caregiver in Aspen, Colorado. "When you travel with them, it's 24 hours. Sometimes it's two or three weeks before you get time off. There's no overtime." . . .

In some cases, such employment can lead to legal status in the United States, but even that has its drawbacks, according to one caregiver. "They seem nice at first. . . . [T]hen when they know they're going to sponsor you they start to treat you differently because they know if you don't work with them you're going to have to start over with someone else again. Some of them treat you like a slave." . . . Caroline Brownell, who directs an employment agency in San Rafael, California, said she recently decided to stop placing caregivers because of the unrealistic demands of "corporate mothers."

. . . [E]fforts are under way to introduce standards. Mary Starkey, who runs a placement agency in Denver, helped found the 300-member International Nanny Association to seek better pay and working conditions. . . . Her efforts are focused partly on drawing attention to the widespread avoidance of such legal requirements that employers face as Social Security payments, workmen's compensation, unemployment insurance, and reporting earnings to the Internal Revenue Service.

In New York, the 92nd Street Y in Manhattan started what may be the first support and education course for caregivers. Roanna Shorofsky, director of the nursery school there, said, "I realized what was happening when I looked down the hallway one day and saw all the caregivers picking up the kids." Of the 150 children enrolled in the nursery school last year, a third had in-home care. Among the caregivers in last year's course were women from Ireland, Haiti, West Germany, Brazil, China and Jamaica. With the prevalence of foreign-born caregivers, many children move in and out of distinctly different cultural worlds.

"There is no Mary Poppins," said a 39-year-old Manhattan advertising sales executive who interviewed 50 women before she found a 50-year-old woman from Trinidad, who has worked for her for seven years and now attends to a 7-year-old and a 4-year-old. "You have to constantly make compromises. . . . This is one of the most important relationships I'll have in my entire life. I work at it all the time." . . .

Sometimes no effort can keep arrangements from falling apart. That was the experience of Ms. Samuelson, 38, a corporate nutritionist who lives in Riverdale with her husband, a college professor, and Zachary, their son. The first woman she hired had taken excellent care of a friend's children but became pregnant in the Samuelson's employ and left after seven months. . . . The second woman, whom Ms. Samuelson found through an advertisement in *The Irish Echo* newspaper, lasted one week. A third woman left after six months to return to her native Jamaica to care for her sick mother. Finally, nearly two years ago, Ms. Samuelson found a 35-year-old Jamaican who was devoted to Zachary. But three months ago the woman announced that she was five months pregnant and not sure she would continue working after she had the baby.

"When child care breaks down," Ms. Samuelson said, "everything else breaks down."

Critical Thinking

What family theory or theories could you use to analyze this situation?

Source: Abridged from Sara Rimer, © New York Times, Dec. 26, 1988a, p. A–1. For additional information on this topic, see Hondagneu-Sotelo 2001; Lipman 1993; MacDonald 1998; Romero 1992.

away from his new job—as a Gulf Bank general manager in Kuwait City. He says he spent the anniversary watching a rented videotape. Judy lives 7,700 miles away in Houston, where she owns a thriving home-interior shop—her first paid job after following her husband around the world for 17 years. She celebrated the anniversary by going out for Italian food with their three college-age children. Later, she cried. (Lublin 1992, p. B1)

"Perhaps reflecting the strong influence of these relationship issues on overall quality of life," commuters were less satisfied with life as a whole than were single-residence couples (Bunker et al. 1992, p. 405).

Couples who have been married for shorter periods of time seem to have more difficulties with commuter marriages. Younger couples who are simultaneously beginning their careers and their relationship often lack not only experience but also information about managing a two-career marriage. Perhaps because of their history of shared time, more "established" couples in commuter marriages have a greater "commitment to the unit" (Gross 1980).

This general discussion of juggling paid and unpaid labor points to the fact that despite the benefits of employment to women and their families, and despite the broad societal pressures and gender-role changes leading to high female employment rates, neither public policy nor families have fully adapted to this change. The next section examines policy issues regarding work and family.

Social Policy, Work, and Family

Our discussions so far show that employment and household labor conflict; that is, "time spent in one sphere means less time spent in another. If commitments to paid labor and household labor call for full-time participation in both, that time must come either at the expense of leisure or else some of the demands of paid labor and household labor must go unmet" (Shelton 1992, p. 143). Corporate policy expert Ellen Galinsky recounts the following, not unusual episode from the life of a working family:

> One father told of a morning when his four-year-old daughter lost her shoes. . . . [H]e and his wife searched everywhere but the shoes were nowhere to be found. The mother began to go through the house a second time while the father made calls to find someone to take over his carpool to the metal factory where he worked. Because his factory had strict time policies . . . he felt frantic, as did his wife who also had a job tied to the time clock. Eventually they settled for last year's too small shoes, put them on their daughter, and they all rushed out the door. Both parents were late for work, and were censored by their supervisors. When they got home from work, they found a note from their daughter's teacher—it asked them please to buy shoes for their child that fit. (Galinsky 1986, pp. 109–110)

This section examines public or social policy issues as society responds (or fails to respond) to today's work–family conflicts. Policy issues center on two questions: "What is needed?" and "Who will provide it?"

What Is Needed to Resolve Work–Family Issues?

Researchers and other work–family experts are in general agreement that single-parent and two-earner families are in need of more adequate provisions for child and elder care, family leave, and flexible employment scheduling.

CHILD CARE Policy researchers define **child care** as the full-time care and education of children under age six, care before and after school and during school vacations for older children, and overnight care when employed parents must travel. Child care may be paid or unpaid and provided by relatives or others, including one of the parents.

In her study of dual-earner couples, sociologist Rosanna Hertz (1997) explored parents' approaches to child care and found they fell into three categories. One was the **mothering approach to child care**, whereby the couple preferred that the wife care for the children. An initial strategy of overtime or a second job for the husband often proved to be unworkable financially or physically, so the wife did have to enter the labor force. But the couple maintained as traditional a division of labor as they could, with the mother working as much as possible during hours the children were sleeping or in school.

In the **parenting approach to child care**, family care was shared by parents, who structured their work to this end. They accepted part-time work, for example, and the lower incomes that went with it. But primarily these were "labor force elites" (Hertz 1997, p. 370), who could be sure of commanding a full-time job when they wanted to, or whose part-time earnings produced substantial income. In blue-collar or lower-income families, shift care (Lawlor 1998) or the periodic unemployment of men produced a parenting approach.

In the **market approach to child care**, career-oriented couples hired other people to care for their children. We now look at child care in this sense.

There are essentially three types of nonrelative child care. Paid care may be provided in the child's home by a **nanny**, an **in-home caregiver** who lives in or comes to the house daily (see "A Closer Look at Family Diversity: Diversity and Child Care"). The term **family child care** refers to care provided in a caregiver's home, often by an older woman or a mother who has chosen to remain out of the labor force to care for her own children. Parents who prefer family day care seem to be seeking a family-like atmosphere, with a smaller-scale, less-routinized setting. Perhaps they also desire social similarity of caregiver and parent to better ensure that their children are socialized according to their own values (Greathouse 1996).

Child-care centers and preschools provide care for many children during the workday. While children may not receive as much adult attention as they might with a single care-giver or with family day care, they benefit from greater interaction with other children and a preschool curriculum.

© Seth Resnick/Stock, Boston

Center care provides group care for a larger number of children in child-care centers. The use of child-care centers has increased rapidly, partly as a result of the growing scarcity of in-home caregivers, as relatives or neighbors who formerly cared for children now join the labor force themselves. Increased use of center care is also due to the perception that it offers greater safety and a strong preschool curriculum.[6]

By the time they enter school, an estimated 80 percent of children have had "regular care" in child-care centers, family day care, nursery schools or preschools, or with relatives (American Academy of Pediatrics 1996). Of children under age three, 27 percent are in parental care (one parent works, they work shifts, or a parent cares for the child while working). Twenty-seven percent are in the care of relatives. Another 17 percent of children are in family child-care homes, 22 percent are in a child-care center, and 7 percent are cared for by a nanny (Ehrle, Adams, and Tout 2001, Figure 1). Of children under age five in non-parental care, 41 percent spend more than thirty-five hours a week in care ("Child Care" 2000).

Now there is extensive research on the developmental outcomes of various child-care arrangements. See "As We Make Choices: Child Care and Children's Outcomes" for a discussion of this research.

An estimated 21 percent of children aged six to twelve (four million children) were in **self-care**—i.e., without adult supervision—for an average of five hours a week (Adams and Tout 2000). Self-care is more common in white upper-middle- and middle-class families than in black, Latino, or low-income settings, perhaps because of differences in neighborhood safety (Casper and Smith 2002).

Low-income, single-parent, rural, and Hispanic parents are especially likely to have relatives take care of their children (Atkinson 1994; Phillips and Adams 2001). Hispanic parents seem to prefer either relative or family day care rather than center care, a choice attributed to wanting a "warm and family-like atmosphere" rather than a "formal and cold" child-care center. Family day care may also be seen as providing a personal relationship for the parent with the caregiver, and perhaps a bilingual setting (Chira 1994a).

African American parents prefer a center for its perceived educational benefits, while white parents' preference for a center is more likely to be for the social interaction experiences it provides for children. Some families may seek a provider of their own racial/ethnic group who will maintain the cultural context children have at home, or at a minimum, a white caregiver or center that will provide "racial safety," will not act in a racist way with their children (Uttal 2004).

Research by the Families and Work Institute has found four sources of parental stress regarding child care: (1) it is difficult to find, (2) some arrangements are of lower quality than others, (3) child care is expensive, and (4) "parents are forced to put together a patchwork

---

6. It is important to note with regard to safety that despite a smattering of confirmed cases, concerns about abuse of children in day care have largely proved unfounded; studies indicate that children are at greater risk of abuse in their own homes (Finkelhor, Hotaling, and Sedlak 1991).

As We Make Choices

Child Care and Children's Outcomes

FOCUS ON CHILDREN

Parents who have to make decisions about child care want to know two things: What are the characteristics of quality child care? And what effect does being in child care have on children?

Psychologist Jay Belsky drew considerable attention, in the media as well as in academic circles, when he reported an early finding that infants in their first year who are in nonparental care for twenty or more hours per week "are at elevated risk of being classified as insecure in their **attachments** to their mothers at 12 or 18 months of age" (Belsky 1990, p. 895).[7] This set off the "day care wars" (Karen 1994), in which Belsky has continued to disagree with most other child-care researchers about whether time in child care

is harmful to children and in what circumstances (2002).

A multiple-site longitudinal study was organized by the National Institute for Child Health and Development and has now followed more than 1,300 children from shortly after birth through the first seven years of life (U.S. National Institute for Child Health and Human Development 1999a, 2002). Professor Belsky was one of the thirty researchers initially involved in the study.

The conclusion first drawn from NICHD research was that children in nonrelative care and children cared for by their own parents differ little in development and emotional stability. At fifteen months, there were no independent effects of child-care quality, amount, age of entry, stability, or type of care on *attachment* (NICHD Early Childhood Research

Network 1997a). The study established that at the three-year point "there is no consistent relation between the hours infants and toddlers spend in child care and these children's cognitive, linguistic, or social development" (U.S. National Institute of Child Health and Human Development 1999b). Mothering is a stronger predictor of child outcomes than child-care time or arrangements (NICHD Early Child Care Research Network 1998).

More favorable outcomes in terms of cognitive and linguistic skills were associated with quality of care, described as "when child care providers talk to children, encourage them to ask questions, respond to children's questions, read to them, challenge them to attend to others' feelings, and to different ways of thinking" (U.S. National Institute of Child Health and Human Development 1999b; NICHD Early Child Care Research Network 1999b). Belsky's concerns about child care were discredited.

Yet, there were some negative effects found by research. Child care did have a negative relationship to maternal sensitivity ("how attuned the mother is to the child's wants and needs") and child engagement ("how connected or involved a child appeared to be when relating to his or her mother"). But that finding did not hold for children in *quality care* (NICHD Early Child Care Research Network 1999a; U.S. National Center of Child

7. "**Attachment** represents an active, affective, enduring, and reciprocal bond between two individuals that is believed to be established through repeated interaction over time" (Coleman and Watson 2000, p. 297, citing Mary Ainsworth et al. 1978).

The concept of *attachment* (also discussed in Chapter 5) is significant in this discussion because child care was associated with "maternal deprivation" by the psychologists who developed the attachment concept (Bowlby 1951; also Ainsworth 1967). Bowlby's perspective that maternal deprivation caused children's insufficient attachment to parents was based on studies of British children who were sent out of London to safety during World War II; they were away from their parents for almost the entirety of the five-year war.

Yet Bowlby extrapolated from this extreme situation to conclude that "maternal deprivation" suffered by children of working mothers would lead to attachment problems for their children. Bowlby did not actually study working mothers, but his views were influential nevertheless in discouraging the employment of mothers of young children and the use of child care.

Aside from the obvious weakness of comparing five years to the time spent away from their children by working mothers, the concept of attachment has been criticized on other grounds (that we do not have time to develop in this textbook; see Eyer 1992). Current psychologists have a much more complex conceptualization of attachment (e.g., Coleman and Watson 2000).

Health and Human Development 1999b).

Later publications reported lower cognitive outcomes for children at three years when mothers entered employment *during the first year of life.* That effect also varied by *quality of care* at home and in child care (Brooks-Gunn, Han, and Waldfogel 2002).

As the children approached age five and entered kindergarten, those who had over time spent longer hours in child care were found to have more behavior problems and conflicts with adults (as reported by parents, teachers, and the children themselves). That was true even when quality and type of care were taken into account. The most recently published research found that "the quantity of nonmaternal care was significantly, even if modestly, associated with less positive adjustment [in child care, at home, and in kindergarten]" (NICHD 2003a, p. 998).

Although the results were made much of by Professor Belsky, his co-researchers argued that these were not serious problems—that, in fact, more serious behavior problems were presented by children who had not been in day care at all. They also pointed to the fact that problem behavior was confined to a minority of day-care children—more than 80 percent of children long in care did *not* exhibit any behavior problems ("Day-Care Researchers" 2001). In this view, the findings had a "lack of clinical significance" (Dworkin 2002, p. 167), meaning that they did not signal a level of trouble that should cause concern.

Moreover, children in high-quality center care outperformed children not in care in measures of cognitive skills and language devel-

opment (NICHD Early Child Care Research Group 2000b). And family background factors and maternal sensitivity were more important in their impact on children's adjustment than time in child care (NICHD Early Child Care Research Group 2003a).

The small size of the negative effects, the good adjustment of the preponderance of children, and the greater importance of parental influence in terms of the effects of extended child care should be reassuring to parents who wish to or must use nonparental child care. Research continues, and

a great many questions remain: What impact does an involved father have? Why are boys more vulnerable? . . . Is there, as some researchers believe, something about the 6-month period, when babies are fearful about separation, which makes it especially difficult for children to adjust to their mother's return to work [during the first year of life]? To what extent does high-quality child care compensate for a depressed mother or a difficult home environment? What effect does the quality of the mother's employment have on the child, both in additional income and additional stress brought home, and in personal growth that may shape the child's development? (Lewin 2002, p. 4)

Child-care researchers are considering the policy implications of the research. Belsky (2002) argues for tax or other policies to support full-time parental care in the home, especially during the first year. Other child-care scholars agree that there should be subsidies to permit parents to cut back hours, but at the

same time urge attention to improving the quality of out-of-home care. They believe child care can make a positive contribution to social development if done well (Maccoby and Lewis 2003).

Meanwhile, some experts worry that individuals will read more into the negative results than is there:

It's not a good idea for parents to take a finding that 3-year-olds' school readiness scores are a few points lower if the mother goes back to work early, and say that means the mother should stay home for a year. . . . [T]he kind of statistical analysis the studies use cannot take account of all the complexities of real life, or of the individual differences that allow one family to thrive in a situation that would create enormous stress, and frayed relationships in another. (Researcher Martha Cox in Lewin 2002, p. 4)

Commentators on the research also find it noteworthy that the focus of the NICHD study is on mothers and "maternal sensitivity." A child is considered to be in care when not with the mother—i.e., care by the father is considered "child care" (U.S. National Institute of Child Health and Human Development 2002).

Critical Thinking

If you were the mother of a new baby, would you find this research useful in making your decision about returning to work? Or would you be more inclined to rely on the advice of family members or other parents—or your children's reactions to child care?

What would you like researchers to find out about children in child care?

system of care that tends to fall apart" (Galinsky and Stein 1990, pp. 369–370). About half of parents using paid care change their arrangements each year because a caregiver quit, the cost was too high, the hours or location were inconvenient, the child was unhappy, or the parent disliked the caregiver (Shellenbarger 1991d). As they struggle to find quality, affordable child care, many parents must make more than one arrangement for each child (Folk and Yi 1994). As they patch together a series of child-care arrangements, the system becomes increasingly unpredictable (Galinsky and Stein 1990; Blau and Robins 1998).

Talk to employed parents of young children for any length of time, and the subject turns to the difficulty of finding child care. Some parents pay providers months in advance to reserve space for babies not yet born. Child care is even more difficult to find for mildly ill youngsters too sick to go to their regular day-care facility, although there are now centers that begin to fill this need (Galinsky and Stein 1990). Then too, family day care and many child-care centers are usually open weekdays only and close by 7 P.M. Some parents, such as single mothers on shift work or those who travel, need access to twenty-four-hour care centers (Curtis 1997).

Adding to the difficulty of finding day care is the fact that parents are looking for *quality child care*. The American Academy of Pediatrics and the American Public Health Association have established guidelines that describe quality child care as having the following features:

1. Adult caregivers who have specialized training or experience in child development

2. A warm, nurturing, attentive, and developmentally appropriate and stimulating learning environment

3. Small groups of children with sufficient numbers of consistent, interactive caregivers who have long-term relationships with the children in their care

4. Good communication between program staff and families and policies that actively involve parents in child-care activities and that try to enhance parenting skills (American Academy of Pediatrics 1996; *www.aap.org/policy*)

"As We Make Choices: Selecting a Child-Care Facility" discusses things that parents should look for in choosing day care.

Quality of care is consistently linked to school readiness, language skills, and the absence of behavior problems. Yet only 10 percent of infant child-care sites and 34 percent of those for three-year-olds completely

"Hey, look -- Mom left us an internal memo."

Some children are in "self-care" after school, increasingly true in middle-class families.

met the standards (NICHD Early Child Care Research Network 1999b). Overall, researchers sponsored by the National Institute of Child Health and Human Development rate the quality of child care in the United States as "fair—neither outstanding nor terrible" (Dr. Cathryn L. Booth, quoted in U.S. National Institute of Child Health and Human Development 1999a). In terms of settings, in-home caregivers (including fathers and grandparents) and only one child provided the most "positive caregiving," with centers with large child–adult ratios providing the lowest level of caregiving. The child–adult ratio and the advantage of in-home care was less important for children aged three and older (NICHD Early Child Care Research Network 2000a).

Meanwhile, paid child care is expensive for parents (Anderson and Vail 1999). For those paying for child care, costs amount to between 10 percent and 35 percent of the family budget ("Facts About Child Care" 1998). Lower-income families pay a disproportionately higher percentage of their earned income than do middle- or upper-income families—often equal to what they pay for housing (Galinsky and Stein 1990; Glass and Estes 1997a). Yet, while child care is expensive for parents, child-care staff are not paid well, and the low pay is an important factor in staff turnover (Zuckerman 2000). Keeping center care affordable may lead to caregiver–child ratios that are too low for quality care (Lewin 1989b; Clinton 1990).

ELDER CARE There are some parallels between workers' responsibility for child care and for elder care. **Elder care** involves providing assistance with daily living activities to an elderly relative who is chronically frail, ill, or disabled (Galinsky and Stein 1990). In a 1990 survey of 7,000 federal workers, nearly half said they cared for dependent adults. Of those, three-quarters had missed some work to do so (Beck 1990, p. 51). About 14 percent of caregivers to the elderly have switched from full- to part-time jobs, and 12 percent have left the work force entirely; another 28 percent have considered quitting their jobs (Galinksy and Stein 1990). Yet it is somewhat unusual for U.S. companies to offer employees help with elderly dependents (Beck 1990). Care of the elderly is discussed in more detail in Chapter 18.

FAMILY LEAVE **Family leave** involves an employee being able to take an extended period of time from work, either paid or unpaid, for the purpose of caring for a newborn, for a newly adopted or seriously ill child, for the care of an elderly parent, or for their own health needs, with the guarantee of a job upon returning. The concept of family leave incorporates maternity, paternity, and elder-care leaves.

The 1993 Family and Medical Leave Act mandates up to twelve weeks of unpaid family leave for workers in companies with at least fifty employees. To date, more than forty million workers have used family leave (Lichtman and Nelson 2003). Unpaid leave will not solve the problem for a vast majority of employees, however, as most working parents need the income.

More employers are now offering paid maternity leave, though, and 43 percent of women who worked during pregnancy took paid leave following the birth; another 11 percent took paid disability leave (Smith, Downs, and O'Connell 2001). The state of California has become the first state to adopt a law mandating paid leave (Broder 2002).

FLEXIBLE SCHEDULING About 28 percent of full-time workers have flexible schedules (U.S. Bureau of Labor Statistics 2002b). **Flexible scheduling** includes options such as **job sharing** (two people share one position), working at home or telecommuting, compressed workweeks, flextime, and personal days (days off for the purpose of attending to a personal matter such as a doctor's appointment or a child's school program). Compressed workweeks allow an employee to concentrate the workweek into three or four, sometimes slightly longer, days. **Flextime** involves flexible starting and ending times, with required core hours.

Flexible scheduling, although not a panacea, can help parents share child care or be at home before and after an older child's school hours. Some types of work do not lend themselves to flexible scheduling (Christensen and Staines 1990), but the practice has become available in the federal government and in some companies because it offers employee-recruiting advantages, prevents turnover, and frees up office space when some employees work at home. Even when not formally offered, it may be possible. In a survey of employees in 1997, almost half reported that they had some choice in when to begin and end the workday, and 19 percent did some work at home (Lewin 1998).

Employees who get flexible hours report enhanced job satisfaction and loyalty to the employer—but they still do not find that flextime alleviates all or even most family–work conflicts. For one thing, women are slightly less likely to have this option, though they are more in need of it given the typical division of labor in the home (Christensen and Staines 1990; U.S. Bureau of Labor Statistics 2002b).

Who Will Provide What Is Needed to Resolve Work–Family Issues?

Policy experts, lawmakers, employers, parents, and citizens disagree over who has the responsibility to provide what is needed regarding various work–family solutions. A principal conflict concerns whether solutions such as child care or family leave should be government policy, or constitute privileges for which a worker must negotiate.

The countries of northwestern Europe, which have a more pronatalist and social-welfare orientation than the United States, tend to view family concerns as a right (Glass and Estes 1997b). There is "the pervasive belief . . . that children are a precious national resource for which society has collective responsibility" (Clinton 1990, p. 25). Putting this belief into practice, most European countries are committed to *paid* maternity (or parental) leave for up to at least six months and usually much longer (Waldfogel 2001). The United States is the only major industrialized nation that does not mandate paid maternity leave; many far-less-wealthy nations provide it (Seager and Olson 1986). Accustomed to a lack of family policy at the federal level, American parents sometimes turn their attention to local schools as a source of help for the care of older children in after-school programs and

As We Make Choices

Selecting a Child-Care Facility

FOCUS ON CHILDREN

Universal, comprehensive, and government-funded day care does not exist in the United States today. While some parents will have access to child-care facilities through government programs or their employers, many parents are on their own in selecting a child-care facility.

Some parents will arrange their work schedules to care for their children, while others will hire a nanny or recruit relatives into this role. Here we make some suggestions to parents who are choosing from commercially available child care.

State laws, which vary in both provisions and enforcement, establish minimal standards, and professional organizations like the American Academy of Pediatrics have developed guidelines for quality child care. Child advocates also offer advice on selecting child care. We outline here some of the things we think parents should consider when exploring and choosing child care for their children. Some are very tangible and specific, like the ratio of children to adults. Some are more qualitative and can best be judged by the parent during visits, including post-placement visits, to the child-care facility. Some are more applicable to center care, while others are relevant to family day care as well:

- *Low staff-to-child ratio.* Positive caregiving is associated with a low staff-to-child ratio, especially for very young children. State guidelines vary, but experts believe they tend to be minimal. Best would be six to eight infants per two caregivers; six to twelve one- to two-year-olds to three teachers; fourteen to twenty children per two teachers for older preschoolers.

- *Stable staff.* Some staff turnover is inevitable, but it should not exceed 25 percent a year. If children must constantly adjust to changes in personnel, they cannot build the warm and trusting relationships that they need with caregivers. It is also important to learn how changes are handled with the children: How much attention is given to preparing them for a caretaker's departure? To helping them adjust to new staff?

- *A well-trained staff.* Trained staff are likely to be more responsive to children, more stimulating, and more creative in their activities with children. Because child-care workers are poorly paid, it is difficult to find centers with highly educated staff or training in early childhood education. Nevertheless, the ideal situation is for staff to be knowledgeable about child development and to participate in workshops or other ongoing training on best practices. Ask about staff education and plans for further training. In family daycare settings, ask whether other family members or others who are not formally "staff" are nevertheless involved in caring for the children.

- *Cultural sensitivity.* Caregivers should be knowledgeable about the diverse racial/ethnic, religious, and social class cultures of this society, as well as that children may come from various types of families, such as traditional nuclear, dual-earner, gay/lesbian, single parent, divorced, or remarried.

- *Other staff qualities.* A warm personality and interpersonal sensitivity are essential. Caregivers who let children express their feelings and who will take their views into account are desirable. Because staff members will have an influence on the child's language acquisition, being verbally fluent and well-spoken is an asset. Some parents may have specific preferences, such as male as well as female caregivers, or minority or bilingual staff. Parents seeking family child care may have a specific type of home environment in mind and should consider how well their values and lifestyle match that of the caretaker.

- *The right kind of attention.* Babies need a responsive adult who coos and talks to them. One-year-olds need a staff member who will name things for them. Two-year-olds need someone who reads to them. Older children need adults as well but can also profit from social interaction and activities with other children. Adults should be responsive to children and interact with them, not limit themselves to a directive, organizing role. Do they greet the child warmly? Do they seem interested in what the child is doing or saying? They should make eye contact and perhaps bend to their level when speaking with children, not brush the child off or have a ho-hum attitude. How staff interact with children can best be ascertained by observation in visits to the center.

- *Age-appropriate and stimulating activities and play spaces.* Experts differ on how academic a preschool program should be, and parents differ in how "educational" a program they are looking for. Look for a facility that also fosters play and community activities such as trips to the zoo or fire station—and one that prepares children for learning rather than offering a first-grade program in preschool. In any case, parents should pick a child-care facility that is a good match for their values in this regard. Parents should find that the staff have a well-thought-out rationale for their program that they can describe to the parent. On the negative side, avoid child-care centers or family day-care environments that seem to provide only custodial care or allow lots of TV watching. What kinds of indoor and outdoor spaces are there for constructive and imaginative child play? What toys, books, and games are available? What are the ages of the other children who will be with your child in care?

- *Discipline.* Inquire about how staff handle the minor behavior problems that inevitably arise with children. "Time out" is typically recommended by child experts, with physical discipline to be avoided. States vary in their laws regarding whether child caretakers are permitted to spank children. Where this is legally permissible, there may be centers or family caretakers who are indeed

committed to the use of physical discipline—of course, parents may vary in terms of whether or not this is acceptable to them. Parents should both inquire and observe how "incidents" are handled, and ascertain whether the child-care facility's policy and practice match what they want for their children. Use of physical discipline suggests that the caretakers are not well trained in how to handle problems and may create a somewhat fearful atmosphere for children as well.

- *A relationship with parents.* This will vary by whether the child is in family day care or a center. Any child-care facility should welcome parental involvement, in the form of visits at a minimum; be wary of facilities that do not allow unannounced visits. Parents should be able to feel they are supported in their parental role by the family caretaker or center staff (rather than distanced or unduly criticized). Parents should feel included in the child's daily life in child care. Especially important is how and how well family caretakers or center staff communicate with parents about problems.

- *Practical and financial considerations.* Parents will be told the basic hours and fees, but also need to know what happens when the child is sick or the family leaves town and the child does not attend as usual. Can arrangements be made to have children arrive earlier or leave later than normal center hours on occasion? Or regularly? Is transportation provided? If so, how costly is it, and how reliable?

- *Recommendations from other parents.* Talk to other parents about

the facility. If you don't know any parents with children in the center, ask for names and phone numbers of parents who have children enrolled there, and talk to them about the facility. If a center declines to give you this information, see if you can determine whether that is barred by a privacy policy adopted by their board to protect parents or whether the management is being elusive and defensive.

- *Visits.* Visit the day-care center as often as you can—and, if possible, unannounced—both before and after selecting a facility.

- *Accreditation.* The National Association for the Education of Young Children (*www.naeyc.org*) is an accrediting agency for child-care centers. If you plan to use center care, you might want to check their website for listings of accredited centers in your state. While not all good child-care centers have taken this step, accreditation by the NAEYC is a good sign.

Critical Thinking

What qualities do you think are most important in choosing a child-care center?

How would you compare in-home care, a family day care, or center care on the qualities you think are important?

Sources: American Academy of Pediatrics 1992; Coordinated Access for Child Care 2001; Find Care 2002; Galinsky 2001; NICHD Early Child Care Research Network 2000a, 2003b; Phillips and Adams 2001; U.S. National Institute of Child Health and Human Development 2002; Watson 1984; Working Moms Refuge 2001.

younger children in preschool programs and all-day kindergarten.

Some large corporations demonstrate interest in effecting **family-friendly workplace policies** that are supportive of employee efforts to combine family and work commitments. Such policies include on-site child-care centers, sick-child care, subsidies for child-care services or child-care locator services, flexible schedules, parental or family leaves, workplace seminars and counseling programs, and support groups for employed parents (Galinsky and Stein 1990).

Because family-friendly policies and programs are voluntary, companies that initiate them tend to have CEOs (often females) who are committed to helping resolve work–family conflicts (Kingston 1990). And they are more common in sectors with a high proportion of female workers. Such research as exists on outcomes for employers suggests that they help in recruitment, reduce employee stress and turnover, enhance morale, and thus increase productivity (Galinsky and Stein 1990; Shellenbarger and Trost 1992b; Glass and Estes 1997b).

But family-friendly policies are hardly available to all American workers. Moreover, according to a 2003 survey by the Society for Human Resources, companies that had maintained family-friendly policies are cutting them back now to cut costs and to take advantage of a labor supply that outnumbers available jobs. Or they have concluded that it is important to have employees work consistently at the office rather than telecommuting (Armour 2003, 2004).

Family-friendly policies are not necessarily available to all employees even within a company that offers them. Companies have tended to leave the administration of work–family policies to the discretion of individual managers or supervisors. Although some managers aggressively promote work–family benefits, others view them less favorably. Thus, many employees, especially men, are reluctant to lobby for child-care benefits or request time off to attend to family needs. Then too, when supervisors approve work-family benefits on a case-by-case basis, they become rewards for prized performers (Galinksy and Stein 1990; Hochschild 1997).

Professionals and managers are much more likely than technical and clerical workers to have access to leave policies, telecommuting, or flexible scheduling (Christensen and Staines 1990). "At the high end, the big corporations are stepping up to provide benefits to help families, and at the lower end, as women leave welfare, there's now much more support for the idea that they deserve help with child care. But the blue-collar families, the K-Mart cashier, get nothing" (work–family policy expert Kathleen Sylvester, quoted in Lewin 2001d).

Single individuals or childless workers have begun to complain about what they see as the privileging of parents of young children when they themselves may have family caregiving needs: for elderly parents, siblings, or friends with whom they maintain caregiving relationships. They may find it onerous to cover for co-workers who are on leave or out of the office. The Family Leave Act and some company benefit policies do provide some coverage of employees' need to take care of elderly parents.

We have devoted attention to work–family policies because these issues so strongly influence the options and choices of individual families. We would like to think that family-friendly companies represent the future of work. After all, "[C]hildren . . . are 'public goods'; society profits greatly from future generations as stable, well-adjusted adults, as well as future employees and tax payers" (Avellar and Smock 2003, p. 605). Nevertheless, these voluntary programs and benefits do depend on cost constraints and corporate self-interest and are not likely to be so available during economic downturns or restructuring. Moreover, family-friendly programs need to be more comprehensive in terms of benefits and more widely available to all echelons of workers. However, keep in mind that most workers need extensive family support only during the period in which they are parenting young children. In that perspective, the challenge looks less daunting (Glass and Estes 1997b).

Entering the political arena to work toward the kinds of changes families want is one aspect of creating satisfying marriages and families. But employed couples also want to know what *they* can do themselves to maintain happy marriages. We now turn to that topic.

■ The Two-Earner Marriage and the Relationship ■

We have been addressing problems associated with two-earner marriages. But research shows that—provided there is enough time to accomplish things—a person's having multiple roles (such as employee/spouse/parent) does not add to stress and in fact may enhance personal happiness (O'Neil and Greenberger 1994; Roxburgh 1997). Research also points to the

A San Francisco choreographer goes back to work, taking her new baby to a ballet rehearsal: another way to combine work and family.

heightened satisfaction, excitement, and vitality that two-earner couples can have because these partners are more likely to have common experiences and shared world views than traditional spouses, who often lead very different everyday lives (Chafetz 1989; Hughes, Galinsky, and Morris 1992). At the same time, conflict may arise in two-earner marriages as couples negotiate the division of household labor and more generally adjust to changing roles (Orbuch and Custer 1995; Hondagneu-Sotelo and Messner 1999; P. Johnson 1998).

Gender Strategies

How a couple allocates paid and unpaid work represents a combination of each partner's **gender strategy**, or way of working through everyday situations that takes into account an individual's beliefs and deep feelings about gender roles, as well as her or his employment commitments (Hochschild 1989). In today's changing society, conscious beliefs and deeper feelings about gender may conflict. For example, a number of men in Hochschild's study of working couples articulated egalitarian sentiments, but had clearly retained gut-level traditional feelings about sex differences.

Tensions exhibited by many of Hochschild's respondents were a consequence of "faster-changing women and slower-changing men" (1989, p. 11). Moreover, even when spouses share similar attitudes about gender, circumstances may not allow them to act accordingly. In one couple interviewed by Hochschild, both partners held the traditional belief that a wife should be a full-time homemaker. Yet because the couple needed the wife's income, she was employed, and they shared housework on a nearly equal basis. How couples manage their everyday lives in the face of contradictions reflects a consciously or unconsciously negotiated gender strategy.

One gender strategy noted by Hochschild (1989) involves a husband's praising his wife's homemaking skills rather than actually sharing the tasks. A more recent study of two-earner couples (Wilkie, Ferree, and Ratcliff 1998) found that a wife's receiving credit for homemaking, and a husband's receiving credit for breadwinning, contribute to both spouses' sense of fairness in their marriage. Another gender strategy, used by wives who would like a husband to do more but know he won't and are reluctant to insist, is to compare their husbands to other men "out there" who apparently are doing even less (Hochschild 1989).

A fairly common gender strategy, according to Hochschild (1989), is to develop **family myths**—"versions of reality that obscure a core truth in order to manage a family tension." For example, when a husband shares housework in a way that contradicts his traditional beliefs and/or feelings, couples may develop a myth alleging the wife's poor health or incompetence in order to protect the man's image of himself. A common family myth defines the wife as an organized and energetic superwoman who has few needs of her own, requires little from her husband, and congratulates herself on how much she can accomplish (Thompson 1991).

Maintaining Intimacy While Negotiating Provider Roles and the Second Shift

There are two kinds of changes involved in moving toward more egalitarian family roles. Women come to share the provider role, while men take greater responsibility for household work. In considering the provider role, we turn to the notion of *meaning* again: Is women's sharing of the provider role a *threat*, so that men fear losing masculine identity, women's domestic services, and power? Or is a woman's sharing the provider role a *benefit*, because men benefit materially from wives' employment and earnings and from a partner's enthusiasm for the wider world? Recent research suggests that men are more apt to see women's employment as a benefit. As a result, there is an "ideological shift of men toward egalitarianism" (Zuo and Tang 2000).

It is household work that seems to be the greater arena for stress and conflict as roles change. Study after study shows that marital satisfaction is greater when wives feel that husbands share fairly in the household work. But a woman's becoming a secondary or co-provider does not necessarily lead to a husband's sharing of household work.

Although husbands may now carry a greater share of the family work than in the past, getting comfortable with transitions in marital roles is not a quick and easy process. But when the transition proceeds from a mutual commitment to achieve an equitable relationship, the result may be greater intimacy. A first step is to address the conflict.

ACCEPT CONFLICT AS A REALITY   The idea that marital partners may sometimes have competing interests departs from the more romanticized view that sees marriages and families as integrated units with shared desires and goals. As a first step toward maintaining intimacy during role changes, partners need to recognize their possibly competing interests and to expect conflict (Paden and Buehler 1995).

ACCEPT AMBIVALENCE   After accepting conflict as a reality, the next step in maintaining intimacy as spouses adjust to two-earner marriages is for both to recognize that each may have ambivalent feelings. The following excerpt from one young husband's essay for his English composition class is illustrative: "I'm in school six days a week. My wife works between 40 to 50 hours a week. So I do the majority of the cooking, cleaning, and laundry. To me this is not right. But am I wrong to think so? I'm lost in my own mind."

Women may also be ambivalent. They want their husbands to be happy, they want their husbands to help and support them, they feel angry about past inequalities, and they feel guilty about their declining interest in housekeeping and husband care and their decreasing willingness to accommodate their husbands' preferences. Furthermore, men who participate have opinions about how child rearing or housework should be done. As a husband begins to pitch in, his wife may resent his intrusion into her traditional domain.

EMPATHIZE   A next step is to empathize. This may be difficult, for it is tempting instead to retaliate for past or current hurts or to continually point out where a partner falls short. But if couples are to maintain intimacy, they must make sure that *both* partners win (see Chapter 14).

It has been suggested that as wives empathize, they try to recognize that a husband's lack of participation is very likely "due to insensitivity, not malice" (Crosby 1991, p. 167). Most husbands underestimate the number of hours that household labor takes (Wilkie, Ferree, and Ratcliff 1998). It is never easy to adjust to new roles, and men especially may feel they have a lot to lose. Men can gain, too, of course: They develop domestic skills, their marriage is enhanced, there is more money, and they benefit from spending time with their children. In Hochschild's study (1989), some fathers who felt they had been emotionally deprived in relationships with their own fathers took great pleasure in creating more satisfying family relationships with and for their children.

As husbands empathize, they need to be aware that their willingness to participate in household tasks is vitally important to wives, especially to employed wives (McHale and Crouter 1992). For one thing, wives doing a second shift value having a "down time" due to a responsive mate's freeing them from overload or from specific tasks they dislike. On another level, a husband's sharing carries a symbolic meaning for a wife, indicating that her work is recognized and appreciated and that her husband cares. Indeed, wives are more inclined to see the division of household labor as fair when their work is obviously appreciated. A husband's participation becomes caring (Thompson 1991; Blair and Johnson 1992).

STRIKE AN EQUITABLE BALANCE Researchers who studied 153 Pennsylvania couples with children in school concluded the following: "Our data imply that the adjustment of individual family members, as well as harmonious family relationships, requires a *balance* among the very different and often conflicting needs and goals of different family members" (McHale and Crouter 1992, pp. 545–546, italics in original). Once equity is habitual, calculation and constant comparison are no longer necessary; some observers point out that the balance need not be an exactly calculated 50–50 split. Such an arrangement, complete with rules and his-and-her chore lists, may seem too impersonal: People find it alienating when others treat them according to some fixed rule rather than as individuals with particular needs and desires. We do not feel so much cared for when others' responsiveness is routinized and rule-bound (Thompson 1991, p. 188).

SHOW MUTUAL APPRECIATION Once partners have committed themselves to striking a balance, they need to create ways to let each know the other is loved. Traditional role expectations were relatively rigid and limiting, but they could be a way of expressing love and caring. When a wife cooked her husband's favorite meal or a husband could pay for family travel, each felt cared about. As spouses relinquish some traditional behaviors, they need to create new ways of letting each other know they care.

Many people have noted the potential of shared work and of shared provider and caregiving roles for enriching a marriage (Beeghley 1996; Risman and Johnson-Sumerford 1998). One important, though small-scale, study of "having it all" couples—who are both employed and who share parenting and related housework—concludes that "Equality is achievable. Although equality may still be the exception in American households, men and women today increasingly

This couple seems happy with their work as welders and happy with each other.

Stewart Cohen/Index Stock Imagery

believe in gender equality. . . . Equal sharers, though rare today, may be our models for tomorrow" (Deutsch 1999, p. 5).

This discussion of the second shift has been framed in terms of marriage, the relationships of husbands and wives as they negotiate this marital challenge. Marriage *is* most likely to draw in cultural expectations of a traditional division of labor. But the second shift exists in other family forms. In heterosexual cohabiting couples, the woman does less household labor and the man more than in marriage, while in gay and lesbian couples the domestic division of labor is rather egalitarian. Single women and men also have work to do to maintain their households, especially if they are parents. Single men tend to do more than married men, while single women do less than married women. Interestingly, remarried couples are more likely to share housework than men and women in a first marriage (Coltrane 2000; Patterson 2000), as are couples who cohabited before marriage (Batalova and Cohen 2002). We should keep in mind that employees are embedded in diverse families and also that partners may come up with a variety of ways of accomplishing providing and caregiving.

The next chapter examines communication and managing conflict in families, skills that can smooth the negotiation of work/family roles.

In Sum

- The labor force is a social invention. Traditionally, marriage has been different for men and women: The husband's job has been as breadwinner, the wife's as homemaker. These roles changed as more and more women entered the work force. Women still remain segregated occupationally, and they earn lower incomes than men, on average.

- We distinguish between two-earner and two-career marriages. In the latter, wives and husbands both earn high wages and work for intrinsic rewards. Even in such marriages, the husband's career usually has priority.

- We have seen that paid work is not usually structured to allow time for household responsibilities and that women, more than men, continue to adjust their time to accomplish both paid and unpaid work. Many wives would prefer shared roles, and negotiation and tension over this issue cast a shadow on many marriages. An incomplete transition to equality at work and at home affects family life profoundly. However, in recent years, men have been increasing their share of the housework.

- We have emphasized that both cultural expectations and public policy affect people's options. As individuals come to realize this, we can expect pressure on public officials and corporations to meet the needs of working families by providing supportive policies: parental leave, child care, and flextime.

- Household work and child care are pressure points as women enter the labor force and the two-earner marriage becomes the norm. To make it work, either the structure of work must be changed, social policy must support working families, or women and men must change their household role patterns—very probably all three.

- To be successful, two-earner marriages will require social policy support and workplace flexibility. But there are some things couples themselves can keep in mind to enable their management of a working-couple family. Recognition of both positive and negative feelings and open communication between partners can help working couples cope with an imperfect social world.

Key Terms

ambivalent provider couple
attachment
center care
child care
commuter marriage
co-provider couple
elder care
family child care
family-friendly workplace policy
family leave
family myth
flexible scheduling
flextime
gender construction perspective
gender strategy
good provider role
househusband
ideological perspective
in-home caregiver
job sharing
labor force
main/secondary provider couple
market approach to child care
motherhood penalty
mothering approach to child care
nanny
occupational segregation
parenting approach to child care
rational investment perspective
reinforcing cycle
resource hypothesis
role-reversed provider couple
second shift
self-care
sequencing mom
shift work
stalled revolution
time availability perspective
trailing spouse
two-career marriage
two-earner marriage
two-person single career
unpaid family work
wage gap

Questions for Review and Reflection

1. Discuss to what extent distinctions between husbands' and wives' work are disappearing.

2. What do you see as the advantages and disadvantages of men being househusbands? Discuss this from the points of view of both men and women.

3. What are some advantages and disadvantages of home-based work? Why are mothers more likely to choose this arrangement, when possible, than fathers?

4. What work–family conflicts do you see around you? Interview some married or single-parent friends of yours for concrete examples and for some suggestions for resolving such conflicts.

5. Policy Question. What "family-friendly" workplace policies would you like to see instituted? Which would you be likely to take advantage of?

Suggested Readings

Crittenden, Ann. 2001. *The Price of Motherhood: Why the Most Important Job in the World Is Still the Least Valued.* New York: Metropolitan. The title speaks to the point that motherhood is economically disadvantaged and insufficiently supported by society. Crittenden argues for more respect and more resources for mothers.

Galinsky, Ellen. 1999. *Ask the Children: What Children Really Think About Working Parents.* New York: Morrow. Reports a survey that gives us the child's viewpoint on work and family.

Hondagneu-Sotelo, Pierrette. 2001. *Doméstica: Immigrant Workers Cleaning and Caring In the Shadow of Affluence.* Berkeley, CA: University of California Press. Known for her work on gender in immigrant Latino families, here Hondagneu-Sotelo provides an in-depth study of the immigrant workers on which so many dual-career families depend.

Landry, Bart. 2000. *Black Working Wives: Pioneers of the American Family Revolution.* Berkeley, CA: University of California Press. This award-winning book traces the history of the black two-earner family. Black two-earner families were common before there were two-earner families visible among whites—hence the term "pioneers."

Families and Work Institute/The Fatherhood Project

http://www.familiesandwork.org

Nonprofit organization devoted to research and policy on work and families. President Ellen Galinksy, an authority on work/family issues, is often quoted in the press. The Fatherhood Project, directed by James Levine, is part of the institute and works to develop "ways to support men's involvement in fatherhood."

U.S. Bureau of Labor Statistics

http://www.bls.gov

Part of the U.S. Labor Department, the BLS maintains statistical data on work and workers. This includes much information on the employment and income of men and women in families. In addition to periodic reports, the BLS publishes the *Monthly Labor Review*—which is accessible on the BLS website. It often contains articles on families.

Virtual Society: The Wadsworth Sociology Resource Center

 Go to the Sociology Resource Center at **http:// sociology.wadsworth.com** for a wealth of online resources, including a companion website for your text that provides study aids such as self-quizzes for each chapter and a practice final exam, as well as links to sociology websites and information on the latest theories and discoveries in the field. In addition, you will find further suggested readings, flash cards, MicroCase online exercises, and appendices on a range of subjects.

Online Study Tool

Marriage & Family ⊗ Now™ Go to **http://sociology .wadsworth.com** to reach the companion website for your text and use the Marriage&FamilyNow access code that came with your book to access this study tool. Take a practice pretest after you have read each chapter, and then use the study plan provided to master that chapter. Afterward, take a posttest to monitor your progress.

Search Online with InfoTrac College Edition

For additional information, exercises, and key words to aid your research, explore InfoTrac College Edition, your online library that offers full-length articles from thousands of scholarly and popular publications. Click on *InfoTrac College Edition* under *Chapter Resources* at the companion website and use the access code that came with your book.

■ Search keywords: *family/families + time.* Explore the Internet to see what research or commentary exists on time pressures, families' time use, and time management.

■ *children's household work.* Do children perform household labor—or not? What specifically do children do to help with housework and child care?

Chapter 13

Communication *and* Managing Conflict *in* Marriages *and* Families

A defining feature of a close relationship is that one partner's psychological states and actions have the capacity to influence those of the other partner.

ANNE THOMPSON AND NIALL BOLGER

When two people always agree, there's no need for one of them anyway.

BEN BROWN, 54, MARRIED 31 YEARS

PROVIDING EMOTIONAL SECURITY AND feelings of belonging is an important function of families today. Partly because of this situation, families are powerful environments. Nowhere else in our society is there such power to support, hurt, comfort, denigrate, reassure, ridicule, hate, and love. It follows that the emotional tone of a couple's everyday communication is very important. Research makes it clear that the expression of positive feelings is a very important determinant of marital and family happiness (Gottman and Levensen 2000; Roberts 2000). Couples who communicate mutual affection create a contagious "spiraling effect" so that the household atmosphere becomes one of emotional support, affecting their children as well (White 1999). Distressed couples, on the other hand, tend toward negative exchanges that put these couples' marriages on a downward spiral (Driver and Gottman 2004; Gottman et al. 1998; Marchand and Hock 2000).

Conflict is a natural part of every relationship. But research shows that unhappily married couples are distinguished by two things: first, their failure to manage conflict, and second, the absence of positive affect, or communications of affection, between them (Booth, Crouter, and Clements 2001; Driver and Gottman 2004). It is imperative to think about how we communicate with our loved ones on a daily basis.

There are several ways to look at couples' communication. For example, psychologists might look at how partners' individual personality characteristics influence their communication and marital satisfaction. One study like this (Bouchard, Lussier, and Sabourin 1999) found that partners who are agreeable, imaginative, intellectually curious, liberal in their attitudes,

and conscientious are more likely to have better communication and marital adjustment (also see Jeffries 2000). On the other side of this coin, depressed and chronically worried or anxious, guilt-ridden, and perfectionist personalities are associated with poorer couple communication and less marital satisfaction (Bouchard, Lussier, and Sabourin 1999; Haring, Hewitt, and Flett 2003; Marchand and Hock 2000). A second way to look at couple communication and satisfaction is through the ecology perspective (see Chapter 3), whereby family interaction is seen as influenced by outside stressors (Sokolski and Hendrick 1999) such as economic uncertainty or racism (Diggs and Paster 1998).

This chapter will focus on couple communication using mainly an interactionist perspective—looking at patterns of interaction between partners. We will discuss some healthy attitudes and propose some guidelines for communicating constructively. Also, we'll see that the sulking that characterizes unhappiness and boredom in intimate relationships often results from partners' attempts to deny or ignore conflict, and we'll examine several other outcomes of refusing to deal openly with conflict. We will explore some guidelines for addressing conflict in ways that can actually enhance the intimate bond between loving partners. To begin, we'll look at family cohesiveness, or cohesion, and see what partners can do to enhance it.

▪ Family Cohesion ▪

A clear implication from the body of research on marital communication is that marriages are held together by positive communication and the expression of feelings on a regular or daily basis (Gottman and Levensen 2000). What can partners and other family members do to create **family cohesion**—the emotional bonding of family members?

In an effort to find out what makes families strong and cohesive, social scientist Nick Stinnett has built a career researching and writing about the characteristics of "strong families." Initially, Stinnett researched 130 "strong families" in rural and urban areas throughout Oklahoma (Stinnett 1979, 1985). Obviously, this limited sample, selected with help from home economics extension agents, has no claim to representativeness. The concept of "strong family" is equally subjective. Various individuals or groups have their own ideas about family strengths that are likely to vary by religion, ethnicity, and political persuasion. Stinnett (1997) has more recently used the term "good families," by which he largely means "resilient" families—ones that are able to face crises and stay supportively together. Meanwhile, Stinnett's interest in strong families has been influential in stimulating research on the specifications and correlates of family solidarity and satisfaction (see, for example, Meredith et al. 1989 on holiday celebrations and other family rituals; see also Bradbury, Fincham, and Beach 2000; Gottman and Notarius 2000).

Research overwhelmingly supports what may be intuitively obvious: The existence or nonexistence of positive feelings is a very important determinant, not only of marital and family happiness (Gottman and Levensen 2000; Roberts 2000; Sacco and Phares 2001) but also of each partner's psychological well-being (Cotton, Burton, and Rushing 2003). When Stinnett made his observations of family strengths, six qualities stood out. First and most important, members often communicated *appreciation for one another*. They "built each other up psychologically" (p. 25). One way of doing this is to express affection for one's partner by touching or hugging (Mackey, Diemer, and O'Brien 2000). Another way of doing this is to really listen to one another, a topic addressed in greater length later in this chapter. Interestingly, research conducted by highly esteemed communication psychologists has found that "The absence of positive affect and not the presence of negative affect . . . was most predictive of later divorcing" (Gottman and Levenson 2000, p. 743). In Stinnett's assessment, "each of us likes to be with people who make us feel good about ourselves" (p. 25); thus, members of a cohesive family *like* being together (Stinnett 2003; see also Canary, Stafford, and Semic 2002).

Stinnett suggests an exercise to help family members express appreciation for one another. Family members sit in a circle. Taking turns, each tells something that he or she likes about the person to her or his left. When they have gone around the circle once or twice, each member then shares something that he or she likes about himself or herself. After that, the direction is reversed, and members say something that they like about the person to their right. The exercise needn't take long, and even when all members are not present, it helps build a sense of family togetherness and appreciation for one another. Studies show that families

maintain more-supportive interaction patterns for a time after the experience. To create togetherness, then, families might use this technique periodically.

Second, Stinnett found that members of strong families *arranged their personal schedules* so that they could do things together or simply be together. Other scholars as well (e.g., Hochschild 2003) emphasize the importance of making time to give and receive emotional nurturance despite—or because of—our increasingly hectic society. In Stinnett's research, the members of some families agreed to save Sundays for one another. Or members might agree to reserve every other weekend strictly for family activities. What families do together at home doesn't have to be routine, habitual, or boring: They might have a winter picnic in front of the fireplace, for example.

Third, members of strong families had a *high degree of commitment* to promoting one another's happiness and welfare and to the family group as a whole. And they "put their money where their mouths were," investing time and energy in the family group. When life got so hectic that members didn't have enough time for their families, they listed the activities they were involved in, found those that weren't worth their time, and scratched them off their lists, leaving more free time for their families (Stinnett 2003). Stinnett comments on the element of knowledgeable decision making in that action:

> This sounds very simple, but how many of us do it? We too often get involved and it's not always because we want to be. We act so often as if we cannot change the situation [but] we do have a choice. . . . [T]here is a great deal that families can do to make life more enjoyable. (Stinnett 1979, p. 28)

A fourth characteristic of the families that Stinnett studied was *spiritual orientation*. Findings from a large national sample show that being *religious* does not necessarily make for happier marriages (Booth et al. 1995). However, some family life educators (Sponsel 2003) offer some evidence to the contrary. Although Stinnett's "strong families" were not necessarily members of an organized religion, they did have a sense of some power and purpose greater than themselves and typically evidenced a "hopeful attitude toward life" (DeFrain 2002). In other words, they had a spiritual orientation.

Fifth, Stinnett found that strong families were able to *deal positively with crises*. Members were able to see something good in a bad situation, even if only gratitude that they had one another and were able to face the crisis together, supporting one another (Stinnett 2003). An example comes from a study of sixty-eight New York couples in which one spouse was studying for the state bar exam—"the final hurdle in the course of legal training, [which] typically evokes high levels of distress in examinees." This research found that the examinee's spouse increasingly made allowances for the partner's irritability—one way of showing support and not increasing marital tension (Thompson and Bolger 1999). (Chapter 15 discusses in detail the process of dealing creatively with stress and crises.) In general, Stinnett's families took the initiative in structuring their lifestyles to enhance family relationships. Instead of drifting into family relationships by default, they played an active part in carrying out their family commitments (see also Olson 1998).

And sixth, Stinnett found that strong families had *positive communication* patterns (Stinnett, Hilliard, and Stinnett 2000). They argued, but they did so openly, sharing their feelings and talking over alternative solutions to their problems. And, more generally—that is, when they were *not* arguing—family members took time to talk with and listen to one another, conveying respect and interest (see also Finkenauer and Engels 2004). In this regard, UCLA psychologist Shelly Gable has studied how one partner responds when something positive happens to the other one, such as a promotion at work (Gable, Reis, Impett, and Asher 2004).

A partner might respond enthusiastically ("That's wonderful, and it's because you've had so many good ideas in the past few months"). But he or she could instead respond in a less-than-enthusiastic manner ("Hmmm, that's nice"), seem uninterested ("Did you see the score of the Yankees game?"), or point out the downsides ("I suppose it's good news, but it wasn't much of a raise.") The only "correct" reaction according to Gable's research—the response that's correlated with intimacy, satisfaction, trust, and continued commitment—is the first response: the enthusiastic, active one (Lawson 2004a).

Now we turn to a necessary component in positive communication—letting the other person know that you are really listening.

Let Your Partner Know You're Listening

Really listening is basic to an emotionally bonded relationship. According to the late sociologist/counselor

Carlfred Broderick, good listening has the following important positive results:

1. The attitude of listening itself shows love, concern, and respect. . . . Any act that expresses a positive attitude is likely to trigger a sequence of positive responses back and forth. . . .

2. The avoidance of interrupting and criticism prevents the sending of negative messages such as "I don't care how you feel or what you think." "You're not worth listening to."

3. You discover how things actually look from your spouse's or partner's point of view. There's a risk, because what you hear may be surprising and even unsettling. But it is nearly always worth it. In fact, it's hard to imagine how any couple can become close without achieving insight into each other's feelings.

4. You lose your status as chief expert on what your spouse really thinks, wants, fears, and feels. Instead, your spouse takes over as the final authority on his or her own feelings. . . . [Furthermore,] if you listen sympathetically to your spouse, he or she is able to develop greater clarity in areas that may have been confused and confusing. . . .

5. You set an example for your spouse to follow in listening to your . . . feelings. (Broderick 1979a, pp. 40–41)

Two communication psychologists have found that predicting a couple's later divorce was possible by examining how well the partners listened to each other when they talked about everyday things:

> In a careful viewing of the videotapes, we noticed that there were critical moments during the events-of-the-day conversation that could be called either "requited" [returned, acknowledged, or reciprocated] or "unrequited" interest and excitement. For example, in one couple, the wife reported excitedly about something their young son had done that day, but she was met with her husband's disinterest. After a time of talking about errands that needed doing, he talked excitedly about something important that happened to him that day at work, but she responded with disinterest and irritation. No doubt this kind of interaction pattern carried over into the rest of their interaction, forming a pattern for "turning away" from one another. (Gottman and Levenson 2000, p. 744)

Thinking about what listening does may help a person listen as well as talk.

WHAT ABOUT "ACTIVE LISTENING"? Over the past several decades, psychologists and marriage counselors have taught and encouraged the "active listening" communication model. There's a good chance you've already heard that term—maybe even been encouraged to practice it.

Active listening involves paying close attention to what the other person is saying, coupled with **giving feedback** and **checking-it-out**. When giving feedback, a partner repeats in her or his own words what the other has said or revealed (Markman, Stanley, and Blumberg 2001). For example, a wife says, "I hate it when you're on the computer for so long in the evenings, when we have so little time together." To give feedback, her husband would respond with something like "I hear you saying that it irritates you when I'm on the computer instead of visiting with you."

Checking-it-out involves asking the other person whether your perception of his or her feelings or of the present situation is accurate. Studies consistently show that partners in distressed marriages seldom understand each other as well as they think they do (Markman, Stanley, and Blumberg 1994; Klein and Johnson 1997; Zak 1998). Checking-it-out often helps avoid unnecessarily hurt feelings. As the following example shows, the procedure can also help partners avoid imagining trouble that may not be there:

HE: I sense you're angry about something. *(checking-it-out)* Is it because it's my class night and I haven't done the dishes?

SHE: No, but I am mad—because I was tied up in traffic an extra half hour on my way home.

Interestingly, however, social psychologist John Gottman, in research described at length later in this chapter, found that few couples—including happy couples—used either feedback or checking-it-out. The researchers' general conclusion was that the active listening model "occurred infrequently in the resolution of marital conflict and was not predictive of different marital outcomes" (Gottman et al. 1998, p. 17). If you are surprised to hear this, you might be interested to know that Gottman and his colleagues were "shocked and surprised" as well. So they reanalyzed all their videotaped data over the past thirteen years. They found that couples seldom paraphrased what their partner said. In addition,

We also found that they were not summarizing their partner's feelings (e.g., "Sounds like this makes you pretty mad"), nor even summarizing the content of their spouse's statements (e.g., "You'd like it if we saved more money each month"). Furthermore, they almost never validated their spouse's feelings (e.g., "I can understand why this would make you upset"). (p. 17)

Gottman concluded that the active listening model may be misguided because

it expects people to be able to be empathetic in the face of negative affect directed at them by their spouses . . . [and] may be expecting a form of emotional gymnastics from people who at that moment in that relationship, are somewhat emotionally disabled by conflict. (p. 18)

Meanwhile, Gottman and his colleagues did find that happy couples typically let each other know they were listening. They did this by using what communication researchers call **listener backchannels**—"the usual brief vocalizations, head nods, and facial movements that convey to the speaker that the listener is tracking" (p. 17).

In conclusion, Gottman's research does not suggest that giving feedback and checking-it-out are harmful communication skills, rather that counselors may be asking too much to expect couples to use them. The alternative suggested by Gottman and his colleagues centers less on communication skills *per se*, and more on each partner's attitudes and motivation to show caring and affection—"a model of gentleness, soothing, and de-escalation of negativity" (p. 17).

Communication and Couple Satisfaction

In his great novel *Anna Karenina* (1886), Leo Tolstoy characterized happy families as being all alike, while suggesting that unhappy families exhibit infinite variety. Scholars of marital communication find that happy families do share some common qualities, especially the expression of positive emotions and affection (Gottman 1994). However, it also appears that Tolstoy was wrong in presuming that all happy marriages are alike.

One prominent researcher on marital communication, Mary Anne Fitzpatrick (1988, 1995), has found variation among happy couples in their marital ideology—ideas about the roles they should play, expectations for closeness and/or distance, and attitudes toward conflict. Some couples expect to engage in conflict

Even the happiest of committed couples experience conflict. The key to staying happily together is not avoiding conflict but dealing with it openly, or directly, and in supportive ways. Doing so involves listening—without judgment, without formulating a response while the other talks, and without interrupting. The goal isn't necessarily agreement, but acknowledgment, insight, and understanding.

© Ronnie Kaufman/CORBIS

only over big issues. Other couples are more open to conflict and argue more often. Still others expect a relationship that largely avoids both conflict and demonstrations of affection.

All of these couples can be satisfied with their relationship. What matters is whether the partners' actual interaction matches their marital ideology. For instance, the marital happiness of the more interdependent couples depends on their level of sharing and disclosure, whereas "separates" are more satisfied if they avoid jarring conflicts. A pivotal task for all marrieds is to balance each partner's need for autonomy with the simultaneous need for intimacy and togetherness. The happiest couples are those who manage to do this—by negotiating personal and couple boundaries through supportive communication (Marks 1989; Scarf 1995).

Meanwhile, Fitzpatrick's research also uncovered "mixed couples." In this case, spouses have dissimilar ideologies of marriage; they differ in their expectations for closeness and attitudes toward conflict (Fitzpatrick 1995; Noller and Fitzpatrick 1991). Not surprisingly, couples who differ in these ways are unlikely to be very satisfied with their marriages (VanLear 1992). Furthermore, unhappy marriages such as these do tend to have some common features: less positive and more negative verbal and nonverbal communication, to-

gether with more reciprocity of negative—but not of positive—communication (Noller and Fitzpatrick 1991; Gottman and Levenson 2000). Among other things, Fitzpatrick's research points out that all couples—even the happiest of them—experience conflict. In the remainder of this chapter, we explore the topic of managing conflict in marriages and other relationships. First, we'll look at the relationship between conflict and love.

▪ Conflict and Love ▪

Marital anger and conflict are necessary forces and a challenge to be met rather than avoided. This is especially true in the early years of marriage, when individuals are often still in the process of getting to know each other (Driver and Gottman 2004). (At this point, a complete lack of conflict might even be cause for concern!) It is also true at points throughout a good relationship (Schechtman and Schechtman 2003).

Sociologist Judith Wallerstein (Wallerstein and Blakeslee 1995) conducted lengthy interviews with fifty predominantly white, middle-class couples in northern California. The shortest marriage was ten years and the longest forty years. In order to participate, both husband and wife had to define their marriage as happy. When discussing what she found, Wallerstein wrote this:

> [E]very married person knows that "conflict-free marriage" is an oxymoron. In reality it is neither possible nor desirable. . . . [I]n a contemporary marriage it is expected that husbands and wives will have different opinions. More important, they can't avoid having serious collisions on big issues that defy compromise. (p. 143)

The couples in Wallerstein's research quarreled on issues such as personal autonomy, who should handle the money and how it ought to be spent, how much a spouse should work, and whether the wife should be employed at all. Some fought over smoking and drinking:

> In one marriage the husband and wife sat in the car to argue, to avoid upsetting the children. She told him that passive smoke was a proven carcinogen, and while the children were young he could not smoke in their home. He could do what he wanted outside. The man admitted that the request was reasonable, but he was furious. He punished her by not talking to her except when absolutely necessary for three months. Then he accepted the injunction on his smoking and they resumed their customary relationship. (p. 148)

Wallerstein concluded that

> The happily married couples I spoke with were frank in acknowledging their serious differences over the years. . . . What emerged from these interviews was not only that conflict is ubiquitous but that these couples considered learning to disagree and to stand one's ground one of the gifts of a good marriage. (p. 144)

Crosby points out that people may misinterpret the idea of working at marriages and other relationships: "Instead of working *at* marriage we may, with all good intentions, end up making work *of* marriage" (Crosby 1991, p. 287). Along with managing conflicts, being married involves play—humor, spontaneity, fun. ("As We Make Choices: Ten Rules for a Successful Relationship" gives some good ideas for positive couple communication.) Being able to feel playful and behave playfully involves feeling safe in the presence of a part-

ner. But how conflicts, which do necessarily arise, are addressed and resolved has much to do with how secure the mates feel in their relationship.

Denying Conflict: Some Results

Many committed couples are reluctant to argue, even to share situations that might lead to an argument or a partner's negative response. For instance, a businessperson may keep her or his failing financial situation from a partner, fearing that the partner might think him or her a failure. But failing to talk about money leaves the spouse in the dark and the partner might continue to spend, driving the couple into bankruptcy that could have been avoided had the two only communicated the truth about the situation (Glink 2001). Reluctance to argue may also have other destructive effects on the partners as individuals and on their relationship, as discussed below.

The majority of us know when we're angry, but many of us may feel uncomfortable about expressing that anger directly. Through years of being socialized to avoid getting mad or letting others know that they are angry, some people learn not to make an issue of things. One result is that they may resort to anger substitutes, rather than dealing directly with their emotions. For instance, feeling bored can be a substitute for anger. As an example, therapists report that one of the most common complaints they hear from married couples these days is that "we don't feel much like having sex anymore" (Masters, Johnson, and Kolodny 1994). Repressing one's anger may contribute to this sexual boredom.

Another substitute for directly expressed anger is **passive-aggression**. When a person expresses anger at someone but does so indirectly rather than directly, that behavior is called passive-aggression. People use passive-aggression for the same reasons they use other anger substitutes—they are reluctant to engage in direct conflict, often because they are afraid of it.

Chronic criticism, nagging, nitpicking, and sarcasm are all forms of passive-aggression. Procrastination, especially when you have promised a partner that you will do something, may be a form of passive-aggression (Ferrari and Emmons 1994). These behaviors create unnecessary distance and pain in relationships. For instance, most people use sarcasm unthinkingly, and they often aren't aware of its effect on a partner. But

As We Make Choices

Ten Rules for a Successful Relationship

Research consistently shows that expressions of positive interest and affection are related to happy marriages. Psychologists Nathaniel Branden and Robert Sternberg, both of whom are mentioned in our discussion about love in Chapter 5, have developed some rules for nourishing a romantically loving relationship. Here are ten:

© PictureQuest

1. *Express your love verbally.* Say "I love you" or some equivalent (in contrast to the attitude, "What do you mean, do I love you? I married you, didn't I?").

2. *Be physically affectionate.* This includes making love sexually as well as hand-holding, kissing, cuddling, and comforting—with a cup of tea, a pillow, or a woolly blanket.

3. *Express your appreciation and even admiration.* Talk together about what you like, enjoy, and cherish in each other.

4. *Share more about yourself with your partner than you do with any other person.* In other words, keep each other primary (see Chapter 8).

5. *Offer each other an emotional support system.* Be there for each other in times of illness, difficulty, and crisis; be generally helpful and nurturing—devoted to each other's well-being.

6. *Express your love materially.* Send cards or give presents, big and small, on more than just routine occasions. Lighten the burden of your partner's life once in a while by doing more than your agreed-upon share of the chores.

7. *Accept your partner's demands and put up with your partner's shortcomings.* We are not talking here about putting up with physical or verbal abuse. But demands and shortcomings are part of every happy relationship, and so is the grace with which we respond to them. Love your partner, not an unattainable idealization of him or her.

8. *Make time to be alone together.* This time should be exclusively devoted to the two of you as a couple. Understand that love requires attention and leisure.

9. *Do not take your relationship for granted.* Make your relationship your first priority and actively seek to meet each other's needs.

10. *Do unto each other as you would have the other do unto you.* Unconsciously, we sometimes want to give less than we get, or to be treated in special ways that we seldom offer our mate. Try to see things from your lover's viewpoint so that you can develop the empathy that underlies every lasting close relationship.

Sources: Branden 1988, pp. 225–228; Sternberg 1988b, pp. 272–277; see also Gottman and Silver 1999; Gottman and DeClaire 2001; Markman, Stanley, and Blumberg 2001.

being the target of a sarcastic remark can be painful; it may also result in partners feeling alienated from each other.

Sex becomes an arena for ongoing conflict when mates habitually withhold it or use it as passive-aggressive behavior. For example, a partner makes a disparaging comment in front of company. The hurt spouse says nothing at the time but rejects the other's sexual advances later that night because "I'm just too tired." It is much better to express anger at the time that an incident occurs. Otherwise, the anger festers and contaminates other areas of the relationship.

Other forms of passive-aggression are sabotage and displacement. In **sabotage**, one partner attempts to spoil or undermine some activity the other has planned. The husband who is angry because his wife invited friends over when he wanted to relax may sabotage her evening by acting bored. In **displacement**, a person directs anger at people or things that the other cherishes. A wife who is angry with her husband for spending too much time and energy on his career may hate his expensive car, or a husband who feels angry and threatened because his wife returned to school may express disgust for her books and "clutter." Sometimes child abuse can be related to displaced aggression felt by a parent. Child abuse is discussed further in Chapter 14.

Another possible consequence of suppressing anger over a long period of time can be indifference toward one's partner, as opposed to either love or hate (Crosby 1991). When partners do not express anger toward each other (in positive—and always nonviolent—ways), their penalty may be emotional detachment: "[P]eople may stay together but become emotionally detached, postponing divorce until their loneliness becomes unbearable and the need to remain married (e.g., to raise children) becomes less compelling" (Gottman and Levenson 2000, p. 738).

Although suppressing anger may be a source of boredom and emotional detachment, partners can of course go too far in the opposite direction and habitually or violently hurt each other in angry outbursts (Berns, Jacobson, and Gottman 1999). Chapter 14 addresses spouse abuse as the extreme of destructive conflict. In this chapter, we look at what some social psychologists and family therapists can teach us about communication and conflict management in general. We turn now to what some recent communication research has to say about resilient unions.

Supportive Couple ■ Communication and ■ Conflict Management

Social psychologist John Gottman (1979, 1994, 1996; Gottman et al. 1998; Gottman and DeClaire 2001; Gottman and Notarius 2000, 2003) has made his reputation in the field of marital communication. In the 1970s, applying an interactionist perspective to partner communication, he began studying newly married couples in a university lab while they talked casually, discussed issues that they disagreed about, or tried to solve problems. Video cameras recorded the spouses' gestures, facial expressions, and verbal pitch and tone.

Since he began this research, Gottman has kept in contact with more than 650 of the couples, some for as many as 14 years. Typically, the couples were videotaped intermittently. More recently, some couples have volunteered for laboratory observation that monitors shifts in their heart rate and chemical stress indicators in their blood and urine as a result of their communicating with each other (Gottman 1996).

Studying marital communication in this detail, Gottman and his colleagues were able to chart the effects of small gestures. For example, early in his career he discovered that when a spouse—particularly the wife—rolls her eyes while the other is talking, divorce is likely to follow sometime in the future, even if the couple is not thinking about divorce at the time (Gottman and Krotkoff 1989).

The Four Horsemen of the Apocalypse

Gottman's research (1994) showed that conflict and anger themselves did not predict divorce, but four processes that he called the **Four Horsemen of the Apocalypse** did.[1] The Four Horsemen of the Apocalypse are contempt, criticism, defensiveness, and stonewalling. Rolling one's eyes indicates **contempt**, a feeling that one's spouse is inferior or undesirable. **Criticism** involves making disapproving judgments or evaluations of one's partner. **Defensiveness** means preparing to defend oneself against what one presumes

---

1. The word *apocalypse* refers to the biblical idea that the world is soon to end, being destroyed by fire. The Four Horsemen are allegorical figures representing war, famine, and death, with the fourth uncertain (*Concise Columbia Encyclopedia* 1994, p. 309). Gottman used the phrase to indicate attitudes and behaviors that foreshadow impending divorce.

is an upcoming attack. **Stonewalling** is resistance, refusing to listen to one's partner, particularly to a partner's complaints. In study after study, these behaviors identified those who would divorce, with an unusually high accuracy of about 90 percent. Later, after more research, Gottman added **belligerence**, "a behavior that is provocative and that challenges the spouse's power and authority. For example: 'What can you do if I do go drinking with Dave? What are you going to do about it?'" (Gottman et al. 1998, p. 6).

In sum, contempt, criticism, defensiveness, stonewalling, and belligerence characterize unhappy marriages and signal impending divorce (Gottman and Levenson 2002). Recently, Gottman and his colleagues have identified a similar pattern among gay and lesbian couples (Gottman, Levenson, Gross, Frederickson, et al. 2003). Supportive communication characterizes happier, stable unions, but what exactly is supportive communication?

What Is Supportive Communication?

In recent research, Gottman and his colleagues videotaped 130 newlywed couples as they discussed for 15 minutes a problem that caused ongoing disagreement in their marriage (Gottman et al. 1998). Each couple's communication was coded in one-second sequences, then synchronized with each spouse's heart-rate data, which was being collected at the same time. The heart-rate data would indicate each partner's physiological stress.

The researchers examined all of the interaction sequences in which one partner first expressed *negative affect:* anger, sadness, whining, disgust, tension and fear, belligerence, contempt, or defensiveness. Belligerence, contempt, and defensiveness (three of Gottman's indicators of impending divorce) were coded as high-intensity, negative affect. The other emotions listed above (anger, sadness, whining, etc.) were coded as low-intensity negative affect.

Next, the researchers watched what happened immediately after a spouse had expressed negative affect or raised a complaint. Sometimes the partner reciprocated with negative affect in kind, either low or high intensity. For example, she whines, and he whines back; he expresses anger, and she responds with tension and fear; or she is contemptuous, and he immediately becomes defensive.

At other times, one partner's first negative expression was reciprocated with an escalation of the nega-

tivity. For example, she whined, and he grew belligerent; or he expressed anger, and she became defensive. Gottman and his colleagues called this kind of interchange *refusing-to-accept-influence*, because the spouse on the receiving end of the other's complaint refuses to consider it and, instead, escalates the fight.

Meanwhile, still other couples were likely to communicate with *positive affect*, responding to each other warmly with interest, affection, or shared (not mean or contemptuous) humor. Positive affect typically de-escalated conflict (Gottman and Levenson 2000, 2002).

What did Gottman and his colleagues find? First, they found that "The only variable that predicted both marital stability and marital happiness among stable couples was the amount of positive affect in the conflict" (p. 17). In stable, happy couples, shared humor and expressions of warmth, interest, and affection were apparent even in conflict situations and, therefore, de-escalated the argument.

Second, the researchers "found no evidence . . . to support the [idea that] anger is the destructive emotion in marriages" (p. 16). Instead, they found that contempt, belligerence, and defensiveness were the destructive attitudes and behaviors. Specifically, they concluded that the interaction pattern that best predicts divorce is a wife's raising a complaint, followed by her husband's refusing-to-accept-influence, followed, in turn, by the wife's reciprocating her husband's escalated negativity, and the absence of any de-escalation by means of positive affect. Gottman and his colleagues went on to make suggestions for better couple communication, and their advice for wives is different than for husbands.

Gender Differences in Couple Communication

Deborah Tannen's book *You Just Don't Understand* (1990) argues that men typically engage in **report talk**, conversation aimed mainly at conveying information. Women, on the other hand, are likely to engage in **rapport talk**, speaking to gain or reinforce rapport or intimacy. The resulting "men and women talking at cross-purposes" (p. 287) that Tannen identifies is played out in marital or other relationship communication: "Gender is a category that will not go away" (p. 287).

A review of research on couple communication in the 1990s (Gottman and Notarius 2000; Bradbury, Fincham, and Beach 2000) strongly suggests that men and women differ in their responses to negative affect

"Of course I'm listening. I'm in a heightened state of alert."

in close relationships. When faced with a complaint from their partner, men tend to withdraw emotionally while women do not. This pattern is so common that therapists have named it: the **"female-demand/male-withdraw pattern."**[2] In distressed marriages, this pattern becomes a repeated cycle of negative verbal expression by a wife and withdrawal by the husband (Kurdek 1995b; Gottman et al. 1998). Which came first is hard to say. One researcher speculates that wives, being more attuned to the emotional quality of a marriage and having less power, attempt to bring conflict out into the open by initiatives that have an attention-getting negative tone. Husbands try to minimize conflict by conciliatory gestures (Real 2002). Ei-

ther a healthy problem-solving dialogue may ensue, or, more likely, the husband's minimization of conflict may seem to the wife to be a lack of recognition of her emotional needs and her concern about the marriage (Noller and Fitzpatrick 1991; Canary and Dindia 1998).

Early in his research, Gottman concluded that wives and husbands have different goals when they disagree: "The wife wants to resolve the disagreement so that she feels closer to the husband and respected by him. The husband, though, just wants to avoid a blowup. The husband doesn't see the disagreement as an opportunity for closeness, but for trouble" (in Gottman 1996). In one husband's words, "I just don't know what she wants. . . . When she comes after me like that, yapping like that, she might as well be hitting me with a bat" (Rubin 1976, p. 113). And as another explained, "I just got mad and I'd take off—go out with the guys and have a few beers or something. When I'd get back, things would be even worse" (p. 77). From his wife's perspective, "The more I screamed, the more he'd withdraw, until finally I'd go kind of crazy. Then he'd leave and not come back until two or three in the

---

2. The vast majority of researchers who study couple communication agree that generally there is a "female-demand/male-withdraw pattern" (Gottman and Levenson 2000, p. 738; Gottman and Notarius 2000, p. 940; Bradbury, Fincham, and Beach 2000, p. 967). However, a minority of researchers argue otherwise. In this alternative view, "it is not gender per se but the nature of the marital discussion—for example, whether it is the wife or the husband who desires a change—that may determine who is demanding and who is withdrawing" (Roberts 2000, p. 702).

morning sometimes" (p. 79). Gottman and his colleagues sought to better understand this female-demand/male-withdraw pattern.

You'll recall that the researchers monitored spouses' heart rates as indicators of physiological stress during conflict. They found that, while the final word is not yet in, "it is likely that the biological, stress-related response of men is more rapid and recovery is slower than that of women, and that this response is related to the greater emotional withdrawal of men than women in distressed families" (p. 19). That is, when confronted with conflict from an intimate, men may experience more intense and uncomfortable physical symptoms of stress than women do. Therefore, men are more likely than women to withdraw emotionally and/or physically.

An alternative—or complementary—view is that men have been socialized to withdraw. You'll recall that Chapter 4 discusses traditional differences in the ways that men and women have been socialized, with men expected to be more instrumental and women expected to be more expressive or relationship oriented. The cultural options for masculinity described in Chapter 4 include "no 'sissy' stuff," according to which men are expected to distance themselves from anything considered feminine. We guess this could include a wife's complaints. In two books on men and communication, the first called *I Don't Want to Talk About It*, therapist Terrence Real (1997, 2002) attributes males' withdrawal to a "secret legacy of depression," brought on by men's traditional socialization, particularly society's refusal to let them grieve over losses (e.g., "Don't cry over nothing"). It is likely that physiology and culture interact to create the female-demand/male-withdraw pattern.

In line with the view that social factors influence divergent communication patterns for men and women is research that compares communication patterns among husbands of various racial/ethnic groups (Mackey and O'Brien 1998). In one such study of sixty non-Hispanic white, African American, and Mexican American couples whose marriages had lasted at least twenty years, social work professors Richard Mackey and Bernard O'Brien found that African American husbands were much less likely to withdraw from conflict than non-Hispanic white or Mexican American husbands. You may recall from Chapter 4 that some research has suggested that black men are more expressive than white men, due to differences in socialization. Mackey and O'Brien speculated that the historical social context of black men has affected their conflict management styles at home:

> It was dangerous for most of these black men to assert themselves in conflict situations with white people. As a consequence, the home may have been one of the few safe places for African American men to deal openly with interpersonal conflict. (p. 138)

WHAT WIVES CAN DO In the following discussion, the term "soothe" indicates things that people do to reduce physical stress symptoms. Although both spouses benefit from being soothed, Gottman and his colleagues go so far as to say that "Marriages will work to the extent that they provide for soothing of the male" (Gottman et al. 1998, p. 20). "Soothing of the male" can involve self-soothing—for example, he takes a timeout or tells his wife that "I just can't talk about it now, but I will later" (and means it). Also, soothing may imply soothing of the male by the female.

This process involves two things: (1) using positive affect, such as shared humor and expressions of affection, to de-escalate negativity; and (2) the wife's softening the way she brings up complaints. Gottman does not mean to discourage wives from raising disagreeable topics, but rather to "soften" their confrontations by using less-negative communication styles. For example, a wife who often voices complaints by whining or with a tone of contempt might try to speak more gently.

WHAT HUSBANDS CAN DO Reminding us that fighting per se ("negative affect reciprocity in kind") is not the problem, Gottman and his colleagues argue that the husband's escalation of negativity is the real problem. The researchers view this escalation as a symptom of the husband's refusal to accept influence from his wife or to share power with her:

> Usually the wife brings marital issues to the table for discussion, and she usually brings a detailed analysis of the conditions in which this problem occurs, its history, and suggestions for a solution. Some men, those whose marriages wind up stable and happy, accept influence from their wives, and some do not. . . . Our data suggest that only newlywed men who accept influence from their wives are winding up in happy and stable marriages. (pp. 18–19)

What can couples do to make conflict management easier on them—and on their relationship? According to John Gottman, wives generally can learn to raise issues in more gentle ways, while husbands generally need to learn to accept their partner's influence rather than escalating the argument. Indeed, both partners need to do what they can to de-escalate the fight—but not to avoid their conflict altogether.

© Royalty-Free/MedioImages/Index Stock Imagery

Unfortunately, newspapers publicized this research with headlines such as "'Honey, just be a yes man'" and "Marriage lasts if husband gives in." But *sharing* power is not the same as how one journalist described it: "Just do what your wife says. Go ahead, give in to her" (Maugh 1998). Sharing power involves the willingness to be influenced—to negotiate or compromise, sometimes giving in and sometimes not (Gottman and DeClaire 2001). The real message to husbands is not to respond to their wife's complaints by escalating the argument with defensiveness, contempt, or belligerence.

WHAT COUPLES CAN DO The general conclusion of Gottman's research on communication and conflict management among married couples is as follows:

1. Partners, especially wives, need to try to be more gentle when they raise complaints.

2. Partners, especially wives, can help soothe their spouse by communicating care and affection.

3. Partners, especially husbands, can learn self-soothing techniques.

4. Partners, especially husbands, need to be willing to accept influence from their wives.

5. Both partners need to do what they can—perhaps using authentic, shared humor, kindness, and

other signs of affection—to de-escalate the argument. (It is important to recognize that this does not mean avoiding the issue altogether.)

Finally, Gottman and his colleagues (1998) suggest that it is probably important for couples to think about communicating with positive affect more often in their daily living, and not just during times of conflict (Gottman and DeClaire 2001). ("As We Make Choices: Ten Rules for a Successful Relationship" suggests ways to do this.) Communicating with positive affect, of course, implies avoiding the Four Horsemen of the Apocalypse.

Avoiding the Four Horsemen of the Apocalypse

Consider the following exchange:

HE: I need more socks.

SHE: What do you mean, you need more socks? Didn't you wash any? Are you accusing me of losing your socks?

HE: No, stupid, I mean I need some new socks.

SHE: So get some.

HE: I thought you could pick them up since you'll be out this afternoon anyway.

SHE: You're just like your father—always ordering somebody around.

HE: So what are you going to do about it? What do you think you can do about it?

SHE: Your father's a bum.

HE: Oh, yeah? Well, at least my mother can cook!

SHE: Well, she's a mess herself! She hasn't had a decent haircut in years.

HE: You ought to do something with *your* hair. It's ridiculous.

SHE: Not that there's room in the bathroom with your stuff scattered all over. . . .

In this scenario, the husband announces that he needs more socks, and a fight ensues. Some might find this couple's exchange humorous. But it is obviously not supportive marital communication, and it's not the kind that helps to bond couples and keep them together. This fight reveals three of Gottman's Four Horsemen of the Apocalypse—contempt, defensiveness, and criticism—along with belligerence, the sign of impending divorce that Gottman added later.

When he says that he needs more socks, she becomes defensive: "What do you mean, you need more socks? . . . Are you accusing me of losing your socks?" At this point, a less distressed couple might stop this negative communication with shared humor or some sign of affection. But he fails to de-escalate the interchange and responds by calling his wife stupid. Name-calling is typically contemptuous; counselors encourage us to avoid it.

He subsequently explains that he thought she could buy the socks "since you'll be out this afternoon anyway." Her reply is contemptuous and critical: "You're just like your father—always ordering somebody around." Again, the couple fails to de-escalate the negative affect. This time he responds with belligerence: "So what are you going to do about it? What do you think you can do about it?"

The couple continues to criticize and show contempt for each other, while neither spouse de-escalates the argument. It probably goes without saying that this is the type of couple interaction we are advised to avoid. Moreover, it appears they've forgotten what the fight is about. In fact, one wonders whether they *know* what the fight is about.

Counselors point out that distressed couples, like the one described here, often do not know what they are really fighting about. Fighting over petty annoyances, such as who should have put gas in the car, is healthy and can even be fun as an essentially harmless way to release tension. But partners sometimes unconsciously allow trivial issues to become decoys so that they evade the real area of conflict and leave it unresolved. For example, an irate husband who complains about how his wife treats their children may really be fighting about his feelings of rejection because he feels that his wife isn't giving him enough attention.

The fight in the above scenario is really about power and work roles in this couple's relationship. He feels comfortable requesting that she purchase his socks; she feels that she is being ordered around and that buying his socks is not her role in the relationship; he believes that she is not adequately performing her role in the union (he finds her cooking unsatisfactory). These are actually serious underlying issues for this couple—the fight is not about socks! Counselors suggest that couples need to try to be clear about what they are really fighting about. This may be a tall order, however, and going to marriage counseling or couple therapy might be recommended.

We turn now to take a closer look at Gottman's fourth Horseman of the Apocalypse—stonewalling, or refusing to listen to a partner's complaints.

STONEWALLING Avoiding or evading a fight is an example of stonewalling. Stonewallers react to their partner's attempts to raise disputed or tension-producing issues by refusing to engage with the partner's initiatives. They fear conflict and hesitate to accept their own and others' hostile or angry emotions. Fight evaders use several tactics to avoid fighting, such as

1. Leaving the house or the scene when a fight threatens
2. Turning sullen and refusing to argue or talk
3. Derailing potential arguments by saying, "I can't take it when you yell at me"
4. Flatly stating, "I can't take you seriously when you act this way"
5. Using the "hit and run" tactic of filing a complaint, then leaving no time for an answer or for a resolution (Bach and Wyden 1970)

Chronic stonewallers may fear rejection or retaliation and therefore hesitate to acknowledge their own or their partner's angry emotions. Examples of stonewalling include saying things like, "I can't take it when you yell at me," or turning sullen and refusing to talk.

© Benelux Press/Index Stock Imagery/Picture Quest

6. Saying "OK, you win," giving in verbally, maybe even promising to "do better next time," but without meaning it

Stonewallers may argue that they avoid conflicts because they don't want to hurt their partners. Often, however, they are really trying to protect themselves: "A great deal of dishonesty that ostensibly occurs in an effort to prevent pain actually occurs as we try to protect and shield ourselves from the agony of feeling our own pain, fear, fright, shame, or embarrassment" (Crosby 1991, pp. 159–160). And stonewalling can make partners who want and need to raise and resolve differences feel worse, not better.

Stonewalling may encourage one's partner to engage in **gunnysacking**: keeping one's grievances secret while tossing them into an imaginary gunnysack that grows heavier and heavier over time. Martyring (see Chapter 5) is typically accompanied by gunnysacking. When marital complaints are toted and nursed along quietly in a gunnysack for any length of time, they "make a dreadful mess when they burst out" (Bach and Wyden 1970, p. 19).

Research psychologists and family counselors agree that strong, or resilient, families are not without conflict. Cohesive families have fights. But arguments do not necessarily pull a union apart. We turn to what may at first seem like a strange idea—that some arguments, or ways to fight, may actually bring a couple or other family members closer together (Lerner 2001).

Bonding Fights— Nine Guidelines

Some goals and strategies can help make conflict management productive rather than destructive. This kind of fighting, which brings people closer rather than pushing them apart, has been called **bonding fighting**. The key to creating a bonding fight is for partners to try to build up, not tear down, each other's self-esteem, even as they argue.

Social groups within the United States vary considerably in the endorsement their cultures give to the open expression of emotion, which may make arguing constructively more or less difficult for people within or across cultures (see, for example, Hirsch 2003). Deborah Tannen's bestselling book *You Just Don't Understand*, which drew wide attention for its comparison of men's and women's communication styles, also points out communication differences among, for example, New York Jews, Californians, New Englanders, and Midwesterners, and among Scandinavians, Canada's native peoples, and Greeks. Nevertheless, there are better (and not-so-good) ways that virtually all couples and family members can resolve differences. Now we turn to nine specific guidelines for constructive conflict management.

Guideline 1: Level with Each Other

Partners need to be as (gently, kindly) candid as possible; counselors call this **leveling**—being transparent,

It may sound impossible to follow rules for fighting fair when you're angry, but they do help, and "practice makes better," if not perfect. Using I-statements, avoiding mixed messages, focusing your anger on specific issues, and being willing to change are some guidelines worth trying.

authentic, and explicit about how one feels, "especially concerning the more conflictive or hurtful aspects" of an intimate relationship (Bach and Wyden 1970, p. 368; Block 2003; Lerner 2001). Leveling is self-disclosure in action.

Various studies indicate that—often because of the mistaken impression that one partner already knows how the other feels—partners overestimate how accurately their mate understands them and then fail to understand their partner. Underlying conflicts often go unresolved because partners fail to voice their feelings, irritations, and preferences—and neither is aware that the other is holding back. The solution to this problem is to air grievances: to candidly explain where one stands and how one feels about a specific situation. Being candid does not mean the same thing as being mean or unnecessarily critical. Leveling is never intentionally hurtful.

Guideline 2: To Avoid Attacks, Use I-Statements When You Can

Attacks are assaults on a partner's character or self-esteem. Needless to say, attacks and assaults do not help to bond a couple. We have already seen that "contemptuous remarks or insults" are destructive fighting tactics (John Gottman, research reported in Goleman 1989, p. 1–B).

A rule in avoiding attack is to use *I* rather than *you* or *why*. The receiver usually perceives I-statements as an attempt to recognize and communicate feel-

ings, but you- and why-statements are more likely to be perceived as attacks—whether or not they are intended as such. For example, instead of asking "Why are *you* late?" a statement such as "*I* was worried because you hadn't arrived" may allow more communication.

I-statements are most effective if they are communicated in a positive way. A partner should express his or her anger directly, but it will seem less threatening if he or she conveys positive feelings at the same time that negative emotions are voiced. The message comes across, but it's not as bitter as when only angry feelings are expressed.

Making I-statements can be difficult, of course, and may be too much to ask in the heat of an argument. One social psychologist has admitted what many of us may already know: "It is impossible to make an 'I-statement' when you are in the 'hating-my-partner, wanting-revenge, feeling-stung-and-needing-to-sting-back' state of mind" (quoted in Gottman et al. 1998, p. 18). Of course, this is partly the point. Keeping in mind the possibility of expressing a complaint—at least *beginning* a confrontation—with an I-statement can discourage partners from getting to that wanting-revenge state of mind in the first place.

Guideline 3: Avoid Mixed, or Double, Messages

A third tip for fighting in a more positive way is to avoid using **mixed, or double, messages**: simultaneous messages that contradict each other.[3] Contradictory messages may be verbal, or one may be verbal and one nonverbal. For example, a spouse agrees to go out to eat with a partner but at the same time yawns and says that he or she is tired and has had a hard day at work. Or a partner insists, "Of course I love you" while picking an invisible speck from her or his sleeve in a gesture of indifference.

Communication also involves both a sender and a receiver. Just as the sender gives both a verbal message and a nonverbal metamessage, so also does a receiver give nonverbal cues about how seriously she or he is taking the message. For example, listening while continuing to do chores sends the nonverbal message that what is being heard is not very important.

Senders of mixed messages may not be aware of what they are doing, and mixed messages can be very subtle. They usually result from just not paying attention to one's relationship or from simultaneously wanting to recognize and to deny conflict or tension. In the latter case, mixed messages allow senders to let other people know they are angry at them and at the same time to deny that they are. A classic example is the *silent treatment.* A spouse becomes aware that she or he has said or done something and asks what's wrong. "Oh, nothing," the partner replies, without much feeling, but everything about the partner's face, body, attitude, and posture suggests that something is indeed wrong (Lerner 2001).

Besides the silent treatment, other ways to indicate that something is wrong while denying it include making a partner the butt of jokes, using subtle innuendos rather than direct communication, and being sarcastic (also defended as "just a joke" by mixed-message senders).

Sarcasm and other mixed messages create distance and cause pain and confusion, for they prevent honest communication from taking place. Expressing anger in as positively a way as possible is better, because it opens the way for solutions.

Guideline 4: Choose the Time and Place Carefully

Fights may be nonconstructive if the complainant raises grievances at the wrong time. One partner may be ready to argue about an issue when the other is almost asleep or working on an important assignment, for instance. At such times, the person who picked the fight may get more than he or she bargained for.

Partners might try to negotiate *gripe hours* by pinning down a time and place for a fight. Fighting by appointment may sound silly and may be difficult to arrange, but it has two important advantages. First, complainants can organize their thoughts and feelings more calmly and deliberately, increasing the likelihood that their arguments will be persuasive. Second, recipients of complaints have time before the fight to prepare themselves for some criticism.

Guideline 5: Focus Anger Only on Specific Issues

Constructive fighting aims at resolving specific problems that are happening *now*—not at gunnysacking. Recipients of complaints need to feel that they can do something specific to help resolve the problem raised. This will be difficult if they feel overwhelmed. Noted marriage communication researcher Andrew Christensen advises that

> If you're angry and resentful, requests for change will be met with resistance and countercharge efforts: "It's not my problem; it's your problem." But if you learn to approach each other with acceptance and empathy, you can create a collaborative context, and often people will make spontaneous changes. ("Loving Your Partner . . ." 2000)

Then too, if things seem to be getting out of hand, call for a timeout.

Guideline 6: Ask for a Specific Change, but Be Open to Compromise

Initially, complainants should be ready to propose at least one solution to the problem. Recipients might come up with possible solutions. If they can keep proposed solutions pertinent to the issue at hand, partners might be able to negotiate alternatives.

Resolving specific issues involves bargaining and negotiation. Partners need to recognize that there are probably several ways to solve a particular problem, and backing each other into corners with ultimatums and counter-ultimatums is not negotiation but attack. John Gottman found that happily married couples

---

3. Communication scholars and counselors point out that there are two major aspects of any communication: *what* is said (the verbal message) and *how* it is said (the nonverbal "metamessage"). The metamessage involves tone of voice, inflection, and body language. In a mixed message, the verbal message does not correspond with the nonverbal metamessage.

reach agreement rather quickly. Either one partner gives in to the other without resentment, or the two compromise. Unhappily married couples tend to continue in a cycle of stubbornness and conflict (Gottman and Krotkoff 1989).

Guideline 7: Be Willing to Change Yourself

Communication, of course, needs to be accompanied by action. One counselor team (Christensen and Jacobson 1999; Jacobson and Christensen 1996) has suggested "acceptance therapy," helping partners accept their spouses as they are instead of demanding change, although they suggest that, paradoxically, acceptance is also the basis for obtaining behavior change. Meanwhile, the romantic belief that couples should accept each other *completely* as they are is often merged with the view that people should be exactly what they choose to be. The result is an erroneous assumption that if a partner loves you, he or she will accept you just as you are and not ask for even minor changes. On the contrary, partners need to be willing to change themselves, to be changed by others, and to be influenced by their partner's feelings and rational arguments. Defensiveness, resentments, and refusing to change are dysfunctional responses that contribute to marital deterioration (Gottman and Silver 1999; Lerner 2001). Every intimate relationship involves negotiation and mutual compromise; partners who refuse to change, or who insist they cannot, are in effect refusing to engage in an intimate relationship.

Guideline 8: Don't Try to Win

Partners must not compete in fights. American society encourages people to see almost everything they do in terms of winning or losing. Yet research clearly indicates that the tactics associated with winning in a particular conflict are also those associated with lower marital satisfaction (Noller and Fitzpatrick 1991; Holmes and Murray 1996; Klein and Johnson 1997; Zak 1998).

Bonding fights, like dancing, can't involve a winner and a loser. If one partner must win, then the other obviously must lose. But losing lessens a person's self-esteem and increases resentment and strain on the relationship. This is why in intimate fighting there can never be one winner and one loser—only two losers.

Both partners lose if they engage in destructive conflict. Both win if they become closer and settle, or at least understand, their differences.

Guideline 9: Remember to End the Argument

The happily married couples that Wallerstein (Wallerstein and Blakeslee 1995) interviewed (described earlier in this chapter) tried to fight only about big issues and knew how and when to stop fighting. However, if a couple cannot designate a winner and a loser, they may be at a loss to know how to end a fight. Ideally, a fight ends when there has been a mutually satisfactory airing of each partner's views. Bach and Wyden suggest that partners question each other to make sure that they've said all they need to say.

Sometimes, when partners are too hurt or frightened to continue, they need to stop arguing before they reach a resolution. Women often cry as a signal that they've been hit below the "beltline" or that they feel too frustrated or hurt to go on fighting. Men experience the same feelings, but they have learned from childhood not to cry. Hence, they may hide their emotions, or they may erupt angrily. In either case, it would help to bargain about whether the fight should continue. The partner who is not feeling so hurt or frightened might ask, "Do you want to stop now or to go on with this?" If the answer is "I want to stop," the fight should be either terminated or interrupted for a time.

We've looked at nine specific guidelines for fighting more positively, even having fights that can bring a couple closer together. Realizing that there are ways to fight that can actually be "bonding" might help to overcome what some of us experience as fear of anger and conflict. The assumption that conflict and anger don't belong in healthy relationships exists in many couples and families. This assumption is based partly on the idea that love is the polar opposite of hate (Crosby 1991). But emotional intimacy necessarily involves feelings of both wanting to be close and needing to be separate, of agreeing and disagreeing (Scarf 1995). Gottman and his colleagues would not have done all their research or spent so much time reporting it both in scholarly journals and in more-popular books if they did not believe that individuals and partners could change their fighting habits for the better. The next section explores this idea.

Learning to express anger and dealing with conflict early in a relationship are challenges to be met rather than avoided. Acknowledging and resolving conflict is painful, but it often strengthens the couple's union in the long run. A key to effective conflict management is to share everyday—and positive—events in friendly, supportive ways so that arguments occur within an overall context of couple satisfaction and mutual trust.

© Myrleen Ferguson/PhotoEdit

Changing Conflict-Management Habits

Social scientist Suzanne Steinmetz traced in fifty-seven intact urban and suburban families the patterns of how families resolve conflict. Her research shows not only that individual families assume consistent patterns or habits for facing conflict but also that these patterns are passed from one generation to the next. Subsequent research has reached similar conclusions (Conger and Conger 2002; VanLear 1992). Parents who resort to physical abuse teach their children, in effect, that such abuse is an acceptable outlet for tension. In this way, the "cycle of violence" is perpetuated (Steinmetz 1977). A similar process takes place as people learn anger substitutes from their parents (Kassorla 1973).

Generational Change

Even though this generalization about the transmission of marital communication patterns from parents to children is correct, it is important to note variations from this pattern. VanLear (1992) found that young married men tend to rebel against their parents' marital conflict style. (Women are more apt to follow their

parents' lead.) VanLear's comparison (in fifty-eight families) of married couples in their late twenties to parental couples in their fifties found that the younger married men tended to choose different conflict styles from their parents. Most often, that meant they evidenced less conflict avoidance. These men also married women very different in conflict style from their own mothers. Moreover, the younger couples also reported more sharing and disclosure than was characteristic of the parental generation (VanLear 1992).

Couple Change

The change in couple communication and conflict management just described is the unplanned outcome of social change and family dynamics. But couples may also consciously act to change marital interaction patterns. A study in Germany found that couples establish conflict resolution styles during the first year of marriage and then gradually make them habitual (Schneewind and Gerhard 2002). However, couples can change. Some training programs in couple empathy and communication, conducted by psychologists, have proven quite effective in helping people change these behaviors (Long, Angera, Carter, Nakamoto, and Kalso

1999). One such program for married couples is ENRICH, developed by social psychologist David Olson (1994) at the University of Minnesota.

A similar important program is PREP (the Prevention and Relationship Enhancement Program), developed by marital communication psychologists Scott Stanley and Howard Markman, with the overall aim of strengthening marriages and preventing divorce (Markman, Stanley, and Blumberg 2001). "Case Study: Making a Marriage Encounter Weekend" describes another program designed to enhance a couple's marriage, although having such a weekend may *not* be a good idea for distressed couples. Marriage Encounter weekends are designed for couples in generally satisfying relationships.

In addition, the federal government has launched the Healthy Marriage Initiative (HMI). According to government publications explaining HMI, a "healthy marriage" is one that is mutually enriching, at least partly because "both partners have a deep respect for each other." One way that HMI fosters healthy marriages is by encouraging community-level programs that teach problem-solving and supportive communication skills to couples (Administration for Children and Families 2004). Meanwhile, the following steps are given to help people work for change on their own.

The first step in changing destructive fighting habits is to accept the reality of conflict. As acceptance therapy founder Christensen puts it, "Acceptance can shorten the recovery time and take the sting out of the battle. But it's not going to create inevitable peace and harmony between two people" (Christenson in "Loving Your Partner . . ." 2000).

A second step is to begin to use the guidelines for bonding fighting that we have described. Often, as partners grow more accustomed to voicing grievances regularly and in more respectful or caring ways, their fights may hardly seem like fights at all: Partners will gradually learn to incorporate many irritations and requests into their normal conversations. Partners adept at constructive fighting often argue in normal tones of voice and even with humor. In a very real sense, their disagreements are essential to their intimacy.

Partners who are just learning to manage their conflicts constructively may be anxious or insecure. One way to begin is by writing letters or using a tape recorder. In this way the complainant is not inhibited or stopped by a mate's interruption or hostile nonverbal cues. Then the mate can read or listen to the other's complaints in privacy when she or he is ready to listen. Letters and tape recorders are no substitute for face-to-face communication, but they don't intimidate either. Once partners become more comfortable with their differences, they can begin to fight face to face.

Another option is to record a fight and play it back later. This exercise can help spouses look at themselves objectively. They can ask themselves whether and where they really listened and stuck to specifics or resorted to hurtful, alienating tactics. Although all the suggestions made in this textbook may help, learning to fight fair is not easy. A good number of fights are even about fighting itself. Sometimes one or both partners feel that they need outside help with their fighting, and they may decide to have a marriage counselor serve as referee. See Appendix H, "Marriage and Close Relationship Counseling," for a discussion of this alternative.

The Myth of Conflict-Free Conflict

By now, so much attention has been devoted to the bonding capacity of intimate fighting that it may seem as if conflict itself can be free of conflict. It can't. Even the fairest fighters hit below the belt once in a while, and it's probably safe to say that all fighting involves some degree of frustration and hurt feelings. After all, anger is anger, and hostility is hostility—even between partners who are very close to each other.

Moreover, some spouses are married to mates who don't want to learn to fight more positively. In marriages in which one partner wants to change and the other doesn't, sometimes much can be gained if just one partner begins to communicate more positively. Other times, however, positive changes in one spouse do not spur growth in the other. Situations like this may end in divorce.

Even when both partners develop constructive habits, all of their problems will not necessarily be resolved (Booth, Crouter, and Clements 2001; Driver and Gottman 2004). Even though a complainant may feel that he or she is being fair in bringing up a grievance and discussing it openly and calmly, the recipient may view the complaint as critical and punitive, and it may be a blow to that partner's self-esteem. The recipient may not feel that the time is right for fighting and may not want to bargain about the issue. Finally, sharing anger and hostilities may violate what the other partner expects of the relationship.

Case Study

Making a Marriage Encounter Weekend

According to its promotional literature, Marriage Encounter is a weekend for couples "who have a good thing going for them, and who want to make it better." Worldwide Marriage Encounter (http://www.wwmc.org) began as a movement devoted to the renewal of the sacrament of matrimony in and for the Catholic church. Today, at least ten other Christian denominations and the Jewish faith offer similar weekends. The movement began in the New York area in 1968. Since then, more than one million couples throughout the United States have made the weekend, and the movement has spread into more than fifty foreign countries. Here, a woman tells about her Marriage Encounter weekend.

We were going along fine. But I think we both had begun to feel we were maybe taking each other pretty much for granted. So we signed up for a Marriage Encounter weekend. Believe me, it was a big step: finding a babysitter and everything just to go *talk*!

Marriage Encounter is an extensive forty-four hours of uninterrupted togetherness. You do nothing else but eat, sleep, and share with each other. There's virtually no socializing with the other couples. It's just the two of you.

You write letters to one another. You write them alone, privately, and then you exchange them. You aren't using your body language while you're writing this, of course, or

being interrupted or interrupting the other person. You have a train of thought. With just trying to talk sometimes, you know, the other person jumps in or tells you what you're saying is positive or negative, and you've gotten off the track. So we would write for ten minutes, picking a topic like, "How do I feel about sex?" Or, "How do I feel about anything really?" And both write.

Then you exchange notebooks and you each read it through twice—once with the heart and once with the head, as they say. And then you what they call dialogue on it for ten minutes. It really leads into neat areas. . . .

I was amazed at how little I had been into feelings, and how much I was into thoughts. And the same for Jerry. It was just really weird how we both thought we were expressing our feelings before the encounter. But we weren't. Not completely anyway. We thought we'd been letting it all hang out, but we weren't. We were expressing our thoughts and our grudges and our hang-ups. But not our true—not all our true—feelings. . . .

I prayed too. I don't want to leave that out. I don't want to minimize that. I want to have the courage to emphasize that I prayed; I prayed hard that weekend, partly because when I went into the room where I was going to write down my feelings about something, I sometimes found myself surprisingly afraid.

And then when we'd start writing, I'd say to myself, "Do I feel like *this*?" I would be surprised at how I felt, and I'd be surprised at how he felt too. It's such a revelation—almost as exciting for you alone as it is for your relationship, because you find out a lot of stuff about yourself that you had no idea about. Anyway I did. And Jerry did too.

When we left that weekend, they gave us a list of ninety topics, suggestions for continuing the dialogue. Things like sex, kids, finances. You can think up anything you want to dialogue about, but we've been more or less going by this list. We recognized, though, that for a while we were skipping around on the list. And then we realized that we were avoiding subjects that we were afraid to talk about. So we've decided—and this took courage, believe me—to go just straight down the list and take the topics as they come. . . .

It's really been a revelation. But maybe the very best thing about it is just that we're making the time to do it.

Critical Thinking

How might weekend encounters such as this one enhance family commitment? What might be some drawbacks or problems with a Marriage Encounter weekend? In what ways does intimacy (described in Chapter 5) affect family cohesion, do you think? Why?

A study comparing mutually satisfied couples with those experiencing marital difficulties found that when couples are having trouble getting along or are stressed, they tend to interpret each other's messages and behavior more negatively. Satisfied partners did not differ from distressed ones in how they intended their behavior to be received by mates. But distressed partners interpreted their spouse's words and behavior as being more harsh and hurtful than was intended (Gottman 1979; Noller and Fitzpatrick 1991).

Not all negative facts and feelings need to be communicated. Before offering negative information, it is important to ask yourself why you want to tell it (to win?) and whether the other person really needs to know the information. Moreover, not every conflict can be resolved, even between the fairest and most mature fighters. If an unresolved conflict is not crucial to either partner, then they have reached a stalemate. The two may simply have to accept their inability to resolve that particular issue.

Communication between mates is addressed throughout this text. Chapter 8 discusses negotiating flexible marriage agreements. Domestic violence, which can be the unfortunate, even tragic, result of poorly managed conflict, is addressed at length in Chapter 14. Like love, fair fighting doesn't conquer

all. But it can certainly help partners who are reasonably well matched and who want to stay together. Success in marriage has much to do with a couple's gentleness—and humor!—in relating to each other—perhaps much more than the social similarity, financial stress, and age at marriage often emphasized by social scientists in earlier studies of marital adjustment (Gottman et al. 1998). Finally, you may recall that Chapter 5 discusses not just discovering love but also keeping it. Keeping love, marital communication research informs us, largely involves letting our loved ones know how much we care about and appreciate them—a task largely accomplished by little gestures of appreciation, such as a touch or hug, and also simply by listening with genuine interest.

In Sum

- Research on couple communication indicates the importance to relationships of both positive communication and the avoidance of a spiral of negativity.
- Stinnett's research on "strong" or "resilient" families suggests that what makes families cohesive are expressing appreciation for each other, doing things together, having positive communication patterns, being committed to the group, having some spiritual orientation, and being able to deal creatively with crises.
- Even though some family interaction tactics may reach the point of pathology, family conflict itself is an inevitable part of normal family life.
- Research psychologists and family counselors are recognizing that to deny conflict may be destructive to both individuals and relationships.
- Although arguing is a normal part of the most loving relationships, there are better and worse ways of managing conflict.
- Alienating practices, such as belligerence and the Four Horsemen of the Apocalypse—contempt, criticism, defensiveness, and stonewalling—should be avoided.
- Bonding fights may often resolve issues and also bring partners closer together by improving communication.
- Bonding fights may be characterized by attitudes of and efforts at gentleness, soothing, and de-escalation of negativity. In bonding fights, both partners win.
- There is no such thing as conflict-free conflict.

Key Terms

belligerence
bonding fighting
checking-it-out
contempt
criticism
defensiveness
displacement
family cohesion
female-demand/male-
  withdraw pattern
Four Horsemen of the
  Apocalypse

giving feedback
gunnysacking
leveling
listener backchannel
mixed, or double, messages
passive-aggression
rapport talk
report talk
sabotage
stonewalling

Questions for Review and Reflection

1. Explain why families are powerful environments. What are the advantages and disadvantages of such power in family interaction?
2. Explain the interactionist theoretical perspective on families, and show how John Gottman's research illustrates this perspective.
3. Describe the Four Horsemen of the Apocalypse. If someone you care for treated you this way in a disagreement, how would you feel? What might you say in response?

4. Discuss your reactions to each of the nine guidelines proposed in this chapter for bonding fights. What would you add or subtract?

5. Policy Question. Besides the suggestions in "As We Make Choices: Ten Rules for a Successful Relationship," what *society-wide* ideas might you offer for keeping love in one's long-term relationship?

Suggested Readings

Diggs, Anita, and Vera Paster. 1998. *Staying Married: A Guide for African-American Couples.* New York: Kensington Books. Advice for and case studies of couples coping with the typical challenges of marriage, as well as the kinds of pressures that black (and other ethnic minority) couples often deal with in a marriage—for example, the impact of racism on financial prospects or helping spouses deal with frustrations sparked by racism.

The Gottman Institute

http://www.gottman.com/

The website of psychologist John Gottman's institute for "researching and restoring relationships" focuses on communication regarding marriages and couples as well as parenting. See also John Gottman's 1995 book, *Why Marriages Succeed or Fail . . . and How You Can Make Yours Last.* New York: Simon and Schuster. This book describes the research discussed in this chapter and is written to appeal to the everyday reader.

Hirsch, Jennifer S. 2003. *A Courtship after Marriage: Sexuality and Love in Mexican Transnational Families.* Berkeley, CA: University of California Press. Qualitative research, presented in an easy-to-read way, that examines the changing Mexican American family as immigrant couples assume the Western cultural pattern of "companionate" marriage and, as a result, couple communication changes its nature and purpose.

Laing, Ronald D. 1971. *The Politics of the Family.* New York: Random House. Psychiatrist Laing analyzes family interaction, particularly the power of the family to shape identity and definitions of the situation. A classic.

Markman, Howard, Scott Stanley, and Susan Blumberg. 2001. *Fighting for Your Marriage.* San Francisco: Jossey-Bass. Readable book by well-known and respected family communication researchers on the general philosophy of communication and conflict in marriages, as well as discussion of communication skills that could help.

Smart Marriages

http://www.smartmarriages.com/

A coalition for marriage, family, and couples education designed for teachers, therapists, and the general public. Covers topics from marital communication to therapy to divorce and "how to fight it."

Virtual Society: The Wadsworth Sociology Resource Center

Go to the Sociology Resource Center at **http://sociology.wadsworth.com** for a wealth of online resources, including a companion website for your text that provides study aids such as self-quizzes for each chapter and a practice final exam, as well as links to sociology websites and information on the latest theories and discoveries in the field. In addition, you will find further suggested readings, flash cards, MicroCase online exercises, and appendices on a range of subjects. You might also want to look at Appendix H, "Marriage and Close Relationship Counseling."

Online Study Tool

Marriage&Family⊛Now™ Go to **http://sociology.wadsworth.com** to reach the companion website for your text and use the Marriage&FamilyNow access code that came with your book to access this study tool. Take a practice pretest after you have read each chapter, and then use the study plan provided to master that chapter. Afterward, take a posttest to monitor your progress.

Search Online with InfoTrac College Edition

For additional information, exercises, and key words to aid your research, explore InfoTrac College Edition, your online library that offers full-length articles from thousands of scholarly and popular publications. Click on *InfoTrac College Edition* under *Chapter Resources* at the companion website and use the access code that came with your book.

- Search keywords: *marital satisfaction, couple communication, marital communication.*

Power *and* Violence *in* Marriages *and* Families

> *To the extent that power is the prevailing force in a relationship — whether between husband and wife or parent and child, between friends or between colleagues — to that extent love is diminished.*
>
> RONALD V. SAMPSON,
> *The Psychology of Power*

- Sarah gets a chance for a promotion at work, but accepting it will mean moving to another city; Sarah's spouse does not want to relocate.
- Antonio wants a new stereo for his truck; his partner would prefer to spend the money on ski equipment.
- Marietta would like to talk to her husband about what he does (and doesn't do) around the house, but he is always too busy to discuss the issue.
- Greg feels that he gives more and is more committed to his marriage than his wife is.

Each of these situations is about power in a relationship. This chapter examines power in relationships, particularly marriage. We will discuss some classic studies of marital decision making, and we will look at what contemporary social scientists say about marital power. We will discuss why playing power politics is harmful to intimacy and explore an alternative. Finally, we will explore one tragic result of the abuse of power in families—family violence. We begin by defining power.

▪ What Is Power? ▪

Power may be defined as the ability to exercise one's will. There are many kinds of power. Power exercised over oneself is *personal power*, or autonomy. Having a comfortable degree of personal power is important to self-development. *Social power* is the ability of people to exercise their wills over the wills of others. Social power may be exerted in different realms, including within the family. Parental power, for instance, operates between parents and children. In this chapter, our discussion of power in families will focus on power

between married partners, as well as power in other intimate-partner relationships. This form of power is termed **marital power**.[1]

What Does Marital Power Involve?

Marital power is complex and has several components. First, marital power involves *decision making:* Who gets to make decisions about everything, from where the couple will live to how they will spend their leisure time. Second, marital power involves the *division of labor:* Who does more work around the house? Third, marital power involves a partner's *sense of empowerment:* feeling free to raise complaints to one's spouse about the relationship (Komter 1989).

In addition to these three components of marital power, the concept involves both *objective measures of power* (who actually makes more—or more-important—decisions, does more housework, and/or feels freer to raise complaints) and a *subjective measure of fairness* in the marriage (Sprecher and Schwartz 1994). These two concepts may be related, but not necessarily. For example, a husband who makes virtually all of the important decisions and does relatively little housework may perceive the relationship as fair, whereas a wife, one who has a larger role in decision making and who has been successful in persuading her husband to share the housework, may nevertheless feel that the relationship is an unfair one.

For the most part, research shows that it is partners' subjective *perception* of fairness (as opposed to objective measures of *actual* equality) that influences marital satisfaction (Kurdek 1998; Wilkie, Ferree, and Ratcliff 1998). Furthermore, when partners perceive themselves as reciprocally respected, listened to, and supported by the other, they are more apt to define themselves as equal partners (Rosenbluth, Steil, and Whitcomb 1998). They are also less depressed (Longmore and DeMaris 1997), generally happier (Steil

---

1. In early research and theory, the term *conjugal power* was used in talking about power in marriage. The term *marital power* is now more commonly used. The analysis of power in couple relationships has been extended to include couples who are not married. We will use the term *intimate-partner power* in referring to unmarried couples or to unmarried and married couples when discussing both together. But since most research on intimate partner power focuses on married couples, we will often characterize that as marital power and the partners as husband and wife.

1997), and more satisfied with their marriage (Rosenbluth, Steil, and Whitcomb 1998). Understanding that marital power is a complex concept, we turn to an examination of the sources of marital power.

Power Bases

Two social scientists (French and Raven 1959) have suggested six bases, or sources, of power: coercive, reward, expert, informational, referent, and legitimate. **Coercive power** is based on the dominant person's ability and willingness to punish the partner either with psychological–emotional abuse or physical violence or, more subtly, by withholding favors or affection. Slapping a mate and spanking a child are examples of coercive power; so is refusing to talk to the other person—the silent treatment. **Reward power** is based on an individual's ability to give material or non-material gifts and favors, ranging from emotional support and attention to financial support or recreational travel.

Expert power stems from the dominant person's superior judgment, knowledge, or ability. Although this is certainly changing, our society has traditionally attributed expertise in such important matters as finances to men. Consequently, wives have been encouraged to assign expert power to husbands more often than the reverse. **Informational power** is based on the persuasive content of what the dominant person tells another individual. A husband may be persuaded to stop smoking by his wife's giving him information on smoking's health dangers.

Referent power is based on the less dominant person's emotional identification with the more dominant individual. In feeling part of a couple or group, such as a family, whose members share a common identity, an individual gets emotional satisfaction from thinking as the more dominant person does or behaving as the "referent" individual wishes. A husband who attends a social function when he'd rather not "because my wife wanted to go and so I wanted to go too" has been swayed by referent power. In happy relationships, referent power increases as partners grow older together (Raven, Centers, and Rodrigues 1975).

Finally, **legitimate power** stems from the dominant individual's ability to claim authority, or the right to request compliance. Legitimate power in traditional marriages involves acceptance by both partners of the husband's role as head of the family.

Throughout the rest of this chapter we will see the various power bases at work. The consistent research finding, for instance, that the economic dependence of one partner on the other results in the dependent partner's being less powerful may be explained by understanding the interplay of both reward power and coercive power: If I can reward you with financial support—or threaten to take it away—then I am more likely to exert power over you.

The Dynamics of Marital Power

We turn now to look more specifically at research on marital power and the theoretical perspectives used to explain couple power relationships.

Classical Perspectives on Marital Power

Research on marital power began in the 1950s with the research of social scientists Robert Blood and Donald Wolfe. At this time—before the feminist movement of the 1970s—interest in marital power was more academic than political. Blood and Wolfe were curious about how married couples made decisions. Their book *Husbands and Wives: The Dynamics of Married Living* (1960) was based on interviews with wives only. Nevertheless, it was a significant piece of research and shaped thinking on marital power for many years.

EGALITARIAN POWER AND THE RESOURCE HYPOTHESIS Blood and Wolfe began with the assumption that although the American family's forebears were patriarchal, "the predominance of the male has been so thoroughly undermined that we no longer live in a patriarchal system" (pp. 18–19). Blood and Wolfe reasoned that the relative power of wives and husbands results from their relative resources. The **resource hypothesis** holds that the spouse with more resources has more power in marriage. Resources include education and earnings; within marriage, a spouse's most valuable resource would be the ability to provide money. Another resource would be good judgment, probably enhanced by education and experience. (Note that the resource hypothesis is a variation on *exchange theory*; see Chapter 3.)

To test their resource hypothesis, Blood and Wolfe interviewed about 900 wives in greater Detroit

Who has power in this relationship? According to the resource hypothesis, the partner with more resources generally has more power. This couple, who are joint owners of a business, appear to be fairly well balanced in terms of their economic resources.

and asked who made the final decision in eight areas, such as what job the husband should take, what car to buy, whether the wife should work, and how much money the family could afford to spend per week on food. From their interviews they drew the conclusion that most families (72 percent) had a "relatively egalitarian" decision-making structure (that is, the spouses held roughly equal power, whether that involved separate areas of decision making or joint decisions). However, there were families in which the husband made the most decisions (25 percent), and a few wife-dominated families (3 percent).

The resource hypothesis was supported by the finding that the relative resources of wives and husbands were important in determining which partner made more decisions. Wage and salary earnings or other individual income was a major source of decision-making power. Older spouses and those with more education made more decisions. Blood and Wolfe also found the relative power of a wife to be greater after she no longer had young children (and so was less dependent on her husband) or when she worked outside the home and thereby gained wage-earning resources for herself. Blood and Wolfe reported little on black families, except to say that black husbands, when compared to white husbands, had more equal decision-making power with their wives.

The Blood and Wolfe study had the important effect of encouraging people to see marital power as shared rather than patriarchal. The power of individual partners was seen as resting on their own attributes or resources rather than on social roles, a perspective that changed the thinking of social scientists. But this study has been strongly criticized.

Criticism of the Resource Hypothesis One criticism concerns Blood and Wolfe's criteria for attributing power to husbands or wives. The decisions made by wives (such as how much to spend on food) were generally less important than those typically made by husbands (in which city should the couple live?): "Having the power to make trivial decisions is not the same as having the power to make important ones" (Brehm et al. 2002, p. 321). And there were important areas of family life that were not included in the Blood and Wolfe study—such as sexual life, how many children to have, and how much freedom partners might have for same- or opposite-sex friendships.

Critics stated that power between spouses involves far more than which partner makes the most *final* decisions—deciding what *alternatives* are going to be considered may be the real decision. Moreover, the person who seems to be making a decision may in fact be acting on a delegation of power from the other partner (Safilios-Rothschild 1970).

Another criticism is that the resource hypothesis has a narrow focus—on individuals' background characteristics and abilities—but does not take into ac-

Native Man and Woman by unidentified Native artist, Chukotka Peninsula, Russia. Artist workshop, Uelen.

© Pat O'Hara/CORBIS

count their personalities and the way they interact (Brehm et al. 2002). And finally, marital power is more than decision making; it also implies the relative autonomy of wives and husbands, along with the division of labor in marriages (Safilios-Rothschild 1970).

Blood and Wolfe came under heaviest fire for their conclusion that a patriarchal power structure had been replaced by egalitarian marriages.

RESOURCES AND GENDER Feminist Dair Gillespie (1971) pointed out that power-giving resources tend to be unevenly distributed between the sexes. Husbands usually earn more money even when wives work, so husbands control more economic resources. Husbands are often older (and at the time of the study were often better educated than their wives). So husbands are more likely to have more status, and they may be more knowledgeable, or seem to be. Even their greater physical strength may be a powerful resource (Collins 1995), although it can be a destructive one, as we will see later in this chapter.

Women are likely to have fewer alternatives to the marriage than their husbands do, especially if wives cannot support themselves or are responsible for the care of young children. Moreover, men can remarry more readily than women. Consequently, according to Gillespie, the resource hypothesis, which presents resources as neutral and power as gender-free, is simply "rationalizing the preponderance of the male sex." Marriage is hardly a "free contract between equals" (p. 449).

Current research tends to support Gillespie's insight that American marriages continue to be inegalitarian even though they are no longer traditional (Rosenbluth, Steil, and Whitcomb 1998; Wilkie, Ferree, and Ratcliff 1998). True, resources make a difference, and an important factor in marital power is whether or not a wife is working. Wage-earning wives have more to say in important decisions (Blumberg and Coleman 1989) and in the division of household labor (Risman and Johnson-Sumerford 1998).

One way in which women come to have fewer resources is through their reproductive roles and resulting economic dependence. Just after marriage the relationship is apt to be relatively egalitarian, with the husband only moderately more powerful than the wife—if at all. Often at this point the wife has considerable economic power in relation to her husband because she is employed and may even have a well-paying career. But relationships tend to become less egalitarian with the first pregnancy and birth (Coltrane and Ishii-Kuntz 1992).

But during the childbearing years of the marriage, the practical need to be married is felt especially strongly by women, who are more often than not the primary caregivers as well as bearers of children (Johnson and Huston 1998). A divorce would likely mean that the woman must parent and support small children alone. Women engaged in reproduction and child rearing may have less energy to resist dominance attempts. On the other hand, a mother may exert power over her husband by threatening to leave and take the infant with her (LaRossa 1979).

As we noted, working contributes to marital power. But working for wages does not necessarily give a wife full status as an equal partner (Risman and

While an older generation may hold to traditional patriarchal power, the next generation may renegotiate and consciously change those roles, especially as women assume more autonomy and make gains in the workplace. In this photo, the classic game of mahjong and the Chinese vase and screen in the background suggest that the grandmother's world is one of tradition. The posture and clothing of the younger family members suggest more casual and democratic family relations.

Johnson-Sumerford 1998; Coltrane 2000). Even though a working wife is less obliged to defer to her husband and has greater authority in making family decisions, she does not necessarily participate equally in decision making and is still unequally burdened with housekeeping and child rearing, as Chapter 12 spells out.

Researchers have come to realize that resource theory does not fully explain marital power. While women's employment rates, occupational status, and income have increased in recent decades, their share of household work has not declined to a similar degree (Coltrane 2000). This "failure of resource and exchange perspectives to explain marital power dynamics in two earner couples" (Tichenor 1999, pp. 638–639) has led scholars to turn to other theoretical perspectives.

All in all, there are a variety of explanations for the general continuation of male marital power in a society that, on the whole, sees marital equality as desirable.

RESOURCES IN CULTURAL CONTEXT The *family ecology* theoretical perspective (see Chapter 3) stresses that family interaction needs to be examined within the context of the society and culture in which it exists. Studies comparing traditional societies with more modern ones suggest that in a traditional society, norms of patriarchal authority may be so strong that they *override personal resources* and give considerable *power to all husbands* (Safilios-Rothschild 1967; Blumberg and Coleman 1989). Put another way, in a traditional society, male authority is *legitimate power*. This perspective is termed **resources in cultural context**.

This situation may be especially true for immigrant families from traditional societies, such as in Asia or Central and South America. A study of Puerto Rican families (Cooney et al. 1982), for example, found that the norms of the parent generation born in Puerto Rico[2] were patriarchal: "[These] norms emphasize the generally superior authority of the man

---

2. All Puerto Ricans are American citizens inasmuch as Puerto Rico is a commonwealth under United States sovereignty. Nevertheless, the experience of migrating from Puerto Rico to the mainland United States is similar in most respects to that of immigration to the United States from any Latin American country.

within the family" (Cooney et al. 1982, p. 622). The specific socioeconomic and personal resources of the husband are irrelevant: He has the power regardless.

Because new immigrants are increasing as a proportion of our population, we may expect a resultant increase in traditional patriarchal families. However, subsequent generations may be expected to adopt the more common American pattern. The generation born in the United States has moved to a "transitional egalitarian society" typical of the rest of the United States, in which "husband–wife relationships are more flexible and negotiated . . . [and] socioeconomic achievements become the basis for negotiation within the family" (p. 622).

Even among native-born Americans, however, we must recognize the continuing salience of tradition and the assumption that it is legitimate for husbands to wield authority in the family (Komter 1989). The continued importance of traditional legitimations of husbands' authority is apparent in religious groups that accept the principle of male headship of the family (see Chapter 2).[3] And although egalitarianism is undoubtedly the most sought after mode among American couples generally, "[e]ven today, female dominance in a heterosexual relationship is less acceptable to both parties than male dominance" (Brehm et al. 2002, p. 323). Cohabiting partners, for example, are more likely to break up if the woman earns more than the man than if the earnings are similar or if the male earns more (Brines and Joyner 1999).

In sum, the cultural context conditions resource theory. Resource theory explains marital power only when there is no overriding **egalitarian norm** or **patriarchal norm** of marital power. Put another way, if traditional norms of male authority are strong, husbands will almost inevitably dominate regardless of personal resources (see Figure 14.1). Similarly, if an egalitarian norm of marriage were completely accepted, then a husband's superior economic achievements would be irrelevant to his decision-making power because both spouses would have equal power (Cooney et al. 1982). It is only in the present **transitional egalitarian situation**, in which neither patriarchal norms nor egalitarian norms are firmly entrenched, that marital power is negotiated by individual couples, and the

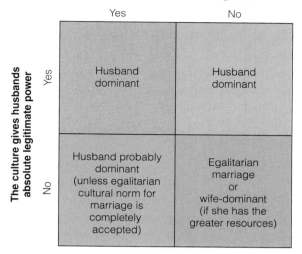

FIGURE 14.1

How resources and legitimate power interact to affect conjugal power.

power of husbands and wives may be a consequence of their resources (Rodman 1972).

LOVE, NEED, AND POWER Some have argued that a primarily economic analysis does not do justice to the complexities of marital power. Perhaps a wife has considerable power through her husband's love for her:

> The relative degree to which the one spouse loves and needs the other may be the most crucial variable in explaining total power structure. The spouse who has relatively less feeling for the other may be the one in the best position . . . to effectively influence the outcome of decisions. Thus, a "relative love and need" theory may be . . . basic in explaining power structure. (Safilios-Rothschild 1970, pp. 548–549)

This theory is congruent with what sociologist Willard Waller termed the **principle of least interest**. The partner with less commitment to the relationship is the one who is more apt to exploit the other. The spouse who is more willing to break up the marriage or to shatter rapport and refuse to be the first to make up can maintain dominance (Waller 1951, pp. 190–192).

Like resource theory, the **relative love and need theory** is a variation of exchange theory. Each partner brings resources to the marriage and receives rewards

---

3. At the same time, as noted in Chapter 4, wives in evangelical families often have more decision-making power than their formal submission to the male family head would indicate (Gallagher and Smith 1999; Bartkowski 2001).

from the other partner, and these may be emotional as well as material resources. The partner who is more dependent on the marriage emotionally is more likely to comply with the other's preferences. The relative love and need theory does not predict whether husbands or wives will generally be more powerful. In other words, it assumes that women are as likely to have power as men are: "The man who desires or values the woman as a mate more than she desires or values him will be in the position of wanting to please her" (Hallenbeck 1966, p. 201).

Generally, however, the wife holds the less powerful position even in this reckoning. How does the relative love and need theory account for a gender difference in power? One explanation offered is that women are more socialized to love and need their husbands than the reverse. They also tend to be more relationship oriented than men are (Tannen 1990; Murstein and Adler 1997). In our society, women are encouraged to express their feelings, men to repress them. Therefore, men are less likely to articulate their feelings for their partners, and "men's dependence on close relationships remains covert and repressed, whereas women's dependence is overt and exaggerated" (Cancian 1985, p. 258). Overt dependency affects power: "A woman gains power over her husband if he clearly places a high value on her company or if he expresses a high demand or need for what she supplies. . . . If his need for her and high evaluation of her remain covert and unexpressed, her power will be low" (p. 258).

But another way of looking at it is that men are less powerful in the private, intimate sphere than they are in the public world because the private world is more likely to be defined by women. Therapists, and mass media, and to an increasing degree the public, support women's desire for more expression of feelings, and men may feel they fall short.

> Insofar as love is defined as the woman's "turf," an area where she sets the rules and expectations, a man is likely to feel threatened and controlled when she seeks more intimacy. Talking about the relationship, like she wants, feels like taking a test that she made up and he will fail. . . . He is blocked from straightforward counterattack insofar as he [also] believes that intimacy is good. (Cancian 1985, p. 260)

Having examined three perspectives on marital power that arose out of the original Blood and Wolfe

research and the responses of critics, we now turn to an examination of marital power as it operates in different social settings.

Social Class, Racial/Ethnic Diversity, and Marital Power

Gender ideologies and practices that affect marital power vary not only with income, religion, and immigration status but also with education, age, and urban/rural residence (McLoyd et al. 2000).

SOCIAL CLASS The majority of Americans, regardless of class, do not see power inequities in their own marriages, although they obviously exist in many marriages. Some studies find middle-class couples to be more egalitarian and attribute that to higher levels of education and less traditional gender ideology. Other studies find working-class couples to be more egalitarian—because husbands are more likely to perceive a working wife's income as necessary and to respond to the practical need for the husband's household labor and child care (Hochschild 1989). Middle-class husbands are more likely than lower-class men to have substantially higher earnings than their wives, which, according to resource theory, should provide them with greater power. In this view, middle-class men *talk* egalitarianism, while working-class men *do* more egalitarian marriage (Coltrane 1996, 2000).

MARITAL POWER IN AFRICAN AMERICAN MARRIAGES American marriages in all racial/ethnic sectors range from patriarchal to relatively egalitarian in their power structure, with wife-dominated marriages rare. Black couples report more-egalitarian relationships than those in other racial/ethnic groups. African American husbands spend more time on domestic work than their Euro-American counterparts, although wives still retain primary responsibility for housework and child care (McLoyd et al. 2000). Moreover, black men do not trade higher earnings for relief from domestic duties, as occurs in other racial/ethnic groups. The division of labor among African American couples—in contrast to Latino and Euro-American couples—is not so easily explained by the resource hypothesis (McLoyd et al. 2000).

The purported egalitarianism of African American families is complex. Although African American husbands are very positive about wives' employment and do more domestic work, at the same time they are more ideologically conservative than Euro-American men about their formal role as head of household and provider (McLoyd et al. 2000).

MEXICAN AMERICANS AND ROLE MAKING
The belief that Mexican American marital relations are unqualifiedly patriarchal is outdated. Migration to the United States has resulted in changed circumstances, notably a need for wives' employment, and this offers opportunity for renegotiation of gender roles and marital power (Hondagneu-Sotelo 1996; Hondagneu-Sotelo and Messner 1999). One study (Williams 1990), based on in-depth interviews and participant observation among Mexican Americans aged twenty-five to fifty in Austin and Corpus Christi, Texas, focused on husbands' and wives' role making as they negotiated and changed their respective roles. Respondents saw themselves as different from their parents in terms of marital power: "My mother *quedaba en la casa* [stayed at home]. She had no voice in family affairs" (p. 85). Today, despite some resistance from husbands, power relationships have changed. As one woman explained,

> I am 44, I've got money, a good car and my kids are behind me. Now, if I am not home in time to make dinner, he can make a sandwich. We've been together a long time and he knows how to make a sandwich. I have had to stand my ground. Two years ago I wanted to go to school to study for a radiologist. He didn't let me. . . . [but] I got my GED. Recently . . . I made a stand that I'm going out and I do. I go out during the day with friends to go out to eat. Not at night. . . . I always felt the obligation that I had to come home to cook. (Williams 1990, p. 94)

MARITAL POWER IN KOREAN AMERICAN FAMILIES While immigration changes family relationships, and women's employment produced some movement away from traditional male dominance in Mexican American families, that has not been the case in Korean American families. True, married women's labor force participation has shown a "phenomenal" increase (Min 2002, p. 201). But the social and cultural context of that work limits the impact that a wife's employment has on her marital power.

Most employed Korean immigrant wives work in small-scale, family-owned businesses. "Korean women who assist their husbands in the family store do not

seem to enjoy the economic and psychological independence that most American wives seem to enjoy" (Min 2002, p. 202). The fact that husbands and wives both work in a segregated sub-economy means that they have little social exposure to the more egalitarian ideas of the wider society. Participation in Korean Christian churches also supports the retention of a patriarchal ideology (Min 2002).

The resource theory of marital power is more applicable to the situation of African American and Mexican American marriages, while the resources in cultural context theory seems operative in Korean American families.

The Future of Marital Power

The preponderance of the evidence indicates that men are more dominant in marital relationships. Yet, power disparities discourage intimacy, which is based on honesty, sharing, and mutual respect. Therefore, attainment of the American ideal of equality in marriage would seem to support the development of intimacy in marital relationships.

Recent research does suggest that women's labor force participation in a dual earner family is associated with increased marital happiness. The researchers attribute this to increased resources (i.e., income) as well as to psychosocial benefits such as self-esteem and to "shifts in the power structure" (Tsang et al. 2003, p. 9).

Equalization of the marital power of men and women may occur in a number of ways. First, women may attain equal status in the public world and develop resources that are truly similar to men's. Despite the persistence of occupational segregation, the trend of the times is in this direction (Nock 2001). White and Rogers (2000) note that "women and men are increasingly similar in their economic roles" (p. 1048). Women's increase in income should "lead to an increased sense of self, sense of control over [their] lives, and expectation of achieving greater bargaining power within the relationship" (Blumberg and Coleman 1989, p. 239).

Family researcher Steven Nock sees the future as one of *mutually economically dependent couples*. He defines that as dual earner couples in which each spouse earns between 40 percent and 50 percent of the family's income. Examining data from the 1999 Current Population Survey, he finds that presently just under one-third of all dual earners (some 20 percent of all couples) are mutually economically dependent. This pattern occurs at all economic levels (Nock 2001).

A second way in which marital power may be equalized is for society to come to value women's resources of caring and emotional expression more highly. Even though women's care of children, the elderly, and other dependents; their creation of a warm, comfortable home; and their emotional support of family and other social bonds have not been much rewarded with either money or status, feminists and conservatives alike forcefully argue the social importance of these contributions. Women's traditional assets could increase in worth in a changed cultural climate.

One impact of feminism on American culture may be the way that women's values *are* increasingly incorporated into the culture. Some men's liberation movements now articulate expressive values as well (see Chapter 4). Sociologist Nock anticipates that, given the important cultural changes we have seen, men's values about marriage will come to resemble women's relational values. Men will recognize the value of women's work in the home and realize the unfairness of unequal responsibility for it (Nock 2001, p. 773).

Finally, norms of equality may come to be so strong that men and women will have equal power in marriage regardless of resources. Equality is an important value in American culture. Today the strength of egalitarian values is uniquely evidenced in evangelical marriages, whose power principle is male headship. Despite the legitimacy of a husband's power in theory, in practice marital power is often negotiated. An emergent doctrine of "mutual submission" (of husband and wife to each other) justifies the shared decision making that characterizes many evangelical marriages (Bartkowski 2001).

Our society might come to endorse norms of equality in marriage as strongly as it endorsed patriarchal authority in the past. The decline in divorce rates since the early 1980s may reflect "the gradual working out of the gender issues first confronted in the 1960s. If so, this implies that young men and women are forming new types of marriages that are based on a new understanding of gender ideals" (Nock 2001, p. 774).

■ Some American Couples ■

Having examined classic research and theoretical perspectives on marital power, along with some thoughts on the future, we now look more closely at some studies of the workings of power in the everyday lives of contemporary couples.

Four Types of Couples Compared

As you may recall from Chapter 6, sociologists Philip Blumstein and Pepper Schwartz (1983)[4] undertook a comparison of four types of couples: heterosexual married couples, cohabiting heterosexual couples, gay male couples, and lesbian couples. Questionnaires were sent to 22,000 couples who responded to media advertisements for participants or to the researchers' solicitation for participants at various events and meetings. More than 12,000 questionnaires were returned, and some 300 couples were interviewed; data were used only if both parties participated. Although this is not a national random sample, the study offers interesting insights. Several other projects or research reviews have undertaken similar comparisons with similar results (Peplau and Cochran 1990; Kurdek 1998).

Blumstein and Schwartz's research illustrates some of our ideas about power in intimate relationships. *The principle of least interest* does seem operative in gay and lesbian relationships, for example (also Patterson 2000, pp. 1053–1054).

Blumstein and Schwartz found gender to be by far the most significant determinant of the pattern of **intimate-partner power**. (We need to add this term to our vocabulary in order to talk about nonmarital relationships.) Married and heterosexual cohabiting couples, composed of a male and a female, tended to be the least egalitarian. The division of labor seems relatively more equal, or at least more flexible, in gay male and lesbian couples, as they tend to share domestic duties, including child rearing (Patterson 2000, p. 1054; see also Peplau, Veniegas, and Campbell 1996).

The impact of gender was apparent, however, even in the comparison of gay and lesbian couples. Gay men tended to be more competitive, very aware of each other's earning power and other signs of status in the public world. Lesbians, with feminine values of cooperation and pleasing others, worked very hard at their relationship and often deferred to each other (Blumstein and Schwartz 1983; see also Kurdek 1998).

---

4. The Blumstein and Schwartz study, published in 1983, is still considered the most extensive study of gay and lesbian couples compared to heterosexual couples and is cited in the latest *Journal of Marriage and the Family* decade review (Christopher and Sprecher 2000).

As resource theory suggests, money was a major determinant of power. Two men or two women are far more likely to have similar incomes and thus to be more equal. However, money affects power even in a same-sex couple (Blumstein and Schwartz 1983; Patterson 2000, p. 1053). High-earning individuals (or the employed partner with an unemployed companion) tended to be excused from tiresome household chores and got to pick leisure activities. The way in which one partner's success in the wider world serves as a basis for claiming relationship benefits is illustrated by the reaction of a gay male partner:

> Our biggest arguments are about what I haven't done lately. . . . I am willing to help out when I can, but my career is not just nine to five and usually I either don't have the time or I'm so tired when I come home that the last thing I'm going to do is clean the kitchen floor. . . . We had this one discussion where he suggested I get up earlier in the morning to help clean up if I'm too tired at night. I blew up and told him that I was the one with the career here and it was my prospects and my salary that gave us his vacations and you just can't be a housewife and a success all at the same time. (Blumstein and Schwartz 1983, pp. 152–153)

Lesbian couples illustrate another principle of intimate-partner power: the importance of norms and the cultural context. Committed to egalitarian and cooperative decision making, lesbian couples were the only ones in the Blumstein and Schwartz study to transcend the principle that economic resources determine decision-making power (see also Peplau and Cochran 1990). Norms of equality were simply so strong that lesbians made strenuous efforts not to let one partner's unemployment or differential earning power affect decision making.

At the same time, the situation may be changing toward greater equality for all types of couples. A majority of both gay and lesbian couples reported egalitarian relationships in later research (Peplau et al. 1996). Heterosexual married couples, as well as gay/lesbian couples, scored high on an equality scale in another study (Kurdek 1998). It may be that the equality norm of couple power is becoming stronger in all sectors.

Returning to the Blumstein and Schwartz study, a final conclusion is that commitment influences the *use*

© Steve Skjold/PhotoEdit

Gay and lesbian couples are more likely to share domestic duties than heterosexual couples, although attainment of an egalitarian ideal eludes many gay/lesbian couples as well. In marriages, men's participation in housework increased in the 1990s, although wives continue to do more.

of power. The formal commitment of marriage represented a barrier to separation that limited the principle of least interest. Because *both* partners would have found it difficult to leave the relationship, both felt secure in the relationship.

In marriage, representing the highest level of commitment, low-resource partners (usually women) felt much freer to spend money earned by the partner than did individuals in a cohabiting relationship. They were likely to view resources as joint ones rather than "yours" and "mine." They also believed, despite periods of inequality, that relative commitment, energy, and the rewards of marriage even out over time. Regardless of actual power in the marriage, it seems that as the years pass, spouses develop an increased sense of identity with each other and therefore are more apt to view marital decisions as joint ones (Schafer and Keith 1981).

Perhaps because of their greater sense of separate identity and of the need to be economically independent if necessary, maintaining equality was very important to individuals in gay, lesbian, and heterosexual cohabiting couples. Resources, rather than a commitment bond, ensured their security and power within the relationship: "Only married couples do not rely on equality to hold them together" (Blumstein and Schwartz 1983, p. 317; see also Brines and Joyner 1999). As couples in nonmarital relationships intensified their commitment over time, however, the partner with fewer resources also gained in power in those relationships (Blumstein and Schwartz 1983).

While some degree of frustration and unhappiness occurred for spouses who tried unsuccessfully to convert a more traditional marriage and unequal relationship into an egalitarian one (1983, p. 324), Blumstein and Schwartz emerged from their project impressed by the advantages of marriage. The stability of a formal commitment enabled couples to survive difficulties and required a sharing and a negotiation of conflict that in the long run strengthened the relationship.

Peer Marriage

Change is hard, Blumstein and Schwartz concluded, because couples "must not only go against everything they have learned and develop new skills, but they have to resist the negative sanction of society" (1983, p. 324; see also Burke and Cast 1997).

Pepper Schwartz (1994, 2001) followed up the earlier research on four types of couples with an exploration of the factors that facilitate **peer marriage**: "I began looking for [more] couples who had worked out no worse than a 60–40 split on childrearing, housework, and control of discretionary funds, and who considered themselves to have 'equal' status or standing in the relationship" (2001, p. 182). The study was based on fifty-seven egalitarian couples, with some additional interviews with couples considered **near peers** and **traditionals** for comparison.

Near peers believed in equality, but the combination of the arrival of children and wanting to maximize income meant that the husband did not participate as much as the couple's egalitarian ideals required. *Tradi-*

tionals were those in which males dominated decision making except regarding children, but both parties were OK with this—the wife did not seek equality.

Peer marriages did not necessarily come from feminist ideology. Only 40 percent of women and 20 percent of men in peer marriages cited feminism as a motive. The rest gave other reasons for wanting a peer marriage: a rejection of negative parental models (women resented their father's dominance of their mothers; men wished for more paternal involvement); a desire to undertake co-parenting; and in some cases, a period of serious tension in the marriage that required renegotiation of roles. However, for men especially, partner's preference was what led their marriage in an egalitarian direction. In an interesting twist on the expressive role of women, "[m]any of these men told me they had always expected a woman to be the emotional architect of a relationship and were predisposed to let her set the rules" (p. 183).

There was "no single blueprint" (p. 189), nor were these peer marriage couples high-earning "yuppies" or academics with flexible schedules. What peer marriage seemed to take in the long run was an intense desire to have such a marriage and a persistent willingness to forgo male career advancement and income. Everyday responsibilities also had to be constantly monitored and renegotiated. Over time, the peer marriage couples evolved strong egalitarian norms that overrode the surrounding structure and typical power processes, much as Blumstein and Schwarz had earlier found in their lesbian couples (and sociologist Barbara Risman [1998] found in her research on "fair" marriages).

The couples' respect for each other as described in Schwartz's study of peer marriage is essentially a "no-power" relationship. We turn now to a discussion of the process of changing power relationships in marriage.

Power Politics Versus No-Power Relationships

Current evidence indicates that equitable relationships are generally more apt to be stable and satisfying (Schwartz 1994; Risman and Johnson-Sumerford 1998). Marriage counselors today are virtually unanimous in asserting that greater intimacy takes place insofar as partners are equal.

"I'm trying to look at it from my point of view."

Social scientist Peter Blau terms this situation *no-power*. **No-power** does not mean that one partner exerts little or no power; it means that both partners wield about equal power. Each has the ability to mutually and reciprocally influence and be influenced by the other (Schwartz 1994; Gottman et al. 1998).

A fair division of household labor—discussed in Chapter 12—is not the only standard by which women and men judge the equality or lack of equality in their marriage. The respect one has for the other's views is extremely important; that is a central element in a no-power conceptualization of marriage and other partner relations. As we use the term, no-power also implies partners' unconcern about exercising their relative power over each other. No-power partners seek to negotiate and compromise, not to win (see Chapter 13). They are able to avoid **power politics**.

Power Politics in Marriage

As gender norms move from traditional toward egalitarian, all family members' interests and preferences gain legitimacy, not only or primarily those of the husband or husband/father. For example, the man's occupation is no longer the sole determining factor in where the family will live or how the wife will spend her time. This means that decisions formerly made automatically, or by spontaneous consensus, must now be consciously negotiated. A possible outcome of such conscious negotiating, of course, is greater intimacy; another is locking into power politics and conflict. If the essential source of marital power is (as the relative love and need theory suggests) "the greater power to go away," then "politics in marriage has to do with suggesting the use of that power to leave the marriage." A spouse plays power politics in marriage by saying, in effect, "this is how it would be if I were not here" (Blumberg and Coleman 1989; Chafetz 1989).

Both equal and unequal partners may engage in a cycle of devitalizing power politics. Partners come to know where their own power lies, along with the particular weaknesses of the other. They may alternate in acting sulky, sloppy, critical, or distant. The sulking partner carries on this behavior until she or he fears the mate will "stop dancing" if it goes on much longer; then it's the other partner's turn. This kind of seesawing may continue indefinitely, with partners taking turns manipulating each other. However, the cumulative effect of such power politics is to create distance and loneliness for both spouses.

Few couples knowingly choose power politics, but this is an aspect of marriage in which choosing by default may occur. Our discussion of power in marriage is designed to help partners become sensitive to these issues so that they can avoid such a power spiral, or reverse one if it has already started.

Alternatives to Power Politics

There are alternatives to this kind of power struggle. Robert Blood and Donald Wolfe (1960) proposed one in which partners grow increasingly separate in their decision making; that is, they take charge of separate domains: one buying the car, perhaps the other taking charge of disciplining their children. This alternative is a poor one for partners who seek intimacy, however, for it enforces the separateness associated with devitalized marriage.

A second, more viable alternative to perpetuating an endless cycle of power politics is for the subordinate spouse to disengage from power struggles, as described in "As We Make Choices: Disengaging from Power Struggles." This includes a third, perhaps best, alternative, which is for the more powerful partner to consciously relinquish some power in order to save or enhance the marriage. We saw in Chapter 13, for instance, that marriage communication expert John Gottman and colleagues (Gottman, Coan, Carrere, and Swanson 1998) advise husbands to be willing to share power with their wives if they want happy, stable marriages (pp. 18–19).

THE IMPORTANCE OF COMMUNICATION Partners who feel free to raise complaints and see themselves as mutually respected, equally committed, and listened to are more likely to see their relationship as egalitarian and are more satisfied overall with their relationship (Rosenbluth, Steil, and Whitcomb 1998; Langhinrichsen-Rohling, Smutzler, and Vivian 1994).

Meanwhile, unequal relationships discourage closeness between partners: Exchange of confidences between unequals may be difficult, especially when self-disclosure is seen to indicate weakness, and men have been socialized not to reveal their emotions (Henley and Freeman 1989). Women, feeling less powerful and more vulnerable, may resort to pretense and the withholding of sexual and emotional response (Blumberg and Coleman 1989).

Nevertheless, trying to change the balance of marital power may bring the risk of devitalizing a relationship, depending on how partners go about it. Sub-

ordinate mates who try to disengage from power struggles, without explaining what they are doing and why, risk estrangement. The reason is that dominant partners may have taken a mate's compliance as evidence of love rather than fear. If this deference is withdrawn, a dominant partner may conclude that "she (or he) doesn't love me anymore" and escalate efforts at control, contributing to a spiral of alienation and estrangement that is not acknowledged or discussed openly. The case study "An Ice-Skating Homemaker in a Me-or-Him Bind" illustrates this pattern.

One wife reported that she had lived ten years in a husband-centered marriage before she returned to school, and when she did return, their power relationship changed. Receiving nourishment for her self-esteem in good grades and new friends, she no longer relied totally on her husband's signs of affection. In subtle ways she showed decreasing attention to his preferences. She felt herself growing toward equality in the marriage, but he "thought she didn't love me anymore. . . . After she went back to school, she stopped doing things for me" (anonymous student).

This couple might have avoided estrangement through mutual self-disclosure. The husband might have shared his anxiety. The wife might have explained that from her point of view, "doing things for him" in a deferential way did not show love. As couples assert their interests and bargain in marriage, communication is especially important in establishing and maintaining trust.

THE CHANGE TO A NO-POWER RELATIONSHIP Even when couples discuss power changes, living through them can be difficult. Changing power patterns can be difficult, even for couples who talk about it, because these patterns usually have been established from the earliest days of the relationship. Although partners may not have discussed them directly, they set up unconscious agreements by sending countless verbal and nonverbal cues. As partners experience recurring subtle messages, they build up predictable behavior patterns. From the interactionist perspective, certain behaviors not only come to be expected but also to have symbolic meaning. For many couples, buying favorite foods or other treats, spending holidays in a certain way, and initiating or responding to sexual overtures symbolize not just who has how much power but love itself. Sociologist William Goode had an insight that continues to be relevant for many

As We Make Choices

Disengaging from Power Struggles

Carlfred Broderick, sociologist and marriage counselor, has offered the following exercise to help people disengage from power struggles. The object of this exercise is to get you out of the business of monitoring everyone else's behavior and free you from the unrewarding power struggles resulting from that assignment. Here is the exercise:

1. Think of as many things as you can that your spouse or children *should do, ought to do,* and *would do if they really cared,* but *don't do* (or do only grudgingly because you are always after them). Write them down in a list.

2. From your list, choose three or four items that are especially troublesome right now. Write each one at the head of a sheet of blank paper. These are the issues that you, considerably more than your spouse, want to resolve (even though he or she, by rights, should be the one to see the need for resolution). Right now you are locked in a power struggle over each one, leading to more resentment and less satisfaction all around.

3. In this step you'll consider, one by one, optional ways of dealing with these issues without provoking a power struggle. Place an *A, B, C,* and *D* on each sheet

of paper at appropriate intervals to represent the four options listed below. Depending on the nature of the issue, some of these options will work better than others, but for a start write a sentence or paragraph indicating how each one might be applied in your case. Even if you feel like rejecting a particular approach out of hand, be sure to write something as positive as possible about it.

Option A: Resign the Crown

Swallow your pride and cut your losses by delegating to the other person full control and responsibility for his or her own life in this area. Let your partner reap his or her own harvest, whatever it is. In many cases your partner will rise to the occasion, but if this doesn't happen, resign yourself to suffering the consequences.

Option B: Do It Yourself

There's an old saying: "If you want something done right, do it yourself." Accordingly, if you want something done, and if the person you feel should do it doesn't want to, it makes sense to do it yourself the way you'd like to have it done. After all, who ever said someone should do something he or she doesn't want to do just because you want him or her to do it?

Option C: Make an Offer Your Partner Can't Refuse

Too many interpret this, at first, as including threats of what will happen if the partner doesn't shape up. The real point, however, if you select this approach, is to find out what your partner would really like and then offer it in exchange for what you want him or her to do. After all, it's your want, not your spouse's, that is involved. Why shouldn't you take the responsibility for making it worth your spouse's while?

Option D: Join with Joy

Often the most resisted task can become pleasant if one's partner shares in it, especially if an atmosphere of play or warmth can be established. This calls for imagination and good will, but it can also be effective in putting an end to established power struggles.

Critical Thinking

Have you ever tried any of these in a couple situation? If so, how did it work out?

Would these principles be useful, do you think, in other relationships, such as with children, extended family, or co-workers?

Source: Broderick 1979a, pp. 117–123.

couples. He wrote about the important change in men's position as women gain equality in society and in the family. According to Goode,

Men have always taken for granted that what they were doing was more important than what the other sex was doing, that where they were,

was where the action was. Their women accepted that definition. Men occupied the center of the stage, and women's attention was focused on them. . . . [But] the center of attention shifts to women more now than in the past. I believe that this shift troubles men far more, and creates more of their resistance, than the women's de-

Case Study

An Ice-Skating Homemaker in a Me-or-Him Bind

Joan is an attractive, full-time homemaker who has been married nineteen years. Recently, she began taking courses at a local university and also became involved in learning to figure-skate.

Interviewer: When did you begin ice-skating?

Joan: Well, I took one year when I was a kid, but I had to ride the bus and the streetcar and all that. . . . And then I didn't skate again until last year. I've been skating for two years now and I just love it. I'm getting better. I can do three turns real well and three of the very basic dances. . . .

I try to skate twice a week. But it's created a problem with Chuck. Last year he was working days during the skating season. But now he works midnight to eight and he just hates for me to go there during the day. . . . I don't know whether it's because I like it real well or what it is. But he doesn't like it. When he works midnight to eight, he knows every time I go. When he was working days and I went, as long as my work was done and I had dinner on the table, there was no problem when he came home from work.

Now he knows every time I leave this house. Every place I go he knows. Every time the garage door opens, it wakes him up. It's almost like being in prison without the doors being locked. . . .

One time I stayed too late. I got home at 5:30. My brother was there—I got home at 5:30 and no dinner or nothing. He told me, he

said, "If you ever do this again—there's no dinner—if you ever do this again, I'm going to cut your skates." Oh boy! So I try to avoid doing that. I come home about four o'clock, so I can get dinner on okay. But the trouble [with the ice-skating] is that I can go there and it's almost like on that ice nothing—I just get totally absorbed in it and I forget I'm a mother, forget I'm a wife, I forget everything, I'm just there. I felt that way about golf and waterskiing too, but those things didn't bother Chuck because I was doing them with him, I think. Skating excludes him. . . .

At first I thought it was jealousy. No, it's not jealousy. It's possessiveness. He wants to control what I do: . . . "This is a possession now; I own this person; I can control her mind and body."

My daughter's starting to want to skate now too. The rink is open for the public this summer and I'm not going to be skating very much because I'd have to go in the evenings and that's just not going to work out with our schedule. But I'll try to go. Like this weekend, Chuck will be out of town, so I'm going to go then. Anyway, my daughter's going to go with me when she's out of school. She's getting so she can skate pretty well and she's starting to like it. So she wants a pair of skates. Now he won't buy her the skates. He says, "No, we're not going to spend the money on something like that." Now I think that's terrible. . . .

I could just go buy them because I definitely bought my own skates. I

just went out and bought them. And then at first I lied to him—this is awful—I told him, "Oh, these are just my sister-in-law's skates. . . ." Then finally once I told him they were my own. He said, "Oh! You can afford those skates and I can't afford a jacket." I said, "You can afford a jacket. Go buy one if you want. . . ."

A lot of times he'll say, "What are you going to do today?" And I say, "Well, it's Tuesday and I skate on Tuesday." He's known that all year, but every time he wants to take me to lunch or go somewhere, it is always on Tuesday. . . . One time I said, "Why can't we do it on Monday or Wednesday?" He said, "Oh, I never thought about that. . . ."

He gets mad about everything I really like. Like when I started bowling and I really liked that, he gave me a hard time. It's really not just the skating. If he took the ice-skating away, and I replaced it with something else I liked equally well, that would be the thing he'd be against.

Whether a spouse is free to spend time in self-actualizing pursuits, how much time is allowed, and which pursuits are allowed depends largely on marital power. Chuck is exercising coercive power in threatening to cut Joan's skates.

Critical Thinking

Do you think these kinds of issues—independent activities for spouses—remain possible areas of conflict in couple relationships? How would you handle this situation?

Partners in a no-power relationship work at doing things on equal terms and seek to negotiate and compromise, thus avoiding deadly power games. By not competing with each other, both partners win.

mand for equal opportunity and pay in employment. (Goode 1982, p. 140)

One small study of twelve fairly equal newlywed couples found that some of them either consciously or unconsciously avoided issues about marital power and developed a "myth of equality" (Knudson-Martin and Mahoney 1998). Sometimes this seems to work—but only for a while. The best way to work through power changes is to openly discuss power and to fight about it fairly, using the techniques and cooperative attitudes described in Chapter 13. The partner who feels more uncomfortable can bring up the subject, sharing his or her anger and desire for change but also stressing that he or she still loves the other. Indeed, recent research suggests that spouses think of their marital relationship as fair when they feel listened to and emotionally supported (Risman and Johnson-Sumerford 1998; Wilkie, Ferree, and Ratcliff 1998).

Meanwhile, partners need to remember that managing conflict about power in a positive way is easier said than done. Attempts at communication—and

open communication itself—do not solve all marital problems. Changing a power relationship is a challenge to any marriage. It can be painful for both partners, though promising a more rewarding relationship in the long run. One option for handling power and gender role change is to seek the help of a qualified marriage counselor or counselor team (see also Appendix H on the *Marriages and Families* website).

The Role That Marriage Counselors Can Play

Today, many marriage counselors are committed to viewing couples as two human beings who need to relate to each other as equals. In other words, they are committed to helping couples develop no-power relationships. They realize that once both spouses admit—to themselves and to each other—that they do in fact love and need each other, the basis for power politics is gone. On this assumption, counselors help spouses learn to respect each other as people and not to engage in coercive withdrawal.

Couples need to be aware that, like everybody in society, marriage counselors have internalized their own perspectives on gender roles—and these may not match the goals of the couple. There may be issues concerning potential racial and cultural bias on the part of therapists (Taylor et al. 1990) or simple lack of awareness of cultural differences in communication style or other matters. Choosing (or retaining) an appropriate counselor should involve an assessment of the counselor's sensitivity to the values, goals, and needs of the couple.

The counselor's gender may be an issue for some couples as they explore power and gender issues. A dominant husband, fearful that "it's going to be two against one," may feel threatened by a female counselor. On the other hand, a wife may fear that a male counselor will be too traditional or unable to relate to her. In this situation, counselors sometimes work as a team, woman and man. In any case, it is important that both partners feel comfortable with a counselor from the beginning.

Whether on their own or with the help of counselors, partners can choose to emphasize no-power over the politics of power. No marriage—indeed, no relationship of any kind—is entirely free of power politics. But as Chapter 13 points out, the politics of love requires managing conflict in such a way that both partners win.

When, on the other hand, power politics triumphs over no-power, one result may be family violence—psychological (emotional) and/or physical.

◾ Family Violence ◾

In addressing family violence in a chapter on power in marriage and families, we assume that "all forms of abuse have at their center the exploitation of a power difference" (Glaser and Frosh 1988, p. 6; Whittaker 1995). The use of physical violence to gain or demonstrate power in a family relationship has occurred throughout history, but only recently has family violence been labeled a social problem.

The identification of child abuse as a social problem in the 1960s was followed in the 1970s by attention to wife abuse. With the 1980s came concern about elder abuse, as well as husband abuse. More recently, attention has been given to youth dating violence, to violence in adult dating and cohabiting relationships, including same-sex relationships, and to sexual coercion in marital and nonmarital relationships.

Major Sources of Data on Family Violence

As attention was drawn to family violence in its many forms, research began and has continued to develop. There are several major sources of data on family violence to point to initially. The work of Murray Straus, Richard Gelles, and their colleagues in their National Family Violence Surveys pioneered the scientific study of family violence. This research group not only collected data, but interpreted it, looking for general patterns and causal factors in family violence.

Initially, the only government data available on family violence were FBI compilations of incidents reported to local law enforcement or child protection agencies—and bear in mind that many, many acts of physical violence go unreported. A supplemental National Crime Victimization Survey began in the 1970s, but questions were not well-suited to the study of domestic violence, nor did family violence receive any special attention in the Department of Justice's analysis of crime data.

But in the 1990s, more questions targeted to domestic violence were included in the survey, and special reports were issued on intimate-partner violence. In addition, the Department of Justice and the Centers for Disease Control and Prevention (violence is considered a public health problem) collaborated in sponsoring a National Violence Against Women Survey.

THE NATIONAL FAMILY VIOLENCE SURVEYS The early and continuing research of Straus, Gelles, and colleagues has shaped the social science study of family violence. This group undertook a household survey in 1975 followed by a 1985 telephone survey; together, the surveys produced data from more than 8,000 husbands, wives, and cohabiting individuals (Straus, Gelles, and Steinmetz 1980; Straus and Gelles 1986, 1988, 1995; Gelles and Straus 1988).

The authors defined violence as "an act carried out with the intention, or perceived intention, of causing physical pain or injury to another person." This definition is synonymous with the legal concept of assault. Researchers developed a measure of family violence termed the **Conflict Tactics Scale**. Respondents were asked about the following acts: threw something at the other; pushed, grabbed, or shoved; slapped or spanked; kicked, bit, or hit with a fist; hit or tried to hit with something; beat up the other; burned or scalded (children) or choked (spouses); threatened with a knife or gun; and used a knife or gun (Straus and Gelles 1988, p. 15). Severe violence was defined as acts that have a relatively high probability of causing an injury. The acts constituting severe violence are kicking, biting, punching, hitting with an object, choking, beating, threatening with a knife or gun, using a knife or gun—and, for violence by parents against children, burning or scalding the child (Straus and Gelles 1988, p. 16). Later modified somewhat (Straus et al. 1996), the Conflict Tactics Scale is different from and broader than the crime categories of assault and homicide that form the basis of criminal justice system statistics.

The 1975 and 1985 National Family Violence Surveys found that in 16 percent of the couples surveyed, at least one of the partners had engaged in a violent act against the other during the previous year. In other words, each year, in about one out of every six couples in the United States, an individual commits at least one violent act against his or her partner. And if the period considered is the entire length of the marriage rather than just the previous year, a violent act occurs in 28 percent of couples. National Family Violence Survey data also yielded information on violence directed toward children by parents and siblings.

The National Family Violence Surveys explored social variation in family violence. We discuss their findings here while also updating them. According to the National Family Violence Surveys and other data (e.g., Bachman and Saltzman 1995), family violence exists in all social classes. However, it is reported more often in blue-collar and lower-class families, a situation partly attributable to the fact that middle-class families have greater privacy than lower-class families and hence are better able to conceal family violence (Fineman and Mykitiuk 1994). Also, middle-class individuals have recourse to friends and professional counselors to help deal with their violent behavior; consequently, their altercations are less likely to become matters for the police (Buzawa and Buzawa 1990).

The National Family Violence Surveys show that unemployed people and high school dropouts are more likely to be violent with their intimates (Straus and Gelles 1995; Gelles 1997). Other research finds that among non-Hispanic whites, Latinos, and African Americans, when men have lower incomes than their wives or women partners, they are more likely to be violent toward them. This pattern fits the *resource theory*, whereby those who lack educational and economic resources may turn to physical violence as a power resource (McLoyd et al. 2000). The finding that women with *higher* incomes than their mates are more violent does not have a ready explanation as of yet (McLoyd et al. 2000). Perhaps you can imagine yourself to be a family violence researcher and try to come up with an explanation for this result.

DEPARTMENT OF JUSTICE STATISTICS ON INTIMATE-PARTNER VIOLENCE The Department of Justice collects two kinds of government data on violence: the National Crime Victimization Survey, conducted twice yearly, and the Uniform Crime Reports, a compilation of crimes reported by local and state law enforcement units. The NCVS is the more important, and it is the primary basis for Bureau of Justice Statistics reports on **intimate-partner violence**— that is, violence committed by spouses, ex-spouses, or current or former boyfriends or girlfriends, including same-sex partners.[5]

According to the National Crime Victimization Survey—which asks respondents about all violence they have experienced whether or not it was reported to the police—there were almost 700,000 (nonfatal) incidents of violence between intimates in 2001: rape/sexual assault, robbery, aggravated assault, and

---

5. The National Crime Victimization Survey is a household survey in which a national random sample of the population is asked about crime victimization during the previous year. Subsets of data are pulled out for special reports on intimate-partner violence. Domestic violence is analyzed in terms of types of crimes—e.g., murder, rape/sexual assault, robbery, aggravated assault, and simple assault. Information on location, perpetrator, and consequences of intimate-partner violence and background data on the victim are also obtained in the survey. The NCVS data are considered more valid than the Uniform Crime Reports. Recent reports (Rennison and Welchans 2002; Rennison 2003) cover the years 1976–2001.

In collaboration with the Department of Justice, the U.S. Centers for Disease Control and Prevention maintains a surveillance of intimate-partner homicide that is based on the Uniform Crime Reports. The latest report in this series covers the years 1981–1998. These data do *not* include ex-boyfriends and ex-girlfriends (Paulozzi et al. 2001).

Estimates are that only about half of intimate-partner violent crimes are reported to the police (Rennison and Welchans 2000). As a result, Uniform Crime Reports data (aggregated by the FBI from crime reports of local jurisdictions) may not be accurate. However, most homicides are reported, so the homicide data are more valid. The Bureau of Justice Statistics also publishes homicide reports that include data on intimate-partner homicides (Fox and Zawitz 2004).

Fifty thousand people participated in this rally at the National Mall in Washington, DC. They gathered to protest all types of violence against women.

simple assault. Eighty-five percent of these violent crimes were against women (Rennison 2003). Among women, it was younger women (aged sixteen to twenty-four) who were the most frequent victims, while among men those twenty-five to thirty-four years old were the most frequently victimized (Rennison and Welchans 2002). The number of violent crimes against women declined by almost half between 1993 and 2001, while intimate violence against men declined by 42 percent during this period (Rennison 2003).

Black men (compared to Hispanic or non-Hispanic whites) and divorced, separated, or never-married men were most likely to be victims of intimate-partner violence, while all those factors, as well as low income and urban residence, were associated with victimization among women (Rennison and Welchans 2002).

In 2000, 1,687 people were killed by intimates, a decline from 1976 (even as the population of the United States has increased). However, women are now three-quarters of intimate-partner homicide victims, compared to around half in 1976 (Rennison 2003). Murders by spouses constitute slightly more than half of intimate-partner homicides, compared to three-quarters in 1976. In other words, spousal homicides have declined much

more than homicides by other intimate partners (Rennison and Welchans 2002).

The decline in the number of intimate-partner murders since 1976 has been dramatic for black men (down 74 percent), white men (down 44 percent), and black women (down 45 percent) but not so great for white women (Rennison and Welchans 2002; see Figure 14.2).

The drop in the male homicide victim rate is attributed to the greater availability of options for abused women. When women kill a partner, it is usually out of desperation to exit a violent relationship. The shelter programs and other resources that now exist have given battered women escape routes, so they are less likely to kill spouses or partners in attempts to stop the violence. When men kill, it is more often out of rage against the partner. Although programs for batterers exist that attempt to address their management of anger, programmatic efforts have not yet been able to reduce intimate homicides of white women to an appreciable degree.

Racial/ethnic gender differences in the decline of intimate-partner homicides are hard to explain. Experts are uncertain as to why the intimate homicide

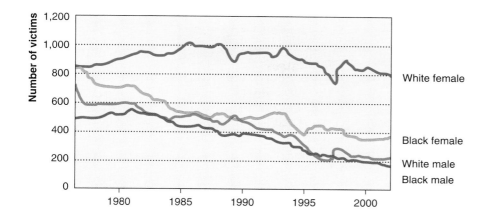

FIGURE 14.2

Number of homicides of intimate partners, by gender and race of the victims, 1976–2002.

Source: Fox and Zawitz 2004 (*Homicide Trends in the United States,* Bureau of Justice Statistics).

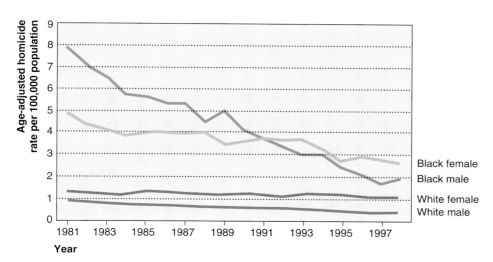

FIGURE 14.3

Intimate-partner age-adjusted homicide rates by victim's race and sex by year—United States, 1981–1998.

Source: Paulozzi et al. 2001, Figure 2 (FBI Uniform Crime Reports, Supplemental Homicide Reports).

victimization of black men and women has declined, while that of white women has not, in that the advocacy of domestic-violence-prevention programs has largely been a white feminist movement.

In discussing gender and racial differences in the decline of the *numbers* of intimate-partner homicides, we should note that *rates* of homicide victimization (murders per 100,000) remain much higher for blacks than for whites (see Figure 14.3).[6]

NATIONAL VIOLENCE AGAINST WOMEN SURVEY A third major source of data on family violence is the National Violence Against Women Survey (Tjaden and Thoennes 1998, 2000), commissioned by the National Institute of Justice and the Centers for Disease Control and Prevention and conducted in 1995–1996. The survey employed a modified version of Straus's Conflict Tactics Scale (rather than asking about "crimes").[7]

According to this survey, women are significantly more likely than men to be victims of intimate-partner violence. *Over a lifetime,* about 25 percent of women

6. *Numbers* of intimate-partner homicides are higher among whites, but the white population is also larger. Data on *rates* tell us about the frequency of a behavior in a given population. Figure 14.3 shows us that blacks are more-frequent victims of intimate-partner homicide relative to the size of the black population, although these rates have declined dramatically. The rate at which white men are victims of intimate-partner homicide has also declined, while that of white women has not shown a significant decline.

7. The National Violence Against Women Survey asks about violence experienced in nonfamily as well as family settings, although we report here only on family violence. It is a victimization survey and does not ask respondents about their possible commission of violent acts.

Table 14.1

	IN LIFETIME Percentage		IN PREVIOUS 12 MONTHS Percentage	
Persons Raped or Physically Assaulted by an Intimate Partner in Lifetime and in Previous 12 Months by Sex of Victim[a]				
Type of Violence	Women (n=8 000)	Men (n=8 000)	Women (n=8 000)	Men (n=8 000)
Rape	7.7[b]	0.3	0.2	–[c]
Physical assault	22.1[b]	7.4	1.3[d]	0.9
Rape and/or physical assault	24.8	7.6	1.5[d]	0.9

a Intimate partner includes current and former spouses, opposite-sex cohabiting partners, same-sex cohabiting partners, dates, and boyfriends/girlfriends.
b Differences between women and men are statistically significant: p-value <= .001.
c The number of men rape victims was insufficient to reliably calculate prevalence estimates.
d Differences between women and men are statistically significant: p-value < = .05.

Source: Tjaden and Thoennes 1998, Exhibit 7 (National Violence Against Women Survey).

and 8 percent of men have been physically assaulted by an intimate partner. (See Table 14.1, which also reports data for the *last twelve months*.)

The researchers also present data on each type of physical assault (see Table 14.2). Women were more likely to be victims in all categories of violence except for "use of knife," where men and women were about equal. Generally, the more serious the act, the greater the difference between men and women (Tjaden and Thoennes 1998).

Racial/Ethnic Diversity, Immigration, and Family Violence

While some data on racial/ethnic diversity are presented in the preceding sections, generally speaking, comparisons among racial/ethnic groups as to the prevalence of family violence cannot be readily made because of the overlap of race/ethnicity with socioeconomic status (Tjaden and Thoennes 1999). That is, while some studies find that minority racial/ethnic groups have higher rates of violence, they also have higher rates of poverty—it is difficult to tell what is the important causative factor (Lockhart 1991). Moreover, men and women in different racial/ethnic groups vary in their definitions of violence or their willingness to acknowledge to researchers that they have been victims of domestic violence. Methodological problems of this sort lead scholars to call for more research be-

fore firm conclusions can be drawn about the relationship between race/ethnicity and family violence (Johnson and Ferraro 2000; McLoyd et al. 2000).

Immigration status is an influence on domestic violence, with one study finding that U.S.-born Puerto Rican and Mexican American men, for example, are *more* likely to be violent toward mates than those who have recently immigrated (McLoyd et al. 2000). Researchers are not sure why this is, but speculate that in traditional country-of-origin settings there is more extended kin control over violence.

Then too, the move to the United States may create cultural conflicts that lead to violent episodes, especially when American values of autonomy lead to resistance to patriarchal authority by wives and children (Min 2002). Relative deprivation—immigrants comparing their standard of living and opportunities to those of middle-class Americans rather than to their former neighbors—could be another factor producing frustration and violence. Immigrants may have come to the U.S. with high hopes, but many men cannot work at their previous occupations in the United States, and so have lost their previous work, status, and income ("Old Ways" 2003). According to social service workers, domestic violence seems to have increased among American Muslims since 9/11, as pressure on the Muslim community from authorities and neighbors was added to stress from the weak economy (Childress 2003).

Table 14.2

Percentage of Persons Physically Assaulted by an Intimate Partner in Lifetime by Type of Assault and Sex of Victim[a]

Type of Assault	Women (n=8,000)	Men (n=8,000)
Total physical assault by intimate partner[b]	**22.1**	**7.4**
Threw something[b]	8.1	4.4
Pushed, grabbed, shoved[b]	18.1	5.4
Pulled hair[b]	9.1	2.3
Slapped, hit[b]	16.0	5.5
Kicked, bit[b]	5.5	2.6
Choked, tried to drown[b]	6.1	0.5
Hit with object[b]	5.0	3.2
Beat up[b]	8.5	0.6
Threatened with gun[b]	3.5	0.4
Threatened with knife[b]	2.8	1.6
Used gun[b]	0.7	0.1
Used knife	0.9	0.8

a Intimate partner includes current or former spouses, opposite-sex cohabiting partners, same-sex cohabiting partners, dates, and boyfriends/girlfriends.
b Differences between women and men are statistically significant: p-value <=.001.

Source: Tjaden and Thoennes 1998, Exhibit 8 (National Violence Against Women Survey).

It does not seem that domestic violence is greater among immigrants than native-born Americans, but certain features of the immigration experience may exacerbate the situation of the abused woman. If the victim is not yet a citizen or legal resident, to seek help carries the risk of deportation; legal status may be dependent on the marriage. A woman may also fear that if she confronts her husband—especially if legal authorities become involved—that her husband may leave the country, taking the children.

Immigrant women may have limited language skills and little access to employment with which to support themselves and their children. They may be socially isolated from family and community. Or they may be living with in-laws who support the abusive husband. For that matter, a woman's own family may urge her to remain in the marriage despite the abuse. Men may exercise extreme patriarchal control over wives, making it difficult for them to leave home or contact others; one husband, for example, kept the mailbox key (Childress 2003; Mehrota 1999; Menjívar and Salcido 2002; Yoshiota et al. 2003).

Programs are beginning to be developed to address issues of family violence in immigrant communities—for example, to meet the needs of South Asian women who are victims of violence (Abraham 1995, 2000). In one New York City community of Bukharan Jews from Central Asia, informal gossip spread the word that wife abuse and harsh physical discipline of children are not the way things are done in America. Community social control thus shifted from protecting abusive husbands to admonishing them ("Old Ways" 2003). Wives sometimes engaged in passive or more direct resistance on their own: neglecting housekeeping, refusing sex, going out surreptitiously, or even destroying their husband's belongings. These tactics were sometimes effective in changing husbands' behavior (Mehrota 1999), though probably not recommended by counselors!

Having presented some major sources of data on family violence, we examine the circumstances and outcomes of spouse or partner abuse in more detail in the next sections.

Wife and Female Partner Abuse

Intimate-partner violence—the physical or emotional abuse of spouses, cohabiting or noncohabiting relationship partners, or former spouses or intimate partners—is a serious and significant problem. First identified in terms of *wife abuse*, the growing practice of cohabitation places many unmarried women in similar situations.[8] Husbands or male partners may also be subject to abuse from intimate partners (to be discussed in a later section).

Physical abuse includes beating, kicking, pushing down stairs, hitting with objects, etc. We focus on physical abuse, but verbal abuse (such as name calling, demeaning verbal attacks, and other vocal assaults) and other kinds of emotional abuse (such as threats to take children away, threats to the victim's extended family or friends, and threats or attacks on pets) virtually always occur along with physical aggression (Stets 1991). Although verbal and emotional aggression are of great psychological importance, we concern ourselves here primarily with repetitive, physically injurious acts.

Physical abuse of wives and other female partners can indeed result in serious injuries. National Crime Victimization Survey data indicate that 5 percent of female victims of intimate-partner abuse and 4 percent of men were seriously injured. More women (42 percent) than men (27 percent) had minor injuries (Rennison and Welchans 2000).

Several recent studies have reported that pregnancy increased the likelihood of physical violence by intimate partners (Burch and Gallup 2004; Martin Harris-Britt, Li, Moracco, Kupper, and Campbell 2004). Neither of these has a representative sample, as was true of some earlier studies reporting a relationship between pregnancy and violence. Other earlier studies using national samples found that when age was controlled, there was no increased risk with pregnancy. Still, the many studies, however imperfect, that have found an association between pregnancy and violence have kept this hypothesis alive, along with a possible explanation—jealousy—specifically that the new baby would interfere with the wife's attention to and care of the man. What is known with more certainty is that those pregnant women who are abused seek medical care later in pregnancy and are more likely to have preterm and low birth weight babies (Kantor and Jasinski 1998, pp. 31–33).

Substance abuse, especially of alcohol, is often cited as a factor in male violence against women. That seems to be true of heavy use of alcohol and binge drinking, though not necessarily for other patterns of alcohol use. Alcohol is implicated in violence through cognitive impairment, impulsivity, and a tendency to perceive threats (Kantor and Jasinski 1998, pp. 20–23; Kaukinen 2004). Drinking may also serve as a rationalization and excuse for violence that would have occurred in any case (Gelles 1974).

MARITAL RAPE Wife and female-partner abuse may take the form of sexual abuse and rape; sexual abuse is often combined with other physical violence. Estimates are that between 10 percent and 14 percent of women experience marital rape (Finkelhor and Yllo 1985; Russell 1990; and see Mahoney and Williams 1998). These sexual assaults often involve other violence as well.

Under traditional common law, **marital rape** was not considered rape at all because the wife was considered her husband's property, and he was entitled to unlimited sexual access. The legal situation has improved since the 1970s as a result of being made an issue by the women's movement. As of 1993, all states have provisions against marital rape in their legal codes[9] ("Marital Rape: A U.S. Study" n.d.). More research is needed in this area; the "lack of empirical and theoretical attention to sexual assault and coercion in marriage . . . is striking" (Christopher and Sprecher 2000, p. 1007).

THE THREE-PHASE CYCLE OF DOMESTIC VIOLENCE Examining the dynamics of intimate-partner violence from the perspective of abused women, experts have found that the initial violent episode usu-

---

8. We will focus primarily on marital violence in analyzing the dynamics of intimate-partner violence, but it is worth noting that the rate of violence between cohabiting partners is higher than that of spouses (Magdol et al. 1998). Overall, cohabitors are younger, less integrated into family and community, and more likely to have psychobehavioral problems such as depression and alcohol abuse—all factors associated with family violence (Stets 1991). As the proportion of cohabiting couples in the population increases, this setting becomes of greater importance in an overall perspective on domestic violence. That is, if cohabiting couples have higher rates of domestic violence and if there come to be more of them, then theories of domestic violence will need to take greater account of cohabitation as well as marriage.

9. There are some exemptions in the laws of thirty-three of the states. One common example is that if a wife is asleep or unconscious, thus legally unable to consent, a husband may be exempt from prosecution ("Marital Rape: A U.S. Study" n.d.).

ally comes as a shock. He promises it will not happen again; she believes him and treats her mate's violence as an exceptional, isolated outburst. She also tries to figure out what she did to cause his reaction so there will be no reason for it to happen again. The likelihood is that it will, however, because of what counselors call the **three-phase cycle of violence**. First, tension resulting from some minor altercations builds over a period of time. Second, the situation escalates, eventually exploding in another violent episode. Third, the husband becomes contrite, treating his wife lovingly. She wants to believe that this change in him will be permanent. The cycle repeats itself, with the violence worsening if nothing is done to change things (Sonkin, Martin, and Walker 1985).

Two questions arise: Why do men beat their wives and partners? And why do women live with it? Both questions may be answered by theories of marital power.

WHY DO MEN DO IT? Richard Gelles (1994, 1997) lists "risk factors" for men who abuse women: those who are between eighteen and thirty years old, unemployed, users of illicit drugs or abusers of alcohol, and high school dropouts. This suggests that men who beat their wives or partners might be attempting to compensate for general feelings of powerlessness or inadequacy—in their jobs, in their marriages, or both. As Chapter 4 indicates, our cultural images and the socialization process encourage men to appear strong and self-sufficient.

Men's feelings of powerlessness may stem from an inability to earn a salary that keeps up with inflation and the family's standard of living—or from the stress of a high-pressure occupation, which is not necessarily a high-status one. Men may use physical expressions of supremacy to compensate for their lack of occupational success, prestige, or satisfaction (Anderson 1997). Research using the National Survey of Households and Families found that financial adequacy reduced the risk of couple violence. Employment in low-status and unpleasant jobs that increased irritability, on the other hand, were associated with man-to-woman violence, a stress explanation of family violence (Fox, Benson, DeMaris, and Van Wyk 2002).

In terms of relative status, a woman's risk of experiencing severe violence is greatest when she is employed and her husband is not. Much research has found violence associated more generally with status

reversal, where the woman is superior in some way to the man in terms of employment, earnings, or education (Kaukinen 2004). A man's loss of status upon immigration—when jobs commensurate with education or expectations do not measure up, economic hardship is the family's lot, and wives, children, and people in general do not accord a male the respect he is accustomed to in a more hierarchical society—can lead to family conflict and violence (Min 2002).

Absent a *reward power* base for family power, some men resort to *coercive* power. "[V]iolence will be invoked by a person who lacks other resources to serve as a basis for power"—it is the "ultimate resource" (Goode 1971, p. 628; Allen and Straus 1980, p. 190, in Fox et al. 2002; see also Pyke 1996). Men may use violence to attempt to maintain control over wives or partners trying to become independent of the relationship (Dutton and Browning 1988). Figure 14.4, developed by staff of a program for male batterers in Duluth, Minnesota (Pence and Paymar 1993), illustrates how a male partner's need for power and control may result in both psychoemotional and physical violence. This type of family violence has been called *patriarchal terrorism* (Johnson 1995) and will be discussed in a subsequent section of this chapter.

WHY DO WOMEN CONTINUE TO LIVE WITH IT? Women do not like to get beaten up. They do not cooperate in their own beatings, and they often try to get away. However, they may stay married to husbands or remain with male partners who beat them repeatedly. For the most part, battered wives leave and/or seek divorce only after a long history of severe violence and repeated conciliation. There are several reasons for this, and they all point to those women's lack of personal resources with which to take control of their own lives.

Fear Battered women's lack of personal power begins with fear (DeMaris and Swinford 1996). "First of all," reports social scientist Richard Gelles, "the wife figures if she calls police or files for divorce, her husband will kill her—literally" (Gelles, quoted in C. Booth 1977, p. 7). This fear is not unfounded. An estimated 75 percent of murders of women by their male partners occurred in response to the woman's attempt to leave (de Santis 1990). Husbands or ex-husbands have shown enormous persistence in stalking, pursuing, and beating or killing women who try to leave an abusive

FIGURE 14.4

The power and control wheel: coercive power that some male partners resort to for power and control.

Source: Domestic Abuse Intervention Program, Duluth Model, Minnesota Program Development Organization, Duluth, MN.

situation (Johann 1994; U.S. Department of Justice 1998b). Fear of reprisals by the batterer continues to be a barrier to seeking police intervention, according to recent studies (Anderson et al. 2003; Wolf, Ly, Hobart, and Kernick 2003).

Cultural Norms Our cultural tradition has historically encouraged women to put up with abuse. English common law, the basis of the American legal structure, asserted that a husband had the right to physically

"chastise" an errant wife. Although the legal right to physically abuse women has long since disappeared, our cultural heritage continues to influence attitudes (Torr and Swisher 1999).[10]

---

10. The influence of culture and social patterns is illustrated by a cross-cultural analysis of domestic violence in ninety different societies. This study found family violence to be virtually absent in sixteen societies that were characterized by equality between the sexes, norms encouraging nonviolence, and intervention by neighbors and kin in domestic disputes (Levinson 1989).

What is true of American culture generally also may be true of immigrant or refugee communities, where "family honor, reputation, and preserving harmony" are primary values. For some women of color, hesitancy to call the police may derive from historic tensions between racial/ethnic communities and the police force (Wolf et al. 2003, p. 124).

Love, Economic Dependence, and Hopes for Reform Women may live with abuse because they love their husbands or partners, depend on their economic resources, and hope they will reform. Battered women who stay with their partners fear the economic hardship or uncertainty that will result if they leave. They hesitate to summon police or to press charges not only out of fear of retaliation but also because of the loss of income or damage to a husband's professional reputation that could result from his incarceration. Fear of economic hardship is heightened when children are involved. For a mother, leaving requires being financially able to take along her children and support them—or leaving them behind, when they may also be in danger.

A new wrinkle in economic dependency has emerged with the passage of welfare reform legislation in 1996. Studies show that 20 percent to 30 percent of women on welfare are in situations of risk for domestic violence. Some men become abusive when the woman gets a job, which may threaten his control. Compliance with the requirement to report paternity of children may also trigger retaliation by a man, who now will be pursued for child support. While the law contains a waiver provision directed at exactly these problems, it is not certain that women are being informed or that the provision is implemented. Some women will find it difficult to comply with welfare requirements because of the objections and control tactics of men in their lives. Cut off from welfare, they become even more dependent on violent men (Ooms 2001; Scott, London, and Meyers 2002).

Apart from such special circumstances, it is possible that while a dramatic rise in women's employment and earnings may prove threatening to low-earning husbands in the short run, in the long run, mutual awareness of a woman's potential economic independence may deter wife abuse by changing the family power dynamic (Blumberg and Coleman 1989).

Gendered Socialization Another factor that helps perpetuate abuse is the cultural mandate that it is primarily a woman's responsibility to keep a marriage or relationship from failing. Believing this, wives are often convinced that their emotional support may lead husbands to reform. Thus, wives often return to violent mates after leaving them (Herbert, Silver, and Ellard 1991).

Childhood Experiences Research suggests that people who experience violence in their parents' home while growing up may regard beatings as part of married life (Torr and Swisher 1999), and this is another factor associated with women's living with abuse. Men, as well as women, are more likely to be victims of intimate-partner violence as adults if they were exposed to child abuse or witnessed parental interpersonal violence as children (Heyman and Slep 2002).

Low Self-Esteem Finally, unusually low self-esteem interacts with fear, depression, confusion, anxiety, feelings of self-blame (Andrews and Brewin 1990), and loss of a sense of personal control (Umberson et al. 1998) to create the **battered woman syndrome**, in which a wife cannot see a way out of her situation (Walker 1988; Johann 1994).

A WAY OUT: SHELTERS AND DOMESTIC VIOLENCE PROGRAMS A woman in such a position needs to redefine her situation before she can deal with her problem, and she needs to forge some links with the outside world to alter her circumstances. This usually occurs over time, with some unsuccessful attempts to leave as part of the process.

Although there are not enough of them, a network of shelters for battered women provides a woman and her children with temporary housing, food, and clothing to alleviate the problems of economic dependency and physical safety. These organizations also provide counseling to encourage a stronger self-concept so that the woman can view herself as worthy of better treatment and capable of making her way in the outside world if need be. Finally, shelters provide guidance in obtaining employment, legal assistance, family counseling, or whatever practical assistance is required for a more permanent solution.

This last service provided by shelters—obtaining help toward more-long-range solutions—is important, research shows. Two face-to-face interviews with the same 155 wife-battery victims (a "two-wave panel study") were conducted within eighteen months during 1982 and 1983 in Santa Barbara, California. Each

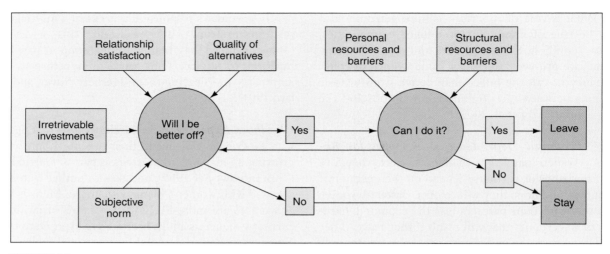

FIGURE 14.5

Conceptual model of abused women's stay/leave decision-making process.

Source: Choice and Lamke 1997, p. 295.

of the women interviewed had sought refuge in a shelter. Findings showed that victims who were also taking other measures (for example, calling the police, trying to get a restraining order, seeking personal counseling or legal help) were more likely to benefit from their shelter experience: "Otherwise, shelters may have no impact or perhaps even trigger retaliation (from husbands) for disobedience" (Berk, Newton, and Berk 1986, p. 488). As the researchers conclude,

> The possibility of perverse shelter effects for certain kinds of women poses a troubling policy dilemma. On the one hand, it is difficult to be enthusiastic about an intervention that places battered victims at further risk. On the other hand, a shelter stay may for many women be one important step in a lengthy process toward freedom, even though there may also be genuine short-run dangers. (p. 488)

As with some other decisions discussed in this text, social scientists have applied *exchange theory* to an abused woman's decision to stay or leave (Choice and Lamke 1997). As Figure 14.5 illustrates, an abused wife weighs such things as her investment in the relationship, her (dis)satisfaction with the relationship, the quality of her alternatives, and her beliefs about whether it is appropriate for her to leave ("subjective norm") against questions such as whether she will be better off if she leaves (might her husband retaliate, for example?) and whether she can actually do it. The

woman's personal resources along with community (structural) resources, such as whether shelters or other forms of assistance are available, further affect her decision. Personal barriers might involve not having either a job with adequate pay or an extended family that could help. Structural barriers might include the lack of community systems for practical help.

Johnson and Ferraro (2000) answer the question "Why do they stay?" with "The truth is, they don't stay." Instead, abused women went "through a process of leaving and returning, each time gaining more psychological and social resources . . . until they escaped from the web (pp. 256–257).

Husband and Male Partner Abuse

Both women and men sometimes resort to violence. A major question regarding family violence is whether female-to-male violence is trivial in numbers and effects or should be regarded as a serious social problem.

The early National Family Violence Surveys reported approximately equal amounts of both minor and serious partner violence on the part of men and women. The NFVS researchers continue to point to comparable levels of male and female intimate-partner violence (Straus 1993, 1999b). A number of other studies and research reviews also find that comparable numbers of males and females have engaged in physical violence (e.g., Anderson 2002; Archer 2000). While the National Family Violence Survey is a na-

Local advocacy groups draw attention to efforts to prevent domestic violence, as well as to the need for more resources. In many localities there are still not enough shelters to meet the needs of battered women and their children

tional sample survey, many of the other studies cited as evidence for gender symmetry are convenience samples, studies of college students, or even clinical samples of couples who have sought help for their marital problems (Kimmel 2002).

Crime victimization data, on the other hand, including carefully done, large sample surveys, indicate that women are overwhelmingly the victims of intimate-partner violence. These conflicting reports set off a dispute, still not resolved, as to whether intimate-partner violence is *asymmetrical*, with women primarily victims of male aggression—or whether couple violence is *symmetrical*—both men and women engage in intimate-partner violence and at similar rates. The first assumption—that violence against partners is primarily perpetrated by males—underlies policy directed toward providing resources for women victims; it is a strongly held feminist perspective. If, on the contrary, women are equally likely to perpetrate intimate-partner violence, then they look less like victims and more like aggressors. Subsidiary issues include methodological critiques of both crime victimization data (which suggest an asymmetrical pattern) and other studies, mostly using the Straus and Gelles

Conflict Tactics Scale (which tend toward gender-symmetrical findings).

Critics of the National Crime Victimization Survey point out that "crime" terminology may dampen reports of less serious female violence because those acts may not seem to be crimes to those interviewed. Questions on the NCVS differ from the Conflict Tactics Scale, so they may simply produce different results since the CTS includes a broader range of actions (Straus 1993, 1999b). On the other hand, sexual assault, a substantial part of male-to-female violence, was not included in the first version of the CTS used in the 1975/1985 National Family Violence Surveys, and that is more likely to be male-to-female violence. (The later modification of the CTS does include sexual assault [Straus et al. 1996].)

The Conflict Tactics Scale, used by many researchers, including those most associated with gender-balanced violence (Archer 2000), has been widely criticized for lack of context. In reporting lifetime or annual incidence of violence, a single, never-repeated act could be equated with a marriage-long pattern of abuse. Feminist critiques assert that the context of violence is ignored in simple counts of male and female violence: Where does a particular violent act fit into the couple relationship? Who initiated the violence? (Kurz 1993; Kimmel 2002)

Recent reviewers of the literature have tried to make distinctions that might explain the contradictory conclusions about who is violent. Definitions and measurement of violence continue to be relevant (Straus 1999b), as does whether a survey asks about victimization only or also asks whether the respondent has been a perpetrator of violence (Tjaden and Thoennes 2000). The most convincing explanations for contradictory findings—that men are the more violent sex (asymmetrical violence) or that men and women are both violent (symmetrical violence)—are (1) sample differences, (2) measures, and (3) typologies of intimate-partner violence (to be discussed momentarily).

Sample composition is important. Studies and research reviews (e.g., Archer 2000) that are dominated by samples of younger people, often college students, may accurately reflect the behavior of that age group. But they cannot claim to be representative of the general adult population in their findings of symmetrical violence. They capture a life course stage in which women are more likely to strike out in an argument and/or to be living in less stable cohabiting relationships (Tjaden and Thoennes 2000). National sample surveys that reach a broader and more representative range of respondents (the National Crime Victimization Survey and the National Violence Against Women Survey) more often find a pattern of much higher rates of victimization and more serious levels of violence directed against women.

The question of whether wives' violence toward husbands is mostly in self-defense, as feminist violence researchers argue, is part of the debate. Kurz (1993) offers evidence that intimate-partner violence by women is largely in self-defense, or at least retaliation, rather than the initiation of a violent attack. Straus (1993) claims that better data indicate that wives often strike out first, that the data do "not support the hypothesis that assaults by wives are primarily acts of self-defense or retaliation" (p. 76). Other data support the defensive character of women's violence against male partners (Kimmel 2002). Kimmel also speculates that women may be inclined to overstate their responsibility for a violent exchange, and men understate it.

In any case, Straus and Gelles find it "distressing" that, "in marked contrast to the behavior of women outside the family, women are about as violent within

the family as men" (1986, p. 470). In responding to the controversy, Straus and Gelles have argued their position, that couple violence is gender symmetrical, as one that ultimately benefits women despite the criticism they have received from feminists:[11]

Let us assume that most of the assaults by women are of the "slap the cad" genre and are not intended to and do not physically injure the husband. The danger to women of such behavior is that it sets the stage for the husband to assault her. [T]he fact that she slapped him provides the precedent and justification for him to hit her when she is being obstinate, "bitchy," or "not listening to reason" as he sees it. Unless women also forsake violence in their relationships with male partners and children, they cannot expect to be free of assault. (Straus and Gelles 1988, pp. 25–26)

Two other well-known researchers of family violence, Neil Jacobson and John Gottman, strongly object to this line of reasoning. In their sample, women rarely initiated a violent sequence. Should a woman do so in the form of punching, pushing, or throwing something, the man quite rightly could defend against it—at the same level of violence. Such minor violence on the part of women should not be taken to be "provocation" of severe violence by men, justification for their battering. Instead, men must be held accountable for their own violence if things are to change (2001, pp. 482–83).

The root explanation for contradictory research results may be that there are two forms of heterosexual violence against women—"patriarchal terrorism" and "common couple violence" (Johnson 1995).[12] **Patriarchal terrorism** refers specifically to abuse that is al-

---

11. Straus has sometimes been verbally harassed when he has presented at professional meetings. Criticism from feminist scholars (see for example Yllo and Bograd 1988) has discouraged some researchers from publishing articles on battered husbands (Gelles and Conte 1990, p. 1046).

12. Johnson now uses the gender-neutral term *intimate terrorism* and points to its existence in lesbian as well as heterosexual couples (Johnson and Ferraro 2000). However, we believe the original term best captures the typical male-to-female abuse represented by this pattern.

Johnson has added two more types that we do not include here as they are not yet fully developed or sufficiently researched (Johnson 2001; Johnson and Ferraro 2000). These are *violent resistance* and *mutual violent control*. Johnson considers the latter to be rare, which we see as confirming the decision to retain a gendered definition of the control-oriented form of intimate-partner violence.

most entirely male and that is oriented to controlling the partner through fear and intimidation. Physical abuse is but one of the tools used by the terrorist; emotional abuse is frequent as well. Patriarchal terroristic violence is not focused on a particular matter of dispute between the partners, but is intended to establish a general pattern of dominance in the relationship. This form of intimate-partner violence typically follows the cycle of violence described earlier and occurs more often in marriage than in cohabitation. It includes more incidents, is likely to escalate, and is more likely to produce serious injury.

Common couple violence refers to mutual violence between partners that often occurs in conjunction with a specific argument. It involves fewer instances, is not likely to escalate, and tends to be less severe in terms of injuries (Johnson 1995; Johnson and Ferraro 2000). Common couple violence appears to be perpetrated by women as well as men, and may be more common than patriarchal terrorism, producing the gender-balanced rates found in some studies.

On the other hand, there is "compelling evidence that men's and women's experiences with violence at the hands of marital and cohabiting partners differ greatly" (Tjaden and Thoennes 2000, p. 56). The overwhelming victimization of women shown by crime victimization data, including data on homicides, suggests that women are victims of the most serious violence. Related research-based points are as follows:

1. Husbands or other male partners have higher rates of inflicting the most dangerous and injurious forms of violence, such as severe beatings (Kurz 1993, p. 90; U.S. Department of Justice 1998a). Female victims report more threats to life and fear of bodily injury (Tjaden and Thoennes 2000).

2. Violence by husbands or male partners does more damage, even if it is an exchange of slaps or punches, because of a man's generally greater physical strength; therefore, the woman is more likely to be seriously injured (Jacobson and Gottman 2001). Women who were physically assaulted were significantly more likely than men to be injured, to receive medical treatment, to be hospitalized, and to lose more time from work (Rennison and Welchans 2000). Moreover, a study that explored the consequences of male and female violence in the context of mutual violence found that "the negative consequences of intimate partner violence [depression and substance abuse] are more likely to be experienced by women" (Anderson 2002, p. 86).

3. Violent acts by men are more frequent, tending to be repeated over time (Straus, Gelles, and Steinmetz 1980; Tjaden and Thoennes 2000).

4. Husbands are more apt to leave an abusive relationship within a short time. Having more resources, men rarely face women's dilemma of choosing between poverty (for their children as well as themselves) and violence (Straus, Gelles, and Steinmetz 1980).

Despite his strong assertion that both men and women may be violent in the family and that we must be attentive to the prevention of violence by women as well as men, Murray Straus takes this position: "[B]ecause of greater physical, financial, and emotional injury suffered, women are the primary victims . . . consequently, first priority in services for victims and in prevention and control must continue to be directed toward assaults by husbands" (Straus 1993, p. 80; see also Tjaden and Thoennes 1998, p. 8).

Yet there may be a need for some programmatic support for male victims of spouse abuse: "Compassion for victims of violence is not a zero sum game" (Kimmel 2002, p. 1354). Kimmel's review of research concludes that couple violence is less than symmetrical, perhaps in a ratio of four to one, male to female. Thus, while the pattern of couple violence is asymmetrical, the distribution of violence would include a significant percentage of women (although a control-oriented pattern of violence is about 90 percent male). "Reasonable people would rationally want to extend compassion, support, and intervention to all victims of violence" (Kimmel 2002, p. 1354). Indeed, the male victim of violence has few resources and often little sympathy (Cose 1994a).

Abuse Among Lesbian, Gay Male, and Bisexual Couples

Domestic violence has long been one of the lesbian and gay communities' "nastiest secrets" (Island and Letellier 1991, p. 36; Obejas 1994, p. 53). Lesbians may have denied the issue because they believe in the inherent goodness of lesbian relationships or are afraid of giving fuel to homophobia. As for violence in the relationships of gay men, there may be even more silence and denial (Island and Letellier 1991).

Research on lesbian, gay male, and bisexual relationship violence was initially scanty, but more research and service-oriented articles and books have appeared in the last few years. Studies done to date suggest that violence between same-sex partners occurs at the same or greater rate as in heterosexual relationships (Potocznik et al. 2003). One large sample study of 499 couples found that 9 percent reported physical violence in current couple relationships, and 32 percent in past relationships (Turrell 2000).

As is also true for straights, domestic violence may be found in all racial/ethnic categories, social classes, education levels, and age groups. Among lesbians, neither "butch/femme" roles nor the women's physical size has been found to figure into violence (Obejas 1994).

Some of the relationship dynamics in same-sex abusive partnerships are similar to those in abusive straight relationships (Kurdek 1994). An "intense dependency" (Renzetti 2001, p. 455) often characterizes the batterer. Batterers may use drugs or alcohol or a history of childhood exposure to violence to enable and excuse attacks on the partner. The abusive partner uses violence or threats of violence to keep the partner from leaving. Furthermore, the couple is likely to deny or minimize the violence, along with believing that the violence is at least partly the victim's fault (Island and Letellier 1991; Renzetti 1992, 2001).

There are other relationship dynamics that are specific to same-sex domestic abuse. It is more difficult to attribute violence to theories of patriarchy and culturally influenced gender roles, the primary perspectives developed to explain men's abuse of women. Lesbians as well as gay men may fight back more often than do heterosexual women, a situation that leads to confusion about who is the battered and who is the batterer. Furthermore, some lesbians and gay men who are battered in one relationship may become batterers in another relationship (Island and Letellier 1991; Obejas 1994; Potocznik et al. 2003).

Lesbian violence is different in still other respects. For one thing, according to psychologist Vallerie Coleman, who works with battered lesbians, heterosexual men tend to feel they have a right to abuse their mates, whereas lesbians do not (Obejas 1994). And a greater proportion of lesbian batterers seek help than do heterosexual male abusers. Lesbians are more likely to go into treatment on their own, according to Coleman: "Heterosexual men go in because they're court-mandated" (quoted in Obejas 1994).

A special problem for lesbian and gay male domestic-violence victims is that few resources exist to serve their needs. The availability of legal protection is problematic in many states. Some states specifically exclude same-sex couples from domestic violence laws, and in many other states the law or its enforcement is ambiguous.

Gay/lesbian/bisexual individuals may be afraid to go to the police—or to use any domestic violence intervention services—for fear of having their gay identity revealed or receiving a hostile response. While lesbians do seek help from the same services as heterosexual women, they find friends, counselors, and relatives the most helpful sources of support. Gay men find friends, counselors, and support groups of greatest help. Domestic violence services oriented to gay men, lesbians, and bisexuals are now somewhat available in larger cities with substantial gay/lesbian communities (Potocznik et al. 2003).

Stopping Relationship Violence

According to one estimate, 32 percent of victimized women will be revictimized within a relatively short time in the absence of intervention (Langan and Innes 1986). Moreover, intimate abuse tends to escalate, growing more severe over time.

The debate over whether women are as violent as men—or not—may be resolved at the practical level by noting that the interests of men as a group converge with those of women in curbing spousal violence—not only in hopes of having viable relationships, but simply for survival. Even though men kill wives and girlfriends at a much higher rate than women kill husbands and boyfriends, some victimized women do murder or seriously injure their male partners. Progress in stopping intimate-partner violence will benefit both sexes.

We have already discussed the shelter movement. Other approaches involve (1) counseling and group therapy directed toward abusive male partners (or the couple) and (2) the criminal justice system.

COUNSELING AND GROUP THERAPY Counseling and group therapy were earlier thought to be ineffective for male abusers. But a number of male batterer intervention programs have now been developed. Many abusing husbands and male partners have difficulty controlling their response to anger and frustration, dealing with problems, and relinquishing their excessive control over their partner. Even though many, perhaps most, abusers are not reachable and may drop out of treatment (Brown, O'Leary, and Feldbau 1997), other men have a sincere desire to stop. Group therapy reduces stigma and provides a setting in which abusers can learn more-constructive ways of both coping with anger and balancing autonomy and intimacy, often another area of difficulty. Some men's therapy groups have emerged in which former batterers help lead male abusers toward recovery (Allen and Kivel 1994).

It is difficult to evaluate the level of success of male batterer intervention programs because of design problems, low response rates, high program dropout rates, and because programs do not always follow the research protocol (Hamby 1998; Jackson et al. 2003). From what we know, it appears that "[o]verall, batterers intervention program outcomes are modest" (Bennett and Williams 1999, p. 242). Two recent and rigorously designed evaluations sponsored by the National Institute of Justice were conducted on intervention programs in Broward County in Florida and in Brooklyn, New York. The researchers concluded that the programs had "little or no effect" (Jackson et al. 2003). But though they may be ineffective on a large scale, such programs may work for some men, and that's all to the good.

In the past decade, some couples' therapy programs have emerged to treat wife abuse (Johannson and Tutty 1998). Typically, such programs counsel husbands and wives—or just husbands—separately over a period of up to six months. After this first treatment phase, couples are counseled together and are taught anger-management techniques, along with communication, problem-solving, and conflict-resolution skills. Couples' therapy programs designed to stop domestic violence are somewhat controversial because they proceed from the premise that a couple's staying together without violence after an abusive past is possible. Feminist scholars have expressed concern that therapists underestimate the danger that women face in violent relationships (Hansen, Harway, and Cervantes 1991). There is some evidence that negative social sanctions from either partner's relatives or friends may help stop wife abuse (Lackey and Williams 1995).

THE CRIMINAL JUSTICE RESPONSE There was little legal protection for battered women in the past. The street wisdom among police, as well as those who worked with battered women, was that calling the police was an ineffective strategy and posed some risk to the woman. Arresting an abusive partner or pressing charges would only aggravate the situation and result in escalating violence later. Officers also felt themselves to be at risk in responding to domestic violence calls.

Police officers typically avoided making arrests for assault that would be automatic if the man and woman involved were not married. The laws themselves contributed to police reluctance: Statutes might require a police officer to witness the act before making an arrest at the scene, or more severe injury might be required for prosecution for battery. In some cases, restraining orders required additional court action before they could be enforced.

However, a sociological experiment in Minneapolis in the 1980s obtained results indicating that mandatory arrest could be an effective deterrent to future violence (Sherman and Berk 1984).[13] As a consequence of this experiment, laws have been changed to make arrests for domestic violence more feasible, and some states or jurisdictions have policies that mandate arrest in certain situations involving family violence (Buzawa and Buzawa 1990, p. 96).

Subsequent replications of the arrest experiment did not all get the same results. It now appears that arrest will deter future violence only on the part of men who are employed and married, men with a "stake in conformity." Other men, those who are unemployed and/or not married to the woman they abused, may react to arrest by *increased* violence (Sherman 1992).

An even more serious problem of the arrest strategy has been that a literal reading of a mandatory arrest law has resulted in the arrest of victims, along with perpetrators, when the victim has resisted with violent force (Goldberg 1999). Women also fear that reporting domestic violence to the police will risk contact with Child Protective Services and the removal of their children from the home. Some women who did contact police reported that the batterer was not arrested, as they had expected, and that the police sometimes trivialized their situation. In some cases women claimed that the perpetrator and the police officer exchange was characterized by "male bonding," in which the perpetrator's story overrode the woman's complaint of violence.

---

13. In the Minneapolis experiment, officers were randomly assigned to respond by arresting the (presumably male) perpetrator, by counseling the parties, or simply by separating them for a cooling-off period. A six-month follow-up by telephone and an examination of police call records indicated that arrest was the most effective response in deterring subsequent violence (Sherman and Berk 1984).

Some women reported positive and protective experiences to researchers:

"[S]o when the police did intervene that night, they made it pretty clear that I didn't deserve it (the abuse). . . . [T]hey talked to me and I filed a report . . . and that's the last I saw of my husband." (Wolf et al. 2003)

We will turn now to another type of family violence in which the more powerful abuse the less powerful—child abuse.

Child Abuse and Neglect

FOCUS ON CHILDREN

Perceptions of what constitutes child abuse or neglect have differed throughout history and in various cultures.[14] Practices that we now consider abusive were accepted in the past as the normal exercise of parental rights or as appropriate discipline. Until the twentieth century, children were mainly considered the property of parents. In colonial Massachusetts and Connecticut, filial disobedience was legally punishable by death.

Today, standards of acceptable child care vary according to culture and social class. What some groups consider mild abuse others consider right and proper discipline. In 1974, however, Congress provided a legal definition of *child maltreatment* in the Child Abuse Prevention and Treatment Act. The act defines child abuse and neglect as the "physical or mental injury, sexual abuse, or negligent treatment of a child under the age of 18 by a person who is responsible for the child's welfare under circumstances that indicate that the child's health or welfare is harmed or threatened" (U.S. Department of Health, Education, and Welfare 1975, p. 3).

People use the term **child abuse** to refer to overt acts of aggression—excessive verbal derogation (emotional child abuse) or physical child abuse such as beating, whipping, punching, kicking, hitting with a heavy object, burning or scalding, or threatening with or

using a knife or gun. (By current American standards, spanking or hitting a child with a paddle, stick, or hair brush is not "abuse," although it is in Sweden and several other countries [Straus and Donnelly 2001], and see Chapter 13 of this text).

Child neglect includes acts of omission—failing to provide adequate physical or emotional care. Physically neglected children often show signs of malnutrition, lack immunization against childhood disease, lack proper clothing, attend school irregularly, and need medical attention for such conditions as poor eyesight or bad teeth. Often these conditions are grounded in parents' or guardians' economic problems (Baumrind 1994; Kruttschnitt, McLeod, and Dornfeld 1994; Brown et al. 1998), but child neglect may also be willful neglect (Gillham et al. 1998).

Emotional child abuse or neglect involves a parent's often being overly harsh and critical, failing to provide guidance, or being uninterested in a child's needs. Emotional child abuse might also include allowing children to witness violence between partners (Carlson 1990; Rubiner 1994). Although emotional abuse may occur without physical abuse, physical abuse results in emotional abuse as well.

Another form of child abuse is **sexual abuse**: a child's being forced, tricked, or coerced into sexual behavior—exposure, unwanted kissing, fondling of sexual organs, intercourse, rape, and incest—with an older person (Gelles and Conte 1990).

Incest involves sexual relations between related individuals. The most common forms are father–daughter incest and incest involving a girl and her stepfather or older brother. The definition of child sexual abuse excludes mutually desired sex play between or among siblings close in age, but coerced sex by strong and/or older brothers is sexual abuse and may be more widespread than parent–child incest (Canavan, Meyer, and Higgs 1992). Incest is the most emotionally charged form of sexual abuse; it is also the most difficult to detect. Incest appears to be in the background of a variety of sexual, emotional, and physical problems among adults who were abused as children (Simons and Whitbeck 1991; Gilgun 1995; Browning and Laumann 1997; Luster and Small 1997; Bell and Belicki 1998).

Sexual abuse by paid caregivers and by mentors such as teachers, coaches, youth program directors, and clergy is also a problem being addressed by policy makers and child-care professionals. Sexual exploitation of homeless children is yet another (Shamin and

---

14. A dramatic example of cultural difference in defining child abuse is the controversy surrounding *female genital mutilation* (FGM). Some sub-Saharan African and Muslim cultures practice FGM, which is the surgical removal of the clitoris and other external female genital organs, and suturing of the vaginal opening until marriage. In those cultures, FGM is an important rite of passage for young girls and considered necessary to make them eligible to marry. (It does not seem to be a Muslim religious teaching, however.) FGM has been brought to the United States by some immigrants as part of their cultural heritage. It has been outlawed in the United States since 1996 and is now prohibited in some African countries. FGM is still practiced clandestinely here (Renteln 2004, pp. 51–53).

Chowdhury 1993). Still, a child's statistical chances of being kidnapped or molested by a stranger are minuscule compared to that same child's statistical chances of being physically or sexually abused by a family member or a friend of the family.

Research by social psychologists finds lower self-esteem and greater incidences of depression among adults who have been victims of child abuse (Downs and Miller 1998; Silvern et al. 1995). A study of nearly 43,000 adolescents found that those who had been physically and/or sexually abused were more prone to binge drinking and thoughts of suicide. However, high levels of supportive interest and monitoring from at least one parent decreased the risk for these outcomes among sexually abused adolescents (Luster and Small 1997).

Sibling violence is often overlooked, yet the National Family Violence Survey found it to be the most pervasive form of family violence (Straus, Gelles, and Steinmetz 1980). Nor was it only of the "harmless" teasing variety (Wiehe 1997; "UF Study" 2004). Moreover, perpetrators of sibling violence are more likely than others to become perpetrators of dating violence, according to a study of more than 500 men and women at a Florida community college. "Siblings learn violence as a form of sibling manipulation and control as they compete with each other for family resources. . . . They carry on these bullying behaviors to dating, the next peer relationship in which they have an emotional investment" (researcher Virginia Noland in "UF Study" 2004). Yet this form of family violence has received comparatively little research attention.[15]

The University of Florida research, which employed the Conflict Tactics Scale, found that more than three-fourths of those responding to the survey had pushed or shoved siblings and in turn had been pushed or shoved themselves. This pattern of somewhat similar percentages of perpetrating sibling violence and being a victim of it also characterized answers to questions about punching and hitting (55 percent and 50 percent), slamming a sibling against a wall (around a quarter of respondents), and using a knife or gun on a sibling (9 percent; 6 percent) (Noland, Liller, McDermott, Coulter, and Seraphine 2004). As with other forms of child abuse, sibling violence leads to depression in child victims and to later

relationship problems. Noland recommends that sibling violence be taken more seriously and that anger management programs be implemented while these violent individuals are still kids ("UF Study" 2004).

HOW EXTENSIVE IS CHILD ABUSE? Interpreting rates of reported child abuse to mean that child abuse is increasing may be inaccurate. For one thing, all states now have compulsory child-abuse reporting laws, so a growing proportion of previously unreported cases comes to the attention of child-welfare authorities. For another, new standards are evolving in respect to how much violence parents may use in child rearing. The definition of child abuse is being gradually enlarged to include acts that were not previously thought of as abusive.

Current estimates from the federal report *Child Maltreatment 2001* (U.S. Department of Health and Human Services 2003) are based on state reports of child abuse. Of the reported cases of child maltreatment, 57 percent are of neglect, 19 percent are of physical abuse, and 10 percent are of sexual abuse. (The remainder are cases that include multiple factors or unspecified maltreatment.) Fifty percent of the victims of child maltreatment were white, 25 percent African American, 15 percent Hispanic, 2 percent American Indian/Alaska Native, and 1 percent Asian/Pacific Islander. When the size of each racial/ethnic group is taken into account, it appears that African American and American Indian children had the highest victimization rates; Hispanics and whites had moderate levels of victimization; and Asian American children had low rates of child maltreatment (Children's Bureau 2000, Table 2–10). The percentages of male (48 percent) and female (52 percent) victims were not very different. The youngest children (through age three) were most vulnerable; 28 percent of victims were in this age group. Maltreatment declined with a child's age (U.S. Health and Human Services 2003).

Almost 60 percent of perpetrators were female, predominantly under thirty. Of children reported to have been maltreated, 84 percent were mistreated by at least one parent (in 41 percent of cases by mother only; in 18 percent of cases by father only; and in 19 percent of cases by both mother and father) (U.S. Health and Human Services 2003). The most common forms of maltreatment by female parents were "neglect" and "medical neglect."

"Physical abuse" was perpetrated by a female parent alone in 36 percent of cases, by a male parent only

15. A November 2001 search of *Sociological Abstracts* produced no recent comprehensive articles on sibling abuse in the United States. A search of the Internet and recent news reports produced the 2004 article cited in this section.

防止虐待兒童會

Against Child Abuse

A C A
CENTRES

Chuk Yuen Centre
107-108, G/F, Wai Yuen House
Chuk Yuen (North) Estate
Wong Tai Sin,
Kowloon
Telephone 2351 6060
Fax 2752 8483

Tuen Mun Centre
409, Ting Cheung House
On Ting Estate
Tuen Mun
New Territories
Telephone 2450 2244
Fax 2457 3782

O P E N I N G
HOURS

Monday to Friday: 9 a.m. to 5 p.m.
(lunch break 1-2 p.m.)
Saturday: 9 a.m. to 1 p.m.

HOTLINE : 2755 1122

After office hour, message will be taken via automatic
telephone tape recording.

A MEMBER AGENCY OF THE COMMUNITY CHEST

Courtesy of Against Child Abuse agency, Hong Kong

Child abuse is not specific to the United States. This pamphlet was produced by social service agencies in Hong Kong.

in 27 percent of cases, or by both parents in 14 percent of cases (U.S. Children's Bureau 2000, Table 3–4).

Estimates of the extent of sexual abuse of children come from various small samples and range from 6 percent to 62 percent of all female children and from 3 percent to 31 percent of all male children. The wide variation in estimates results from different definitions of sexual abuse used in various studies and from methodological factors, such as the conditions under which people are interviewed (Gelles and Conte 1990; Finkelhor et al. 1996). Although boys are also victimized, it appears that girls are between two and five times more likely to be sexually abused (U.S. Department of Justice 1996).

Sexual abuse was almost entirely perpetrated by male parents or male relatives, according to a recent government report (U.S. Children's Bureau 2000). Re-

search has found that only a very small proportion of sexual abusers are female—at most 4 percent when the victims are girls, and 20 percent when the victims are boys (Glaser and Frosh 1988, p. 13). Other data on sexual exploitation indicate that 47 percent of sexual assaults on children were by relatives; 49 percent by others such as teachers, coaches, or neighbors; and only 4 percent by strangers (Hernandez 2001).

Abused children live in families of all socioeconomic levels, races, nationalities, and religious groups, although child abuse is reported more frequently among poor and nonwhite families than among middle- and upper-class whites. This situation may be due to some of the same reasons (discussed earlier) that spouse abuse is reported to police more frequently in the poorer classes. Another reason may be unconscious discrimination on the part of physicians and others who report abuse and neglect (Lane, Rubin, Monteith, and Christian 2002).

ABUSE VERSUS "NORMAL" CHILD REARING
One writer has observed that "a culturally defined concept of caregivers as legitimate users of physical force appears to be an essential component of child abuse" (Garbarino 1977, p. 725). It is all too easy for parents to go beyond reasonable limits when angry or distraught or to have limits that include as discipline what most observers would define as abuse (Baumrind 1994; Whipple and Richey 1997). Hence, child abuse must be seen as a potential behavior in many families—even those we think of as "normal" (Straus 1994).

Immigrant families may come from cultures where rather severe physical punishment is considered necessary for good child rearing. Those parents may not even be aware that what they are doing by way of parental discipline is illegal in this country. They may instead view themselves as very responsible parents (Renteln 2004, pp. 54–57).

RISK FACTORS FOR CHILD ABUSE Consider the following society-wide beliefs and conditions that, when exaggerated, may encourage even well-intentioned parents to mistreat their children:

- A belief in physical punishment is a contributing (but not sufficient) factor in child abuse. Abusive parents have learned—probably in their own childhood—to view children as requiring physical punishment (Gough and Reavey 1997; Whipple and Richey 1997).

- Parents may have unrealistic expectations about what the child is capable of; often, they lack awareness and knowledge of the child's physical and emotional needs and abilities (Gough and Reavey 1997). For example, slapping a bawling toddler to stop her or his crying is completely unrealistic, as is too-early toilet-training.

- Parents who abuse their children were often abused or neglected themselves as children. Violent parents are likely to have experienced and thereby learned violence as children. Whether victims of child abuse or witnesses of adult interpersonal violence, those exposed to family violence in childhood are more likely than others to abuse their own children, and their wives as well (Heyman and Slep 2002).

  This does *not* mean that abused children are predetermined to be abusive parents or partners. The highest rate of intergenerational transmission of violence reported by Straus and colleagues was 20 percent (Straus, Gelles, and Steinmetz 1980), while a more recent national sample study found "[t]he most typical outcome for individuals exposed to violence in their families of origin is to be nonviolent in their adult families. This is the case for both men and women. . . ." (Heyman and Slep 2002, p. 870; see also Johnson and Ferraro 2000, p. 958).

- Parental stress and feelings of helplessness play a significant part in child abuse (Rodriguez and Green 1997). "Economic adversity and worries about money pervade the typical violent home" (Gelles and Straus 1988, p. 85). Overload, so often related to family problems, also creates stress that may lead to child abuse (Brown et al. 1998). Other causes of parental stress are children's misbehavior, changing lifestyles and standards of living, and a parent's feeling pressure to do a good job but being perplexed about how to do it.

- Families have become more private and less dependent on kinship and neighborhood relationships (Berardo 1998). Hence, parents and children are alone together, shut off at home from the "watchful eyes and sharp tongues that regulate parent–child relations in other cultures" (Skolnick 1978, p. 82). In neighborhoods that have support systems and tight social networks of community-related friends—where other adults are somewhat involved in the activities of the family—child abuse and neglect are much more likely to be noticed and stopped (Gelles and Straus 1988).

- Other circumstances that are statistically related to child maltreatment include parental youth and inexperience, marital discord and divorce, and unusually demanding or otherwise difficult children (Baumrind 1994; Brown et al. 1998). Other risk factors involve parental abuse of alcohol or other substances (Fleming, Mullen, and Bammer 1996), a mother's cohabiting with her boyfriend (who is more likely than a child's male relative to abuse the child) (Margolin 1992), and having a stepfather (because stepfathers are more likely than biological fathers to abuse their children) (Daly and Wilson 1994).

COMBATING CHILD ABUSE Two major approaches to combating child abuse and willful neglect are the punitive approach, which views abuse and neglect as crimes for which parents should be punished, and the therapeutic approach, which views abuse as a family problem requiring treatment. We may also consider a third, social welfare approach.

The Criminal Justice Approach Those who favor the punitive approach believe that one or both parents should be held legally responsible for abusing a child.

A complicated issue emerging with regard to this approach involves holding battered women criminally responsible for failing to act to prevent such abuse at the hands of their male partners. Feminist legal advocates have begun to question whether the law should hold a battered woman responsible for failing to prevent harm to her children when, as a battered woman, she cannot even defend herself:

> When the law punishes a battered woman for failing to protect her child against a batterer, it may be punishing her for failing to do something she was incapable of doing. . . . She is then being punished for the crime of the person who has victimized her. (Erickson 1991, pp. 208–209)

Legal experts note that fathers are typically *not* held accountable for child abuse committed by female partners (Liptak 2002).

The Therapeutic Approach All states have criminal laws against child abuse. But the approach to child protection has gradually shifted from punitive to therapeutic. Not all who work with abused children are happy with this shift. These critics prefer to hold one or both parents clearly responsible. They reject the family system approach to therapy because it implies distribution of responsibility for change to all family members (Stewart 1984). Nevertheless, social workers and clinicians—rather than the police and the court system—increasingly investigate and treat abusive or neglectful parents.

The therapeutic approach involves two interrelated strategies: (1) increasing parents' self-esteem and their knowledge about children and (2) involving the community in child rearing (Goldstein, Keller, and Erne 1985). One voluntary program, Parents Anonymous (PA), holds regular meetings to enhance self-esteem and educate abusive parents. Another voluntary association, CALM, attempts to reach stressed parents before they hurt their children. Among other things, CALM advocates obligatory high school classes on family life, child development, and parenting, and it operates a 24-hour hotline for parents under stress.

Involving the community means getting people other than parents to help with child rearing. One form of relief for abused or neglected children is to remove them from their parents' homes and place them in foster care. This practice is itself controversial (Ingrassia 1995b) as foster parents have been abusive in some cases, and in many regions of the country there are not enough foster parents to go around (Weisman 1994; see also Gelles 1996). More and more, people are choosing alternatives, such as *supplemental mothers*, who are available to babysit regularly with potentially abused children. Another community resource is the *crisis nursery*, where parents may take their children when they need to get away for a few hours. Ideally, crisis nurseries are open twenty-four hours a day and accept children at any hour without prearrangement.

The Social Welfare Approach This approach overlaps with the therapeutic approach, but takes note of the social, cultural, and economic context of child maltreatment to provide services and parent education that may make child abuse less likely. Housing assistance and subsidized child care, for example, might prevent a low-income or socially isolated parent's taking the risk of leaving children alone while working.

Parent education directed toward new immigrant parents might mitigate the development of situations that end in removal of children from the home. For example, if some immigrant families come to the U.S. not realizing that their traditional disciplinary practices constitute criminal child abuse in the United States, parent education offered through refugee service centers could anticipate that problem. The same is true regarding leaving children alone at home. This may be customary and perfectly safe in a small tribal village, but not so safe in the United States, and moreover, illegal (Gonzalez and O'Connor 2002; Renteln 2004, pp. 54–58).

COMMERCIAL SEXUAL EXPLOITATION OF CHILDREN We close this section on child maltreatment with a look at a form of child abuse that is not, strictly speaking, family violence, but which is often set in motion by developments in seriously troubled families—that is the commercial sexual exploitation of children. Researchers Richard J. Estes and Neil Weiner of the University of Pennsylvania go beyond family violence per se to look at society-wide organized sexual exploitation of children. Based on their research, they estimate that as many as 300,000 to 400,000 children a year may be molested or used in pornography or prostitution.

For the most part this is commercial sexual exploitation, not abuse within the family, but family dynamics often place children in harm's way. Typically, victims of organized sexual exploitation are runaways, "throwaways," (children who have been kicked out of the home by parents), or other homeless children who trade or sell sex to meet their basic survival needs. Some sexually exploited children live at home but are offered for sexual purposes by their families in exchange for money, drugs, or other benefits (Hernandez 2001; Memmott 2001). The study was based on interviews with victims and child welfare workers in twenty-eight cities in the United States, Mexico, and Canada (Estes and Weiner 2002; Hernandez 2001; Memmott 2001).

We turn now to another topic that is gaining more and more attention in the context of family violence: elder abuse and neglect.

Elder Abuse and Neglect

Parallel to child abuse and neglect, **elder abuse** involves overt acts of aggression, whereas **elder neglect** involves acts of omission or failure to give adequate care. Elder abuse by family members may include physical assault, emotional humiliation, purposeful social isolation (for example, forbidding use of the telephone), or material exploitation and theft (Tatara and Blumerman 1996; Henningson 1997).

As with other forms of domestic abuse, the development of accurate statistics has been a gradual process, as formal reports to state agencies miss the many unreported instances of elder abuse. Various studies have concluded that between 1 percent and 10 percent of individuals over age sixty are abused or neglected. In 1996, the federal government sponsored the National Elder Abuse Incidence Study, a random sample survey of counties, which combined reports from Adult Protective Services with interviews with "sentinels," people in the community who have contact with the elderly. Estimates from this study are that 450,000 individuals over sixty living in domestic settings were abused or neglected; if self-neglect is included, the total rises to 551,011 (U.S. Administration on Aging 1998). Neglect is the most common form of elder maltreatment (55 percent in the 1996 study); 15 percent experienced physical abuse, 12 percent exploitation, 8 percent emotional abuse, and 0.3 percent sexual abuse (Tatara, Kuzmeskus, and Duckhorn 1997).

The emerging profile of the abused or neglected elderly person is of a female, seventy years old or older, who has physical, mental, and/or emotional impairments and is dependent on the abuser/caregiver for both companionship and help with daily living activities. Studies have found that the *neglected* elderly are older and have more physical and mental difficulties (and hence are more burdensome to care for) than are elder *abuse* victims (Pillemer 1986; Whittaker 1995).

There are many parallels between elder maltreatment and other forms of family violence. In fact, "there is reason to believe that a certain proportion of elder abuse is actually spouse abuse grown old" (Phillips 1986, p. 212). In some cases, marital violence among the elderly involves abuse of a caregiving partner by a spouse who has become ill with Alzheimer's disease (Pillemer 1986). Spouses, though, are 16 percent of abusers, while adult children make up 37 percent of perpetrators. Males and females appear equally likely to abuse the elderly (Tatara et al. 1997).

The social context of elders who are abused by family members or others includes stress from outside sources, such as financial problems or a caregiver's job conflicts, and social isolation of the elderly person (lack of connectedness with friends and community). As we have seen, these factors are also associated with child abuse.

Elder-abuse victims, in contrast to the neglected, are relatively healthy and able to meet their daily needs. The common denominators in cases of physical elder abuse are shared living arrangements, the abuser's poor emotional health (often including alcohol or drug problems), and a pathological relationship between victim and abuser (Anetzberger, Korbin, and Austin 1994). Indeed, data from one study of 300 cases of elder abuse in the Northeast found that an abuser (frequently an adult son) was likely to be financially dependent on the elderly victim. Abusive acts may be "carried out by abusers to compensate for their perceived lack or loss of power" (Pillemer 1986, p. 244). Moreover, "In many instances, both the victim and the perpetrator were caught in a web of interdependency and disability, which made it difficult for them to seek or accept outside help or to consider separation" (Wolf 1986, p. 221, 1996).

Researching and combating elder abuse generally proceed from either of two models: the *caregiver model* or the *domestic violence model*. The **caregiver model of elder abuse and neglect** views abusive or neglectful caregivers as individuals who are simply overwhelmed by the requirements of caring for their elderly family members. (See Chapter 18 for more discussion of aging.) In contrast, the **domestic violence model** views elder abuse and neglect as one form of family violence and focuses both on characteristics of abusers and on situations that put potential victims at increased risk (see Finkelhor and Pillemer 1988; Whittaker 1995) and on a possible criminal justice response (Brownell 1998).

In discussing it here, we have placed elder abuse within the context of family violence. And we have noted the interplay between power and violence that is at work in some situations of elder abuse. Elders are vulnerable, with little power. Those financially dependent on their elders sometimes try to assert power over them by violent means.

Generally, we see any form of family violence as more likely to occur in situations of unequal rather than equal power. We close this chapter with a reminder of everyone's basic right to be respected—and not to be physically, emotionally, or sexually abused—in any relationship.

In Sum

- Power, the ability to exercise one's will, may rest on cultural authority, economic and personal resources that are gender-based and/or involve love and emotional dependence, interpersonal dynamics, or physical violence.

- Marital power or power in other intimate-partner relationships includes decision making, the division of household labor, and a sense of empowerment in the relationship. American marriages experience a tension between male dominance and egalitarianism, with a transitional egalitarian model probably the most common.

- The relative power of a husband and wife in a marriage varies by education, social class, religion, race/ethnicity, age, immigration status, and other factors. It varies by whether or not the wife works and with the presence and age of children. Studies of married couples, cohabiting couples, and gay and lesbian couples illustrate the significance of economically based power and of norms about who should have power.

- Couples can consciously work toward more-egalitarian marriages or intimate-partner relationships and relinquish "power politics." Changing gender roles, as they affect marital and intimate-relationship power, necessitate negotiation and communication.

- Physical violence is most commonly used in the absence of other resources.

- Researchers do not agree as to whether intimate-partner violence is primarily perpetrated by males or whether males and females are equally likely to abuse their partners. The effects of intimate-partner violence indicate that victimization of women is the more crucial social problem, and it has received the most programmatic attention. Recently, some programs have been developed for male abusers. Studies indicating that arrest is *sometimes* a deterrent to further wife abuse illustrate the importance of public policies in this area.

- Economic hardships and other factors (among parents of all social classes and races) can lead to physical and/or emotional child abuse as can lack of understanding of children's developmental needs and abilities. One difficulty in eliminating child abuse is drawing a clear distinction between "normal" child rearing and abuse. Criminal justice, therapeutic, and social welfare approaches are ways of addressing the problem of child maltreatment.

- Elder abuse and neglect are relatively new areas of investigation into family violence. Data suggest that abused elderly are often financially independent and abused most frequently by dependent adult children or by elderly spouses.

Key Terms

battered woman syndrome
caregiver model of elder abuse and neglect
child abuse
child neglect
coercive power
common couple violence
Conflict Tactics Scale
domestic violence model (of elder abuse and neglect)
egalitarian norm (of marital power)
elder abuse
elder neglect
emotional child abuse or neglect
expert power
incest
informational power
intimate-partner power
intimate-partner violence
legitimate power
marital power
marital rape
near peer marriage (Schwartz's typology)
no-power
patriarchal norm (of marital power)
patriarchal terrorism
peer marriage (Schwartz's typology)
power
power politics
principle of least interest
referent power
relative love and need theory
resource hypothesis
resources in cultural context
reward power
sexual abuse
sibling violence
three-phase cycle of violence
traditionals (Schwartz's typology)
transitional egalitarian situation (of marital power)

Questions for Review and Reflection

1. How is gender related to power in marriage? How do you think recent social change will affect power in marriage?

2. Do you think that power in a marriage or other couple relationship depends on who earns how much money? Or does it depend on emotions? Is it possible for a couple to develop a no-power relationship?

3. Looking at domestic violence, why might women remain with the men who batter them? Do you think that shelters provide an adequate way out for these women? What about arresting the abuser? Should intimate-partner violence against men receive more attention in the form of social programs? Why or why not?

4. What factors might play a role when well-intentioned parents abuse their children?

5. **Policy Question.** What can we as a society do to combat child neglect that is really due to family poverty?

Suggested Readings

Goetting, Ann. 1999. *Getting Out: Life Stories of Women Who Left Abusive Men.* New York: Columbia University Press. Narratives about "battered women who safely and permanently leave their abusers." These stories give us a sense of the process of leaving an abuser—advances, retreats, and eventual safety.

Loseke, Donileen R., Richard J. Gelles, and Mary M. Cavanaugh (Eds.). 2004. *Current Controversies on Family Violence,* 2nd ed. Newbury Park, CA: Sage. Various topics, such as husband abuse and the battered woman syndrome, are presented in a debate format. Well-known experts and researchers are the authors of these paired articles.

Miller-Perrin, Cindy L., Robin D. Perrin, and Ola W. Barnett. 2004. *Family Violence Across the Life Span: An Introduction,* 2nd ed. Thousand Oaks, CA: Sage. Articles on many aspects of family violence, organized around the life course.

Straus, Murray A., and Denise Donnelly. 2001. *Beating the Devil Out of Them: Corporal Punishment in American Families and Its Effect on Children.* New Brunswick, NJ: Transaction. Straus and Donnelly argue that corporal punishment, including spanking, is family violence and that its effect is to increase aggressiveness in children. This is not a popular position in our society, but worth considering.

Wallace, Harvey (Ed.). 2004. *Family Violence: Legal, Medical, and Social Perspectives,* 4th ed. Boston: Allyn and Bacon. Comprehensive source on many aspects of family violence, including in families working in such occupations as the police and the military.

Journal of Family Violence. Begun in 1985, this journal is dedicated to research on family violence.

Violence Against Women. A well-respected journal dedicated to research on this topic.

Virtual Society: The Wadsworth Sociology Resource Center

 Go to the Sociology Resource Center at **http://sociology.wadsworth.com** for a wealth of online resources, including a companion website for your text that provides study aids such as self-quizzes for each chapter and a practice final exam, as well as links to sociology websites and information on the latest theories and discoveries in the field. In addition, you will find further suggested readings, flash cards, MicroCase online exercises, and appendices on a range of subjects.

Online Study Tool

Marriage&Family ⊛ Now™ Go to **http://sociology.wadsworth.com** to reach the companion website for your text and use the Marriage&FamilyNow access code that came with your book to access this study tool. Take a practice pretest after you have read each chapter, and then use the study plan provided to master that chapter. Afterward, take a posttest to monitor your progress.

Search Online with InfoTrac College Edition

For additional information, exercises, and key words to aid your research, explore InfoTrac College Edition, your online library that offers full-length articles from thousands of scholarly and popular publications. Click on *InfoTrac College Edition* under *Chapter Resources* at the companion website and use the access code that came with your book.

- Search keywords: *dating violence, relationship violence.* See what is available on violence in couple relationships that are not at a commitment stage.

- Search keywords: *sibling violence.* What is available on this very common form of family violence? Is it the focus of much research? Judging by the research that does exist, is this a significant form of violence that should receive more attention? Or is it "kids being kids"?

Family Stress, Crises, *and* Resilience

God, grant me the serenity to accept the things I cannot change, the courage to change the things I can, and the wisdom to know the difference.

The Serenity Prayer

BENJAMIN FRANKLIN SAID THE ONLY things a person can be sure of in this world are death and taxes. It should be noted that a third sure thing exists. This third reality is family stress . . ." (National Ag Safety Database n.d.). As sociologist Pauline Boss (1997) reminds us,

> Perhaps the first thing to realize about stress is that it's not always a bad thing to have in families. In fact it can make family life exciting—being busy, working, playing hard, competing in contests, being involved in community activities, and even arguing when you don't agree with other family members. Stress means change. It is the force exerted on a family by demands. (p. 1)

Family stress exists within the family as a group or unit. We can think of the family as a group that is continually balancing the demands put on it against its capacity to meet those demands. **Family stress** is a state of tension that arises when demands test, or tax, a family's capabilities. Moving to a different neighborhood, taking on a new job, and bringing a baby home are examples of situations that create family stress. Responding to the needs of aging parents is stressful for a family, and making eldercare decisions may often be defined as a crisis situation (see Chapter 18).

Furthermore, family stress might be caused by financial pressures such as finding adequate housing on a poverty budget or financing children's education on a middle-class income. A family member's injury or illness or a death in the family is a source of family stress. You may have noticed something from these examples: Situations that we think of as good, as well as those that we think of as bad, are all capable of creating stress in our families. Family stress calls for family adjustment (Patterson 2002b). In response to financial pressures, for instance, middle-class family members might adjust their budget, cutting back spending on

clothing, recreation, travel, or eating out. They might cope with time pressures by reducing their responsibilities or by arranging for someone outside the immediate family to help.

When adjustments are not easy to come by, family stress can lead to a **family crisis**: "a situation in which the usual behavior patterns are ineffective and new ones are called for immediately" (National Ag Safety Database n.d., p. 1; Patterson 2002b). We can think of a family crisis as a sharper jolt to a family than more ordinary family stress.

The definition of crisis encompasses three interrelated ideas:

1. Crises necessarily involve change.
2. A crisis is a turning point with the potential for positive effects, negative effects, or both.
3. A crisis is a time of relative instability.

Family crises share these characteristics. They are turning points that require some change in the way family members think and act in order to meet a new situation (Hansen and Hill 1964; McCubbin and McCubbin 1991; Patterson 2002b). In the words of social worker and crisis researcher Ronald Pitzer,

> *Crisis* occurs when you or your family face an important problem or task that you cannot easily solve. A crisis consists of the problem and your reaction to it. It's a turning point for better or worse. Things will never be quite the same again. They may not necessarily be worse; perhaps they will be better, but they will definitely be different. (Pitzer 1997a, p. 1)

We point out in several places throughout this text that families are more likely to be happy when they work toward mutually supportive relationships—and when they have the resources to do so. Nowhere does this become more apparent than in a discussion of how families manage stress and crises. This chapter examines how families cope with stress and crises—and how they can do so more creatively. We'll discuss what precipitates family stress or crisis, then look at how families define or interpret stressful situations and how their definitions affect the course of a family crisis. To begin, we'll review some theoretical perspectives on the family and see how these can be applied to family stress and crises.

Theoretical Perspectives on Family Stress and Crises

We see in Chapter 3 that there are various theoretical perspectives concerning marriages and families. Throughout this chapter, we will apply several of these theoretical perspectives to family stress and crises. Here we give a brief review of several theoretical perspectives that are typically used when examining family stress and crises.

You may recall that the *structure–functional* perspective views the family as a social institution that performs essential functions for society—raising children responsibly and providing economic and emotional security to family members. From this point of view, a family crisis threatens to disrupt the family's ability to perform these critical functions (Patterson 2002b).

The *family development*, or *family life course*, perspective sees a family as changing in predictable ways over time. This perspective typically analyzes **family transitions**—expected or *predictable* changes in the course of family life—as family stressors that can precipitate a family crisis (Carter and McGoldrick 1988). For example, having a first baby or sending the youngest child off to college taxes a family's resources and brings about significant changes in family relationships and expectations. Over the course of family living, people may form cohabiting relationships, marry, become parents, divorce, remarry, redivorce, remarry again, and make transitions to retirement and widowhood or widowerhood. All these transitions are stressors. Many are discussed in detail elsewhere in this text.

In addition, this perspective focuses on the fact that predictable family transitions, such as an adult child's becoming financially independent, are expected to occur within an appropriate time period (see, for example, Furstenberg et al. 2004). Transitions that are "outside of expected time" create greater stress than those that are "on time" (Hagestad 1996; Rogers and Hogan 2003).

The *family ecology* perspective explores how a family influences and is influenced by the environments that surround it. From this point of view, many causes of family stress originate outside the family—in the family's neighborhood, workplace, national or international environment (Boss 2002). Living in a violent neighborhood causes family stress and has potential for sparking a family crisis (Fox 2000; Koblinsky 2001).

Conflict between work and family roles that is largely created by workplace demands is another example of an environmental factor that may cause family stress (Voydanoff 2002). Changes in the national welfare laws have caused stress or crisis for many families (Blalock, Tiller, and Monroe 2004; Dyk 2004; London, Scott, Edin, and Hunter 2004). The September 11, 2001, attacks on New York City and Washington, DC, were environmental factors that dramatically affected our families, creating family stress. Furthermore, as we'll see later in this chapter, our family's external environment offers or denies us resources for dealing with stressors.

The *family systems* theoretical framework looks at the family as a system—like a computer system or an organic system, such as a living plant or the human body. In a system, each component or part influences all the other parts. For example, changing a piece of code in a computer program will affect the entire program. Similarly, one family member's changing her or his role requires all the family members to adapt and change as well. For instance, when a family member becomes addicted to alcohol, the entire family system is affected. Among other negative consequences, spousal or parental alcoholism is associated with other family members' depression (El-Sheikh and Flanagan 2001), spouse abuse (Hutchison 1999), children's overall poor behavioral adjustment (El-Sheikh and Flanagan 2001), adolescents' drinking (Hill and Yuan 1999), suicide among children aged ten through fourteen as well as adolescents (Fernquist 2000), and unusually high levels of stress among college students (Fischer et al. 2000). ("Issues for Thought: Sudden Health: The Experience of Families with a Member Who Has Surgery to Correct Epilepsy" illustrates families as systems.)

Furthermore, any system has boundaries; an observer can tell what is in the system and what is outside the system. Family systems theorists point out that a family needs to know "who is in and who is outside the family" (Boss 1997, p. 4). Some family stresses and crises involve renegotiating in this regard.

Finally, exploring the discussions, gestures, and actions that go on in families, the interactionist perspective views families as shaping family traditions and family members' self-concepts and identities. By interacting with one another, family members gradually create shared family meanings that define stressful or potentially stressful situations—for example, as good or bad, disaster or challenge, someone's fault or no

Issues for Thought

Sudden Health: The Experience of Families with a Member Who Has Surgery to Correct Epilepsy

People may think of family demands, or stressors, as negative events, but family systems theory tells us that even good changes in a family's daily living experiences may create challenges and the need for adjustment. In this regard, two medical school professors investigate families' responses to an epileptic family member's sudden cure through surgery. Here is what they have to say about their research.

. . . Persons with epilepsy may lose their faculties numerous times each day, speak incoherently, and become incontinent. They may not be able to go for a walk alone or boil water, not to mention hold a job, complete an education, drive a car, or maintain intimate relationships. . . . Unfortunately, despite aggressive medical treatment, approximately [one-third] of all persons with epilepsy live with intractable seizures that cannot be controlled through [drugs]. . . .

For those who are eligible . . . surgery is remarkably successful, with 70 percent of patients being completely cured. We became

interested in this population of patients and their families. We wondered what their post-surgery experience was since in most cases the families had lived with epilepsy for an extended period of time, often decades.

Six Families

To explore the experience of these patients and families we conducted a qualitative pilot study in which six families were examined in depth. The family member with epilepsy in each of these families had suffered from the disease for an average of more than fifteen years. The study included a married father with three children; a single mother with one son and a supportive father; a wife with two teenaged children; a single woman living with her aunt and a friend; an adult daughter living with her parents; and a young man in his twenties who moved back home to live with his mother, stepfather, and siblings.

Each of these families agreed to be interviewed and videotaped in their homes twice, once just before

the surgery and a second time six to eight months after the surgery. We learned that epilepsy has a profound effect on families in the long period before surgery. Many family roles are organized around epilepsy, with seizures being significant events that are seldom discussed. Families struggle with the stigma of epilepsy and try to establish a sense of "normal" life even though they readily admit that their lives don't feel normal.

Family Responses to Epilepsy

We found that families in the study responded to epilepsy in one of two primary ways. Families with a member whose onset of epilepsy was in late adolescence or early adulthood responded to the seizure disorder like trauma teams who saw the seizures as out-of-the-ordinary events that must be addressed so that they could return to their normal daily living. . . .

In families in which the onset of epilepsy was in childhood, long before the person married or had children, we found a nesting phe-

---

one's fault. As we will explore later in this chapter, "a family's shared meanings about the demands they are experiencing can render them more or less vulnerable in how they respond" (Patterson 2002b, p. 355).

What Precipitates a Family Crisis?

Demands put upon a family cause stress and sometimes precipitate a family crisis. Social scientists call such demands **stressors**—a precipitating event or

events that create stress. Stressors vary in both kind and degree, and their nature is one factor that affects how a family responds. In general, stressors are less difficult to cope with when they are expected, are brief in duration, and gradually improve over time.

Types of Stressors

There are several types of stressors, as Figure 15.1 shows. We will briefly examine seven of them here.

ADDITION OF A FAMILY MEMBER Adding a member to the family—through birth, adoption (Bird,

nomenon in which the family organized themselves in such a way that they could hold and protect the member who had epilepsy. . . .

Dealing with "Sudden Health"

The post-surgery interviews revealed that each of these families had to deal with a new set of challenges brought on by their experience of "sudden health." In each case, the surgery was successful, with only one patient reporting a single seizure. That was the good news. But what was unexpected was the difficulty that several families had in making the adjustment to the absence of seizures from their daily life. This was particularly challenging for the nesting families because much of their structure was organized around epilepsy as a normative experience in their lives. For them, the transition to having a "new" person in their midst was often difficult.

In one family, the father had surgery. He had been emotionally absent throughout his marriage. His wife reported that she didn't like the fact that now he was "barking orders at my kids." This family also struggled with personality changes in the father who was known as taciturn at best. Now he talked all the time, something that was annoying to several family members. . . .

Similar processes occurred in other families. One woman received angry phone messages from her boyfriend because she was out so often when he called. When she was having seizures she never left home and he always knew where she was. Her son found it hard to go to school because his mother had returned to work and wasn't as available to him as she was when she was having seizures.

In another family, the husband realized that he steadfastly ignored positive changes in his wife's personality after surgery because he "never expected her to change."

No More Excuses

In yet another family, conflict escalated to near violence between the formerly ill member and his brother. When the family discussed the matter, they realized that they had endured the formerly ill member's angry outburst before the surgery because they didn't want to upset him and they wondered if his anger was related to his epilepsy. When the angry outbursts continued long after the surgery, the family confronted him with the need to change or move out. The young man acknowledged that he had "used" his seizures as an "excuse" to get angry in the past, because he knew that his family wouldn't abandon him no matter what he did.

While this is a preliminary exploratory study that cannot be generalized to all families, it still raises important questions about how families become organized around chronic illnesses and what happens in those families when they are faced with apparent good news in the form of health. The counterintuitive finding that families may face significant adjustment difficulties when an illness abates points to the need for further research of this phenomenon. It also points to the need for health care professionals to work with whole families around the place that an illness may have in their lives and how to adjust when an ill member becomes well.

Critical Thinking

Why do you suppose that the researchers characterize their findings as "unexpected"? Are *you* surprised at what these researchers found? How does this research illustrate family systems theory? How do the six families that took part in this research illustrate the diversity of family forms, described in Chapter 1?

Source: Quoted/excerpted in near entirety from David B. Seaburn and Giuseppe Erba, "Sudden Health: The Experience of Families with a Member Who Has Surgery to Correct Epilepsy." *Family Focus*, December 2002: F8–F10.

Peterson, and Miller 2002), marriage, remarriage, or the onset of cohabitation, for example—is a stressor. You may recall the discussion in Chapter 11 on why the transition to parenthood is typically stressful. The addition of adult family members may bring into intimate social contact people who are very different from one another in values and life experience. Then, too, not only are in-laws (and increasingly stepparents, stepgrandparents, and stepsiblings) added through marriage but also a whole array of *their* kin come into the family. Adding a family member is stressful because doing so involves family boundary changes; that

is, family boundaries have to shift to include or "make room for" new people or to adapt to the loss of a family member (Boss 1980).

LOSS OF A FAMILY MEMBER The loss of a family member either permanently, such as through death, or temporarily, such as through hospitalization, is a stressor (Greeff and Human 2004). The likelihood of death in our society influences how we define a death in the family. Under the mortality conditions that existed in this country in 1900, half of all families with three children could expect to have one die before reaching age

| Addition of a family member | Loss of a family member | Ambiguous loss | Sudden change | Conflict over family roles | Caring for a disabled or dependent family member | Demoralizing event | Daily family hassles |

FIGURE 15.1

Types of stressors.

fifteen. Social historians have argued that parents defined the loss of a child as almost natural or predictable and, consequently, may have suffered less emotionally than do parents today (Wells 1985, pp. 1–2). Family members who lose a child today do so "outside of expected time," a situation that exacerbates, or adds to, their grief. Moreover, when an only child dies, parents must adjust to the sudden loss of an important role as well as grieving their child (Talbot 1996, 1997). The long-term effects of grieving such a loss may negatively affect marital intimacy (Gottlieb, Lang, and Amsel 1996).

Loss of potential children through miscarriage or stillbirth has the possible added strain of family disorientation. Attachment to the fetus may vary substantially so that the loss may be grieved greatly or little. Add to that the generally minimal display of bereavement customary in the United States and the omission of funerals or support rituals for perinatal (birth process) loss, and "all these ambiguities mean that a family may have to cope with sharply different feelings among family members . . . [and] the family as a whole may have to cope with the fact that they as a family have a very different reaction to loss than do the people around them" (Rosenblatt and Burns 1986, p. 238).

In fact, a study of fifty-five instances of perinatal loss found that grief was still felt by some parents forty years later, whereas the majority reported no long-term grief; some had always defined their loss as a medical problem rather than a child's death. Men and women may have different reactions to their pregnancy loss and a different sensibility about the expression of feelings (Stinson et al. 1992). As with the addition of a family member, loss also involves the additional stress of negotiating family boundary changes (Boss 1980).

AMBIGUOUS LOSS Negotiating family boundary changes is particularly difficult when the loss of a family member is *ambiguous*—when it is uncertain whether the family member is "really" gone. For instance, a spouse, parent, grandparent, or in-law can become physically absent (at least a lot of the time) through divorce but may still remain a part of the family psychologically, socially, and economically (Boss 1999; Cole and Cole 1999). The ambiguity of postdivorce family boundaries can be stressful, as Chapters 15 and 16 illustrate. As other examples, having a family member who is in the military, stationed in Iraq, or who is missing in action (MIA) are situations of ambiguous loss (Pittman, Kerpelman, and McFadyen 2004; Tubbs and Boss 2000). In addition, a family member may be physically present but psychologically absent, as in the case of alcoholic or chemically ill family members (see Figure 15.2).

From the family systems perspective, ambiguous loss is uniquely difficult to deal with because it creates **boundary ambiguity** in a family:

> In simple terms, that means not knowing who is in and who is out of the family. . . . If someone has run away, is missing, or is constantly drunk, the family is in limbo. The family is unable to grieve the loss because they don't know if the person is "in or out of the family." (Boss 1997, pp. 2–3)

SUDDEN CHANGE A sudden change in the family's income or social status may also be a stressor. Most people think of stressors as being negative, and some sudden changes are, such as traffic accidents. But positive changes, such as winning the lottery (don't you wish?) or getting a significant promotion may cause

High Boundary Ambiguity	
Physical Absence	Physical Presence
Psychological Presence	Psychological Absence
Examples: physically missing family members. There is a preoccupation with thinking of the absent member. The process of grieving and re-structuring cannot begin because the facts surrounding the loss of the person are not clear.	Examples: alcoholic/chemically ill family members. Families where a member is physically there but not emotionally avail-able to the system. The family is intact, but a member is psychologically preoccupied with something outside the system.

FIGURE 15.2

High boundary ambiguity—two forms: (1) a family member's physical absence, coupled with psychological presence and (2) a family member's physical presence, coupled with psychological absence. "Sometimes a family experiences an event or situation that makes it difficult—or even impossible—for them to determine precisely who is in their family system."

Source: Boss 1997, pp. 2–3.

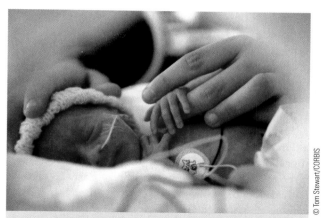

Sometimes a situation may be classified as more than one type of stressor. Due to advancing medical technology, for instance, more newborns today survive low birth weight or birth defects but may need ongoing remedial attention. Therefore, adding a baby to the family may also mean caring for a medically fragile child.

stress too. One author of this text knows a family that became suddenly wealthy when a product they had invented and manufactured on a small scale became nationally popular. This family hired a consultant to teach them how to behave in their new social circumstances. Deciding such matters as whether it would be appropriate for the children to continue to take babysitting jobs occupied a great deal of family energy.

ONGOING FAMILY CONFLICT Ongoing, unresolved conflict among members may be a stressor (Hammen, Brennan, and Shih 2004). For example, deciding how children should be disciplined may bring to the surface divisive differences over parenting roles. The role of an adult child living with parents is often unclear and can be a source of unresolved conflict. If children of teenagers or of divorced adult children are involved, the situation becomes even more challenging. For a grandmother, watching her married child go through family conflict may be a stressor (Hall and Cummings 1997).

CARING FOR A DEPENDENT, ILL, OR DISABLED FAMILY MEMBER Caring for a dependent or disabled family member is a stressor (Patterson 2002a). Being responsible for an adult child or a sibling with mental illness or retardation is an example (Lustig 1999; Seltzer, Greenberg, Krauss, Gordon, and Judge 1997). Parents' raising a mentally or physically disabled child is another example (Rogers and Hogan 2003). Due mainly to advancing medical technology, the number of dependent people and the severity of their disabilities have steadily increased over recent decades. For instance, more babies today survive low birth weight and birth defects (Auslander, Netzer, and Arad 2003). Also, more people now survive serious accidents, and many seriously injured soldiers in Iraq have survived. These family members may require ongoing care and medical attention.

Then too, parents may be raising children with chronic physical conditions, such as asthma, cerebral palsy, diabetes, or epilepsy, for example. Families may need to see their children through bone marrow, kidney, or liver transplants, sometimes requiring several months' residence at a medical center away from home (LoBiondo-Wood, Williams, and McGhee 2004). Adults with advanced AIDS may return home to be taken care of by family members. Caring for a terminally ill family member is, of course, another stressor—for young children, who may exhibit behavior problems as a response, as well as for adults in the household (LeClere and Kowalewski 1994; Seltzer and Heller 1997).

DEMORALIZING EVENTS Stressors may be demoralizing events—those that signal some loss of family morale. Demoralization can accompany the stressors already described (see, for example, Early, Gregoire, and McDonald 2002). But, among other things, this category also includes job loss, unwanted pregnancy, poverty, homelessness, having one's child placed in foster care, juvenile delinquency or criminal prosecution, scandal, family violence, mental illness, alcoholism, drug abuse, incarceration, or suicide (Arditti 2003; Blalock 2003; Dolan, Braun, and Murphy 2003). Being the brunt of racist treatment is potentially demoralizing (Murry, Brown, Brody, Cutrona, and Simons 2001; "Poor People" 2003). Chapter 11 addresses grandparents' raising grandchildren, a situation that is often associated with demoralizing events (Warren 2003).

Physical, mental, or emotional illnesses or disorders can be demoralizing, especially when they carry possible attributions of family dysfunction—attention deficit hyperactivity disorder (Wells et al. 2000), anorexia nervosa, or bulimia, for example—or are socially stigmatized—AIDS, for example. Sexually transmitted diseases with less serious health implications may nevertheless present a threat to the marriage. Alzheimer's disease or head injury, in which a beloved family member seems to have become a different person, can be heartbreaking.

DAILY FAMILY HASSLES Finally, daily family hassles are stressors. Examples are balancing employment against family demands (Grzywacz, Almeida, and McDonald 2002; Voydanoff 2002); working odd hours (Coles 2004); arranging child care or transportation to work among low-income families (Roy, Tubbs, and Burton 2004); or protecting children from danger, especially in neighborhoods characterized by violence (Jarrett and Jefferson 2004). Although we may tend to think of work–family tensions as a middle-class issue, research points to serious stress involved in balancing working and family caregiving among the working poor as well (Blalock 2003; Dolan, Braun, and Murphy 2003, Reschke 2003).

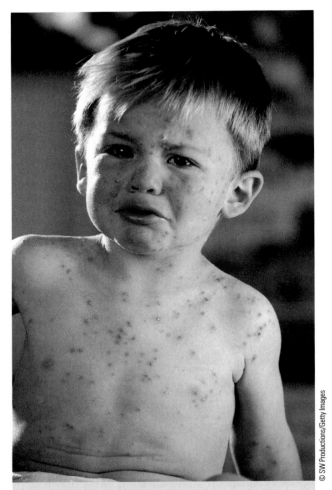

Daily family hassles, such as a child coming down with chicken pox, put demands on a family. Sometimes everyday hassles pile up to result in what social scientists call "stressor overload." This is especially true when a new stressor is added to already difficult daily family life.

Recently scholars have begun to investigate everyday stressors that are unique to certain professions. For instance, especially in recent years military families "are subjected to unique stressors, such as repeated relocations that often include international sites, frequent separations of service members from families, and subsequent reorganizations of family life during reunions" (Drummet, Coleman, and Cable 2003, p. 279; see also Bowen et al. 2003). And families of protestant clergy experience not only the stressors of

ministry demands but also family criticism and situations in which members of the congregation "intrusively assume that the minister will fulfill their expectations without due consideration of the minister's priorities" (Lee and Iverson-Gilbert 2003, p. 251). "Facts About Families: Some Examples of Everyday Family Stressors" lists some examples of common family stressors.

You may have noted as you read this section that sometimes a single event can be classified as more than one type of stressor. For instance, the September 11, 2001, attack on New York City and Washington, DC, was an event that can be classified as a sudden change in our family environments—a change that, among other things, sparked parents' need to consider how to talk with their children about terrorism (Myers-Walls 2001; Walsh 2002b). For many, the attack was a demoralizing event. For others of us, the event was not only sudden and demoralizing, but also sadly marked the loss of one or more family members.

Stressor Overload

A family may be stressed not just by one serious, chronic problem but also by a series of large or small, related or unrelated stressors that build on one an-

other too rapidly for the family members to cope effectively (McCubbin, Thompson, and McCubbin 1996). This situation is called stressor overload, or pile-up:

> Even small events, not enough by themselves to cause any real stress, can take a toll when they come one after another. First an unplanned pregnancy, then a move, then a financial problem that results in having to borrow several thousand dollars, then the big row with the new neighbors over keeping the dog tied up, and finally little Jimmy breaking his arm in a bicycle accident, all in three months, finally becomes too much. (Broderick 1979b, p. 352)

Characteristically, stressor overload creeps up on people without their realizing it. Even though it may be difficult to point to any single precipitating factor, an unrelenting series of relatively small stressors can add up to a major demoralizing crisis. In today's economy, characterized by longer working hours, two-paycheck marriages, fewer high-paying jobs, fewer benefits, and less job security, stressor overload may be more common than in the past. ("A Closer Look at Family Diversity: Stressor Pile-Up Among Single-Mother Families in Homeless Shelters" illustrates stressor overload.) Another example of stressor overload is the addition of depression to an earlier stressor, such as chronic poverty or an adolescent family member's living with epilepsy (Dunn, Austin, and Huster 1999; Seaton and Taylor 2003). We'll return to the idea of stressor pile-up shortly. Now, however, with an understanding of the various kinds of events that cause family stress and can precipitate a family crisis, we turn to a discussion of the course of a family crisis.

The Course of a Family Crisis

Family stress "is simply pressure put on the family"; in a family crisis, there is an "imbalance between pressure and supports" (Boss 1997, p. 1). A family crisis ordinarily follows a fairly predictable course, similar to the truncated roller coaster shown in Figure 15.3. Three distinct phases can be identified: the event that causes the crisis, the period of disorganization that follows, and the reorganizing or recovery phase after the family reaches a low point. Families have a certain level of organization before a crisis; that is, they function at a certain level of effectiveness—higher for some families, lower for others. Families that are having difficulties or functioning less than effectively before the onset of additional stressors or demands are said to be **vulnerable**; families capable of "doing well in the face of adversity" are called **resilient** (Patterson 2002b, p. 350).

In the period of disorganization following the crisis, family functioning declines from its initial level. Families reorganize, and after the reorganization is complete, (1) they may function at about the same level as before; (2) they may have been so weakened by the crisis that they function only at a reduced level—more often the case with vulnerable families; or (3) they may have been stimulated by the crisis to reor-

ganize in a way that makes them more effective—a characteristic of resilient families.

At the onset of a crisis, it may seem that no adjustment is required at all. A family may be confused by a member's alcoholism or numbed by the new or sudden stress and, in a process of denial, go about their business as if the event had not occurred. Gradually, however, the family begins to assimilate the reality of the crisis and to appraise the situation. Then the **period of family disorganization** sets in.

The Period of Disorganization

At this time, family organization slumps, habitual roles and routines become nebulous and confused, and members carry out their responsibilities with less enthusiasm. Although not always, this period of disorganization may be "so severe that the family structure collapses and is immobilized for a time. The family can no longer function. For a time no one goes to work; no one cooks or even wants to eat; and no one performs the usual family tasks" (Boss 1997, p. 1). Typically, and legitimately, family members may begin to feel angry and resentful.

Expressive relationships within the family change, some growing stronger and more supportive perhaps, and others more distant. Sexual activity, one of the most sensitive aspects of a relationship, often changes sharply and may temporarily cease. Parent–child relations may also change.

Relations between family members and their outside friends, as well as the extended kin network, may also change during this phase. Some families withdraw from all outside activities until the crisis is over; as a result, they may become more private or isolated than before the crisis began. As we shall see, withdrawing from friends and kin often weakens rather than strengthens a family's ability to meet a crisis.

FIGURE 15.3

Patterns of family adaptation to crisis.

Source: Adapted from Hansen and Hill 1964, p. 810.

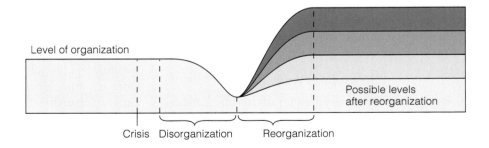

Level of organization

Possible levels after reorganization

Crisis　Disorganization　Reorganization

At the **nadir**, or low point, of family disorganization, conflicts may develop over how the situation should be handled. For example, in families with a seriously ill member, the healthy members are likely either to overestimate or to underestimate the sick person's incapacitation and, accordingly, to act either more sympathetically or less tolerantly than the ill member wants (Conner 2000; Pyke and Bengtson 1996; Strauss and Glaser 1975). Reaching the optimal balance between nurturance and encouragement of the ill person's self-sufficiency may take time, sensitivity, and judgment.

During the period of disorganization, family members face the decision of whether to express or to smother any angry feelings they may have. As Chapter 13 points out, people can express their anger either in primarily bonding ways or in alienating ways. Expressing anger as blame will almost always sharpen hostilities; laying blame on a family member for the difficulties being faced will not help to solve the problem and will only make things worse (P. Stratton 2003). At the same time, when family members opt to repress their anger, they risk allowing it to smolder, thus creating tension and increasingly strained relations. How members cope with conflict at this point will greatly influence the family's overall level of recovery.

Recovery

Once the crisis hits bottom, things often begin to improve. Either by trial and error or (when possible) by thoughtful planning, family members usually arrive at new routines and reciprocal expectations. They are able to look past the time of crisis to envision a return to some state of normalcy and to reach some agreements about the future.

Some families do not recover intact, as today's high divorce rate illustrates. Divorce (or the breakup of a cohabiting relationship) can be seen both as an adjustment to family crisis and as a family crisis in itself (Figure 15.4).

Other families stay together, although at lower levels of organization or mutual support than before the crisis. As Figure 15.3 shows, some families remain at a very low level of recovery, with members continuing to interact much as they did at the low point of disorganization. This interaction often involves a series of circles in which one member is viewed as deliberately causing the trouble and the others blame and nag him or her to stop. This is true of many families in which one member is an alcoholic or otherwise chemically dependent, an overeater, or a chronic gambler, for example. Rather than directly expressing anger about being blamed and nagged, the offending member persists in the unwanted behavior.

Some families match the level of organization they had maintained before the onset of the crisis, whereas others rise to levels above what they experienced before the crisis (McCubbin 1995). For example, a family member's attempted suicide might motivate all family members to reexamine their relationships.

Reorganization at higher levels of mutual support may also result from less dramatic crises. For instance, partners in midlife might view their boredom with their relationship as a challenge and revise their lifestyle to add some zest—by traveling more or planning to spend more time together rather than in activities with the whole family, for example.

Now that we have examined the course of family crises, we will turn our attention to a theoretical model specifically designed to explain family stress, crisis, adjustment, and adaptation.

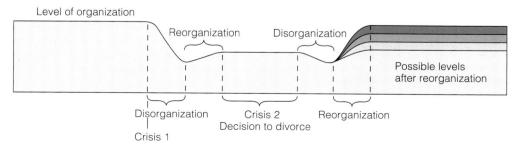

FIGURE 15.4

Divorce as a family adjustment to crisis and as a crisis in itself.

Family Stress, Crisis, Adjustment, and Adaptation: A Theoretical Model

Several decades ago, sociologist Reuben Hill proposed the ABC-X family crisis model, and much of what we've already noted about stressors is based on the research of Hill and his colleagues (Hill 1958; Hansen and Hill 1964). The **ABC-X model** states that **A** (the stressor event) interacting with **B** (the family's ability to cope with a crisis, their crisis-meeting resources) interacting with **C** (the family's appraisal of the stressor event) produces **X** (the crisis) (see Sussman, Steinmetz, and Peterson 1999). In Figure 15.5, *A* would be the demands put upon a family, *B* would be the family's capabilities—resources and coping behaviors, and *C*

would be the meanings that the family creates to explain the demands.

As Figure 15.5 illustrates, families continuously balance the demands put upon them against their capabilities to meet those demands. When demands become heavy, families engage their resources to meet them while also appraising their situation—that is, they create meanings to explain and address their demands. When demands outweigh resources, family adjustment is in jeopardy, and a family crisis may develop. Through the course of a family crisis, some level of adaptation occurs (Patterson 2002b).

Stressor Pile-Up

Building on the ABC-X model, Hamilton McCubbin and Joan Patterson (1983) advanced the *double* ABC-X model to better describe family adjustment to crises. In Hill's original model, the "A" factor was the stressor event; in the double ABC-X model, A becomes "Aa," or "family pile-up." **Pile-up** includes not just the stressor but also previously existing family strains and future hardships induced by the stressor event.

When a family experiences a new stressor, prior strains that may have gone unnoticed—or been barely managed—come to the fore. Prior strains might be any residual family tensions that linger from prior unresolved stressors or are inherent in ongoing family

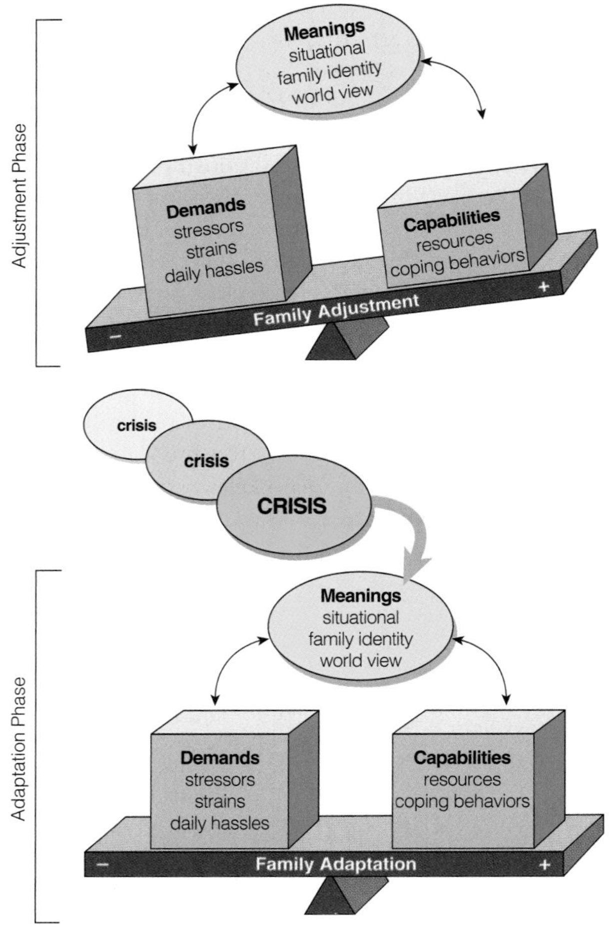

FIGURE 15.5

Family Stress, Crisis, Adjustment, and Adaptation. Families continuously balance the demands put upon them against their capabilities to meet those demands. When demands become heavy, families engage their resources to meet them while also appraising their situation—that is, they create meanings to explain and address their demands. When demands outweigh resources, family adjustment is in jeopardy, and a family crisis may develop. Through the course of a family crisis, some level of adaptation occurs (Patterson 2002b).

Source: Joan M. Patterson, "Integrating Family Resilience and Family Stress Theory," *Journal of Marriage and Family* 64 (2), p. 351.

Note: Previously adapted from "Families Experiencing Stress: The Family Adjustment and Adaptation Response Model," by J. M. Patterson, 1988, *Family Systems Medicine* 6 (2), pp. 202–237. Copyright © 1988 by Families, Systems & Health, Inc.

roles, such as being a single parent or a spouse in a two-career family. For example, ongoing-but-ignored family conflict may intensify when parents or stepparents must deal with a child who is underachieving in school, has joined a criminal gang, or is abusing drugs. As another example, financial and time constraints typical of single-parent families may assume crisis-inducing importance with the addition of a stressor, such as caring for an injured child.

An example of future demands precipitated by the stressor event would be a parent's losing a job, a stressor followed by unpaid bills. One recent study about parenting a disabled child found that the child's rehabilitation often led to parental job changes, severe financial problems, and sleep deprivation (Rogers and Hogan 2003; Porterfield 2002). ("A Closer Look at Family Diversity: Stressor Pile-Up Among Single-Mother Families in Homeless Shelters" further illustrates stressor pile-up.)

The pile-up concept of family-life demands, or stressors (similar to the concept of stressor overload described earlier), is important in predicting family adjustment over the course of family life. Social scientists believe that, generally, an excessive number of life changes and strains occurring within a brief time, perhaps a year, are more likely to disrupt a family.[1] Put another way, pile-up renders a family more vulnerable to emerging from a crisis at a lower level of effectiveness (McCubbin and McCubbin 1989).

This family has survived a flood that greatly damaged their home. Families with strong crisis-meeting resources appraise their situation in a way that encourages them to find the potential positive amidst their troubles and work together so as not to make the demands that they are confronting even worse.

© Kevin Fleming/CORBIS

---

1. The Holmes–Rahe Social Readjustment Ratings Scale, developed in 1967, provides a way to measure an individual adult's or child's stress level. Many of the scale items, such as death of a spouse, death of a parent, divorce, divorce of parents, marital separation, death of a close family member, marriage, marital reconciliation, change in health of a family member, pregnancy, fathering an unwed pregnancy, gaining a new family member, child leaving home, and trouble with in-laws, are actually family stressors and result not only in individual stress but also in family stress or crisis.

The authors rank various life events according to how difficult they are to cope with. For instance, death of a spouse, the most stressful life event on the adult scale, is equivalent to 100 *life change units*. Getting married, the most stressful life event on the scale designed for children age 18 and under, is equivalent to 101 life change units. For adults, divorce is equivalent to 73 life change units, while trouble with in-laws is equivalent to 29. For children, divorce of parents is equivalent to 77 life change units, while hospitalization of a parent is equivalent to 55 life change units and loss of a job by a parent is equivalent to 46. You can find the Holmes–Rahe Social Readjustment Ratings Scale on the Internet; see "Suggested Readings" at the end of this chapter.

We have examined various characteristics of stressor demands put upon a family. Next we will look at how the family makes meaning of, defines, or appraises those demands. We'll look at crisis-meeting resources and coping behaviors after that.

Appraising the Situation

From an interactionist perspective, the meaning that a family gives to a situation—how family members appraise, define, or interpret a crisis-precipitating event—can have as much or more to do with the family's ability to cope as does the character of the event itself (McCubbin and McCubbin 1991; Patterson 2002a, 2002b). For example, a study of families faced with caring for an aging family member (Pyke and Bengston 1996) found that some families felt more ambivalent or negative about having to provide care than did others, who saw caregiving as one more chance to bring the family together.

A Closer Look at Family Diversity

Stressor Pile-Up Among Single-Mother Families in Homeless Shelters

Homeless families, mostly single mothers with children, constitute about one-third of the U.S. homeless population. Up to one-half of these families became homeless when the mothers fled abusive relationships. Other causes include job loss, eviction due to inability to pay rent or other conflicts with landlords, mother's or partner's substance abuse, and conflict with relatives or friends with whom the family was staying prior to becoming homeless.

The average age of children in homeless families is six years. While the majority are preschoolers, many school-age children are homeless as well. Many homeless mothers have not graduated from high school and have inconsistent work histories, along with high rates of depression. Typically, they have had traumatic childhoods: Homeless mothers are more likely than other low-income women to have lived in foster care, a group home, or an institution; run away from home; been physically or sexually abused; and lived on the street or other public places: "They also tend to have small social networks that they turn to and exhaust before entering shelters" (Lindsey 1998, p. 244; Torquati 2002).

Social scientist Elizabeth Lindsey (1998) analyzed interviews from seventeen Georgia and North Carolina mothers who had stayed in a homeless shelter with at least one of their children: "The sample size was determined by the criterion of redundancy, that is, interviewing stopped when additional interviews ceased to generate new data" (p. 245).

Participants ranged in age from nineteen to fifty-two years. Twelve were African American, and five were white. The families had from one to five children, between six months and sixteen years of age; they had stayed in shelters between two weeks and eight months. Some had been homeless more than once.

Lindsey noted that while these families had many past and present stressors, they also evidenced important strengths: pride, determination, a positive orientation, clarity of focus, commitment to parenting and other personal relationships, finding purpose in helping others, and a moral structure used to guide their lives: "It is also important to note that women who enter shelters with their children have managed to maintain enough stability to avoid having the children placed into foster care" (p. 244).

These families obviously benefited from being sheltered. However, shelter life itself often added stress, partly because shelters usually hold families to the same rules as singles. For example, the mothers objected strongly to requirements that they and their children leave the shelter during the day, regardless of the weather: "How can this mother go out and look for a job or even look for a place to live when she's got three kids, and it's raining, or it's cold?" (p. 248).

Other problematic rules involved bedtimes, mealtimes, keeping their children quiet, and the requirement that children be with their parents at all times:

> They have a bedtime for the children, 8:00. . . . And if you can't get them in the bed, they require

Several factors influence how family members define a stressful situation.[2] One is the nature of the stressor itself. For instance, sometimes in the case of ambiguous loss, families do not know whether a missing family member will ever return or whether a chronically ill or a chemically dependent family member will ever recover. Being in limbo this way is very difficult.

In addition to the nature of the stressor itself, a second factor is the degree of hardship or the kind of problems the stressor creates. Temporary unemployment is less a hardship than is a layoff in an area where there are few job prospects or a loss of a job at age

---

2. Although we are discussing the family's definition of the situation, it is important to remember the possibility that each family member experiences a stressful event in a unique way: "These unique meanings may enable family members to work together toward crisis resolution or they may prevent resolution from being achieved. That is, an individual's response to a stressor may enhance or impede the family's progress toward common goals, may embellish or reduce family cohesion, may encourage or interfere with collective efficacy" (Walker 1985, pp. 832–833).

that you put them in the room if you can, and keep them occupied until they're sleepy. Which, you know, they need those rules with that many people. (p. 249)

We had to eat the main meal at 4:00 . . . [and you] couldn't bring any food in there. . . . Little boys eat all the time, and they don't eat their main meal of the day at 4:00, 4:30 in the evening. (p. 248)

[My son] was more or less suffocated because you couldn't really be a child. . . . You could sit there and play with their toys, look at their books, and watch TV up to a point, but just to get wild, like a child likes to do, you couldn't do it. . . . Basically, they were to be seen and not heard. (p. 248)

It was tough on him, it was real tough on him. My son's ADD [diagnosed with attention deficit disorder], and there he had to be quiet and still, play quietly in the bedrooms, no running around. (p. 250)

The kids is supposed to be with you at all times. [Even] at 15, they supposed to be with you at all times. . . . You're supposed to know where your kid is at all times, but it's very hard to do, . . . to keep your child 24-7 when you're here. (p. 247)

Other stressors occurred as well. One mother told of a single male

resident's "getting fresh with my older girl" (p. 249). Another mother expressed concern about changes in her son:

My 12-year-old, oh gosh! He was so depressed. . . . His personality changed, and I had to learn how to deal with that. And it was so tough because he had always been such a sweet child . . . but his attitude became rotten. He was fed up with the rules. . . . (p. 250)

However, Lindsey found that perhaps the most troublesome aspect of shelters for the mothers was the prohibition against any type of corporal punishment: "Parents were expected to make their children behave but were not allowed to use their main form of discipline. At times, shelter staff corrected the mothers in front of their children, undermining their parental authority" (p. 248).

Some mothers described the stress they felt. One said she was

in a daze. . . . I really didn't know where to turn. My nerves were gone. I couldn't sleep. I was about afraid to close my eyes, and I didn't feel safe when I first got there. . . . I had a 3-year-old, and I was like panicking. "What am I going to do?" (p. 249)

Beginning in their own childhoods, these mothers' stresses had gradually piled up, or accumulated.

Lindsey's findings were not all negative. Many of the younger children liked the security and attention they received from shelter residents and staff. Some mothers said that they and their children had grown closer at the shelter. Nevertheless, this research shows that shelter life itself can add to stressor pile-up for homeless families.

Suggestions for lessening family stress while at homeless shelters include allowing parents as much control as possible over bedtimes and eating arrangements, as well as offspring day care and keeping shelters open to families during the day. Furthermore, since "punitive approaches toward parents who rely on corporal punishment do not necessarily prevent parents from spanking," shelter staff need to be supportive in helping parents learn and use other forms of discipline (Lindsey 1998, p. 251; see also Torquati 2002).

From "The Impact of Homelessness and Shelter Life on Family Relationships," by Elizabeth W. Lindsey. Family Relations, 9807, vol. 47:3, p. 251. Copyright © 1998 by the National Council on Family Relations.

fifty-five. Being victimized by a crime is always a stressful event, but coming home to find one's house burglarized may be less traumatic than being robbed at gunpoint.

A third factor is the family's previous successful experience with event crises, particularly those of a similar nature. If family members have had experience in nursing a sick member back to health, they will feel less bewildered and more capable of handling a new, similar situation. Believing from the start that de-

mands are surmountable, and that collectively the family has the ability to cope, may make adjustment somewhat easier (Pitzer 1997b; Wells, Widmer, and McCoy 2004). Family members' interpretations of a crisis event shape their responses in subsequent stages of the crisis. Meanwhile, the family's crisis-meeting resources affect its appraisal of the situation.

A fourth, related factor that influences a family's appraisal of a stressor involves the adult family members' legacies from their childhoods (Carter and

McGoldrick 1988).[3] For example, growing up in a family that tended to define anything that went wrong as a catastrophe or a "punishment" from God might lead the family to define the current stressor more negatively. On the other hand, growing up in a family that tended to define demands simply as problems to be solved or as challenges might mean defining the current stressor more positively.

Crisis-Meeting Resources

A family's crisis-meeting capabilities—resources and coping behaviors—constitute its ability to prevent a stressor from creating severe disharmony or disruption. We might categorize a family's crisis-meeting resources into three types: personal/individual, family, and community.

The personal resources of each family member (for example, intelligence, problem-solving skills, and physical and emotional health) are important. At the same time, the family *as family* or family system has a level of resources, including bonds of trust, appreciation, and support (family harmony); sound finances and financial management and health practices; positive communication patterns; healthy leisure activities; and overall satisfaction with the family and quality of life (Boss 2002; Patterson 2002b).

Rituals may be family resources. A study of alcoholic families found that adult children of alcoholics who came from families that had maintained family dinner and other rituals (or who married into families that did) were less likely to become alcoholics themselves (Bennett, Wolin, and Reiss 1988; Goleman 1992b).

And, of course, money is a family resource (Seaton and Taylor 2003). For instance, the breadwinner's losing his or her job is less difficult to deal with when the family has substantial savings (Bryant 2001). In a qualitative study among U.S. working-poor rural families, one respondent explained that, "I had absolutely nothing after I paid my bills to feed my kids. I scrounged just so that they could eat something, and I had to short change my landlord so that I could feed them,

too, which put me behind in rent." Another said, "I felt overwhelmed and stressed because every time I get paid, I just don't have money for everything . . . because I have two . . . children [with medical problems]" (Dolan, Braun, and Murphy 2003, p. F14).

The family ecology perspective alerts us to the fact that community resources are consequential as well. Increasingly aware of this, medical and family practice professionals have in recent years designed a wide variety of community-based programs to help families adapt to medically related family demands, such as a partner's cancer or a child's diabetes, congenital heart disease, and other illnesses (Peck 2001; Tak and McCubbin 2002). In fact, in many instances family members have become community activists, working to create community resources to aid them in dealing with a particular family stressor or crisis. Parents have been "a driving force" in shaping services and laws related to individuals with mental retardation (Lustig 1999). As a second example, parent groups helped to pass the Americans with Disabilities Act (Turnbull and Turnbull 1997).

VULNERABLE VERSUS RESILIENT FAMILIES Ultimately the family either successfully adapts or becomes exhausted and vulnerable to continuing crisis. Family systems may be high or low in vulnerability, a situation that affects how positively the family faces demands; this enables us to predict or explain the family's poor or good adjustment to stressor events (Patterson 2002b).

More prone to poor adjustment from crisis-provoking events, vulnerable families evidence a lower sense of common purpose and feel less in control of what happens to them. They may cope with problems by showing diminished respect or understanding for one another. Vulnerable families are also less experienced in shifting responsibilities among family members and are more resistant to compromise. There is little emphasis on family routines or predictable time together (McCubbin and McCubbin 1991).

From a social psychological point of view, resilient families tend to emphasize mutual acceptance, respect, and shared values. Family members rely on one another for support. Generally accepting difficulties, they work together to solve problems with members, feeling that they have input into major decisions. It may be apparent that these behaviors are less difficult to foster when a family has sufficient economic re-

---

3. In their model of family stress and crisis, social workers Betty Carter and Monica McGoldrick (1988) see "family patterns, myths, secrets [and] legacies" as *vertical stressors*—because they come down from the previous generations. These authors call the type of stressors that we have been discussing in this chapter *horizontal stressors* (p. 9).

A positive outlook, spiritual values, supportive communication, adaptability, informal social support—all these, along with an extended family and community resources—are factors in family resilience, or meeting a crisis creatively.

© Bruce Ayers/Getty Images

sources. The next section discusses factors that help families to meet crises creatively.

▪ Meeting Crises Creatively ▪

Meeting crises creatively means that after reaching the nadir in the course of the crisis, the family rises to a level of reorganization and emotional support that is equal to or higher than that which preceded the crisis. For some families—for example, those experiencing the crisis of domestic violence—breaking up may be the most beneficial (and perhaps the only workable) way to reorganize. Other families stay together and find ways to meet crises effectively. What factors differentiate resilient families that reorganize creatively from those that do not?

A Positive Outlook

In times of crisis, family members make many choices, one of the most significant of which is whether to blame one member for the hardship (Judge 1998). Casting blame, even when it is deserved, is less productive than viewing the crisis primarily as a challenge (P. Stratton 2003).

Put another way, the more that family members can strive to maintain a positive outlook, it helps a person or a family to meet a crisis constructively. Electing to work toward developing more open, supportive family communication—especially in times of conflict—also helps individuals and families meet crises constructively. Families that meet a crisis with an accepting attitude, focusing on the positive aspects of their lives, do better than those that feel they have been singled out for misfortune. For example, many chronic illnesses have downward trajectories, so both partners may realistically expect that the ill mate's health will only grow worse. Some couples are remarkably able to adjust to this, "either because of immense closeness to each other or because they are grateful for what little life and relationship remains" (Strauss and Glaser 1975, p. 64).

Spiritual Values and Support Groups

Some researchers have found that strong religious faith is related to high family cohesiveness (Stinnett 2003) and helps people manage demands or crises, partly because it provides a positive way of looking at suffering (Wiley, Warren, and Montanelli 2002). A spiritual outlook may be fostered in many ways, including through Buddhist, Christian, Muslim, and other religious or philosophical traditions. Self-help groups, such as Al-Anon for families of alcoholics, can also help people take a positive approach to family crises.

Open, Supportive Communication

Families whose members interact openly and supportively meet crises more creatively (Orthner, Jones-Sanpei, and Williamson 2004). For one thing, free-flowing communication opens the way to understanding. As an example, research shows that expressions of support from parents help children to cope with daily stress (Valiente, Fabes, Eisenberg, and Spinrad 2004). As another example, the better-adjusted husbands with multiple sclerosis believed that even though they were embarrassed when they fell in public or were incontinent, they could freely discuss these situations with their families and feel confident that their families understood (Power 1979). And as a final example, talking openly and supportively with an elderly parent who is dying about what that parent wants—in terms of medical treatment, hospice, and burial—can help (Fein 1997).

Knowing how to indicate the specific kind of support that one needs is important at stressful times. For example, differentiating between—and knowing how to request—just listening as opposed to problem-solving discussion can help reduce misunderstandings among family members—and between family members and others as well (Perlman and Rook 1987; Tannen 1990).

Adaptability

Adaptable families are better able to respond effectively to crises (Boss 2002; Kosciulek and Lustig 1998). And families are more adaptable when they are more democratic and when conjugal power is fairly egalitarian. In families in which one member wields authoritarian power, the whole family suffers if the authoritarian leader does not make effective decisions during a crisis—and allows no one else to move into a position of leadership (McCubbin and McCubbin 1994). A partner who feels comfortable only as the family leader may resent his or her loss of power, and this resentment may continue to cause problems when the crisis is over.

Family adaptability in aspects other than leadership is also important (Burr, Klein, and McCubbin 1995). Families that can adapt their schedules and use of space, their family activities and rituals, and their connections with the outside world to the limitations and possibilities posed by the crisis will cope more effectively than families that are committed to preserving sameness. For example, a study of mothers of children with developmental disabilities found that mothers who worked part time had less stress than those who worked full time or were not employed at all (Gottlieb 1997). Having multiple roles, along with time flexibility, seemed to help.

Informal Social Support

It's easier to cope with crises when a person doesn't feel alone (see, for example, Bowen et al. 2003; Tak and McCubbin 2002). It may go without saying that spouses do better when they feel supported or validated by their partners (Franks, Hong, Pierce, and Ketterer 2002; Owens and Qualls 1997). A study of military families who had a member deployed during Operation Desert Storm or Desert Shield found that practical and emotional help from a "supportive unit culture" made things easier (Pittman, Kerpelman, and McFadyen 2004). Families may find helpful support in times of crisis from kin, good friends, neighbors, and even acquaintances such as work colleagues. These various relationships provide a wide array of help—from lending money in financial emergencies to helping with child care to just being there for emotional support. Even continued contact with more-casual acquaintances may be helpful, as often they offer useful information, along with enhancing one's sense of community (Orthner, Jones-Sanpei, and Williamson 2004).

An Extended Family

Sibling relationships and other kin networks can be a valuable source of support in times of crisis (Johnson 2000; Weaver, Coleman, and Ganong 2003). Grandparents, aunts, or other relatives may help with health crises or with more common family stressors, like child rearing in two-career families. Families going through divorce often fall back on relatives for practical help and financial assistance. In other crises, kin provide a shoulder to lean on—someone who may be

Many—although not all—turn to their extended family for social support in times of stress. This may be less true than researchers once thought, but kin may provide emotional support, monetary support, and practical help.

asked for help without causing embarrassment—which can make a crucial difference in a family's ability to recover.

Even though extended families as residential groupings represent a small proportion of family households, kin ties remain salient (Kamo 2000). One aspect of all this that is just beginning to get research attention is reciprocal friendship and support among adult siblings (White and Riedmann 1992; Weaver, Coleman, and Ganong 2003). In times of family stress or crisis, new immigrants (as well as African Americans) may rely on **fictive kin**—relationships based not on blood or marriage but rather on "close friendship ties that replicate many of the rights and obligations usually associated with family ties" (Ebaugh and Curry 2000).

We need to be cautious, though, not to overestimate or romanticize the extended family as a resource. Along with some previous research, a small study of low-income families living in two trailer parks along the mid-Atlantic coast concluded that "low-income families do not share housing and other resources within a flexible and fluctuating network of extended and fictive kin as regularly as previously assumed" (Edwards 2004, p. 523; see also Roschelle 1997). Extended family members may not get along, or individuals may be too embarrassed to ask their kin for help. One woman explained that neither her parents nor any one of her five siblings could help her because "they all have problems of their own." A Hispanic mother told the interviewer, "I know you've probably heard that Hispanic families are close-knit, well, hmmph! No, we take care of ourselves" (Edwards 2004, p. 523). Then, too, among some recent immigrant groups, such as Asians or Hispanics, expectations of the extended family may clash with the more-individualistic values of Americanized family members (Kamo and Zhou 1994).

Community Resources

The success with which families meet the demands placed upon them also depends on the community resources available to help:

Community-based resources are all of those characteristics, competencies and means of persons, groups and institutions outside the family which the family may call upon, access, and use

It's important to remember that not all stressors are unhappy ones. Happy events, such as moving into a new house, can be family stressors too.

to meet their demands. This includes a whole range of services, such as medical and health care services. The services of other institutions in the family's . . . environment, such as schools, churches, employers, etc. are also resources to the family. At the more macro level, government policies that enhance and support families can be viewed as community resources. (McCubbin and McCubbin 1991, p. 19)

Among others, community resources include social workers and family welfare agencies; foster child care; church programs that provide food, clothing, or shelter to poor or homeless families; twelve-step and other support programs for substance abusers and their families; programs for crime or abuse victims and their families; support groups for people with serious diseases such as cancer or AIDS; support groups for parents and other relatives of disabled or terminally ill children; support groups for caregivers of disabled family members or those with cancer or Alzheimer's disease; and community pregnancy prevention and/or parent education programs.

A unique example of the latter is parent education programs for federal prison inmates, mandated by the U.S. government in 1995. Parent inmates learn general skills, such as how to talk to their child. They also learn ways to create positive parent–child interaction from prison—such as games they can play with a child through the mail—as well as suggestions on what to do when returning home upon release (Coffman and Markstrom-Adams 1995). ("Issues for Thought: When a Parent Is in Prison" further describes some of these programs.)

A more familiar community resource is marriage and family counseling. Counseling can help families after a crisis occurs; it can also help when families foresee a family change, or future new demands. For instance, a couple might visit a counselor when expecting or adopting a baby, when deciding about work commitments and family needs, when the youngest child is about to leave home, or when a partner is about to retire. Increasingly, counselors and social workers emphasize empowering families toward the goal of enhanced resilience—that is, emphasizing and building upon a family's strengths (Power 2004; Walsh 2002a, 2004). Family counseling is not just for relationships that are in trouble but is also a resource that can help to enhance family dynamics (see Appendix H).

We also need to note here the countless resources available online. Indeed, families with an infinite variety of stressors—from involuntary infertility (resolve. org); to having a disabled child (childrenwithdisabilities. ncjrs.org); to experiencing the death of a child (*compassionatefriends.org*); to having a family member in prison (*prisontalk.com*)—can participate in web-based virtual communities and access information from experts as well as from others who are experiencing similar family demands. Unfortunately, many families feel stigmatized by the stressors that they are experiencing (such as epilepsy, money problems, or a diagnosis of mental illness, for example) and therefore are reluctant to seek informal and community support (Arditti 2003; Edwards 2004; Hinshaw 2003; Seaburn and Erba 2002). Because people can seek help anonymously, online resources may be especially helpful in this situation.

Crisis: Disaster or Opportunity?

A family crisis is a turning point in the course of family living that requires members to change how they have been thinking and acting (McCubbin and McCubbin 1991, 1994). We tend to think of *crisis* as synonymous with *disaster*, but the word comes from the Greek for *decision*. Although we cannot control the occurrence of many crises, we can decide how to cope with them.

Most crises—even the most unfortunate ones—have the potential for positive as well as negative ef-

fects. For example, Professor Joan Patterson, a recognized expert in the field of family stress, has observed that many parents who are raising children with "complex and intense" medical needs "seem to find new meaning for their life.

Having a child with such severe medical needs and such a tenuous hold on life shatters the expectations of most parents for how life is supposed to be. It leads to a search for meaning as a way to accept their circumstances. When families get to this place, they not only accept their child and their family's life, but they often experience a kind of gratitude that those of us who have never faced this level of hardship can't really understand. (2002a, p. F7)

Whether a family emerges from a crisis with a greater capacity for supportive family interaction depends at least partly on how family members choose to define the crisis. A major theme of this text is that, given the opportunities and limitations posed by society, people create their families and relationships based on the choices they make. Families whose members choose to be flexible in roles and leadership meet crises creatively.

However, even though they have options and choices, family members do not have absolute control over their lives (Coontz 1997b; Kleber et al. 1997). Many family troubles are really the results of public issues. For example, the serious family disorganization that results from poverty is as much a social as a private problem. Then too, most American families have some handicaps in meeting crises creatively. The typical American family is under a high level of stress at all times. Providing family members with emotional security in an impersonal and unpredictable society is difficult even when things are running smoothly. Family members are trying to do this while holding jobs and managing other activities and relationships.

Moreover, many family crises are more difficult to bear because communities lack adequate resources to help families meet them (Coontz 1997b; Mason, Skolnick, and Sugarman 1998). When families act collectively toward the goal of obtaining the resources they need for effectively meeting the demands placed upon them, family adjustment can be expected to improve overall.

When a Parent Is in Prison

Some children have parents who are in jail or prison—a demoralizing family stressor event, coupled with boundary ambiguity. Incarceration rates began to increase dramatically in the 1970s and have risen even more sharply since 1990 (Arditti 2003). Rates are especially high for young minority men but have increased more rapidly for women than for men (Mumola 2000).

"The impact of strict and severe sentencing has meant that increasing numbers of children are affected by the imprisonment of their parents" (Enos 2001, p.1). Estimates are that about a million and a half children have parents behind bars, about half of whom had lived with their incarcerated parent. Some 78 percent of women prisoners and 64 percent of men are parents. But there is a crucial gender difference. Prior to imprisonment, 79 percent of mothers were living with their children compared to 53 percent of fathers, and mothers were usually the primary caretakers (Federal Resource Center for Children of Prisoners 2004; Mumola 2000).

While mothers were in prison, 35 percent of white children, 24 percent of Hispanic children, and 19 percent of African American children lived with their fathers. Grandparents cared for 57 percent of black children, 55 percent of Hispanic children,

and 41 percent of white children. White children were more likely to be in nonfamily foster care (see Chapter 11's discussion on foster parenting) than African American or Hispanic children (13 percent compared to 6 percent). This may be because black and Hispanic communities have had more of a tradition of shared care of children (e.g., Stack 1974), a situation facilitating making arrangements that place children with adult relatives who feel an obligation to care for them. White parenthood has been more "privatized," so white mothers have fewer resources in a crisis situation (Enos 2001, especially p. 38).

Children's visiting an incarcerated parent can be expensive and otherwise difficult to arrange, since prisons are often far from the homes of children. One study found that half of children of women prisoners did not visit at all during their mother's incarceration. However, including phone calls and letters, 78 percent of mothers and 62 percent of fathers had at least monthly contact with children (Mumola 2000).

Then too, the children's caregivers often:

feel compelled to lie about their loved one's whereabouts. If the children are young, their mother

may explain the father's absence by saying that "Daddy's away on a long trip" or "He's working on a job in another state." One caregiver . . . explained to her nephews that their father was away at "super-hero school." Older children who know the truth may feel that they are careful not to discuss it at school or with friends. (Arditti 2003, p. F15)

More and more, policy makers have realized that disrupted family ties have a severe and negative impact on the next generation (Arditti 2003). Consequently, a number of correctional systems, including the Federal Bureau of Prisons, have developed visitation programs to facilitate parent–child contact. Many correctional facilities have returned to an earlier practice of permitting babies born in prison to remain with their mothers for a time. Although visitation programs were initially oriented solely to mothers, prisons have more recently developed programs for fathers as well (Amnesty International 1999; Enos 2001).

Visitation programs try to normalize parent–child contact. The Nebraska women's correctional facility, for instance, permits overnight stays of five days for children aged one through eight. In an Indiana women's prison day camp,

Having a family member in prison or jail is a crisis faced by a small but growing number of families today. Family stress and adjustment experts tell us that virtually all family crises have some potential for positive as well as negative effects. Can you think of any possible positive effects in this case? What community supports might help this family? What might be some alternatives to incarcerating parents who have been actively involved in raising their children?

[Visiting] children snack on snow cones, line up for pony rides, and bond with their families. . . . But [these activities] can't hide razor-wire fences and uniformed guards at the Indiana Women's Prison, where a summer day camp strives to preserve family ties among inmates and their loved ones. ("Prison Day Camp" 2001)

Since there may be opposition to benefiting parents who have been convicted of crimes, it is important to note that the effect of parent-in- prison programs is to improve behavior in prison and to reduce recidivism after release, and also to provide hope for the next generation: "It's about the children bonding with their parents [said one mother] . . . more so than the parents bonding with the children" (Goldyn 2001, p. 17).

We focus here on children's needs, but imprisonment demoralizes spouses and other family members as well and usually has a negative economic impact on all family members, not only when the prisoner has been an essential breadwinner but also due to costs associated with visiting the prisoner and long-distance family telephone calls, among others (Arditti, Lambert-Shute, and Joest 2003). Moreover, due to "the stigma of incarceration, families of prisoners receive little social support" (Arditti 2003, p. F15).

However, strong marital and family bonds seem to reduce deviant behavior, while "incarceration can undermine social bonds, strain marital and other family relationships. . . . Without assistance for families disrupted by incarceration, the negative social effects of the penal system may aggravate the problems it was designed to solve" (Western and McLanahan 2000, p. 323). A family member's imprisonment is damaging to white-collar families as well as to those at lower social levels (Mason 2000, p. 335).

Policy analysts close to this topic argue that, "An overreliance on incarceration as punishment, particularly for nonviolent offenders, is not good family policy" (Arditti 2003, p. F17). They propose alternatives to incarceration, such as home confinement with work-release. Meanwhile, some officials have begun to act on the idea that it is important for society to make family relations as good as they can be under the circumstances of incarceration and to aid with the parenting of the 2 percent of America's children who have parents in prison (Cose 2000; Enos 2001; Gardiner et al. 2002).

© Joel Gordon

In Sum

- Throughout the course of family living, *all* families are faced with demands, transitions, and stress.

- Family stress is a state of tension that arises when demands test, or tax, a family's resources.

- A sharper jolt to a family than more-ordinary family stress, a family crisis encompasses three interrelated ideas: (1) family change, (2) a turning point with the potential for positive and/or negative effects, and (3) a time of relative instability.

- Demands, or stressors, are of various types and have varied characteristics. Generally, stressors that are expected, brief, and improving are less difficult to cope with.

- The predictable changes of individuals and families—parenthood, midlife transitions, post-parenthood, retirement, and widowhood and widowerhood—are all family transitions that may be viewed as stressors.

- A common pattern can be traced in families that are experiencing family crisis. Three distinct phases can be identified: (1) the stressor event that causes the crisis, (2) the period of disorganization that follows, and (3) the reorganizing or recovery phase after the family reaches a low point.

- The eventual level of reorganization a family reaches depends on a number of factors, including the type of stressor, the degree of stress it imposes, whether it is accompanied by other stressors, the family's appraisal or definition of the crisis situation, and the family's available resources.

- Meeting crises creatively means resuming daily functioning at or above the level that existed before the crisis.

- Several factors can help families meet family stress and/or crises more creatively: a positive outlook, spiritual values, the presence of support groups, high self-esteem, open and supportive communication within the family, adaptability, counseling, and the presence of a kin network.

Key Terms

ABC-X model
boundary ambiguity
family crisis
family stress
family transitions
fictive kin
nadir of family
 disorganization
period of family
 disorganization
pile-up (stressor overload)
resilient families
stressor
vulnerable families

Questions for Review and Reflection

1. Compare the concepts *family stress* and *family crisis*, giving examples and explaining how a family crisis differs from family stress.

2. Differentiate among the types of stressors. How are these single events different from stressor overload? How might living in poverty cause stressor overload?

3. Discuss issues addressed in other chapters of this text (e.g., work–family issues, parenting, divorce, and remarriage) in terms of the ABC-X model of family crisis.

4. What factors help some families recover from crisis while others remain in the disorganization phase?

5. **Policy Question.** In your opinion, what, if anything, could/should government do to help families in stress? In crisis?

Suggested Readings

Boss, Pauline. 2002. *Family Stress Management*, 2nd ed. Newbury Park, CA: Sage. A textbook on this topic by a foremost expert in this field.

Boss, Pauline, and Carol Mulligan (Eds.). 2003. *Family Stress: Classic and Contemporary Readings*. Thousand Oaks, CA: Sage. An anthology, or "reader," that includes twenty-three major articles—both classic and current— from the family stress and adaptation literature. This collection was designed to go with Boss's textbook, described above. However, put together by recognized experts in the field, the anthology is a valuable resource on its own.

Doka, Kenneth J. (Ed.). 2002. *Disenfranchised Grief: New Directions, Challenges, and Strategies for Practice.* Disenfranchised grief is grief that goes unacknowledged by society—whether it's over the loss of a cherished pet or the death of an ex-spouse (whom you shouldn't need to grieve because you're divorced, right?). This collection of readings is highly recommended by others who've experienced disenfranchised grief.

Fincannon, Joy L., and Katherine V. Bruss. 2003. *Couples Confronting Cancer: Keeping Your Relationship Strong.* Atlanta: American Cancer Society. A realistic—and positive—how-to book for couples confronting cancer. Chapters include, among others, "Evaluating Your Relationship," "Lifestyle Factors," "Improving Communication," and "Support Services."

Holmes–Rahe Social Readjustment Ratings Scale

http://www.education.umd.edu

Scale designed to measure an individual's stress level but also applicable to family stress and crisis. You can use this scale to measure your personal or family stress level. This site, maintained by the College of Human Ecology at the University of Minnesota, also has several articles by Minnesota professors on family stress.

Journal of Health and Social Behavior. Academic journal that reports many studies of relationships among life events, stress, social supports, and other coping mechanisms, and physical and mental health.

Sorensen, Elaine Shaw. 1993. *Children's Stress and Coping: A Family Perspective.* New York: Guilford. Focuses on the obvious—but often neglected—point that babies and older children suffer from family stress too, and discusses what may be done about it.

Westberg, Granger E. 1971. *Good Grief: A Constructive Approach to the Problem of Loss.* Philadelphia: Fortress.

A classic full of information and advice on the mourning process.

Virtual Society: The Wadsworth Sociology Resource Center

 Go to the Sociology Resource Center at **http:// sociology.wadsworth.com** for a wealth of online resources, including a companion website for your text that provides study aids such as self-quizzes for each chapter and a practice final exam, as well as links to sociology websites and information on the latest theories and discoveries in the field. In addition, you will find further suggested readings, flash cards, MicroCase online exercises, and appendices on a range of subjects.

Online Study Tool

Marriage & Family ⊛ Now™ Go to **http://sociology .wadsworth.com** to reach the companion website for your text and use the Marriage&FamilyNow access code that came with your book to access this study tool. Take a practice pretest after you have read each chapter, and then use the study plan provided to master that chapter. Afterward, take a posttest to monitor your progress.

Search Online with InfoTrac College Edition

For additional information, exercises, and key words to aid your research, explore InfoTrac College Edition, your online library that offers full-length articles from thousands of scholarly and popular publications. Click on *InfoTrac College Edition* under *Chapter Resources* at the companion website and use the access code that came with your book.

- Search keywords: *family stress, resilient family, vulnerable family.*

Divorce:
Before and After

You cannot imagine how much we hoped in the beginning.

LIV ULLMAN
Changing

DIVORCE HAS BECOME A COMMON experience in the United States for all social classes, age categories, and religious and ethnic groups. Between 40 percent and 50 percent of recent first marriages are likely to end in divorce (Amato 2001; Kreider and Fields 2002). In this chapter, we'll examine factors that affect people's decisions to divorce, the experience itself, and ways the experience may be made less painful and become the prelude to the future, alone or in a new marriage. We'll also analyze why so many couples in our society decide to divorce and examine the debate over whether a divorce should be harder to get than it is today. We'll begin by looking at current divorce rates in the United States, which are among the highest in the world.

Today's High U.S. Divorce Rate

The frequency of divorce increased sharply throughout most of the twentieth century, as Figure 16.1 shows, with dips and upswings surrounding historical events such as the Great Depression and major wars. Before we examine divorce further, we need to understand how divorce rates are calculated and what data on divorce are available. "Facts About Families: How Divorce Rates Are Reported" describes the various divorce rates and discusses the availability and usefulness of each.

Let us look at what we know about divorce trends. Between 1960 and a peak in 1979, the *refined divorce rate* more than doubled, most of the increase taking place between 1965 and 1975. Since then the refined divorce rate has declined; see Figure 16.1 (U.S. National Center for Health Statistics 1990a, 1998). We can extend the time line to 2003 if we use the *crude divorce rate* (see Figure 16.2). The crude divorce rate has declined about 28 percent since 1979. The same general trends in rates have occurred in all race and age groups.

Most divorces occur relatively early in marriage. The median length of a first marriage that ends in divorce is about eight years. At the five-year point, 10 percent have divorced; at the fifteen-year point, 43 percent. The proportion of divorces for couples married twenty years or more has increased, however (Bramlett and Mosher 2001; Kreider and Fields 2002; U.S. National Center for Health Statistics 2004, Table A; Wu and Penning 1997).

Most observers conclude that the divorce rate has stabilized for the time being. One reason is that fewer people are marrying at the vulnerable younger ages—

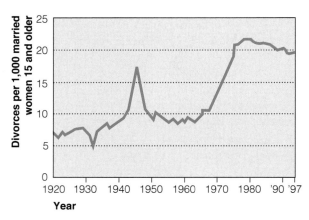

FIGURE 16.1

Divorces per 1,000 married women aged fifteen and older in the United States, 1920–1997. The NCHS has not recalculated the *refined divorce rate* since 1997.

Source: U.S. National Center for Health Statistics 1990; 1998, p. 3.

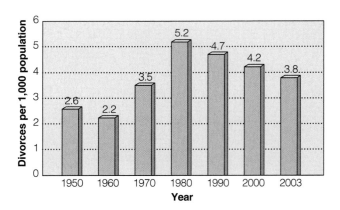

FIGURE 16.2

Divorces per 1,000 population, 1950 to 2003 (*crude divorce rate*).

Source: U.S. Census Bureau 2003a, Table 83; U.S. National Center for Health Statistics 2004, Table A.

Facts About Families
How Divorce Rates Are Reported

Divorce rates are reported in many forms, and these data vary in validity and availability. The implications of measures of divorce are frequently misunderstood when they are read in media reports.

- *Number of divorces per year.* The number of divorces recorded per year is not a good measure of the divorce rate because it does not take into account the increase in population. There may be more divorces simply because there are more people.

- *Ratio of current marriages to current divorces.* This measure is faulty because the marriages have all taken place in the current year, whereas the divorces are from marriages that took place earlier, in many different years. Moreover, if the number of marriages goes down, the tendency to divorce will appear to rise even if the number of divorces remains constant.

- *Lifetime records of marriage and divorce.* A cohort of married couples could be followed over a lifetime and their rate of divorce calculated. This sort of longitudinal study is unlikely ever to be done because of the expense and the length of time it would require. Furthermore, a divorce rate calculated on couples reaching their later years would

not necessarily apply to younger couples, who are living their married years in a changed social setting.

- *Crude divorce rate.* The **crude divorce rate** is the number of divorces per 1,000 population. This measure takes population size into account, but includes portions of the population—children and the unmarried—who are not at risk for divorce. Despite its limitations, the crude divorce rate is used for comparisons among states and regions over time because it is a simple statistic for which data are usually available. And now that the *refined divorce rate* is no longer available, it is the only measure we have with which to track national divorce trends.

- *Refined divorce rate.* The **refined divorce rate** is the number of divorces per 1,000 married women over age fifteen. This measure compares the number of divorces to the total number of women eligible for divorce (adult married women) and hence is a more valid indicator of the propensity to divorce than *the crude divorce rate.*

  However, the National Center on Health Statistics—the federal agency responsible for marriage and divorce statistics—discontinued

compilation of this divorce statistic or other detailed divorce statistics in the mid-nineties in a budget-cutting measure (Broome 1995). Consequently, you will notice that much of the detailed information about divorce presented in this chapter is based on older data, including sample surveys and the crude divorce rate used to track long-term trends.

- *National sample surveys.* We must now rely on national sample surveys—including the U.S. Census Bureau's annual Current Population Survey—for individuals' reports of their current or cumulative experience of divorce. The data themselves are rather good, and scholars have used them to estimate the likelihood of divorce over a lifetime or at certain lengths of marriage. But questions on marital history are included in the Current Population Survey only every five years. The National Survey of Family Growth was last conducted in 1995. All in all, the federal government's withdrawal from this area of vital statistics is a loss to scholars, policy makers, and students—and to the general public interested in information about divorce (Ooms 1999; Wetzstein 1999).

it is marrying before age twenty that carries the highest risk (Bramlett and Mosher 2001, pp. 5–6; Heaton 2002). But the fact remains that since the 1970s, divorce rates are higher than they have ever been in our society. Then too, some demographers argue that informal separation is underreported, so real marital dissolution rates may be higher than official divorce statistics indicate (Bumpass, Raley, and Sweet 1995).

Historians, however, point to the fact that marriage can be dissolved by death as well as divorce. Until the mid-to-late 1970s, increasing divorce and decreasing mortality canceled each other out. The longer lifespan attained in the twentieth century gives people who remain married more time together. Married couples are now much more likely to reach their fortieth anniversary than they were at the beginning of the twentieth century, and children less likely to be bereft of both parents (Skolnick 2001).

Still, the continuation of a high incidence of divorce and separation contributes to the increased prevalence of single-parent families. Between 1970 and 2000, married-couple families declined from 87 percent to 69 percent of families with children. Single-mother families increased from 12 percent to 26 percent of families with children, and single-father households increased from 1 percent to 5 percent (Fields and Casper 2001, p. 7).

Single-father households may have increased as a result of judges becoming more favorable to father custody, but there are no definitive studies on whether fathers are now winning more contested custody cases.[1] It may be the case that mothers have become less inclined to insist on sole custody. Fatherhood scholar James Levine thinks that "We're seeing some weakening of the constraints on women to feel they can only be successful if they are successful mothers," so they are more willing to concede custody to willing fathers (quoted in Fritsch 2001b, p. 4–4). In any case, as of 2002, 56 percent of custodial fathers were divorced or separated, while 20 percent were never married and 25 percent widowed or still legally married (Grall 2003).

The general increase in single-mother families is largely a result of two other factors besides divorce: rising nonmarital birth rates and a greater tendency for unmarried mothers to establish independent households. In 2002, 44 percent of custodial single mothers were divorced or separated, while 31 percent were never married and 25 percent widowed or currently married (Grall 2003). White women were much more likely to become single parents through divorce (50 percent) than through nonmarital childbearing (30 percent). But for African American and Hispanic women, single parenthood was more often due to nonmarital childbearing. Both black and Hispanic single mothers are more likely than white single mothers to live with larger family groupings rather than establishing separate households (Fields and Casper 2001, pp. 8–9 and Table 4).

Children's living arrangements vary greatly by race and ethnicity, as Figure 16.3 indicates. Asian and white non-Hispanic children are most apt to be living

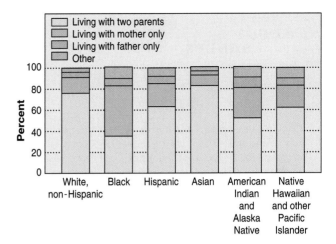

FIGURE 16.3

Living arrangements of children under eighteen by race/ethnicity, 2000. *Other* includes children who are living in the homes of relatives, in foster homes, or with other nonrelatives, or who are heads of their own households.

Source: Adapted from Lugaila and Overturf 2004, Table PHC-T-30b.

in two-parent families (with biological parents or a parent and stepparent). A majority of Hispanic, American Indian, and Hawaiian/Pacific Islander children live with two parents, while just under a majority of black children are living in a single-mother household (Lugaila and Overturf 2004).

We need to note in summing up the statistics that the high divorce rate does not mean that Americans have given up on marriage. It means that they find an unhappy marriage intolerable and hope to replace it with a happier one (Glenn 1996). But a consequence of remarriages—which have higher divorce rates than first marriages (Goldstein 1999, p. 410)—is an emerging trend of **redivorce**. Consequently, many who divorce—and their children—can expect several rapid and emotionally significant transitions in family structure and lifestyle. They will experience stress and the need for adjustment. The stability of remarriages is addressed in greater detail in Chapter 17, and the general topic of family stress is the focus of Chapter 15.

▪ Why Are Couples Divorcing? ▪

Various factors can bind marriages and families together: economic interdependence; legal, social, and

---

1. One study of appealed custody cases found that by 1995, court decisions were almost equalized, with 45 percent of mothers and 42 percent of fathers awarded sole custody and 9 percent sharing custody in disputed cases (Mason and Quirk 1997).

moral constraints; and the spouses' relationship itself. The binding strength of some of these factors has lessened, however. "[A]ll Western [and some non-Western] countries have been moving toward a less familistic set of attitudes and toward greater individual investments in self, career, and even personal growth and goals" (Goode 1993, p. 81).[2]

Economic Factors

Traditionally, as we've seen, the family was a self-sufficient productive unit. Survival was far more difficult outside of families, so members remained economically bound to one another. But today, because family members no longer need one another for basic necessities, they are freer to divorce than they once were (Coontz 1997b).

Families are still somewhat interdependent economically. As long as marriage continues to offer practical benefits, economic interdependence will help hold marriages together. The economic practicality of marriages varies according to several conditions. We'll look briefly at two: income level—and how it relates to divorce—and wives' employment.

DIVORCE AND SOCIAL CLASS A positive relationship generally exists between marital stability and education and family income, particularly men's earnings. Home ownership reduces the risk of divorce. The higher the social class as defined in these terms, the less likely a couple is to divorce, while income loss has been found to increase the likelihood of divorce (White and Rogers 2000). Both the stress of living with inadequate finances and the failure to meet expectations for economic or educational attainment seem to contribute to marital instability (White 1990). This situation, together with the tendency of low-income groups to marry relatively early, helps explain why less-well-off families have the highest rates of marital disruption, including divorce, separation, and desertion.

WIVES IN THE LABOR FORCE The upward trend of divorce and the upward trend of women in the labor force have accompanied each other historically (Sayer and Bianchi 2000). But are they causally connected? Many other changes have occurred during the same time period.

Much research, though not all, indicates that wives' employment in itself makes no difference in marital quality (Rogers 1999; Sayer and Bianchi 2000). As Chapter 12 points out, whether husbands are supportive of their wives' employment and share in housework *does* relate to wives' marital satisfaction. *Conflict theorists* would notice that marital conflict might increase if women go into the job market but their husbands do not take over an equitable share of the domestic tasks.

Although it may not affect marital quality, employment might nevertheless contribute to a divorce by giving an unhappily married woman the economic power, the increased independence, and the self-confidence to help her decide on divorce—called the **independence effect** (Sayer and Bianchi 2000; Schoen, Astone, Rothert, Standish, and Kim 2002). In *exchange theory* terms (see Chapter 3), an employed woman has alternatives to the marriage in that she can now better support herself should she divorce.

Some economists and sociologists posit that marriages are most stable and cohesive when husbands and wives have different and complementary roles—the husband the primary earner, while the wife bears and rears children and is the family's domestic and emotional specialist. Drawing on *exchange theory*, they assert that economic interdependency in marriage is a strong bond holding a marriage together; women's economic independence threatens the viability of the marriage (Becker 1991; Oppenheimer 1997b).

But much recent research does *not* support the premise that specialized roles and economic interdependence are necessary to marital stability (Schoen et al. 2002). Moreover, there is an **income effect** to women's employment. That is, among low-income couples, a wife's earnings may actually help to hold the marriage together by counteracting the negative effects of poverty on marital stability (Ono 1998; Heckert, Nowak, and Snyder 1998). In an era of stagnating male wages and economic insecurity, the income effect may be stronger and more pervasive (Sayer and Bianchi 2000).

The effects of women's employment on marriage may depend on gender ideology. For couples today, expectations of role sharing are common. And shared experiences of employment are more likely to foster

2. Some non-Western countries (e.g., Indonesia, Japan, some Arab countries, and Taiwan) traditionally had stable, relatively high divorce rates. Those have declined with modernization and industrialization; a companionate marriage pattern has somewhat replaced the sharp separation of husbands and wives and polygamous marriage of traditional culture (Goode 1993, p. 329).

© Royalty-Free/CORBIS

Deciding to divorce is difficult. Couples struggle with concerns about the impact on children and feelings about their past hopes and current unhappiness.

intimacy in a relationship than are divergent everyday lives. To explore whether wives' employment has positive or negative effects on divorce proneness, researchers Sayer and Bianchi (2000) analyzed a national sample survey based on 3,339 female respondents interviewed around 1988 and again around 1994. When gender ideology, features of the marriage, and other variables related to likelihood of divorce were taken into account, there was no direct effect of women's employment on divorce. This result was even more true of higher-earning couples even though the wife would have a higher absolute level of income should she divorce. The desirability of the marriage relationship was a much more important factor in predicting divorce in this study.

Another researcher (South 2001), who used a different data set and time frame (1969–1993), got different results, however. He had hypothesized that some features of the present-day context of women's market work might connect women's employment to divorce. Institutional supports for working mothers would enable mothers who divorce to anticipate coping better with employment than they might have in the past. Shift work is especially disruptive to marriages. And the workplace provides a possible locus for the formation of extramarital relationships that may threaten a marriage. Finally, given the support that changing gender roles and women's employment now have in the culture, contemporary employed women may feel less concerned about the impact of their outside work on the marriage and less inclined than earlier employed women to compensate by doing more housework or being deferential.

While South recognized that women's employment offered some positive benefits to marriage, all in all, what he found in his research is that over the last twenty-five years, the more hours of employment women engage in and the more their income increases relative to that of their husbands, the more likely the couple is to divorce.

These two studies have opposite results. Sayers and Bianchi, who find no effect of wives' employment, have probably done the better job of accounting for other factors. South has covered more ground in terms of time. That two well-done studies differ leaves us uncertain about the impact of women's employment as a possible contributing factor to current rates of divorce.

It is probably the case that there is considerable variety in the impact of women's employment and earnings on a marriage. For example, Brennan, Barnett, and Gareis (2001), in a study conducted in the Boston area, found that some men were disturbed when their wives had higher earnings, while others were not. Men who placed a great importance on their own earning power had higher marital quality when their earnings increased relative to their wives' earnings. Women generally—and those men who didn't care that much about relative earnings—were not affected when wives earned more than husbands did. The researchers concluded that "times have changed and the theories may need to change" (p. 179)—role specialization is no longer so important to couples. Moreover, women's recent educational gains seem to be a stabilizing factor in marriage (Heaton 2002).

High Expectations of Marriage

Many observers attribute our high divorce rate to the view that Americans' expectations are too high these days. People increasingly expect marriage to provide a happy, emotionally supportive relationship. This is an essential family function, yet too-high expectations for intimacy between spouses may push the divorce rate upward (Glenn 1996; also VanLaningham, Johnson, and Amato 2001). Research has found that couples whose expectations are more practical are more satisfied with their marriages than are those who expect completely loving and expressive relationships (Troll, Miller, and Atchley 1979; see also White and Booth 1991). Although many couples part for serious and specific reasons, others may do so because of unrealized (often unrealistic) expectations and general discontent.

The Changed Nature of Marriage

To say that societal constraints against divorce no longer exist would be an overstatement; nevertheless, barriers have weakened (Knoester and Booth 2000). Virtually no respondents in a study of marital cohesion mentioned stigma or disapproval as a barrier to divorce (Previti and Amato 2003). Some social scientists believe that as divorce has increased, marriage has been redefined as a nonpermanent—or, at best, a semipermanent or hopefully permanent relationship (Safilios-Rothschild 1983).

Marriage was originally a social institution directed toward the practical purposes of economic support and responsible child rearing. We now see marriage as a *relationship*. Emphasis on the emotional relationship over the institutional benefits of marriage results in its being defined as not necessarily permanent (Glenn 1996; Cowan and Cowan 1998). As Frederick Engels, a colleague of Karl Marx and an early family theorist, noted: "If only the marriage based on love is moral, then also only the marriage in which love continues." Engels went on to argue—as have some counselors and others over the past three decades—that "if affection definitely comes to an end or is supplanted by a new passionate love, separation is a benefit for both partners as well as for society" (Engels 1942 [1884], p. 73). The changing nature of marriage is a worldwide phenomenon, as far as the industrialized world is concerned (Giddens 2003).

The impetus to divorce when love declines is more likely to be expressed in a world in which indi-

viduals live longer and so have a longer period of time in which to maintain their feelings for each other. Thus, some scholars have explained the current high divorce rate in terms of increasing longevity (Skolnick 2001). This explanation is widely accepted, but as sociologist Norval Glenn points out, in the past, those who survived long enough to have children also lived to later ages. Deaths were concentrated in the very young and very old portions of the population (Glenn 1997b, pp. 204–205).

SELF-FULFILLING PROPHECY Defining marriage as semipermanent can become a self-fulfilling prophecy (Becker 1991, p. 329). Increasingly, spouses may enter the union with reservations, making "no definitive gift" of themselves (Durkheim 1951, p. 271). If partners behave as if their marriage could end, it is more likely that it will. Experts on the family who had at first remained optimistic even as divorce rates rose are now concerned about what they see as eroding family commitment (Glenn 1996). Others speculate that whatever cultural change is producing the current stability, the decline in divorce rates could "break the momentum" of the self-fulfilling prophecy (Goldstein 1999, p. 414).

MARITAL CONVERSATION—MORE STRUGGLE AND LESS CHITCHAT Besides being visibly less permanent, marriage has changed in another way. Structural changes such as increased economic inequality and work–family conflict, cultural changes regarding gender roles, and individualism versus familism "have made marriage a more difficult arrangement since 1980" (VanLaningham, Johnson, and Amato 2001, p. 1335). No longer are the normative role prescriptions for wives, husbands, or children taken for granted. Consequently, marriage entails continual negotiation and renegotiation among members about trivial matters as well as important ones.

When family roles were culturally agreed on, members were likely to "share the indifferent 'intimacies' of the day" (Simmel 1950, p. 127)—in other words, to engage in relatively inconsequential conversation about events outside the family. Today, however, as family roles are less precisely defined, "marital conversation is more struggle and less chitchat. . . . The conversation turns inward, to the question of defining the makeup of the family, . . . [to the] forging and fighting for identities" (Wiley 1985, pp. 23, 27). As one divorced woman put it,

It had taken Howard and me only about ten minutes to pronounce the "I do's," but we would spend the next ten years trying to figure out who, exactly, was supposed to do what: Who was responsible for providing child care, finding babysitters and tutors, driving car pools, for which periods and where? (Blakely 1995, p. 37)

One result is that, increasingly, marriage and family living feel like work, and living alone may look restful by comparison.

Decreased Social, Legal, and Moral Constraints

Another important influence on the divorce rate has been that the social constraints that once kept unhappy partners from separating operate less strongly now. The official posture of many—though not all—religions in the United States has changed to be less critical of divorce than in the past.[3] *No-fault divorce* laws, which exist in all fifty states,[4] have eliminated legal concepts of guilt and are a symbolic representation of how our society now views divorce. But it does not appear that changes in the law have themselves led to more divorce. Rather, legal change seems to have followed the trajectory of cultural attitudes and behavioral practice regarding divorce.[5]

A related factor may be the rise of individualistic values. Americans increasingly value personal freedom and happiness over commitment to the family (Glenn 1996; Whitehead 1997). They believe marriages ought to be happy if they are to continue. Poll data indicate

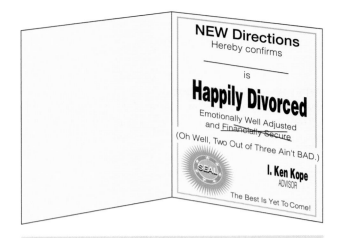

With greeting cards like this one in our everyday (popular) culture, it is clear that the stigma associated with divorce in the past has decreased. Consumer items such as this are marketed to the divorced and their friends, but their presence in the culture also helps to legitimize divorce.

that four-fifths of young people (age thirty-one in 1993) find divorce acceptable even when children are affected (Thornton and Young-DeMarco 2001, p. 1019).

At the same time, the American public holds somewhat ambivalent attitudes about divorce. In one poll, one-half of those surveyed thought divorce should be harder to get (Thornton and Young-DeMarco 2001, p. 1021; specific proposals to make divorce harder to obtain are addressed later in this chapter). It also appears that some unhappily married individuals postponed divorce until their children were older. An

---

3. The Roman Catholic church has retained its prohibition on divorce and remarriage. Communicants may obtain a legal divorce for practical purposes, but are not permitted to remarry in the church or maintain a nonmarital cohabiting or sexual relationship. However, they may apply for a church annulment, which would treat the marriage as having been flawed from its inception (Paulson 2001). An annulment permits Catholics to leave a marriage and form a new one, remaining in good standing in the church. The number of annulments obtained by Catholics has risen dramatically, to more than 55,000 worldwide in 2002 (most annulments are granted in the United States) (Allen 2004). The annulment process has been sharply criticized, most notably by spouses who have opposed an annulment of their own marriage (e.g., Kennedy 1997, p. 19) and by the Pope (Kurson 1998).

4. Some authorities say that "most states" have no-fault divorce laws (Buehler 1995), while others cite all fifty states (Nakonezny et al. 1995). There is a gray area in that some "no-fault" divorces may require a specific period of separation rather than only a declaration by one of the parties that the marriage is over.

Some states have retained fault divorce alongside no-fault. In those states, a spouse may choose to file for divorce under a fault provision, alleging that the other partner has committed whatever statutory faults are relevant to the state's marital dissolution laws. New York is a particularly difficult venue to categorize in that no-fault divorce is available in principle, but only if the parties file for a formal separation first and then are in complete agreement on all of the provisions of the anticipated divorce (Fritsch 2001c).

5. Nakonezny, Shull, and Rodgers (1995) published an article purporting to prove that no-fault divorce laws have played a causative role in increasing divorce rates. Sociologist Norval Glenn (1997a) responded with an effective critique of their methodology, concluding that "the adoption of no-fault divorce in itself had very little direct effect on divorce rates" (p. 1023; and see Rodgers, Nakonezny, and Shull's 1997 response). Further research supports the view that the passage of divorce laws does not account for divorce trends (Wolfers 2004).

AARP (2004) survey of 1,147 men and women aged forty to seventy-nine found that 58 percent of the men and 37 percent of the women said they had postponed seeking a divorce for five years or more because of concerns about children (AARP 2004).

Intergenerational Transmission of Divorce

Having parents who divorced increases the likelihood of divorcing (Amato and DeBoer 2001; Teachman 2002). Researchers are not certain of the reasons for this. It is possible that (1) divorcing parents are models of divorce as a solution to marital problems or that (2) children of divorced parents are more likely to exhibit personal behaviors that interfere with maintaining a happy marriage (Amato 1996). There is also evidence that children of divorced parents marry at younger ages and are more likely to experience premarital co-habitation and births; these factors are associated with higher divorce rates (Heaton 2002; Teachman 2002).

In a test of the two major hypotheses about **intergenerational transmission of divorce**, using longitudinal data, Amato and DeBoer (2001) found support for the *commitment to marriage* hypothesis. When parents remained married, they served as models of optimism about solving marital problems.

A hypothesis about the importance of *parents as models of relationship skills and interpersonal behavior* was not supported in this study (although there is other evidence for it—e.g., Amato 1996). The conclusion of Amato and DeBoer's study is that "it is actual termination of the marriage rather than the disturbed family relationships that affects children. Divorce, rather than conflict, undermines children's faith in marriage" (p. 1049).

As more parents divorce, more offspring would seem to be vulnerable to the intergenerational transmission of divorce. Yet research spanning the period 1973–1996 finds a decline of almost 50 percent of the rate of intergenerational transmission of divorce. It may be that acceptance of divorce is now so widespread that having parental models is less significant for marital stability (Wolfinger 1999).

Other Factors Associated with Divorce

So far in this section we have looked at socio-historical, cultural, and intrafamilial factors that encourage high divorce rates. Another way to think about divorce is to recognize that certain demographic and behavioral factors are related to divorce rates. These include the following:

- As we have already seen, *remarried mates are more likely to divorce.*
- *Premarital sex and cohabitation before marriage increase the likelihood of divorce, but only when these take place with someone other than the future marital partner* (Wu and Penning 1997; Heaton 2002).
- *Premarital pregnancy and childbearing increase the risk of divorce in a subsequent marriage* (Heaton 2002; Teachman 2002).
- Young children stabilize marriage (Hetherington 2003). Hence, *remaining child-free is associated with a higher likelihood of divorce.*
- *Race and ethnicity are differentially associated with the chances of divorcing.* A government survey reported that as of 1996 (latest detailed data) blacks had the highest cumulative divorce percentage (48 percent of first marriages), with non-Hispanic whites and Hispanics at about 40 percent and Asian/Pacific Islanders with a much lower cumulative divorce percentage (24 percent) (Kreider and Fields 2002, p. 18).

  Even among those who are similarly educated and/or earning similar incomes, African Americans are more likely than non-Hispanic whites to divorce (Lawson 1999). At the same time, economic and educational factors seem to play a much more significant role in marital stability among African Americans than in other racial/ethnic groups (Sweeney and Phillips 2004). All in all, the difference in marital stability among blacks and whites remains a puzzle (White and Rogers 2000).

- Not surprisingly, when marital partners are emotionally mature and possessed of good interpersonal communication skills "they are better able to deal with the bumps along the road to marital survival" (Hetherington 2003, p. 322).

So far we have been discussing social, economic, cultural, and interpersonal communication factors associated with divorce. Now we will look at some of the common marital complaints voiced by divorcing couples—their own accounts of why they have decided to end their marriages.

Common Marital Complaints

Marital complaints given by the divorced include the partner's infidelity, alcoholism, drug abuse, jealousy, moodiness, violence, and, much less often, homosexuality, as well as perceived incompatibility and growing apart (White 1990; Amato and Rogers 1997; Amato and Wallin 2001). A more general conclusion to be drawn from research is that deficiencies in the emotional quality of the marriage lead to divorce (Martin and Luke 1991).

Probably the most systematic study of marital complaints at time of divorce was done by Gay Kitson (1992), who asked some 200 white and black residents of suburban Cleveland "What caused your marriage to break up?" Blacks and whites did not differ in their tendency to offer the most common complaints.

The complaint most frequently mentioned by both men and women was "lack of communication or understanding" (by 27 percent of men and 32 percent of women). "Joint conflict over roles" was ranked second by men (21 percent). Men's third-ranked "explanation" was "not sure" (18 percent). ("Not sure" was offered as a complaint by less than 2 percent of divorcing women—gender differences in communication and emotional processes would seem at work here.) "Different backgrounds" and "change in interests" made up the remainder of men's top five complaints.

For women, complaints about "alcohol," men being "untrustworthy and immature," going "out with the boys," and "extramarital sex" were most common after communication problems (Kitson 1992, pp. 118–131, and Table 5.3). Infidelity, incompatibility, drinking and drug use, and growing apart continue to be major explanations offered for their divorce (Amato and Wallin 2001).

Social scientists and counselors vary in their reactions to the explanations given by those who divorce. It is "striking . . . that so few empirical studies of divorce take these individual complaints seriously" (White 1990, p. 908). On the other hand, counselors suggest that some common complaints—about money, sex, and in-laws, for example—are really arenas for acting out deeper conflicts, such as who will be the more powerful partner, how much autonomy each partner should have, and how emotions are expressed.

The personal decision about divorce involves a process of balancing alternatives against the practical and emotional satisfactions of one's present union.

▪ Thinking About Divorce: ▪ Weighing the Alternatives

Not everyone who thinks about divorce actually gets one. As divorce becomes a more available option, spouses may compare the benefits of their union to the projected consequences of not being married (Kurdek 1998).

Marital Happiness, Barriers to Divorce, and Alternatives to the Marriage

One model of deciding about divorce, derived from exchange theory (see Chapter 3) by social psychologist George Levinger, posits that spouses assess their marriage in terms of the *rewards* of marriage, *alternatives* to the marriage (possibilities for remarriage or fashioning a satisfying single life), and *barriers* to divorce (for example, religious beliefs against divorce, parental pressure to stay married, common friendship networks, joint economic investments, and consideration of children's interests) (Levinger 1965). Let's look at what research has to say about this theory of divorce.

Respondents to the Marital Instability Across the Life Course surveys named children, along with religion and lack of financial resources, as *barriers* to divorce in open-ended interviews (Previti and Amato 2003). In quantitative data from these surveys, researchers (Knoester and Booth 2000) found that concern about a child's suffering from divorce, fear of losing the child, and religious beliefs were perceived to be barriers to divorce by at least 40 percent of those interviewed several times between 1983 and 1992. Dependence on spouse was reported as a barrier by about 30 percent, and (concerns about) financial security seen as a barrier by 24 percent.

When the researchers examined the relationship between actual divorces and these perceived barriers, they found that only three of nine barriers studied were associated with a lower likelihood of divorce: (1) when wife's income was a smaller percentage of the family income, (2) when church attendance was high, or (3) when there was a new child (Knoester and Booth 2000). It may be that individuals who remain married and those who divorce are not always aware of the factors influencing their decisions.

There is considerable research evidence that young children do serve as a barrier to divorce (Heaton 2002). Affection for their children and con-

When parents consider divorce, they often think about the potential impact on their children—and that is a barrier to divorce.

cern about the children's welfare after divorce discourages some parents from dissolving their marriage.

Long marriages are less likely to end in divorce. One reason for this, in addition to the marital bond itself, is that common economic interests and friendship networks increase over time and help stabilize the marriage at times of tension (White and Booth 1991; Kurdek 1998). When divorce does occur in a longer marriage, it may be partly related to dissatisfaction with one's marital relationship at the onset of the empty nest, when the couple's grown children leave home (Hiedemann, Suhomlinova, and O'Rand 1998).

While some barriers do seem to have an impact on decisions to divorce, it is the *rewards* of marriage—love, respect, friendship, and good communication—that are most effective in keeping marriages together

(Previti and Amato 2003). "Generally, marriages that have built up positive emotional bank accounts through respect, mutual support, and affirmation of each person's worth are more likely to survive" (Hetherington 2003, p. 322).

Alternatives, the third element of Levinger's theory, was found to be the least important in decisions to divorce (Previti and Amato 2003).

"Would I Be Happier?"

Yet, some married people may ask themselves whether they would be happier if they were to divorce. This is not an easy question to answer. Some people may prefer to stay single after divorce, but many partners probably weigh their chances for a remarriage. Waite and Gallagher (2000) report that marital status is an important correlate of happiness, as 40 percent of marrieds are "very happy," compared to 18 percent of divorced people (p. 67). Married people also have better physical and emotional health.

One study of 1,755 whites in Detroit found an interesting wrinkle, however. Higher levels of depression among the divorced were not apparent among those who saw themselves as escaping marriages with serious, long-term problems (Aseltine and Kessler 1993). Other research (Ross 1995) used data from a national sample of 2,031 adults to compare depression levels among those with no partners and those in relationships of varying quality. As Figure 16.4 shows, people without a partner are likely to be depressed—but those in unhappy relationships are likely to be even more depressed. Compared to unhappily married people, divorced individuals display generally better physical and emotional health and higher morale (Wickrama, Lorenz, Conger, and Elder 1997).

Marriage can and often does provide emotional support, sexual gratification, companionship, and economic and practical benefits, including better health. But unhappy marriages do not provide all (or in some cases, any) of these benefits (Wickrama et al. 1997) and may be a factor in poorer health (Elias 2004). "In short, it appears that at any particular point in time most marriages are 'good marriages' and that such marriages have a strong positive effect on well-being and that 'bad marriages' have a strong negative effect on well-being" (Gove, Style, and Hughes 1990, p. 14).

Still, in some cases, partners might be happier trying to improve their relationship rather than divorc-

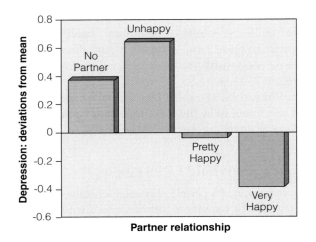

FIGURE 16.4

Depression levels of people with no partner and in relationships of varying quality. Depression is measured by a modified Center for Epidemiological Studies Depression Scale (CES-D), and scores are calculated in terms of deviation from the mean (average) rating of depression in the sample. Married and unmarried partners' scores were similar for each relationship status, so they were combined. Those with *unhappy* relationships were more depressed than those with *no partner,* while those in *very happy* relationships had the lowest levels of depression.

Source: From "Reconceptualizing Marital Status as a Continuum of Social Attachment" by C. E. Ross, 1995, *Journal of Marriage and the Family, 57,* pp. 129–140, fig. 2. Copyright © 1995 by the National Council on Family Relations. Reprinted by permission of the authors and the National Council on Family Relations, 3989 Central Avenue, N.E. Suite 550, Minneapolis, MN 55421.

ing. In a recent interview, sociologist Linda Waite reports that couples may be in the lowest grouping on marital satisfaction, yet, if they don't divorce, five years later two-thirds of the unhappily married describe themselves as "very happy." Those who divorce do not report themselves as very happy later: "If you are playing the odds in favor of happiness, . . . 'staying married is the better bet'" (Waite, quoted in Peterson 2001, p. 8D).

Improvements in these marriages came about through the passage of time (children got older, job or other problems improved); because partners' efforts to work on problems, make changes, and communicate better were effective; or because individual partners made personal changes (travel, work, hobbies, or emotional disengagement) that enabled them to live relatively happily despite an unsatisfying marriage (Waite et al. 2002).

One must decide whether divorce represents a healthy step away from an unhappy relationship that cannot be satisfactorily improved or is an illusory way to solve what in reality are personal problems. Going to a marriage counselor may help partners become more aware of the consequences of divorce so that they can make this decision more knowledgeably.

MARITAL SEPARATION Some marital partners who have separated do make efforts to reconcile. Little research has been done on marital separation. But "each year [it appears] that a substantial number of separated women try to save their marriage" (Wineberg 1996, p. 308). Wineberg's study, using a sample of white women from the 1987 National Survey of Families and Households, found that 44 percent of the separated women attempted reconciliation. Half of the resumptions of marriage that followed took place within a month, suggesting that those separations may have been impulsive and soon regretted. Virtually no marriages were resumed after eight months of separation.

Only one-third of the reconciliations "took," that is, resulted in a continued marriage (Wineberg 1996). For a majority of individuals, first separation from the spouse denotes permanent dissolution (Binstock and Thornton 2003). Researcher Wineberg cautions that "not all separated couples should be encouraged to reconcile since a reconciliation does not ensure a happy marriage or that the couple will be married for very long" (p. 308).

Is Divorce a Temporary Crisis or a Permanent Stress?

Initially, studies portrayed divorce as a temporary crisis, with adjustment completed in two to four years. Some scholars now consider divorce to be a lifetime chronic stress for both children and adults (Wallerstein, Lewis, and Blakeslee 2000). While outcomes vary, divorce researcher Mavis Hetherington maintains that 70 percent of those who obtain a divorce have a "good enough" postdivorce adjustment (Hetherington and Kelly 2002).

It appears likely that both temporary crisis and chronic stress are outcomes of divorce—some divorced people are rather permanently derailed from an economically and emotionally comfortable life, while others are mostly recovered after several years. Of the latter, those who may be considered "recovered," some have diminished well-being in some respects, while others arrive at a higher level of life satisfaction (Amato 2000, 2003a; Hetherington and Kelly 2002). Difficulties and adjustments don't seem to vary much by race or ethnicity (Amato 2000).

■ Getting the Divorce ■

One of the reasons it feels so good to be engaged and newly married "is the rewarding sensation that out of the whole world, you have been selected. One of the reasons that divorce feels so awful is that you have been de-selected" (Bohannan 1970b, p. 33). Sociologist Paul Bohannan (1970b) analyzed the divorce experience in terms of six different facets, or "stations": the emotional, the legal, the community, the psychic, the economic, and the co-parental divorce. Experience in each of these realms varies from one individual to another; some stations, such as the co-parental, do not characterize every divorce. Yet the six stations capture the complexity of the divorce experience. In this section, we will examine the first four stations listed above; we will explore the economic and co-parental aspects of divorce in greater detail later in this chapter.

The Emotional Divorce

Emotional divorce involves withholding positive emotions and communications from the relationship (Vaughan 1986), typically replacing these with alienating actions and words. Partners no longer reinforce but rather undermine each other's self-esteem through endless large and small betrayals: responding with blame rather than comfort to a spouse's disastrous day, for instance, or refusing to go to a party given by the spouse's family, friends, or colleagues. As emotional divorce intensifies, betrayals become greater.

In a failing marriage, both spouses feel profoundly disappointed, misunderstood, and rejected (Brodie 1999). Because the other's very existence and presence is a symbol of failure and rejection, the spouses continually grate on each other. The couple may want the marriage to continue for many reasons—continued attachment, fear of being alone, obligations to children, the determination to be faithful to marriage vows—yet they may hurt each other as they communicate their frustration by look, posture, and tone of voice.

Not all divorced people wanted or were ready to end their marriage, of course. It may have been their spouse's choice. Not surprisingly, research shows that the degree of trauma a divorcing person suffers usually depends on whether that person or the spouse wanted the dissolution, at least partly because the one feeling "left" experiences a greater loss of control (Wilder and Chiriboga 1991) and has much mourning yet to do— the divorce-seeking spouse may have already worked through his or her sadness and distress (Amato 2000). Even for those who actively choose to divorce, however, divorce and its aftermath may be unexpectedly painful.

The Legal Divorce

A **legal divorce** is the dissolution of the marriage by the state through a court order terminating the marriage. The principal purpose of the legal divorce is to dissolve the marriage contract so that emotionally divorced spouses can conduct economically separate lives and be free to remarry.

Two aspects of the legal divorce make marital breakup painful. First, divorce, like death, creates the need to grieve. But the usual divorce in court is a rational, unceremonial exchange that takes only a few minutes. Lawyers have been trained to solve problems logically and to deal with clients in a detached, businesslike manner. Although divorcing spouses might need and want them to, very few divorce attorneys view their role as helping with the grieving process. Also, the divorcing individuals may feel frustrated by their lack of control over a process in which the lawyers are the principals. In one study of divorced women, virtually all had complaints about their lawyers and the legal system (Arendell 1986).

A second aspect of the legal divorce that aggravates the misery is the adversary system. Under our judicial system, a lawyer advocates his or her client's interest only and is eager to "get the most for my client" and "protect my client's rights." Opposing attorneys are not trained to and ethically are not even supposed to balance the interests of the parties and strive for the outcome that promises most mutual benefit.

NO-FAULT DIVORCE A major change in the legal process of divorce has been the introduction of **no-fault divorce**. This revision of divorce law was intended to reduce the hostility of the partners, as well as to permit an individual to end a failed marriage readily. Before the 1970s, the fault system predominated. A party seeking a divorce had to prove that she or he had "grounds" for divorce (that is, a reason within a state's divorce law), such as the spouse's adultery, mental cruelty, or desertion. A fault divorce required a determination that one party was guilty and the other innocent; if both were at fault, the divorce was not granted. The one judged guilty rarely got custody of the children, and the judgment largely influenced property settlement and alimony awards, as well as the opinion of friends and family (Weitzman 1985). Such a protracted legal battle of adversaries—with at least one party trying to prove that the other was in some respects a bad person and responsible for the break-up—increased hostilities and diminished chances for cooperative negotiation, not to mention a civil post-divorce relationship and successful co-parenting.

Beginning with California in 1970 and continuing until all states passed no-fault legislation,[6] divorce was redefined as "marital dissolution" and no longer required proof and a legal finding of a "guilty" party and an innocent one. Under no-fault divorce, a marriage is legally dissolvable when it is "irretrievably broken." But approaching marital breakdown and dissolution in neutral terms is emotionally difficult. One result, observers suspect, is that those divorcing spouses who are bent on blaming the other may fight the same court battle, but as a child-custody suit or support issue instead.

A final note on the legal divorce is that, by definition, it applies only to marriage. There is no legal forum in which cohabitants, whether heterosexual or gay/lesbian, may obtain a divorce. Some couples may be cohabiting precisely to avoid the prospect of going to court should their relationship sour. However, they are likely to find that the absence of a venue in which to resolve separation-related disputes in a standardized way is also a problem. ("The Legal Side of Living Together" is discussed in more detail in Chapter 9.) Cohabiting couples may be able to avail themselves of mediation services.

DIVORCE MEDIATION **Divorce mediation** is an alternative, nonadversarial means of dispute resolution by which a couple, with the assistance of a mediator or mediators (frequently a lawyer–therapist team), nego-

tiate the terms of their settlement of custody, support, property, and visitation issues. The couple work out a settlement best suited to the needs of their family. In the process, it is hoped that they learn a pattern of dealing with each other that will enable them to resolve future disputes.

Divorce mediation is a fairly recent development in the United States. Research indicates that couples who use divorce mediation have less relitigation, feel more satisfied with the process and the results, and report better relationships with ex-spouses (Marlow and Sauber 1990) and children (Beck and Blank 1997). However, various women's advocacy groups have noted that mediation as it is currently practiced may be biased against females, who report being labeled "unladylike" or "vindictive" if they refuse to give in on a point (Lonsdorf 1991; Woo 1992b). Moreover, sociologist Judith Wallerstein (1998) points out that the positive effects of divorce mediation for children may be overstated:

> What protects children in the divorced family is cooperative, civilized coparenting. The resolution of conflict may represent a necessary step along the road, but resolution of legally defined conflict, alone, which has been the central concern of the courts and the mediation movement, is not sufficient to protect the child. (p. 79)

The Community Divorce

Marriage is a public announcement to the community that two individuals have joined their lives. Marriage usually also joins extended families and friendship networks and simultaneously removes individuals from the world of dating and mate seeking. The **community divorce** refers to ruptures of relationships and changes in social networks that come about as a result of divorce. These changes in social networks may be disappointing or embittering, and are often confusing. At the same time, divorce also provides the opportunity for forming new ties.

KIN NO MORE? Given the frequency of divorce, most extended families find themselves touched by it. Grandparents fear losing touch with grandchildren, and this does happen. In response, states have passed statutes authorizing grandparents to seek visitation rights in some circumstances. All fifty states now have grandparent visitation laws (which vary in whether

---

6. See Footnotes 4 and 5.

Divorce affects the extended family as well as the nuclear one. In some families, grandparents may lose touch with grandchildren, while in others they may become more central figures of support and stability.

© Paul Barton/CORBIS

they apply to death, divorce, or intact marriage). However, a Supreme Court decision struck down Washington's grandparent visitation law (*Troxel v. Granville* 2000). The status of other states' laws, which may differ in important respects, is now uncertain. At present, courts do not seem to issue grandparent visitation orders in the face of parental objections (Henderson and Moran 2001; Hsia 2002).

Where involvement of grandparents does not encounter legal resistance, grandparents very commonly become closer to grandchildren, as adult children turn to grandparents for help (Coleman, Ganong, and Cable 1997) or grandchildren seek emotional support (Spitze et al. 1994). Researchers and therapists have concluded that

> these relationships work best when family members do not take sides in the divorce and make their primary commitment to the children.
>
> Grandparents can play a particular role, especially if their marriages are intact: symbolic generational continuity and living proof to children that relationships can be lasting, reliable, and dependable. Grandparents also convey a sense of tradition and a special commitment to the young. . . . Their encouragement, friendship, and affection has special meaning for children of divorce; it specifically counteracts the children's sense that all relationships are unhappy and transient.

> For the fortunate children in our study who could rely on their extended families, the world seemed a more stable, predictable place. (Wallerstein and Blakeslee 1989, p. 111)

Indeed, children who were close to their grandparents had fewer problems adjusting to their parents' divorce (Lussier, Deater-Deckard, Dunn, and Davies 2002). Of course, more and more grandparents' own marriages are not intact today. Nevertheless, one can assume that even a loving, divorced grandparent could add to the support system of a grandchild of divorce.

Women are more likely than men to retain in-law relationships after divorce, particularly if they had been in close contact before the divorce and if the in-law approves of the divorce (Serovich, Price, and Chapman 1991). Relationships between former in-laws are more likely to continue when children are involved.

One study looked at the general character of postdivorce extended-kin relationships. This study found that in half of the cases, the kinship system included **relatives of divorce** and *relatives of remarriage* (Johnson 1988, p. 168; see also Stacey 1990; remarriage is discussed in Chapter 17). This was most likely to occur with paternal relatives, who, of course, needed to keep in touch in order to see grandchildren living with custodial mothers. When fathers had custody, they too were likely to have contact with their former spouse's extended family. But the most commonly retained tie was between a grandmother and her former daughter-in-law. Still, relationships between former in-laws may deteriorate or vanish (Ambert 1988). In any case, grandchildren were more likely to remain closest to maternal grandparents, as mothers typically grew closer to and relied more on their parents after divorce (Lussier et al. 2002).

After their divorce, adult children's relationships with their own parents may change. According to one study:

> Members of both generations had to revise their expectations of the other, and members of the older generation found themselves in a situation of having to give more of themselves to a child than they had expected to do at their stage of life. They were often forced into a parenting role, and this greater involvement provided more opportunity to observe and comment on their adult child's life. . . .
>
> Even so, there was extensive contact between generations, which did not decrease over time. . . . Nevertheless, there appeared to be incongruity in their expectations. Adult children were more likely to feel that parents should be available to help them with their emotional problems than their parents felt was appropriate. Divorcing children did not want their parents to interfere in childrearing or offer unsolicited advice, while their parents felt they could voice their concerns. (Johnson 1988, pp. 190–191)

There was considerable variation in these relationships within the sample of fifty-two adult–child dyads followed over several years in Johnson's study. But most older parents espoused "modern values of personal freedom and self-fulfillment" (p. 191); that is, they did not criticize the decision to divorce from a traditional perspective.

Couples who divorce later in life and/or after long marriages often find socioemotional support from their adult children (Gander 1991), but this is not always the case and may be truer for mothers than for fathers (Wright and Maxwell 1991).

FRIENDS NO MORE? Important changes in one's lifestyle almost invariably mean changes in one's community of friends. When they marry, people usually replace their single friends with couple friends. When couples divorce, they also change communities. Separating from one's former community of friends and in-laws is part of the pain of divorce. More than three-quarters of the women in one study reported losing friends during or after the divorce (Arendell 1986).

Divorced people may feel uncomfortable with their friends who are still married because activities are done in pairs. Conversely, a married couple may find that a friend's divorce challenges them to take another look at their own marriage, an experience that may cause them to feel anxious and uncomfortable with the divorced friend. Also, couple friends may be reluctant to become involved in a conflict over allegiances and often experience their own sense of loss and grief. A common outcome is a mutual withdrawal, during which the divorced person feels heightened loneliness.

Like many newly married people, those who are newly divorced must find new communities to replace old friendships that are no longer mutually satisfying. The initiative for change may in fact come not only from rejection or awkwardness in old friendships but also from the divorced person's finding friends who share with him or her the new concerns and emotions of the divorce experience. Priority may also go to new relationships with people of the opposite sex; for the majority of divorced and widowed people, building a new community involves dating again.

The Psychic Divorce

Psychic divorce refers to the regaining of psychological autonomy through emotional separation from the personality and influence of the former spouse. In the process, one learns to feel whole again and to have faith in one's ability to cope with the world (Brodie 1999). In psychic divorce, one must distance oneself from the still-loved aspects of the spouse, from the hated aspects, and "from the baleful presence that led to depression and loss of self-esteem" (Bohannan 1970b, p. 53).

Not all divorced people fully succeed at psychic divorce: "The 'graph' of divorce recovery is typically jagged rather than straight, and each forward step is likely to be matched by a retreat" (Sprenkle 1989, p. 175). But counselors point out that this stage is a necessary prerequisite to a satisfying remarriage.

To be successful, a psychic divorce requires a period of mourning. The experience of loss is real (Brodie 1999). Just as a gradual process of emotional estrangement starts long before the actual legal event of divorce, the partners' emotional involvement often continues long after. This "persistence of attachment"

(Weiss 1975) is real for both spouses and should be understood and addressed.

There are at least three stages in the mourning process. The first, which typically occurs before the legal divorce, is denial. Sometimes, a person's inability to accept the divorce manifests itself in physical illnesses, accidents, or even suicide attempts. Eventually, however, the frustration of emotional divorce leads partners to face facts. They may say to each other, "We can't go on like this."

A second stage, characterized by anger and depression, follows this realization. These feelings often alternate, so recently divorced people feel confused. Sometimes one's feelings resemble those of an ex-wife, who asked a counselor, "How come I miss so terribly someone I couldn't stand?" (Framo 1978, p. 102).

In the third stage, ex-spouses take responsibility for their own part in the demise of the relationship, forgive themselves and the mate, and proceed with their lives: The psychic divorce is then complete. As long as one views the ex-spouse as an object of ongoing anger and is preoccupied with the emotional residue of the marriage, the psychic divorce has not been accomplished. Counseling can help—personal counseling or the divorce workshops that are provided by social service agencies, religious groups, or other community organizations.

Deciding knowledgeably whether to divorce means weighing what we know about the consequences of divorce. The next section examines the economic consequences of divorce.

The Economic Consequences of Divorce

Increasingly, social scientists and policy makers worry about the economic consequences of divorce, especially for children, but also for women.

Divorce, Single-Parent Families, and Poverty

Figure 16.5 displays the proportions of children who were living in poverty in 2000 for the largest racial/ethnic groups, comparing poverty rates by family type. As you can see, 33 percent of all children who reside in mother-only, single-parent families live in poverty. This compares to 6 percent of those living in married-couple families. Among Hispanics and blacks, 41 percent of children in mother-headed, single-parent families live in poverty, compared to 6 percent in black married-couple families and 17 percent in Hispanic married-couple families.

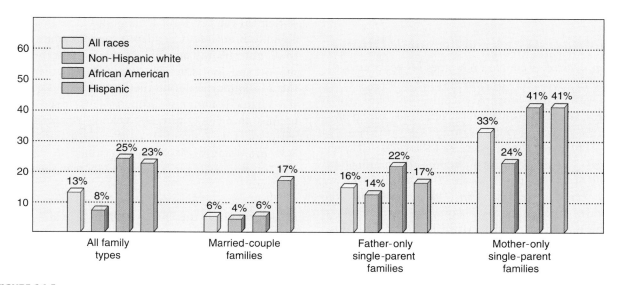

FIGURE 16.5

Percentage of families with incomes below the poverty level. Poverty status of families with children under eighteen by race/ethnicity and type of family, 2000.

Source: Dalaker 2001. Annual Demographic Supplement. Historical Poverty Tables, Table 4.

The relationship between racial/ethnic minority status and poverty is consistent across family types: Non-Hispanic whites are much less likely than other racial/ethnic groups to be poor. At the same time, the relationship between family type and poverty is consistent across racial/ethnic categories: Children in mother-headed single-parent families are significantly more likely to live in poverty than children in married-couple households. Children in father-only families are less likely to be poor than children in mother-only families but are not as well off as children in married-couple families (with the exception of Hispanic families, where father-only and married-couple families have the same rate of poverty).

Looking at such figures, some policy makers argue that single-parent families are the major cause of poverty. Opponents of this view argue that financial deprivation exists (although to a lesser extent) even in married-couple families and that racial/ethnic discrimination and low wages, particularly for women, account for poverty (Mauldin 1990; Lichter and Eggebeen 1994; Lichter and Landale 1995). Still others point out that for many individuals—those who have experienced family violence, for example—divorce is the lesser of two evils.

Meanwhile, a consistent research finding is that divorce is related to a woman's (but not always to a man's) lowered economic status (Arditti 1997). Why is this the case?

Husbands, Wives, and Economic Divorce

Upon divorce, a couple undergoes an **economic divorce** in which they become distinct economic units, each with its own property, income, control of expenditures, and responsibility for taxes, debts, and so on.

WOMEN LOSE FINANCIALLY IN DIVORCE Sociologist Lenore Weitzman addressed the financial plight of divorced women and their children in her book *The Divorce Revolution* (1985), comparing the postdivorce economic decline of women with children to the improved standard of living of ex-husbands.[7] Research continues to present a consistent picture of postdivorce economic decline for women (Peterson

1996; Smock, Manning, and Gupta 1999; McManus and DiPrete 2001). A study that compared former spouses in terms of their postdivorce economic situations found that wives with custody had only 56 percent of the income-relative-to-needs that noncustodial fathers had (Bianchi, Subaiya, and Kahn 1999).

What accounts for this situation? A fundamental reason for the income disparity between ex-husbands and their former wives is men's and women's unequal wages and different work patterns (Smock 1993). Despite women's greater participation in the labor force, their reduction in employment during childbearing and child-rearing years means they have foregone opportunities for career development. "[A]lthough women are moving toward greater equality with men in the labor market, they remain more economically vulnerable when marriages end" (Bianchi, Subaiya, and Kahn 1991, p. 196).

It is also the case that women who are custodial parents must depend on child support from the other parent to meet their new single-parent family's expenses. Child support amounts are set relatively low, and much child support remains unpaid (as discussed in a later section of this chapter) (Teachman and Paasch 1993).

A third reason has to do with the typical division of property in divorce. Most state laws require a division of property that is specified as "equitable" (Buehler 1995). Behind the idea of a fair property settlement run two legal assumptions: The first is that a family is an interdependent economic unit. A man could not earn the money he earns without the moral support and domestic work of his wife, whether or not she was employed during the marriage. A minority of states have community property laws based on the premise that family property belongs equally to both partners. The remaining states, the majority, have laws promising a divorced wife either an equitable (fair) or an equal (exactly the same) share of the marital property.

But a second assumption is that property consists of such tangible items as a house or money in the bank, or other investments. Yet, except for very wealthy people, the valuable "new property" (Glendon 1981) in today's society is the earning power of a professional degree, a business or managerial position, work experience, a skilled trade, or other "human capital." When property is divided in divorce, the wife may get an equal share of tangible property, such as a house or savings, but usually that does not put her on an equal

---

7. Weitzman's book brought attention to the different economic outcomes of divorce for men and women. Her figures later proved to be erroneous, but a reanalysis of her data still showed a substantial loss for divorced women compared to a slight gain for men (Peterson 1996).

footing with her former husband for the future. An even split of the marital property may not be truly equitable if one partner has stronger earning power and benefits, but the other does not, and if the parent with custody of the children has a heavier child support burden. Put another way, dividing property may be easy compared to ensuring that both partners and their children will have enough to live on comfortably after divorce or at least will be on a similar financial footing.

This situation partially results from the assumption of legislators and the courts that women and men have—or soon would have—equal earning power. When divorce laws were reformed in the 1970s, a presumptive goal of self-support for both parties was included (Buehler 1995). Some financially dependent spouses have been awarded short-term **spousal support** or *maintenance*[8] in the form of *rehabilitative alimony*, in which the ex-husband pays his ex-wife "just enough cash to put her back on her feet, or at least in a word-processing class" (Stern 1994). But in many, perhaps most cases, this is not truly enough to enable the woman to reestablish herself financially, and it is not that commonly awarded in any case. Courts award spousal support in only 10 percent to 20 percent of all divorce cases, and in the majority of cases the amount awarded is low (Buehler 1995, p. 110).

Full-time homemakers, often older, who suddenly find themselves divorced and without adequate support (called **displaced homemakers**) are particularly disadvantaged by this system (Coontz 1997a, p. 23). Many have few or no marketable skills, no employment record, and no pension. Nor are they in a position to pursue education or job training followed by long-term employment. The results of divorce may be devastating for them. Some activists have argued that many

© Jeff Greenberg/PhotoEdit

Women and their children experience a substantial decline in their standard of living after a divorce. They may need to move to less-expensive—and less-desirable—housing and away from former neighborhood, school, and friends.

wives—particularly those who left the labor force to raise children or to help with their husband's career—deserve not alimony but an *entitlement*, the equivalent of severance pay for work done at home during the length of a marriage (Weitzman 1985). Social Security provisions now do allow an ex-wife who had been married at least ten years to collect 50 percent of the amount paid her ex-husband, which is the same rate at which still-married spouses collect Social Security.

Families of women and children would be much better off after divorce, of course, if they received the child support due them. For many years, the child support awarded to the **custodial parent**, usually the mother, was often not received, and states made little effort to collect it on her behalf. A series of federal laws mandating state-level action have changed that situation considerably, though it is not yet perfect (child support will be discussed in more detail later in the chapter). Meanwhile, the bottom line is that "Most women would have to make heroic leaps in the labor or marriage market to keep their losses as small as the losses experienced by the men from whom they separate" (McManus and DiPrete 2001, p. 266).

---

8. These terms have replaced *alimony* to describe a former spouse's support payment to his or her ex-spouse following divorce. Historically, alimony was a payment of husband to wife resting on the assumption that the contract of marriage included a husband's lifetime obligation to support his wife and children. Traditionally, of course, the wife had not been employed, but instead had primary responsibility for making a home and bearing and raising children. Popular myth had it that ex-wives lived comfortably on high alimony awards. But in fact, courts awarded alimony to only a small minority of wives.

In 1979 the U.S. Supreme Court determined that laws against sex discrimination should make alimony gender-neutral—in essence, transforming the basis for spousal support from the common-law tradition of husbands' and wives' specialized roles into an economic partnership model. Along with this and the reform of other divorce-related laws came a presumption that spouses should be self-supporting after divorce (Buehler 1995, pp. 102–111).

In the future, more women who are divorced will have a history of employment and a current job, although they will still be likely to have the heavier expenses of a custodial parent.

SOME MEN WIN, MOST LOSE FINANCIALLY IN DIVORCE The postdivorce economic situation of men has undergone some rethinking, as circumstances have changed since the 1970s. Men and women are now more economically interdependent in marriage because married women are likely to be in the labor force. A study covering the years 1980–1993 (McManus and DiPrete 2001) found that except for those who earned 80 percent of their family's predivorce income, men also lose economically in divorce (or in a separation from a cohabiting union). The chief reason for their declining standard of living is the loss of the partner's income. A secondary reason is that most men are required to provide child support for their children.[9] This was always true in principle, but only in recent years have government authorities been more successful at securing payment, and at standardized amounts that are often higher than what was previously the case. Moreover, many men at all income levels voluntarily contribute more than is required.

Thus, while there are no women "winners" in divorce, a majority of men lose too. Only men with 1950s-type marriages gain economically in divorce. "Studies that focus on women's outcomes have yet to unearth any comparable core of women who gain financially following union dissolution" (McManus and DiPrete 2001, p. 266).

Child Support

Child support involves money paid by the noncustodial to the custodial parent to support the children of a now-ended marital, cohabiting, or sexual relationship. Because mothers retain custody in the preponderance of cases, the vast majority of those ordered to pay child support are fathers.

During the 1980s and 1990s, the federal government made sweeping changes in child support award

and collection policies and procedures. Before that, child support was negotiated as part of each individual divorce/separation agreement or paternity case. Payment was difficult to enforce, and collection of past-due amounts depended on the custodial parent's coming forward to prove delinquency.

Policy and procedural changes in child support were prompted by four separate but overlapping concerns:

1. The move to privatize support obligations for children in an effort to lessen welfare spending ("Child Support Enforcement" 1996).

2. Concern about the growing proportion of children in female-headed, single-parent households.

3. Alarm about the growing proportion of children living in poverty.

4. Public recognition of the inequitable economic consequences of divorce for women, compared to men.

The Child Support Amendments (1984) to the Social Security Act, together with the Family Support Act (1988) and the child support provisions of the Personal Responsibility and Work Opportunity Reconciliation Act (1996), did the following: (1) encouraged the establishment of paternity and consequent child support awards, (2) required states to develop numerical guidelines for determining child support, (3) required periodic review of the award levels so that they could be amended to keep up with inflation and to ensure that the noncustodial parent continued to pay an appropriate share of his or her income, and (4) enforced payments through locator services to find nonpaying noncustodial parents and collect the support due. States were required to implement automatic wage withholding of child support, and some states imposed penalties such as driver's license revocation, seizing a delinquent payer's assets, or garnishing his or her wages ("Child Support Collected" 1995; Pirog-Good and Amerson 1997; Garfinkel, Meyer, and McLanahan 1998).

These policies have yielded some positive results in terms of increased child support. In 2002, 59 percent of custodial parents had child support awards, and three-fourths of those received payments. Only 45 percent received full payment of what was due, however, and the amounts involved are not very impressive. Child support awards have historically been and

---

9. Income loss runs about one-third for white married men who separate from their households. While their income decreases, there are fewer people to be supported, so that per-capita income may actually increase. However, child support and loss of the partner's income explain why men's as well as women's standard of living often declines even though the income men control may not (McManus and DiPrete 2001).

continue to be small. Custodial mothers received $3,200 in 2002; custodial fathers received $2,900. Some parents do make additional contributions in the form of gifts, clothes, food, medical costs (beyond health insurance), and camp or child care (Grall 2003).

Some research suggests that the principal reason for a noncustodial parent's failure to pay is unemployment or underemployment (Meyer and Bartfeld 1996). Among families in which the absent parent has been employed during the entire previous year, payment rates are 80 percent or more. Not so when unemployment is involved. Hence,

> coercive child-support collection policies, such as automatic wage withholding, will have only limited success. Divorced fathers (perhaps in distinction to never married fathers) appear to pay quite well if they are fully employed. . . . The key to reducing poverty thus appears to be the old and unglamorous one, of solving un- and underemployment, both for the fathers and the mothers. (Braver, Fitzpatrick, and Bay 1991, pp. 184–185)

The child support issue is complex. Some noncustodial fathers provide support in ways other than money (Teachman 1991), such as child care: "In some cases attempts to locate and require payments from such fathers may result in severing these ties" (Peterson and Nord 1990, p. 539). Compliance may be related to the noncustodial parent's involvement in the child's life. Seventy-seven percent are in compliance when they have either joint custody or visitation arrangements, only 56 percent when the parent has neither (Grall 2003).

Two suggested alternative solutions are guaranteed child support and a children's allowance. Both are based on the principle of society-wide responsibility for investing in all children. With **guaranteed child support**, a policy adopted in France and Sweden, the government sends to the custodial parent the full amount of support awarded to the child, even though this sum may not have been received from the noncustodial parent. It then becomes the government's responsibility to collect the money from the parent who owes it (Salt 1991). A second alternative, a **children's allowance**, provides a government grant to all families—married or single-parent, regardless of income—based on the number of children they have. All industrialized countries except the United States have

some version of a children's allowance. However, the present political and economic climate in the United States makes it unlikely that such measures would be adopted.

As another approach to securing payment of child support, both the federal government and some states are targeting low-income fathers with special programs. Low-income fathers are typically expected to pay a higher portion of their income in child support than middle-class fathers, resulting in a spiral of expanded debt and often withdrawal from their children (Bianchi, Suybaiya, and Kahn 1999; Harden 2002). With the encouragement of grants from the federal government, some states have begun experimenting with "responsible fatherhood" programs. Recognizing that there are low-income fathers who want to provide support for their children, but lack the income to do so, these multifaceted programs provide employment services, family support, and mediation services.

Thus far there are only modest results. There is some increase in child support payments, though not the dramatic improvement in the lives of men and their children that program designers had hoped for (Johnson, Levine, and Doolittle 1999; Pearson et al. 2003; Reichert 1999). The programs have barely begun, however, and their future potential is not yet known.

We turn now from examining the economics of post-divorce family support to a broader examination of the aftermath of divorce for children.

▪ Divorce and Children ▪

FOCUS ON CHILDREN More than half of all divorces involve children under eighteen, and about 40 percent of children born to married parents will experience marital disruption (Amato 2000). How do separation and divorce affect children? There is strong disagreement on the answer to this question. In fact, just by reading media interviews with researchers and policy makers, it is easy to spot the "polemical nature of divorce scholarship" (Amato 2000, p. 1270).

Experiences and outcomes of children depend on the circumstances before and after the divorce. While the divorce experience is psychologically stressful and, in most cases, financially disadvantageous for children, children in high-conflict marriages seem to benefit from a divorce. Living in an intact family characterized by unresolved tension and alienating conflict can cause as great or greater emotional stress and a lower sense of self-worth in children than living in a supportive single-parent family (L'Heureax-Dube 1998). On the other hand, when the conflict level in the home is low, children have poorer outcomes. They are likely taken by surprise by a divorce and seem to suffer more emotional damage, partly because it is difficult for them to see the divorce as necessary in this situation—the more common one today (Amato and Booth 1997; Booth and Amato 2001; Morrison and Coiro 1999).

The Various Stresses for Children of Divorce

During and for a period of time after divorce, children typically feel guilty, depressed, and anxious (Hetherington 1973; Wallerstein and Kelly 1980). In one longitudinal study of children's postdivorce adjustment, psychologists Judith Wallerstein and Joan Kelly interviewed all of the members of some sixty families with one or more children who entered counseling at the time of the parents' separation in 1971. Wallerstein and her colleagues reinterviewed children at one year, two years, five years, ten years, and in some cases, fifteen years later and finally again at the twenty-five-year point (Wallerstein et al. 2000).

In the initial aftermath of the divorce, children appeared worst in terms of their psychological adjustment at one year after separation, many having declined significantly since their parents' separation. By two years postdivorce, households had generally stabilized. At five years, many of the 131 children seemed to have come through the experience fairly well; 34 percent "coped well"; 29 percent were in a middle range of adequate, though uneven, functioning; while 37 percent were not coping well, with anger

playing a significant part in the emotional life of many of them (Wallerstein and Kelly 1980). If the middle group is considered to be well enough adjusted, one can say that two-thirds of these children emerged from the divorce intact. (In Figures 16.6 and 16.7, children's drawings suggest the ways the children have discovered to accommodate their parents' divorce.)

After following her sample of children of divorce for ten years, Wallerstein and colleagues found the majority to be approaching economic self-sufficiency, to be enrolled in educational programs, and, in general, to be responsible young adults. Even so, at that point and later, the overall impression left by the Wallerstein research is one of loss. Children may lose fathers, who become uninterested and detached; they may lose mothers, who are overwhelmed by the task of supporting the family and managing a household alone and who either see little chance of happiness for themselves or are busy pursuing their "second chance." Children of divorce experience the loss of daily interaction with one of their parents, and they get less help with homework (Astone and McLanahan 1991). Boys were particularly lost, seeming to find it difficult to establish themselves educationally, occupationally, or maritally (Wallerstein and Blakeslee 1989).

One of Wallerstein's findings is that girls, who seemed, as in other studies, far better adjusted than boys in the early postdivorce years, evidenced a "sleeper effect," which surfaced as they reached adolescence and young adulthood (Wallerstein and Lewis 1998). They were beset with "lingering sorrow" and seemed hesitant about marriage and childbearing. Said one of Wallerstein's respondents, "How can you expect commitment when anyone can change his mind?" The "sleeper effect" described by Wallerstein has not been generally supported by other studies (e.g., Dunlop and Burns 1995; and see Coontz 1997a). But other

FIGURE 16.6

This drawing reveals the creative coping of a child whose parents are divorcing. She has figured out a way to include her father as well as keep within the bounds of reality as she knows it.

Source: From *The Difficult Divorce*, by Marla Beth Isaacs et al. Copyright © 1986 by Basic Books, Inc. Reprinted by permission of Basic Books, a member of Perseus Books, L.L.C.

Harriet · Sister · Mother / Father / Harriet Sister

Sister   Susan   Mother   Father

FIGURE 16.7

The sister of the child who drew Figure 16.6 used a jagged line to separate her father from the rest of the family.

Source: From *The Difficult Divorce*, by Marla Beth Isaacs et al. Copyright © 1986 by Basic Books, Inc. Reprinted by permission of Basic Books, a member of Perseus Books, L.L.C.

researchers have come to think, like Wallerstein, that divorce has long-term effects (Cherlin 2000; Amato 2000; Amato and Sobolewski 2001). Divorce is a "risk factor for multiple problems in adulthood" (Amato 2000, p. 1279). ("Issues for Thought: How It Feels When Parents Divorce" illustrates many points raised in this section.)

Sociologist Paul Amato expected the negative effects of divorce to lessen as more families got divorces and schools and community groups instituted programs to help children cope with their parents' divorce. But instead, reviewing research done in the 1990s, he finds that children of divorce continue to have lower outcomes than children from intact families in the areas of academic success, conduct, psychological adjustment, social competence, and self-concept, and they have more troubled marriages and weaker ties to parents, especially fathers, as well (Amato 2003b; also Kelly and Emery 2003). The "small but persistent gap in well-being observed in earlier decades persisted into the 1990s" (Amato 2000, p. 1278).

CHILDREN OF REDIVORCE In some cases, a new stepparent can prove a stabilizing and supportive influence, and so a parent's divorce from the stepparent may be a blow to the child. Counselors—who now encounter children who have experienced divorce more than once—encourage divorced stepparents to maintain contact with their former stepchildren. Wallerstein found that half of the children in her study had experienced a second divorce of one or both parents.

LESS MONEY, LESS EDUCATION, MORE PROBLEMS Children whose parents have divorced will more than likely have less money available for their needs. This is especially significant because some of

the negative impact of divorce can be attributed to economic deprivation (McLanahan and Sandefur 1994).

We may think here in terms of children at the lower end of the socioeconomic scale, but Wallerstein found considerable deprivation among middle-class children compared to what they could have expected had their parents remained married. Because divorce settlements seldom include arrangements to pay for children's college education[10] and family savings are often eroded by the costs related to divorce, financing higher education may be especially problematic for children of divorced parents (Wallerstein and Blakeslee 1989; also Powers 1997). Wallerstein, who followed her sample into young adulthood, was surprised at the extent of their educational downward mobility. Sixty percent of the study children were likely to receive less education than their fathers; 45 percent were likely to receive less than their mothers. Even divorced fathers who had retained close ties, who had the money or could save it, and who ascribed importance to education seemed to feel less obligated to support their children through college. Along with this came a favoring of boys over girls. In Wallerstein's study, fathers who helped with college were twice as likely to help sons (Wallerstein et al. 2000).

---

10. Some states have passed laws that require divorced parents who are financially able (this would usually be a father) to pay for college, and in other states, courts have made decisions in individual cases to require parental support for college. They have taken the position that parents must provide a level of support that the child would have received had they stayed married (Schembari 2003). Those arguing against requiring divorced parents to pay for college point out that married parents are not similarly obliged to cover college expenses for children. One must also consider that the children themselves may not have established a good precollege record.

How It Feels When Parents Divorce

In the following excerpts, five children of divorce tell their own stories. As you will see, they talk about issues raised in this chapter.

Zach, Age 13

Even though I live with my Dad and my sister lives with my Mom, my parents have joint custody, which means we can switch around if we feel like it. I think that's the best possible arrangement because if they ever fought over us, I know I would have felt I was like a check in a restaurant—you know, the way it is at the end of a meal when two people are finished eating and they both grab for the check and one says, "I'll pay it," and the other one says, "No, this one is mine," and they go back and forth, but secretly neither one really wants it, they just go on pretending until someone finally grabs it, and then that one's stuck. . . .

My parents knew they couldn't live together, but they also knew it was nobody's fault. It was as if they were magnets—as if when you turn them the opposite way they can't touch. . . . Neither of them ever blamed the other person, so they worked it out the best they could—for their sakes and ours, too.

Nevertheless, it's very sad and confusing when your parents are divorced. I think I was five when they separated. . . .

When my parents first split up, it affected me a lot. . . . I got real fat and my grades went way down, so I went to a psychologist. She made me do a lot of things which seemed dumb at the time—like draw pictures and answer lots of silly questions. . . . My school work suffered because I was so distracted

thinking about my situation that I couldn't listen very well, and for a long time I didn't work nearly as hard as I should have. Everyone told me I was an underachiever, and my parents tell me I still am, but I don't think so. What I do think is that I am a lot more independent—a go-out-and-do-it-yourself person. . . .

I've heard about kids who are having all these problems because their parents are getting divorced, but I can't understand what the big deal is. I mean, it's upsetting, sure, but just because your parents are separated it doesn't mean you're going to lose anybody. . . . It's not something I talk about very much. Most of my friends would rather talk about MTV than talk about divorce.

Ari, Age 14

When my parents were married, I hardly ever saw my Dad because he was always busy working. Now that they're divorced, I've gotten to know him more because I'm with him every weekend. And I really look forward to the weekends because it's kind of like a break—it's like going to Disneyland because there's no set schedule, no "Be home by five-thirty" kind of stuff. It's open. It's free. And my father is always buying me presents.

My mom got remarried and divorced again, so I've gone through two divorces so far. And my father's also gotten remarried—to someone I don't get along with all that well. It's all made me feel that people shouldn't get married—they should just live together and make their own agreement. Then, if things get bad, they don't have to get divorced and hire lawyers and sue each other.

And, even more important, they don't have to end up hating each other.

I'd say that the worst part of the divorce is the money problem. It's been hard on my Mom because lots of times she can't pay her bills, and it makes her angry when I stay with my father and he buys me things. She gets mad and says things like, "If he can buy you things like this, then he should be able to pay me." And I feel caught in the middle for two reasons: First, I can't really enjoy whatever my Dad does get for me, and second, I don't know who to believe. My Dad's saying, "I don't really owe her any money," and my Mom's saying he does. Sometimes I fight for my Mom and sometimes I fight for my Dad, but I wish they'd leave me out of it completely.

Jimmy, Age 10

My mother divorced my father when I was two and a half. My Mom took me to live with her, but she couldn't cope, and so she was going to put me up for adoption. There was a big scene because my Dad didn't want that to happen, and so I went to live with him . . . for the next three years—until the first "snatch." . . .

One weekend while I was visiting [my mother], she and Don [my mother's boyfriend] packed up their car with a lot of stuff and we all piled in. I kept asking her, "Where are we going?" And finally she said, "Take a wild guess." I guessed a couple of places and finally I said Florida because that was the one place she had talked about a lot—she had some relatives who lived there. I didn't have any idea how far away

Florida was, so I asked her how long it would take us to get there, and she said about two days. All I could think of was, "Wow! We're going to Florida!" I remember asking her, "What about Daddy?" And she just said, "Don't worry about it."

After we got there she put me in school, but since she didn't want to send for my school records, she started me in first grade instead of putting me in second grade, where I belonged. And I had to have all three of my shots over again, which I hated. The reason she couldn't write for my school records is because then my father might find out where I was and she didn't want that to happen.

School was really easy for me and I'd just sit there being bored. It seems like all we did was learn the alphabet, which I already knew, and play with blocks and do dumb things like that. I didn't have to stay for long, though, because one day my mother decided we were going to move without paying our next rent. We packed up all our belongings, climbed out the window, got in the car, and drove off. We slept in the car that night, and the next day we found a nice apartment. I went to another school, which was better because at least I was in second grade, where I belonged, but I didn't stay there for very long, either. One morning the principal came into my classroom and told me to pick up my stuff—to take some crayons and paper—because some man had come to pick me up. The man told me he was a detective and showed me a picture of my father. . . . Before I knew what was happening we were driving off in his car. . . .

That night [my father and I] went out to eat with the detective, and the next day my father said he had two surprises for me. The first surprise was that we were going bowling, and later on he said that the second surprise was that we were all going to go on a big airplane. That's how I got to take my first plane ride—which was a lot of fun! The three of us flew back to New York and then went to my Dad's house—my old home—and that night we had a big party with lots of balloons and cake. Everyone was there—all my father's relatives and friends came and everyone was hugging me. The next week, my father won custody again, and this time he actually got to keep me because my mother didn't even try to get me back. It's hard to believe, but I haven't seen her since then, which is about four years now. At first I was glad because I was so happy to settle down and be in a good school, but then I started feeling sad, too, because I missed my mother. I still miss her.

Caleb, Age 7

My parents aren't actually divorced yet. But they're getting one soon. They stopped living together when I was one and a half, and my Dad moved next door. Then, when I was five, he moved to Chicago, and that hurt my feelings because I realized he was really leaving and I wouldn't be able to see him every day. My father's an artist, and when he lived next door to us in New York, I used to go to his studio every day and watch him when he was welding. I had my own goggles and tools, and we would spend many an hour together. I remember when I first heard the bad news that he was moving away, because I almost flipped my lid. My father said he would be divorcing my Mom but that he wouldn't be divorcing me and we'd still see each other a lot—but not as often. I started crying then and there, and ever since then I've been hoping every single second that he'd move back to New York and we'd all live together again. I don't cry much anymore because I hold it back, but I feel sad all the same.

I get to visit my father quite often. And Shaun. He's my collie. My cat lives in New York with me and Mom. Whenever I talk with Daddy on the phone I can hear Shaun barking in the background. The hardest thing for me about visiting my father is when I have to leave, and that makes me feel bad—and mad—inside. I still wish I could see him every day like I did when I was little. It's hard to live with just one person, because you don't have enough company, though my Mom has lots of great babysitters and that helps a little.

Tito, Age 11

It seems like my parents were always fighting. The biggest fight happened one night when we were at a friend's house. Mommy was inside the house crying, and Daddy was out on the sidewalk yelling and telling my mother to come down, and my little sister, Melinda, and I were outside with a friend of my father's. We were both crying because we were so frightened. Then Daddy tried to break the door down, so Mommy came downstairs. And then the police cars came and Daddy begged Mommy to stay quiet and not say anything and to give him another chance, but she was so unhappy that she got into one of the cars. I was only four but I remember everything.

We stayed with our cousin for about two months, and during this time I saw my father whenever he visited us at my grandmother's house. . . . I was always happy to see him, but sometimes it made me feel sad, too, because I would look forward to our visits so much, and then when we were together it

continued

could never be as perfect as I was hoping it would be. He was still so angry at Mommy's leaving him that it was hard for him to feel anything else for anybody. . . .

About the time of the divorce I started to get into fights with other kids, and my mother got worried. She thought I must be feeling very angry and having a hard time expressing my feelings, so she took me to a therapist. . . . We got really close and he'd talk to me about my problems with my Dad. This went on for about two years, and during that time he helped me realize that the divorce was better for me in the long run because our home was

more relaxed and there wasn't so much tension in the air.

The other thing that happened around this time was that my mother found out about an organization called Big Brothers, where I could have another male figure in my life. . . . They paired me off with a guy named Pat Kelly, and we've been getting together every weekend for a couple of years. . . . Pat and I do a lot of things like play baseball or video games and eat hot dogs. But the best thing we do is talk—like when I do something good in school I can tell him, and if I feel sad I can talk about that, too. His parents got divorced when he

was twelve, and so we have a lot of the same feelings.

Critical Thinking

The families that people grow up in and their social class influence their life options. How is that point evident in these children's stories? Overall, do you see these stories as hopeful, dismaying, or both? Why? Were there any particular points that you found surprising or interesting?

Source: Excerpts from *How It Feels When Parents Divorce*, by Jill Krementz, 1984. Copyright © 1984 by Jill Krementz. Reprinted by permission of Alfred A. Knopf, Inc.

Children of divorce feel less protected economically; unlike children from intact families, whose parents usually continue to support them through college and sometimes even beyond. . . . Many children of divorce cannot help but feel that when child support stops, something else stops in the social contract between parent and child. (Wallerstein and Blakeslee 1989, p. 157)

We've given considerable attention to the research of Wallerstein and colleagues because it has been very influential. "Judith Wallerstein's research on the long-term effects of divorce on children has had a profound effect on scholarly work, clinical practice, social policy, and the general public's views of divorce" (Amato 2003b, p. 332). But in fact, this is not a definitive study, and the strongly negative conclusions about divorce that Wallerstein sometimes presents seem overstated. "Many of Wallerstein's conclusions about the longterm consequences of dissolution on children are more pessimistic than the evidence warrants" (Amato 2003b, p. 332).

A frequently noted bias of the study (e.g., Ahrons 1994, p. 273) is that these families were specifically invited to obtain counseling in exchange for participation in the study and may have been more troubled than other families going through a divorce. Because the Wallerstein study is based on a small sample of children whose parents responded to an offer of free

counseling, it has been challenged by studies with more-representative samples. These studies reach less negative conclusions.

The absence of a comparison group in the Wallerstein study design to tell us how children in intact homes are faring renders the study inconclusive. Whenever possible, Wallerstein referred to other studies, and her latest book (Wallerstein, Lewis, and Blakeslee 2000), done at the twenty-five-year point past separation, does include a comparison group selected and interviewed recently. But this is not the same as a comparison to children of nondivorced parents made in conjunction with the longitudinal study. The lack of a control group remains a point of criticism of the Wallerstein research.

Critics of Wallerstein's research—or of how it has been presented to the public—point to a disconnect between her first book, *Surviving the Break-Up* (Wallerstein and Kelly 1980), and her two later books (Wallerstein and Blakeslee 1989; Wallerstein et al. 2000) and other public statements. *Now* she attributes the adult problems of her research participants to their parents' divorce. Earlier she described the inadequate mental health and parental functioning that characterized many of the families prior to divorce and the adjustment difficulties of their children that had already been observed (Ahrons 1994, p. 76, footnote 16; Cherlin 1999, p. 423; 2000). Some have also noted that in the early 1970s, when the study began, women were less likely to be in the labor force than they are now. The need for an inexperienced mother to enter the labor force created an adjustment problem in the 1970s that would be less of a stress now. Another methodological problem, although one shared by other longitudinal studies, is that continual interviewing of children about the impact of the divorce might create a mindset in which any problems are given a divorce-generated interpretation (Coontz 1997a; and see Ahrons 1994, pp. 273–276).

However, concern that children of divorce are disadvantaged does not rest solely on Wallerstein's small sample and what many see as her exaggerated presentation of the dangers of divorce (Cherlin 1999). In fact, "the main point of contention between Wallerstein and her critics involves the pervasiveness and strength" of the effects of divorce. A "persuasive body of evidence supports a moderate version of [her] thesis" (Amato 2003b, pp. 338–339).

REASONS FOR NEGATIVE EFFECTS OF DI-VORCE ON CHILDREN Besides differing on the overall impact of divorce, researchers and theorists offer a variety of explanations for why and how divorce could adversely affect children. Amato (1993) has summarized five theoretical perspectives found in the literature concerning the reasons for negative outcomes. We present his typology below, along with some relevant research by others:

1. The **life stress perspective** assumes that, just as divorce is known to be a stressful life event for adults, it must also be so for children. Furthermore, divorce is not one single event but a process of associated events (Morrison and Cherlin 1995; Lorenz et al. 1997) that may include moving—often to a poorer neighborhood (South, Crowder, and Trent 1998)—changing schools, giving up pets, and losing contact with grandparents and other relatives, which may be distressing for children. This perspective holds that an accumulation of negative stressors results in problems for children of divorce.

2. The **parental loss perspective** assumes that a family with both parents living in the same household is the optimal environment for children's development. Both parents are important resources, providing children love, emotional support, practical assistance, information, guidance, and super-

vision, as well as modeling social skills such as cooperation, negotiation, and compromise. Accordingly, the absence of a parent from the household is problematic for children's socialization.

3. The **parental adjustment perspective** notes the importance of the custodial parent's psychological adjustment. Put another way, the quality of parenting is an important element in children's adjustment to divorce. Supportive and appropriately disciplining parents facilitate their children's well-being. However, the stress of divorce is compounded for parents by the associated stressors that follow, such as lower economic well-being. Such stress may lead to parental depression (Lorenz et al. 1997), which may impair a parent's child-rearing skills, with probably negative consequences for children. Divorced parents do spend less time with children. Divorced parents, compared to married parents, are "less supportive, have fewer rules, dispense harsher discipline, provide less supervision, and engage in more conflict with their children" (Amato 2000, p. 1279).

4. The **economic hardship perspective** assumes that economic hardship brought about by marital dissolution is primarily responsible for the problems faced by children whose parents divorce (Entwisle and Alexander 1995; Amato 2000). Indeed, economic circumstances do condition diverse outcomes for children—perhaps accounting for one-half of the differences between children in divorced compared to intact two-parent families. But differences in outcomes exist *within* social class groupings. Moreover, children in better-off remarried or single-parent families still lag behind children from two-parent families on various outcome indicators (McLanahan and Sandefur 1994; Parke 2003).

5. The **interparental conflict perspective** holds that conflict between parents prior to, during, and after the divorce is responsible for the lowered well-being of children of divorce. Many studies, including that of Wallerstein, indicate that some negative results for children may not be simply the result of divorce per se, but also are affected by exposure to parental conflict prior to, during, and subsequent to the divorce (Wallerstein and Kelly 1980; Amato and Booth 1996; Dawson 1991; Morrison and Cherlin 1995; Cherlin,

Chase-Lansdale, and McRae 1998; Hetherington 1999; Amato 2000). There are studies that find even when this is so, divorce nevertheless augments the problems (Morrison and Coiro 1999) or conclude that interparental conflict and divorce have independent negative effects (Hanson 1999).

From studies that reach different conclusions about overall outcomes, we can still learn much that is potentially useful about what postdivorce circumstances are most beneficial to children's development and what pitfalls to avoid. A good mother–child (or custodial parent–child) bond and competent parenting by the custodial parent seem to be the most significant factors (Wallerstein and Blakeslee 1989; Tschann et al. 1989). Another highly important factor in children's adjustment to divorce is the divorced parents' relationship with each other (Ahrons 2004; Kelly and Emery 2003; Wallerstein 1998). And good nonresident parental relationships are also a positive influence on outcomes (Amato and Gilbreth 1999).

FIGHTING THROUGH THE CHILDREN In the Wallerstein study, more than half of eight- and twelve-year-old children were asked by one parent to spy on the other—to go through bureau drawers and the like. Even though married partners may be angry and feel vindictive about something, they do not usually draw children openly into the spousal wars in the way that ex-spouses do.

Visitation is one frequent arena of paternal disputes: The child isn't ready to go when visitation time starts, or the visiting parent brings the child home late, for instance. Visitation can be an arena in which ex-spouses continue the basic conflicts they experienced before the divorce. Counselors urge ex-spouses to work out irritations and conflict directly with each other rather than through their children. They encourage the attitude: "We had our problems, but that doesn't mean he (or she) is bad or that I'm bad." Some jurisdictions sponsor "visitation support groups," in which parents and stepparents discuss their problems with others, or provide court-supported conciliation of visitation disputes.

Experts agree that adjusting to divorce is easier for children *and* parents when former spouses cooperate. Maintenance of the child's ties with the noncustodial parent is also important.

One of the more difficult and recurring moments in life after divorce is the transfer of the child from one parent to another. It is easier for both children and parents when former spouses cooperate over custody and financial issues.

A MORE POSITIVE SET OF FINDINGS E. Mavis Hetherington has been studying divorcing families for about the same length of time as Judith Wallerstein, but she has a much more optimistic view of the outcomes for children—and adults.

Starting in 1974 in Virginia with forty-eight divorced and forty-eight married-couple families, parents of four-year-olds, Hetherington ultimately studied 1,400 stable and dissolved marriages and the children of those marriages, some for almost thirty years. Hetherington found that 25 percent of the children of divorce that she studied had long-term social, emotional, or psychological problems, compared to 10 percent of those whose parents had not divorced. However, in assessing children of divorce, she would emphasize the 75 percent to 80 percent of children who are coping reasonably well. In looking at outcomes for divorced parents, she finds 70 percent with "good enough" adjustment (Hetherington and Kelly 2002).

Another summary of the research literature on children of divorce concludes:

> Researchers have clearly demonstrated that, on average, children benefit from being raised in two biological or adoptive parent families rather than separated; divorced; or never married single-parent households. . . . But within groups [two parent versus single parent households], there is considerable variability, and the differences between groups, while significant, are relatively small. Indeed, despite the well-documented risks associated with separation and divorce, the majority of divorced children as young adults enjoy average or better social and emotional adjustment (Kelly and Lamb 2003, p. 195; citations omitted; also Kelly and Emery 2003).

All in all, divorce researchers seem to be moving to a middle ground in which they acknowledge that children of divorce are disadvantaged compared to those of married parents—and that those whose parents were not engaged in serious marital conflict have especially lost the advantage of an intact parental home. But many have moved away from simplistic or overly negative views of the outcomes of divorce:

> On one side are those who see divorce as an important contributor to many social problems. On the other side are those who see divorce as a largely benign force that provides adults with a second chance for happiness and rescues children from dysfunctional and aversive home environments. . . . Based on . . . research . . . it is reasonable to conclude that. . . . [d]ivorce benefits some individuals, leads others to experience temporary decrements in well-being that improve over time, and forces others on a downward cycle from which they might never fully recover. (Amato 2000, p. 1282)

We now turn to issues of custody, the setting in which children will live after the divorce.

Custody Issues

As we noted earlier, more than half of couples who divorce have children under age eighteen. A basic issue for them is determining which parent will take **custody**—that is, assume primary responsibility for caring for the children and making decisions about their upbringing and general welfare.

CUSTODY AFTER DIVORCE As formalized in divorce decrees, child custody is most commonly an extension of the basic exchange, and indeed of traditional gender roles (Finley 2004). Divorced fathers have legal responsibility for financial support while divorced mothers continue the physical, day-to-day care of their children.

Custody patterns and preferences have changed over time. As part of a patriarchal system of law, fathers were automatically given custody in the United States until the mid-nineteenth century. Then the first wave of the women's movement made mothers' parental rights an important issue, and emerging developmental theories of childhood well-being lent support to a presumption that mother custody was virtually always in the child's best interest, the so-called "tender years" doctrine (Depner 1993; Erickson and Babcock 1995).

In the 1970s, states' reforms of divorce law, incorporating new ideas about gender and parenthood, changed the situation again, and custody criteria were made specifically gender neutral. Under current laws, a father and a mother who want to retain custody have theoretically equal chances, and judges try to assess the relationship between each parent and the child on a case-by-case basis. However, because mothers are typically the ones who have physically cared for the child, and because many judges still have traditional attitudes about gender, some courts continue to give preference to mothers (Bauserman 2002). The "best interests of the child" or the more recent "primary caretaker" standard was often assumed by judges to signal a choice of the mother (Erickson and Babcock 1995). In 2002, 84 percent of mothers were custodial parents, but only 16 percent of fathers were (Grall 2003).

When both parents seek custody, the odds of father custody are slightly higher when the children are older, especially when the eldest child is male and when the father is the plaintiff in the divorce (Fox and Kelly 1995). Generally, studies have found nothing to preclude father custody or to prefer it (Rosenthal and

Keshet 1980; Luepnitz 1982; Buchanan, Maccoby, and Dornbusch 1996). Neither does whether or not the custodial parent is the same sex as the child seem to make a difference in a child's adjustment (Powell and Downey 1997).

NONCUSTODIAL MOTHERS With unpromising economic prospects and in the context of changing attitudes about gender roles, some mothers are voluntarily relinquishing custody and more fathers are seeking custody. There are more than two million noncustodial mothers, of varying backgrounds, but concentrated in the twenty-five to forty-five age range and lower- to middle-class economic level. Some of those mothers have lost custody of children due to their abuse or neglect, while others have voluntarily surrendered custody or lost a custody contest to the other parent (Eicher-Catt 2004).

In an earlier study of noncustodial mothers based on interviews with more than 500 mostly white women in forty-four states, only 9 percent reported losing their children in a court battle or ceding custody to avoid a custody fight. The others voluntarily agreed to father custody and gave as reasons: money (30 percent), child's choice (21 percent), difficulty in handling the children (12 percent), avoidance of moving the children (11 percent), and self-reported instability or problems (11 percent) (Greif and Pabst 1988, p. 88; also Depner 1993). "Issues for Thought: How It Feels When Parents Divorce" includes one child's story (Jimmy's) in which the father eventually won custody, presumably following the mother's financial and perhaps emotional instability.

More than 90 percent of mothers in the Greif and Pabst study reported that the experience of becoming the noncustodial parent was stressful. So is maintaining a relationship with the child. The minority of mothers in Eicher-Catt's qualitative study whose custody was abrogated by the courts are restricted in various ways, perhaps permitted only supervised visitation. The larger group who voluntarily relinquished custody find it hard to achieve a workable relationship with the child, as well. They are unable to be traditional mothers, but find a "mother-as-friend" role insufficient and uncomfortable. Eicher-Catt advises noncustodial mothers to focus on building a relationship, rather than thinking in terms of the traditional maternal role (Eicher-Catt 2004).

A small but growing number of fathers are seeking, and are awarded, custody.

Judith Fisher, who also studied noncustodial mothers, believes that women should not relinquish custody because they feel inadequate in comparison to their successful husbands. At the same time, she strongly supports the freedom of men and women to make choices about custody—including the woman's choice to live apart from her children—without guilt or stigma. She urges

(1) the negation of the unflattering stereotypes of noncustody mothers; (2) sensitivity to the demands society places on mothers . . . and to the needs of all family members; (3) supportiveness of the woman's choice when it appears to have been well thought out; and (4) . . . prohibitions against blaming the mother when others (the children, the children's father, the courts) decide that the children should live apart from her. (Fisher 1983, p. 357)

THE VISITING PARENT To date, most research and discussion on visiting parents has been about fathers, but one study did compare the two sexes. Nonresidential mothers are more apt to telephone and to engage in extended visits with children. But nonresidential mothers and fathers had essentially similar levels of visitation in terms of frequency and activities during the visit. Both were more likely to engage in only leisure activities with their children—42 percent of fathers and 38 percent of mothers—rather than spending time helping with homework or going to school activities. Those who did the latter were more likely to live closer, had lived with the children, and were providing support to them. In reality, less frequent and more recreational visitation seems to be a result of structural factors: the difficulty of finding an appropriate setting for the visit and the wish not to engage in conflict or disciplinary actions in the limited time spent with the child (Stewart 1999).

Fathers without custody experience a sense of extreme loss. There is some evidence that, ironically, the more emotionally involved fathers may cope with this loss by visiting their children less often than fathers who had less emotional involvement before the divorce (Kruk 1991). Often, fathers become increasingly frustrated with their loss of influence over the children's upbringing, and they let themselves drift away from the children (Wallerstein 1998, p. 75). Noncustodial fathers, like noncustodial mothers, find it difficult to construct a satisfying parent–child relationship. During the marriage, a father's authority in the family gave weight to his parental role, but this vanishes in a nonresidential situation. Geographical distance and conflict with the mother are also barriers to frequent contact with children (Leite and McKenry 2002).

The situation of noncustodial fathers seems to have improved since earlier research found that many had detached from their children. Noncustodial fathers now spend more time with their children, and 35 percent to 40 percent have at least weekly contact. Few drop out entirely (Kelly and Lamb 2003, pp. 195–196; citations omitted), and about a quarter of fathers in one study increased their visitation over time. In Ahrons' longitudinal study of postdivorce families, 62 percent of the now-adult children reported that their relationships with their father got better or at least stayed the same over the twenty years since the divorce (Ahrons and Tanner 2003).

A new marriage or cohabiting relationship was not itself a factor in decreasing visitation, but the presence of children in a new family, particularly biological children, did lead to a decline. Fathers seemed to find it difficult to parent their children across two families (Manning and Smock 1999).

A father's decreased visiting may be painful for children. In the Wallerstein study, fathers visited their children with more regularity than other research found at that time, but they were often psychologically detached. In one case, "Almost always, there would be other adults around or adult activities planned. Carl watched hundreds of hours of television at his father's house, feeling more and more alone and removed from his earlier visions of family life" (Wallerstein and Blakeslee 1989, p. 79). Children often forgave geographically distant fathers who did not appear frequently but were very hurt by those nearby fathers who rarely visited. When, as is likely, the lack of divorced-father–child contact persists into and throughout the child's adulthood, this situation reduces the probability that a divorced father can think of his children as potential sources of support in times of need (Amato 1994a; Aquilino 1994b; Cooney 1994; Lawton, Silverstein, and Bengston 1994).

The visitation of fathers does not always affect children positively (Marsiglio, Amato, Day, and Lamb 2000).[11] When the father enacts an authoritative parenting style (see Chapter 11) and when the visit does not lead to conflict between the parents, it has a favorable impact on the child's adjustment. The most recent studies do show a higher level of paternal parenting skills, so perhaps younger divorced fathers have been more involved with children in the marriage and have a better mastery of parenting during visitation. Good relationships with noncustodial fathers foster better outcomes for children (White and Gilbreth 2001). Studies generally indicate that an involved, caring father benefits his children in many ways (Harris, Furstenberg, and Marmer 1998).

CHILD SNATCHING At the other extreme from dissociating from children is **child snatching**: kidnapping one's children from the other parent. A 1988–1989 study by the Justice Department reports that 163,200 children were taken in a year by noncustodial parents who took them to another state and/or intended to keep them (Fass 2003b).

---

11. In extreme cases—where there is verbal, physical, or sexual abuse—father contact may actually be damaging to children (King 1994). We've seen that some divorces are precipitated by alcoholism, drug abuse, or domestic violence; in such cases, visitation is not necessarily in the best interest of a child. In some communities, courts and social workers have developed programs to offer **supervised visitation** between a noncustodial parent and his or her offspring. In this situation, parent–child contact occurs only in the presence of a third party, such as a social worker or a court employee.

Child snatching is frightening and confusing for the child, may be physically dangerous, and is usually detrimental to the child's psychological development (Wallerstein and Blakeslee 1989; Fass 2003b). Yet for years the snatching of a child by a biological parent (without custody) was not legally considered kidnapping—or at least not prosecuted as such. Now, however, due to the passage of the Uniform Child Custody Jurisdiction Act by all states and the federal Parental Kidnapping Prevention Act of 1980, states must recognize out-of-state custody decrees and do more to find the child and prosecute offenders (Fass 2003b).

Parents who snatch their children may be either mothers or fathers. Child snatchers may have the help of a social network or underground dissident group. Interviews indicate they do not think that their act is immoral. Child snatching is an extreme act, but it points up the frustration involved in arrangements regarding sole custody, or, in some cases, a lack of attention to the noncustodial parent's allegations of child abuse (Johnston and Girtner 2001). "Issues for Thought: How It Feels When Parents Divorce" tells the story of Jimmy, who was snatched by each parent in turn.

JOINT CUSTODY In **joint custody**, both divorced parents continue to take equal responsibility for important decisions regarding the child's general upbringing. When parents live close to each other and when both are committed, joint custody can bring the experiences of the two parents closer together, providing advantages to each. Both parents may feel they have the opportunity to pass their own beliefs and values on to their children. In addition, neither parent is overloaded with sole custodial responsibility and its concomitant loss of personal freedom.

There are two variations in joint custody agreements. One is *joint legal and physical custody*, in which parents or children move periodically so that the child resides with each parent in turn on a substantially equal basis. The second variation is *joint legal custody*—in which both parents have the right to participate in important decisions and retain a symbolically important legal authority—with physical custody (that is, residential care of the child) going to just one parent. Parents with higher incomes and education are more likely to have joint custody (Seltzer 1991b; Wallerstein 1998).

An important predictor of mothers' preference for joint custody is faith in their ex-husband's parenting competence (Wilcox, Wolchik, and Braver 1998).

"So what's your custody deal?"

Table 16.1 lists advantages and disadvantages of joint custody from a father's perspective. Shared custody gives children the chance for a more realistic and normal relationship with each parent (Arditti and Keith 1993). The parents of Zach, whose story is included in "Issues for Thought," have joint custody; this may be one reason for his conclusion that "just because your parents are separated it doesn't mean you're going to lose anybody."

The high rate of geographic mobility in the U.S. can make joint physical custody difficult. Even without that, some children who have experienced joint custody report feeling "torn apart," particularly as they get older (Simon 1991). Although some youngsters appreciate the contact with both parents and even the "change of pace" (Krementz 1984, p. 53), others don't. The following account from eleven-year-old Heather shows both sides:

> The way it works now is we switch houses every seven days—on Friday night at five-thirty. At first we tried switching every three days and that was crazy, and then we tried five days and that was still too confusing. . . . And switching on school nights was awful. Friday nights are perfect because we don't have to worry about homework, and if Matthew [her brother] and I both have after-school activities it doesn't matter because my Dad can take me and Mom can drive Matt. Another reason it works out well is because each of our parents likes to help us with our homework and when we stay with them for a week at a time it's easier for them to keep up with what we're doing. . . .

Table 16.1

Advantages and Disadvantages of Joint Custody from a Father's Perspective

ADVANTAGES	DISADVANTAGES
Fathers can have more influence on the child's growth and development—a benefit for men and children alike.	Children lack a stable and permanent environment, which can affect them emotionally.
Fathers are more involved and experience more self-satisfaction as parents.	Children are prevented from having a relationship with a "psychological parent" as a result of being shifted from one environment to another.
Parents experience less stress than sole-custody parents.	Children have difficulty gaining control over and understanding of their lives.
Parents do not feel as overburdened as sole-custody parents.	Children have trouble forming and maintaining peer relationships.
Generally, fathers and mothers report more friendly and cooperative interaction in joint custody than in visitation arrangements, mostly because the time with children is evenly balanced and agreement exists on the rules of the system.	Long-term consequences of joint custody arrangements have not been systematically studied.
Joint custody provides more free social time for each single parent.	
Relationships with children are stronger and more meaningful for fathers.	
Parental power and decision making are equally divided, so there is less need to use children to barter for more.	

Source: Adapted from *The Developing Father: Emerging Roles in Contemporary Society* by B. E. Robinson and R. L. Barret, 1986, p. 89. Copyright © 1986 Guildford Publications. Adapted by permission.

And as long as they're divorced, I don't see any alternative because it wouldn't seem right to live with either parent a hundred percent of the time and only see the other one on weekends. But switching is definitely the biggest drag in my life—like it's just so hard having two of everything. My rooms are so ugly because I never take the time to decorate them—I can't afford enough posters and I don't bother to set up my hair stuff in a special way because I know that I'll have to take it right back down and bring it to the next house. Now I'm thinking that I'll try to make one room my real room and have the other one like camping out. I can't buy two of everything, so I might as well have one good room that's really mine. (quoted in Krementz 1984, pp. 76–78)

Joint custody is expensive. Each parent must maintain housing, equipment, toys, and often a separate set of clothes for the children and must sometimes pay for travel between homes if they are geographically distant. Mothers, more than fathers, would find it difficult to maintain a family household without child support, which is often not awarded when custody is shared.

Research does not support the presumption that joint custody is always best for children of divorced parents because there may be situations—an abusive parent or extremely high levels of parental conflict, for example—where sole custody is preferable, and other situations where continued contact by a supportive noncustodial parent may offset the one-sidedness of the custodial arrangement.

Nevertheless, a review of thirty-three studies of joint and sole custody (Bauserman 2002) found that children in joint custody arrangements had superior adjustment. In fact, "joint custody and intact family children did not differ in adjustment" in terms of general adjustment, family relationships, self-esteem, emotional and behavioral adjustment, and divorce-specific adjustment (p. 98). This finding of the advantages of joint custody applies to *legal joint custody* as well as to *legal and physical joint custody*. Sole custody was not necessarily bad, but joint custody was simply better in terms of child outcomes.

WHEN A CUSTODIAL PARENT WANTS TO MOVE The desire of a joint custodian or a parent with sole custody to move and take the children "is the hottest issue in the divorce courts at the moment," according to Judith Wallerstein (Eaton 2004, p. A-1). Some divorce degrees mandate judicial consent and/or the consent of the other parent for a move to another locality. Other cases have gone to court as a result of a parent's initiating legal action to prevent a move.

In deciding these cases, judges in different jurisdictions have rendered varying decisions; they have difficult issues to sort out: "Does the parent who wants to move have a compelling reason, or is she just trying to keep the child away from the father? Does the parent who opposes the move really want to be involved with the child, or is he just trying to control his ex-wife" (Eaton 2004).

Some find that a custodial parent who wishes to move is harming the child or the other parent, and they require a choice between relinquishing custody and staying put. Other judges see a constitutional issue in the right to move, or they wish to balance the needs of all family members and consider the benefits, as well as costs, involved in a parent's relocation—a child may benefit from a parent's increased earning power, for example, or may gain a two-parent family if the move is related to remarriage (LaFrance 1995–1996; Downey 2000).

Some state laws or court decisions have prohibited custodial parents from moving. Meanwhile, there are extraordinary situations resulting from legal prohibitions on moving. One remarried mother, whose second husband lost his job, shuttles between her husband and the child of that marriage, who live in California, and her first child in New York (Eaton 2004). Still, courts are now more inclined to permit moves for remarriage or economic reasons than they were in the 1980s and 1990s (Kelly and Lamb 2003).

Social scientists have begun to weigh in on this question. Judith Wallerstein, who favors a custodial parent's freedom to relocate, has appeared in court in support of relocating parents and her opinion has proven very influential. She takes the position that the well-being of the custodial parent and that parent's relationship with the child are the most important factors in adjustment, trumping the question of contact with the other parent. Another divorce researcher, Richard Warshak, presents the opposite point of view in advocating that attention be paid to the importance of a child's maintaining contact with each parent (Eaton 2004).

There is little research to date on the issue of parental relocation. Braver, Ellman, and Fabricius (2003) comment that as of a 1998 review of the literature, "not a single empirical study could be found . . . on the effects of parental moves on the well-being of children of divorce" (p. 209). Their later study of a sample of college students in psychology classes at Arizona State University found that those children of divorce whose parents had moved more than an hour from each other after the divorce had worse outcomes in terms of financial support and support for college; inner turmoil and distance from parents; rapport with parents; and parents as role models. But the differences were small, and there were no differences between the two groups on friendship and dating behavior, substance abuse, and general life satisfaction (Braver et al. 2003). The Braver et al. study has been criticized for its failure to control for the context of divorce: for example, how old the child was when the divorce took place, whether parents remarried, and the financial circumstances of the family (Glenn and Blankenhorn 2003). There is no research yet on the adjustment of young children to parental relocation.

UNMARRIED PARENTS AND CHILD CUSTODY Another relatively new arena for court determination of child custody is that of children of unmarried parents who separate. Some courts are treating nonmarital relationships, whether same-sex or heterosexual, as "sufficiently marriagelike" for marital law to apply (Judge Heather Van Nuys in "Court Treats" 2002). In making these custody (and property, child support, and visitation) decisions, courts may disregard actual biological relationship to a child ("Court Treats" 2002; Finz 2003; "Lesbian May Have to Pay Child Support"; Biskupic 2003; Strawley 2002; *V.C. v. M.J.B.* 2000; American Civil Liberties Union 2004b). In a California case, for example, a nonmarital partner was awarded custody over a biological mother's claim. He was considered a more responsible parent than the biological mother, while the biological father was declared "unfit" (Janofsky 2002).

Not all courts make such rulings, and there is substantial opposition to the courts' becoming involved in the custody issues of unmarried parents. However, as the dean of the Duke University Law School, Katherine Bartlett, remarked: "Courts aren't trying to contribute to the demise of traditional families. But they recognize the reality of families today and functional parents" (Biskupic 2003, p. 2A).

Parent Education for Co-Parenting Ex-Spouses

Earlier in this chapter we saw that much of the pain and disorganization suffered by children of divorce results from parents' hostility toward each other before the divorce and continuing thereafter. Many courts in several states have begun to offer or require parent education for divorcing parents. Information and education about what types of behaviors to expect from a child and what the child needs during the divorce process are part of the curriculum, along with techniques in conflict management. Programs of this kind usually involve a series of lectures or workshops offered by a mediator or mental health professional and are sometimes followed by small-group discussions. In some communities, the children also meet in groups with a teacher or mental health professional (Lewin 1995; Geasler and Blaisure 1998).

Although many parents have been reluctant to participate, evaluation forms completed after the sessions have shown predominantly positive responses. But "there has been no evaluation of whether the information provided is actively employed by parents in their relationship with each other or with the child or whether, indeed, there is any change in the child's well-being" (Wallerstein 1998, p. 85; see also Lewin 1995 and Emery, Kitzmann, and Waldron 1999).

Other developments in terms of programs directed toward divorcing spouses and their children may help facilitate co-parenting and the adjustment of children. School-based therapeutic interventions are now offered to children in some locations, although we do not have any data on their effects in reducing stress. We do know that divorce mediation tends to result in more cooperative parenting. Parents in many states are now required to negotiate a "parenting plan" before their divorce is approved; again, we have no research yet as to the effectiveness of this requirement in facilitating cooperative postdivorce parenting.

This discussion of mothers' and fathers' custody issues suggests that being divorced is in many ways a very different experience for men and women. Just as sexually segregated or traditional roles may lead to

"his" and "her" marriages (Bernard 1982), so also may they result in "his" and "her" divorces.

▪ His and Her Divorce ▪

We have seen that gender roles diminish communication and understanding between women and men. Perhaps nowhere is the lack of understanding more evident than in the debate over which partner—the ex-wife or the ex-husband—is the victim of divorce. Both are affected by the divorce.

The first year after divorce is especially stressful for both ex-spouses. Divorce wields a blow to each one's self-esteem. Both feel they have failed as spouses and, if there are children, as parents (Brodie 1999). They may question their ability to get along well in a remarriage. Yet each has particular difficulties that are related to the sometimes different circumstances of men and women.

Her Divorce

Women who were married longer, particularly those oriented to traditional gender roles, lose the identity associated with their husband's status. Getting back on their feet may be particularly difficult for older women. They have few opportunities for meaningful career development and limited opportunities to remarry (Choi 1992).

Divorced mothers who retain sole custody of their children also experience difficulties. They often undergo severe overload as they attempt to provide not only for financial self-support but also for the day-to-day care of their children (Campbell and Moen 1992). Their difficulties are aggravated by discrimination in promotion and salaries, by the high cost of child care, and often by their less extensive work experience and training. All in all, custodial mothers frequently feel alone as they struggle with money, scheduling, and discipline problems. Objective difficulties are reflected in decreased psychological well-being (Doherty, Su, and Needle 1989; Ross 1995). An encouraging note, though, is that the poverty rate of single custodial mothers dropped by 30 percent between 1993 and 2002, although at 25 percent, it still remains higher than that of custodial fathers, whose poverty rate is 15 percent (Grall 2003).

While those experiencing marital dissolution are less happy than those who are married, another com-

"Her" divorce often involves financial worries and task and emotional overload as she tries to be the complete parent for the children.

parison gives us a picture of "her" divorce that is a bit brighter. A majority of women respondents to the National Survey of Families and Households (1992–1993) who compared their lives before and after marital separation perceived improvement in overall happiness, home life, social life, and parenting, though not in finances or job opportunities (Furstenberg 2003, Figure 1, p. 172).

His Divorce

Divorced men miss their families and children. In some ways, divorced noncustodial fathers have more radical readjustments to make in their lifestyles than do custodial mothers. In return for the responsibilities and loss of freedom associated with single parenthood, custodial mothers escape much of the loneliness that the loss of family status might otherwise cause and are somewhat rewarded by social approval for rearing their children (Myers 1989). In fact, many children of divorce, especially daughters, developed closer relationships with their mothers after the divorce (Amato 2000).

Custodial fathers, like custodial mothers, are under financial stress. Noncustodial fathers often retain the financial obligations of fatherhood while experiencing few of its joys (Arendell 1995). Whether it takes place in the children's home, the father's residence, or at some neutral spot, visitation is typically awkward and superficial. And the man may worry that if his ex-wife remarries, he will lose even more influence over his children's upbringing. For many individ-

uals, parenthood plays an important role in adult development: "Removed from regular contact with their children after divorce, many men stagnate" (Wallerstein and Blakeslee 1989, p. 143).

Ex-husbands' anger, grief, and loneliness may be aggravated by the traditional male gender role, which discourages them from sharing their pain with other men (Arendell 1995). Sociologist Catherine Ross (1995) compared levels of psychological distress for men and women in four different categories: marrieds, cohabitors, those who were dating, and those with no partner. Ross found that divorced men had the lowest levels of emotional support of any group, while emotional support among divorced women was "not that much lower than married women's" (p. 138).

At least some men are angry that their efforts seem to go unrecognized. One noncustodial father wrote the following in a letter to "Dear Abby":

I'm concerned that [noncustodial fathers] (including myself) are getting a bad rap. I take my children to weekly counseling sessions, due in part to an ex-wife who constantly tells them what a "jerk" their father is. Not only do I send the required child-support payments on time, I send an amount over the required legal minimum. I also help their mother with religious-school tuition, summer camp expenses and assorted other child-care expenses—gifts, sports and extracurricular activities. . . . I attend my kids' school and extra-curricular activities with enthusiasm (when

Maintaining the parent–child bond is significant in a child's adjustment to divorce.

© Lawrence Migdale/Stock, Boston

I'm notified about them) and call the kids regularly. Regrettably, I have only the legally minimum visitation opportunities, which their mother tried to deny me. ("Divorced Dad Tries" 1996, p. E7)

Many ex-husbands feel shut out and lost because women seem to have a monopoly on emotional nurturance and may also have a stronger influence on children (Thomas and Forehand 1993). Yet for most women, men still hold the keys to economic security, and ex-wives suffer financially more than do ex-husbands. The fact is that both men's and women's grievances could be at least somewhat alleviated by eliminating the economic discrimination faced by women and the gender role expectations that create husbands' and wives' divorces. This leads us to a consideration of how divorce affects the families of the future.

Forming Families: The Next Generation

We have talked about the general effect of divorce on children, but what do we specifically know about how a parental divorce affects adult children's married and

family lives? Sociologists have paid particular attention to the effects of parental divorce on two broad areas regarding adult children's family lives: (1) the quality of intergenerational relationships between adult children and their divorced parents, and (2) the marital stability of adult children of divorced parents.

Adult Children of Divorced Parents and Intergenerational Relationships

There is evidence that adult children of divorced parents have probably come to accept their parents' divorce as a desirable alternative to ongoing family conflict (Amato and Booth 1991; Ahrons 2004). Nevertheless, a number of studies point to one conclusion: Ties between adult children and their parents are generally weaker (less close or supportive) when the parents are highly conflicted and "divorce prone," even if they are still together (Booth and Amato 1994b) or when the parents are divorced (Aquilino 1994a, 1994b; Cooney 1994; White 1994; Furstenberg, Hoffman, and Shrestha 1995; Lye et al. 1995; Marks 1995; Szinovacz 1997). The effect for divorced parents is stronger for fathers, who were usually the noncustodial parent, but the relationship has been found for mothers as well.

Sociologist Lynn White (1994) analyzed data from 3,625 National Survey of Families and Households respondents to examine the long-term consequences of childhood family divorce for adults' relationships with their parents. Using a broad array of indicators of family solidarity—relationship quality, contact frequency, and perceived and actual social support (doing favors, lending and giving money, feeling that one can call on the parent for help in an emergency)—White found that those raised by single parents reported lowered solidarity with them. As adults, they saw their parents less often, had poorer-quality relationships, felt less able to count on parents for help and emotional support, and actually received less support. White found these negative effects to be stronger regarding noncustodial parents (usually the father) but not limited to them.

In another study, sociologist William Aquilino (1994a) analyzed National Survey of Families and Households data from 3,281 young adults between ages nineteen and thirty-four who grew up in intact families and had therefore lived with both biological parents from birth to age eighteen. Aquilino separated his sample into three categories: those whose parents were still married, those whose parents had divorced (about 20 percent of the sample), and those whose parent had been widowed. Aquilino found that parental divorce did not reduce the amount of help that adult children gave their parents, but it did reduce the amount of help and money that the divorced parents gave their sons (though not their daughters). Furthermore, Aquilino found that even when parents divorce after the child is eighteen, the divorce seems to negatively affect the quality of their relationship. Children of divorced parents were in contact with their parents less often and reported lower relationship quality overall. These findings applied to both mothers and fathers, although the effect was much stronger for fathers.

Generally, evidence suggests that adult children of divorced parents feel less obligation to remain in contact with them and are less likely to receive help from them or to provide help to them. Social scientists (Lye et al. 1995) have posited four reasons for these findings:

1. Children raised in divorced, single-parent families may have received fewer resources from their custodial parent than did their friends in intact families, and thus they may feel less obliged to reciprocate.

2. Strain in single-parent families, deriving from the single parent's emotional stress and/or economic hardship, may weaken subsequent relations between adult children and their parents.

3. The reciprocal obligations of family members in different generations may be less clear in single-parent, postdivorce families—a situation that may also tend to weaken intergenerational relations in later life.

4. Adult children raised in divorced, single-parent families may still be angry, feeling that their parents failed to provide a stable, two-parent household.

Remarriage and stepfamily relationships may generate similar tensions (remarriage and stepfamilies are discussed in Chapter 17).

Marital Stability for Adult Children of Divorced Parents

Studies show that children of divorced parents do, in fact, have higher divorce rates than children from stable households. On average, adult children of divorced parents have acquired less education, marry sooner, and are more likely to cohabit and/or to have children before marriage. All these factors are associated with the increased likelihood of divorce.

But not all studies find parental divorce to be the long-term family handicap that we might expect. The primary problem seems to be the likelihood that a child of divorce will marry early, at a riskier age than those from intact families. When, however, a child of divorce marries a supportive, well-adjusted partner, there is no difference in marital stability (Hetherington 2003). Moreover, although adult children whose parents divorced may be more negative about their families of origin, they seem little different from children of intact marriages in their goals and attitudes toward marriage and families—only perhaps a little more realistic (Amato and Booth 1991). While they are "aware of [marriage's] limitations and tolerant toward its alternatives," at the same time, they value marriage, believe that it should be forever, believe that partners should be monogamous, and believe that one's truly important relationships are in families (Amato 1988, pp. 453, 460). It would be nice to conclude on that hopeful note. But we need to go on to consider the policy debate that arises out of optimistic and pessimistic assessments of the impact of divorce.

Should Divorce Be Harder to Get?

Some family scholars argue that our high divorce rate signals "the decline of the American family" (see Chapter 1). To address this situation, policy makers have proposed changes in state divorce laws so that divorces would be more difficult to get than they have been since the 1970s.[12] An assumption behind this movement is that making divorces harder to get would foster a renewed "culture of marriage" in the United States (Council on Families in America 1996) and "encourage people to take marriage more seriously" (Wagner 1998).

As noted earlier, with no-fault divorce laws, a marriage can be dissolved simply by *one* spouse's testifying in court that the couple has "irreconcilable differences" or that the marriage has suffered an "irretrievable breakdown." No-fault divorce is sometimes termed "unilateral divorce" because a spouse not desiring a divorce has no control over the matter.

Concerned about the sanctity of marriage, the impact on children of marital impermanence, and what seems to some a lack of fairness toward the spouse who would like to preserve the marriage, some states have developed—or at least considered—laws and policies that would make divorce harder to obtain. As of 2004, three states—Louisiana, Arizona, and Arkansas—have enacted covenant marriage laws, and they have been proposed, though not as yet passed, in at least twenty additional states.

Covenant marriage is an alternative to standard marriage that couples may select at the time of marriage or later. It is essentially a return to fault-based divorce because it requires spouses to prove fault (adultery, physical or sexual abuse, imprisonment for a felony, or abandonment) and/or to live apart for a substantial length of time in order to obtain a divorce. Premarital counseling and counseling directed toward saving the marriage are also required. While a poll indicates that one-half of Americans say they support covenant marriage, and two-fifths would consider it as an option for themselves (Thornton and Young-DeMarco 2001), only a small minority of couples in covenant marriage states have chosen this option— 2 percent in Louisiana and fewer than that in Arkansas ("More Binding Marriage" 2004; Nock 2003b; Sanchez, Nock, Wright, and Gager 2002; Schemo 2001).

Those who believe divorce is too readily available have proposed other restrictions on divorce or postdivorce arrangements. Proposals have included restoration of fault for all divorces; a waiting period of as long as five years; a two-tier divorce process, with a more extensive process for divorces involving children; prioritization of children's needs in postdivorce financial arrangements; requirement of a "parenting plan" to be negotiated prior to granting a divorce; requiring or encouraging premarital counseling; and publicizing research that would convince the public of the risks of divorce (Galston 1996; Hewlett and West 1998, pp. 242–243; Waite and Gallagher 2000, pp. 188–199; Whyte 2000).

Many states and cities have established premarital counseling, marriage education, and/or marriage counseling as either required or voluntary for couples. Some locales require divorcing parents to attend a parent education program. Few object to such programs when voluntary, though some have objected to their being required. Research is lacking on their effectiveness in preventing divorce (Lewin 1995; Belluck 2000).

Criticism and opposition to covenant marriage or other restrictions on divorce center around various points: First, divorce is not always or necessarily bad for children. Second, some marriages—those involving physical violence and/or overt conflict—are harmful to children and to one or both spouses. Divorce provides an escape from marital behaviors, such as a parent's alcoholism or drug abuse, that may be more harmful than divorce itself (Riley 1991; Coontz 1997a). In fact, an interesting study by economists Betsey Stevenson and Justin Wolfers found that no-fault divorce was associated with a decline in suicide rates for women, as well as a decline in domestic violence against both men and women, and a decline in intimate-partner homicides of women. The existence of an escape route seems to change the balance of power and reduce violence (Stevenson and Wolfers 2004; also Chapman 2004).

It also appears to be the case that staying married would not necessarily provide economic stability for

---

12. The laws of marriage and divorce are the province of state governments, so they vary from state to state. Despite the fact that family law is the domain of the states, Congress has passed laws which regulate marriage and divorce, notably the Defense of Marriage Act and the child support enforcement statutes. The latter are imposed on the states "by purchase"; that is, states are required to incorporate certain provisions in state law or lose some federal funding.

women and children: "If policies were in place to en-courage people to remain in their marriages, the over-all [economic] benefits of marriage would probably be smaller than currently observed" (Smock et al. 1999). Those women who obtain divorces would be better off economically if they remained married, but they would not be as well off as that portion of the popula-tion that at present has not divorced; there are differ-ences between the two groups in economic resources quite apart from divorce.

Those who oppose restoration of fault divorce point to the fraudulent practices that characterized the divorce process under fault statutes. Seldom was either party truly "innocent" of contributing to the marital difficulties, although one party had to pose as such. "Mental cruelty" was the most easily proven grounds for divorce, but the "evidence" for this was often exag-gerated at best and completely trumped up at worst. In New York state—where adultery was the only grounds for divorce—"adultery" was often staged, in a drama organized by lawyers and colluded in by both spouses.

Is Divorce Necessarily Bad for Children?

Having thoroughly reviewed the literature and con-ducted longitudinal research on the subject, sociolo-gists Amato and Booth (1997) conclude that children whose parents were continuously and happily married are indeed the most successful in adulthood. Children of divorce or those whose parents remained unhappily married were less successful. Amato and Booth note the significant role that level of parental conflict plays in conclusions about benefit or harm to children from divorce. They divide divorce outcomes into two classes: In one-third of the cases, marital conflict is so serious and so affects children that they are much bet-ter off if the parents divorce. But in two-thirds of the cases—in these researchers' opinion—conflict is low-level and not very visible to children. Then the chil-dren seem better off if the parents remain married. Amato and Booth present their conclusions as infor-mative, not as advocacy for legal restrictions on divorce.

Is Making Divorce Harder to Get a Realistic Idea?

Noting that divorce is "an American tradition" that began in colonial times and has grown more prevalent with industrialization and urbanization, family histo-rian Glenda Riley, among others, argues that making divorce harder to get will not change this trend (Riley 1991; Coontz 1997b; Skolnick 1997; Sugarman 1998). Interestingly, a recent poll found most people saying that they do want divorce laws to be tougher—but not when the divorce is their own ("The Divorce Dilemma" 1996): "We can watch Ozzie and Harriet reruns as long as we like, but we cannot return to the world it evokes, even if we wish to" (Stacey 1999, p. 489). Given the likelihood that the restrictions on divorce that some reformers would like to see put in place are unlikely to become law, what else may be done to address the negative consequences of divorce for children, and to help postdivorce families more generally?

▪ Surviving Divorce ▪

Judith Wallerstein's initial research report on the often negative consequences of divorce for children was titled *Surviving the Break-Up* (Wallerstein and Kelly 1980). The passage of time has brought attention to some positive developments. There is some reconsid-eration of just how negative divorce is for children, as well as studies in other countries that suggest policy remedies. And there is research on "the good divorce," one that provides a workable family in the aftermath of divorce.

What Can Be Done to Address the Negative Consequences of Divorce for Children?

A cross-cultural study gives insight into what the wider U.S. society might do to help. Sociologists Sharon Houseknecht and Jaya Sastry (1996) conducted re-search to examine the relationship between "family decline" and child well-being in four industrialized countries: Sweden, the United States, the former West Germany, and Italy. These researchers' measures of family decline included nonmarital birth and divorce rates, the proportion of one-parent households with children, and the percentage of employed mothers with children under three years old. Child well-being was measured by six factors: educational performance, the percentage of children in poverty, infant deaths from child abuse, teenage suicide rates, juvenile delin-quency rates, and juvenile drug offense rates. The re-searchers found the following:

Sweden, which has the highest family decline score, does not demonstrate a high level of negative outcomes for children compared with other countries with lower levels of family decline. It looks much better than the U.S., which ranks the lowest on child well-being. Having said this, though, we must acknowledge that Italy, ranking lowest on family decline, looks the best of all the countries as far as child well-being is concerned. (p. 736)

What makes the difference between child well-being in the United States and that in Sweden? Sweden's welfare policies are "egalitarian and generous" when compared to those of the United States (p. 737). Sweden's society-wide willingness to support children's needs by paying relatively high taxes translates into significantly less child poverty, fewer working hours for parents, and more family support programs, such as paid parental leave (see Chapter 12). This situation results in relatively high levels of child well-being despite high proportions of nonmarital births, mother employment, divorces, and single-parent households. A review of policies and outcomes in Nordic countries by sociologist William Goode reached similar conclusions (Goode 1993).

The Good Divorce

Is there such a thing as a "good divorce"? That depends on expectations. Against the assumption that divorce is a disaster and solidifies a lasting enmity between the partners, to the detriment of their children, one can instead find a different pattern whereby couples maintain civility and cooperative parenting. "Case Study: The Post-Divorce Family as a Child-Rearing Institution" describes a couple that continued to parent their children after divorce, with the assistance of a counselor and after some turmoil.

THE BINUCLEAR FAMILY STUDY The Binuclear Family Study, led by sociologist Constance Ahrons (1994), interviewed ninety-eight divorcing couples approximately one year after their divorce. Ninety percent of them were followed to the five-year point, in a total of three interviews each. These were primarily white, middle-class couples from one Wisconsin county.

At the one-year point, 50 percent of the ex-spouses had amicable relations while the other 50 percent did not. In half the cases, the divorce was a bad

one, and harmful to family members; in the other half, the divorcing spouses had "preserved family ties and provided children with two parents and healthy families" (p. 16):

> In a good divorce a family with children remains a family. The family undergoes dramatic and unsettling changes in structure and size, but its functions remain the same. The parents—as they did when they were married—continue to be responsible for the emotional, economic, and physical needs of their children. (Ahrons 1994, p. 3)

The ninety-eight couples represented a broad range of postdivorce relationships. In 12 percent of the cases, couples were what Ahrons termed *Perfect Pals*—friends who called each other often and brought their common children and new family ties together on holidays or for outings or other activities. This was a minority pattern among the "good divorces." More often (38 percent), the couples were *Cooperative Colleagues*, who worked well together as co-parents, but did not attempt to share holidays or be in constant touch—occasionally, they might share children's important occasions such as birthdays. Ex-spouses might talk about extended family, friends, or work. They still had areas of conflict but were able to compartmentalize them and keep them out of the collaboration that they wanted to maintain for their children (Ahrons 1994). "As We Make Choices: Ten Keys to Successful Co-Parenting" provides some general guidelines for divorcing parents who want to cooperate in parenting their children.

Other divorcing couples were the *Angry Associates* (25 percent) or *Fiery Foes* (25 percent) that we often think of in conjunction with divorce. Over time, one-quarter of the Collaborative Colleagues drifted into one of these more antagonistic categories.[13]

Ahrons's overall point is that the "good divorce" does not end a family but instead produces a **binuclear family**—two households; one family. She argues that we must "recognize families of divorce as legitimate." To encourage more "good divorces," it is important to dispel the "myth that only in a nuclear family can we

---

13. Ahrons (1994) identified a fifth type of postdivorce couple relationship, the *Dissolved Duo*. These are couples who have completely lost touch with each other. Since Ahrons's specification of her sample required that a divorced couple have children and be in touch, there were no instances of Dissolved Duos in her sample.

Case Study

The Post-Divorce Family as a Child-Rearing Institution

Jo Ann is thirty-eight and has been divorced for six years. She has five children. Gary, nineteen, her oldest, lives with his father, Richard. At the time of this interview, Jo Ann and Richard and their children had recently begun family counseling. The purpose, Jo Ann explained, was to create for their children a more cooperative and supportive atmosphere. Jo Ann and Richard do not want to renew an intimate relationship, but they and their children are still in many ways a family fulfilling traditional family functions.

We've been going to family counseling about twice a month now. The whole family goes—all five kids, Richard, and me. The counselor wants to have a videotaping session. He says it would help us gain insights into how we act together. The two older girls don't want any part of it, but the rest of us decided it might be really good for Joey to see how he acts. [Joey's] the reason we're going in the first place. At the first counseling sessions, he sat with his coat over his head. . . .

Joey's always been a problem. He's used to getting his own way. Some people want all the attention.

They will do anything to get it. I guess I never knew how to deal with this. . . . He drives us nuts at home. He calls me and the girls names. . . . He was disrupting class and yelling at the teacher. And finally they expelled him. . . . Joey gets anger and frustration built up in him.

So I took him to a psychologist, and the psychologist said he'd like the whole family to come in, including Richard. Well, Richard still lives in this city and sees all the kids, so I asked him about it. And he said okay. . . .

In between sessions, the counselor wants us to have family conferences with the seven of us together. One day I called Richard and asked him over for supper. In the back of my mind I thought maybe we could get this family conferencing started.

Well, after dinner Joey, our eleven-year-old, started acting up. So I went for a walk with him. We must have walked a mile and a half, and Joey was angry the whole time. He told me I never listen to him; I never spend time with him. Then he started telling me about how he was mad at his dad because his dad won't listen to him.

He said his dad tells all these dumb jokes that are just so old, but he just keeps telling them and telling them. So when he got home, I saw Richard was still there, and I asked Joey, "Would you like to have a family conference? Maybe tell your dad some of the things that are bothering you?" And he said, "Could we?" . . . [During the conference] Joey talked first. Then everybody had a chance to say something. There was one time I was afraid it was going to get out of hand. Everybody was interrupting everybody else. But the counselor had told me you have to set up ground rules. This is where we learned that we got some neat kids because when I said "Let somebody else talk," everybody did! So it went real well. . . . And then finally Richard said, "I think it's time for us to come to a conclusion." I said, "Well, you're right."

Critical Thinking

How might this divorced family differ from the same family before divorce? How is it the same? Even though Jo Ann and Richard's family is no longer intact, what functions does it continue to perform for its members? For society?

raise healthy children" (p. 4). People often find what they expect, and social models of a functional postdivorce family have been lacking.

Ahrons (2004) recently reinterviewed 173 children from eighty-nine of the original families in her Binuclear Family Study. Now averaging thirty-one years of age, they had been six through fifteen at the time of the marital separation. At present—twenty years later—79 percent think that their parents' decision to divorce was a good one, and 78 percent feel that they are either better off than they would have been, or else not that affected. Twenty percent, however, did not do so well, with "emotional scars that didn't heal" (p. 44). Ahrons judges that the prime factor affecting outcomes was how the parents related to each other, in terms of avoiding conflict, that is. She concludes from her research that it is possible for families of divorce to still function as families. The title of

As We Make Choices

Ten Keys to Successful Co-Parenting

Melinda Blau, author of *Families Apart: Ten Keys to Successful Co-Parenting,* observes that "Divorce ends a marriage—it does not end a family; we got divorced; our children didn't" (1993, p. 16). Below are her general guidelines for those who hope to accomplish the "heroic feat" of co-parenting after divorce (1993, pp. 16–17):

Key #1: Heal yourself—so that you can get on with your life without leaning on your kids.

Key #2: Act maturely—whether or not you really *feel* it; you and your co-parent are the adults, with the responsibility to care for your kids and to act in their best interest.

Key #3: Listen to your children; understand their needs.

Key #4: Respect each other's competence as parents and love for the children.

Key #5: Divide parenting time—somehow, in some way, so that the children feel they still have two parents.

Key #6: Accept each other's differences—even though one of you is a health-food nut and the other eats Twinkies, one is laid-back and the other a disciplinarian, one's fanatically neat, the other is a slob.

Key #7: Communicate about (and with) the children directly, not *through* them.

Key #8: Step out of traditional gender roles. Mom learns how to fix a bike and knows what the "first down" is if her son's into

football, and Dad can take his daughter shopping and talk with her about dates.

Key #9: Recognize and accept that change is inevitable and therefore can be anticipated.

Key #10: Know that co-parenting is forever; be prepared to handle holidays, birthdays, graduations, and other milestones in your children's lives with a minimum of stress and encourage your respective extended families to do the same.

Critical Thinking

Do you agree or disagree with the advice presented here?

Source: Blau 1993.

Ahrons' most recent book—*We're Still Family* (2004)—characterizes the positive outcomes of divorce that she has found among the families she studied.

Ahrons offers a number of suggestions that she believes would contribute to good divorce outcomes and successful binuclear families. One piece of advice is for the parent to "accept that your child's family will expand to include nonbiological kin" (p. 252). Indeed, divorce and the new relationships that follow can produce a *divorce-extended family.*

THE DIVORCE-EXTENDED FAMILY A surprising phenomenon encountered by those who do research on divorced families is the expansion of the kinship system that is produced by links between ex-spouses and their new spouses and significant others and on beyond to *their* extended kin. Sociologist Judith Stacey (1990) speaks of a **divorce-extended family** (p. 61) and quotes writer Delia Ephron's apt observation:

It occurred to me . . . that the extended family is in our lives again. . . . Your basic extended family today includes your ex-husband or -wife, your ex's new mate, your new mate, possibly your new mate's ex, and any new mate that your new mate's ex has acquired. It consists entirely of people who are not related by blood, many of whom can't stand each other. (Ephron 1988, frontleaf)

Ephron's version may be out of date in one respect. Some postdivorce extended families find they can enjoy and benefit from connections to one another even when there had earlier been conflict, and tensions sometimes resurface (Kleinfield 2003). Stacey's research describes a Silicon Valley family that functioned as a mutual aid society in times of crisis and happily shared good times and special occasions as well.

Therapists claim to see "a new norm" of rapport and social contact among the divorce-extended family

A man, his wife, and his son, along with his former wife and their daughters, celebrate the holidays together.

© James Estrin/NYT Pictures

that is "becoming part of the culture" (Dr. Harvey Ruben, professor of clinical psychiatry at Yale School of Medicine, quoted in Kuczynski 2001, pp. 9–1, 9–6). In this spirit, "No longer are the names of exes unmentioned at the dinner table. No longer are the details of passing children between homes confined to emotionless e-mail messages. Family therapists, sociologists, and journalists note that 'family members who 25 years ago might not have had anything to do with one another are finding it desirable to stay connected'" (Kuczynski 2001, p. 9–1).

To the extent that relationships between exspouses are cordial and the ties of a divorce-extended family come to seem natural, tension for children moving between families should be reduced. Familial

occasions such as graduations and weddings that bring everyone together should be less strained. New research finds that good relationships between children and noncustodial fathers *and* with residential stepfathers make independent contributions to good child outcomes (White and Gilbreth 2001). If the therapists are right about "new norms," what we could see in the future would be an institutionalization of the "good divorce"—perhaps not attainable for all, but recognized as "normal" for those who do.

That change involves incorporating remarriage bonds into the original family. We turn in Chapter 17 to a consideration of that common step for many divorced people: remarrying.

In Sum

- Divorce rates rose sharply in the twentieth century, and divorce rates in the United States are now the highest in the world. Since around 1980, however, they have declined somewhat.

- Reasons why more people are divorcing now have to do with changes in society. Economic interdependence and legal, moral, and social constraints are lessening. Expectations for intimacy have risen, while expectations of permanence are declining.

- People's personal decisions to divorce involve weighing marital complaints—most often problems with communication or the emotional quality of the relationship—against the possible consequences of divorce.

- Two consequences that receive a great deal of consideration are how a divorce will affect children, if there are any, and whether it will cause serious financial difficulties.

- Bohannan has identified six ways in which divorce affects people. These six "stations of divorce" are the emotional divorce, the legal divorce, the community divorce, the psychic divorce, the economic divorce, and the co-parental divorce. The psychic divorce involves a healing process that individuals must complete before they can fully enter new intimate relationships.

- The economic divorce is typically more disastrous for women than for men, and this is especially so for custodial mothers. Over the past twenty-five years, child support policies have undergone sweeping changes. The results seem to be positive, with more child support being collected.

- Researchers have proposed five possible theories to explain negative effects of divorce on children. These include the life stress perspective, the parental loss perspective, the parental adjustment perspective, the economic hardship perspective, and the interparental conflict perspective.

- Husbands' and wives' divorce experiences are typically different. Both the task overload and financial decline that characterize the wife's divorce and the loneliness that often accompanies the husband's, especially when there are children, might be lessened in the future by less gender-differentiated postdivorce arrangements. Joint custody offers the opportunity of greater involvement by both parents.

- Meanwhile, debate has emerged among family scholars and policy makers concerning how important a threat divorce is to children today. Some call for return to a fault system of divorce or other restrictions on divorce. Others see divorce as part of a set of broad social changes, the implications of which must be addressed in ways other than hoping to turn back the clock.

- At the same time, new norms and new forms of the family are developing. Some postdivorce families can share family occasions and attachments and work together civilly and realistically to foster a "good divorce" and a binuclear family.

Key Terms

binuclear family
child snatching
child support
children's allowance
community divorce
covenant marriage
crude divorce rate
custodial parent
custody
displaced homemaker
divorce-extended family
divorce mediation
economic divorce
economic hardship perspective (on children's adjustment to divorce)
emotional divorce
guaranteed child support
income effect
independence effect
intergenerational transmission of divorce
interparental conflict perspective (on children's adjustment to divorce)
joint custody
legal divorce
life stress perspective (on children's adjustment to divorce)
no-fault divorce
parental adjustment perspective (on children's adjustment to divorce)
parental loss perspective (on children's adjustment to divorce)
psychic divorce
redivorce
refined divorce rate
relatives of divorce
spousal support
supervised visitation

Questions for Review and Reflection

1. What factors bind marriages and families together? How have these factors changed, and how has the divorce rate been affected?

2. How is "his" divorce different from "her" divorce? How are these differences related to society's gender expectations? In your observation, are the descriptions given in this chapter accurate assessments of divorce outcomes for men and women today?

3. In what situation(s), in your opinion, would divorce be the best option for a family and its children?

4. Do you think couples are too quick to divorce? What are your reasons for thinking so?

5. **Policy Question.** Should divorced parents with children be required to remain in the same community? Permitted to move only by court authorization? Be free to choose whether to be geographically mobile?

Suggested Readings

Ahrons, Constance. 2004. *We're Still Family: What Grown Children Have to Say about Their Parents' Divorce*. New York: HarperCollins. This book continues the author's Binuclear Family Study by reporting interviews with now-grown children of divorced parents. It is a readable presentation of divorce research with a quite hopeful outlook on the postdivorce life of families.

Amato, Paul R., and Alan Booth. 1997. *A Generation at Risk: Growing Up in an Era of Family Upheaval*. Cambridge, MA: Harvard University Press. Important analysis of the well-being of American children in the late twentieth century, based on the authors' and others' research. Presents some gains as well as losses. Assesses the impact of divorce on children, comparing low-conflict to high-conflict marriages.

Harvey, John H., and Mark A. Fine. 2004. *Children of Divorce: Stories of Loss and Growth*. Mahwah, NJ: Erlbaum. College student voices are the substance of this book. Students' commentaries written in Professor Harvey's classes on "Close Relationships" and "Loss and Trauma." The book contains a discussion of theory and research that includes the Wallerstein/Hetherington "debate" on outcomes of divorce.

Hetherington, E. Mavis, and John Kelly. 2002. *For Better or For Worse: Divorce Reconsidered*. New York: Norton. This book, by one of the foremost researchers on divorce, sums up several decades of research and presents us with a relatively optimistic view of the outcomes of divorce.

Lawson, Erma Jean, and Aaron Thompson. 2000. *Black Men and Divorce*. Thousand Oaks, CA: Sage. Sociological treatment of marriage and divorce among black men, along with some discussion of coping strategies. Challenges stereotypes of black men from a cultural variant perspective. This book assumes a special importance, as the major studies of divorce by Wallerstein, Hetherington, and Ahrons are all based on middle-class whites.

Riley, Glenda. 1991. *Divorce: An American Tradition*. New York: Oxford University Press. An historical analysis of American values, attitudes, and behaviors regarding divorce since the establishment of the United States.

Argues that traditional American values of independence, freedom, and individualism are much in keeping with high divorce rates.

Wallerstein, Judith S., Julia M. Lewis, and Sandra Blakeslee. 2000. *The Unexpected Legacy of Divorce: A 25 Year Landmark Study*. New York: Hyperion. A major figure in divorce research and the debate about divorce, Wallerstein sums up her research and its implications for parents and policy in a mostly negative view of divorce.

Virtual Society: The Wadsworth Sociology Resource Center

Go to the Sociology Resource Center at **http://sociology.wadsworth.com** for a wealth of online resources, including a companion website for your text that provides study aids such as self-quizzes for each chapter and a practice final exam, as well as links to sociology websites and information on the latest theories and discoveries in the field. In addition, you will find further suggested readings, flash cards, MicroCase online exercises, and appendices on a range of subjects.

Online Study Tool

Marriage & Family ⊛ Now™ Go to **http://sociology.wadsworth.com** to reach the companion website for your text and use the Marriage&FamilyNow access code that came with your book to access this study tool. Take a practice pretest after you have read each chapter, and then use the study plan provided to master that chapter. Afterward, take a posttest to monitor your progress.

Search Online with InfoTrac College Edition

For additional information, exercises, and key words to aid your research, explore InfoTrac College Edition, your online library that offers full-length articles from thousands of scholarly and popular publications. Click on *InfoTrac College Edition* under *Chapter Resources* at the companion website and use the access code that came with your book.

- Search keywords: *joint custody*. See what current research has to say about the merits of joint custody.

- Search keywords: *same-sex partners—separation, divorce, custody, or visitation*. The U.S. has not established same-

sex marriage as legally valid, but same-sex couples who dissolve their relationship must find a way to regularize their newly separate status in terms of property, and especially regarding the children of their gay/lesbian family. Is there any research on this in social science or law journals?

17

Remarriages

and Stepfamilies

WEDDINGS FOR PEOPLE GETTING remarried are big business, with web magazines, such as *Bride Again*, and specialized jewelry meant to symbolize a newly blended family (*www.brideagain.com*; "Twice As Nice" 2000). Stepparents Day has been proposed as a new national holiday (Bruno 2001). Many Americans choose to marry more than once, usually after being divorced. Today, remarriages make up approximately half of all marriages (Coleman, Ganong, and Fine 2000). And "one in three Americans are now stepparents, stepchildren, stepsiblings, or living in a stepfamily" (Miller 2004). Indeed, "It may be that eventually the majority of people will be married more than once during their lifetime" (Ihinger-Tallman and Pasley 1997, p. 24).

Many remarried people are happy with their relationships and lives. Much of what we have said throughout this book—about good parenting practices, for example, and about positive ways for couples to communicate or how best to handle family stress—applies to remarried families. At the same time, partners and children in stepfamilies experience unique challenges, because stepfamilies are different from first-marriage families in several important ways (Ganong and Coleman 2004). This chapter explores remarriages and stepfamilies. More and more stepfamilies today result from cohabitation rather than from legal remarriage, but relatively little research has been done on how cohabiting stepfamilies function (Coleman, Ganong, and Fine 2000; Ganong and Coleman 2004). Consequently, the vast majority of researchers' findings and therapists' suggestions in this chapter were meant to apply only to remarried families. The extent to which they may be applied to cohabiting stepfamilies is uncertain.

In this chapter, we will discuss choosing a remarriage partner, noting some social factors that influence that choice. We'll examine happiness and stability in remarriage, as well as the adjustment and well-being of

About half of all marriages today are remarriages, a fact that greeting card companies acknowledge.

"Well, the children are grown up, married, divorced, and remarried. I guess our job is done."

children in stepfamilies. We'll examine two challenging areas in remarriages: stepchildren and finances. Finally, we will explore ideas for creating happy and supportive remarriages and stepfamilies. We'll begin with an overview of remarriage in the United States today.

Remarriage: Some Basic Facts

Unfortunately, the U.S. Census Bureau stopped compiling remarriage statistics in 1988, and other sources of detailed remarriage statistics are not current either. As a result, in many cases we can only estimate today's situation, based on prior data. We do know, though, that **remarriages** (marriages in which at least one partner had previously been divorced or widowed) are increasingly frequent in the United States today, compared to the middle decades of the twentieth century. The remarriage rate rose sharply during World War II, peaking as the war ended. During the 1950s, both the divorce rate and the remarriage rate declined and remained relatively low until the 1960s, when they began to rise again. The remarriage rate peaked again

in about 1975 but declined slightly after that (Bianchi and Casper 2000, Figure 2).

One reason for the slight decline in remarriage rates is that many divorced people who would have remarried in the past are now cohabiting (Coleman, Ganong, and Fine 2000; Stewart 2001). A second reason for the decline may be economic constraints and uncertainties, which discourage divorced men, in particular, who may already be paying child support, from assuming financial responsibility for a new family.[1]

Nevertheless, 75 percent of divorced women remarry within ten years, and 83 percent do so after fifteen years (Bramlett and Mosher 2001, Table 7). Some people divorce, remarry, redivorce, then remarry again. But a majority of remarriages are second marriages. ("Facts about Families: Remarriages and Race/Ethnic Diversity" gives further statistics regarding remarriages.)

---

1. Some states, concerned about child support, passed legislation in the 1970s designed to prevent the remarriage of people whose child support was not paid up. But the Supreme Court ruled in *Zablocki v. Redhail* (1978) that marriage—including remarriage—was so fundamental a right that it could not be abridged in this way.

Facts About Families

Remarriages and Race/Ethnic Diversity

The average divorced person who remarries does so within four years after divorce; 30 percent do so within one year (Coleman, Ganong, and Fine 2000). However, rapidity—and overall probability—of remarriage vary for women of different ethnic origins. About 42 percent of non-Hispanic white women remarry within three years after divorce, compared with 23 percent of non-Hispanic black women and 29 percent of Latinas. Analogous percentages for five years after dissolution are 58 percent for non-Hispanic whites, 32 percent for non-Hispanic blacks, and 44 percent for Latinas (Bramlett and Mosher 2001, Table 8).

The living arrangements of children who are residing with two parents are also differentially distributed by race and Hispanic origin.* Among African American children who live in two-parent families, nearly 64 percent reside with both biological parents and another 31 percent live with their biological mother and a stepfather. These figures compare to 81.5 percent and 14.6 percent, respectively, for all races taken together. The higher proportion of African American children living with a stepfather reflects the higher divorce rate among African Americans as well as the lower life expectancy for African American men.

* Note that this discussion is about the distribution of children, not in *all* households with children, but only in *two-parent* households.

Remarriages have always been fairly common in the United States, but in the past this was due to high mortality and low divorce rates. Well into the twentieth century almost all remarriages followed widowhood. Today, the vast majority of remarrieds have been divorced (U.S. Census Bureau 2000, Table 145). Remarriage is much more likely to occur, age for age, among divorced women than among widowed women (Talbott 1998). Figure 17.1 contrasts the marriage rates of divorced and widowed men and women with those of never-married people and illustrates change over time.

Single-parent and remarried families are still stereotyped as neither as "normal" nor as functional as first-marriage, nuclear families (Ganong and Coleman 2004). But there is no question that their increased incidence and visibility have led to somewhat greater social and cultural acceptance of remarriage and stepfamilies.

Remarriage, Stepfamilies, and Children's Living Arrangements

FOCUS ON CHILDREN

One result of the significant number of remarriages today (as well as the growing incidence of cohabitation after divorce) is that more Americans are parenting other people's children. Put another way, more children are living with other than their biological parents. In U.S. households, a little over 5 percent of children under age eighteen are stepchildren, and almost 6 percent of adult children (eighteen years old and over) who are living "at home" are doing so in stepfamily households (Kreider 2003, Table 1). As you can see in Figure 17.2, 88 percent of children under age eighteen in married-couple or cohabiting households are the biological offspring of both parents. Another 7 percent of children in two-parent households are the biological offspring of the mother and stepchildren of the father. About 2 percent of children in two-parent households are biological children of the father and stepchildren of the mother (Fields 2001).

Figure 17.2 points up the fact that stepfamilies are not all alike: A stepparent may be mother or father (although usually, the father). Furthermore, a stepfamily may or may not contain biological children of both remarried parents. At least 4 percent and perhaps up to 10 percent of households with children are *joint biological-step*; i.e., at least one child is a *mutual child*—the biological child of both parents—and at least one other child is the biological child of one parent and the stepchild of the other parent (U.S. Census Bureau

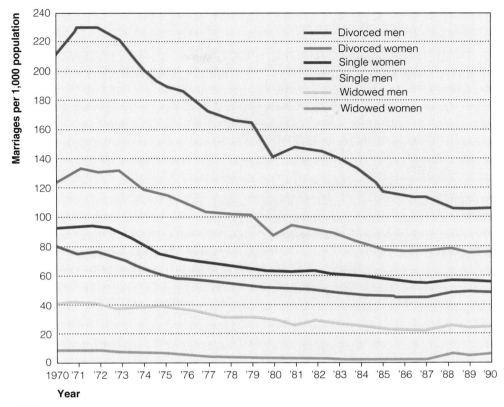

FIGURE 17.1

Marriage rates of never-married, divorced, and widowed men and women, 1970–1990. Marriage rates presented here are number of marriages per 1,000 population in the specified marital status category. These data are from the 1990 national census—the latest statistics available.

Sources: U.S. National Center for Health Statistics 1990b, Table 5; Clarke 1995a, Table 6.

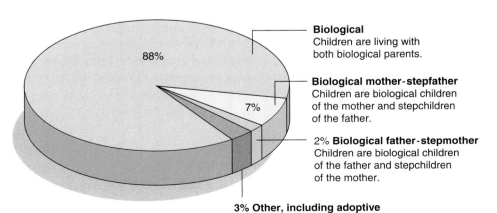

FIGURE 17.2

Children under age eighteen living with two parents, by their biological, step, and adoptive status, 1996—the latest statistics available.

Source: Fields 2001, Table 2.
See also Kreider 2003, Table 8.

1994a, Table 78; Kreider 2003, Table 8). In some step-families, both parents are stepparents to their spouse's biological children.

Then, too, as we have already mentioned, step-families do not always result from remarriage: "Approximately 25% of the 3.7 million cohabiting couples in the United States are households in which at least one adult brings children from prior relationships, thereby creating cohabiting stepfamily households" (Coleman, Ganong, and Fine 2000, p. 1290; see also Simmons and O'Connell 2003, Table 4).

The remainder of this chapter explores what family life is like for children—and their parents—who are living in stepfamilies. We begin with a question about courtship before remarriage. Do people choose partners differently the next time around?

Choosing Partners ■ the Next Time: ■ Variations on a Theme

It goes without saying that spouses are older at the time of remarriage than at first marriage. In 1990, the latest data available, the mean age of remarriage was 34.2 for previously divorced brides and 37.8 for previously divorced grooms—about ten years older than for first marriages (U.S. Census Bureau 1999, Table 158). Researchers note that people who ended troubled first marriages through divorce are often still experiencing personal conflicts (Hetherington 1989; Bray 1999) that they need to resolve before they can expect to fashion a supportive, stable second marriage. Consequently, counselors advise waiting until one has worked through grief and anger over the prior divorce before entering into another serious relationship (Marano 2000).

Meanwhile, courtship before remarriage may differ in many respects from courtship before first marriage. It may proceed much more rapidly, with the people involved viewing themselves as mature adults who know what they are looking for—or it may be more cautious, with the partners needing time to recover from their previous marital experience or being wary of repeating it. A second courtship is likely to have an earlier, more open sexual component—which may be hidden from the children through a series of complex arrangements. It may include both outings with the children and evenings at home as partners seek to

recapture their accustomed domesticity (Rodgers and Conrad 1986): "A common courtship pattern is as follows: (a) male partner spends a few nights per week in the mother's household, followed by (b) a brief period of full-time living together, followed by (c) remarriage" (Coleman, Ganong, and Fine 2000, p. 1290).

Courtship for remarriage has not been a major topic for research. Almost twenty years ago, Canadian sociologists Roy Rodgers and Linda Conrad posed several hypotheses for future testing. Generally, the hypotheses point up the complicated interrelationships among courting parents, their respective children, and their ex-spouses. For example, if one ex-spouse begins courtship while the other does not, conflict between the former spouses may escalate. Moreover, the noncourting partner may try to interfere with the ex-spouse's new relationship. Not only ex-spouses but children, too, may react negatively to a parent's dating. Generally, "the more the custodial parent's new partner displaces the child as a source of emotional support for the parent, the greater the probability of a negative reaction of the child to the new partner," and the more that problems are likely to arise (Rodgers and Conrad 1986, p. 771).

Unfortunately, little has been done to test these hypotheses.[2] Meanwhile, they suggest that courtship toward remarriage differs from that for first marriages in important ways. Nevertheless, the basic structure of the remarrying process has much in common with first marriages. We'll look at two topics that we first examined in Chapter 7 with regard to first marriages: the relative advantages of remarriage for men and for women, and homogamy.

Remarriage Advantages for Women and Men

Economists and other social scientists point out that, as a group, ex-wives, but not ex-husbands, are likely to gain financially by being remarried. Indeed, "stepfamily relationships are important in lifting single-parent families out of poverty" (Mason 1998, p. 114). A longitudinal study by sociologists Donna Morrison and Amy Ritualo (2000) used National Longitudinal Survey of Youth (NLSY) data to track the financial well-

---

2. Looking for a research topic? Going to graduate school in family studies someday? These hypotheses proposed by Rodgers and Conrad (1986) would make a nice research project.

being of children of divorced mothers and their custodial children. The children had been born to a married couple who later divorced. Some of the custodial mothers remained single, others remarried, and still others formed cohabiting stepfamilies. The finances of mothers who remarried greatly improved. Mothers who began cohabiting also saw an increase in finances, although not as great. We can conclude that, in general, remarriage is financially advantageous to divorced mothers and their children. Furthermore, "in absolute terms, remarriage is economically more advantageous than cohabitation." Nevertheless, "cohabitation and remarriage are equivalent in their ability to restore family income to prior levels [because] cohabiting mothers start off in a weaker economic position prior to divorce" (Morrison and Ritualo 2000, p. 560). This situation would change, of course, if women's earnings were to catch up with men's. Chapter 16 addresses the economic plight of divorced women in more detail.

Meanwhile, the following account by a single male in his late twenties illustrates that women typically have more to gain financially from being remarried than men do:

> She was eyeing me and eyeing my house as a nice place to live with her son. It was the first thing she did. We went to my house one night and she says, "Boy, you've really got a nice backyard and a nice house here." And I'm thinking, "Why is she saying that?" It didn't click at the time, but she told this buddy of mine that her plan was to move in here with her kid—whatever his name was. Jason, that was the name, Jason. I could not stand that kid at all. So when I found this out, that I was her meal ticket, I thought, "Hea-a-a-vy." And that was the last time I saw her. She had great plans for me, but then I thought "Nah." (personal interview)

This uneven situation—that is, that remarrying women, on average, benefit financially more than do remarrying men—is one reason that women's remarriage rate is considerably lower than men's. (In part, this statistic is a consequence of the very low remarriage rate of widows, for whom few partners are available in later life. But even comparing only divorced people, men's remarriage rates are substantially higher, particularly after age thirty.) At least two factors work against women's remarriage.

CHILDREN AND THE ODDS OF REMARRIAGE

"Children lower the likelihood of remarriage for both men and women, but the impact of children is greater on women's probability of remarriage" (Coleman, Ganong, and Fine 2000, p. 1289). As we see in Chapter 16, the woman usually retains custody of children from a previous marriage. As a result, a prospective second husband may look on her family as a financial—and also an emotional and psychological—liability. Then too, children are often strongly loyal to the first family and may oppose or have strong reservations about the divorce and a parent's possible remarriage for as long as five years afterward.

AGE AND THE ODDS OF REMARRIAGE

A second factor, age, may work against women in several ways. Figure 17.3 shows the remarriage rates for divorced women in six age categories. While the pattern of remarriage since 1960 has been similar for all age categories, the remarriage rate for younger women has been consistently higher. As discussed in Chapters 7 and 9, women live longer, on average, than men do: By age 65, there are about 80 men for every 100 women (U.S. Census Bureau 2000, Table 12; and see Figure 9.3 in this textbook). The *double standard of aging*, de-

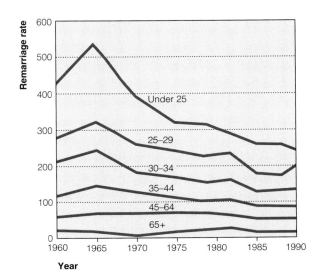

FIGURE 17.3

Remarriage rates per 1,000 divorced and widowed women over age fifteen, by age at remarriage, 1960–1990—the latest statistics available.

Source: Clarke 1995a, Table 6.

As Americans live longer, many of them are finding that love and intimacy can occur at any age. People tend to choose partners differently the second time around, and although remarriage rates are relatively low for those over sixty-five, some do find happiness in a late remarriage.

scribed in Chapter 7, works against women in the remarriage market. In our society, women are considered to be less physically attractive with age, and they may also be less interested in fulfilling more-traditional gender-role expectations.

Remarriages increased among older adults over the past several decades. Currently about a half million people over age sixty-five remarry annually, and about 4 percent of older adults who do not remarry choose to cohabit (Coleman, Ganong, and Fine 2000, p. 1290). Nevertheless, age may work against both women's and men's remarriage. For instance, older people may face considerable opposition to remarriage—both from restrictive pension and Social Security regulations and from their friends and children. Although some peers or grown children may be supportive of a remarriage, others may find it inappropriate. Adult children may worry about the biological parent's continued interest in them, or, ultimately, they may be concerned about their inheritance (Pasley 1998b; Rosenfeld 1997).

Homogamy in Remarriage

Homogamy has traditionally been a second important factor influencing marriage choices. We see in Chapter 7 that homogamy may be important in both the choice of a first marriage partner and in subsequent marital stability. Does homogamy play a similar role in remarriages? The answer to that question is, on the whole, no. Older people, particularly those who are widowed, are likely to remarry homogamously. Sometimes the new partner is someone who reminds them of their first spouse or is someone they've known for years. But this rule does not apply to middle-aged or younger people who choose remarriage partners.

Choosing a remarriage partner differs from making a marital choice the first time inasmuch as there is a smaller pool of eligibles with a wider range on any given attribute. As prospective mates move from their late twenties into their thirties, they affiliate in occupational circles and interest groups that assemble people from more diverse backgrounds. As a result, remarriages are less homogamous than first marriages, with partners differing more in age, educational background (U.S. National Center for Health Statistics 1990b), and religion.

Because homogamy increases the likelihood of marital stability, the increased heterogamy characteristic of remarriage has been offered as a partial explanation for the fact that the divorce rate is higher for remarriages (Booth and Edwards 1992). The next section discusses stability and happiness in remarriage.

Spouses' Happiness/ ▪ Satisfaction and Stability ▪ in Remarriage

As pointed out elsewhere in this text, marital happiness, or satisfaction, and marital stability are not the same. *Marital happiness* and *marital satisfaction* are synonymous phrases that refer to the quality of the marital relationship whether or not it is permanent; *marital stability* refers simply to the duration of the union. We'll look at both ways of evaluating remarriage.

Happiness/Satisfaction in Remarriage

In general, research shows little difference in spouses' overall well-being (Demo and Acock 1996b) or in marital happiness between first and later unions (Ihinger-Tallman and Pasley 1997; Skinner, Bhar, Crane, and Call 2002). For one thing, we see in Chapters 12 and 14 that wives' satisfaction with the division of household labor is important to marital satisfaction. There is evidence that there is more equity, or fairness, in remarriages than in first marriages (Buunk and Mutsaers 1999) because remarried husbands contribute somewhat more to housework than do husbands in first marriages. (Interestingly, one study found that this appears to have more to do with an ex-wife's less-than-satisfactory experience in her first marriage, and subsequent partner selection for remarriage, than with remarried men's resolution to do more around the house than they did in their first marriage [Sullivan 1997].)

However, considerable research shows that remarrieds experience more tension and conflict than do first marrieds, usually on issues related to stepchildren—discipline or how resources should be distributed to stepchildren (Coleman, Ganong, and Fine 2000). Nevertheless, it is probably safe to conclude that support from friends and families of origin and supportive family communication are more important to marital satisfaction than whether the union is a first marriage or a remarriage (Kurdek 1989a; Golish 2003).

The Stability of Remarriages

"Remarriages dissolve at higher rates than first marriages, especially for remarried couples with stepchildren" (Coleman, Ganong, and Fine 2000, p. 1291; Bramlett and Mosher 2001). According to the Stepfamily Association of America, about 60 percent of remarriages end in divorce, compared with about half of all first marriages ("Stepfamily Facts" 2003). As a result, a "conservative estimate is that between 20 percent and 30 percent of stepchildren will, before they turn eighteen, see their custodial parent and stepparent divorce" (Mason 1998, p. 99).

There are several reasons for the generally lower stability of remarriages. First, people who divorce in the first place are disproportionately from lower-middle- and lower-class groups, which generally have a higher tendency to divorce. Second, people who remarry after divorce are, as a group, more accepting of divorce and may have already demonstrated that they are willing to choose divorce as a way of resolving an unsatisfactory marriage. Third, remarrieds receive less social support from their families of origin and are generally less integrated with parents and in-laws, thus not having the advantage of relationships that can act as a barrier to divorce (Booth and Edwards 1992; Coleman, Ganong, and Fine 2000).

Finally, remarriages present some special stresses on a couple, stresses that are not inherent in first marriages. Our culture has not yet fully evolved norms or traditions that provide remarried partners and their families with models for appropriate behavior (Ganong and Coleman 2004). As we gain experience with the special challenges of remarriage, which are discussed throughout this chapter, remarriages may become more stable.

Perhaps the most significant factor in the comparative instability of remarriages is the presence of stepchildren. One important study on a national sample of black and white couples concluded that stepchildren are *not* necessarily associated with more frequent marital conflict. Moreover, it's important to note that the negative impact of stepchildren declines with the length of the remarriage (MacDonald and DeMaris 1995). "Case Study: My (Step)Family" illustrates these points. However, sociologists Lynn White and Alan Booth interviewed a national sample of more than 2,000 married people under age fifty-five in 1980 and reinterviewed four-fifths of them in 1983. During that interval, **double remarriages**, in which both partners had been married before, were twice as likely to have broken up as those of people in their first marriage. **Single remarriages**, in which only one partner had been previously married, did not differ significantly from first marriages in their likelihood of divorce.

It is estimated that about one-fifth of all marriages today are double remarriages. Approximately another one-fifth of all marriages are single remarriages (Clarke 1995a, p. 4). In White and Booth's study, double remarriage increased the probability of divorce by 50 percent over what it would have been otherwise,

Case Study

My (Step)Family

The following essay was written for a marriage and family course by a young college student named David.

I'm writing this paper about my family. My family is made up of my family that I reside with and then my dad, stepmother, and half-sister that I visit. My family I reside with is who I consider my real family. We are made up of five girls and three boys, a cat and a dog, my mom and stepfather. The oldest is Harry, then down the line goes Diane, Barbara Ann, Kathy, Debi, Mel, Sharon, and myself. My sister Debi and I are the only kids from my mom's original marriage, so as you can see my mom was taking a big step facing six new kids. (My mom has guts!)

I still consider my dad "family," but I don't come into contact with him that much now. I would like to concentrate on my new "step-family," but I really don't like that word for it. My family is my family.

My brothers and sisters are *all* my brothers and sisters whether they are step or original. My stepfather, although I don't call him "dad," is my father. My grandparents, step or original, are my grandparents. I can honestly say I love them all the same.

It all began when I was four. I don't remember much about my parents' divorce. The one real memory I have is sleeping with my dad downstairs while my sister slept upstairs with my mom. . . .

My mom met my stepfather, Harry, through mutual friends who went to our church. I was in first grade, and I don't really remember much about their dating. All I knew was either these strange kids came over to my house or I went over to theirs. They were married in March 1976. I was five. At the reception I got to see all my relatives, old and new. When my parents left for their honeymoon, I began to cry. My aunt did a good job of consoling me.

After my parents got married, we moved. We didn't move into my stepfather's and his kids' house but to a new house altogether for everyone. I still live there. I love it there and probably will live in that area all my life.

I remember when we first went to look at the house. We live on a golf course. Mel, my brother (step), and sister (step), and I went out on this big sand trap to get a look around. The next thing I remember is getting pushed off and swallowing sand and not being able to breathe. I don't know if this was just an older brother thing or a new stepbrother thing. In any event, Mel came over and helped me get my breath back and all was fine. That was just the first of our many childhood altercations. There were lots of other fights over things from broken toys to slap shots in the face.

Well, we moved into our new house, and I had to change schools.

and having stepchildren in the home increased it an additional 50 percent. Although the presence of stepchildren did not make so much difference in single remarriages, double remarriages involving stepchildren have a very elevated risk of dissolution. Of course, these are the most-complex family types in a society that has not yet developed a normative structure for stepfamilies.

Nevertheless, White and Booth found that *marital quality* does not vary greatly between first marriages and single or double remarriages. It is *satisfaction with family life* that is generally affected:

> Since they report only modestly lower marital happiness, we interpret this as evidence that the stepfamily, rather than the marriage, is stress-

ful. . . . These data suggest that . . . if it were not for the children these marriages would be stable. The partners manage to be relatively happy despite the presence of stepchildren, but they nevertheless are more apt to divorce because of child-related problems. (White and Booth 1985b, p. 696)

Negative Stereotypes and Remarital Satisfaction and Stability

Remarital satisfaction is influenced by the wider society through the negative stereotyping of remarriages (Ganong and Coleman 2004). Some religions, such as Catholicism, do not recognize a remarriage after divorce unless the first marriage has been annulled

I had to leave all my old friends and make some new ones. I did make new friends, and what was neat was that our two football teams played each other every year. So I got to play against my old friends with my new friends. When I got into high school, we were all united again. So I had gotten a new family, a new house, and a new school with new friends. I would have to say it was a major life transition.

As I grew up there were some tough times. I got picked on, but the youngest always does. But as I got older, it got to be less and less. And by the time I made it into high school, my long-time adversary, Mel, was beginning to be my best friend. I owe him a lot. During my childhood, my stepfather was extremely busy with work, and my dad was seldom around. It was Mel who taught me how to ride a bike and play basketball, baseball, and football. He also watched out for the younger kids, me and Sharon. I owe him a lot and would do anything for him.

Both my parents agreed about most issues (discipline, for example), and this led to smooth communication between our parents and us

kids. The only thing detrimental I can think of that came out of being in a large family was that I had poor study habits as a young child. The problem was my stepfather can watch TV, listen to the radio, and prepare a balance sheet all at the same time. So he let his kids listen to the radio or watch TV while they did their homework. My mom didn't agree with this, but it was too hard for her to enforce not watching TV with so many kids already used to doing it. . . .

I love all my brothers and sisters very much and would do anything for them. It is neat to see them get married and have kids. I have three nieces and five nephews. It is very exciting to get the whole family together. A lot of my family, nuclear and extended, live in our area. My grandparents, aunts, and uncles, cousins, three sisters and their kids all live within twenty minutes of our house. Having roots and strong family connections are two things I'm very thankful for. These are things I received from my stepfather because if I lived with my dad, I would be on what I consider his nomadic journey: he moves about every three years.

I think I'm very lucky. I had a solid upbringing and relatively few problems. I owe my stepfather a lot. He has given me clothes and food, taught me important lessons, instilled in me a good work ethic, and seen to it that I get a good education—all the way through college. Without him a lot of these things would not be possible; I am grateful for everything he has done for me. I'm happy with the way things turned out, and I love my family dearly.

Critical Thinking

What might be a reason that David does not like to apply the term *stepfamily* to his own family? How does David's essay illustrate some potential problems specific to stepfamilies? Do you think David's parents have a stable marriage? Why or why not? Divorce and remarriage may be thought of as transitions and/or crises, the subjects of Chapter 15. In what ways does David's essay illustrate meeting crises creatively, as discussed in that chapter? If you live in a stepfamily, how does David's experience compare to your own? (See also Freisthler, Svare, and Harrison-Jay 2003).

(Hornik 2001). Historically (Phillips 1997), and today, society is beset with such potentially harmful myths as "A stepfamily can never be as good a family in which children live with both natural parents" (Kurdek and Fine 1991, p. 567). In an interesting small study, 211 university students were asked to examine an eight-year-old child's report card. All the students saw the same report card, but some were told that the child lived with his biological parents while others were told that he lived with his mother and stepfather. Asked about their impressions of the child, male (but not female) students rated stepchildren less positively than biological children with respect to social and emotional behaviors (Claxton-Oldfield et al. 2002).

In other words, the stigma associated with stepfamilies may influence our appraisal of stepfamily

members' functioning (Jones and Galinsky 2003).[3] Furthermore, "When stepfamilies are not stigmatized, they are often invisible to social systems—the policies and practices of schools and youth organizations create barriers to participation by stepfamily members because they are based on models of first-marriage families" (Coleman, Ganong, and Fine 2000, p. 1299).

In a study of thirty-one white, middle-class spouses in stepfather families, researchers found, especially among the wives, that believing in none or very few of these negative myths and having high optimism about

3. As a unique form of stepfamilies, many gay and lesbian families are "triple-stigmatized" for being (1) gay, (2) gay parents, and (3) stepfamilies (Berger 2000; Erera and Fredriksen 1999; Lynch and Murray 2000).

the remarriage were related to high family, marital, and personal satisfaction (Kurdek and Fine 1991). Therapist Anne Bernstein (1999) proposes that we all begin "deconstructing the stories of failure, insufficiency, and neglect" and, instead, "collaboratively reconstruct stories that liberate steprelationships" from this legacy (p. 415). Meanwhile, an important reason that stepfamilies may not be as stable is that, although they are increasingly prevalent, remarried families remain a "normless norm."

Remarried Families: A Normless Norm

When neither spouse enters a remarriage with children, the couple's union is usually very much like a first marriage. But when at least one spouse has children from a previous marriage, family life often differs sharply from that of first marriages. A primary reason for this is that our society offers members of **remarried families** no **cultural script**, or set of socially prescribed and understood guidelines, for relating to each other or for defining responsibilities and obligations (Ganong and Coleman 2000). Because of the cultural ambiguity of stepfamily relationships, social scientist Andrew Cherlin (1978) twenty-five years ago called the remarried family an **incomplete institution**. For the most part, researchers continue to view the situation this way (Ganong and Coleman 2004; Marsiglio 2004a). Social

work professor Irene Levin (1997) argues that "the nuclear family has a kind of model monopoly when it comes to family forms" (p. 123). According to this **nuclear-family model monopoly**, the first-marriage family is the "real" model for family living, with all other family forms "seen as deficient alternatives." This "prejudice" affects everyone's understanding of stepfamilies—researchers and stepfamily members alike—so that we incorrectly expect a second marriage to be "more or less the same as the first" (p. 124).

Although society tends to broadly apply the rules and assumptions of first marriages to remarriages, these rules often ignore the complexities of remarried families and leave many questions unanswered (Kheshgi-Genovese and Genovese 1997; Ganong and Coleman 2004). The next section explores three areas in which remarriage as an incomplete institution, or a "normless norm," is most apparent: (1) within the remarried families themselves, (2) in relationships with kin, and (3) in family law.

Characteristics of Remarried Families

"I come from a family that has two sets of stepfamilies," wrote one of our students in a recently assigned essay. The complexity of stepfamily structure, which affects family relationships, is further illustrated in Table 17.1. The table compares stepfamilies with the original nuclear family and with the single-parent family, which often is a stage between former marriages and remarriages. ("A Closer Look at Family Diversity:

Table 17.1

Major Structural Characteristics of Three American Family Patterns

STEPFAMILIES	NUCLEAR (INTACT) FAMILIES	SINGLE-PARENT FAMILIES
Biological parent is elsewhere.	Both biological parents are present.	Biological parent is elsewhere.
Virtually all members have recently sustained a primary relationship loss.	————	All members have recently sustained a primary relationship loss.
An adult couple is in the household.	An adult couple is in the household.	————
Relationship between one adult (parent) and child predates the marriage.	Spousal relationship predates parental ones.	Parental relationship is the primary family relationship.
Children are members in more than one household.	Children are members in only one household.	Children may be members in more than one household.
One adult (stepparent) is not legally related to a child (stepchild).	Parents and child(ren) are legally related.	Parents and child(ren) are legally related.

Source: Adapted with permission from *Stepfamilies: A Guide to Working with Stepparents and Stepchildren* by Emily B. Visher and John S. Visher, 1979. Copyright © 1979 by Brunner/Mazel. Used by permission.

Immigrant Stepfamilies" explores an even more complex stepfamily system.) The sequential transitions from one family structure to another create a prolonged period of upheaval and stress. Yet enough adjustment to a single-parent household is likely to have occurred so that a new adaptation to a two-parent remarried family may be all the more difficult.

STEPFAMILIES ARE OF VARIOUS TYPES Remarried families are of various types. The simplest is one in which a divorced or widowed spouse with one child remarries a never-married childless spouse. In the most complex type, both remarrying partners bring children from previous unions and also have a mutual child or children together. If a remarriage is followed by redivorce and a subsequent remarriage, the new remarried family structure is even more complex (Trost 1997). Moreover,

[E]x-spouses remarry, too, to persons who have spouses by previous marriages, and who also have mutual children of their own. This produces an extraordinarily complicated network of family relationships in which adults have the roles of parent, stepparent, spouse, and ex-spouse; some adults have the role of custodial parent and others have the role of noncustodial, absent parent. The children all have roles as sons or daughters, siblings, residential stepsiblings, nonresidential stepsiblings, residential half-siblings, and nonresidential half-siblings. There are two subtypes of half-sibling roles: those of children related by blood to only one of the adults, and the half-sibling role of the mutual child. Children also have stepgrandparents and ex-stepgrandparents as well as grandparents. (Beer 1989, p. 8)

Stepgrandparents are addressed in Chapter 18.

DIFFERENCES BETWEEN FIRST MARRIAGES WITH CHILDREN AND STEPFAMILIES We can point to the following differences between stepfamilies and first marriages with children:

1. "There are different structural characteristics" (see Table 17.1). Therefore, the first-married, nuclear family model is not valid.
2. "There is a complicated 'supra family system,'" including family members from one or more previous marriages.
3. "Children [may] have more than two parenting figures."
4. "There [may be] less family control because there is an influential parent elsewhere or in memory."
5. "There [may be] preexisting parent–child coalitions."
6. "There have been many losses for all individuals."
7. "There are ambiguous family boundaries with little agreement as to family history."

A Closer Look at Family Diversity

Immigrant Stepfamilies

Social scientists typically research the topics of remarriage and immigration separately, but social work professor Roni Berger (1997) points out that the two situations can occur simultaneously, making for extra family stress.

In the transition from their country of origin to the new society, immigrants experience loss of a familiar physical, social and cultural environment, destruction of significant relationships, and a loss of language, belief system, and socioeconomic status. Immigration often means also the bitter loss of a dream because of discrepancies between pre-immigration expectations and the reality of life in the new country. . . .

Immigration and remarriage are similar in that both involve multiple losses, discrepancy between expectations and reality, and integration of two cultures within one unit.

Therefore, both processes shake the individual and family foundation of identity and require flexibility in adapting to a totally new situation. . . .

In immigration the family culture may serve as a support and in remarriage the cultural context may do the same. However, when remarriage and immigration coincide, families lose the stability of their anchors and the stresses exacerbate each other. For example, it has been recognized that one source of difficulty in remarriage stems from reactivation of previous losses caused by divorce or death. Immigration is an additional link in the chain of losses that intensifies the already heavy history of losses typical to all stepfamilies. . . .

Case Example

Igor, 15, was referred by the school he attends because of acting out behaviors in school. At the time of

his referral the boy had been in the United States for six months and lived with his divorced and subsequently remarried mother, his stepfather, his four-year-old half-sister, and his maternal grandparents. All these six people are crowded in a one bedroom apartment.

Igor's biological parents lived in Moscow. They married when both of them were 29, . . . and they eventually divorced when Igor was five years old. However, they continued to live in the same apartment because of housing difficulties. As both parents worked, Igor's maternal grandmother was the main parenting figure, a common practice in Soviet families.

When Igor was nine his father moved in with another woman, a single mother of a boy the same age as Igor. They had together two daughters, married, and emigrated

---

8. At least initially, "there is little or no family loyalty."

9. "There is a long integration period . . ."

10. Prior to possible integration, family members must recover from previous transitional stresses.

11. Because "society compares stepfamilies negatively to first-married families," individuals need validation as members of a worthwhile family unit.

12. The balance of power is different: Stepparents have relatively little authority initially and children generally wield more power than in first-married families.

13. A good couple relationship does not necessarily make for good stepparent–stepchild relationships (Visher and Visher 1996, pp. 41–42).

Throughout this chapter, we address many of these characteristics and what can be done to meet the challenges they create.

Kin Networks in the Remarried Family

Relationships with kin outside the immediate remarried family are complex and uncharted as well (Ganong and Coleman 2004). We have few mutually accepted ways of dealing with the new extended and ex-kin relationships that result from remarriage. One indication of this situation is that our language has

to the United States, where Igor's biological father secured a high engineering position and is financially very successful. For five years Igor had no contact with his biological father and his new family. His mother remarried and had a daughter with her new husband, who had never been married before. A year ago the family renewed the contact with Igor's biological father, who sponsored their emigration. Igor's stepfather has been unemployed for most of the last year and Igor's mother works off the books in child care.

His mother and stepfather reported that until the immigration Igor was a "model child." He excelled in school, was popular with friends, involved in extra-curricular activities, played the violin, [was] active in sports and was cooperative and pleasant. During all these years Igor's grandmother remained the major parental figure while practically no relationship developed between him and his stepfather. The troubles started a short time after the family came to the United States. Igor was enrolled in a public school with mostly immigrant Black and Hispanic students. He excelled in mathematics and physics which he studied in a bilingual program and in sports. His language skills were very limited and so were his social relationships. The family's squeezed housing conditions fostered tension and conflicts. Igor's grandmother does not speak any English and could not therefore continue to negotiate with school and social agencies for him anymore, forcing his mother to take on more of a parental role.

The main issues that Igor brought up with the therapist related to his natural father and to his parents' divorce which he returned to time and again. His mother and stepfather were annoyed with his behavior, blamed him for being ungrateful, and used him as a target for all their frustrations and disappointments with the hardships in the new land. Igor felt rejected, idealized his biological father, and blamed his mother and stepfather of being unjust and not understanding. Everybody in the family felt deprived, treated unfairly, disappointed, and angry.

It seemed that while the divorce occurred 15 years earlier and the actual separation four years later, family stresses related to the remarriage of both parents and the birth of the half-sibling gradually piled up. Subsequently the immigration reactivated the experiences of loss and triggered reactions of mourning, accusation, anger, and guilt that have been building up for a long time. . . .

Igor's situation reveals multiple forces operating simultaneously. . . . Systematic research is much needed to study the combined effects of immigration and step-relationships, the issues caused by this combination of stresses, coping mechanisms that help families with this pile up of stresses, and effective strategies to promote the welfare and well being of immigrant stepfamilies. (pp. 362, 364–369)

Source: Roni Berer. "Immigrant Stepfamilies." *Contemporary Family Therapy.* Sept. 1997, vol. 19, Issue 3, pp. 360–370. Copyright © 1997 Kluwer Academic Publishers. Reprinted by permission of Springer-Verlag.

not caught up with the proliferation of new family roles.[4] As family members separate and then join new families formed by remarriage, the new kin do not so much *replace* as *add* to kin from the first marriage (White and Riedmann 1992). What are the new relatives to be called? There may be stepparents, stepgrandparents, and stepsiblings, but what, for instance, does a child call the new wife that her or his noncustodial father has married? (Ganong and Coleman 1997, pp. 89–90).

Or if a child alternates between the new households or remarried parents in a joint-custody arrangement, what does he or she call "home," and where is his or her "family"? According to sociologist William Beer (1989), "I began my in-depth interviewing of one stepfamily with a question about who the family members were. The response was a confused look and the question, 'Well, when do you mean?'" (p. 9). A further symptom of the incompleteness of remarriage as a so-

---

4. Stepmother Beth Bruno (2001) tells of her experience shortly after her marriage to a man with two daughters:

> We hated the words that described our connection after their dad and I married; the words "stepmother" and "stepdaughter" seemed like flashing neon signs that said, "not-real-mother" and "not-real-daughter." It had been much easier for them to introduce me as their Dad's friend, Beth, and for me to introduce them as Gordon's daughters, Terry and Cindy. Yet I was proud to be legally related to these two wonderful children, who have enriched my life since the day we met. . . . We've come to terms with these complexities over the years.

cial institution is the lack of the legal definitions for roles and relationships.

Family Law and the Remarried Family

Because family law assumes that marriages are first marriages, there are few legal provisions for several remarried-family challenges—as examples, balancing husbands' financial obligations to their spouses and children from current and previous marriages, and defining a wife's obligations to husbands and children from the current and the former marriages. For instance, in the absence of family legislation for things such as providing stepchildren with health insurance, stepfamilies are left to draft individual solutions based on expediency:

> Children receive medical benefits from whichever parent has the more generous plan, or any plan at all. Sometimes, it is the noncustodial parent who offers this advantage, and in one case, it was the cohabiting girlfriend of the noncustodial parent whose plan somehow included the nonresidential children of her partner. Still, a number of stepchildren have currently or at some point in the past been considered dependents of their stepparents for these purposes. (Mason, Harrison-Jay, Svare, and Wolfinger 2002, p. 516)

Incidentally, research suggests that, while remarrieds often share their economic resources, they also take care to protect their individual interests and those of their biological children (Mason 1998; Mason et al. 2002).

Moreover, in some states, stepparents do not have the authority to see the school records of stepchildren or make medical decisions for them. The preservation of stepparent–stepchild relations when death or divorce severs the marital tie is also a serious issue. Visitation rights (and corresponding support obligation) of stepparents are just beginning to be legally clarified (Hans 2002; Mason, Fine, and Carnochan 2001). When a custodial, biological parent dies, the absence of custodial preference for stepparents over extended kin may result in children's being removed from a home in which they had close psychological ties to a stepparent. If a stepparent dies without a will, stepchildren are not legally entitled to any inheritance. The only way to be certain that situations like these do not occur is for the stepparent to legally adopt the stepchild, and this situation may be virtually impossible due to the noncustodial, biological parent's objec-

tions (Mason et al. 2002).[5] We turn now to a topic of considerable research over the last decade: children's well-being in stepfamilies.

Children's Well-Being in Stepfamilies

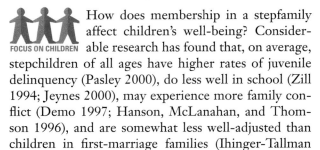

FOCUS ON CHILDREN

How does membership in a stepfamily affect children's well-being? Considerable research has found that, on average, stepchildren of all ages have higher rates of juvenile delinquency (Pasley 2000), do less well in school (Zill 1994; Jeynes 2000), may experience more family conflict (Demo 1997; Hanson, McLanahan, and Thomson 1996), and are somewhat less well-adjusted than children in first-marriage families (Ihinger-Tallman and Pasley 1997; Coleman, Ganong, and Fine 2000; Hetherington 1999).

However, sociologist Paul Amato (1994b) has pointed out that the differences found in these and other studies are fairly small. Since many of the small, negative outcomes for stepchildren are also associated with divorce (see Chapter 16),

> it is difficult to know the relative contribution of parental remarriage to poor child adjustment. It may well be that most of the negative effects can be attributed to predivorce conditions . . . or postdivorce effects (e.g., reduced income, multiple transitions that accompany divorce), of which parental remarriage is only one. (Ihinger-Tallman and Pasley 1997, p. 31)

Some social scientists have asked whether remarriage can lessen some of the negative effects of divorce for children. One researcher has concluded that "Children of stepfamilies don't do better than children of mothers who never marry" (McLanahan and Sandefur 1994, p. 51). However, other researchers (Zill, Morrison, and Coiro 1993) have concluded that remarriage lessens some negative effects for children—but only for those who experienced their parents' divorce at an

---

5. Stepchild adoption generally requires the waiver of parental rights by the biological parent, who may be actively involved with the child and—understandably!—may not want to do so. When the nonresident parent is actively involved, adoption is seldom given serious consideration by either the remarried adults or the children (Pasley 1998a). Children above a certain age, perhaps fourteen, may or must give their consent to stepparent adoption in some states, and even younger children need to agree to the adoption (which they may not).

early age and when the remarriage remained intact (see also Arendell 1997b, pp. 186–188). Additional research shows that younger children adjust better to a parent's remarriage than do older children, especially adolescents (Coleman, Ganong, and Fine 2000).

While we note the above findings, we also recognize another aspect of this story. According to several studies, family structure (whether the family is a first-marriage, cohabiting, divorced, or remarried) is not as important to stepchildren's well-being or future outcomes as is the quality of the communication and relationships among family members (Davis and Friel 2001; White and Gilbreth 2001). Furthermore, the extent to which parents or stepparents monitor their children's comings and goings is probably more important to positive child outcomes than is family structure itself (Fisher, Leve, O'Leary, and Leve 2003). But we have seen that there may be more conflict in stepfamilies than in first-marriage families (Demo 1997). Furthermore, parents may more diligently monitor their children in two-parent biological families than in stepfamilies (Fisher, Leve, O'Leary, and Leve 2003). Hence, the quality of family interaction and of parental monitoring may be statistically associated with remarriage.

Just as social scientists debate whether the family is in "decline" (see Chapters 1 and 5), they disagree on how to interpret findings about stepchildren's well-being (Cherlin 1999): "In recent years, a new rationale for the superiority of the nuclear family model has emerged" (Ganong and Coleman 1997, p. 87). Social scientists working from a biosocial perspective (see Chapter 3) argue that biological forces make genetically related families more functional for children than other family types (Popenoe 1996). According to this view, bioevolutionary forces encourage parents to favor their genetic offspring. This situation puts stepchildren at risk and perhaps even jeopardizes their safety. For instance, there is evidence that the incidence of child abuse, including sexual abuse, is higher for stepfathers than for biological fathers (Giles-Sims 1997).[6] From this perspective, characterized by family

law expert Mary Ann Mason (1998) as *negativist*, the formation of stepfamilies should be discouraged (Popenoe 1998).

However, the vast majority of social scientists reject the idea that stepfamily formation should be discouraged. Sociologist Jean Giles-Sims (1997) points out that although child abuse rates are higher among stepfamilies, this situation assuredly "does not mean that all stepfamilies are at risk" (p. 227). In fact, "a low percent of stepchildren are physically or sexually abused" (p. 220; Claxton-Oldfield 2003).

In sum, research findings can hardly be characterized as rosy, but we can still conclude that most children "eventually adapt to life in a stepfamily and emerge as reasonably competent individuals" (Hetherington and Jodl 1994, p. 76). Then too, "Understanding how families manage change and supporting all families to provide good enough parenting is likely to be a better investment for children than cataloguing disadvantages and difficulties and denigrating different family structures" (De'Ath 1996, p. 82).

Stepparenting: A Challenge in Remarriage

Although they are developing, cultural norms do not clearly indicate how stepparents should play their role (Ganong and Coleman 2004). With few clear guidelines or norms regarding what responsibilities a stepparent has, it may not be surprising that for a remarried spouse, stepchildren and finances present the greatest challenges (Visher and Visher 1996).

Some Reasons Stepparenting Is Difficult

"Crucial to children's overall well-being and development in remarriage and stepparent families, as in divorced and intact families as well, is the *quality* of parenting" (Arendell 1997b, p. 187). Meanwhile, there are special difficulties associated with bringing families together under the same roof. For one thing, it is likely that children are influenced not only by their residential parents but also by their relationship with their noncustodial biological parent (Stewart 2003). For another thing, stepsiblings may not get along with each other (Bernstein 1997; Ganong and Coleman 2004).

Over the past thirty years, researchers and family therapists have consistently reported an array of challenges specific to stepfamilies. For instance, ties with

---

6. "Unfortunately, given how abuse data are recorded, it is sometimes difficult to determine whether the perpetrator of child abuse is a stepparent or another adult. For example, mothers' boyfriends and legally remarried stepfathers are often categorized as one group. Children are more at risk for abuse if they live in a household with an adult who is not their genetic parent, but the extent to which stepchildren are at greater risk for being abused by a step-parent continues to be debated" (Ganong, Coleman, and Fine 2000, p. 1295).

the noncustodial parent may create a triangle effect that makes the spouse's previous marriage seem "more real" than the second union. The children, upset after visits with the noncustodial parent, may make life difficult for everyone else. Stepchildren in joint-custody arrangements (see Chapter 16) may regularly move back and forth between two households with two sets of rules.

Family-rule differences, along with disruptions associated with one or more family members' coming and going, may be stressful (Kheshgi-Genovese and Genovese 1997). And the biological parents may feel caught between loyalties to their biological child and the desire to please their partner (Visher and Visher 1996; Bray 1999)—and between other loyalties as well. As one stepparent puts it,

> When you become a stepparent, you find yourself not just playing Piggy in the Middle between your partner and his/her children, but often between your partner and his/her ex, your partner and your ex, your partner and your children, your children and your partner's children. The combinations are endless! (Andersen 2004)

Three major parenting challenges can be identified in remarried families with stepchildren: financial strains, role ambiguity, and negative feelings of the children, who often don't want the new family to work (Kheshgi-Genovese and Genovese 1997).

FINANCIAL STRAINS The particular challenges that characterize stepfamilies often begin with the previous divorce. This is especially evident in the case of finances (Mason, Fine, and Carnochan 2001). Frequently, money problems arise from two sources: financial obligations from first marriages and stepparent role ambiguity.

A remarried spouse (usually the husband) generally is financially accountable by law for children from the first union *and* financially responsible—sometimes legally[7]—for stepchildren (Hans 2002; Manning,

Stewart, and Smock 2003). Whether legally required to or not, "many stepparents do in fact help to support the stepchildren with whom they reside, either through direct contributions to the child's personal expenses or through contributions to general household expenses such as food and shelter" (Mahoney 1997, p. 236; see also Mason et al. 2002).[8] Even though disproportionately more second wives are employed outside their homes than are first wives, remarried husbands report feeling caught between the often impossible demands of both their former family and their present one.

Meanwhile, stepmothers often spend their own money on stepchildren—usually for incidentals during visitation periods (Engel 2000). Then too, mothers with children from a former marriage worry about receiving regular child support from their ex-husband (Manning, Stewart, and Smock 2003; Mason et al. 2002). Some second wives—more often, those without children of their own—feel resentful about the portion of the husband's income that goes to his first wife to help support his children from that marriage (Engel 2000). Or a second wife may feel guilty about the burden of support that her own children place on their stepfather (Barash 2000). For some remarried couples, the financial stress associated with stepchildren's expenses is a determining factor in the decision not to have a mutual child (Engel 2000).

ROLE AMBIGUITY Relatively low role ambiguity has been associated with higher remarital satisfaction, especially for wives, and with greater parenting satisfaction, especially for stepfathers (Kurdek and Fine 1991). Hence, another challenge to remarried families is that roles of stepchild and stepparent are not well defined, clearly understood, or fully agreed upon by the stepfamily members themselves (Bray 1999; Ganong, Coleman, and Fine 2000). "The role of the stepparent is precarious; the relationship between a stepparent and stepchild only exists in law as long as

---

7. A minority of states (about seventeen) "have ratified a wide assortment of laws that hold stepparents responsible for the support of stepchildren during marriage. . . . They range from Hawaii's situation-specific support statute:

> A stepparent who acts *in loco parentis* is bound to provide, maintain, and support the stepparent's stepchild during the residence of the child with the stepparent if the legal parents desert the child or are unable to support the child, thereby reducing the child to destitute and necessitous circumstances. (Hawaii Review Statutes, 1999)

"to a much broader support statute, such as Missouri's:

> A stepparent shall support his or her stepchild to the same extent that a natural [sic] or adoptive parent is required to support his or her child so long as the stepchild is living in the same home as the stepparent. (Missouri Review Statutes, 1999)." (Hans 2002, p. 303)

8. Even though the stepfamily may come to rely on it, if the remarriage ends in divorce, the stepparent is not legally responsible for child support unless he or she has formally adopted the stepchildren or signed a written promise to pay child support in the event of divorce (Mahoney 1997).

Conflicting expectations concerning a stepfather's—or stepmother's—role may make it stressful. When stepparents can ignore the myths and negative images of the role and maintain optimism about the remarriage, they are more likely to have high family, marital, and personal satisfaction.

the biological parent and stepparent are married" (Beer 1989, p. 11).

Although some stepchildren certainly do maintain relations with a stepparent after a stepparental divorce, doing so requires forging personalized ways to do this in the absence of commonly understood norms (Dickinson 2002). Legally, the stepparent is a nonparent with no prescribed rights or duties (Mason, Fine, and Carnochan 2001). Indeed, the term *stepparent* originally meant a person who replaces a dead parent, not an *additional* parent figure (Bray 1999).

Uncertainties arise when the role of parent is shared between stepparent and the noncustodial natural parent (MacDonald and DeMaris 2002). Stepparents aren't "real" parents, but "the culture so far provides no norms to suggest how they are different"

(Bohannan 1970a, p. 119; Fine, Coleman, and Ganong 1999). One result of role ambiguity is that society—and hence the members of the stepfamily itself—seems to expect stepparents and children to love one another in much the same way as biologically related parents and children do. In reality, however, this is not often the case, and therapists point out that stepparents and stepchildren should not expect to feel the same as they would if they were biologically related (Visher and Visher 1996; Barash 2000). Therapists advise—and research shows—that a stepparent's waiting through a period of family adjustment before becoming an active disciplinarian is usually a good idea (Visher and Visher 1996; Ganong, Coleman, and Fine 2000). Of course, children's attitudes as well as their power can have an impact on the new marriage.

STEPCHILDREN'S HOSTILITY A third reason for the difficulty in stepparent–child relationships lies in children's lack of desire to see them work. After age two or three (Gamache 1997), children often harbor fantasies that their original parents will reunite (Burt and Burt 1996; Bray 1999). Children who want their natural parents to remarry may feel that sabotaging the new relationship will help achieve that goal (Kheshgi-Genovese and Genovese 1997).

Furthermore, "Stepchildren may feel they are betraying their biological parent of the same sex as the stepparent if they form a friendly relationship with the stepparent" (Kheshgi-Genovese and Genovese 1997, p. 256). As one of our students wrote in an essay for this chapter: "Since I [had] idolized my father for so many years, I didn't want to accept my stepfather. I didn't like the fact that someone else was sleeping with my mother and touching her." In the case of remarriage after widowhood, children may have idealized, almost sacred, memories of the parent who died and may not want another to take his or her place (Andersen 2002; Barash 2000).

Then too, many adolescents blame their parents or themselves, or both, because the first marriage broke up. The stepparent becomes a convenient scapegoat for their hostilities (Warshak 2000). As a result, stepchildren, especially adolescents, may prove to be hostile adversaries. Our discussion of power in Chapter 14 focuses on marital power, but we're reminded that adolescent stepchildren wield considerable family power (Kurdek and Fine 1995; Visher and Visher 1996). Then too, the desire of the remarried parents to create a cohesive family may conflict with an adolescent's normal need to express independence (Kheshgi-Genovese and Genovese 1997). Adolescents seem to have less power in stepfamilies of greater longevity, reflecting either the breakup of the most troubled families or a gradual consolidation of the new stepfamily, which is evident over time in some (though not all) research (Papernow 1993).

Sociologists Lynn White and Alan Booth's (1985b) analysis of stability in remarriages, discussed earlier, considered one additional point: that family tension may be resolved by the child's rather than the partner's exit from the home. Speculating that children might be moved out by sending them to live with the other parent or forcing them to become independent, White and Booth found that older teenage and young adult children in stepfamilies do indeed leave home at significantly lower ages than do teens in intact families. White and Booth were working from the perspective of the married parents; qualitative data from Wallerstein's study of divorced families suggest that stepchildren often feel excluded and out of place in their new household, shut out by the tight bond between the remarried couple. Some reported a sense of rejection as they perceived the largest share of the parent's attention and energy going to the new marriage (Wallerstein and Blakeslee 1989). Subsequent research supports the finding that stepchildren are likely to move away from home at younger ages than are children in first-marriage families, "especially to independence, cohabitation, or relatively early marriage" (Goldscheider and Goldscheider 1998, p. 743; Ganong, Coleman, and Fine 2000). ("As We Make Choices: Some Stepparenting Tips" contains advice that can make stepparenting easier.)

Although stepchildren, their biological parents, and stepparents may be uncomfortable with aspects of their family roles, certain difficulties are more likely to trouble stepmothers, and others are more common to stepfathers. We'll look at each of these roles and the problems associated with them in more detail.

Stepmothers

A small study asked 265 stepmothers about their expectations of the stepmother role. The researchers found that stepmothers expect to be included in stepfamily activities but certainly do not see themselves as replacing the stepchild's mother. The more time a stepmother spent with her stepchildren, the more she expected to be included in stepfamily functions and decisions, and the more she behaved as concerned parent, rather than friend (Orchard and Solberg 2000). The stepmother role is thought by social scientists to be more difficult than the stepfather role (Coleman and Ganong 1997; White 1994). One important reason for this is a contradiction in expectations for the stepmother role:

> Whether mothers or stepmothers, . . . the women's roles are very similar. Irrespectively, they take care of children and housework. The *step-mother* role does not expect her to do such tasks. On the contrary; the stepparent role expects a certain distance, the female role the opposite. Between the two roles there is a dilemma. One cannot be distant and close at the same time. (Levin 1997, p. 187)

The stepmother role has been described as the **stepmother trap**: On the one hand, society seems to expect romantic, almost mythical loving relationships between stepmothers and children (Raphael 1978; Smith 1990). On the other hand, stepmothers are seen and portrayed as cruel, vain, selfish, competitive, and even abusive (remember Snow White's, Cinderella's, and Hansel and Gretel's).

Maureen McHugh (2004) is a stepmother who writes for the website *Second Wives Café: Online Support for Wives and Stepmothers* (http:stepmotherscafe.com). Here's an excerpt from her online article "The Evil Stepmother":

> My nine-year-old stepson Adam and I were coming home from Kung Fu. "Maureen," Adam said—he calls me "Maureen" because he was seven when Bob and I got married and that was what he had called me before. "Maureen," Adam said, "are we going to have a Christmas Tree?"
>
> "Yeah," I said, "of course." After thinking a moment, "Adam, why didn't you think we were going to have a Christmas Tree?"
>
> "Because of the new house," he said, rather matter-of-fact. "I thought you might not let us."
>
> It is strange to find that you have become the kind of person who might ban Christmas Trees. (retrieved 9/20/04)

Some stepmothering situations can make the role especially complicated (Coleman and Ganong 1997). Special problems accompany the role of *part-time* or "weekend" *stepmother* when women are married to noncustodial fathers who see their children regularly. The part-time stepmother may try to establish a loving relationship with her husband's children only to be openly rejected, or she may feel left out by the father's ongoing relationship with his offspring. Part-time stepmothers may also feel left out by the father's continued relationship with his ex-wife (Barash 2000). Noncustodial fathers may spend long hours on the telephone with their ex-wives discussing their children's school problems, orthodontia, illnesses, and even household maintenance and repairs.

Meanwhile, *residential stepmothers* may face somewhat different challenges. Social worker and stepmother Emily Bouchard tells her story:

> When I moved in with my husband and his two teenage daughters, he had a real "hands off" approach. . . . Sparks began to fly as soon as I asserted what I needed to be different . . . For example, when I noticed that my car had been "borrowed" (the odometer was different) without my knowledge or permission, I had to show up as a parent the way I needed to parent—setting limits, confronting the greater issues of lying and sneaking, and asserting the natural consequences for unacceptable behavior. This method was foreign to their family, and there were reactions all the way around! Thankfully, my husband supported me in front of his daughter, and then we discussed our differences privately and came to a mutual understanding about how to handle parenting together from then on. (Bouchard n.d.)

One explanation for the greater difficulty of the residential stepmother role involves the fact that stepmother families, more than stepfather families, begin after difficult custody battles and/or have a history of particularly troubled family relations. Consequently, residential stepmothers tend to be more stressed, anxious, and depressed than other mothers (Santrock and Sitterle 1987) and also more stressed than residential stepfathers (Pasley and Ihinger-Tallman 1988).

Stepfathers

Men who decide to marry a woman with children come to their new responsibilities with varied emotions, typically far different from those that motivate a man to assume responsibility for his biological children. "I was really turned on by her," said one stepfather of his second wife. "Then I met her kids." This sequence is a fairly common "situation of many stepparents whose primary focus may be the marriage rather than parenting" (Ceballo, Lansford, Abbey, and Stewart 2004, p. 46). A new husband may have negative reactions, such as fright, as well as positive feelings. About half of stepfathers find it somewhat or definitely true that "having stepchildren is just as satisfying as having your own children" (Marsiglio 1992, p. 204).

Research into the stepfather role shows that many children do have positive relationships with their stepfathers and that a good relationship is associated with better child outcomes (White and Gilbreth 2001). Children and their stepfathers are more likely to feel positive about their relationship when the role expectations are clear; when the stepfather assumes, or "claims," a parental identity; when his parenting behavior meets his own and other family members' expectations; and when his parental demands are not challenged by the presence of an involved nonresidential, biological father (Coleman, Ganong, and Fine 2000; MacDonald and DeMaris 2002; Marsiglio 2004a).

However, when a mother and her children make up a single-parent family, the woman tends to learn autonomy and self-confidence, and her children may do more work around the house and take more responsibility in family decisions than do children in two-parent households. These are positive developments, but to enter such a family, a stepfather must work his way into a closed group (Cherlin and Furstenberg 1994). For one thing, the mother and children share a common history, one that does not yet include a new stepfather.

The **hidden agenda** is one of the first difficulties a stepfather encounters: The mother, her children, or both may have expectations about what the stepfather will do but may not think to give the new husband a clear picture of what those expectations are. The step-

As We Make Choices

Some Stepparenting Tips

Preparing to Live in Step

In a stepfamily, at least three (and usually more) individuals find themselves struggling to form new familial relationships while still coping with reminders of the past. Each family member brings to the situation expectations and attitudes that are as diverse as the personalities involved. The task of creating a successful stepfamily, as with any family, will be easier for all concerned if each member tries to understand the feelings and motivations of the others as well as his or her own.

It is important to discuss the realities of living in a stepfamily before the marriage, when problems that are likely to arise can be foreseen and examined theoretically. If you are contemplating entering a steprelationship, here are some key points to consider:

1. Plan ahead! Some chapters of Parents Without Partners conduct "education for remarriage" workshops. Contact your local chapter or write to Parents Without Partners.

2. Examine your motives and those of your future spouse for marrying. Get to know him or her as well as possible under all sorts of circumstances. Consider the possible impact of contrasting lifestyles.

3. Discuss the modifications that will be required in bringing two families together. Compare similarities and differences in your concepts of child rearing.

4. Explore with your children the changes remarriage will bring: new living arrangements, new family relationships, the effect on their relationship with their noncustodial parent.

5. Give your children ample opportunity to get to know your future spouse well. Consider your children's feelings, but don't allow them to make your decision about remarriage.

6. Discuss the disposition of family finances with your future spouse. An open and honest review of financial assets and responsibilities may reduce unrealistic expectations and resultant misunderstandings.

7. Understand that there are bound to be periods of doubt, frustration, and resentment.

---

father may have a hidden agenda of his own. For example, he may see his new stepchildren as unruly and decide they need discipline. In a time of increased ethnic and cultural diversity, as well as increasing inter-ethnic and inter-religious marriages, a new stepfather may feel out of place not only because of his different background but also because he has a different perspective on family life.

A part of the stepchildren's hidden agenda involves the extent to which they will let the new husband play the father role. Here's an example from a student essay:

[When my stepfather] tried to discipline us children, my mom would yell at him, telling him to leave us alone. That made me respect him less because he had no authority over us when my mom was around. The thing that won us over, I feel, was his support of everything that we did.

Whenever we went to any of our sporting events, he was there to help us. (Murphy 2004)

Children may be adamant in their distaste for or jealousy of the stepfather, or they may be ready and anxious to accept the stepfather as a new dad. This last is particularly true of young children.

Research shows that both stepmothers and stepfathers play their roles with more distance than do biological parents—as more like friends than monitoring parents (Ganong, Coleman, and Fine 2000). Meanwhile, stepfathers tend to be more distant and detached than stepmothers, especially when they have biological children of their own (Coleman and Ganong 1997). Young adult children tend to think of the new addition to the family primarily as their mother's husband rather than as a stepfather.

Discipline is likely to be a particularly tricky aspect of both the children's and the parents' hidden

Living in Step

Any marriage is complex and challenging, but the problems of remarriage are more complicated because more people, relationships, feelings, attitudes, and beliefs are involved than in a first marriage. The two families may have differing roles, standards, and goals. Because its members have not shared past experiences, the new family may have to redefine rights and responsibilities to fit both individual and combined needs.

Time and understanding are key allies in negotiating the transition from single-parent to stepfamily status. Consideration of the following points may ease the transition process:

1. Let your relationship with stepchildren develop gradually. Don't expect too much too soon—from the children or yourself. Children need time to adjust, accept, and belong. So do parents.
2. Don't try to replace a lost parent; be an additional parent.

Children need time to mourn the parent lost through divorce or death.

3. Expect to deal with confusing feelings—your own, your spouse's, and the children's. Anxiety about new roles and relationships may heighten competition among family members for love and attention; loyalties may be questioned. Your children may need to understand that their relationship with you is valued but different from that of your relationship with your spouse and that one cannot replace the other. You love and need them both, but in different ways.
4. Recognize that you may be compared to the absent partner. Be prepared to be tested, manipulated, and challenged in your new role. Decide, with your mate, what is best for your children, and stand by it.
5. Understand that stepparents need support from natural par-

ents on child-rearing issues. Rearing children is tough; rearing someone else's is tougher.

6. Acknowledge periods of cooperation among stepsiblings. Try to treat stepchildren and your own with equal fairness. Communicate! Don't pretend that everything is fine when it isn't. Acknowledge problems immediately, and deal with them openly.
7. Admit that you need help if you need it. Don't let the situation get out of hand. Everyone needs help sometimes. Join an organization for stepfamilies; seek counseling.

Source: U.S. Department of Health, Education, and Welfare 1978; Van Pelt 1985; see also Jeannette Lofas, "Ten Steps for Steps." The Stepfamily Foundation (http://www.stepfamily.org/tensteps.html). See also Judy Lavin, "Smoothing the Step-Parenting Transition" (http://www.selfgrowth.com/articles/Lavin1.html, n.d.

agendas. A few challenges are notable (Isaacs, Montalvo, and Abelsohn 1986). First, there are now two parents rather than one to establish house rules and to influence children's behavior, but the parents may not agree. A second challenge may be the holdover influence of the biological father. To the new father, there may sometimes seem to be *three* parents instead of two—especially if the noncustodial father sees the children regularly—with the biological father wielding more influence than the stepfather. A third challenge may be the development of children's responsibility and participation in decision making in single-parent families. The children may be unwilling to go back to being "children"—that is, dependent on and subject to adult direction. The new parent may view them as spoiled and undisciplined rather than mature.

A stepfather may react to these difficulties in finding a place in a new family in one of four ways. First, the stepfather may be driven away. Second, he may

take control, establishing himself as undisputed head of the household, and force the former single-parent family to accommodate his preferences. Third, he may be assimilated into a family with a mother at its head and have relatively little influence on the way things are done. And fourth, the stepfather, his new wife, and her children may all negotiate new ways of doing things (Isaacs, Montalvo, and Abelsohn 1986, pp. 248–264). This is the most positive alternative for everyone, and it is further addressed in the final section of this chapter. First, though, we'll look at what the research has to say about having a mutual child.

Having a Mutual Child

Some, especially older, men make it a condition of their remarriage to a younger woman that she relinquish the idea of having children together (Brooke

Some older men make it a condition of their remarriage to a younger woman that they not have children together. However, some remarried couples do decide to have one or more mutual children together, often with the hope of strengthening the remarriage bond. While some experts have expressed concern about introducing a mutual child to a remarriage that is already complicated, having a mutual child seems to be associated with both increased happiness and marital stability.

2002). However, some remarried couples do decide to have one or more children together, a decision addressed in Chapter 10. Research shows that a principal reason for choosing to have a child together involves hope that the mutual child will "cement" the remarriage bond. Some women with children feel obliged to give a childless husband a son or daughter of his own. Another cause is perceived social pressure to be like "a normal family." Couples who choose not to have a mutual child explain that they are too old, are concerned about finances, or feel that they already have enough children (Pasley and Lipe 1998).

Research shows that having a mutual child is associated with increased happiness and marital stability

(Pasley and Lipe 1998; White and Booth 1985b). However, some experts have expressed concern about the impact on remarriage of having a child early in what is bound to be a complex adjustment (Bernstein 1997). Believing that they will now be ignored by the stepparent—or seeing the mutual child as having a privileged place in the family—the stepchildren may feel threatened, jealous, or resentful (Barash 2000; Pasley and Lipe 1998). "But the scant literature shows that parents who had a mutual child saw the decision as a positive influence on their relationship with their stepchildren" (Pasley and Lipe 1998). We turn now to a look at what family therapists can tell us more generally about creating supportive stepfamilies.

This family portrait is of a mother and stepfather of two full sisters, along with a baby son from the new union. The remarried family structure, which is complex and has many unique characteristics, has no accepted cultural script. When all members are able to work thoughtfully together, adjustment to a new family life can be easier.

Creating Supportive Stepfamilies

Creating a supportive stepfamily is not automatic, partly because getting remarried typically involves other stress-inducing changes as well. Findings from a qualitative study of 426 women who are members of the Stepfamily Association of America showed that almost half moved to a new city or state when they remarried. One-quarter of the women quit a job, and more than that began a new job. Many reported considerable stress, and some even indicated that they had second-guessed their decision. But others agreed with the respondent who wrote, "I wouldn't change anything" (Engel 2000).

One stepfamily scholar (Papernow 1993) has suggested a **seven-stage model of stepfamily development**:

1. Fantasy—adults expect a smooth and quick adjustment while children expect that the stepparent will disappear and their parents will be reunited.

2. Immersion—tension-producing conflict emerges between the stepfamily's two biological "subunits."

3. Awareness—family members realize that their early fantasies are not becoming reality.

4. Mobilization—family members initiate efforts toward change.

5. Action—remarried adults decide to form a solid alliance, family boundaries are better clarified, and there is more positive stepparent–stepchild interaction.

6. Contact—the stepparent becomes a significant adult family figure, and the couple assumes more control.

7. Resolution—the stepfamily achieves integration and appreciates its unique identity as a stepfamily.

Therapists agree that creating a supportive stepfamily takes time—from four to seven years!—and "is one of the most difficult tasks that families can face" (Wark and Jobalia 1998, p. 69; Bray 1999; Gamache

From Stepfather to Father— Creating a Resilient Stepfamily

At the groom's dinner the night before my marriage to Jack, there was much good-natured bantering. My children were happy that my grief over the death of their father had finally run its course. They savored the sight of their mother filled with joy over a new love.

Jack, a genuine, never-been-married bachelor, received their mock gratitude for taking me off their hands. They congratulated him on his good fortune in acquiring them as family now that they were all grown up rather than during their teen years when they had been really rotten. I laughed with them, remembering those earlier times. At the nuptial Mass the next morning, I thanked God for this man and all he would bring to the family.

Honeymoon's End

Jack was elated over this new family of his—a wife, four children aged nineteen to twenty-four, a son-in-law, and two grandchildren—though he did wince the first few times the little ones called him "Grumpa." That discomfort eased when I reminded him that he would now be sharing his life with a grandmother.

The new relationship between Jack and his stepfamily began smoothly enough. We left the off-spring behind at their various apartments and campuses when we relocated from Minnesota to Houston because of Jack's job. But a series of harried phone calls caused the rosy family picture to fade. One of the brood had spent tuition money repairing a car that she had not maintained. Then another neglected to wrap water pipes at the family homestead before a fierce storm. The frozen lines ruptured, requiring major replacement work.

Another's car died. Though I would have preferred to send flowers, a loan was more to the point. We weren't optimistic about repayment. As each new problem unfolded, I saw the light dim in Jack's eyes. These kids he had gotten so easily were *not* all grown up.

Meanwhile, the tales he brought home about co-workers' children bore a common thread: achievement! One father, with all due modesty, reported on the winning touchdown made by his high school junior, whose coach, of course, saw potential for the pros. Another's daughter had graduated Phi Beta Kappa and was breezing through a prestigious M.B.A. program.

Before Jack became part of the "Dad Derby," such tales hadn't affected him. But as a new parent, he was listening to the daily achievement litany as other parents paraded the most recent honors bestowed upon brilliant kids. And Jack had no one to brag about. I felt responsible both for my kids' failures and for his disillusionment.

The Truth

In despondent moments I thought about family friends back home. They had all had problems similar to mine with nearly-adult children. How did I know that? I wondered. Ah, yes, I'd heard the misadventures from other mothers—not fathers.

The next time we dined with friends of Jack's, I paid close attention. It was the men who reported accomplishments. Mothers mostly remained quiet or cautiously changed the subject. On another dinner date, the conversation predictably progressed to children, theirs then mine—"*our* children," I hastily corrected. But what wondrous tale could I spin about my splendid, overachieving children? What story could I tell that would make Jack glow with pride over his new heirs?

A little voice in my heart said, "Forget it, Mary. It won't work." So I told the truth—the latest dumb thing that had happened back home.

There was just the briefest moment of silence, a collective sigh, and then came the response. "You think that's bad? Well, wait till you hear about *our* kids' latest exploits." I sat back and enjoyed watching Jack's stunned expression as the stories spilled across the table. See, I wanted to say, mine aren't so bad. At least they're normal. I finally felt vindicated.

Family Triangle

There was still a bumpy road ahead for this family. My kids were my kids. Jack was accepting them as that and was beginning to acknowledge that they really were pleasant young people. And they thought he was great as Mom's husband. But there remained distance.

Toward the end of the first year, one son quit college and decided that Houston, where Mom and Jack lived, had better job potential than the old hometown. He was taking us up on the promise that our home would always be his. This was the kid who had quit talking to the family for five years when he reached thirteen. The same one who couldn't wait to be old enough to get away from his parents.

Now there was a triangle in the house, a disruption of the still-delicate relationship Jack and I were working out together. I felt caught between the two males, serving as a messenger, carrying subtle little missives between them. When the star boarder found a good job within a few weeks, I was relieved. But, of course, he had to stay on for a bit to build financial reserves. I finally gave him a little nudge; it was time he settled into a place of his own. I had been struggling on the family bridge long enough.

Trial by Fire

Two years later the same son was stricken with a rare form of meningitis. It was scary watching his body and his mind atrophy while neurologists struggled to diagnose him. Meanwhile, I fell into near despair, terrified that his brain would be destroyed before they found a treatment.

Jack, a fitness buff, decided that disuse had caused the wasting away of his stepson's body and mind. "He needs to get out of that hospital bed and move around to regain strength in his muscles." But he was unable to stand or sit unsupported. "He needs to make himself eat to rebuild his stamina." But he couldn't hold a fork anymore; he vomited whatever he could swallow.

We were with him and his future bride the evening his neurologist came in with the final test results, which we all hoped would bring an answer. But the tests hadn't isolated his specific kind of meningitis.

"We have come to the wall," the doctor said. "We have no choice but to schedule a cranial biopsy for tomorrow morning." We were stunned. The surgery would involve drilling a hole the size of a quarter through his skull to reach the meninges, the membranes surrounding the brain, for tissue samples.

After reading and signing the papers, I looked at Jack. He had moved to the bedside. He was looking down, oblivious to the tears dripping off his cheeks, at my son— *our* son. I saw nothing short of pure love in his face, his touch, his heart. Jack became a dad that night.

Real Love

The surgery solved the mystery, and medication miraculously brought on a quick return of full brain function, though it was several years before our son's body returned to normal. Meanwhile, there were other minor crises with each child. And each time, sharing both the problem and the solution created deeper bonds. Through these experiences, Jack has learned and taught both of our sons that it is okay to cry and to hug another man—their stepdad and each other, for starters.

The whole gang has learned to trust this man, knowing they can rely on him without doubt or fear. We know that Jack loves us all, even with our many warts.

We are a family.

Critical Thinking

What principles discussed in this chapter are illustrated in this woman's essay? What factors helped to make this remarried family a resilient one?

Source: From "From Stepfather to Father," by Mary Zimmeth Shomaker, 1994, *Liguoria.* (June) pp. 54–55. Copyright © 1994 by Liguoria Publications. Reprinted by permission.

1997). The transition to successful remarriage requires considerable adjustment on the part of everyone involved. From a family systems perspective,

> shifting roles and relationships is necessary when a new member is introduced into the family system by remarriage. The family has to struggle with the role of the new family member while allegiances, loyalties, and daily relationship patterns undergo transition. For many families, just as they are adjusting to one new member, the other ex-spouse remarries, which causes another transition requiring a shift in the family's tentative equilibrium. (Ahrons and Rodgers 1997, p. 187)

The unrealistic "urge to blend the two biological families as quickly as possible" may lead to disappointment when one or more adult or child members "resist connecting" (Wark and Jobalia 1998, p. 70).[9]

A principal challenge in creating supportive stepfamilies stems from society's nuclear-family model monopoly, discussed earlier in this chapter. Remarrieds often unconsciously try to approximate the nuclear-family model, but "this model does not work for most remarried families" (Wark and Jobalia 1998, p. 70) because, as we have seen, stepfamilies differ from first-marriage families in some important ways (Ganong and Coleman 2004). It may help to think of a stepfamily as a **binuclear family**—a new family type that includes members of the two (or more) families that existed before the divorce and remarriage (Ahrons 2004).

As "Case Study, "From Stepfather to Father—Creating a Resilient Stepfamily" illustrates, people can and do create supportive, resilient remarriages and stepfamilies (Ahrons 2004). For instance, the Binuclear Family Research Project (Ahrons and Miller 1993) collected data from ninety-eight pairs of Wis-

consin families at one, three, and five years after divorce. At three years, remarried biological parents and their new partners had high rates of **co-parenting**—shared decision making and parental supervision in such areas as discipline and schoolwork or shared holidays and recreation—with 62 percent of stepmothers and 73 percent of stepfathers reporting joint involvement in seven of ten areas of child rearing.

Meanwhile, counselors remind remarrieds not to forget their couple relationship (Lofas n.d.). Because stepfamilies—once called "instant families" (Phillips 1997)—have children from the start, spouses have little time or privacy to adjust to each other as partners. Furthermore, the relationship between biological parent and child predates the remarriage and may be stronger than the marital relationship. Therefore, "the couple relationship needs to be a priority in the family's life" (Kheshgi-Genovese and Genovese 1997, p. 260). In many locations, prospective spouses can participate in remarriage preparatory courses to alert remarrying couples to common problems and to help them find ways to discuss inevitable conflicts. Openly discussing upcoming changes prior to the remarriage can help (Manczak 1999).

In a clever play on words, online columnist and stepmother Dawn Miller titled one of her essays "Don't Go Nuclear—Negotiate." Chapter 8 presents some things for couples to talk about when forging an adaptable, supportive marriage relationship. Many of those questions also apply to remarriages. But there are additional things to talk about regarding stepfamilies. For instance, the rights of stepparents to visitation or even custody of a stepchild in the event of death or divorce from the child's parent are a crucial issue when so many people become closely attached to stepchildren—and vice versa. Some stepparents do continue relationships with their stepchildren after divorce (Dickinson 2002); law in this area—case law and legislation—is rapidly changing. Although it does not seem likely—and with good reason—that biological parents will be legally replaced by stepparents, it is important to indicate in a will or other statement that the biological parent would like his or her children's relationship with a stepparent preserved through visitation, if that is the case (Mahoney 1997). The general point here is that people who remarry should not assume that they may do some of these things without checking with a

---

9. You may have noticed that we have not used the once-familiar term "blended family" in this chapter. That's because family therapists and other stepfamily experts have concluded that stepfamilies do not readily "blend." In fact, Dr. Marjorie Engel (2003), president of the Stepfamily Association of America, warns that "Couples with 'blended' as their objective tend to have the most problematic households and those are the couples most likely to leave the stepfamily because some or all of the members won't buy into the blended concept." Playing with the language, stepmother and online columnist Dawn Miller refers to stepfamily living as "life in a blender" (Dawn Miller, "Surviving" n.d.).

lawyer. Other things to discuss involve house rules in the binuclear family, expectations for a stepparent's financial support of stepchildren, questions of inheritance, and perhaps whether there will be a mutual child or children.

Chapter 15 points out that life transitions, such as remarriage or the transition to stepparent, are family stressors. That chapter explains that resilient families deal with family transitions creatively by emphasizing mutual acceptance, respect, and shared values (Ahrons 2004). You may also recall that Chapter 13 presents several guidelines for bonding fights—all applicable in remarriages and binuclear families. We'll note here that one of these guidelines is to "choose the time and place carefully." Columnist Dawn Miller applies this advice to the stepfamily situation: "[T]here's a lot to be said for using a demilitarized zone for some negotiations. Talking with my husband's ex-wife about a switch in the custody schedule would not be best in our home, or hers. That's better handled on neutral turf." (Miller, "Don't Go Nuclear" n.d.).

As the number of stepfamilies increases, they have access to more resources than in the past. For instance, several online websites by stepfamily counselors and well-respected researchers are designed to give advice and report research findings concerning stepfamilies.

Examples are thestepfamilylife.com, secondwivescafe.com, and the website of the Stepfamily Association of America (www.saafamily.org). There are also more and more books written by psychologists and others for remarrieds and stepfamily members. One of these, directed to teens, is *Stepliving for Teens: Getting Along with Step-Parents, Parents and Siblings* (Block and Bartell 2001). And stepfamily enrichment programs, support groups, and various other group-counseling resources for stepfamilies are becoming available in more and more communities (Jones 2004; Michaels 2000).

In general, counselors and other stepfamily experts advise the following: "Don't resent the custody situation—deal with it. Form realistic expectations, and don't be afraid to establish new traditions" (Miller, "Surviving" n.d.). Researchers and family therapists tend to agree that "it is neither the structural complexity nor the presence/absence of children in the home *per se* that impacts the marital relationship. Rather, the ways in which couples interact around these issues are the key to understanding marital relationships in general and marital relationships in remarriages specifically" (Ihinger-Tallman and Pasley 1997, p. 25). Interacting in positive ways in remarriages and stepfamilies involves making knowledgeable choices.

In Sum

- Remarriages have always been fairly common in the United States but are far more frequent now than they were earlier in this century, and they follow divorce more often than widowhood.

- The courtship process by which people choose remarriage partners has similarities to courtship preceding first marriages, but the basic exchange often weighs more heavily against older women, and homogamy tends to be less important.

- Remarriages are usually about as happy as first marriages, but they tend to be slightly less stable.

- One reason for relative remarital instability is lack of a cultural script for living in remarriages or stepfamilies.

- Relationships in immediate remarried families and with kin are often complex, yet there are virtually no social prescriptions and few legal definitions to clarify roles and relationships.

- The lack of cultural guidelines is most apparent in the stepparent role.

- Stepparents are often troubled by financial strains, role ambiguity, and stepchildren's hostility.

- Marital happiness and stability in remarried families are greater when the couple has strong social support, high expressiveness, a positive attitude about the remarriage,

- low role ambiguity, and little belief in negative stereotypes and myths about remarriages or stepfamilies.
- ■ "Stepfamily therapists now use a model that assumes that stepfamilies are normal and can be successful in a variety of ways, enriching the lives of their members" (Burt and Burt 1996, p. 182).

Key Terms

binuclear family
co-parenting
cultural script
double remarriages
hidden agenda
incomplete institution
nuclear-family model
 monopoly

remarriages
remarried families
seven-stage model of stepfamily development
single remarriages
stepmother trap

Questions for Review and Reflection

1. Discuss the similarities and differences between courtship before remarriage and courtship before first marriage.
2. The remarried family has been called an incomplete institution. What does this mean? How does this affect the people involved in a remarriage? Include a discussion of kin networks and family law. Do you think this situation is changing?
3. What evidence can you gather from observation and/or your own personal experience to show that stepfamilies (a) may be more culturally acceptable today than in the past and (b) remain negatively stereotyped as not as functional or as normal as first-marriage, nuclear families?
4. What are some problems faced by both stepmothers and stepfathers? What are some problems faced particularly by stepfathers? Why might the role of stepmother be more difficult than that of stepfather? How might these problems be resolved or alleviated?
5. **Policy Question.** In terms of social policy, what might be done to increase the stability of remarriages?

Suggested Readings

Barash, Susan Shapiro. 2000. *Second Wives: The Pitfalls and Rewards of Marrying Widowers and Divorced Men.* Far Hills, NJ: New Horizon. A self-help, "how-to" book with good advice.

Booth, Alan, and Judy Dunn (Eds.). 1994. *Stepfamilies: Who Benefits? Who Does Not?* Hillsdale, NJ: Erlbaum. A collection of papers on stepfamilies by recognized authorities in the field.

Deal, Ron L. 2002. *The Smart Stepfamily.* Minneapolis: Bethany House. Deal is a licensed marriage and family therapist as well as a family life minister for the Church of Christ. His advice is based on family psychology, and the book has some, although not pronounced, (Christian) spiritual flavor.

Ganong, Lawrence H., and Marilyn Coleman. 2004. *Stepfamily Relationships: Development, Dynamics, and Interventions.* New York: Kluwer Academic/Plenum Publishers. Comprehensive, readable review of the literature to date by two of the foremost recognized researcher-experts in this field.

Gillespie, Natalie Nichols. 2004. *The Stepfamily Survival Guide.* Grand Rapids, MI: Revell. Down-to-earth, good advice for supportive and successful stepfamily living.

Marsiglio, William. 2004b. *Stepdads: Stories of Love, Hope, and Repair.* Boulder, CO: Rowman and Littlefield.

Rogers, Fred. 1997. *Stepfamilies.* New York: Putnam. By public television's "Mr. Rogers," in the "Let's Talk About It" series for children.

Stepfamily Association of America.

http://www.saafamily.org

Website produced by recognized experts in the field, offering research findings, advice, and chatrooms for stepfamily members.

The Stepfamily Foundation.

http://www.stepfamily.org

Another website overseen by recognized experts in the field, offering research findings, advice, and helpful e-booklets for sale. Examples of the latter are "Your Stepchildren are Visiting: Plan It, Manage It" and "The 'Demons' of Stepfamily Life and the Strategies to Conquer Them." This chapter's "As We Make Choices: Some Stepparenting Tips" is adapted from this website.

Virtual Society: The Wadsworth Sociology Resource Center

 Go to the Sociology Resource Center at **http:// sociology.wadsworth.com** for a wealth of online resources, including a companion website for your text that provides study aids such as self-quizzes for each chapter and a practice final exam, as well as links to sociology websites and information on the latest theories and discoveries in the field. In addition, you will find further suggested readings, flash cards, MicroCase online exercises, and appendices on a range of subjects.

Online Study Tool

Marriage & Family ⊛ Now™ Go to **http://sociology .wadsworth.com** to reach the companion website for your text and use the Marriage&FamilyNow access code that came with your book to access this study tool. Take a practice pretest after you have read each chapter, and then use the study plan provided to master that chapter. Afterward, take a posttest to monitor your progress.

Search Online with InfoTrac College Edition

For additional information, exercises, and key words to aid your research, explore InfoTrac College Edition, your online library that offers full-length articles from thousands of scholarly and popular publications. Click on *InfoTrac College Edition* under *Chapter Resources* at the companion website and use the access code that came with your book.

- Search keywords: *remarriage, stepfamily.*

Chapter **18**

Aging Families

The increasing prevalence and importance of multigenerational bonds represents a valuable new resource for families in the 21st century.

VERN L. BENGSTON

IN A CLEVER PLAY ON WORDS, *NEWSWEEK* magazine announced in 1999 that America was becoming the "home of the gray." "The Senior Boom is coming," wrote the article's author (Peyser 1999, p. 50). Besides "home of the gray," the aging of the American population has been termed a "demographic avalanche" and an "age wave" (Conner 2000, p. 6). More and more family members are living longer. This chapter examines families in later life. We will look at living arrangements of older Americans and at marriage relationships in later life. We will discuss the grandparent role, then explore issues concerning giving care to older family members. To begin, we'll examine some facts about our aging population.

▪ Our Aging Population ▪

The number of older people in the United States (and all other industrialized nations) is growing remarkably. In 1980 there were 25.5 million Americans aged 65 or older; today nearly 35 million Americans are aged 65 or older, and that number is expected to double over the next twenty-five years. Regarding Americans aged 75 and older, in 1980 there were close to 10 million; by 2002 there were more than 17 million. Of those aged 85 and above, there were 2.2 million in 1980, compared to more than 4.5 million today. Projections are that by the year 2050, there will be nearly 87 million Americans aged 65 and older and close to 21 million Americans aged 85 and over (U.S. Census Bureau 2003a, tables 11 and 12).

Not just the *number* of elderly has increased, but also their *proportion* of the total U.S. population. This is especially true for those in the "older-old" (aged 75–84) and the "old-old" (85 and over) age groups. Those aged 75 and above rose from 4.4 percent in 1980 to 6 percent in 2002, while the proportion of Americans aged 85 and older rose from 1.0 percent to 1.6 percent over those same years (U.S. Census Bureau 2003a, Table 11).

Aging Baby Boomers

Between 1946 and 1964, in the aftermath of World War II, more U.S. women married and had children than ever before. The high birth rate created what is commonly called the **baby boom**.[1] Now baby boomers are beginning to retire, and within the next twenty years they will comprise a dramatically large elderly population (see Figure 18.1). Meanwhile, the number of children under age 18 is about the same today as it has been for several decades (about 70 million). So children now make up a smaller proportion—and older Americans a larger proportion—of the population.[2] The changing American age structure is indicated by the nation's median age; it was 35.7 in 2002—up from 28.0 in 1970 (U.S. Census Bureau 2000, Table 11; U.S. Census Bureau 2003a, Table 13). Along with the impact of the baby boomers' aging and the declining proportion of children in the population, longer life expectancy has contributed to the aging of our population.

Longer Life Expectancy

People are living to very old ages. In fact, Americans are now living long enough that demographers divide the aging population into three categories: the "young-old" (aged 65–74), the "older-old" (aged 75–84), and the "old-old" (aged 85 and over). Life expectancy at birth increased from 70.8 in 1970 (67.1 for men and 74.7 for women) to 77.2 in 2001 (74.4 for men and 79.8 for women) (U.S. Census Bureau 2003a, Table 105).

Women, on average, live about five and one-half years longer than men. Consequently, the make-up of the elderly population differs by gender. In 2002, there were 20.8 million women aged 65 and older, compared to 14.8 million men. For Americans over age 84, there are 3.2 million women and about 1.4 million men (U.S. Census Bureau 2003a, Table 11). In addition to differing by gender, life expectancy also differs by

---

1. The baby boom "was a product of complicated and powerful social forces surrounding the end of World War II, the beginning of the cold war, and the dawn of the nuclear age. . . . The family became the central focus in the lives of most Americans and was the place where many found a sense of security" (Conner 2000, p. 7).
2. The proportion of the U.S. population under age 18 was about 36 percent in 1960, compared to about 28 percent in 2002 (U.S. Census Bureau 2003a, Table 11).

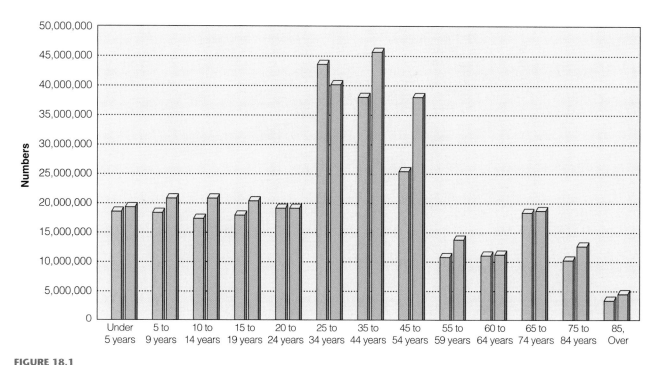

FIGURE 18.1

Number of Americans in Population Age Groups, 1990 and 2000.

The baby boom cohort is represented by the central bars. As this cohort continues to age, we will see a dramatic increase in the elderly population.

Source: www.seniorjournal.com/news/features/05-16-01popgraphs.htm. Reprinted with permission.

race/ethnicity, with Asians and whites having the longest life expectancy.[3]

Demographers point to two general family-related consequences of our living longer. First, because more generations are alive at once, we increasingly have opportunities to maintain ties with grandparents, great-grandparents, and even great-great-grandparents (Beng-

ston 2001). A second consequence of longer life expectancy is that, on average, Americans spend more years near the end of their lives with chronic health problems (Crimmins 2001).[4] As Americans get older, more and more of us will be called upon to provide care for a parent or other aging relative (Garey, Hansen, Hertz, and MacDonald 2002). We will return to issues surrounding giving care to aging family members later in this chapter. At this point, we'll look at the racial/ethnic composition of the older American population.

---

3. In 2001 the white male life expectancy at birth was 75.0, compared to 68.6 for black males. Among women, the figure was 80.2 for whites, compared to 75.5 for blacks (U.S. Census Bureau 2003a, Table 105). Much of this difference is associated with whites having, on average, higher incomes and lower poverty rates than blacks. Higher incomes, along with higher education levels, are associated with better health and longer life expectancy, largely because people in higher socioeconomic groups have access to better preventive health care and are less likely to work in hazardous environments: "Their educational advantage may also make them more avid consumers of the vast amounts of information available on improving health" (Conner 2000, p. 16). Some of the racial/ethnic difference in life expectancy may also be explained genetically and by discrimination in health care.

---

4. Indeed, we can think not just in terms of overall life expectancy but also in terms of **active life expectancy**—the period of life free of disability in activities of daily living, after which may follow a period of being at least somewhat disabled. Today, an American man who is 65 can expect to live actively for about another fourteen years, with two years after that at least partly disabled. For females aged 65, the numbers are about sixteen more years of active life with about seven additional years at least partly disabled (Manton and Land 2000).

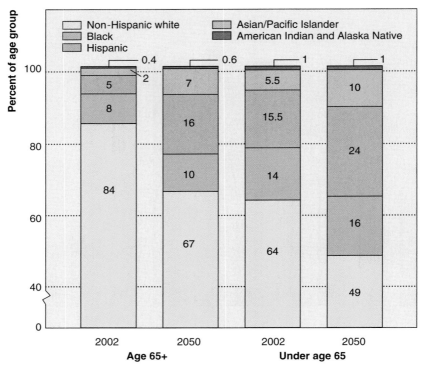

FIGURE 18.2

U.S. elderly and nonelderly population by race/ethnicity, 2002 and 2050.

Note: Hispanic may be of any race.

Sources: del Pinal and Singer 1997; Lee 1998; and calculated from U.S. Census Bureau 2003a, Table 13.

Racial/Ethnic Composition of the Older American Population

As a group, non-Hispanic whites in the United States are older than other racial/ethnic categories. Twenty percent of the total population is currently over age 65, while 24.5 percent of non-Hispanic whites are over 65. This figure compares to just 12.4 percent of blacks, 14 percent of Asians and Pacific Islanders, and 7.5 percent of Hispanics (U.S. Census Bureau 2003a, Table 13).

Figure 18.2 looks at the nation's age distribution by race/ethnicity in another way. As you can see from Figure 18.2, about 84 percent of the U.S. population over age 64 is non-Hispanic white. Another 8 percent is African American, with another 5 percent Hispanic. However, the older population is becoming more ethnically and racially diverse as members of racial/ethnic minority groups grow older. As described in Chapter 2, due to immigration and to relatively high birth rates of ethnic and racial minority groups, Hispanic, African

American, and Asian populations are growing faster than non-Hispanic whites (del Pinal and Singer 1997; Lee 1998). By 2050, the non-Hispanic white share of the elderly population is projected to fall to 67 percent: "Some senior centers already offer *tai chi* exercise classes or serve tamales for lunch, a reflection of greater ethnic diversity" (Treas 1995, p. 8).

Living Arrangements of Older Americans

Table 18.1 shows that about one-quarter of U.S. households are made up of people living alone. As is evident from Figure 9.4, many of them are older people. This situation represents a growing trend since about 1940. Among Americans aged 65 and older, approximately 31 percent live alone. Due to the increased likelihood of being widowed, nearly 40 percent of people over age 75

"Good news, honey—seventy is the new fifty."

live by themselves (U.S. Census Bureau 2003a, Table 64). In the future, an increasing proportion of older Americans is projected to live alone (U.S. Senate Special Committee on Aging 2001, 2004).[5]

One review of historical trends in family living arrangements (Haber and Gratton 1994) notes the long-term preference for separate households in American society. Some older Americans move to retirement communities in the "Sun Belt"—Florida and the Southwest (Frey 1999). However, for the most part, both adult children and their parents prefer to live near one another, although not in the same residence (Rosenmayr 1977).

Gender Differences in Older Americans' Living Arrangements

Table 18.1 shows the living arrangements of older Americans by gender. Due mainly to differences in life expectancy, older men are much more likely to be living with their spouse than are older women (73 percent of men aged 65 and older, compared to 41 percent of women). This pattern persists into the older ages: Among those aged 75 and over, 67 percent of men live with a spouse while just 29 percent of women do.

Again, due to life expectancy differences, older women are more likely than men to be widowed.

Table 18.1

Living Arrangements Of Persons 65 Years Old and Over, by Gender, 2000			
	LIVING ARRANGEMENT	MEN (%)	WOMEN (%)
65 years old and over	Alone	17	40
	With spouse	73	41
	With other persons	10	19
65–74 years old	Alone	14	31
	With spouse	77	53
	With other persons	10	16
75 years old and over	Alone	21	49
	With spouse	67	29
	With other persons	12	22

Source: Adapted from Fields and Casper 2001, Table 6.

---

5. The future increase in the proportion of elderly living alone will be due largely to three factors: first, the relatively high divorce rate for people who are now middle-aged (see Chapter 16); second, an increase in the number of people who never marry (see Chapter 9); and third, a decline in the proportion of older people living with their adult children due to decreasing economic incentive to share living space (Novak 1997; Bianchi and Casper 2000)—unless there is a very significant and prolonged downturn in our economy.

Therefore, older women are more than twice as likely to live alone than older men (40 percent of women, compared to 17 percent of men aged 65 and older). Of those 75 and over, 49 percent of women live by themselves, compared to 21 percent of men.

Finally, from Table 18.1, we can see that older women are significantly more likely than older men to live with people other than their spouse (19 percent of women aged 65 and older, compared to 10 percent of men)—a pattern that persists into old-old age (Fields and Casper 2001, Table 6). We can conclude from these figures that

> Men generally receive companionship and care from their wives in the latter stages of life, while women are more likely to live alone, perhaps with assistance from grown children, to live with other family members, or to enter a nursing home. (Bianchi and Casper 2000, p. 10)

Besides gender, race and ethnicity also affect the living arrangements of older Americans.

Racial/Ethnic Differences in Older Americans' Living Arrangements

Due to economic and cultural differences, the living arrangements of older Americans vary according to race and ethnicity. For instance, Asian and Central and South American immigrant parents are more likely than non-Hispanic whites to reside with adult children who provide most of the household income (Glick and Hook 2002). Table 18.2 compares the living arrangements of white, black, and Hispanic adults aged 65 and older (see also Figure 9.2). One generalization that we can make from the statistics in Table 18.2 is that African Americans and Hispanics are much more likely (indeed, more than twice as likely) as whites to live with people other than their spouse—grown children, siblings, or other relatives. Partly as a result of economic necessity, coupled with social norms involving family members' obligations to one another (Bianchi and Casper 2000), older blacks and Hispanics are less likely than whites to live alone. This is true even though blacks and Hispanics are also less likely than whites to live with a spouse.[6]

Table 18.2

Living Arrangements Of Persons 65 Years Old and Over, by Race/Ethnicity, 2002

	LIVING ARRANGEMENT	65–74 YEARS OLD (%)	75 AND OLDER (%)
Total Population[a]	Alone	27	40
	With spouse	65	45
	With other persons	11	15
White	Alone	23	40
	With spouse	67	46
	With other persons	9.5	14
Black	Alone	29.5	39
	With spouse	49	30
	With other persons	22	31
Hispanic Origin[b]	Alone	16	25
	With spouse	60	45
	With other persons	24	30

a Includes other races and persons not of Hispanic origin, not shown separately.
b Persons of Hispanic origin may be of any race.

Source: Calculated from U.S. Census Bureau 2003a, Table 64.

Among older Americans without partners, living arrangements depend on a variety of factors, including the status of one's health, the availability of others with whom to reside, social norms regarding obligations of other family members toward their elderly, personal preferences for privacy and independence, and economics (Bianchi and Casper 2000). We will look at all these factors in various sections of this chapter. Here we note that older Americans with better health and higher incomes are more likely to live independently, a situation that suggests strong personal preferences for privacy and independence. Meanwhile, those in financial need are more likely to live with relatives (Bianchi and Casper 2000).

▪ Aging in Today's Economy ▪

Today's older Americans live on a combination of Social Security benefits, private pensions from employers, personal savings, and social welfare programs

---

6. There are two reasons that older African Americans and Hispanics are less likely than whites to live with a spouse. First, due to differences in patterns of marriage and divorce (U.S. Census Bureau 2003a, Table 61), African Americans are more likely than whites to enter older

ages without a spouse. Second, gender differences in life expectancy (with women living longer than men) are slightly higher among blacks and Hispanics (a little over eight years) than among whites (about 7.6 years) (U.S. Census Bureau 2003a, Table 105).

designed to meet the needs of the poor and disabled. About 40 percent of the income of people aged 65 and older is from Social Security benefits and related federal programs, such as Medicare, Medicaid, and Supplemental Security Income (SSI).[7] Social security benefits are the only source of income for one-fifth of Americans over age 65 (U.S. Social Security Administration 2003).

Growth in Social Security benefits has resulted in dramatic changes in U.S. poverty rates over the last several decades. Before Social Security and Medicare were initiated, the elderly were disproportionately poor (Meyer and Bellas 2001). But poverty has declined sharply for those aged 65 and over—from 36 percent in 1959 to about 10 percent today (see Figure 11.3). Due largely to older Americans' organization and lobbying to protect Social Security benefits, the poverty rate for those over age 64 is now about one-half that of children (U.S. Census Bureau 2003a, Table 697).

Largely due to Social Security pensions and Medicare health insurance, "today we have the most affluent generation of older people America has ever seen" (Conner 2000, p. 10). Then, too, older Americans today benefit from a generally stable or rising economy during most of their working years and have also gained from the appreciated value of their homes. Overall, the improvements in the financial status, as well as the health, of older Americans over the past

several decades have resulted in "a revolution in lifestyles and living arrangements among the elderly" (Bianchi and Casper 2000, p. 9).

However, having noted that today's older Americans are better off than generations preceding them, we need to acknowledge that, on average, their income declines by up to one-half upon retirement and that the retired spend considerably more of their incomes on health care (DeNavas-Walt, Cleveland, and Webster 2003, Table 3; "Spending Patterns" 2000). Health costs are rising dramatically, and health insurance programs, including Medicaid and Medicare, are unlikely to keep up (Meyer and Bellas 2001). Serious illness can erode the savings and income of the elderly and their families. Furthermore, one-tenth of older adults *are* living in poverty. They, along with the "near poor" (those with incomes at or below 125 percent of the poverty level), and many others with relatively low incomes are hardly enjoying the RV lifestyle we might think of when we imagine retirement.[8]

Older Women's Finances

Older men are considerably better off financially than are older women. In 2002, the median income of individual Americans aged 65 and older was $19,436 for males and $11,406 for females (U.S. Administration on Aging 2003). This situation is partly due to the fact that throughout their employment years, men averaged higher earnings than women did (see Chapter 12). Consequently older women have smaller (if any) pensions from employers. Furthermore, older women on average did not begin to save for retirement as early as did men (Even and Macpherson 2004).

Moreover, women's Social Security benefits average about 76 percent of men's. Maximum Social Security benefits (about $1,600 monthly) are available only to workers with lengthy and continuous labor force participation in higher-paying jobs. This situation works against older women today, who either did not participate in the labor force at all or are likely to have dropped in and out of the labor force while taking lower-paying jobs (Vartanian and McNamara 2002). "Thus, women are penalized for conforming to a role that they are strongly encouraged to assume—unpaid

---

7. During the Depression of the 1930s, millions of Americans lost their jobs and savings. In response, the federal government passed the 1935 Social Security Act, a dramatically new program designed to assist the elderly. The Social Security Act established the collection of taxes on income from one generation of workers to pay monthly pensions to an older generation of nonworkers. Initially, only those who contributed to Social Security were eligible to receive benefits, but over the years the U.S. Congress has extended coverage to spouses and to the widowed, as well as to the blind and permanently disabled.

Medicare, begun in 1965, is a compulsory federal program that provides health care insurance and benefits to the aged, blind, and permanently disabled. Before the program began, just 56 percent of the aged had hospital insurance. In 1992, at least 97 percent of all older people in the United States had coverage because all who qualify for Social Security are eligible for Medicare.

In 1965, intending to provide health care to poor Americans of all ages, Congress created the Medicaid program in conjunction with Medicare. Eligibility for Medicaid is based on having virtually no family assets (saving and checking accounts, stocks, bonds, mutual funds, and any form of property that can be converted to cash) and very little income. In 1972, Congress created the federal Supplemental Security Income program (SSI), a "welfare" program that provides monthly income checks to poverty-level older Americans and the disabled (Meyer and Bellas 2001).

8. For instance, Medicaid recipients (see Footnote 7) living in nursing homes are wards of the state. Hence, their entire monthly incomes, except for a small personal-needs allowance, goes toward nursing home costs (Meyer and Bellas 2001).

Social Security and Medicare have raised the incomes of older Americans, beginning in 1940, so that today the proportion of elderly in the United States living in poverty has declined and is less than that of children. Nevertheless, 10 percent of older Americans—disproportionately the unmarried and women—are living in poverty. Among nonmarrieds aged 65 and over, 14 percent of men and 18 percent of women live in poverty (U.S. Social Security Administration 2003, p. 8).

household worker—and their disadvantaged economic position is carried into old age" (Meyer and Bellas 2001, p. 193). An older wife married for at least ten years to a now-retired worker can receive a spousal "allowance," but it is equal to one-half of her husband's benefits.[9]

Compared to widows, divorced and separated women are worse off, and many need to work for sev-

9. Employed women may qualify on the basis of both their own and their husband's work records, although they cannot receive benefits under both categories. It is a statement of the gendered inequality in earnings, described in Chapter 12, that about half of women who are dually entitled today receive greater benefits from qualifying as their husband's spouse than on their own work history (Meyer and Bellas 2001).

eral years after traditional retirement age. Ex-spouses qualify for one-half the amount of their ex's Social Security benefits, provided the marriage lasted at least ten years. Nevertheless, "Poorly constructed divorce settlements and short-term thinking—trying to hang onto a dream home that took two incomes to support, for instance—can cripple [divorced] women's finances" (Block 2000, p. 1B).

Having looked at the economic situation of older Americans, together with their living arrangements, we turn to an examination of marriage and other family relationships in later life.

Marriage Relationships in Later Life

Only about 4 percent of women and of men over 65 today have never married (Fields and Casper 2001). Some later-life marriages are remarriages, but the vast majority of older married couples have been wed for quite some time—either in first or second marriages.

Most older married couples place intimacy as central to their lives and describe their unions as happy (Walker, Manoogian-O'Dell, McGraw, and White 2001; Szinovacz and Schaffer 2000). A study of love styles (see Chapter 5) found high endorsement of both *eros* (passionate love) and of *storge* (friendship or companionship love) among marrieds of all ages. However, those in later life were more likely to value the practical benefits of their marriage (*pragma*) as well (Montgomery and Sorell 1997).

Older Americans continue to be interested in sex, even into old-old age and even in nursing homes (Talbott 1998; Purdy 1995). According to sociologist Andrew Greeley, "It may be that the last great American taboo is passion among the elderly" (quoted in "Happiest Couples in Study" 1992). However, the fact that the large baby boom cohort is aging means that we now see many more books about sex in later life. And the overall conclusion of these books is that—as one author titles hers—the old folks are "still doing it" (Sachs 2001).

In general, health is an important factor in morale in later life, and it has a substantial impact on marital quality as well as other social contacts (Atchley 1997; Wickrama et al. 1997). Chapter 6 points out that while health does affect sexual performance, sex does indeed continue into late life. A national survey sponsored by the American Association of Retired People (AARP) of Americans aged 45 and older asked respondents what would most improve their sex lives. People aged 45–59 most often said "less stress" and "more free time." "Better health" headed the list for men 60 and older, "better health for partner" headed for women 60–74, and "finding a partner" was the most frequent answer for women 75 and older.[10] The survey found that more than half of men and women with partners in all age groups had regular sexual intercourse. Even including those aged 75 and older, more than half of men and 85 percent of women said that their sex lives were unimpaired by illness (Jacoby 1999).

This is not to say that there are no sexual problems in later marriages. There can be, of course. A husband's having difficulty with erection, which can begin to happen in late middle age, may decrease his sexual motivation. However, it is also true that a husband's having difficulty with erection may result in his slowing down sexually and making sex more exciting for his partner (Sachs 2001).

As discussed in Chapter 6, long-term partners have to deal with habituation, or declining interest in sex due to greater accessibility. But habituation effects seem to be more prevalent in the first year of marriage. Indeed, marrieds of all ages tend to report high satisfaction with their sex lives, perhaps because increasingly they see sex as a "pleasure bond" (see Chapter 6). According to psychiatrist Stephen Levine, "Over age 50, the quality of sex depends much more on the overall quality of a relationship than it does for young couples" (quoted in Jacoby 1999, p. 42).

The Postparental Period and Retirement

Older married-couple households without children residing therein constitute an increasing proportion of American households (Bianchi and Casper 2000).[11] Postparental unions have the potential for high satisfaction because, on average, older couples report having fewer disagreements, and marital happiness often increases when couples have the time, energy, and financial resources to invest in their couple relationship (Binstock and George 1996; Hatch and Bulcroft 2004). Still, a frequent strain on couples at this time results from serious new family responsibilities due to the failing health of their own aging parents—a situation that may last well into a couple's retirement years.[12]

We tend to think of retirement as an abrupt event, but many people retire gradually by steadily reducing their work hours or intermittently leaving, then returning to the labor force before retiring completely (Elder and Pavalko 1993; Atchley 1997). Even when it is not an abrupt event, retirement represents an important change for individuals and couples.

One small study of 228 couples (Smith and Moen 1998) found that the decision to retire is influenced by one's spouse—although for both husbands and wives, personal satisfaction in retirement is associated with *not* having been influenced by one's partner. Interestingly—and in line with traditionally gendered power relations in marriage—wives more often than husbands are motivated to retire by their spouse's wanting them to do so (Smith and Moen 2004).

We know most about the retirement experience of men. A retired husband may choose to devote more attention to family roles such as being a companionate husband and grandparent; he might spend more time in homemaking tasks, especially if his wife is still employed (Szinovacz 2000). However, doing this can be problematic for men who cling to the traditional masculine role that highly values work and achievement

---

10. While older and elderly women may be interested in sex, the lack of a partner is the problem (Talbott 1998). Jacoby (1999) refers to this situation as the "partner gap." We have seen that, as they age, women are far more likely than men to be widowed. Moreover, as they grow older, women are adversely affected by the *double standard of aging* (Sontag 1976); that is, men aren't considered old or sexually ineligible as soon as women are. In our culture, being physically attractive is far more important in attracting a mate for women than for men. Beauty, "identified, as it is for women, with youthfulness, does not stand up well to age" (Sontag 1976, p. 352). So in our society, women become sexually ineligible much earlier than men do. An attractive man can remain eligible well into old age and is considered an acceptable mate for a younger woman. For older single women, this situation can exacerbate more general feelings of loneliness.

11. The postparental stage of family life first came to attention about thirty-five years ago through the value-laden term *empty nest* (Bart 1972). It was assumed that (full-time) mothers would feel lonely and depressed once their children had grown and left home. However, current cohorts of women are likely to have employment and other outside interests and activities. The old stereotype of the depressed empty-nest mother is also ironic because fathers can have transition pains, too (Robinson and Barret 1986).

12. Although most older people retire, some do not—and many of those who don't are employed into their seventies and eighties. Not wanting to retire is one reason for continuing to work. Another reason, particularly applicable to divorced older women, is being unable to afford to retire (Atchley 1997), as noted earlier in this chapter.

A retired husband may choose to spend more time doing homemaking tasks and give increased attention to being a companionate spouse. Role sharing and supportive communication predict good adjustment for retiring couples, including those who adhered to more-traditional gender roles in their younger years.

(Aldous 1978). A husband's retirement requires homemaking wives to adjust as well. Full-time homemakers may find it difficult to share the house that had become their exclusive territory during the day. This may be partly why some research has found that husbands are happier with wives' retirement than vice versa (Smith and Moen 2004). When both partners are employed, simultaneous retirement or the retirement of the wife before the husband may cause fewer relationship problems (Davey and Szinovacz 2004; Brubaker 1991).

For both wives and husbands, role flexibility is important to successful adjustment, and "both husbands and wives are happier in the aging period when they emphasize mutual help, companionship, and affection rather than trying to maintain the segregation of daily role activities characteristic of the preretirement period" (Aldous 1978, p. 204; see also Brubaker 1991).

Later-Life Divorce and Widowhood

Although the majority of couples who divorce do so before their retirement years, some couples do divorce in later life. Older-age divorces may be prompted by a husband's falling in love with a younger woman or by an older wife's tiring of being what she considers an unappreciated caregiver (Springen 2000a). Little research has been done on the topic, but we might hypothesize that later-life divorces are not necessarily easy on the couple's adult children. For one thing, family rituals, such as birthday parties or Thanksgiving dinner are disrupted (Pett, Lang, and Gander 1992). Then too, adult children of divorcing parents may worry about having to become full-time caregivers to an aging parent in the absence of the parent's spouse.

Although some later-life marriages end in divorce, the vast majority do so with the death of a spouse.

Widowhood and Widowerhood

Adjustment to widowhood or widowerhood is an important and common family transition in later life. We saw earlier in this chapter that, because women's life expectancy is longer and older men remarry far more often than women do, widowhood is significantly more common than widowerhood in our society. As Table 18.1 shows, nearly three-quarters of men aged 65 and over live with their spouse, but fewer than half (41 percent) of women live with theirs. Widowhood is usually a permanent status for older women. Indeed, for some women, widowhood may last longer than the child-rearing stage of life. Nevertheless, we are reminded that widowhood does not, of course, happen only to women (Atchley 1997). In 2000, for instance, nearly one-third of men aged 75 and older were widowed (Fields and Casper 2001, Table 6).

Typically, widowhood and widowerhood begin with **bereavement**, a period of mourning, followed by gradual adjustment to the new, unmarried status and to the loss. Bereavement manifests itself in physical, emotional, and intellectual symptoms (Figley et al. 1998). Recently widowed people perceived their health as declining and reported depressive symptoms (Brubaker 1991). Both men and women experience emotional reactions—anger, guilt, sadness, anxiety, and preoccupation with thoughts of the dead spouse—but these responses tend to diminish over time (Doka, Breaux, and Gordon 2002). Social support, adult children's help with housework and related tasks, and activities with friends, children, and siblings help (Atchley 1997; Utz, Reidy, Carr, Nesse, and Wortman 2004).

There is some evidence that being single in old age is more detrimental, physically and emotionally, for men than for women (Peters and Liefbroer 1997). As pointed out in Chapter 9, women more often have social support outside the family, whereas men are typically more dependent on family for support. But

> men and women experience similar physical and emotional difficulties initially, but after a time seem to cope with the loss of a spouse. . . . [B]oth establish new [single] lifestyles based on their

past patterns of interaction. For both, their financial [and health] situation is related to their feelings of well-being. (Brubaker 1991, p. 233)

A spouse's death brings the conjugal unit to an end—often a profoundly painful event. During later life, morale and well-being frequently derive from relations with siblings, as well as from friends, neighbors, and other social contacts (Atchley 1997; Eriksen and Gerstel 2002; Wickrama et al. 1997). Furthermore, particularly for women, relationships with adult children and grandchildren continue to be important.

Older Parents, ▪ Adult Children, ▪ and Grandchildren

More often than spousal relationships, those between parents and their children last a lifetime (Kaufman and Uhlenberg 1998). In this section, we examine older parent–adult child and grandparent relations.

Older Parents and Adult Children

Chapter 11 mentions that adults' relationships with their parents can be classified as *tight-knit*, *sociable*, *obligatory*, *intimate but distant*, or *detached*. Here we will expand our discussion of this typology. Sociologists Merril Silverstein and Vern L. Bengston (2001) developed six indicators of relationship solidarity, or connection: geographical proximity, contact between members in a relationship, emotional closeness, similarity of opinions, providing care, and receiving care. Based on survey evidence and using these six indicators, they developed a typology of five kinds of parent–adult child relations (see Table 18.3).

Parent–adult child relations vary depending on how family members combine—or, in the case of the detached relationship style, do not combine—the six indicators. For instance, in tight-knit relations, the parent and the adult child live near each other (geographical proximity), feel emotionally close, share similar opinions, and help each other (give and receive assistance). Sociable relations involve all of these characteristics except that the parent and adult child do not exchange assistance.

Table 18.3

Types of Intergenerational Relations	
CLASS	**DEFINITION**
Tight-knit	Adult children are engaged with their parents based on geographical proximity, frequency of contact, emotional closeness, similarity of opinions, providing and receiving assistance.
Sociable	Adult children are engaged with their parents based on geographic proximity, frequency of contact, emotional closeness, and similarity of opinions but not based on providing or receiving assistance.
Obligatory	Adult children are engaged with their parents based on geographic proximity and frequency of contact but not based on emotional closeness and similarity of opinions. Adult children are likely to provide and/or receive assistance.
Intimate but distant	Adult children are engaged with their parents based on emotional closeness and similarity of opinions but not based on geographic proximity, frequency of contact, providing assistance, and receiving assistance.
Detached	Adult children are not engaged with their parents based on any of these six indicators of solidarity.

Source: Adapted from Silverstein and Bengston 2001, p. 55.

Obligatory relations between parent and adult child involve geographical proximity, frequency of contact, and, often, mutual assistance. However, the relationship is not emotionally close, nor do the parent and adult child share similar opinions. Helping each other depends more on family norms of reciprocal obligation and a sense of duty than on feeling close emotionally.

In intimate-but-distant relationships, parent and adult child are emotionally close and share opinions but do not live near each other. Having infrequent contact, they do not exchange help or assistance. Detached parent–adult child relations evidence none of these characteristics.

Research shows that there is no one typical model for parent–adult child relationships (Silverstein and Bengston 2001). Furthermore, parent–adult child relations might change over time, moving from one relationship type to another depending on the parent's and the adult child's respective ages, the parent's changed marital status, and the presence or absence of grandchildren, among other factors. For instance, to be nearer to their aging parents, adult children sometimes return to the area in which they grew up, or retired grandparents may decide to relocate in order to be near their grandchildren. Both of these situations could move an intimate-but-distant relationship to a tight-knit one. Then too, a parent–adult child relationship might change depending only on emotional factors, such as when an adult child chooses to forgive an aging parent for some past transgression, or vice versa.

Using national survey data from a sample of 971 adult children who had at least one surviving non-coresident parent, Silverstein and Bengston (2001) made the following findings (among others):

- The majority of relations were neither tight-knit nor distant, but "variegated"—one of the three relationship styles in between (see Table 18.3). Variegated relations characterized 62 percent of adult children's interaction with their mothers and 53 percent with their fathers.

- Tight-knit relations are more likely to occur among lower socioeconomic groups and racial/ethnic minorities.

- Non-Hispanic whites were more likely than African Americans to have detached relationships with their parents and more likely than blacks or Hispanics to have obligatory relationships with their mothers.

- The most common relationship between a mother and her adult child was tight-knit (31 percent). The next most common was sociable (28 percent), followed by intimate-but-distant (19 percent), obligatory (16 percent), and, finally, detached (7 percent).

- The most common relationship between a father and his adult child was detached (27 percent), followed by sociable (23 percent), tight-knit (20 percent), obligatory (16 percent), and intimate-but-distant (14 percent). Almost four times as many adult children reported being detached from their fathers as from their mothers.

- Daughters were more likely than sons to have tight-knit relations with their mothers.

- Sons were more likely than daughters to have obligatory relations with their mothers.

- Adult children were more likely to have obligatory or detached relations with divorced or separated mothers than with married mothers.

Adults' relationships with a parent can be of several types: tight-knit, sociable, obligatory, intimate-but-distant, or detached. In tight-knit relationships, such as this one of a mother and her two sons, the brothers live near their mother, feel emotionally close to her, and share similar opinions with her. In addition, the mother and her sons help each other out when necessary.

© 2002 Zigy Kaluzny/Stone/Getty Images

- Adult children were more likely to have detached relations with divorced or separated fathers than with married fathers: "indeed, relations with divorced [as opposed to married] fathers are 33 percent more likely to be detached" (p. 57).

We can conclude from these findings that daughters are more likely than sons to have close relationships with their parents, especially with their mothers—patterns demonstrating that "adult intergenerational solidarity is stronger with mothers than with fathers" (Silverstein and Bengston 2001, p. 56). Even among mothers, a parent's divorce or separation often weakens the bond with adult children. However, the effect of parental divorce on the likelihood of having detached relations with one's adult children is nearly five times greater for fathers than for mothers. Partly, at least, this is because a divorced father is less likely than either a married father or a divorced mother to live with his biological children and more likely to remarry (Silverstein and Bengston 2001).

In some families, the reality of past abuse, a conflict-filled divorce, or simply fundamental differences in values or lifestyles make it seem unlikely that parents and children will spend time together (Kutner 1990a; Kaufman and Uhlenberg 1998). Money matters can also cause tension (Kutner 1990c). Overall, however, adult children's relations with their parents, while not necessarily tight-knit, continue to be meaningful.

Grandparenthood

Partly due to longer life expectancy, which creates more opportunity for the role, grandparenting (and great-grandparenting) became increasingly important to families throughout the twentieth century (Bengston 2001). This is true despite urbanization changing the grandparent role somewhat, with rural grandchildren more likely than urban ones to have regular contact with and to receive various kinds of help from their grandparents (King, Silverstein, Elder, Bengston, and Conger 2003). Among both rural and urban grandparents, some are raising grandchildren, as explored in Chapter 11. However, the discussion in this section focuses on grandparents who are not primarily responsible for raising their grandchildren.

Due to declining birth rates—and the fact that people tend not to have children over a long period of time—grandparenting is less likely to overlap with the parenting role than in previous decades (Conner 2000). However, because blacks tend to be younger than whites when they have their first child, they are likely to become grandparents at a younger age than whites and—unlike whites—simultaneously play the roles of active parent, grandparent, and even great-grandparent (Perry 1999).

Living longer now than in the past, grandparents are likely to proceed from young-old to older-old and, finally, to old-old grandparents. Young-old grandpar-

Many grandfathers, including those who may have been pressured for time when their own children were young, welcome the chance to be involved with their grandchildren.

© Robert Rathe/Stock, Boston

time to spend with them. Grandmothers were more likely to say that older people had more resources these days, especially money, so they could do more things with their grandchildren today (Cunningham-Burley 2001).

Many grandparents find the role deeply meaningful: Grandchildren give personal pleasure and a sense of immortality. Some grandfathers see the role as an opportunity to be involved with babies and very young children, an activity discouraged when their own children were young (Cunningham-Burley 1987, 2001). Overall, the grandparent role is mediated by the parent; not getting along with the parent dampens the grandparent's contact and hence the relationship with her or his grandchildren (Whitbeck, Hoyt, and Huck 1993). In a nonrepresentative sample survey conducted by AARP, nearly 90 percent of grandparents said that their grandchildren's parents encouraged phone calls and visits; about 7 percent reported e-mailing back and forth with grandchildren, while another 15 percent exchanged written letters (Baker 2001).

Grandparents continue to provide practical help (King et al. 2003). They may serve as valuable "family watchdogs," ready to provide assistance when needed (Troll 1985). In low-income and minority families, parents and children readily rely on grandparents and other kin. Even among white, middle-class families, it is not unusual for grandparents to help with child care or contribute to the cost of a grandchild's tuition, wedding, or first house. If an adult child of divorced parents becomes divorced, assistance may be more readily available from a grandparent (Vandell, McCarthy, Owen, Booth, and Clarke-Stewart 2003).

Grandparents often adopt a grandparenting style similar to the one they experienced as grandchildren with their own grandparents (King and Elder 1997). Of course, grandparenting styles are also shaped by the grandparent's age, health, employment status, and personality (Silverstein and Marenco 2001). Among those who are not playing parentlike roles to their grandchildren, three general styles of grandparenting have been identified: remote, companionate, and involved (Cherlin and Furstenberg 1986). About one-third of grandparents have *remote* relationships with their grandchildren, often because they live far away. About half of grandparent–grandchild relationships are *companionate*. In this case, grandparents do things with their grandchildren but exercise little authority and allow the parent to control access to the youth. Com-

ents are typically employed and often married, while old-old grandparents may be physically disabled, so younger grandparents' experiences with their grandchildren are typically quite different from those of older grandparents (Silverstein and Marenco 2001). Meanwhile, declining birth rates have decreased the number of available grandchildren (Conner 2000).

Besides (and in accordance with) these demographic changes, this century has seen increased emphasis on affection and companionship with grandparents. In one recent small study, eighteen working-class couples between ages 42 and 55 were interviewed over a period of one year, once before and twice after the birth of their first grandchild. Grandfathers often stressed today's different family environment and how this meant that you had fewer grandchildren and more

panionate grandparents are often involved in work, leisure, or social activities of their own. Other grandparents are more *involved*, probably living with or near their grandchildren and frequently initiating interaction with their grandchild.

A grandparent may have different relationship styles with different grandchildren. Although some of them prefer to interact with their teenage grandchildren, grandparents generally are most actively involved with preadolescents, particularly preschoolers. Preschoolers are more available and respond most enthusiastically to a grandparent's attention. There is also evidence that after a typically uninterested adolescence, adults renew relationships with grandparents (Cherlin and Furstenberg 1986). Also, race affects grandparenting (Hunter 1997). In one study, 87 percent of black grandparents felt free to correct a grandchild's behavior, compared to 43 percent of white grandparents. As one black grandmother said of her fourteen-year-old grandson, "He can get around his mother, but he can't get around me so well" (quoted in Cherlin and Furstenberg 1986, p. 128; see also Flaherty, Facteau, and Garver 1999).

How does an adult child's divorce affect the grandparent relationship? Evidence suggests that the news hits hard, and grandparents worry over whether to intervene on behalf of the grandchildren. As might be expected, effects of the divorce are different for the **custodial grandparent** (parent of the custodial parent) than for the **noncustodial grandparent** (parent of the noncustodial parent), with noncustodial grandparents significantly less likely to see their grandchildren as often as they had before the divorce (Cherlin and Furstenberg 1986; Spitze et al. 1994). With the current trends in child custody, the most common situation is for maternal grandparent relationships to be maintained or enhanced while paternal ones diminish (Mills, Wakeman, and Fea 2001). Because of pressure from noncustodial grandparents, all fifty states have passed laws intended to give grandparents the right to seek legalized visitation rights, but courts are reluctant to do so when parents object (Henderson and Moran 2001).

Then, too, remarriages (and re-divorces) create stepgrandparents (and ex-stepgrandparents) (Ganong and Coleman 2004). There is very little information on stepgrandparents, but what data there are suggest that stepgrandparents tend to distinguish their "real" grandchildren from those of remarriages, while younger

"You're real good with kids, Grandma... you ought to have some of your own."

© George Crenshaw 1995. Reprinted by permission.

stepgrandchildren and those who live with the grandparent's adult child are more likely to develop ties with the stepgrandparent (Cherlin and Furstenberg 1986; Coleman, Ganong, and Cable 1997).

To close this section, we quote sociologist Vern L. Bengston (2001) as he notes the importance of grandparents to younger family members' well-being:

Grandparents provide many unacknowledged functions in contemporary families. They are important role models in the socialization of grandchildren. They provide economic resources to younger generation family members. They contribute to cross-generational solidarity and family continuity over time. They also represent a bedrock of stability for teenage moms raising infants [as well as other family members]. (p. 7)

We turn now to an examination of caregiving to aging family members.

Aging Families and Caregiving

When we associate caregiving with the elderly, we may tend to think only in terms of older generations as care recipients and younger generations as caregivers. However, older Americans give to their communities and assist their adult children financially and in many other ways as well (Ingersoll-Dayton, Neal, and Hammer 2001). Having pointed this out, in this section we focus on eldercare.

Eldercare (care provided to older people) involves emotional support, a variety of services, and, sometimes, financial assistance. A growing number of tax-funded, charity, and for-profit services provide eldercare. Nevertheless, the persisting social expectation in the United States is that family members will either care for elderly relatives personally or organize and supervise the care provided by others (Conner 2000). At least one eldercare giver resides in one-fourth of all U.S. households (Gavin 2003).

Being concerned about an elderly family member might involve nothing more than a daily phone call to make sure that he or she is OK or stopping by for a weekly visit. However, **gerontologists**—social scientists who study aging—more specifically define **caregiving** as "assistance provided to persons who cannot, for whatever reason, perform the basic activities or instrumental activities of daily living for themselves" (Uhlenberg 1996, p. 762).

Caregiving may be short term (taking care of someone who has recently had joint-replacement surgery, for example) or long term. The majority of the young-old need almost no help at all, but as an elderly person continues to age, she or he may require ongoing help with tasks such as paying bills and, later, eating or bathing. Severely ill or disabled older people often need a great deal of care over a long period of time.[13] Almost one-quarter of American households are involved in eldercare to some extent, with the average caregiver providing eighteen hours of assistance each week (Cancian and Oliker 2000). The vast majority of eldercare is **informal caregiving**—unpaid and provided personally by a family member as a form of unpaid family work, discussed in Chapter 12.

Gerontologists point to two models of family caregiving: the **care provider model** and the **care manager model**. In the first, the caregiver personally provides the required care; in the second, the caregiver-manager coordinates paid service providers to meet the care receiver's needs. Family members who live nearby are more likely to use the care provider model; those living farther away are more likely to employ the care manager model.

A second factor that affects which model is used is the extent to which family members can afford to pay service providers (Uhlenberg and Hammill 1998; Greider 1999). We may also think of these two family-caregiving models as opposite points on a continuum, with caregivers combining elements of both models. In this **eldercare team approach**, some care is personally provided by family members while other care is managed (Allen, Blieszner, and Roberto 2000). "As We Make Choices: Community Resources for Eldercare" describes eldercare options.

A number of eldercare givers are relatively young—in their thirties, with some in their twenties, partly because children born to older parents begin eldercare at younger ages (Dellmann-Jenkins, Blankemeyer, and Pinkard 2000; "When Elder Care Falls" 2001). However, the mean age for caregivers is 57; more than one-third (35 percent) are over age 65 and may themselves be in poor health or beginning to suffer from age-related disabilities (Himes 2001b). The National Long-Term Care survey conducted in 1982 by the federal Department of Health and Human Services found that most long-term caregivers had provided help for between one and four years, and 20 percent had been caring for the disabled person for five years or more. Almost all caregivers in this survey provided assistance seven days a week for an average of four hours daily (Cancian and Oliker 2000).

Which family members more often provide eldercare and how much they provide depend on the care receiver's preference as well as the family's understanding of who is primarily responsible for giving the care. The first choice for a caregiver is an available spouse, followed by adult children, siblings, grandchildren, nieces and nephews, neighbors and friends, and, finally, a formal service provider (Cantor 1979; Horowitz 1985).[14]

The old-old especially, who may have survived the deaths of their spouse, siblings, many friends, and even one or more of their children, may engage in **kin upgrading**—elevating a niece, for instance, or a goddaughter to "like a daughter." They may also engage in **kin conversion**—redefining long-time friends as kin: "Maria is like a sister" (Johnson and Barer 1997).

Then, too, care receivers may prefer caregivers based on the kind of help needed. In this **task speci-**

---

13. About 54 percent of those over age 85 need assistance in meeting their daily needs. This compares to 22 percent of those between 75 and 84, and 8 percent of those 65 to 74 (Conner 2000).

14. Cantor (1979) termed this system of elderly care receivers' preference for caregivers the *hierarchical compensatory model* of caregiving.

Aging and failing health can create stress both individually and within a marriage, but many spouses draw on deep reserves of affection and love to find the patience and willingness to care for the other.

ficity model, family members are preferred for help with tasks such as shopping or housekeeping. Community service providers are more often preferred for assistance with activities that require more technical competence than family members have. Friends as well as siblings are likely to be called on for emotional support (Connidis and Campbell 2001).

Older Americans provide a considerable amount of eldercare to one another. Up to 40 percent of eldercare is provided by the elderly care receiver's spouse (Novak 1997). Caregiving and receiving are expected components of the marital relationship for most of today's older couples, who have developed a relationship of mutual exchange over many years (Huyck 1996; Machir 2003). A qualitative study of seventy-five spouse caregivers found that those in longer, emotionally close marriages with little ongoing conflict evidenced better overall well-being (Townsend and Franks 1997).

After spouses, adult children are most likely to be providing eldercare. Especially for the unmarried and child-free, an older American's siblings are important in mutual caregiving (Eriksen and Gerstel 2002).

Adult Children as Eldercare Providers

Motivated by both **filial responsibility** (a child's obligation to parents) and, often, by affection, adult children care for their folks "because they're my parents" (Stein et al. 1998). Adults who care for aging parents often provide the vast majority of care themselves, but they also enlist their siblings when possible and/or engage the care manager model, seeking assistance from formal service providers (Wolf, Freedman, and Soldo 1997).

A small study of 387 elderly parents in Florida found that principles of reciprocity are at work regarding family eldercare. Parents expected help from their adult children in proportion to the aid that the parents had once given to their children (Lee, Netzer, and Coward 1994). In other research, adult children who had received considerably more financial help from their parents were more likely than their siblings to be engaged in caring for the parent in old age (Henretta, Hill, Soldo, Wei, and Wolf 1997).

Today it's often the case that siblings have geographically moved away from each other and from

As We Make Choices

Community Resources for Eldercare

Financial resources enhance options when dealing with the stress or crisis of providing eldercare. Today, more older Americans and their care providers are turning to professional eldercare service providers for help. A few will arrange a house call from a dentist or look after the cat when you go to the hospital. Nurses provide medical care; home health aides assist with personal care like bathing (Shapiro 2001b, p. 61). With growing numbers of elderly today, there are more and more community services for eldercare and, consequently, more options (Greenwald 1999). The table in this box describes several options. We can also look at advice given by experts on steps in coping with an aging parent:

1. "Don't wait." Exploring options before they're needed helps all family members know what to expect and begin to prepare for the future (Greenwald 1999, p. 53).

2. "Seek support." Eldercare givers need to seek all the help they can get. For example, geriatric social workers can help to assess an elderly person's needs and develop action plans: "Such people may be especially helpful in those painful cases when children must take needed steps in spite of the objections of mentally declining parents" (Greenwald 1999, p. 53).

3. Shop around. Most providers of senior housing are businesses,

THE OPTIONS	HOME CARE	ADULT DAY CARE	CONGREGATE HOUSING
What Is It?	Services ranging from shopping and transportation, to health aides who give baths, to nurses who provide medical care, to physical therapy brought to the home	Places to get meals and spend the day, usually run by not-for-profit agencies	A private home within a residential compound, providing shared activities and services
Whom Is It For?	Seniors who are able to continue living at home but need some help	Seniors who need a day out and caregivers who need a day off	Seniors in good health who want both independence and companionship
What Does It Offer?	Independence at home, but can be costly depending on level of care needed	Occasional respite (time off) for caregivers and a place to socialize for the care receiver	The advantages of home, plus services like 24-hour security and laundry

Sources: Greenwald 1999, pp. 54–55; Shapiro 2001a, 2001b.

not charities, and their products should be scrutinized for cost and quality. Families should visit as many facilities as they can on different days of the week and hours of the day. Ask for references (Shapiro 2001b, p. 60).

There are now several types of help for seniors, as the table shows. These services include home care, services ranging from shopping and transportation to physical therapy brought to the home, for seniors who are able to continue living at home but need some help; congregate care, a private home within a residential compound, providing shared activities and services, for seniors in good health who want both independence and companionship; assisted living arrangements, residential units offering private rooms, meals, 24-hour supervision, and other assistance for seniors who may need help with bathing, dressing, medication, etc., but who otherwise want to live on their own; continuing care facilities, a variety of housing options and a continuum of services all in one location, for seniors who want to provide for health needs as they age without having to relocate; and nursing homes, residential medical care for the aged who need continual attention, for seniors with deteriorating mental or physical abilities or great difficulty with daily activities (Greenwald 1999, pp. 54–55).

ASSISTED LIVING	CONTINUING CARE FACILITIES	NURSING HOMES
Residential units offering private rooms, meals, 24-hour supervision, and other assistance	A variety of housing options and a continuum of services all in one location	Residential medical care for the aged who need continual attention
Seniors who may need help with bathing, dressing, medication, etc.	Seniors who want to provide for health needs as they age without having to relocate	Seniors with deteriorating mental or physical abilities or great difficulty with daily activities
A greater level of care while maintaining some independence	Guaranteed care as a resident ages—at a relatively high price	About the only option for those who need constant care

their aging parents. Even when siblings live near an elderly parent, however, the burden of eldercare does not always fall upon each equally—a situation that causes added stress for the principal or sole caregiver. A study based on forty focus groups asked eldercare givers with siblings to describe how they felt about this situation (Ingersoll-Dayton, Neal, Ha, and Hammer 2003). "Siblings who described an imbalance in caregiving responsibilities reported feeling considerable distress. . . . One participant confessed that she was straddling a 'real thin line between just taking her [barely participating sister's] head off some day, because I'm so mad at the inequity of it'" (p. 205). Participants reported alerting brothers or sisters when their parent needed help and offering suggestions about how to be more involved. Said one about her brother, "I have to kick him in the pants every once in a while" (p. 206).

In addition, the participants sought to define the situation as more-or-less fair. To do so, they took into account such things as a sibling's geographical distance from the aging parent, employment responsibilities, and other family obligations. Interestingly, some participants (both men and women) called upon gendered expectations to help justify women's inequitable eldercare responsibilities. "I guess it's my gender," said a woman whose brother did little to help. "It's just natural." Participants also explained that their parents preferred the help of their daughters. As a son-in-law explained his wife's caring for her mother this way: "I think gender has a lot to do with it . . . that's traditionally . . . been the way it goes. Mom just, I think, calls on her more, so that's the way . . . It's not that the brothers wouldn't help at all, but it's just . . . she gets called on more" (p. 207).

Gender Differences in Providing Eldercare

Of the caregivers in the 1982 National Long-Term Care survey, 72 percent were women (Stone, Cafferata, and Sangl 1987). An analysis of Internet hits on the Michigan Aging Services website found that, even when using e-mail to request information, women are more active in eldercare (Ellis 1999). Today, women spend more years in eldercare than in caring for young children (Abel 1991).

Among marrieds, about one-quarter of informal caregivers are wives and approximately 13 percent are

husbands. This difference is mostly due to women's living longer; feelings of obligation to care for an elderly disabled spouse are fairly equal between husbands and wives. Husband-caregivers may see their role as an extension of the traditionally masculine one of provider and protector (Bowers 1999). However, gender makes a significant difference in adult children's caregiving obligations (Cancian and Oliker 2000).

Norms in many Asian American families designate the oldest son as the responsible caregiver to aging parents (Lin and Liu 1993; Kamo and Zhou 1994). Except in this case, the adult child involved in a parent's care is more likely to be a daughter (or even a daughter-in-law) than a son. This situation—one that raises issues of gender equity similar to those of parenting and domestic work discussed in Chapters 11 and 12—is partly due to ongoing employment differences between women and men (Sarkisian and Gerstel 2004).

Then too, in accordance with the findings (discussed earlier) that parent–daughter relations are more often tight-knit than parent–son relations, research has found that married sons feel almost equally obligated to help both their own parents and their aging in-laws, while daughters feel responsible primarily to their own parents. However, in practice, sons tend to provide eldercare only in the absence of available daughters (Lee, Spitze, and Logan 2003). Nevertheless, the proportion of sons involved in eldercare is expected to increase in the relatively near future due to the growing number of only-child sons, smaller sibling groups from which to draw care providers, and changing gender roles that make caregiving an expectation for adult male behavior (Harris 1998). The case study "Looking After: A Son's Memoir" is one son-caregiver's story.

When siblings share in caring for aging parents, daughters do more than sons, on average, as measured by time spent. Furthermore, men and women tend to provide care differently—in ways that reflect socially gendered expectations (see Chapters 4 and 12) and increase females' caregiver fatigue (Raschick and Ingersoll-Dayton 2004). Sons, grandsons, and other male caregivers (although not husbands) tend to perform a more limited range of occasional tasks, such as cleaning gutters or mowing the lawn, while daughters more often provide consistently required routine services like housekeeping, cooking, or doing laundry.

A son is more likely than a daughter to enlist help from his spouse, the eldercare receiver's daughter-in-law. Furthermore, sons more often employ the care manager model; they serve as organizers, negotiators, supervisors, and intermediaries between the care receiver and formal service providers (Dwyer and Coward 1991; Raschick and Ingersoll-Dayton 2004). "Providing intimate, hands-on care is culturally defined as feminine, [and the] dirty parts of care work are mainly women's work" (Isaksen 2002, pp. 806, 809).

The Sandwich Generation

Many daughter-caregivers have children under age 18 living at home. Indeed, it looks as if "the presence of children in the household connects parents to kin," including aging parents who may need eldercare (Gallagher and Gerstel 2001, p. 272). National surveys show that 37 percent of Americans between ages 53 and 61 have at least one living parent and one dependent child. More than one-quarter have a grandchild as well (Kolata 1993). A decade or more ago, journalists and social scientists took note of an emerging **sandwich generation**: middle-aged (or older) individuals, usually women—although not always (Harris and Bichler 1997)—who are sandwiched between the simultaneous responsibilities of caring for their dependent children and aging parents. Although some demographers believe that the popular press has exaggerated the burdens of the sandwich generation (Bengston, Rosenthal, and Burton 1996), the sandwich generation does indeed experience all the hectic task juggling discussed in Chapters 11 and 12 (Kaplan-Leiserson 2003). Stress builds as family members handle not only employment and child care but also parent care (Ingersoll-Dayton, Neal, and Hammer 2001).

Eldercare as a Family Process

"Contrary to the myth that Americans are increasingly abandoning older people to institutional care," write sociologists Francesca Cancian and Stacey Oliker (2000), "families continue to provide most care for frail or disabled elders, except for financial support. Only 5 percent of all older people live in nursing homes, and the figure was only slightly lower in the 1950s" (p. 65).

In accordance with the interactionist theoretical perspective, we can envision eldercare as an interactive process during which family members struggle to negotiate various caregiving decisions. Social scientists have noted a **caregiving trajectory** through which the process of eldercare proceeds.

The majority of elderly Americans maintain their own homes. However, many of the frail elderly depend upon, or live with, family members. While care is often given with fondness and love, it can also bring stress, conflicting emotions, and great demands on time, energy, and finances.

First, the caregiver becomes concerned about an aging family member, and often she or he expresses this concern to others, although not necessarily to the older family member. Later, still concerned, the caregiver begins to give advice to the older family member, such as "Don't forget to take your medicine" or "You should get an appointment for new glasses." Still later, the caregiver takes action to provide needed services (Cicirelli 2000). Throughout this trajectory, family members may be called upon for advice and counsel in making medical or other significant decisions (Roberto 1999). A family's decision to move an elderly parent to a nursing home is particularly painful, with concern for the aged parent continuing thereafter (Keefe and Fancey 2000).

As they make decisions about the elderly family member's condition, disagreements may arise between the caregiver(s) and the receiver as well as among family caregivers themselves (Mills and Wilmoth 2002; Roberto 1999). Issues such as whether the elderly family member is able to drive safely or should undergo major surgery are examples. And families "are often forced to make urgent, complex decisions for loved ones in intensive care units" (Siegel 2004). All else being equal, the caregiving experience is more positive

Case Study

Looking After: A Son's Memoir

Females are far more likely to be caregivers than males, and daughters more likely than sons. When sons do provide eldercare, they are more likely to help with other-than-intimate care, such as filling out forms or managing finances. However, some men do give more personal or intimate kinds of care (nonnormative care for them), and more often they do so when the care receiver lives in the same home that they do (Campbell and Martin-Matthews 2000). In the following essay, author John Daniel describes providing intimate care for his elderly mother.

"I never looked forward to helping my mother with her shower. She wasn't the least self-conscious about baring her body in my presence, but something in me shrank from it. To be with her in her nakedness seemed too intimate for a grown son. And some other part of me, the child who wants always to be cared for and never burdened with responsibility, felt put upon and put out. Why was I having to do this? It seemed an indignity, and it touched an open wound. I had no child to bathe, to make faces at, to splash and laugh with. Most likely I never would. What I had was a frail and failing old woman who couldn't take a shower on her own.

"Talking her into it was the first challenge. 'Oh, I don't need a shower,' she would say. 'I just had one yesterday, didn't I?'

"'You haven't had one for a week.'

"'But I don't *do* anything. Why do I need a shower?'

"It wasn't only bad memory and lapsing judgment that made her resist, of course. It was also that the shower was strenuous for her, and she didn't want to acknowledge, or couldn't, that she needed help with anything so simple. In her own mind, the mind I believe she inhab-ited most of the time, she was perfectly capable of taking a shower by herself if she wanted to. In this mind she was still the woman she had been five years ago, a woman who came and went and drove a car, a woman who lived on her own on the coast of Maine and was only temporarily exiled in a distant place. This woman was honestly perplexed when we bought her a cane and asked her, over and over again, to use it. . . . Somewhere inside her she was not only an able-bodied woman but still a Sea Scout, climbing the rigging in a bright clear wind.

"But in her present mind she knew, whenever she leaned far forward in a chair and tried to stiff-arm herself to her feet, whenever she steadied herself with a hand on the wall as she shuffled to the bathroom, just how incapable she had become. She knew, and she hated it. How could she not have hated it? And if she had to bear it, she didn't

---

when family members can come to agreement on issues such as these (Conner 2000). Put another way, families that have developed a shared understanding of the caregiving situation make more effective caregiving teams (Pruchno, Burant, and Peters 1997).

Caregiving parent–child relations—like some other family relationships—might best be characterized by ambivalence (Connidis and McMullin 2002a; Fingerman, Hay, and Birditt 2004; Luscher 2002; Willson, Shuey, and Elder 2003). Older people are often uncomfortable and sometimes angry or stubborn about receiving help, for it represents a threat to their autonomy and self-esteem, especially if the caregiver is controlling or if earlier conflicts reemerge (Brubaker, Gorman, and Hiestand 1990).

Parents may become more controlling as they grow older, a common reaction to loss of bodily and social power with aging and retirement, although one in-depth study suggests that adult-children caregivers may expect a certain amount of deference, or courteous submission to their opinions and decisions, from the aging parent for whom they are caring—and when this does not occur, "intergenerational relations become strained, and children are likely to set limits on their caregiving" (Pyke 1999, p. 661). Meanwhile, frail and fearful parents may make unreasonable demands.

CAREGIVER STRESS Providing eldercare may enhance one's sense of purpose and overall life satisfaction due to the self-validating effects of helping another person, enhanced intimacy, and the belief that helping others may result in assistance with one's own needs when the time arrives (Krause, Herzog, and Baker 1992; Marks, Lambert, and Choi 2002).

want me . . . to have to bear it. She wanted to carry herself on her own stooped shoulders. . . . Standing for any length of time was hard for my mother, and so the shower was a kind of siege. She would grip the soap tray with both hands as I got the water temperature right— *'Aaant!'* she would holler, 'too cold!'—and soaped a washcloth to scrub her sway-spined back. Even the soap met resistance.

"'Sai Baba says not to use soap,' she informed me early on. 'It's just one more thing that has to come off.'

"'Well, it does come off,' I answered, peeling open a bar of Dial. 'It rinses off.'

"'My dear, it leaves a *residue.* Plain water is enough.'

"'Mother, for God's sake. This isn't the ashram. You need soap to get clean.'

"'Yes, Father,' she said with a scowl.

"Eventually we worked out a mulish compromise. We used Ivory, which we both agreed was the most natural. . . .

"As I lathered shampoo into her wet white curls, her head would bow from the pressure of my fingers. I'd ask her to hold it up and she would for a second or two, then it would slowly sink again. . . .

"She squeezed her eyes shut as I rinsed her hair in the shower stream. She scrunched up her face, stuck her lips out, and sputtered through the soapy runoff. It was in that recurring moment of her life with us, her hair flattened to her head, darkened a little with the soaking spray, that I could almost see my mother as a girl—swimming the cold swells off Hancock Point, splashing and laughing, shouting something toward shore, laying into the water with strong even strokes that would take her where she wanted to go.

"She would let me stop rinsing only when she could rub a bit of her hair between finger and thumb and make it squeak. Then I would steady her out of the shower stall, her two hands in mine. It felt at that moment like a kind of dance, a dance that maybe I knew how to do and needed to do.

"I let my mother down into the straight-backed chair and left her in the bathroom with towels, clean underwear, and a little space heater to keep her warm. . . . No matter how hard she might have resisted the idea, a bath or shower always seemed to renew her: Soap or no soap, the old woman came forth cleaner of spirit.

"'She was pure as the driven snow,' she usually quoted, gaily, then a pause: 'But she drifted.'

"I guess I came out of the bathroom cleaner of spirit myself. Soap or no soap, whatever the tenor of our conversation, I appreciate now what a privilege it was to help my mother with her shower. I wish I'd seen it more clearly at the time. We don't get to choose our privileges, and the ones that come to us aren't always the ones we would choose, and each of them is as much burden as joy. But they do come, and it's important to know them for what they are. . . ."

Source: From *Looking After: A Son's Memoir* by John Daniel. Copyright © 1997 by John Daniel. Reprinted by permission of Counterpoint Press, a member of Perseus Books, L.L.C.

Nevertheless, caregiving is stressful and can be financially and emotionally costly. Employed caregivers not only spend their own money but (especially women) may also pass up promotions or take extended time off from work or take early retirement to engage in eldercare (Cancian and Oliker 2000; Dentinger and Clarkberg 2002). In addition, providing eldercare may be socially isolating, often brings on depression, and may further strain one's own health (Machir 2003; Marks, Lambert, and Choi 2002). Younger caregivers experience limitations on dating and other relationships. As one twenty-six-year-old explained to a research team, "I would like to go camping with my husband once in a while, but I can't just get up and go away, because of taking care of my grandparents" (in Dellmann-Jenkins, Blankemeyer, and Pinkard 2000, p. 181).

Caregiver stress among Americans results partly from the fact that ours is an individualist, rather than a collectivist, culture (see Chapter 7), where adult children are expected to establish lives apart from their parents and to achieve success as individuals rather than (or as well as) working to benefit the family system (Killian and Ganong 2002). "The most problematic aspect of individualism and caregiving is that there is no formal mechanism to ensure that there will be support, and expectations are vague at best" (Fry 1996, p. 124). Interestingly, adult-child caregivers who in childhood were exposed to traditional, extended households tend to have more positive attitudes about taking an aging parent into their own home (Szinovacz 1997).

Furthermore, because the chronically ill or disabled of all ages are decreasingly cared for in hospitals, today's informal caregivers are asked to perform complicated care regimens that have traditionally been handled only in hospitals by health care professionals. This situation places added demands on a family caregiver's time, energy, and emotional stamina, a situation that not infrequently leads to caregiver depression (Dwyer, Lee, and Jankowski 1994).

Elder abuse in families, discussed in Chapter 14 as a family-power issue, often—although not always—results from caregiver stress (Conner 2000). Burdens associated with caring for an older person may sometimes cause the caregiver to lose control and verbally or physically abuse the receiver. Professional care providers employed by community agencies are often trained to recognize potentially abusive family situations and can work to reduce dangerous levels of caregiver stress that may trigger abuse.

A study of caregivers to AIDS patients found that when the relationship feels more reciprocal, with the caregiver feeling that he or she is getting something in return, the caregiver is less often depressed (LeBlanc and Wright 2000). Furthermore, receiving adequate training and learning specific caregiver skills lessens caregiver stress, as do various forms of social support—including finding information and connecting with other caregivers on the Internet (Colvin, Chenoweth, Bold, and Harding 2004; "Learning Skills" 2003). Research with 100 African American wife caregivers found that receiving support from their churches lessened their stress and helped their marriage relationships (Chadiha, Rafferty, and Pickard 2003).

Then too, some employers now offer services particularly designed for employees engaged in family eldercare. Ford Motor Company's free house calls by geriatric care managers is an example (Gavin 2003). We have examined providing eldercare as a general process. We turn next to a discussion of racial/ethnic diversity and eldercare.

Racial/Ethnic Diversity and Family Eldercare

Adult children of all races and ethnicities feel responsible for their aging parents (Eggebeen and Davey 1998) and to their siblings, with whom they may share eldercare obligations (Stein et al. 1998). However, racial/ethnic differences do exist regarding eldercare. For instance, as we see in Chapter 8, Asians (as well as

many Hispanics) tend to emphasize the centrality of filial obligations over conjugal relationships (Burr and Mutchler 1999). As another example, older blacks are more likely than non-Hispanic whites to expect their adult children to personally care for them in old age (Lee, Peek, and Coward 1998). Blacks and Hispanics are more likely than non-Hispanic whites to expect to share a residence if necessary (Burr and Mutchler 1999), and Table 18.2 shows that they do.

Usually associated with the African American family, **fictive kin** (family-like relationships that are not based on blood or marriage but on close friendship ties) are often resources for eldercare-giving help among Hispanics and some other ethnic minorities as well (Johnson and Barer 1990; Ebaugh and Curry 2000). Meanwhile, racial/ethnic minorities are not as likely as non-Hispanic whites to use community-based services, such as senior centers, or to receive government assistance, because of language barriers (U.S. House of Representatives Select Committee on Aging 1992), because they don't know that they qualify for government-funded services, or because they are reluctant to include paid service providers as members of their caregiving team (Treas 1995; Riekse and Holstege 1996).

Partly as a result of differences like these, the cultural assumption, or myth, exists that minority ethnic communities rely only on their own family members for support. We may have an idealized view of minority families' providing eldercare with little stress or need for public or community assistance (Connor 2000). However, research shows that this is an exaggerated stereotype. Minority families providing eldercare do experience stresses and often need to rely on community services (Dilworth-Anderson, Williams, and Cooper 1999). For instance, Asian Americans have been held up as examples of those who "take care of their own," but many of them do indeed need formal agency assistance (Koh and Bell 1987). As a second example, Native Americans highly value the extended family while emphasizing respect for the elderly. Although elderly Native Americans on reservations typically rely on family members for eldercare, those living off the reservations, typically in urban areas, are likely to depend on community services to meet their needs (Riekse and Holstege 1996).

Assumptions that ethnic minorities take care of their own with little need for community assistance may be used by the larger community to relieve itself of responsibility for providing access to services and designing services to meet the needs of the minority community. [These stereotypical assumptions] can also give a false sense that older people in these communities do not need care and attention from the larger society and result in further isolation and alienation of minority group Americans. (Conner 2000, p. 164)

Moreover, among many immigrant ethnic groups, **acculturation** (the process whereby immigrant groups adopt the beliefs, values, and norms of their new culture) affects norms of filial obligation. Among immigrant groups, younger generations are more likely than their elders to become acculturated—a situation that creates the potential for intergenerational conflict (Silverstein 2000, p. F9). A study on grandparent–grandchild relationships among Mexican Americans found that differential rates of acculturation across generations can socially and emotionally distance grandchildren from their grandparents (Silverstein and Chen 1999).

A study of older Puerto Ricans found that filial obligation has declined in the younger generations. Hence, older Puerto Ricans in this study "strive to retain some measure of self-management and to more flexibly integrate informal and formal services, creating a dynamic and individualized plan of care for themselves" (Zsembik and Bonilla 2000, p. 652). And research on ethnic Chinese immigrant families in California found that sons often outsourced elder care:

> "I told her that I hire you to help me achieve my filial duty," Paul Wang, a 60-year-old Taiwanese immigrant owning a software company in Silicon Valley, California, described . . . his conversation with the in-home care worker he employed for his mother suffering from Alzheimer's disease. (Lan 2002, p. 812)

Acculturation has also meant that more elderly immigrants today than in the past live in housing designed for the elderly, rather than with their grown children: "As norms change, more retirement homes have miso soup on the menu" (Kershaw 2003, p. A10).

To close this chapter, we turn to a discussion of eldercare in the future, given that American families are changing.

The Changing American Family and Eldercare in the Future

As America ages, providing eldercare has become "a central feature of American family life" (Conner 2000, p. 88). At the same time, the American family is changing in structure and form, as we have seen throughout this text. Because these changes could result in a diminishing caregiver "kin supply" (Bengston 2001, p. 5), many policy makers have become concerned about the family's capability to provide eldercare in the future (U.S. Senate Special Committee on Aging 2002).

For one thing, women's increased participation in the labor force decreases the time that women, the principal providers of eldercare, have available to engage in eldercare. Furthermore, the greater geographical mobility of family members is likely to negatively affect family members' face-to-face support (Himes 2001b). A small study based on in-depth interviews with twelve individuals who had migrated to the United States from Australia showed that they felt considerable stress as they cared for their aging parents from a distance, and some of them were considering returning to Australia (Baldock 2000).

Moreover, families on average are smaller today than in the past (see Chapter 10, and Chapter 1's "Issues for Thought: Some Facts About Families in the United States Today"). Hence, the ratio of adult children to elderly parents is declining (Bengston 2001). Research shows that the more living children a person has, the more care from family members he or she is likely to receive (Spitze and Logan 1990). Further, more siblings ease the burden of each one because they can share in the caregiving (Wolf, Freedman, and Soldo 1997).

However, today and increasingly in the future, there are and will be fewer adult siblings available to share in the care of their elderly parents. Furthermore, today's older Americans are likely to have siblings who can help them, but as more younger parents today choose to have fewer or only children, more elderly in the future will have fewer or no siblings.

Policy makers' concerns about providing eldercare involve other family-structure changes as well, such as higher rates of individuals' remaining single and/or child-free and higher rates of divorce. The child-free and unmarried populations will increase among future elderly generations, and being child-free

Many older Americans remain active even into old-old age, as has this water-skier, who is 82. Nonetheless, the aging of the American population raises concerns about how a changing family structure will be able to care for them and to what extent community and government resources can or will be engaged to help.

or without a spouse "eliminates the two most important caregiving resources—spouse and adult child" (Conner 2000, p. 14).

According to some observers, divorce has several potentially negative impacts on providing family eldercare. First, a divorce that is not followed by remarriage means being without a spouse, a most important eldercare resource. Then, too, divorced caregivers lack a partner with whom to share the burdens of caregiving (Conner 2000).

Moreover, a high sense of filial obligation in a family has been positively related to actual caregiving and support (Ikkink, Tilburg, and Knipscheer 1999). But divorce among the older generation seems to reduce the younger generation's feelings of filial obligation. Research suggests that a daughter's being divorced does *not* decrease her help to her parents—although divorce probably does decrease help from an ex-daughter-in-law (Spitze et al. 1994). Meanwhile, research also shows that—particularly for fathers—being divorced reduces parents' intergenerational exchanges with adult children. Exchanges at the end of the life course continue to be negatively affected (Pezzin and Schone 1999). Put another way, divorce in the parental generation lessens the care that the parent receives in old age. This is particularly true for divorced fathers (Silverstein and Bengston 2001).

There is evidence that people without a spouse or adult children get less personal eldercare and have a higher rate of nursing-home residency than do elderly people with children (Conner 2000). However, singles in the future may be increasingly creative in providing alternatives for themselves. Partly so as not to be separated from their partners by well-meaning relatives who may put them in separate nursing homes, gay men and lesbian couples have begun to create old-age and retirement communities of their own (Nystrom and Jones 2003; Price 2000; Rosenberg 2001). Then, too, siblings, nieces, and nephews can fulfill the obligations of children for the child-free elderly (Penning 1990). We can also imagine that, especially among women (see Chapter 8), child-free and single elderly will fashion "families" of mutually caring friends. The extent to which one's cohabiting partner participates in eldercare is a matter for future research.

Although many policy analysts express concern, some demographers conclude that intergenerational relations "generally possess the potential to serve their members' needs" (Silverstein and Bengston 1997). They point to the **latent kin matrix**, defined as "a web of continually shifting linkages that provide the potential for activating and intensifying close kin relationships" (Riley 1983, p. 441). An important feature of the latent matrix is that family relations, although they may remain dormant for long periods of time, emerge as a resource when the need arises (Silverstein and Bengston 2001).

Moreover, while family structure and forms become increasingly diverse, so may ways that members of the postmodern family (see Chapter 3) deal with eldercare. For instance, in research involving in-depth interviews with forty-five older respondents, a sixty-seven-year-old separated wife, whose husband had become diabetic and asthmatic and had heart trouble, reported that she still loved him very much: "If something happened to him and this gal [his new romantic partner] didn't take care of him, I would go and take care of him myself" (quoted in Allen, Blieszner, Roberto, Farnsworth, and Wilcox 1999, p. 154).

Toward Better Caregiving

Family sociologist and demographer Andrew Cherlin (1996) distinguishes between the **"public"** and the **"private"** face of families. The family's private face "provides individuals with intimacy, emotional support, and love" (p. 19). The family's public face produces public goods and services by educating their children, caring for their ill, and helping their elderly members: "While serving each other, members of the 'public' family also serve the larger community" (Conner 2000, p. 36; Gross 2004). Recognizing this, the United States Congress enacted the National Family Caregiver Support Act in 2000, providing $125 million for training, counseling, and periodic relief, or respite services to informal family caregivers (Conway-Giustra, Crowley, and Gorin 2002). The public family saves millions of dollars annually for the taxpayer. In this context, sociologist Arlie Hochschild (1997, p. 168) has suggested that family and friends may be considered "as an informal domestic 'welfare system.'"

Meanwhile, the costs of providing good care for ill and disabled family members are often too high for family caregivers to manage without government help. People who are not poor enough to receive Medicaid and are not wealthy may be the most strapped. Then, too, people who are ill or disabled may also need special care that the family cannot provide. Furthermore, caregiving, as we have seen, is stressful. Many point to their need for services that temporarily replace the caregiver, such as transportation, personal care services, and adult day care. However, existing centers in the United States can be expensive, and they are not subsidized by Medicare (Cancian and Oliker 2000).

Unlike other Western democracies, the United States restricts its social insurance programs to elderly people. Social Security and Medicare have indeed improved the economic status of the aged, as we saw earlier in this chapter. However, it is estimated that Medicare pays for less than half of all old-age health care costs: "A fragmented old-age welfare state places much of the responsibility for the care of older people on the shoulders of family members, mainly women" (Meyer and Bellas 2001, p. 199).

Sociologists and policy analysts Francesca Cancian and Stacey Oliker (2000) argue that men ought to be encouraged to be as responsible as women for eldercare. Also, they ask rhetorically whether the wider community, as well as individual families, is not responsible for eldercare. They have proposed the following strategies for moving our society toward better eldercare coupled with greater gender equity in providing eldercare:

1. Provide government funds that support more care outside the family, such as government-funded day care centers for the elderly and respite (time-off) services for caregivers.
2. Increase social recognition of caregiving—both paid and unpaid—as productive and valuable work.
3. Make caregiving more economically rewarding or, at least, less economically costly to caregivers. (p. 130)

How these policy changes might be accomplished may be difficult to imagine, but this fact does not negate the utility of the vision. Across the world and throughout history, families have been expected to provide eldercare, and they did so until about the twentieth century in industrialized countries without help from government or community services or resources. However, at least in the industrialized world, that time has passed (Conway-Giustra, Crowley, and Gorin 2002). Eldercare (as well as child care) is indeed a responsibility not only of individual families but of an entire society.

In Sum

- The *number* of elderly, as well as their *proportion* of the total U.S. population, is growing.

- Along with the impact of the baby boomers' aging and the declining proportion of children in the population, longer life expectancy has contributed to the aging of our population.

- For the most part, both adult children and their parents prefer to live near each other, although not in the same residence.

- Due mainly to differences in life expectancy, older men are much more likely to be living with their spouse than are older women.

- Among older Americans without partners, living arrangements depend on one's health, the availability of others with whom to reside, social norms regarding obligations of other family members toward their elderly, personal preferences for privacy and independence, and economics.

- Growth in Social Security benefits has resulted in dramatic reductions in U.S. poverty rates for the elderly over the last several decades, although 11 percent of older adults are living in poverty.

- Due to differences in work patterns, wage differentials, and Social Security regulations, older men are considerably better off financially than are older women.

- Most older married couples place intimacy as central to their lives, describe their unions as happy, and continue to be interested in sex, even into old age.

- Even when it is not an abrupt event, retirement represents a great change for individuals and couples, particularly for males who have embraced the traditional masculine gender role.

- Adjustment to widowhood or widowerhood is an important family transition that often must be faced by married couples in later life. Bereavement manifests itself in physical, emotional, and intellectual symptoms.

- Daughters are more likely than sons to have close relationships with their parents, especially with their mothers. However, even among mothers, a parent's divorce or separation often weakens the bond with adult children.

- Partly due to longer life expectancy, grandparenting (and great-grandparenting) became increasingly important to families throughout the twentieth century.

- As members of our families age, eldercare is becoming an important feature in family life, with women providing the bulk of it.

- After spouses, adult children (usually daughters) are a preferred choice of an older family member as eldercare providers.

- Eldercare in families typically follows a caregiving trajectory as the care receiver ages, and involves not only benefits, but also stresses, for the caregiver(s).

- There are empirically noted racial/ethnic differences in eldercare, but this does not negate that racial/ethnic minorities—as well as non-Hispanic whites—need community and government assistance in providing eldercare.

- Changes in the American family lead some policy analysts to be concerned that families will have greater difficulty in the future providing eldercare. However, others point out that family relationships, while latent for long periods of time, can be activated when needed.

- Better eldercare in the future will necessitate involving more men as caregivers and developing more community services to assist families in providing eldercare.

Key Terms

acculturation	filial responsibility
active life expectancy	gerontologist
baby boom	informal caregiving
bereavement	kin conversion
care manager model	kin upgrading
care provider model	latent kin matrix
caregiving	noncustodial grandparent
caregiving trajectory	private face of family
custodial grandparent	public face of family
eldercare	sandwich generation
eldercare team approach	task specificity model
fictive kin	

Questions for Review and Reflection

1. Discuss ways that society's age structure today affects American families.

2. Describe the living arrangements of older Americans today, and give some reasons for these arrangements.

3. Give some facts concerning family relationships—for example, between spouses or between older parents and their adult children—in later life.

4. Apply the exchange, interactionist, functionalist, or ecological perspective (Chapter 3) to the process of providing eldercare.

5. **Policy Question.** Describe two suggestions for policy changes that would make family eldercare less difficult.

Suggested Readings

Administration on Aging

http://www/aoa.gov

United States government administration agency with information about kinds of care for the elderly, as well as other information.

Cancian, Francesca M., and Stacey J. Oliker. 2000. *Caring and Gender.* Walnut Creek, CA: AltaMira. Explores the causes, consequences, and ramifications of the relationship between gender and caregiving in our society, as well as society-level solutions.

Doka, Kenneth J., John Breaux, and Jack D. Gordon. 2002. *Living with Grief: Loss in Later Life.* Washington, DC: Hospice Foundation of America. Helpful facts and encouragement on dealing with old-age infirmities, illness and, ultimately, death, published by the Hospice Foundation of America, a highly respected nonprofit service for dying individuals and their families.

Generations United

http://www.gu.org

Resources for intergenerational caregivers and care receivers.

Harris, Phyllis B., and Joyce Bichler. 1997. *Men Giving Care: Reflections of Husbands and Sons.* New York: Garland. Report of a qualitative study of thirty husbands and thirty sons who are caregivers to a relative with dementia.

Olson, Laura K. 2001. *Age Through Ethnic Lenses: Caring for the Elderly in a Multicultural Society.* Lanham, MD: Rowman & Littlefield. A collection of readings on this topic that covers many sorts of diversity, such as racial/ethnic minorities; some ethnic groups of European origin; socioreligious groups, such as Mormons, Amish, and Arab Americans; as well as diversity related to sexual orientation and to region (rural elderly).

Virtual Society: The Wadsworth Sociology Resource Center

 Go to the Sociology Resource Center at **http://sociology.wadsworth.com** for a wealth of online resources, including a companion website for your text that provides study aids such as self-quizzes for each chapter and a practice final exam, as well as links to sociology websites and information on the latest theories and discoveries in the field. In addition, you will find further suggested readings, flash cards, MicroCase online exercises, and appendices on a range of subjects.

Online Study Tool

Marriage & Family ⊛ Now™ Go to **http://sociology.wadsworth.com** to reach the companion website for your text and use the Marriage&FamilyNow access code that came with your book to access this study tool. Take a practice pretest after you have read each chapter, and then use the study plan provided to master that chapter. Afterward, take a posttest to monitor your progress.

Search Online with InfoTrac College Edition

For additional information, exercises, and key words to aid your research, explore InfoTrac College Edition, your online library that offers full-length articles from thousands of scholarly and popular publications. Click on *InfoTrac College Edition* under *Chapter Resources* at the companion website and use the access code that came with your book.

- Search keywords: *aging family, elderly caregiving.*

How to Find the Appendices

The following appendices are available in full color on the Ninth Edition's book companion site at **http://sociology.wadsworth.com/lamanna_riedmann9e/**. To access the appendices, click on "Appendices" from the left navigation bar.

Glossary

AAMFT (American Association for Marital and Family Therapy) Membership requires a graduate degree in medicine, law, social work, psychiatry, psychology, or the ministry; special training in marriage or family therapy or both; and at least three years of clinical training and experience under a senior counselor's supervision.

ABC-X model A model of family crisis in which A (the stressor event) interacts with B (the family's resources for meeting a crisis) and with C (the definition the family formulates of the event) to produce X (the crisis).

abortion The expulsion of the fetus or embryo from the uterus either naturally (*spontaneous abortion* or *miscarriage*) or medically (*induced abortion*). The discussion of abortion as a social issue in Chapter 10 is with reference to induced abortion.

abstinence The standard that maintains that, regardless of the circumstances, nonmarital intercourse is wrong for both women and men. Many religions espouse abstinence as a moral imperative.

acculturation The process whereby immigrant groups adopt the beliefs, values, and norms of their new culture and lose their traditional values and practices.

acquaintance rape Forced or unwanted sexual contact between people who know each other, often—although not necessarily—taking place on a date.

active life expectancy The period of life free of disability in activities of daily living, after which may follow a period of being at least somewhat disabled.

adoption A parent–child relationship that is established legally rather than through biological reproduction.

adoption reunion The meeting of a birth parent (most often the mother) with a now-adult biological child who was given up for adoption.

A-frame relationship A relationship style (symbolized by the capital letter A) in which partners have a strong couple identity but little self-esteem; therefore, they are dependent on each other rather than interdependent.

afterbirth The placenta, amniotic sac, and the remainder of the umbilical cord, all of which are expelled during delivery after the birth of the baby.

agape The love style that emphasizes unselfish concern for the beloved, in which one attempts to fulfill the other's needs even when that means some personal sacrifice.

agentic (instrumental) character traits Traits such as confidence, assertiveness, and ambition that enable persons to accomplish difficult tasks or goals.

agreement reality Knowledge based on agreement about what is true.

ambivalent provider couple A couple in which the wife's providing responsibilities are not clearly acknowledged.

amniotic fluid Salty, watery fluid that surrounds the developing fetus within the mother's uterus, cushioning and protecting it; also called *amnion*.

androgyny The social and psychological condition in which individuals can think, feel, and behave in ways that express both instrumental and expressive character traits. Androgyny is the combination of both masculine and feminine qualities in one individual.

anger "insteads" Ways that people deal with their anger rather than expressing it directly. Some substitutes for open anger are overeating, boredom, depression, physical illness, and gossip.

anthropomorphism Thinking of and treating nonhumans such as pets as though they were human.

archival family function The creating, storing, preserving, and passing on of particular objects, events, or rituals that family members consider relevant to

their personal identities and to maintaining the family as a unique existential reality or group.

areolae The pigmented areas of the breasts surrounding the nipples.

arranged marriage Unions in which parents choose their children's marriage partners.

artificial insemination A process in which a physician or other person injects sperm into a woman's vagina when she is ovulating in an attempt to achieve pregnancy. The sperm may be from her husband or partner or from a donor.

assisted reproductive technologies (ART) Advanced reproductive technologies such as artificial insemination or in vitro fertilization that enable infertile couples or individuals, including gay and lesbian couples, to have biological children.

assortive mating Social psychological filtering process in which individuals gradually filter out those among their pool of eligibles who they believe would not make the best spouse.

attachment "An active, effective, enduring, and reciprocal bond between two individuals that is believed to be established through repeated action over time" (Coleman and Watson 2000, p. 297, citing Mary Ainsworth et al. 1978).

attachment disorder An emotional disorder in which a person defensively shuts off the willingness or ability to make future attachments to anyone.

attachment theory A psychological theory that holds that, during infancy and childhood, a young person develops a general style of attaching to others; once an individual's attachment style is established, she or he unconsciously applies that style to later, adult relationships. The three basic styles are secure, insecure/anxious, and avoidant.

attribution Assigning or attributing character traits to other people. Attributions can be positive or negative, such as when a spouse is told that he or she is an interesting or a boring person.

authoritarian parenting style All decision making is in parents' hands, and the emphasis is on compliance with rules and directives. Parents are more punitive than supportive, and use of physical punishment is likely.

authoritative parenting style Parents accept child's personality and talents and are emotionally supportive. At the same time, they consciously set and enforce rules and limits, whose rationale is usually explained to the child. Parents provide guidance and direction and state expectations for the child's behavior. Parents are in charge, but child is given responsibility and must take the initiative in completing schoolwork and other tasks and in solving child-level problems.

avoidant attachment style One of three attachment styles in attachment style theory, this style avoids intimacy either by evading relationships altogether or by establishing considerable distance in intimate situations.

baby boom The unusually large cohort of U.S. children born after the end of World War II, between 1946 and 1964.

backstage The private sphere, where we can be informal, relaxed, and authentic.

balanced connection Relationship type in which a partner sometimes focuses on her or his private self and needs quiet time; at other times, the partners focus on each other; at still other times, they focus on some outside interest.

battered woman syndrome A circumstance in which a battered woman feels incapable of making any change in her way of living.

belligerence A negative communication/relationship behavior that challenges the partner's power and authority.

bereavement A period of mourning after the death of a loved one.

binational family An immigrant family in which some members are citizens or legal residents of the country they migrate to, while others are *undocumented*; that is, they are not legal residents.

binuclear family One family in two household units. A term created to describe a postdivorce family in which both parents remain involved and children are at home in both households.

biosocial perspectives Theoretical perspective based on concepts linking psychosocial factors to physiology, genetics, and evolution.

bisexual A person who is sexually attracted to both males and females.

blocking strategies Strategies used by some when dating interracially/interethnically by which negative responses from others are psychologically/emotionally deflected, or blocked.

bonding fighting Fighting that brings intimates closer together rather than leaving them just as far apart or pushing them even farther apart.

borderwork Interaction rituals that are based on and reaffirm boundaries and differences between girls and boys.

boundaries Barriers which mark off the family from the rest of the world. Boundaries can be physical or psychological.

boundary ambiguity When applied to a family, a situation in which family members do not know who is in and who is out of the family.

breech presentation In childbirth, a delivery in which the baby's buttocks, shoulder, foot, or face emerge first. This makes for a more difficult delivery than the vertex presentation.

bride price Money or property that the future groom pays the future bride's family so that he can marry her.

care manager model One of two caregiving models. In this case, the care receiver's needs are identified, and paid service providers are engaged to meet those needs. See also *care provider model*.

care provider model One of two caregiving models. In this case, the needs of the care receiver are identified, and the care provider personally provides the required care. See also *care manager model*.

caregiver model of elder abuse and neglect A view of elder abuse or neglect that highlights stress on the caregiver as important to the understanding of abusive behavior.

caregiving "Assistance provided to persons who cannot, for whatever reason, perform the basic activities or instrumental activities of daily living for themselves" (Cherlin 1996, p. 762).

caregiving trajectory The process through which eldercare proceeds, according to which, first, the caregiver becomes concerned about an aging family member, then later begins to give advice to the older family member, and still later takes action to provide needed services.

case study A written summary and analysis of data gained by psychologists, psychiatrists, counselors, and social workers when working directly with individuals and families. Case studies are often used as sources in scientific investigation.

center care Group child care provided in day-care centers for a relatively large number of children.

cervix At the top of the vagina in the female, the neck of the uterus.

cesarean section A surgical operation in which a physician makes an incision in the mother's abdomen and uterine wall to remove the infant. Named after Julius Caesar, who was supposedly delivered this way.

checking-it-out A communication or fighting technique in which a person asks the other whether her or his perceptions of the other's feelings or thoughts are correct.

child abuse Overt acts of aggression against a child, such as excessive verbal derogation, beating, or inflicting physical injury. Sexual abuse is a form of physical child abuse. See also *emotional child abuse or neglect*.

child care The care and education of children by persons other than their parents. Child care may include before and after school care for older children and overnight care when employed parents must travel, as well as day care for preschool children.

child neglect Failure to provide adequate physical or emotional care for a child. See also *emotional child abuse or neglect*.

child snatching Kidnapping one's own children from the other parent after divorce.

child support Money paid by the non-custodial to the custodial parent to financially support children of a separated marital, cohabiting, or sexual relationship.

children's allowance A type of child support that provides a government grant to all families—married or single-parent, regardless of income—based on the number of children they have.

Chodorow's theory of gender A theory of gender socialization that combines psychoanalytic ideas about identification of children with parents with an awareness of what those parents' social roles are in our society.

choosing by default Making semiconscious or unconscious choices when one is not aware of all the possible alternatives or when one pursues the path of least resistance. From this perspective, doing nothing about a problem or issue, or making no choice, is making a serious choice—that is, the choice to do nothing.

choosing knowledgeably Making choices and decisions after (1) recognizing as many options or alternatives as possible, (2) recognizing the social pressures that can influence personal choices, (3) considering the consequences of each alternative, and (4) becoming aware of one's own values.

circumcision Surgical removal of the foreskin, a membrane that covers the glans of the penis.

Civil Union Act Vermont state legislation that allows any two single adults—including same-sex partners or blood relatives, such as siblings or parent and adult child—to have access to some (though not all) legal rights on the state level, but none on the federal level.

clitoris Part of the female genitalia: female erectile tissue, consisting of an internal shaft and a tip, or glans, which contains concentrations of nerve endings and is highly sensitive.

closed marriage A synonym for static marriage.

co-dependents "Persons who gravitate toward relationships with exploitative or abusive partners around whom they organize their lives and to whom they remain strongly committed despite the absence of any identifiable rewards or

personal fulfillment for themselves" (Wright and Wright 1999, p. 528).

co-parenting Shared decision making and parental supervision in such areas as discipline and schoolwork or shared holidays and recreation.

coercive power One of the six power bases, or sources of power. This power is based on the dominant person's ability and willingness to punish the partner either with psychological–emotional or physical abuse, or with more subtle methods of withholding affection.

cohabitation Living together in an intimate, sexual relationship without traditional, legal marriage. Sometimes referred to as living together or marriage without marriage. Cohabitation can be a courtship process or an alternative to legal marriage, depending on how partners view it.

collectivist society A society in which people identify with and conform to the expectations of their relatives or clan, who look after their interests in return for their loyalty. The group has priority over the individual.

commitment (to intimacy) The determination to develop relationships in which experiences cover many areas of personality, problems are worked through, conflict is expected and seen as a normal part of the growth process, and there is an expectation that the relationship is basically viable and worthwhile.

commitment (Sternberg's triangular theory of love) The short-term decision that one loves someone and the long-term aspect—the commitment to maintain that love; one dimension of the triangular theory of love.

common couple violence Mutual violence between partners in conjunction with a specific argument.

common law marriage A legal concept whereby cohabiting partners are considered legally married if certain requirements are met, such as showing intent to enter into a marriage and living together as husband and wife for a certain period of time. Most states have dropped common law marriage, but cohabiting relationships may sometimes have a similar effect on property ownership and custody rights.

communal (expressive) character traits Traits that foster relationships with others, such as warmth, sensitivity, the ability to express tender feelings, and placing concern about others' welfare above self-interest.

commune A group of adults and perhaps children who live together, sharing aspects of their lives. Some communes are group marriages, in which members share sex; others are communal families, with several monogamous couples, who share everything except sexual relations and their children.

community divorce Ruptures of relationships and changes in social networks that come about because of divorce.

commuter marriage A marriage in which the two partners live in different locations and commute to spend time together.

conception The moment in which an ovum (egg) joins with a sperm cell and a fetus begins to develop.

conflict perspective Theoretical perspective that emphasizes social conflict in a society and within families. Power and dominance are important themes.

Conflict Tactics Scale A scale developed by sociologist Murray Straus to assess how couples handle conflict. Includes detailed items on various forms of physical violence.

Confucian training doctrine Concept used to describe Asian and Asian American parenting philosophy that emphasizes blending parental love, concern, involvement, and physical closeness with strict and firm control.

congestion The engorgement of blood vessels, which causes the affected tissues to swell. Occurs to the genitals during the excitement phase of sexual response.

conjoint marital counseling Counseling in which the counselor sees the husband and wife together rather than one at a time.

conjugal power See *marital power*.

conjugal relatives/kin Term used to define relationships acquired through marriage (spouses and in-laws), as opposed to consanguineous relatives/kin (parents and grandparents), who are blood related.

consanguineous relatives/kin Term used to define blood-related kin (parents and grandparents), as opposed to conjugal relatives/kin (spouses and in-laws), who are related through marriage.

consensual marriage Heterosexual, conjugal unions that have not gone through a legal marriage ceremony.

consensual validation The process whereby people depend on others, especially significant others, to help them affirm their definitions of and attitudes and feelings about reality. Consensual validation is important in modern society because social reality is no longer just taken for granted as the way things are.

consummate love A complete love, in terms of Sternberg's triangular theory of love, in which the components of passion, intimacy, and commitment come together.

contempt One of the Four Horsemen of the Apocalypse (which see), in which a partner feels that his or her spouse is inferior or undesirable.

continuum of social attachment A conception of social attachment developed by Catherine Ross that emphasizes the quality of the attachment and its relationship to happiness or depression. Her research found that singles are not all socially unattached, isolated, or disconnected, and that people who are in relationships that are unhappy are more depressed than people who are alone and without a partner.

contraceptives Techniques and devices that prevent conception.

co-provider couple A relationship in which both partners have a primary responsibility for the family's economic support.

corona A crownlike ridge at the base of the glans on the penis.

couple-centered connection Relationship type in which the couple is romantically fused, focusing on their relationship.

courtly love Popular during the twelfth century and later, courtly love is the intense longing for someone other than one's marital partner—a passionate and sexual longing that ideally goes unfulfilled. The assumptions of courtly love influence our modern ideas about romantic love.

courtship The process whereby a couple develops a mutual commitment to marriage.

covenant marriage A type of legal marriage in which the bride and groom agree to be bound by a marriage contract that will not let them get divorced as easily as is allowed under no-fault divorce laws.

criticism One of the Four Horsemen of the Apocalypse (which see) that involves making disapproving judgments or evaluations of one's partner.

cross-cultural researcher A researcher who compares cultures around the world.

cross-national marriage Marriage in which spouses are from different countries.

crude birthrate The number of births per thousand population. See also *total fertility rate.*

crude divorce rate The number of divorces per 1 thousand population.

cultural broker A person who mediates between two cultures, explaining customs and meanings to individuals who must undertake transactions that cross cultural boundaries.

cultural deviant A theoretical framework that emphasizes those features of racial/ethnic minority families that distinguish them from white, usually middle-class, families. Those different qualities of minority families are viewed negatively.

cultural equivalent A theoretical framework that emphasizes those features that racial/ethnic minority families have in common with majority white families.

cultural script Set of socially prescribed and understood guidelines for relating to others or for defining role responsibilities and obligations.

cultural variant A theoretical approach that calls for making contextually relevant interpretations of racial/ethnic minority families. Minority families are studied on their on terms, as opposed to making comparisons, favorable or unfa-

vorable, to white families. Instead, within group comparisons are explored.

custodial grandparent A parent of a divorced, custodial parent.

custodial parent The parent who has legal responsibility for a child after parents divorce or separate. In sole custody, the child resides with the custodial parent. In joint custody, the child may reside primarily with one parent or may live part of the time with each.

custody Primary responsibility for making decisions about the children's upbringing and general welfare.

cyberadultery Marital infidelity or adultery on the Internet.

date rape Forced or unwanted sexual contact between people who are on a date.

Defense of Marriage Act Federal statute declaring marriage to be a "legal union of one man and one woman," denying gay couples many of the civil advantages of marriage, and also relieving states of the obligation to grant reciprocity, or "full faith and credit," to marriages performed in another state.

defensiveness One of the Four Horsemen of the Apocalypse (which see) that means preparing to defend oneself against what one presumes is an upcoming attack.

delivery The second phase (after labor) of childbirth, lasting from the time the cervix is completely dilated until the baby is expelled.

demographers Social scientists who study fertility, mortality, morbidity (illness), race/ethnicity, and age structure of a population.

dependence The general reliance on another person or on several others for continuous support and assurance, coupled with subordination to that other. A dependent partner probably has low self-esteem and is having illegitimate needs met by the partner on whom he or she is dependent. See also *independence, interdependence.*

dependency-distancing couples Couples in which one partner focuses on the marriage, or relationship, while the other partner puts most of his or her energy outside the relationship.

developmental task Challenges that must be mastered in one stage of the family life cycle for a successful transition to the next.

displaced homemaker A full-time housewife who, through divorce or widowhood, loses her means of economic support.

displacement A passive–aggressive behavior in which a person expresses anger with another by being angry at or damaging people or things the other cherishes. See also *passive-aggression*.

divorce extended family Kinship ties that form in the wake of a divorce. Can include former in-laws, new spouses of one's ex-spouse, and that person's children and kin as part of one kinship system.

divorce mediation A nonadversarial means of dispute resolution by which the couple, with the assistance of a mediator or mediators (frequently a lawyer–therapist team), negotiate the terms of their settlement of custody, support, property, and visitation issues.

domestic partner Partner in an unmarried couple who have registered their partnership with a civil authority and then enjoy some (although not necessarily all) rights, benefits, and entitlements that have traditionally been reserved for marrieds.

domestic violence model of elder abuse and neglect A model that conceptualizes elder abuse as a form of family violence.

dominant dyad A centrally important twosome that symbolizes the culture's basic values and kinship obligations. In white, middle-class America, the husband–wife dyad is expected to take precedence over any others.

donor eggs Eggs, or ova, donated by one woman and used by another to become pregnant through in vitro fertilization.

donor insemination (DI) A form of artificial insemination in which the man providing the sperm is not the husband or partner of the woman. In medical settings, the donor is typically anonymous, but some donors may be family members or otherwise known to the prospective parents. In "do-it-yourself"

artificial insemination, the donor is likely to be known.

double ABC-X model A variation of the ABC-X model of family crises that emphasizes the impact of unresolved prior crises. In this model, A becomes Aa and represents not only the current stressor event but also family pile-up, or residual strains from prior crises.

double message See *mixed message*.

double remarriage A remarriage in which both partners were previously married.

double standard The standard according to which premarital sex is more acceptable for males than for females. Reiss subdivided the double standard into orthodox and transitional.

dowry A sum of money or property brought to the marriage by the female.

dyspareunia Painful sexual intercourse.

economic divorce The separation of the couple into separate economic units, each with its own property, income, control of expenditures, and responsibility for taxes, debts, and so on.

economic hardship perspective One of the five theoretical perspectives concerning the negative outcomes among children of divorced parents. From this perspective, the economic hardship brought about by marital dissolution is primarily responsible for the problems faced by children.

economic maturity Quality of an individual who demonstrates the ability to support himself and a partner if necessary.

egalitarian norm (of marital power) The norm (cultural rule) that husband and wife should have equal power in a marriage.

ejaculation The rhythmic discharge of seminal fluid containing sperm from the penis during orgasm.

elder abuse Overt acts of aggression toward the elderly, in which the victim may be physically assaulted, emotionally humiliated, purposefully isolated, or materially exploited.

elder neglect Acts of omission in the care and treatment of the elderly.

eldercare Care provided to older generations.

eldercare team approach One approach to eldercare giving in which some care is personally provided by family members while other care is managed.

embryo adoption An arrangement by which one couple's unneeded frozen embryos are used by another couple to have a child through implantation of the embryo.

embryo transplant The implantation of a fertilized egg, donated by a fertile woman, into an infertile woman. See also *ovum transplant*.

embryonic stage The period of pregnancy after the first two weeks (germinal period) until about eight weeks, during which the fetal head, skeletal system, heart, and digestive system begin to form.

emerging adulthood The youth and young adult stage of life, which is a period of frequent change and exploration. See also *transition to adulthood*.

emotion A strong feeling arising without conscious mental or rational effort, such as joy, reverence, anger, fear, love, or hate. Emotions are neither bad nor good and should be accepted as natural. People can and should learn to control what they *do about their emotions*.

emotional child abuse or neglect A parent or other caregiver's being overly harsh and critical, failing to provide guidance, or being uninterested in a child's needs.

emotional divorce Withholding any bonding emotions and communication from the relationship, typically replacing these with alienating feelings and behavior.

emotional maturity Quality of an individual who has enough sense of self-worth to permit a satisfying degree of intimacy and interdependence in a relationship.

empty nest An old (some say outdated) sociological term referring to the postparental stage of family life. With the contracting economy, the trend to stay single longer, and the high divorce rate, more and more parents are complaining that their nests won't seem to empty.

endogamy Marrying within one's own social group. See also *exogamy*.

endometrium The lining of the uterus, which thickens with a layer of tissue and blood in order to nourish an embryo should an egg become fertilized. If no egg is fertilized, the endometrial tissue and blood are discarded during menstruation.

erectile dysfunction A sexual dysfunction in which a male is unable to produce or maintain an erection.

erectile tissue Genital tissue that becomes engorged with blood during sexual arousal, causing it to increase in size. In women, erectile tissue composes the clitoris; in men, it composes the penis.

eros The love style characterized by intense emotional attachment and powerful sexual feelings or desires. See also *agape, ludus, mania, pragma, storge*.

ethnicity A group's identity based on a sense of a common culture and language.

Euro-American families Families whose members are of European ethnic background.

exchange balance Balance of rewards and costs in a relationship.

exchange theory Theoretical perspective that sees relationships as determined by the exchange of resources and the reward–cost balance of that exchange. This theory predicts that people tend to marry others whose social class, education, physical attractiveness, and even self-esteem are similar to their own.

excitement phase One of the four phases of sexual arousal described by Masters and Johnson. The excitement phase begins when people begin to feel sexually aroused and is characterized by increased breathing, blood pressure, and pulse rates; vasocongestion of the penis and clitoris; and vaginal lubrication in women.

exogamy Marrying a partner from outside one's own social group. See also *endogamy*.

expectations of permanence One component of the marriage premise, according to which individuals enter marriage expecting that mutual affection and commitment will be lasting.

experiential reality Knowledge based on personal experience.

experiment One tool of scientific investigation, in which behaviors are carefully monitored or measured under controlled conditions.

expert power One of the six power bases, or sources of power. This power stems from the dominant person's superior judgment, knowledge, or ability.

expressive sexuality The view of human sexuality in which sexuality is basic to the humanness of both women and men, all individuals are free to express their sexual selves, and there is no one-sided sense of ownership.

extended family Family including relatives besides parents and children, such as aunts or uncles. See also *nuclear family*.

extramarital sex Sex by a married person with a person who is not her or his spouse.

fallopian tubes The tubes that connect a female's uterus with her ovaries. Named after sixteenth-century Italian anatomist Gabriel Fallopius, who first described them.

la familia In Hispanic families, "the family" means the extended family as well as the nuclear family.

familism Placing family well-being over individual interests and preferences.

family Any sexually expressive or parent–child or other kin relationship in which people live together with a commitment in an intimate interpersonal relationship. Family members see their identity as importantly attached to the group, which has an identity of its own. Families today take several forms: single-parent, remarried, dual-career, communal, homosexual, traditional, and so forth. See also *extended family, nuclear family*.

family boundary changes A situation in which family boundaries have to shift to include new people or to adapt to the loss of a family member.

family-centered connection Relationship type in which partners focus on a shared family interest, such as parenting and/or relations with extended kin.

family child care Child care provided in a caregiver's home.

family cohesion That intangible emotional quality that holds groups together and gives members a sense of common identity.

family crisis A situation (resulting from a stressor) in which the family's usual behavior patterns are ineffective and new ones are called for.

family "decline," family "change" Some family scholars and policy makers characterize late-twentieth-century developments in the family as "decline," while others describe "change." Those who take the family "decline" perspective view such changes as increases in the age at first marriage, divorce, cohabitation, and nonmarital births and the decline in fertility as disastrous for the family. Those who point to family "change" consider that the family has varied over time and space; they argue that family and society can adapt to recent changes.

family development perspective Theoretical perspective that gives attention to changes in the family over time.

family ecology perspective Theoretical perspective that explores how a family influences and is influenced by the environments that surround it. A family is interdependent first with its neighborhood, then with its social–cultural environment, and ultimately with the physical–biological environment. All parts of the model are interrelated and influence one another.

family foster care Foster care that takes place in a trained and licensed foster parent's home.

family-friendly workplace policies Workplace policies that are supportive of employee efforts to combine family and work commitments.

family function Activities performed by families for the benefit of society and of family members.

family gamble A family's decision to "give up on" a missing family member and begin to grieve their loss.

family leave A leave of absence from work granted to family members to care for new infants, newly adopted children, ill children, or aging parents, or to meet similar family needs or emergencies.

family life cycle Stages of family development defined by the addition and subtraction of family members, children's stages, and changes in the family's connection with other social systems.

family myths Versions of reality that obscure a core truth in order to manage a family's tension.

family of orientation The family in which an individual grows up. Also called family of origin.

family of procreation The family that is formed when an individual marries and has children.

family policy All the actions, procedures, regulations, attitudes, and goals of government that affect families.

family power Power among family members.

family stress State of tension that arises when demands tax a family's resources.

family structure The form a family takes, such as nuclear family, extended family, single-parent family, stepfamily, etc.

family systems theory An umbrella term for a wide range of specific theories. This theoretical perspective examines the family as a whole. It looks to the patterns of behavior and relationships within the family, in which each member is affected by the behavior of others. Systems tend toward equilibrium and will react to change in one part by seeking equilibrium by restoring the old system or creating a new one.

family transitions Expected or predictable changes in the course of family life that often precipitate family stress and can result in a family crisis.

family values Values that focus on the family group as a whole and on maintaining family identity and cohesiveness. See also *familism*.

fecundity Reproductive capacity; biological capability to have children.

female-demand/male-withdraw communication pattern A cycle of negative verbal expression by a wife and withdrawal by the husband in the face of his partner's demands. In other words, women tend to deal with problems by bringing them into the open through initiatives that have an attention-getting negative tone. Men tend to withdraw emotionally from the disagreement or conflict.

female orgasmic dysfunction Inability of a woman to reach orgasm during sexual activity.

female sexual arousal disorder A female sexual dysfunction in which a woman experiences very little if any erotic pleasure from sexual stimulation.

femininities Culturally defined ways of being a woman. The plural conveys the idea that there are varied models of appropriate behavior.

feminist perspective Feminist theories are conflict theories. The primary focus of the feminist perspective is that male dominance in families and society is oppressive to women. The mission of this perspective is to end this oppression of women (or related pattern of subordination based on social class, race/ethnicity, age, or sexual orientation) by developing knowledge that confronts this disparity. See also *conflict perspective*.

fertility Births to a woman or category of women.

fertilization The joining of an ovum (egg) with a sperm cell.

fetal period The period of pregnancy lasting from about eight weeks until birth.

fictive kin Family-like relationships that are not based on blood or marriage but on close friendship ties.

filial responsibility A child's obligation to a parent.

flexible marriage One that allows and encourages partners to grow and change both as individuals and in the relationship. A synonym is *open marriage*.

flexible scheduling A type of employment scheduling that includes scheduling options such as job sharing or flextime.

flextime A policy that permits an employee some flexibility to adjust working hours to suit family needs or personal preference.

foreskin A thin membrane that covers the glans of the penis at birth and is sometimes removed by circumcision.

formal kinship care Out-of-home placement with biological relatives of children who are in the custody of the state.

foster care Care provided to children by other than their parents as a result of state intervention.

Four Horsemen of the Apocalypse Contempt, criticism, defensiveness, and stonewalling—marital communication behaviors delineated by John Gottman that often indicate a couple's future divorce.

free-choice culture Culture or society in which individuals choose their own marriage partners, a choice usually based at least somewhat on romance.

frenum The place where the foreskin is or was connected to the penis.

gamete intrafallopian transfers (GIFT) An in vitro fertilization procedure in which eggs are collected from the ovaries, put into a catheter outside the body, and then placed (along with sperm) inside a woman's fallopian tubes.

gay Homosexual; a person whose sexual attraction is to persons of the same sex. Used especially for males, but may also include both sexes.

gender Attitudes and behavior associated with and expected of the two sexes. The term *sex* denotes biology, while *gender* refers to social role.

gender construction perspective An analysis that looks to the *meaning* of housework to explain a gendered division of household labor. The type of household task a person performs can function to affirm gender identity.

gender identity The degree to which an individual sees herself or himself as feminine or masculine based on society's definition of appropriate gender roles.

gender-linked characteristics and roles Traits and roles that are associated with males or females in a given society.

gender roles Masculine and feminine prescriptions for behavior. The masculine gender role demands instrumental character traits and behavior, whereas the feminine gender role demands expressive character traits and behavior. Traditional gender roles are giving way to androgyny, but they're by no means gone.

gender schema A framework of knowledge and beliefs about differences or similarities between males and females.

gender strategy A way of working through everyday family situations that takes into account an individual's beliefs and deep feelings about gender roles, as well as her or his employment and other nonfamily commitments.

gendered The way every aspect of people's lives and relationships is influenced by gender, by whether we are male or female.

generating strategies Strategies used by some when dating interracially/interethnically in which the dating individual does not react directly to any specific encounter but develops ways to generate more empowered feelings about the relationship.

germinal period The first two weeks of pregnancy.

gerontologist A social scientist who studies aging and the elderly.

gestation The entire period of pregnancy during which the fertilized egg develops into the baby that will be born.

gestational mother The woman who bears and delivers a child. In the context of assisted reproductive technology, this describes a woman who receives an embryo transplant and bears a child for someone else to parent.

getting together A courtship process different from dating, in which groups of women and men congregate at a party or share an activity.

giving feedback A recommended communication behavior in which a partner repeats in her or his own words what the other has said or revealed.

glans The sensitive tip at the end of the clitoris in women and of the penis in men.

globalization The interdependency or connection across national borders of people, organizations, or governments.

gonads Sex glands, or glands secreting sex hormones: the ovaries in women, the testicles in men.

good provider role A specialized masculine role that emerged in this country in about the 1830s and that emphasizes the husband as the only or the primary economic provider for his family.

grandparent families Families in which a grandparent acts as primary parent to grandchildren.

group home One type of foster-care setting in which several children are

cared for round-the-clock by paid professionals who work in shifts and live elsewhere.

guaranteed child support Type of child support, used in France and Sweden, in which the government sends to the custodial parent the full amount of support awarded to the child.

gunnysacking An alienating fight tactic in which a person saves up, or gunnysacks, grievances until the sack gets too heavy and bursts, and old hostilities pour out.

habituation The decreased interest in sex that results from the increased accessibility of a sexual partner and the predictability in sexual behavior with that partner over time.

hermaphrodite See *intersexual*.

heterogamy Marriage between partners who differ in race, education, religious background, or social class. Compare with *homogamy*.

heterosexism The taken-for-granted system of beliefs, values, and customs that places superior value on heterosexual behavior (as opposed to homosexual) and denies or stigmatizes nonheterosexual relations. This tendency also sees the heterosexual, or straight, family as standard.

heterosexuals Individuals who prefer sexual partners of the opposite sex.

H-frame relationship Relationships that are structured like a capital H: Partners stand virtually alone, each self-sufficient and neither influenced much by the other. An example would be a devitalized, dual-career marriage. See also *A-frame relationship, M-frame relationship*.

hidden agenda Associated with stepfathers who, with remarriage, join a single-parent family of a mother and her children. The former single-parent family may have a hidden agenda, or assumptions and expectations about how the stepfather will behave—expectations and assumptions that are often not passed on to the new stepfather.

hierarchical parenting Concept used to describe a Hispanic parenting philosophy that blends warm emotional support for children with demand for significant respect for parents and other authority

figures, including older extended-family members.

HIV/AIDS HIV is human immunodeficiency virus, the virus that causes AIDS, or acquired immune deficiency syndrome. AIDS is a sexually transmitted disease involving breakdown of the immune system defense against viruses, bacteria, fungi, and other diseases.

holistic view of sex The view that conjugal sex is an extension of the whole marital relationship, which is not chopped into compartments, with sex reduced to a purely physical exchange.

homogamy Marriage between partners of similar race, age, education, religious background, and social class. See also *heterogamy*.

homophobia Fear, dread, aversion to, and often hatred of homosexuals.

homosexuals People who are sexually attracted to individuals of the same sex.

horizontally extended family Family members from the same generation or other related lines, such as uncles, brothers, sisters, and aunts, who live and work together.

hormonal processes Chemical processes within the body regulated by such hormones as testosterone (a "male" hormone) and estrogen (a "female" hormone). Hormonal processes are thought to shape behavior, as well as physical development and reproductive functions, although experts disagree as to their impact on behavior.

hormones Chemical substances secreted into the bloodstream by the endocrine glands.

household As a Census Bureau category, *household* is any group of persons residing together.

househusband A man who takes a full-time family care role, rather than being employed; the male counterpart to a housewife.

Huber's theory of gender stratification A theory which posits that gender inequality in a society is a consequence of the type of economy in that society: foraging, agricultural, or industrial.

human-built environment The environment that is created when nature is altered by human action.

hymen In the female, a ring of tissue that partly covers the vaginal opening.

hypergamy A marriage in which a person gains social rank by marrying someone of higher rank.

hypogamy Marrying a partner with lower social and/or economic status than one's own.

identity A sense of inner sameness developed by individuals throughout their lives. They know who they are throughout their various endeavors and pursuits, no matter how different these may be.

ideological perspective A perspective used in explaining the division of household labor in families that points to the impact of cultural expectations on household labor.

illegitimate needs Needs that arise from feelings of self-doubt, unworthiness, and inadequacy. Loving partners cannot fill each other's illegitimate needs no matter how much they try. One fills one's illegitimate needs best by personally working to build one's self-esteem. A first step might be doing something nice for oneself rather than waiting for somebody else to do it.

immigrant stock A demographic category that includes immigrants and children of immigrants.

implantation The process in which the fertilized egg, or zygote, embeds itself in the thickened lining of the uterus.

impotence See *erectile dysfunction.*

in vitro fertilization (IVF) A process in which a baby is conceived outside a woman's body, in a laboratory dish or jar, but develops within the woman's uterus.

incest Sexual relations between closely related individuals.

inclusive fitness In evolutionary theories of human behavior, the propensity to advance preservation of one's genes either through direct reproduction (one's own offspring) or through facilitating the reproduction of close relatives.

income effect Occurs when an increase in income contributes to the stability of a marriage by giving it a more adequate financial basis.

incomplete institution Cherlin's description of a remarried family due to cultural ambiguity.

independence Self-reliance and self-sufficiency. To form lasting intimate relationships, independent people must choose to become interdependent.

independence effect Occurs when an increase in income leads to marital dissolution because the partners are better able to afford to live separately.

individualistic orientation Seeking primarily personal—as opposed to communal, or group—happiness and goals.

individualistic society Society in which the main concern is with one's own interests (which may or may not include those of one's immediate family).

individualistic values Values that encourage self-fulfillment, personal growth, doing one's own thing, autonomy, and independence. Individualistic values can conflict with family values.

infant mortality rate The number of deaths of infants under one year per 1,000 live births.

infecundity Technical term for the physical inability to have children.

informal adoption Children are taken into a home and considered to be children of the parents, although the "adoption" is not legally formalized.

informal caregiving Unpaid caregiving, provided personally by a family member.

informational power One of the six power bases, or sources of power. This power is based on the persuasive content of what the dominant person tells another individual.

in-home caregiver A caregiver who provides child care in the child's home, either coming in by the day or as a live-in caregiver.

insecure/anxious attachment style One of three attachment styles in attachment style theory, this style entails concern that the beloved will disappear, a situation often characterized as "fear of abandonment."

institution See *social institution.*

interactional relationship pattern Relationship pattern in which partners expect companionship and intimacy as well as more practical benefits. See also *parallel relationship pattern.*

interactionist perspective Theoretical perspective that focuses on internal family dynamics; the ongoing action and response of family members to one another.

interactionist perspective on human sexuality A perspective, derived from symbolic interaction theory, which holds that sexual activities and relationships are shaped by sexual scripts available in a culture.

intercourse The insertion of the penis into the vagina; also called coitus.

interdependence A relationship in which people who have high self-esteem make strong commitments to each other, choosing to help fill each other's legitimate, but not illegitimate, needs.

interethnic marriage Marriage between spouses who are not defined as of different races but do belong to different ethnic groups.

intergenerational transmission of divorce The tendency for children of divorced parents to have a greater propensity to divorce than children from intact families.

internalize The process of making a cultural belief, value, or attitude one's own. When internalized, an attitude becomes a part of us and influences how we think, feel, and act.

interparental conflict perspective One of the five theoretical perspectives concerning the negative outcomes among children of divorced parents. From the interparental conflict perspective, the conflict between parents prior to, during, and after the divorce is responsible for the lowered well-being of the children of divorce.

interpersonal exchange model of sexual satisfaction A view of sexual relations, derived from exchange theory, that sees sexual satisfaction as shaped by the costs, rewards, and expectations of a relationship and the alternatives to it.

interracial marriage Marriage of a partner of one (socially defined) race to someone of a different race.

intersexual A person whose genitalia, secondary sex characteristics, hormones, or other physiological features are not unambiguously male or female.

intimacy Committing oneself to a particular other and honoring that commitment in spite of some personal sacrifices while sharing one's inner self with the other. Intimacy requires interdependence.

intimacy (Sternberg's triangular theory of love) Close, connected, and bonded feelings in loving relationships, including sharing oneself with the loved one; one dimension of the triangular theory of love.

intimate partner power Power in a relationship, whether of married or unmarried intimate partners.

intimate partner violence Violence against current or former spouses, cohabitants, or sexual or relationship partners.

involuntary infertility Situation of a couple or individual who would like to have a baby, but cannot. Involuntary infertility is medically diagnosed when a woman has tried for twelve months to become pregnant without success.

involuntary stable singles Older divorced, widowed, and never-married people who wanted to marry or remarry, but have not found a mate and have come to accept being single as a probable life situation.

involuntary temporary singles Singles who would like, and expect, to marry. These can be younger never-marrieds who do not want to be single and are actively seeking mates, as well as somewhat older people who had not previously been interested in marrying but are now seeking mates.

jealousy Emotional pain, anger, and uncertainty arising when a valued relationship is threatened or perceived to be threatened. Research has shown that men and women experience and react differently to jealousy.

job sharing Two people sharing one job.

joint custody A situation in which both divorced parents continue to take equal responsibility for important decisions regarding their child's general upbringing.

kin conversion Redefining long-time friends as kin.

kin scripts framework A theoretical framework for studying ethnic minority families that includes three culturally relevant family concepts: kin-work, kin-time, and kin-scription. Kin scripts theorizing helps to make theory and research less biased and more relevant to minority families. In addition, it can be applied to mainstream white families.

kin upgrading Psychologically elevating a more distant relative, such as a niece, to a closer family relationship, such as "like a daughter."

labia majora Two rounded folds of skin, the external lips in the female genitalia.

labia minora Latin for "lesser lips"; two folds of tissue with the labia majora in the female genitalia.

labor In childbirth, the process by which the baby is propelled from the mother's body.

labor force A social invention that arose with the industrialization of the nineteenth century, when people characteristically became wage earners, hiring out their labor to someone else.

laissez-faire parenting Overly permissive parenting. Children set their own standards for behavior, with little or no parental guidance or authority. Parents are indulgent, but not necessarily involved in a supportive way with the child's everyday activities and problems.

latent kin matrix "A web of continually shifting linkages that provide the potential for activating and intensifying close kin relationships" (Riley 1983, p. 441).

legal divorce The dissolution of a marriage by the state through a court order terminating the marriage.

legitimate needs Needs that arise in the present rather than out of the deficits accumulated in the past.

legitimate power One of the six power bases, or sources of power. This power stems from the more dominant individual's ability to claim authority, or the right to request compliance.

lesbian A homosexual woman; one who is sexually attracted to other women.

leveling Being transparent, authentic, and explicit about how one truly feels, especially concerning the more conflictive or hurtful aspects of an intimate relationship. Among other things, leveling between intimates implies self-disclosure and commitment (to intimacy).

life chances The opportunities that exist for a social group or individual to pursue education and economic advancement, to secure medical care and preserve health, to marry and have children, to have material goods and housing of desired quality, etc.

life expectancy The number of years, or amount of time, that an individual is expected to live.

life stress perspective One of the five theoretical perspectives concerning the negative outcomes among children of divorced parents. From the life stress perspective, divorce involves the same stress for children as for adults, and divorce is not one single event but a process of stressful events—moving, changing schools, and so on.

longitudinal study One technique of scientific investigation, in which researchers study the same individuals or groups over an extended period of time, usually with periodic surveys.

looking-glass self The concept that people gradually come to accept and adopt as their own the evaluations, definitions, and judgments of themselves that they see reflected in the faces, words, and gestures of those around them.

loose connection Relationship type in which both partners focus mainly (although not exclusively) on their separate careers, hobbies, or friends.

love A deep and vital emotion resulting from significant need for satisfaction, coupled with a caring for and acceptance of the beloved, and resulting in an intimate relationship. Love may make the world go 'round, but it's a lot of work too.

love style A distinctive character or personality that loving or lovelike relationships can take. One social scientist has distinguished six: agape, eros, ludus, mania, pragma, and storge.

ludus The love style that focuses on love as play and on enjoying many sexual partners rather than searching for one serious relationship. This love style emphasizes the recreational aspect of sexuality. See also *agape, eros, mania, pragma, storge.*

machismo A cultural complex involving extreme male dominance and male privilege, including greater sexual freedom for males.

main/secondary provider couple Husband provides family's primary economic support; wife contributes to the family income, but her earnings are seen as inessential. She takes primary responsibility for homemaking.

male dominance The cultural idea of masculine superiority; the idea that men exercise the most control and influence over society's members.

mania The love style that combines strong sexual attraction and emotional intensity with extreme jealousy and moodiness, in which manic partners alternate between euphoria and depression. See also *agape, eros, ludus, pragma, storge.*

manipulating Seeking to control the feelings, attitudes, and behavior of one's partner or partners in underhanded ways rather than by assertively stating one's case.

marital power Power exercised between spouses.

marital rape A husband's compelling a wife against her will to submit to sexual contact that she finds offensive.

market approach to child care Childcare arrangement of working parents; other people are hired to care for children while parents are at their jobs.

marriage gradient The sociological concept that men marry down in educational and occupational status and women marry up. As a result, never-married women may represent the cream of the crop, whereas never-married men may be the bottom of the barrel. The marriage gradient is easy to observe in the way American couples match their relative heights and ages, with the men slightly taller and older.

marriage market The sociological concept that potential mates take stock of their personal and social characteristics and then comparison shop or bargain for the best buy (mate) they can get.

marriage premise By getting married, partners accept the responsibility to keep each other primary in their lives and to work hard to ensure that their relationship continues. See also *primariness.*

martyring Doing all one can for others while ignoring one's own legitimate needs. Martyrs often punish the person to whom they are martyring by letting her or him know "just how much I put up with."

masculinities Culturally defined ways of being a man. The plural conveys the idea that there are varied models of appropriate behavior.

masked Term sometimes used to indicate the situation in which individuals involved in interracial relationships are not recognized as such when out in public but not together.

meaning What a given activity or statement conveys symbolically. For example, a woman's domestic work may symbolize love and family caring or it may symbolize a subservient social status. Meanings can be culturally agreed upon or be the attributions of individuals.

meatus The opening at the tip of the penis.

menstruation The (about monthly) process of discarding an unfertilized ovum, unused tissue, and blood through the vaginal opening.

M-frame relationship Relationship based on couple interdependence. Each partner has high self-esteem, but they mutually influence each other and experience loving as a deep emotion. See also *A-frame relationship, H-frame relationship.*

Miller's typology of urban Native American families: bicultural: Families that develop a successful blend of native beliefs and practices with those adaptive to living in urban settings; **marginal:** Urban families that have become alienated from both Indian and mainstream American cultures; **traditional:** Families that retain primarily Indian ways in their urban environment; **transitional:** Families that are tending to assimilate to the white working class.

minority group, minority A group that experiences disadvantage, exclusion, and/or discrimination in the larger society. A minority group can be of any size relative to the total population; it is not necessarily a numerical minority.

mixed message Two simultaneous messages that contradict each other, also called a double message. For example, society gives us mixed messages regarding family values and individualistic values and about premarital sex. People, too, can send mixed messages, as when a partner says, "Of course I always like to talk with you" while turning up the TV.

modern family The traditional nuclear family—husband, wife, and children living in one household.

modern sexism Sexism that takes the form of (a) denying the existence of discrimination against women, (b) resentment of complaints about discrimination, and (c) resentment of "special favors" for women.

monogamy The sexually exclusive union of a couple.

mons veneris The female pubic mound, an area of fatty tissue above the pubic bone.

motherhood penalty The lifetime earnings disadvantage that results from motherhood.

mothering approach to child care A family's child-care arrangement that gives preference to the mother's caregiving role. A couple balances nonemployment of the mother with extra jobs or hours for the father; or if the mother must work to maintain the family economically, her employment role is minimized.

multiorgasmic Capable of experiencing several successive orgasms during one sexual encounter.

myotonia Increased muscle tension, often as a result of sexual arousal.

nadir of family disorganization Low point of family disorganization when a family is going through a family crisis.

nanny An in-home child-care worker, who cares for a family's children either on a live-in basis or by the day; may include traveling with the family.

narcissism Concern chiefly or only with oneself, without regard for the well-being of others. Narcissism is selfishness, not self-love. People with high self-esteem care about and respect themselves *and* others. Narcissistic, or selfish, people, on the other hand, have low self-esteem, are insecure, and therefore worry unduly about their own well-being and very little about that of others.

natural childbirth Management of childbirth to minimize medical and technological intervention. Usually involves minimization of anesthesia; no electronic monitoring or use of medical interventions such as forceps or surgical episiotomy. Usually includes prebirth training and presence of husband or other labor partner in the delivery room.

natural physical–biological environment The natural environment of climate, soil, plants, animals, etc.

naturalistic observation A technique of scientific investigation in which a researcher lives with a family or social group or spends extensive time with them, carefully recording their activities, conversations, gestures, and other aspects of everyday life.

Near Peer Marriage (Schwartz) Couples who believe in partner equality, but fall short of a 60/40 division of household labor, usually because of the need for the husband's higher earnings.

neo-sexism Same as modern sexism.

no-fault divorce The legal situation in which a partner seeking a divorce no longer has to prove grounds. Virtually all states now have no-fault divorce.

noncustodial grandparent A parent of a divorced, noncustodial parent.

no-power A situation in which partners are equally able to influence each other and, at the same time, are not concerned about their relative power vis-à-vis each other. No-power partners negotiate and compromise instead of trying to win.

nuclear family A family group comprising only the wife, the husband, and their children. See also *extended family*.

nuclear-family model monopoly The cultural assumption that the first-marriage family is the "real" model of family living, with all other family forms viewed as deficient.

occupational segregation The distribution of men and women into substantially different occupations. Women are overrepresented in clerical and service work, for example, whereas men dominate the higher professions and the upper levels of management.

open adoption An adoption process in which there is direct contact between the biological and adoptive parents, ranging from one meeting before the child is born to lifelong friendship.

opportunity costs (of children) The economic opportunities for wage earning and investments that parents forgo when rearing children.

orgasm The climax in human sexual response during which sexual tension reaches its peak and is suddenly discharged. In men, ejaculation almost always accompanies orgasm.

orgasmic phase The third of four progressive phases of sexual arousal described by Masters and Johnson. The orgasmic phase is characterized by extremely pleasurable sexual sensations and by involuntary rhythmic contractions in the vagina and penis.

ova Plural of ovum.

ovaries Two female gonads, or sex glands, that produce reproductive cells called ova, or eggs.

ovulation The process by which the ovary produces an ovum, or egg. Usually, the two ovaries alternate so that only one ovulates each month.

ovum An egg produced by the female ovary. Usually the two ovaries alternate in producing one ovum each month in a process called ovulation.

ovum transplant A process in which a fertilized egg is implanted into an infertile woman. See also *embryo transplant*.

parallel relationship pattern A pattern noted by sociologist Jesse Bernard among working-class marriages (as opposed to the interactional pattern among middle-class marriages) in which the husband was expected to be a hardworking provider and the wife a good housekeeper and cook. See also *interactional relationship pattern*.

para-parent An unrelated adult who informally plays a parentlike role for a child.

parental adjustment perspective One of the five theoretical perspectives concerning the negative outcomes among children of divorced parents. From the parental adjustment perspective, the parent's child-rearing skills are impaired

as a result of the divorce, with probable negative consequences for the children.

parental loss perspective One of the five theoretical perspectives concerning the negative outcomes among children of divorced parents. From the parental loss perspective, divorce involves the absence of a parent from the household, which deprives children of the optimal environment for their emotional, practical, and social support.

parenting approach to child care In this approach, child care is shared by the parents on as equal a basis as possible. Working parents try to restructure their employment arrangements to make this possible.

parenting style A general manner of relating to and disciplining children.

passion (Sternberg's triangular theory of love) The drives that lead to romance, physical attraction, sexual consummation, and so, on in a loving relationship; one dimension of the triangular theory of love.

passive-aggression Expressing anger at some person or situation indirectly, through nagging, nitpicking, or sarcasm, for example, rather than directly and openly. See also *displacement, sabotage*.

patriarchal norm (of marital power) The norm (cultural rule) that the man should be dominant in a marital relationship.

patriarchal sexuality The view of human sexuality in which men own everything in the society, including women and women's sexuality, and males' sexual needs are emphasized while females' needs are minimized.

patriarchal terrorism A man's systematic use of verbal or physical violence to gain or maintain control over his female partner.

Peer Marriage (Schwartz) Couples who have a close-to-equal split of household chores and money management and who consider themselves to have equal status in the marriage or cohabiting union.

penis The penis and the scrotum together make up the external male genitalia. The penis is composed of an erectile shaft and a sensitive tip, or glans.

perineum In the female, the area between the vestibule and the vagina and the anus. In the male, the area between the scrotum and the anus.

period of family disorganization That period in a family crisis, after the stressor event has occurred, during which family morale and organization slump and habitual roles and routines become nebulous.

permissiveness with affection The standard that permits premarital sex for women and men equally, provided they have a fairly stable, affectionate relationship.

permissiveness without affection The standard that allows premarital sex for women and men regardless of how much stability or affection there is in their relationship. Also called the "recreational standard."

personal marriage agreement An articulated, negotiated agreement between partners about how each will behave in many or all aspects of the marriage. Personal marriage contracts need to be revised as partners change. A synonym is *relationship agreement.*

pile-up Concept from family stress and crisis theory that refers to the accumulation of family stressors and prior hardships.

placenta Tissue and membrane that hold the fetus in place inside the uterus and function in nourishment; discharged in childbirth.

plateau phase The second phase of sexual arousal, during which the bodily changes begun during the excitement phase intensify, and pelvic thrusting, which begins voluntarily, grows more rapid and becomes involuntary, especially among men.

play As a term used in social theory, *play* references the symbolic interaction theory of George Herbert Mead. Play is not idle time, but a vehicle through which children develop appropriate concepts of adult roles, as well as images of themselves, through acting out social roles and engaging in social interaction.

pleasure bond The idea, from Masters and Johnson's book by the same name, that sexual expression between intimates is one way of expressing and strengthening the emotional bond between them.

pleasuring Spontaneously doing what feels good at the moment during a sexual encounter; the opposite of spectatoring.

polyamory Marriages in which one or both spouses retain the option to sexually love others in addition to their spouses.

polyandry A marriage system in which a woman has more than one spouse.

polygamy A marriage system in which a person takes more than one spouse. Polygyny describes one man with multiple wives, while a marriage of a woman with plural husbands is termed polyandry.

polygyny A marriage system in which a man has more than one spouse.

pool of eligibles A group of individuals who, by virtue of background or birth, are most likely to make compatible marriage partners.

population pyramid A figure that shows the proportion of the population in each age group.

postindustrial Describes an economy and society characterized by information-based and service work and the social structures and patterns that go with it.

postmodern family As a result of progressively increasing family diversity, today's family has little or no objective reference to a particular structure. In the postmodern perspective, there is tremendous variability of family forms in contemporary society, leading some theorists to conclude that the concept of "family" no longer has any objective meaning.

power The ability to exercise one's will. Personal power, or autonomy, is power exercised over oneself. Social power is the ability to exercise one's will over others.

power politics Power struggles between spouses in which each seeks to gain a power advantage over the other; the opposite of a no-power relationship.

pragma The love style that emphasizes the practical, or pragmatic, element in human relationships and involves the rational assessment of a potential (or actual) partner's assets and liabilities. See also *agape, eros, ludus, mania, storge.*

premature ejaculation A sexual dysfunction in which a man is unable to control his ejaculatory reflex.

prepuce Part of the female genitalia; the fold of skin that sometimes covers the clitoris, formed where the labia minora join; the clitoral hood.

primariness Commitment to keeping one's partner the most important person in one's life. See also *commitment (to intimacy).*

primary group A group, usually relatively small, in which there are close, face-to-face relationships. The family and a friendship group are primary groups. See also *secondary group.*

primary parent Parent who takes full responsibility for meeting child's physical and emotional needs by providing the major part of the child's care directly and/or managing the child's care by others.

principle of least interest The postulate that the partner with the least interest in the relationship is the one who is more apt to exploit the other.

private family The aspect of the family that provides individuals with intimacy, emotional support, and love; also called the "private face" of families.

pronatalist bias A cultural attitude that takes having children for granted.

prostate A male internal reproductive organ that, along with the seminal vesicles, produces semen.

psychic divorce Regaining psychological autonomy after divorce; emotionally separating oneself from the personality and influence of the former spouse.

psychic intimacy The sharing of people's minds and feelings. Psychic intimacy may or may not involve sexual intimacy.

public family The aspect of the family that produces public goods and services; also called the "public face" of families.

quasi-kin Anthropologist Paul Bohannan's term for the person one's former spouse remarries. The term is also used more broadly to refer to former in-laws and other former and added kin resulting from divorce and remarriage.

quickening The first fetal movements apparent to the pregnant woman.

race A group or category that is thought of as representing a distinct biological heritage. In reality, there is only one human race; "racial" categories and differences are social constructs. The so-called races do not differ significantly in terms of basic biological make-up.

rape myth Belief about rape that functions to blame the victim and exonerate the rapist.

rapport talk In Deborah Tannen's terms, this is conversation engaged in by women aimed primarily at gaining or reinforcing rapport or intimacy. See also *report talk*.

rational investment perspective Theory arguing that couples attempt to maximize the family economy by trading off between time and energy investments in paid market work and unpaid household labor.

Reciprocal Beneficiaries Law Hawaii state legislation that allows any two single adults—including same-sex partners or blood relatives, such as siblings or parent and adult child—to have access to some (though not all) legal rights on the state level, but none on the federal level.

recreational standard See *permissiveness without affection*.

redivorce An emerging trend in U.S. society. Redivorces take place more rapidly than first divorces so that many who divorce (and their children) can expect several rapid and emotionally significant transitions in lifestyle and family unit.

referent power One of the six power bases, or sources of power. This power is based on the less dominant person's emotional identification with the more dominant individual.

refined divorce rate Number of divorces per thousand married women over age fifteen.

refractory period A time after orgasm during which a man cannot become sexually aroused; it usually lasts at least twenty minutes and may be considerably longer, particularly in older men.

reinforcing cycle A cycle regarding women's earnings and paid and unpaid family work in which cultural expectations and persistent discrimination result in employed males receiving higher average earnings than women

employed full time, and hence in women's doing more unpaid family work.

relationship agreement See *personal marriage agreement*.

relationship maturity Quality of an individual who demonstrates skill of communicating with a partner; this includes the ability to understand the partner's point of view, make decisions about changing behavior a partner doesn't like, explain one's points of view to the partner, and ask for changes in the partner's behavior when this seems appropriate.

relative love and need theory Theory of conjugal power that holds that the spouse with the least to lose if the marriage ends is the more powerful in the relationship.

relatives of divorce Kinship ties established by marriage, but retained after the marriage is dissolved—for example, the relationship of a former mother-in-law and daughter-in-law.

remarriages Marriages in which at least one partner has already been divorced or widowed. Remarriages are becoming increasingly common for Americans.

remarried family A family consisting of a husband and wife, at least one of whom has been married before, and one or more children from the previous marriage of either or both spouses. There are more remarried families in the United States today, and they usually result from divorce and remarriage.

report talk In Deborah Tannen's terms, this is conversation engaged in by men aimed primarily at conveying information. See also *rapport talk*.

representative sample Survey samples that reflect, or represent, all the people about whom social scientists want to know something.

resiliency model of family stress, adjustment, and adaptation Complex model of family stress and adaptation developed from the double ABC-X model.

resilient families Families that emphasize mutual acceptance, respect, and shared values; members rely on one another for emotional support.

resolution phase The final phase of sexual arousal described by Masters and

Johnson, during which partners' bodies return to their unstimulated state. See also *excitement phase, plateau phase, orgasmic phase*.

resource hypothesis Hypothesis by Blood and Wolfe that because conjugal power was no longer distributed according to sex, the relative power between wives and husbands would result from their relative resources (for example, age, education, job skills) as individuals.

resources in cultural context The effect of resources on marital power depends on the cultural context. In a traditional society, norms of patriarchal authority may override personal resources. In a fully egalitarian society, a norm of intimate partner and marital equality may override personal resources as well. It is in a transitional society that the resource hypothesis is most likely to shape marital power relations.

retarded ejaculation A sexual dysfunction in which a man, although sexually aroused, cannot trigger orgasm.

reward power One of the six power bases, or sources of power. This power is based on an individual's ability to give material or nonmaterial gifts and favors.

role making Improvising a course of action and fitting it to that of others. In role making we use our acts to alter the traditional expectations and obligations associated with a role.

role reversal A change or reversal of the usual role relationships. An example would be the situation of immigrant families in which a child assumes family leadership because of greater knowledge of the host language and culture, displacing the parents.

role-reversed provider couple A couple in which the wife or female partner is the principal breadwinner, while the man has primary responsibility for housework and children.

sabotage A passive–aggressive action in which a person tries to spoil or undermine some activity another has planned. Sabotage is not always consciously planned. See also *passive-aggression*.

safer sex Use of protective methods (such as latex or plastic condoms) or strategies (careful selection of partners) in sexual activity. Use of the term *safer* rather than *safe* points to the risk of sexually transmitted disease that remains even when these methods and strategies are used.

sandwich generation Middle-aged (or older) individuals, usually women, who are sandwiched between the simultaneous responsibilities of caring for their dependent children (sometimes young adults) and aging parents.

scientific investigation The systematic gathering of information—using surveys, experiments, naturalistic observation, and case studies—from which it is often possible to generalize with a significant degree of predictability.

scrotum A sac behind the penis that holds the two male gonads, or sex glands, the testicles.

second shift Sociologist Arlie Hochschild's term for the domestic work that employed women must perform after coming home from a day on the job.

secondary group A group, often large, characterized by distant, practical relationships. An impersonal society is characterized by secondary groups and relations. See also the opposite, *primary group*.

secure attachment style One of three attachment styles in attachment style theory, this style involves trust that the relationship will provide necessary and ongoing emotional and social support.

self-care An approach to child care for working parents in which the child is at home or out without an adult caretaker. Parents may be in touch by phone.

self-concept The basic feelings people have about themselves, their abilities, and their worth; how people think of or view themselves.

self-disclosure Letting others see one as one really is. Self-disclosure demands authenticity.

self-esteem Feelings and evaluations people have about their own worth.

self-identification theory of gender A theory of gender socialization, developed by psychologist Lawrence Kohlberg, that begins with a child's categorization of self as male or female. The child goes on to identify sex-appropriate

behaviors in the family, media, and elsewhere, and to adopt those behaviors.

semen The milky fluid that carries the sperm through the urethra and out the meatus.

seminal vesicles Internal male reproductive glands that, with the prostate, produce semen, the milky fluid that carries the sperm through the urethra and out the meatus.

separate spheres The Victorian era doctrine that men and women are essentially different and should occupy different social roles and spheres—women the private sphere of the home and men the public sphere of jobs and political authority.

sequencing mom A mother who chooses to leave paid employment in order to spend some years at home raising children, but who plans to return to work eventually.

seven-stage model of stepfamily development Model of stepfamily progression that proceeds through the following stages: fantasy, immersion, awareness, mobilization, action, contact, and resolution.

sex Refers to biological characteristics, that is, male or female anatomy or physiology. The term *gender* is used to refer to the social roles, attitudes, and behavior associated with males or females.

sex flush A rash that appears on the skin during sexual arousal, especially common in women.

sex ratio The number of men per 100 women in a society. If the sex ratio is above 100, there are more men than women; if it is below 100, there are more women than men.

sexual abuse A form of child abuse that involves forced, tricked, or coerced sexual behavior—exposure, unwanted kissing, fondling of sexual organs, intercourse, rape, and incest—between a young person and an older person.

sexual arousal The process of awakening, stirring up, or exciting sexual desires and feelings in ourselves or others.

sexual dysfunction Sexual dysfunction can be defined in objective terms as "a specific chronic disorder involving sexual performance." It can also be defined subjectively as "a chronic inability to re-

spond sexually in a way one finds satisfying" (Greenberg et al. 2002, p. 515).

sexual exclusivity Expectations for strict monogamy in which a couple promise or publicly vow to have sexual relations only with each other.

sexual intimacy A level of interpersonal interaction in which partners have a sexual relationship. Sexual intimacy may or may not involve psychic intimacy.

sexual orientation The attraction an individual has for a sexual partner of the same or opposite sex.

sexual responsibility The assumption by each partner of responsibility for his or her own sexual response.

sexual script A *script* is a culturally written pattern or "plot" for human behavior. A sexual script offers reasons for having sex, designates who should take the sexual initiative, how long an encounter should last, what positions are acceptable, etc.

sexually related diseases Diseases or infections that may be transmitted through or in conjunction with sexual activity, although they may also be acquired in other ways.

sexually transmitted diseases (STDs) Contagious diseases transmitted from one person to another through sexual contact. They are also termed *sexually transmitted infections*.

shared parenting Mother and father (or two homosexual parents) who both take full responsibility as parents.

shift work As defined by the Bureau of Labor Statistics, any work schedule in which more than half of an employee's hours are before 8 A.M. or after 4 P.M.

sibling violence Family violence that takes place between siblings (brothers and sisters).

significant others People whose opinions about one are very important to one's self-esteem. Good friends are significant others, as are family members.

single Any person who is divorced, widowed, or never-married.

single-mothers-by-choice Women who planfully become mothers, although they are not married or with a partner. They are typically older, with economic and educational resources that enable them to be self-supporting.

single-parent family A family consisting of a never-married, divorced, or widowed parent and one or more biological or adopted children. The majority of single-parent families in the United States today are headed by women.

single remarriage A remarriage in which only one of the partners is previously married.

social capital perspective (on parenthood) Motivation for parenthood in anticipation of the links parenthood provides to social networks and their resources.

social class Position in the social hierarchy, such as "upper class," "middle class," "working class," or "lower class." Can be viewed in terms of such indicators as education, occupation, and income, or analyzed in terms of status and respect or lifestyle.

social–cultural environment Consists of cultural products and social institutions.

social institution A system of patterned and predictable ways of thinking and behaving—beliefs, values, attitudes, and norms—concerning important aspects of people's lives in society. Examples of major social institutions are: the family, religion, government, the economy, and education.

social learning theory According to this theory, children learn gender roles as they are taught by parents, schools, and the media.

Social Security Social insurance whose chief purpose is financial support of the elderly. Based on employer–employee contributions, it is available at a minimum age of 62 to formerly employed persons or their spouses. Payments to current beneficiaries far exceed their actual contributions. Other Social Security programs provide support to minor children whose parents have died and to the disabled.

socialization The process by which society influences members to internalize attitudes, beliefs, values, and expectations.

spectatoring A term Masters and Johnson coined to describe the practice of emotionally removing oneself from a sexual encounter in order to watch oneself and see how one is doing.

sperm Male reproductive cells.

spousal support Economic support of a separated spouse or ex-spouse by the other spouse ordered by a court following separation or divorce.

stalled revolution As used by sociologist Arlie Hochschild, the juxtaposition of women's entry into the paid labor force without men's doing more unpaid family work.

static (closed) marriage A marriage that does not change over the years and does not allow for changes in the partners. Static marriage partners rely on their formal, legal bond to enforce permanence and sexual exclusivity. Static marriages are more inclined to become devitalized than are flexible marriages.

status exchange hypothesis Regarding interracial/interethnic marriage, the argument that an individual might trade his or her socially defined superior racial/ethnic status for the economically or educationally superior status of a partner in a less privileged racial/ethnic group.

stepmother trap The conflict between two views: Society sentimentalizes the stepmother's role and expects her to be unnaturally loving toward her stepchildren but at the same time views her as a wicked witch.

sterility See *infecundity*.

Sternberg's triangular theory of love Psychologist Robert Sternberg's formulation of love, in which a variety of types of love are constructed from the three basic dimensions of passion, intimacy, and commitment.

stimulus–values–roles (SVR) The three-stage filtering sequence couples undergo to determine whether they are appropriately matched. The first stage involves physical attraction. The second stage assesses values consensus on a range of issues. The final stage explores role compatibility, wherein couples test and negotiate how they will play out their marital roles.

stonewalling One of the Four Horsemen of the Apocalypse (which see) that involves refusing to listen to a partner's complaints.

storge An affectionate, companionate style of loving. See also *agape, eros, ludus, mania, pragma*.

stressor A precipitating event that causes a crisis—it is often a situation for which the family has had little or no preparation. See also *ABC-X model, double ABC-X model*.

stressor overload A situation in which an unrelenting series of small crises adds up to a major crisis.

structural antinatalism The structural, or societal, condition in which bearing and rearing children is discouraged either overtly or—as may be the case in the United States—covertly through subtle economic discrimination against parents.

structural constraints Established and customary rules, policies, and day-to-day practices that affect a person's life chances.

structure–functional perspective Theoretical perspective that looks to the functions that institutions perform for society and the structural form of the institution.

subfecundity Involuntary infertility experienced by those who have previously had a biological child.

supervised visitation A situation in which contact between a child and a visiting noncustodial parent occurs only in the presence of a third party, such as a social worker or a court employee.

suppression of anger Repression—the involuntary, unconscious blocking of painful thoughts, feelings, or memories from the conscious mind—as it applies to anger. Repressed feelings of anger often come out in other ways, such as overeating and feeling bored or depressed.

surrogate mother A woman who carries within her uterus a developing fetus for a couple who cannot conceive and carry an infant naturally. The surrogate mother delivers the infant, then turns it over to the couple.

survey A technique of scientific investigation using questionnaires or brief face-to-face interviews or both. An example is the United States census.

swinging A marriage agreement in which couples exchange partners in order to engage in purely recreational sex.

symbiotic relationship A relationship based on the mutual meeting of illegitimate needs. See also *legitimate needs*.

task specificity model Model of elder-care giving in which, based on the kind of help they need, care receivers may prefer family members, community professionals, or friends as caregivers.

Temporary Assistance for Needy Families (TANF) Federal legislation that replaces Aid to Families with Dependent Children and whereby government welfare assistance to poor parents is limited to five years for most families, with most adult recipients required to find work within two years.

testicles Male gonads, or sex glands, that hang in the scrotum behind the penis and produce male reproductive cells (sperm) and the hormone testosterone.

theoretical perspective A way of viewing reality, or a lens through which analysts organize and interpret what they observe. Researchers on the family identify those aspects of families that are of interest to them, based on their own theoretical perspective.

theory of complementary needs Theory developed by social scientist Robert Winch suggesting that we are attracted to partners whose needs complement our own. In the positive view of this theory, we are attracted to others whose strengths are harmonious with our own so that we are more effective as a couple than either of us would be alone.

three-phase cycle of violence A relationship-violence cycle in which (1) tension builds between two parties; (2) the situation escalates, exploding in a violent episode; and (3) the violent person becomes contrite, apologizing and treating the other lovingly. Predictably, the cycle continually repeats itself.

time availability perspective Theory explaining a couple's division of domestic labor in terms of the time available to each partner.

total fertility rate For a given year, the number of births that women would have over their reproductive lifetimes if all women at each age had babies at the rate for each age group that year.

traditional sexism Beliefs that men and women are essentially different and should occupy different social roles, that women are not as fit as men to perform certain tasks, and that differential treatment of men and women is acceptable.

traditionals (Schwartz) Marriages or domestic partnerships in which the man dominates all areas of decision making except children. He is the primary breadwinner and she is the primary homemaker, even if employed. In Schwartz's typology, both spouses favor this arrangement.

trailing spouse The spouse of a relocated employee who moves with him or her.

transforming strategies Strategies used by some when dating interracially/interethnically by which negative responses from others are reinterpreted in order to define them differently.

transgendered A person who has adopted a gender identity that differs from sex/gender of birth.

transition to adulthood Period of transition between adolescence and adulthood. See also *emerging adulthood*.

transition to parenthood The circumstances involved in assuming the parent role.

transitional egalitarian situation (of marital power) Marriages or domestic partnerships in which neither patriarchal nor egalitarian norms prevail. The couple negotiates relationship power, with the relative resources of each individual playing an important role in the outcome.

transnational family A family of immigrants or immigrant stock that maintains close ties with the sending country. Identity and behavior connect the immigrant family to the new country and the old, and their social networks cross national boundaries.

transsexual Individuals who have begun life identified as a member of one sex, but later come to believe they belong to the other sex. The person may undertake surgical reconstruction to attain a body type closer to that of the desired sex.

tubal ligation Cutting or scarring the fallopian tubes between a woman's ovaries and uterus so that eggs cannot pass into the tubes to be fertilized.

two-career marriage Marriage in which both partners have a strong commitment to the lifetime development of both careers. Also called *dual-career couple* or *dual-career family*.

two-earner marriage Marriage in which the wife as well as the husband is employed, but her work is not viewed as a lifetime career. His may be viewed as a "job" rather than a career, as well. Sometimes termed *two-paycheck marriage* or *dual-earner couple*.

two-person single career The situation in which one spouse, usually the wife, encourages and participates in the other partner's career without direct recognition or personal remuneration.

two-stage marriage An alternative to more formal dating proposed by the late anthropologist Margaret Mead. Americans would first enter into individual marriages involving no children but a serious though not necessarily lifelong commitment. Couples who were compatible in individual marriages might choose to move into the second stage, parental marriage, which would presume lifelong commitment and the ability to cooperatively support and care for a child or children.

umbilical cord Tube that connects the abdomen of a fetus to the placenta inside the mother's uterus.

undocumented immigrant The preferred term for "illegal" immigrants, those who are present in a country but not citizens or legal residents. The implication of the term "undocumented" (compared to "illegal") is that immigrants may or should have legitimate claims to asylum or residence even if these have not been formally recognized.

unpaid family work The necessary tasks of attending to both the emotional needs of all family members and the practical needs of dependent members, such as children or elderly parents, and maintaining the family domicile.

urethra The opening in women and men through which urine passes from the bladder to the outside.

uterus A cavity inside the female in which a fetus grows until birth; also called womb.

vagina The passageway in the female from the uterus to the outside; the birth canal.

vaginismus A sexual dysfunction in which anatomically normal vaginal muscles involuntarily contract whenever a sex partner attempts penetration so that intercourse is impossible.

value maturity Quality of an individual who recognizes and feels confident about her or his personal values.

value of children perspective (on parenthood) Motivation for parenthood because of the rewards, including symbolic rewards, that children bring to parents.

vasectomy Tying the tubes (vas deferens) between the testicles and the penis so that sperm will not be included in a man's ejaculation of semen.

vertically extended family Three or more generations sharing housing and resources.

vestibule Entryway to the vagina.

voluntary childlessness The deliberate choice not to become a parent.

voluntary stable singles Singles who are satisfied to have never married, divorced people who do not want to remarry, cohabitants who do not intend to marry, and those whose lifestyles preclude marriage, such as priests and nuns.

voluntary temporary singles Younger never-marrieds and divorced people who are postponing marriage or remarriage. They are open to the possibility of marriage, but searching for a mate has a lower priority than do other activities, such as career.

vulnerable families Families that have a low sense of common purpose, feel in little control over what happens to them, and tend to cope with problems by showing diminished respect and/or understanding for each other.

vulva The female external genitalia.

wage gap The persistent difference in earnings between men and women.

wheel of love An idea developed by Ira Reiss in which love is seen as developing through a four-stage, circular process, including rapport, self-revelation, mutual dependence, and personality need fulfillment.

zygote A fertilized ovum (egg). See also *embryonic stage, fetal period, germinal period.*

zygote intrafallopian transfer (ZIFT) An in vitro fertilization process in which fertilized eggs are implanted in a woman's fallopian tubes while the fertilized egg is still a single cell, or zygote.

References

AAUW (American Association of University Women). 1992. *The AAUW Report: How Schools Shortchange Girls.* New York: Marlowe.

AAUW Educational Foundation. 1999. *Gender Gaps: Where Schools Still Fail Our Children.* New York: Marlowe.

Abelson, Reed. 1998. "Part-Time Work for Some Adds up to Full-Time Job." *New York Times.* November 2: A1–A16.

"Abnormalities Cause New In Vitro Concern." 2003. *Omaha World-Herald (LA Times).* Jan. 24.

Abraham, Margaret. 1995. "Ethnicity, Gender, and Marital Violence: South Asian Women's Organizations in the U.S." *Gender and Society* 9: 450–68.

Abraham, Margaret. 2000. *Speaking the Unspeakable: Marital Violence among South Asian Immigrants in the United States.* New Brunswick NJ: Rutgers.

Abraham, Yvonne, and Rick Klein. 2004. "Free To Marry: Historic Date Arrives for Same-sex Couples in Massachusetts." *The Boston Globe.* May 17.

Ackerman, Brian P., Kristen Schoff D'Eramo, Lina Umylny, David Schultz, and Carroll E. Izard. 2001. "Family Structure and the Externalizing Behavior of Children from Economically Disadvantaged Families." *Journal of Family Psychology* 15 (2): 288-301.

ACLU. 2001. "An ACLU Lesbian Gay Rights Project Update on the Status of Sodomy Laws." www.aclu.org/issues/gay/sodomy-update.html.

"Across the USA: Indiana." 2003. *USA Today.* Mar. 20.

Adams, Bert N. 1971. *On the American Family: A Sociological Interpretation.* Chicago: Markham Publishing Company.

Adams, Brooke. 2003. "The Old Schoolyard Jingle about Marriage—First Comes Love, Then Comes Marriage, Then Comes Baby in a Baby Carriage—May Need A Rewrite." *Salt Lake Tribune.* June 29.

Adams, Gina, and Kathryn Tout. 2000. *Child Care Patterns for School-Age Children with Employed Mothers.* Washington, DC: The Urban Institute.

Adams, Karen L., and Norma C. Ware. 1995. "Sexism and the English Language: The Linguistic Implications of Being a Woman." Pp. 331–46 in *Women: A Feminist Perspective*, 5th ed., edited by Jo Freeman. Mountain View, CA: Mayfield.

Adler, Jerry. 1993. "Sex in the Snoring '90s." *Newsweek.* Apr. 26: 55–57.

———. 1996a. "Adultery: A New Furor Over an Old Sin." *Newsweek.* Sept. 30: 54–60.

———. 1996b. "Building a Better Dad." *Newsweek.* June 17: 58–64.

———. 1997a. "A Matter of Faith." *Newsweek.* Dec. 15: 49–54.

———. 1997b. "How Kids Mourn." *Newsweek.* Sept. 22: 58–61.

———. 1998. "Tomorrow's Child." *Newsweek.* Nov. 2: 54–64.

Adler, Nancy E., Henry P. David, Brenda N. Major, Susan H. Roth, Nancy Felipe Russo, and Gail E. Wyatt. 1992. "Psychological Factors in Abortion: A Review." *American Psychologist* 47: 1194-1204.

Administration for Children and Families. 2004. *The Healthy Marriage Initiative (HMI).* U.S Department of Health and Human Services. http://www.acf.hhs.gov/healthymarriage.html

Ager, Susan. 2004. "Christians, Where Is Your Tolerance?" *Knight Ridder/Tribune News Service.* March 3.

Ahmed, Ashraf Uddin. 1993. "Marriage and Its Transition in Bangladesh." Pp. 74–83 in *Next of Kin: An International Reader on Changing Families*, edited by Lorne Tepperman and Susannah J. Wilson. Englewood Cliffs, NJ: Prentice Hall.

Ahrons, Constance. 1994. *The Good Divorce: Raising Your Family Together When Your Marriage Comes Apart.* New York: HarperCollins.

———. 2004. *We're Still Family: What Grown Children Have to Say about Their Parents' Divorce.* New York: HarperCollins.

Ahrons, Constance, and Jennifer L. Tanner. 2003. "Adult Children and Their Fathers: Relationship Changes 20 Years after Parental Divorce." *Family Relations* 52: 340-351.

Ainsworth, Mary D. S. 1967. *Infancy in Uganda: Infant Care and the Growth of Attachment.* Baltimore: Johns Hopkins University.

Ainsworth, Mary D. S., M. C. Blehar, E. Waters, and S. Wall. 1978. "Patterns of Attachment: A Psychological Study of the Strange Situation." Hillsdale NJ: Erlbaum.

Aksamit, Nichole. 2001. "Bellevue Police Rush to Learn About Culture of New Neighbors." *Omaha World-Herald.* Aug. 24.

Alan Guttmacher Institute. 2000. "Contraceptive Use." www.guttmacher.org.pubs/fb_contr_use.html.

Albert, Alexa, and Kris Bulcroft. 1988. "Pets, Family, and the Life Course." *Journal of Marriage and the Family* 50: 543-552.

Albrecht, Carol M., and Don E. Albrecht. 2001. "Sex Ratio and Family Structure in the Nonmetropolitan United States." *Sociological Inquiry* 71 (1): 67–84.

Albrecht, Carol M., Mark A. Fossett, Cynthia M. Cready, and K. Jill Kiecolt. 1997. "Mate Availability, Women's Marriage Prevalence, and Husbands' Education." *Journal of Family Issues* 18 (4): 429–52 .

Albrecht, Chris, and Jay D. Teachman. 2003. "Childhood Living Arrangements and the Risk of Premarital Intercourse." *Journal of Family Issues* 24 (7): 867-894.

Aldous, Joan. 1978. *Family Careers: Developmental Change in Families.* New York: Wiley.

———. 1996. *Family Careers: Rethinking the Developmental Perspective.* Thousand Oaks, CA: Sage.

Alexander, C. S., and B. Guyer. 1993. "Adolescent Pregnancy: Occurrence and Consequences." *Pediatric Annals* 22: 85–88.

Alexander, Deborah. 2003. "Money Spent on Pets Is Nothing to Growl At." *Omaha World-Herald.* May 27.

Alexander, Pamela C., Sharon Moore, and Elmore R. Alexander III. 1991. "What Is Transmitted in the Intergenerational Transmission of Violence?" *Journal of Marriage and Family* 53 (3): 657–68.

Allen, C. M., and M.A. Straus. 1980. "Resources, Power, and Husband Wife Violence." Pp. 188-208 in *The Social Causes of Husband-Wife Violence*, edited by Murray A. Straus and Gerald T. Hotaling. Minnesota: University of Minnesota.

Allen, Cheryl. 2001. "Doing the Dad Thing: Real Men Stay at Home." *The Greenville News.* August 6.

Allen, John L., Jr. 2004. "The Word from Rome." *National Catholic Reporter.* Sept. 24.

Allen, Karen. 2002. "Companion Animals as Part of a Healthy Family Environment." www.deltasociety.org.

Allen, Katherine R. 1997. "Lesbian and Gay Families." Pp. 196–218 in *Contemporary Parenting: Challenges and Issues*, edited by Terry Arendell. Thousand Oaks, CA: Sage.

Allen, Katherine R., Rosemary Blieszner, and Karen A. Roberto. 2000. "Families in the Middle and Later Years: A Review and Critique of Research in the 1990s." *Journal of Marriage and Family* 62 (4): 911–26.

Allen, Katherine R., Rosemary Blieszner, Karen A. Roberto, Elizabeth B. Farnsworth, and Karen L. Wilcox. 1999. "Older Adults and Their Children: Family Patterns of Structural Diversity." *Family Relations* 48 (2): 151–57.

Allen, Mike, and Alan Cooperman. 2004. "Bush Plans to Back Marriage Amendment." *Washington Post.* February 11.

Allen, Robert L., and Paul Kivel. 1994. "Men Changing Men." *Ms.* Sept./Oct.: 50–53.

Allen, Sarah M., and Alan J. Hawkins. 1999. "Maternal Gatekeeping: Mothers' Beliefs and Behaviors That Inhibit Greater Father Involvement in Family Work." *Journal of Marriage and Family* 61: 199–212.

Allgeier, E. R. 1983. "Sexuality and Gender Roles in the Second Half of Life." Pp. 135–37 in *Changing Boundaries: Gender Roles and Sexual Behavior*, edited by Elizabeth Rice Allgeier and Naomi B. McCormick. Palo Alto, CA: Mayfield.

Alper, Gerald. 2003. *Knowing If It's the Real Thing: Discovering the Roots of Intimacy.* Lanham: Taylor Trade Publishers.

Altman, Irwin, and Dalmas A. Taylor. 1973. *Social Penetration: The Development of Interpersonal Relations.* New York: Holt, Rinehart & Winston.

Altman, Lawrence K. 2002. "Many Americans with H.I.V. Don't Know It or Don't Seek Care, Study Shows." *New York Times.* Feb. 26.

———. 2003. "Panel Finds No Connection Between Cancer and Abortion." *New York Times.* Mar. 30.

———. 2004a. "Genital Herpes Decline 17% Surveys Show." *New York Times.* Mar. 9.

———. 2004b. "Study Finds That Teenage Virginity Pledges Are Rarely Kept." *New York Times.* Mar. 10.

Alvardo, Donna. 1992. "Children Having Children." *San Jose Mercury News.* July 1: 1D, 6D.

Alvarez, Lizette. 2003. "Arranged Marriages Get a Little Rearranging." *The New York Times.* June 21.

Alvord, Valerie. 2003a. "Some Troops Freeze Sperm Before Deploying." *USA Today* Jan. 27.

———. 2003b. "Webcam Helps Military Kids Ease Pain of Separation." *USA Today* April 1.

Amatenstein, Sherry. 2002. *Love Lessons from Bad Breakups.* New York: Perigee Publishers.

Amato, Paul R. 1988. "Parental Divorce and Attitudes Toward Marriage and Family Life." *Journal of Marriage and Family* 50: 453–61.

———. 1993. "Children's Adjustment to Divorce Theories, Hypotheses, and Empirical Support." *Journal of Marriage and Family* 55 (1): 23–28.

———. 1994a. "Father–Child Relations, Mother–Child Relations, and Offspring Psychological Well-Being in Early Adulthood." *Journal of Marriage and Family* 56 (4): 1031–42.

———. 1994b. "The Implications of Research Findings on Children in Stepfamilies." Pp. 81–88 in *Stepfamilies: Who Benefits? Who Does Not?* edited by Alan Booth and Judy Dunn. Hillsdale, NJ: Erlbaum.

———. 1996. "Explaining the Intergenerational Transmission of Divorce." *Journal of Marriage and Family* 58 (3): 628–40.

———. 2000. "The Consequences of Divorce for Adults and Children." *Journal of Marriage and Family* 62: 1269–87.

———. 2001. "Children of Divorce in the 1990s: An Update of the Amato and Keith (1991) Meta-Analysis." *Journal of Family Psychology* 15: 355–370.

———. 2003a. "The Consequences of Divorce for Adults and Children." Pp. 190–213 in *Family in Transition*, 12th ed., edited by Arlene S. Skolnick and Jerome H. Skolnick. Boston: Allyn and Bacon.

———. 2003b. "Reconciling Divergent Perspectives: Judith Wallerstein, Quantitative Research, and Children of Divorce." *Family Relations* 52: 332–330.

Amato, Paul R., and Alan Booth. 1991. "The Consequences of Divorce for Attitudes Toward Divorce and Gender Roles." *Journal of Family Issues* 12 (3): 306–22.

———. 1996. "A Prospective Study of Divorce and Parent–Child Relationships." *Journal of Marriage and Family* 58 (2): 356–65.

———. 1997. *A Generation at Risk: Growing Up in an Era of Family Upheaval.* Cambridge, MA: Harvard University Press.

Amato, Paul R., and Danelle B. DeBoer. 2001. "The Transmission of Marital Instability Across Generations: Relationship Skills or Commitment to Marriage?" *Journal of Marriage and Family* 63: 1038–51.

Amato, Paul R., and Frieda Fowler. 2002. "Parenting Practices, Child Adjustment, and Family Diversity." *Journal of Marriage and Family* 64 (3)+ 703-716.

Amato, Paul R., and Joan G. Gilbreth. 1999. "Nonresident Fathers and Children's Well-Being: A Meta-Analysis." *Journal of Marriage and the Family* 61: 557-573.

Amato, Paul R., David R. Johnson, Alan Booth, and Stacy J. Rogers. 2003. "Continuity and Change in Marital

Quality Between 1980 and 2000." *Journal of Marriage and Family* 65 (1): 1-22.

Amato, Paul R., Sandra J. Rezac, and Alan Booth. 1995. "Helping Between Parents and Young Adult Offspring: The Role of Parental Marital Quality, Divorce, and Remarriage." *Journal of Marriage and Family* 57 (2): 363–74.

Amato, Paul R., and Fernando Rivera. 1999. "Paternal Involvement and Children's Behavior Problems." *Journal of Marriage and Family* 61 (2): 375–84.

Amato, Paul R., and Stacy J. Rogers. 1997. "A Longitudinal Study of Marital Problems and Subsequent Divorce." *Journal of Marriage and Family* 59 (3): 612–24.

Amato, Paul R., and Juliana M. Sobolewski. 2001. "The Effects of Divorce and Marital Discord on Children's Well-Being." *American Sociological Review* 66: 900–21.

Amato, Paul R., and Denise Wallin. 2001. "People's Reasons for Divorce: Gender, Social Class, the Life Course, and Adjustment." Paper presented at the annual meeting of the National Council on Family Relations. Rochester, NY. Nov. 10.

Ambert, Anne-Marie. 1988. "Relationships with Former In-laws After Divorce: A Research Note." *Journal of Marriage and Family* 50: 679–86.

———. 1994. "A Qualitative Study of Peer Abuse and Its Effects: Theoretical and Empirical Implications." *Journal of Marriage and Family* 56 (1): 119–30.

Ambroz, Juliann R. 1995. "Keeping Love Alive: How Couples Counseling Can Work for You." *Mothering* (Fall): 75–80.

American Academy of Pediatrics. 1992. *Caring for Our Children: National Health and Safety Performance Standards as Guidelines for Out-of-Home Child Care Programs.* Elk Grove Village, IL: American Public Health Association and American Academy of Pediatrics.

———. 1996. "Universal Access to Good-Quality Education and Care of Children from Birth to 5 Years: Policy Statement." *Pediatrics* 97: 417–19.

American Academy of Pediatrics. 1999. "Circumcision Policy Statement." *Pediatrics* 103: 686-693.

American Association for Marital and Family Therapy. http://www.aamft.org

American Association of Retired Persons (AARP). 2001. *In the Middle: A Report on Multicultural Boomers Coping with Family and Aging Issues.* Washington, DC: AARP.

———. 2004. *A Report of Multicultural Boomers Coping with Family and Aging Issues.* Washington DC: American Association of Retired Persons.

American Civil Liberties Union. 2000. "Federal Court Rejects HIV-Based Job Discrimination, Ties Employment to Individual Capabilities, Not Bias." March 10. www.aclu.org.

———. 2004a. "In A Six-To-Six Vote, Federal Appeals Court Declines to Reconsider Decision Upholding Florida's Anti-Gay Adoption Law." July 22. www.aclu.org.

———. 2004b. "Washington Appeals Court Allows Non-biological Mother in Same-Sex Relationship to Seek Parental Rights after Breakup." Press release. www.aclu.org.

AmeriStat Staff. 2001. "Racial Identity in the U.S. Hispanic/Latino Population." www.prb.org June.

———. 2003a. "Americans Increasingly Opting Out of Marriage." www.ameristat.org. March.

———. 2003b. "Diversity, Poverty Characterize Female-Headed Households." www.ameristat.org. March.

———. 2003c. "Marriage Boosts Individual Earnings." www.ameristat.org. March

———. 2003d. "More Women Out Earning Their Husbands." www.ameristat.org. March.

———. 2003e. "Solitaire Set Continues to Grow." www.ameristat.org March.

———. 2003f. "Traditional Families Account for Only 7 Percent of U.S. Households." www.ameristat.org. March.

"American Indians by the Numbers." 1992. *New York Times.* Feb. 26.

American Psychological Association. 2001. "Answers to Your Questions About Sexual Orientation and Homosexuality." *APA Online.* www.apa.org/pubinfo/orient.html.

American Psychological Association. Committee on Lesbian and Gay Concerns. 1991. "Avoiding Heterosexual Bias in Language." *American Psychologist* 46: 973-74.

"American Public Opinion about Gay and Lesbian Marriage." 2004. The Gallup Organization: Gallup Poll News Service. January 27. http://www.gallup.com

"American Sperm, As Hardy As Ever." 2000. *New York Times.* Mar. 28.

Ames, Katherine. 1992. "Domesticated Bliss." *Newsweek.* Mar. 23.

Amnesty International. 1999. *"Not Part of My Sentence": Violations of the Human Rights of Women in Custody.* New York: Amnesty International.

"Amniocentesis." 2004. WebMD. www.webmd.com.

Andersen, Jan. 2004. "Stepfamilies— How to Live in Harmony." Self-Growth.com. http://www.selfgrowth.com Retrieved 9/21/2004.

Andersen, Julie Donner. 2002. "His Kids: Becoming a W.O.W. Stepmother." SelfGrowth.com. http://www.selfgrowth.com/articles/Andersen3.html.

Andersen, Margaret L. 1988. *Thinking about Women: Sociological Perspectives on Sex And Gender,* 2nd ed. New York: Macmillan.

Andersen, Margaret L., and Patricia Hill Collins, eds. 2004. *Race, Class, and Gender,* 5th ed. Belmont CA: Wadsworth.

Anderson, Diane. 2000. "Suspicions Confirmed." *Newsweek.* Oct. 2: 74.

Anderson, Kristin L. 1997. "Gender, Status, and Domestic Violence: An Integration of Feminist and Family Violence Approaches." *Journal of Marriage and Family* 59 (3): 655–69.

Anderson, Kristin L. 2002. "Perpetrator or Victim: Relationships between Intimate Partner Violence and Well-being." *Journal of Marriage and the Family* 64: 851-863.

Anderson, Michael A., Paulette Marie Gillig, Marilyn Sitaker, Kathy Mc-Closkey, Katherine Malloy, and Nancy Grigsby. 2003. "'Why Doesn't She Just Leave?' A Descriptive Study of Victim Reported Impediments to Her Safety." *Journal of Family Violence* 18: 151–155.

Andrews, Bernice, and Chris R. Brewin. 1990. "Attributions of Blame for Marital Violence: A Study of Antecedents and Consequences." *Journal of Marriage and Family* 52 (3) (Aug.): 757–67.

Andrews, Lori. 1991. "Sperminators: When Dead Men Become Dads." *Ottawa Citizen* Apr. 19.

———. 1999. *The Clone Age: Adventures in the New World of Reproductive Technology.* New York: Henry Holt.

Anetzberger, Georgia, Jill Korbin, and Craig Austin. 1994. "Alcoholism and Elder Abuse." *Journal of Interpersonal Violence* 9 (2): 184–93.

Angier, Natalie. 1998. "Men. Are Women Better Off with Them, or Without Them?" *New York Times.* June 21.

Anti-Defamation League of B'nai Brith. 1981. "The American Story: The Hernandez Family." New York: Anti-Defamation League. Video.

Appleby, Julie. 2001. "Pricey Infertility Care Sparks Insurance Clash." *USA Today.* Dec. 19.

Aquilino, William S. 1994a. "Later Life Parental Divorce and Widowhood: Impact on Young Adults' Assessment of Parent–Child Relations." *Journal of Marriage and Family* 56 (4): 908–22.

———. 1994b. "Impact of Childhood Family Disruption on Young Adults' Relationships with Parents." *Journal of Marriage and Family* 56 (2): 295–313.

———. 1997. "From Adolescent to Young Adult: A Prospective Study of Parent–Child Relations During the Transition to Adulthood." *Journal of Marriage and Family* 59: 670–86.

Archer, John. 2000. "Sex Differences in Aggression Between Heterosexual Partners: A Meta-Analytic Review." *Psychological Bulletin* 126: 651–80.

Arditti, Joyce A. 1997. "Women, Divorce, and Economic Risk." *Family and Conciliation Courts Review* 35 (1): 79–92.

———. 2003. "Incarceration Is a Major Source of Family Stress." *Family Focus.* June: F15-F17.

Arditti, Joyce A., and Timothy Z. Keith. 1993. "Visitation Frequency, Child Support Payment, and the Father–Child Relationship Postdivorce." *Journal of Marriage and Family* 55 (3): 699–712.

Arendell, Terry. 1986. *Mothers and Divorce: Legal, Economic, and Social Dilemmas.* Berkeley: University of California Press.

———. 1995. *Fathers and Divorce.* Thousand Oaks, CA: Sage.

———. 1997. "Divorce and Remarriage." Pp. 154–95 in *Contemporary Parenting: Challenges and Issues,* edited by Terry Arendell. Thousand Oaks, CA: Sage.

Arias, Elizabeth. 2004. "United States Life Tables , 2001." *National Vital Statistics Reports* 52 (14). Hyattsville, MD: National Center for Health Statistics. Feb. 11.

Ariès, Phillipe. 1962. *Centuries of Childhood: A Social History of Family Life.* New York: Knopf.

Armour, Stephanie. 2001a. "Pressures on Firms to Ban Discrimination Against Gays." *USA Today.* Aug. 13.

———. 2001b. "Telecommuting Gets Stuck in the Slow Lane." *USA Today.* June 25.

———. 2002. "More Moms Make Kids Their Career of Choice." *USA Today.* Mar. 12.

———. 2003. "More Men Train to Be Nurses, Midwives, Secretaries." *USA Today.* July 11.

———. 2004. "Moms Find It Easier to Pop Back into Work Force." *USA Today.* Sept. 23.

Armstrong, Larry. 2003. "Your Mouse Knows Where Your Car Is." *Business Week:* 16.

Arnett, Jeffrey Jensen. 2000. "High Hopes in a Grim World: Emerging Adults' Views of Their Futures and 'Generation X.'" *Youth and Society* 31: 267-286.

Aron, Arthur, Christina C. Norman, Elaine N. Aron, Colin McKenna, and Richard E. Heyman. 2000. "Couples' Shared Participation in Novel and Arousing Activities and Experienced Relationship Quality." *Journal of Personality and Social Psychology* 78 (2): 273–84.

Aronson, Pamela. 2003. "Feminists or 'Postfeminists'? Young Women's Attitudes Toward Feminism and Gender Relations." *Gender and Society* 17: 903–922.

Artis, Julie E., and Eliza K. Pavalco. 2003. "Explaining the Decline in Women's Household Labor: Individ-

ual Change and Cohort Differences." *Journal of Marriage and the Family* 65: 746-761.

Aseltine, Robert H., Jr., and Ronald C. Kessler. 1993. "Marital Disruption and Depression in a Community Sample." *Journal of Health and Social Behavior* 34 (Sept.): 237–51.

Astone, Nan Marie, and Sara S. McLanahan. 1991. "Family Structure, Parental Practices and High School Completion." *American Sociological Review* 56 (June): 309–20.

Atchley, Robert C. 1997. *Social Forces and Aging.* Belmont, CA: Wadsworth. "At-Home Workers Are Vanishing." 2003. *Omaha World-Herald (Wall Street Journal).* Aug. 4.

Atkinson, Alice M. 1994. "Rural and Urban Families' Use of Child Care." *Family Relations* 43: 16–22.

Aune, Krystyna S., and Jamie Comstock. 2002. "An Exploratory Investigation of Jealousy in the Family." *Journal of Family Communication* 2 (1): 29-39.

Avellar, Sarah, and Pamela J. Smock. 2003. "Has the Price of Motherhood Declined Over Time? A Cross-Cohort Comparison of the Motherhood Wage Penalty." *Journal of Marriage and the Family* 65: 597-607.

Avery, Rosemary J. 1997. *Adoption Policy and Special Needs Children.* Westport, CT: Auborn House.

Axinn, William G., and Arland Thornton. 1993. "Mothers, Children, and Cohabitation: The Intergenerational Effects of Attitudes and Behavior." *American Sociological Review* 58 (2): 233–45.

Babbie, Earl. 1992. *The Practice of Social Research,* 6th ed. Belmont, CA: Wadsworth.

———. 2003. *The Practice of Social Research,* 10th ed. Belmont CA: Wadsworth.

Baca Zinn, Maxine, Pierette Hondagneu-Sotelo, and Michael A. Messner. 2004. "Gender through the Prism of Difference." Pp. 166-174 in *Race, Class, and Gender,* 5th ed. Belmont CA: Wadsworth.

Baca Zinn, Maxine, and Angela Y.H. Pok. 2002. "Tradition and Transition in Mexican-Origin Families." Pp. 79–100 in *Minority Families in the United States,* 3rd ed., edited by

Ronald L. Taylor. Upper Saddle River NJ: Prentice-Hall.

Baca Zinn, Maxine, and Barbara Wells. 2000. "Diversity Within Latino Families: New Lessons for Family Social Science." Pp. 252–73 in *Handbook of Family Diversity*, edited by David H. Demo, Katherine R. Allen, and Mark Fine. New York: Oxford.

Bach, George R., and Peter Wyden. 1970. *The Intimate Enemy: How to Fight Fair in Love and Marriage.* New York: Avon.

Bachman, Ronet, and Linda S. Saltzman. 1995. "Violence Against Women: Estimates from the Redesigned Survey August 1995." *U.S. Department of Justice Special Report NCJ–154348.* Washington, DC: U.S. Bureau of Justice Statistics Clearinghouse. www.ojp.usdoj.gov

Bachrach, Christine, Patricia F. Adams, Soledad Sambrano, and Kathryn A. London. 1990. "Adoption in the 1980's." U.S. National Center for Health Statistics, Advance Data, No. 181, Jan. 5.

Bachu, Amara. 1999. "Is Childlessness Among American Women on the Rise?" Population Division Working Paper No. 37. May. Washington, DC: U.S. Census Bureau.

Bachu, Amaru, and Martin O'Connell. 2000. *Fertility of American Women: June 1998.* Current Population Reports P20–526. Washington, DC: U.S. Census Bureau. September.

Bailey, J. Michael, David Bobrow, Marilyn Wolfe, and Sarah Mikach. 1995. "Sexual Orientation of Adult Sons of Gay Fathers." *Developmental Psychology* 31: 124–29.

Baker, Beth. 2001. "Grandparents Speak Out." *San Francisco Chronicle Sunday Magazine.* April.

Baldock, Cora Vellekoop. 2000. "Migrants and Their Parents: Caregiving from a Distance." *Journal of Family Issues* 21: 205–24.

Balli, Sandra J., David H. Demo, and John F. Wedman. 1998. "Family Involvement with Children's Homework: An Intervention in the Middle Grades." *Family Relations* 47 (2): 149–57.

Bancroft, John, Jeni Loftus, and J. Scott Long. 2003. "Distress about Sex: A National Survey of Women in Heterosexual Relationships." *Archives of Sexual Behavior* 32: 193-208.

Bankston, Carl L. III. 1998. "Sibling Cooperation and Scholastic Performance Among Vietnamese-American Secondary School Students: An Ethnic Social Relations Theory." *Sociological Perspectives* 41 (1): 167–84.

Barash, Susan Shapiro. 2000. *Second Wives: The Pitfalls and Rewards of Marrying Widowers and Divorced Men.* Far Hills, NJ: New Horizon.

Barbach, Lonnie. 1980. *Women Discover Orgasm: A Therapist's Guide to a New Treatment Approach.* New York: Free Press.

———. 1991 [1975]. *For Yourself: The Fulfillment of Female Sexuality.* New York: New American Library.

Barbell, K. 1996. "Foster Care Today." Washington, DC: Child Welfare League of America.

Bart, Pauline. 1972. "Depression in Middle-Aged Women." Pp. 163–86 in *Women in Sexist Society: Studies in Power and Powerlessness*, edited by Vivian Gornick and Barbara K. Moran. New York: New American Library.

Barth, Richard P., and Marianne Berry. 1988. *Adoption and Disruption: Rates, Risks, and Responses.* New York: Aldine.

Bartholet, Elizabeth. 1993. *Family Bonds: Adoption and the Politics of Parenthood.* Boston: Houghton Mifflin.

Bartkowski, John P. 2001. *Remaking the Godly Family: Gender Negotiation in Evangelical Families.* Piscataway NJ: Rutgers University Press.

Barton, Sharon J. 1999. "Promoting Family-Centered Care with Foster Families." *Pediatric Nursing* 25 (1): 57–62.

Basow, Susan H. 1991. "The Hairless Ideal: Women and Their Body Hair." *Psychology of Women Quarterly* 15: 83–96.

———. 1992. *Gender: Stereotypes and Roles*, 3d ed. Pacific Grove, CA: Brooks/Cole.

Batalova, Jeanne A., and Philip N. Cohen. 2002. "Premarital Cohabitation and Housework: Couples in Cross-National Perspective." *Journal of Marriage and the Family* 64: 743–755.

Baum, Angela C., Sedahlia Jasper Crase, and Kirsten Lee Crase. 2001. "Influences on the Decision to Become or Not Become a Foster Parent." *Families in Society* 82 (2): 202–21.

Baumrind, Diana. 1978. "Parental Disciplinary Patterns and Social Competence in Children." *Youth and Society* 9: 239–76.

———. 1994. "The Social Context of Child Maltreatment." *Family Relations* 43 (4) (Oct.): 360–68.

Bauserman, Robert. 2002. "Child Adjustment in Joint-Custody Versus Sole Custody Arrangements: A Meta-Analyic Review." *Journal of Family Psychology* 16: 91-102.

Bayles, Fred. 2004. "Mass. Legislators Revisit Gay-Marriage Debate." *USA Today.* March 11.

Beach, B. 1989. *Integrating Work and Family Life: The Home-working Family.* Albany: SUNY.

Beaman, Lori G. 2001. "Molly Mormons, Mormon Feminists and Moderates: Religious Diversity and the Latter Day Saints Church." *Sociology of Religion* 62: 65-86.

Bean, Frank, and Marta Tienda. 1987. *The Hispanic Population of the United States.* New York: Russell Sage.

Bearman, Peter S., and Hannah Brückner. 2001. "Promising the Future: Virginity Pledges and First Intercourse." *American Journal of Sociology* 106: 859–912.

Becerra, Rosina M. 1998. "The Mexican-American Family." Pp. 153–71 in *Ethnic Families in America: Patterns and Variations*, edited by Charles H. Mindel, Robert W. Haberstein, and Roosevelt Wright, Jr. Upper Saddle River, NJ: Prentice Hall.

Beck, Melinda. 1990. "Trading Places." *Newsweek.* July 16: 48–54.

Beck, Peggy, and Nancee Blank. 1997. "Broadening the Scope of Divorce Mediation to Meet the Needs of Children." *Mediation Quarterly: Journal of the Academy of Family Mediators* 14 (3): 179–85.

Becker, Gary S. 1991. *A Treatise on the Family*, 2d ed. Cambridge, MA: Harvard University Press.

Becker, Gay. 1990. *Healing the Infertile Family.* New York: Bantam.

———. 2000. *The Elusive Embryo: How Men and Women Approach Reproductive Technology.* Berkeley and Los Angeles: University of California Press.

Bedard, Marcia E. 1992. *Breaking with Tradition: Diversity, Conflict, and Change in Contemporary Families.* Dix Hills, NY: General Hall.

Beeghley, Leonard. 1996. *What Does Your Wife Do? Gender and the Transformation of Family Life.* Boulder, CO: Westview.

Beer, William R. 1989. *Strangers in the House: The World of Stepsiblings and Half Siblings.* New Brunswick, NJ: Transaction.

Begley, Sharon. 1998. "You're OK, I'm Terrific: 'Self-Esteem' Backfires." *Newsweek.* July 13: 69.

Belcastro, Philip A. 1985. "Sexual Behavior Differences Between Black and White Students." *The Journal of Sex Research* 21 (1): 56–67.

Belge, Kathy. 2004. "Lesbian and Gay Marriage: What's the Big Deal?" *About Lesbian Life.* http://lesbianlife.about.com

Belkin, Lisa. 2000. "The Making of an 8-Year Old Woman." *New York Times Magazine.* Dec. 24: 38–43.

———. 2001. "The Made-To-Order Savior." *New York Times Magazine:* 36–43; 48; 62.

———. 2003. "The Opt-Out Revolution." *The New York Times Magazine.* Oct. 26. Pp. 42-47; 58; 85-86.

Bell, Alan P., Martin S. Weinberg, and Sue Kiefer Hammersmith. 1981. *Sexual Preference: Its Development in Men and Women.* Bloomington: University of Indiana Press.

Bell, Diane, and Kathy Belicki. 1998. "A Community-Based Study of Well-Being in Adults Reporting Childhood Abuse." *Child Abuse & Neglect* 22 (7): 681–85.

Bell, Maya. 2003. "More Gays and Lesbians Than Ever Are Becoming Parents." Knight Ridder/Tribune News Service. October 1.

Bell, Richard Q. 1974. "Contributions of Human Infants to Caregiving and Social Interaction." Pp. 11–19 in *The Effect of the Infant on Its Care Giver: Origins of Behavior Series,* vol. 1, edited by Michael Lewis and Leonard A. Rosenblum. New York: Wiley.

Bellafante, Ginia. 2004. "Two Fathers, with One Happy to Stay at Home." *New York Times.* Jan. 12.

Bellah, Robert N., Richard Madsen, William M. Sullivan, Ann Swidler, and Steven M. Tipton. 1985. *Habits of the Heart: Individualism and Commitment in American Life.* Berkeley and Los Angeles: University of California Press.

Belluck, Pam. 2000. "States Declare War on Divorce Rates Before Any 'I Dos.'" *New York Times.* Apr. 21.

———. 2004. "Gays Win the Right to Marry." *Oakland Tribune.* February 5.

Belsky, Jay. 1990. "Parental and Nonparental Child Care and Children's Socioemotional Development: A Decade in Review." *Journal of Marriage and Family* 52 (4): 885–903.

———. 1991. "Parental and Non-Parental Child Care and Children's Socioemotional Development." Pp. 122–40 in *Contemporary Families: Looking Forward, Looking Back,* edited by Alan Booth. Minneapolis: National Council on Family Relations.

———. 2002. "Quantity Counts: Amount of Child Care and Children's Socioemotional Development." *Developmental and Behavioral Pediatrics* 23: 167-170.

Belsky, Jay, and K. H. Hsieh. 1998. "Patterns of Marital Change During the Early Childhood Years: Parent Personality, Coparenting, and Division-of-Labor Correlates." *Journal of Family Psychology* 12: 511–26.

Bem, Sandra Lipsitz. 1975. "Androgyny vs. the Tight Little Lives of Fluffy Women and Chesty Men." *Psychology Today* 9: 58–62.

———. 1981. "Gender Schema Theory: A Cognitive Account of Sex Typing." *Psychological Review* 88: 354–64.

Bengtson, Vern L. 2001. "Beyond the Nuclear Family: The Increasing Importance of Multigenerational Bonds." *Journal of Marriage and Family* 63 (1): 1–16.

Bengtson, Vern L, Timothy J. Biblarz, and Robert E.L. Roberts. 2002. *How Families Still Matter: A Longitudinal Study of Youth in Two Generations.* Cambridge UK: Cambridge University Press.

Bengtson, Vern L., C. Rosenthal, and L. Burton. 1996. "Paradoxes of Families and Aging." Pp. 245–53 in *Handbook of Aging and the Social Sciences,* edited by R. H. Binstock and L. K. George. New York: Academic.

Bennett, Larry W., and Oliver J. Williams. 1999. "Men Who Batter." Pp. 227–59 in *Family Violence: Prediction and Treatment,* 2nd ed., edited by Robert L. Hampton. Thousand Oaks, CA: Sage.

Bennett, Linda A., Steven J. Wolin, and David Reiss. 1988. "Deliberate Family Process: A Strategy for Protecting Children of Alcoholics." *British Journal of Addiction* 83: 821–29.

Benoit, D., and K. Parker. 1994. "Stability and Transmission of Attachment Across Three Generations." *Child Development* 65: 1444–56.

Berardo, Felix M. 1998. "Family Privacy." *Journal of Family Issues* 19 (1): 4–19.

Berg, Barbara. 1984. "Early Signs of Infertility." *Ms.* May: 68ff.

Berg, S. J., and K. E. Wynne-Edwards. 2001. "Changes in Testosterone, Cortisol, and Estradiol Levels in Men Becoming Fathers." *Mayo Clinic Proceedings* 76: 582-92.

Berger, Leslie. 2002. "Quest for Male Pill Is Gaining Momentum." *New York Times.* Dec. 10.

Berger, Peter L., Brigitte Berger, and Hansfried Kellner. 1973. *The Homeless Mind: Modernization and Consciousness.* New York: Random House.

Berger, Peter L., and Hansfried Kellner. 1970. "Marriage and the Construction of Reality." Pp. 49–72 in *Recent Sociology No. 2,* edited by Hans Peter Dreitzel. New York: Macmillan.

Berger, Roni. 1997. "Immigrant Stepfamilies." *Contemporary Family Therapy* 19 (3): 361–70.

———. 2000. "Gay Stepfamilies: A Triple-Stigmatized Group." *Families in Society* 81 (5): 504–16.

Bergman, Mike. 2004. "Census Bureau Projects Tripling of Hispanic and Asian Populations in 50 Years; Non-Hispanic Whites May Drop to Half the Total Population." Press release. U.S. Census Bureau. Mar. 18.

Bergstein, Brian. 2002. "Woman to Meet Sperm Donor Dad." *Washington Post.* Jan. 30.

Berk, Richard A., Phyllis J. Newton, and Sarah Fenstermaker Berk. 1986. "What a Difference a Day Makes: An Empirical Study of the Impact of Shelters for Battered Women." *Journal of Marriage and Family* 48: 481–90.

Berk, Sarah Fenstermaker. 1985. *The Gender Factory: The Apportionment of Work in American Households.* New York: Plenum.

Berke, Debra L. 2003. "Coming Home Again: The Challenges and Rewards of Home-Based Self-Employment." *Journal of Family Issues* 24: 513-546.

Bernard, Jessie. 1964. "The Adjustment of Married Mates." Pp. 675–739 in *The Handbook of Marriage and the Family,* edited by Harold T. Christensen. Chicago: Rand McNally.

———. 1982 [1972]. *The Future of Marriage,* 2d ed. New York: Bantam.

———. 1986. "The Good-Provider Role: Its Rise and Fall." Pp. 125–44 in *Family in Transition: Rethinking Marriage, Sexuality, Child Rearing, and Family Organization,* 5th ed., edited by Arlene S. Skolnick and Jerome H. Skolnick. Boston: Little, Brown.

Berns, Sara B., Neil S. Jacobson, and John M. Gottman. 1999. "Demand–Withdraw Interaction in Couples with a Violent Husband." *Journal of Consulting and Clinical Psychology* 67 (5): 666–74.

Bernstein, Anne C. 1997. "Stepfamilies from Siblings' Perspectives." Pp. 153–75 in *Stepfamilies: History, Research, and Policy,* edited by Irene Levin and Marvin B. Sussman. New York: Haworth.

———. 1999. "Reconstructing the Brothers Grimm: New Tales for Stepfamily Life." *Family Process* 38 (4): 415–30.

Bernstein, Fred A. 2004. "On Campus, Rethinking Biology 101." *New York Times.* Mar. 7.

Bernstein, Robert. 2002. "1-in-5 U.S. Residents Either Foreign-born or First-Generation, Census Bureau Reports." Press release. Washington, DC U.S. Census Bureau. Feb. 7.

———. 2003. "Two Married Parents the Norm." Press release. Washington DC: U.S. Census Bureau Jan. 12.

Bernstein, Robert, and Mike Bergman. 2003. "Hispanic Population Reaches All-Time High of 38.8 Million, New Census Bureau Estimates Show." Press release. Washington DC: U.S. Census Bureau.

Berry, Judy O., and Julie Meyer Rao. 1997. "Balancing Employment and Fatherhood." *Journal of Family Issues* 18 (4): 386–402.

Beutel, Ann M., and Margaret Mooney Marini. 1995. "Gender and Values." *American Sociological Review* 60 (3): 436–49.

Bianchi, Suzanne. 2000. "Maternal Employment and Time with Children: Dramatic Change or Surprising Continuity?" *Demography* 37: 401–14.

Bianchi, Suzanne M., and Lynne M. Casper. 2000. "American Families." *Population Bulletin* 55 (4). Washington, DC: Population Reference Bureau.

Bianchi, Suzanne M., Lekha Subaiya, and Joan P. Kahn. 1999. "The Gender Gap in the Economic Well-being of Nonresident Fathers and Custodial Mothers." *Demography* 36: 185-203.

Billingsley, Andrew. 1992. *Climbing Jacob's Ladder: The Enduring Legacy of African-American Families.* New York: Simon and Schuster.

Billy, J. O. G., K. Tanfer, W. R. Grady, and D. H. Kepinger. 1993. "The Sexual Behavior of Men in the U.S." *Family Planning Perspectives* 25: 52–60.

Binstock, Georgina, and Arland Thornton. 2003. "Separations, Reconciliations, and Living Apart in Cohabiting and Marital Unions." *Journal of Marriage and the Family* 65: 432-443.

Binstock, Robert H., and Linda K. George. 1996. *Handbook of Aging and the Social Sciences,* 4th ed. San Diego: Academic.

Bird, Chloe E. 1997. Gender Differences in the Social and Economic Burdens of Parenting and Psychological Distress." *Journal of Marriage and Family* 59 (4): 809–23.

Bird, Chloe E., and Catherine E. Ross. 1993. "Houseworkers and Paid Workers: Qualities of the Word and Effects on Personal Control." *Journal of Marriage and Family* 55 (Nov.): 913–25.

Bird, Gloria W., Rick Peterson, and Stephanie Hotta Miller. 2002. "Factors Associated with Distress among Support-Seeking Adoptive Parents." *Family Relations* 51 (3): 215-220.

Biskupic, Joan. 2003. "Same-sex Couples Are Redefining Family Law in USA." *USA Today.* Feb. 18.

Bjornsen, Sally. 2005. *The Single Girl's Guide to Marrying a Man, His Kids, and His Ex-Wife: Becoming a Stepmother with Humor and Grace.* New York: New American Library.

Black, Dan, Gary Gates, Seth Sanders, and Lowell Taylor. 2000. "Demographics of the Gay and Lesbian Population in the United States: Evidence from Available Systematic Data Sources." *Demography* 37: 139–54.

"Black Parents Fight Racial Discrimination in Schools." 2004. *PR Web.* July 27. http://www.prweb.com/releases/2004

Blackwell, Debra L. 1998. "Marital Homogamy in the United States: The Influence of Individual and Paternal Education." *Social Science Research* 27 (2): 159–64.

Blair, Sampson Lee, and Michael P. Johnson. 1992. "Wives' Perceptions of the Fairness of the Division of Household Labor: The Intersection of Housework and Ideology." *Journal of Marriage and Family* 54 (3): 570–81.

Blakely, Mary Kay. 1995. "An Outlaw Mom Tells All." *Ms.* January/February: 34–45.

Blalock, Lydia B. 2003. "Poverty Exacerbates Work/Family Tensions." *Family Focus.* June: F11-F13.

Blalock, Lydia L., Vicky R. Tiller, and Pamel A. Monroe. 2004. " 'They Get You Out of Courage:' Persistent Deep Poverty among Former Welfare-Resilient Women." *Family Relations* 53 (2): 127-137.

Blankenhorn, David. 1995. *Fatherless America: Confronting Our Most Urgent Social Problem.* New York: Basic.

Blau, David M., and Philip K. Robins. 1998. "A Dynamic Analysis of Turnover in Employment and Child Care." *Demography* 35 (1): 83–96.

Blau, Melinda. 1993. *Families Apart: Ten Keys to Successful Co-Parenting.* New York: Perigee.

Blecher, Michele. 2001. "Cutting to the Point on Circumcision." *WebMD Medical News.* Sept. 26. http://my.webmd.com/content/article/3609.107.

Blinn-Pike, Lynn. 1999. "Why Abstinent Adolescents Report They Have Not Had Sex: Understanding Sexually Resilient Youth." *Family Relations* 48: 295–301.

Block, Joel D. 2003. *Naked Intimacy: How To Increase True Openness in Your*

Relationship. Chicago: Contemporary Books.

Block, Sandra. 2000. "Golden Years Bleak for Divorcees." *USA Today.* Aug. 8.

———. 2002. "Pet Insurance Can Save Owners from Wrenching Decisions." *USA Today.* Feb. 19.

———. 2003. "Adopting Can Be Expensive, But Tax Credit Jumped to $10,000 in 2002." *USA Today.* Apr. 8.

Blood, Robert O., Jr., and Donald M. Wolfe. 1960. *Husbands and Wives: The Dynamics of Married Living.* New York: Free Press.

Bloomberg News. 2004. "Colorado Reinstates Football Coach Despite Scandal." *New York Times.* May 25.

Bluestone, Cheryl, and Catherine S. Tamis-LeMonda. 1999. "Correlates of Parenting Styles in Predominantly Working- and Middle-Class African American Mothers." *Journal of Marriage and Family* 61 (4): 881–93.

Blum, Deborah. 1997. *Sex on the Brain: The Biological Differences Between Men and Women.* New York: Penguin.

Blumberg, Rae Lesser, and Marion Tolbert Coleman. 1989. "A Theoretical Look at the Gender Balance of Power in the American Couple." *Journal of Family Issues* 10: 225–50.

Blumstein, Philip, and Pepper Schwartz. 1983. *American Couples: Money, Work, Sex.* New York: Morrow.

Bly, Robert. 1990. *Iron John: A Book About Men.* Reading, MA: Addison-Wesley.

Bock, Jane D. 2000. "'Doing the Right Thing?' Single Mothers by Choice and the Struggle for Legitimacy." *Gender and Society* 14: 62-86.

Bogenschneider, Karen. 2000. "Has Family Policy Come of Age? A Decade Review of the State of U.S. Family Policy in the 1990s." *Journal of Marriage and Family* 62: 1136–59.

———. 2002. *Family Policy Matters: How Policymaking Affects Families and What Professionals Can Do.* Mahwah, NJ: Lawrence Erlbaum.

Bogert, Carroll. 1994. "Bringing Back Baby." *Newsweek.* Nov. 21: 78–79.

Bohannan, Paul. 1970a. "Divorce Chains, Households of Remarriage, and Multiple Divorces." Pp. 113–23 in *Divorce and After,* edited by Paul Bohannan. New York: Doubleday.

———. 1970b. "The Six Stations of Divorce." Pp. 29–55 in *Divorce and After,* edited by Paul Bohannan. New York: Doubleday.

Boland, Ed. 2000. "In Modern E-Mail Romances, 'Trash' Is Just a Click Away." *New York Times.* Oct. 19.

Bold, Mary. 2001. "Impact of Computer-Mediated Communication on Families." *Family Focus* (Mar.): F16–F17.

Booth, Alan, and Paul R. Amato. 1994a. "Parental Gender Role Nontraditionalism and Offspring Outcomes." *Journal of Marriage and Family* 56 (4): 865–77.

———. 1994b. "Parental Marital Quality, Parental Divorce, and Relations with Parents." *Journal of Marriage and Family* 56 (1): 21–34.

———. 2001. "Parental Predivorce Relations and Offspring Post-Divorce Well-Being." *Journal of Marriage and the Family* 63: 197-212.

Booth, Alan, Karen Carver, and Douglas A. Granger. 2000. "Biosocial Perspectives on the Family." *Journal of Marriage and Family* 62 (4): 1018–34.

Booth, Alan, and Ann C. Crouter. 2002. *Just Living Together: Implications of Cohabitation for Children, Families, and Social Policy.* Mahwah, NJ: Lawrence Erlbaum.

Booth, Alan, Ann C. Crouter, and Mari Clements. 2001. *Couples in Conflict.* Mahwah, NJ: Lawrence Erlbaum.

Booth, Alan, Ann C. Crouter, and Michael J. Shanahan. 1999. *Transition to Adulthood in a Changing Economy: No Work, No Family, No Future?* Westport, CT: Praeger

Booth, Alan, and James Dabbs. 1993. "Testosterone and Men's Marriages." *Social Forces* 72: 463–77.

Booth, Alan, and John N. Edwards. 1992. "Starting Over: Why Remarriages Are More Unstable." *Journal of Family Issues* 13 (2) (June): 179–94.

Booth, Alan, David R. Johnson, Lynn K. White, and John N. Edwards. 1985. "Predicting Divorce and Separation." *Journal of Family Issues* 6: 331–46.

———. 1995. "Marital Instability over the Life Course [United States]: A Three Wave Panel Study 1980- 88." (2nd ICPSR ed.) Computer file. Ann Arbor MI: Interuniversity Consor-

tium for Political And Social Research.

Booth, Alan, and Ann C. Crouter, editors. 1998. *Men in Families: When Do They Get Involved? What Difference Does It Make?* Mahwah, NJ: Erlbaum.

———. 2001. *Does It Take A Village?: Community Effects on Children, Adolescents, and Families.* Mahwah NJ: Lawrence Erlbaum.

———. 2002. *Just Living Together: Implications of Cohabitation on Families, Children, and Social Policy.* Mahwah NJ: Lawrence Erlbaum.

Booth, Alan, Ann C. Crouter, and Michael J. Shanahan, editors. 1999. *Transitions to Adulthood in a Changing Economy: No Work, No Family, No Future?* Westport, CT: Praeger.

Booth, Cathy. 1977. "Wife-Beating Crosses Economic Boundaries." *Rocky Mountain News.* June 17.

Boraas, Stephanie, and William R. Rodgers, III. 2003. "How Does Gender Play A Role In the Earnings Gap? An Update." *Monthly Labor Review.* Mar. 2003: 9-15.

Borello, Gloria M., and Bruce Thompson. 1990. "A Note Regarding the Validity of Lee's Typology of Love." *Journal of Psychology* 124: 639–44.

"Born Again Adults Less Likely to Cohabit, Just as Likely to Divorce." 2001. Ventura, CA: Barna Research Group (Barna Research Online). Aug. 6. www.barna.org/ cgi-binPagePressRelease.

"Born Again Adults Remain Firm in Opposition to Abortion and Gay Marriage." 2001. Ventura, CA: Barna Research Group (Barna Research Online). July 23. www.barna.org/cgi-bin/PagePressRelease

Bornstein, Marc H., and Robert H. Bradley (eds.). 2003. *Socioeconomic Status, Parenting, and Child Development.* Mahwah, NJ: Lawrence Erlbaum.

Boss, Pauline. 1997. "Ambiguity: A Factor in Family Stress Management." University of Minnesota Extension Service. http://www.extension.umn.edu.

———. 1980. "Normative Family Stress: Family Boundary Changes Across the Lifespan." *Family Relations* 29: 445–52.

———. 1999. *Ambiguous Loss: Learning to Live with Unresolved Grief.* Cambridge, MA: Harvard University Press.

———. 2002. *Family Stress Management, 2nd edition.* Newbury Park, CA: Sage.

Boss, Pauline, and Carol Mulligan (Eds.). 2003. *Family Stress: Classic and Contemporary Readings.* Thousand Oaks, CA: Sage.

Bossard, James H., and E. S. Boll. 1943. *Family Situations.* Philadelphia: University of Pennsylvania Press.

Bost, Kelly K., Martha J. Cox, and Chris Payne. 2002. "Structural and Supportive Changes in Couples' Family and Friendship Networks Across the Transition to Parenthood." *Journal of Marriage and Family* 64 (2): 517–531.

Boss, Pauline G., William J. Doherty, Ralph La Rossa, Walter R. Schumm, and Suzanne K. Steinmentz, editors. 1993. *Sourcebook of Family Theories and Methods.* New York: Plenum.

Boston Women's Health Book Collective. 1998. *Our Bodies, Ourselves for the New Century.* New York: Touchstone/Simon & Schuster.

Bouchard, Emily. Nd. "Navigating Parenting Differences." SelfGrowth.com. http://www.selfgrowth.com/articles/Bouchard2.html. Retrieved 9/21/04.

Bouchard, Genevieve, Yvan Lussier, and Stephane Sabourin. 1999. "Personality and Marital Adjustment: Utility of the Five-Factor Model of Personality." *Journal of Marriage and Family* 61 (3): 651–60.

Bould, Sally. 2003. "Caring Neighborhoods: Bringing Up the Kids Together." *Journal of Family Issues* 24: 427-447.

Bouton, Katherine. 1987. "Fertility and Family." *Ms.* April: 92.

Bowen, Gary L., Jay A. Mancini, James A. Martin, William B. Ware, and John P. Nelson. 2003. "Promoting the Adaptation of Military Families: An Empirical Test of a Community Practice Model." *Family Relations* 52 (1): 33-44.

Bower, Bruce. 1995. "Depression: Rates in Women, Men . . . and Stress Effects Across Sexes." *Science News* 147 (22): 346.

Bowers v. Hardwick. 1986. 478 U.S. 186, 92 L.Ed.2d 140, 106 S. Ct. 2841.

Bowers, Susan P. 1999. "Gender Role Identity and the Caregiving Experience of Widowed Men." *Sex Roles* 41 (9/10): 645–55.

Bowlby, John. 1951. *Maternal Care and Mental Health.* Geneva: World Health Organization.

———. 1969. *Attachment and Loss.* New York: Basic.

———. 1982. *Attachment and Loss*, 2nd ed. New York: Basic.

Bowser, Benjamin P. 1999. "African-American Male Sexuality Through the Early Life Course." Pp. 127–50 in *Sexuality Across the Life Course*, edited by Alice S. Rossi. Chicago: University of Chicago Press.

Bradbury, Thomas N., Frank D. Fincham, and Steven R. H. Beach. 2000. "Research on the Nature and Determinants of Marital Satisfaction: A Decade in Review." *Journal of Marriage and Family* 62 (4): 964–80.

Bragonier, David, and Debbie Bragonier. 2003. *Getting Your Financial House in Order: A Floorplan for Managing Your Money.* Nashville, TN: Broadman & Holman.

Bramlett, Matthew D., and William D. Mosher. 2001. "First Marriage Dissolution, Divorce, and Remarriage: United States." Advance Data from Vital and Health Statistics, no. 323. Hyattsville, MD: National Center for Health Statistics.

Branden, Nathaniel. 1988. "A Vision of Romantic Love." Pp. 218–31 in *The Psychology of Love*, edited by Robert J. Sternberg and Michael L. Barnes. New Haven, CT: Yale University Press.

———. 1994. *Six Pillars of Self-Esteem.* New York: Bantam.

Braschi v. Stahl Associates Company. 1989. 74 N.Y. 2d 201.

Braver, Sanford E., Ira M. Ellman, and William V. Fabricius. 2003. "Relocation of Children after Divorce and Children's Best Interests: New Evidence and Legal Considerations." *Journal of Family Psychology* 17: 206–219.

Braver, Sanford L., Pamela J. Fitzpatrick, and R. Curtis Bay. 1991. "Noncustodial Parent's Report of Child Support Payments." *Family Relations* 40 (2): 180–85.

Bray, James H. 1999. "From Marriage to Remarriage and Beyond." Pp. 253–71 in *Coping with Divorce, Single Parenting and Remarriage*, edited by E. Mavis Hetherington. Mahwah, NJ: Erlbaum.

Brazelton, T. Berry. 1997. "Building A Better Self-Image." *Newsweek Special Issue.* (Spring/Summer): 76–79.

Brazelton, T. Berry, and Stanley Greenspan. 2000. "Our Window to the Future." *Newsweek Special Issue.* Fall/Winter: 34–36.

Brehm, Sharon S., Rowland S. Miller, Daniel Perlman, and Susan M. Campbell. 2002. *Intimate Relationships*, 3rd ed. New York: McGraw-Hill.

Brennan, Robert T., Rosalind Chait Barnett, and Karen C. Gareis. 2001. "When He Earns More Than She Does: A Longitudinal Study of Dual Earner Couples." *Journal of Marriage and Family* 63: 168–80.

Brickley, Margie, Aimee Gelnaw, Hilary Marsh, and Daniel Ryan. 1999. *Opening Doors: Lesbian and Gay Parents and Schools.* Educational Advocacy Committee of the Family Pride Coalition. http://www.familypride.org

Brien, Michael J., Lee A. Lillard, and Linda J. Waite. 1999. "Interrelated Family-Building Behaviors: Cohabitation, Marriage, and Nonmarital Conception." *Demography* 36 (4): 535–51.

Brind, Joel. 2002. "Abortion and Breast Cancer: National Cancer Institute's Disinformation Halted." *National Right to Life News.* July. P. 12.

Brines, Julie. 1994. "Economic Dependency, Gender, and the Division of Labor at Home." *American Journal of Sociology* 100 (3): 652–88.

Brines, Julie, and Kara Joyner. 1999. "The Ties That Bind: Principles of Cohesion in Cohabitation and Marriage." *American Sociological Review* 64: 333–55.

Britner, Preston. 2004. "Stress and Coping: A Comparison of Self-report measures of Functioning in Families of Young Children with Cerebral Palsy or no Medical Diagnosis." *Journal of Child and Family Studies* 12 (3): 355–348.

Brock, Fred. 2005. *Live Well on Less Than You Think: The New York Times Guide to Achieving Your Financial Freedom.* New York: Times Books.

Brockman, Erin Schoen. 2000. "The Baby and the Bathwater: Birth Methods Then and Now." *New York Times.* June 25.

Broder, John M. 2002. "Family Leave in California Now Includes Pay Benefit." *New York Times.* Sept. 24.

Broderick, Carlfred B. 1979a. *Couples: How to Confront Problems and Maintain Loving Relationships.* New York: Simon & Schuster.

———. 1979b. *Marriage and the Family.* Englewood Cliffs, NJ: Prentice-Hall.

Brodie, Deborah. 1999. *Untying the Knot: Ex-Husbands, Ex-Wives, and Other Experts on the Passage of Divorce.* New York: St. Martin's Griffin.

Brody, Charles J., and Lala Carr Steelman. 1985. "Sibling Structure and Parental Sex-Typing of Children's Household Tasks." *Journal of Marriage and Family* 47 (2): 265–73.

Brody, Jane E. 1991. "Better Conduct? Train Parents, Then Children." *New York Times.* Dec. 3.

———. 2001. "V.I.P. Medical Treatment Adds Meaning to a Dog's (or Cat's) Life." *New York Times.* Aug. 14.

———. 2002. "What Women Must Know about Fertility." *New York Times.* Jan. 1.

———. 2003a. "As Cases of Induced Labor Rise, So Do Experts' Concerns." *New York Times.* Jan. 14.

———. 2003b. "Empowering Children to Thwart Abductors." *New York Times.* Jan. 28.

———. 2003c. "Fact of Life: Condoms Can Keep Disease at Bay." *New York Times.* Jan. 21.

———. 2004a. "Abstinence-Only: Does It Work?" *New York Times.* June 3.

———. 2004b. "Prenatal Tests: More Information, Less Risk." *New York Times.* July. 27.

———. 2004c. "The Politics of Emergency Contraception." *New York Times.* Aug. 24.

———. 2004d. "The Risks and Demands about Pregnancy after 20." *The New York Times.* May 11.

Brody, Leslie. 1999. *Gender, Emotion, and the Family.* Cambridge, MA: Harvard University Press.

Brodzinsky, David M., Daniel. W. Smith, and Anne B. Brodzinsky. 1998. *Children's Adjustment to Adoption.* Thousand Oaks, CA: Sage.

Brooke, Jill. 2002. "A Promise to Love, Honor, and Bear No Children." *New York Times.* Oct. 13.

———. 2004. "Close Encounters With A Home Barely Known." *New York Times.* July 22.

Brooks, Clem. 2002. "Religious Influence and the Politics of Family Decline Concern: Trends, Sources, and U.S. Political Behavior." *American Sociological Review* 67: 191-211.

Brooks, Robert, and Sam Goldstein. 2001. *Raising Resilient Children: Fostering Strength, Hope, and Optimism in Your Child.* New York: Contemporary.

Brooks-Gunn, Jeanne, Wen-Jui Han, and Jane Waldfogel. 2002. "Maternal Employment and Child Cognitive Outcomes in the First Three Years of Life: The NICHD Study of Early Child Care." *Child Development* 73: 1052-1072.

Broome, Claire V. 1995. "Change in the Marriage and Divorce Data Available from the National Center for Health Statistics." *Federal Register* 60, No. 241: 64437–38. Dec. 15.

Brown, David. 2002. "Studies: Test-Tube Babies Face Higher Health Risks." *Washington Post.* Mar. 7.

Brown, Jocelyn, Patricia Cohen, Jeffrey G. Johnson, and Suzanne Salzinger. 1998. "A Longitudinal Analysis of Risk Factors for Child Maltreatment: Findings of a 17-Year Prospective Study of Officially Recorded and Self-Reported Child Abuse and Neglect." *Child Abuse & Neglect* 22 (11): 1065–78.

Brown, Pamela D., K. Daniel O'Leary, and Shari R. Feldbau. 1997. "Dropout in a Treatment Program for Self-Referring Wife Abusing Men." *Journal of Family Violence* 12 (4): 365–87.

Brown, Patricia Leigh. 2001. "Heavy Lifting Required: The Return of Manly Men." *New York Times.* Oct. 28.

Brown, Susan L. 2000. "Fertility Following Marital Dissolution: The Role of Cohabitation." *Journal of Family Issues* 21: 501–524.

———. 2003. "Relationship Quality Dynamics of Cohabiting Unions." *Journal of Family Issues* 24 (5): 583–601.

———. 2004. "Family Structure and Child Well-Being: The Significance of Parental Cohabitation." *Journal of Marriage and Family* 66 (2): 351–367.

Brownell, Patricia J. 1998. *Family Crimes against the Elderly: Elder Abuse and the Criminal Justice System.* New York: Taylor and Francis.

Browning, Christopher R., and Edward O. Laumann. 1997. "Sexual Contact Between Children and Adults: A Life Course Perspective." *American Sociological Review* 62: 540–60.

Brownridge, Douglas A., and Shiva Halli. 2002. "Understanding Male Partner Violence Against Cohabiting and Married Women: An Empirical Investigation with a Synthesized Model." *Journal of Family Violence* 17 (4): 341-361.

Brubaker, Ellie, Mary Anne Gorman, and Michele Hiestand. 1990. "Stress Perceived by Elderly Recipients of Family Care." Pp. 267–81 in *Family Relationships in Later Life,* 2d ed., edited by Timothy H. Brubaker. Newbury Park, CA: Sage.

Brubaker, Timothy H. 1991. "Families in Later Life: A Burgeoning Research Area." Pp. 226–48 in *Contemporary Families: Looking Forward, Looking Back,* edited by Alan Booth. Minneapolis: National Council on Family Relations.

Bruno, Beth. 2001. "A New National Holiday: Stepparents Day." Self-Growth.com. http://www.selfgrowth.com/articles/Bruno1.html

Bryant, Adam. 2001. "Drowning in a Sea of Debt." *Newsweek.* Feb. 5: 43.

Bryant, Chalandra M., Rand D. Conger, and Jennifer M. Meehan. 2001. "The Influence of In-Laws on Change in Marital Success." *Journal of Marriage and Family* 63 (3): 614–626.

Bryson, Ken, and Lynne M. Casper. 1999. "Coresident Grandparents and Grandchildren." *Current Population Reports* P23-198. Washington, DC: U.S. Census Bureau.

Bubolz, Margaret M., and M. Suzanne Sontag. 1993. "Human Ecology Theory." Pp. 419–48 in *Sourcebook of Family Theories and Methods: A Contextual Approach,* edited by Pauline G. Boss, William J. Doherty, Ralph LaRossa, Walter R. Schumm, and Suzanne K. Steinmetz. New York: Plenum.

Buchanan, Christy M., Eleanor E. Maccoby, and Sanford M. Dornbusch.

1996. *Adolescents After Divorce.* Cambridge, MA: Harvard University Press.

Budd, Ken. 2002. "Egg Beaters." *AARP* May/June. P. 15.

Budget & Save: Six Steps to Help You Make the Most of Your Income. 2003.Washington, DC: Kiplinger.

Budig, Michelle J., and Paula England. 2001. "The Wage Penalty for Motherhood." *American Sociological Review* 66: 204–55.

Buehler, Cheryl. 1995. "Divorce Law in the United States." Pp. 99–120 in *Families and Law,* edited by Lisa J. McIntyre and Marvin B. Sussman. New York: Hayworth.

Buehler, Cheryl, and Jean M. Gerard. 2002. "Marital Conflict, Ineffective Parenting, and Children's and Adolescents' Maladjustment." *Journal of Marriage and Family* 64 (1)+ 78–92.

Buehler, Cheryl, Ambika Krishnakumar, Gaye Stone, Christine Anthony, Sharon Pemberton, Jean Gerard, and Brian K. Barber. 1998. "Interpersonal Conflict Styles and Youth Problem Behaviors." *Journal of Marriage and Family* 60 (1): 119–32.

Bulanda, Ronald E. 2004. "Paternal Involvement with Children: Influence of Gender Ideologies." *Journal of Marriage and Family* 66 (1: 40–45.

Bulcroft, Kris, Linda Smeins, and Richard Bulcroft. 1999. *Romancing the Honeymoon: Consummating Marriage in Modern Society.* Thousand Oaks, CA: Sage.

Bulcroft, Richard. 2000. "The Management and Production of Risk in Romantic Relationships: A Postmodern Paradox." *Journal of Family History* 25 (1): 63–92.

Bulcroft, Richard, and Jay Teachman. 2004. "Ambiguous Constructions: Development Of a Childless or Child-Free Life Course." Pp. 116–135 in *Handbook of Contemporary Families: Considering the Past: Contemplating the Future,*edited by Marilyn Coleman and Lawrence H. Ganong. Thousand Oaks CA: Sage.

Bumpass, Larry L., and Hsien-Hen Lu. 2000. "Trends in Cohabitation and Implications for Children's Family Contexts in the United States." *Population Studies* 54: 29–41.

Bumpass, Larry L., R. K. Raley, and J. Sweet. 1995. "The Changing Character of Stepfamilies: Implications of Cohabitation and Nonmarital Childbearing." *Demography* 32 (3): 425–36.

Bumpass, Larry L., and James A. Sweet. 1989. "National Estimates of Cohabitation." *Demography* 26:615–625.

Bumpass, Larry L., James A. Sweet, and Andrew Cherlin. 1991. "The Role of Cohabitation in Declining Rates of Marriage." *Journal of Marriage and Family* 53 (4): 913–27.

Bunker, Barbara B., Josephine M. Zubek, Virginia J. Vanderslice, and Robert W. Rice. 1992. "Quality of Life in Dual-Career Families: Commuting Versus Single-Residence Couples." *Journal of Marriage and Family* 54 (3): 399–407.

Burbach, Mary, and Mary Ann Lamanna. 2000. "The Moral Mother: MotherhoodDiscourse in Biological Father and Third Party Cases." *Journal of Law and Family Studies* 2: 153–197.

Burch, Rebecca, and Gordon G. Gallup, Jr. 2004. "Pregnancy as a Stimulus for Domestic Violence." *Journal of Family Violence* 19: 243–247.

Burchell, R. Clay. 1975. "Self-Esteem and Sexuality." *Medical Aspects of Human Sexuality* (Jan.): 74–90.

Burgess, Ernest, and Harvey Locke. 1953 [1945]. *The Family: From Institution to Companionship.* New York: American.

Buriel, Raymond, and Terri DeMent. 1997. "Immigration and Sociocultural Change in Mexican, Chinese, and Vietnamese American Families." Pp. 165–200 in *Immigration and the Family,* edited by Alan Booth, Ann C. Crouter, and Nancy Landale. Mahwah, NJ: Erlbaum.

Burke, Peter J., and Alicia D. Cast. 1997. "Stability and Change in the Gender Identities of Newly Married Couples." *Social Psychology Quarterly* 60 (4): 277–90.

Burns, A., and R. Homel. 1989. "Gender Division of Tasks by Parents and Their Children." *Psychology of Women Quarterly* 13: 113–25.

Burr, Jeffrey A., and Jan E. Mutchler. 1999. "Race and Ethnic Variation in Norms of Filial Responsibility Among Older Persons." *Journal of Marriage and Family* 61 (3): 674–87.

Burr, Wesley R., Shirley Klein, and Marilyn McCubbin. 1995. "Reexamining Family Stress: New Theory and Research." *Journal of Marriage and Family* 57 (3): 835–46.

Burt, Marla S., and Roger B. Burt. 1996. *Stepfamilies: The Step by Step Model of Brief Therapy.* New York: Brunner/Mazel.

Burton, Linda M., and Robin L. Jarrett. 2000. "In the Mix, Yet on the Margins: The Place of Families in Urban Neighborhood and Child Development Research." *Journal of Marriage and Family* 62 (4): 1114–35.

Buscaglia, Leo. 1982. *Living, Loving, and Learning.* New York: Holt, Rinehart & Winston.

Bushman, Brad J., and Roy F. Baumeister. 1998. "Threatened Egoism, Narcissism, Self-Esteem, and Direct and Displaced Aggression: Does Self-Love or Self-Hate Lead to Violence?" *Journal of Personality and Social Psychology* 75 (1): 219–30.

Buss, D. M. 1994. *The Evolution of Desire: Strategies of Human Mating.* New York: Basic.

Buss, D. M., Todd K. Shackelford, Lee A. Kirkpatrick, and Randy J. Larsen. 2001. "A Half Century of Mate Preferences: The Cultural Evolution of Values." *Journal of Marriage and Family* 63 (2): 491–503.

Bussey, K., and A. Bandura. 1999. "Social Cognitive Theory of Gender Development and Differentiation." *Psychological Review* 106: 676–713.

Buttry, Stephen. 2001a. "Girl Embraces America, Refusing to Marry at 11." *Omaha World-Herald.* Mar. 11.

———. 2001b. "An Unhappy Marriage: Sudanese Custom, U.S. Law." *Omaha World-Herald.* Mar. 11.

Buunk, Bram. 1991. "Jealousy in Close Relationships: An Exchange Theoretical Perspective." Pp. 148–77 in *The Psychology of Jealousy and Envy,* edited by Peter Salovey. New York: Guilford.

Buunk, Bram, and Wim Mutsaers. 1999. "Equity Perceptions and Marital Satisfaction in Former and Current Marriage: A Study Among the Remarried." *Journal of Social and Personal Relationships* 16 (1): 123–32.

Butz, Tim. 2004. "Marital Amendment Would Discriminate." *Omaha World-Herald.* March 12.

Buxton, Amity Pierce. 1991. *The Other Side of the Closet: The Coming–Out Crisis for Straight Spouses.* Santa Monica, CA: IBS.

Buzawa, Eve S., and Carl G. Buzawa. 1990. *Domestic Violence: The Criminal Justice Response.* Newbury Park, CA: Sage.

Byers, E. S., S. Demmons, and K. Lawrance. 1998. "Sexual Satisfaction in Dating Relationships: A Test of the Interpersonal Exchange Model of Sexual Satisfaction." *Journal of Social and Personal Relationships* 15: 257–67.

Cahan, Vicky. 2001. "Dramatic Decline in Disability Continues for Older Americans." Bethesda MD: National Institute on Aging. May 7.

Caldera, Y. M., A. C. Huston, and M. O'Brien. 1989. "Social Interactions and Play Patterns of Parents and Toddlers with Feminine, Masculine, and Neutral Toys." *Child Development* 60: 70–76.

Caldwell, John, Indra Gajanayake, Bruce Caldwell, and Pat Caldwell. 1993. "Marriage Delay and the Fertility Decline in Sri Lanka." Pp. 140–46 in *Next of Kin: An International Reader on Changing Families,* edited by Lorne Tepperman and Susannah J. Wilson. Englewood Cliffs, NJ: Prentice Hall.

Call, Vaughn, Susan Sprecher, and Pepper Schwartz. 1995. "The Incidence and Frequency of Marital Sex in a National Sample." *Journal of Marriage and Family* 57 (3): 639–52.

Camarena, Phame M., Kris Minor, Theresa Melmer, and Cheryl Ferrie. 1998. "The Nature and Support of Adolescent Mothers' Life Aspirations." *Family Relations* 47 (2): 129–37.

Campbell, Marian L., and Phyllis Moen. 1992. "Job–Family Role Strain Among Employed Single Mothers of Preschoolers." *Family Relations* 41 (2) (Apr.): 205–11.

Campbell, Susan. 1991. "Male Day-Care Workers Face Prejudice." *Omaha World-Herald.* July 14.

———. 2004. *Truth in Dating: Finding Love by Getting Real.* Tiburon, CA: H.J. Kramer/ New World Library.

Canary, D. J., and K. Dindia. 1998. *Sex Differences and Similarities in Communication.* Mahwah, NJ: Erlbaum.

Canary, D. J., and Tara M. Emmers-Sommer. 1997. *Sex and Gender Differences in Personal Relationships.* New York: Guilford.

Canary, D. J., Laura Stafford, and Beth A. Semic. 2002. "A Panel Study of the Associations Between Maintenance Strategies and Relational Characteristics." *Journal of Marriage and Family* 64 (2): 395–406.

Canavan, Margaret M., Walter J. Meyer, III, and Deborah C. Higgs. 1992. "The Female Experience of Sibling Incest." *Journal of Marital and Family Therapy* 18 (2): 129–42.

Cancian, Francesca M. 1985. "Gender Politics: Love and Power in the Private and Public Spheres." Pp. 253–64 in *Gender and the Life Course,* edited by Alice S. Rossi. New York: Aldine.

———. 1987. *Love in America: Gender and Self-Development.* New York: Cambridge University Press.

Cancian, Francesca M., and Stacey J. Oliker. 2000. *Caring and Gender.* Walnut Creek, CA: AltaMira.

Canedy, Dana. 2001. "Often Conflicted, Hispanic Girls Are Dropping Out at High Rates." *New York Times.* Mar. 25.

Cann, Arnie, Jessica L. Mangum, and Marissa Wells. 2001. "Distress in Response to Relationship Infidelity: The Roles of Gender Attitudes about Relationships." *The Journal of Sex Research* 38 (3): 186–191.

Cannon, Angie. 2004. "A Legal Maze—And More to Come." *U.S. News & World Report.* March 8.

Cano, Annmarie, and K. Daniel O'Leary. 1997. "Romantic Jealousy and Affairs: Research and Implications for Couple Therapy." *Journal of Sex & Marital Therapy* 23 (4): 249–75.

Cantor, M. H. 1979. "Neighbors and Friends: An Overlooked Resource in the Informal Support System." *Research on Aging* 1: 434–63.

Caputo, Richard K. 2001. "Grandparents and Coresident Grandchildren in a Youth Cohort." *Journal of Family Issues* 22 (5): 541–56.

Carey v. Population Services International. 1977. 431 U.S. 678, 52 L.Ed.2d 675, 97 S.Ct. 2010.

Carlson, Margaret. 1990. "Abortion's Hardest Cases." *Time.* July 9: 22–25.

Carnoy, Martin, and David Carnoy. 1995. *Fathers of a Certain Age: The Joys and Problems of Middle-Aged Fatherhood.* Minneapolis: Fairview Press.

Carpenter, Laura M., Constance A. Nathanson, and J. Kim Young. 2002. "Gender and Sexual Satisfaction in Midlife." Paper presented at the annual meeting of the American Sociological Association. Chicago. August 17.

Carter, Betty. 1991. "Children's TV, Where Boys Are King." *New York Times.* May 1: A1, C18.

Carter, Betty, and Monica McGoldrick. 1988. *The Changing Family Life Cycle: A Framework for Family Therapy,* 2nd ed. New York: Gardner.

———. (Eds.). 1999. *The Expanded Family Life Cycle: Individual, Family, and Social Perspectives,* 3rd ed. Boston: Allyn and Bacon.

Carter, Steven. 2001. *This Is How Love Works: 9 Essential Secrets You Need to Know.* NY: M. Evans and Co.

Casey, Terri. 1998. *Pride and Joy: The Lives and Passions of Women Without Children.* Hillsboro OR: Beyond Words.

Casper, Lynne M., and Martin O'Connell. 1998. "Work, Income, the Economy, and Married Fathers as Child-Care Providers." *Demography* 35 (2): 243–50.

Casper, Lynne M., and Kristen E. Smith. 2002. "Dispelling the Myths: Self-Care, Class, and Race." *Journal of Family Issues* 23: 716–727.

Cass, Vivienne C. 1984. "Homosexuality Identity Formation: Testing a Theoretical Model." *Journal of Sex Research* 20: 143–67.

Castro Martin, Teresa, and Larry Bumpass. 1989. "Trends in Marital Disruption." *Demography* 26: 37–52.

Ceballo, Rosario, Jennifer E. Lansford, Antonia Abbey, and Abigail J. Stewart. 2004. "Gaining a Child: Comparing the Experiences of biological Parents, Adoptive parents, and Stepparents." *Family Relations* 53 (1): 38-48. "Census Data in 2 States Show More Same-Sex Couple Homes." 2001. *Omaha World-Herald.* June 13.

Center for the Advancement of Women. 2003. *Progress and Perils: New Agenda for Women.* www.advancewomen.org.

Chadiha, Letha A., Jane Rafferty, and Joseph Pickard. 2003. "The Influence of Caregiving Stressors, Social Support, and Caregiving Appraisal on Marital Functioning Among African American Wife Caregivers." *Journal of Marital and Family Therapy* 29 (4): 479–490.

Chafetz, Janet Saltzman. 1988. "The Gender Division of Labor and the Reproduction of Female Disadvantage: Toward an Integrated Theory." *Journal of Family Issues* 9: 108–31.

———. 1989. "Marital Intimacy and Conflict: The Irony of Spousal Equality." Pp. 149–56 in *Women: A Feminist Perspective*, 4th ed., edited by Jo Freeman. Mountain View, CA: Mayfield.

Chambers, Veronica. 2003. *Having It All? Black Women and Success.* New York: Doubleday.

Chan, Raymond W., Barbara Raboy, and Charlotte J. Patterson. 1998. "Psychosocial Adjustment among Children Conceived Via Donor Insemination by Lesbian and Heterosexual Mothers." *Child Development* 69: 443–457.

Chandra, Anjani, Joyce Abma, Penelope Maza, and Christine Bachrach. 1999. *Adoption, Adoption Seeking, and Relinquishment for Adoption in the United States.* Advance Data No. 306. May 11. Hyattsville, MD: National Center for Health Statistics.

Chandra, Anjani, and Elizabeth Hervey Stephen. 1998. "Impaired Fecundity in the United States: 1982–1995." *Family Planning Perspectives* 30 (1): 35–42.

Chang, True See. 1999. "Analytical Paper—Classical Theory: Gemeinschaft to Gesellschaft." Unpublished student paper.

Chao, R. K. 1994. "Beyond Parental Control and Authoritarian Parenting Style: Understanding Chinese Parenting Through the Cultural Notion of Training." *Child Development* 65 (4): 1111–19.

Chapman, Steve. 2004. "Surprise: No Fault Divorce May Strengthen Marriage." *Chicago Tribune.* April 2.

Chappell, Crystal Lee Hyun Joo. 1996. "Korean-American Adoptees Organize for Support." *Minneapolis Star Tribune.* Dec. 29: E7.

Chavez, L. R. 1992. *Shadowed Lives: Undocumented Immigrants in American Society.* Fort Worth, TX: Holt, Rinehart, Winston.

Cherlin, Andrew J. 1978. "Remarriage as Incomplete Institution." *American Journal of Sociology* 84: 634–50.

———. 1981. *Marriage, Divorce, Remarriage.* Cambridge, MA: Harvard University Press.

———. 1999. "Going to Extremes: Family Structure, Children's Well-Being, and Social Science." *Demography* 36: 421–28.

———. 2000. "Generation Ex-." *The Nation.* Dec. 11. www.thenation.com.

Cherlin, Andrew J., and Aphichat Chamratrithirong. 1993. "Variations in Marriage Patterns in Central Thailand." Pp. 84–89 in *Next of Kin: An International Reader on Changing Families*, edited by Lorne Tepperman and Susannah J. Wilson. Englewood Cliffs, NJ: Prentice Hall.

Cherlin, Andrew J., and Frank F. Furstenberg, Jr. 1986. *The New American Grandparent: A Place in the Family, A Life Apart.* New York: Basic.

———. 1994. "Stepfamilies in the United States: A Reconsideration." *Annual Review of Sociology* 20: 359–81.

Chiang, Harriet, and Steve Rubenstein. 2004. "Mad Dash to Get Hitched at City Hall." *San Francisco Chronicle.* February 14.

"Child Care." 2000. *Time.* Apr. 17.

"Child Care NOW." 1998. Children's Defense Fund. Mar. 9. http.www.childrensdefense.org.

Child Support Amendments. 1984. PL 98-378. Washington DC: U.S. Congress.

"Child Support Collected: DHHS Press Release." 1995. *Family Law List.* Familylaw 1@1awlib.wuacc.edu

"Child Support Enforcement: A Fact Sheet for Personal Responsibility and the Work Opportunity Act of 1996 (HR 3734)." 1996. Stanislaus County, CA: Stanislaus County Community Summit.

Children's Defense Fund. 1998. *The State of America's Children, Yearbook 1998.* Washington, DC: CDF.

Childress, Sarah. 2003. "9/11's Hidden Toll." *Newsweek.* Aug. 4. P. 37.

Chilman, Catherine Street. 1978. "Families of Today." Paper presented at the Building Family Strengths Symposium, University of Nebraska, Lincoln, May.

Chira, Susan. 1994. "Hispanic Families Avoid Using Day Care, Study Says." *New York Times.* Apr. 6.

———. 2002. "Woman's Work." *New York Times Book Review.* June 9. P. 16.

Chivers, C. J. 1999. "Fighting Trend, Women Choose to Bear with Pain." *New York Times.* Oct. 18.

Chodorow, Nancy. 1978. *The Reproduction of Mothering: Psychoanalysis and the Sociology of Gender.* Berkeley: University of California Press.

Choi, Namkee G. 1992. "Correlates of the Economic Status of Widowed and Divorced Elderly Women." *Journal of Family Issues* 13 (1): 38–54.

Choice, Pamela, and Leanne K. Lamke. 1997. "A Conceptual Approach to Understanding Abused Women's Stay/Leave Decisions." *Journal of Family Issues* 18: 290–314.

"Chorionic Villus Sampling." WebMD. www.webmd.com.

Christensen, Andres, and Neil Jacobson. 1999. *Reconcilable Differences.* London: Guilford Press.

———. 2004. Reconsilable Differences. NY: Guilford Press.

Christensen, Kathleen E., and Graham L. Staines. 1990. "Flextime: A Viable Solution to Work/Family Conflict?" *Journal of Family Issues* 11 (4): 455–76.

Christiansen, Shawn L., and Rob Palkovitz. 2001. "Why the 'Good Provider' Role Still Matters: Providing as a Form of Paternal Involvement." *Journal of Family Issues* 22: 84–106.

Christopher, F. Scott, and Susan Sprecher. 2000. "Sexuality in Marriage, Dating, and Other Relationships." *Journal of Marriage and Family* 62: 999–1017.

Ciaramigoli, Arthur P., and Katherine Ketcham. 2000. *The Power of Empathy: A Practical Guide to Creating Intimacy, Self-Understanding, and Lasting Love in Your Life.* New York: Dutton.

Cicirelli, Victor G. 2000. "An Examination of the Trajectory of the Adult Child's Caregiving for an Elderly Parent." *Family Relations* 49 (2): 169–75.

"Civil Marriage and Freedom of Religion." 2003. Gay & Lesbian Advocates & Defenders (GLAD). http://www.glad.org/Publications/CivilRightsProject/

Clarke, Sally C. 1995. "Advance Report of Final Marriage Statistics, 1989 and 1990." *Monthly Vital Statistics Report* 43 (12), July 14. U.S. Department of Health and Human Services, National Center for Health Statistics.

Claxton-Oldfield, Stephen. 2003. "Child Abuse in Stepfather Families." *Journal of Divorce and Remarriage* 40 (1): 17–35.

Claxton-Oldfield, Stephen, Carla Goodyear, Tina Parsons, and Jane Claxton-Oldfield. 2002. "Some Possible Implications of Negative Stepfather Stereotypes." *Journal of Divorce and Remarriage.* Spring-Summer: 77–89.

Clayton, Obie, and Joan Moore. 2003. "The Effects of Crime and Imprisonment on Family Formation." Pp. 84–201 in *Black Fathers in Contemporary American Society: Strengths, Weaknesses, and Strategies for Change*, edited by Obie Clayton, Ronald B. Mincy, and David Blankenhorn. New York: Russell Sage.

Clemetson, Lynette. 2000. "Love Without Borders." *Newsweek.* Sept. 18: 62.

———. 2003. "Poor Workers Finding Modest Housing Unaffordable, Study Says." *New York Times.* Sept. 9.

Climo, Jacob. 1992. *Distant Parents.* New Brunswick, NJ: Rutgers University Press.

Clinton, Hillary Rodham. 1990. "In France, Day Care Is Every Child's Right." *New York Times.* Apr. 7.

Cloud, John. 2004. "The Battle over Gay Marriage." *Time.* February 16: 56–64.

Clymer, Adam. 2002. "U.S. Revises Sex Information, And A Fight Goes On." *New York Times.* December 27.

Cobb, Nathan P. Jeffry H. Larson, and Wendy L. Watson. 2003. "Development of the Attitudes about Romance and Mate Selection Scale." *Family Relations* 52 (3): 222–231. Coburn, Jennifer. 1999. "Motherhood a Key Feminist Issue." *Omaha World-Herald.* Apr. 9.

Cochran, Susan D., and Vicki M. Mays. 1999. "Sociocultural Factors in the Black Gay Male Experience." Pp. 349–56 in *The Black Family: Essays and Studies*, 6th ed., edited by Robert Staples. Belmont, CA: Wadsworth.

Coffman, Ginger, and Carol Markstrom-Adams. 1995. "A Model for Parent Education Among Incarcerated Adults." Paper Presented at the Annual Meetings of the National Council on Family Relations, Portland, Ore., November 15–19.

Cohan, Catherine L., and Stacey Kleinbaum. 2002. "Toward a Greater Understanding of the Cohabitation Effect: premarital Cohabitation and Marital Communication." *Journal of Marriage and Family* 64 (1): 180–192.

Cohen, Joyce. 2001a. "He-Mails, She-Mails: Where Sender Meets Gender." *New York Times.* May 17.

———. 2001b. "On the Internet, Love Really Is Blind." *New York Times.* Jan. 18.

Cohen, Philip N., and Lynne M. Casper. 2002. "In Whose Home? Multigenerational Families in the United States, 1998–2000." *Sociological Perspectives* 45 (1): 1–20.

Cole, Charles Lee, and Anna L. Cole. 1999. "Boundary Ambiguities That Bind Former Spouses Together After the Children Leave Home in Post-Divorce Families." *Family Relations* 48 (3): 271–72.

Cole, Thomas. 1983. "The 'Enlightened' View of Aging." *Hastings Center Report* 13: 34–40.

Coleman, Marilyn, and Lawrence H. Ganong. 1997. "Stepfamilies from the Stepfamily's Perspective." Pp. 107–22 in *Stepfamilies: History, Research, and Policy*, edited by Irene Levin and Marvin B. Sussman. New York: Haworth.

Coleman, Marilyn, Lawrence H. Ganong, and Susan M. Cable. 1997. "Beliefs About Women's Intergenerational Family Obligations to Provide Support Before and After Divorce and Remarriage." *Journal of Marriage and Family* 59 (1): 165–76.

Coleman, Marilyn, Lawrence Ganong, and Mark Fine. 2000. "Reinvestigating Remarriage: Another Decade of Progress." *Journal of Marriage and Family* 62: 1288–1307.

Coleman, Priscilla, and Anne Watson. 2000. "Infant Attachment as a Dynamic System." *Human Development* 43: 295–313.

Coles, Clifton. 2004. "Odd Working Hours Cause Family Stress: Need for Night and Weekend Shift Workers Continues to Rise." *The Futurist* 38 (3): 9-10.

Collaborative Group on Hormonal Factors in Breast Cancer. 2004. "Breast Cancer and Abortion: Collaborative Reanalysis of Data from 53 Epidemiological Studies, including 83,000 Women with Breast Cancer from 16 Countries." *Lancet* 363 (9414): 1007–1016.

Collins, Nancy L., and Brooke C. Feeney. 2000. "A Safe Haven: An Attachment Theory Perspective on Support Seeking and Caregiving in Intimate Relationships." *Journal of Social and Personal Relationships* 78 (6): 1053–73.

Collins, Patricia Hill. 1999. "Shifting the Center: Race, Class, and Feminist Theorizing About Motherhood." Pp. 197–217 in *American Families: A Multicultural Reader*, edited by Stephanie Coontz. New York: Routledge.

Collins, Randall, and Scott Coltrane. 1995. *Sociology of Marriage and the Family: Gender, Love, and Property*, 4th ed. Chicago: Nelson-Hall.

Collins, W. A. 1990. "Parent–Child Relationships in the Transition to Adolescence: Continuity and Change in Interaction, Affect and Cognition." Pp. 85–106 in *From Childhood to Adolescence: A Transitional Period? Advances in Adolescent Development*, vol. 2, edited by R. Montemayor, G. R. Adams, and T. P. Gullotta. Newbury Park, CA: Sage.

Colombo, Luann. 1999. *How to Have Sex in the Woods.* New York: Random House.

Coltrane, Scott. 1990. "Birth Timing and the Division of Labor in Dual-Earner Families: Exploratory Findings and Suggestions for Further Research." *Journal of Family Issues* 11: 157–81.

———. 1996. *Family Man: Fatherhood, Housework, and Gender Equity.* New York: Oxford.

———. 2000. "Research on Household Labor: Modeling and Measuring the Social Embeddedness of Routine

Family Work." *Journal of Marriage and Family* 62: 1208–33.

Coltrane, Scott, and Masako Ishii-Kuntz. 1992. "Men's Housework: A Life Course Perspective." *Journal of Marriage and Family* 54 (2): 43–57.

Colvin, Jan, Lillian Chenoweth, Mary Bold, and Cheryl Harding. 2004. "Caregivers of Older Adults: Advantages and Disadvantages of Internet-based Social Support." *Family Relations* 53 (1): 49-57. "Communal Living Returns, This Time with Yuppie Flair." 1998. Associated Press. Feb. 19.

Concise Columbia Encyclopedia. 1994. New York: Columbia University Press.

Condor, Bob. 2000. "Perfect Male: Now Men Are Falling Victim to Media Images of Perfect Bodies." *Chicago Tribune.* Oct. 11.

Conger, Rand D., and Katherine J. Conger. 2002. "Resilience in Midwestern Families: Selected Findings from the First Decade of a Prospective, Longitudinal Study." *Journal of Marriage and Family* 64 (2): 361–373.

Congregation for the Doctrine of the Faith. 1988. "Instruction on Respect for Human Life in Its Origin and on the Dignity of Procreation. Pp. 325–331 in *Moral Issues and Christian Response,* 4th ed. edited by Paul Jersild and Dale A. Johnson. New York: Holt, Rinehart, Winston.

Conlin, Michelle. 2001. "Look Who's Barefoot in the Kitchen." *Business Week. September 17.*

———. 2003a. "The New Gender Gap." *Business Week.* May 26: 75–82.

———. 2003b. "Unmarried America." *Business Week.* Oct. 20: 106–116.

Connell, Joan. 1993. "For Some Muslims, the Holiday Is Difficult." Newhouse News Service. Dec. 18.

Connell, R. W. 1995. *Masculinities.* Berkeley: University of California Press.

Conner, Karen A. 2000. *Continuing to Care: Older Americans and Their Families.* New York: Falmer.

Connidis, Ingrid A. 2001. *Family Ties & Aging.* Thousand Oaks, CA: Sage.

Connidis, Ingrid A., and Lori D. Campbell. 2001. "Closeness, Confiding, and Contact Among Siblings in Middle and Late Adulthood." Pp. 149–55 in *Families in Later Life: Connections and Transitions,* edited by Alexis J. Walker, Margaret Manoogian-O'Dell, Lori A. McGraw, and Diana L. G. White. Thousand Oaks, CA: Pine Forge.

Connidis, Ingrid A., and Julie A. McMullin. 2002a. "Ambivalence, Family Ties, and Doing Sociology." *Journal of Marriage and Family* 64 (3): 594–601.

———. 2002b. "Sociological Ambivalence and Family Ties: A Critical Perspective." *Journal of Marriage and Family* 64 (3): 558–567.

Conway-Giustra, Francine, Ann Crowley, and Stephen H. Gorin. 2002. "Crisis in Caregiving: A Call To Action." *Health and Social Work* 27 (4): 307–312.

Cooley, Charles Horton. 1902. *Human Nature and the Social Order.* New York: Scribner's.

Cooney, Rosemary, Lloyd H. Rogler, Rose Marie Hurrel, and Vilma Ortiz. 1982. "Decision Making in Intergenerational Puerto Rican Families." *Journal of Marriage and Family* 44: 621–31.

Cooney, Teresa M. 1997. "Parent–Child Relations across Adulthood." Pp. 451–68 in *Handbook of Personal Relationships: Theory, Research, and Interventions,* edited by Steve Duck, 2nd edition. New York: Wiley.

Coontz, Stephanie. 1992. *The Way We Never Were: American Families and the Nostalgia Trap.* New York: Basic Books.

———. 1997a. "Divorcing Reality." *The Nation.* Nov. 17: 21–24.

———. 1997b. *The Way We Really Are: Coming to Terms with America's Changing Families.* New York: Basic.

Coordinated Access for Child Care. 2001. "Choosing Quality Child Care." www.cafcc.on.ca.

Corliss, Richard, and Sonia Steptoe. 2004. "The Marriage Savers." *Time.* January 19:

Cose, Ellis. 1994a. "Truths About Spouse Abuse." *Newsweek.* Aug. 8: 49.

———. 1994b. "The Year of the Father." *Newsweek.* Oct. 31: 61.

———. 2000. "The Prison Paradox." *Newsweek.* Nov. 13: 42–49.

Cotton, Sheila R. 1999. "Marital Status and Mental Health Revisited: Examining the Importance of Risk Factors and Resources." *Family Relations* 48 (3): 225–33.

Cotton, Sheila, R., Russell Burton, and Beth Rushing. 2003. "The Mediating Effects of Attachment to Social Structure and Psychosocial Resources on the Relationship Between Marital Quality and Psychological Distress." *Journal of Family Issues* 24 (4): 547–577.

Cottrell, Ann Baker. 1993. "Cross-National Marriages." Pp. 96–103 in *Next of Kin: An International Reader on Changing Families,* edited by Lorne Tepperman and Susannah J. Wilson. New York: Prentice Hall.

Council on Families in America. 1996. "Marriage in America: A Report on the Nation." Pp. 293–318 in *Promises to Keep: Decline and Renewal of Marriage in America,* edited by D. Popenoe, J. B. Elshtain, and D. Blankenhorn. Lanham, MD: Rowman and Littlefield.

"Court Treats Same-sex Breakup as Divorce." 2002. *Seattle Times.* Nov. 3.

"Covenant Marriages Ministry." 1998. http://www.covenantmarriages.com/index2.html.

Coverman, Shelly. 1985. "Explaining Husbands' Participation in Domestic Labor." *Sociological Quarterly* 26 (1): 81–97.

Cowan, C. P., and P. A. Cowan. 1992. *When Partners Become Parents: The Big Life Change for Couples.* New York: Basic.

Cowan, Gloria. 2000. "Beliefs About the Causes of Four Types of Rape." *Sex Roles* 42 (9/10): 807–23.

Cowan, Ruth Schwartz. 1983. *More Work for Mother: The Ironies of Household Technology from the Open Hearth to the Microwave.* New York: Basic.

Cowley, Geoffrey. 1996. "The Biology of Beauty." *Newsweek.* June 3: 61–66.

———. 2000. "For the Love of Language." *Newsweek Special Issue.* Fall/Winter: 12–15.

Cowley, Geoffrey, and Anne Underwood. 1997. "Why Ebonie Can't Breathe." *Newsweek.* May 26: 57–64.

Craig, Stephen. 1992. "The Effect of Television Day Part on Gender Portrayals in Television Commercials: A Content Analysis." *Sex Roles* 26 (5/6): 197–211.

Cramer, Duncan. 2000. "Relationship Satisfaction and Conflict Style in Romantic Relationships." *Journal of Psychology* 134 (3): 337–42.

———. 2003. "Facilitativeness, Conflict, Demand for Approval, Self-esteem, and Satisfaction with Romantic Relationships." *The Journal of Psychology* 137 (1): 85-94.

Cravens, Hamilton. 1997. "Postmodernist Psychobabble: The Recovery Movement for Individual Self-Esteem in Mental Health Since World War II." *Journal of Policy History* 9 (1): 141–53.

Crawford, Duane W., Renate M. Houts, Ted L. Huston, and Laura J. George. 2002. "Compatibility, Leisure, and Satisfaction in Marital Relationships." *Journal of Marriage and Family* 64 (2): 433–449.

Creasey, Gary, Kathy Kershaw, and Ada Boston. 1999. "Conflict Management with Friends and Romantic Partners: The Role of Attachment and Negative Mood Regulation Expectancies." *Journal of Youth and Adolescence* 28 (5): 523–637.

Crittenden, Ann. 2001. *The Price of Motherhood: Why the Most Important Job in the World Is Still Undervalued.* New York: Metropolitan.

Crockett, Roger O. 2003. "For Blacks, Progress without Parity." *Business Week.* July14. www.businessweek.com.

Crohn, Joel. 1995. *Mixed Matches: How to Create Successful Interracial, Interethnic, and Interfaith Relationships.* New York: Fawcett Columbine.

Crosbie-Burnett, Margaret, and Edith Lewis. 1999. "Use of African-American Family Structure and Functioning to Address the Challenges of European-American Post-Divorce Families." Pp. 455–68 in *American Families: A Multicultural Reader*, edited by Stephanie Coontz. New York: Routledge.

Crosby, Faye J. 1991. *Juggling: The Unexpected Advantages of Balancing Career and Home for Women and Their Families.* New York: Free Press.

Crosby, John F. 1991. *Illusion and Disillusion: The Self in Love and Marriage*, 4th ed. Belmont, CA: Wadsworth.

Crosnoe, Robert. 2004. "Social Capital and the Interplay of Families and Schools." *Journal of Marriage and Family* 66 (2): 267–280.

Crossen, Cynthia. 1990. "Baby Ads Spark Debate Over Ethics." *Wall Street Journal.* Dec. 26.

Crouter, Ann C., and Alan Booth. 2003. *Children's Influence on Family Dynamics: The Neglected Side of Family Relationships.* Mahway, NJ: Lawrence Erlbaum Associates.

———. 2004. *Work-Family challenges for Low-Income Parents and Their Children.* Mahway, NJ: Lawrence Erlbaum Associates.

Crouter, Ann C., and Heather Helms-Erikson. 1997. "Work and Family from a Dyadic Perspective: Variations in Inequality." Pp. 487–503 in *Handbook of Personal Relationships: Theory, Research, and Interventions*, edited by Steve Duck, 2nd edition. New York: Wiley.

Crowder, Kyle D., and Stewart E. Tolnay. 2000. "A New Marriage Squeeze for Black Women: The Role of Racial Intermarriage by Black Men." *Journal of Marriage and Family* 62 (3): 792–807.

Crowley, M. Sue. 1998. "Men's Self-perceived Adequacy as the Family Breadwinner: Implications for Their Psychological, Marital, and Work–Family Well-Being." *Journal of Family and Economic Issues* 19 (1): 7–23.

Cuber, John, and Peggy Harroff. 1965. *The Significant Americans.* New York: Random House. (Published also as *Sex and the Significant Americans.* Baltimore: Penguin, 1965.)

Cue, Kelly L., William H. George, and Jeanette Norris. 1996. "Women's Appraisals of Sexual-Assault Risk in Dating Situations." *Psychology of Women Quarterly* 20: 487–504.

Cullen, Lisa T. 2004. "Cupid Academy." *Time.* February 16: 67.

Cummings, E. Mark, Marcie C. Goeke-Morey, Lauren M. Papp, and Tammy L. Dukewich. 2002. "Children's Responses to Mothers' and Fathers' Emotionality and Tactics in Marital Conflict in the Home." *Journal of Family Psychology* 16 (4): 478–492.

Cunningham-Burley, Sarah. 1987. "The Experience of Grandfatherhood." Pp. 91–105 in *Reassessing Fatherhood: New Observations on Fathers and the Modern Family*, edited by Charles Lewis and Margaret O'Brien. Newbury Park, CA: Sage.

———. 2001. "The Experience of Grandfatherhood." Pp. 92–96 in *Families in Later Life: Connections and Transitions*, edited by Alexis J. Walker, Margaret Manoogian-O'Dell, Lori A. McGraw, and Diana L. G. White. Thousand Oaks, CA: Pine Forge.

Curtis, Carla M. 1997. "Factors Influencing Parents' Perceptions of Child Care Services." *Journal of Black Studies* 27 (6): 768–82.

Curtis, Kristen Taylor, and Christopher G. Ellison. 2002. "Religious Heterogamy and Marital Conflict." *Journal of Family Issues* 23 (4): 551–576.

DadStaysHome.com. nd. http://www.dadstayshome.com

Dahms, Alan M. 1976. "Intimacy Hierarchy." Pp. 85–104 in *Process in Relationship: Marriage and Family*, 2d ed., edited by Edward A. Powers and Mary W. Lees. New York: West.

Dailard, Cynthia. 2002. "Abstinence Promotion and Teen Family Planning: The Misguided Drive for Equal Funding." *The Guttmacher Report on Public Policy* 5(1).

———. 2003. "Understanding 'Abstinence': Implications for Individuals, Programs and Policies." *The Guttmacher Report* 6(5). December. www.agi-usa.org.

Dalaker, Joseph. 2001. *Poverty in the United States: 2000.* Current Population Reports P60–214. September. Washington, DC: U.S. Census Bureau.

Dalley, Timothy J. 2004. "Homosexual Parenting: Placing Children at Risk." Family Research Council. March 25. http://www.frc.org

Dalphonse, Sherri. 1997. "Childfree by Choice." *The Washingtonian* 32 (5): 48–57.

Daly, Martin, and Margo I. Wilson. 1994. "Some Differential Attributes of Lethal Assaults on Small Children by Stepfathers Versus Genetic Fathers." *Ethology and Sociobiology* 15: 207–17.

———. 2000. "The Evolutionary Psychology of Marriage and Divorce." Pp. 91–110 in *The Ties That Bind: Perspectives on Marriage and Cohabitation*, edited by Linda J. Waite. New York: Aldine de Gruyter.

Daniel, John. 2001. "Looking After: A Son's Memoir." Pp. 107–109 in *Families in Later Life: Connections and Tran-*

sitions, edited by Alexis J. Walker, Margaret Manoogian-O'Dell, Lori A. McGraw, and Diana L. G. White. Thousand Oaks, CA: Pine Forge.

Daniels, Pamela, and Kathy Weingarten. 1980. "Postponing Parenthood: The Myth of the Perfect Time." *Savvy.* May: 55–60.

D'Antonio, W.V., D.R. Hoge, K. Meyer, and J.D. Davidson. 1999. "American Catholics." *Catholic Reporter.* October 29: 20.

D'Antonio, W.V., James D. Davidson, Dean R. Hoge, and Ruth A. Wallace. 1996. *Laity—American and Catholic—Transforming the Church.* Kansas City: Sheed and Ward.

"The Dark Side of Cyber Romance." 1997. http://www.cvp.com/cyber/badlove. html.

Davey, Adam, and Maximiliane E. Szinovacz. 2004. "Dimensions of Marital Quality and Retirement." *Journal of Family Issues* 25 (4): 431-464.

Davidson, Beverly. 1997. "Service Needs of Relative Caregivers: A Qualitative Analysis." *Families in Society* 78 (5): 502–11.

Davidson, James E., Andrea S. Williams, Richard A. Lamanna, Jan Stenftenagel, Kathleen Maas Weigert, William J. Whalen, and Patricia Wittberg, S.C. 1997. *The Search for Common Ground: What Unites and Divides Catholic Americans.* Huntington, IN: Our Sunday Visitor Publications.

Davidson, Jeannette R. 1992. "Theories About Black–White Interracial Marriage: A Clinical Perspective." *Journal of Multicultural Counseling and Development* 20 (4): 150–57.

Davis, Deborah, and Michael L. Vernon. 2002. "Sculpting the Body Beautiful: Attachment Style, Neuroticism, and the Use of Cosmetic Surgeries. *Sex Roles* 47 (3/4): 129-138.

Davis, Erin Calhoun, and Lisa V. Friel. 2001. "Adolescent Sexuality: Disentangling the Effects of Family Structure and Family Context." *Journal of Marriage and Family* 63 (3): 669–81.

Davis, Fred. 1991. [1963]. *Passage Through Crisis: Polio Victims and Their Families*, 2d ed. New Brunswick, NJ: Transaction.

Davis, James. 1991. *Who Is Black? One Nation's Definition.* University Park: Pennsylvania State University Press.

Dawkins, Richard. 1976. *The Selfish Gene.* New York: Oxford.

Dawson, Deborah A. 1991. "Family Structure and Children's Health and Well-Being: Data from the 1988 National Health Interview Survey on Child Health." *Journal of Marriage and Family* 53 (3): 573–84.

Day, Jennifer Cheeseman, and Eric C. Newburger. 2002. "The Big Payoff: Educational Attainment and Synthetic Estimates of Work-Life Earnings." *Current Population Reports* P23-210. Washington DC: U.S. Census Bureau. July.

Day, Randal D., Gary W. Peterson, and Coleen McCracken. 1998. "Predicting Spanking of Younger and Older Children by Mothers and Fathers." *Journal of Marriage and Family* 60 (1): 79–94.

"Day-Care Researchers in Retreat." 2001. *Omaha World-Herald.* Apr. 26.

de la Cruz, Patricia, and Angela Brittingham. 2003. "The Arab Population: 2000." *Census 2000 Brief* C2KBR 23. Dec.

Deal, Ron L. 2002. *The Smart Step-Family*. Minneapolis, Minn.: Bethany House.

Dear, Greg E., and Clare M. Roberts. 2002. "The Relationships between Codependency and Femininity and Masculinity." *Sex Roles* 46 (5/6): 159–165.

De'Ath, Erica. 1996. "Family Change: Stepfamilies in Context." *Children & Society* 10: 80–82.

Declercq, Eugene, Fay Menacker, and Marian MacDormand. 2004. "Rise in 'No Indicated Risk' Primary Caesareans in the United States, 1991–2001: Cross Sectional Analysis." *British Medical Journal.* doi: 10.1136/bmj.38279.705336OB. *Online First BMJ.com.* Nov. 19.

Deenen, A. A., L. Gijs, and A. X. van Naerssen. 1994. "Intimacy and Sexuality in Gay Male Couples." *Archives of Sexual Behavior* 23 (4): 421–31.

DeFrain, John. 2002. *Creating a Strong Family: American Family Strengths Inventory*. Nebraska Cooperative Extension NF01-498.

http://ianrpubs.unl.edu/family/ nf498.htm

DeLamater, John, and William N. Friedrich. 2002. "Human Sexual Development." *Journal of Sex Research* 39: 10–14.

De Lisi, R., and L. Soundranayagam. 1990. "The Conceptual Structure of Sex Stereotypes in College Students." *Sex Roles* 23: 593–611.

DeMaris, Alfred. 2001. "The Influence of Intimate Violence on Transitions out of Cohabitation." *Journal of Marriage and Family* 63 (1): 235–246.

DeMaris, Alfred, and Steven Swinford. 1996. "Female Victims of Spousal Violence: Factors Influencing Their Level of Fearfulness." *Family Relations* 45 (1): 98–106.

Demian. 2001. "Quick Facts on Legal marriage for Same-Sex Couples." Partners Task force for Gay & Lesbian Couples. http://buddybuddy.com.

———. 2002. "Life Partnerships: The German Approach." Partners Task Force for Gay & Lesbian Couples. http://www.buddybuddy.com/d-p-germ.html

———. 2003a. "Common-Law Marriage States." Partners Task Force for Gay & Lesbian Couples. http://www. buddybuddy.com/common.html

———. 2003b. "Legal Precautions to Protect Your Relationship." Partners Task Force for Gay & Lesbian Couples. http://www.buddybuddy.com/ protect.html

———. 2004a. "Where to Get a Religious Blessing: Gay-Welcoming Denominations in the United States." Partners Task Force for Gay & Lesbian Couples. http://www. buddybuddy.com/blessing.html

———. 2004b. "Legal Marriage Report: Global Status of Legal Marriage." Partners Task Force for Gay & Lesbian Couples. http://www. buddybuddy.com/mar-repo.html

———. 2004c. "Civil Marriage Disobedience: Revolution Starts with a Kiss—the San Francisco Wed-In." Partners Task Force for Gay & Lesbian Couples. http://www. buddybuddy.com/civil-01.html

———. 2004d. "Canada Offers Legal Marriage." Partners Task Force for

Gay & Lesbian Couples. http://www.buddybuddy.com/ civil-01.html

———. 2004e. "Domestic Partner Benefits: Philosophy and Provider List." Partners Task Force for Gay & Lesbian Couples. http://www. buddybuddy.com/d-p-2.html

D'Emilio, John, and Estelle B. Freedman. 1988. *Intimate Matters: A History of Sexuality in America.* New York: Harpers.

Demo, David H. 1997. "Family Type and Adolescent Adjustment." *Research Findings.* Stepfamily Association of America. http://www.saafamilies.org

Demo, David H., and Alan C. Acock. 1996. "Singlehood, Marriage, and Remarriage: The Effects of Family Structure and Family Relationships on Mothers' Well-Being." *Journal of Family Issues* 17 (3): 388–407.

Demo, David H., and Martha J. Cox. 2000. "Families with Young Children: A Review of Research in t the 1990s." *Journal of Marriage and Family* 62 (4): 876-895.

DeNavas-Walt, Carmen, Robert W. Cleveland, and Bruce H. Webster, Jr. 2003. "Income in the United States: 2002." *Current Population Reports* P60–221. Washington DC: U.S. Census Bureau. Sept.

DeNavas-Walt, Carmen, Bernadette D. Proctor, and Robert J. Mills. 2004. "Income, Poverty, and Health Insurance Coverage in the United States: 2003." *Current Population Reports* P60–226. Washington DC: U.S. Census Bureau. August.

Denizet-Lewis, Benoit. 2003. "Double Lives on the Down Low." *New York Times Magazine.* August 3. Pp. 28ff.

———. 2004. "Friends, Friends with Benefits, and the Benefits of the Local Mall." *New York Times.* May 30.

Dentinger, Emma, and Marin Clarkberg. 2002. "Informal Caregiving and Retirement Timing Among Men and Women." *Journal of Family Issues* 23 (7): 857–879.

Depner, Charlene E. 1993. "Parental Role Reversal: Mothers as Nonresidential Parents." Pp. 37–57 in *Nonresidential Parenting: New Vistas in Family Living,* edited by Charlene E. Depner and James H. Bray. Newbury Park CA: Sage.

de Santis, Marie. 1990. "Hate Crimes Bill Excludes Women." *Off Our Backs.* June.

Detzner, Daniel F., and Blong Xiong. 1999. "Southeast Asian Families Straddle Two Worlds." *NCFR Report* (June): 14–15.

Deutsch, Anthony. 2000. "Netherlands Gives Gays Right to Marry, Adopt." *San Francisco Chronicle.* Sept. 13.

Deutsch, Francine M. 1999. *Halving It All: How Equally Shared Parenting Works.* Cambridge, MA: Harvard.

De Valle, Elaine. 2004. "Adoption Loss Has Gays Reeling." *Miami Herald.* January 30.

De Vise, Daniel. 2004. "Living with Parents Lets Young Adults Build Careers, Savings." Knight Ridder/ Tribune Business News. January 11.

Dickinson, Amy. 2002. "An Extra-Special Relation." *Time.* Nov. 18: A1+.

Diekmann, A., and H. Engelhardt. 1999. "The Social Inheritance of Divorce: Effects of Parent's Family Type in Postwar Germany." *American Sociological Review* 64: 783–93.

Diggs, Anita D., and Vera S. Paster. 1998. *Staying Married: A Guide for African-American Couples.* Kensington.

Dilworth-Anderson, Peggy, Linda M. Burton, and Eleanor Boulin Johnson. 1993. "Reframing Theories for Understanding Race, Ethnicity, and Families." Pp. 627–46 in *Sourcebook of Family Theories and Methods: A Contextual Approach,* edited by Pauline G. Boss, William J. Doherty, Ralph LaRossa, Walter R. Schumm, and Suzanne K. Steinmetz. New York: Plenum.

Dilworth-Anderson, Peggy, Sharon Wallace Williams, and Theresa Cooper. 1999. "The Contexts of Experiencing Emotional Distress Among Family Caregivers to Elderly African Americans." *Family Relations* 48 (4): 391–96.

DiNatale, Marisa, and Stephanie Boraas. 2002. "The Labor Force Experience of Women From 'Generation X.'" *Monthly Labor Review.* March: 3-15.

Dinkmeyer, Don, Sr., Gary D. McKay, and Don Dinkmeyer, Jr. 1997. *The Parent's Handbook: Systematic Training for Effective Parenting.* Circle Pines, MN: American Guidance Service.

"Divorced Dad Tries to Give Children His Full Support." 1996. "Dear Abby." *Minneapolis Star Tribune.* Jan. 8: E7.

Doherty, William J. 1992. "Private Lives, Public Values." *Psychology Today* 25 (3): 32-39.

Doherty, William J., Edward F. Kouneski, and Martin Erickson. 1998. "Responsible Fathering: An Overview and Conceptual Framework." *Journal of Marriage and Family* 60 (2): 277–92.

Doherty, William J., Susan Su, and Richard Needle. 1989. "Marital Disruption and Psychological Well-Being: A Panel Study." *Journal of Family Issues* 10: 72–85.

Doka, Kennneth J., editor. 1989. *Disenfranchised Grief: Recognizing Hidden Sorrow.* Lexington MA: Lexington Books.

Doka, Kenneth J., John Breaux, and Jack D. Gordon. 2002. *Living with Grief: Loss in Later Life.* Washington, DC: Hospice Foundation of America.

Dolan, Elizabeth M., Bonnie Braun, and Jessica C. Murphy. 2003. "A Dollar Short: Financial Challenges of Working-Poor Rural Families." *Family Focus.* June: F13–F15.

Dolgin, Janet L. 1997. *Defining the Family: Law, Technology and Reproduction in an Uneasy Age.* New York: NYU Press.

Dollahite, David C. 2002. Review of *Remaking the Godly Marriage. Journal of Marriage and the Family* 64: 817–818.

Domitrz, Michael J. 2003. *May I Kiss You?: A Candid Look at Dating, Communication, Respect, and Sexual assault Awareness.* Greenfield, WI: Awareness Publications.

"Donor-Egg Pregnancies Called Safe After Age 50." *New York Times.* Nov. 13.

Dowd, James J., and Nicole R. Pallotta. 2000. "The End of Romance: The Demystification of Love in the Postmodern Age." *Sociological Perspectives* 43 (4): 549–80.

Dower, Catherine. 1999. "Task Force Urges Inclusion of Midwifery in Managed Care Plans." www.futurehealth.ucsd.edu/press_ releases/midwifery.html.

Downey, Douglas B. 1995. "When Bigger Is Not Better: Family Size, Parental Resources, and Children's

Educational Performance." *American Sociological Review* 60: 746–61.

Downey, Sarah. 2000. "The Moving-Van Wars." *Newsweek.* Feb. 28: 53.

Downs, Barbara. 2003. "Fertility of American Women: June 2002." *Current Population Reports* P20–548. Washington DC: U.S. Census Bureau. Oct.

Downs, William R., and Brenda A. Miller. 1998. "Relationships Between Experiences of Parental Violence During Childhood and Women's Self-Esteem." *Violence and Victims* 13 (1): 63–74.

Doyle, J. 1989. *The Male Experience.* Dubuque, IA: Brown.

Driver, Janice L., and John M. Gottman. 2004. "Daily Marital Interactions and Positive Affect During Marital Conflict among Newlywed Couples." *Family Process* 43 (3): 301–314.

Drummet, Amy R., Marilyn Coleman, and Susan Cable. 2003. "Military Families Under Stress: Implications for Family Life Education." *Family Relations* 52 (3): 279–287.

Duck, Steve. 1998. *Human Relationships,* 3rd ed. Thousand Oaks, CA: Sage.

———. 1999. *Relating to Others,* 2nd ed. Philadelphia: Open University Press.

Duenwald, Mary. 2003. "After 25 Years, New Ideas in the Prenatal Test Tube." *New York Times.* Sept. 21.

Duggan, Lisa. 2004. "Holy Matrimony!" *The Nation* 278 (10).

Dugger, Celia W. 1996. "Immigrant Cultures Raising Issues of Child Punishment." *New York Times.* Feb. 29: A1, A12.

———. 1998. "In India, an Arranged Marriage of 2 Worlds." *New York Times.* July 20: A1, A10.

Dukes, Howard. 2003. "In Parents' Hands, Children's Development Influenced Profoundly by Marital Conflict, ND Researcher Points Out." *South Bend Tribune.* July 8.

Duncan, Greg J., and Jeanne Brooks-Gunn. 2002. "Family Poverty, Welfare Reform, and Child Development." *Child Development* 71: 188–196.

Duncan, Stephen F., Gabrielle Box, and Benjamin Silliman. 1996. "Racial and Gender Effects on Perceptions of Marriage Preparation Programs

Among College Educated Young Adults." *Family Relations* 45 (1): 80–90.

Dunlop, Rosemary, and Ailso Burns. 1995. "The Sleeper Effect—Myth or Reality?" *Journal of Marriage and Family* 57: 375–86.

Dunn, David W., Joan K. Austin, and Gertrude A. Huster. 1999. "Symptoms of Depression in Adolescents with Epilepsy." *Journal of the American Academy of Child and Adolescent Psychiatry* 38 (9): 1132–39.

Dunne, John E., E. Wren Hudgins, and Julia Babcock. 2000. "Can Changing the Divorce Law Affect Post-Divorce Adjustment?" *Journal of Divorce & Remarriage* 33 (3): 35-55.

Dunnewind, Stephanie. 2003. "Book Helps Impart Coping Skills, Self-Esteem to Multiracial Children." Knight Ridder/Tribune News Service. August 5.

Dunphy v. Gregor. 1994. 136 N.J. 99.

Durkheim, Émile. 1911. Contribution to discussion of "L'Education sexuelle." *Bulletin de la Societé française philosophie* XL: pp. 33-38; 44–47.

———. 1951. *Suicide,* translated by John A. Spaulding and George Simpson. Glencoe, IL: Free Press.

Durm, Mark W., Angela Giddens, and Melissa Blankenship. 1997. "Parental Marital Status and Self-Esteem of Boys and Girls." *Psychological Reports* B1 (1): 125–37.

Dush, Claire M. Kamp, Catherine L. Cohan, and Paul R. Amato. 2003. "The Relationship Between Cohabitation and Marital Quality and stability: Change Across Cohorts?" *Journal of Marriage and Family* 65 (3): 539–549.

Dutton, Donald G. 2003. *The Abusive Personality: Violence and Control in Intimate Relationships.* New York: Guilford Press.

Dutton, Donald G., and James J. Browning. 1988. "Concern for Power, Fear of Intimacy, and Aversive Stimuli for Wife Assault." Pp. 163–75 in *Family Abuse and Its Consequences: New Directions in Research,* edited by Gerald T. Hotaling, David Finkelhor, John T. Kirkpatrick, and Murray A. Straus. Newbury Park, CA: Sage.

Duvall, Evelyn M., and Brent C. Miller. 1985. *Marriage and Family Develop-*

ment, 6th ed. New York: Harper and Row.

Dworkin, Paul H. 2002. "Editor's Note." *Journal of Developmental and Behavioral Pediatrics* 23: 167.

Dwyer, J. W., and R. T. Coward. 1991. "A Multivariate Comparison of the Involvement of Adult Sons Versus Daughters in the Care of Impaired Parents." *Journal of Gerontology* 46: S259–69.

Dwyer, J. W., Gary R. Lee, and Thomas B. Jankowski. 1994. "Reciprocity, Elder Satisfaction, and Caregiver Stress and Burden: The Exchange of Aid in the Family Caregiving Relationship." *Journal of Marriage and Family* 56 (1): 35–43.

Dyk, Patricia H. 2004. "Complexity of Family Life Among the Low-Income and Working Poor: Introduction to the Special Issue." *Family Relations* 53 (2): 122–126.

Dziech, Billie Wright. 2003. "Sexual Harassment on College Campuses." Pp. 147–71 in *Academic and Workplace Sexual Harassment: A Handbook of Cultural, Social Science, Management, and Legal Perspectives,* edited by Michele Paludi and Carmen A. Paludi, Jr. Westport CT: Praeger.

Eagles, Michelle. 2002. *From Heaven to Earth: Soft Landing Your Family Budget: 14 Steps to Manage Downsizing Family Finances in Downsizing Times.* New York: Writers Club Press.

Eagly, Alice H. 1995. "The Science and Politics of Comparing Women and Men." *American Psychologist* 50 (1): 164–68.

Early, Theresa J, Thomas K. Gregoire, and Thomas P. McDonald. 2002. "Child Functioning and Caregiver Well-Being in Families of Children with Emotional Disorders." *Journal of Family Issues* 23 (3): 374–391.

Easterlin, Richard. 1987. *Birth and Fortune: The Impact of Numbers on Personal Welfare,* 2d rev. ed. Chicago: University of Chicago Press.

Eaton, Leslie. 2004. "Divorced Parents Move, and Custody Gets Trickier." *New York Times.* Aug. 8.

Ebaugh, Helen Rose, and Mary Curry. 2000. "Fictive Kin as Social Capital in New Immigrant Communities." *Sociological Perspectives* 43 (2): 189–209.

Economic Policy Institute. http://www.epinet.org

"Education of Homeless Children and Youth." 2001. National Coalition for the Homeless. Fact sheet #10. http://www.nationalhomeless.org/edchild.html

Edwards, Margie L. K. 2004. "We're Decent People: Constructing and Managing Family Identity in Rural Working-Class Communities." *Journal of Marriage and Family* 66 (2): 515–529.

Edwards, Mark Evan. 2001. "Uncertainty and the Rise of the Work-Family Dilemma." *Journal of Marriage and the Family* 63: 183–196.

Egan, Timothy. 1993. "A Cultural Gap May Swallow a Child." *New York Times*. Nov. 12.

Egelko, Bob. 2004. "Top State Court Voids S.F.'s Gay Marriages." *San Francisco Chronicle*. August 13.

Eggebeen, David J., and Adam Davey. 1998. "Do Safety Nets Work? The Role of Anticipated Help in Times of Need." *Journal of Marriage and Family* 60 (4): 939–50.

Ehrenberg, Marion F., Margaret Gearing-Small, Michael A. Hunter, and Brent J. Small. 2001. "Childcare Task Division and Shared Parenting Attitudes in Dual-Earner Families with Young Children." *Family Relations* 50 (2): 143–53.

Ehrenfeld, Temma. 2002. "Infertility: A Guy Thing." *Newsweek*. Mar. 25. Pp. 60-61.

Ehrenreich, Barbara. 1983. *The Hearts of Men: American Dreams and the Flight from Commitment*. Garden City, NY: Anchor/Doubleday.

———. 2001. *Nickel and Dimed: On (Not) Getting By in America*. N.Y.: Henry Holt & Co.

———. 2004. "Do Women Need A Viagra?" *Time*. Jan. 19. P. 154.

Ehrensaft, Diane. 1990. *Parenting Together: Men and Women Sharing the Care of Their Children*. Urbana: University of Illinois Press.

Ehrle, J., G. Adams, and T. Tout. 2001. *Who's Caring for Our Youngest Children?: Child Care Patterns of Infants and Toddlers*. Washington, DC: The Urban Institute.

Eicher-Catt, Deborah. 2004. "Noncustodial Mothers and Mental Health:

When Absence Makes the Heart Break." NCFR *Family Focus* March: F7-F8.

Eisenstadt v. *Baird*. 1972. 405 U.S. 398.

Elder, Glen H., Jr. 1974. *Children of the Great Depression: Social Change in Life Experience*. Chicago: University of Chicago Press.

Elder, Glen H., Jr., and Eliza K. Pavalko. 1993. "Work Careers in Men's Later Years: Transitions, Trajectories, and Historical Change." *Journal of Gerontology: Social Sciences* 48 (4): S180–S191.

Elias, Marilyn. 2003. "Women's Sex Problems May Be Overstated." *USA Today*. Nov. 15.

———. 2003a. "Children on Heightened Alert." *USA Today*. March 24.

———. 2004. "Marriage Taken to Heart." *USA Today*. March 4.

Elkind, David. 1988. *The Hurried Child: Growing Up Too Fast Too Soon*. Reading, MA: Addison-Wesley.

———. 1994. *Ties That Stress: The New Family Imbalance*. Cambridge, MA: Harvard University Press.

Ellis, R. Darin. 1999. "Patterns of E-Mail Requests by Users of an Internet-Based Aging-Services Information System." *Family Relations* 48 (1): 15–21.

El Nasser, Haya. 2004. "For More Parents, 3 Kids Are A Charm." *USA Today*. Mar. 10.

El-Sheikh, Mona, and Elizabeth Flanagan. 2001. "Parental Problem Drinking and Children's Adjustment: Family Conflict and Parental Depression as Mediators and Moderators of Risk." *Journal of Abnormal Child Psychology* 29 (5): 417–35.

Emery, R. E., K. M. Kitzmann, and M. Waldron. 1999. "Psychological Interventions for Separated and Divorced Families." Pp. 323–44 in *Coping with Divorce, Single Parenting, and Remarriage: A Risk and Resiliency Perspective*, edited by E. Mavis Hetherington. Mahwah, NJ: Erlbaum.

Emlen, Stephen T. 1995. "An Evolutionary Theory of the Family." *Proceedings of the National Academy of Sciences* 92: 8092–99.

"Emotional Intimacy More Important than Sex According to National Survey: What Do Men Really Want?" 2003. *PR Newswire*. Nov. 30.

Enda, Jodi. 1998. "Women Have Made Gains, Seek More." Washington Bureau in *Saint Paul, Minneapolis Pioneer Press*, Early Edition. July 19: 1A, 4A.

Engel, Marjorie. 2000. "The Financial (In)Security of Women in Remarriages." *Research Findings*. Stepfamily Association of America. http://www.saafamilies.org

Engels, Friedrich. 1942 [1884]. *The Origin of the Family, Private Property, and the State*. New York: International.

English-Lueck, J. A. 2001. "Technology and Social Change: The Effects on Family." *Family Focus* (Mar.): F1–F2, F5.

Enos, Sandra. 2001. *Mothering from the Inside: Parenting in a Women's Prison*. Albany: SUNY Press.

Entwisle, Doris R., and Karl L. Alexander. 1995. "A Parent's Economic Shadow: Family Structure Versus Family Resources as Influences on Early School Achievement." *Journal of Marriage and Family* 57 (2): 399–409.

Ephron, Delia. 1988. *Funny Sauce: Us, the Ex, the Ex's New Mate, the New Mate's Ex, and the Kids*. New York: Penguin.

Epstein, Norma, Lynda Evans, and John Evans. 1994. "Marriage." Pp. 115–25 in *Encyclopedia of Human Behavior*, vol. 3, edited by V.S. Ramachandran. New York: Academic.

Erel, O., and B. Burman. 1995. "Interrelatedness of Marital Relations and Parent–Child Relations: A Meta-Analytic Review." *Psychological Bulletin* 118: 108–32.

Erera, Pauline, and Karen Fredriksen. 1999. "Lesbian Stepfamilies: A Unique Family Structure." *Families in Society* 80 (3): 263–70.

Erickson, Nancy S. 1991. "Battered Mothers of Battered Children: Using Our Knowledge of Battered Women to Defend Them Against Charges of Failure to Act." *Current Perspectives in Psychological, Legal, and Ethical Issues*, vol. 1A: Children and Families: Abuse and Endangerment: 197–218.

Erickson, Rebecca J., and Ginna M. Babcock. 1995. "Men and Family Law: From Patriarchy to Partnership." Pp. 31–54 in *Families and Law*, edited by Lisa J. McIntyre and Marvin B. Sussman. New York: Haworth.

Eriksen, Shelley, and Naomi Gerstel. 2002. "A Labor of Love or Labor Itself: Care Work Among Brothers and Sisters." *Journal of Family Issues* 23 (7): 836-856.

Estes, Richard, and Neil Weiner. 2002. *The Commercial Sexual Exploitation of Children in the U.S., Canada, and Mexico.* Web-published paper. Philadelphia: University of Pennsylvania. www.ssw.upenn.edu/~restes/CSEC.htm.

"Estimated Median Age at First Marriage, by Sex: 1890 to the Present." 1999. U.S. Census Bureau. www.census.gov/population/socdemo/ms-la/tabms-2.txt.

Etzioni, Amitai. 1997. "Marriage with No Easy Outs." *New York Times.* Aug. 13.

Eveld, Edward M. 2003. "At-home Dads Create Support Systems." *Omaha World-Herald.* Sept. 4.

Even, William E., and David A. Macpherson. 2004. "When Will the Gender Gap in Retirement Income Narrow?" *Southern Economic Journal* 71 (1): 182–201.

Eyer, Diane E. 1992. *Mother–Infant Bonding: A Scientific Fiction.* New Haven, CT: Yale University Press.

Faber, Adele, and Elaine Mazlish. 1982. *How to Talk So Kids Will Listen and Listen So Kids Will Talk.* New York: Avon.

"Facts About Child Care in America." 1998. Children's Defense Fund. July 18. http.www.childrensdefense.org.

Fagan, Jay. 2000. "Head Start Fathers' Daily Hassles and Involvement with Their Children." *Journal of Family Issues* 21 (3): 329–46.

Fagan, Jay, and Marina Barnett. 2003. "The Relationship Between Maternal Gatekeeping, Paternal Competence, Mothers' Attitudes about the Father Role, and Father Involvement." *Journal of Family Issues* 24 (8): 1020–1043.

Falbo, T. 1976. "Does the Only Child Grow Up Miserable?" *Psychology Today* 9: 60–65.

Family Support Act. 1988. PL100-628. Washington DC: U.S. Congress.

Family Science Network. 1998. "Corporal Punishment Debate: The Play of Values and Perspectives." familysci@lsv.uky.edu.

Fanshel, David. 1972. *Far from the Reservation: The Transracial Adoption of American Indian Children.* Metuchen NJ: Scarecrow.

Farkas, Steve, Jean Johnson, and Ann Duffett. 2002. *A Lot Easier Said Than Done: Parents Talk about Raising Children in Today's America.* Public Agenda: Report prepared for State Farm Insurance Companies.

Farrell, Betty G. 1999. *Family: The Making of an Idea, an Institution, and a Controversy in American Culture.* Boulder, CO: Westview Press.

Farver, Jo Ann M., Barbara Welles-Nystrom, Dominick L. Frosch, Supra Wimbarti, and Sigfried Hoppe-Graff. 1997. "Toy Stories: Aggression in Children's Narratives in the United States, Sweden, Germany, and Indonesia." *Journal of Cross-Cultural Psychology* 28 (4): 393–420.

Fass, Paula S. 2003a. Review of *Anxious Parents.* www.amazon.com.

———. 2003b. "A Sign of Family Disorder? Changing Representations of Parental Kidnapping." Pp. 170–195 in *All Our Families: New Policies for A New Century*, 2nd ed., edited by Mary Ann Mason, Arlene Skolnick, and Stephen D. Sugarman. New York: Oxford.

Fausto-Sterling, Anne. 2000. "The Five Sexes Revisited." *The Sciences* (July/August): 19–23.

———. 2000. *Sexing the Body: Gender Politics and the Construction Of Sexuality.* New York: Basic.

Feagin, Joe R., and Melvin P. Sikes. 1994. *Living with Racism: The Black Middle-Class Experience.* Boston: Beacon.

Fears, Darryl. 2003. "Race Divides Hispanics, Report Says." *Washington Post. July 13.*

Fears, Darryl, and Claudia Dean. 2001. "Biracial Couples Report Tolerance: Most Are Accepted by Families." *Washington Post.* July 6.

Febring, Richard, and Andrea Martovina Schmidt. 2001. "Trends in Contraceptive Use Among Catholics in the United States: 1988–1995. *Linacre Quarterly* (May): 170–185.

Federal Interagency Forum. 2004. *America's Children 2004.* Federal Interagency Forum on Child and Family Statistics, Washington, DC: U.S. Government Printing Office. http://ChildStats.gov.

Federal Resource Center for Children of Prisoners. 2004. "Overview of Statistics." http://www.cwla.org/programs/incarcerated/cop_fact-sheet.htm

"Feel Like A Natural Woman?" 2000. *Family Planning Perspectives* 32: 55.

Feigelman, W. 2000. "Adjustments of Transracially and Inracially Adopted Young Adults. *Child and Adolescent Social Work Journal* 17: 165–83.

Fein, Esther B. 1997. "Failing to Discuss Dying Adds to Pain of Patient and Family." *New York Times.* March 5: A1, A14.

Feldman, Robert S. 2003. *Development across the Life Span*, 3rd ed. Upper Saddle River NJ: Prentice-Hall.

Feldt, Gloria. 1998. "New Abortion Statistics Confirm Effectiveness of Prevention Programs." *Planned Parenthood.* Dec. 11. www.ppfa.org.

Felson, Richard B., and Natalie Russo. 1988. "Parental Punishment and Sibling Aggression." *Social Psychology Quarterly* 51 (1): 11–18.

Felstead, A., and J. Jewson. 2000. *In Work, at Home: Toward an Understanding of Home-working.* London: Routledge.

Fernandez, Marilyn. 1998. "Asian Indian Americans in the Bay Area and the Glass Ceiling." *Sociological Perspectives* 41 (1): 119–50.

Fernquist, Robert M. 2000. "Problem Drinking in the Family and Youth Suicide." *Adolescence* 35 (1): 551–62.

Ferrante, Joan. 2000. *Sociology: The United States in a Global Community*, 4th ed. Belmont, CA: Wadsworth.

Ferrari, J. R., and R. A. Emmons. 1994. "Procrastination As Revenge: Do People Report Using Delays as a Strategy for Vengeance?" *Personality and Individual Differences* 17 (4): 539–42.

Fields, Jason. 2001. *Living Arrangements of Children: 1996.* Current Population Report P70–74. Washington, DC: U.S. Census Bureau. April.

———. 2003. "Children's Living Arrangements and Characteristics: March 2003." *Current Population Reports* P20-547. Washington DC: U.S. Census Bureau.

Fields, Jason, and Lynne M. Casper. 2001. *America's Families and Living Arrangements: March 2000.* Current

Population Report P20–537. Washington, DC: U.S. Census Bureau.

Fierstein, Harvey. 2003. "The Culture of Disease." *New York Times*. July 31.

Figley, Charles, Brian Bride, Nicholas Mazza, and Marcia Egan. 1998. "Death and Trauma: The Traumatology of Grieving." *Health and Social Work* 23 (1): 186–98.

"Financial Agreements without Saying 'I Do': Publications Outline Options for Same-Sex Couples." 2004. *US Newswire*. March 4.

Fincannon, Joy L., and Katherine V. Bruss. 2003. *Couples Confronting Cancer: Keeping Your Relationship Strong*. Atlanta, GA: American Cancer Society.

Find Care. 2002. "Choosing Quality Child Care." www/cafcc.on.ca.

Fine, Mark. 1997. "The Role of Stepparent: How Similar are the Views of Stepparents, Parents, and Stepchildren?" *Research Findings*. Stepfamily Association of America. http://www.saafamilies.org

Fine, Mark, Marilyn Coleman, and Lawrence H. Ganong. 1999. "A Social Constructionist Multi-Method Approach to Understanding the Stepparent Role." Pp. 273–94 in E. Mavis Hetherington (Ed.). *Coping with Divorce, Single Parenting, and Remarriage*. Mahwah, NJ: Erlbaum.

Fineman, Martha Albertson. 1991. *The Illusion of Equality: The Rhetoric and Reality of Divorce Reform*. Chicago: University of Chicago Press.

Fineman, Martha Albertson, and Roxanne Mykitiuk. 1994. *The Public Nature of Private Violence: The Discovery of Domestic Abuse*. New York: Routledge.

Finer, Lawrence B., Jacqueline E. Darroch, and Jennifer J. Frost. 2003. "Services for Men at Publicly Funded Family Planning Agencies, 1998–1999." *Perspectives on Sexual and Reproductive Health* 35: 202-207.

Fingerman, Karen L., Elizabeth L. Hay, and Kira S. Birditt. 2004. "The Best of Ties, the Worst of Ties: Close, Problematic, and Ambivalent Social Relationships." *Journal of Marriage and Family* 66 (3): 792–808.

Fink, Paul J. 2003. "Fink! Still at Large: Low Self-esteem and Narcissism." *Clinical Psychiatry News* 31 (1): 25.

Finkelhor, David, David Moore, Sherry L. Hamby, and Murray A. Straus. 1996. "Sexually Abused Children in a National Survey of Parents: Methodological Issues." *Child Abuse & Neglect* 21 (1): 1–9.

Finkelhor, David, and Karl Pillemer. 1988. "Elder Abuse: Its Relationship to Other Forms of Domestic Violence." Pp. 244–54 in *Family Abuse and Its Consequences: New Directions in Research*, edited by Gerald T. Hotaling, David Finkelhor, John T. Kirkpatrick, and Murray A. Straus. Newbury Park, CA: Sage.

Finkelhor, David, and Kersti Yllo. 1985. *License to Rape: Sexual Abuse of Wives*. New York: Holt.

Finkenauer, Catrin, Rutger C.M.E. Engels, Susan J.T. Branje, and Wim Meeus. 2004. "Disclosure and Relationship Satisfaction in Families." *Journal of Marriage and Family* 66 (1): 195–209.

Finley, Gordon E. 2000. "Adoptive Families: Dramatic Changes Across Generations." (NCFR) *Family Focus*. June. Pp F10; F12.

———. 2004. "Divorce Inequalities." (NCFR) *Family Focus*. Sept. F9-F10.

Finz, Stacy. 2003. "Estranged Lesbians Battle for Custody of Twins." *San Francisco Chronicle*. Dec. 5.

Fischer, Kathy E., Mark Kittleson, Roberta Ogletree, Kathleen Welshimer, Paula Woehlke, and John Benshoff. 2000. "The Relationship of Parental Alcoholism and Family Dysfunction to Stress Among College Students." *Journal of American College Health* 48 (4): 151–63.

Fisher, Judith L. 1983. "Mothers Living Apart from Their Children." *Family Relations* 32: 351–57.

Fisher, Philip A., Leslie D. Leve, Catherine C. O'Leary, and Craig Leve. 2003. "Parental Monitoring of Children's Behavior: Variation Across Stepmother, Stepfather, and Two-Parent Biological Families." *Family Relations* 52 (1): 45–52.

Fishman, Katherine Davis. 1992. "Problem Adoptions." *The Atlantic Monthly* 270 (3): 37–69.

Fitzpatrick, Mary Anne. 1988. *Between Husbands and Wives: Communication in Marriage*. Newbury Park, CA: Sage.

———. 1995. *Explaining Family Interactions*. Thousand Oaks, CA: Sage.

"Five Years after Their Own or Their Husband's Sterilization, Few Women Regret the Decision." 2002. *Perspectives on Sexual and Reproductive Health* 34: 265.

Flaherty, Julie. 2001. "A Patch for Family Bonds Put Asunder." *New York Times*. May 10.

Flaherty, Sr. Mary Jean, Lorna Facteau, and Patricia Garver. 1999. "Grandmother Functions in Multigenerational Families: An Exploratory Study of Black Adolescent Mothers and Their Infants." Pp. 223–31 in *The Black Family: Essays and Studies*, edited by Robert Staples. Belmont, CA: Wadsworth.

Flanagan, Caitlin. 2002. "What Price Valor?" *Atlantic Monthly*. June: 108–110.

Fleming, Julian, Paul Mullen, and Cabriele Bammer. 1996. "A Study of Potential Risk Factors for Sexual Abuse in Childhood." *Child Abuse & Neglect* 21 (1): 49–58.

Fletcher, Garth. 2002. *The New Science of Intimate Relationships*. Malden, MA: Blackwell Publishers.

Foley, Lara, and James Fraser. 1998. "A Research Note on Post-Dating Relationships." *Sociological Perspectives* 41 (1): 209–19.

Folk, Karen, and Yunae Yi. 1994. "Piecing Together Child Care with Multiple Arrangements: Crazy Quilt or Preferred Pattern for Employed Parents of Preschool Children?" *Journal of Marriage and Family* 56 (3): 669–80.

Fong, Colleen, and Judy Yung. 1995. "In Search of the Right Spouse: Interracial Marriage Among Chinese and Japanese Americans." *Amerasia Journal* 21 (3): 77–84.

Forman, Robert. 1996. *Drug Induced Infertility and Sexual Dysfunction*. Cambridge, MA: Cambridge University Press.

Formichelli, Linda. 2001. "Baby Blues." *Psychology Today*. March/April: 24.

Forste, Renata. 2002. "Where Are All the Men: A Conceptual Analysis of the Role of Men in Family Formation." *Journal of Family Issues* 23 (5): 579-600.

Foster Care Project. 1998. "The Foster Care Project: What You May Not

Know." http://www.kidscampaigns.org/fostercare.

Foster, E. Michael, Damon Jones, and Saul D. Hoffman. 1998. "The Economic Impact of Nonmarital Childbearing: How Are Older, Single Mothers Faring?" *Journal of Marriage and Family* 60 (1): 163–74.

Foust, Michael. 2004. "Another Town Bows to Pressure to Halt Same-sex 'Marriages'." *BPNews*. March 10. http://www.bpnews.net/

Fox, Greer Litton. 2000. "No Time for Innocence, No Place for Innocents: Children's Exposure to Extreme Violence." Pp. 163–81 in *Families, Crime, and Criminal Justice*, edited by Greer Litton Fox and Michael L. Benson. New York: Elsevier Science.

Fox, Greer L., Michael L. Benson, Alfred A. DeMaris, and Judy Van Wyk. 2002. "Economic Distress and Intimate Violence: Testing Family Stress and Resources Theory." *Journal of Marriage and the Family* 64: 793–807.

Fox, Greer L., Carol Bruce, and Terri Combs-Orme. 2000. "Parenting Expectations and Concerns of Fathers and Mothers of Newborn Infants." *Family Relations* 49 (2): 123–31.

Fox, Greer L., and Robert F. Kelly. 1995. "Determinants of Child Custody Arrangements at Divorce." *Journal of Marriage and Family* 57 (3): 693–708.

Fox, James Alan, and Marianne W. Zawitz. 2004. *Homicide Trends in the U.S.* Washington DC: U.S. Bureau of Justice Statistics. www.ojp.usdoj.gov/bjs

Fox-Genovese, E. 1991. *Feminism Without Illusions: A Critique of Individualism.* Chapel Hill: University of North Carolina Press.

Fracher, Jeffrey, and Michael S. Kimmel. 1992. "Hard Issues and Soft Spots: Counseling Men About Sexuality." Pp. 438–50 in *Men's Lives*, 2d ed., edited by Michael S. Kimmel and Michael A. Messner. New York: Macmillan.

Framo, James L. 1978. "The Friendly Divorce." *Psychology Today* 11: 77–80, 99–102.

Francoeur, Robert T., and William J. Taverner. 2002. *Taking Sides: Clashing Views On Controversial Issues in Human Sexuality*, 7th ed. McGraw Hill/Duskin.

Frankenberg, Ruth. 1993. *White Women, Race Matters: The Social Construction of Whiteness.* Minneapolis: University of Minnesota Press.

Franklin, Donna L. 1997. *Ensuring Inequality: The Structural Transformation of the African American Family.* New York: Oxford.

Franks, Melissa M., Tantina B. Hong, Linda S. Pierce, and Mark W. Ketterer. 2002. "The Association of Patients' Psychosocial Well-Being with Self and Spouse Ratings of Patient Health." *Family Relations* 51 (1):22–27.

Freeman, Arthur, and Jon Carlson. 2004. *Cognitive-behavioral Couples Therapy.* Washington, DC: American Psychological Association.

Freisthler, Bridget, Gloria M. Svara, and Sydney Harrison-Jay. 2003. "It Was the Best of Times, It Was the Worst of Times: Young Adult Children Talk about Growing Up in a Stepfamily." *Journal of Divorce and Remarriage* 38 (3-4): 83-102.

French, J. R. P., and Bertram Raven. 1959. "The Basis of Power." In *Studies in Social Power*, edited by D. Cartwright. Ann Arbor: University of Michigan Press.

Frey, Kurt, and Mahzad Hojjat. 1998. "Are Love Styles Related to Sexual Styles?" *Journal of Sex Research* 35 (3): 265–72.

Frey, William H. 1999. " 'New Sun Belt' Metros and Suburbs Are Magnets for Retirees." *Population Today* 27 (9): 1–3.
———. 2002. "The New White Flight." *American Demographics* 24: 20–23.

Friedan, Betty. 1963. *The Feminine Mystique.* New York: Dell.

Friedman, Joel, Marcia M. Boumil, and Barbara Ewert Taylor. 1992. *Date Rape: What It Is, What It Isn't, What It Does to You, What You Can Do About It.* Deerfield Beach, FL: Health Communications.

Friedrich, William N., Jennifer Fisher, Daniel Broughton, Margaret Houston, and Constance R. Shafran. 1998. "Normative Sexual Behavior in Children: A Contemporary Sample." *Pediatrics* 104 (April): E9. www.pediatrics.org.

Friend, Tim. 2003. "Blueprint for Life." *USA Today* Jan. 27.

Frisco, Michelle L., and Kristi Williams. 2003. "Perceived Housework Equity, Marital Happiness, and Divorce in Dual Earner Families." *Journal of Family Issues* 24: 51–73.

Fritsch, Jane. 2001a. "Matrimony: The Magic's Still Gone." *New York Times.* May 20.
———. 2001b. "A Rise in Single Dads." *New York Times.* May 20.
———. 2001c. "Where Breaking Up Is Harder to Do." *New York Times.* July 29.

Fromm, Erich. 1956. *The Art of Loving.* New York: Harper & Row.

Fry, C. L. 1996. "Age, Aging, and Culture." Pp. 26–34 in *Handbook of Aging and the Social Sciences*, edited by R. H. Binstock and L. K. George. New York: Academic.

Frye, Marilyn. 1992. "Lesbian 'Sex.' " Pp. 109–19 in *Essays in Feminism 1976–1992*, edited by Marilyn Frye. Freedom, CA: Crossing.

Fu, Xuanning, and Tim B. Heaton. 2000. "Status Exchange in Intermarriage Among Hawaiians, Japanese, Filipinos and Caucasians in Hawaii: 1983–1994." *Journal of Comparative Family Studies* 31 (1): 45–64.

Fulighi, Andrew J., and Vivian Tseng. 1999. "Attitudes toward Family Obligations Among American Adolescents with Asian, Latin American, and European Backgrounds. " *Child Development* 70: 1030–1044.

Fuller, T. L., and F. D. Fincham. 1997. "Attachment Style in Married Couples: Relation to Current Marital Functioning, Stability Over Time, and Method of Assessment." *Personal Relationships* 2: 17–34.

Fullilove, Mindy Thompson, Robert E. Fullilove, Katherine Haynes, and Shirley Gross. 1990. "Black Women and AIDS Prevention: A View Toward Understanding the Gender Roles." *Journal of Sex Research* 27: 47–64.

Furman, W., and A. S. Flanagan. 1997. "The Influence of Earlier Relationships on Marriage: An Attachment Perspective." Pp. 179–202 in *Clinical Handbook of Marriage and Couples Interventions*, edited by W. K. Halford and H. J. Markman. Chichester, UK: Wiley.

Furstenberg, Frank F., Jr. 1992. "Good Dads—Bad Dads: Two Faces of Fatherhood." Pp. 342–62 in *Families in Transition*, 7th ed., edited by Arlene S. Skolnick and Jerome H. Skolnick. New York: Harper.

———. 2000. "The Sociology of Adolescence and Youth in the 1990s: A Critical Commentary." *Journal of Marriage and Family* 62 (4): 896–910.

———. 2001a. "The Fading Dream: Prospects for Marriage in the Inner City." Pp. 224–246 in Elijah Anderson and Douglas S. Massey (Eds.). *Problem of the Century: Racial Stratification in the United States*. New York: Russell Sage.

———. 2001b. "Managing to Make It." *Journal of Family Issues* 22 (2): 150–62.

———. 2003. "The Future of Marriage." Pp. 171-177 in Arlene S. Skolnick and Jerome H. Skolnick, eds. *Family in Transition*, 12th edition. Boston: Allyn and Bacon.

Furstenberg, Frank F., Jr., J. Brooks-Gunn, and S. Philip Morgan. 1987. *Adolescent Mothers in Later Life*. New York: Cambridge University Press.

Furstenberg, Frank F., Jr., Saul D. Hoffman, and Laura Shrestha. 1995. "The Effect of Divorce on Intergenerational Transfers: New Evidence." *Demography* 32 (3): 319–33.

Furstenberg, Frank F., Jr., and Mary Elizabeth Hughes. 1995. "Social Capital and Successful Development Among At-Risk Youth." *Journal of Marriage and Family* 57 (3): 580–92.

Furstenberg, Frank F., Jr., Sheela Kennedy, Vonnie C. McLloyd, Rubén Rumbaut, and Richard A. Settersten, Jr. 2003. "Between Adolescence and Adulthood: Expectations about the Timing of Adulthood." Research Network Working Paper No. 1. Network on Transitions to Adulthood and Public Policy. www.macfound.org/ research/hcd/cyd/ transitions_ adulthood.htm.

Furstenberg, Frank F., Jr., Sheela Kennedy, Vonnie C. McLoyd, Ruben G. Rumbaut, and Richard A. Settersten, Jr. 2004. "Growing Up Is Harder To Do." *Contexts* 3 (3).

Gable, Shelly L., Harry T. Reis, Emily A. Impett, and Evan R. Asher. 2004. "Interpersonal Relations and Group Processes—What Do You Do when Things Go Right? The Intrapersonal and Interpersonal Benefits of Sharing Positive Events." *Journal of Personality and Social Psychology* 87 (2): 228–245.

Gager, Constance T., and Laura Sanchez. 2003. "Two As One? Couples' Perceptions of Time spent Together, Marital Quality, and the Risk of Divorce." *Journal of Family Issues* 24 (1): 21–50.

Gagnon, John H., and William Simon. 2005. *Sexual Conduct: The Social Sources of Human Sexuality (Social Problems and Social Issues)*, 2nd ed. New Brunwwick NJ: Transaction Publishers.

Galinsky, Ellen. 1986. "Family Life and Corporate Policies." Pp. 109–45 in *In Support of Families*, edited by Michael W. Yogman and T. Berry Brazelton. Cambridge, MA: Harvard University Press.

———. 1999. *Ask The Children: What America's Children Really Think About Working Parents*. New York: Morrow.

———. 2001. "Parent Tips." Families and Work Institute. www. familiesandwork.org/ParentTips.htm.

Galinsky, Ellen, and Peter J. Stein. 1990. "The Impact of Human Resource Policies on Employees: Balancing Work/Family Life." *Journal of Family Issues* 11 (4): 368–83.

Gallagher, Sally K., and Naomi Gerstel. 2001. "Connections and Constraints: The Effects of Children on Caregiving." *Journal of Marriage and Family* 63 (1): 265–275.

Gallagher, Sally K., and Christian Smith. 1999. "Symbolic Traditionalism and Pragmatic Egalitarianism: Contemporary Evangelicals, Families, and Gender." *Gender and Society* 13: 211–33.

Galston, William A. 1996. "Children Are Victims of No-Fault Divorce: Law Needs to Make It More Difficult for Mom and Dad to Call It Quits." *Minneapolis Star Tribune*. Jan. 3: A11.

Gamache, Susan J. 1997. "Confronting Nuclear Family Bias in Stepfamily Research." *Marriage and Family Review* 26 (1–2): 41–50.

Gander, Anita Moore. 1991. "After the Divorce: Familial Factors That Predict Well-Being for Older and Younger Persons." *Journal of Divorce and Remarriage* 15 (1/2): 175–92.

Ganong, Lawrence H. and Marilyn Coleman. 1997. "How Society Views Stepfamilies." Pp. 85–106 in *Stepfamilies: History, Research, and Policy*, edited by Irene Levin and Marvin B. Sussman. New York: Haworth.

———. 2004. *Stepfamily Relationships: Development, Dynamics, and Interventions*. NY: Kluwer Academic/Plenum Publishers.

Ganong, Lawrence, Marilyn Coleman, A. K. McDaniel, and T. Killian. 1998. "Attitudes Regarding Obligations to Assist an Older Parent or Stepparent Following Later Life Remarriage." *Journal of Marriage and Family* 60: 595–610.

Gans, Herbert J. 1982. [1962]. *The Urban Villagers: Group and Class in the Life of Italian-Americans*, updated and expanded edition. New York: Free Press.

———. 1996. *The War Against the Poor*. New York: Basic.

Garbarino, James. 1977. "The Human Ecology of Child Maltreatment: A Conceptual Model for Research." *Journal of Marriage and Family* 39: 721–35.

García Coll, Cynthia, and Katherine Magnuson. 1997. "The Psychological Experience of Immigration: A Developmental Perspective." Pp. 91–131 in *Immigration and the Family*, edited by Alan Booth, Ann C. Crouter, and Nancy Landale. Mahwah, NJ: Erlbaum.

Gardiner, Karen N., Michael E. Fishman, Plamen Kikolov, Asaph Glosser, Stephanie Laud. 2002. *State Policies to Promote Marriage: Final Report*. Washington DC: U.S. Department of Health and Human Services. Sept. http://aspe.hhs.gov/hsp/marriage02f

Gardyn, Rebecca. 2002. "Animal Magnetism." *American Demographics* 24 (May): 30-37.

Garey, Anita I., Karen V. Hansen, Rosanna Hertz, and Cameron MacDonald. 2002. "Care and Kinship." *Journal of Family Issues* 23 (6): 703–715.

Garfinkel, Irwin, Daniel R. Meyer, and Sara S. McLanahan. 1998. "A Brief History of Child Support Policies in the U.S." Pp. 14–30 in *Fathers Under Fire: The Revolution in Child Support Enforcement*, edited by Irwin Garfinkel, Sara S. McLanahan, Daniel

R. Meyer, and Judith A. Seltzer. New York: Russell Sage.

Gates, Gary J. 2001. "Domestic Partner Benefits Won't Break the Bank." *Population Today* 29 (3): 1, 4.

Gaughan, Monica. 2002. "The Substitution Hypothesis: The Impact of Premarital Liaisons and Human Capital on Marital Timing." *Journal of Marriage and Family* 64 (2): 407–419.

Gavazzi, Stephen M., Patrick C. McKenry, Jill A. Jacobson, Teresa W. Julian, and Brenda Lohman. 2000. "Modeling the Effects of Expressed Emotion, Psychiatric Symptomology, and Marital Quality Levels on Male and Female Verbal Aggression." *Journal of Marriage and Family* 62 (3): 669–82.

Gavin, Molly R. 2003. "Elder Care Targeted As Top Employee Benefit." *Healthcare Review* 16 (2): 11–13.

"Gay Marriage Issue Puts Oregonians' Tolerance to Test." 2004. *Knight Ridder/Tribune Business News*. March 4.

"Gays Want the Right, But Not Necessarily the Marriage." 2004. *The Christian Science Monitor*. February 12.

Geary, David C., and Mark V. Flinn. 2001. "Evolution of Human Parental Behavior and the Human Family." *Parenting Science and Practice* 1: 5–61.

Geasler, Margie J., and Karen R. Blaisure. 1998. "A Review of Divorce Education Program Materials." *Family Relations* 47 (2): 167–75.

Gelles, Richard J. 1974. *The Violent Home: A Study of Physical Aggression between Husbands and Wives*. Beverly Hills CA: Sage.

———. 1994. "Ten Risk Factors." *Newsweek*. July 4: 29.

———. 1996. *The Book of David: How Preserving Families Can Cost Children's Lives*. New York: Basic.

———. 1997. *Intimate Violence in Families*, 3rd ed. Thousand Oaks, CA: Sage.

Gelles, Richard J., and Jon R. Conte. 1990. "Domestic Violence and Sexual Abuse of Children: A Review of Research in the Eighties." *Journal of Marriage and Family* 52 (4): 1045–58.

Gelles, Richard J., and Murray A. Straus. 1988. *Intimate Violence: The Definitive Study of the Causes and Consequences of Abuse in the American Family*. New York: Simon & Schuster.

"Gender Differences in Life Expectation at Birth, United States, Selected Years, 1900–1999." 2001. *Population Today*. August/September: 11.

"Genetically, Race Doesn't Exist." 2003. *Washington University Magazine*. Fall. P. 4.

Geronimus, Arline T. 1991. "Teenage Childbearing and Social and Reproductive Disadvantage: The Evolution of Complex Questions and the Demise of Simple Answers." *Family Relations* 40 (4): 463–71.

Gerson, Kathleen. 1985. *Hard Choices: How Women Decide About Work, Career, and Motherhood*. Berkeley: University of California Press.

———. 1993. *No Man's Land: Men's Changing Commitments to Family and Work*. New York: HarperCollins, Basic Books.

———. 1997. "The Social Construction of Fatherhood." Pp. 119–53 in *Contemporary Parenting: Challenges and Issues*, edited by Terry Arendell. Thousand Oaks, CA: Sage.

Gibbs, Nancy R. 1991. "Marching Out of the Closet." *Time*. Aug. 19: 14–15.

———. 1993. "Bringing Up Father." *Time*. June 28: 53–61.

Giddens, Anthony. 2003. "The Global Revolution in the Family and Personal Life." Pp.17-23 in *Family in Transition*, 12th ed.,edited by Arlene S. and Jerome H. Skolnick. Boston: Allyn and Bacon.

Gilbert, Lucia Albino, Sarah J. Walker, Sherry McKinney, and Jessica L. Snell. 1999. "Challenging Discourse Theories Reproducing Gender in Heterosexual Dating: An Analog Study." *Sex Roles* 41: 753–74.

Gilbert, Neil. 1998. "Working Families: Hearth to Market." Pp. 193–216 in *All Our Families: New Policies for a New Century*, edited by Mary Ann Mason, Arlene Skolnick, and Stephen D. Sugarman. New York: Oxford University Press.

Gilbert, Susan. 1997. "2 Spanking Studies Indicate Parents Should Be Cautious." *New York Times*. Aug. 20.

Giles-Sims, Jean. 1997. "Current Knowledge About Child Abuse in Stepfamilies." Pp. 215–30 in *Stepfamilies: History, Research, and Policy*, edited by Irene Levin and Marvin B. Sussman. New York: Haworth.

Gilgun, Jane E. 1995. "We Shared Something Special: The Moral Discourse of Incest Perpetrators." *Journal of Marriage and Family* 57 (2): 265–81.

Gillespie, Dair. 1971. "Who Has the Power? The Marital Struggle." *Journal of Marriage and Family* 33: 445–58.

Gillespie, Natalie Nichols. 2004. *The Stepfamily Survival Guide*. Grand Rapids, Michigan: Revell.

Gillespie, Rosemary. 2003. "Childfree and Feminine: Understanding the Gender Identity of Voluntarily Childless Women." *Gender and Society* 17: 122–136.

Gillham, Bill, Gary Tanner, Bill Cheyne, Isobel Freeman, Martin Rooney, and Allan Lambie. 1998. "Unemployment Rates, Single Parent Density, and Indices of Child Poverty: Their Relationship to Different Categories of Child Abuse and Neglect." *Child Abuse & Neglect* 22 (2): 79–90.

Gilmartin, B. 1977. "Swinging: Who Gets Involved and How." Pp. 161–85 in *Marriage and Alternatives*, edited by R. W. Libby and R. N. Whitehurst. Glenview, IL: Scott, Foresman.

Ginott, Haim G., Alice Ginott, and Wallace Goddard. 2003. *Between Parent and Child: The Bestselling Classic that Revolutionized Parent-Child Communication*. New York: Three Rivers Press. Gladding, Samuel T. 2004. *Counseling: A Comprehensive Profession*, 5th edition. Upper Saddle River, NJ: Pearson/Merrill/Prentice Hall.

Gladstone, James, and Anne Westhues. 1998. "Adoption Reunions: A New Side to Intergenerational Family Relationships." *Family Relations* 47 (2): 177–84.

Glaser, Danya, and Stephen Frosh. 1988. *Child Sexual Abuse*. Chicago: Dorsey.

Glass, Jennifer. 1992. "Housewives and Employed Wives: Demographic and Attitudinal Change, 1972–1986." *Journal of Marriage and Family* 54: 559–69.

———. 1998. "Gender Liberation, Economic Squeeze, or Fear of Strangers: Why Fathers Provide Infant Care in Dual-Earner Families." *Journal of Marriage and Family* 60 (4): 821–32.

Glass, Jennifer, and Sarah Beth Estes. 1997a. "Employment and Child Care." Pp. 254–88 in *Contemporary*

Parenting: Challenges and Issues, edited by Terry Arendell. Thousand Oaks, CA: Sage.

———. 1997b. "The Family Responsive Workplace." *Annual Review of Sociology* 23: 289–313.

Glass, Jennifer, and Tetsushi Fujimoto. 1994. "Housework, Paid Work, and Depression Among Husbands and Wives." *Journal of Health and Social Behavior* 35: 179–91.

Glass, Shirley. 1998. "Shattered Vows." *Psychology Today* 31 (4): 34–52.

Glass, Shirley, and Jean C. Staeheli. 2003. *Not Just Friends: Protect Your Relationship from Infidelity and Heal the Trauma of Betrayal*. New York: Free Press.

Glasser, William. 2001. *Counseling with Choice Therapy, the New Reality Therapy*. Alexandria, VA: American Counseling Association.

Glassboro v. Vallorosi. 1990. 117 N.J. 421.

Glassner, Barry. 1999. *The Culture of Fear: Why Parents Are Afraid of the Wrong Things*. New York: Basic.

Glendon, Mary Ann. 1981. *The New Family and the New Property*. Toronto: Butterworths.

Glenn, Norval. 1987. "Continuity Versus Change, Sanguineness Versus Concern: Views of the American Family in the Late 1980s." Introduction to a special issue of the *Journal of Family Issues* 8: 348–54.

———. 1990. "Quantitative Research on Marital Quality in the 1980s: A Critical Review." *Journal of Marriage and Family* 52 (November): 818–31.

———. 1996. "Values, Attitudes, and the State of American Marriage." Pp. 15–33 in *Promises to Keep: The Decline and Renewal of Marriage in America*, edited by David Popenoe, Jean Bethke Elshtain, and David Blankenhorn. Lanham, MD: Rowman and Littlefield.

———. 1997a. "A Reconsideration of the Effect of No-Fault Divorce on Divorce Rates." *Journal of Marriage and Family* 59 (4): 1023–30.

———. 1997b. "A Critique of Twenty Family and Marriage and Family Textbooks." *Family Relations* 46 (3): 197–208.

———. 1998. "The Course of Marital Success and Failure in Five American 10-Year Marriage Cohorts." *Journal of Marriage and Family* 60 (3): 569–76.

———. 2001. "Is the Current Concern about American Marriage Warranted?" *The Virginia Journal of Social Policy & the Law* 9 (1): 5–47.

———. 2002. "A Plea for Greater Concern About the Quality of Marital Matching." Pp. 45–58 in Alan J. Hawkins, Lynn D. Wardle, and David Orgon Coolidge (eds.). *Revitalizing the Institution of Marriage for the Twenty-first Century*. Westport, Connecticut: Praeger.

Glenn, Norval, and David Blankenhorn. 2003. "Does Moving After Divorce Damage Kids?" www.americanvalues.org Sept. 11.

Glenn, Norval, and Charles N. Weaver. 1988. "The Changing Relationship of Marital Status to Reported Happiness." *Journal of Marriage and Family* 50: 317–24.

Glick, Jennifer E., Frank D. Bean, and Jennifer Van Hook. 1997. "Immigration and Changing Patterns of Extended Family Household Structure in the United States: 1970–1990." *Journal of Marriage and Family* 59: 177–91.

Glick, Jennifer E., and Jennifer Van Hook. 2002. "Parents' Coresidence with Adult Children: Can Immigration Explain racial and Ethnic Variation?" *Journal of Marriage and Family* 64 (1): 240–253.

Glick, Paul C., and Sung-Ling Lin. 1986a. "More Young Adults Are Living with Their Parents: Who Are They?" *Journal of Marriage and Family* 48: 107–12.

———. 1986b. "Recent Changes in Divorce and Remarriage." *Journal of Marriage and Family* 48 (4): 737–47.

Glick, Paul C., and Arthur J. Norton. 1979. "Marrying, Divorcing, and Living Together in the U.S. Today." *Population Bulletin* 32 (5). Washington, DC: Population Reference Bureau.

Glink, Ilyce R. 2001. *50 Simple Things You Can Do To Improve Your Personal Finances*. NY: Three Rivers Press.

Globerman, Judith. 1996. "Motivations to Care: Daughters- and Sons-in-Law Caring for Relatives with Alzheimer's Disease." *Family Relations* 45 (1): 37–45.

Godecker, Amy L., Elizabeth Thomson, and Larry L. Bumpass. 2001. "Union Status, Marital History and Female Contraceptive Sterilization in the United States." *Family Planning Perspectives* 33: 35–41; 49.

Goetting, Ann. 1999. *Getting Out: Life Stories of Women Who Left Abusive Men*. New York: Columbia University Press.

Goffman, Erving. 1959. *The Presentation of Self in Everyday Life*. Garden City, NY: Doubleday.

Gold, J. M., and J. D. Rogers. 1995. "Intimacy and Isolation: A Validation Study of Erikson's Theory." *Journal of Humanistic Psychology* 35 (1): 78–86.

Gold, Steven J. 1993. "Migration and Family Adjustment: Continuity and Change Among Vietnamese in the United States." Pp. 300–14 in *Family Ethnicity: Strength in Diversity*, edited by Harriette Pipes McAdoo. Newbury Park, CA: Sage.

Goldberg, Carey. 1998. "After Girls Get the Attention, Focus Shifts to Boys' Woes." *New York Times*. Apr. 23.

———. 1999. "Crackdown on Abusive Spouses, Surprisingly, Nets Many Women." *New York Times*. Nov. 23.

Goldman, Ari L. 1992. "Catholics Are at Odds with Bishops." *New York Times*. June 18.

Goldner, Virginia. 1993. "Feminist Theories." Pp. 623–25 in *Sourcebook of Family Theories and Methods: A Contextual Approach*, edited by Pauline G. Boss, William J. Doherty, Ralph LaRossa, Walter R. Schumm, and Suzanne K. Steinmetz. New York: Plenum.

Goldscheider, Frances K. 1997. "Recent Changes in U.S. Young Adult Living Arrangements in Comparative Perspective." *Journal of Family Issues* 18 (6): 708–24.

Goldscheider, Frances K., and Calvin Goldscheider. 1998. "Effects of Childhood Family Structure on Leaving and Returning Home." *Journal of Marriage and Family* 60: 745–56.

———. 1999. *The Changing Transition to Adulthood: Leaving and Returning Home*. Thousand Oaks, CA: Sage.

Goldstein, Arnold P., Harold Keller, and Diane Erne. 1985. *Changing the Abusive Parent*. Champaign, IL: Research Press.

Goldstein, Joshua R. 1999. "The Leveling of Divorce in the United States." *Demography* 36: 409–14.

Goldstein, Joshua R., and Catherine T. Kenney. 2001. "Marriage Delayed or Marriage Foregone? New Cohort Forecasts of First Marriage for U.S. Women." *American Sociological Review* 66: 506–519.

Goldyn, Cheryl. 2001. "The Mother and Child Reunion." *The Reader.* June 13: 14–17.

Goleman, Daniel. 1985. "Patterns of Love Charted in Studies." *New York Times.* Sept. 10.

———. 1988a. "Adding the Sounds of Silence to the List of Health Risks." *New York Times.* Aug. 4.

———. 1988b. "The Lies Men Tell Put Women in Danger of AIDS." *New York Times.* Aug. 14.

———. 1989. "For a Happy Marriage, Learn How to Fight." *New York Times.* Feb. 21.

———. 1992a. "Gay Parents Called No Disadvantage." *New York Times.* Dec. 21.

———. 1992b. "Family Rituals May Promote Better Emotional Adjustment." *New York Times.* Mar. 11.

Golish, T.D. 2003. "Stepfamily Communication Strengths: Understanding the Ties that Bind." *Human Communication Research* 29 (1): 41–80.

Golombok, Susan., A. Brewaeys, M. T. Giavazzi, D. Guerra, F. MacCallum, and J. Rust. 2002. "The European Study of Assisted Reproduction Families: The Transition to Adolescence." *Human Reproduction* 17: 830–40.

Golombok, Susan, Rachel Cook, Alison Bish, and Clare Murray. 1995. "Families Created by the New Reproductive Technologies: Quality of Parenting and Social and Emotional Development of the Children." *Child Development* 66: 285–298.

Golombok, Susan, Fiona MacCallum, and Emma Goodman. 2001. "The 'Test-Tube' Generation: Parent–Child Relationships and the Psychological Well-Being of In Vitro Fertilization Children at Adolescence." *Child Development* 72: 599–608.

Golombok, Susan, Fiona MacCallum, Emma Goodman, and Michael Rutter. 2002. "Families with Children Conceived by Donor Insemination: A Follow-up at Age Twelve." *Child Development* 73: 952–968.

Golombok, Susan, and Fiona Tasker. 1996. "Do Parents Influence the Sexual Orientation of Their Children? Findings from a Longitudinal Study of Lesbian Families." *Developmental Psychology* 32: 3–11.

Gomes, Charlene. 2003. "Partners as Parents: Challenges Faced by Gays Denied Marriage." *The Humanist* 63 (6): 14–20.

Gonzalez, Cindy, and Michael O'Connor. 2002. "Dialogue Key in Blending Cultures." *Omaha World- Herald.* May 4.

Goode, Erica. 2002. "Deflating Self-Esteem's Role in Society's Ills." *New York Times*. October 1. Retrieved 1/14/04 from http://web.lexis-nexis.com.

Goode, William J. 1959. "The Theoretical Importance of Love." *American Sociological Review* 24: 38–47.

———. 1968. "The Theoretical Importance of Love." *American Sociological Review* 33: 750–60.

———. 1971. "Force and Violence in the Family." *Journal of Marriage and The Family* 33: 624–636.

———. 1982. "Why Men Resist." Pp. 131–50 in *Rethinking the Family: Some Feminist Questions*, edited by Barrie Thorne and Marilyn Yalom. New York: Longmans.

———. 1993. *World Changes in Divorce Patterns.* New Haven, CT: Yale University Press.

Goodman, Brenda. 2004. "Forgiveness Is Good, up to a Point." *Psychology Today*. January/February: 16.

Goodman, Catherine Chase, and Merril Silverstein. 2001. "Grandmothers Who Parent Their Grandchildren." 2001. *Journal of Family Issues* 22 (5): 557–78.

Gordon, Thomas. 2000. *Parent Effectiveness Training: The Proven Program for Raising Responsible Children.* New York: Three Rivers Press.

Gorman, Jean Cheng. 1998. "Parenting Attitudes and Practices of Immigrant Chinese Mothers of Adolescents." *Family Relations* 47 (1): 73–80.

Gottlieb, Alison Stokes. 1997. "Single Mothers of Children with Developmental Disabilities: The Impact of Multiple Roles." *Family Relations* 46 (1): 5–12.

Gottlieb, Annie. 1979. "The Joyful Marriage." *Redbook*. November: 29, 194–96.

Gottlieb, Laurie N., Ariella Lang, and Rhonda Amsel. 1996. "The Long-Term Effects of Grief on Marital Intimacy Following an Infant's Death." *Omega* 33 (1): 1–9.

Gottman, John M. 1979. *Marital Interaction: Experimental Investigations.* New York: Academic.

———. 1994. *Why Marriages Succeed or Fail.* New York: Simon and Schuster.

———. 1996. *What Predicts Divorce?: The Measures.* Hillsdale, NJ: Erlbaum.

Gottman, John M., James Coan, Sybil Carrere, and Catherine Swanson. 1998. "Predicting Marital Happiness and Stability from Newlywed Interactions." *Journal of Marriage and Family* 60 (1): 5–22.

Gottman, John M., and Joan DeClaire. 2001. *The Relationship Cure: A Five-Step Guide for Building Better Connections with Family, Friends, and Lovers.* New York: Crown Publishers.

Gottman, John M., and L. J. Krotkoff. 1989. "Marital Interaction and Satisfaction: A Longitudinal View." *Journal of Consulting and Clinical Psychology* 57: 47–52.

Gottman, John M., and Robert W. Levenson. 2000. "The Timing of Divorce: Predicting When a Couple Will Divorce Over a 14-Year Period." *Journal of Marriage and Family* 62 (3): 737–45.

———. 2002. "A Two-Factor Model for Predicting When a Couple Will Divorce: Exploratory Analyses Using 14-Year Longitudinal Data." *Family Process* 41 (1): 83–96.

Gottman, John M., Robert W. Levenson, James Gross, Barbara Frederickson, Leah Rosenthal, Anna Ruef, and Dan Yoshimoto. 2003. "Correlates of Gay and Lesbian Couples' Relationship Satisfaction and Relationship Dissolution." *Journal of Homosexuality* 45 (1): 23-45.

Gottman, John M., and Clifford I. Notarius. 2000. "Decade Review: Observing Marital Interaction." *Journal of Marriage and Family* 62 (4): 927–47.

———. 2003. "Marital Research in the 20th Century and a Research Agenda for the 21st Century." *Trends in Marriage, Family, and Society* 25 (2): 283–297.

Gottman, John M., and Nan Silver. 1999. *The Seven Principles for Making Marriage Work.* New York: Crown Publishers.

Gough, Brendan, and Paula Reavey. 1997. "Parental Accounts Regarding the Physical Punishment of Children: Discourses of Dis/empowerment." *Child Abuse & Neglect* 21 (5): 417–30.

Gove, Walter R., and Michael Hughes. 1983. *Overcrowding in the Household: An Analysis of Determinants and Effects.* New York: Academic.

Gove, Walter R., Carolyn Briggs Style, and Michael Hughes. 1990. "The Effect of Marriage on the Well-Being of Adults." *Journal of Family Issues* 11 (1): 4–35.

Grady, Denise. 2002. "Vaccine Appears to Prevent Cervical Cancer." *New York Times.* Nov. 21.

———. 2004. "Trying to Avoid Second Caesarean, Many Find Choice Isn't Theirs." *New York Times.* Nov. 29.

Graefe, Deborah R., and Daniel T. Lichter. 1999. "Life Course Transitions of American Children: Parental Cohabitation, Marriage, and Single Motherhood." *Demography* 36 (2): 205–17.

Grall, Timothy. 2000. *Child Support for Custodial Mothers and Fathers.* Washington, DC: U.S. Census Bureau.

———. 2003. *Custodial Mothers and Fathers and Their Child Support: 2001.* Current Population Reports P60-225. Oct.

Grant, Linda, Layne A. Simpson, Xue Lan Rong, and Holly Peters-Golden. 1990. "Gender, Parenthood, and Work Hours of Physicians." *Journal of Marriage and Family* 52 (2): 39–49.

Gray, John. 1995. *Mars and Venus in the Bedroom.* New York: HarperCollins.

Gray, Marjory Roberts, and Laurence Steinberg. 1999. "Unpacking Authoritative Parenting: Reassessing a Multidimensional Construct." *Journal of Marriage and Family* 61 (3): 574–87.

Greathouse, Ann N. 1996. "Quality Child Care from a Parental Perspective." Unpublished M.A. thesis. Omaha, NE: University of Nebraska at Omaha.

Greeff, Abraham, and Berquin Human. 2004. "Resilience in Families in Which a Parent Has Died." *American Journal of Family Therapy* 32 (1): 27–42.

Greeley, Andrew. 1989. "Protestant and Catholic." *American Sociological Review* 54: 485–502.

———. 1991. *Faithful Attraction: Discovering Intimacy, Love, and Fidelity in American Marriage.* New York: Doherty.

Greenberg, Jerrold S., Clint E. Bruess, and Debra W. Hafner. 2002. *Exploring the Dimensions of Human Sexuality.* Sudbury, MA: Jones and Bartlett.

Greenblatt, Cathy Stein. 1983. "The Salience of Sexuality in the Early Years of Marriage." *Journal of Marriage and Family* 45: 289–99.

Greene, Melissa Fay. 2000. "The Orphan Ranger." *New Yorker.* July 17: 38–45.

Greenfield, Patricia M., and Lalita K. Suzuki. 2001. "Culture and Parenthood." Pp. 20–33 in *Parenthood in America,* edited by Jack C. Westman. Madison: University of Wisconsin Press.

Greenfield, Sidney J. 1969. "Love and Marriage in Modern America: A Functional Analysis." *Sociological Quarterly* 6: 361–77.

Greenstein, Gregg A. 2001. "Relationships Made Easy by Marital and Cohabitation Agreements." http://www.frascona.com.

Greenstein, Theodore N. 2001. *Methods of Family Research.* Thousand Oaks CA: Sage.

Gregg, Gail. 1986. "Putting Kids First." *New York Times Magazine.* Apr. 13: 47ff.

Greider, Linda. 1999. "Caring for Parents from Faraway: Host of New Services Relieves Burden on Family Members." *Modern Maturity.* September–October: 18–20.

Greif, Geoffrey, and Mary S. Pabst. 1988. *Mothers Without Custody.* Lexington, MA: Heath.

Grieco, Elizabeth, and Rachel Cassidy. 2001. "Census 2000 Shows America's Diversity." Press Release. Washington, DC: U.S. Census Bureau.

Grimm-Thomas, Karen, and Maureen Perry-Jenkins. 1994. "All in a Day's Work: Job Experiences, Self-Esteem,

and Fathering in Working-Class Families." *Family Relations* 43: 174–81.

Grimsley, Kristen Downey. 2000. "Family a Priority for Young Workers." *Washington Post.* May 3.

Griswold v. *Connecticut.* 1965. 381 U.S. 479, 14 L.Ed.2d 510, 85 S.Ct. 1678.

Groat, Theodore, Peggy Giordano, Stephen Cernkovich, M. D. Puch, and Steven Swinford. 1997. "Attitudes Toward Childbearing Among Young Parents." *Journal of Marriage and Family* 59: 568–81.

Gross, Harriet Engel. 1980. "Dual-Career Couples Who Live Apart: Two Types." *Journal of Marriage and Family* 42: 567–76.

Gross, Jane. 1991a. "A Milestone in the Fight for Gay Rights: A Quiet Suburban Life." *New York Times.* June 30.

———. 1991b. "More Young Single Men Clinging to Apron Strings." *New York Times.* June 16.

———. 1992a. "Collapse of Inner-City Families Creates America's New Orphans." *New York Times.* Mar. 29.

———. 1992b. "Divorced, Middle-Aged and Happy: Women, Especially, Adjust to the 90's." P. 10 in *The New York Times, Themes of the Times.* Englewood Cliffs, NJ: Prentice-Hall.

———. 2001. "A Difference of Generations: Reactions to a World Gone Awry." *New York Times.* Nov. 14.

———. 2004. "Alzheimer's in the Living Room: How One Family Rallies to Cope." *The New York Times.* September 16.

Grote, Nancy K., Kristen E. Naylor, and Margaret S. Clark. 2002. "Perceiving the Division of Family Labor to Be Unfair: Do Social Comparison, Enjoyment, and Competence Matter?" *Journal of Family Psychology* 16: 510–522.

"Groups Opposing Gay marriage Vow to challenge Oregon Decision." 2004. *Knight Ridder/Tribune Business News.* March 4.

Grow, Brian. 2004. "Hispanic Nation: Is America Ready?" *Business Week.* Mar. 15: 58-70.

Groze, V. 1996. *Successful Adoptive Families: A Longitudinal Study.* Westport, CT: Praeger.

Grzywacz, Joseph G., David M. Almeida, and Daniel A. McDonald. 2002. "Work-Family Spillover and

Daily Reports of Work and Family Stress in the Adult Labor Force." *Family Relations* 51 (1): 28–36.

Guelzow, Maureen G., Gloria W. Bird, and Elizabeth H. Koball. 1991. "An Exploratory Path Analysis of the Stress Process for Dual-Career Men and Women." *Journal of Marriage and Family* 53 (1): 151–64.

Gueorguieva, Ralitza V., Randy L. Carter, Mario Ariet, Jeffrey Roth, Charles S. Mahan, and Michael B. Resneck. 2001. "Effect of Teenage Pregnancy on Educational Disabilities in Kindergarten." *American Journal of Epidemiology* 154: 212–20.

Guernsey, Lisa. 2001. "Cyberspace Isn't So Lonely After All." *New York Times.* July 26.

Gurian, Michael. 1996. *The Wonder of Boys: What Parents, Mentors and Educators Can Do to Shape Boys into Exceptional Men.*

Haas, Kurt, and Adalaide Haas. 1993. *Understanding Sexuality*, 3d ed. St. Louis: Mosby.

Haber, C., and B. Gratton. 1994. *Old Age and the Search for Security.* Bloomington: Indiana University Press.

Hacker, Andrew, Ed. 1983. *U/S: A Statistical Portrait of the American People.* New York: Viking.

Haddad, Yvonne Y., and Jane I. Smith. 1996. "Islamic Values Among American Muslims." Pp. 19–40 in *Family and Gender Among American Muslims: Issues Facing Middle Eastern Immigrants and their Descendants*, edited by Barbara C. Aswad and Barbara Bilgé. Philadelphia: Temple University Press.

Hafen, Elder Bruce C. 1998. "Covenant Marriage." July 7. http://www.mormons.org/conferences/96oct/Hafen-Marriage.html.

Hafner, Katie. 2000. "Hi Mom. At the Beep, Leave a Message." *New York Times.* Mar. 16.

Hagar, Laura. 1995. "Why Has AIDS Education Failed?" *Express: The East Bays' Weekly.* June 23: 1, 10–16.

Hagenbaugh, Barbara. 2002. "More Men Just Say No to Working." *USA Today.* Feb. 20.

Hagestad, G. 1996. "On-time, off-time, out of time? Reflections on Continuity and Discontinuity from an Illness Process." Pp. 204–222 in V.L.

Bengston (ed.). *Adulthood and Aging.* New York: Springer.

Haiken, Elizabeth. 2000. "Virtual Virility, or, Does Medicine Make the Man?" *Men and Masculinities* 2 (4): 388–409.

Haines, James and Margery Neely. 1987. *Parents' Work Is Never Done.* Far Hills, NJ: New Horizon.

Haines, Michael R. 1996. "Long-Term Marriage Patterns in the United States from Colonial Times to the Present." *The History of the Family: An International Quarterly* 1 (1): 15–39.

Hall, Edie Jo, and E. Mark Cummings. 1997. "The Effects of Marital and Parent–Child Conflicts on Other Family Members: Grandmothers and Grown Children." *Family Relations* 46 (2): 135–43.

Hall, Elaine J. 2000. "Developing the Gender Relations Perspective: The Emergence of A New Conceptualization of Gender in the 1990s." *Current Perspectives in Social Theory* 20: 91–123.

Hall, Elaine J., and Marnie Salupo Rodriguez. 2003. "The Myth of Postfeminism." *Gender and Society* 17: 878–902.

Hallenbeck, Phyllis N. 1966. "An Analysis of Power Dynamics in Marriage." *Journal of Marriage and Family* 28: 200–203.

Halpern, Sue. 1989a. "AIDS: Rethinking the Risk." *Ms.* May: 80–87.

———. 1989b. "And Baby Makes Three." *Ms* Jan.–Feb.: 151.

Hamachek, Don E. 1971. *Encounters with the Self.* New York: Holt, Rinehart & Winston.

———. 1992. *Encounters with the Self,* 4th ed. New York: Holt, Rinehart & Winston.

Hamby, Sherry L. 1998. "Partner Violence: Prevention and Intervention." Pp. 210–258 in *Partner Violence: A Comprehensive Review of 20 Years of Research*, edited by Jana L. Jasinski and Linda M. Williams. Thousand Oaks CA: Sage.

Hamer, Dean, and Peter Copeland. 1998. *Living with Our Genes.* New York: Doubleday.

Hamer, Jennifer. 2001. *What it Means to Be Daddy: Fatherhood for Black Men Living Away from Their Children.* New York: Columbia University Press.

Hamilton, Brady E., Joyce A. Martin, and Paul D. Sutton. 2003. "Births: Preliminary Data for 2002." *National Vital Statistics Reports* 51(11). June 25.

Hamilton, Brady E., Joyce A. Martin, and Paul D. Sutton. 2004. "Births: Preliminary Data for 2003." *National Vital Statistics Reports* 53(9). Hyattville MD: Nov. 23.

Hamilton, W. D. 1964. "The Genetical Evolution of Social Behavior. II." *Journal of Theoretical Biology* 7: 17–52.

Hammen, Constance, Patricia A. Brennan, and Josephine H. Shih. 2004. "Family discord and Stress Predictors of Depression and Other Disorders in Adolescent Children of Depressed and Nondepressed Women." *Journal of the American Academy of Child and Adolescent Psychiatry* 43 (8): 994–1003.

Hanash, Kamal A. 1994. *Perfect Lover: Understanding and Overcoming Sexual Dysfunction.* New York: SPI.

Hanawalt, Barbara. 1986. *The Ties That Bound: Peasant Families in Medieval England.* New York: Oxford University Press.

Hancock, LynNell. 1995. "Breaking Point." *Newsweek.* Mar. 6: 56–62.

Hans, Jason D. 2002. "Stepparenting after Divorce: Stepparents' Legal Position Regarding Custody, Access, and Support." *Family Relations* 51 4): 301–307.

Hansen, Donald A., and Reuben Hill. 1964. "Families Under Stress." Pp. 782–819 in *The Handbook of Marriage and the Family*, edited by Harold Christensen. Chicago: Rand McNally.

Hansen, Gary L. 1985. "Perceived Threats and Marital Jealousy." *Social Psychology Quarterly* 48 (3): 262–68.

Hansen, M., M. Harway, and N. Cervantes. 1991. "Therapists' Perceptions of Severity in Cases of Family Violence." *Violence and Victims* 6: 225–35.

Hanson, Thomas L. 1999. "Does Parental Conflict Explain Why Divorce Is Negatively Associated with Child Welfare?" *Social Forces* 77: 1283–1315.

Hanson, Thomas L., Sara S. McLanahan, and Elizabeth Thomson. 1996. "Double Jeopardy: Parental Conflict and Stepfamily Outcomes for Children." *Journal of Marriage and Family* 58 (1): 141–54.

"Happiest Couples in Study Have Sex After 60." 1992. *New York Times National Sunday*. Oct. 4: 13.

Haraway, Donna. 1989. *Primate Visions: Gender, Race, and Nature in the World of Modern Science*. New York: Routledge, Chapman and Hall.

Harden, B. 2001. "Bible Belt Couples 'Put Asunder' More, Despite New Efforts." *New York Times*. May 21.

———. 2002. " 'Dead Broke' " Dads' Child-Support Struggle." *New York Times*. Nov. 29.

Harden, B., and S. Sengupta. 2001. "Some Passengers Singled Out for Exclusion by Flight Crew." *New York Times*. Sept. 22.

Haring, Michelle, Paul L. Hewitt, and Gordon L. Flett. 2003. "Perfectionism, Coping, and Quality of Intimate Relationships." *Journal of Marriage and Family* 65 (1): 143–158.

Harmon, Amy. 1998. "Guess Who's Going on Line." *New York Times*. Mar. 26.

———. 2003. "Lost? Hiding? Your Cellphone is Keeping Tabs." *New York Times*. Dec. 21.

Harris, B. 1998. "Listening to Caregiving Sons: Misunderstood Realities." *The Gerontologist* 38: 342–52.

Harris, Christine R. 2002. "Sexual and Romantic Jealousy in Heterosexual and Homosexual Adults." *Psychological Science* 13 (1):7–12.

———. 2003a. "A Review of Sex Differences in Sexual Jealousy, Including Self-Report Data Psychophysiological Responses, Interpersonal Violence, and Morbid Jealousy." *Personality and Social Psychology Review* 7 (2): 102–108.

———. 2003b. "Factors Associated with jealousy over Real and Imagined Infidelity." *Psychology of Women Quarterly* 27 (4): 319–329.

Harris, Gardiner. 2003. "Levitra, A Rival with Ribald Ads, Gains on Viagra." *New York Times*. Sept. 18.

———. 2004. "Pfizer Gives Up Testing Viagra on Women." *New York Times*. Feb. 28.

Harris, Kathleen M., Frank F. Furstenberg Jr., and Jeremy K. Marmer. 1998. "Paternal Involvement with Adolescents in Intact Families: The Influence of Fathers Over the Life Course." *Demography* 35 (2): 201–16.

Harris, Phyllis B., and Joyce Bichler. 1997. *Men Giving Care: Reflections of Husbands and Sons*. New York: Garland.

Harrist, Amanda W., and Ricardo C. Ainslie. 1998. "Marital Discord and Child Behavior Problems." *Journal of Family Issues* 19 (2): 140–63.

Harry, Joseph. 1983. "Gay Male and Lesbian Relationships." Pp. 216–34 in *Contemporary Families and Alternative Lifestyles: Handbook in Research and Theory*, edited by Eleanor D. Macklin and Roger H. Rubin, Newbury Park, CA: Sage.

Hartog, Henrik. 2000. *Man and Wife in America: A History*. Cambridge MA: Harvard.

Harvey, Elizabeth. 1999. "Short-Term and Long-Term Effects of Early Parental Employment on Children of the National Longitudinal Survey of Youth." *Developmental Psychology* 35: 445–59.

Harvey, John H., and Mark A. Fine. 2004. *Children of Divorce: Stories of Loss and Growth*. Mahwah NJ: Erlbaum.

Harvey, Kay. 2002. "Help for Parents a Call Away: Specialists Coach Moms, Dads." *Omaha World Herald*. November 10: E-5.

Hatch, Laurie R., and Kris Bulcroft. 2004. "Does Long-Term Marriage Bring Less Frequent Disagreements?" *Journal of Family Issues* 25 (4): 465–495.

"Hatchet Job on the Federal Marriage Amendment?" 2004. Family Research Council. March 25. http://www.frc.org

Hatfield, Larry D. 1996. "Same-Sex Marriages Assailed in Congress." *San Francisco Examiner*. May 8. A–1.

Hawke, Sharryl, and David Knox. 1978. "The One-Child Family: A New Lifestyle." *Family Coordinator* 27: 215–19.

Hawkins, Alan J., Steven L. Nock, Julia C. Wilson, Laura Sanchez, and James D. Wright. 2002. "Attitudes about Covenant Marriage and Divorce: Policy Implications from a Three-State Comparison." *Family Relations* 51 (2): 166–175.

Hayden, Dolores. 1981. *The Grand Domestic Revolution: A History of Feminist Designs for American Homes, Neighborhoods, and Cities*. Cambridge, MA: MIT Press.

Hayden, Thomas. 2000. "A Sense of Self." *Newsweek Special Issue*. Fall/Winter: 57–62.

Hayes, Cheryl D. (Ed.). 1987. *Risking the Future: Adolescent Sexuality, Pregnancy, and Childbearing*, vol. 1. Washington, DC: National Academy Press.

Haynes, Faustina E. 2000. "Gender and Family Ideals: An Exploratory Study of Black Middle Class Americans." *Journal of Family Issues* 21: 811–37.

Hays, Sharon. 1996. *The Cultural Contradictions of Motherhood*. New Haven, CT: Yale University Press.

Hazen, C., and P. Shaver. 1994. "Attachment As an Organizing Framework for Research on Close Relationships." *Psychological Inquiry* 5: 1–22.

"Hearing Tomorrow in Alaska's Gay Marriage 'Catch 22' Could Impact Other States That Tie Benefits to Marriage." 2001. American Civil Liberties Union press release. Apr. 16. http://www.aclu.org/news/2001.

Heaton, Tim B. 2002. "Factors Contributing to Increasing Marital Stability in the United States." *Journal of Family Issues* 23 (3): 392–409.

Heaton, Tim B., Cardell K. Jacobson, and Kimberlee Holland. 1999. "Persistence and Change in Decisions to Remain Childless." *Journal of Marriage and Family* 61: 531–39.

Heaton, Tim B., and Edith L. Pratt. 1990. "The Effects of Religious Homogamy on Marital Satisfaction and Stability." *Journal of Family Issues* 11 (2): 191–207.

Heckert, D. Alex, Thomas C. Nowak, and Kay A. Snyder. 1998. "The Impact of Husbands' and Wives' Relative Earnings on Marital Disruption." *Journal of Marriage and Family* 60 (3): 690–703.

Hedges, Chris. 2000. "Translating America for Parents and Family." *New York Times*. June 19.

Heiman, Julia R., aand Joseph Lopiccolo. 1992. *Becoming Orgasmic: A Sexual and Personal Growth Program for Women*. New York: Simon and Schuster.

Heimdal, Kristen R., and Sharon K. Houseknecht. 2003. "Cohabiting and Married Couples' Income Organization: Approaches in Sweden and the United States." *Journal of Marriage and Family* 65 (3): 525–538.

Heiss, Jerold. 1991. "Gender and Romantic Love Roles." *Sociological Quarterly* 32: 575–92.

Helgeson, Vicki S. 1994. "Relation of Agency and Communion to Well-Being: Evidence and Potential Explanations." *Psychological Bulletin* 116 (3): 412–29.

Hellstrom, Wayne J. 1997. *Male Infertility and Sexual Dysfunction.* New York: Springer.

Helms, Heather M., Ann C. Crouter, and Susan M. McHale. 2003. "Marital Quality and Spouses' Marriage Work with Close Friends and Each Other." *Journal of Marriage and Family* 65 (4): 963–977.

Henderson, Mark, and Patrick Barkham. 2002. "Biological Clock Strikes for Men Too—At Age 35." *The Times* (London). Oct. 15.

Henderson, Tammy L., and Patricia B. Moran. 2001. "Grandparent Visitation Rights." *Journal of Family Issues* 22 (5): 619–38.

Hendrick, Clyde, Susan S. Hendrick, and Amy Dicke. 1998. "The Love Attitudes Scale: Short Form." *Journal of Social and Personal Relationships* 15 (2): 147–59.

Hendrick, Susan S. 2000. "Links Between Sexuality and Love as Contributors to Relationship Satisfaction." Paper presented at the annual meeting of the National Council on Family Relations, Minneapolis, MN, Nov. 10–13.

Henley, Nancy, and Jo Freeman. 1989. "The Sexual Politics of Interpersonal Behavior." Pp. 457–69 in *Women: A Feminist Perspective*, 4th ed., edited by Jo Freeman. Mountain View, CA: Mayfield.

———. 1995. "The Sexual Politics of Interpersonal Behavior." Pp. 79–91 in *Women: A Feminist Perspective*, 5th ed. Mountain View, CA: Mayfield.

Henningson, Ellen. 1997. "Financial Abuse of the Elderly." Wisconsin Department of Health and Family Services. www.dhrs.state.wi.us.

Henretta, J. C., M. S. Hill, W. Lei, B. J. Soldo, and D. A. Wolf. 1997. "Selection of Children to Provide Care: The Effect of Early Parental Transfers." *Journal of Gerontology* 52B: 110–19.

Henshaw, Stanley K. 1998. "Unintended Pregnancy in the United States." *Family Planning Perspectives* 30: 24–29; 46.

Herbert, Bob. 2003. "The Big Chill at the Lab." *New York Times.* Nov. 3.

Herbert, Tracy Bennett, Roxane Cohen Silver, and John H. Ellard. 1991. "Coping with an Abusive Relationship: I. How and Why Do Women Stay?" *Journal of Marriage and Family* 53 (2): 311–25.

Herel, Suzanne. 2004. "29-Day Drama." *San Francisco Chronicle*. March 12.

Hernandez, Raymond. 2001. "Children's Sexual Exploitation Underestimated, Study Finds." *New York Times.* Sept. 10.

Hertz, Frederick. 2001. *Living Together: A Legal Guide for Unmarried Couples.* Berkeley, CA: Nolo Press.

Hertz, Rosanna. 1986. *More Equal Than Others: Women and Men in Dual Career Marriages.* Berkeley: University of California Press.

———. 1997. "A Typology of Approaches to Child Care." *Journal of Family Issues* 18 (4): 355–85.

Hetherington, E. Mavis. 1973. "Girls Without Fathers." *Psychology Today* 6: 47–52.

———. 1989. "Coping with Family Transitions: Winners, Losers, and Survivors." *Child Development* 60: 1–14.

———. (Ed.). 1999. *Coping with Divorce, Single Parenting, and Remarriage: A Risk and Resiliency Perspective.* Mahwah, NJ: Erlbaum.

———. 2003. "Intimate Pathways: Changing Patterns in Close Personal Relationships across Time." *Family Relations* 52: 318–331.

Hetherington, E. Mavis, and K. M. Jodl. 1994. "Stepfamilies as Settings for Child Development." Pp. 55–80 in *Stepfamilies: Who Benefits? Who Does Not?*, edited by Alan Booth and J. Dunn. Hillsdale, NJ: Erlbaum.

Hetherington, E. Mavis, and John Kelly. 2002. *For Better or for Worse: Divorce Reconsidered.* New York: Norton.

Hewlett, Sylvia Ann. 1986. *A Lesser Life: The Myth of Women's Liberation in America.* New York: Morrow.

———. 2002. *Creating A Life: Professional Women and The Quest for Children.* New York: Hyperion.

Hewlett, Sylvia Ann, and Cornell West. 1998. *The War Against Parents: What We Can Do for America's Beleaguered Moms and Dads.* Boston: Houghton Mifflin.

Heyman, Richard A., and Amy M. Smith Slep. 2002. "Do Child Abuse and Interparental Violence Lead to Adulthood Family Violence?" *Journal of Marriage and the Family* 64: 864–870.

Heywood, Leslie, and Jennifer Drake. 1997. "Introduction." Pp. 1–20 in *Third Wave Agenda: Being Feminist, Doing Feminism*, edited by Leslie Heywood and Jennifer Drake. Minneapolis: University of Minnesota Press.

Hiedemann, Bridget, Olga Suhomlinova, and Angela M. O'Rand. 1998. "Economic Independence, Economic Status, and Empty Nest in Midlife Marital Disruption." *Journal of Marriage and Family* 60 (1): 219–31.

Hein, Holly. 2000. *Sexual Detours: Infidelity and Intimacy at the Crossroads.* New York: St. Martin's Press.

Hill, C. A., and L. K. Preston. 1996. "Individual Differences in the Sexual Experience of Sexual Motivation: Theory and Measurement of Dispositional Sexual Motive." *Journal of Sex Research* 33: 27–45.

Hill, Jeffrey E., Alan J. Hawkins, and Brent C. Miller. 1996. "Work and Family in the Virtual Office: Perceived Influences of Mobile Telework." *Family Relations* 45 (3): 293–301.

Hill, Miriam R., and Volker Thomas. 2000. "Strategies for Racial Identity Development: Narratives of Black and White Women in Interracial Partner Relationships." *Family Relations* 49 (2): 193–200.

Hill, Nancy E., Cynthia Ramirez, and Larry E. Dumka. 2003. "Early Adolescents' Career Aspirations: A Qualitative Study of Perceived Barriers and Family Support Among Low-Income Ethnically Diverse Adolescents." *Journal of Family Issues* 24 (7):934–959.

Hill, Reuben. 1958. "Generic Features of Families Under Stress." *Social Casework* 49: 139–50.

Hill, Shirley Y., and Huixing Yuan. 1999. "Familial Density of Alcoholism and Onset of Adolescent Drinking." *Journal of Studies on Alcohol* 60 (1): 7–10.

Himes, Christine L. 2001a. "Elderly Americans." *Population Bulletin* 56 (4).

Washington DC: Population Reference Bureau.

———. 2001b. "Social Demography of Contemporary Families and Aging." Pp. 47–50 in *Families in Later Life: Connections and Transitions*, edited by Alexis J. Walker, Margaret Manoogian-O'Dell, Lori A. McGraw, and Diana L. G. White. Thousand Oaks, CA: Pine Forge.

Hinck, Shelly Schaefer, and Richard W. Thomas. 1999. "Rape Myth Acceptance in College Students: How Far Have We Come?" *Sex Roles* 40 (9/10): 815–32.

Hines, Melissa, Susan Golombok, John Rust, Katie J. Johnston, Jean Golding, and the Avon Longitudinal Study of Parents and Children Study Team. 2002. "Testosterone During Pregnancy and Gender Role Behavior of Preschool Children: A Longitudinal Population Study." *Child Development* 73: 1678–1687.

Hinshaw, Stephen P. 2003. "A Family Perspective on Mental Disorder: Silence, Stigma, Diagnosis, Treatment, and Resilience." *The ADHD Report* 11 (6): 1–4.

Hirsch, Jennifer S. 2003. *A Courtship after Marriage: Sexuality and Love in Mexican Transnational Families.* Berkeley: University of California Press.

"Hispanic Nation—Myth and Reality." 2004. *Business Week.* Mar. 15: 128.

"Hispanics Back Big Government and Bush Too." 2003. *New York Times.* Aug. 3.

Hitt, Jack. 2000. "The Second Sexual Revolution." *New York Times Magazine.* Feb. 20: 34; 36–41; 50; 62; 64; 68–69.

Hochschild, Arlie. 1989. *The Second Shift: Working Parents and the Revolution at Home.* New York: Viking/Penguin.

———. 1997. *Time Bind: When Work Becomes Home and Home Becomes Work.* New York: Henry Holt.

———. 2003. *The Commercialization of Intimate Life: Notes from Home and Work.* Berkeley, CA: University of California Press.

Hofferth, Sandra L. and John F. Sandberg. 2001. "How American Children Spend Their Time." *Journal of Marriage and Family* 63 (2): 295–308.

Hoffman, Lois W., and Jean B. Manis. 1979. "The Value of Children in the United States: A New Approach to the Study of Fertility." *Journal of Marriage and Family* 41: 583–96.

Hogben, Matthew, and Caroline K. Waterman. 2000. "Patterns of Conflict Resolution Within Relationships and Coercive Sexual Behavior of Men and Women." *Sex Roles* 43 (5/6): 341–57.

Holloway, Lynette. 1994. "A Grandmother Fights for Her 2d Generation." *New York Times.* Dec. 12: 59.

Holmes, Ivory H. 1983. *The Allocation of Time by Women Without Family Responsibilities.* Lanham, MD: University Press of America.

Holmes, J. G., and S. L. Murray. 1996. "Conflict in Close Relationships." Pp. 622–54 in *Social Psychology: Handbook of Basic Principles*, edited by E. T. Higgins and A. Kruglanski. New York: Guilford.

Holmes, Jeremy. 1997. "Attachment, Autonomy, Intimacy: Some Clinical Implications of Attachment Theory." *British Journal of Medical Psychology* 70 (3): 231–43.

"Homeless Families with Children." 2001. National Coalition for the Homeless, Fact Sheet #7. http://www.nationalhomeless.org/families.html

Hondagneu-Sotelo, Pierrette. 1996. "Overcoming Patriarchal Constraints: The Reconstruction of Gender Relations Among Mexican Immigrant Women and Men." Pp. 184–205 in *Race, Class, and Gender*, edited by Esther Ngan-Ling Chow, Doris Wilkinson, and Maxine Baca Zinn. Newbury Park, CA: Sage.

———. 2001. *Doméstica: Immigrant Workers Cleaning and Caring in the Shadows of Affluence.* Berkeley: U. of California Press.

Hondagneu-Sotelo, Pierrette, and E. Avila. 1997. "I'm Here But I'm There: The Meaning of Transnational Motherhood." *Gender and Society* 11: 548–71.

Hondagneu-Sotelo, Pierrette, and Michael A. Messner. 1994. "Gender Displays and Men's Power: The 'New Man' and the Mexican Immigrant." Pp. 200–18 in *Theorizing Masculinity*, edited by Harry Brod and Michael Kaufman. Newbury Park, CA: Sage.

———. 1999. "Gender Displays and Men's Power: The 'New Man' and the Mexican Immigrant Man." Pp. 342–58 in *American Families: A Multicultural Reader*, edited by Stephanie Coontz. New York: Routledge.

Hood, Jane C. 1986. "The Provider Role: Its Meaning and Measurement." *Journal of Marriage and Family* 48: 349–59.

Hook, Misty K., Lawrence H. Gerstein, Lacy Detterich, and Betty Gridley. 2003. "How Close Are We? Measuring Intimacy and Examining Gender Differences." *Journal of Counseling and Development* 81 (4): 462–473.

Hooks, bell. 2000. *All About Love.* New York: HarperCollins.

Hornik, Donna. 2001. "Can the Church Get in Step with Stepfamilies?" *U.S. Catholic* 66 (7): 30–41.

Horowitz, A. 1985. "Sons and Daughters as Caregivers to Older Parents: Differences in Role Performance and Consequences." *The Gerontologist* 25: 612–17.

Horowitz, June Andrews. 1999. "Negotiating Couplehood: The Process of Resolving the December Dilemma Among Interfaith Couples." *Family Process* 38: 303–23.

Houseknect, Sharon K., and Jaya Sastry. 1996. "Family 'Decline' and Child Well-Being: A Comparative Assessment." *Journal of Marriage and Family* 58 (3): 726–39.

Houts, Renate M., Elliot Robins, and Ted L. Huston. 1996. "Compatibility and the Development of Premarital Relationships." *Journal of Marriage and Family* 58: 7–20.

Howard, J. A. 1988. "Gender Differences in Sexual Attitudes: Conservatism or Powerlessness?" *Gender and Society* 2: 103–14.

Hsia, Annie. 2002. "Considering Grandparents' Rights and Parents' Wishes: 'Special Circumstances' Litigation Alternatives." *The Legal Intelligencer* 227, No. 83. Oct. 28. P. 7.

Hsu, F. L. K. 1971. *Kinship and Culture.* Chicago: Aldine.

Huber, Joan. 1980. "Will U.S. Fertility Decline Toward Zero?" *Sociological Quarterly* 21: 481–92.

———. 1986. "Trends in Gender Stratification, 1970–1985." *Sociological Forum* 1: 476–95.

———. 1989. "A Theory of Gender Stratification." Pp. 110–19 in *Feminist Frontiers II*, edited by Laurel Richardson and Verta Taylor. New York: Random House.

Hughes, Diane, Ellen Galinsky, and Anne Morris. 1992. "The Effects of Job Characteristics on Marital Quality: Specifying Linking Mechanisms." *Journal of Marriage and Family* 54 (1): 31–42.

Hughes, Robert, Jr., and Jason D. Hans. 2001. "A Review of the Role New Technology Plays in Family Life." *Journal of Family Issues* 22: 776–90.

Human Rights Campaign. 2003. "Study Shows Continued Spread of Laws Prohibiting Gay, Lesbian, Bisexual, Transgender Workplace Discrimination." Press release. May 16. www.hrc.org

———. 2004. "Domestic Partner Benefits." www.hrc.org. Feb. 16.

Hummer, Robert A., Kimberly A. Hack, and R. Kelly Raley. 2004. "Retrospective Reporting of Pregnancy Wantedness and Child Well-Being in the United States. *Journal of Family Issues* 25: 404- 428.

Hunt, Janet G., and Larry L. Hunt. 1977. "Dilemmas and Contradictions of Status: The Case of the Dual-Career Family." *Social Problems* 24: 407–16.

———. 1986. "The Dualities of Careers and Families: New Integrations or New Polarizations?" Pp. 275–89 in *Family in Transition: Rethinking Marriage, Sexuality, Child Rearing, and Family Organization*, 5th ed., edited by Arlene S. Skolnick and Jerome H. Skolnick. Boston: Little, Brown.

Hunt, Mary. 2003. *Debt-proof Your Marriage: How to Achieve Financial Harmony*. Grand Rapids, MI: Fleming H. Revell.

Hunter, Andrea G. 1997. "Counting on Grandmothers: Black Mothers' and Fathers' Reliance on Grandmothers for Parenting Support." *Journal of Family Issues* 18 (3): 251–69.

Hunter, Andrea G., and Sherrill L. Sellers. 1998. "Feminist Attitudes Among African American Women and Men." *Gender and Society* 12: 81–99.

Hunter, Melanie. 2004. "Massachusetts Court Urged to Stay Same-Sex 'Marriage' Ruling." *CNSNEWS.COM*. April 20. http://www.cnsnews.com

Hurtado, Aída. 2003. *Voicing Chicana Feminisms: Young Women Speak Out on Sexuality and Identity*. New York: NYU Press.

Hurwitt, Sam. 2004. "Meet the Quirkyalones." *East Bay Express*. March 17.

Huston, A. C., V. C. McLoyd, and C. G. Coll. 1994. "Children and Poverty: Issues in Contemporary Research." *Child Development* 65 (2): 275–82.

Hutchinson, Ray, and Miles McNall. 1994. "Early Marriage in a Hmong Cohort." *Journal of Marriage and Family* 56 (3): 579–90.

Hutchison, Ira W. 1999. "Alcohol, Fear, and Woman Abuse." *Sex Roles* 40 (11): 893–906.

Huyck, M. H. 1996. "Marriage and Close Relationships of the Marital Kind." Pp. 56–67 in *Aging and the Family*, edited by R. Blieszner and V. H. Bedford. London: Praeger.

Hwang, Sean-Shong, and Benigno E. Aguirre. 1997. "Structural and Assimilationist Explanations of Asian American Intermarriage." *Journal of Marriage and Family* 59: 758–72.

Hwang, Sean-Shong, and Rogelio Saenz. 1997. "Fertility of Chinese Immigrants in the U.S.: Testing a Fertility Emancipation Hypothesis." *Journal of Marriage and Family* 59: 50–61.

Hyde, Janet Shibley, Elizabeth Fennema, and Susan Lamon. 1990. "Gender Differences in Mathematics Performance: A Meta-analysis." *Psychological Bulletin* 106: 139–55.

Ihinger-Tallman, Marilyn, and Kay Pasley. 1997. "Stepfamilies in 1984 and Today—A Scholarly Perspective." *Marriage and Family Review* 26 (1-2): 19–41.

Ikkink, Karen Klein, Theo van Tilburg, and Kees Knipscheer. 1999. "Perceived Instrumental Support Exchanges in Relationships Between Elderly Parents and Their Adult Children: Normative and Structural Explanations." *Journal of Marriage and Family* 61 (4): 831–44.

"Illegal Immigrant Population." 2001. *New York Times*. July 26.

In Re-Petition of L. S. and V. L. for the Adoption of T. and of M. Sup. Ct. D.C.,

Fam. Div. Adoption Nos. A–269–90 and A–270–90.

"Infertile Black Couples." 1999. *Omaha World-Herald*. July 11.

Ingersoll-Dayton, Berit, Margaret B. Neal, Jung-Hwa Ha, and Leslie B. Hammer. 2003. "Redressing Inequity in Parent Care Among Siblings." *Journal of Marriage and Family* 65 (1): 201–212.

Ingersoll-Dayton, Berit, Margaret B. Neal, and Leslie B. Hammer. 2001. "Aging Parents Helping Adult Children: The Experience of the Sandwiched Generation." *Family Relations* 50 (3): 262–71.

Ingoldsby, Bron B. 1995a. "Marital Structure." Pp. 117–37 in *Families in Multicultural Perspective*, edited by Bron B. Ingoldsby and Susanna Smith. New York: Guilford.

———. 1995b. "Mate Selection and Marriage." Pp. 143–60 in *Families in Multicultural Perspective*, edited by Bron B. Ingoldsby and Susanna Smith. New York: Guilford.

Ingoldsby, Bron B., and Suzanna Smith (Eds.). 1995. *Families in Multicultural Perspective*. New York: Guilford.

Ingoldsby, Bron B., and Suzanne R. Smith, eds. 2005. *Families in Global and Multicultural Perspective*, 2nd ed. Thousand Oaks CA: Sage.

Ingoldsby, Bron B., Suzanne R. Smith, and J. Elizabeth Miller. 2004. *Exploring Family Theories*. Los Angeles: Roxbury.

Ingrassia, Michele. 1995a. "Ordered to Surrender." *Newsweek*. Feb. 6: 44–45.

———. 1995b. "On the Side of the Child." *Newsweek*. Feb. 20: 63.

Institute for Social Research. University of Michigan. 2002. "U.S. Husbands Are Doing More Housework While Wives Are Doing Less." Press release. Mar. 12.

Iovine, Julie V. 2002. "Fido Is Having a Senior Moment." *New York Times*. Dec. 1.

Isaacs, Maria Beth, Braulio Montalvo, and David Abelsohn. 1986. *The Difficult Divorce: Therapy for Children and Families*. New York: Basic.

Isaksen, Lise W. 2002. "Toward a Sociology of (Gendered) Disgust." *Journal of Family Issues* 23 (7): 791–811.

Ishii-Kuntz, Masako. 2000. "Diversity Within Asian American Families."

Pp. 274–92 in *Handbook of Family Diversity*, edited by David H. Demo, Katherine R. Allen, and Mark Fine. New York: Oxford.

Ishii-Kuntz, Masako, and Karen Seccombe. 1989. "The Impact of Children Upon Social Support Networks Throughout the Life Course." *Journal of Marriage and Family* 51 (3): 777–90.

Island, David, and Patrick Letellier. 1991. *Men Who Beat the Men Who Love Them: Battered Gay Men and Domestic Violence.* New York: Haworth

Jackson, Maggie. 2002. "Using Technology to Add New Dimensions to Nightly Call Home." *New York Times.* Oct. 22.

Jackson, Shelly, Lynette Feder, David R. Forde, Robert C. Davis, Christopher D. Maxwell, and Bruce G. Taylor. 2003. *Batterer Intervention Programs: Where Do We Go From Here?* Washington DC: U.S. National Institute of Justice.

Jacobson, Neil S., and Andrew Christensen. 1996. *Integrative Couple Therapy: Promoting Acceptance and Change.* New York: W. W. Norton.

Jacobson, Neil S., and John M. Gottman. 2001. "Anatomy of A Violent Relationship." Pp. 475–487 in *Family in Transition*, 11th ed., edited by Jerome and Arlene Skolnick. Boston: Allyn and Bacon.

Jacobvitz, Deborah, and Neil F. Bush. 1996. "Reconstructions of Family Relationships: Parent–Child Alliances, Personal Distress, and Self-Esteem." *Developmental Psychology* 32 (4): 732–43.

Jacoby, Susan. 1999. "Great Sex: What's Age Got to Do with It?" *Modern Maturity.* September–October: 41–47.

Jain, Anju, and Jay Belsky. 1997. "Fathering and Acculturation: Immigrant Indian Families with Young Children." *Journal of Marriage and Family* 59 (4): 873–83.

Jaksch, Mary. 2002. *Learn to Love: A Practical Guide to Fulfilling Relationships.* San Francisco, CA: Chronicle Books.

Jana, Reena. 2000. "Arranged Marriages, Minus the Parents." *New York Times.* Aug. 17.

Janofsky, Michael. 2001. "Conviction of a Polygamist Raises Fears Among Others." *New York Times.* May 24.

———. 2002. "Custody Case in California Paves Way for Fathers." *New York Times.* June 8.

Jarrett, Robin L., and Stephanie M. Jefferson. 2004. "Women's Danger Management Strategies in an Inner-City Housing Project." *Family Relations* 53 (2): 138–147.

Jayokody, R. and A. Kalil. 2002. "Social Fathering in Low-Income, African American Families with Preschool Children." *Journal of Marriage and Family* 64 (2): 504–516.

J.B. v. M.B. and C.C. 2001. 170 N.J. 9

Jeffries, Vincent. 2000. "Virtue and Marital Conflict: A Theoretical Formulation and Research Agenda." *Sociological Perspectives* 43 (2): 231–46.

Jendrick, Margaret Platt. 1993. "Grandparents Who Parent Their Grandchildren: Effects on Lifestyle." *Journal of Marriage and Family* 55 (3): 609–21.

Jenkins, Jennifer M. 2000. "Marital Conflict and Children's Emotions: The Development of an Anger Organization." *Journal of Marriage and Family* 62 (3): 723–36.

Jenks, R. L. 1998. "Swinging: A Review of the Literature." *Archives of Sexual Behavior* 27: 507–21.

Jepsen, Lisa. K., and Christopher A. Jepsen. 2002. "An Empirical Analysis of the Matching Patterns of Same-Sex and Opposite-Sex Couples?" *Demography* 39 (3): 435–453.

Jervey, Gay. 2004. "The Bad Mother." *Good Housekeeping.* August: 132–182.

Jeynes, William. 2000. "A Longitudinal Analysis on the Effects of Remarriage Following Divorce on the Academic Achievement of Adolescents." *Journal of Divorce and Remarriage* 33 (1/2): 131–48.

Jezl, D. R., C. E. Molidor, and T. L. Wright. 1996. "Physical, Sexual and Psychological Abuse in High School Dating Relationships: Prevalence Rates and Self-Esteem Issues." *Child and Adolescent Social Work Journal* 13 (1): 69–74.

Johann, Sara Lee. 1994. *Domestic Abusers: Terrorists in Our Homes.* Springfield, IL: Thomas.

Johannson, Melanie A., and Leslie M. Tutty. 1998. "An Evaluation of After-Treatment Couples' Groups for Wife Abuse." *Family Relations* 47 (1): 27–35.

John, Daphne, Beth Anne Shelton, and Kristen Luschen. 1995. "Race, Ethnicity, and Perceptions of Fairness." *Journal of Family Issues* 16: 357–79.

John, Robert. 1998. "Native American Families." Pp. 382–421 in *Ethnic Families in America: Patterns and Variations*, edited by Charles H. Mindel, Robert W. Haberstein, and Roosevelt Wright, Jr. Upper Saddle River, NJ: Prentice Hall.

Johnson, Colleen L. 1988. *Ex Familia: Grandparents, Parents, and Children Adjust to Divorce.* New Brunswick, NJ: Rutgers University Press.

Johnson, Colleen L., and B. M. Barer. 1990. "Families and Networks Among Older Inner-City Blacks." *The Gerontologist* 30: 726–33.

———. 1997. *Life Beyond 85 Years: The Aura of Survivorship.* New York: Springer.

Johnson, Dirk. 1990. "Chastity Organizations: Starting Over in Purity." *New York Times.* Jan. 28.

———. 1991. "Polygamists Emerge from Secrecy, Seeking Not Just Peace but Respect." *New York Times.* Apr. 9.

———. 1995. "Home on the Range (and Lonely Too)." *New York Times.* Dec. 12.

———. 2002. "Until Dust Do Us Part." *Newsweek.* Mar. 25. P. 41.

Johnson, Earl S., Ann Levine, and Fred Doolittle. 1999. *Fathers' Fair Share: Helping Poor Men Manage Child Support and Fatherhood.* New York: Russell Sage.

Johnson, Elizabeth M., and Ted L. Huston. 1998. "The Perils of Love, or Why Wives Adapt to Husbands During the Transition to Parenthood." *Journal of Marriage and Family* 60 (1): 195–204.

Johnson, Jason B. 2000. "Something Akin to Family: Struggling Parents, Kids, Move in with Their Mentors." *San Francisco Chronicle.* November 10.

Johnson, Kirk. 1998. "Self-Image Is Suffering from Lack of Esteem." *New York Times.* May 5: B12.

Johnson, Michael P. 1995. "Patriarchal Terrorism and Common Couple Violence: Two Forms of Violence Against Women." *Journal of Marriage and Family* 57 (2): 283–94.

———. 2001. "Conflict and Control: Images of Symmetry and Asymmetry in Domestic Violence. Pp. 95–104 in *Couples in Conflict*, edited by Alan Booth, Ann C. Crouter, and M. Clements. Hillsdale, NJ: Erlbaum.

Johnson, Michael P., and Kathleen J. Ferraro. 2000. "Research on Domestic Violence in the 1990s: Making Distinctions." *Journal of Marriage and Family* 62 (4): 948–63.

Johnson, Michael P., Ted L. Huston, Stanley D. Gaines, Jr., and George Levinger. 1992. "Patterns of Married Life Among Young Couples." *Journal of Social and Personal Relationships* 9: 343–64.

Johnson, Suzanne M., and Elizabeth O'Connor. 2002. *The Gay Baby Boom: The Psychology of Gay Parenthood.* New York: New York University Press.

Johnson, Walter R., and D. Michael Warren. 1994. *Inside the Mixed Marriage: Accounts of Changing Attitudes, Patterns, and Perceptions of Cross-Cultural and Interracial Marriages.* New York: University Press of America.

Johnston, Janet, and Linda K. Girtner. 2001. "Family Abductions, Descriptive Profiles, and Preventive Interventions." *Juvenile Justice Bulletin.* January.

Jones, A.J., and M. Galinsky. 2003. "Restructuring the Stepfamily: Old Myths, New Stories." *Social Work* 48 (2): 228–237.

Jones, Anne C. 2004. "Transforming the Story: Narrative Applications to a Stepmother Support Group." *Families in Society: The Journal of Contemporary Human Services* 85 (1): 29–39.

Jones, Charisse. 2001. "An Agonizing Road for Kids of Sept. 11." *USA Today.* Oct. 19.

Jones, Nicholas A., and Amy Symens Smith. 2001. "The Two or More Races Population: 2000." *Census 2000 Brief* C2KBR/01-6. Nov.

Jones, Rachel K., Jacqueline E. Darroch, and Stanley K. Henshaw. 2002. "Patterns in The Socioeconomic Characteristics of Women Obtaining Abortions in 2000–2001." *Perspectives on Sexual and Reproductive Health* 34: 226–235.

Jong-Fast, Molly. 2003. "Out of Step and Having a Baby." *New York Times.* Oct. 5.

Joseph, Elizabeth. 1991. "My Husband's Nine Wives." *New York Times.* May 23.

Jourard, Sidney M. 1976. "Reinventing Marriage." Pp. 231–37 in *Process in Relationship: Marriage and Family*, 2nd ed., edited by Edward A. Powers and Mary W. Lees. New York: West.

Joy, Kevin. 2004. "A Battle Just Begun for Both Supporters, Foes." *The Boston Globe.* March 30.

Judge, Sharon L. 1998. "Parental Coping Strategies and Strengths in Families of Young Children with Disabilities." *Family Relations* 47 (3): 263–68.

Julian, Teresa W., Patrick C. McKenry, and Mary W. McKelvey. 1994. "Cultural Variations in Parenting." *Family Relations* 43: 30–37.

Kader, Samuel. 1999. *Openly Gay, Openly Christian.: How the Bible Really Is Gay Friendly.* Leyland Publications.

Kaiser Family Foundation. 2001. *Inside-OUT: A Report on the Experiences of Lesbians, Gays, and Bisexuals in American and the Public's Views on Issues and Policies Related to Sexual Orientation.* Menlo Park CA: Kaiser Family Foundation.

———. 2003. "Sexually Transmitted Diseases in the U.S." Fact Sheet. Menlo CA: Kaiser Family Foundation. June. www.kff.org.

Kalb, Claudia. 2001. "Should You Have Your Baby Now?" *Newsweek.* Aug. 13: 40–48.

———. 2004. "Brave New Babies." *Newsweek.* Jan. 26. Pp. 45–52.

Kalish, Susan. 1995. "Multiracial Births Increase as U.S. Ponders Racial Definitions." *Population Today* 23 (4): 1–2.

Kalmijn, Matthijs. 1998. "Differentiation and Stratification—Intermarriage and Homogamy: Causes, Patterns, and Trends." *Annual Review of Sociology* 24: 395–427.

Kalof, Linda, and Timothy Cargill. 1991. "Fraternity and Sorority Membership and Gender Dominance Attitudes." *Sex Roles* 25 (7/8): 417–23.

Kamo, Yoshinori. 2000. "Racial and Ethnic Differences in Extended Family Households." *Sociological Perspectives* 43 (2): 211–29.

Kamo, Yoshinori, and Min Zhou. 1994. "Living Arrangements of Elderly Chinese and Japanese in the United States." *Journal of Marriage and Family* 56 (3): 544–58.

Kane, Emily W. 2000. "Racial and Ethnic Variations in Gender-related Attitudes." *Annual Review of Sociology* 26: 416–439.

Kann, Mark E. 1986. "The Costs of Being on Top." *Journal of the National Association for Women Deans, Administrators, and Counselors* 49: 29–37.

Kantor, David and William Lehr. 1975. *Inside the Family: Toward a Theory of Family Process.* San Francisco: Jossey-Bass.

Kantor, Glenda Kaufman, and Jana L. Jasinski. 1998. "Dynamics and Risk Factors In Partner Violence." Pp. 1–43 in *Partner Violence: A Comprehensive Review of 20 Years of Research*, edited by Jana L. Jasinski and Linda M. Williams.. Thousand Oaks CA: Sage.

Kantrowitz, Barbara, and Claudia Kalb. 1998. "Boys Will Be Boys." *Newsweek.* May 11: 54–60.

Kantrowitz, Barbara, and Pat Wingert. 2001. "The Parent Trap." *Newsweek.* Jan. 29: 49–53.

Kaplan, Helen Singer. 1974. *The New Sex Therapy: Active Treatment of Sexual Dysfunctions.* New York: Brunner/Mazel.

———. 1995. *The Sexual Desire Disorders: Dysfunctional Regulation of Sexual Motivation.* New York: Brunner/Mazel.

Kaplan, Marion A. (Ed.). 1985. *The Marriage Bargain: Women and Dowries in European History.* New York: Harrington Park.

Kaplan-Leiserson, Eva. 2003. "Generation Sandwich." American Society for Training and Development: *T&D* 57 (2): 16–18.

Karen, R. 1994. *Becoming Attached: Unfolding the Mystery of the Infant–Mother Bond and Its Impact on Later Life.* New York: Warner.

Kaschak, Ellyn, and Leonore Tiefer, eds. 2002. *A New View of Women's Sexual Problems.* Binghamton New York: Haworth.

Kassorla, Irene. 1973. *Putting It All Together.* New York: Brut Publications; Hawthorn/Dutton.

Katz, Jon. 2003. *The New Work of Dogs: Tending to Life, Love, and The Family.* New York: Villard.

Katz, Lillian G. 1998. *Distinction Between Self-Esteem and Narcissism: Implications for Practice.* http://ericps.ed.uiuc.edu/eeec/pubs./books/selfe.html.

Katz, Lynn F., and Erica M. Woodin. 2002. "Hostility, Hostile Detachment, and Conflict engagement in Marriages: Effects on Child and Family Functioning." *Child Development* 73 (2): 636–652.

Kaufman, Gayle. 2000. "Do Gender Role Attitudes Matter? Family Formation and Dissolution Among Traditional and Egalitarian Men and Women." *Journal of Family Issues* 21: 128–144.

Kaufman, Gayle, and Peter Uhlenberg. 1998. "Effects of Life Course Transitions on the Quality of Relationships Between Adult Children and Their Parents." *Journal of Marriage and Family* 60 (4): 924–38.

———. 2000. "The Influence of Parenthood on the Work Effort of Married Men and Women." *Social Forces* 78: 931–49.

Kaukinen, Catherine. 2004. "Status Compatibility, Physical Violence, and Emotional Abuse in Intimate Relationships." *Journal of Marriage and the Family* 66: 452–471.

Keefe, Janice, and Pamela Fancey. 2000. "The Care Continues: Responsibility for Elderly Relatives Before and After Admission to a Long Term Care Facility." *Family Relations* 49 (3): 235–44.

Keith, Carolyn. 1995. "Family Caregiving Systems: Models, Resources, and Values." *Journal of Marriage and Family* 57 (1): 179–89.

Kelly, Joan B., and Robert E. Emery. 2003. "Children's Adjustment Following Divorce: Risk and Resiliency Perspectives." *Family Relations* 52: 352–362.

Kelly, Joan B., and Michael E. Lamb. 2003. "Developmental Issues in Relocation Cases Involving Young Children: When, Whether, and How? *Journal of Family Psychology* 17: 193-205.

Kennedy, Sheila Rauch. 1997. *Shattered Faith: A Woman's Struggle to Stop the Catholic Church from Annulling Her Marriage.* New York: Pantheon.

Kennelly, Ivy, Sabine N. Merz, and Judith Lorber. 2001. "What Is Gender?" *American Sociological Review* 66: 598–605.

Kenney, Catherine. 2004. "Cohabiting Couple, Filing jointly? Resource Pooling and U.S. Poverty Policies." *Family Relations* 53 (2): 237–247.

Kephart, William. 1971. "Oneida: An Early American Commune." Pp. 481–92 in *Family in Transition: Rethinking Marriage, Sexuality, Child Rearing, and Family Organization*, edited by Arlene S. Skolnick and Jerome H. Skolnick. Boston: Little, Brown.

Kern, Louis J. 1981. *An Ordered Love: Sex Roles and Sexuality in Victorian Utopias—The Shakers, the Mormons, and the Oneida Community.* Chapel Hill: University of North Carolina Press.

Kershaw, Sarah. 2003. "Many Immigrants Decide to Embrace Homes for Elderly." *The New York Times.* October 20: A1, A10.

Khaleque, Abdul, and Ronald P. Rohner. 2002. "Perceived Parental Acceptance-Rejection and Psychological Adjustment: A Meta-Analysis of Cross-Cultural and Intracultural Studies." *Journal of Marriage and Family* 64 (1): 54–64.

Kheshgi-Genovese, Zareena, and Thomas A. Genovese. 1997. "Developing the Spousal Relationship Within Stepfamilies." *Families in Society* 78 (3): 255–64.

Kibria, Nazli. 2000. "Race, Ethnic Options, and Ethnic Binds: Identity Negotiations of Second-Generation Chinese and Korean Americans." *Sociological Perspectives* 43 (1): 77–95.

Kiecolt, K. Jill, and Mark A. Fossett. 1995. "Mate Availability and Marriage Among African Americans: Aggregate and Individual Level Analyses." Pp. 121–35 in *The Decline in Marriage Among African Americans: Causes, Consequences, and Policy Implications*, edited by Belinda Tucker and Claudia Mitchell-Kernan. New York: Russell Sage.

Kilborn, Peter T. 1990. 1992a. "Lives of Unexpected Poverty in Center of a Land of Plenty." *New York Times.* July 7.

———. 1992b. "Sad Distinction for the Sioux: Homeland Is No. 1 in Poverty." *New York Times.* Sept. 29.

———. 2002. "Census Shows Bigger Houses and Incomes, But Not For All." *New York Times.* May 15.

Kilborn, Peter T., and Lynette Clemetson. 2002. "Gains of 90s Did Not Lift All, Census Shows." *New York Times.* June 5.

Kilbourne, Jean. 1994. "Gender Bender' Ads: Same Old Sexism." *New York Times.* May 15: F–13.

Killian, Timothy, and Lawrence H. Ganong. 2002. "Ideology, Context, and Obligations to Assist Older Persons." *Journal of Marriage and Family* 64 (4): 1080–1088.

Kim, K. Hyoun, and Patrick C. McKenry. 2002. "The Relationship Between Marriage and Psychological Well-Being." *Journal of Family Issues* 23 (8): 885–911.

Kimmel, Michael S. 1995. "Misogynists, Masculinist Mentors, and Male Supporters: Men's Responses to Feminism." Pp. 561–72 in *Women: A Feminist Perspective*, 5th ed., edited by Jo Freeman. Mountain View, CA: Mayfield.

———. 2000a. *The Gendered Society.* New York: Oxford.

———. 2000b. "What About the Boys?" *WEEA Digest.* November: 1–4.

———. 2001. "Manhood and Violence: The Deadliest Equation." *Newsday.* Mar. 8: p. A–41.

———. 2002. "Gender Symmetry' in Domestic Violence." *Violence Against Women* 8: 1332–1363.

Kimmel, Michael S., and Michael A. Messner. 1998. *Men's Lives*, 4th ed. Boston: Allyn And Bacon.

Kindlon, Dan, and Michael Thompson. 1998. *Raising Cain: Protecting the Emotional Life of Boys.* London: Michael Joseph.

King, Rosalind Berkowitz. 1999. "Time Spent in Parenthood Status among Adults in the United States." *Demography* 36: 377-385.

King, Valerie. 1994. "Variation in the Consequences of Nonresident Father Involvement for Children's Well-Being." *Journal of Marriage and Family* 56 (3): 963–72.

King, Valerie, and Glen H. Elder, Jr. 1997. "The Legacy of Grandparenting: Childhood Experiences with Grandparents and Current Involvement with Grandchildren." *Journal of Marriage and Family* 59 (4): 848–59.

King, Valerie, Merril Silverstein, Glen H. Elder, Jr., Vern L. Bengston, and Rand D. Conger. 2003. "Relations with Grandparents: Rural Midwest Versus Urban Southern California." *Journal of Family Issues* 24 (8): 1044–1069.

Kingsbury, Nancy, and John Scanzoni. 1993. "Structural-Functionalism." Pp. 195–217 in *Sourcebook of Family Theories and Methods: A Contextual Approach*, edited by Pauline G. Boss, William J. Doherty, Ralph LaRossa, Walter R. Schumm, and Suzanne K. Steinmetz. New York: Plenum.

Kingston, Paul W. 1990. "Illusions and Ignorance About the Family-Responsive Workplace." *Journal of Family Issues* 11 (4): 438–54.

Kinsey, Alfred, Wardell B. Pomeroy, and Clyde E. Martin. 1948. *Sexual Behavior in the Human Male*. Philadelphia: Saunders.

———. 1953. *Sexual Behavior in the Human Female*. Philadelphia: Saunders.

Kirby, David. 2004. "Party Favors: Pill Popping As Insurance." *New York Times*. June 21.

Kirby, Douglas. 2001. *Emerging Answers*. Washington, DC: National Campaign to Prevent Teen Pregnancy.

———. 2002. "Effective Approaches to Reducing Adolescent Unprotected Sex, Pregnancy, and Childbearing." *Journal of Sex Research* 39:51–57.

Kirn, Walter. 2000. "The Love Machines." *Time*. Feb. 14: 73–74.

Kirn, Walter, and Wendy Cole. 2001. "What Ever Happened To Play?" *Time*. April 30: 54056.

Kitano, Harry, and Roger Daniels. 1995. *Asian Americans: Emerging Minorities*, 2d ed. Englewood Cliffs, NJ: Prentice-Hall.

Kitson, Gay C. 1992. *Portrait of Divorce: Adjustment to Marital Breakdown*. New York: Guilford.

Klebanov, Pamela Kato, Jeanne Brooks-Gunn, and Greg Duncan. 1994. "Does Neighborhood and Family Poverty Affect Mothers' Parenting, Mental Health, and Social Support?" *Journal of Marriage and Family* 56 (2): 441–55.

Kleber, Rolf J., Charles R. Figley, P. R. Barthold, and John P. Wilson. 1997. "Beyond Trauma: Cultural and Societal Dynamics." *Contemporary Psychology* 42 (6): 516–27.

Kleiman, Carol. 2003. "Working Moms See Pay Take A Hit." *Omaha World-Herald*. May. 4

Klein, Marjorie H., Janet S. Hyde, Marilyn J. Essex, and Roseanne Clark. 1998. "Maternity Leave, Role Quality, Work Involvement, and Mental Health One Year After Delivery." *Psychology of Women Quarterly* 22 (2): 239–66.

Klein, R. C., and M. P. Johnson. 1997. "Strategies of Couple Conflict." Pp. 14–39 in *Handbook of Personal Relationships: Theory, Research, and Interventions*, 2nd ed., edited by S. Duck. New York: Wiley.

Klein, Rick. 2004. "Vote Ties Civil Unions to Gay-Marriage." *Boston Globe*. March 30.

Kleinfield, N.R. 2002. "In Nightmares and Anger, Children Are Paying a Hidden Price for 9/11." *New York Times*. May 14.

———. 2003. "Around Tree, Smiles Even for Wives No. 2 and 3." *New York Times*. Dec. 24.

Kliman, Jodie, and William Madsen. 1999. "Social Class and the Family Life Cycle." Pp. 88–105 in *The Expanded Family Life Cycle: Individual, Family, and Social Perspectives*, 3rd ed. Boston: Allyn and Bacon.

Kline, Marsha, Jeanne M. Tschann, Janet R. Johnston, and Judith Wallerstein. 1989. "Children's Adjustment in Joint and Sole Physical Custody Families." *Developmental Psychology* 25: 430–38.

Klohnen, Eva C., and Gerald A. Mendelsohn. 1998. "Partner Selection for Personality Characteristics: A Couple-Centered Approach." *Personality & Social Psychology Bulletin* 24 (3): 268–277.

Kluger, Jeffrey. 2004. "The Power of Love." *Time*. January 19.

Kluwer, Esther S., Jose A.M. Heesink, and Evert Van de Vliert. 2002. "The division of Labor Across the Transition to Parenthood: A Justice Perspective." *Journal of Marriage and Family* 64 (4): 930–943.

Knapp, Caroline. 1999. *Pack of Two: The Intricate Bond between People and Dogs*. New York: Doubleday/Broadway.

Knoester, Chris, and Alan Booth. 2000. "Barriers to Divorce: When Are They Effective? When Are They Not?" *Journal of Family Issues* 21: 78–99.

Knox, David H., Jr. 1975. *Marriage: Who? When? Why?* Englewood Cliffs, NJ: Prentice-Hall.

Knox, Noelle. 2004. "Orphans Caught in the Middle." *USA Today*. May 18.

Knudson-Martin, Carmen, and Anne Rankin Mahoney. 1998. "Language and Processes in the Construction of Equality in New Marriages." *Family Relations* 47 (1): 81–91.

Koblinsky, Sally A. 2001. "A Peaceful Village: Protecting Young Children from Community Violence." *Family Focus*. Sept.: F10.

Koch, Joanne, and Lew Koch. 1976. "A Consumer's Guide to Therapy for Couples." *Psychology Today* 9: 33–38.

Kochanek, Kenneth D., and Betty L. Smith. 2004. "Deaths: Preliminary Data for 2002." *National Vital Statistics Reports* 52 (13). Hyattsville MD: National Center for Health Statistics. Feb. 11.

Koh, J., and W. K. Bell. 1987. "Korean Elders in the United States: Intergenerational Relations and Living Arrangements." *The Gerontologist* 27: 66–71.

Kohlberg, Lawrence. 1966. "A Cognitive–Developmental Analysis of Children's Sex-Role Concepts and Attitudes." Pp. 82–173 in *The Development of Sex Differences*, edited by Eleanor E. Maccoby. Palo Alto, CA: Stanford University Press.

Kohn, M. L. 1977. *Class and Conformity: A Study in Values*. Chicago: University of Chicago Press.

Kolata, Gina. 1993. "Family Aid to Elderly Very Strong, Study Shows." *New York Times*. May 3.

———. 1997. "Clinics Enter a New World of Embryo 'Adoption.'" *New York Times*. Nov. 23.

———. 2001. "Doubters Fault Theory Finding Earlier Puberty." *New York Times*. Feb. 20.

———. 2002a. "Parenthood Help for Men with H.I.V." *New York Times*. April 30.

————. 2002b. "Treatments for Fertility Are Studied for Problems." *New York Times* Mar. 7.

————. 2004. "The Heart's Desire." *New York Times.* May 11.

Komter, A. 1989. "Hidden Power in Marriage." *Gender and Society* 3: 187–216.

Konner, Melvin. 1990. "Women and Sexuality." *New York Times Magazine.* Apr. 29: 24, 26.

Koop, C. Everett. n.d. *Surgeon General's Report on Acquired Immune Deficiency Syndrome.* Washington, DC: U.S. Department of Health and Human Services.

Korte, Diana. 1995. "Midwives on Trial." *Mothering* (Fall): 52–63.

Kosciulek, J. F., and D. C. Lustig. 1998. "Predicting Family Adaptation from Brain Injury-Related Family Stress." *Journal of Applied Rehabilitation Counseling* 29 (1): 8–19.

Kost, Kathleen A. 2001. "The Function of Fathers: What Poor Men Say about Fatherhood." *Families in Society: The Journal of Contemporary Human Services* 82 (5): 499-515.

Kozol, Jonathan. 2000. *Ordinary Resurrections: Children in the Years of Hope.* New York: Crown.

Kraus, L. A., M. H. Davis, D. Bazzini, M. B. Church, and C. M. Kirchman. 1993. "Personal and Social Influences on Loneliness: The Mediating Effect of Social Provisions." *Social Psychology Quarterly* 56: 37–53.

Krause, N., A. R. Herzog, and E. Baker. 1992. "Providing Support to Others and Well-Being in Later Life." *Journal of Gerontology* 47: P300–P311.

Kreider, Rose M. 2003. "Adopted Children and Stepchildren: 2000. *Census 2000 Special Reports* CENSR-6. Washington DC: U.S. Census Bureau. Aug.

Kreider, Rose M., and Jason M. Fields. 2002. "Number, Timing, and Duration of Marriages and Divorces: 1996." *Current Population Reports* P70-80. Washington DC U.S. Census Bureau. February.

Kreider, Rose M., and Tavia Simmons. 2003. "Marital Status: 2000." *Census 2000 Brief* C2KBR-30. Washington DC: U.S. Census Bureau.

Krementz, Jill. 1984. *How It Feels When Parents Divorce.* New York: Knopf.

Kreppner, Kurt. 1988. "Changes in Parent–Child Relationships with the Birth of the Second Child." *Marriage and Family Review* 12 (3–4): 157–81.

Krishnakumar, Ambika, and Cheryl Buehler. 2000. "Interparental Conflict and Parenting Behaviors: A Meta-Analytic Review." *Family Relations* 49 (1): 25–44.

Kroska, Amy. 1997. "The Division of Labor in the Home: A Review and Reconceptualization." *Social Psychology Quarterly* 60 (4): 304–22.

————. 2004. "Division of Domestic Work: Revising and Expanding the Theoretical Explanations." *Journal of Family Issues* 25: 900–932.

Krueger, Alan. B. 2004. "Economic Scene." *New York Times.* Apr. 29.

Krueger, Joachim. 2003. "Self-esteem as a Social Dilemma." Knight Ridder/Tribune News Service. May 13.

Kruk, Edward. 1991. "Discontinuity Between Pre- and Post-Divorce Father–Child Relationships: New Evidence Regarding Paternal Disengagement." *Journal of Divorce and Remarriage* 16 (3/4): 195–227.

Kruttschnitt, Candace, Jane D. McLeod, and Maude Dornfeld. 1994. "The Economic Environment of Child Abuse." *Social Problems* 41 (2): 299–315.

Kuczynski, Alex. 2001. "Guess Who's Coming to Dinner Now?" *New York Times.* Dec. 23.

Kuhn, Manfred. 1955. "How Mates Are Sorted." In *Family, Marriage, and Parenthood,* edited by Howard Becker and Reuben Hill. Boston: Heath.

Kulczycki, Andrzej, and Arun Peter Lobo. 2002. "Patterns, Determinants, and Implications of Intermarriage Among Arab Americans." *Journal of Marriage and Family* 64 (1): 202–210.

Kumpfer, Karol, and Connie Tait. 2000. "Family Skills Training for Parents and Children." *Juvenile Justice Bulletin.* April.

Kurdek, Lawrence A. 1989a. "Relationship Quality for Newly Married Husbands and Wives: Marital History, Stepchildren, and Individual-Difference Predictors." *Journal of Marriage and Family* 51 (4): 1053–64.

————. 1989b. "Relationship Quality in Gay and Lesbian Cohabiting Couples: A 1-Year Follow-up Study." *Journal of Social and Personal Relationships* 6: 35–59.

————. 1991. "The Relations Between Reported Well-Being and Divorce History, Availability of a Proximate Adult, and Gender." *Journal of Marriage and Family* 53 (1): 71–78.

————. 1994. "Areas of Conflict for Gay, Lesbian, and Heterosexual Couples: What Couples Argue About Influences Relationship Satisfaction." *Journal of Marriage and Family* 56 (4): 923–34.

————. 1995a. "Assessing Multiple Determinants of Relationship Commitment in Cohabiting Gay, Cohabiting Lesbian, Dating Heterosexual, and Married Heterosexual Couples." *Family Relations* 44: 261–66.

————. 1995b. "Predicting Change in Marital Satisfaction from Husbands' and Wives' Conflict Resolution Styles." *Journal of Marriage and Family* 57 (1): 153–64.

————. 1998. "Relationship Outcomes and Their Predictors: Longitudinal Evidence from Heterosexual Married, Gay Cohabiting, and Lesbian Cohabiting Couples." *Journal of Marriage and Family* 60 (3): 553–68.

Kurdek, Lawrence A., and Mark A. Fine. 1991. "Cognitive Correlates of Satisfaction for Mothers and Stepfathers in Stepfather Families." *Journal of Marriage and Family* 53 (3): 565–72.

————. 1995. "Mothers, Fathers, Stepfathers, and Siblings as providers of Supervision, Acceptance, and Autonomy to Young Adolescents." *Journal of Family Psychology* 9 (1): 95–99.

Kurson, Bob. 1998. "Pope Talks Tough on Annulment: Cites 'Divorce Under Different Name.'" *Chicago Sun-Times.* Oct. 18.

Kurtz, Stanley. 2004. "End of Marriage As We Know It." *San Francisco Chronicle.* February 29.

Kurz, Demie. 1993. "Physical Assaults by Husbands: A Major Social Problem." Pp. 88–103 in *Current Controversies on Family Violence,* edited by Richard J. Gelles and Donileen R. Loseke. Newbury Park, CA: Sage.

————. 1997. "Doing Parenting: Mothers, Care Work, and Policy." Pp. 68–91 in *Contemporary Parenting: Challenges and Issues,* edited by Terry Arendell. Thousand Oaks, CA: Sage.

———. 2002. "Poor Mothers and the Care of Teenage Children." Pp. 23–36 in *Child Care and Inequality: Rethinking Care Work for Children and Youth*, edited by Francesca Cancian, Demie Kurz, Andrew S. London, Rebecca Reviere, and Mary C. Tuominen. New York: Routledge.

Kutner, Lawrence. 1988a. "Parent & Child: Parents Change: Children Must Too." *New York Times*. Mar. 24.

———. 1988b. "Parent and Child: Working at Home; or, The Midday Career Change." *New York Times*. Dec. 8.

———. 1990a. "Parent & Child: Chasms of Pain and Growth: When Generation Gaps Are Too Wide to Leap." *New York Times*. Mar. 8.

———. 1990b. "Parent & Child: Confronting Mother and Father About Their Battles and the Effect It Has on the Family." *New York Times*. Mar. 29.

———. 1990c. "Parent & Child: Money Matters, for Some as Confidential as Sex, Are Often a Stressful Subject." *New York Times*. Jan. 11.

———. 1990d. "Parent & Child: When a Child Marries: The Pride and the Pitfalls." *New York Times*. May 10.

Lackey, Chad, and Kirk R. Williams. 1995. "Social Bonding and the Cessation of Partner Violence Across Generations." *Journal of Marriage and Family* 57 (2): 295–305.

Ladner, Joyce A. 1984. "Providing a Healthy Environment for Interracial Children." *Interracial Books for Children Bulletin* 15 (6): 7–9.

LaFrance, Arthur B. 1995–1996. "Child Custody and Relocation: A Constitutional Perspective." *Journal of Family Law* 34: 1–158.

LaGuardia, Jennifer G., Richard M. Ryan, Charles E. Couchman, and Edward L. Deci. 2000. "Within-Person Variation in Security of Attachment: A Self-Determination Theory Perspective on Attachment, Need Fulfillment, and Well-Being." *Journal of Personality and Social Psychology* 79 (3): 367–84.

Laing, Ronald D. 1971. *The Politics of the Family*. New York: Random House.

Lally, Catherine F., and James W. Maddock. 1994. "Sexual Meaning Systems of Engaged Couples." *Family Relations* 43: 53–60.

Lamanna, Mary Ann. 1977. "The Value of Children to Natural and Adoptive Parents." Ph.D. dissertation, Department of Sociology, University of Notre Dame.

———. 2002. *Emile Durkheim on the Family*. Thousand Oaks CA: Sage.

Lamb, Kathleen A., Gary R. Lee, and Alfred DeMaris. 2003. "Union Formation and Depression: Selection and Relationship Effects." *Journal of Marriage and Family* 65 (4): 953–962.

Lan, Pei-Chia. 2002. "Subcontracting Filial Piety: Elder Care in Ethnic Chinese Immigrant Families in California." *Journal of Family Issues* 23 (7): 812–835.

Landry, Bart. 2000. *Black Working Wives: Pioneers of the American Family Revolution*. Berkeley: U. of California.

Landry, David J., Jacqueline E. Darroch, Susheela Singh, and Jenny Higgins. 2004. "Factors Associated with the Content of Sex Education in U.S. Public Secondary Schools." *Perspectives on Sexual and Reproductive Health* 35: 261–69.

Landry-Meyer, Laura. 1999. "Research into Action: Recommended Intervention Strategies for Grandparent Caregivers." *Family Relations* 48 (4): 381–89.

Lane, Wendy G., David. M. Rubin, Ragin Monteith, and Cindy Christian. 2002. "Racial Differences in the Evaluation of Pediatric Fractures for Physical Abuse." *Journal of the American Medical Association* 288, No. 13. Oct. 2. www.jama.org

Laner, Mary Riege. 2003. "A Rejoinder to Mark Cresswell." *Sociological Inquiry* 73: 152–56.

Langan, P., and C. Innes. 1986. *Preventing Domestic Violence Against Women*. Bureau of Justice Statistics. Washington, DC: Department of Justice.

Langhinrichsen-Rohling, Jennifer, Russel E. Palarea, Jennifer Cohen, and Martin L. Rohling. 2000. "Breaking Up Is Hard to Do: Unwanted Pursuit Behaviors Following the Dissolution of a Romantic Relationship." *Violence and Victims* 15 (1): 73–90.

Lankford, Kimberly. 2002. "What's Love Got To Do with It?" *Kiplinger's Personal Finance Magazine* 56 (5): 100–104. "Large Proportions of Men and Women with HIV Have Sex without Telling Partners They Are Infected." *Perspectives on Sexual and Reproductive Health* 35: 235-6.

LaRossa, Ralph. 1979. *Conflict and Power in Marriage: Expecting the First Child*. Newbury Park, CA: Sage.

LaRossa, Ralph, and Donald C. Reitzes. 1993. "Symbolic Interactionism and Family Studies." Pp. 135–63 in *Sourcebook of Family Theories and Methods: A Contextual Approach*, edited by Pauline G. Boss, William J. Doherty, Ralph LaRossa, Walter R. Schumm, and Suzanne K. Steinmetz. New York: Plenum.

Larson, Jeffry H., and Thomas B. Holman. 1994. "Premarital Predictors of Marital Quality and Stability." *Family Relations* 43 (2): 228–242.

Larson, Jeffry H., Shannon M. Anderson, Thomas B. Holman, and Brand K. Niemann. 1998. "A Longitudinal Study of the Effects of Premarital Communication, Relationship Stability, and Self-Esteem on Sexual Satisfaction in the First Year of Marriage." *Journal of Sex & Marital Therapy* 24: 193–206.

Larson, R., and M. Ham. 1993. "Stress and 'Storm and Stress' in Early Adolescence: The Relationship of Negative Events with Dysphoric Affect." *Developmental Psychology* 29: 130–40.

Larzelere, Robert E., Paul R. Sather, William N. Schneider, David B. Larson, and Patricia L. Pike. 1998. "Punishment Enhances Reasoning's Effectiveness As a Disciplinary Response to Toddlers." *Journal of Marriage and Family* 60 (2): 388–403.

Laslett, Peter. 1971. *The World We Have Lost: England Before the Industrial Age*, 2d ed. New York: Scribner's.

Laumann, Edward, John H. Gagnon, Robert T. Michael, and Stuart Michaels. 1994. *The Social Organization of Sexuality: Sexual Practices in the United States*. Chicago: University of Chicago Press.

Laumann, Edward, Anthony Paik, and Raymond C. Rosen. 1999. "Sexual Dysfunction in the United States: Prevalence and Predictors." *Journal of the American Medical Association* 281: 537–544.

Lareau, Annette. 2002. "Invisible Inequality: Social Class and Childrearing in Black and White Families."

American Sociological Review 67: 747-776.

———. 2003a. "The Long-Lost Cousins of the Middle Class." *New York Times.* Dec. 20.

———. 2003b. *Unequal Childhoods: Class, Race, and Family Life.* Berkeley: University of California Press.

Lauro, Patricia Winters. 2000a. "Advertising: The Subject of Divorce Is Becoming More Common as Another Backdrop in Campaigns." *New York Times.* Oct. 12.

———. 2000b. "New Campaigns Geared to Parents Replace Stodgy with Cool." *New York Times.* Jan. 3.

Lavee, Yoav, and Ruth Katz. 2002. "Division of Labor, Perceived Fairness, and Marital Quality: The Effect of Gender Ideology." *Journal of Marriage and the Family* 64:27–39.

Lavin, Judy. Nd. "Smoothing the Step-Parenting Transition." SelfGrowth.com. http://www.selfgrowth.com/articles/Lavin1.html Retrieved 9.21.04.

Lawlor, Julia. 1998. "For Many Blue-Collar Fathers, Child Care Is Shift-work Too." *New York Times.* Apr. 26.

Lawrance, K., and E. S. Byers. 1995. "Sexual Satisfaction in Long-Term Heterosexual Relationships: The Interpersonal Exchange Model of Sexual Satisfaction." *Personal Relationships* 2: 267–85.

Lawrence et al. v Texas. 2003. 539 U.S. 558.

Lawson, Carol. 1990. "Fathers, Too, Are Seeking a Balance Between Their Families and Careers." *New York Times.* Apr. 12.

Lawson, Erma Jean. 1999. "Black Men After Divorce: How Do They Cope?" Pp. 112–27 in *The Black Family: Essays and Studies,* edited by Robert Staples. Belmont, CA: Wadsworth.

Lawson, Erma Jean, and Aaron Thompson. 1999. *Black Men and Divorce.* Thousand Oaks CA: Sage.

Lawson, Willow. 2004a. "Encouraging Signs: How Your Partner Responds to Your Good News Speaks Volumes." *Psychology Today.* January/February: 22.

———. 2004b. "The Glee Club: Positive Psychologists Want to Teach You to be Happier." *Psychology Today.* January/February: 34–40.

Lawton, Leora, Merril Silverstein, and Vern Bengston. 1994. "Affection, Social Contact, and Geographic Distance Between Adult Children and Their Parents." *Journal of Marriage and Family* 56 (1): 57–68.

"Learning Skills Greatly Limits stress for Family Caregivers, Says Stanford Study." 2003. *Mental Health Weekly Digest.* October 13.

LeBlanc, Allen J., and Richard G. Wright. 2000. "Reciprocity and Depression in AIDS Caregiving." *Sociological Perspectives* 43 (4): 631–49.

LeClere, Felicia B., and Brenda M. Kowalewski. 1994. "Disability in the Family: The Effects on Children's Well-Being." *Journal of Marriage and Family* 56 (2): 457–68.

Lee, Cameron, and Judith Iverson-Gilbert. 2003. "Demand, Support, and Perception in Family-Related Stress among Protestant Clergy." *Family Relations* 52 (3): 249–257.

Lee, Ellie. 2003. *Abortion, Motherhood, and Mental Health: Medicalizing Reproduction in the United States and Great Britain.* Hawthorne NY: Aldine.

Lee, Eunju, Glenna Spitze, and John R. Logan. 2003. "Social Support to Parents-in-Law: The Interplay of Gender and Kin Hierarchies." *Journal of Marriage and Family* 65 (2): 396–403.

Lee, F. R. 2001. "Trying to Soothe the Fears Hiding Behind the Veil." *New York Times.* Sept. 23.

Lee, Felicia. 1994. "AIDS Toll on Elderly." *New York Times.* Nov. 21.

Lee, Gary R., Julie K. Netzer, and Raymond T. Coward. 1994. "Filial Responsibility Expectations and Patterns of Intergenerational Assistance." *Journal of Marriage and Family* 56 (3): 559–65.

Lee, Gary R., Chuck W. Peek, and Raymond T. Coward. 1998. "Race Differences in Filial Responsibility Expectations among Older Parents." *Journal of Marriage and Family* 60 (2): 404–12.

Lee, John Alan. 1973. *The Colours of Love.* Toronto: New Press.

———. 1981. "Forbidden Colors of Love: Patterns of Gay Love." Pp. 128–39 in *Single Life: Unmarried Adults in Social Context,* edited by Peter J. Stein. New York: St. Martins.

Lee, Sharon M. 1998. *Asian Americans: Diverse and Growing.* Population Bulletin 53 (2). Washington, DC: Population Reference Bureau.

Leigh, Suzanne. 2004. "Fertility Patients Deserve to Know the Odds—and Risks." *USA Today.* July 7.

Leinwand, Donna. 2002. "Kidnapping Problem 'Impossible' to Quantify." *USA Today.* Aug. 15.

Leitch, M. Laurie. 1998. "Contextual Issues in Teen Pregnancy and Parenting: Refining Our Scope of Inquiry." *Family Relations* 47 (2): 145–47.

Leite, Randall W., and Patrick C. McKenry. 2002. "Aspects of Father Status and Post-Divorce Father Involvement with Children" *Journal of Family Issues* 23: 601–623.

Leland, John. 1997. "A Pill for Impotence?" *Newsweek.* Nov. 17: 62–8.

———. 1999. "Bad News in the Bedroom." *Newsweek,* Feb. 22: 47.

———. 2000. "The Science of Women and Sex." *Newsweek,* May 29: 48–54.

LeMasters, E. E., and John DeFrain. 1989. *Parents in Contemporary America: A Sympathetic View,* 5th ed. Belmont, CA: Wadsworth.

Leonhardt, David. 2001. "Recession, Then a Boom? Maybe Not This Time." *New York Times.* Dec. 30.

Lerner, Harriet. 2001. *The Dance of Connection: How to Talk to Someone When You're Mad, Hurt, Scared, Frustrated, Insulted, Betrayed, or Desperate.* NY: HarperCollins.

Lerner, Sharon. 2003. "Making New Efforts to Convince Youths They're Not Invulnerable to H.I.V." *New York Times.* August 5.

"Lesbian and Gay Rights in the 107th Congress." 2001. American Civil Liberties Union. http://www.aclu.org/issues/gay.

"Lesbian May Have to Pay Child Support." 2002. *Omaha World-Herald.* Feb. 14.

"Lesbian Survivor May Lose Home." 2002. *off our backs.* January-February: 7.

Letiecq, Bethany L, and Sally A. Koblinsky. 2001. "African American Fathers' Strategies for Protecting Young Children in Violent Neighborhoods." *NCFR Family Focus* (Sept.): F7-F8.

———. 2004. "Parenting in Violent Neighborhoods: African American

Families Share Strategies for Keeping Children Safe." *Journal of Family Issues* 25: 715–734.

LeVay, S., and D. H. Hamer. 1994. "Evidence for a Biological Influence in Male Homosexuality." *Scientific American* (May).

Levin, Irene. 1997. "Stepfamily as Project." Pp. 123–33 in *Stepfamilies: History, Research, and Policy*, edited by Irene Levin and Marvin B. Sussman. New York: Haworth.

Levine, Judith. 1994. "White Like Me." *MS.* Mar./Apr.: 22–24.

Levine, Robert, Suguru Sato, Tsukasa Hashimoto, and Jyoti Verma. 1995. "Love and Marriage in Eleven Cultures." *Journal of Cross-Cultural Psychology* 26 (5): 554–71.

Levine, Stephen B. 1998. "Extramarital Sexual Affairs." *Journal of Sex & Marital Therapy* 24: 207–16.

Levinger, George. 1965. "Marital Cohesiveness and Dissolution: An Integrative Review." *Journal of Marriage and Family* 27: 19–28.

Levinson, David. 1989. *Family Violence in Cross-Cultural Perspective.* Newbury Park, CA: Sage.

Levinson, Deborah. 2001. "2000—The Year in Review." *Gay/Lesbian Issues.* http://www.gayissues.about.com.

Lev-Wiesel, Rachel, and Marianne Amir. 2003. "The Effects of Similarity Versus Dissimilarity of Spouses' Traumatic Childhood Events on Psychological Well-being and Marital Quality." *Journal of Family Issues* 24 (6): 737–752.

Levy, Barrie (Ed.). 1991. *Dating Violence: Young Women in Danger.* Seattle: Seal.

Lewin, Tamar. 1989a. "Family or Career? Choose, Women Told." *New York Times.* Mar. 8.

———. 1989b. "Small Tots, Big Biz." *New York Times Magazine.* Jan. 29: 30–31, 89–92.

———. 1995. "Now Divorcing Parents Must Learn How to Cope with Children's Needs." *New York Times.* Apr. 24.

———. 1998. "Men Assuming Bigger Share at Home, New Survey Shows." *New York Times.* Apr. 15.

———. 2001a. "Confusion Ensued After Census Report on Two-Parent Families." *New York Times.* Apr. 21.

———. 2001b. "In Genetic Testing for Paternity, Law Often Lags Behind Science." *New York Times.* Mar. 11.

———. 2001c. "Report Looks at a Generation, and Caring for Young and Old." *New York Times.* July 11.

———. 2001d. "Study Says Little Has Changed." *New York Times.* Sept. 10.

———. 2002. "A Child Study Is A Peek: It's Not the Whole Picture." *New York Times.* July 21.

———. 2003a. "For More People in Their 20's and 30's, Going Home Is Easier Because They Never Left." *New York Times.* Dec. 22.

———. 2003b. "Parents' Role Is Narrowing Generation Gap on Campus." *New York Times.* Jan. 6.

Lewis, Thomas, M.D., Fari Amini, M.D., and Richard Lannon, M.D. 2000. *A General Theory of Love.* New York: Random House.

Lewontin, Richard C. 1992. *Biology as Ideology: The Doctrine of DNA.* New York: Harper.

L'Heureax-Dube, Claire. 1998. "A Response to Remarks by Dr. Judith Wallerstein on the Long-Term Impact of Divorce on Children." *Family and Conciliation Courts Review* 36 (3): 384–86.

Libby, Roger W. 1976. "Social Scripts for Sexual Relationships." In *Sexuality Today and Tomorrow*, edited by Sol Gordon and Roger W. Libby. North Scituate, MA: Duxbury.

Lichter, Daniel T., and Martha L. Crowley. 2002. "Poverty in America: Beyond Welfare Reform." *Population Bulletin* 57(2). Washington DC: Population Reference Bureau. June.

Lichter, Daniel T., and David J. Eggebeen. 1994. "The Effect of Parental Employment on Child Poverty." *Journal of Marriage and Family* 56 (3): 633–45.

Lichter, Daniel T., Deborah Roempke Graefe, and J. Brian Brown. 2003. "Is Marriage A Panacea? Union Formation among Economically Disadvantaged Unwed Mothers." *Social Problems* 50: 60–86.

Lichter, Daniel T., Felicia B. LeClere, and Diane K. McLaughlin. 1991. "Local Marriage Markets and the Marital Behavior of Black and White Women." *American Journal of Sociology* 96 (4): 843–67.

Lichtman, Judith L, and Charlotte B. Nelson. 2003. "Paid Family Leave Is A Logical Next Step for Nation's Workers." *Omaha World-Herald.* August. 5.

Lieblich, Julia. 1998. "Non-Christian Summer Camps for Kids Combine Fun, Faith." *Saint Paul Pioneer Press.* July 19: 3G.

Liebow, Elliot. 1967. *Tally's Corner.* Boston: Little, Brown.

Lin, Chien, and William T. Liu. 1993. "Relationships Among Chinese Immigrant Families." Pp. 271–86 in *Family Ethnicity: Strength in Diversity*, edited by Harriette Pipes McAdoo. Newbury Park, CA: Sage.

Lindsey, Elizabeth W. 1998. "The Impact of Homelessness and Shelter Life on Family Relationships." *Family Relations* 47 (3): 243–52.

Lindsey, Eric W., and Jacquelyn Mize. 2001. "Interparental Agreement, Parent–Child Responsiveness, and Children's Peer Competence." *Family Relations* 50 (4): 348–54.

Lino, Mark. 2002. "Expenditures on Children by Families, 2001." *Annual Report.* Washington DC: U.S. Department of Agriculture. Center for Nutrition Policy and Promotion. Miscellaneous Publication No. 1528-2001.

Linton, Sally. 1971. "Woman the Gatherer: Male Bias in Anthropology." In *Women in Cross-Cultural Perspective*, edited by Lenore Jacobs. Champaign-Urbana: University of Illinois Press.

Lipman, Joanne. 1993. "The Nanny Trap." *Wall Street Journal.* April 14: A1, A8.

Lips, Hilary M. 1995. "Gender-Role Socialization: Lessons in Femininity." Pp. 128–48 in *Women: A Feminist Perspective.* 5th ed., edited by Jo Freeman. Mountain View, CA: Mayfield.

Liptak, Adam. 2002. "Judging A Mother for Someone Else's Crime." *New York Times.* Nov. 27.

———. 2004. "Bans on Interracial Unions Offer Perspective on Gay Ones." *The New York Times.* March 17.

Liu, Chien. 2000. "A Theory of Marital Sexual Life." *Journal of Marriage and Family* 62 (2): 363–74.

Liu, William T., Mary Ann Lamanna, and Alice Murata. 1979. *Transition to*

Nowhere: Vietnamese Refugees in America. Nashville, TN: CharterHouse.

"Living in Poverty." 2002. *New York Times.* April 13.

Lobb, Annelena. 2002. "Does Mom Need A Raise? The Market Value of Mom's Work Could Cause Sticker Shock." CNN Money. May 8. www.cnnfn.com.

LoBiondo-Wood, Geri, Laurel Williams, and Charles McGhee. 2004. "Liver Transplantation in Children: Maternal and Family Stress, Coping, and Adaptation." *Journal of the Society of Pediatric Nurses* 9 (2): 59–67.

Lobo, Susan, ed. 2001. *American Indians and the Urban Experience.* Thousand Oaks CA: Altamira.

Lockhart, Lettie L. 1991. "Spousal Violence: A Cross-Racial Perspective." Pp. 85–101 in *Black Family Violence,* edited by Robert L. Hampton. Lexington, MA: Lexington.

Lofas, Jeannette. n.d. "Ten Steps for Steps." The Stepfamily Foundation. http://www.stepfamily.org/tensteps.html.

Loftus, Jeni. 2001. "America's Liberalization in Attitudes Toward Homosexuality, 1973 to 1998." *American Sociological Review* 66: 762–82.

London, Andrew S., Ellen K. Scott, Kathryn Edin, and Vicki Hunter. 2004. "Welfare Reform, Work-Family Tradeoffs, and Child Well-Being." *Family Relations* 53 (2): 148–158.

London, Rebecca A. 1998. "Trends in Single Mothers' Living Arrangements from 1970 to 1995: Correcting the Current Population Survey." *Demography* 35 (1): 125–31.

Long, Colleen. 2002. "Surveillance Devices Help Keep An Eye on Mom." AP. Sept. 23.

Long, Edgar C. J., Jeffrey J. Angera, Sara Jacobs Carter, Mindy Nakamoto, and Michelle Kalso. 1999. "Understanding the One You Love: A Longitudinal Assessment of an Empathy Training Program for Couples in Romantic Relationships." *Family Relations* 48 (3): 235–42.

Long, Janie K., and Julianne M. Serovich. 2003. "Incorporating Sexual Orientation into MFT Training Programs: Infusion and Inclusion." *Journal of Marital and Family Therapy* 29 (1): 59–67.

Longman, Phillip J. 1998. "The Cost of Children." *U.S. News & World Report.* Mar. 30: 51–58.

Longmore, Monica A. 1998. "Symbolic Interactionism and the Study of Sexuality." *Journal of Sex Research* 35 (1): 44–57.

Longmore, Monica A., and Alfred Demaris. 1997. "Perceived Inequality and Depression in Intimate Relationships: The Moderating Effect of Self-Esteem." *Social Psychology Quarterly* 60 (2): 172–81.

Longmore, Monica A., Wendy D. Manning, and Peggy C. Giordano. 2001. "Preadolescent Parenting Strategies and Teens' Dating and Sexual Initiation: A Longitudinal Analysis." *Journal of Marriage and Family* 63 (2): 322–35.

Lonsdorf, Barbara J. 1991. "The Role of Coercion in Affecting Women's Inferior Outcomes in Divorce: Implications for Researchers and Therapists." *Journal of Divorce and Remarriage* 16 (1/2): 69–106.

Lorenz, Frederick O., Ronald L. Simons, Rand D. Conger, and Glen H. Elder Jr. 1997. "Married and Recently Divorced Mothers' Stressful Events and Distress: Tracing Change Across Time." *Journal of Marriage and Family* 59 (1): 219–32.

Losh-Hesselbart, Susan. 1987. "Development of Gender Roles." Pp. 535–64 in *Handbook of Marriage and the Family,* edited by Marvin B. Sussman and Suzanne K. Steinmetz. New York: Plenum.

Louv, Richard, 1996. "What Do Mothers Really Want." *Parents.* May: 38–40.

Love, Pamela. 2001. *The Truth About Love.* New York: Simon & Schuster.

Loving v. Virginia. 1967. 388 U.S. 1, 87 S. Ct. 1817, 18 L. Ed. 2d 1010.

"Low Self-esteem More Damaging than Annoying Habits." 2003. *Health & Medicine Week.* Sept. 8: 724.

Lubell, Sam. 2004. "The Womb As Photo Studio." *New York Times.* Sept. 30.

Lublin, Joann S. 1992. "Spouses Find Themselves Worlds Apart as Global Commuter Marriages Increase." *Wall Street Journal.* Aug. 19: B1, B6.

Luepnitz, Deborah Anne. 1982. *Child Custody: A Study of Families After Divorce.* Lexington, MA: Lexington.

Lugaila, Terry, and Julia Overturf. 2004. "Children and the Households They Live In: 2000." *Census Special Report* CENSR-14. Feb.

Lugaila, Terry A.. 2003a. "A Child's Day: 2000: Selected Indicators of Child Well-Being." *Current Population Reports* P70-89. August.

Luke, Carmen. 1994. "White Women in Interracial Families: Reflections on Hybridization, Feminine Identities, and Racialized Othering." *Feminist Issues* 14 (2): 49–72.

Lukemeyer, Anna, Marcia K. Meyers, and Timothy Smeeding. 2000. "Expensive Children in Poor Families: Out-of-Pocket Expenditures for the Care of Disabled and Chronically Ill Children in Welfare Families." *Journal of Marriage and Family* 62 (2): 399–415.

Luker, Kristin. 1984. *Abortion and Politics of Motherhood.* Berkeley: University of California Press.

Luscher, Kurt. 2002. "Intergenerational Ambivalence: Further Steps in Theory and Research." *Journal of Marriage and Family* 63 (3): 585–593.

Lussier, Gretchen, Kirby Deater-Deckard, Judy Dunn, and Lisa Davies. 2002. "Support Across Two Generations: Children's Closeness to Grandparents following Parental Divorce and Remarriage." *Journal of Family Psychology* 16: 363-376.

Luster, Tom, Laura Bates, Hiram Fitzgerald, Marcia Vanderbelt, and Judith Peck Key. 2000. "Factors Related to Successful Outcomes Among Preschool Children Born to Low-Income Adolescent Mothers." *Journal of Marriage and Family* 62 (1): 133–46.

Luster, Tom, Kelly Rhoades, and Bruce Haas. 1989. "The Relation Between Parental Values and Parenting Behavior: A Test of the Kohn Hypothesis." *Journal of Marriage and Family* 51: 139–47.

Luster, Tom, and Stephen A. Small. 1997. "Sexual Abuse History and Problems in Adolescence: Exploring the Effects of Moderating Variables." *Journal of Marriage and Family* 59 (1): 131–42.

Lustig, Daniel C. 1999. "Family Care-giving of Adults with Mental Retardation: Key Issues for Rehabilitation Counselors." *Journal of Rehabilitation* 65 (2): 26–45.

Lye, Diane N., Daniel H. Klepinger, Patricia Davis Hyle, and Anjanette Nelson. 1995. "Childhood Living Arrangements and Adult Children's Relations with Their Parents." *Demography* 32 (2): 261–80.

Lynch, Jean M., and Kim Murray. 2000. "For the Love of the Children: The Coming Out Process for Lesbian and Gay Parents and Stepparents." *Journal of Homosexuality* 39 (1): 1–24.

Lytton, H., and D. M. Romney. 1991. "Parents' Differential Socialization of Boys and Girls: A Meta Analysis." *Psychological Bulletin* 109: 267–296.

Maccoby, Eleanor E.. 1998. *The Two Sexes: Growing Up Apart; Coming Together.* Cambridge, MA: Belknap/Harvard.

Maccoby, Eleanor E., and Carol Nagy Jacklin. 1974. *The Psychology of Sex Differences.* Stanford, CA: Stanford University Press.

Maccoby, Eleanor E., and Catherine C. Lewis. 2003. "Less Day Care or A Different Day Care?" *Child Development* 74: 1069–1075.

MacDonald, Cameron L. 1998. "Manufacturing Motherhood: The Shadow Work of Nannies and Au Pairs." *Qualitative Sociology* 21 (1): 25–53.

MacDonald, William L., and Alfred DeMaris. 1995. "Remarriage, Stepchildren, and Marital Conflict: Challenges to the Incomplete Institutionalization Hypothesis." *Journal of Marriage and Family* 57 (2): 387–98.

———. 2002. "Stepfather-stepchild Relationship Quality: The Stepfather's Demand for Conformity and the Biological Father's Involvement." *Journal of Family Issues* 23 (1): 121–137.

Machir, John. 2003. "The Impact of Spousal Caregiving on the Quality of Marital Relationships in Later Life." *Family Focus.* September: F11–F13.

Mackey, Richard A. 1997. *Gay and Lesbian Couples: Voices from Lasting Relationships.* Westport, CT: Praeger.

Mackey, Richard A., Matthew A. Diemer, and Bernard A. O'Brien. 2000. "Psychological Intimacy in the Lasting Relationships of Heterosexual and Same-Gender Couples." *Sex Roles.* August: 201–15.

Mackey, Richard A., and Bernard A. O'Brien. 1998. "Marital Conflict Management: Gender and Ethnic Differences." *Social Work* 43 (2): 128–41.

Macklin, Eleanor D. 1983. "Nonmarital Heterosexual Cohabitation: An Overview." Pp. 49–74 in *Contemporary Families and Alternative Lifestyles: Handbook on Theory and Research*, edited by Eleanor D. Macklin and Roger H. Rubin. Newbury Park, CA: Sage.

———. 1987. "Nontraditional Family Forms." Pp. 317–53 in *Handbook of Marriage and the Family*, edited by Marvin B. Sussman and Suzanne K. Steinmetz. New York: Plenum.

Madrick, Jeff. 2002. "Economic Scene." *New York Times.* Dec. 26.

Magdol, Lynn, Terrie E. Moffitt, Avshalom Caspi, and Phil A. Silva. 1998. "Hitting Without a License: Testing Explanations for Differences in Partner Abuse Between Young Adult Daters and Cohabitors." *Journal of Marriage and Family* 60 (1): 41–55.

Maheu, Marlene M., and Rona Subotnik. 2001. *Infidelity on the Internet: Virtual Relationships and Real Betrayal.* Naperville, Ill: Sourcebooks.

Mahoney, Margaret M. 1997. "Stepfamilies from a Legal Perspective." Pp. 231–47 in *Stepfamilies: History, Research, and Policy*, edited by Irene Levin and Marvin B. Sussman. New York: Haworth.

Mahoney, P., and L. Williams. 1998. "Sexual Assault in Marriages: Prevalence, Consequences, and Treatment of Wife Rape." Pp. 113–162 in *Partner Violence: A Comprehensive Review of 20 Years of Research*, edited by Jana L. Jasinski and Linda M. Williams.. Thousand Oaks CA: Sage

Maier, Thomas. 1998. "Everybody's Grandfather." *U.S. News & World Report.* Mar. 30: 59.

Main, M. 1996. "Introduction to the Special Section on Attachment and Psychopathology: Overview of the Field of Attachment." *Journal of Consulting Clinical Psychology* 64: 237–43.

Mainemer, Henry, Lorraine C. Gilman, and Elinor W. Ames. 1998. "Parenting Stress in Families Adopting Children from Romanian Orphanages." *Journal of Family Issues* 19 (2): 164–80.

Majors, Richard G., and Janet M. Billson. 1992. *Cool Pose: The Dilemmas of Black Manhood in America.* Lexington, MA: Heath.

Makepeace, James M. 1981. "Courtship Violence Among College Students." *Family Relations* 30: 97–102.

———. 1986. "Gender Differences in Courtship Violence Victimization." *Family Relations* 35: 383–88.

"Male Contraceptive Proves Effective." 2003. *USA Today.* Oct. 8.

Malec, Karen. 2003. "The Abortion-Breast Cancer Link: How Politics Trumped Science And Informed Consent." *Journal of American Physicians and Surgeons* 8: 41–45.

Maneker, Jerry S., and Robert P. Rankin. 1993. "Religious Homogamy and Marital Duration Among Those Who File for Divorce in California, 1966–1971." *Journal of Divorce and Remarriage* 19 (1–2): 233–41.

Manisses Communications Group. 2000. "When It Comes to Handling Your Hard-to-Handle Child, Are You An Authoritative, Authoritarian or Permissive Parent?" *The Brown University Child and Adolescent Behavior Letter* 16 (3): S1–S2.

Manlove, Jennifer, Suzanne Ryan, and Kerry Franzetta. 2003. "Patterns of Contraceptive Use Within Teenagers' First Sexual Relationships." *Perspectives on Sexual and Reproductive Health* 35: 246–255.

Manning, Wendy D. 1993. "Marriage and Cohabitation Following Premarital Conception." *Journal of Marriage and Family* 55 (3): 839–50.

———. 2001a. "Childbearing in Cohabiting Unions: Racial and Ethnic Differences." *Family Planning Perspectives* 33 (5): 217–234.

———. 2001b. "Childbearing in Cohabiting Unions: Racial and Ethnic differences." *Family Planning Perspectives* 33 (5): 217–234.

Manning, Wendy D., and Kathleen A. Lamb. 2003. "Adolescent Well-Being in Cohabiting, Married, and Single-Parent Families." *Journal of Marriage and Family* 65 (4): 876–893.

Manning, Wendy D., and Nancy S. Landale. 1996. "Racial and Ethnic Differences in the Role of Cohabitation in

Premarital Childbearing." *Journal of Marriage and Family* 58 (1): 63–77.

Manning, Wendy D., and Pamela J. Smock. 1996. "Why Marry? Race and the Transition to Marriage among Cohabitors." *Demography* 32: 509–20.

———. 1999. "New Families and Non-resident Father–Child Visitation." *Social Forces* 78: 87–116.

———. 2002. "First Comes Cohabitation and Then Comes Marriage?" *Journal of Family Issues* 23 (8): 1065–1087.

Manning, Wendy D., Susan D. Stewart, and Pamela J. Smock. 2003. "The Complexity of Fathers' Parenting Responsibilities and Involvement with Nonresident Children." *Journal of Family Issues* 24 (5): 645–667.

Mannis, Valerie S. 1999. "Single Mothers by Choice." *Family Relations* 48 (2): 121–28.

Mansnerus, Laura. 1998. "Market Puts Price Tags on the Priceless." *New York Times.* Oct. 26.

———. 2001. "Couples Looking to Adopt Find a Shifting Spotlight." *New York Times.* Sept. 26.

Manton, Kenneth G., and Kenneth C. Land. 2000. "Active Life Expectancy Estimates for the U.S. Elderly Population: A Multidimensional Continuous-Mixture Model of Functional Change Applied to Completed Cohorts, 1982–1996." *Demography* 37 (3): 253–65.

Marano, Hara E. 2000. "Divorced? (Remarriage in America)." *Psychology Today* 33 (2): 56–60.

Marano, Hara Estroff. 1997. "Puberty May Start at 6 as Hormones Surge." *New York Times.* July 1: B1, B12.

March, Karen. 1997. "The Dilemma of Adoption Reunion: Establishing Open Communication Between Adoptees and Their Birth Mothers." *Family Relations* 46 (2): 99–105.

Marchand, Jennifer F., and Ellen Hock. 2000. "Avoidance and Attacking Conflict-Resolution Strategies Among Married Couples: Relations to Depressive Symptoms and Marital Satisfaction." *Family Relations* 49 (2): 201–206.

Mare, Robert D. 1991. "Five Decades of Educational Assortative Mating." *American Sociological Review* 56: 15–32.

Marecek, Jeanne. 1995. "Gender, Politics, and Psychology's Ways of Knowing." *American Psychologist* 50 (3): 162–64.

Marech, Rona. 2004a. "To Wed or Not to Wed." *San Francisco Chronicle Magazine.* January 18.

———. 2004b. "Nearly Weds." *San Francisco Chronicle.* March 13.

———. 1992. "Child Abuse by Mothers' Boyfriends: Why the Overrepresentation?" *Child Abuse & Neglect* 16: 541–51.

Marin, Rick. 2000. "At-home Fathers Step Out to Find They Are Not Alone." *New York Times.* Jan. 12.

"Marital Rape—A U.S. Study." N.d. *The New Criminologist* 1. www.thecriminologist.com/new .

Markman, Howard, Scott Stanley, and Susan L. Blumberg. 1994. *Fighting for Your Marriage: Positive Steps for Preventing Divorce and Preserving a Lasting Love.* San Francisco: Jossey-Bass.

Marks, Nadine F. 1995. "Midlife Marital Status Differences in Social Support Relationships with Adult Children and Psychological Well-Being." *Journal of Family Issues* 16 (1): 5–28.

Marks, Nadine F., James D. Lambert, and Heejeong Choi. 2002. "Transitions to Caregiving, Gender, and Psychological Well-Being: A Prospective U.S. National Study." *Journal of Marriage and Family* 64 (3): 657–667.

Marks, Stephen R. 1989. "Toward a Systems Theory of Marital Quality." *Journal of Marriage and Family* 51: 15–26.

———. 2001. "Teasing Out the Lessons of the 1960s: Family Diversity and Family Privilege." Pp. 66–79 in *Understanding Families in the New Millennium: A Decade in Review,* edited by Robert M. Milardo. Lawrence, KS: National Council on Family Relations.

Marlow, Lenard, and S. Richard Sauber. 1990. *The Handbook of Divorce Mediation.* New York: Plenum.

"Marriage Wanes as American Families Enter New Century, University of Chicago Research Shows." 1999. Chicago: University of Chicago News Release. Nov. 24. www.news.uchicago.edu/releases/99.

"Married Households Rise Again among Blacks, Census Finds." 2003. AP. April 25.

Marriott, Michel. 1995. "Living in 'Lockdown'." *Newsweek.* Jan. 23: 56–7.

Marshall, Susan E. 1995. "Keep Us on the Pedestal: Women Against Feminism in Twentieth-Century America." Pp. 547–60 in *Women: A Feminist Perspective,* 5th ed., edited by Jo Freeman. Mountain View, CA: Mayfield.

Marsiglio, William. 2003. "Making Males Mindful of Their Sexual and Procreative Identities: Using Self-Narratives in Field Settings." *Perspectives on Sexual and Reproductive Health* 35: 229–232.

———. 1992. "Adolescent Males' Orientation Toward the Reproductive Realm: Paternity and Contraception." Paper presented at the annual meeting of the Population Association of America. Denver, May 1.

———. 2004a. *Stepdads: Stories of Love, Hope, and Repair.* Boulder, CO: Rowman and Littlefield.

———. 2004b. "When Stepfathers Claim Stepchildren: A Conceptual Analysis." *Journal of Marriage and Family* 66 (1): 22–39.

Marsiglio, William, Paul Amato, Randal Day, and Michael E. Lamb. 2000. "Scholarship on Fatherhood in the 1990s and Beyond." *Journal of Marriage and Family* 62: 1173–91.

Marsiglio, William, and Sally Hutchison. 2002. *Sex, Men, and Babies: Stories of Awareness and Responsibility.* New York: NYU Press.

Martin, C. L. 1989. "Children's Use of Gender-Related Information in Making Social Judgments." *Developmental Psychology* 25: 80–88.

Martin, Joyce A., Brady E. Hamilton, Paul D. Sutton, Stephanie Ventura, Fay Menacker, and Martha Munson. 2003. "Births: Final Data for 2002." *National Vital Statistics Report* 52 (10), Hyattsville MD: National Center for Health Statistics. Dec. 17.

Martin, Joyce A., Brady E. Hamilton, and Stephanie J. Ventura. 2001. *Births: Preliminary Data for 2000.* National Vital Statistics Report 49 (5). July 24. Hyattsville, MD: National Center for Health Statistics.

Martin, Joyce A., Brady E. Hamilton, Stephanie J. Ventura, Fay Menacker,

Melissa M. Park, and Paul D. Sutton. 2002. "Births: Final Data for 2001." *National Vital Statistics Report* 51(2). Hyattsville MD: National Center for Health Statistics. Dec. 18.

Martin, Joyce A., and Melissa M. Park. 1999. *Trends in Twin and Triplet Births.* National Vital Statistics Reports 47 (24). Sept. 14. Hyattsville, MD: National Center for Health Statistics.

Martin, Peter, and Landy Luke. 1991. "Divorce and the Wheel Theory of Love." *Journal of Divorce and Remarriage* 15 (1/2): 3–22.

Martin, Philip, and Elizabeth Midgley. 2003. "Immigration: Shaping and Reshaping America." *Population Bulletin* 58(2). Washington DC: Population Reference Bureau. June.

Martin, Sandra L., April Harris-Britt, Yun Li, Kathryn E. Moracco, Lawrence L. Kupper, and Jacquelyn C. Campbell. 2004. "Change in Intimate Partner Violence During Pregnancy." *Journal of Family Violence* 19: 243–247.

Martin, Teresa Castro. 2002. "Consensual Unions in Latin America: Persistence of a Dual Nuptiality System." *Journal of Comparative Family Studies* 33 (1): 35–56.

Marvin v. Marvin. 1976. 18 Cal.3d 660, 134 Cal.Rptr. 815, 557 P.2d 106.

Maslow, Abraham H. 1943. "A Theory of Human Motivation." *Psychological Review* 50: 370–96.

Mason, Karen A. 2000. "They Do Time Too: The Effects of Imprisonment on the Families of White-Collar Offenders." Pp. 325–27 in *Families, Crime, and Criminal Justice*, edited by Greer Litton Fox and Michael L. Benson. New York: Elsevier Science.

Mason, Mary Ann. 1988. *The Equality Trap.* New York: Simon & Schuster.

———. 1998. "The Modern American Stepfamily: Problems and Possibilities." Pp. 95–116 in *All Our Families: New Policies for a New Century*, edited by Mary Ann Mason, Arlene Skolnick, and Stephen D. Sugarman. New York: Oxford University Press.

Mason, Mary Ann, Mark A. Fine, and Sarah Carnochan. 2001. "Family Law in the New Millennium: For Whose Families?" *Journal of Family Issues* 22 (7): 859–81.

Mason, Mary Ann, Sydney Harrison-Jay, Gloria Messick Svare, and Nicholas H. Wolfinger. 2002. "Stepparents: De Facto Parents or Legal Strangers?" *Journal of Family Issues* 23 (4): 507–522.

Mason, Mary Ann, and Ann Quirk. 1997. "Are Mothers Losing Custody? Read My Lips: Trends in Judicial Decision-Making in Custody Disputes—1920, 1960, 1990, and 1995." *Family Law Quarterly* 31: 215–36.

Mason, Mary Ann, Arlene Skolnick, and Stephen D. Sugarman. 1998. *All Our Families: New Policies for a New Century.* New York: Oxford University Press.

Masters, William H., and Virginia E. Johnson. 1966. *Human Sexual Response.* Boston: Little, Brown.

———. 1970. *Human Sexual Inadequacy.* Boston: Little, Brown.

———. 1973. "Orgasm, Anatomy of the Female." In *The Encyclopedia of Sexual Behavior*, edited by Albert Ellis and Albert Abarbanel. New York: Aronson.

———. 1976. *The Pleasure Bond: A New Look at Sexuality and Commitment.* New York: Bantam.

Masters, William H., Virginia E. Johnson, and Robert C. Kolodny. 1994. *Heterosexuality.* New York: HarperCollins.

Matthews, Jan M., and Alan M. Hudson. 2001. "Guidelines for Evaluating Parent Training Programs." *Family Relations* 50 (1): 77–86.

Matthews, J.J., Fay Menacker, and Marian F. MacDorman. 2003. "Infant Mortality Statistics from the 2001 Period Linked Birth/Infant Death Data Set." *National Vital Statistics Reports* 52(2). Hyattsville MD: National Center for Health Statistics. Sept. 14.

Matthews, Ralph, and Anne Martin Matthews. 1986. "Infertility and Involuntary Childlessness: The Transition to Nonparenthood." *Journal of Marriage and Family* 48: 641–49.

Maugh, Thomas H. 1998. "'Honey, Just Be a Yes Man'—Study: Marriage Lasts if Husband Gives In." *Los Angeles Times.* Feb. 21.

Mauldin, Teresa A. 1990. "Women Who Remain Above the Poverty Level in Divorce: Implications for Family Policy." *Family Relations* 39 (2): 141–46.

Mauldon, Jane. 2003. "Families Started by Teenagers." Pp. 40-65 in *All Our Families*, 2nd ed., edited by Mary Ann Mason, Arlene Skolnick, and Stephen D. Sugarman. New York: Oxford.

Maxwell, Lorraine E. 1996. "Multiple Effects of Home and Day Care Crowding." *Environment and Behavior* 28: 494–511.

May, Elaine Tyler. 1997. *Barren in the Promised Land: Childless Americans and the Pursuit of Happiness.* Cambridge, MA: Harvard University Press.

May, Rollo. 1969. *Love and Will.* New York: Norton.

———. 1975. "A Preface to Love." Pp. 114–19 in *The Practice of Love*, edited by Ashley Montagu. Englewood Cliffs, NJ: Prentice-Hall.

Mayer, Susan E. 1997. *What Money Can't Buy: Family Income and Children's Life Chances.* Cambridge, MA: Harvard.

Mays, Vickie M., and Susan D. Cochran. 1999. "The Black Woman's Relationship Project: A National Survey of Black Lesbians." Pp. 59–66 in *The Black Family: Essays and Studies*, 6th ed., edited by Robert Staples. Belmont, CA: Wadsworth.

McAdoo, Harriette Pipes. 2003. "Religion in African American Families." *Family Focus.* December: F9-F11.

McBride-Chang, Catherine, and Lei Chang. 1998. "Adolescent–Parent Relations in Hong Kong: Parenting Styles, Emotional Autonomy, and School Achievement." *Journal of Genetic Psychology* 159 (4): 421–35.

McCary, James Leslie. 1979. *Human Sexuality*, 2nd ed. New York: Van Nostrand.

McClusky, Tom. 2004. "Thirty Years of Marriage on Trial." Family Research Council. March 25. http://www.frc.org

McCormick, Richard A., S. J. 1992. "Christian Approaches: Catholicism." Paper presented at the Surrogate Motherhood and Reproductive Technologies Symposium, Creighton University, Jan. 13.

McCubbin, Hamilton I., and Marilyn A. McCubbin. 1991. "Family Stress Theory and Assessment: The Resiliency Model of Family Stress, Adjustment and Adaptation." Pp. 3–32 in *Family Assessment Inventories for Research and*

Practice, 2nd ed., edited by Hamilton I. McCubbin and Anne I. Thompson. Madison: University of Wisconsin, School of Family Resources and Consumer Services.

———. 1994. "Families Coping with Illness: The Resiliency Model of Family Stress, Adjustment, and Adaptation." Chapter 2 in *Families, Health, and Illness.* St. Louis: Mosby.

McCubbin, Hamilton I., Anne I. Thompson, and Marilyn A. McCubbin, eds.. 1996. *Family Assessment: Resiliency, Coping and Adaptation: Inventories for Research and Practice.* Madison: University of Wisconsin Publishers.

McCubbin, Marilyn A. 1995. "The Typology Model of Adjustment and Adaptation: A Family Stress Model." *Guidance and Counseling* 10 (4): 31–39.

McCubbin, Marilyn, Karla Balling, Peggy Possin, Sharon Frierdich, and Barbara Byrne. 2002. "Family Resiliency in Childhood Cancer." *Family Relations* 51 (2): 103–111.

McCubbin, Marilyn A., and Hamilton I. McCubbin. 1989. "Theoretical Orientations to Family Stress and Coping." Pp. 3–43 in *Treating Families Under Stress,* edited by Charles Figley. New York: Brunner/Mazel.

McCurdy, Karen, and Deborah Daro. 2001. "Parent Involvement in Family Support Programs: An Integrated Theory." *Family Relations* 50 (2): 113–21.

McCurdy, Karen, Robin A. Gannon, and Deborah Daro. 2003. "Participation Patterns in Home-Based Family Support Programs: Ethnic Variations." *Family Relations* 52 (1): 3–11.

McDonald, Katrina Bell, and Elizabeth M. Armstrong. 2001. "De-Romanticizing Black Intergenerational Support: The Questionable Expectations of Welfare Reform." *Journal of Marriage and Family* 63: 213–23.

McFalls, Joseph A., Jr. 2003. "Population: A Lively Introduction." *Population Bulletin* 58 (4). Washington, DC: Population Reference Bureau.

McGinnis, Sandra L. 2003. "Cohabiting, Dating, and Perceived Costs of Marriage: A Model of Marriage Entry." *Journal of Marriage and Family* 65 (1): 105–116.

McGrew, Kathryn B. 1998. "Daughters' Caregiving Decisions: From an Impulse to a Balancing Point of Care." *Journal of Women and Aging* 10 (2): 49–65.

McHale, Susan M., W. T. Bartko, Ann C. Crouter, and M. Perry-Jenkins. 1990. "Children's Housework and Psychological Functioning: The Mediating Effects of Parents' Sex-Role Behaviors and Attitudes." *Child Development* 61: 1413–26.

McHale, Susan M., and Ann C. Crouter. 1992. "You Can't Always Get What You Want: Incongruence Between Sex-Role Attitudes and Family Work Roles and Its Implications for Marriage." *Journal of Marriage and Family* 54 (3): 537–47.

McHugh, Maureen F. 2004. "The Evil Stepmother." *Second Wives Café: Online Support for Second Wives and Stepmothers.* http://secondwivescafe.com

McIntosh, Peggy. 2004. "White Privilege: Unpacking the Invisible Knapsack." Pp. 103-108 in *Race, Class, and Gender,* 5th ed., edited by Margaret L. Andersen and Patricia Hill Collins. Belmont, CA: Wadsworth.

McKee, Mike, and Michael Booth. 1999. "1st District to Hear Gay Adoption Case." *The Recorder.* Mar. 17. Web.lexis-nexis.com/universe.

McKee, Tom. 2004. "Ohio House Approves Defense of Marriage Act." February 3. http://www.wcpo.com/news/2004/local/02/03/marriage_passed.html

McKinnon, Jesse. 2003. "The Black Population of the United States: March 2002." *Current Population Reports* P-20-541. April.

McLanahan, Sara, Irwin Garfinkel, Nana E. Reichman, and Julien O. Teitler. 2001. "Unwed Parents or Fragile Families? Implications for Welfre and Child Support Policy." Pp. 202–228 in *Out of Wedlock: Causes and Consequences of Nonmarital Fertility,* edited by Lawrence L. Wu and Barbara Wolfe. New York: Russell Sage.

McLanahan, Sara, and Gary Sandefur. 1994. *Growing Up with A Single Parent: What Hurts, What Helps?* Cambridge MA: Harvard.

McLaughlin, Diane K., and Daniel T. Lichter. 1997. "Poverty and the Mari-

tal Behavior of Young Women." *Journal of Marriage and Family* 59: 582–94.

McLoyd, Vonnie C., Ana Mari Cauce, David Takeuchi, and Leon Wilson. 2000. "Marital Processes and Parental Socialization in Families of Color: A Decade Review of Research." *Journal of Marriage and Family* 62: 1070–93.

McMahon, Catherine A., Frances Gibson, Garth Leslie, Jennifer Cohen, and Christopher Tennant. 2003. "Parents of 5-Year-Old In Vitro Fertilization Children: Psychological Adjustment, Parenting Stress, and the Influence of Subsequent In Vitro Fertilization Treatments." *Journal of Family Psychology* 17: 361–369.

McManus, Patricia A., and Thomas DiPrete. 2001. "Losers and Winners: The Financial Consequences of Separation and Divorce for Men." *American Sociological Review* 66: 246–68.

McNicholas, J., and G. M. Collis. 2004. "Children's Representations of Pets in Their Social Networks." *Child: Care, Health and Development* 27: 279–294.

McQuillan, Julia, Arthur L. Greil, Lynn White, and Mary Casey Jacob. 2003. "Frustrated Fertility: Infertility and Psychological Distress among Women." *Journal of Marriage and the Family* 65: 1007–1018.

Mead, Margaret. 1949. *Male and Female: A Study of the Sexes in a Changing World.* New York: Morrow.

———. 1966. "Marriage in Two Steps." *Redbook.* July.

Means-Christensen, Adrienne J., Douglas K. Snyder, and Charles Negy. 2003. "Assessing Nontraditional Couples: Validity of the Marital Satisfaction Inventory—Revised with Gay, Lesbian, and Cohabiting Heterosexual Couples." *Journal of Marital and Family Therapy* 29 (1):69–83.

Meckler, Laura. 1999. "Welfare Reform Hurts Poorest." Associated Press. Aug. 22.

Medeiros, Daniel M. 2003. "Get Used to It!" *Archives of Sexual Behavior* 32 (5): 490–492.

Mehrota, Meela. 1999. "The Social Construction of Wife Abuse: Experiences of Asian Indian Women in the United States." *Gender and Society* 16: 898–920.

Meilander, Gilbert. 1992. "Christian Approaches: Protestantism." Paper presented at the Surrogate Motherhood and Reproductive Technologies Symposium, Creighton University, Jan. 13.

Memmott, Mark. 2001. "Sex Trade May Lure 325,000 U.S. Kids." *USA Today.* Sept. 10.

Menaghan, Elizabeth, and Morton Lieberman. 1986. "Changes in Depression Following Divorce: A Panel Study." *Journal of Marriage and Family* 48: 319–28.

Menjívar, Cecilia, and Olivia Salcido. 2002. "Immigrant Women and Domestic Violence: Common Experiences in Different Countries." *Gender and Society* 16: 898–920.

"Men, Women, and HIV." 2004. *Perspectives on Sexual and Reproductive Health*: 36: 49.

Meredith, William H., Douglas A. Abbott, Mary Ann Lamanna, and Gregory Sanders. 1989. "Rituals and Family Strengths: A Three Generation Study." *Family Perspectives* 23: 75–83.

Merkle, Erich R., and Rhonda A. Richardson. 2000. "Digital Dating and Virtual Relating: Conceptualizing Computer Mediated Romantic Relationships." *Family Relations* 49 (2): 187–92.

Mertensmeyer, Carol, and Mark Fine. 2000. "ParentLink: A Model of Integration and Support for Parents." *Family Relations* 49 (3): 257–65.

Messner, Michael A. 1997. *The Politics of Masculinity: Men in Movements.* Thousand Oaks, CA: Sage.

Metropolitan Life Insurance Company. 1997. *The Metropolitan Life Survey of the American Teacher, 1997: Examining Gender Issues in the Public Schools.* New York: Metropolitan Life Insurance Company.

Meyer, Daniel R., and Judi Bartfeld. 1996. "Compliance with Child Support Orders in Divorce Cases." *Journal of Marriage and Family* 58 (1): 201–12.

Meyer, Madonna H., and Marcia L. Bellas. 2001. "U.S. Old-Age Policy and the Family." Pp. 191–201 in *Families in Later Life: Connections and Transitions*, edited by Alexis J. Walker, Margaret Manoogian-O'Dell, Lori A. McGraw, and Diana L. G. White. Thousand Oaks, CA: Pine Forge.

Michael, Robert T., John H. Gagnon, Edward O. Laumann, and Gina Kolata. 1994. *Sex in America: A Definitive Survey.* Boston: Little, Brown.

Michaels, Marcia L. 2000. "The Stepfamily Enrichment Program: A Preliminary Evaluation Using Focus Groups." *American Journal of Family Therapy* 28 (1): 61–73.

"Middle Ranks Lack Women, Research Says." 1999. *Omaha World-Herald.* Nov. 21.

Milkie, Melissa A., Marybeth Mattingly, Kei M. Nomaguchi, Suzanne M. Bianchi, John D. Robinson. 2004. "The Time Squeeze: Parental Statuses and Feelings about Time with Children." *Journal of Marriage and the Family* 66: 739-761.

Miller, Brent C., Xitao Fan, Mathew Christensen, Harold Grotevant, and Manfred van Dulmen. 2000. "Comparisons of Adopted and Nonadopted Adolescents in a Large, Nationally Representative Sample." *Child Development* 71: 1458–1473.

Miller, Claudia. 2003. "When It's Good to go Bananas: Oakland Nonprofit Has Been Helping Families Stay Sane for 30 Years." *San Francisco Chronicle.* October 19.

Miller, Dawn. 2004. "From the Author." TheStepfamilyLife: A Column from Life in the Blender." http://www.thestepfamilylife.com.

———. Nd. "Don't Go Nuclear—Negotiate." SelfGrowth.com. http://www.selfgrowth.com/articles/Miller. Retrieved 9/21/04.

———. Nd. "Surviving the Blended Family Holiday: Five Tips for the Stressed Out." SelfGrowth.com. http://www.selfgrowth.com/articles/Miller. Retrieved 9/21/04.

Miller, Dorothy. 1979. "The Native American Family: The Urban Way." Pp. 441–84 in *Families Today: A Research Sampler on Families and Children*, edited by Eunice Corfman. Washington, DC: Government Printing Office.

Miller, Eleanor, and Carrie Yang Costello. 2001. "The Limits of Biological Determinism." *American Sociological Review* 66: 592–98.

Miller, Elizabeth. 2000. "Religion and Families over the Life Course." Pp. 173–186 in *Families Across Time: A Life Course Perspective*, edited by Sharon J. Price, Patrick C. McKenry, and Megan J. Murphy. Los Angeles: Roxbury.

Miller, Richard B., and Jennifer Glass. 1989. "Parent–Child Attitude Similarity Across the Life Course." *Journal of Marriage and Family* 51: 991–97.

Miller, Timothy. 1999. *The 60s Communes: Hippies and Beyond.* New York: Syracuse University Press.

Miller-Perrin, Cindy, Robin D. Perrin, and Ola W. Barnett, eds. 2004. *Family Violence Across the Life Span*, 2nd ed. Thousand Oaks CA: Sage.

Mills, C. Wright. 1973 [1959]. *The Sociological Imagination.* New York: Oxford University Press.

Mills, Terry L., Melanie A. Wakeman, and Christopher B. Fea. 2001. "Adult Grandchildren's Perceptions of Emotional Closeness and Consensus with Their Maternal and Paternal Grandparents." *Journal of Family Issues* 22 (4): 427–55.

Mills, Terry L., and Janet M. Wilmoth. 2002. "Intergenerational Differences and Similarities in Life-Sustaining Treatment Attitudes and Decision Factors." *Family Relations* 51 (1): 46–54.

Milner, Jan. 1990. "Strangers in a Strange Land: Housewives in the 1980's." Paper presented at the annual meeting of the Midwest Sociological Society, Chicago, Apr. 14.

Min, Pyong Gap. 2002. "Korean American Families." Pp. 193–211 in *Minority Families in the United States: A Multicultural Perspective*, 3rd ed., edited by Ronald L. Taylor. Upper Saddle River NJ: Prentice-Hall.

Minino, Arialdi M., and Betty Smith. 2001. *Deaths: Preliminary Data for 2000.* National Vital Statistics Reports 49(12). Hyattsville, MD: National Center for Health Statistics.

Mink, Gwendolyn. 1998. "Feminists, Welfare Reform, Justice." *Social Justice* 25 (1): 146–58.

Minnis, Alexandra M., and Nancy S. Padian. 2001. "Choice of Female-Controlled Barrier Methods among Young Women and Their Male Sexual Partners." *Family Planning Perspectives* 33: 28–34.

Mintz, Steven, and Susan Kellogg. 1988. *Domestic Revolutions: A Social History of*

American Family Life. New York: Free Press.

Molyneux, Guy. 1995. "Losing by the Rules." *Los Angeles Times*. Sept. 3: M1, M3.

Money, John. 1995. *Gendermaps: Social Constructionism, Feminism, and Sexosophical History*. New York: Continuum.

"Monogamy: Is It for Us?" 1998. *The Advocate*. June 23: 29.

Monroe, Michael, Richard C. Baker, and Samuel Roll. 1997. "The Relationship of Homophobia to Intimacy in Heterosexual Men." *Journal of Homosexuality* 33 (2): 23–37.

Monroe, Pamela A., and Vicky V. Tiller. 2001. "Commitment to Work Among Welfare-Reliant Women." *Journal of Marriage and Family* 63 (3): 816–28.

Montgomery, Marilyn J., and Gwendolyn T. Sorell. 1997. "Differences in Love Attitudes Across Family Life Stages." *Family Relations* 46: 55–61.

Moore, David W. 2004. "Modest Rebound in Public Acceptance of Homosexuals." May 20. www.gallup.com

Moore, Kathleen A., Marita P. McCabe, and Roger B. Brink. 2001. "Are Married Couples Happier in Their Relationships Than Cohabiting Couples? Intimacy and Relationship Factors." *Sexual and Relationship Therapy* 16 (1): 35–46.

Moore, Kristin A., Margaret C. Simms, and Charles L. Betsey. 1986. *Choice and Circumstance: Racial Differences in Adolescent Sexuality and Fertility*. New Brunswick, NJ: Transaction.

Moore, Teresa. 1993. "Pain of Color-Coded Child Rearing." *San Francisco Chronicle*. Feb. 15: B3.

Moran, Rachel F. 2001. *Interracial Intimacy: The Regulation of Race & Romance*. Chicago, ILL: University of Chicago Press.

"More Binding Marriage Gets A Governor's Participation." 2004. *Omaha World-Herald*. Nov. 14.

Moretti, Robb. 2002. "The Last Generation to Live on the Edge." *Newsweek*. Aug. 5.

Morin, Richard, and Megan Rosenfeld. 1998. "The Politics of Fatigue." *Washington Post National Weekly Edition*. Apr. 20: 6–7.

Morris, A.S., J.S. Silk, L. Steinberg, F.M. Sessa, S. Avenevoli, and

M.J. Essex. 2002. "Temperamental Vulnerability and Negative Parenting as Interacting Predictors of Child Adjustment." *Journal of Marriage and Family* 64 (2):461–471.

Morris, Bonnie Rothman. 1999a. "Webcams Focus on Day Care." *New York Times*. Dec. 2.

———. 1999b. "You've Got Romance: Seeking Love on the Line." *New York Times*. Aug. 26.

Morrison, Donna R., and Andres J. Cherlin. 1995. "The Divorce Process and Young Children's Well-Being: A Prospective Analysis." *Journal of Marriage and Family* 57 (3): 800–12.

Morrison, Donna R., and Mary Jo Coiro. 1999. "Parental Conflict and Marital Disruption: Do Children Benefit When High Conflict Marriages Are Dissolved?" *Journal of Marriage and Family* 61: 626–37.

Morrison, Donna R., and Amy Ritualo. 2000. "Routes to Children's Economic Recovery After Divorce: Are Cohabitation and Remarriage Equivalent?" *American Sociological Review* 65 (4): 560–80.

Morrow, Lance. 1992. "Family Values." *Time*. Aug. 31: 22–27.

Mosher, William D., Gladys M. Martinez, Anjana Chandra, Joyce C. Abma, and Stephanie J. Wilson. 2004. "Use of Contraception and Use of Family Planning Services in the United States: 1982–2002." *Advance Data from Vital and Health Statistics*. No. 350. Hyattsville MD. Dec. 10.

Mosher, William D., and William F. Pratt. 1990. "Contraceptive Use in the United States, 1973–88." *Advance Data*, No. 182, Mar. 20. Hyattsville, MD: National Center for Health Statistics.

Mui, Ada C. 1996. "Depression Among Elderly Chinese Immigrants: An Exploratory Study." *Social Work* 41: 633–45.

Mulcahy, John J. 1997. *Diagnosis and Management of Male Sexual Dysfunction*. New York: Igaku-Shoin.

Muller, Chandra. 1995. "Maternal Employment, Parent Involvement, and Mathematics Achievement Among Adolescents." *Journal of Marriage and Family* 57 (1): 85–100.

Mulrine, Anna. 2003. "Love.com." *U.S. News & World Report*. September 29: 52–58.

"Multnomah County, Ore., to Grant Marriage Licenses to Same-Sex Couples." 2004. *Knight/Ridder/Tribune Business News*. March 4.

Mumola, Christopher J. 2000. *Incarcerated Parents and Their Children*. Washington, DC: U.S. Bureau of Justice Statistics.

Murkoff, Heidi. 2000. "The Real Parenting Expert Is . . .You." *Newsweek Special Issue*. Fall/Winter: 20–21.

Murphy, Josh. 2004. "Stepfamily Chapter Essay Question." Unpublished manuscript.

Murphy, Mike, Karen Glaser, and Emily Grundy. 1997. "Marital Status and Long-Term Illness in Great Britain." *Journal of Marriage and Family* 59: 156–64.

Murray, Sandra L., John G. Holmes, and Dale W. Griffin. 2000. "Self-Esteem and the Quest for Felt Security: How Perceived Regard Regulates Attachment Processes." *Journal of Personality and Social Psychology* 78 (3): 478–98.

Murry, Velma M., Gene H. Brody, Anita Brown, Joseph Wisenbaker, Carolyn E. Cutrona, and Ronald L. Simons. 2002. "Linking Employment Status, Maternal Psychological Well-Being, Parenting, and Children's attributions about Poverty in Families Receiving Government Assistance." *Family Relations* 51 (2): 112–120.

Murry, Velma M., P. Adama Brown, Gene H. Brody, Carolyn E. Cutrona, and Ronald L. Simons. 2001. "Racial Discrimination as a Moderator of the Links among Stress, Maternal Psychological Functioning, and Family Relationships." *Journal of Marriage and Family* 63 (4): 915–926.

Murstein, Bernard I. 1980. "Mate Selection in the 1970s." *Journal of Marriage and Family* 42: 777–92.

———. 1986. *Paths to Marriage*. Newbury Park, CA: Sage.

Murstein, Bernard I., and E. R. Adler. 1997. "Gender Differences in Power and Self-Disclosure in Dating and Married Couples." *Personal Relationships* 2: 199–209.

Musick, Kelly. 2002. "Planned and Unplanned Childbearing among Unmarried Women." *Journal of Marriage and the Family* 64 (4): 915–929.

"Muslim Women's Veils Should Be More Than Anti-Western Protest." *Omaha World-Herald.* Dec. 8.

Myers, David G. 2002. *Social Psychology,* 7th ed. New York: McGraw-Hill.

Myers, Michael F. 1989. *Men and Divorce.* New York: Guilford.

Myers, Robert. 2004. "Gay Marriages Fit into This Adaptable Institution." *USA Today.* March 15.

Myers-Walls, Judy. 2002. "Talking to Children about Terrorism and Armed Conflict." *The Forum for Family and Consumer Issues* 7(1). www.ces.ncsu.edu./depts/fcs/pubs

———. 2001. "Talking to Children About Terrorism: By the Numbers." Purdue Extension: Knowledge to Go. http://www.ces.purdue.edu/ terrorism/.

Nachman, Patricia. 1997. *You and Your Only Child: The Joys, Myths and Challenges of Raising an Only Child.* New York: HarperCollins.

Nakazawa, Donna Jackson. 2003. *Does Anybody Else Look Like Me? A Parent's Guide to Raising Multiracial Children.*

Nakonezny, P. A., R. D. Shull, and J. L. Rodgers. 1995. "The Effect of No-Fault Divorce Law on the Divorce Rate Across the 50 States and Its Relation to Income, Education, and Religiosity." *Journal of Marriage and Family* 57 (2): 477–88.

Nanji, Azim A. 1993. "The Muslim Family in North America." Pp. 229–42 in *Family Ethnicity: Strength in Diversity,* edited by Harriette Pipes McAdoo. Newbury Park, CA: Sage.

Nannini, Dawn K., and Lawrence S. Meyers. 2000. "Jealousy in Sexual and Emotional Infidelity: An Alternative to the Evolutionary Explanation." *The Journal of Sex Research* 37 (2): 117–125.

Nash, J. Madeleine. 1997. "Special Report: Fertile Minds." *Time.* Feb. 3: 48–56.

Nason, Ellen M., and Margaret M. Poloma. 1976. *Voluntarily Childless Couples: The Emergence of a Variant Life Style.* Newbury Park, CA: Sage.

National Ag Safe Database. n.d. "From Family Stress to Family Strengths: Stress, Lesson 5." http://www.cec.gov/niosh/nasd.

National Conference of State Legislatures. 2004a. "50 States Summary of Legislation Related to Insurance Coverage for Infertility Therapy." June. www.ncsl.org.

———. 2004b. "Marriage and Divorce / Same Sex Marriage." http://www.ncsl.org/programs/cyf/ samesex.htm

National Public Radio (NPR)/Kaiser Family Foundation/ Kennedy School of Government. 2004. *Sex Education in America Survey.*Menlo CA: Kaiser Family Foundation. Jan. www.kff.org

"Navajo Tribal Court Supported by Utah Court in Adoption Case." 1988. *New York Times.* Dec. 15.

Navarro, Mireya. 2001. "Consensus Is Lacking on Bilingual Education." *New York Times.* Feb. 24.

———. 2004. "Conservative Agenda is Curtailing Sexual Health and Research." *New York Times.* July 11.

Nazario, Sonia L. 1990a. "Midwifery Is Staging Revival as Demand for Prenatal Care, Low-Tech Births Rises." *Wall Street Journal.* Sept. 25.

———. 1990b. "Identity Crisis: When White Parents Adopt Black Babies, Race Often Divides." *Wall Street Journal.* Sept. 20.

Neimark, Jill. 2003. "All You Need Is Love: Why It's Crucial to Your Health—and How to Get More in Your Life." *Natural Health* 33 (8): 109–113.

"NE-UNL Study Finds Wages Benefitted from Immigrants." 2003. *Lincoln Journal Star.* April 17.

"N.Y. Gay-Marriage Mayor Charged with 19 Counts." Associated Press. March 3. http://www.foxnews.com/

Newburger, Eric. 2001. *Home Computers and Internet Use in the United States: August 2000.* Current Population Report P23–207. Washington, DC: U.S. Census Bureau.

Newman, Katherine. 1993. *Declining Fortunes: The Withering of the American Dream.* New York: Basic.

Newman, Louis. 1992. "Jewish Approaches." Paper presented at the Surrogate Motherhood and Reproductive Technologies Symposium, Creighton University, Jan. 13.

Newport, Frank. 1999. "Americans Agree That Being Attractive Is a Plus in American Society." *The Gallup Organization Poll Releases.* Sept. 15. http://www.gallup.com/poll/releases.

———. 2001. "American Attitudes Toward Homosexuality Continue to Become More Tolerant." *Poll Analyses.* June 4. http://www.gallup.com.

———. 2003a. "Public Shifts to More Conservative Stance on Gay Rights." July 30. www.gallup.com.

———. 2003b. "Six Out of 10 Americans Say Homosexual Relations Should be Legal." May 15. www.gallup.com

———. 2004a. "Constitutional Amendment Defining Marriage Lacks 'Supermajority' Support." The Gallup Organization: Gallup News Service. February 25. http://www.gallup.com

———. 2004b. "Americans Evenly Divided on Constitutional Amendment: Majority Oppose Same-sex Marriage in Principle." The Gallup Organization: Gallup News Service. February 11. http://www.gallup.com

Newport, Frank, David W. Moore, and Lydia Saad. 1999. "Long-Term Gallup Poll Trends: A Portrait of the American Public." www.gallup.com.

NICHD Early Child Care Research Network. 1997a. "The Effects of Infant Child Care on Infant–Mother Attachment Security: Results of the NICHD Study of Early Child Care." *Child Development* 68: 860–79.

———. 1997b. "Familial Factors Associated with the Characteristics of Nonmaternal Care for Infants." *Journal of Marriage and Family* 59: 389–408.

———. 1998. "Early Child Care and Self-Control, Compliance, and Problem Behavior at Twenty-Four and Thirty-Six Months." *Child Development* 69: 1145–70.

———. 1999a. "Child Care and Mother–Child Interaction in the First Three Years of Life." *Developmental Psychology* 35: 1399–1413.

———. 1999b. "Child Outcomes When Child Care Center Classes Meet Recommended Standards for Quality." *American Journal of Public Health* 89: 1072–77.

———. 2000a. "Characteristics and Quality of Child Care for Toddlers and Preschoolers." *Applied Developmental Science* 4: 116–135.

———. 2000b. "The Relation of Child Care to Cognitive and Language Development." *Child Development* 71: 960–980.

NICHD Early Child Care Research Network. 2003a. "Does the Amount of Time Spent in Child Care Predict Socioemotional Adjustment During the Transition to Kindergarten?" *Child Development* 74: 976–1005.

———. 2003b. "Does Quality of Child Care Affect Child Outcomes at Age 4?" *Developmental Psychology* 39: 451–469.

Nie, Norman H., D. Sunshine Hillygus, and Lutz Erbring. 2002. "Internet Use, Interpersonal Relations, and Sociability." Pp. 215-243 in *The Internet in Everyday Life*, edited by Barry Wellman and Caroline Haaythornethwaite. Malden MA: Blackwell.

Niebuhr, Gustave. 1998. "Southern Baptists Declare Wife Should 'Submit' to Her Husband." *New York Times.* June 10.

Nippert-Eng, Christena E. 1996. *Home and Work: Negotiating Boundaries Through Everyday Life.* Chicago: University of Chicago Press.

Noble, Lynne Steyer. 1997. "The Face of Foster Care." *Educational Leadership* 54 (7): 26–29.

Nock, Steven L. 1998a. "The Consequences of Premarital Fatherhood." *American Sociological Review* 63: 250–263.

———. 1998b. "Too Much Privacy?" *Journal of Family Issues* 19: 101–18.

———. 1998c. *Marriage In Men's Lives.* New York: Oxford.

———. 2001. "The Marriages of Equally Dependent Spouses." *Journal of Family Issues* 22: 755–775.

———. 2003a. "Marriage and Fatherhood in the Lives of African American Men." Pp. 30–42 in *Black Fathers in Contemporary American Society: Strengths, Weaknesses,and Strategies for Change*, edited by Obie Clayton, Ron Mincy, and David Blankenhorn. New York: Russell Sage.

———. 2003b. "Marriage Movements Today; The Politics of Matrimony—Covenant Marriage." Washington DC: Council on Contemporary Families. www.contemporaryfamilies.org.

Noland, Virginia J., Karen D. Liller, Robert J. McDermott, Martha Coulter, Anne E. Seraphine. 2004. "Is Adolescent Sibling Violence a Precursor to Dating Violence." *American Journal of Health Behavior* 28: Supp. 1: 813–823).

Noller, Patricia, and Mary Anne Fitzpatrick. 1991. "Marital Communication in the Eighties." Pp. 42–53 in *Contemporary Families: Looking Forward, Looking Back*, edited by Alan Booth. Minneapolis: National Council on Family Relations.

Nomaguchi, Kei M., and Melissa A. Milkie. 2003. "Costs and Rewards of Children: The Effects of Becoming A Parent on Adults' Lives." *Journal of Marriage and the Family* 65: 356–374.

Noonan, David. 2001. "Stop Stressing Me." *Newsweek.* Jan. 29: 54–55.

Nordin, Rhonda K. 2000. *After the Baby: Making Sense of Marriage after Childbirth.* Dallas, TX: Taylor Publishers.

"Not in Our House: Oh no?" 2001. *Time.* October 8.

Novak, M. 1997. *Issues in Aging.* New York: Longman.

Nystrom, Nancy M., and Teresa C. Jones. 2003. "Community Building with Aging and Old Lesbians." *American Journal of Community Psychology* 31 (3-4): 293–301.

Obejas, Achy. 1994. "Women Who Batter Women." *Ms.* (Sept./Oct.): 53.

O'Connell, Martin. 2001. "Labor Force Participation for Mothers of Infants Declines for First Time, Census Bureau Reports." Revised press release CB–01–170. Oct. 18. Washington, DC: U.S. Census Bureau.

Oglesby, Christy. 2004. "Survey: Adults Still Skip Condom Use." www.cnn.com. Apr. 6.

O'Hare, William P. 2001a. *The Child Population: First Data from the 2000 Census.* Washington, DC: Annie E. Casey Foundation and Population Reference Bureau.

———. 2001b. "The Rise—and Fall—of Single-Parent Families." *Population Today* 29 (5): 1, 4.

O'Hare, William, and Mark Mather. 2003. *The Growing Number of Kids in Severely Distressed Neighborhoods: Evidence from the 2000 Census.* Washington, DC: Annie E. Casey Foundation and Population Reference Bureau. Sept. http://www.kidscount.org; http://www.ameristat.org.

"Old Ways Bring Tears in a New World." 2003. *New York Times.* Mar. 7.

"Older Americans Month Celebrated in May." 2004. Press release. U.S. Census Bureau. April 20.

"Older Moms' Birth Risks Called Greater." 1999. *Omaha World-Herald.* Jan. 2.

Olmsted, Maureen E., Judith A. Crowell, and Everett Waters. 2003. "Assortive Mating Among Adult Children of Alcoholics and Alcoholics." *Family Relations* 52 (1): 64-71.

Olson, David H. 1994. *Prepare, Enrich: Counselor's Manual.* Minneapolis: Prepare-Enrich.

Olson, Jeremy. 2002. "Couple Knows What's Riding on the Number of Embryos Used." *Omaha World-Herald.* Mar. 3.

Olson, Laura K. 2001. Age Through Ethnic Lenses: Caring for the Elderly in a Multicultural Society. Lanham, MD: Rowman & Littlefield.

Olson, Walter. 1998. "Free To Commit." *Reason Online Magazine.* October. http://www.reasonmag.com/9710/col.olson.html.

O'Malley, Jaclyn. 2002. "Abortion Grief Not Etched in Stone." *Omaha World-Herald.* Oct. 16.

"One Hundred Questions and Answers about Arab Americans." Nd. *Detroit Free Press.* Retrieved on April 1, 2004 from http://www.bintjbeil.com/E/news/100q/family.html

O'Neil, Robin, and Ellen Greenberger. 1994. "Patterns of Commitment to Work and Parenting: Implications for Role Strain." *Journal of Marriage and Family* 56 (1): 101–18.

O'Neill, Nena, and George O'Neill. 1974. *Shifting Gears: Finding Security in a Changing World.* New York: M. Evans.

Ono, Hiromi. 1998. "Husbands' and Wives' Resources and Marital Dissolution." *Journal of Marriage and Family* 60 (3): 674–89.

Ooms, Theodora. 1999. "The Lamentable Status of Marriage and Divorce Statistics." *Around the Coalition.* Apr. 23. www.smartmarriages.com.

———. 2001. "Policy Responses to Couple Conflict and Domestic Violence: A Framework for Discussion." Pp. 227-239 in *Couples in Conflict*, edited by Alan Booth, Ann C. Crouter, and Mari Clements. Mahwah NJ: Erlbaum.

"Opposition to Gay Marriage Grows." 2003. CBSNews.com. December 21. http://www.cbsnews.com

Orbuch, Terri L., and Lindsay Custer. 1995. "The Social Context of Married Women's Work and Its Impact on Black Husbands and White Husbands." *Journal of Marriage and Family* 57 (2): 333–45.

Orbuch, Terri L., and Sandra L. Eyster. 1997. "Division of Household Labor Among Black Couples and White Couples." *Social Forces* 75: 301–32.

Orchard, Ann L., and Kenneth B. Solberg. 2000. "Expectations of the Stepmother's Role." *Journal of Divorce and Remarriage* 31 (1/2): 107–24.

Orenstein, Peggy. 1994. *School Girls: Young Women, Self-Esteem, and the Confidence Gap.* New York: Doubleday.

———. 1998. "Almost Equal." *New York Times Magazine.* Apr. 5: 42–43; 45; 47–48.

Oropesa, R. S. 1996. "Normative Beliefs About Marriage and Cohabitation: A Comparison of Non-Latino Whites, Mexican Americans, and Puerto Ricans." *Journal of Marriage and Family* 58: 49–62.

Oropesa, R. S., and Bridget K. Gorman. 2000. "Ethnicity, Immigration, and Beliefs About Marriage as a 'Tie That Binds.'" Pp. 188–211 in *The Ties That Bind: Perspectives on Marriage and Cohabitation,* edited by Linda J. Waite. New York: Aldine de Gruyter.

Oropesa, R. S., Daniel T. Lichter, and Robert N. Anderson. 1994. "Marriage Markets and the Paradox of Mexican American Nuptiality." *Journal of Marriage and Family* 56 (4): 889–907.

Orthner, Dennis K., Hinckley Jones-Sanpei, and Sabrina Williamson. 2004. "The Resilience and Strengths of Low-Income Families." *Family Relations* 53 (2): 159–167.

Osmond, Marie Withers, and Barrie Thorne. 1993. "Feminist Theories: The Social Construction of Gender in Families and Society." Pp. 591–623 in *Sourcebook of Family Theories and Methods,* edited by Pauline Boss et al. New York: Plenum.

Oswald, Ramona F., and Linda S. Culton. 2003. "Under the Rainbow: rural Gay Life and Its Relevance for Family

Providers." *Family Relations* 52 (1): 72–81.

Owens, Stephen J., and Sara H. Qualls. 1997. "Family Stress at the Time of a Geopsychiatric Hospitalization." *Family Relations* 46 (2): 179–85.

Owo, Yvette. 2004. "African-Americans Still Face Discrimination in Schools." *The Daily Texan.* April 30.

Paden, Shelley L., and Cheryl Buehler. 1995. "Coping with Dual-Income Lifestyle." *Journal of Marriage and Family* 57 (1): 101–10.

Page, Susan. 2003. "Poll Shows Backlash on Gay Issues." *USA Today.* July 28.

Page, Susan, and Richard Benedetto. 2004. "Bush Backs Gay-Marriage Ban." *USA Today.* February 24.

Page, Jessica R., Heather B. Stevens, and Shelley L. Galvin. 1996. "Relationships between Depression, Self-Esteem, and Self-Silencing Behavior." *Journal of Social and Clinical Psychology* 15 (4): 381–390.

Pan, Esther. 1999. "Not Mother Nature's Way." *Newsweek.* Nov. 29.

Papernow, P. 1993. *Becoming a Stepfamily: Patterns of Development in Remarried Families.* San Francisco: Jossey-Bass.

Parcel, Toby L., and Mikaela J. Dufur. 2001. "Capital at Home and at School: Effects on Child School Adjustment." *Journal of Marriage and Family* 63 (1): 32–47.

Park, Kristin. 2002. "Stigma Management among the Voluntarily Childless." *Sociological Perspectives* 45: 21–45.

Parke, Mary. 2003. "Are Married Parents Really Better for Children? What Research Says about the Effects of Family Structure on Child Well-Being. CLASP Policy Brief. Washington DC: Center for Law and Social Policy. Brief No. 3. May.

Parnes, Francine. 2001. "Online Sites Match Religious Singles." *New York Times.* Dec. 22.

Parsons, Talcott. 1943. "The Kinship System of the Contemporary United States." *American Anthropologist* 45: 22–38.

———. 1955. "The American Family: Its Relationship to Personality and Social Structure." Pp. 1–33 in *Family Socialization and Interaction Process,* edited by Talcott Parsons and Robert F. Bales. Glencoe, IL: Free Press.

Parsons, Talcott, and Robert F. Bales. 1955. *Family, Socialization, and Interaction Process.* Glencoe, IL: Free Press.

Partners Task Force for Gay & Lesbian Couples. 1998a. "Legislative Reactions to Legal Marriage." http.//www.buddybuddy.com/t-line-2.html.

———. 1998b. "Restraining Order Availability by State: 1997." http://www.buddybuddy.com.

———. 1999. "Marriage Law Status." Jan. 20. http://www.buddybuddy.com.

———. 2000a. "Reciprocal Beneficiaries: The Hawaiian Approach." http://www.buddybuddy.com.

———. 2000b. "Registration for Domestic Partnership." http://www.buddybuddy.com.

———. 2001. "Civil Unions: The Vermont Approach." http://www.buddybuddy.com.

Paset, Pamela S., and Ronald D. Taylor. 1991. "Black and White Women's Attitudes toward Interracial Marriage." *Psychological Reports* 69: 753–54.

Pasley, Kay. 1998a. "Contemplating Stepchild Adoption." *Research Findings.* Stepfamily Association of America. http://www.saafamilies.org

———. 1998b. "Divorce and Remarriage in Later Adulthood." *Research Findings.* Stepfamily Association of America. http://www.saafamilies.org

———. 2000. "Does Living in a Stepfamily Increase the Risk of Delinquency in Children?" *Research Findings.* Stepfamily Association of America. http://www.saafamilies.org

Pasley, Kay, Ted G. Futris, and Martie L. Skinner. 2002. "Effects of Commitment and Psychological Centrality on Fathering." *Journal of Marriage and Family* 64 (1): 130–138.

Pasley, Kay, and Marilyn Ihinger-Tallman. 1988. "Remarriage and Stepfamilies." Pp. 204–21 in *Variant Family Forms,* edited by Catherine S. Chilman, Elam W. Nunnally, and Fred M. Cox. Newbury Park, CA: Sage.

Pasley, Kay, and Emily Lipe. 1998. "How Does Having a Mutual Child Affect Stepfamily Adjustment?" *Research Findings.* Stepfamily Association of America. http://www.saafamilies.org

Passno, Diane. 2000. "The Feminist Mistake." *Focus on the Family.* September: 12–13.

Patterson, Charlotte. 2000. "Family Relationships of Lesbians and Gay Men." *Journal of Marriage and Family* 62 (4): 1052–69.

Patterson, Joan M. 2002a. "Family Caregiving for Medically Fragile Children." *Family Focus.* December: F5–F7.

———. 2002b. "Integrating Family Resilience and Family Stress Theory." *Journal of Marriage and Family* 64 (2): 349–360.

Pattillo-McCoy, Mary. 1999. *Black Picket Fences: Privilege and Peril among the Black Middle Class.* Chicago: University of Chicago Press.

Paul, Pamela. 2001. "Childless by Choice." *American Demographics.* Nov.: 45–50.

Paulozzi, Leonard J., Linda E. Saltzman, Marlie P. Thompson, and Patricia Holmgreen. 2001. *Surveillance for Homicide Among Intimate Partners—United States, 1981–1998.* Morbidity and Mortality Weekly Report Surveillance Summaries. Oct. 12: 1–16. www.cdc.gov/mmwr/preview/mmwrhtml/ss5003a1.htm.

Paulson, Michael. 2001. "A Vow to Move On: Catholic Church Updates the Annulment Process." *Boston Globe.* Nov. 4.

Pearlin, Leonard I. 1975. "Status Inequality and Stress in Marriage." *American Sociological Review* 40: 344–357.

Pearson, Jessica, Nancy Thoennes, Lanae Davis, Jane C. Venohr, David A. Price, and Tracy Griffith. 2003. *OCSE Responsible Fatherhood Programs: Client Characteristics and Program Outcomes.* Washington DC: U.S. Office of Child Support Enforcement; Denver: Center for Policy Research and Policy Studies Institute..

Peck, M. Scott, 1978. *The Road Less Traveled: A New Psychology of Love, Traditional Values and Spiritual Growth.* New York: Simon & Schuster.

Peck, Peggy. 2001. "Cancer Hard on Marriages." WebMD Medical News Archive. http://my.webmd.com

Pence, E., and M. Paymar. 1993. *Education Groups for Men Who Batter: The Duluth Model.* New York: Springer.

Penning, M. J. 1990. "Receipt of Assistance by Elderly People: Hierarchical Selection and Task Specificity." *The Gerontologist* 30: 220–27.

"People: Gender." 2003. American FactFinder. U.S. Census Bureau. http://factfinder.census.gov

Peplau, Leticia A. 1981. "What Homosexuals Want in Relationships." *Psychology Today* 15: 28–38.

Peplau, Leticia A., and S. D. Cochran. 1990. "A Relationship Perspective on Homosexuality." Pp. 321–47 in *Homo-sexuality/Heterosexuality: Concepts of Sexual Orientation,* edited by David P. McWhirter, Stephanie A. Sanders, and June M. Reinisch. New York: Oxford.

Peplau, Leticia A., Rosemary C. Veniegas, and Susan Miller Campbell. 1996. "Gay and Lesbian Relationships." Pp. 250–73 in *The Lives of Lesbians, Gays, and Bisexuals: Children to Adults,* edited by Ritch C. Savin-Williams and Kenneth M. Cohen. New York: Harcourt.

Peres, Judy. 1997. "Sperm-Donor's Case Challenges Old Laws." *Chicago Tribune.* Aug. 12: 1, 8.

Perez, Lisandro. 2002. "Cuban American Families." Pp. 114-133 in *Minority Families in the United States,* 3rd ed., edited by Ronald L. Taylor. Upper Saddle River NJ: Prentice-Hall.

Perlman, Daniel, and Karen S. Rook. 1987. "Social Support, Social Deficits, and the Family." Pp. 17–44 in *Family Processes and Problems: Social Psychological Aspects. Applied Social Psychology Annual,* vol. 7, edited by Stuart Oskamp. Newbury Park, CA: Sage.

Perrin, Ellen C. 2002. *Sexual Orientation in Child and Adolescent Health Care.* New York, NY: Kluwer Academic/Plenum Publishers.

Perry, Charlotte. 1999. "Extended Family Support Among Older Black Females." Pp. 70–76 in *The Black Family: Essays and Studies,* 6th ed., edited by Robert Staples. Belmont, CA: Wadsworth.

Perry, JoAnn, and Deborah O'Connor. 2002. "Preserving Personhood: (Re)Membering the Spouse with Dementia." *Family Relations* 51 (1): 55–62.

Personal Mvelopes: The simple, smarter budgeting system. http://www.mvelopes.com.>

Personal Responsibility and Work Opportunity Reconciliation Act. 1996. PL 104-193. Washington DC: U.S. Congress.

Pertman, Adam. 2000. *Adoption Nation: How the Adoption Revolution is Transforming America.* New York: Basic.

"Pet Lovers Find Emotional Support from Others Who Share Their Grief." 2002. *Omaha World Herald.* April 14.

Peters, Arnold, and Aart C. Liefbroer. 1997. "Beyond Marital Status: Partner History and Well-Being in Old Age." *Journal of Marriage and Family* 59 (3): 687–99.

Peters, Marie Ferguson, and Harriette P. McAdoo. 1983. "The Present and Future of Alternative Lifestyles in Ethnic American Cultures." Pp. 288–307 in *Contemporary Families and Alternative Lifestyles: Handbook on Research and Theory,* edited by Eleanor D. Macklin and Roger H. Rubin. Newbury Park, CA: Sage.

Petersen, Larry R. 1994. "Education, Homogamy, and Religious Commitment." *Journal for the Scientific Study of Religion* 33 (2): 122–28.

Peterson, James L., and Christine Winquist Nord. 1990. "The Regular Receipt of Child Support: A Multistep Process." *Journal of Marriage and Family* 52 (2): 539–51.

Peterson, Karen S. 2001. "The Good in a Bad Marriage." *USA Today.* June 21.

———. 2002. "'Market Work, Yes; Housework, Hah'" *USA Today.* Mar. 13.

———. 2003a. "Adoption Groups Opening Doors To Gays, Report Says." *USA Today.* Oct. 29.

———. 2003b. "Adoptions Reflect Diversity." *USA Today.* Aug. 25.

Peterson, Richard R. 1989. *Women, Work, and Divorce.* New York: State University of New York Press.

———. 1996. "a Re-evaluation of the Economic Consequences of Divorce." *American Sociological Review.* 61: 528–36.

Peterson, Richard R., and Kathleen Gerson. 1992. "Determinants of Responsibility for Child Care Arrangements Among Dual-Earner Couples." *Journal of Marriage and Family* 54 (3): 527–36.

Pett, Marjorie A., Nancy Lang, and Anita Gander. 1992. "Late-Life Divorce: Its Impact on Family Rituals." *Journal of Family Issues* 13: 526–53.

Peyser, Marc. 1999. "Home of the Gray." *Newsweek*. Mar. 1: 50–53.

Pew Health Professions Commission and the University of California, San Francisco Center for the Health Professions. 1999. *The Future of Midwifery*. San Francisco: The Center for the Health Professions, University of California. April.

Pezzin, Liliana E., and Barbara Steinberg Schone. 1999. "Parental Marital Disruption and Intergenerational Transfers: An Analysis of Lone Elderly Parents and Their Children." *Demography* 36 (3): 287–97.

Phillips, Deborah, and Gina Adams. 2001. "Child Care and Our Youngest Children." *The Future of Children* 11: 35–51.

Phillips, Linda R. 1986. "Theoretical Explanations of Elder Abuse: Competing Hypotheses and Unresolved Issues." Pp. 197–217 in *Elder Abuse: Conflict in the Family*, edited by Karl A. Pillemer and Rosalie S. Wolf. Dover, MA: Auburn.

Phillips, Roderick. 1997. "Stepfamilies from a Historical Perspective." Pp. 5–18 in *Stepfamilies: History, Research, and Policy*, edited by Irene Levin and Marvin B. Sussman. New York: Haworth.

Pietropinto, Anthony, and Jacqueline Simenauer. 1977. *Beyond the Male Myth: What Women Want to Know About Men's Sexuality, A National Survey*. New York: Times Books.

Pillemer, Karl A. 1986. "Risk Factors in Elder Abuse: Results from a Case-Control Study." Pp. 239–64 in *Elder Abuse: Conflict in the Family*, edited by Karl A. Pillemer and Rosalie S. Wolf. Dover, MA: Auburn.

Pillemer, Karl, and J. Jill Suitor. 2002. "Explaining Mothers' Ambivalence Toward Their Adult Children." *Journal of Marriage and Family* 64 (3): 602–613.

Pines, Maya. 1981. "Only Isn't Lonely (or Spoiled or Selfish)." *Psychology Today* 15: 15–19.

Pink Weddings. 2004. retrieved 3/29/04 from http://www.pinkweddings.biz

Pirog-Good, Maureen A., and Lydia Amerson. 1997. "The Long Arm of Justice: The Potential for Seizing the Assets of Child Support Obligors." *Family Relations* 46 (1): 47–54.

Pittman, Joe F., Jennifer L. Kerpelman, and Jennifer M. Mc Fadyen. 2004. "Internal and External Adaptation in Army Families: Lessons from Operations Desert Shield and Desert Storm." *Family Relations* 53 (3): 249–260.

Pitzer, Ronald L. 1997a. "Change, Crisis, and Loss in Our Lives." University of Minnesota Extension Service. http://www.extension.umn.edu.

———. 1997b. "Perception: A Key Variable in Family Stress Management." University of Minnesota Extension Service. http://www.extension.umn.edu.

Planned Parenthood Federation of America. 2002. "Fact Sheet: Nonoxynol-9." New York: Planned Parenthood Federation. www.plannedparenthood.org.

———. 2004a. "Birth Control: Your Contraceptive Choices." New York: Planned Parenthood Federation. www.plannedparenthood.org.

———. 2004b. "Facts about Birth Control: Comparison of Effectiveness." New York: Planned Parenthood Federation. www.plannedparenthood.org.

———. 2004c. "Facts about Birth Control: Reversible Prescription Methods—Progestin Only Implant." New York: Planned Parenthood Federation. www.plannedparenthood.org.

"Playing Catch-up with Career." 2004. *Omaha World-Herald (Wall Street Journal)*. May 10.

Pleck, Elizabeth H. 2000. *Celebrating the Family: Ethnicity, Consumer Culture, and Family Rituals*. Cambridge MA: Harvard.

Pleck, Joseph H. 1977. "The Work–Family Role System." *Social Problems* 24: 417–27.

———. 1992. "Prisoners of Manliness." Pp. 98–107 in *Men's Lives*, 2nd ed, edited by Michael S. Kimmel and Michael A. Messner. New York: Macmillan.

Poe, Marshall. 2004. "The Other Gender Gap." *Atlantic Monthly*. Feb.: 137.

Pollack, Andrew. 2004. "More Data Sought on Drug for Sex Drive." *New York Times*. Dec. 3.

Pollack, William. 1998. Real Boys: Rescuing Our Sons from the Myths of Boyhood. New York: Random House.

Pollak, Michael. 2000. "Searching the Web as a Matter of Life and Death." *New York Times*. June 1.

Pollard, Kelvin M., and William P. O'Hare. 1999. *America's Racial and Ethnic Minorities*. Population Bulletin 54 (3). Washington, DC: Population Reference Bureau.

Pollitt, Katha. 2002. "Backlash Babies." *The Nation*. May 13: 10.

Pomerleau, A., D. Bolduc, G. Malcuit, and L. Cossetts. 1990. "Pink or Blue: Environmental Stereotypes in the First Two Years of Life." *Sex Roles* 22: 359–67.

Poniewozik, James. 2002. "The Cost of Starting Families." *Time*. Apr. 15: 56–58.

Popenoe, David. 1994. "The Evolution of Marriage and the Problem of Stepfamilies: A Biosocial Perspective." Pp. 3–28 in *Stepfamilies: Who Benefits? Who Does Not?*, edited by Alan Booth and Judy Dunn. Hillsdale, NJ: Erlbaum.

———. 1996. *Life Without Father: Compelling New Evidence That Fatherhood and Marriage Are Indispensable for the Good of Children and Society*. New York: Martin Kessler.

———. 1998. "The Decline of Marriage and Fatherhood." Pp. 312–19 in *Seeing Ourselves: Classic, Contemporary, and Cross-Cultural Readings in Sociology*, 4th edition, edited by John J. Macionis and Nijole V. Benokraitis. Upper Saddle River, NJ: Prentice Hall.

Popenoe, David, and Barbara Dafoe Whitehead. 2000. *The State of Our Unions 2000: The Social Health of Marriage in America*. New Brunswick, NJ: Rutgers University, National Marriage Project.

Population Information Program. Center for Communication Programs. Johns Hopkins School of Public Health. 2005. "Do You Know Your Population Choices?" Wall chart. Baltimore: Johns Hopkins University.

Population Reference Bureau. 2001. *2001 World Population Data Sheet*.

Washington, DC: Population Reference Bureau.

———. 2002. *Kids Count International Data Sheet.* Washington DC: Population Reference Bureau.

———. 2003. *World Population Data Sheet.* Washington DC: Population Reference Bureau.

Porter, Sylvia. 1976. *Sylvia Porter's Money Book.* New York: Avon.

Porterfield, Ernest. 1982. "Black-American Intermarriages in the United States." Pp. 17–34 in *Intermarriages in the United States,* edited by Gary Crester and Joseph J. Leon. New York: Haworth.

Porterfield, Shirley L. 2002. "Work Choices of Mothers in Families with Children with Disabilities." *Journal of Marriage and Family* 64 (4): 972–981.

Potoczniak, Michael J., Jon Etienne Mourot, Margaret Crosbie-Burnett, and Daniel A. Potoczniak. 2003. "Legal and Psychological Perspectives on Same-Sex Domestic Violence: A Multisystemic Approach." *Journal of Family Psychology* 17: 252-259.

Potuchek, Jean L. 1997. *Who Supports the Family? Gender and Breadwinning in Dual-Earner Marriages.* Stanford, CA: Stanford University Press.

Powell, Brian, and Douglas Downey. 1997. "Living in Single-Parent Households: An Investigation of the Same-Sex Hypothesis." *American Sociological Review* 62: 521–39.

Powell, John. 1969. *Why Am I Afraid to Tell You Who I Am?* Niles, IL: Argus Communications.

Power, Kathryn. 2004. "Resilience and Recovery in Family Mental Health Care." *Family Focus.* March: F1–F2.

Power, Paul W. 1979. "The Chronically Ill Husband and Father: His Role in the Family." *Family Coordinator* 28: 616–21.

Powers, Mike. 1997. "The Hidden Costs of Divorce." *Human Ecology Forum* 25 (1): 4–15.

Pozzetta, George E. (Ed.). 1991. *Immigrant Family Patterns: Demography, Fertility, Housing, Kinship, and Urban Life.* New York: Garland.

Presser, Harriet B. 2000. "Nonstandard Work Schedules and Marital Instability." *Journal of Marriage and Family* 62: 93–110.

Preston, Anne E. 2003 [2000]. "Sex, Kids, and Commitment to the Workplace: Employers, Employees, and the Mommy Track." Unpublished Paper. Haverford College. Haverford PA.

Preves, Sharon E. 2002. "Sexing the Intersexed: An Analysis of Sociocultural Responses To Intersexuality." *Signs* 27: 523–556.

———. 2003. *Intersex and Identity: The Contested Self.* New Brunswick NJ: Rutgers.

Previti, Denise, and Paul R. Amato. 2003. "Why Stay Married? Rewards, Barriers, and Marital Stability." *Journal of Marriage and the Family* 65: 561–573.

Price, Deb. 2000. "It's Time To Treat Gay Elders with Respect." Partners Task Force for Gay and Lesbian Couples. <www.buddybuddy.com/price-2.html>

Prinstein, Mitchell J., Christina S. Meade, and Geoffrey L. Cohen. 2003. "Adolescent Oral Sex, Peer Popularity, and Perception of Best Friends' Sexual Behavior." *Journal of Pediatric Psychiatry* 28: 243–249.

"Prison Day Camp Extends Family Ties Behind Bars." 2001. *Omaha World-Herald.* Aug. 6.

Proctor, Bernadette D., and Joseph Dalaker. 2003. "Poverty in the United States: 2002." *Current Population Reports* P60-222. Washington DC: United States Census Bureau.

Pruchno, R. A., C. J. Burant, and N. D. Peters. 1997. "Typologies of Caregiving Families: Family Congruence and Individual Well Being." *The Gerontologist* 37: 157–67.

Prue, Lisa. 2003. "Forging Harmony When Cultures Clash."

Public Interest. 1994. "Unnecessary Cesarean Sections: Curing A National Epidemic." www.citizen.org/publications/release.cfm?ID=6930.

Purdum, Todd S. 1996. "Heat on Clinton for Gay Marriage Ruling." *San Francisco Examiner.* Sept. 22: A–2.

Purdy, Matthew. 1995. "A Sexual Revolution for the Elderly: At Nursing Homes, Intimacy Is Becoming a Matter of Policy." *New York Times.* Nov. 6.

Purkayastha, Bandana. 2002. "Rules, Roles, and Realities: Indo-American Families in The United States." Pp. 212–226 in *Minority Families in the United States,* 3rd ed., edited by Ronald L. Taylor. Upper Saddle River NJ: Prentice-Hall.

Purnine, Daniel M., and Michael P. Carey. 1998. "Age and Gender Differences in Sexual Behavior Preferences: A Follow-Up Report." *Journal of Sex & Marital Therapy* 24: 93–102.

Pyke, Karen D. 1996. "Class-Based Masculinities: The Interdependence of Gender, Class, and Interpersonal Power." *Gender and Society* 10: 527–49.

———. 1999. "The Micropolitics of Care in Relationships Between Aging Parents and Adult Children: Individualism, Collectivism, and Power." *Journal of Marriage and Family* 61 (3): 661–72.

———. 2003. "The 'Normal American Family' as An Interpretive Structure of Family Life among Grown Children of Korean and Vietnamese Immigrants." Pp. 436-457 in *Family in Transition,* 12th ed., edited by Arlene S. and Jerome H. Skolnick. Boston: Allyn and Bacon.

Pyke, Karen D., and Vern L. Bengston. 1996. "Caring More or Less: Individualistic and Collectivist Systems of Family Eldercare." *Journal of Marriage and Family* 58 (2): 379–92.

Qian, Zhenchao. 1997. "Breaking the Racial Barriers: Variations in Interracial Marriage Between 1980 and 1990." *Demography* 34 (2): 263–76.

———. 1998. "Changes in Assortive Mating: The Impact of Age and Education, 1970–1980." *Demography* 35 (3): 279–92.

Quindlen, Anna. 2001. "Our Tired, Our Poor, Our Kids." *Newsweek.* Mar. 12: 80.

"Race and Ethnicity in 2001." 2001. Washington DC: Washington Post/Kaiser Family Foundation/Harvard.

Raley, R. Kelly. 1995. "Black–White Differences in Kin Contact and Exchange Among Never Married Adults." *Journal of Family Issues* 16 (1): 77–103.

———. 1996. "A Shortage of Marriageable Men? A Note on the Role of Cohabitation in Black–White Differences in Marriage Rates." *American Sociological Review* 61: 973–83.

———. 2001. "Increasing Fertility in Cohabiting Unions: Evidence for the

Second Demographic Transition in the United States?" *Demography* 38 (1): 59–66.

Raley, R. Kelly, and Jennifer Bratter. 2004 "Not Even if You Were the Last Person on Earth! How Marital Search Constraints Affect the Likelihood of Marriage." *Journal of Family Issues* 25 (2): 167–181.

Raley, R. Kelly, and Elizabeth Wildsmith. 2004. "Cohabitation and Children's Family Instability." *Journal of Marriage and the Family* 66 (1): 210-219.

Ramirez, Robert R., and G. Patricia de la Cruz. 2003. "The Hispanic Population of the United States: March 2002. *Current Population Reports* P-20-545. Washington DC: U.S. Census Bureau. June.

Rane, Thomas R., and Brent A. McBride. 2000. "Identity Theory as a Guide to Understanding Fathers' Involvement with Their Children." *Journal of Family Issues* 21 (3): 347–66.

Raney, Rebecca Fairley. 2000. "Study Finds Internet of Social Benefit to Users." *New York Times.* May 11.

Raschick, Michael, and Berit Ingersoll-Dayton. 2004. "Costs and Rewards of Caregiving Among Aging Spouses and Adult Children." *Family Relations* 53 (3): 317–325.

Rauch, Jonathan. 2002. "The Marrying Kind: Why Social Conservatives Should Support Same-Sex Marriage." *Atlantic Monthly* 289 (5): 24–25.

Raven, Bertram, Richard Centers, and Arnoldo Rodrigues. 1975. "The Bases of Conjugal Power." Pp. 217–32 in *Power in Families*, edited by Ronald E. Cromwell and David H. Olson. Beverly Hills, CA: Sage.

Ravo, Nick. 1993. "With a New Kind of Housing, Togetherness Is Built Right In." *New York Times.* Feb. 25.

Raymond, Joan. 2002. "Gray Market for Gadgets." *Newsweek.* Sept. 23. P. 52.

Real, Terrence. 1997. *I Don't Want to Talk about It: Overcoming the Secret Legacy of Male Depression.* New York: Scribner.
———. 2002. *How Can I Get Through to You? Reconnecting Men and Women.* New York: Scribner.

Rector, Robert E., and Melissa G. Pardue. 2004. *Understanding the President's Healthy marriage Initiative.*

Heritage Foundation. http://www.heritage.org/Research/Family/bg1741.cfm

Reeves, Terrance, And Claudette Bennett. 2003. "The Asian and Pacific Islander Population in the United States: March 2002." *Current Population Reports* P-20-540. U.S. Census Bureau. May.

Regan, Pamela C., and Carla S. Dreyer. 1999. "Lust? Love? Status? Young Adults' Motives for Engaging In Casual Sex." *Journal of Psychology and Human Sexuality* 11: 1–24.
———. 2003. *The Mating Game: A Primer on Love, Sex, and Marriage.* Newbury Park, CA: Sage.

"Regional Variations in the Traditional American Household." 2001. www.prb.org.

Reichert, Dana. 1999. *Broke but Not Deadbeat: Reconnecting Low-Income Fathers and Children.* Washington, DC: National Conference of State Legislatures.

Reimann, Renate. 1997. "Does Biology Matter?: Lesbian Couples' Transition to Parenthood and Their Division of Labor." *Qualitative Sociology* 20 (2): 153–85.

Reiss, David, Sandra Gonzalez, and Norman Kramer. 1986. "Family Process, Chronic Illness, and Death: On the Weakness of Strong Bonds." *Archives of General Psychiatry* 43: 795–804.

Reiss, Ira L. 1976. *Family Systems in America*, 2d ed. Hinsdale, IL: Dryden.
———. 1986. *Journey into Sexuality: An Exploratory Voyage.* Englewood Cliffs, NJ: Prentice-Hall.

Reiss, Ira L., and G. L. Lee. 1988. *The Family System in America*, 4th ed. New York: Holt, Reinhart & Winston.

"Religious Leaders Descend on California's Capitol in Support of Equality California's Same-sex Marriage Legislation." 2004. Equality California Press Release. April 19. http://www.eqca.org

Remez, L. 2000. "As Many Lesbians Have Had Sex with Men, Taking a Full Sexual History Is Important." *Family Planning Perspectives* 32: 97–98.

Rendall, Michael S. 1999. "Entry or Exit? A Transition–Probability Approach to Explaining the High Prevalence of Single Motherhood Among

Black Women." *Demography* 36 (3): 369–76.

Rennison, Callie Marie. 2003. *Intimate Partner Violence 1993-2001.* BJS Crime Data Brief. Washington DC: U.S. Bureau of Justice Statistics.

Rennison, Callie Marie, and Sarah Welchans. 2000. *Intimate Partner Violence.* Bureau of Justice Statistics Special Report. NCJ 178247. May. Washington, DC: U.S. Department of Justice.
———. 2002. *Intimate Partner Violence.* BJS Special Report. Washington DC: U.S. Bureau of Justice Statistics.

Renteln, Alison Dundes. 2004. *The Cultural Defense.* New York: Oxford.

Renzetti, Claire M. 1992. *Violent Betrayal: Partner Abuse in Lesbian Relationships.* Newbury Park, CA: Sage.
———. 2001. "Toward a Better Understanding of Lesbian Battering." Pp. 454–66 in *Shifting the Center*, 2nd ed., edited by Susan J. Ferguson. Mountain View, CA: Mayfield.

Reschke, Kathy L. 2003. "Difficult Choices: Low-Income Mothers Struggle to Balance Caregiving and Employment." *Family Focus.* June: F8–F10.

Reynolds v. *United States.* 1878. 98 U.S. 145, 25 L.Ed. 244.

Reynolds, Meredith, L. Schieve, G. Jeng., and H.B. Peterson. 2003. "Does Insurance Coverage Decrease the Risk for Multiple Births Associated with Assisted Reproductive Technology?" *Fertility and Sterility* 80: 1–15.

Rice, Tom W., and Diane L. Coates. 1995. "Gender Role Attitudes in the Southern United States." *Gender and Society* 9: 744–756.

Rich, Jason. 2004. *Make Your Paycheck Last: How to Create a Budget You Can Live With.* Franklin Lakes, NJ: The Career Press.

Riche, Martha Farnsworth. 2000. *America's Diversity and Growth: Signposts for the 21st Century.* Population Bulletin 55 (2). Washington, DC: Population Reference Bureau.

Ridley, Carl, Dan J. Peterman, and Arthur W. Avery. 1978. "Cohabitation: Does It Make for a Better Marriage?" *Family Coordinator* 27: 129–36.

Riekse, R. J., and H. Holstege. 1996. *Growing Older in America.* New York: McGraw-Hill.

Riggs, D. S. 1993. "Relationship Problems and Dating Aggression: A Potential Treatment Target." *Journal of Interpersonal Violence* 8: 18–35.

Riley, Glenda. 1991. *Divorce: An American Tradition*. New York: Oxford University Press.

Riley, Matilda W. 1983. "The Family in an Aging Society: A Matrix of Latent Relationships." *Journal of Marriage and Family Issues* 4: 439–54.

Rimer, Sara. 1988a. "Child Care at Home: 2-Women, Complex Roles." *New York Times*. Dec. 26.

———. 1988b. "Women, Jobs and Children: A New Generation Worries." *New York Times*. Nov. 27.

———. 2003. "Love on Campus." *New York Times*. Oct. 1.

Rindfleisch, Nolan. 1999. "Foster Parents More Likely to Continue Role with Encouragement and Support from Social Workers." *Brown University Child and Adolescent Behavior Letter* 15 (9): 2.

Riordan, Teresa. 1999. "Viagra's Success Has Brought to Light A Second Big Market for Sexual Dysfunction Therapies: Women." *New York Times*. April 26.

Risman, Barbara J. 1998. *Gender Vertigo: American Families in Transition*. New Haven, CT: Yale University Press.

———. 2001. "Calling the Bluff of Value-Free Science." *American Sociological Review* 66: 605–11.

Risman, Barbara J., and Danette Johnson-Sumerford. 1998. "Doing It Fairly: A Study of Postgender Marriages." *Journal of Marriage and Family* 60 (1): 23–40.

Risman, Barbara, and Pepper Schwartz. 2002. "After the Sexual Revolution: Gender Politics in Teen Dating." *Contexts* (Spring): 16–23.

Ritter, Raymond A. Sr., M.D. 1990. *A Healing Life: Memoirs of a Missouri Doctor*. Cape Girardeau MO: Concord Publishing House.

Robbins, Jim. 2001. "Where Adoption Is An Open Book." *New York Times*. May 17.

Roberts, Linda J. 2000. "Fire and Ice in Marital Communication: Hostile and Distancing Behaviors as Predictors of Marital Distress." *Journal of Marriage and Family* 62 (3): 693–707.

Roberts, Nicole A., and Robert W. Levenson. 2001. "The Remains of the Workday: Impact of job Stress and Exhaustion on Marital Interaction in Police Couples." *Journal of Marriage and Family* 63 (4): 1052–1067.

Robinson, B.E., and R.L. Barret. 1986. *The Developing Father: Emerging Roles in Contemporary Society*. New York: Guilford.

Rockquemore, Kerry Ann, and David L. Brunsma. 2001. *Beyond Black: Biracial Identity in American*. Thousand Oaks CA: Sage.

Rodgers, Joseph Lee, Paul A. Nakonezny, and Robert D. Shull. 1997. "The Effect of No-Fault Divorce Legislation on Divorce Rates: A Response to a Reconsideration." *Journal of Marriage and Family* 59: 1020–30.

Rodgers, Roy H., and Linda M. Conrad. 1986. "Courtship for Remarriage: Influences on Family Reorganization After Divorce." *Journal of Marriage and Family* 48: 767–75.

Rodgers, Roy H., and James M. White. 1993. "Family Development Theory." Pp. 225–54 in *Sourcebook of Family Theories and Methods: A Contextual Approach*, edited by Pauline G. Boss, William J. Doherty, Ralph LaRossa, Walter R. Schumm, and Suzanne K. Steinmetz. New York: Plenum.

Rodier, Danielle N. 2000. "Court: 'De Facto' Parent May Not Adopt Same-Sex Partner's Child." *Legal Intelligencer*. Nov. 9.

Rodman, Hyman. 1971. *Lower Class Families: The Culture of Poverty in Rural Trinidad*. New York: Oxford.

———. 1972. "Marital Power and the Theory of Resources in Cultural Context." *Journal of Comparative Family Studies* 3: 50–69.

Rodriguez, Christina M., and Andrea J. Green. 1997. "Parenting Stress and Anger Expression As Predictors of Child Abuse Potential." *Child Abuse & Neglect* 21 (4): 367–77.

Rogers, Fred. 1997. *Stepfamilies*. New York: Putnam.

Rogers, Lesley. 2001. *Sexing the Brain*. New York: Columbia University Press.

Rogers, Michelle L., and Dennis P. Hogan. 2003. "Family Life with Children with Disabilities: The Key Role

of Rehabilitation." *Journal of Marriage and Family* 65 (4): 818-833.

Rogers, Stacy J. 1999. "Wives' Income and Marital Quality: Are There Reciprocal Effects?" *Journal of Marriage and Family* 61: 123–32.

Rogers, Stacy J., and Paul R. Amato. 2000. "Have Changes in Gender Relations Affected Marital Quality." *Social Forces* 79: 731–753.

Romano, Lois, and Jacqueline Trescott. 1992. "Love in Black & White." *Redbook*. February: 88–94.

Romero, Mary. 1992. *Maid in the U.S.A.* New York: Routledge.

Romney, Lee. 2004. "In S.F., a Test Case for Gays." *Los Angeles Times*. February 11.

Ronfeldt, Heidi M., Rachel Kimerling, and Ilena Arias. 1998. "Satisfaction with Relationship Power and the Perpetuation of Dating Violence." *Journal of Marriage and Family* 60: 70–78.

Roos, Patricia A., and Catherine W. Jones. 1993. "Shifting Gender Boundaries. Women's Inroads into Academic Sociology." *Work and Occupations* 20: 395–428.

Roschelle, A.R. 1997. *No More Kin: Exploring Race, Class, and Gender in Family Networks*. Thousand Oaks, CA: Sage.

Rose, Stephen J., and Heidi I. Hartmann. 2004. *Still A Man's Labor Market: The Long- Term Earnings Gap*. Washington D C: Institute for Women's Policy Research.

Roseamilia, Carrie, and Marieke Van Willigen. 2002. "To Spank or Not to Spank: Explaining Regional Differences in Parenting Styles." Paper presented at the annual Meeting of the American Sociological Society. Chicago. August.

Rosenberg, Debra. 2001. "A Place of Their Own." *Newsweek*. Jan. 15: 54–55.

———. 2004. "Generation Ambivalent." *Newsweek*. Apr. 26. P. 29.

Rosenblatt, Paul C., and Linda Hammer Burns. 1986. "Long-Term Effects of Perinatal Loss." *Journal of Family Issues* 7: 237–54.

Rosenbluth, Susan C. 1997. "Is Sexual Orientation a Matter of Choice?" *Psychology of Women Quarterly* 21: 595–610.

Rosenbluth, Susan C., Janice M. Steil, and Juliet H. Whitcomb. 1998. "Marital Equality: What Does It Mean?" *Journal of Family Issues* 19 (3): 227–44.

Rosenfeld, Alvin, and Nicole Wise. 2001. *The Over-Scheduled Child: Avoiding the Hyper-Parenting Trap.* NY: St. Martin's Griffin Press.

Rosenfeld, Jeffrey P. 1997. "Will Contests: Legacies of Aging and Social Change." Pp. 173–91 in *Inheritance and Wealth in America*, edited by Robert K. Miller, Jr., and Stephen J. McNamee. New York: Plenum.

Rosenmayr, L. 1977. "The Family—A Source of Hope for the Elderly." Pp. 72–86 in *Family, Bureaucracy and the Elderly*, edited by E. Shanas and M. Sussman. Durham, NC: Duke University Press.

Rosenthal, Elisabeth. 1991. "As More Tiny Infants Live, Choices and Burdens Grow." *New York Times.* Sept. 29.

Rosenthal, Kristine, and Harry F. Keshet. 1980. *Fathers Without Partners.* New York: Rowman & Littlefield.

Rosenthal, M. Sara. 2003. *The Gynecological Sourcebook*, 4th ed. New York: McGraw-Hill.

Roskoff, Allen. 2004. "New York and Gay Marriage." *Gotham Gazette.* March 8. http://www.gothamgazette.com

Ross, Catherine E. 1987. "The Division of Labor at Home." *Social Forces* 65 (3): 816–33.

———. 1995. "Reconceptualizing Marital Status as a Continuum of Social Attachment." *Journal of Marriage and Family* 57 (1): 129–40.

Ross, Catherine E., John Mirowsky, and Patricia Ulrich. 1983. "Distress and the Traditional Female Role." *American Journal of Sociology* 89: 670–82.

Rossi, Alice S. 1973. *The Feminist Papers.* New York: Bantam.

Rotenberg, Ken J., George B. Schaut, and Brian O'Connor. 1993. "The Roles of Identity Development and Psychosocial Intimacy in Marital Success." *Journal of Social and Clinical Psychology* 12 (2): 198–213.

Rothman, Barbara Katz. 1982. *In Labor: Women and Power in the Birthplace.* New York: Norton.

———. 1989. *Recreating Motherhood: Ideology and Technology in a Patriarchal Society.* New York: Norton.

———. 1999. "Comment on Harrison: The Commodification of Motherhood." Pp. 435–38 in *American Families: A Multicultural Reader*, edited by Stephanie Coontz. New York: Routledge.

Rothman, Ellen K. 1984. *Hands and Hearts: A History of Courtship in America.* New York: Basic.

Roxburgh, Susan. 1997. "The Effect of Children on the Mental Health of Women in the Paid Labor Force." *Journal of Family Issues* 18 (3): 270–89.

Roy, Kevin M., Carolyn Y. Tubbs, and Linda M. Burton. 2004. "Don't Have No Time: Daily Rhythms and the Organization of Time for Low-Income Families." *Family Relations* 53 (2): 168-178.

Rubin, Lillian. 2004. "Is This A White Country or What?" Pp. 410–418 in *Race, Class, And Gender*, 5th ed., edited by Margaret L. Andersen and Patricia Hill Collins. Belmont CA: Wadsworth.

———. 1976. *Worlds of Pain: Life in the Working-Class Family.* New York: Basic.

———. 1997. *The Transcendent Child: Tales of Triumph Over the Past.* New York: HarperPerrenial.

———. 1999. "Excerpts from *Families on the Fault Line: America's Working Class Speaks About the Family, the Economy, Race, and Ethnicity.*" Pp. 273–86 in *American Families: A Multicultural Reader*, edited by Stephanie Coontz. New York: Routledge.

Rubin, Rita. 2001. "Circumcision Rate Increases in Midwest, Drops in West." *USA Today.* August 21.

———. 2003. "A Wrinkle on Motherhood." *USA Today.* Jan. 22.

———. 2004. "Birthing Study Reexamines Risks." *USA Today.* Dec. 15.

Rubin, Roger H. 2001. "Alternative Lifestyles Revisited, or Whatever Happened to Swingers, Group Marriages, and Communes?" *Journal of Family Issues* 22 (6): 711–26.

Rubiner, Betsy. 1994. "The Hidden Damage." *Des Moines Register.* Oct. 9: 2E.

Rubinstein, Robert L., Baine B. Alexander, Marcene Goodman, and Mark Luborsky. 1991. "Key Relationships of Never Married, Childless Older Women: A Cultural Analysis." *Journal of Gerontology* 46 (5): 270–81.

Ruefli, Terry, Olivia Yu, and Judy Barton. 1992. "Brief Report: Sexual Risk Taking in Smaller Cities." *Journal of Sex Research* 29 (1): 95–108.

Rugel, Robert P., and Zoran Martinovich. 1997. "Dealing with the Problem of Low Self-Esteem: Common Characteristics and Treatment in Individual, Marital/Family and Group Psychotherapy." *Contemporary Psychotherapy* 42 (1): 69–76.

Ruggles, Steven. 1994. "The Origins of African-American Family Structure." *American Sociological Review* 59: 136–51.

Rumbaut, Rubén G. 1999a. "Children of Immigrants: Noteworthy Achievement and Resilient Ambition." *NCFR Report* (June): 10–12.

———. 1999b. "'Immigrant Stock' Numbers One Fifth of U.S. Population." *NCFR Report* (June): 8–9.

Russell, Diana E. H. 1990. *Rape in Marriage*, 2nd ed. New York: Macmillan.

Russo, Francine. 1997. "Can the Government Prevent Divorce?" *Atlantic Monthly.* October. http.//www.theatlantic.com/issues/97oct/divorce.html.

Russo, Nancy Felipe. 1985. "Editorial: Forging New Directions in Gender Role Measurement." *Psychology of Women Quarterly* 21 (1): i–ii.

Russo, Nancy Felipe, and Amy J. Dabul. 1997. "The Relationship of Abortion to Well-Being: Do Race and Religion Make a Difference?" *Professional Psychology: Research and Practice* 28: 23–31.

Russo, Nancy Felipe, and Kristin L. Zierk. 1992. "Abortion, Childbearing, and Women's Well-Being." *Professional Psychology: Research and Practice* 23: 269–280.

Ryan, Jim, and Anne Ryan. 1995. "Dating in the Nineties: Courtship Makes a Comeback." *Focus on the Family.* November: 11–12.

Ryan, Sarah. 1999. "Management by Stress: The Reorganization of Work Hits Home in the 1990s." Pp. 332–41 in *American Families: A Multicultural Reader*, edited by Stephanie Coontz. New York: Routledge.

Ryan, Suzanne, Jennifer Manlove, and Kerry Franzetta. 2003. *The First Time: Characteristics of Teens' First Sexual Relationships.* Washington DC: ChildTrends. August. www.childtrends.org.

Saad, Lydia. 1995. "Children, Hard Work Taking Their Toll on Baby Boomers." *The Gallup Poll Monthly.* April: 21–24.

———. 2001a. "Majority Consider Sex Before Marriage Morally Okay." Gallup Poll News Service. May 24. www.gallup.com/poll.

———. 2001b. "Women See Room for Improvement in Job Equity." Gallup News Service. June 29. www.gallup.com/poll/releases/pr010629.asp

———. 2002. "Public Opinion about Abortion: An In-Depth Review." Gallup News Service. Jan. 22. www.gallup.com/poll.

———. 2003. "Roe v. Wade Has Positive Public Image." Gallup News Service. Jan. 20. www.gallup.com/poll

———. 2004. "No Time for R & R." *Gallup Poll Tuesday Briefing.* May 11. www.gallup.com

Sabatelli, Ronald M., and Constance L. Shehan. 1993. "Exchange and Resources Theories." Pp. 385–411 in *Sourcebook of Family Theories and Methods,* edited by Pauline Boss et al. New York: Plenum.

Sacco, William P., and Vicky Phares. 2001. "Partner Appraisal and Marital Satisfaction: The Role of Self-Esteem and Depression." *Journal of Marriage and Family* 63 (2): 504–513.

Sachs, Andrea. 1990. "When the Lullaby Ends." *Time.* June 4: 82.

Sachs, Andrea, Dorian Solot, and Marshall Miller. 2003. "Happily Unmarried." *Time.* March 3.

Sachs, Susan. 2001. "Indians Abroad Get Pitch on Gender Choice." *New York Times.* Aug. 15.

Sadker, M., and D. Sadker. 1994. *Failing at Fairness: How America's Schools Cheat Girls.* New York: Scribner's. *Perspectives on Sexual and Reproductive Health* 36: 98–105.

Safilios-Rothschild, Constantina. 1967. "A Comparison of Power Structure and Marital Satisfaction in Urban Greek and French Families." *Journal of Marriage and Family* 29: 345–52.

———. 1970. "The Study of Family Power Structure: A Review 1960–1969." *Journal of Marriage and Family* 32: 539–43.

———. 1983. "Toward a Social Psychology of Relationships." Pp. 306–12 in *Family in Transition: Rethinking Marriage, Sexuality, Child Rearing, and Family Organization,* 4th ed., edited by Arlene S. Skolnick and Jerome H. Skolnick. Boston: Little, Brown.

Sage, Alexandria. 2004. "Papers Filed to Fight Ban on Polygamy." Associated Press. January 13.

Salholz, Eloise. 1993. "For Better or For Worse." *Newsweek.* May 24: 69.

Salt, Robert. 1991. "Child Support in Context: Comments on Rettig, Christensen, and Dahl." *Family Relations* 40 (2): 175–78.

Saluter, Arlene F., and Terry A. Lugaila. 1998. *Marital Status and Living Arrangements: March 1996.* U.S. Bureau of the Census, Current Population Reports, Series P20–496. Washington, DC: U.S. Government Printing Office.

"Same-Sex Marriage." 2004. National Conference of State Legislatures. February 27. Retrieved 3/5/04 from http://www.ncsl.org/programs/cyf/samesex.htm

Samuelson, Robert J. 1997. "The Two-Earner Myth." *Washington Post.* Jan. 22.

Sanchez, Laura, Steven L. Nock, James D. Wright, and Constance T. Gager. 2002. "Setting the Clock Forward or Back? Covenant Marriage and the 'Divorce Revolution.'" *Journal of Family Issues* 23: 91–120.

Sanchez, Rene. 2002. "A City Combats AIDS Complacency." *Washington Post.* May 12.

Sander, Peter J. 2003. *The Everything Personal Finance Book: Manage, Budget, Save, and Invest Your Money Wisely.* Avon, MA: Adams Media Corp.

Sanders, Cheryl. 1992. "Gender and Racial Perspectives: The Black Community." Paper presented at the Surrogate Motherhood and Reproductive Technologies Symposium, Creighton University, Jan. 13.

Sanders, Joshunda. 2004. "Breaking Free from the Tired Old Dating Game: Quirky Singles Forge New Attitudes on Relationships." *San Francisco Chronicle.* February 8.

Santelli, John, Roger Rochat, Kendra Hatfield-Timajchy, Brenda Colley Gilbert, Kathryn Curtis, Rebecca Cabral, Jennifer S. Hirsch, Laura Shieve, and Other Members of the Unintended Pregnancy Working Group. 2003. "The Measurement and Meaning of Unintentional Pregnancy." *Perspectives on Social and Reproductive Health* 35: 94–101.

Santelli, John S., Laura Duberstein Lindberg, Joyce Abma, Clea Sucoff McNeely, and Michael Resnick. 2000. "Adolescent Sexual Behavior: Estimates and Trends from Four Nationally Representative Surveys." *Family Planning Perspectives* 32: 156–65, 194.

Sarkisian, Natalia, and Naomi Gerstel. 2004. "Explaining the Gender Gap in Help to Parents: The Importance of Employment." *Journal of Marriage and Family* 66 (2): 431–451.

Sassler, Sharon, and Frances Goldscheider. 2004. "Revisiting Jane Austen's Theory of Marriage Timing: Changes in Union Formation among Men in the Late 20th Century." *Journal of Family Issues* 25 (2): 139–166.

Satir, Virginia. 1972. *Peoplemaking.* Palo Alto, CA: Science and Behavior Books.

Savage, Jill. 2003. *Is There Really Sex after Kids?* Grand Rapids, Michigan: Zondervan Press.

"Save the Date: Relationships Ward Off Disease and Stress." 2004. *Psychology Today.* January/February: 32.

Sax, Leonard. 2002. "How Common Is Intersex? A Response to Anne Fausto-Sterling." *Journal of Sex Research* 39: 174–178.

Sayer, Liana, and Suzanne M. Bianchi. 2000. "Women's Economic Independence and the Probability of Divorce." *Journal of Family Issues* 21: 906–42.

Scannapieco, Maria, Rebecca Hegar, and Catherine McAlpine. 1997. "Kinship Care and Foster Care: A Comparison of Characteristics and Outcomes." *Families in Society* 78 (5): 480–89.

Scanzoni, John H. 1972. *Sexual Bargaining: Power Politics in the American Marriage.* Englewood Cliffs, NJ: Prentice-Hall.

————. 2001. "Reconnecting Household and Community." *Journal of Family Issues* 22 (2): 243–64.

Scanzoni, John H.. 2001a. *The Household in Its Neighborhood and Community.* Special issue of *Journal of Family Issues* 22(2).

————. 2001b. "Reconnecting Household and Community." *Journal of Family Issues* 22: 243-264.

Scarf, Maggie. 1995. *Intimate Worlds: Life Inside the Family.* New York: Random House.

Schafer, Robert B., and Patricia M. Keith. 1981. "Equity in Marital Roles Across the Family Life Cycle." *Journal of Marriage and Family* 43: 359–67.

Schechtman, Morris R., and Arleah Schechtman. 2003. *Love in the Present Tense: How to Have a High Intimacy, Low Maintenance Marriage.* Boulder, CO: Bull Publishing Co.

Schembari, James. 2003. "When It Comes to Child Custody, Who Pays for Yale?" *New York Times.* July 27.

Schemo, Diana Jean. 2000a. "Survey Finds Parents Favor More Detailed Sex Education." *New York Times.* Oct. 4.

————. 2000b. "Virginity Pledges by Teenagers Can Be Highly Effective, Federal Study Finds." *New York Times.* Jan. 4.

————. 2001. "In Covenant Marriage, Forging Ties That Bind." *New York Times.* Nov. 10.

————. 2003. "Rate of Rape at the Academy Is Put at 12% in Survey." *New York Times.* Aug. 29.

Scheuble, Laurie, and David R. Johnson. 1993. "Marital Name Change: Plans and Attitudes of College Students." *Journal of Marriage and Family* 55 (3): 747–54.

Schieve, Laura et al. 2002. "Low and Very Low Birth Weight in Infants Conceived with Use of Assisted Reproductive Technology." *New England Journal of Medicine* 346: 731–737.

Schmidley, Dianne. 2003. "The Foreign-Born Population in the United States: March 2002." *Current Population Reports* P-20-539. Washington DC: U.S. Census Bureau. February.

Schneewind, Klaus A., and Anna-Katharina Gerhard. 2002. "Relationship Personality, Conflict Resolution, and Marital Satisfaction in the First 5 Years of Marriage." *Family Relations* 51 (1): 63–71.

Schneider, Barbara, Linda Waite, and Nicholas P. Dempsey. 2000. "Teenagers in Dual-Career Families." *Family Focus* (December): F11, F13.

Schneider, Jodi. 2003. "Living Together." *U.S. News & World Report.* March 24.

Schnittger, Maureen H., and Gloria W. Bird. 1990. "Coping Among Dual-Career Men and Women Across the Family Life-Cycle." *Family Relations* 39 (2): 199–205.

Schnittler, Jason, Jeremy Freese, and Brian Powell. 2003. "Who Are the Feminists and What Do They Believe? The Role of Generations." *American Sociological Review* 68: 607-622.

Schoen, Robert, Nan Marie Astone, Kendra Rothert, Nicola J. Standish, and Young J. Kim. 2002. "Women's Employment, Marital Happiness, and Divorce." *Social Forces* 81: 643–662.

Schoen, Robert, and Paula Tufis. 2003. "Precursors of Nonmarital Fertility in the United States. *Journal of Marriage and the Family* 65: 1030–1040.

Schoen, Robert, and Robin M. Weinick. 1993. "Partner Choice in Marriages and Cohabitations." *Journal of Marriage and Family* 55 (2): 408–14.

Scholl, Richard W. 2002. "Attribution Theory." <htto://www.cba.uri.edu/Scholl/Notes/Attribution.html> Revised September 15.

Schor, Juliet B. 1991. *The Overworked American: The Unexpected Decline of Leisure.* New York: Basic.

Schouten, Fredreka. 2003. "Internet Leaves Schoolkids Nowhere to Hide." *USA Today.* Nov. 26.

Schwartz, Pepper. 1994. *Peer Marriage: How Love Between Equals Really Works.* New York: Free Press.

————. 2001. "Peer Marriage: What Does It Take to Create a Truly Egalitarian Relationship?" Pp. 182–89 in *Families in Transition,* 11th ed., edited by Arlene S. and Jerome H. Skolnick. Boston: Allyn and Bacon.

Schwartz, Pepper, and Virginia Rutter. 1998. *The Gender of Sexuality.* Thousand Oaks, CA: Pine Forge.

Schwartz, Richard D. 1954. "Social Factors in the Development of Legal Control." *Yale Law Journal* 63: 471–91.

Schwartz, Seth J., and Howard A. Liddle. 2001. "The Transmission of Psychopathology from Parents to Offspring: Development and Treatment in Context." *Family Relations* 50 (4): 301–307.

Scott, Ellen K., Andrew S. London, and Nancy A. Meyers. 2002. "Dangerous Dependencies: The Intersection of Welfare Reform and Domestic Violence." *Gender and Society* 16: 878–897.

Scott, Janny. 2001a. "Boom of the 1990s Missed Many in Middle Class, Data Suggest." *New York Times.* Aug. 31.

————. 2001b. "Rethinking Segregation Beyond Black and White." *New York Times.* July 29.

Scott, Joseph W. 1980. "Black Polygamous Family Formulation." *Alternative Lifestyles* 3: 41–64.

————. 1999. "From Teenage Parenthood to Polygamy: Case Studies in Black Polygamous Family Formation." Pp. 339–38 in *The Black Family: Essays and Studies,* 6th ed., edited by Robert Staples. Belmont, CA: Wadsworth.

Scott, Niki. 1992. "Irate Husband Vents His Side of the Story." *Working Woman.* Apr. 13.

Seaburn, David B., and Giuseppe Erba. 2002. "Sudden Health: The Experience of Families with a Member Who Has Surgery to Correct Epilepsy." *Family Focus.* December: F8-F10.

Seager, Joni, and Ann Olson. 1986. *Women in the World: An International Atlas.* New York: Simon & Schuster.

Seals, Brenda. 1990. Personal communication.

Seaton, Eleanor K., and Ronald D. Taylor. 2003. "Exploring Familial Processes in Urban, Low-Income African American Families." *Journal of Family Issues* 24 (5): 627–644.

Seccombe, Karen. 1991. "Assessing the Costs and Benefits of Children: Gender Comparisons Among Childfree Husbands and Wives." *Journal of Marriage and Family* 53 (1): 191–202.

————. 2000. "Families in Poverty in the 1990s: Trends, Causes, Consequences, and Lessons Learned." *Journal of Marriage and Family* 62 (4): 1094–1113.

Second Wives Café. http://secondwivescafe.com

Seelye, Katherine Q. 1998. "Specialists Report Rise in Adoptions That Fail." *New York Times.* Mar. 24.

Seery, Brenda L., and M. Sue Crowley. 2000. "Women's Emotion Work in the Family: Relationship Management and the Process of Building Father–Child Relationships." *Journal of Family Issues* 21 (1): 100–27.

Segura, Denise A., and Beatriz M. Pesquera. 1995. "Chicana Feminisms: Their Political Context and Contemporary Expressions." Pp. 617–31 in *Women: A Feminist Perspective,* 5th ed., edited by Jo Freeman. Mountain View, CA: Mayfield.

Seidler, Victor J. 1992. "Rejection, Vulnerability, and Friendship." Pp. 15–34 in *Men's Friendships: Research on Men and Masculinities,* edited by Peter M. Nardi. Newbury Park, CA: Sage.

Seidman, Steven. 2003. *The Social Construction of Sexuality.* New York: W. W. Norton.

Seltzer, Judith A. 1991a. "Relationships Between Fathers and Children Who Live Apart: The Father's Role After Separation." *Journal of Marriage and Family* 53 (1): 79–101.

———. 1991b. "Legal Custody Arrangements and Children's Economic Welfare." *American Journal of Sociology* 96: 895–929.

———. 2000. "Families Formed Outside of Marriage." *Journal of Marriage and Family* 62 (4): 1247–68.

Seltzer, Marsha, Jan Greenberg, Wyngaarden Krauss, Rachel Gordon, and Katherine Judge. 1997. "Siblings of Adults with Mental Retardation or Mental Illness: Effects on Lifestyle and Psychological Well-Being." *Family Relations* 46 (4): 395–405.

Seltzer, Marsha, and Tamar Heller (Eds.). 1997. "Family Caregiving for Persons with Disabilities." *Family Relations* Special Issue 46 (4). October.

Sengupta, Somini. 1997. "College Freshmen Adopting Stricter Views, Survey Finds." *New York Times.* Jan. 13.

Serovich, Julianne M., Sharon J. Price, and Steven F. Chapman. 1991. "Former In-Laws as a Source of Support." *Journal of Divorce and Remarriage* 17 (1/2): 17–26.

Shalit, Wendy. 1999. *A Return to Modesty: Discovering the Lost Virtue.* New York: Free Press.

Shamin, Ishrat, and Quamrul Ahsan Chowdhury. 1993. *Homeless and Powerless: Child Victims of Sexual Exploitation.* Dhaka, Bangladesh: University of Dhaka Press.

Shanahan, Michael J. 2000. "Pathways to Adulthood in Changing Societies: Variabilities and Mechanisms in Life Course Perspective." *Annual Review of Sociology* 26: 667–697.

Shapiro, Joseph P. 2001a. "The Assisted-Living Dilemma." *U.S. News & World Report.* May 21: 64–66.

———. 2001b. "Growing Old in a Good Home." *U.S. News & World Report.* May 21: 57–61.

Shatzmiller, Maya. 1996. "Marriage, Family, and the Faith: Women's Conversion to Islam." *Journal of Family History* 21 (3): 235–46.

Sheehan, Constance L., E. Wilbur Bock, and Gary R. Lee. 1990. "Religious Heterogamy, Religiosity, and Marital Happiness: The Case of Catholics." *Journal of Marriage and Family* 52: 73–79.

Shellenbarger, Sue. 1991a. "Child-Care Setups Still Fall Apart Often." *Wall Street Journal.* Sept. 26.

———. 1991b. "Companies Team Up to Improve Quality of Their Employees' Child-Care Choices." *Wall Street Journal.* Oct. 17: B1, B4.

———. 1991c. "Leaving Infants for Work Boosts Child-Care Costs." *Wall Street Journal.* July 22.

———. 1991d. "More Job Seekers Put Family Needs First." *Wall Street Journal.* Nov. 15: B1, B6.

Create Patchwork of Family-Leave Laws." *Wall Street Journal.* July 28.

———. 1998. "Families, Communities Can Benefit from Rise in Home-Based Work." *Wall Street Journal.* May 13: B1.

———. 2002. "As Moms Earn More, More Dads Stay Home." *Wall Street Journal.* Feb. 20.

Shellenbarger, Sue, and Cindy Trost. 1992a. "Annual List of Family-Friendly Firms Is Issued by *Working Mother* Magazine." *Wall Street Journal.* Sept. 22: A2, A4.

———. 1992b. "Partnership of 109 Companies Aims to Improve Care Nationwide for Children and the Elderly." *Wall Street Journal.* Sept. 11: A12.

Shelton, Beth Anne. 1990. "The Distribution of Household Tasks: Does Wife's Employment Status Make a Difference?" *Journal of Family Issues* 11 (2): 115–35.

———. 1992. *Women, Men and Time.* New York: Greenwood.

———. 2000. "Understanding the Distribution of Housework Between Husbands and Wives." Pp. 343–55 in *The Ties That Bind: Perspectives on Marriage and Cohabitation,* edited by Linda Waite. New York: de Gruyter.

Shelton, Beth Anne, and Daphne John. 1993. "Ethnicity, Race, and Difference: A Comparison of White, Black, and Hispanic Men's Household Labor Time." Pp. 131–50 in *Men, Work, and Family,* edited by Jane C. Hood. Newbury Park, CA: Sage.

———. 1996. "The Division of Household Labor." *Annual Review of Sociology* 22: 299–322.

Sherif-Trask, Bahira. 2003. "Marriage from a Cross-Cultural Perspective." *National Council on Family Relations Report* 48 (3): F13–F14.

Sherman, Lawrence W. 1992. *Policing Domestic Violence: Experiments and Dilemmas.* New York: Free Press.

Sherman, Lawrence W., and Richard A. Berk. 1984. "Deterrent Effects of Arrest for Domestic Assault." *American Sociological Review* 49: 261–72.

Sherman, Paul J., and Janet T. Spence. 1997. "A Comparison of Two Cohorts of College Students in Responses to the Male–Female Relations Questionnaire." *Psychology of Women Quarterly* 21 (2): 265–278.

Shihadeh, Edward S. 1991. "The Prevalence of Husband-Centered Migration: Employment Consequences for Married Mothers." *Journal of Marriage and Family* 53 (2): 432–44.

Shomaker, Mary Zimmeth. 1994. "From Stepfather to Father," *Liguorian.* June: 54–56.

Shorter, Edward. 1975. *The Making of the Modern Family.* New York: Basic.

Shostak, Arthur. 1987. "Singlehood." Pp. 355–67 in *Handbook of Marriage and the Family,* edited by Marvin B. Sussman and Suzanne K. Steinmetz. New York: Plenum.

Siegel, Deborah. 2004. "The New Trophy Wife." *Psychology Today.* January/February: 52–58.

Siegel, Judith P. 2000. *What Children Learn from Their Parents' Marriage.* NY: HarperCollins.

Siegel, Mark D. 2004. "To the Editor: Making Decisions About How to Die." *The New York Times. October 3.*

Sigle-Rushton, Wendy, and Sara McLanahan. 2002. "The Living Arrangements of New Unmarried Mothers." *Demography* 39 (3): 415–434.

Siller, Sidney. 1984. "National Organization for Men." Privately printed pamphlet.

Silvern, Louise, Jane Karyl, Lynn Waelde, William F. Hodges, and Joanna Starek. 1995. "Retrospective Reports of Parental Partner Abuse: Relationships to Depression, Trauma Symptoms and Self-Esteem Among College Students." *Journal of Family Violence* 10 (2): 177–86.

Silverstein, Merril. 2000. "The Impact of Acculturation on Intergenerational Relationships in Mexican American Families." *National Council on Family Relations Report* 45 (2): F9.

Silverstein, Merril, and Vern L. Bengston. 1997. "Intergenerational Solidarity and the Structure of Adult Child–Parent Relationships in American Families." *American Journal of Sociology* 103 (2): 429–60.

———. 2001. "Intergenerational Solidarity and the Structure of Adult Child–Parent Relationships in American Families." Pp. 53–61 in *Families in Later Life: Connections and Transitions,* edited by Alexis J. Walker, Margaret Manoogian-O'Dell, Lori A. McGraw, and Diana L. G. White. Thousand Oaks, CA: Pine Forge.

Silverstein, Merril, and Xuan Chen. 1999. "The Impact of Acculturation in Mexican American Families on the Quality of Adult Grandchild–Grandparent Relations." *Journal of Marriage and Family* 61 (1): 188–98.

Silverstein, Merril, and Anne Marenco. 2001. "How Americans Enact the Grandparent Role Across the Family Life Course." *Journal of Family Issues* 22 (4): 493–522.

Simmel, Georg. 1950. *The Sociology of Georg Simmel,* translated and edited by Kurt H. Wolfe. Glencoe, IL: Free Press.

Simmons, Roberta G. 1991. "Altruism and Sociology." *Sociological Quarterly* 32: 1–22.

Simmons, Tavia, and Martin O'Connell. 2003. "Married-couple and Unmarried Partner Households: 2000." *Census Special Report* CENSR-5 Washington DC: U.S. Census Bureau.

Simmons, Tavia, and Grace O'Neill. 2001. "Households and Families: 2000. *Census 2000 Brief* C2KBR/ 01-8. Washington D.C. U.S. Census Bureau.

Simmons, Ronald L., Kuei-Hsiu Lin, Leslie C. Gordon, Gene H. Brody, and Rand D. Conger. 2002. "Community Differences in the Association Between Parenting and Child Conduct Problems." *Journal of Marriage and Family* 64 (2): 331–345.

Simon, Barbara Levy. 1987. *Never Married Women.* Philadelphia: Temple University Press.

Simon, Rita J. 1990. "Transracial Adoptions Can Bring Joy: Letters to the Editor." *Wall Street Journal.* Oct. 17.

Simon, Rita J., and Howard Altstein. 2000. *Adoption Across Borders: Serving the Children in Transracial and Intercountry Adoptions.* Oxford, England: Rowman and Littlefield.

———. 2002. *Adoption, Race, & Identity: From Infancy To Young Adulthood.* New Brunswick NJ: Transaction Publishers.

Simon, Stephanie. 1991. "Joint Custody Loses Favor for Increasing Children's Feeling of Being Torn Apart." *Wall Street Journal.* July 15: B1.

Simons, Ronald L., Kuei-Hsiu Lin, and Leslie C. Gordon. 1998. "Socialization in the Family of Origin and Male Dating Violence: A Prospective Study." *Journal of Marriage and Family* 60: 467–78.

Simons, Ronald L., and Les B. Whitbeck. 1991. "Sexual Abuse as a Precursor to Prostitution and Victimization Among Adolescent and Adult Homeless Women." *Journal of Family Issues* 12 (3): 361–79.

Simpson, J., and R. Rholes. 1998. *Attachment Theory and Close Relationships.* New York: Guilford.

Singer v. Hara. 1974. 11 Wash. App. 247, 522 P 2d 1187.

Sink, Mindy. 2000. "Going Online to Build a Family." *New York Times.* Dec. 18.

Skinner, Kevin B., Stephen J. Bahr, D. Russell Crane, and Vaughn A. Call. 2002. "Cohabitation, Marriage, and Remarriage: A Comparison of Relationship Quality over Time." *Journal of Family Issues* 23 (1): 74–90.

Skolnick, Arlene S. 1978. *The Intimate Environment: Exploring Marriage and Family,* 2nd ed. Boston: Little, Brown.

———. 1997. "A Response to Glenn: The Battle of the Textbooks: Bringing in the Culture Wars." *Family Relations* 46 (3): 219–22.

———. 2001. "The Life Course Revolution." Pp. 23–31 in *Families in Transition,* 11th ed., edited by Arlene S. Skolnick and Jerome H. Skolnick. Boston: Allyn & Bacon.

Slater, Lauren. 2002. "The Trouble with Self-Esteem." *New York Times.* February 3: Section 6, p. 44.

Slater, Suzanne. 1995. *The Lesbian Family Life Cycle.* New York: Free Press.

Slowlane.com: The Online Resource for Stay At Home Dads. Nd. http://slowlane.com

Smalley, Gary. 2000. *Secrets to Lasting Love: Uncovering the Keys to Life-Long Intimacy.* New York: Simon & Schuster.

Smith, David M., and Gary J. Gates. 2001. *Gay and Lesbian Families in the United States: Same-Sex Unmarried Partner Households.* Washington DC: Human Rights Campaign.

Smith, Deborah B., and Phyllis Moen. 1998. "Spousal Influence on Retirement: His, Her, and Their Perceptions." *Journal of Marriage and Family* 60 (3): 734–44.

———. 2004. "Retirement Satisfaction for Retirees and Their Spouses: Do Gender and the Retirement Decision-Making Process Matter?" *Journal of Family Issues* 25 (2): 262–285.

Smith, Donna. 1990. *Stepmothering.* New York: St. Martin's.

Smith, Kristin, Barbara Downs, and Martin O'Connell. 2001. *Maternity Leave and Employment Patterns: 1961–1995.* Current Population Report P70–79. Nov. Washington, DC: U.S. Census Bureau.

Smith, Tom W. 1999. *The Emerging 21st Century American Family*. GSS Social Change Report No. 42. Chicago: University of Chicago, National Opinion Research Center.

———. 2003a. "American Sexual Behavior: Trends, Socio-Demographic Differences, and Risk Behavior." General Social Survey Topical Report No. 25, updated. Chicago: National Opinion Research Center, University of Chicago. April.

———. 2003b. "Coming of Age in 21st Century America: Public Attitudes towards the Importance and Timing of Transitions to Adulthood." GSS Topical Report No. 35. Chicago: NORC.

Smits, Jeroen, Wout Ultee, and Jan Lammers. 1998. "Educational Homogamy in 65 Countries: An Explanation of Differences in Openness Using Country-Level Explanatory Variables." *American Sociological Review* 63 (2): 264–75.

Smock, Pamela J. 1993. "The Economic Costs of Marital Disruption for Young Women Over the Past Two Decades." *Demography* 30 (3): 353–71.

———. 2000. "Cohabitation in the United States: An Appraisal of Research Themes, Findings, and Implications." *Annual Review of Sociology* 26: 1–20.

Smock, Pamela J., and Sanjiv Gupta. 2002. "Cohabitation in Contemporary North America." Pp. 53- 84 in *Just Living Together: Implications of Cohabitation on Families*, edited by Alan Booth and Ann C. Crouter. Mahwah NJ: Erlbaum.

Smock, Pamela J., Wendy D. Manning, and Sanjiv Gupta. 1999. "The Effect of Marriage and Divorce on Women's Economic Well-Being." *American Sociological Review* 64: 794–812.

Smolka, Angie. 2001. "That's the ticket: A New Way of Defining Family." *Cornell Journal of Law and Public Policy* 10 (3): 62ff.

Smolowe, Jill. 1996a. "The Unmarrying Kind." *Time*. Apr. 29: 68–69.

———. 1996b. "Parenting on Trial." *Time*. May 20: 50.

Snipp, C. Matthew. 2002. *American Indian and Alaska Native Children in the 2000 Census*. Washington DC: Annie E. Casey Foundation/Population Reference Bureau.

Sokolski, Dawn M., and Susan S. Hendrick. 1999. "Fostering Marital Satisfaction." *Journal of the California Graduate School of Family* 26 (1): 39–47.

Soler, Hosanna, David Quadagno, David F. Sly, Kara S. Riehman, Isaac W. Eberstein, and Dianna F. Harrison. 2000. "Relationship Dynamics and Condom Use Among Low-Income Women." *Family Planning Perspectives* 32: 82-88; 101.

Solis, Dianne, and Charlene Oldham. 2001. "Women Break Glass Ceiling by Starting Own Businesses." *Dallas Morning News*. June 18.

"Some Groups Are Wary Over Government's Promotion of 'Embryo Adoption.'" *Omaha World-Herald* (AP). Aug. 22.

"Some Noses More to the Grindstone Than Others." *New York Times*. July 7.

Somers, Marsha D. 1993. "A Comparison of Voluntarily Childfree Adults and Parents." *Journal of Marriage and Family* 55 (3): 643–50.

Sommers, Christina Hoff. 2000a. *The War Against Boys*. New York: Simon and Schuster.

———. 2000b. "The War Against Boys." *Atlantic Monthly*. May: 59–75.

Sonkin, Daniel Jay, Del Martin, and Lenore E. Auerbach Walker. 1985. *The Male Batterer: A Treatment Approach*. New York: Singer.

Sontag, Susan. 1976. "The Double Standard of Aging." Pp. 350–66 in *Sexuality Today and Tomorrow*, edited by Sol Gordon and Roger W. Libby. North Scituate, MA: Duxbury.

Sorensen, Elaine Shaw. 1993. *Children's Stress and Coping: A Family Perspective*. New York: Guilford.

Soukhanov, Anne H. 1996. "Watch." *Atlantic Monthly*. August: 96.

South, Scott J. 1993. "Racial and Ethnic Differences in the Desire to Marry." *Journal of Marriage and Family* 55 (2): 357–70.

———. 1995. "Do You Need to Shop Around?" *Journal of Family Issues* 16 (4): 432–49.

———. 2001. "Time-Dependent Effects of Wives' Employment on Marital Dissolution." *American Sociological Review* 66: 226–43.

South, Scott J., Kyle D. Crowder, and Katherine Trent. 1998. "Children's Residential Mobility and Neighborhood Environment Following Parental Divorce and Remarriage." *Social Forces* 77: 667–93.

South, Scott J., and Kim M. Lloyd. 1992a. "Marriage Markets and Non-Marital Fertility in the U.S." *Demography* 29: 247–64.

———. 1992b. "Marriage Opportunities and Family Formation: Further Implications of Imbalanced Sex Ratios." *Journal of Marriage and Family* 54: 440–51.

"Spending Patterns by Age." 2000. *Issues in Labor Statistics*. Summary 00–16. August. U.S. Department of Labor, Bureau of Labor Statistics.

Spiro, Melford. 1956. *Kibbutz: Venture in Utopia*. New York: Macmillan.

Spitz, G., and J. Logan. 1990. "More Evidence on Women (and Men) in the Middle." *Research on Aging* 12 (2): 182–196.

Spitze, Glenna, John R. Logan, Glenn Deane, and Suzanne Zerger. 1994. "Adult Children's Divorce and Intergenerational Relationships." *Journal of Marriage and Family* 56 (2): 279–93.

Sponsel, Leanne M. 2003. "Spirituality and Family Resilience." *Family Focus*. December: F5-F6.

Spragins, Ellyn. 2002. "Full-Time Fathers Are Still Finding Their Way." *New York Times.*" May 5.

Spraggins, Renee E. 2001. "U.S. Census Bureau Releases Profile of Nation's Women." News Release. Washington, DC: U.S. Census Bureau. Mar. 15.

———. 2003. "Women and Men in the United States: March 2002." *Current Population Reports* p20- 544. Washington DC: United States Census Bureau.

Sprecher, Susan. 1989. "Premarital Sexual Standards for Different Categories of Individuals." *Journal of Sex Research* 26: 232–48.

———. 2002. "Sexual Satisfaction in Premarital Relationships: Associations with Satisfaction Love, Commitment, and Stability." *Journal of Sex Research:* 39:190–196.

Sprecher, Susan, Kathleen McKinney, and Terri Orbuch. 1987. "Has the Double Standard Disappeared?: An Experimental Test." *Social Psychology Quarterly* 50: 24–31.

Sprecher, Susan, and P. C. Regan. 1996. "College Virgins: How Men and Women Perceive Their Sexual Status." *Journal of Sex Research* 33: 3–15.

Sprecher, Susan, and Pepper Schwartz. 1994. "Equity and Balance in the Exchange of Contributions in Close Relationships." Pp. 89–116 in *Entitlement and the Affectional Bond: Justice in Close Relationships*, edited by M. J. Lerner and G. Mikula. New York: Plenum.

Sprecher, Susan, and Maura Toro-Morn 2002."A Study of Men and Women from Different Sides of Earth to Determine if Men Are from Mars and Women Are from Venus in Their Beliefs about Love and Romantic Relationships." *Sex Roles: A Journal of Research* (March): 131–148.

Sprenkle, Douglas H. 1989. "The Clinical Practice of Divorce Therapy." Pp. 171–95 in *The Divorce and Divorce Therapy Handbook*, edited by Martin Textor. Northvale, NJ: Jason Aronson.

———. 2003. "Effectiveness Research in Marriage and Family Therapy." *Journal of Marital and Family Therapy* 29 (1): 85–96.

Springen, Karen. 2000a. "Feeling the 50-Year Itch." *Newsweek*. Dec. 4: 56–57.

———. 2000b "The Right to Choose." *Newsweek*. Dec 4: 73.

Springer, S., and G. Deutsch. 1994. *Left Brain/Right Brain*, 4th edition. New York: Freeman.

Stacey, Judith. 1990. *Brave New Families: Stories of Domestic Upheaval in Late Twentieth Century America*. New York: Basic.

———. 1996. *In the Name of the Family: Rethinking Family Values in the Postmodern Age*. Boston: Beacon.

———. 1999. "The Family Values Fable." Pp. 487–90 in *American Families: A Multicultural Reader*, edited by Stephanie Coontz. New York: Routledge.

Stacey, Judith, and Timothy J. Biblarz. 2001. "(How) Does the Sexual Orientation of Parents Matter?" *American Sociological Review* 66: 159–83.

Stack, Carol B. 1974. *All Our Kin: Strategies for Survival*. New York: Harper & Row.

Stack, Steven, and Ira Wasserman. 1993. "Marital Status, Alcohol Consumption, and Suicide: An Analysis of National Data." *Journal of Marriage and Family* 55: 1018–24.

Stamler, Bernard. 2004. "Now That There Are Choices, How to Choose?" *New York Times*. June 21.

Stanley v. Illinois. 1972. 405 U.S. 645, 92 S.Ct. 1208, 31 L.Ed.2d 551.

Stanley, Scott M. 2001. "Making a Case for Premarital Education." *Family Relations* 50: 272–80.

Staples, Robert. 1985. "Changes in Black Family Structure: The Conflict Between Family Ideology and Structural Conditions." *Journal of Marriage and Family* 47: 1005–13.

———. 1994. *The Black Family: Essays and Studies*, 5th ed. Belmont, CA: Wadsworth.

———. 1999a. *The Black Family: Essays and Studies*, 6th ed. Belmont, CA: Wadsworth.

———. 1999b. "Interracial Relationships: A Convergence of Desire and Opportunity." Pp. 129–36 in *The Black Family: Essays and Studies*, 6th ed., edited by Robert Staples. Belmont, CA.: Wadsworth.

———. 1999c. "Patterns of Change in the Postindustrial Black Family." Pp. 281–90 in *The Black Family: Essays and Studies*, 6th ed., edited by Robert Staples. Belmont, CA: Wadsworth.

Stark, Steven. 1997. "Alliance Sees Pure Sense in Abstaining from Sex." *Chicago Tribune*. July 26: 1–5.

Stattin, H., and G. Klackenberg. 1992. "Discordant Family Relations in Intact Families: Developmental Tendencies Over 18 Years." *Journal of Marriage and Family* 54: 940–56.

Stearns, Peter N. 2003. *Anxious Parents: A History of Modern Childrearing In America*. New York: NYU Press.

Steil, Janice M. 1997. *Marital Equality: Its Relationship to the Well-Being of Husbands and Wives*. Thousand Oaks CA: Sage.

Stein, Arlene. 1989. "Three Models of Sexuality: Drives, Identities, and Practices." *Sociological Theory* 7: 1–13.

Stein, Catherine H., Virginia A. Wemmerus, Marcia Ward, Michelle E. Gaines, Andrew L. Freeberg, and Thomas C. Jewell. 1998. "Because They're My Parents': An Intergenerational Study of Felt Obligation and Parental Caregiving." *Journal of Marriage and Family* 60 (3): 611–22.

Stein, Peter J. 1976. *Single*. Englewood Cliffs, NJ: Prentice-Hall.

———. (Ed.). 1981. *Single Life: Unmarried Adults in Social Context*. New York: St. Martin's.

———. 2001. Personal communication/Review of seventh edition of this textbook.

Stein, Rob. 2003. "Elective Caesareans Judged Ethical." *Washington Post*. Oct. 30.

Steinberg, L. 1990. "Interdependency in the Family: Autonomy, Conflict, and Harmony in the Parent–Adolescent Relationship." In *At the Threshold: The Developing Adolescent*, edited by S. Feldman and G. Elliot. Cambridge, MA: Harvard University Press.

Steinhauer, Jennifer. 1995. "Living Together Without Marriage or Apologies." *New York Times*. July 6.

Steinmetz, Suzanne K. 1977. *The Cycle of Violence: Assertive, Aggressive, and Abusive Family Interactions*. New York: Praeger.

Stepfamily Association of America. http://www.saafamily.org

"Stepfamily Facts." 2003. Stepfamily Association of America. http://www.saafamily.org/faqs/index.html>

Stephens, William N. 1963. *The Family in Cross-Cultural Perspective*. New York: Holt, Rinehart & Winston.

Stern, Gabriella. 1991. "Young Women Insist on Career Equality, Forcing the Men in Their Lives to Adjust." *Wall Street Journal*. Sept. 16: B1, B3.

Stern, Gary. 2003. "Jewish Intermarriage Still Up, but Rate Slowing." *The Journal News*. September 11.

Stern, Linda. 1994. "Money Watch: Divorce." *Newsweek*. June 6: 58.

Sternberg, Robert J. 1988a. "Triangulating Love." Pp. 119–38 in *The Psychology of Love*, edited by Robert J. Sternberg and Michael L. Barnes. New Haven, CT: Yale University Press.

———. 1988b. *The Triangle of Love: Intimacy, Passion, Commitment*. New York: Basic.

Sternberg, Steve. 2001. "Report: Little Proof of Condom Protection against Some STDS." *USA Today*. July 20.

Stets, Jan E. 1991. "Cohabiting and Marital Aggression: The Role of Social Isolation." *Journal of Marriage and Family* 53 (3): 669–80.

Stevens, Daphne, Gary Kiger, and Pamela J. Riley. 2001. "Working Hard and Hardly Working: Domestic Labor and Marital Satisfaction in Dual Earner Couples." *Journal of Marriage and the Family* 63: 514–526.

Stevens, Gillian. 1991. "Propinquity and Educational Homogamy." *Sociological Forum* 6 (4): 715–26.

Stevenson, Betsey, and Justin Wolfers. 2004. "Bargaining in the Shadow of the Law: Divorce Laws and Family Distress." National Bureau of Economic Research Working Paper 10175. Cambridge MA: National Bureau of Economic Research. Oct. 4.

Stewart, Mary White. 1984. "The Surprising Transformation of Incest: From Sin to Sickness." Paper presented at the annual meeting of the Midwest Sociological Society, Chicago, Apr. 18.

Stewart. Susan. 2001. "Contemporary American Stepparenthood: Integrating Cohabiting and Nonresident Stepparents." *Population Research and Policy Review* 20 (4): 345–64.

———. 1999. "Disneyland Dads, Disneyland Moms?" *Journal of Family Issues* 20: 539–56.

———. 2002. "The Effect of Stepchildren on Childbearing Intentions and Births." *Demography* 39: 181–197.

———. 2003. "Nonresident Parenting and Adolescent Adjustment." *Journal of Family Issues* 24 (2): 217–244.

Stinnett, Nick. 1979. "In Search of Strong Families." Pp. 23–30 in *Building Family Strengths: Blueprints for Action*, edited by Nick Stinnett, Barbara Chesser, and John DeFrain. Lincoln: University of Nebraska Press.

———. 1985. *Secrets of Strong Families*. New York: Little, Brown.

———. 1997. *Good Families*. New York: Doubleday.

———. 2003. *Fantastic Families: 6 Proven Steps to Building a Strong Family*. Princeton, NJ: Sound Recording.

Stinnett, Nick, Donnie Hilliard, and Nancy Stinnett. 2000. *Magnificent Marriage: 10 Beacons Show the Way to Marriage Happiness*. Montgomery, AL: Pillar Press.

Stinson, Kandi M., Judith N. Lasker, Janet Lohmann, and Lori J. Toedter. 1992. "Parents' Grief Following Pregnancy Loss: A Comparison of Mothers and Fathers." *Family Relations* 41: 218–23.

Stock, Robert W. 1997. "When Older Women Contract the AIDS Virus." *New York Times*. July 31: B1.

Stokes, Randall, and Albert Chevan. 1996. "Female-Headed Families: Social and Economic Context of Racial Differences." *Journal of Urban Affairs* 18: 245–68.

Stolberg, Sheryl Gay. 1997a. "For the Infertile: A High Tech Treadmill." *New York Times*. Dec. 14.

———. 1997b. "U.S. Publishes First Guide to Treatment of Infertility." *New York Times*. Dec. 19.

———. 2000. "New Way to Have Children: Adoption of Frozen Embryos." *New York Times*. Feb. 25.

———. 2001a. "Another Academic Salvo from a 'Mommy Wars' Veteran." *New York Times*. Apr. 21.

———. 2001b. "Researchers Find a Link Between Behavioral Problems and Time in Child Care." *New York Times*. Apr. 19.

———. 2001c. "A Risk Is Found in Natural Birth after Cesarean." *New York Times*. July 5.

———. 2002. "Study Says Premature Babies Fare Better Than Expected." *New York Times*. Jan. 17.

Stolzenberg, Ross M., Mary Blair-Loy, and Linda J. Waite. 1995. "Religious Participation in Early Adulthood: Age and Family Life Cycle Effects on Church Membership." *American Sociological Review* 60: 84–103.

Stone, Brad. 1999. "Valley of the Doll-less." *Newsweek*. Aug. 16: 59.

———. 2001. "Love Online." *Newsweek*. Feb. 19: 46–51.

Stone, Lawrence. 1980. *The Family, Sex, and Marriage in England, 1500–1800*. New York: Harper & Row.

Stone, R. I., G. I. Cafferata, and J. Sangl. 1987. "Caregivers of the Frail Elderly: A National Profile." *The Gerontologist* 505–10.

Strand, Erik. 2004. "Out of Touch?" *Psychology Today*. January/February: 24.

Stratton, Kelly. 2003. "Squeeze Your Main Squeeze: Stress-proof Your Whole Day." *Prevention* 55 (8): 42.

Stratton, Peter. 2003. "Causal Attributions During Therapy: Responsibility and Blame." *Journal of Family Therapy* 25 (2): 136–160.

Straus, Murray A. 1993. "Physical Assaults by Wives: A Major Social Problem." Pp. 67–87 in *Current Controversies on Family Violence*, edited by Richard J. Gelles and Donileen R. Loseke. Newbury Park, CA: Sage.

———. 1994. *Beating the Devil Out of Them: Corporal Punishment in American Families*. New York: Lexington.

———. 1996. "Presentation: Spanking and the Making of a Violent Society." *Pediatrics* 98: 837–49.

———. 1999a. "The Benefits of Avoiding Corporal Punishment: New and More Definitive Evidence." Paper No. CP40–59/CP41B.P. University of New Hampshire: Family Research Laboratory.

———. 1999b. "The Controversy Over Domestic Violence by Women: A Methodological, Theoretical, and Sociology of Science Analysis." Pp. 17–44 in *Violence in Intimate Relationships*, edited by Ximena B. Arriaga and Stuart Oskamp. Thousand Oaks, CA: Sage.

Straus, Murray A., and Denise A. Donnelly. 2001. *Beating the Devil Out of Them: Corporal Punishment in American Families and Its Effect on Children*, 2nd ed. New Brunswick NJ Transaction.

Straus, Murray A., and Richard J. Gelles. 1986. "Societal Change and Change in Family Violence from 1975 to 1985 as Revealed by Two National Surveys." *Journal of Marriage and Family* 48: 465–79.

———. 1988. "How Violent Are American Families? Estimates from the National Family Violence Resurvey and Other Studies." Pp. 14–36 in *Family Abuse and Its Consequences: New Directions in Research*, edited by Gerald T. Hotaling, David Finkelhor, John T. Kirkpatrick, and Murray A. Straus. Newbury Park, CA: Sage.

———. 1995. *Physical Violence in American Families: Risk Factors and Adaptations to Violence in 8,145 Families*. New Brunswick, NJ: Transaction.

Straus, Murray A., Richard J. Gelles, and Suzanne K. Steinmetz. 1980. *Behind*

Closed Doors: Violence in the American Family. New York: Doubleday.

Straus, Murray A., Sherry L. Hambey, Sue Boney-McCoy, and David B. Sugarman. 1996. "The Revised Conflict Tactics Scales (CTS2): Development and Preliminary Psychometric Data." *Journal of Family Issues* 17: 283–316.

Straus, Murray A., and Vera E. Mouradian. 1998. "Impulsive Corporal Punishment by Mothers and Antisocial Behavior and Impulsiveness of Children." *Behavioral Sciences & the Law* 16 (3): 353–62.

Straus, Murray A., and Julie H. Stewart. 1999. "Corporal Punishment by American Parents: National Data on Prevalence, Chronicity, Severity, and Duration, in Relation to Child and Family Characteristics." *Clinical Child and Family Psychology Review* 2 (2): 55–70.

Straus, Murray A., and Carrie L. Yodanis. 1996. "Corporal Punishment in Adolescence and Physical Assaults on Spouses Later in Life: What Accounts for the Link?" *Journal of Marriage and Family* 58 (4): 825–924.

Strauss, Anselm, and Barney Glaser. 1975. *Chronic Illness and the Quality of Life*. St. Louis: Mosby.

Strauss, Robert. 2002. "Dad's 50, Junior's 8. What's The Plan?" *New York Times*. Mar. 12.

Strawley, George. 2002. "Lesbian Partner Must Pay Child Support." *Philadelphia Inquirer*. Dec. 19.

Strobe, W., and M. Strobe. 1996. "The Social Psychology of Social Support." Pp. 597–621 in *Social Psychology: Handbook of Basic Principles*, edited by E. T. Higgins and A. Kruglanski. New York: Guilford.

Strömberg, B., G. Dahlquist, A. Ericson, O. Finnström, M. Köster, and K. Stjernquist. 2002. "Neurological Sequaelae in Children Born after In Vitro Fertilization: A Population-Based Study." *The Lancet* 395: 461-465.

Struening, Karen. 2002. *New Family Values: Liberty, Equality, and Diversity*. Lanham MD: Rowman and Littlefield.

"Study: Male Puberty Commencing Sooner." 2001. *Omaha World-Herald*. Sept. 19.

"Study: Multiple Test-Tube Babies Declining." 2004. CNN. April 26. www.cnn.health.

Suarez, Liza M., and Bruce L. Baker. 1997. "Child Externalizing Behavior and Parents' Stress: The Role of Social Support." *Family Relations* 46 (4): 373–81.

Sudarkasa, Niara. 1981. "Interpreting the African Heritage in Afro-American Family Organization." In *Black Families*, edited by Harriette Pipes McAdoo. Beverly Hills, CA: Sage.

———. 1993. "Female-Headed African American Households: Some Neglected Dimensions." Pp. 81–89 in *Family Ethnicity: Strength in Diversity*, edited by Harriette Pipes McAdoo. Newbury Park, CA: Sage.

Sugarman, Stephen D. 1998. "Single-Parent Families." Pp. 13–38 in *All Our Families: New Policies for a New Century*, edited by Mary Ann Mason, Arlene Skolnick, and Stephen D. Sugarman. New York: Oxford University Press.

Sugrue, Thomas J. 1999. "Poor Families in an Era of Urban Transformation: The 'Underclass' Family in Myth and Reality." Pp. 243–57 in *American Families: A Multicultural Reader*, edited by Stephanie Coontz. New York: Routledge.

Sullivan, Oriel. 1997. "The Division of Housework Among Remarried Couples." *Journal of Family Issues* 18 (2): 205–23.

Sullivan, Teresa A., Elizabeth Walker, and Jay Lawrence Westbrook. 2000. *The Fragile Middle Class: Americans in Debt*. New Haven, CT: Yale University Press.

Suro, Roberto. 1992. "Generational Chasm Leads to Cultural Turmoil for Young Mexicans in U.S." *New York Times*. Jan. 20.

Surowiecki, James. 2003. "Leave No Parent Behind." *New Yorker*. Aug. 18/25: 48.

Surra, Catherine A. 1990. "Research and Theory on Mate Selection and Premarital Relationships in the 1980s." *Journal of Marriage and Family* 52: 844–65.

Surra, Catherine A., and Debra K. Hughes. 1997. "Commitment Processes in Accounts of the Development of Premarital Relationships."

Journal of Marriage and Family 59: 5–21.

Sussman, Marvin B., Suzanne K. Steinmetz, and Gary W. Peterson. 1999. *Handbook of Marriage and the Family*, 2nd ed. New York: Plenum.

Swartz, Susan. 2004. "Singular Lives: SSU Sociologist Kay Trimberger Is Documenting a New Trend of Unmarried Women Who Are Not Only Content, but Happy To Be Single." *The Press Democrat*. February 29.

Sweeney, Megan, and Julie A. Phillips. 2004. "Understanding Racial Differences in Marital Disruption: Recent Trends and Explanations." *Journal of Marriage and the Family* 66: 639–650.

Sweet, James, Larry Bumpass, and Vaughn Call. 1988. *The Design and Content of the National Survey of Families and Households* (Working Paper NSFH–1). Madison: University of Wisconsin, Center for Demography and Ecology.

Swim, Janet K. 1994. "Perceived Versus Meta-analytic Effect Sizes: An Assessment of the Accuracy of Gender Stereotypes." *Journal of Personality and Social Psychology* 66 (1): 21–37.

Swim, Janet K., K. J. Aikin, W. S. Hall, and B. A. Hunter. 1995. "Sexism and Racism: Old-Fashioned and Modern Prejudices." *Journal of Personality and Psychology* 68: 199–214.

Swim, Janet K., and Laurie L. Cohen. 1997. "A Comparison Between the Attitudes Toward Women and Modern Sexism Scales." *Psychology of Women Quarterly* 21 (1): 103–18.

"Syphilis Through Oral Sex On the Rise." 2004. Reuters. Oct. 21. www.reuters.co.uk.

Szabo, Liz. 2004a. "American's First 'Test-Tube Baby.'" *USA Today*. May 13.

———. 2004b. "Study Gives Male Contraceptive A Shot." *USA Today*. Nov. 12.

Szasz, Thomas S. 1976. *Heresies*. New York: Doubleday/Anchor.

Szinovacz, Maximiliane. 1997. "Adult Children Taking Parents into Their Homes: Effects of Childhood Living Arrangements." *Journal of Marriage and Family* 59: 700–17.

———. 2000. "Changes in Housework After Retirement: A Panel Analysis."

Journal of Marriage and Family 62 (1): 78–92.

Szinovacz, Maximiliane, and Anne Schaffer. 2000. "Effects of Retirement on Marital Conflict Tactics." *Journal of Family Issues* 21 (3): 376–89.

Taffel, Selma. 1987. "Characteristics of American Indian and Alaska Native Births: United States, 1984." *Monthly Vital Statistics Report* 36 (3), Suppl., U.S. National Center for Health Statistics, June 19.

Tak, Young Ran, and Marilyn McCubbin. 2002. "Family Stress, Perceived Social Support, and Coping Following the Diagnosis of a Child's Congenital Heart Disease." *Journal of Advanced Nursing* 39 (2): 190-198.

Takagi, Dana Y. 2002. "Japanese American Families." Pp. 164-180 in *Multicultural Families in the United States*, 3rd ed., edited by Ronald L. Taylor. Upper Saddle River NJ: Prentice-Hall.

Talbot, Margaret. 1999. "Pay on Delivery." *New York Times Magazine*. Oct. 31: 19–20.

———. 2001. "Open Sperm Donation." *New York Times Magazine*. Dec. 8: 88.

———. 2002a. "Homing Devices for Your Kids." *New York Times Magazine*. Dec. 15. P. 96.

———. 2002b. "Jack or Jill?" *Atlantic Monthly*. March. P. 25.

Talbott, Maria M. 1998. "Older Widows' Attitudes Towards Men and Remarriage." *Journal of Aging Studies* 12 (4): 429–49.

Tanfer, Koray, and Lisa A. Cubbins. 1992. "Coital Frequency Among Single Women: Normative Constraints and Situational Opportunities." *Journal of Sex Research* 29 (2): 221–50.

Tannen, Deborah. 1990. *You Just Don't Understand*. New York: Morrow.

Targ, Dena B., and Mary Brintnall-Peterson. 2001. "Grandparents Raising Grandchildren." *Journal of Family Issues* 22 (5): 579–93.

Tatara, Toshio, and Lisa Blumerman. 1996. *Summaries of the Statistical Data on Elder Abuse in Domestic Settings: An Exploratory Study of State Statistics for FY 93 and FY 94*. Washington, DC: National Center on Elder Abuse.

Tatara, Toshio, and Lisa M. Kuzmeskus with Edward Duckhorn. 1997. *Trends in Elder Abuse in Domestic Settings*. Elder Abuse Information Series No. 2. Washington DC: National Center on Elder Abuse.

Tavris, Carol. 1992. *The Mismeasure of Woman*. New York: Simon & Schuster.

Taylor, Robert J., Linda M. Chatters, M. Belinda Tucker, and Edith Lewis. 1990. "Developments in Research on Black Families: A Decade Review." *Journal of Marriage and Family* 52: 993–1014.

———. 1991. "Developments in Research on Black Families: A Decade Review." Pp. 274–96 in *Contemporary Families Looking Forward, Looking Back*, edited by Alan Booth. Minneapolis: National Council on Family Relations.

Taylor, Ronald L. 1997a. "Who's Parenting? Trends and Patterns." Pp. 68–91 in *Contemporary Parenting: Challenges and Issues*, edited by Terry Arendell. Thousand Oaks, CA: Sage.

———. 1997b. *Minority Families in the United States: A Multicultural Perspective*, 2nd ed. Englewood Cliffs, NJ: Prentice Hall.

———. 2000. "Diversity Among African American Families." Pp. 232–51 in *Handbook of Family Diversity*, edited by David H. Demo, Katherine R. Allen, and Mark A. Fine. New York: Oxford.

———. 2002a. "Black American Families." Pp. 19-47 in *Minority Families In the United State: A Multicultural Perspectives*, 3rd ed., edited by Ronald L. Taylor. Upper Saddle River NJ: Prentice-Hall.

———. 2002b. "Minority Families and Social Change." Pp. 252–300 in *Minority Families in the United States: A Multicultural Perspective*, 3rd ed. Upper Saddle River NJ: Prentice-Hall.

———. 2002c. *Minority Families in the United States: A Multicultural Perspective*, 3rd ed. Upper Saddle River NJ: Prentice Hall.

———. 2003. "Diversity within African American Families." Pp. 365–388 in *Family in Transition*, 12th ed., edited by Arlene S. and Jerome H. Skolnick. Boston: Allyn and Bacon.

Taylor, Ronald L., M. Belinda Tucker, and C. Mitchell-Kernan. 1999. "Ethnic Variations in Perceptions of Men's Provider Role." *Psychology of Women Quarterly* 23: 741–761.

Teachman, Jay. 2003. "Premarital Sex, Premarital Cohabitation, and the Risk of Subsequent Marital Dissolution among Women." *Journal of Marriage and the Family* 65: 444–455.

Teachman, Jay D. 1991. "Who Pays? Receipt of Child Support in the United States." *Journal of Marriage and Family* 53 (3): 759–72.

———. 2000. "Diversity of Family Structure: Economic and Social Influences." Pp. 32–58 in *Handbook of Family Diversity*, edited by David H. Demo, Katherine R. Allen, and Mark A. Fine. New York: Oxford.

———. 2002. "Childhood Living Arrangements and the Intergenerational Transmission of Divorce." *Journal of Marriage and the Family* 64: 717–729.

———. 2003. "Premarital Sex, Premarital Cohabitation, and the Risk of Subsequent Marital Dissolution Among Women." *Journal of Marriage and Family* 65 (2): 444–455.

———. 2004. "The Childhood Living Arrangements of Children and the Characteristics of Their Marriages." *Journal of Family Issues* 25 (1): 86–111.

Teachman, Jay D., and Kathleen Paasch. 1993. "The Economics of Parenting Apart." Pp. 61-86 in *Nonresidential Parenting: New Vistas in Family Living*, edited by Charlene E. Depner and James H. Bray. Newbury Park CA: Sage.

Teachman, Jay D., Lucky M. Tedrow, and Kyle D. Crowder. 2000. "The Changing Demography of America's Families." *Journal of Marriage and Family* 62 (4): 1234–1246.

Tepperman, Lorne, and Susannah J. Wilson (Eds.). 1993. *Next of Kin: An International Reader on Changing Families*. New York: Prentice Hall.

Terry, Elizabeth, and Jennifer Manlove. 2004. "Trends in Sexual Activity and Contraceptive Use among Teens." Washington DC: ChildTrends. www.childtrends.org.

Teti, Douglas M., and Michael Lamb. 1989. "Socioeconomic and Marital Outcomes of Adolescent Marriage, Adolescent Childbirth, and Their Co-occurrence." *Journal of Marriage and Family* 51: 203–12.

"The Divorce Dilemma." 1996. *U.S. News & World Report.* Sept. 30: 58–62.

"The Quest Is On for Male Version of The 'Pill.'" *Omaha World-Herald* (AP). Apr. 25.

"The Self-fulfilling Prophecy or Pygmalion Effect." 2004. Accel-Team.com. http://www.accel-team.com/pygmalion/prophecy_01.html

Thibaut, John W., and Harold H. Kelley. 1959. *The Social Psychology of Groups.* New York: Wiley.

"Third of New HIV Cases Acquired Heterosexually." 2004. *Omaha World-Herald.* Feb. 20.

Thomas, Amanda, and Rex Forehand. 1993. "The Role of Paternal Variables in Divorced and Married Families." *American Journal of Orthopsychiatry* 63 (1): 154–68.

Thompson, Anne, and Niall Bolger. 1999. "Emotional Transmission in Couples Under Stress." *Journal of Marriage and Family* 61 (1): 38–48.

Thompson, Linda. 1991. "Family Work: Women's Sense of Fairness." *Journal of Family Issues* 12 (2): 181–96.

Thompson, Linda, and Alexis J. Walker. 1991. "Gender in Families." Pp. 76–102 in *Contemporary Families: Looking Forward, Looking Back,* edited by Alan Booth. Minneapolis: National Council on Family Relations.

Thompson, Michael, and Dan Kindlon. 1999. *Raising Cain: Protecting the Emotional Life of Boys.* New York: Ballantine.

Thomson, Elizabeth, and Ugo Colella. 1992. "Cohabitation and Marital Stability: Quality or Commitment?" *Journal of Marriage and the Family* 54 (2): 368–78.

Thomson, Elizabeth, Jane Mosley, Thomas L. Hanson, and Sara S. McLanahan. 2001. "Remarriage, Cohabitation, and Changes in Mothering Behavior." *Journal of Marriage and Family* 63 (2): 370–380.

Thorne, Barrie. 1992. "Girls and Boys Together . . . But Mostly Apart: Gender Arrangements in Elementary School." Pp. 108–23 in *Men's Lives,* 2nd ed., edited by Michael S. Kimmel and Michael A. Messner. New York: Macmillan.

Thornton, Arland, and Deborah Freedman. 1983. *The Changing American Family.* Population Bulletin 38. Washington, DC: Population Reference Bureau.

Thornton, Arland, and Linda Young-DeMarco. 2001. "Four Decades of Trends in Attitudes Toward Family Issues in the United States: The 1960s Through the 1990s." *Journal of Marriage and Family* 63: 1009–37.

Throsby, Karen, and Rosalind Gill. 2004. "'It's Different for Men': Masculinity and IVF." *Men and Masculinity* 6: 330-348.

Thurman, Judith. 1982. "The Basics: Chodorow's Theory of Gender." MS. (Sept.): 35–36.

Tichenor, Veronica Jaris. 1999. "Status and Income as Gendered Resources: The Case of Marital Power." *Journal of Marriage and Family* 61: 638–50.

Tiger, Lionel. 1969. *Men in Groups.* New York: Vintage.

Tjaden, Patricia, and Nancy Thoennes. 1998. *Prevalence, Incidence, and Consequences of Violence Against Women: Findings from the National Violence Against Women Survey.* November. Washington, DC: National Institute of Justice/Centers for Disease Control and Prevention.

———. 1999. *Extent, Nature, and Consequences of Intimate Partner Violence: Findings from the National Violence Against Women Survey.* Washington, DC: National Institute of Justice/ Centers for Disease Control and Prevention.

———. 2000. "Prevalence and Consequences of Male-to-Female and Female-to-Male Intimate Partner Violence as Measured by the National Violence Against Women Survey." *Violence Against Women* 6: 142–61.

Toledo, Sylvie de, and Doborah Edler Brown. 1995. *Grandparents as Parents: A Survival Guide for Raising a Second Family.* New York: Guilford.

Tolstoy, Leo. 1886. *Anna Karenina.* New York: Crowell.

Tonelli, Bill. 2004. "Thriller Draws on Oppression of Italians in Wartime U.S." *New York Times.* Aug. 2.

Toohey, Bill, and Mary Toohey. 2001. *The Average Family's Guide to Financial Freedom: How You Can Save a Small Fortune on a Modest Income.* New York: Wiley.

Toppo, Greg. 2003. "Troubling Days at U.S. Schools." *USA Today.* Oct. 21.

Torquati, Julia C. 2002. "Personal and Social Resources as Predictors of Parenting in Homeless Families." *Journal of Family Issues* 23 (4): 463–485.

Torr, James D., and Karin Swisher. 1999. *Violence Against Women.* San Diego, CA: Greenhaven.

Torres, Zenia. 1997. "Interracial Dating." Unpublished student paper.

Toth, J. 1997. *Orphans of the Living.* New York: Simon and Schuster.

Tough, Suzanne E., Christine Newburn-Cook, David M. Johnston, Lawrence W. Swenson, Sara Rose, and Jacques Belik. 2002. "Delayed Childbearing and Its Impact On Population Rate Changes in Lower Birth Weight, Multiple Birth, and Preterm Delivery." *Pediatrics* 109: 399–403.

Townsend, Aloen L., and Melissa M. Franks. 1997. "Quality of the Relationship Between Elderly Spouses: Influence on Spouse Caregivers' Subjective Effectiveness." *Family Relations* 46 (1): 33–39.

"Tracing Jewish History Through Genes." 2003. *Native New Yorker.* May 16.

Treas, Judith. 1995. *Older Americans in the 1990s and Beyond.* Population Bulletin 50 (2). Washington, DC: Population Reference Bureau.

———. 2004. "Sex and Family: Changes and Challenges." Pp. 397–415 in *The Blackwell Companion to the Sociology of the Family,* edited by Jacqueline Scott, Judith Treas, and Martin Richards. Malden MA: Blackwell.

Treas, Judith, and Deirdre Giesen. 2000. "Sexual Infidelity Among Married and Cohabiting Americans." *Journal of Marriage and Family* 62 (1): 48–60.

Trent, Katherine, and Scott J. South. 2003. "Spousal Alternatives and Marital Relations." *Journal of Family Issues* 24 (6): 787–810.

Troiden, Richard R. 1988. *Gay and Lesbian Identity: A Sociological Analysis.* New York: General Hall.

Troll, Lillian E. 1985. "The Contingencies of Grandparenting." Pp. 135–50 in *Grandparenthood,* edited by Vern L. Bengston and Joan F. Robertson. Newbury Park, CA: Sage.

Troll, Lillian E., Sheila J. Miller, and Robert C. Atchley. 1979. *Families in Later Life*. Belmont, CA: Wadsworth.

Trost, Jan. 1997. "Step-Family Variations." Pp. 71–84 in *Step-Families: History, Research, and Policy*, edited by Irene Levin and Marvin B. Sussman. New York: Haworth.

Troxel v. Granville. 2000. 530 U.S. 57.

Tsang, Laura Lo Wa, Carol D. H. Harvey, Karen A. Duncan, and Reena Sommer. 2003. "The Effects of Children, Dual Earner Status, Sex Role Traditionalism, and Marital Structure on Marital Happiness over Time." *Journal of Family and Economic Issues* 24: 5–26.

Tubbs, Carolyn Y., and Pauline Boss. 2000. "Dealing with Ambiguous Loss." *Family Relations* 49 (3): 285–86.

Tucker, Corinna J., Susan M. McHale, and Ann C. Crouter. 2003. "Conflict Resolution: Links with Adolescents' Family Relationships and Individual Well-Being." *Journal of Family Issues* 24 (6): 715–736.

Tucker, Judith E., Ed. 1993. *Arab Women: Old Boundaries, New Frontiers*. Bloomington: Indiana University Press.

Tucker, M. Belinda. 2000. "Marital Values and Expectations in Context: Results from a 21-City Survey." Pp. 166–87 in *The Ties That Bind: Perspectives on Cohabitation and Marriage*, edited by Linda J. Waite. New York: Aldine de Gruyter.

Tuller, David. 2001. "Adoption Medicine Brings New Parents Answers and Advice." *New York Times*. Sept. 4.

Turnbull, A., and H. Turnbull. 1997. *Families, Professionals, and Exceptionality: A Special Partnership*, 3rd ed. Upper Saddle River, NJ: Merrill.

Turley, Riuth N. Lopez. 2003. "Are Children of Young Mothers Disadvantaged Because of Their Mother's Age or Family Background?" *Child Development* 74: 465–474.

Turner, Josephine. 2001. *Show Me The Money: Lessons 1 Through 5*. University of Florida Extension: Institute of Food and Agricultural Sciences. http://edis.ifas.ufl.edu

Turner, Ralph H. 1976. "The Real Self: From Institution to Impulse." *American Journal of Sociology* 81: 989–1016.

Turow, Joseph, and Andrea L. Kavanaugh. 2002. *The Wired Homestead: An MIT Press Sourcebook on the Internet and the Family*. Boston: MIT Press.

Turrell, Susan C. 2000. "A Descriptive Analysis of Same-Sex Relationship Violence for A Diverse Sample." *Journal of Family Violence* 15: 281–293.

Twenge, Jean M. 1997a. "Attitudes Toward Women, 1970–1995: A Meta-Analysis." *Psychology of Women Quarterly* 21 (1): 35–51.

———. 1997b. "Mrs. His Name': Women's Preferences for Married Names." *Psychology of Women Quarterly* 21 (3): 417–30.

Twenge, Jean.M., W. Keith Campbell, and Craig Foster. 2003. "Parenthood and Marital Satisfaction: A Meta-Analytic Review." *Journal of Marriage and the Family* 65: 574–583.

"Twice As Nice: No Longer Merely a Quick Visit to the City Hall, the Second Wedding Is Getting to Be As Extravagant As the First." *Time*. June 19: 53.

Two Brides. 2004. Retrieved 3/29/04 from http://www.twobrides.com

Tyre, Peg. 2004. "A New Generation Gap." *Newsweek*. Jan. 19. Pp. 68–71.

Tyre, Peg, and Daniel McGinn. 2003. "She Works, He Doesn't." *Newsweek*. May 12. Pp. 45-52.

Uchitelle, Louis. 1998a. "Even the Rich Can Buffer from Income Inequality." *New York Times*. Nov. 15.

———. 1998b. "Downsizing Comes Back, But the Outcry Is Muted." *New York Times*. Dec. 7.

———. 2001. "Unemployment Jumps to 5.4%, a 5-year High." *New York Times*. Nov. 3.

———. 2002. "Job Track or 'Mommy Track'? Some do Both in Phases." *New York Times*. July 5.

Udry, J. Richard. 1974. *The Social Context of Marriage*, 3rd ed. Philadelphia: Lippincott.

———. 1994. "The Nature of Gender." *Demography* 31 (4): 561–73.

———. 2000. "The Biological Limits of Gender Construction." *American Sociological Review* 65: 443–57.

———. 2001. "Feminist Critics Uncover Determinism, Positivism, and Antiquated Theory." *American Sociological Review* 66: 611–18.

"UF Study: Sibling Violence Leads to Battering in College Dating." *UF News*. Gainesville: University of Florida.

Uhlenberg, Peter. 1996. "Mortality Decline in the Twentieth Century and Supply of Kin Over the Life Course." *The Gerontologist* 36: 681–85.

Uhlenberg, Peter, and Bradley G. Hammill. 1998. "Frequency of Grandparent Contact with Grandchild Sets: Six Factors That Make a Difference." *The Gerontologist* 38 (3): 276–86.

Umberson, Debra, Kristin Anderson, Jennifer Glick, and Adam Shapiro. 1998. "Domestic Violence, Personal Control, and Gender." *Journal of Marriage and Family* 60 (2): 442–52.

"United Nations Drops Gay Civil Rights." 2004. *365Gay.com Newscenter Staff*. March 29. Retrieved 3/29/04 from http://www.sodomylaws.org/world/wonews023.htm>

Updegraff, Kimberly, Susan McHale, Ann Crouter, and Kristina Kupanoff. 2001. "Parents' Involvement in Adolescents' Peer Relationships: A Comparison of Mothers' and Fathers' Roles." *Journal of Marriage and Family* 63 (3): 655–68.

U.S. Administration on Aging. 1998. *The National Elder Abuse Incidence Study: Final Report*. Sept. Washington, DC: U.S. Administration on Aging. www.aoa.dhhs.gov/abuse/report.

———. 2003. *A Profile of Older Americans: 2003*. http://www.aoa.gov/prof/Statistics. Retrieved 10/15/04.

U.S. Bureau of Labor Statistics. 2002a. *Work at Home in 2001*. USDL 02-107. Washington DC: U.S. Bureau of Labor Statistics. Mar. 1.

———. 2002b. *Workers on Flex and Shift Schedules in 2001*. USDL 02-225. Washington DC: U.S. Bureau of Labor Statistics. Apr. 18.

———. 2003a. *Highlights of Women's Earnings in 2002*. Report 972. Washington DC: U.S. Bureau of Labor Statistics. Sept.

———. 2003b. *A Profile of the Working Poor, 2001*. Report 968. June. Washington DC: U.S. Bureau of Labor Statistics.

———. 2003c. *Work Experience of the Population in 2002*. USDL 03-911. Washington DC: U.S. Bureau of Labor Statistics.

———. 2004a. *"Employment Characteristics of Families in 2003.* USDL 04-713. Washington DC: Bureau of Labor Statistics.

———. 2004b. "Time Use Survey— First Results Announced by BLS." Washington DC: U.S. Bureau of Labor Statistics.

———. 2004c. *Usual Weekly Earnings of Wage and Salary Workers: Second Quarter 2004.* Washington DC: U.S. Bureau of Labor Statistics. July 20.

U.S. Census Bureau. 1988. *Households, Families, Marital Status, and Living Arrangements, March 1988: Advance Report.* Current Population Reports, Series P–20, No. 432. Washington, DC: U.S. Government Printing Office.

———. 1989a. *Statistical Abstract of the United States,* 109th ed. Washington, DC: U.S. Government Printing Office.

———. 1989b. *Fertility of American Women: June 1988.* Current Population Reports, Population Characteristics Series P–20, No. 436. Issued May 1989.

———. 1994a. *Statistical Abstract of the United States.* Washington, DC: U.S. Government Printing Office.

———. 1994b. "How We're Changing: Demographic State of the Nation 1995." *Current Population Reports,* Special Studies Series P–23, No. 188. Washington, DC: U.S. Government Printing Office.

———. 1995. *Statistical Abstract of the United States.* Washington, DC: U.S. Government Printing Office.

———. 1998. *Statistical Abstract of the United States, 1998.* Washington, DC: U.S. Government Printing Office.

———. 1999. *Statistical Abstract of the United States.* Washington, DC: U.S. Government Printing Office.

———. 2000. *Statistical Abstract of the United States,* 120th ed. Washington, DC: Government Printing Office. www.census.gov/stat_abstract.

———. 2001. *Technical Note on Same-Sex Unmarried Partner Data from the 1990 and 2000 Censuses.* June 29. www.census.gov/population/www/cen2000/samesex/html.

———. 2002. *Statistical Abstract of the United States: 2002.* Washington DC: U.S. Census Bureau.

———. 2003a. *Statistical Abstract of the United States; 2003.* Washington, D.C: U.S. Census Bureau.

———. 2003b. "U.S. Census Bureau Guidance on the Presentation and Comparison of Race and Hispanic Origin Data." Washington DC: U.S. Census Bureau. June 12.

———. 2003c. "Income in the United States: 2002." Current Population Reports # P60-221.

———. 2004. "Facts for Features. Special Edition: National Adoption Month November." Press release CB04-FFSE. 12. Sept. 20.

U.S. Centers for Disease Control and Prevention. 2001a. "HIV/AIDS and U.S. Women Who Have Sex with Women (WSW)." Fact Sheet. www.cdc.gov/hivpubs/facts/wsw.htm.

———. 2001b. *HIV/AIDS Surveillance Report* 12 (2). Aug. 10. www.cdc.gov/hiv/statshasr1202/htm.

———. 2001c. *Tracking the Hidden Epidemics: Trends in STDs in the United States: 2000.* Atlanta: U.S. Centers for Disease Control and Prevention. www.cdc.gov.

———. 2002. "Cytomegalovirus (CMV) Infection." Atlanta GA: U.S. Centers for Disease Control and Prevention. www.cdc.gov.

———. 2003 "Male Latex Condoms and Sexually Transmitted Diseases." Atlanta GA: U.S. Centers for Disease Control and Prevention. Jan. 23.

———. 2004a. *Bacterial Vaginosis Fact Sheet.* Atlanta GA: U.S.Centers for Disease Control and Prevention. May 2004.

———. 2004b. *Chlamydia Fact Sheet.* Atlanta GA: U.S. Centers for Disease Control and Prevention. May 2004.

———. 2004c. *Genital Herpes Fact Sheet.* Atlanta GA: U.S. Centers for Disease Control and Prevention. May 2004.

———. 2004d. *Genital HPV Infection Fact Sheet.* Atlanta GA: U.S. Centers for Disease Control and Prevention. May 2004.

———. 2004e. *Gonorrhea Fact Sheet.* Atlanta GA: U.S. Centers for Disease Control and Prevention. May 2004.

———. 2004f. *Hepatitis B Fact Sheet.* Atlanta GA: U.S. Centers for Disease Control and Prevention. May 2004.

———. 2004g. *HIV/AIDS Surveillance Report.* V. 15. Atlanta GA: U.S. Centers for Disease Control and Prevention.

———. 2004h. *HIV/AIDS Surveillance Supplementary Report* 10(1). Atlanta GA: U.S. Centers for Disease Control and Prevention.

———. 2004i. *Pelvic Inflammatory Disease Fact Sheet.* Atlanta GA: Centers for Disease Control and Prevention. May 2004.

———. 2004j. *STD Surveillance 2003.* Atlanta GA: U.S. Centers for Disease Control and Prevention. Nov. 15.

———. 2004k. *Syphilis Fact Sheet.* Atlanta GA: U.S. Centers for Disease Control and Prevention. May 2004.

———. 2004l. "Trends in Reportable Sexually Transmitted Diseases in the United States, 2003." Press release. Atlanta GA: U.S. Centers for Disease Control and Prevention. Nov. 15.

———. 2004m. *Trichomoniasis Fact Sheet.* Atlanta GA: U.S. Centers for Disease Control and Prevention. May 2004.

———. 2004n. "Youth Risk Behavior Surveillance: United States, 2003." Surveillance Summaries. *Morbidity and Mortality Weekly Report* 53: No. SS-2. May 21.

U.S. Children's Bureau. 2000. *Fact Sheet: Child Maltreatment 1999.* www.acf.dhhs.gov/programs/cb/publications/cm99.

U.S. Department of Health and Human Services. 1997. "HHS Invests in America's Children Fact Sheet." DHHS Publication No. 97–0917. Washington, DC: U.S. Government Printing Office.

———. 2003. *Child Maltreatment 2001.* Washington DC: Administration for Children, Youth, and Families.

U.S. Department of Health, Education, and Welfare. 1975. *Child Abuse and Neglect: Volume I, An Overview of the Problem.* Publication #(OHD) 75–30073. Washington, DC: U.S. Government Printing Office.

U.S. Department of Health, Education, and Welfare, National Institute of Mental Health. 1978. *Yours, Mine, and Ours: Tips for Stepparents.* Washington, DC: U.S. Government Printing Office.

U.S. Department of Justice. 1996. "Child Victimizers: Violent Offender and Their Victims—Executive Summary." Bureau of Justice Statistics. March. No. NCJ–158625. Washington, DC: U.S. Government Printing Office. www.ojp.usdoj.gov.

———. 1998a. "Violence by Intimates: Analysis of Data on Crimes by Current or Former Spouses, Boyfriends, and Girlfriends." Bureau of Justice Statistics Selected Findings: Domestic Violence. March. No. NCJ–167237. Washington, DC. U.S. Government Printing Office. www.ojp.usdoj.gov.

———. 1998b. *Stalking and Domestic Violence: The Third Annual Report to Congress Under the Violence Against Women Act.* Washington, DC: Violence Against Women Grants Office.

U.S. Federal Interagency Forum on Child and Family Statistics. 1998. *America's Children: Key National Indicators of Well-Being, 1998.* Washington, DC: Government Printing Office.

———. 2001. *America's Children: Key National Indicators of Wellbeing.* Washington, DC: Government Printing Office.

———. 2003. *America's Children: Key National Indicators of Well-Being 2003.* Washington DC: Federal Interagency Forum on Child and Family Statistics. February.

———. 2004. *America's Children in Brief 2004.* http://childstats.gov.

"U.S. Fertility Rates Higher Among Minorities." 2001. Washington, DC: Population Reference Bureau. www.prb.org/AmeristatTemplate.

"U.S. Fertility Trends: Boom and Bust and Leveling Off." 2001. Washington, DC: Population Reference Bureau. www.prb.org/AmeristatTemplate.

U.S. General Accounting Office. 1997. Letter to The Honorable Henry J. Hyde. Office of the General Counsel. January 31. http://www.frwebgate.access.gpo.gov/cgi-bin/useftp.cgi/

———. 2003. *Women's Earnings: Work Patterns Partially Explain Differences between Men's and Women's Earnings.* GAO-04-35. Washington DC: General Accounting Office. October.

U.S. House of Representatives Select Committee on Aging. 1992. *Insurmountable Barriers: Lack of Bilingual Services at Social Security Administration Offices.* Washington, DC: U.S. Government Printing Office.

U.S. National Cancer Institute. 2003. *Summary Report: Early Reproductive Events and Breast Cancer Workshop."* Bethesda MD: National Cancer Institute. Mar. 23.

U.S. National Center for Chronic Disease Prevention and Health Promotion. 2003. *2001 Assisted Reproductive Technology Success Rates.* Washington DC: Department of Health And Human Services.

U.S. National Center for Education Statistics. 2001. "Fall Staff 1999." Washington DC: U.S. National Center for Education Statistics. http://nces.ed.gov.

———. 2002. "Fall Enrollment in Institutions of Higher Education Surveys and Post-Secondary Educational Data System." 2002. Washington DC: U.S. National Center for Education Statistics. http://nces.ed.gov

———. 2004. "Indicators of School Crime and Safety." Washington DC: U.S. National Center for Educational Statistics. http://nces.ed.gov.

U.S. National Center for Health Statistics. 1990a. "Advance Report of Final Divorce Statistics," 1987. *Monthly Vital Statistics Report* 38 (12), Suppl., Apr. 3.

———. 1990b. "Advance Report of Final Marriage Statistics," 1987. *Monthly Vital Statistics Report* 38 (12), Suppl., Apr. 3.

———. 1998. "Births, Marriages, Divorces, and Deaths for 1997." *Monthly Vital Statistics Report* 46 (12). July 28.

———. 2002. "Trends in Circumcisions among Newborns." Press release. Hyattsville MD: U.S. National Center for Health Statistics. June 21.

———. 2004. "Births, Marriages, Divorces, and Deaths: Provisional Data for March 2003." *National Vital Statistics Reports* 52(22). June 10.

U.S. National Institute of Child Health and Human Development. 1999a. "NICHD Child Care Study Investigators to Report on Child Care Quality: Higher Quality Care Related to Less Problem Behavior." News Release. Jan. 26. www.nichd.nih.gov/new/release/daycar99.

———. 1999b. "Only Small Link Found Between Hours in Child Care and Mother–Child Interaction." News Release. Nov. 7.

www.nichd.nih.gov/new/release/daycar99.

———. 2002. "The NICHD Study of Early Child Care." Bethesda MD: U.S. Institute of Health and Human Development.

U.S. Office of Management and Budget. 1999. *Revisions to the Standards for Classification of Federal Data on Race and Ethnicity.* Apr. 1. Washington, DC: U.S. Census Bureau.

"U.S. Rejects Rights Plan for Women." 2004. *Omaha World-Herald.* Oct. 14.

"U.S. Scraps Study of Teen-Age Sex." 1991. *New York Times.* July 25.

U.S. Senate Special Committee on Aging. 2002. *Long-Term Care Report.* Washington D.C. U.S. Government Printing Office.

———. 2004. *Findings from Committee Hearings of the 107th Congress.* Washington D.C. U.S. Government Printing Office.

U.S. Social Security Administration. 2003. *Some Facts and Figures About Social Security.* Washington, DC: SSA Publication No. 13-11785. www.socialsecurity.gov/policy

U.S. Surgeon General. 2001. *The Surgeon General's Call to Action to Promote Sexual Health and Responsible Sexual Behavior.* Hyattsville, MD: U.S. Surgeon General. July 9.

Uttal, Lynet. 1999. "Using Kin for Child Care." *Journal of Marriage and Family* 61: 845–57.

———. 2004. "Racial Safety and Cultural Maintenance: The Child Care Concerns of Employed Mothers of Color." Pp. 295–304 in *Race, Class, and Gender,* 5th ed., edited by Margaret L. Andersen and Patricia Hill Collins. Belmont CA: Wadsworth.

Utz, Rebecca L., Erin B. Reidy, Deborah Carr, Randolph Nesse, and Camille Wortman. 2004. "The Daily Consequences of Widowhood." *Journal of Family Issues* 25 (5): 683–712.

Valiente, Carlos, Richard A. Fabes, Nancy Eisenberg, and Tracy L. Spinrad. 2004. "The Relations of Parental Expressivity and Support to Children's Coping with Daily Stress." *Journal of Family Psychology* 18 (1): 97–107.

Van den Haag, Ernest. 1974. "Love or Marriage." Pp. 134–42 in *The Family: Its Structures and Functions,* 2nd ed., edited by Rose Laub Coser. New York: St. Martin's.

Van Pelt, Nancy L. 1985. *How to Turn Minuses into Pluses: Tips for Working Moms, Single Parents, and Stepparents.* Washington, DC: Review and Herald, Better Living Series.

Vance, Lisa M. 1998. "Reaction Paper, Chapter 13." Unpublished student paper.

Vandell, Deborah L., Kathleen McCarthy, Margaret T. Owen, Cathryn Booth, and Alison Clarke-Stewart. 2003. "Variations in Child Care by Grandparents During the First Three Years." *Journal of Marriage and Family* 65 (2): 375–381.

Vander Ven, Thomas M., Francis T. Cullen, Mark A. Carrozza, and John Paul Wright. 2001. "Home Alone: The Impact of Maternal Employment on Delinquency." *Social Problems* 48: 236–57.

Vanderkam, Laura. 2003. "New Umbilical Cords Tie Young Adults to Parents." *New York Times.* Aug. 26.

VanLaningham, Jody, David R. Johnson, and Paul Amato. 2001. "Marital Happiness, Marital Duration, and the U-Shaped Curve: Evidence from a Five-Wave Panel Study." *Social Forces* 79: 1313–41.

VanLear, C. Arthur. 1992. "Marital Communication Across the Generations: Learning and Rebellion, Continuity and Change." *Journal of Social and Personal Relationships* 9: 103–23.

Vannoy, Dana. 1991. "Social Differentiation, Contemporary Marriage, and Human Development." *Journal of Family Issues* 12: 251–67.

Vartanian, Thomas P., and Justine M. McNamara. 2002. "Older Women in Poverty: The Impact of Midlife Factors." *Journal of Marriage and Family* 64 (2): 532–548.

Vaughan, Diane. 1986. *Uncoupling: Turning Points in Intimate Relationships.* New York: Oxford University Press.

V. C. v. M.J.B. 2000. 163 NJ 2000.

Veevers, Jean E. 1980. *Childless by Choice.* Toronto: Butterworths.

Vega, William A. 1990. "Hispanic Families in the 1980s: A Decade of Research." *Journal of Marriage and Family* 52 (4): 1015–24.

———. 1995. "The Study of Latino Families: A Point of Departure." Pp.

3–17 in *Understanding Latino Families: Scholarship, Policy, and Practice*, edited by Ruth E. Zambrana. Thousand Oaks, CA: Sage.

"Venous Thromboembolism Risk Is Sharply Elevated for Users of Combined Pill." *Perspectives On Sexual and Reproductive Health* 36: 217.

Ventura, Stephanie J., and Christine A. Bachrach. 2000. *Nonmarital Childbearing in the United States, 1940–99.* National Vital Statistics Reports 48 (16). Hyattsville, MD: National Center for Health Statistics. Oct. 18.

Ventura, Stephanie J., Brady E. Hamilton, and Paul D. Sutton. 2003. "Revised Birth and Fertility Rates for the United States, 2000 and 2001." *National Vital Statistics Report* 51(4). Hyattsville MD: National Center for Health Statistics. Feb. 6.

Ventura, Stephanie J., Joyce A. Martin, Sally C. Curtin, and Brady E. Hamilton. 2001. *Births: Final Data for 1999.* National Vital Statistics Report 49 (1). Hyattsville, MD: National Center for Health Statistics. Apr. 17.

Ventura, Stephanie J., Joyce A. Martin, Sally C. Curtin, and T. J. Mathews. 1998. "Report of Final Natality Statistics, 1996." *Monthly Vital Statistics Report* 46 (11), Supp. Hyattsville, MD: National Center for Health Statistics.

Ventura, Stephanie J., Joyce A. Martin, Sally C. Curtin, Fay Menacker, and Brady E. Hamilton. 2001. *Births: Final Data for 1999.* National Vital Statistics Report 49 (1). Hyattsville, MD: National Center for Health Statistics. Apr. 17.

Ventura, Stephanie J., T. J. Mathews, and Brady E. Hamilton. 2001. *Births to Teenagers in the United States, 1940–2000.* National Vital Statistics Report 49 (10). Hyattsville, MD: National Center for Health Statistics. Sept. 25.

"Verbal and IQ Scores Improve As Premature Infants Grow, Yale Researchers Report." 2003. Yale News Release. Feb. 11. www.yale.edu/opa.

"Views on Homosexuality and Gay Marriage." 2003. NYT/CBS News Poll. *New York Times.* Dec. 21.

Vig, Pooja. 2003. "Surgeons in China Do First Whole Ovary Transplant." Reuters. Apr. 11.

Villarosa, Linda. 2001. "Women Now Look Beyond H.I.V. to Children and Grandchildren." *New York Times.* Aug. 7.

———. 2002a. "Making An Appointment with The Stork." *New York Times.* June 23.

———. 2002b. "Once-Invisible Sperm Donors Get to Meet The Family." *New York Times.* May 21.

———. 2002c. "Rescued H.I.V. Babies Face New Problems as Teenagers." *New York Times* Mar. 5.

———. 2003. "Raising Awareness about AIDS and the Aging." *New York Times.* July 8.

Visher, Emily B., and John S. Visher. 1979. *Stepfamilies: A Guide to Working with Stepparents and Stepchildren.* New York: Brunner/Mazel.

———. 1996. *Therapy with Stepfamilies.* New York: Brunner/Mazel.

Voydanoff, Patricia. 2002. "Linkages Between the Work-Family Interface and Work, Family and Individual Outcomes." *Journal of Family Issues* 23 (1): 138–164.

Wadyka, Sally. 2004. "For Women Worried about Fertility, Egg Bank Is A New Option." *New York Times.* Sept. 21.

Wagner, David G., and Joseph Berger. 1997. "Gender and Interpersonal Task Behaviors: Status Expectation Accounts." *Sociological Perspectives* 40 (1): 1–32.

Wagner, David M. 1998. "Divorce Reform: New Directions." *Current.* Feb. 1: 7–10.

Wagner-Raphael, Lynne I., David Wyatt Seal, and Anke A. Ehrhardt. 2001. "Close Emotional Relationships with Women Versus Men." *Journal of Men's Studies* 9 (2): 243–56.

Waite, Linda J. 1995. "Does Marriage Matter?" *Demography* 32 (4): 483–507.

———. 2001. "The Family as Social Organization: Key Ideas for the Twenty-First Century." *Contemporary Sociology* 29: 463–499.

Waite, Linda J., Don Browning, William J. Doherty, Maggie Gallagher, Ye Luo, and Scott M. Stanley. 2002. "Does Divorce Make People Happy? Findings from A Study of Unhappy Marriages." New York: Institute for American Values.

Waite, Linda J., and Maggie Gallagher. 2000. *The Case for Marriage: Why Married People Are Happier, Healthier, and Better Off Financially.* New York: Doubleday.

Waite, Linda J., and Kara Joyner. 2001. "Emotional and Physical Satisfaction with Sex In Married, Cohabiting, and Dating Sexual Unions: Do Men and Women Differ?" Pp. 239–269 in *Sex, Love, and Health in America,* edited by Edward O. Laumann and Robert T. Michael. Chicago: University of Chicago.

Waldfogel, Jane. 1997. "The Effect of Children on Women's Wages." *American Sociological Review* 62: 209–17.

———. 1998. "Understanding the 'Family Gap' in Pay for Women With Children." *Journal of Economic Perspectives* 12: 137–56.

———. 2001. "International Policies Toward Parental Leave and Child Care." *The Future of Children* 11: 99–111.

Walker, Alexis J. 2001. "Refracted Knowledge: Viewing Families Through the Prism of Social Science." Pp. 52–65 in *Understanding Families in the New Millennium: A Decade in Review,* edited by Robert M. Milardo. Lawrence, KS: National Council on Family Relations.

Walker, Alexis J., Margaret Manoogian-O'Dell, Lori A. McGraw, and Diana L. G. White. (Eds.). 2001. *Families in Later Life: Connections and Transitions.* Thousand Oaks, CA: Pine Forge.

Walker, Karen E., and Frank F. Furstenberg, Jr. 1994. "Neighborhood Settings and Parenting Strategies." Paper presented at the annual meeting of the American Sociological Association. Los Angeles. August.

Walker, Lenore E. 1988. "The Battered Woman Syndrome." Pp. 139–48 in *Family Abuse and Its Consequences: New Directions in Research,* edited by Gerald T. Hotaling, David Finkelhor, John T. Kirkpatrick, and Murray A. Straus. Newbury Park, CA: Sage.

Walker, Lou Ann. 1985. "When a Parent Is Disabled." *New York Times.* June 20.

Walker, Susan K., and David A. Riley. 2001. "Involvement of the Personal Social Network as a Factor in Parent Education Effectiveness." 2001. *Family Relations* 50 (2): 186–93.

Wallace, Harvey, ed. 2004. *Family Violence: Legal, Medical, and Social Perspectives,* 4th ed. Boston: Allyn and Bacon.

Wallace, Pamela M., and Ian H. Gotlib. 1990. "Marital Adjustment During the Transition to Parenthood: Stability and Predictors of Change." *Journal of Marriage and Family* 52: 21–29.

Waller, Willard. 1937. "The Rating and Dating Complex." *American Sociological Review* 2: 727–34.

———. 1951. *The Family: A Dynamic Interpretation.* New York: Dryden. (Revised by Reuben Hill.)

Wallerstein, Judith S. 1998. "Children of Divorce: A Society in Search of Policy." Pp. 66–94 in *All Our Families: New Policies for a New Century,* edited by Mary Ann Mason, Arlene Skolnick, and Stephen D. Sugarman. New York: Oxford University Press.

Wallerstein, Judith S., and Sandra Blakeslee. 1989. *Second Chances: Men, Women, and Children a Decade After Divorce.* New York: Ticknor & Fields.

———. 1995. *The Good Marriage: How and Why Love Lasts.* Boston: Houghton Mifflin.

Wallerstein, Judith S., and Joan Kelly. 1980. *Surviving the Break-Up: How Children Actually Cope with Divorce.* New York: Basic.

Wallerstein, Judith S., and Julia Lewis. 1998. "The Long-Term Impact of Divorce on Children: A First Report from a 25-Year Study." *Family and Conciliation Courts Review* 36 (3): 368–79.

Wallerstein, Judith S., Julia M. Lewis, and Sandra Blakeslee. 2000. *The Unexpected Legacy of Divorce: A 25 Year Landmark Study.* New York: Hyperion.

Wallis, Claudia. 2004. "The Case for Staying Home." *Time.* March 22: 51–59.

Wallis, Rev. Jim. 1999. "A Look at Welfare Reform." *San Francisco Chronicle.* Mar. 2: A19.

Walsh, Froma. 2002a. "A Family Resilience Framework: Innovative Practice Applications." *Family Relations* 51 (2): 130-137.

———. 2002b. "Bouncing Forward: Resilience in the Aftermath of September 11." *Family Process* 41 (1): 34–36.

———. 2004. "Family Resilience: A Framework for Clinical Practice." *Family Process* 42 (1): 1–18.

Walsh, Wendy. 2002. "Spankers and Nonspankers: Where They Get Information on Spanking." *Family Relations* 51 (1): 81-88.

Walster, Elaine H., and G. William Walster. 1978. *A New Look at Love.* Reading, MA: Addison-Wesley.

Walter, Carolyn Ambler. 1986. *The Timing of Motherhood.* Lexington, MA: Heath.

Ward, J. 1998. "Specialized Foster Care: One Approach to Retaining Good Foster Homes." http://www.westworld.com/~barbara.

Ward, Margaret. 1997. "Family Paradigms and Older-Child Adoption: A Proposal for Matching Parents' Strengths to Children's Needs." *Family Relations* 46 (3): 257–62.

Waring, E. M., B. Schaefer, and R. Fry. 1994. "The Influence of Therapeutic Self-Disclosure on Perceived Marital Intimacy." *Journal of Sex and Marital Therapy* 20 (2): 135–41.

Wark, Linda, and Shilpa Jobalia. 1998. "What Would It Take to Build a Bridge? An Intervention for Stepfamilies." *Journal of Family Psychotherapy* 9 (3): 69–77.

Warren, Chris, and Crescy Cannan. 1997. *Social Action with Children and Families: A Community Approach to Child and Family Welfare.* New York: Routledge.

Warren, Elizabeth, and Amelia Warren Tyagi. 2003. *The Two-Income Trap: Why Middle- Class Mothers and Fathers Are Going Broke.* New York: Basic.

Warren, Gloria. 2003. "A Way Outa' No Way: Grandparents Raising Grandchildren." *Family Focus.* June: F19-F20.

Warshak, Richard. 2000. "Remarriage as a Trigger of Parental Alienation Syndrome." *American Journal of Family Therapy* 28 (3): 229–41.

Waters, Mary C. 1997. "Immigrant Families at Risk: Factors That Undermine Chances of Success." Pp. 79–87 in *Immigration and the Family,* edited by Alan Booth, Ann C. Crouter, and Nancy Landale. Mahwah, NJ: Erlbaum.

Watson, Russell. 1984. "Five Steps to Good Day Care." *Newsweek.* Sept. 10: 21.

Watt, Toni T. 2002. "Marital and cohabiting Relationships of Adult Children of Alcoholics." *Journal of Family Issues* 23 (2): 246–265.

Wax, Amy L. 1998. "Bargaining in the Shadow of the Market: Is There a Future for Egalitarian Marriage?" *Virginia Law Review* 84 (4): 509–36.

Wax, Naomi. 2001. "Not to Worry: Real Men Can Cry." *New York Times.* Oct. 28.

Weaver, Shannon E., Marilyn Coleman, and Lawrence H. Ganong. 2003. "The Sibling Relationship in Young Adulthood." *Journal of Family Issues* 24 (2): 245–263.

Webster, Tia. 2002. "Condom Error Common Among College Men." *Emory Report.* Sept. 30. www.emory.edu.

Weeks, John R. 2002. *Population: An Introduction to Concepts and Issues*, 8th ed. Belmont, CA: Wadsworth.

Weigert, Andrew, and Ross Hastings. 1977. "Identity Loss, Family and Social Change." *American Journal of Sociology* 28: 1171–85.

Weinberg, Daniel H. 2004. "Evidence from Census 2000 about Earnings by Detailed Occupation for Men and Women." *Census 2000 Special Reports* CENSR-15. May.

Weinberg, Martin S., and Colin J. Williams. 1988. "Black Sexuality: A Test of Two Theories." *Journal of Sex Research* 25: 197–218.

Weiner, B. 1986. *An Attribution Theory of Motivation and Emotion.* NY: Springer-Verlag.

Weisberg, D. Kelly. 1993. "The Equality Debate: Equal Treatment Versus Special Treatment." Pp. 121–27 in *Feminist Legal Theory*, edited by D. Kelly Weisberg. Philadelphia: Temple University Press.

Weise, Elizabeth. 2003. "Science Peers Behind the Veil of the Unborn." *USA Today.* Mar. 3.

Weisman, Mary-Lou. 1994. "When Parents Are Not in the Best Interests of the Child." *Atlantic Monthly.* July: 43–63.

Weiss, Rick. 2002. "Multiple Fears about IVF Births: Study: In-Vitro Twins, Triplets Prone to Brain Disorders." *Washington Post.* Feb. 12.

———. 2003a. "400,000 Human Embryos Frozen in U.S." *Washington Post.* May 8.

———. 2003b. "Scientists Produce Human Embryos of Mixed Gender." *Washington Post* July 3.

Weiss, Robert S. 1975. *Marital Separation: Managing After a Marriage Ends.* New York: Basic.

Weitzman, Lenore J. 1981. *The Marriage Contract: Spouses, Lovers, and the Law.* New York: Free Press.

———. 1985. *The Divorce Revolution: The Unexpected Social and Economic Consequences for Women and Children in America.* New York: Free Press.

Wells, Karen C., Jeffery Epstein, Stephen Hinshaw, C. Keith Conners, John Klaric, Howard Abikoff, Ann Abramowitz, L. Eugene Arnold, Glenn Elliott, Laurence Greenhill, Lily Hechtman, Betsy Hoza, Peter Jensen, John March, William Pelham, Linda Pfiffner, Joanne Severe, James Swanson, Benedetto Vitiello, and Tim Wigal. 2000. "Parenting and Family Stress Treatment Outcomes in Attention Deficit Hyperactivity Disorder (ADHD): An Empirical Analysis in the MTA Study." *Journal of Abnormal Child Psychology* 28 (6): 543–59.

Wells, Marolyn, Cheryl Glickauf-Hughes, and Rebecca Jones. 1999. "Codependency: A Grass Roots Construct's Relationship to Shame-Proneness, Low Self-Esteem, and Childhood Parentification." *American Journal of Family Therapy* 27: 63–71.

Wells, Mary S., Mark A. Widmer, and J. Kelly McCoy. 2004. "Grubs and Grasshoppers: Challenge-Based Recreation and the Collective Efficacy of Families with At-Risk Youth." *Family Relations* 53 (3): 326–333.

Wells, Robert V. 1985. *Uncle Sam's Family: Issues in and Perspectives on American Demographic History.* Albany: State University of New York Press.

Wentzel, Jo Ann. 2001. "Foster Kids Really Are Ours." http://www.fosterparents.com.

Werner, Emmy E. 1992. "The Children of Kauai: Resilience and Recovery in Adolescence and Adulthood." *Journal of Adolescent Health* 13: 262–68.

Werner, Emmy E., and Ruth S. Smith. 2001. *Journeys from Childhood to Midlife: Risk, Resiliency, and Recovery.* Ithica, NY: Cornell University Press.

West, Carolyn M. 2003. "'Feminism Is A Black Thing'? Feminist Contributions to Black Family Life." *State of Black America 2003.* Washington DC: National Urban League.

Westberg, Granger E. 1971. *Good Grief: A Constructive Approach to the Problem of Loss.* Philadelphia: Fortress.

Western, Bruce, and Sara McLanahan. 2000. "Fathers Behind Bars: The Impact of Incarceration on Family Formation." Pp. 309–24 in *Families, Crime, and Criminal Justice*, edited by Greer Litton Fox and Michael L. Benson. New York: Elsevier Science.

Wetzstein, Cheryl. 1999. "Researchers Deplore the Dearth of Statistics About Marriage." *Washington Times.* Aug. 31.

"What Do I Need to Know about Getting Married in Canada?" 2004. Gay & Lesbian Advocates & Defenders (GLAD). Retrieved 3/30/04 from http://www.glad.org/marriage/canadianmarriage/

"What Happened to the Wedding Bells? Cohabitation Is On the Rise, New Data from Census Reveals." 2003. *Forecast* 23 (4): 1–4.

"What Is Dignity?" Retrieved 3/29/04 from http://www.dignityusa.org.

"When Elder Care Falls to the Young." 2001. National Public Radio. Aug. 29. http://www.npr.org/programs/morningfeatures.

"Where America Stands." 2004. USA Today/CNN/Gallup Poll. February 24. http://www.keepmedia.com

Whipple, Ellen E., and Cheryl A. Richey. 1997. "Crossing the Line from Physical Discipline to Child Abuse: How Much Is Too Much?" *Child Abuse & Neglect* 21 (5): 431–44.

Whitbeck, Les B., Danny R. Hoyt, and Shirley M. Huck. 1993. "Family Relationship History, Contemporary Parent–Grandparent Relationship Quality, and the Grandparent–Grandchild Relationship." *Journal of Marriage and Family* 55 (4): 1025–35.

Whitchurch, Gail G., and Larry L. Constantine. 1993. "Systems Theory." Pp. 325–52 in *Sourcebook of Family Theories* and Methods, edited by Pauline Boss et al. New York: Plenum.

"White House Distances Itself from Sex-Education Report." 2001. Omaha World-Herald. June 29.

White, Jack E. 1993. "Growing Up in Black and White." Time. May 17: 48–49.

White, James M., and David M. Klein. 2002. Family Theories: Second Edition. Thousand Oaks, CA: Sage.

White, Lynn. 1999. "Contagion in Family Affection: Mothers, Fathers, and Young Adult Children." Journal of Marriage and Family 61 (2): 284–94.

White, Lynn, and Joan G. Gilbreth. 2001. "When Children Have Two Fathers: Effects of Relationships with Stepfathers and Noncustodial Fathers on Adolescent Outcomes." Journal of Marriage and Family 63: 155–67.

White, Lynn, and Stacy J. Rogers. 2000. "Economic Circumstances and Family Outcomes: A Review of the 1990s." Journal of Marriage and Family 62: 1035–51.

White, Lynn K. 1990. "Determinants of Divorce: A Review of Research in the Eighties." Journal of Marriage and Family 52: 904–12.

———. 1994. "Growing Up with Single Parents and Stepparents: Long-Term Effects on Family Solidarity." Journal of Marriage and Family 56 (4): 935–48.

White, Lynn K., and Alan Booth. 1985a. "The Transition to Parenthood and Marital Quality." Journal of Family Issues 6 (4): 435–49.

———. 1985b. "The Quality and Stability of Remarriages: The Role of Stepchildren." American Sociological Review 50: 689–98.

———. 1991. "Divorce Over the Life Course: The Role of Marital Happiness." Journal of Family Issues 12: 5–21.

White, Lynn K., Alan Booth, and John N. Edwards. 1986. "Children and Marital Happiness." Journal of Family Issues 7 (2): 131–47.

White, Lynn K., and Bruce Keith. 1990. "The Effect of Shift Work on the Quality and Stability of Marital Relations." Journal of Marriage and Family 52: 453–62.

White, Lynn K., and Agnes Riedmann. 1992. "When the Brady Bunch Grows Up: Step/Half- and Full-Sibling Rela-

tionships in Adulthood." Journal of Marriage and Family 54 (1): 197–208.

White, Lynn K., and Stacy J. Rogers. 1997. "Strong Support But Uneasy Relationships: Coresidence and Adult Children's Relationships with Their Parents." Journal of Marriage and Family 59 (1): 62–76.

Whitehead, Barbara Dafoe. 1997 [1996]. The Divorce Culture. New York: Knopf.

Whitehead, Barbara Dafoe, and David Popenoe. 2001. Who Wants to Marry a Soul Mate? New Survey Findings on Young Adults' Attitudes About Love and Marriage. Piscataway, NJ: Rutgers University. National Marriage Project. http://marriage.rutgers.edu/TEXTSOOU2001.htm.

Whitman, David. 1997. "Was It Good For Us?" U.S. News & World Report. May 19: 56–64.

Whittaker, Terri. 1995. "Violence, Gender and Elder Abuse: Towards a Feminist Analysis and Practice." Journal of Gender Studies 4 (1): 35–45.

"Who Is Homeless?" 2004. National Coalition for the Homeless, Fact Sheet #3. http://www.nationalhomeless.org/who.html

"Who Needs Doctors? The Boom in Home Testing." 1998. Newsweek. July 20: 14.

"Why Interracial Marriages Are Increasing." 1996. Jet. June 3: 12–15.

Whyte, Martin King. 1990. Dating, Mating, and Marriage. New York: Aldine de Gruyter.

———. (Ed.). 2000. Marriage in America: A Communitarian Perspective. Lanham, MD: Rowman and Littlefield.

Wickrama, K. A. S., Frederick O. Lorenz, Rand D. Conger, and Glen H. Elder. 1997. "Marital Quality and Physical Illness: A Latent Growth Curve Analysis." Journal of Marriage and Family 59 (1): 143–55.

"A Widening Gulf in School . . . Leads More and More to a Girls' Club in College." 2003. Business Week. May 26: 76–77.

Wiederman, Michael W. 1997. "Extramarital Sex: Prevalence and Correlates in a National Survey." Journal of Sex Research 34 (2): 167–174.

Wiederman, Michael W., and Shannon R. Hurst. 1998. "Body Size, Physical Attractiveness, and Body Image

Among Young Adult Women: Relationships to Sexual Experience and Sexual Esteem." Journal of Sex Research 35 (3): 272–81.

Wiehe, Vernon R. 1997. Sibling Abuse: Hidden Physical, Emotional, and Sexual Trauma. Thousand Oaks, CA: Sage.

Wilcox, Kathryn L., Sharlene A. Wolchik, and Sanford L. Braver. 1998. "Predictors of Maternal Preference for Joint or Sole Legal Custody." Family Relations 47 (1): 93–101.

Wilcox, W. Bradford. 1998. "Conservative Protestant Childrearing: Authoritarian or Authoritative?" American Sociological Review 63: 796–809.

———. 2002. "Religion, Convention, and Paternal Involvement." American Sociological Review 64: 780–792.

Wilder, H. B., and David A. Chiriboga. 1991. "Who Leaves Whom: The Importance of Control." Pp. 224–47 in Divorce: Crisis, Challenge or Relief? edited by David A. Chiriboga and Linda S. Catron. New York: New York University Press.

Wiley, Angela R., Henriette B. Warren, and Dale S. Montanelli. 2002. "Shelter in a Time of Storm: Parenting in Poor Rural African American Communities." Family Relations 51 (3): 265–273.

Wiley, Norbert. 2003. "The Self as Self-Fulfilling Prophecy." Symbolic Interaction 26 (4): 501–513.

———. 1985. "Marriage and the Construction of Reality: Then and Now." Pp. 21–32 in The Psychosocial Interior of the Family, 3d ed., edited by Gerald Hantel. Hawthorne, NY: Aldine.

Wilkie, Jane Riblett. 1991. "The Decline in Men's Labor Force Participation and Income and the Changing Structure of Family Economic Support." Journal of Marriage and Family 53 (1): 111–22.

Wilkie, Jane Riblett, Myra Marx Ferree, and Kathryn Strother Ratcliff. 1998. "Gender and Fairness: Marital Satisfaction in Two-Earner Couples." Journal of Marriage and Family 60 (3): 577–94.

Wilkinson, Doris. 1993. "Family Ethnicity in America." Pp. 15–59 in Family Ethnicity: Strength in Diversity, edited by Harriette Pipes McAdoo. Newbury Park, CA: Sage.

———. 2000. "Rethinking the Concept of 'Minority': A Task for Social Scientists and Practitioners." *Journal of Sociology and Social Welfare* XXVII: 115–132.

Willetto, Angela A. A., and Charlotte Goodluck. 2004. "Economic, Social and Demographic Losses and Gains among American Indians." www.prb.org. Jan.

Willetts, Marion C. 2003. "An Exploratory Investigation of Heterosexual Licensed Domestic Partners." *Journal of Marriage and Family* 65 (4): 939–952.

Williams, Lee. M., and Michael G. Lawler. 2003. "Marital Satisfaction and Religious Heterogamy." *Journal of Family Issues* 24 (8): 1070–1092.

Williams, Patricia J. 2003. "Code Orange." *The Nation*. Mar. 3. P. 9.

———. 2004. "Wedlockstep." *The Nation* 278 (9): 10.

William Petschek National Jewish Family Center of the National Jewish Committee. 1986. "Intermarriage." *Newsletter* 6 (1).

Williams, Linda S. 1992. "Adoption Actions and Attitudes of Couples Seeking In Vitro Fertilization." *Journal of Family Issues* 13 (1): 99–113.

Williams, Norma. 1990. *The Mexican American Family: Tradition and Change.* Dix Hills, NY: General Hall.

Willing, Richard. 2002. "More States Allowing Trust Funds for Pets." *USA Today*. Aug. 16.

Willson, Andrea E., Kim M. Shuey, and Glen H. Elder, Jr. 2003. "Ambivalence in the Relationship of Adult Children to Aging Parents and In-Laws." *Journal of Marriage and Family* 65 (4): 1055–1072.

Wilson, James Q. 2001. "Against Homosexual Marriage." Pp. 123–27 in *Debating Points: Marriage and Family Issues,* edited by Henry L. Tischler. Upper Saddle River, NJ: Prentice Hall.

Wilson, William Julius. 1987. *The Truly Disadvantaged: The Inner City, The Underclass, and Public Policy.* Chicago: University of Chicago Press.

Winch, Robert F. 1958. *Mate Selection: A Study of Complementary Needs.* New York: Harper & Row.

Wineberg, Howard. 1994. "Marital Reconciliation in the United States: Which Couples Are Successful?" *Journal of Marriage and Family* 56 (1): 80–88.

———. 1996. "The Resolutions of Separation: Are Marital Reconciliations Attempted?" *Population Research and Policy Review* 15: 297–310.

Wineberg, Howard, and James Mc-Carthy. 1998. "Living Arrangements After Divorce: Cohabitation Versus Remarriage." *Journal of Divorce and Remarriage* 29 (1/2): 131–46.

Winkler, Anne E. 1998. "Earnings of Husbands and Wives in Dual-earner Families." *Monthly Labor Review* 121: 42–48.

Winston, Kimberly. 1998. "A Test of Faith." *San Francisco Chronicle*. Apr. 5: A–1, A–11.

Wise, Nicole. 2000. "Parents Shouldn't Be on Call All the Time." *Newsweek*. Aug. 7: 15.

Witchel, Alex. 2001. "Voices of the Past; We've Been There, Done That." *New York Times*. Oct. 14.

Wittenauer, Cheryl. 2004. "1st U.S. Transplant of Ovary Successful." AP. Oct. 16.

Witt, April, and Dennis Roberts. 1997. "Mission for Islam: Muslims Try to Educate Americans About Their Religious Practices." *Modesto Bee*. Jan. 25: G–1, G–2.

Wolf, D. A., V. Freedman, and B. J. Soldo. 1997. "The Division of Family Labor: Care for Elderly Parents." *Journal of Gerontology* 52B: 102–109.

Wolf, Marsha E., Uyen Ly, Margaret A. Hobert, and Mary A. Kernic. 2003. "Barriers To Seeking Police Help for Intimate Partner Violence." *Journal of Family Violence* 18: 121–129.

Wolf, Rosalie S. 1986. "Major Findings from Three Model Projects on Elderly Abuse." Pp. 218–38 in *Elder Abuse: Conflict in the Family,* edited by Karl A. Pillemer and Rosalie S. Wolf. Dover, MA: Auburn.

———. 1996. "Elder Abuse and Family Violence: Testimony Presented Before the U.S. Senate Special Committee on Aging." *Journal of Elder Abuse & Neglect* 8 (1): 81–96.

Wolfers, Justin. 2004. "Did Unilateral Divorce Raise Divorce Rates? A Reconciliation and New Results." National Bureau of Economic Research Working Paper 10014. Cambridge MA: National Bureau of Economic Research.

Wolfinger, Nicholas H. 1999. "Trends in the Intergenerational Transmission of Divorce." *Demography* 36: 415–20.

"Women Still Lag White Males in Pay." 2004. CNNMoney. Apr. 20.

———. 2000. "Beyond the Intergenerational Transmission of Divorce: Do People Replicate the Patterns of Marital Instability They Grew Up With?" *Journal of Family Issues* 21 (8): 1061–1086. http://cnnmoney.com

Wong, Paul, Chienping Faith Lai, Richard Nagazawa, and Tieming Lin. 1998. "Asian Americans as a Model Minority: Self-Perceptions and Perceptions by Other Racial Groups." *Sociological Perspectives* 41 (1): 95–118.

Woo, Junda. 1992a. "Adoption Suits Target Agencies for Negligence." *Wall Street Journal*. July 9: A1, A6.

———. 1992b. "Mediation Seen as Being Biased Against Women." *Wall Street Journal*. Aug. 4: B1, B9.

Wood, Wendy, and Alice H. Eagly. 2002. "A Cross-Cultural Analysis. Of Behavior of Women and Men: Implications for the Origins of Sex Differences." *Psychology Bulletin* 128: 699–727.

Woodward, Kenneth L. 1997. "Was the Pope Wrong?" *Newsweek*. June 16: 48.

———. 2001. "A Mormon Moment." *Newsweek*. Sept. 10: 44–51.

Working Group on A New View of Women's Sexual Problems. 2003. *The Manifesto: A New View Of Women's Sexual Problems.* www.fsd-alert.org.

Working Moms Refuge. 2001. "Factors to Consider When Selecting A Child Care Center." www.momsrefuge.com/newmoms/tips/childcare_centers.html.

Workman, Jane E., and Elizabeth W. Freeburg. 1999. "An Examination of Date Rape, Victim Dress, and Perceiver Variables Within the Context of Attribution Theory." *Sex Roles* 41 (3/4): 261–77.

"World's Smallest Baby Ready to Go Home." 2004. *USA Today*.Dec. 21.

Wright, Carol L., and Joseph W. Maxwell. 1991. "Social Support During Adjustment to Later-Life Divorce: How Adult Children Help Parents." *Journal of Divorce and Remarriage* 15 (3/4): 21–48.

Wright, Paul H., and Katherine D. Wright. 1999. "The Two Faces of Codependent Relating: A Research-Based Perspective." *Contemporary Family Therapy* 21 (4): 527–43.

Wright, Robert. 1994a. *The Moral Animal: Evolutionary Psychology and Everyday Life.* New York: Pantheon.

———. 1994b. "Our Cheating Hearts." *Time.* August 15: 44–52.

Wright, Victoria Clay, Laura A. Schieve, Meredith A. Reynolds, Gary Jeng, and Dmitry Kissin. 2004. "Assisted Reproductive Technology Surveillance—United States, 2001." *Mortality and Morbidity Weekly Report.* 53, No. SS-1: 1-10. April 30.

Wright, William. 1998. *Born That Way.* New York: Knopf.

Wu, Lawrence L. 2001. "Introduction." Pp. viii-xxii in *Out of Wedlock: Causes And Consequences of Nonmarital Fertility,* edited by Lawrence L. Wu and Barbara Wolfe. New York: Russell Sage.

Wu, Zheng, and Margaret J. Penning. 1997. "Marital Instability After Midlife." *Journal of Family Issues* 18 (5): 459–78.

Wyatt, Gail E., Hector F. Myers, Kimlin Ashing-Giwa, and Ramani Durvasula. 1999. "Sociocultural Factors Affecting Sexual Risk-Taking in African American Men and Women: Results from Two Empirical Studies." Pp. 45–58 in *The Black Family: Essays and Studies,* 6th ed., edited by Robert Staples. Belmont, CA: Wadsworth.

Wyeth Medical Communications. 2005. Personal communication. March 31.

Yancey, George, and Sherelyn Yancey. 1998. "Interracial Dating." *Journal of Family Issues* 19 (3): 334–48.

Yarrow, Andrew L. 1987. "Older Parents' Child: Growing Up Special." *New York Times.* Jan. 26.

Yellowbird, Michael, and C. Matthew Snipp. 1997. "American Indian Families." Pp. 226–48 in *Minority Families in the United States: A Multicultural Perspective,* edited by Ronald L. Taylor. Upper Saddle River, NJ: Prentice-Hall.

———. 2002. "American Indian Families." Pp. 227-249 in *Multicultural Families in the United States,* 3rd ed., edited by Ronald L. Taylor. Upper Saddle River NJ: Prentice-Hall.

Yeung, W. Jean, John Sandberg, Pamela Davis-Kean, and Sandra Hofferth. 2001. "Children's Time with Fathers in Intact Families." *Journal of Marriage and Family* 63 (1): 136–54.

Yllo, Kersti, and Michele Bograd, eds. 1988. *Feminist Perspectives on Wife Abuse.* Newbury Park, CA: Sage.

Yorburg, Betty. 2002. *Family Realities: A Global View.* Upper Saddle River NJ: Prentice Hall.

Yoshihama, Mieko, Asha L. Parekh, and Doris Boyington. 1991. "Dating Violence in Asian/Pacific Communities." Pp. 184–95 in *Dating Violence: Young Women in Danger,* edited by Barrie Levy. Seattle: Seal.

Yoshioka, Marianne R., Louisa Gilbert, Nabila El-Bassel, and Malahat Baig-Amin. 2003. "Social Support and Disclosure of Abuse.: Comparing South Asian, African American, and Hispanic Battered Women." *Journal of Family Violence* 18: 171–180.

Zabin, Laurie Schwab, Rebeca Wong, Robin M. Weinick, and Mark R. Emerson. 1992. "Dependency in Urban Black Families Following the Birth of an Adolescent's Child." *Journal of Marriage and Family* 54 (3): 496–507.

Zablocki v. Redhail. 1978. 434 U.S. 374, 54 L.Ed.2d 618, 98 S.Ct. 673.

Zak, A. 1998. "Individual Differences in Perception of Fault in Intimate Relationships." *Personality and Individual Differences* 24: 131–33.

Zelizer, Viviana K. 1985. *Pricing the Priceless Child: The Changing Social Value of Children.* New York: Basic.

Zeng-Yin, Chen, and Howard B. Kaplan. 2001. "Intergenerational Transmission of Constructive Parenting." *Journal of Marriage and Family* 63 (1): 17–31.

Zernike, Kate. 2003a. "Many Women Gleeful at Old Friend's Encore." *New York Times.* Mar. 7.

———. 2003b. "30 Years after Abortion Ruling, New Trends But The Old Debate." *New York Times.* Jan. 20.

Zhao, Yilu. 2002. "Immersed in 2 Worlds, New and Old." *New York Times.* July 22.

Zilbergeld, Bernie. 1999. *The New Male Sexuality,* rev. ed. New York: Bantam.

Zill, Nicholas. 1994. "Understanding Why Children in Stepfamilies Have More Learning and Behavior Problems Than Children in Nuclear Families." Pp. 97–106 in *Stepfamilies: Who Benefits? Who Does Not?,* edited by Alan Booth and Judy Dunn. Hillsdale, NJ: Erlbaum.

Zimmerman, Eilene. 2004. "Bragging Rights: The 'Gifted' Label May Mean Too Much to Parents." *Psychology Today.* January/February: 20.

Zimmerman, Jeffrey, and Elizabeth Thayer. 2004. *Adult Children of Divorce: How to Overcome the Legacy of Your Parents' Breakup and Enjoy Love, Trust and Intimacy.* Oakland, CA: Hi Marketing Publishers.

Zsembik, Barbara A., and Zobeida Bonilla. 2000. "Eldercare and the Changing Family in Puerto Rico." *Journal of Family Issues* 21 (5): 652–74.

Zuang, Yuanting. 2004. "Why Foreign Adoption?" Paper presented at the annual Meeting of the American Sociological Association. San Francisco. Aug. 15.

Zuckerman, Diana. 2000. "Child Care Staff: The Low Down on Salaries and Stability." Washington, DC: National Center for Policy Research for Women and Families. www.cpr4womenandfamilies.org/wwf2.html.

Zuo, Jiping, and Shengming Tang. 2000. "Breadwinner Status and Gender Ideologies of Men and Women Regarding Family Roles." *Social Forces* 43: 29–43.

Zvonkovic, Anisa M., Kathleen M. Greaves, Cynthia J. Schmiege, and Leslie D. Hall. 1996. "The Marital Construction of Gender Through Work and Family Decisions: A Qualitative Analysis." *Journal of Marriage and Family* 58 (1): 91–100.

Credits

This page constitutes an extension of the copyright page. We have made every effort to trace the ownership of all copyrighted material and to secure permission from copyright holders. In the event of any question arising as to the use of any material, we will be pleased to make the necessary corrections in future printings. Thanks are due to the following authors, publishers, and agents for permission to use the material indicated.

Excerpts

Chapter 4. 101: Excerpt from Hard Choices: How Women Decide about Work, Career and Motherhood, by Kathleen Gibson, 1985, pp. 18–19. University of California Press, copyright © 1985 The Regents of the University of California. Reprinted by permission. **105:** Excerpt from "The Costs of Being on Top," by Mark E. Kann, Journal of the National Association for Women Deans, Administrators, and Counselors, 49 (Summer). Copyright © 1986 by the National Association for Women Deans, Administrators and Counselors. Reprinted by permission. **Chapter 12. 354, 358:** From The Second Shift by Arlie Hochschild and Ann Machung, copyright © 1989, 2003 by Arlie Hochschild. Used by permission of Viking Penguin, a division of Penguin Group (USA) Inc. **Chapter 13. 384:** Excerpt reprinted with the permission of Simon & Schuster, from Couples: How to Confront Problems and Maintain Loving Relationships, by Carlfred B. Broderick, pp. 40–41. Copyright © 1979 by Carlfred B. Broderick. **Chapter 14. 419, 421:** Excerpt from "Why Men Resist" by William J. Goode, 1982, p. 140. In Barrie Thorne and Marilyn Yalom, [Eds.] Rethinking the family: Some Feminist Questions. Longman Publishing Group. Reprinted by permission of Marilyn Yalom, Stanford University. **Chapter 16. 488:** Excerpt from Ex. Familia: Grandparents, Parents, and Children Adjust to Divorce, by Colleen Leahy Johnson, 1988, pp. 190–191. Copyright © 1988 by Rutgers, The State University. Used with permission of Rutgers University Press. **Chapter 17. 534–535:** Roni Berer, "Immigrant Stepfamilies." Contemporary Family Therapy, September 1997, Vol. 19, Issue 3, pp. 361–370. © 1997 Kluwer Academic Publishers. Reprinted by permission of Springer-Verlag. **533–534:** Adapted with permission from Therapy with Stepfamilies by Emily B. Visher and John S. Visher, 1996, pp. 41–42. Copyright © 1996 by Taylor & Francis.

Photographs

Chapter 1. xxx: © Kayte M. Deioma/PhotoEdit **2:** right, © Ron Chapple/Getty Images **2:** left, © Austin MacRae **4:** © Jeff Greenberg/PhotoEdit **9:** © Michael Heron/CORBIS **10:** bottom, Courtesy of John Hancock Financial Services and Agencies, CNA and Commercial Talent **10:** top, Courtesy of Mitchell Gold and Trone Advertising **11:** © Ken Benjamin **13:** © Michael Newman/PhotoEdit **15:** © Curtis Willocks/Brooklyn Image Group **17:** © Mark Romaine/Stock Connection **19:** © AP/Wide World Photos **Chapter 2. 22:** © Myrleen Ferguson Cate/PhotoEdit **25:** © Alfred Eisenstaedt/Getty Images **28:** © Charles Thatcher/Getty Images **34:** © Royalty Free/Getty Images **36:** © Phil Schermeister/CORBIS **39:** © AP/Wide World Photos **40:** © Sergio Dorantes/CORBIS **41:** © Ed Lallo/Index Stock Imagery/PictureQuest **Chapter 3. 52:** © Wolfgang Kaehler/CORBIS **57:** © Tony Freeman/PhotoEdit **61:** © Sybil Shackman **62:** © Elyse Lewin Studio, Inc./Getty Images **65:** © Lawrence Migdale **69:** © Martin Rodgers/Stock, Boston **Chapter 4. 78:** © Tom & Dee Ann McCarthy/CORBIS **81:** © Davis Factor/CORBIS **86:** © Carol Halebian **90:** © J. Pat Carter **93:** © David Young-Wolff/PhotoEdit **95:** Courtesy Deb Glover and Celeste Wheeler **97:** © Cassy Cohen/PhotoEdit **Chapter 5. 110:** © Austrian Archives, Osterreichsche Galerie, Vienna, Gustav Klimt/CORBIS **113:** © Jack Hollingsworth/Index Stock Imagery **114:** © Ghislain & Marie David de Lossy/Getty Images **116:** © David Young-Wolff/PhotoEdit **120:** © Arthur Tilley/Getty Images **125:** © Ronnie Kaufman/CORBIS **128:** © Scott T. Baxter/Getty Images **Chapter 6. 132:** © Alexandra Michaels/Getty Images **138:** © "Morning on the Cape," 1935. Leon Kroll, American, 1884–1974. Oil on canvas, 36 × 58" in Carnegie Museum of Art, Pittsburgh; Patrons

Author Index

Names followed by italicized letters indicate footnotes (*n*), tables (*f* or *t*), cases (*c*), or boxed material (*b*)

Subject Index

Names followed by italicized letters indicate footnotes (*n*), tables (*f* or *t*), cases (*c*), or boxed material (*b*)

Relative love and need theory, 411
Relatives of divorce, 487–488
Relatives of remarriage, 487–488
Religion
  families and, 38–41
  male dominance in, 86–87
  marriage and, 180–181
Remarriages, 523–526. *See also* Stepfamilies
  advantages of, 526–527
  age and odds of, 527–528
  children and, 527
  choosing partners, 526–528
  divorce and, 481
  double, 529
  happiness and satisfaction in, 528–532
  homogamy in, 528
  negative stereotypes, 530–531
  race/ethnicity and, 524*b*
  rates, 7*b*, 523
  relatives of, 487–488
  sexuality and, 152
  single, 529
  stability of, 529–532
  stepfamilies and children's living arrangements, 524–526
  stepparenting in, 537–544
Remarried families, 532–536
  family law and, 536
  kin networks in, 534–536
Report talk, 390
Representative sample, 71, 148
Reproduction, commercialization of, 290–291
Reproductive technology, 287–292
  test tube babies, 293*b*
  in vitro fertilization (IVF), 293*b*
Residence, cohabitation legalities and, 253*b*
Resilient children, 315–316
Resilient families, 456
Resilient stepfamilies, 548*b*–549*b*
Resilient versus vulnerable families, 462–463
Resource hypothesis, 356
  criticisms of, 408–409
  egalitarian power and, 407–409
  family violence and, 423
  marital power and, 407–409
Resources
  in cultural context, 410–411
  gender and, 408–409
Retirement, 561–562
Reward power, 407, 429
Rewards, 93
Reynolds v. United States, 211*b*
Roe v. Wade, 286
Role ambiguity, stepfamilies and, 538–539
Role compatibility, 189

Role making, 224
  Mexican Americans and, 413
Role reversal, 32*b*
Role-reversed provider couple, 339

Sabotage, 389
Same-sex marriage, 214–223
  Alaska, 217
  arguments for, 220–221
  civil disobedience, 220*b*–221*b*
  debate over, 218–222
  dissenting arguments from lesbians and gay men, 221–222
  Hawaii, 217
  legal issues, 216–218
  Massachusetts, 216–217
  public opinion on, 222–224
  Vermont, 217
Same-sex partner households, 6*b*
  regional differences in, 42*b*–43*b*
Sandwich generation, 304, 573
Sarcasm, 397
Schools, socialization in, 96–100
Scientific investigation, 70–71
Secondary group, 3*n*
Second shift of unpaid family work, 354–355
  maintaining intimacy while negotiating provider roles and, 376–378
Secure attachment style, 126
Selection hypothesis, 193
Self-care, 367
Self-concept, 64
Self-disclosure, 127
Self-esteem, 122*n*
  See also Self worth
  emotional interdependence and, 123–125
  low self-esteem as reason for tolerating family violence, 431
  personal relationships and, 123
  sexual pleasure and, 153
Self-fulfilling prophecy, 479
Self-identification theory, 93–94
Self-love, narcissism distinguished from, 123
Self-revelation, 127
Self worth
  See also Self-esteem
  as a consequence, 123
  enhancing, 123, 124*b*
  as prerequisite to love, 122–126
Sense of empowerment, 406
Sensitization stage (of homosexual identity construction), 142
Separate spheres, 91
Separation, marital, 484
September 11th terrorist attacks, 25, 55, 58*b*, 59*b*, 83, 316, 449, 455
Sequencing moms, 350–351

Seven-stage model of stepfamily development, 545
Severe violence, 423
Sex, 80
Sexism
  modern, 80
  traditional, 80
Sex ratio, 29, 237–240
Sexual abuse, 438
Sexual coercion, 194
Sexual development, 134–135
  children's, 134–135
  theoretical perspectives on, 136–144
Sexual dimorphism, 88*n*
Sexual education, 160–162
Sexual exclusivity. *See also* Affairs; Extramarital sex
  cohabitation and, 208
  marriage premise and, 208
  subcultures with norms contrary to, 210*b*–211*b*
Sexual intimacy, 115–116
Sexuality, 134
  cultural scripts, 138–144
  elderly and, 560–561
  first-marrieds compared to remarrieds and cohabitators, 152
  political controversy influencing. *See* Politics
  regional differences in views on, 42*b*
  throughout marriage, 147–152
Sexually transmitted diseases (STDs), 143–144, 156. *See also* specific disease
  sexual responsibility, 162–163
Sexually transmitted infections (STIs) *See* Sexually transmitted diseases (STDs)
Sexual orientation, 135–136
Sexual responsibility, 152, 162–163
Sexual revolution, 139–140
Sexual scripts, 137
Sexual sharing, principles for, 154–155
Shared parenting, 308
Shelters, 431–432
Shift work, 349
Short-term affairs, 227
Sibling rivalry, 311*n*
Sibling violence, 439
Silent treatment, 397
Singer v. Hara, 216
Singlehood. *See also* Nonmarrieds; Unmarrieds
  African Americans and, 242–244
  changing attitudes toward, 240–242
  choice and, 259
  cohabitation. *See* Cohabitation
  desire for, 240*f*
  divorced persons. *See* Divorce
  factors in, 236–237, 240